THE

BOOK OF NATURE:

AN ELEMENTARY INTRODUCTION

TO

THE SCIENCES OF

PHYSICS,	GEOLOGY,
ASTRONOMY,	BOTANY,
CHEMISTRY,	ZOOLOGY, AND
MINERALOGY,	PHYSIOLOGY.

BY

FRIEDRICH SCHOEDLER, PH. D.,

PROFESSOR OF THE NATURAL SCIENCES AT WORMS, AND FORMERLY ASSISTANT IN THE CHEMICAL LABORATORY OF GIESSEN.

FIRST AMERICAN EDITION,

WITH A GLOSSARY, AND OTHER ADDITIONS AND IMPROVEMENTS

FROM

THE SECOND ENGLISH EDITION,

TRANSLATED FROM THE SIXTH GERMAN EDITION

BY

HENRY MEDLOCK, F.C.S.,

DIRECTOR OF THE MARLBOROUGH STREET LABORATORY AND SCHOOL OF PRACTICAL CHEMISTRY, LECTURER ON CHEMISTRY AND NATURAL PHILOSOPHY AT THE BRIGHTON COLLEGE, AND FORMERLY SENIOR ASSISTANT IN THE ROYAL COLLEGE OF CHEMISTRY, LONDON.

ILLUSTRATED BY

SIX HUNDRED AND SEVENTY-NINE ENGRAVINGS ON WOOD.

NEW YORK:

SHELDON & COMPANY, PUBLISHERS,

498 & 500 BROADWAY.

1870.

PUBLISHERS' ADVERTISEMENT.

UNDER the title of "The Book of Nature" the present work has attained a wide reputation in Europe, as evinced by the demand for repeated editions in Germany and England. In its present improved form, therefore, with the thorough revisions and numerous additions of the American editor, the publishers confidently claim for it a place in the library of every family where there is a desire to understand and appreciate the facts and principles of the visible world around them.

PHILADELPHIA, *January*, 1854.

PREFACE TO THE SECOND ENGLISH EDITION.

In preparing the Second Edition of the Book of Nature, I have incorporated the additions and improvements introduced by the Author into the Sixth German Edition, which has been recently issued from the Press.

In the section on Physics a more convenient arrangement has been adopted; and a new chapter on the Mechanism of the Clock and of the Flour-mill added.

The section on Astronomy has been almost entirely re-written, and rendered more uniform in language and style of treatment with the rest of the work.

The section devoted to Chemistry is considerably extended; and a new chapter on Organic Radicals introduced.

In revising the proof-sheets, and making the copious Index, I have received the valuable assistance of my friends Dr. Philip W. Hofmann and Mr. Charles Harwood Clarke, to whom my best thanks are especially due.

H. MEDLOCK.

20 *Great Marlborough Street*,
March 1853.

PREFACE

In the present rapidly advancing state of society, the study of the Natural and Physical Sciences has become an essential branch of a liberal education. The advantage of such pursuits is universal; for all men are partakers of the bounties of Nature, and all should possess some knowledge of the manifold operations on which their own enjoyments, and even their existence, depend.

Enlarged views of Nature are more especially requisite for those who watch over the progress of mental development, and whose object and duty it is to direct the tendencies of the progressive spirit of the age, and to counteract the evils of prejudiced and illiberal views either of Natural or of Moral Phenomena. Hence the Artist and the Philosopher, the Poet and the Divine, need a deep insight into Nature, and an enlarged apprehension of her economy and her laws. The Manufacturer, the Husbandman, and the Merchant, whose avocations may be prosecuted with the aid of a knowledge of those branches of Natural and Physical Science which are indispensable to their special pursuits, are likely to be more uniformly successful when acting upon principles derived from a thorough comprehension of the relation of Nature's laws to one another.

It may hence be inferred that the Natural and Physical Sciences are of the highest importance to all classes of the community, and that they ought to form an especial branch of study in every institution devoted to the instruction of youth.

The Author's object has been to render the Book of Nature a Manual that may be appropriately placed in the hands of pupils in all educational institutions where the importance of a general knowledge of the Natural and Physical Sciences is recognised. Founded on a scientific basis, and composed with simplicity and clearness, it presents a general and comprehensive view of all the principal branches of the Natural and Physical Sciences.

The composition of the various sections by the same author is intended to secure the advantage of a uniformity of style and treatment; to avoid the repetition of numerous general statements; to exclude all varying and contradictory views; and, finally, to avoid all inadequate explanations and expressions, which so greatly retard the progress of the student in the perusal of scanty outlines of the several sciences composed by different authors.

The estimation in which the BOOK OF NATURE is held by the Germans, who have justly been styled a "Nation of Thinkers," is testified by the sale of upwards of twenty thousand copies in the short space of five years, and by the high encomiums of some of the most eminent Professors of the individual branches of science on which it treats.

The work has received many new illustrations, some of them original, and others copied from Regnault's *Cours Elémentaire de Chimie*, and from the *Cours Elémentaire d'Histoire Naturelle*, par MM. Milne-Edwards, A. de Jussieu et Beudant, which were placed at my disposal by the Publishers, and which have enhanced its beauty and usefulness.

H. MEDLOCK.

Royal College of Chemistry, London,
October **1851.**

CONTENTS.

PHYSICS—*continued.*

ASTRONOMY — 139.

CHEMISTRY — 203.

CHEMISTRY—*continued.*

MINERALOGY AND GEOLOGY—313.

I. MINERALOGY—314.

MINERALOGY AND GEOLOGY—*continued.*

II. GEOLOGY—353.

BOTANY—417.

BOTANY—*continued.*

ZOOLOGY — 515.

INTRODUCTION.

THE BOOK OF NATURE has, for thousands of years, been displayed to the gaze, the admiration, and the delight of mankind. In great and glorious characters, it testifies to the wonderful power and goodness of its Divine Author: — even the meanest or the uncomeliest thing in existence declares the infinite wisdom of its Creator.

In all times and in all places man has sought to understand the language of Nature; and thousands have applied themselves to its study with perseverance, energy, and profound attention. The exertions of the most intellectual and ingenious of men have been exercised in rendering the contents of this great volume intelligible and accessible to those who seek in its wonderful page for instruction and wisdom.

These labours, however, have not been crowned with complete success: there are in this Book still many marks and signs, even whole pages, which we do not understand, which appear so doubtful or obscure, that we can only guess at their meaning, or conjecture what may be their connexion with other portions of the same perfect work.

But as it is only after we have deciphered the separate characters that we discover the meaning of an ancient inscription, so we progressively advance from the knowledge of individual facts and simple objects, to the recognition and comprehension of the general laws of Nature on which they depend.

The efforts of the earlier students of Nature were solitary, interrupted, and uncombined, and therefore they led to no important results. A subject so full of marvel and mystery can only be successfully prosecuted when men are in the possession of leisure, and when they enjoy the blessings of peace. But these circumstances we rarely find to have been the lot of the learned and the wise, the distinguished men of ancient times. In the history of the earlier nations and empires we learn that the few who directed the destinies of the people at large, were so much occupied either in acquiring or in adjusting political power, that only a limited number of favoured individuals, here and there, had leisure to cast a few hasty glances on Nature.

People were then fully engaged in providing for their mere physical wants; civil order had to be established, and life and property to be secured. When wars and other calamities left them a breathing-time, this was chiefly and necessarily spent in the performance of their legislative and religious functions.

Hence the sciences cultivated in the more ancient times, were those of civil polity, law and, religion; and to all these, but especially to the last, the fine arts were more conducive than natural science, and were consequently more successfully cultivated.

Our sketch of the progress of science is divided into that of the earliest, the middle, the modern, and the present age.

EARLIEST AGES.

The ancients were content to use and to enjoy the gifts of Nature, but had little desire to know their causes or their effects. They had everything to learn. Their usual employments were hunting and fishing, and to these were subsequently added the tending of cattle and the tillage of the soil—occupations which supplied food and clothing, the prime necessaries of life. Hence, in consequence of their daily intercourse with Nature, they noticed many facts and phenomena which, individually and collectively, were useful to their successors.

The Chinese and the Egyptians, who, even at this early period, had formed themselves into well-organized communities, are the earliest nations among which we meet with a large amount of artistic knowledge, as well as regulations which evince that they enjoyed an intimate intercourse with Nature. Yet both of these nations had only attained to intelligence of some individual words or passages of this Book; but to an understanding of its spirit and unity, or even to an intelligent apprehension of its less obscure chapters and pages, they never reached.

MIDDLE AGES.

The Greeks, the most civilized people of antiquity, were surrounded by the bounties of Nature, which almost spontaneously yielded up to them all the necessaries of life. And thus, not being compelled to wrest from Nature her treasures by incessant labour and patient attention, they entered less deeply into her mysteries than might have been anticipated. It was the spirit of Nature collectively, and of the human mind specially, that formed the main objects of their observation and reflection; and thus the intellectual, moral and political sciences were more successfully cultivated than those of Nature.

The powerful people of Rome desired only conquest and dominion; their principal occupations were war and legislation; they had no inclination for science, which never thrives unless embraced with love, and nursed in the lap of peace. This nation, which made all kingdoms tributary to itself, never dived into the kingdom of Nature; and whilst it prescribed laws to all people, it had no idea of the eternal, immutable laws of Nature which overrule the transitory laws of men.

After the overthrow of the great Roman Empire, a stormy period succeeded. Prodigious swarms of turbulent people forsook their rugged homes, in quest of new and more congenial habitations. These brought war and desolation in their train: like a destructive flood, they destroyed everything which lay in their track. Art and science bade farewell to Europe, and sought and found an asylum in the more peaceful countries of Asia. While Europe was torn to pieces by savage wars, science was cultivated and expanded in Arabia, and much valuable knowledge was brought thence by the Crusaders.

MODERN AGES.

Both the external and internal circumstances of Europe became gradually more favourable to the promotion of science. The Christian faith, strengthened and cemented by the testimony and the blood of martyrs, united the nations in defence of their country and common religion, assailed by the irruptions of foreign barbarians. The Empire of Germany, founded on the ruins, and composed of the relics of Roman power and civilization, grew up into a permanent and powerful refuge for art and science. Wars and warlike expeditions were still frequent, yet in the seclusion of the monastic establishments, and within the walls of strong, fortified cities, science and art, trade and manufactures, found a safe abode, aud were cultivated with energy and success. As men were connected by the bond of proximity and interest, their wants multiplied as their means of supplying them were increased; and the effects of combination and concentration were a more abundant supply of the treasures of Nature. There were, besides, other causes co-operating in the ampler diffusion of natural science. The discovery of printing afforded the facility of preserving and transmitting every invention, experiment, and observation; and the discovery of America not only displayed to the wondering inhabitants of Europe a multitude of curious and remarkable objects, which not merely excited their curiosity, but enkindled the passionate desire of more extensive discovery and more accurate examination. In England, Scotland, Italy, France, and Germany, they founded Universities, establishments in which all the sciences were sedulously cultivated by the most distinguished scholars of that age. The connexion of medical and physical science was especially favourable to the promotion of the latter, which, from the earliest ages, has been considered as the sure foundation of medical knowledge and practice.

PRESENT AGE.

Armed with the experience of the past, and favoured by a lengthened duration of peace, the present age is more distinguished for scientific pursuits than any former period of the world's history. The more important nations of Europe, during the greater part of half a century, have sheathed their swords, so long drawn against themselves; and England, France, and Germany no longer emulate each other in the bloody works of destruction, but strive for the mastery in science, arts, and manufactures.

Many of the most eminent and ingenious men have applied themselves exclusively to the study of Nature. They were endowed with a keen perception of the essential importance of the physical sciences in philosophy, medicine, agriculture, arboriculture, and manufactures. Under a combination of favourable circumstances and of associated efforts, science has lately made gigantic progress.

In Germany, the General Association of Naturalists was first established; and every year they meet to excite and encourage each other in their labours to extend the empire of science and the love and knowledge of Nature. The British Association for the Encouragement of Science meets annually for similar purposes. From neighbouring nations, and even from the most distant parts of the world, there is a continual intercourse or scientific commerce carried on, which has a direct tendency to awaken the energies of men, as well as to enlarge their knowledge and excite their curiosity.

The science of the present day has no mysterious secrets which she carefully or churlishly conceals; freely and generously bubble unceasingly her fountains for every one who approaches her with the noble thirst of knowledge.

Happy youths of the present age, whose cradle was rocked under the shadow of the peaceful olive, take advantage of the favourable circumstances of the time, and acquaint yourselves with Nature! For, as the man who learned a new language was believed by the ancients to become possessed of a new soul, so man acquires a new sense with the acquisition of every new branch of natural science.

"*Thus Nature addresses herself to the recognised, the misused, and unknown senses; thus, by thousands of phenomena, she speaks with herself and to us; to the attentive listener she is nowhere dead, never silent.*"

With these words of GOETHE, we recommend to your acceptance and study THE BOOK OF NATURE.

1.

By the term Nature we understand the tenor or the united totality of all that can be perceived by the senses.

We *feel* that which is in immediate contact with our own bodies; we *see* whatever is presented to the eye, whether at a greater or a less distance; we *hear* the varieties of sound around us; we *smell* the fragrance of the flowers; and we *taste* the peculiar savours of different things.

Our senses are therefore the essential media between mind and Nature. They alone give information to the mind of the presence of that which is external to it; so that it is only through the senses that the mind has any conviction of an external world.

It is impossible for the mind to form a conception of any one part of Nature, unless it be perceptible to the senses. The blind, by the sense of touch, can, it is true, form a conception of the shape of an object, but they cannot form the least idea of the different colours; and it is impossible to convey any notion of this by mere description. Blue and red can no more be described than can a sound or taste.

Consequently, if the mind wishes to become acquainted with Nature, it must employ the senses as principal guides; it must despatch these its servants into the unknown domains of Nature, and form its conceptions and ideas in conformity with the information obtained through the means of the senses. Futile will be the endeavours of the most ingenious mind, which attempts to investigate or expound Nature either as a whole or in individual parts, on purely reflective or logical principles. We must refer constantly to the evidence of our senses: for the history of scientific progress clearly proves that those who have neglected or despised the guidance of their senses, and who would comprehend Nature on purely intellectual principles, have been led farthest astray.

2.

Though we justly attach a high importance to the perception of the senses in the investigation of Nature, it is not by itself adequate to the attainment of this knowledge. The child and the imbecile, as well as the savage, are susceptible of impressions, yet they make no advancement in the knowledge of Nature, for they are not in possession of a correspondingly-developed understanding, which alone is capable of rightly apprehending and judging, of arranging and comparing, the facts communicated through the medium of the senses. The mind alone is able to combine the different observations, and thus, conducted by the senses, to obtain a deeper insight into Nature.

The attentive consideration of Nature we call *observation*, and to observe with the view of understanding is called *investigation*. When we ourselves perform certain operations, or fulfil certain conditions, in order to observe an appearance more accurately, or so that we may be able to repeat or continue the operation, this action is called an *investigation* or *experiment*.

3.

All appearances or perceptions do not make an equal impression on our senses. That which is perceptible at once, both to sight and to feeling, is called an *Object.* Thus, Stones, Plants, and Animals, are Objects. That we are justified in classing with objects the atmosphere and the heavenly bodies, will only become perfectly clear on a closer acquaintance with Nature.

On the other hand, we name *Phenomena* all such appearances as are of themselves and at the same time, perceptible or revealed to us by only one of our senses. Thus, heat is apprehended only by the feeling, light by the eye, sound by the ear; hence, heat, light, and sound are designated by the term *Natural Phenomena.*

Certain perceptions, such as those of the colour, the smell, and the taste of many bodies, are usually called *Properties.*

Objects occupy *Space,* and can be measured and compared; phenomena fill up a portion of *Time,* and divide it by their succession, and repetition.

Nature is therefore revealed in objects and phenomena.

4.

If we attentively consider an object, we are sensible that it does not always present the same appearance. Certain changes are easily perceptible. Sometimes it changes its place, sometimes its figure, sometimes its colour; in a word, every object is to be seen under a greater or less striking variety of accidents or aspects.

What is the origin or foundation of these appearances, — whence arise these mutations to which objects are constantly subject?

We will endeavour to answer this question by an example.

There lies a stone on the ground. Suppose we lay hold of it and lift it up.

The stone by this action evidently changes its position, and we perceive that a motion is communicated to it. The stone is the *Object,* and the motion is the *Phenomenon.*

What now was the ground or the cause of this phenomenon of motion?

Nobody will, in this case, doubt that it was the will, the individual act, which by the laying hold of, and the lifting up of the stone, communicated the motion, and caused the change of place.

But what happens if we now leave the elevated stone to itself, by opening and withdrawing the hand? Does the stone retain the same position?

By no means, it remains neither suspended nor hovering in the air; but the moment we withdraw the hand, it falls to the ground.

Moreover, we have here again a phenomenon of motion which is certainly independent of our will. For if, at the very instant the stone is relinquished, we express the most decided desire for its remaining where we leave it, it will fall to the ground notwithstanding.

It is indifferent, as experience proves, to what height we may lift up the stone; under similar conditions, all objects will manifest the same phenomenon.

There must necessarily be a cause present, which produces in the most dissimilar objects the same phenomenon of falling—a cause altogether independent of human volition — a cause which is invisibly united to every object, and belongs to its existence.

Such a cause of a phenomenon independent of human will, we call a *Force,* or *Natural Force.* For example, the power which we consider as the cause of the falling of bodies, is called *Attraction,* or the *Force of Gravitation.*

As Nature exhibits a great number of very different phenomena, it might easily be supposed that many different forces are constantly active in producing these different results.

This, however, is not the case. Attentive observation has proved that a single force is adequate to the production of a multitude of different phenomena. It is probable that, taken on the whole, there are only a few final causes, or forces in existence, whereby all the phenomena surrounding us are occasioned.

In the observation of Nature, we have therefore, in the first place, to comprehend *Objects*, and the *Phenomena* which they manifest. We have then to account for the *Causes* or the *Forces* which produce these phenomena. The complete account of this scientific knowledge we call the *Knowledge of Nature*, or *Natural Science.*

5.

Let us now behold Nature.

The most suitable means of attaining this end will be to take a walk, and consider well whatever presents itself to our senses. We directly perceive many and very various objects. The fields and commons are covered with plants and grass; the distant hills are crowned with broom, or woods, or forests. In the vale at their feet the sparkling brook glides along, while in the atmosphere the clouds chase each other in rapid succession. Complete rest and stillness are nowhere to be seen. Leaves rustle, branches wave, the flowing water eddies and ripples, everywhere we meet with the most varied forms of animal life in incessant impulsive activity. What a multitude of objects! what a multiplicity of phenomena! Where shall we commence our research? How shall we comprehend the individual object in the constantly-moving panorama of Nature?

Indeed the multitude distracts us: we feel discouraged in our efforts to obtain a right apprehension of what we behold; we return home little instructed by our walk.

But even here, within our four walls, how manifold and multiform are the objects capable of arresting our attention! The warmth radiating from the grate, the disappearance of the wood consumed by the fire, the hissing and bubbling of the water boiling in the tea-urn—all these are phenomena which claim our observation. What remarkable properties are exhibited by the glass-furnishings of the room! Whilst the window-panes permit unaltered the appearance of external objects, our spectacles increase their apparent magnitude, and the mirror presents a faithful likeness of ourselves.

These are, in truth, things which we daily see, and with which every one is acquainted; but if we inquire into the proximate causes of such phenomena, we perceive that it is not easy to extemporize a satisfactory solution.

Thus with the materials and objects of investigation, we are always and everywhere supplied. It is only requisite now to show how to proceed to attain a comprehension, and to survey Nature in her multiform aspects and manifold phenomena. To study all at once would be impossible. With this view, we adopt a systematic treatment of the various subjects, making the sciences follow one another in a natural sequence.

6.

Thus then we are under the necessity of *subdividing* the natural sciences. It is not possible to do so with absolute precision; for though certain natural divisions readily present themselves, yet in the richness of Nature every subject is always more or less intimately connected with every other.

It is, moreover, difficult to afford a systematic view of the whole Natural Sciences to one who is totally unacquainted with their details, or who only knows them superficially; for a clear comprehension of the whole can only be attained by him who knows precisely its constituent parts. If, notwithstanding, we make an effort to divide the great kingdom of Nature into different provinces, it is chiefly with the view to point out the course by which we mean to pursue our journey through it.

We have already shown that Nature is revealed partly in *Objects*, and partly in *Phenomena;* and hence the entire science separates itself into two primary divisions — the science of objects and the science of phenomena.

7.

The Science of OBJECTS, which is commonly termed NATURAL HISTORY, is divided into three parts or divisions. The principles on which this division is founded will be most easily rendered intelligible by examples.

From the thousands of objects with which we are surrounded, we choose a piece of Sandstone, Chalk, or Granite; and pieces of Sulphur, Coal, common Potter's clay, white Pipe-clay, and yellow Tripoli.

These objects are certainly very different from one another, yet they present this property in common, that every one of them is homogeneous (similar) in its whole mass. If we break off a fragment from the piece of Sandstone, or Chalk, or Coal, we have in this bit, the same Sandstone, the same Coal, the same Chalk, only of smaller size. We can thence convey to any one as accurate a knowledge of the essential qualities of one of these bodies, by presenting him with a small piece, as if we showed him an entire mountain of it.

In none of these objects do we perceive any individual portion which exhibits an essential difference from the other portions. We cannot infer that any one portion is more necessary to the existence of a piece of sandstone than is any other, or that the one particle has a different function or another destination than the other. The minutest atom of chalk adhering to the finger, is as perfect a bit of chalk, as the mass of this substance which constitutes the stratum of a mountain.

Even the Granite, which appears, indeed, to be a composition of different materials, forms an exception rather in appearance than in reality, for on the whole it is homogeneous. As will be shown in a subsequent part, Granite is a uniform mixture of Quartz, Mica, and Felspar, and it is indifferent whether it be only of the size of a cherry-stone, or of as ample dimensions as the huge Granite-block which supports the equestrian statue of Peter the Great, or of the still greater mass that forms the peaked mountain of Goatfell, in Arran. All are equally perfect pieces of Granite.

Thus, therefore, there are objects which are homogeneous in their mass, and in which no parts specially formed for special purposes can be distin-

guished. These are termed MINERALS, *and that branch of natural science which treats of them is called* MINERALOGY.

The case is altogether different if we submit to consideration a tree, or a shrub, or even a flower, a leaf, or a root.

How different are here the individual parts in *form*, *colour*, and *density!* It is easy to be observed that the peculiarly formed parts of a tree have special functions and destinations; for suppose it to be deprived of its root, its bark, or its leaves, we soon are sensible that it is going rapidly to decay. From a part of a tree we can form no adequate conception of it as a whole, when the whole is previously unknown to us.

But still more remarkable is that which, by the help of the microscope, we are able to see in the interior of the root, the bark, and the leaves of a tree. We perceive the sap it contains is in motion, ascending and descending, the liquids in it evaporating or being assimilated. On the outside of the tree, shrub, or herb, we are not sensible of any motion communicated from within, or occasioned by itself. It is true that the wind shakes the branches and top of the oak, but of itself, not even a single leaflet is in a condition to move. The wind and the forester scatter its seeds over the ground, but the stem remains immovably fixed where it first took root in the soil.

Objects with parts specially adapted for certain functional purposes, without voluntary external movements, are termed PLANTS, *and the science which treats of them*, BOTANY.

There is still another group of objects which coincide with plants in being provided with peculiarly constructed parts, to which special functions are assigned, and in possessing an internal movemement, but which are, nevertheless, not plants.

They are distinguished from plants by their capability of voluntary external movements, whereby they can not only change the posture and attitude of their individual parts, but they can move from one place to another.

Objects endowed with specially formed parts, adapted for the fulfilling of certain functions, and are besides capable of voluntary external motion, are called ANIMALS, *and the science which treats of them is called* ZOOLOGY.

All objects, consequently, are either similar or homogeneous, like minerals, or they are dissimilar or heterogeneous, like plants and animals. The latter have peculiarly constructed parts, adapted for certain functional purposes; these parts are termed *Organs.* The united activity of all the organs of a plant or an animal, we call *Life*, and hence plants and animals are designated *animate* objects, while minerals are called *inanimate* objects.

8.

The Science of PHENOMENA, which is sometimes termed PHYSICS, or NATURAL PHILOSOPHY, is also divisible into three parts.

We are taught by observation, that all natural phenomena form three primary groups or divisions, each one distinguished by peculiar characteristics These we will now render comprehensible by examples.

If we strike a bell with a hammer, we hear a sound. The same will take place on the drawing of a bow across tightened strings. A lens of polished glass apparently enlarges the magnitude of every object viewed through it: with the same lens we can intercept and concentrate the sun's rays into a focus or point, and thereby kindle any combustible object; in every body elevated above the surface of the earth and then relinquished, we observe the phenomenon of falling; by the drawn bowstring we can communicate a swift motion to the arrow; the water which we heat is changed into steam; and when the steam is cooled, it again becomes water.

Thus we produce very different phenomena,—*sound, magnifying effect, combustion, falling, motion,* and the *formation of steam.*

Though these phenomena differ greatly, they have still something in common: all objects in which they are made to appear, or by which they are produced, undergo no essential change in consequence.

The sounding-bell and the string, the burning-glass, the falling stone, and the bow-string, all remain unchanged. Even the water, which has been converted into steam, resumes its original condition whenever the temperature is reduced sufficiently to admit of another change, without its suffering the least alteration of its essential qualities.

The heavenly bodies and their motions are also phenomena for our present consideration: accompanied as they are by no perceptible change, they are arranged among the above-mentioned phenomena.

Phenomena without essential change of the objects contributing thereto are termed PHYSICAL PHENOMENA, *and the science which treats of these is called* PHYSICS, or NATURAL PHILOSOPHY.

The case, however, is totally different with another series of phenomena which we have next to consider.

When we burn a piece of coal, of wood, or of sulphur; the coal, the wood, and the sulphur, entirely disappear. They pass into another condition, having entirely lost their former properties. When sand and potash are mixed together and exposed to strong and continued heat, both bodies melt together and become *glass;* in which new combination the original materials cannot be perceived. Still more striking is it when sulphur and mercury are heated together. Both substances entirely disappear, and instead of the yellow sulphur and the shining silvery mercury, we obtain the beautiful red vermilion. Of similar examples, thousands could be given, wherein the objects which we select for the production of such phenomena experience an essential change, and in their place objects appear with totally different qualities.

Phenomena accompanied with essential change of the objects applied thereto are called CHEMICAL PHENOMENA, *and the science which treats of them,* CHEMISTRY.

Finally, we have remaining a third group of peculiar phenomena, called vital phenomena, because they only appear in animate objects, viz., in plants, and animals. These are, for example, their growth, the motion of the different fluids in their interior parts, the reception and appropriation of the nourishing media, &c.

The phenomena of animated objects are called PHYSIOLOGICAL PHENOMENA, *and the science which treats of them,* PHYSIOLOGY.

Tabular View of the foregoing Divisions of the entire subject of Natural Science.

A — Science of Phenomena.			B — Science of Objects.		
1. Without change in the objects,	**2.** With change in the objects,	**3.** In animated objects,	**4.** Which are homogeneous in their mass,	**5.** Which are heterogeneous in mass, and without voluntary motion,	**6.** Which are heterogeneous in mass, and endowed with voluntary motion
Physics.	Chemistry.	Physiology.	Mineralogy.	Botany.	Zoology.

9.

The sequence or order in which these different branches of natural science are to be pursued is not a matter of indifference. For such as are of riper years and experience, the most advantageous course is, in the first place, to acquire a knowledge of general phenomena and their laws, which are almost incessantly repeated by nearly every object. It is easier and more agreeable to the developed understanding to survey, in the first place, the great outlines and general principles, rather than labour at the comprehension of many dissimilar individual forms. In this case the most suitable plan of study is to begin with *Physics* and *Astronomy*, to be succeeded by *Chemistry* and *Mineralogy* as their indispensable complement. These four sciences contain the fundamental knowledge necessary to the thorough comprehension of animal and vegetable life. Then follow *Botany* and *Zoology*, of which *Physiology* is generally reckoned a branch; unless it be intended to handle that subject more profoundly and with higher scientific aims.

This is the arrangement adopted in The Book of Nature, with the express intention of making every earlier division more or less introductory to that which follows.

Another course must, however, be followed, if it be wished to initiate the young into the knowledge of Nature. The child more easily comprehends the relations of external forms, the magnitude of objects, their qualities, and other characteristics, than he does the forces and the laws whereby phenomena are regulated. On these branches it is difficult for a child to acquire just notions, or even clear perceptions.

With children, we may first begin to direct their attention to the animal kingdom; and of all animals insects offer the richest and most interesting materials, which may everywhere and at all seasons be obtained in the living state. When they become more expert in observing and comprehending, with advancing age and frequent practice, they may be introduced through the vegetable to the mineral kingdom.

The study of physics and chemistry cannot usually be undertaken with advantage earlier than the age of fifteen.

In fine, a repeated survey will complete the whole picture of Nature, and make it appear in that intimate connexion which we ought not materially to derange. But every teacher may choose his own way, if he be only able to walk securely himself, to awaken the desire for the study, and to preserve the zeal of his pupils.

All ways, then, tend to the same end, but he who would reach the end must not avoid the way.

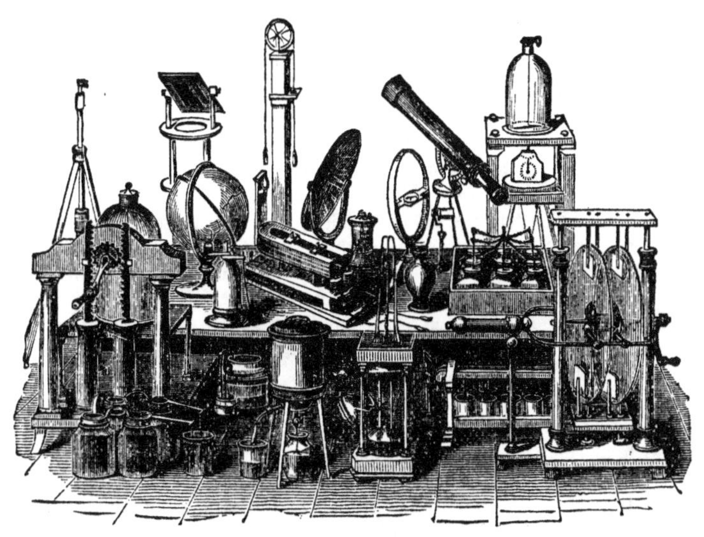

PHYSICS.

"Thou hast ordered all things in measure and number and weight, for thou canst show Thy great strength at all times when thou wilt, and who may withstand the power of Thine arm?"—*Wisdom of Solomon*, xi. 20, 21.

1. PHYSICS is that branch of Natural Science which treats of such phenomena as are unaccompanied by any *important changes* in the objects in which the phenomena are observed, or which serve for their production.

Such phenomena as these are — the falling of a stone, the sounding of a bell, or the magnifying effect of spectacles, as the objects by which they are produced undergo no change. As little do the rays of light affect a window-pane as they pass through it, and even heat produces only a temporary change in the condition of bodies.

In distinguishing physical phenomena an apparent difficulty can only arise when they occur simultaneously with other phenomena.

The heat disengaged in the combustion of coal belongs to the physical class of phenomena, while the *metamorphosis* which the coal undergoes must be classed under the head of *chemical* phenomena.

2. Man, from his earliest age, by observation, by the eye, the sense of touch, and still more distinctly by the motion of his body from one place to another, arrives at a conception of the relative position of surrounding objects, or, in other words, at the idea of *magnitude* or *form*.

It is not the sense of vision alone that endows him with this conception. A young child as often grasps at distant objects, at the moon for instance, as it does at those within its reach. A person born blind, who acquires his sense of vision by operation only, in after years, is unable at first to judge by the eye either of distance or of magnitude. All objects appear to him equally distant, and he is incapable of judging of their size. It is only by moving about and feeling the objects which are visible, that he is enabled to distinguish between vicinity and distance, or to recognise a difference in size. It is to the habit of observing from our early youth with both senses, that we are indebted for our ability of judging correctly, with the eye alone, of magnitude and distance.

Experience also teaches us that magnitude may be followed out in three directions, which we distinguish by the terms *Length*, *Breadth*, and *Depth*.

That which is conceived as extending in three directions is *Space*. As we can imagine either of these three directions to be carried out *ad infinitum*, we may likewise define space as the infinite universe surrounding us. It is, however, much more easy for us to form a conception of any limited space than of the illimitable expanse of Heaven.

3. In like manner every man is endowed unconsciously with a conception of *Number*, by the variety and the repetition of the objects surrounding him; and with an idea of *Time*, by the succession of phenomena or even by the mere train of his own thoughts. Certain points of departure, as well as an acquired practice, are essential to the formation of a judgment of time and number; without them we should be as little capable of forming accurate conceptions of these subjects as we should of space. The act of breathing, the beating of the pulse, the alternations of day and night, and of the seasons, are the kind of phenomena that aid us in measuring and dividing time.

Space, Number, and Time, are, therefore, the generalities which force themselves upon our minds by every observation, and are of special importance in the study of most natural phenomena. The more accurate observation of space and number forms the subject of a special science, which is called *Mathematics*.

4. That which fills space is *Matter*. If all space were filled with matter, the latter, like the former, would be infinite, and space and matter would, therefore, be the same. But this is not the case. Matter exists only in certain portions of space, and is always limited in extent. Matter, as a limited, finite substance, is termed *Body* or *Object*.

The celestial bodies, as well as the earth, are such limited portions of matter, or bodies, existing in space. Their dimension is extremely small when compared with that of space.

5. If we examine matter in the various forms in which it has yet been defined, we can perceive no reason for its undergoing any change. As matter, it should ever be alike, and remain in the same state, and the same place. It would, therefore, be perfectly unchangeable, fixed and motionless, and would not attract and occupy our attention by the change in the phenomena observable in connexion with it. Such a condition of matter we express by the term *vis inertiæ*. Every phenomenon, therefore, is produced by the overcoming of this inertia by some particular cause.

Hence we must assume that in addition to matter, there exists a special cause of the phenomena which are exhibited, a cause which is termed *Force*. Two ideas may be formed of the relation between force and matter. We may either consider force to be independent of matter, separable from it, and influencing it, perhaps, in the manner in which we conceive that the Deity influences the universe as its Creator and Ruler; or force may be considered as being inseparable from matter, as is the body and soul in the living being

Such general views are, however, the more indistinct and indefinite the less we know of the facts upon which they must be grounded. It is, therefore, advisable to become first thoroughly acquainted with individual natural phenomena, and afterwards to endeavour to form more general views, and to denote them by suitable expressions.

General Properties of Matter.

6. The following are the general properties of bodies: 1. *Magnitude and Form;* 2. *Impenetrability;* 3. *Inertia;* 4. *Divisibility;* 5. *Porosity;* 6. *Compressibility;* 7. *Elasticity;* 8. *Expansibility.*

Observation teaches us that the above-mentioned properties are possessed by every substance, without exception, whilst of the numerous distinctive marks which we perceive in every individual object, the greater part of them are observed only in particular objects, and are, therefore, called *special* properties, as for example, colour, form, &c.

7. As matter occupies a certain portion of space, it must be possessed of *magnitude*, and in describing physical phenomena, we have so frequently to refer to it, that it appears to us desirable to point out here the means of arriving at a correct idea of magnitude, or, in other words, of measuring it.

If we follow magnitude only in one unchangeable direction, as a straight line, the means of determining it is called a *measure of length.* It will be readily seen that it is of the greatest importance for scientific observation, as well as for commerce, to possess a universal, unchangeable measure of length; and it is particularly important to determine the unit of the measure of length in such a manner, that in the event of its being lost or falsified, it can easily be again found.

Several scientific men in France were commissioned to discover a unit of length. After having most accurately measured the fourth-part of the largest circle passing through the poles of the earth (the meridian), and divided it into ten millions of equal parts, they adopted one such part as a measure of length and called it a *meter.* The length of the meter is 39·37079 English inches.

The meter is divided into smaller parts according to the following plan:—

Meter; M.		Decimeter; Dm.		Centimeter; Cm.		Millimeter; Mm.
1	=	10	=	100	=	1000
		1	=	10	=	100
				1	=	10

Here, therefore, the millimeter is the smallest measure, and having been once determined, it may be conveniently employed for the comparison of other measures. It is equal to very nearly $\frac{1}{25}$ English inch.

In most other countries the unit of measure is the foot, which is divided into ten or twelve inches. In England the imperial yard of 36 inches, or three feet, is the legal standard of length.

The inch is divided into ten or twelve parts, which are called lines:—

COMPARISON OF MEASURES OF DIFFERENT COUNTRIES.

	Foot.		Inches.		Lines.		Millimeters.
England	1	=	12	=	144	=	304
Prussia (Rhenish foot)	1	=	12	=	144	=	313
Parisian or old French foot	1	=	12	=	144	=	324
Austria	1	=	12	=	144	=	316
Hesse Darmstadt	1	=	10	=	100	=	250
Saxony	1	=	12	=	144	=	283
Frankfort-on-the-Maine	1	=	12	=	144	=	284
Brunswick	1	=	12	=	144	=	285
Wurtemburg and Hamburg	1	=	10	=	100	=	286
Electorate of Hesse	1	=	12	=	144	=	287
Bavaria	1	=	12	=	144	=	291
Hanover	1	=	12	=	144	=	292
Baden	1	=	10	=	100	=	300

Those measures which are divided into ten equal parts, as the meter, are called *decimal measures*, as fig. 1, which is a square inch divided into one hundred square lines, and fig. 2, which represents a cubic inch divided into cubic lines.

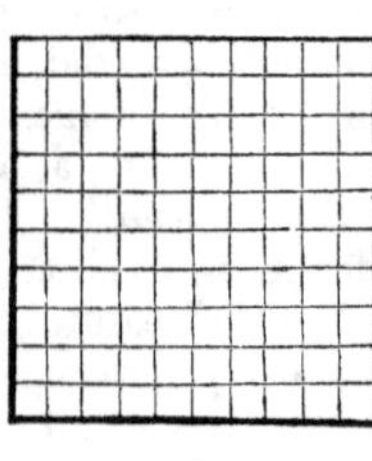

1.

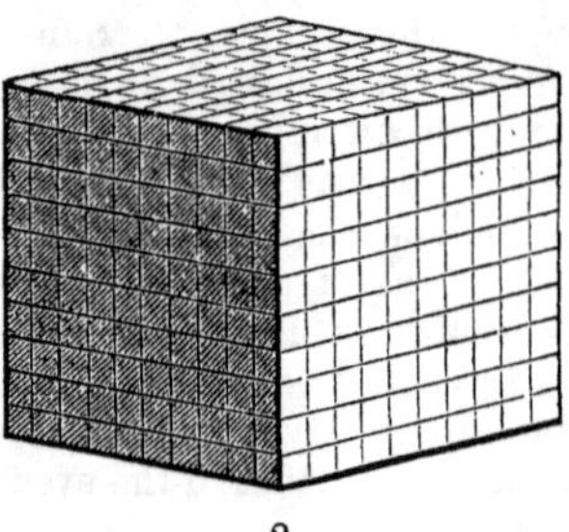

2.

Duodecimal measures, which are most commonly used in this country, are divided into twelve equal parts. A square foot is a plane measuring twelve inches in length and in breadth, whilst a cubic foot measures twelve inches in length, breadth, and depth.

8. The occupation of space by matter is rendered manifest to us by its *impenetrability*. In the same space which the earth occupies there can be no other celestial body at the same time, and daily experience teaches us, that in the space occupied by a mountain, a tree, or by our own bodies, no other material substance can be simultaneously present.

The impediments we should encounter by moving forward in one direction, result from the impenetrability of the substances we meet with in our way.

The *air* likewise occupies space; it is impenetrable, and is, therefore, considered as a body or a portion of matter. This requires a more positive proof. If we immerse an ordinary drinking-glass, with its opening downwards, in water, no sensible quantity of water will enter the glass, unless it be immersed to a considerable depth, when the pressure of the superincumbent liquid will compress the air into a smaller space. This depends upon the *impenetrability* of the air contained in the glass, which does not allow the water to occupy its place. The possibility of descending to a great depth in the sea, by means of a *diving-bell,* depends partly upon the impenetrability of the air which it contains.

A vessel which, in common language, is called *empty,* is, in reality, not empty, but filled with air; and it is not until this is displaced, that we can introduce another body, for instance, water, into the space which the air previously occupied.

All kinds of matter do not offer an equal resistance to the motion of our bodies, but we perceive, in this respect, a great difference. For example, those objects which we term *solid* are much more difficult to displace than those which are *liquid:* and in the case of *gaseous* bodies we scarcely feel that they oppose a resistance to our movements; they are mobile in the highest degree. Matter, therefore, presents itself in three different states, which are called *states of aggregation,* namely, *solid, liquid,* and *gaseous.* These we shall subsequently consider more minutely.

9. It has been shown that matter presents to us various phenomena only when influenced by the forces of nature: when it is uninfluenced by any of these forces, and remains in a state of rest, its condition is called its *inertia.* As this general property of matter is most remarkably displayed by the phenomena of motion, the consideration of it will be discussed more minutely when we treat of motion generally.

10. All substances may be divided into small particles by suitable means. Stones and grains of corn may be ground to fine dust, or flour; metals reduced to small particles by means of files, beaten into thin leaves by the hammer, or drawn into wires finer than hairs. Water contained in a vessel may be easily divided into single drops, and each drop may be spread over a large surface by a brush. The surface thus moistened becomes dry after a short time, owing to the evaporation of the water, which is converted into extremely small particles, no longer perceptible to the eye.

Divisibility is, therefore, a general property of bodies: their division is effected either by the proper implements, in which case they suffer *mechanical* division; or by natural forces, when they are said to undergo *physical* division.

The extent to which division may be carried is best shown by examples. The little line (-) shows the length measure, which is termed a *millimeter.* (See § 7.) The silk-worm spins filaments, 100 of which must be placed side by side to occupy the space of a millimeter (about $\frac{1}{25}$ inch). But metals have been drawn out into wires of such fineness, that one hundred and forty of them have together only the thickness of one silk filament, and fourteen thousand of them placed together occupy the space only of one millimeter.

Bodies may, however, be divided to a much greater extent by physical means. If, for instance, a grain of salt be dissolved in a glassful of water, every drop of the solution that can be taken up on the point of a needle contains a particle of the salt.

However minute are the particles into which matter may be divided, we are led to infer, by a number of phenomena, that the divisibility of matter cannot be continued *ad infinitum,* at least not with the means and natural forces at our command.

Every substance is, therefore, assumed to be an aggregate of smaller particles, which we term *atoms* or *molecules.* We have glasses magnifying from

1200 to 1600 times, but chemistry teaches us that the atoms must be still less than the smallest particle visible by means of these glasses.

If this view be followed out, we must conclude that the mass of a body depends on the number of its atoms, and that its properties are dependent on the constitution and arrangement of them.

We shall have opportunities of seeing these conclusions more or less confirmed, by results arrived at in the study of Nature.

11. The small openings in the skin, through which the perspiration escapes, are termed *pores*. Hence all bodies that are easily penetrated by air or water are termed *porous;* and as most bodies possess this property, we class *porosity* among the general properties of matter.

Sponge, wood, and charcoal, bread-crumbs, &c., are very porous bodies; the numerous and large pores they contain may be perceived at a glance; but the porosity of other bodies is only perceptible under certain circumstances. If, for instance, hollow balls, constructed of gold, iron, or other dense metals, be filled with water, closed tightly and submitted to great pressure, the water will exude in small drops through the pores of the metal.

Glass, and a few other substances, do not admit the passage of air and water under any circumstances. Although there may be reasons for believing even these substances to contain interstices or pores, still it is customary to consider only those bodies as porous that possess, under ordinary circumstances, the above-named properties.

12. It may be concluded, from the foregoing remarks, that *compressibility* also belongs to the general properties of matter. For, whenever a mass of matter contains spaces or interstices, it is capable of compression, provided we have at command the requisite amount of force to effect it. Indeed, no body has as yet been discovered that could not be made to occupy a smaller space by the application of pressure.

It is obvious that the density of a body will increase in proportion to the amount of pressure to which it is subjected, and that the resistance offered by a body against farther compression increases proportionately to the increase of the pressure applied.

The air is indisputably the most compressible of all bodies, while it is singular that water and other fluids can only be compressed to a very small extent. If, for example, 20 cubic inches of water were introduced into a cannon, the sides of which were three inches thick, and an attempt were made to compress the water into a space of 19 cubic inches, the cannon would burst before this compression could be effected.

Very porous bodies naturally admit of considerable compression, but metals likewise occupy a much smaller space when hammered or coined, and even glass may be compressed to a certain extent; hence it must likewise contain pores, though they are too minute to be visible.

13. When a body is compressed by the application of an external force, its particles will evince a tendency to resume their original position. The term *elasticity* has been given to this property, and the bodies are therefore called *elastic.*

This property is possessed by bodies in very different degrees. A certain quantity of air, to whatever extent and however frequently it may be compressed, will always return to its original volume, immediately the pressure is removed. Air is, therefore, perfectly elastic.

Amongst the highly elastic substances may be mentioned caoutchouc, feathers and hairs, whalebone, many kinds of wood and metals, and particularly steel.

In many substances, such as fluids, clay, &c., elasticity is scarcely perceptible, or at least only under peculiar conditions: such bodies as these are, on the contrary, termed *non-elastic.*

If an ivory ball be laid gently on a marble slab, coated with lamp-black, it will only receive a small black speck at the point on which it rests on the slab. But if the ball be allowed to fall from a height upon the slab, it will receive a round black spot, increasing in size proportionately to the height from which the ball falls. This experiment proves that the ball is flattened at the moment it touches the slab, but that, being elastic, it immediately regains its spherical form. The bow, the cross-bow, and the projectile apparatus of the ancients owe their power to elasticity. This property is most extensively made available in mechanics, and it is especially the elasticity of wires and strips of brass and steel, termed *springs*, which, as a moving power, are very generally employed. Such springs are used for gun-locks, door-locks, and pocket-knives; and it is the *spiral* springs which give to some kinds of sofas and beds their elasticity; carriages also owe their easy and characteristic movement to springs. The importance of elasticity, however, will be more readily understood, when we show, in the following pages, that watches and clocks can be set in motion by springs without the use of weights.

14. By *expansibility* of bodies we understand their property of increasing in size, and consequently of occupying a greater space when they are heated.

The space occupied by a body may be assumed to increase proportionately as the latter is heated.

Expansibility is, therefore, observed most distinctly, and to the greatest extent, in many of those substances which are not destroyed by the highest temperatures we can subject them to, as is the case with air and water. One cubic foot of water, when completely converted by heat into vapour, at the temperature of 212° F., occupies in that condition a space of 1696 cubic feet.

Classification of Physical Phenomena.

15. As physical phenomena are very numerous and various, it is expedient to class them into larger groups. It is evident that the characters of these groups can only be perfectly understood when we are familiar with their contents; we shall, therefore, limit ourselves at present to a brief exposition.

The first group embraces those phenomena only, the ultimate cause of which is the mutual *attraction* existing between the particles of matter.

In the second group are comprised the phenomena, arising from a peculiar motion, which we term *vibration.*

The third group consists of a series of phenomena, based on the existence of certain currents, of which we shall speak farther at the proper place.

This arrangement will be rendered more intelligible by the following table:—

I. Group.	II. Group.	III. Group.
Phenomena of Attraction.	Phenomena of Vibration.	Phenomena of Currents.
1. Cohesion. 2. Gravity. 3. Equilibrium and Motion.	1. Sound. 2. Heat. 3. Light.	1. Electricity. 2. Magnetism.

I. PHENOMENA OF ATTRACTION.

16. All the smallest particles of matter attract each other mutually. This inherent power is, however, displayed in *three* ways, differing considerably from each other.

In the first case only those particles attract each other which are in immediate contact, a more or less powerful connexion being thereby established between them, whence this kind of attraction has received the name of *Cohesion.*

Secondly, we have to deal with the mutual attraction of particles, even when they are not in actual contact, and, indeed, when they are situated at a great distance from each other. This power is called *Gravitation* or *Gravity.*

By the third kind of attraction, which is termed chemical attraction, or *affinity*, the properties of the cohering particles are *altered;* these phenomena form a particular branch of natural science, termed *Chemistry.*

I. Cohesion.

17. A more or less powerful resistance is always met with in the endeavour to separate the particles of any substance from each other. We ascribe the adhesion of these particles with a certain strength to a peculiar kind of attraction, to which the name *Cohesion* has been given.

This power has been found, upon closer examination, to possess the peculiarity of being called into action only at *immeasurably small distances.*

If wood, metal, or glass be broken, the cohesive power is destroyed at the fractures, and cannot be restored, even if the two surfaces be placed close together very carefully. It is only with bodies the particles of which are exceedingly mobile, such as fluids, that the disjointed surfaces can come into sufficiently close contact to be made again to cohere.

The force with which the particles of a body cohere is entirely dependent upon heat, the existing cohesive force decreasing proportionately to the increase of temperature.

Assuming the entire matter composing the earth to be several thousand times hotter than boiling water, the attraction between the particles of matter would cease altogether. If, on the contrary, the temperature of the earth were a few thousand times less, all particles of matter would cohere so powerfully that it would be impossible to separate them by mechanical means.

The state of things at the ordinary temperature of our earth, however, is very different. Substances are met with, the particles of which can be separated only with difficulty; these are termed *solid* substances. Of others, the particles may be easily separated, or their position altered; such bodies are called *fluids.* Finally, there exists a class of bodies, whose particles are so far removed from each other by heat, that their cohesion appears to be entirely suspended; these are the *aëriform bodies*, or *gases.*

18. Next to heat, the *arrangement* of the particles of matter exerts its influence over the force of cohesion. Wood is known to be more easily cleavable lengthways than across the fibres; cast-steel is more brittle than wrought-steel.

Such expressions as are commonly used to denote the various degrees of cohesion, as hard, brittle, tough, soft, ductile, plastic, semi-fluid, fluid, &c., need no farther explanation.

It is of importance, for many purposes, to be able to compare the power with which various bodies maintain their cohesion. To attain this end, pieces of the substances, of equal length and thickness, are loaded with weights, which are gradually increased, until the bodies break. The cohesion is of course the greater the more weight that is required to overcome it.

Thus, for example, 120 lbs. are required to tear asunder an iron wire of $\frac{1}{25}$ inch diameter; wires of equal thickness, made of the following metals, require the weights mentioned with each to overcome the cohesion of their particles: bar iron 90 lbs., steel 60 to 80 lbs., cast-iron 28 lbs., brass wire 60 to 120 lbs., copper wire 42 lbs., lead wire 2½ lbs., glass tube, or rod, 5 lbs.

19. A great peculiarity in the cohesive force of bodies is its continual tendency to arrange the ultimate particles of matter with a certain regularity, so as to produce bodies limited by planes, edges, and angles, which we term *crystals*. Salt and sugar-candy are well-known examples of the result of this property.

There are a number of causes, and more particularly some other natural forces, that exert an influence adverse to the formation of crystals. Hereafter we shall make ourselves better acquainted with the conditions necessary for crystallisation.

20. If two smooth and even plates of glass or metal be laid upon each other, they will adhere together with a certain amount of force, so that the lower plate may be lifted up by means of the upper one.

Observation teaches us that, in general, when two bodies come in contact with each other, they will cohere with more or less force.

This phenomena is explained by the attraction exercised by the particles of the surface of the one body for those of the other body. This attraction increases in strength, therefore, in proportion to the number of particles that come into contact with each other. Indeed two balls that touch only at one point have no perceptible attraction for each other, while plates will adhere together with a strength increasing proportionately to the size and smoothness of their surfaces.

The attraction thus exercised on the surfaces of two different bodies is termed *adhesion*, and likewise exists only at infinitely small distances. This attractive force is not confined to solids alone, but is exercised between solid, fluid, and gaseous bodies, particularly air, which adheres with great obstinacy to the surface of solid bodies. The adhesion of fluids to solids is termed *wetting*. Painting, white-washing, pasting, glueing, cementing, &c., are instances of the application of adhesion to practical purposes.

21. On the other hand, it is remarkable that many fluids do not adhere either to solids or to other fluids. If a glass rod be dipped into water or oil, some particles of each liquid will adhere to it; this would not be the case with mercury. If the rod be coated with grease previously to immersion, no water will adhere, since oil and water do not mix. In fact, the oil and water, or the mercury and glass, not only appear to be devoid of this attraction, but to possess rather a repulsive force, which is ascribed to a particular power, termed *repulsion*. If, however, the mutual cohesion of the particles of water and oil be assumed as exceedingly great compared with the adhesive

power of the one liquid to the other, the above phenomena may be explained without the necessity of assuming any repulsive force.

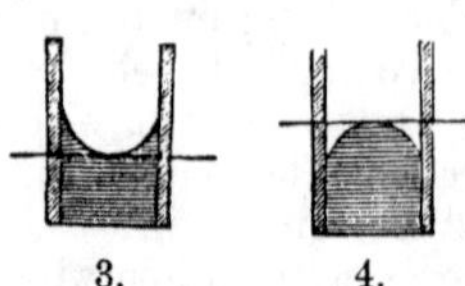
3. 4.

22. If, therefore, a glass tube be dipped into water, and another into mercury, the two liquids in the tubes will not exhibit perfectly plane surfaces; the water ascends the sides of the glass tube, by virtue of its attraction for the latter, a concave surface being thus produced, as shown in fig. 3; while the mercury, which possesses no attraction for the glass, forms a convex surface in the tube (fig. 4).

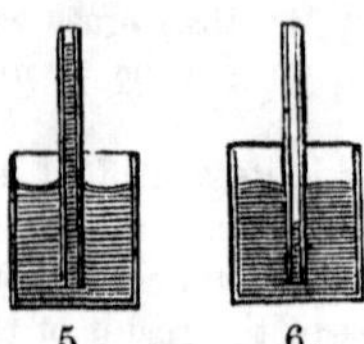
5. 6.

If this experiment be made with very narrow tubes, the water will not only rise at the sides, but in the entire tube; while the surface of the mercury inside the other tube will be lower than that of the mercury outside (figs. 5 and 6).

Very narrow tubes are called *hair* or *capillary* tubes, and the force with which fluids ascend these tubes is termed *capillary force.*

The narrower the capillary tubes, the higher fluids ascend in them, and it is immaterial of what substance they are, so long as the surface is moistened by the liquid employed. Hence porous bodies attract and retain fluids with great force, as the pores may be considered as an infinite number of irregularly aggregated capillary tubes.

Similar phenomena are exhibited by white sugar, wood, sandstone, or even a heap of sand or ashes. Walls and porous stones that are situated on damp ground always remain damp. A heap of dry sand under the same circumstances will become rapidly saturated with water to the very top. . The property of lamp-wicks and filtering-paper of absorbing oil and water, and a number of other phenomena, may be explained by the same kind of attraction.

II. Gravity (Gravitation).

23. Gravity is the mutual attraction between different portions of matter, which acts at all distances, and the force of which corresponds to the mass of the attracting bodies.

Let us suppose the two balls A and B (fig. 7) which are of equal magnitude,

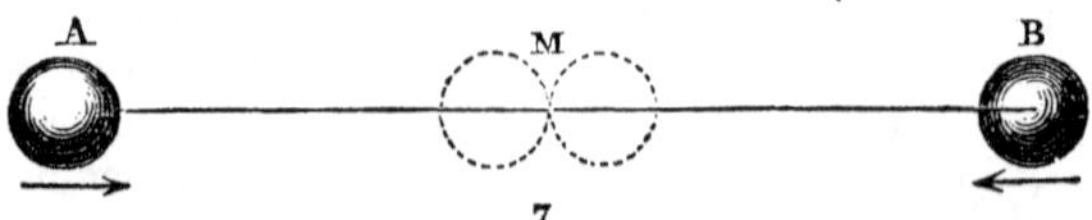

7.

and therefore attract each other with equal force, unless influenced by any other opposing force, it is evident that both balls, following their attraction, will approach each other with equal velocity until they come in contact at the point M, which is exactly in the centre of their original distance. But if, as in fig. 8, the ball B is as large again as A, the attraction that B exercises towards A will be double that which A exercises towards B; and as the two balls approach, A will advance with double the velocity of B, and consequently pass over double the distance. Both balls must therefore mee at the point D, which is situated at one-third of the entire distance. We thus see that the smaller ball passes over the greater distance, and this is

8.

even more evident when the difference in the size of the two balls is still greater, as in fig. 9, where A is supposed to equal 1, and B equal 100.

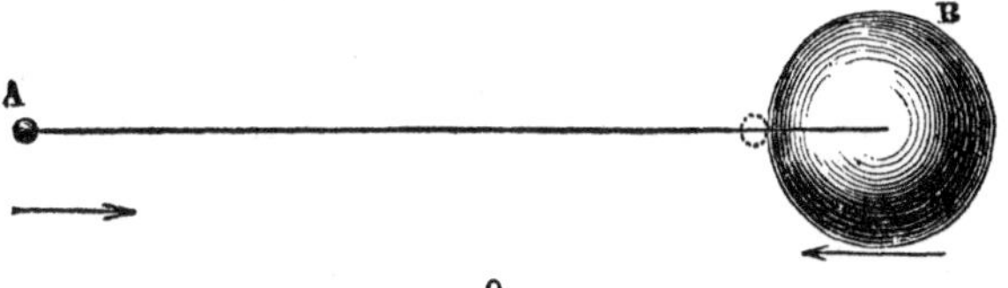

9.

In this case the motion of B is so small that it apparently remains at rest while the smaller ball A advances with great velocity to the greater ball. This affords us an explanation of one of the most common phenomena, namely, the *falling* of bodies, since all bodies existing on the surface of the earth are comparatively exceedingly small, and are attracted by it with considerable force. Hence, gravity is the cause of the *falling* of bodies, and observation has shown that when the time a body occupies in falling amounts to a second, it passes through a space of 16 feet.

If a heavy body, for example, a leaden bullet, be suspended to a thread, it will certainly not be able to fall, but will draw the thread in a position which indicates the direction of gravitation (fig. 10). This position is termed *vertical*, and the simple instrument which serves to indicate it is called a plummet. The direction which intersects the vertical line at right angles is called the *horizontal* direction. The surface of water when at rest is always in a horizontal position.

10.

24. If we suppose the direction which a plummet takes to be prolonged, we obtain a line extending to the centre of the earth, and as this is the same at every point of the earth's surface, the entire attraction of the earth E (fig. 11) appears to be concentrated at the centre c. Every object on the surface of the earth is, therefore, situated from the centre of gravity at a distance equal to the radius r of the earth, and is there attracted with a force producing a velocity in falling bodies of 16 feet in a second. The attraction is not equal at greater distances from the earth,

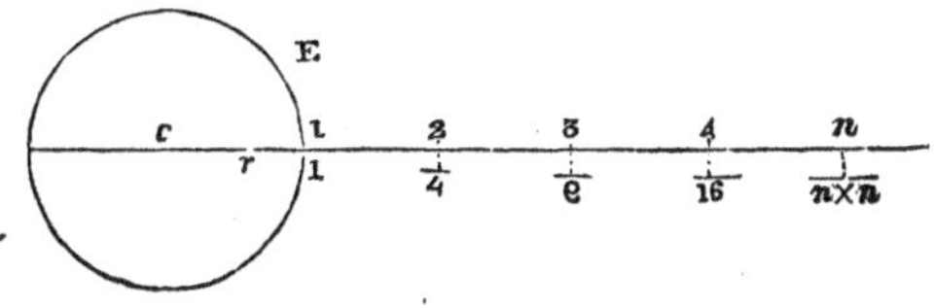

11.

but becomes weaker in proportion to the distance of the body attracted, from the centre of the earth. This decrease in the force of gravity follows a particular law, which may be expressed as follows: the force of gravity in the distance 1 from the centre of the earth being represented by the space of 16 feet, two is equal to $\frac{16}{4}$, three to $\frac{16}{9}$, and four equal to $\frac{16}{16}$, &c. The force of gravity at any distance from the earth may be expressed by a fraction whose numerator is 16, and the denominator of which is obtained by multiplying the number of the distance by itself; or, more shortly, *the gravity decreases in proportion to the square of the distance.*

It may now be imagined that, on very high mountains, the space through which a body is carried in a second, by the force of gravity, would be less than 16 feet. But the highest mountains on the face of the earth are too small in size when compared to the latter, to have any perceptible influence over the velocity of motion resulting from the force of gravity.

25. As gravity has equal influence over one particle of matter as over several together, all bodies must fall with equal velocity, however large or small they may be.

A piece of paper, a feather, or a straw, are, however, observed to fall less rapidly than a stone or a leaden bullet: the only reason of this is the greater resistance of the air against the former; if, therefore, the above-named bodies were to be placed in a *vacuum* and allowed to fall, they would all do so with equal velocity.

26. The motion of a falling body is continually accelerated; for if we assume a body to receive, through the force of gravity, a certain velocity for a particular period, it will retain this velocity unaltered for every succeeding period, even if gravity had no longer any influence over it. We know, however, that the latter continues to exercise its force and to increase the velocity of the motion unceasingly. If, therefore, a body falls 16 feet in the first second, the distance it travels in the first half of that time must necessarily be less than that which it describes in the second half, and at the end of the second the velocity of its motion must be greater than at any preceding time. Hence it follows that a body must attain a rapidly increasing velocity for every succeeding second that it falls; according to a law established by calculation as well as observation the space through which a body falls in a certain number of seconds may be found by squaring the number of seconds, and multiplying the result by 16. The law of falling bodies must therefore be expressed thus: *the space through which a body falls increases in proportion to the square of the time it occupies in falling.*

If a stone be thrown into a well, and four seconds elapse before it is heard to touch the bottom, the depth of the well will be $4 \times 4 \times 16 = 256$ feet.

The Pendulum.

27. A heavy body, such as a ball or disc of metal, fastened to the end of a string, represents a pendulum.

If we bring the pendulum from its vertical position or equilibrium, *f l*, fig. 12, so that the ball be situated at *b*, and then leave it to itself, it will fall to the point *l*, and then rise on the opposite side to *a*, which is situated, almost imperceptibly, lower than *b*. When the ball has arrived at *a* it will again fall, and rise once more on the other side, without, however, reaching exactly to the point *b*; and thus the motion, which is termed the oscillation of the pendulum, will continue, each oscillation being slightly less than the preceding one, until at last the pendulum will be once more at rest. More accurate observation shows that oscillations of the pendulum are dependent upon gravity, and are only slightly changed motions of falling. Attracted by the earth, on the one side to *b*, and on the other side maintained in one unchangeable distance from the point of suspension by the thread, it is drawn by these two forces in a circular course, in which the pendulum, according to the law enunciated at § 26, falls with increasing velocity towards the lowest point *l*. The pendulum would remain at rest in the position *f l*, which is the direction of gravity, if it had not acquired a certain velocity by falling from *b* to *l*. With this velocity, continually diminishing by the influence of gravity, it now rises on the other side, until it is overcome, when the pendulum again begins to fall from the point *a*. Were it not for the friction at the point of suspension, and the resistance of the atmosphere, which together bring it at last to rest, the oscillations of the pendulum would continue for ever.

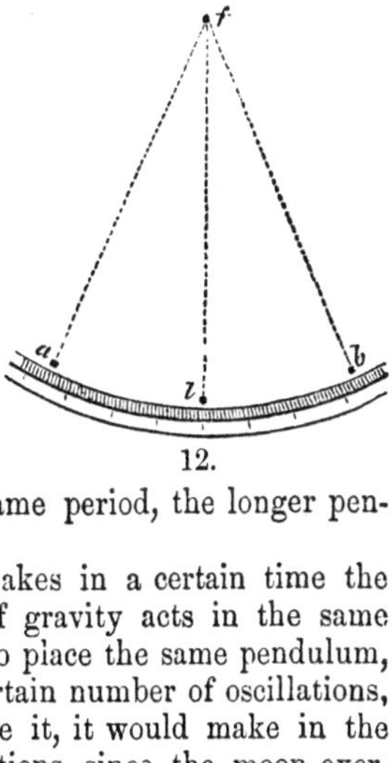

Some laws concerning the oscillations of the pendulum have been deduced, of which the most important points are expressed in the following:—

(1.) The single oscillations of one and the same pendulum are of *equal duration*, whether the rise be greater or smaller, supposing that the arc *a b* does not amount to more than five degrees.

(2.) Two pendulums of equal length perform an equal number of oscillations in the same period.

12.

(3.) Two pendulums of unequal length perform an unequal number of oscillations in the same period, the longer pendulum performing the smallest number.

(4.) One and the same pendulum always makes in a certain time the same number of oscillations, when the force of gravity acts in the same manner and with equal power. If we were able to place the same pendulum, which on the earth makes in a definite time a certain number of oscillations, upon the moon and the sun, and there observe it, it would make in the former fewer and in the latter many more oscillations, since the moon exercises fifty times less, and the sun nearly one and a half million times greater, attraction than the earth.

28. These laws have led to applications of this simple instrument, which render it one of great importance. In the first place, the pendulum serves in clocks to rectify the unequal motion which is produced either by weights or springs, and likewise to furnish a measure of definite and unalterable length.

29. The *seconds' pendulum* is one that describes exactly sixty oscillations in one minute, each oscillation having the duration of a second. It is obvious, from what has just now been stated, that this pendulum must be of a certain length; for if it were too short it would describe more than sixty oscillations in a minute, and a smaller number if it were longer.

Hence the seconds' pendulum of any particular place may be used as a certain, invariable measure of length. In Paris this pendulum must have exactly the length of three Parisian feet and eight lines. It is, therefore, only two and two-thirds lines shorter than the meter. In London the length of the seconds' pendulum is 39·13929 inches.

30. The observation that one and the same seconds' pendulum did not perform an equal number of oscillations in one minute at all parts of the surface of the earth, created a great deal of surprise amongst philosophers. On taking the Parisian seconds' pendulum, three feet eight lines in length, to the equator, for instance, it was found to perform a smaller number of oscillations than sixty in one minute, whereas, in the neighbourhood of the North Pole, it performed a larger number.

As the movements of the pendulum are dependent on the force of gravity, and as the latter force decreases (§ 24) as the distance from the centre of the earth increases, the observations with the pendulum led to the conclusion, that a point at the equator must be more distant from the centre of the earth than a point at the poles. Hence the earth can be no perfect sphere, but appears to be somewhat depressed at the poles, as shown at fig. 13. The diameter of the earth at the equator is 7935 miles, at the poles it is only 7900 miles. The centrifugal force which the earth receives from its revolutions, likewise contributes to the decreasing of the oscillations of the pendulum at the equator.

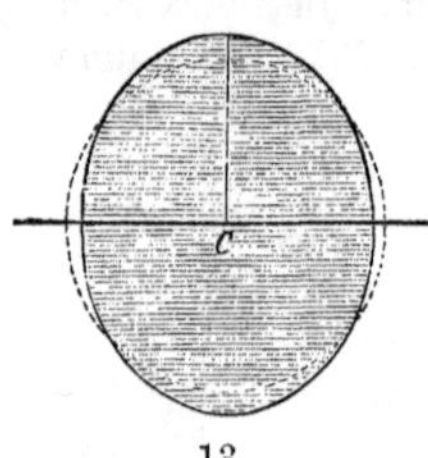

13.

Weight.

31. As every particle of a body is attracted by the earth, it must necessarily exercise a certain amount of pressure upon any support on which it may be placed. The total pressure of all the particles of a body on its *horizontal* support is termed its *weight.* Hence the greater the *mass* of a body (*i. e.* the larger the number of particles of which it consists) the greater is its weight.

The masses or weights of two bodies may be compared by suspending them to the two ends of an equal-armed lever. If the latter remains in equilibrium, the weight of the two bodies is equal. If the two weights are unequal, the heavier one is denoted by an inclination downwards of that arm to which it is suspended.

An arrangement of this description for the comparison of weights is termed a *balance.*

32. By *weights* are also meant the various units of masses, employed in different countries to weigh with, *i. e.* to determine and express the masses of bodies in general.

The *gramme* (15½ grains) is the comparative unit of weight most generally employed in scientific researches. It is represented accurately by the amount of water, at a temperature of 4° C. (39·2 F.), required to fill a vessel in the form of a cube, whose sides are one centimeter (0·39 inch) in length, and which, therefore, contains one cubic centimeter (0·061 cubic inch) of water.

If, therefore, a certain substance is said to weigh 80 grammes, we mean thereby, that if it be placed in one pan of a balance, 80 cubic centimeters of water will be required in the other pan to maintain it in equilibrium. It is obviously far more convenient to substitute for the water small pieces of metal, each of which corresponds exactly to one cubic centimeter of the former.

33. The general unit of weight in commerce is the pound. It would be exceedingly convenient if this weight were equal in all countries: this is, however, by no means the case, as will be seen by the following table:—

1 pound is equal	to	453	grammes in	England.
1 kilogramme	"	1000	"	France.
1 pound	"	560	"	Austria and Bavaria.
1 "	"	500	"	Hesse Darmstadt and Baden. This is the pound adopted by the German Zollverein.
1 "	"	484	"	Hamburg.
1 "	"	467	"	Prussia, Saxony, Hanover, Wurtemberg, Electorate of Hesse, Brunswick, and Frankfort-on-the-Maine. This pound is also called the *Cologne* light pound.

Density.

34. It might be expected that, on placing a cubic inch of water in one pan of a balance and a cubic inch of lead in the other, these two substances would hold each other in equilibrium, their masses being of equal extent. This, however, is well known not to be the case; indeed, as many as 11 cubic inches of water are required to retain one cubic inch of lead in equilibrium. If mercury were substituted for lead, 13 cubic inches of water would be required; and one cubic inch of gold would even require 19 cubic inches of water to maintain it in equilibrium.

If the same experiment be made with one cubic inch of water and the same quantity of alcohol, it will be found, on the contrary, that the quantity of spirit must be increased, or that of the water diminished, in order to obtain equilibrium. Oil of turpentine, poppy-oil, and other oils, stand to water in a similar relation.

These facts clearly prove that different bodies contain a different number of atoms in an equal space. This may be easily imagined, if we conceive the atoms to be placed more or less closely together. One cubic inch of lead contains undoubtedly eleven times the mass of one cubic inch of water, and, therefore, weighs eleven times as much as the latter. Turpentine and other oils are, on the contrary, not so heavy as water.

The densities of most fluids and solid bodies have been compared with that of water; and the number expressing the amount that one cubic inch of a body is heavier or lighter than the same amount of water, is called the density or the *specific gravity* of the body. The following are the specific gravities of a few well-known bodies:—

Substance.	Specific Gravity.	Substance.	Specific Gravity.	Substance.	Specific Gravity.
Cork	0·24	Milk	1·030	Chromium	5·900
Poplar wood	0·38	Oak wood	1·170	Antimony	6·712
Lime-tree wood	0·439	Phosphorus	1·770	Zinc	7·037
Pine wood	0·555	Sulphuric acid	1·848	Iron (wrought)	7·788
Nut-tree wood	0·677	Ivory	1·917	Steel	7·816
Ether	0·713	Sulphur	2·03	Copper (wrought)	8·878
Alcohol	0·793	Quartz	2·6	Bismuth	9·820
Oil of Turpentine	0·872	Basalt	2·66	Silver	10·474
Poppy oil	0·929	Bottle-glass	2·60	Lead	11·852
Ice	0·916	Granite	2·80	Mercury	13·598
Water	1·000	Diamond	3·52	Gold	19·325
Sea-water	1·026	Heavy spar	4·426	Platinum	22·100

35. The advantage to be derived from a knowledge of the above numbers may be easily proved.

For instance, as every substance invariably possesses a uniform density under equal conditions, we arrive at one of the most important means of recognising a body. In purchasing pure silver, each cubic inch should weigh 5·237 ounces. Should its density be less, the silver may be assumed to contain copper; if it be greater, lead may be present. If a structure of oak weighs 1,170 lbs., a similar one, of exactly the same cubic contents, made of deal, would weigh only 555 lbs. A bottle, capable of containing 10 lbs. of water, will hold 18 lbs. of sulphuric acid, the latter being nearly twice as heavy as the former.

In every-day language those bodies are termed *light* that occupy a comparatively large space and contain a small amount of mass, as, for instance, cork, and several other substances.

Air is far lighter than all solid and liquid bodies. It will be seen hereafter in what manner the density of gaseous bodies is determined.

III. Equilibrium and Motion.

36. A body is said to be in *motion* when it occupies different positions at different times. It must thus continually change its place in relation to surrounding objects, and this enables us to recognise the motion. The hand of the clock traverses from number to number, the ship passes by valleys and hills, the railway train hurries through town and country;—these bodies are in motion, since we observe that they pass by neighbouring objects, and approach those which are in the distance.

On the other hand, the mighty mountain appears to us fixed and motionless, the mass of a building immovable, and the tree firmly rooted in the ground. This motionless condition of a body and its members remaining always at the same distance from surrounding objects we call *rest*.

37. From what has been said, it is essential to the perception of motion that certain objects should appear as being at rest: because if all objects were moving at the same velocity, they would all appear to be at rest, since their relative position would remain unchanged, as we perceive by gazing at the star-bespangled heavens, the mountains, forests, and towns, on the surface of the earth.

But observation teaches us that all the heavenly bodies, even the fixed stars, which by reason of their inconceivable distance appear to us as being motionless, are in perpetual movement, and we may with safety assume that not a single particle of the universe is ever at perfect rest. We know by the daily rotation of the earth, that mountains, forests, and cities, participate in this motion.

There is hence no *absolute*, but only *relative* rest. When travelling in a vessel, our bodies, in relation to objects immediately surrounding us, as the masts, tables, and chairs, may be at rest, whilst a single glance at the objects on the shore, which one by one disappear from our view, convinces us that the vessel and all it contains are in rapid motion.

38. If we inquire into the causes of motion, they are numerous. The force of gravity is the only, or at least the co-operating cause of most phenomena of motion. Other moving powers are electric and magnetic attrac-

tion, the influence of heat, and finally that power by means of which men and animals are enabled to set in motion not only their own bodies, but also other objects, and which cause the peculiar vital phenomena in plants and animals. But, for the general consideration of the laws of motion, it is quite immaterial on which cause these motions depend.

39. As the first and most important law of the science of motion, or *mechanics* of inanimate matter, is the following:—

1. *A body at rest cannot impart motion to itself.*

2. *A body in motion cannot by itself change or annihilate this condition of motion.*

Both these principles convey a more accurate expression of the *inertia* of matter, already alluded to in § 9.

40. If any body be set in motion, it would, according to the second principle, continue the motion imparted to it unimpaired *ad infinitum*, as is actually the case with the heavenly bodies. But within the sphere of the earth's influence, we cannot impart to any object such a continuous motion. If, for example, we fire a ball, with the strongest charge of powder, into the air, or roll it over a smooth surface of ice with a velocity the eye can scarcely follow, its motion will become gradually slower, and at last cease altogether. In both cases the ball does not of itself come to a state of rest, but there are other forces, such as the resistance of the air and the attraction of the earth, which put an end to the motion.

41. In the farther consideration of motion, we have first to consider its relation to space and time, namely, its *direction* and *velocity*.

The distance from the point at which the motion of a body begins to that where it ceases, is termed its way, or course, and the line which indicates this way is called its *direction*. This is either a continually unchanged *straight* line, or it is a *crooked* line. The circular motion which the points of a body describe around itself is called *rotation*.

42. By a comparison of the distance with the time which the body requires to describe it, we arrive at the *velocity* of motion.

There is a great variety in the degrees of velocity. For instance, the minute-hand of a watch describes the same distance in one hour which the hour-hand accomplishes in twelve. In one second a snail travels one line, a rapid runner 25 feet, a race-horse 50 feet, a gale of wind 124 feet, a cannon-ball 600 feet, sound 1000 feet, and light 195,000 miles.

43. The velocity of *molecular motion* is inappreciable. We often find that the individual particles of a body describe a distance so exceedingly small, that we are not enabled to take cognizance of their motion, although we perceive the changes in the object which are the result of this motion. This occurs when a body is expanded or contracted by the influence of heat, by crystallization, by chemical combinations, and by the development of plants and animals. As the smallest particles of bodies are termed *molecules*, the force extending only to those particles which are in immediate proximity and acting at immeasurably small distances, has received the name of *molecular force*.

44. Investigation teaches us that velocity is either *equal* or *unequal*.

In the case of equal velocity, the same distance is traversed in the same space of time, be the space ever so small. If, therefore, a body traverses a mile in one hour, it must traverse the sixtieth part of a mile in a minute, and the three thousand six hundredth part of a mile in a second.

Equal motion requires that the moving body be under the influence of a continuous moving power, which accurately counterbalances opposing forces, so that the original velocity remains unchanged.

The velocity of a body in motion is said to be *unequal* if it increases or decreases at every consecutive moment; hence in the first case it is called *increased* or *accelerated*, and in the second *decreased* or *retarded* velocity.

Accelerated velocity occurs when, on a body already in motion, a force acts continually in the same direction, as in the case of falling bodies (§ 26), and the descending pendulum (§ 27). In the case of retarded motion, a force continually opposes the body in motion, for example, as the force of gravity opposes the motion of a stone when thrown into the air, and that of the rising pendulum.

45. From what has been said, it follows that a body which moves with accelerated velocity during one minute, has in the second second of time a greater velocity than in the first, and in the third second greater than in the second second, &c. If at any part of the time that the body is in motion the accelerating force ceases to act, the body continues its motion uniformly with that velocity which it had at the moment of interruption, and which is called its *final velocity*. On the other hand, we understand by the term *mean velocity*, that velocity which a body would have if we suppose the accelerating power to be removed exactly in half the time the body is in motion. If a body fall during the space of a second, it attains a final velocity of thirty-two feet, and its mean velocity is sixteen feet. If it had had this latter velocity at first, and had continued it *uniformly*, it would have described the same distance in one second, as the body falling with accelerated motion would have traversed in the same space of time, namely, sixteen feet.

46. The power of a force is shown by its action. Let us suppose a strong strip of elastic steel, similar to those which are employed for cross-bows: the farther the force is capable of bending the steel, the greater will be its power. Indeed, elastic metallic strips are employed in the manufacture of *dynamometers*, by means of which various powers may be compared, as, for example, that of men and horses, with weights. We also frequently judge of power by the weight of a mass which is lifted or moved. But in the latter case we must also take into consideration the velocity, two forces being equal if they impart to corresponding masses the same velocity, or if the masses are in an inverse ratio to the velocity imparted to them. This is the case when the numbers obtained by multiplying each mass with its velocity are equal: for example, a mass represented by 4 has a velocity 2, and the mass 2 has the velocity 4. In both cases the product of multiplication = 8. The product obtained by multiplying the mass of a body, which is moved, by its velocity, is generally called its *momentum*.

If a body in motion come in contact with another, a *blow* is the result. Thus numerous phenomena may arise, according to the substance, the size, the direction, and the velocity of the bodies in question. It may in general be said that soft unelastic substances receive a permanent, and elastic bodies only a transitory flattening, and that a blow exercises its entire force only when directed against the centre of gravity of the object which is struck.

The behaviour of hard bodies when struck may be exhibited in a very beautiful manner with balls of ivory suspended by threads.

47. If a body in motion come in contact with a second body of equal size at rest, the motion of the first will cease completely, while the second body will move with a velocity equal to that of the first. If the mass of the body at rest be larger than that of the one originally in motion, the velocity imparted to the former will be less than that possessed by the latter, and *vice versâ*. A large mass, moving with a small degree of velocity, will, therefore, impart to a small mass a high degree of velocity, and, on the other hand, a very small ball, moving with extraordinary velocity, will, if it meet with a large ball, scarcely set it in motion.

Such small bodies are hailstones and shot, which acquire their destructive properties solely from the velocity with which they travel.

If an object fall perpendicularly upon a plane *s s'* (fig. 14), it will, in consequence of the mutual elasticity, rebound in the same direction; but, on the other hand, if the blow takes place at an acute angle *r l*, the striking object will rebound at an equal angle *l d*. A practical application of this is frequently seen in playing at billiards, and in the ricochet firing of artillery.

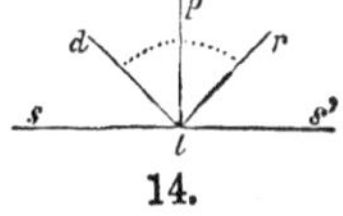

14.

48. Motion is not imparted simultaneously to every particle of a body, but at first only to the particles which are directly exposed to the influence of the force, for instance, of a blow. From these particles it spreads to the rest. A slight blow is sufficient to smash a whole window-pane, while a shot from a gun will only make a small round hole in it, because in the latter case the particles of glass that receive the blow are torn away from the remainder with such rapidity, that the motion imparted to them has no time to spread any farther.

On this also depends the method of fastening a hammer upon its handle, by knocking the latter on the ground, and the well-known trick of placing a small coin on a ring perpendicularly over the mouth of a bottle (fig. 15). If the ring be rapidly pushed from under it, the coin will fall into the bottle.

15.

49. If several forces act simultaneously upon an object, without producing the slightest change in its condition, their actions completely neutralize each other, and in this case the forces are said to *maintain each other in equilibrium*, or in other words, the body is in equilibrium. In this case it is perfectly indifferent whether the body be in a state of rest or in motion. If a locomotive engine, proceeding at a uniform rate, arrive at an ascent, and its steam-power is increased at a rate corresponding to this impediment, the engine continues its way at its previous speed, — both powers being, as it were, not in existence, since they maintain each other in equilibrium.

We must, however, distinguish this *equilibrium of forces* from the equilibrium of bodies,—that is, the position which solid, liquid, and gaseous bodies assume under the influence of gravity, and to which we shall refer at a subsequent page.

50. If two or more forces, not in equilibrium with each other, are brought to bear upon one body, a motion will be imparted to it. It must be borne

in mind that a body always moves in *one* direction only, whatever may be the number of forces that are brought into operation.

This point may be most easily comprehended by assuming a body to be under the influence of *two* forces. In this case, the body does not move in the direction of either force, but in one that lies between these two directions. This kind of motion is termed *compound*, and the line which indicates the direction of this motion is termed the *mean* or *resultant*.

The *resultant* of two forces is easily found. In fig. 16 we have two forces acting simultaneously on the point *a* in two directions, *a x* and *a y*. The lines *a b* and *a c* represent the directions and distances which the body would have travelled under the influence of each separate force. Let the lines *c r* and *b r* be drawn from the terminating points *c* and *b*, parallel to the direction of the forces. The line from the point *r*, where the two lines intersect each other, to *a*, is the mean or resultant of the forces *a b* and *a c*, and denotes not only the direction of the force, but also the distance described by the body under its influence.

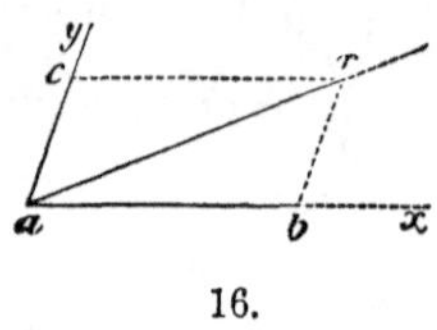

16.

Figure 17 furnishes us with an illustration of this compound motion. A ship urged obliquely across a river from A to B by the action of wind and

17.

rudder, is propelled, however, by the stream from A to C. If the two parallels B D and C D be drawn, the line A D denotes the direction and distance which the vessel really describes.

From these examples, it will be seen that by this process a parallelogram is each time formed by the given lines which represent the forces, the diagonal of which is the mean; hence it is also called the *parallelogram of forces.*

The point to which a body arrives, under the influence of two forces, may also be found by dividing the time during which they act into two equal parts, and by assuming that in the first half of the time one force exclusively acts, and in the second half the other force only is in operation. It will be readily seen that each given force may be substituted or decomposed by two other forces acting in a suitable manner. If, as in fig. 16, the two forces *c a* and *b a* may be substituted by their mean *r a*, it follows, on the other hand, that if the force *r a* be given, its action might be substituted by the two forces *c a* and *b a*.

51. Curvilinear motions generally arise if several forces act on a body

simultaneously and continuously. As, for instance, a body propelled with a certain velocity, in a horizontal direction, is simultaneously acted upon by the force which moves it in this direction, and by gravity, which draws it vertically to the earth. The course resulting from these forces is *curvilinear*, and deviates more or less from the horizontal direction, according to the ratio in which the two forces stand to each other.

It is well known that a marksman who fires at a distant object, aims rather higher, to counteract the influence of gravity upon the ball.

52. If a blow be given to a ball, *m*, fig. 18, suspended to a thread, it would move in a horizontal direction if it were not attached to the thread and drawn by the latter towards the point *c*. The resulting motion of the ball will be circular.

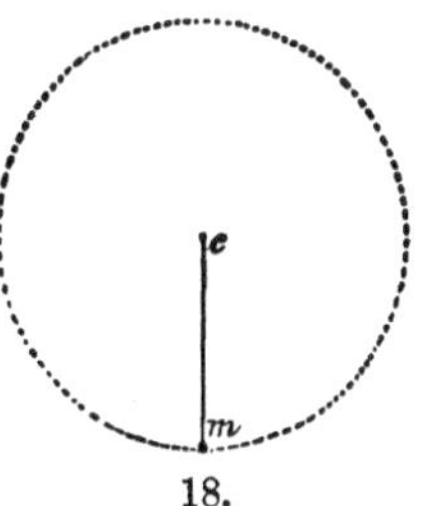

18.

It is obvious that if any other force, in place of the thread, attract *m* continually to *c*, the result will be always a similar circular motion.

The force that acts towards the central point *c* may be termed *centripetal*, and that which exerts its influence at right angles with the latter, the *tangential force*. The line of motion described by a body under the simultaneous influence of these two forces is obviously dependent on their mutual relation. In circular motion, the following is the relation between the forces: the square of the tangential velocity must be equal to the diameter of the circle multiplied by the central velocity. If the first product were greater than the second, the resulting curved motion would not be circular but *elliptic;* if it were exactly twice as great as the second product, the motion would be *parabolic;* and if the first product were even larger still, the body in motion would describe a *hyperbola.* These are all different forms of curved motion, which will be more minutely described at a future period.

The most stupendous examples of these various kinds of motion are afforded us by the paths described by the celestial bodies. Thus the moon is always under the simultaneous influence of two forces, namely, the attractive force of the earth, and a second acting at right angles to the former and propelling the moon at the rate of about 200,000 feet in one minute. If the attractive force of the earth were alone active, the moon would approach it, in a vertical direction, 15 feet in the above space of time. The resultants of *both* forces is the elliptical path which the moon describes.

53. The science that treats of the celestial bodies and their motions is called *Astronomy.* It is, properly speaking, a branch of Physics; but the great number and high importance of astronomical phenomena render it, however, necessary to devote a special section of this work to their consideration.

54. In the case of the *oblique plane*, it is necessary to resolve one force into two others (§ 50). But before we investigate this subject, some preliminary remarks are necessary.

It has been stated in § 31 that the pressure a body exercises upon a *horizontal* plane, in consequence of gravity, is called the *weight* of that body. If in this case we move the object, it is by no means its weight that we have to overcome, as this is supported by the horizontal plane, but only the friction of the object on the plane, and the smoother the two surfaces the smaller the friction will be. In the following observations we shall entirely disregard the friction, and assume that it is of no influence, but which never in reality is the fact. In this case even a very small force must be sufficient to move a body, the weight of which is borne by its support.

The small weight G, for example, may be just sufficient to move the body L (fig. 19), upon the plane A B, on which the line *a b* represents the entire pressure which L exercises upon A B. But if we give this plane the inclined position represented in fig. 20, the weight G is by no means sufficient to move the object L in the direction A B. The object will, on the contrary, slide down in the opposite direction towards A, exactly as if a force

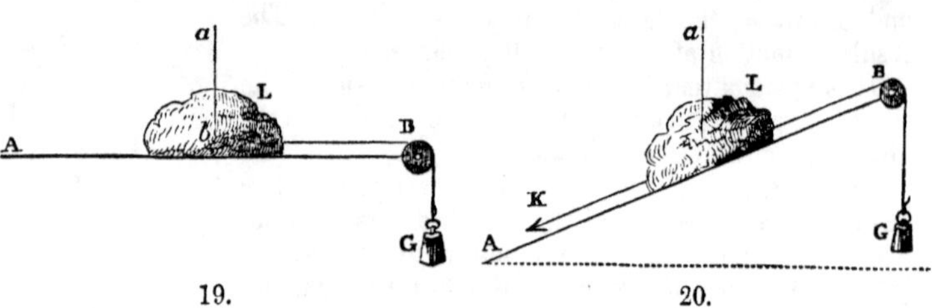

19. 20.

at K drew it down in a direction parallel to the plane. From this it follows that the plane no longer sustains the entire weight of the object, and that, consequently, the pressure which it bears must no longer be represented by the line *a b*, but by one that is shorter. But as the body remains intact, and has lost nothing of its weight, it is clear that that portion of its weight which no longer acts as pressure upon the plane manifests itself as a force which pulls down the object in a direction parallel to the plane.

The force *a b* with which the body L presses upon the horizontal plane A B (fig. 19), is, therefore, in the case of the oblique plane A B (fig. 21), resolved into two forces, namely, into the force *a c*, which acts as a vertical pressure upon A B, and into the force *c b*, which is directed downwards parallel to A B.

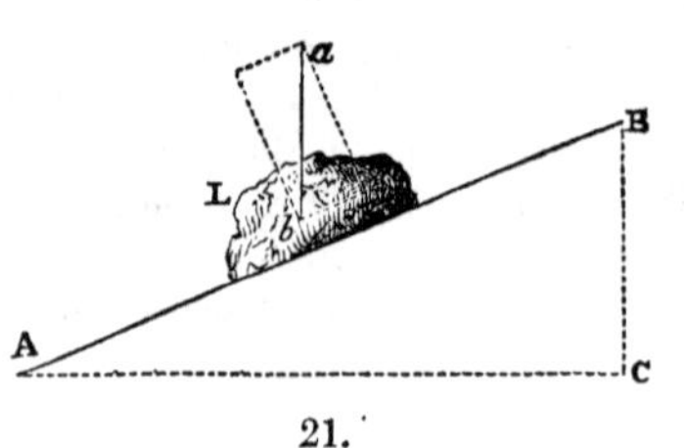

21.

If we call A B the length and B C the height of the inclined plane A B, it can be proved by the laws of geometry, from the similarity of the triangles *a b c* and A B C that the downward propelling force *b c* is in the same proportion to the weight of the body *a b* as the height B C of the inclined plane is to its length A B. If, therefore, the height B C be the fourth, fifth, or sixth part of the length A B, the force *b c* will be equal to the fourth, fifth, or sixth part of the weight of the body.

55. The application of the laws of the inclined plane is seen in the lifting of heavy weights to a certain height, in ascending and descending mountains, in architecture, &c., and the facility thus afforded is the greater the less the height is in comparison with the length, or, as it is generally expressed, the smaller the *incline*, which ought not to exceed 5 per cent. in roads and ⅓rd of a per cent. in railways.

Besides the inclined plane has found application in a number of our instruments and tools. The blades of knives, chisels, and axes consist of two inclined planes joined together, as is also the case with the *Wedge.*

An inclined plane wound round a cylinder is termed a *Screw.* Gimlet corkscrews, the Archimedean screw, and the screw that has lately been applied in propelling steam-vessels, are all applications of the inclined plane. The more minute examination of these screws belongs to *Mechanics.*

56. If a ball, *m*, attached to a thread, be set in rapid circular motion round the central point *c*, and the thread be then suddenly severed, the ball will fly off from the central point. The direction taken by the ball is described by a line, the position of which is at right angles to the direction of the thread at the moment when the ball flies off. If, for instance, the ball be situated just at the point *m* when it flies off, it will move in the direction *m x*.

22.

The velocity with which the ball moves, on being detached from the thread, is in direct ratio to the velocity of the original circular motion.

This force is often made use of by children in throwing balls attached to a string to a great height.

A still more general application of this phenomenon is seen in bodies which *rotate*, or in other words, turn on their own axes. In this case all those parts of such a body, which do not lie in its axis, describe circles round it, and acquire a tendency to fly off from the axis, which is called *centrifugal force.* As in such rotations all particles describe their way round the axis in the *same time*, the particles farthest distant must have a greater velocity, and consequently a stronger centrifugal tendency than those which are nearer to the axis. Such a body is the *earth*, which rotates round an axis, the terminating points of which are called the *poles.* Hence it follows that those portions of the earth which are situated near the equator must possess a greater centrifugal force than those which are nearer to the poles.

The action of the centrifugal force can be manifested only when it is greater than the cohesion of the rotating body, particularly, therefore, in those the mass of which is soft, or which possesses movable particles. By means of the *centrifugal machine* (fig. 23), a series of beautiful experiments may be made to illustrate these facts, and the cause of the flattening of the earth in particular may be shown by an elastic brass hoop *a b*. (Comp. § 30.)

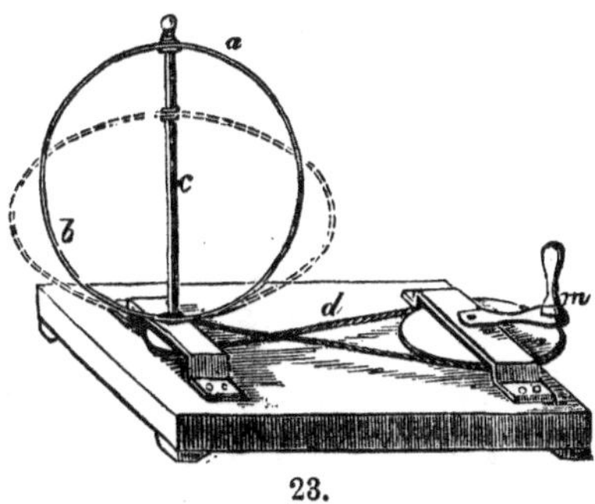

23.

PARALLEL FORCES.

57. We meet with a series of interesting phenomena which are of particular practical importance in investigating the results which take place when parallel forces act upon a body.

The forces employed in the following examples are weights, which act in the first place at right angles upon a straight and inflexible line. We use for this purpose a rod, which is suspended by its centre c (fig. 24). The action of the force is best represented if we leave out of consideration the influence of gravity upon the rod, and this is counterbalanced by fastening to the string passing over a pulley a weight a, equal to that of the rod. We call the horizontal position which the rod now has the *position of equilibrium*, and the point to which it is fastened its *fulcrum*.

24.

If we allow the two forces b b to act at equal distances from the fulcrum, they will, of course, draw down the rod with a power equal to $2\,b$. But this effect will be completely neutralized if we allow a weight equal to $2\,b$ to act on the other side of the pulley in an opposite direction. Neither the horizontal position of the rod, nor its situation, suffers the slightest change, hence the forces acting upon it are in perfect equilibrium. The same will be the case if we now allow the two forces b and b to act on the centre of the rod.

From these experiments we draw the following important conclusions:—

(1.) The effect of two equal forces upon a line is neutralized by a force equal to their sum, acting at the centre in an opposite direction.

(2.) The effect of two equal forces, acting on a line, may be substituted by a force equal to their sum acting at their common centre.

(3.) Two equal forces, acting at corresponding distances from the fulcrum, maintain each other in equilibrium.

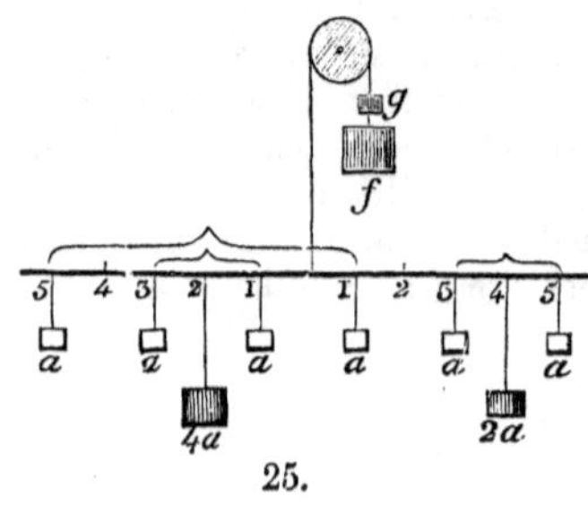

25.

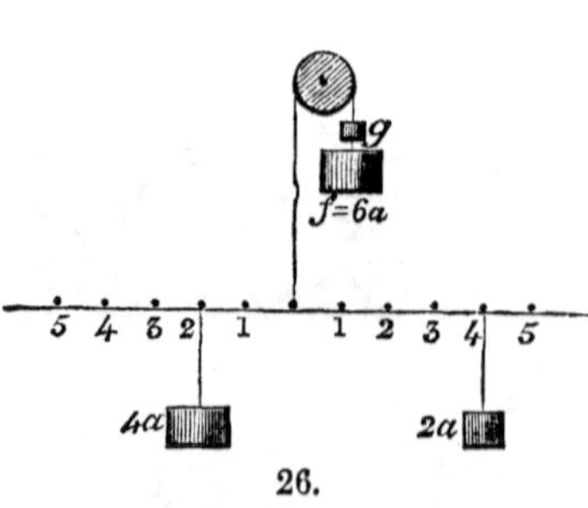

26.

58. Figure 25 represents another rod, the weight of which is counterbalanced by the weight g. The six equal and parallel forces a act at equal distances upon the different points, and are counterbalanced by the weight f, which is equal to $6\,a$.

Without destroying the equilibrium of this arrangement in the slightest degree, the weights 3 and 5 may be removed from the one side, and combined in the central point at 4 (according to § 57, 2). In like manner the weights 1 on the one side, and 5 on the other side, together with 1 and 3 on the one side of the rod, may be combined at their mutual central point 2, from which, therefore, $4\,a$ are suspended.

We will now take into consideration figure 26. The weights with which the rod is loaded, and their distances from its central point, are unequal, and yet the whole is in equilibrium.

It will, however, be observed, directly on examining the figure, that the smaller force $2\,a$ acts at a distance of 4 from the central point, while the larger force $4\,a$ only acts at the distance 2. The distances 4 and 2 bear an inverse ratio to the forces $2\,a$ and $4\,a$.

Unequal forces, acting parallel on a straight line, retain each other, therefore, in equilibrium, if their distances from the fulcrum bear an inverse ratio to the forces; or, in other words, if the force and distance on the one side, multiplied by each other, are equal to the power on the other side, multiplied by its distance.

In the above example, $2 \times 4 = 8$, and $4 \times 2 = 8$.

It will now be easily understood that a large weight, near to the central point of a rod, may be moved by a very small force applied on the other side, at a great distance from the centre.

The above is the case in the application of the *Lever*, which is nothing more than a rod placed on a solid point of support, or *fulcrum*, while two other points are acted upon by the load and the force. The following kinds of levers are distinguished by the relative position of these points.

(1.) The *equal-armed lever* (fig. 27). Its fulcrum lies in the centre at *c*. The arms *b c* and *c a*, being equal, a small weight cannot in this case maintain a larger one in equilibrium. The principal applications of this lever are in the balance and pulley.

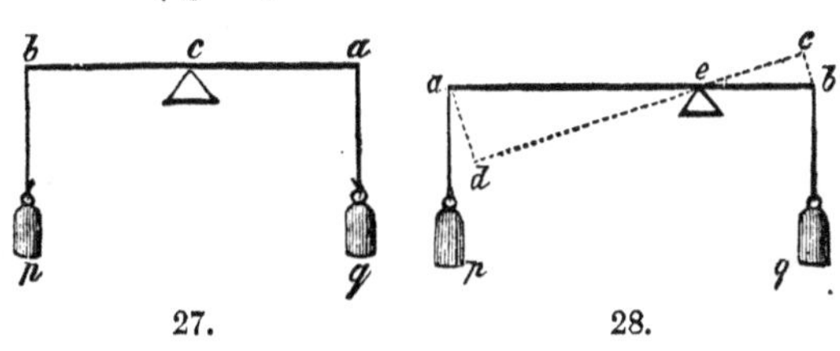

27. 28.

(2.) The *unequal-armed lever* (fig. 28), of which the arm *a e* is longer than the other, is applied in various ways, for moving great weights with a smaller power. One of the most familiar examples of the principles of this lever is that of two boys of unequal size wishing to swing upon a board; in order to accomplish this, the *lighter* boy chooses the *longer* end.

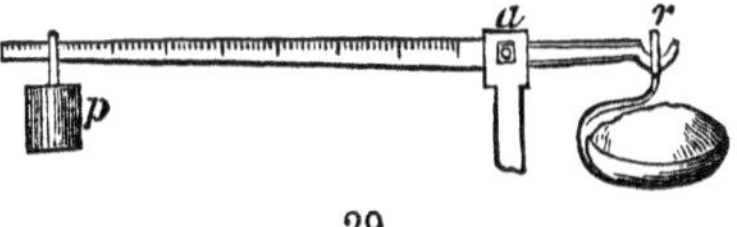

29.

Other applications of this lever are: the ordinary lever, the crow-bar, the windlass, the reel, the steel-yard with sliding weights (fig. 29), the weighing machine, the wheel and axle, the crane, borers, keys, scissors, &c. By due examination the principle of this lever may be traced in all these instruments.

(3.) The *single-armed lever* (fig. 30) differs somewhat from those already considered, the fulcrum *c* being situated at the end of the lever. The forces *k* and *w* act on the unequal arms *b c* and *a c*, but in contrary directions, for *k* acts *upwards*, and *w* draws *downwards*. Equilibrium is likewise established in this case if $k \times b\,c = w \times a\,c$.

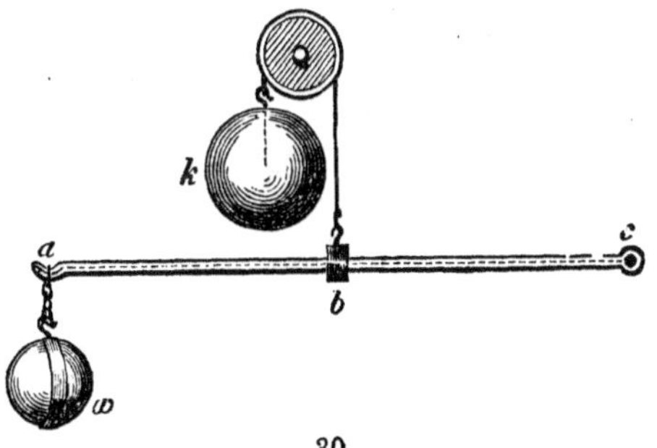

30.

Applications of the one-armed lever are found in the chopping-blade, the nut-crackers, in most lever presses, in the force-pump (fig. 31), and in many safety valves (fig. 32), wheel-barrows, &c.

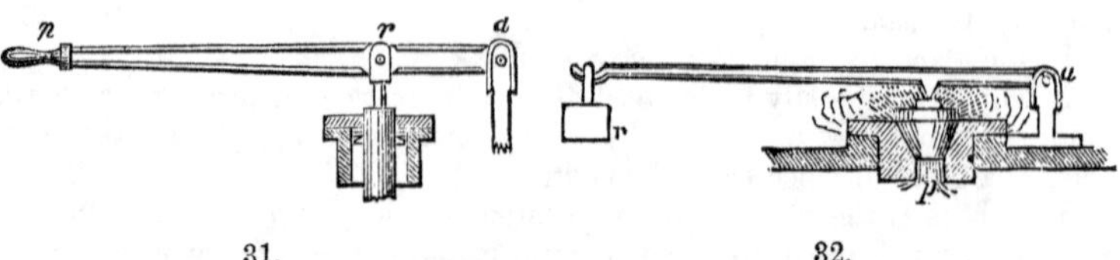

31. 32.

60. In the *fixed* pulley (fig. 33), the forces p and q act at the points a and b, and the line $a\ c\ b$ represents nothing more than an equal-armed lever, whose point of support is at c. No power is gained, therefore, in employing the fixed pulley; it is only of use in permitting the application of the force at the most appropriate point, as, for instance, when applied to a draw-well.

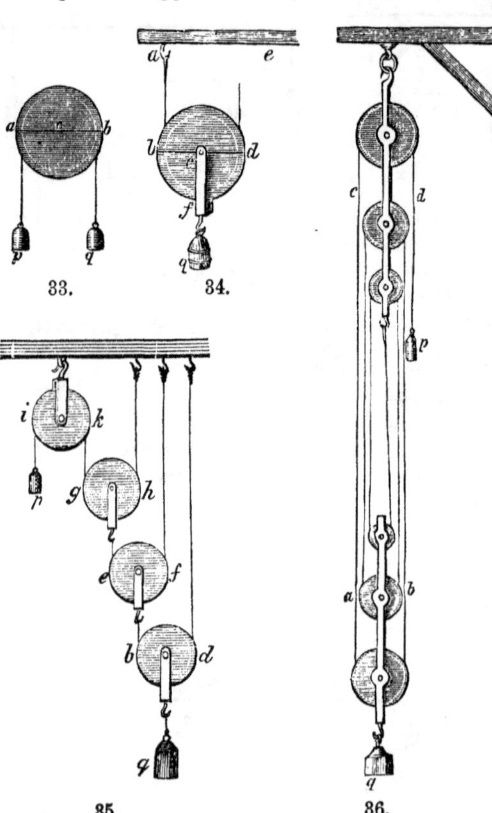

33. 34. 35. 36.

The *moveable* pulley (fig. 34) represents a one-armed lever (compare § 59), the fulcrum of which is situated at b, while the force q draws downwards at the distance 1, and the force e upwards at the distance 2 and at the point d. As, however, the latter force acts at double the distance, it is only required to be half as great as the force q, in order to maintain the equilibrium. If, therefore, a weight of 4 lbs. be suspended on the hook of the moveable pulley, a force equal to 2 lbs. applied at e will be sufficient to raise it, and the least excess of power will be sufficient to set the load in motion.

By combining a number of moveable pulleys, as seen in fig. 35, we are enabled to raise a considerable weight by the application of a small amount of force. On suspending the weight *q*, equal to 8 lbs., to a system of three moveable pulleys, 1 lb. will be found sufficient to maintain it in equilibrium.

As was shown at fig. 34, the weight of the suspended load decreases one-half for every additional moveable pulley.

The most convenient arrangement for raising weights by means of moveable pulleys, is shown at fig. 36. In this system the three upper pulleys are stationary, and the three lower ones moveable; and, therefore, the advantage in its application is, likewise, that the load *q* may be counterbalanced by the application of one-eighth of its weight at *p*.

It might be expected that by the application of a great number of pulleys, we should be enabled to raise enormous weights with ease. But the results obtained fall short of expectation, partly because, by the addition of every pulley, the distance to which the load may be raised is diminished, while the friction, which is, as we shall presently find, a great impediment to motion, is proportionably increased.

Centre of Gravity.

61. The body *m* (fig. 37) may be considered as composed of the three parts, *a*, *b*, *b*. Each of these parts is attracted to the earth in the direction of the arrows in the figure, which it will be seen are parallel to each other. We have seen at § 57, that the action of two equal parallel forces on a line may be counterbalanced by the application of a force acting in the opposite direction, and possessing a power equal or superior to that of the combined forces; we are able, therefore, to prevent the body *m* from obeying the force of gravity, *i. e.* from falling, by suspending or supporting it at the point *a*.

b	*a*	*b*
↓	↓	↓

37.

It follows from this that we are likewise able to counteract the whole of the forces acting on each single part of the body *n* (fig. 38) by supporting the part *a*; and it is found not only by theory but also by experience that one point must exist in every body, of whatever form it may be, in which the sum of the forces of gravity, acting on all the particles, may be considered as united. This particular point is called the *centre of gravity* of the body.

e	*d*	*c*	*b*	*a*	*b*	*c*	*d*	*e*
↓	↓	↓	↓	↓	↓	↓	↓	↓

38.

When the centre of gravity of a body is supported it cannot fall, and is, therefore, in a state of equilibrium.

62. In bodies of regular form, such as a ball, a cube, a cylinder, or a prism, the centre of gravity is always identical with the mathematical central point of the body. In irregularly formed bodies it is always situated near the largest portion of the mass. In pyramids and cones the largest mass is evidently at their bases. In these bodies the centre of gravity is consequently found to be at one-fourth of their height.

63. The centre of gravity of a body is supported, as long as a line drawn

vertically from that point (the line of direction) falls within the base, *i. e.* the surface with which the body touches the ground.

An inclined stone or beam of wood, in which, as at fig. 39, the vertical line drawn from the centre of gravity falls within the base, cannot fall. If, however, it had the size marked out by the dotted lines, the centre of gravity would be situated at *b*, and the mass must necessarily fall.

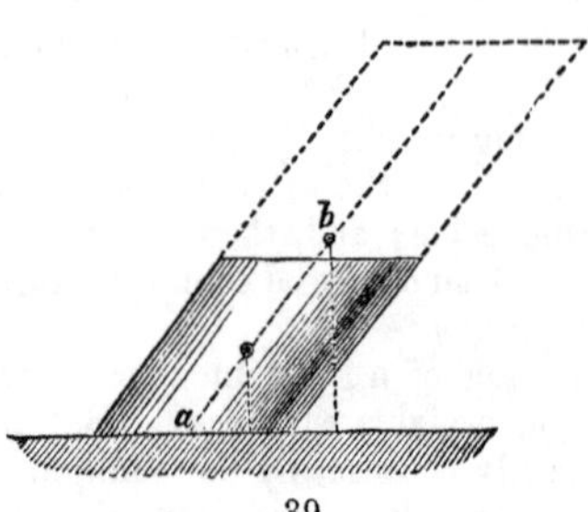

39.

The larger the base of a body, and the nearer its principal mass is to the base, the firmer the body will stand. It is probable that the Egyptians chose the form of the pyramid on this account for their stupendous structures, which have stood for thousands of years.

The bodies of men and animals, the different parts of which are moveable, are continually altering the position of their centre of gravity. A man

40.

41.

carrying a load on his back (fig. 40), will lean forwards; if he has it in his left hand (fig. 41), he will stretch out the right arm; and any person who is in danger of falling on one side will instinctively endeavour to save himself by stretching out his arm in the opposite direction.

Friction.

64. A great impediment to motion is *Friction.* It arises from the circumstance that no body exists with a perfectly plane surface. If the smoothest substances, such as polished steel, be examined under the microscope, their surfaces will be found to consist of elevations and depressions.

Therefore, in propelling one body along the surface of another, the elevations on the one must be continually lifted over the inequalities on the surface of the other, as is shown in fig. 42. The smaller these elevations are, that is, the smoother the surface, the less friction will there be. In fluids the friction is comparatively slight, the particles being easily displaced. The friction between two bodies may be considerably diminished by filling the cavities on their surfaces with fluids, such as oil or fat, or with very fine powders, such as graphite. Hence these substances are employed for smearing axletrees and various parts of machinery.

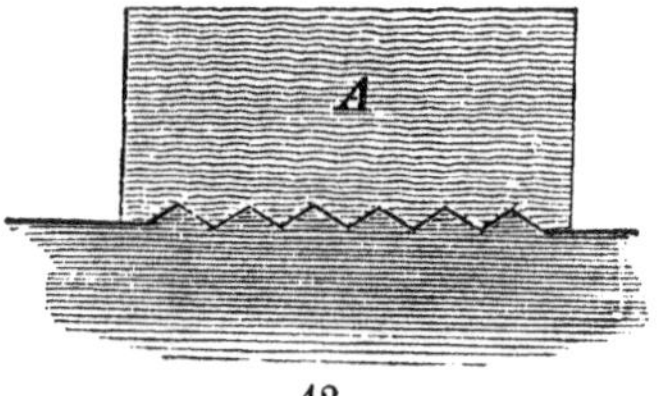

42.

The amount of friction is, moreover, dependent upon the weight of the body to be moved. The greater the weight the stronger the friction. The extent of the rubbing surfaces exercises no influence, since to move, for example, 100 lbs. of iron upon a surface of metal a force of 27·7 lbs. is required, whether the mass of iron be in the form of a flat plate or of a square block.

Mechanics.

65. *Mechanics* is the science which treats of *forces* and of *motion*. It is the province of the practical engineer to produce any motion that may be required, at the least expense of power. He accomplishes this by suitable instruments, which are called *machines*. It is not the object of the present work to exhaust the wide field of mechanical appliances. It seems, however, desirable to pay some attention to those instruments which have become of so much importance.

66. A distinction is made between *simple* and *compound* machines. With the first we have already become, in some measure, acquainted; such, for example, are the lever, the inclined plane, the pulley, and its different forms, and all our common working tools; and in the section devoted to Anatomy, we shall find that most of the motions of the limbs are effected in accordance with the laws of the lever.

Compound machines are produced by the co-operative action of several simple machines, and however difficult it may, at first sight, appear to understand them, they may, nevertheless, all be traced back to the simple machines above alluded to.

67. The *wheel* and *axle* is a simple machine, very frequently employed: it consists of a cylinder, called an *axle*, furnished with pivots at both ends, which in the case of the horizontal axle rest in a groove, and in the vertical axle in holes, so that the axle may rotate round its longer axis. A wheel is connected with the axle in such a manner that its centre lies in the axis of the cylinder, and that the axle must rotate as soon as the wheel is set in motion, and *vice versâ*.

The windlass (figs. 43 and 44,) furnishes an example of the application of this principle. It consists of a cylinder or axle *a*, the pivots of which rest in notches at the top of two supports; the weight R is suspended by a rope coiled round the axle, and the latter is made to rotate by forces applied to the levers or handle, W. It will be readily seen that two forces, R and W,

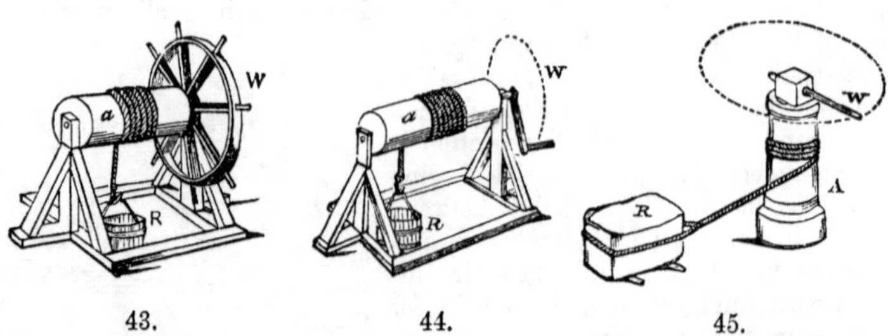

43. 44. 45.

endeavour here to turn the cylinder in opposite directions, but that the force W acts on the longer arm of the lever, and the weight R on the shorter arm. The force W may, therefore, be smaller than the weight R, in the ratio of the radius of the axle to the length of the levers, to maintain the latter in equilibrium. The levers which move the axle act, consequently, more effectually, the greater their length in relation to the diameter of the axle.

[The capstan (fig. 45) differs only from the windlass, by having its revolving axle placed vertically; and thus a comparatively small force is required at W to move the weight R.]

68. *Transmission of Motion.*—According to the nature of the machine, we distinguish three principal parts, namely: the first, on which the motive power acts; the second, on which the resistance to be overcome is exercised; and lastly, the part between these two, which is the means of transmitting the force. In simple machines, for example, the crow-bar, these various parts consist generally of one piece, and are in close proximity.

But in compound machines a considerable number of intermediate contrivances are necessary to transmit the power to the actual working parts, as, for instance, from the water-wheel of a mill to the grinding-stones. In order to transmit the motion, transmission axles, endless bands, and toothed wheels are generally employed.

69. If we enter a cotton factory, we witness on the right and the left of the passages of the long rooms series of machines in full activity, but we do not see the parts which are acted on directly by the moving power. If, however, we look towards the ceiling of the room, we perceive a rotating axle, extending along its entire length, entering by an opening in the wall, and also frequently passing into the adjoining room to transmit the power to other machines. The mules are united to this transmission axle by suitable contrivances,—motion being imparted to the axle either by a water-wheel or steam-engine.

70. The *endless band* is employed when motion is to be transmitted from one rotating axle to another in the same plane, but at some distance from it, as, for instance, from the above-mentioned transmission-axle to the mules. For this purpose there are fastened on different parts of the axle *rollers*, called also drums, which rotate with the axle, and have on their circumference, a rope or leather band, the ends of which are united. One of these bands passes over a corresponding roller on one of the mules and sets the latter in motion. Fig. 46 represents an axle A B, which communicates motion to a grindstone. If it be desired to arrest the motion, the band is transferred to an adjoining loose roller by means of the lever C D E. The

loose roller is not connected with the axis of the grindstone, but is merely movable round it, so that this roller, only, rotates while the grindstone remains at rest. Such an arrangement is called a live and dead pulley.

46.

The endless band is either open, as at fig. 46, or it is crossed, as in the common spinning-wheel, or in the centrifugal machine, fig. 23. In reference to the action of the endless band, it must be remarked that the part of the band which is called the driving-side, has a greater tension than the other, since no rotation could be produced if the tension were equally distributed throughout the whole of the band.

If the diameter of the two wheels A and B, over which the endless band passes, are equal, and A is set in motion, it imparts to B the same velocity of rotation. But if the wheel A, which is set in motion, be larger than the second wheel B, it will impart to the latter a greater velocity in the ratio of the diameter of the wheels; so that in this manner an exceedingly great velocity of rotation may be produced, for instance, as in the bobbin on the spinning-jenny, the centrifugal machine, &c.

If we conceive the idea of two wheels A and B, connected by an endless band, and a given force acting by a winch on the smaller wheel A, the diameter of which may be $\frac{1}{2}$, $\frac{1}{3}$, $\frac{1}{4}$, $\frac{1}{n}$th of that of the second wheel B, this power produces the same effect as if the force were acting directly on the axle of the larger wheel B by a winch of the 2, 3, 4, or n-times the length.

71. The *wheel-works* so much employed in mechanics consist of *toothed wheels*, which transmit the motion from one axle to another, which is either parallel to the first or forms with it an angle. On their circumference are alternate teeth and spaces, which accurately correspond and fit in each other in such a manner that one wheel cannot be moved without turning the other in the opposite direction.

The remarks we have made in reference to endless bands apply also to toothed wheels, inasmuch as wheels of equal diameter transfer the motion unchanged from one axle to another; but if the first wheel be of larger size, it imparts to the second a velocity as many times greater as the number of its teeth exceed those of the latter. The second wheel is capable of imparting motion to a third, and this to a fourth, and so on, of continually decreasing size, and in this manner we may obtain any convenient, and if requisite, extraordinary velocity.

It is also to be remarked that if a given force F acts on the axle of a smaller wheel C by the winch B (fig. 47), and the diameter of the smaller wheel C is, as here represented, one-third, or $\frac{1}{4}$, $\frac{1}{5}$, $\frac{1}{n}$th of that of the larger wheel D, the force F exercises the same action as if it acted directly on the axle A of the larger wheel D by a lever-arm B′ of 3, 4, 5, or n-times the length. But as winches of such length are very inconvenient, or scarcely manageable, a combination of several toothed wheels are employed with advantage. The smallest wheel which is directly set in motion is called a *pinion* C (fig. 43).

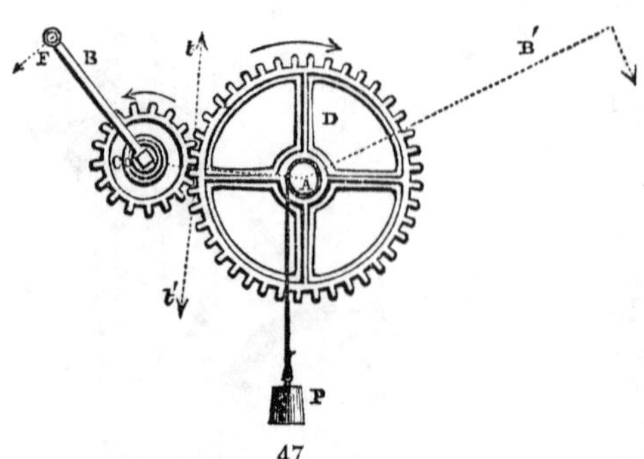

47.

It will readily be seen that the motion produced takes place in a reversed sense if the motion be transferred from a larger to a smaller toothed wheel, and that the effect of wheel-works is considerably impaired by friction.

72. The *bevelled-wheel* (fig. 48), and the crown-wheel (fig. 49), transfer the motion from a horizontal to a vertical axis, or *vice versâ*, and the remarks we have made in reference to toothed wheels generally are in every respect applicable to these wheels.

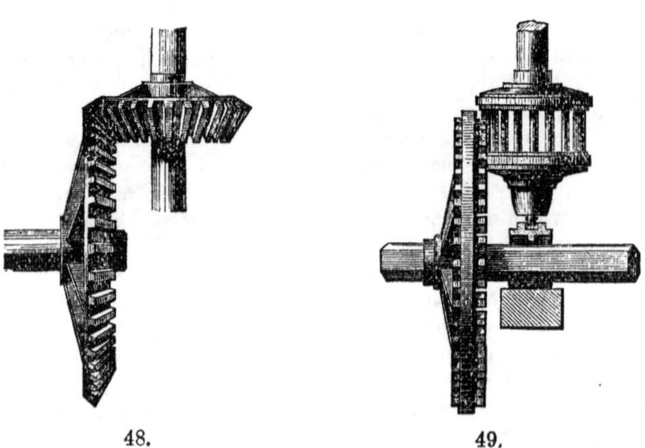
48. 49.

73. The disturbances arising to a machine from the irregular action of the moving power would render the generality of operations impossible if no means were adopted to counterbalance these disturbing influences.

To accomplish this a large heavy wheel of cast-iron, called a *fly-wheel*, is fixed to the axle, and rotates with it. If a sudden increase of force takes place, this excess of power acts also on the heavy fly-wheel, and the effect of the increase of power on the whole arrangement is rendered less perceptible; if, on the other hand, the moving power be decreased or even temporarily interrupted, the motion of the whole of the machinery is thus only slightly diminished, since, according to the laws of inertia (§ 39), the fly-wheel retains, at least for a short time, its velocity, and keeps the rest of the machinery in motion until the moving power again acts in a suitable manner. Fly-wheels are employed in rolling-mills, mints, in stationary steam-engines, watches, and in grinding machines.

74. Amongst the numberless mechanical arrangements employed for the most varied purposes, there are two which we consider as especially worthy of a more minute description, since their applications are intimately connected with our most necessary wants; these are the *flour-mill* and the *clock*. A knowledge of their construction appears as attractive as it is useful.

The Flour-Mill.

75. Most of our flour-mills are moved by water-power. The water either exerts its force on the float-boards, which are situated on the under part of the wheel (*undershot-wheel*), or it flows into the buckets at half the height of the wheel (*breast-wheel*), or else it is conducted in a channel over the wheel and falls into similar buckets on the front, in which case the wheel is called an *overshot-wheel*. In the under-shot wheel the water acts by its velocity, and in the breast-wheel it produces rotation by its weight and force, whilst in the overshot-wheel it acts chiefly by its weight. The adoption of either of these wheels depends on the quantity and on the fall of the water at command.

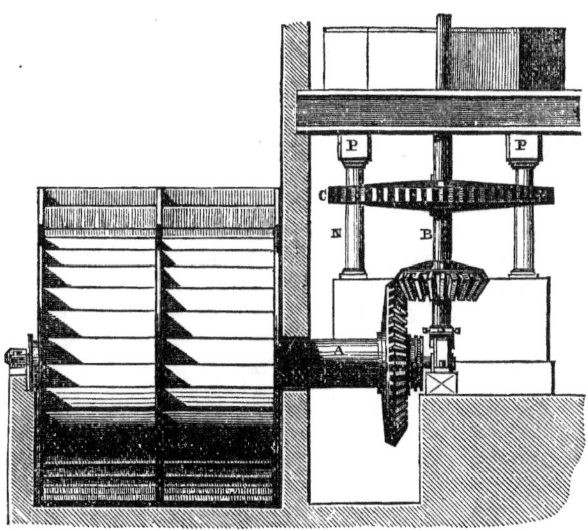

50.

In fig. 50 we have given a representation of an overshot wheel which turns the axle A. This axle extends to the mill, and by means of two bevelled wheels transfers its rotatory motion to the vertical axle B.

In fig. 51 the wheel C is employed to turn two pairs of millstones, of the first of which we have given a sectional and of the second a front view. For

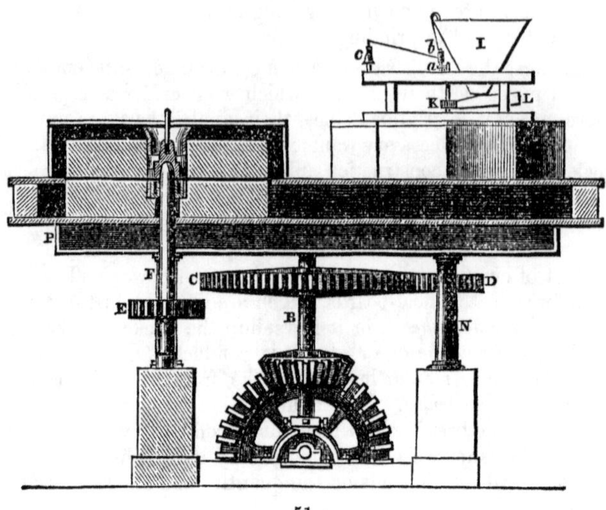

51.

this purpose two toothed wheels E and D are movable on the vertical axles F and N, and may be regulated in such a manner as to work into the crown-wheel C, and in this case the stones are set in motion. In the figure the stones on the right are supposed to be in motion, while those on the left hand are at rest. From the latter we will pursue the interior arrangement. The axle F rests below by a peg in a groove, and passes above through the floor P and through the millstone which rests upon it, and which is called the *under-stone.* On its upper conical end this axle carries the second mill-stone, called the *runner,* which is fastened to it by the mill-iron, and is, therefore, turned round with the axle. Between the two millstones only a very small space intervenes, and it is of the greatest importance that the runner rests exactly on its centre of gravity, in order to preserve a uniform distance on all sides.

The hole in the centre of the runner is not perfectly closed by the mill-iron, but there are some openings left which allow the corn to fall down between the stones, where it is ground into flour and bran by the rotation of the runner. In order perfectly to crush the grain, shallow furrows are cut in the opposite surfaces of the stones, and act in a similar manner to the blades of a pair of scissors. By the centrifugal motion the ground corn is removed from between the two stones to a room closed on all sides, and thence carried through a room to the bolting apparatus. This arrangement, which serves to separate the flour from the bran, is not represented in the figure; it is set in motion by a prolongation of the axle B.

The corn which is to be ground is introduced into a funnel-shaped box I, called a *hopper,* the lower opening of which is nearly closed by a little inclined box L, called the *shoe*. On a prolongation of the axle which supports the runner are several pegs K, which, in turning, repeatedly shake the shoe, so that the corn gradually slides down and falls into the aperture of the runner.

A bell C is made to ring, to inform the miller when the hopper is nearly empty. A string passes from the bell to the peg *b*, and thence over a pulley into the hopper. To the end of the string is attached a large but light piece of wood, which on filling the hopper is buried by the miller beneath the corn, so that the peg *b* is at such a height that it cannot be touched by the peg *a* during the rotation. The quantity of corn, however, soon becomes so small that it is no longer sufficient to retain the piece of wood in the same position, and the peg *b* descends so far that the peg *a* causes the bell to ring by touching *b* at each rotation.

The diameter of a millstone is generally about 4 feet, the runner makes about 70 rotations in a minute, and a pair of millstones grind in 24 hours from 500 lbs. to 600 lbs. of corn.

The Clock.

76. If we succeed in imparting to an object a perfectly uniform motion, so that it describes an equal distance in the same time, the motion may be employed as a measure of time, and it is this which we expect of a good clock. This problem would be easily solved if we had at command a force acting with perfect uniformity. This, however, is by no means the case, since the descending *weight*, as well as the *spring*, which are employed most advantageously to set our clocks in motion, exert an action which is unequal.

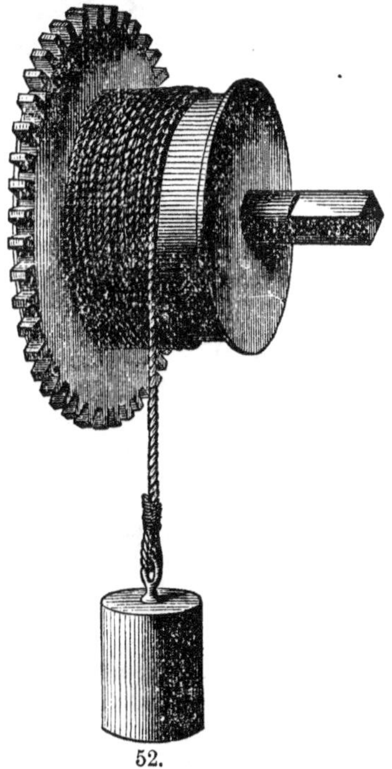

52.

If the cord (fig. 52) to which a weight is suspended, be wound on a cylinder furnished with a toothed wheel to transmit the motion, the cylinder is set in rotation by the descending weight, slowly at first, but soon increasing, because the weight, as a falling body (§ 26), quickly acquires an accelerated velocity.

We may employ for the same purpose a *spring* (fig. 53), of highly-elastic steel, which is fastened by its external extremity to a fixed point, and by its inner end to an axis which is capable of rotating round itself.* If the spring be now wound up and left to

* This is the arrangement adopted in Geneva watches. Fig. 56 represents the English construction.—Ed.

itself, it must, by virtue of its elasticity, cause the axis to rotate in an opposite direction (fig. 54). In the first moment, when the spring is strongly contracted, the rotation is very rapid; it soon, however, becomes slower, and finally ceases when the spring has regained its original form. Toothed wheels, which are thus set in motion by weights and springs, would attain a motion much too irregular to cause the hand on the dial, which is set in motion, to traverse over equal spaces every hour.

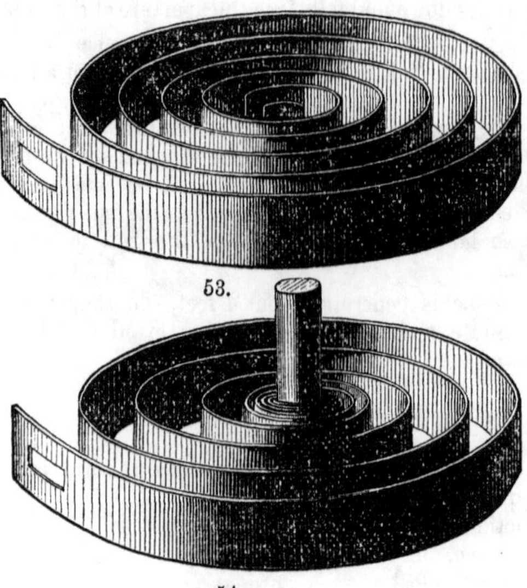
53.

54.

77. If, however, we check the unwinding of the cord, which is caused by the descending weight, by means of a regular resistance acting at very short intervals, it is evident that the weight cannot attain an accelerated velocity, consequently the cord is unrolled slowly and regularly, and imparts to the cylinder on which it is fastened, and also to the works connected with it, a corresponding movement. If, moreover, a wound-up spring be fastened by means of its axis to a combination of wheels, which likewise receives a transient check at very short intervals, the spring cannot be relaxed suddenly, but its force will be divided over a longer space of time.

These facts led to the use of such an arrangement, called an *escapement*, being adopted in all our clocks.

The escapement movement is most perfectly accomplished by the aid of the pendulum, since, as we have seen in § 27, that within a certain limit described by the pendulum all its oscillations are of equal duration.

Fig. 55 represents a toothed wheel connected with the axis, on which the weight acts, and above it is suspended a pendulum, the upper part of which, called the *beam*, is furnished with pallets *a* and *b*, for the purpose of catching the teeth of the wheel. It will be readily seen that when the pendulum is set in motion, its pallets on the right and left alternately drop in the teeth of the wheel, and must produce a short and transitory interruption, thus transforming the accelerating velocity of the falling weight into a uniform velocity. If the beam have a horizontal position, both teeth would simultaneously drop and entirely interrupt the rotation of the toothed wheel; hence it is that we may entirely stop a pendulum clock by holding the pendulum for some seconds in a vertical position, and again set it in motion by moving it gently on one side

78. Greater difficulties are presented in the regulation of a watch, since a pendulum cannot, of course, be employed. It was originally endeavoured to compensate the action of the spring by means of the *fusee* (fig. 56), an arrangement which is frequently seen in English watches.

55.

The conical wheel (fusee) D, which has on the upper part a spiral plane, is turned round by the watch-key. By means of a linked chain this wheel is connected with the barrel A, on which the chain is fastened and wound. To the inner side of the barrel one end of the spring is fastened, and its other end is held by an immovable pin. In winding up the watch the chain from the barrel is wound upon the circumference of the fusee, the box-wheel makes several rotations and contracts the spring, which, as soon as the works are left to themselves, again opens and causes the barrel A to rotate in an opposite direction. In this rotation the barrel imparts, by means of the chain, a motion to the fusee, the teeth of which set the whole of the works in motion. Immediately after the watch is wound up, and the spring most strongly contracted, it acts by means of the chain on the highest plane of the fusee, which is of the smallest diameter, and in the same degree as the spring is unrolled and its tension relaxed, the planes increase in size, so that the continually-decreasing force acts on a continually-increasing lever arm. In this manner the inequality of the motion receives a suitable compensation.

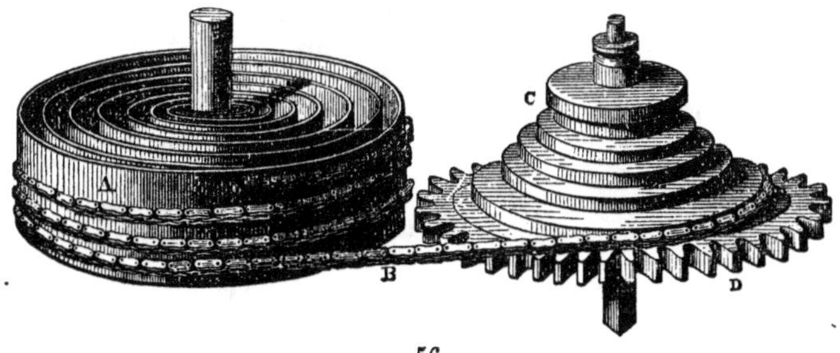

56.

The arrangement just described, however, is insufficient to produce a perfect regulation, and is entirely omitted in watches furnished with the improved escapement, as may be seen in the following figure, which represents

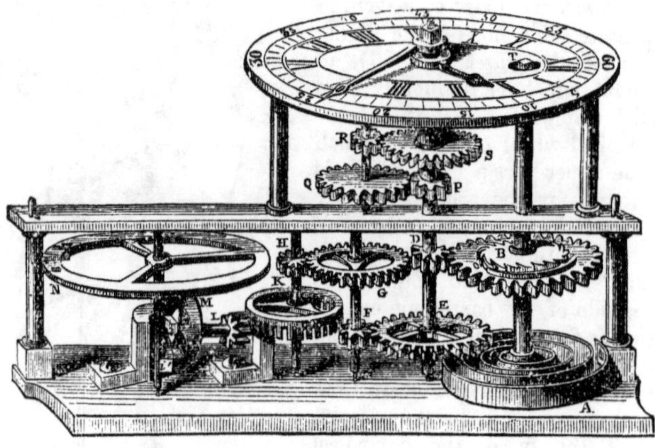

57.

the entire works of a watch, and in which all the axes furnished with wheels are made longer than they are in reality for the sake of greater perspicuity.* It should be mentioned that the wheels P Q R S form the hand-work, and all the other the working train of the watch.

By means of the winding square T, the spring A is contracted, or, in other words, the watch is *wound up*, when the elasticity of the spring causes its own axis to rotate in an opposite direction, as well as the toothed-wheel C, which is fastened upon it, and which is called the *great wheel.*

The great wheel catches first in the pinion D, and in this manner moves the hand-works. The tension of the spring and the action of the escapement, to be described hereafter, should be regulated in such a manner that the axis of the small wheel P, which is called the *minute-wheel,* turns round once in an hour. On the end of this axis and on the surface of the dial the minute-hand is fastened, which in twelve hours describes the same number of rotations. The hour-hand, however, must only make one rotation in twelve hours. It should first be observed that the axis of the hour-hand is in the form of a hollow tube, moveable round the axis of the minute-hand, and has fastened to its extremity the wheel S. Let us now see in what manner the twelve rotations of the minute-wheel P are, by means of toothed-wheels (§ 71), converted into one rotation of the hour-wheel S. For this purpose the minute-wheel is furnished with eight teeth, and catches in the other wheel Q, which has twenty-four teeth; hence the axis of the latter, together with the pinion R which is fastened to it, makes only *three* rotations in twelve hours.

The pinion R has eight teeth, which catch in the thirty-two teeth on the

* The arrangement with regard to the spring (fig. 57) is that of modern Geneva watches, while the escapement is the old vertical escapement of ordinary English watches.—Ed.

hour-wheel S, which, consequently, turns round only once, whilst R makes four rotations and the minute-wheel twelve.

If we now consider the entire works, we observe that the movement is propagated and the contrate-wheel K set in rotation by means of the *intermediate wheel* E E, the pinion F, the third wheel G, the pinion H; the contrate-wheel K imparts its motion, by means of pinion L, to a horizontal axis, with its peculiarly toothed escapement-wheel M. In the front of the escapement-wheel we observe a vertical axis, called the *verge*, which carries on its upper part a fly-wheel N, which is also called a *balance-wheel* (§ 73), whilst lower down there are two little plates of steel or pallets, *i i'*, the mutual distance of which is equal to the diameter of the escapement-wheel M, and which in reference to their position with the verge are at right angles to each other. The last-mentioned parts form, with the escapement-wheel, the *escapement* of the watch.

If a tooth on the upper part of the escapement-wheel M meet the upper pallet *i*, it imparts to the latter a slight backward motion; but immediately afterwards the other pallet *i'* meets with an under tooth of M, and is driven by it forwards, so that as long as the escapement-wheel is in motion the pallets *i i'* are alternately driven backwards and forwards. It will be readily seen that in this manner the spindle, together with the balance-wheel, receive a corresponding alternate rotation, describing an arc of a circle. But as often as a pallet comes in contact with a tooth of the escapement-wheel, it receives a backward push from the balance, since this does not lose the whole of its velocity by the encounter, by which means the balance-wheel is somewhat retarded.

If the above-described oscillations of the balance-wheel were, like those of the pendulum, of equal duration, the resulting retardations would also be of equal duration, and the movements of the watch would be regular. This, however, is not the case, because the spring itself is the moving power which primarily causes the oscillations of the balance and keeps it perpetually in motion, so that the inequalities of the moving force are propagated to the balance.

If we employ on the balance another very small spring, these irregularities receive an important compensation. Such a contrivance, which is also termed a *balance*, or *pendulum-spring*, may, like the pendulum, be set in oscillations of almost equal duration by a slight blow, with this difference, however, that in the former they take place in a vertical and in the latter in a horizontal plane, and that with the former the oscillations are maintained by gravitation, and in the latter case by the elasticity of the spring. In this manner it has been possible to produce a regular escapement in the movements of the watch, which attained to the greatest exactness since the adoption of the balance-spring.

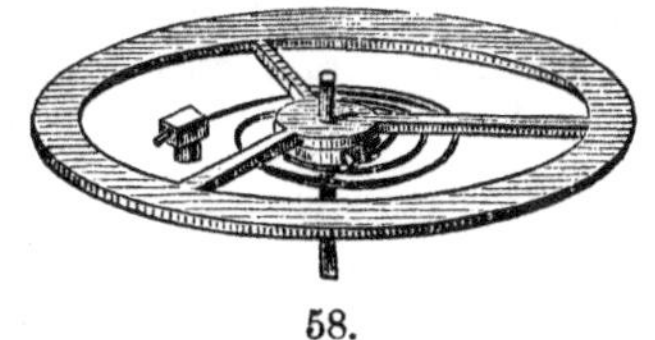

58.

Since, according to what has been stated, the watch is regulated by the oscillations of the balance, these must be of certain duration. The watch would go too fast if the oscillations were too quick, and in the opposite case, too slow; we must, therefore, adopt a means of imparting to the oscillations of the balance-wheel the required duration. This is done by making the spring shorter or longer, according to circumstances, since it is easily to be seen that its tension will be increased by shortening and decreased by lengthening, and in the same proportion the number of oscillations within a certain time will increase or decrease.

Such a contrivance is called the *regulator* (fig. 59). The spiral fastened to the stud C is inserted at B in a groove of the arm A, which is made in one piece with the toothed circular section. The result of this is, that only from the point B the elasticity of the spiral exerts its influence. If now the hand D is moved in either the one or the other direction, a corresponding motion of the arm A is produced by the catching of the teeth, the stationary portion B C of the spiral becomes shortened or lengthened, and in this manner the oscillations are made of the required duration.

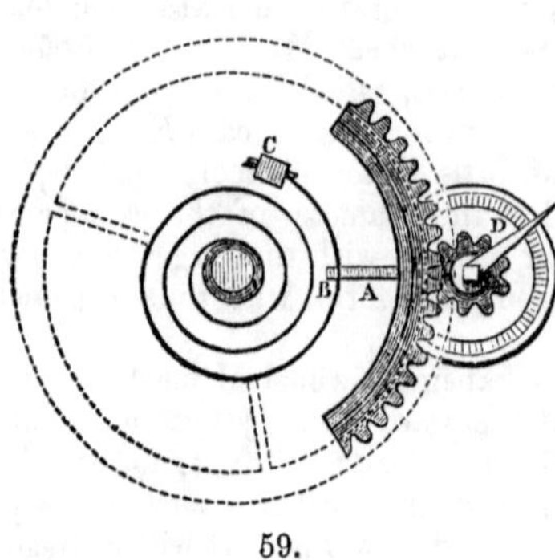

59.

79. Cylinder watches are distinguished from the above-described lever watches, by the escapement in the latter being performed by the vertical wheel M (fig. 57), whilst in the cylinder watches the teeth of a horizontal wheel catch in the hollow and peculiarly-cut axis of the balance, which is called a *cylinder*. This arrangement has the advantage that the cylinder watches can be made very flat, becoming thereby more convenient to carry, and which may be recognised even by their exterior.

80. Regarding the history of clocks, it may be remarked that wheel clock-work was unknown to the ancients, and in reference to the time and by whom the discovery was first made much uncertainty prevails. Artificial wheel-works, especially those employed for astronomical purposes, were first found in convents, and in these also the first clocks moved by weights might have existed.

The discovery of the watch is generally ascribed to *Peter Hele* in 1500, and his watches, in consequence of their shape, were called Nuremberg eggs.

On the other hand, it is certain that the requisite exactness in the going of clocks was first attained by the distinguished Dutch philosopher *Huygens* in 1657, who first carried out the idea of employing the pendulum and the spiral to the regulation of time-pieces.

Equilibrium of Fluids (Hydrostatics).

81. A fluid is in a state of equilibrium when all the particles on its surface are equidistant from the centre of the earth. Hence the surface of a fluid in a state of rest must have the form of the segment of a globe. This is really the case, as may be observed with large masses of water,—for instance, the surface of the sea. Smaller surfaces of fluids appear, however, when in equilibrium, as perfect planes at right angles with the direction of gravity.

If a higher position be given to one portion of a liquid than to another, the consequence of the slight disarrangement of the particles is a continuous motion, until the state of equilibrium is re-established. The flowing of rivers towards the sea is owing to the tendency of the water on the surface of the earth to maintain itself in equilibrium.

As a consequence of the ratio of equilibrium in fluids, the surfaces of liquids, contained in vessels having one part wider than the other, or in different vessels in communication, invariably stand at equal heights from the bases of the vessels. Thus in watering-pots, tea-pots, or oil-lamps, the liquid is always found to stand as high in the narrow spouts as it does in the wider portions of the vessels. If a stream of water be conducted from a height to a plane, the reservoir will form, as it were, a vessel connected with the spring by the conducting pipes, and the water will attain a similar height in both parts. This phenomenon familiarly explains the formation of *fountains*. The *sides* of vessels containing liquids also suffer a pressure, which for equal parts of the walls is the greater the nearer these parts are situated to the bottoms of the vessels. That this pressure may be employed as a motive power may be shown by suitable arrangements, as in Segner's wheel and in the *turbine*.

82. The amount of pressure sustained by the bottom of a vessel filled with a liquid, does not depend on the amount of liquid, but upon its height in the vessel and the extent of the vessel's base. It may be proved by decisive experiments that if the heights and the bases of different vessels are equal, as is the case with those represented by figs. 60, 61, 62, and 63,

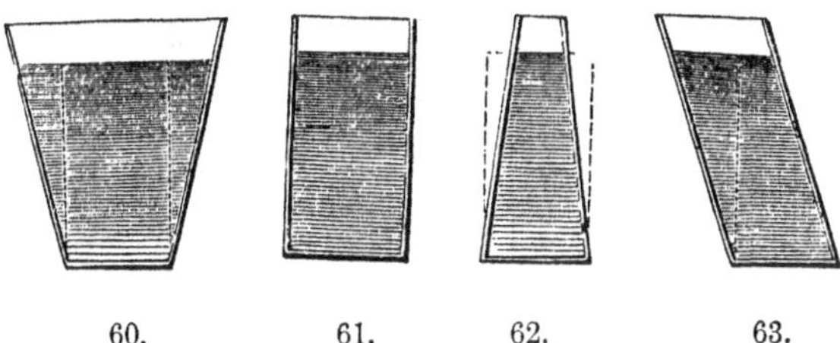

60. 61. 62. 63.

the pressure sustained by the bottoms of the vessels will be in all cases perfectly equal, although the amount of liquid they contain varies to a considerable extent, as shown by the figures. A very great pressure may, therefore, be obtained with a very small amount of liquid, if it be poured into a very narrow and high tube, widening considerably towards the base. The amount of pressure obtained is the same as if the tube were of equal width the whole way up.

If a cubic inch of water weighs $\frac{1}{2}$ oz., the base of the vessel measures 32 square inches, and the height of the liquid 1 inch, the base sustains a pressure of 1×32 cubic inches, equal therefore to 1 lb. of water.

Assuming the height of the column of liquid to be 100 inches, the pressure sustained by the base is 100×32 cubic inches, or 100 lbs. of water.

83. If one portion of the surface of a liquid be exposed to a certain pressure, the pressure becomes equally dispersed in all directions.

In illustration of this, a vessel, closed on all sides, is provided with two openings, each a square inch in diameter, one at the top and another at the side. The latter opening is closed with a cork: the vessel is then filled completely with water, and the liquid is pressed upon by a piston, through the upper opening, with a force equal to 100 lbs. Every portion of the sides of the vessel, measuring 1 square inch, has now to bear 100 lbs. pressure. If the surface of the vessel is 60 square inches, the total pressure on its sides will amount to $60 \times 100 = 6000$ lbs. The cork in the lateral opening has to bear a pressure of 100 lbs. If it cannot withstand this, it is of course forced out. Supposing the lateral opening to be 2 square inches in size and to be closed by a plate, the latter must be pressed against the opening from the outside with a force of 200 lbs., in order to counterbalance the inward pressure.

84. The hydraulic press is constructed upon the above principles.

In fig. 64, A B represents the bottom of a hollow cylinder, into which is fitted the piston P: into the bottom of this cylinder there is introduced a pipe C leading from the forcing pump D; water is supplied to this pump by a cistern below, from which is led the pipe E, furnished with a valve opening upwards at the point where it is joined to the pump-barrel. Where the pipe C enters into the pump-barrel there is also a valve opening outwards into the pipe; consequently when the piston D rises this valve shuts, the valve of the cistern-pipe opens, and the fluid rises into the pump-barrel. When the piston begins to descend, the cistern-valve closes, and the water is forced through the pipe C into the large cylinder A B; and by the law of fluids above alluded to, whatever pressure may be exerted by the piston D on the surface of the water in the pump will be repeated on the piston of the large cylinder A B, as many times as the area of the small piston D is contained in the area of the large piston A B; that is, if the area of the pump-piston were 1 square inch, and that of the cylinder 100 inches, and if the piston were forced down with a pressure of 10 lbs., then the whole pressure on the bottom of the piston A B would be $10 \times 100 = 1000$ lbs.

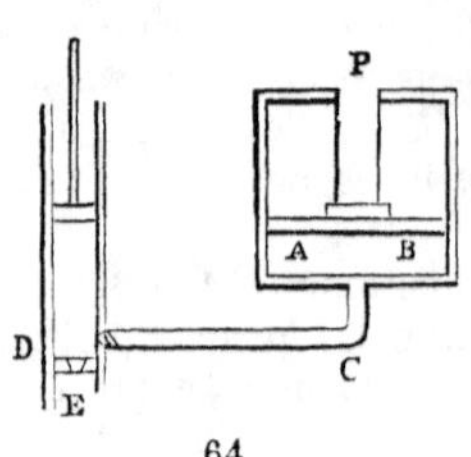

64.

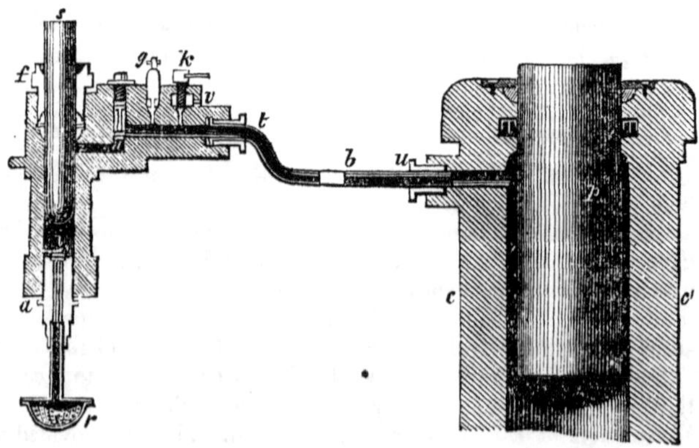

65.

Figs. 65 and 66 give a correct idea of the most improved construction of the press. Fig. 65 is a section, and fig. 66 a complete representation on a small scale of the hydraulic press. The piston *s* is raised by the lever *l*, and the water of the reservoir *b*, pressing through the perforated vessel *r*

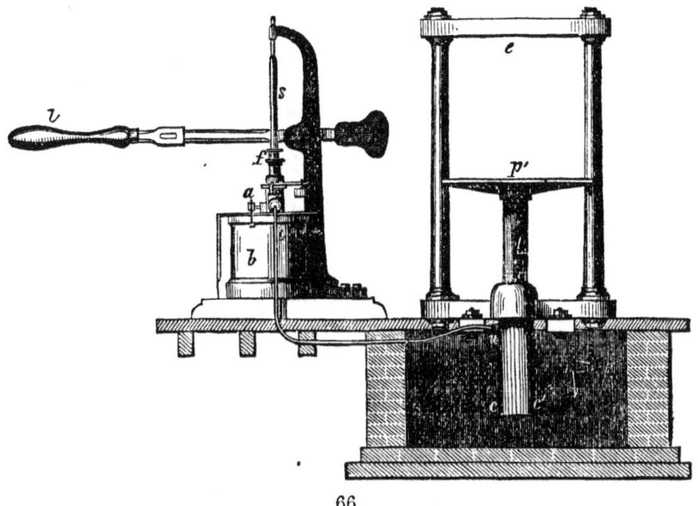

66.

lifts the valve *i*, and thus gets beneath the piston *s*. If we press down the lever *l*, the piston *s* goes down, the water is forced back, closes the valve *i*, raises the valve *d*, and runs through the tube *t b u* into the cylinder *c c'* of the press; here it presses against the piston *p*, which it lifts with the plate *p'*, and thus the body to be acted on is compressed between *p'* and the fixed plate *e*.

To prevent the machine from bursting, a safety-valve, capable of overcoming a given pressure, is employed, and for the purpose of admitting the water, or drawing it from the large cylinder, the press is furnished with a stop-cock. From the facility of operating with this machine, and its great power, it is now applied to many purposes.

85. Let us picture to ourselves, in a vessel filled with a liquid, in a state of perfect equilibrium, a certain portion of this liquid, situated in the centre of the whole, and submit it to a closer examination. The dark part *h'*, in fig. 67, may be considered to represent this portion. Now, it would certainly not occupy the position that it does, if it were not maintained there by the pressure exerted on all sides by the remaining liquid. It is evidently pressed downwards by the upper portion of the fluid, but, as it does not sink, the liquid situated below it must necessarily exert an equal upward pressure. It is retained equally in equilibrium by the portions of liquid pressing at the sides. The portion *h'* is, therefore, kept in perfect equilibrium by the liquid surrounding it; its tendency to sink, by the force of its gravity, being counteracted by the pressure from below. If it were possible to suspend it by a thread to the beam of a balance, the equilibrium of the latter would be as

67.

little disturbed as if it were connected by a thread to a weight lying upon, and therefore supported by, a table.

If this portion h' of the liquid were replaced by another body of equal weight and volume, this would obviously bear the same relation to the surrounding liquid, and would be, therefore, just as completely supported.

Suppose the body immersed to have the same volume, but to be lighter or heavier than the liquid displaced — even then, the pressure exerted by the surrounding liquid is the same in every case; if the body is lighter than the water displaced, it will not retain its equilibrium, and will, therefore, rise to the surface; but if it is heavier, the surrounding liquid will certainly counterbalance a portion of its weight, but not the whole, and the body will consequently sink to the bottom.

86. The following law was established by Archimedes: *If a body be immersed in a fluid, a portion of its weight will be sustained by the fluid, equal to the weight of the fluid displaced.*

A few common examples will serve as proofs of this theorem. A pail filled with water may be lifted about with ease as long as it is immersed in water, its whole weight being supported by the latter. But if the pail be taken out of the water, an amount of force, equal to its entire weight, will be required to lift it. In the same manner a man may be lifted and moved about in the water with the force of one finger.

87. One cubic inch of water weighs about half an ounce (more exactly, 252½ grains). Any other substance, for instance, a piece of lead, is weighed first in air, as usual, and found to weigh 11 ozs. If it is then weighed while

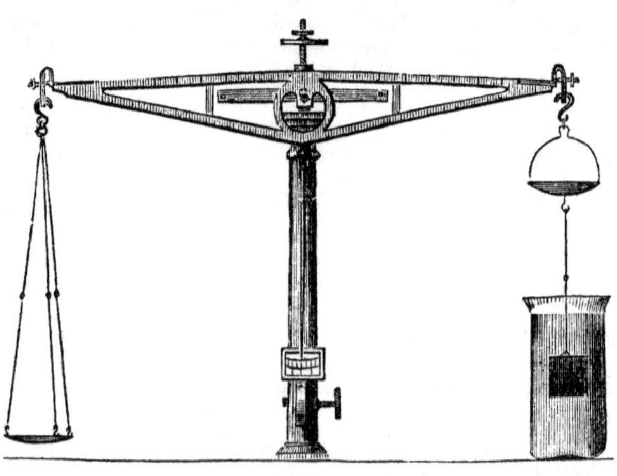

68.

immersed in water, as shown at fig. 68, the latter will be found to support about 1 oz. of its weight. This experiment shows that 11 ozs. of lead occupy the same space as 1 oz. of water (or nearly 2 cubic inches). From this we conclude, that lead is eleven times heavier than water.

This is the method generally adopted for determining the density or specific gravity of bodies.

88. It may be easily conceived that the heavier a fluid is, the greater will be the weight of a body immersed therein, that it is capable of supporting.

According to the table, § 34, the relations of the densities of alcohol, water, and sulphuric acid, are expressed by the figures 0·79 : 1 : 1·85.

A glass tube, similar in shape to that represented by fig. 69, which is loaded at the bottom with a little mercury or a few shot, to give it a vertical position when immersed, will evidently not sink to an equal depth in all three of these liquids. If it sinks to half its length when immersed in water, it will sink still lower in alcohol, that liquid being lighter than the former, while in sulphuric acid, which is so much heavier than water, it will not sink nearly so deep.

These instruments, which are termed *hydrometers* or *areometers*, are particularly adapted for comparing the densities of different fluids: they are employed under different names, according to the purposes to which they are applied.

69.

Equilibrium of Gases.

89. We have become acquainted, at §§ 8 and 17, with the properties by which aeriform bodies or gases are so easily distinguished from fluids and solids.

In our examination of these properties we shall, for our examples, generally select the air that surrounds us, as everything that may be remarked as to its general properties holds good equally with the other gases.

The particles of air are maintained at such a distance by heat, that their mutual attraction appears to cease altogether. The particles *a a a a* (fig. 70), existing within a certain space, do not appear to have any tendency to approach in the direction denoted by the arrows, on the contrary they exhibit an inclination to increase the distance between each other, by moving in the course shown by the arrows in fig. 71.

70. 71.

Gases are, therefore, considered to be bodies, the particles of which exhibit a tendency to move away from each other continually: this property is ascribed to the action of a peculiar kind of force, termed *repulsion*.

90. We will now see what deductions may be made from this property of gaseous bodies. If the same space of air be assumed as enclosed in a vessel (fig. 72), the particles *a*, possessing the tendency to move away from each other, will exert a pressure on the sides of the vessel.

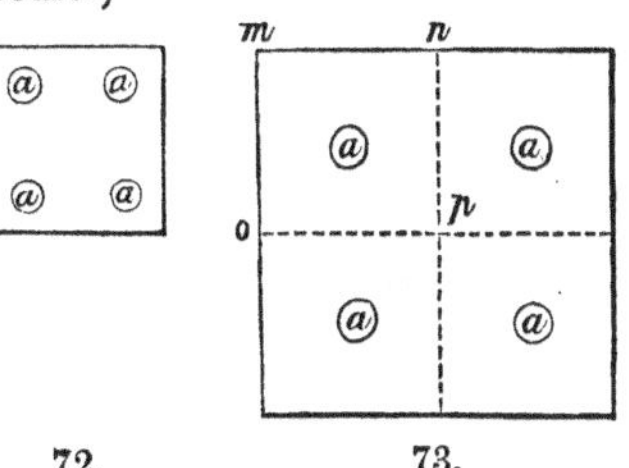

72. 73.

This expansive property of gases is called their *elasticity* or *tension.*

If we imagine the vessel (fig. 72) expansible to four times its size, by a peculiar construction of its sides, as shown in fig. 73, the particles *a* will in consequence move to a greater distance from each other. While, therefore, the sides of the vessel (fig. 72) had to sustain a pressure of 4 *a*, a portion of the vessel (fig. 73), marked *m n o p*, equal in size to the former vessel, has to withstand only one-fourth of that pressure, or 1 *a*.

74. 75.

On reversing this experiment, by compressing the air, as in fig. 74, to such an extent that it occupies only one-fourth of its original space (fig. 75), it is evident that the sides of the vessel (fig. 75), will have to sustain a pressure of 4 *a*, while a portion of the vessel, *m n o p* (fig. 74), equal in size to the former, will have to sustain only a fourth part of that pressure, or 1 *a*.

91. In the foregoing examples we had the same quantity of air existing in different states of expansion and elasticity; and we saw clearly that its elasticity decreases with increasing expansion, whilst, on the other hand, it gains in elasticity when compressed into a smaller space.

This relation between expansion and elasticity obeys a certain law, which may be expressed thus: *the elasticity of a gas stands in inverse ratio to the space it occupies.*

With the same amount of air, therefore—

Occupying the space of	1	$\frac{1}{2}$	$\frac{1}{3}$	$\frac{1}{4}$	$\frac{1}{5}$	$\frac{1}{6}$	....	$\frac{1}{100}$	$\frac{1}{n}$
The tension is	1	2	3	4	5	6	....	100	n

92. Hence, by compressing air into a very small space, by means of proper apparatus, we can increase its tension to such an extent as to apply it to the production of powerful effects.

The *air-gun* (fig. 76) is an example of the application of this power, but a still more familiar one is the *pop-gun*, a well-known toy (fig. 77.) The

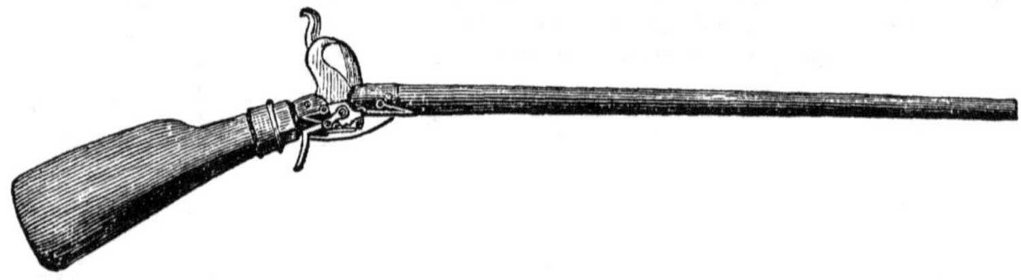

76.

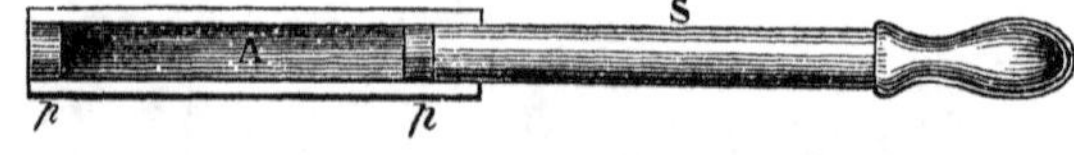

77.

space A is enclosed by the two stoppers *p p*. On the stopper *p* nearest to the piston being pushed farther into the cylinder by the rod S, the air contained in the space A is compressed until its tension becomes so great as to drive out the stopper at the mouth of the cylinder with great force, accompanied by a report. The stopper *p* may be considered as a moveable side of the vessel A.

93. The tendency of the particles of gases to repel each other would soon cause the air to be dispersed over the whole universe if it were not influenced and retained by the attractive force of the earth. The latter is, therefore, surrounded by the air, as a kind of covering, which we term *atmosphere*, and which has a height of about 30 or 40 miles.

Another result of the attraction of air by the earth is the pressure which the former exercises upon every substance on which it rests. This pressure may be measured, or, in other words, the weight of the air may be determined.

For this purpose, a hollow glass globe is filled with air and accurately weighed. The air is then removed from the globe by means of the air-pump, and the globe again weighed. The difference between the two results is the weight of the air contained in the globe.

The density of the air has been found, by this method, to be 770 times less than that of water. Supposing the globe with which the experiment is made to contain exactly 1 oz. of air, it would, when filled with water, hold exactly 770 ozs. of the latter; 770 cubic inches of air weigh, therefore, as much as 1 cubic inch of water.

94. We are acquainted with several gases besides atmospheric air which are possessed of different densities: thus, for instance, hydrogen is 14 times lighter than air; the density of chlorine gas is 2½ times, and that of carbonic acid gas 1½ times, greater than that of air.

The application of gases lighter than air to *aerostatics* will be described hereafter.

95. The pressure exerted by the air may be indicated and determined even without the use of the balance.

The bent glass tube (fig. 78, A) is supposed to contain mercury. As we have seen at § 81, the surfaces of the liquid must be equally high in both arms; hence it is evident that the column of mercury *a b* holds the column *c d* in perfect equilibrium.

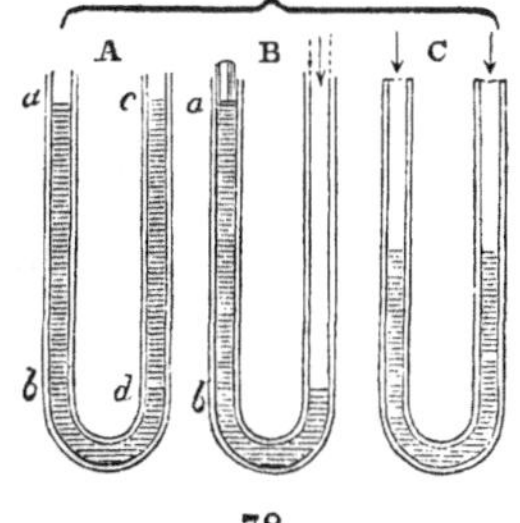

78.

The opening *a* is now closed air-tight by means of a cork, and one-half of the mercury is removed from the tube by inclining and shaking it. The mercury will now be found not to stand equally high in both arms, but to remain in the one arm, as shown at fig. 78, B. What is it that now holds the column of mercury in equilibrium? Evidently nothing else than the column of air pressing into the other arm, and which we may imagine as extending upwards to the confines of the atmosphere.

On removing the cork from the opening *a*, the mercury will immediately fall and stand at an equal height in both arms of the tube, as seen at C. The air, pressing equally on both openings of the tube, once more maintains the equilibrium (comp. § 49).

96. The result of the experiment is slightly different if a glass tube of

considerable length is employed, each arm being about 36 inches high. It will be found, on conducting the experiment as above, that the mercury will not remain perfectly stationary in the one arm, but will fall to a certain point *c* (fig. 79). In measuring the height of the column of mercury remaining in the arm, from *b* to *c*, it will be found to be 29·9 inches or 760 millimeters in height.

97. This clearly proves that the air cannot maintain in equilibrium a column of mercury of any indefinite height.

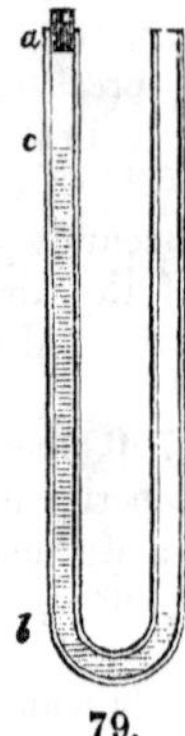

79.

Assuming that the tube employed measures one square inch in the bore, the two forces that maintain each other in equilibrium are, on the one side, a column of mercury, 1 square inch in thickness and 29·9 inches high, consisting therefore of 29·9 cubic inches of mercury, and, on the other side, a column of air, 1 square inch in thickness, but of the height of the atmosphere.

The weight of the above column of mercury is about $14\frac{4}{5}$ lbs. (see § 33); a column of air of 1 square inch in thickness, and of the height of the atmosphere, must therefore likewise weigh $14\frac{4}{5}$ lbs. As the air surrounds the earth and every object thereon, and as the pressure of the atmosphere acts in all directions similar to that of water (comp. § 83), every square inch (fig. 80) of the surface of a body situated in the air has continually to sustain a pressure of $14\frac{4}{5}$ lbs.

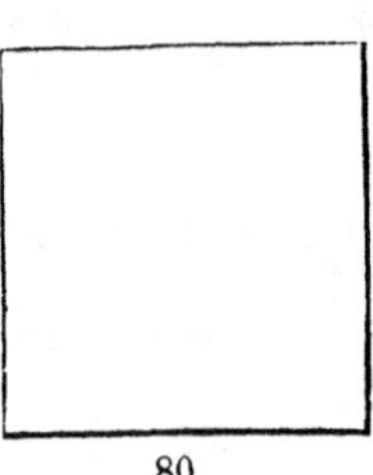
80.

Supposing the surface of a table to measure 1 square meter = 1550 square inches, it would have to sustain a pressure of 1550 × 14·8 = 22,940 lbs.

The surface of the body of a grown person measures about 1 square meter. The atmospheric pressure that such a person has continually to sustain is, therefore, equal to the enormous weight of 22,940 lbs. We are, however, not in the least sensible of this pressure, as the air, pressing equally on all sides, maintains itself in equilibrium. If the atmospheric pressure could be suddenly removed from the one side of a man, he would receive a blow on the other side equal to 11,470 lbs., a force which no human strength could withstand.

81.

98. The barometer (fig. 81) is the most simple instrument for measuring the atmospheric pressure. It consists of a glass tube several lines in width and from 36 to 40 inches in height, and sealed at one end. It is filled perfectly with mercury, its open end being closed with the finger, and then, as in fig. 81, immersed in mercury, and again opened. The mercury in the tube will now fall to the point *s*, which is 30 inches above the surface of the mercury in the vessel *a*. This distance is called the *height of the barometer*. In this case also, the column of mercury is evidently maintained in equilibrium by the atmospheric pressure acting upon the surface *a*.

The question now arises, what does that portion of the tube above the column of mercury contain? Nothing but a perfectly *empty space*, which has been named, after the discoverer, the *Torricellian vacuum*.

For a good barometer, the tube employed should not be too narrow; its bore should be at least three or four lines in diameter. The glass and mercury must be perfectly clean and pure, and the vacuum must of course not contain a trace of air, as the latter would exert its tension in overcoming a portion of the atmospheric pressure. In order to prevent the possibility of the presence of any air, the mercury is for some time heated or boiled in the tube, or before it is poured into it.

99. Observation has shown that the mercury in one and the same barometer does not at all times stand at an equal height; hence it follows that the pressure of the atmosphere is not always and everywhere the same.

The variations in the height of the barometer are termed its *rising* and *falling*.

If a barometer stands at 30 inches at the sea-side, and if it be afterwards taken to the top of a mountain, the column of mercury will no longer stand at the same height. The higher the place of observation, the lower will the barometer fall.

This is easily accounted for. The distance from the summit of a mountain to the confines of the atmosphere is evidently less than from the sea-shore. The column of air pressing upon the barometer at a certain height is shorter in proportion to this height: the force of its pressure is, therefore, less.

The barometer is consequently an instrument of the greatest importance for determining altitudes: it may be constructed for travellers so as to be transportable, and has, in this state, already been taken by natural philosophers to the highest summits of the Alps, the Andes, and the Cordilleras.

100. The height of the barometer is, however, influenced by other causes, besides the altitude of the place of observation, which frequently render it subject to certain variations. Severe tempests, which arise from great disturbances in the equilibrium of the air, and earthquakes, are generally preceded by a considerable fall of the barometer.

If the air contain much aqueous vapour, as it generally does in fine and warm weather, the pressure of the air is increased by the tension of the vapour: at such times the barometer will stand very high.

But when, on the cooling down of the air, the vapours lose their tension, the pressure of the atmosphere will of course decrease, and the barometer fall. The condensed vapours soon render themselves visible in the form of clouds and rain.

As the barometer indicates these changes long before the clouds and rain make their appearance, it may be considered as a prophet of the weather, and is to be found in that capacity in many houses.

101. The atmosphere is not equally dense at every height. Its density is greatest at the surface of the earth, the lower strata of air having to sustain the pressure of those above.

The decrease of atmospheric pressure is observed to be considerable even on the summits of very high hills. If a bottle, filled with air and well corked, be taken to a great height, the cork will be forced out of the bottle. The blood is driven, by the action of the heart, with a certain force, into the finest and most delicate veins in the extremities of the human body, which are, however, capable, under the ordinary pressure, of withstanding this force. At altitudes of 24,000 and 26,000 feet, however, where the atmospheric pressure on the surface of the body is much lessened, these small blood-vessels burst, the blood forcing its way through them. The air at these heights is likewise no longer sufficiently dense for perfect respiration.

102. The tension, or the expansive property, of the air, affords us a means of rarefying it in closed vessels, to such an extent that the latter may be almost considered as free from air. The instruments used for this purpose are called *air-pumps*.

Let us examine the construction of such an instrument (fig. 82). In a cylinder *a*, which must be perfectly well finished, the piston *b* moves by means of the rod *c*, which must be perfectly air-tight, no air being able to escape between the piston and the cylinder. In the piston there is a valve *s*, which must move easily, and open upwards. It rises when the pressure from below is greater than from above, but otherwise remains hermetically closed. The rod *e d* is the valve for the cylinder. If the piston be raised, the whole rod is lifted up, but *d* soon strikes the upper plate of the cylinder, and the piston moves with some friction along the whole rod. As soon as the piston descends, the truncated cone *e* is pressed into the conical opening below it, so that the upper surface of the cone *e* and the bottom of the cylinder form a plane surface, and the piston may, therefore, rest perfectly on this bottom.

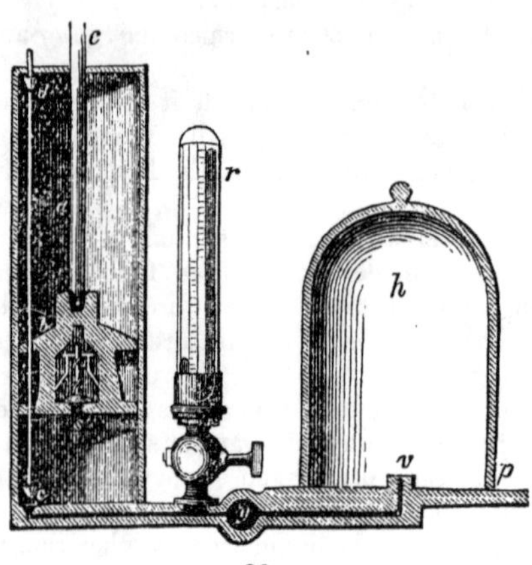

82.

From the above-mentioned conical opening a canal goes on to *v*. Here there is a screw, to which may be attached the balloons or receivers that are to be exhausted.

The screw *v* is in the middle of a plate *p*, on which the bell *h* may be placed. Let us assume that the piston is on the lower plate of the cylinder. If then it be raised, a *vacuum* will be formed, provided all the valves remain shut; but the valve *e* is opened, and air from the bell passes partly over to the cylinder.

But, by this means, the air in the bell and in the canal of the bell is rarefied, and, consequently, the valve *s* in the piston must remain closed. On the descent of the piston the valve at *e* is shut, and all passage closed for the return of the air from the cylinder into the bell. The air thus shut in will escape through the valve *s*, until the piston reaches the bottom of the cylinder. Another upward stroke of the piston produces a fresh rarefication in the bell.

By repeating this operation, the air is continually rarefied until its tension no longer suffices to lift the valve *e;* in which case no farther rarefication can be produced.

We now proceed to illustrate this remarkable phenomenon.

The bell now no longer contains any air, the tension of which would counteract the pressure of the external atmosphere upon the bell. The latter is, therefore, pressed down with such power upon the plate, that it cannot be removed by the application of considerable force. It is only after admission of air into the bell by means of a stop-cock, that we are once more enabled to remove it with ease.

103. Of the many remarkable experiments that may be made by means of the air-pump, we will mention one in particular that has attained historical celebrity.

Otto von Guerike in Magdeburg, the inventor of the air-pump, constructed two hollow hemispheres of copper, the edges of which fitted accurately to each other (fig. 83). The latter were rubbed over with grease, pressed tightly together, and the globe was then exhausted of air, through the cock *c*. The two hemispheres, that fell asunder before exhaustion, were now pressed together by the external air with such force that several horses, attached to the ring of each hemisphere, could not exert sufficient force to separate them.

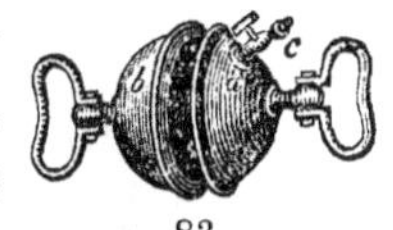

83.

This beautiful experiment was performed, in the year 1650, to the great astonishment of all beholders, at the Imperial Diet at Ratisbon, in the presence of the Emperor Ferdinand III. and a number of princes and nobles.

84.

It may be shown, by means of the air-pump, that all bodies fall with equal velocity when in a vacuum, and that animals cannot exist therein; and a number of other phenomena are produced by the aid of this instrument, of which mention can be made only hereafter.

104. Many phenomena, such as respiration and suction, and many important instruments, as the suction-pump and fire-engine, depend upon the pressure of the atmosphere and the production of rarefied spaces.

By enlarging the space of the cavity of the chest, by means of particular muscles, the air contained therein is rarefied, and a fresh portion enters from the atmosphere; thus *inhalation* is produced. On the contraction of the sides of the chest by the muscles, the air contained in the cavity is compressed and escapes; this is termed *exhalation*.

On immersing one end of a glass tube, the stem of a pipe, or a reed, into water, and applying suction to the other end, the air will become rarefied, and the water will be forced upwards by the pressure of the external air.

An arrangement for effecting suction by means of the air-pump, instead of the mouth, is termed a *pump*.

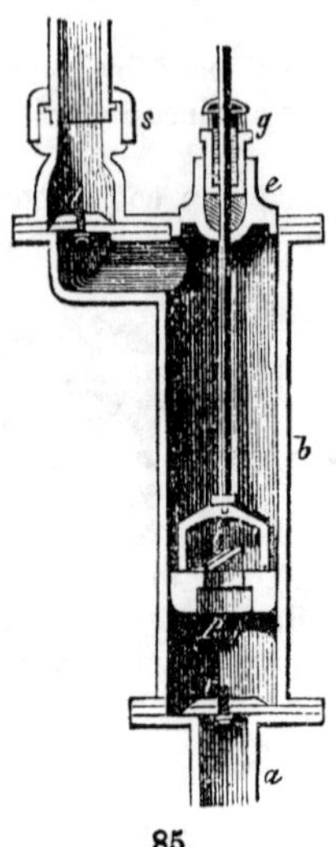

85.

105. The pump consists of a *reservoir* (fig. 85), generally speaking, an underground cistern, into which extends the *suction-pipe a*, which may be closed by the valve *r*. Above this are situated the *cylinder b*, and an upper pipe *s*, but more frequently a *spout*. The cylinder contains the *piston p*.

On raising the piston the air in the space beneath is rarefied, and causes the valve *t* to remain closed; while *r* opens and admits the water from the suction-pipe into the cylinder. On the piston being depressed the valve *r* is closed; the water that has been raised above it forces open the valve *t*, and passing thereby through the piston, reaches the upper portion of the cylinder, whence it flows out when it arrives at the spout, or passes into the upper pipe *s*, through the valve *l*. The number of strokes to be made with the piston before the water flows out of the spout of the pump, depends upon the relative size of the various parts of the instrument.

106. Water cannot, however, be raised to any height by means of the suction-pump; because the pressure of the atmosphere is incapable of forcing water higher than about 32 feet. We have ascertained (§ 96) that it is capable of maintaining in equilibrium a column of mercury 30 inches in height; water being thirteen times lighter than mercury, a column of water 13×30 inches in height is required to counterbalance the pressure of the column of mercury, or the pressure of the atmosphere.

The height of the first valve above the surface of the liquid should, therefore, not exceed 30 feet. It is still possible to raise the water in the cylinder, but not to a much greater height, as the operation of pumping becomes too laborious.

If, therefore, water is to be raised from a considerable depth, or to a great height, *forcing-pumps* of peculiar construction are substituted for the suction-pump.

107. The action of the *fire-engine* (fig. 86) depends principally on the increased tension of compressed air. The various parts of this machine are situated in a large vessel or cistern, which is kept continually filled with water. In its centre is fixed a strong receiver, *a*, called the *air-chamber*, in which the tube *g* reaches nearly to the bottom. When the engine is about to be used, this tube is first closed at *g*, by means of a cock. Water is now pumped into the air-chamber by means of the two suction-pumps *e e*, and as the air cannot escape from the former, it becomes more and more compressed therein, as fresh quantities of water are introduced. When the pressure has attained a certain force, the cock at *g* is opened, and the compressed air at the top of the chamber immediately drives out a jet of water with great

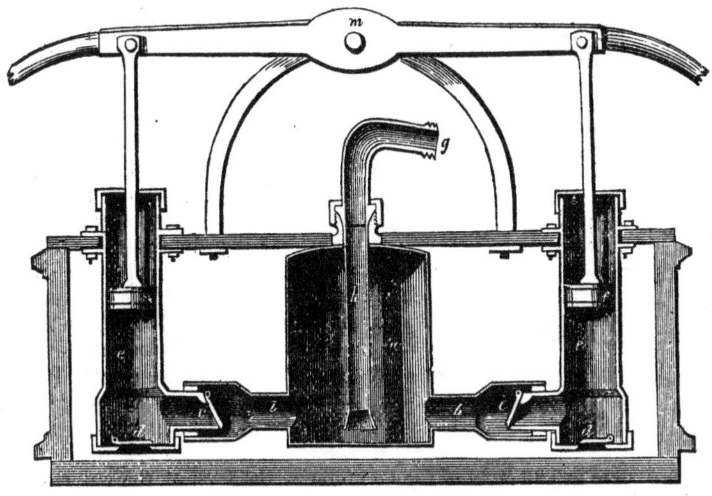

86.

force through the opening of the pipe. As water is continually pumped into the air-chamber, an uninterrupted jet is thus obtained.

The manner in which the air-chamber acts may be easily shown by half-filling a little bottle with water, corking it up, and fitting a small glass tube, or the stem of a pipe, air-tight, into the cork, so as to reach nearly to the bottom of the bottle. On blowing forcibly into the tube with the mouth, the air in the vessel becomes compressed, and as soon as the external pressure at the mouth of the tube is removed, a jet of water will be forced out of the glass. (Fig. 87.)

108. If a tumbler be perfectly filled with water, the surface covered with a piece of paper, and the glass then inverted, the water will not flow out, being prevented from so doing by the pressure of the atmosphere against the external surface of the paper. The use of the paper is merely to enable the experimenter to invert the glass, and to prevent any water from running out at the sides, or particles of air from entering in its place. If the lower opening is sufficiently narrow to prevent the efflux of the water, as is the case with the dipping-syphon, the paper is no longer required. The *dipping-syphon* (fig. 88) is a tubular vessel, somewhat contracted above and below, and open at both extremities. If it be immersed in a liquid it will become entirely filled, and, by closing the upper orifice with the thumb, the syphon may be lifted up without any of the fluid contained in it escaping.

87.

A modification of the common syphon, known as Mitscherlich's syphon (fig. 89), consists of a bent tube $b\ b'$, whose legs are of unequal length, the shorter one being sometimes curved upwards, for the purpose of drawing a liquid from above downwards, and thus removing it with more facility from a precipitate. If, after the shorter leg is plunged into the solution, the whole tube be filled by closing with the finger the lower aperture *b'*, and sucking out the air at *t*, the liquid, on removal of the finger, will continue to run out at the end of the longer leg *b'*, and may thus be perfectly separated without disturbing the precipitate. The action of the syphon is readily explained: the column of liquid in the longer leg, and that reaching in the shorter leg from the curve to the surface of the fluid in the vessel, have both a tendency to obey the law of gravity. This tendency, however, is opposed on both sides by atmospheric pressure, acting on the one side at the aperture *b'*, and on the other upon the surface of the liquid in the vessel; thus preventing, in the interior of the tube, the formation of a vacuum which would take place at the curve if the two columns ran down on both sides. By the pressure of the atmosphere acting with equal force, a perfect equilibrium would be established if the columns of water were equally high in both legs; that is, if the opening were at the elevation of the level of the water in the vessel; as soon, however, as *b'* lies deeper than *b*, the column in the longer leg preponderates, and, in proportion as the liquid escapes, a fresh portion is forced into the tube on the other side by the pressure of the air, so that the liquid continues to flow out at *b'* until the level has fallen to the height of the aperture *b*.

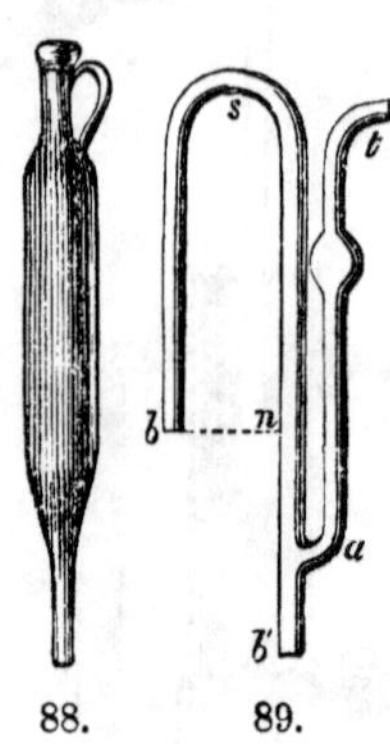

88. 89.

II. PHENOMENA OF VIBRATION.

109. We are now about to enter upon the consideration of a class of phenomena differing widely from those already examined, both by their impressions upon our senses, and by the manner in which we arrive at a conception of their origin and nature.

However much the most zealous and ingenious philosophers have enriched us with their experiments and the deductions they have arrived at, it still remains a difficult task to form a clear and definite idea of the nature of these phenomena.

110. We have become acquainted with *matter* as something occupying space, obeying the laws of mutual attraction, and under every form possessing weight. It is now necessary to enter upon the consideration of a class of phenomena which are independent of weight.

The term *Ether* has been adopted to express something opposite to matter; something that is not accumulated, like the latter, into bodies in different parts of the universe, but distributed over the whole in a state of infinite subtlety. Ether, therefore, penetrates even matter; and we cannot conceive an idea of substance without every particle thereof being surrounded by ether. As it does not occupy space in the same manner as matter, and is not influenced by attraction, it exists equally in the rarefied space of the air-pump and in the perfect vacuum of the barometer. It exists in everything, just as though the whole universe had been immersed in ether, and had become completely and eternally penetrated by it.

But how are we to recognise the presence of that in which all the properties by which we distinguish material bodies are absent? Ether also pos sesses its peculiar properties, by which alone we are enabled to form a conception of it.

Besides being possessed of exceeding *subtlety*, ether is also endowed with the highest *mobility*, and only becomes evident to our senses when in motion. Its slightest vibration distributes itself, therefore, over a great distance, until, as it reaches our senses, it produces sensations which we describe as *heat* and *light*. Other kinds of motion of ether render themselves perceptible to us by the production of phenomena which we comprise under the names of *Electricity* and *Magnetism*.

Scientific men naturally hesitated in adopting a conception of ether; for it is one of the most important principles in science to assume the existence of that only which may be made directly perceptible to the senses. Although this has not been possible as yet with regard to ether, we are enabled to increase our belief in its reality by calling to our aid that which is most similar to it, and which renders its existence more probable.

No man doubts the existence of the *mind* or the *soul*. Though invisible and incomprehensible to us, we are convinced of the presence of the soul by the wonderful and manifold actions of which it is capable on the slightest impulse.

And why should it be a matter of such difficulty to exalt our ideas to the conception of ether as something supermaterial, of exceeding fineness, after having become acquainted with water existing as a solid, a liquid, and a gas? There was a time when the conception of air as a body, presented to the mind a greater difficulty than does now the assumption of the presence of ether in the universe.

Our belief in the existence of ether finds its principal support in the fact that through this assumption we are enabled to form connected and sensible ideas of a variety of phenomena, and, indeed, to predict them, and confirm such by experiment, that we could not otherwise satisfactorily account for in any manner. It should, however, be observed here, that this physical ether must, by no means, be confounded with the fluid known in chemistry by the same name.

Vibrations in General.

111. A peculiar vibratory motion may be imparted to matter as well as to ether. The vibrations of matter produce in us the sensation of *sound;* while those of ether render them perceptible as *heat* and *light*.

As the clearest conception can be formed of vibrations by comparing them to the waves produced by throwing a stone into smooth water, the term *undulatory* or *wave motion* has been adopted in general to express the phenomena of vibrations.

A distinction is made between *standing* waves and *moving* or *progressing* waves. The former are produced by taking hold of a stretched cord or string in the centre, drawing it on one side, and then leaving it to itself. Progressing waves are formed by throwing a stone into water, or giving a blow to a tightly-stretched cord. The difference between these waves depends upon the following principles:—

When the state of rest or *equilibrium* of a stretched cord is disturbed, by imparting to the latter an undulatory motion, every portion of the cord returns for an instant, at each vibration or wave that it describes, to the position of equilibrium; or, in other words, the position of equilibrium is passed. Progressing waves differ particularly from standing waves in the circumstance that, with the former, the various vibrating parts will only pass the position of equilibrium one after the other, while it is simultaneously performed by the vibrating points of a standing wave.

The waves of water are well known to spread themselves in uniformly-increasing circles over the whole surface, so that the most distant portions of the water are gradually set in motion. Water-waves consist of alternate elevations and depressions. The whole number of waves, produced by throwing a stone into the water, is termed a system of waves.

The meeting of two different systems of waves, produced, for instance, by throwing two stones into the water, is accompanied by very peculiar phenomena. On their coming in contact, the elevations of the one system may meet with those of the other, and the wave depressions of the two systems may likewise come in simultaneous contact with each other, the result being the production of higher elevations and deeper depressions; or an elevation of one system may meet a depression of the other, in which case it is obvious that the two waves will counteract each other, and the undulatory motion will cease. This so-called *interference* of wave-systems produces *points of repose* or *nodes;* several of these, situated side by side, form lines of repose or *nodal lines.*

On progressing waves meeting with a sufficient impediment, their farther progress is not only prevented, but they are also thrown back. If, therefore, the waves moving along from one end of a cord meet with others coming in the opposite direction, nodal lines are also easily produced, the cord being divided by them into a number of standing waves.

Undulatory motions are most powerful at the point where they originate, and at the moment when they commence. They become smaller and decrease in power with every succeeding fraction of time, the farther they spread from the point where they originated. Sound, heat, and light, therefore, decrease in strength the farther we are distant from the point of their origin; this decrease of power stands in direct ratio to the squares of the distance.

The waves of a vibrating string proceed only in the direction of its axis. The waves of water spread in circles, which increase in size from the point of origin on the horizontal plane of the surface. But in order to understand the vibrations of air and ether, we must avail ourselves of another illustration. The point, for instance, at which a sound commences, we may consider as the centre of an infinite number of strata of air which surround that point in the form of hollow spheres of gradually increasing magnitude. The sound is farther spread, from the inner to the outer, by the progressive vibrations of all these spherical strata of air. These vibrations consist of the alternate approaching and receding of the strata of air, by means of which condensations and rarefactions are produced. By the same laws, heat and light diffuse themselves from the point of origin in *all directions.*

Straight lines which proceed from the centre through the circles of water waves, or through the spherical surfaces of vibrating air, are called *wave-rays*, and hence we speak of rays of sound, heat, and light.

A *difference* may, however, exist among the vibrations, according to the length or height of the waves, originally set in motion, as also according to their direction and velocity, *i. e.*, the number of vibrations occurring within a certain time. It will be seen that these differences exercise considerable influence over the phenomena resulting from undulatory motion.

We have now endeavoured to arrive at a general conception of the nature of sound, heat, and light; we must not, however, omit to state that the above is not the only view by which these natural phenomena, so remarkable in their appearance and effects, are accounted for.

It is not so much our object in this work to enter into the investigation of theories, or to compare the views of different philosophers, as to arrive at a knowledge of the most important facts which have been gleaned from nature by scientific men. It is our intention to communicate these, making use only of the most popular expressions, even if they should not always agree exactly with the view entered into above. *Muller's undulatory disc* is of great assistance for attaining a proper conception of wave motion.

I. Sound.

112. Daily experience teaches us that scarcely any motion of surrounding objects can take place without producing an audible sound. We may say with certainty, that every sound is the result of the vibrations of a portion of matter, and the nature of the tone or sound depends only on the manner in which these vibrations arise. Sounds generally reach our ears through the air, as waves of sound. These are produced by the alternate condensation and rarefaction of the air at certain points. With wires, bells, and tuning-forks, it is the bodies themselves that produce the sound which the air only serves to convey. In wind instruments and the human voice, it is the vibrating columns of air that sound.

The following remarks hold good in general with regard to sound: the height or depth of a tone depends on the number of vibrations made by the sounding body in a given time. The smaller the number of vibrations, the deeper is the tone, and *vice versâ*. The length of the different sound-waves stands in the closest relation to the tone produced. The deeper notes are produced by the longer, and the higher ones by the shorter sound-waves.

The deepest tone that can be produced results from vibrations, of which 14 or 15 are performed in one second. The deepest note that is applied in music, is that obtained by the organ-pipe of 16 feet length, closed at its upper end, which produces sound-waves of 32 feet. On the other hand, there exist high notes, the vibrations of which number 48,000 in a second. The wave-length of the highest musical notes is 18 lines. Higher or lower tones than the above-named can no longer be clearly distinguished by the ear, and are, therefore, not accepted as notes.

113. The phenomena of vibrating strings may be most conveniently examined by means of a string or wire (fig. 90), which may be lengthened or shortened by a movable bridge, and stretched more or less forcibly by weights attached to one end.

It may be easily proved by means of an arrangement of this description, that the number of vibrations of a string is the *greater*, the *shorter*, and the *thinner* it is, and the *tighter* it is *stretched*, and lastly, the smaller the *density* of it is. Such strings consequently produce the highest tones.

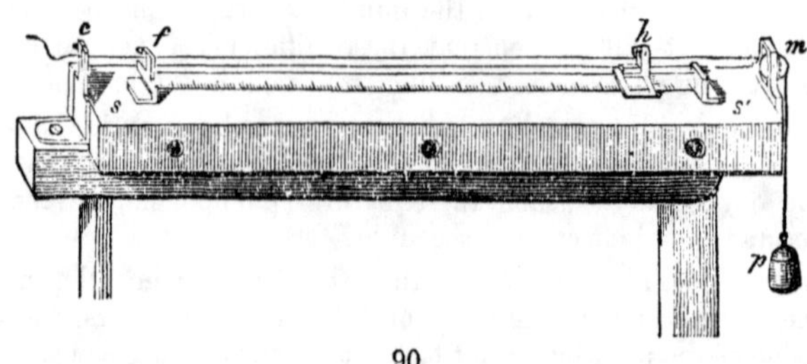

90.

The depth of tone of a string increases, therefore, with its thickness, density, and length, and with the decrease of the tension. The strings of the piano or harp are examples of this. Those strings which are to produce the deepest tones, on the violin and double bass, for instance, are covered with metallic wire, whereby their specific gravity is increased. Strings of equal length may possess different tones, according to their comparative thickness, or the unequal force with which they are stretched.

114. If we now notice a tone which has a certain number of vibrations, and call it, for instance *c;* the note that makes just double the number of vibrations in the same space of time, is called the *higher octave*, and the one that only performs half the vibrations, the *lower octave*, of C. Between every note and its octave, there are six other notes, the names and vibrations of which are as follows :—

Key note.	Second.	Third.	Fourth.	Fifth.	Sixth.	Seventh.	Octave.
c	*d*	*e*	*f*	*g*	*a*	*b*	*c*
1	$\frac{9}{8}$	$\frac{5}{4}$	$\frac{4}{3}$	$\frac{3}{2}$	$\frac{5}{3}$	$\frac{15}{8}$	2

These relations of the numbers of vibration are the same through all octaves and for all notes, by whatever instrument they may be produced. If the deep note C produced by the 16-feet pipe makes 32 single or 16 double vibrations in a second, its octave will make 64, its third 40, its fifth 48, &c.

The ratios between the numbers of each of two consecutive notes in this series are not alike. In the following list, the fraction placed by the letter denotes than how much greater the number of vibrations of each following note is, that of the preceding one:—

c		*d*		*e*		*f*		*g*		*a*		*b*		*c*
	$\frac{1}{8}$		$\frac{1}{9}$		$\frac{1}{15}$		$\frac{1}{8}$		$\frac{1}{9}$		$\frac{1}{8}$		$\frac{1}{15}$	

d therefore makes $1\frac{1}{8}$ times as many vibrations as *c* in a given time, *e* $1\frac{1}{9}$ times as many as *d*, *f* $1\frac{1}{15}$ times as many as *e*, &c.

The intervals from *c* to *d*, from *d* to *e*, from *f* to *g*, from *g* to *a*, and from *a* to *b*, are called *whole tones*, and measure either $\frac{1}{8}$ or $\frac{1}{9}$. On the other hand, the intervals from *e* to *f*, and from *b* to *c*, are called *semi-tones*, as they measure only about one-half of the above spaces, namely, $\frac{1}{15}$. In order, however, to be able to proceed from any note, with the intervals as they are given above, it becomes necessary first to introduce semitones between *c* and *d*, *f* and *g*, *g* and *b*, giving to them the names *c* sharp, *d* sharp, *f* sharp, *g* sharp, *a* sharp.

The key-note always forms with its octave, third, or fifth, a *consonance*, with all together a *concord;* and with its second, or seventh, a *discord.*

115. If a stretched wire be supported in its centre by the bridge, and the one half-stroked with the bow, the other half will also vibrate: this may be proved by placing small paper *riders* on the latter, which will be thrown off by the vibrations.

If the string be supported by the bridge at one-third its length, and the other two-thirds be covered with paper riders, they will all fall off on the first-third of the string being stroked with the bow, with the exception of those which are situated exactly on the second-third of the string. This point consequently does not participate in the vibrations of the string, and is, therefore, termed the *nodal* point. On supporting the string at one-fourth of its length, it is divided into four vibrating parts, with two nodes or points of repose, and so on.

When discs, bells, or plates are sounded, the vibratory motion is likewise not imparted equally to all parts. This, for instance, may be rendered perceptible by strewing a glass plate with fine sand, laying hold of it at one point and stroking its edge with the bow. The vibrating portions of the glass will cast the sand on to those points of repose which will form nodal lines in various mutual directions.

By employing square or round plates of glass, and by altering the point of support, the place where the vibratory motion is imparted, or the force with which it is imparted, a variety of *sound figures* may be produced, such as are shown in figs. 91 and 92.

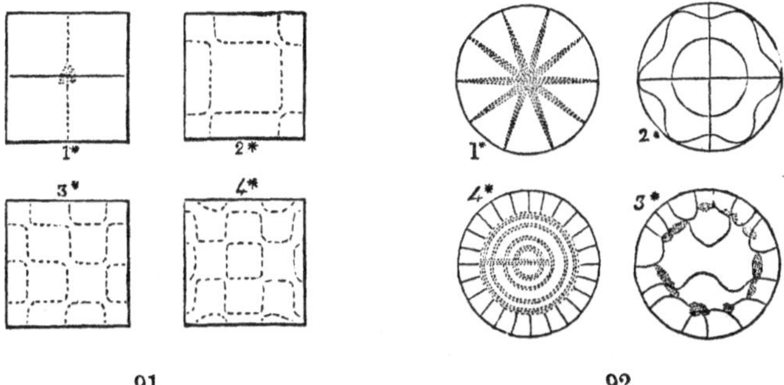

91. 92.

116. Sound distributes itself in all directions, the vibratory motion being imparted from one particle to those which surround it. This proceeds with great velocity, for it has been observed that sound travels, in the ordinary atmosphere, at a rate of 1,050 feet in a second. Its velocity is, however, far surpassed by that of light, as may be observed when a gun is fired off at a distance. The fire and smoke are first seen, and the report is heard only some time afterwards. We see the lightning before we hear the thunder that is produced simultaneously, and we judge correctly of the distance of the storm by the interval that elapses between the observation of both.

It is remarkable that sound passes much more rapidly through denser bodies than it does through those which are of less density. It is well known that the roar of cannon, the trampling of horses, &c., may be heard at a much greater distance by holding the ear to the earth, than merely by listening in the open air. Water also conducts sound to a great distance: and fish will hear the sound of a bell or fife summoning them to be fed.

At considerable altitudes, where the air is less dense, the sound of the voice is more feeble, and the report of a musket is not audible at so great a distance.

If, however, the sounding vibrations are imparted to a body in vacuo, they cannot communicate beyond that body, and will, therefore, not be heard. This experiment may be easily made by means of the air-pump. A bell, suspended and struck in a vacuum, will not be audible. As soon, however, as air is admitted into the space, the sound will be distinctly heard.

117. When the sound rays, passing through the air in a straight direction, meet with denser objects, the direction of their course will be more or less altered. They may indeed, if they meet with a solid obstacle, be perfectly repelled or reflected like the water-waves on the sea-shore. The phenomenon of reflected sound is called *echo.* In order to hear an echo of one syllable, the observer must be at least 60 feet from the surface where the sound is reflected; for an echo of more syllables the distance must be from 116 to 120 feet.

Speaking-tubes are employed for the conveyance of sound, particularly of language. They are tin tubes, about one inch in diameter, and extending from one story or room to another, or from the mast-head to the deck of a vessel. A word spoken into one end of the tube will be distinctly heard at the other end, the sound-waves being prevented from dispersing.

The *speaking-trumpet* is a cone-shaped instrument, likewise serving to retain the sound-waves more together, by which means they may be directed with particular force in one direction. On the other hand, a similar instrument is employed as a *hearing-trumpet,* the wide opening of which collects the waves of sound, and conducts them to the ear.

Heat.

118. The conditions which we term *hot, warm,* or *cold,* appear to be the results produced by certain vibrations of matter. These conditions are not really opposed to each other, but may be regarded as different degrees of one general phenomenon which we call *heat,* and which, besides rendering itself sensible to our feelings through the above conditions, always exerts an influence on the expansion of bodies.

On inquiring into the proximate causes of heat, they will be found to be various. Heat renders itself sensible when two bodies are rubbed or knocked together. It is well known that savages obtain fire by the friction of two pieces of wood, and that the smith can make a nail red-hot by the proper management of his hammer. A great quantity of heat is likewise disengaged in the turning or boring of metals. When bodies are reduced to a higher degree of density, a considerable evolution of heat takes place; as, for instance, by the rapid and powerful compression of air, and by the slacking of lime.

Various and important phenomena of heat are the results of *chemical* combinations which are unceasingly proceeding in Nature. The best known of these is the process of combustion, which is commonly applied by us to the production of heat for our own purposes. Even the chemical decomposition of food continually proceeding in the human body is an abundant source of heat. Electricity likewise produces considerable heat, as is proved by the effects of lightning.

The earth, moreover, possesses in itself a certain amount of heat, which is but slightly perceptible on its surface, but becomes more sensible to us at some depth, so that we have reason to assume the existence of a considerable degree of heat in the interior of the earth.

Finally, we regard the sun as the principal source of the heat felt on the surface of the earth, as rays of heat, besides those of light, are daily imparted by it. If the earth were not under the influence of solar heat, it would differ widely in its nature from its present state.

Whatever may be the source whence heat is derived, it always exhibits the same phenomena in its relation to other objects.

Expansion by Heat.

119. One of the most common phenomena produced by heat, which is sensible to the eye, is the expansion of bodies. It has already been shown (§ 17) that the solid, fluid, or gaseous state of matter is entirely dependent on the influence exercised thereon by heat.

Examples of this expansion may be easily found. A metallic ball, which is a little too large to pass through a ring of metal, will, on the latter being heated, fall through it with ease, the ring being expanded by the heat.

If a vessel be filled completely with a liquid, and the latter heated gradually, it will soon flow over the edge of the vessel, in consequence of its expansion.

A bladder, pressed together, with the opening firmly tied up, but containing still a little air, will, on being warmed, assume the same form as if it were inflated with the mouth, in consequence of the expansion of the enclosed air.

120. The expansion of bodies furnishes a very valuable means of comparing the effects of heat, and likewise of measuring its increase. Heat, as far as it exerts its influence on the comparative expansion of bodies, is termed *temperature*, and the instrument employed for measuring the latter is called a *thermometer* (fig. 93).

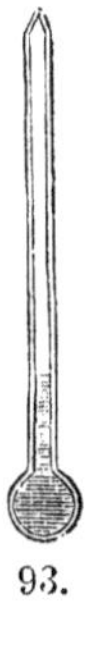

The thermometer, like other important philosophical instruments, as the pendulum and barometer, possesses the advantage of great simplicity.

A glass tube is chosen for the construction of the thermometer, the bore of which is perfectly uniform throughout, having about the width of a moderate-sized needle. A small bulb is blown at one end, and then filled with pure mercury. The mercury is now heated, upon which it expands, and fills the whole tube, which is from 6 to 10 inches in length. As soon as the mercury is at the point of protruding from the tube, the latter is sealed, so that it now contains no air whatever,

93.

but only the mercury, which on cooling again contracts, so as to stand to about one-third or one-fourth of the height of the tube.

When a tube thus prepared is immersed in melting ice, the column of mercury will stand at a certain height, which is accurately noted by a mark made on the glass tube. The thermometer is then placed for some time in boiling water, and the height to which the mercury rises likewise marked.

Whenever the thermometer is introduced into melting ice or boiling water, the mercury will stand at exactly the heights already noted, which shows that a body always occupies the same space at an equal temperature, and that this space decreases proportionately as the body becomes colder.

The point to which the mercury sinks, when the thermometer is immersed in melting ice, is indicated by a *naught*, and is called the *freezing-point.* That point to which the mercury rises, when the thermometer is plunged into boiling water, is called the *boiling-point.*

When, therefore, the thermometer is placed in any other position, we can judge of the surrounding temperature from the point at which the mercury stands in the tube. We call the temperature *high* if the mercury is near to the boiling-point, and *low* if it approaches the freezing-point.

In order to give greater accuracy to such determinations of temperature, the space between the two points above mentioned is divided into a number of equal parts, which are called *degrees.* This division of the tube is also extended beyond the freezing- and boiling-points; those degrees that are situated above the former are termed *heat-degrees,* and are denoted by the sign +, while those below the freezing-point are called *degrees of cold,* and are indicated by the mark —.

121. In some thermometers the distance between the freezing- and boiling-points is divided into 80 equal parts. This scale of divisions was first made by Reaumur, after whom it has been named: this kind of thermometer is most frequently employed in Germany. In France, and in scientific works, a thermometer, with a scale of 100 divisions, or the *Centigrade* thermometer, is adopted, in which the boiling-point stands at 100°. But in this country, and in England, a thermometer, with a perfectly different scale, constructed by *Fahrenheit,* is most generally employed. The following comparative table will most clearly show the relation existing between the different scales :—

Fahrenheit Scale.	Centigrade.	Reaumur.	——
— 4°	— 20°	— 16°	Every 5 degrees on the Centigrade scale are here seen to be equal to 4 degrees on the Reaumur scale. In order to prevent mistakes in the statement of temperatures, it is customary to describe particularly the scale employed. Thus, for instance, + 15° F. signifies 15 heat degrees on the Fahrenheit scale; or — 16° C. is equal to 16 degrees of cold on the Centigrade scale.
+ 14	— 10	— 8	
32	0	0	
50	+ 10	+ 8	
68	20	16	
86	30	24	
104	40	32	
122	50	40	
140	60	48	
158	70	56	
176	80	64	
194	90	72	
212	100	80	

122. The following is a Table of a number of Temperatures worthy of notice :—

——	Fahrenheit.	Centigrade.	Reaumur.
Freezing-point of spirit of wine.........	— 68°	— 90°	— 72°
Freezing-point of mercury	— 40	— 40	— 32
Temperature at the Polar regions......	—32·8 to —40	— 36 to — 40	— 28 to — 32
Lowest winter temperature..............	10·4 to — 4	— 12 to — 20	— 10 to — 16
Freezing-point of water.	32	0	0
Greatest density of water................	39·2	+ 4	+ 3·1
Temperature of the bodies of fishes, } Dependent on the surrounding medium.	59 to 77	15 to 25	12 to 20
Temperature of the bodies of many amphibious animals, } Dependent on the surrounding medium.	59 to 86	15 to 30	12 to 24
Mean temperature of Frankfort-on-the-Maine.......................................	48·2	9	7
Mean temperature of a room...........	68	20	16
General summer heat.......................	68 to 77	20 to 25	15 to 20
Higher summer heat........................	75·2 to 96·8	24 to 36	19 to 28
Mean temperature of the Equator......	84·2	29	23
Temperature of the human body, or blood heat	98·6	37	29
Boiling-point of ether......................	95	35	28
Temperature of the bodies of birds....	107·6	42	34
Melting-point of wax........................	154·4	68	54
Temp'ture at which phosphorus ignites	167	75	60
Boiling-point of alcohol...................	172·4	78	62
Boiling-point of water.......................	212	100	80
Melting-point of sulphur..................	226·4	108	86
Melting-point of lead.......................	611·6	322	257
Boiling-point of sulphuric acid..........	618·8	326	260
Boiling-point of mercury..................	680	360	288
Melting-point of silver......................	1832	1000	800
Melting-point of cast-iron.................	2192	1200	980
Melting-point of gold.......................	2282	1250	1000
Melting-point of bar-iron..................	2912	1600	1280

It is very remarkable, in the preceding series of temperatures, that water at + 4° C. (39° F.) is denser than ice. It is, however, owing to this exception, that in winter the waters of our rivers are not frozen to the ground.

123. As mercury freezes at —40° C. (—40° F.), we employ, for the determination of very low temperature, thermometers filled with alcohol, coloured red. Degrees of heat, situated near or above the boiling-point of mercury, can likewise be no longer determined by a mercury thermometer. The various methods employed for the determination of such high temperatures are all attended with difficulties; the expansion of air presents the means upon which most reliance can be placed.

The expansion of solid bodies, particularly of steel, is applied to the construction of other kinds of thermometers, which find, however, but little application.

124. The force with which bodies are expanded by heat is exceedingly great. The strongest vessels, when filled with water or air, tightly closed and heated, are often incapable of withstanding the force of expansion. Ir

is of great importance in many respects, particularly in the construction of machinery, to know the extent to which solid bodies expand at certain differences of temperature: determinations of this description have been made with the greatest accuracy.

The fracture of solid bodies in consequence of unequal expansion, such as the cracking of a tumbler when placed on a stove, is of very frequent occurrence, and admits of a simple explanation. The lower particles of the glass become heated and expanded sooner than the upper ones, which still remain in their original state. Hence a tension or pressure is produced in the glass, frequently causing it to crack. The thinner the glass, or the more gradually it is heated, for instance, by placing paper under it, the less likely will there be an unequal expansion, and consequently, danger of fracture.

125. A second result of the expansion of bodies by heat is the decrease of their density. This is particularly perceptible with fluid and gaseous bodies. If water is heated in a vessel, the lower strata, which become heated first and are thereby rendered less dense, rise to the surface, while the colder portions sink to the bottom of the vessel. A motion is thus produced in the water which is perceptible on the introduction of a fine powder into it. This motion continues until the whole mass of water has attained an equal temperature, and, therefore, uniform density.

A still more rapid motion is imparted to the air by heat. In warmed rooms, the lower stratum of air is frequently quite cold, while the upper portion is already thoroughly warmed. The so-called draughts in stoves are caused only by the ascent of air heated by the fire. The ascending of warm air may be rendered visible by a very pretty little contrivance. A piece of card-board is cut into a spiral form, and one end is fixed on the point of a knitting-needle, the other end of which is stuck into a piece of soft wood. On standing this upon the top of a stove, the heated air as it ascends will make the card-strip revolve round the needle, thus giving it the appearance of a snake. If a good-sized globe of thin paper be inflated with air, which is rapidly heated, the globe will ascend to a considerable height, and may even be made to remain a long time in the atmosphere, by suspending to its opening, at the bottom, a vessel containing burning spirit.

126. *Winds* are, generally speaking, nothing more than currents of air, produced in consequence of the unequal temperature of different parts of the atmosphere. This is most regularly shown by the *trade-winds*, which are produced by the ascent of heated air from the equator, and its replacement by dense cold currents of air from the poles. The revolution of the earth, however, tends to give them a direction parallel with the equator, so that, in the northern hemisphere, the trade-winds follow the mean of the two directions, namely, north-east.

The prevailing land and sea breezes on the coasts are also very regular. After sunrise, a wind sets in from the sea to the land, the latter becoming much more rapidly heated by the sun than the water, so that the warm air ascending from the land is replaced by currents of air coming from the water. After sunset the reverse is the case. The land cools down more rapidly; in consequence of which currents of air pass from it to the sea. A similar phenomenon is observed at the entrance of valleys.

Storms are winds of tremendous velocity, travelling at the rate of 120 feet in a second. They are the results of the sudden condensation of aqueous vapour contained in the atmosphere. The air rushes with great force from all sides into the rarefied space thus produced. The circumstance, that the appearance of storms is always accompanied by a fall of the barometer, has led to the above explanation of these phenomena.

If violent winds or storms meet from opposite directions, they produce *whirlwinds*, which often tear away with them all movable objects to which they impart a circular motion. On land they give rise to columns of sand, and at sea they produce *water-spouts* (fig. 94).

94.

127. In speaking of the density of a body, it is always understood to bear reference to a certain temperature, at which the density was determined. The densities of solid and liquid bodies vary, however, only slightly with small differences of temperature. The determinations of density are generally made at a temperature of 12° to 15° C. (53° to 59° F.).

Slight differences of temperature, however, greatly affect the density of gaseous bodies. According to the most accurate observations, all gases expand to $\frac{1}{273}$ of their volume for every degree on the Centigrade scale, corresponding to an expansion of $\frac{1}{492}$ of their volume for each Fahrenheit degree; 273 cubic inches of air at 15° C. (59° F.) occupy therefore a space of 274 cubic inches if their temperature is increased to 16° C. (60·8° F.), whereas at 14° C. (57·2° F.), they will only occupy a space of 272 cubic inches.

Besides the thermometer, the barometer also shows us that the density of the air is not always the same. For when the barometer stands high, the density of the air is not the same as when its position is low, as air, when charged with aqueous vapour, has naturally a different density from dry air.

These circumstances have, however, been carefully regarded and allowed for, in the determination of the density of gases; when it is, therefore, said (§ 93) that 770 cubic inches of atmospheric air weigh $\frac{1}{2}$ oz., or, what is the same, that air is 770 times lighter than water, it is understood that the density determination was made with dry air at a barometric height of 30 inches, and at the temperature of 0° C. (32° F.). The same conditions hold good for the statements regarding the density of all the other gases.

As we know, however, from § 91, that the spaces occupied by gases bear an inverse ratio to the pressure exerted upon them, and as we are acquainted with the extent to which gases expand for every degree of the thermometer, we may easily find by calculation the density of a gas for any pressure and temperature.

It is now perfectly intelligible why a balloon, filled with warm, and therefore lighter, air, ascends in the atmosphere. We are as little surprised at this as at the rising of a cork to the surface of water.

The circumstance that vines and other plants occasionally are not frozen on high hills, while they perish in valleys, is likewise accounted for by the ascent of the warm air.

EBULLITION—EVAPORATION.

128. If various bodies are exposed to a high temperature, they are either destroyed, as is the case with vegetable and animal productions, or they suffer merely a change of condition.

Solid bodies become fluid at a certain temperature. At § 122 the fusing or melting-points of various bodies have been enumerated; we have only to add that the same body always melts at a certain temperature; lead, for instance, at 322° C. (611° F.).

If a fused body be continuously heated, a certain point will at last be attained, when its particles will, by the influence of heat, assume the properties of gases. Solid and fluid bodies, when in this state, are called *vapours*. Most bodies may be converted into vapour, although many require a very high temperature to attain that state; but, under these conditions, even such metals as iron, copper, or platinum may be vaporized.

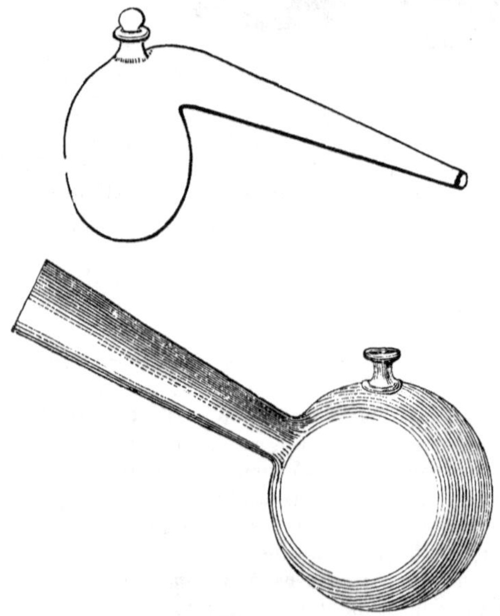

95.

Such bodies as may be converted into vapour at a comparatively low temperature are called *volatile* bodies.

All vapours remain in that state as long as the temperature by which they were formed continues. As soon, however, as it decreases, the body condenses to a liquid, which may afterwards solidify.

129. Two important technical and chemical operations, namely, *sublimation* and *distillation*, are based upon the property which bodies possess of assuming, under the influence of heat, the form of vapour.

The first of these consists in the conversion of *solid* bodies into vapour, and the condensation of the latter in appropriate vessels. The condensed substance is generally deposited as a fine pulverulent body, which is called a *sublimate.* The most simple way of effecting sublimation is by placing a substance, such as camphor, at the sealed end of a glass tube, and applying heat. The camphor will soon be converted into white vapours, which will condense as a fine powder at the upper, cool portion of the tube.

Distillation has found far more frequent application than sublimation. It is employed for the separation of a volatile body from other substances that are not volatile, or only very slightly so. Thus, for instance, at brandy distilleries the volatile spirit in the fermented wash is separated from the remainder by distillation.

A distilling apparatus generally consists of three parts; the still or retort in which the liquid is heated, the condenser in which the vapours are condensed, and the receiver in which the distillate is collected.

For chemical operations the distilling apparatus usually consists of a glass retort and receiver (fig. 95); but if the vapours are very volatile other means are required to cool and condense them perfectly, otherwise a considerable portion would escape into the air and thus be lost.

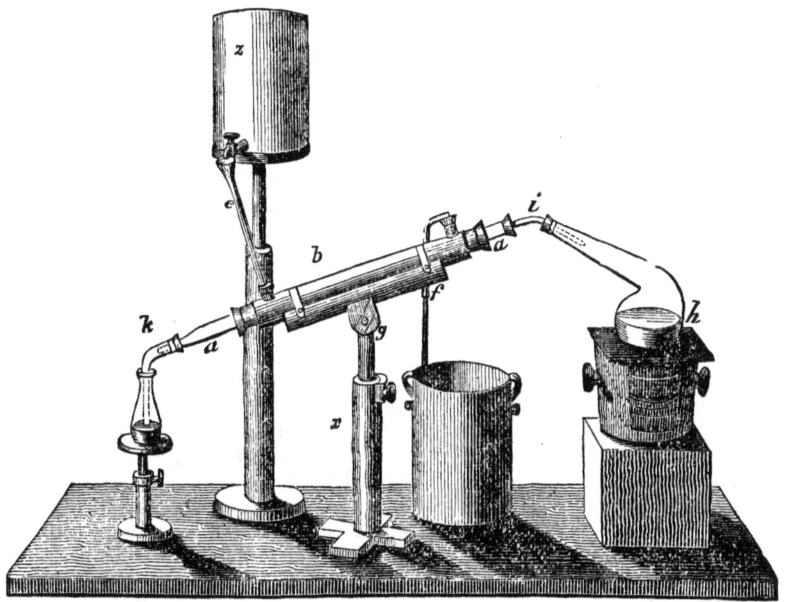

96.

In such cases the arrangements shown in fig. 96 answer exceedingly well for small operations. The vapours generated in the distilling flask pass into the long glass-tube, *a a*, which is encased in a wider one of tin-plate or zinc *b*. The space between the two tubes is filled with cold water, which is introduced by the funnel-tube *e*, whilst the warm water flows out from the tube *f*. By this arrangement the vapours are perfectly condensed, and may be collected in a receiver.

An apparatus similar to that shown in fig. 97 is employed for distilling brandy and spirits of wine. It consists of a copper still A mounted in a brick furnace, and to which is adapted a dome-shaped head B. The head of the still, terminating in the bent tube *b c d*, communicates with the worm O, which is enclosed in a large cylinder of metal *p q r j*, kept continually

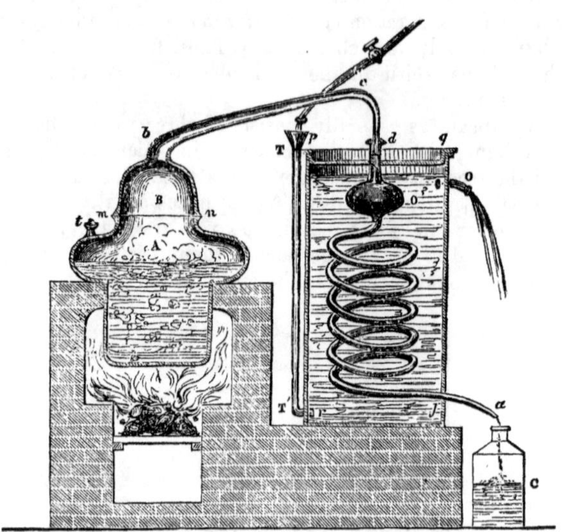

97.

filled with water. The fermented liquid is introduced at the tubulure *t*. As the water in the cylinder becomes heated by the condensation of the vapours in the worm, it is necessary from time to time to renew it. This is most conveniently effected by allowing a stream, from a reservoir of cold water, to run slowly through the funnel-tube T T′, which communicates with the bottom of the cylinder. The heated water rises to the surface, and escapes by the tube *o*, whilst the condensed spirit passes out at the inferior extremity of the worm *a*, and is collected in the receiver at C.

It must, however, be remarked that there exists an innumerable variety of arrangements for distilling, which all correspond in the most important points with the apparatus just described, whatever may be their form.

130. When water is heated in an open vessel, its conversion into vapour is opposed by two forces, viz., the cohesion of its own particles and the pressure of the atmosphere, by which they are compressed together. These impediments must, therefore, both be overcome in the formation of vapour.

By the continued heating of water, till it attains the temperature of 100° C. (212° F.), its particles at last acquire a tendency to separate, which is greater than the counteracting forces. From the moment that temperature is attained, bubbles of vapour will be seen to form at the lowest portion of the vessel, to rise to the surface of the water, imparting to it an undulatory motion, and finally to escape into the air. This phenomenon is termed *ebullition* or *boiling;* the tension of the vapour forming the bubbles is equal to the pressure of the atmosphere, otherwise, of course, they could not be formed. In this manner any quantity of water may be perfectly converted into vapour, and it will be observed that, during the entire period that ebullition continues, the thermometer will not rise above 100° C. (212° F.), however large may be the fire applied to the bottom of the vessel. All the heat in this case goes over to the vapours produced, as will be presently shown.

If water be heated to ebullition on the top of a high mountain, and a thermometer introduced, it will be found that the latter will not rise to 100° C. (212° F.). The reason of this may be easily explained. The pressure of the air upon the water is less at this height, consequently the latter must boil at a lower temperature than it would at the common level. On the high plane of Quito, which lies 8,724 feet above the level of the sea, water boils at 90° C. (194° F.). An egg cannot, therefore, be boiled hard there in an open vessel. If the air in a vessel, containing a little water, be highly rarefied or almost entirely removed by the air-pump or other means, the water may be made to boil even by the heat of the hand.

131. When water is exposed in the open air it vaporizes even without the application of heat. This spontaneous evaporation proceeds but slowly, and is called *vaporization.* The rapidity with which a certain amount of water evaporates is proportionate to the extent of its surface in contact with the air, to the dryness and warmth of the latter, and to the rapidity with which fresh layers of air are allowed to pass over its surface.

132. The *amount of moisture* contained in the air is regulated by atmospheric temperature, and by the quantity of available water. A certain amount of air contains more water, if taken from over the surface of the sea in hot climates, than if obtained from the cold steppes of Northern Asia, or the hot and dry sandy deserts of Africa. The air is *saturated* with moisture, when it contains quite as much water as corresponds to the temperature. When the air approaches to this state it is called *damp*, and when it contains much less water than corresponds to its temperature it is termed *dry* air. This explains why air which is called dry, for instance, in Italy, may, notwithstanding, contain more water than what is termed damp air in colder countries.

When the air is saturated with moisture it can no longer take up fresh quantities, hence water when brought in contact with it will not evaporate or decrease in quantity. As soon, however, as its temperature is increased, it is capable of taking up more moisture. Various means are employed to ascertain the amount of aqueous vapour contained in air. Thus there are many solid substances, as chloride of sodium or common salt, that attract the water from damp air, and become moist, or even assume the liquid form, as is the case with potassa.

Other substances only change their form in attracting water. To these belong the porous bodies, particularly those consisting of capillary tubes, as hairs, portions of plants, wool, or strings. Ladies' hair, for example, that curls so beautifully in dry weather, will become perfectly straight in damp atmospheres. Wood swells, musical instruments are put out of tune, and many other phenomena are due to the same cause. An apparatus has been constructed in which a human hair, as it stretches or shrinks, sets an index in motion, whereby a very accurate idea may be formed of the amount of moisture in the air. Numerous other *hygrometers* or *psychrometers* have been constructed, which we shall, however, refrain from describing.

133. If air, saturated with aqueous vapour, be cooled down, for instance, by winds, it will of course no longer retain the same amount of water. A portion of the latter is, therefore, condensed, and, if the condensation takes place close to the surface of the earth, becomes visible to the eye as *fog*, or as *clouds* if the vapours separate at a greater height. The formation of fog may be observed on a small scale at every breath we take, when the warm air, saturated with aqueous vapour as it proceeds from our lungs, is exhaled into a colder medium.

Fogs and clouds consist of an immense number of exceedingly small *hollow* globules of water. Although heavier than the air, they do not fall to the earth immediately upon their formation, but, like soap-bubbles, are retained, often for a considerable length of time, in suspension by the action of currents of air, and are driven from one place to another.

Various names have been given to the clouds, according to their form and mass: thus there are the *feathery cloud* or *cirrus*, the *dense cloud* or *cumulus*, and *stratified clouds* or *stratus*, which again merge into a variety of others, such as the *cirro-cumulus*, *cumulo-stratus*, &c.

134. *Rain* is produced when the clouds, unimpeded by winds, sink down to the lower strata of air, which are saturated with moisture, so that the globules of water increase in size, by the condensation of fresh particles, until they at last form drops of rain, which rapidly increase as they descend to the earth.

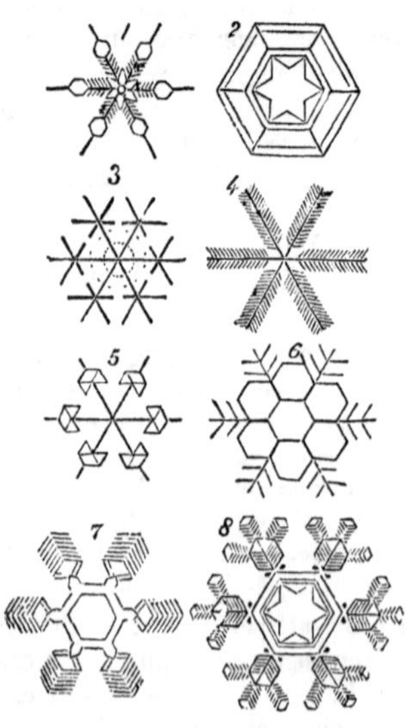

98.

The formation of snow is not so easily explained. If we assume damp currents of air to come from warmer regions to much colder ones, the aqueous vapour they contain may form itself into very minute particles of ice, instead of into globules of water, thus producing snow-clouds, from which these particles of ice descend in flakes of various sizes and forms. By the aid of the microscope the flakes of snow are observed to consist of a large number of regular six-sided prisms, elongated, and grouped around a centre, in such a manner as to form always angles of 60° or 120°. Nos. 2, 3, 4, 5, 6, 7, and 8 (fig. 98) represent some of the most simple groups. But frequently it presents itself in less complicated forms, and sometimes we recognise perfectly regular six-sided plates, as shown in No. 1.

The formation of *hail* is one of those natural phenomena, of which we are as yet unable to furnish a sufficiently satisfactory explanation. It is more particularly difficult to conceive how these pieces of ice are produced, in the height of summer, at no very great altitudes. They are frequently met with of considerable size, weighing upwards of an ounce, and some even from a quarter to half a pound. The destruction effected by hail renders it one of the most fearful scourges to agriculturists. Thus, in the year 1788, a hail-storm passed over the whole of France from the Pyrenees to Holland, destroying in about six hours the crops of 1,039 communities: the loss sustained amounted to upwards of a million pounds.

Dew and *Hoar-frost.*—After sunset the surface of the earth radiates towards the sky the heat which is absorbed during the day. It is often cooled down thereby to such an extent that the vapours contained in the lower strata of air are condensed into water, which is deposited as dew upon all the objects on the surface of the earth. As plants, and particularly grasses, possess a stronger radiating power than earth and stones, they are first covered with dew. When the sky is clouded, the nocturnal radiation is impeded by the clouds, and in that case no dew is formed. Thus, dew is likewise not deposited under tents, tables, or other coverings, placed in the open air.

If those bodies on which the dew is deposited, have cooled down to below the freezing-point, it is converted into ice, and is then called *hoar-frost.*

135. If common salt, sugar, or other substances are dissolved in water, their solutions must be heated above 100° C. (212° F.) before they will enter into ebullition. Most kinds of food, as they are boiled, possess a higher temperature, and, therefore, such liquids will produce more serious scalds than boiling water alone.

136. If water be heated in a close vessel, so that the steam as it is formed cannot escape, the temperature of the water increases continually, and the vapours acquire a greater tension, the force of which becomes at last tremendous. Strong iron vessels are therefore generally taken for such experiments.

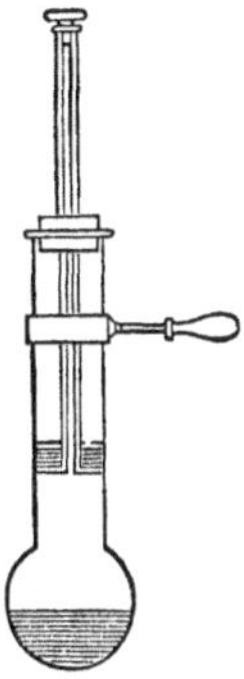

99.

On heating some water in a Wollaston's bulb (fig. 99), the opening of which is hermetically closed by the piston, the tension of the aqueous vapour will soon raise the piston in the tube. If the vessel be now immersed in cold water, by which the steam is suddenly condensed, a rarefied space will of course be produced below the piston, into which the latter will again be forced by the outer pressure of the air.

This simple experiment, by forcing up and down the piston, illustrates the principle of the *steam-engine.*

The Steam-Engine.

137. In the introduction to this work, the invention of the art of printing was spoken of as an event which had secured to science an eternal duration, and furnished it with auxiliary means, without which it would never have attained its present exalted position.

The invention of the steam-engine is of similar importance to the arts

It furnishes man with power equal to hundreds of thousands of hands and numberless horses and beasts of burden. It renders the mariner independent of wind and tide, and sets our mills in motion, whether the streams be dried up or frozen by the winter cold — it overcomes with ease the heaviest weights, and accomplishes the greatest distances with the velocity of the wind.

And as every important alteration in the external conditions of man has an influence on his inward state, so the power of steam has also had an important influence over the condition of his mind.

If it is the office of the printing-press to establish and extend ideas and thoughts, it is also an important function of the steam-engine to work out ideas and establish facts; if by the former centuries are brought into connexion, the latter serves to connect and link together men of the present age.

A space should, therefore, be more particularly set aside in this work for the contemplation of the steam-engine, in order that its power may not appear to us as something supernaturally wonderful, but that it may serve us as a wonderful example of the forces of Nature being made subservient to the mind of man.

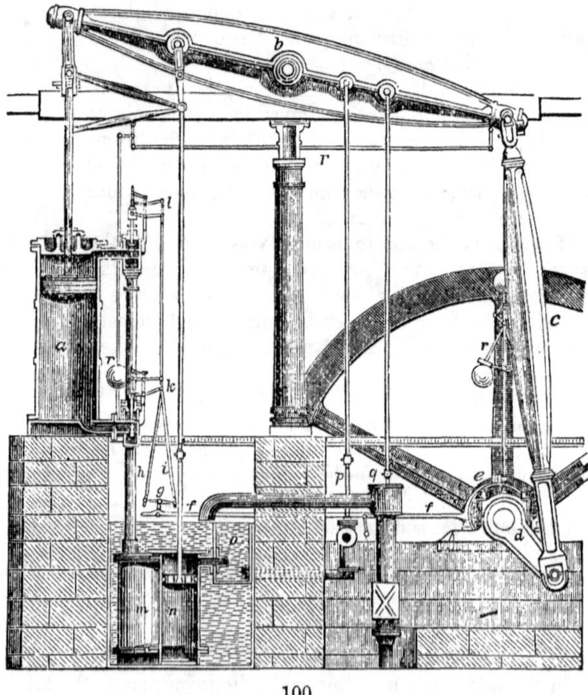

100.

138 The steam-engine derives its power from the tension of confined aqueous vapour heated above the temperature of boiling water. Steam is

applied either to *stationary* engines, for steam-mills or steam-vessels, or to *movable* engines, or *locomotives*, which are used on railways. The construction of these two kinds of engines differs in many respects.

In examining the stationary engine we have first to consider the generation of the steam, and afterwards its application as a motive power.

The steam is generated in an iron *steam-boiler*. There are various forms of boilers, but the main point in their construction is always the exposure of the greatest possible surface to the action of the fire. The general form of the boiler is that of a tube closed at both ends, and perfectly surrounded by the fire. By this means a great quantity of water may be rapidly converted into steam. The latter is conducted by means of a pipe from the boiler into the engine, which we shall now proceed to describe.

Fig. 100 represents a modern double-acting low-pressure engine, which is particularly adapted for impelling machinery. The piston, being acted on by the steam within the cylinder *a*, communicates its required motion to *b* through the medium of the piston-rod and the parallel motion which connects it to the beam. To the opposite end of the beam is attached the connecting rod *c*, the lower end of which being jointed to the crank *d*, a rotatory motion is thus imparted to the wheel; the crank being properly supported on plummer blocks. Affixed to the crank-shaft and behind the crank is what is termed an eccentric wheel *e;* so styled from the circumstance of the wheel not being concentric with the shaft upon which it is fixed. The eccentric wheel, which it will be seen is merely a convenient substitute for a short crank, has a groove or depression turned round its edge into which a corresponding metal hoop or strap, joined together in two halves, is fitted so as to allow the wheel to revolve easily within it. Fastened to one side of the hoop, and projecting from it horizontally, is the eccentric rod, as it is termed,

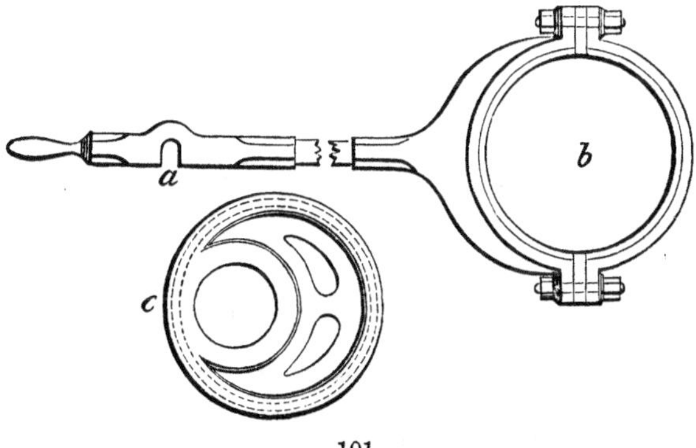

101.

f f, which embraces a pin on the end of a lever at *g*. In fig. 101, *a b* represent the eccentric rod, and *c* the eccentric wheel, each enlarged and detached from each other. It will be observed that the part of the rod, where it embraces the pin of the lever, is indented below into a circular hollow, so that it may be disengaged from the lever by being simply raised. Whilst the engine is in action, the eccentric wheel, as it revolves, imparts a reciprocating movement, by means of the eccentric rod, to the lever at *g*, the axis of which, termed the rocking or wiper shaft, has on opposite sides of it two other levers; these operate on the valves through the medium of the rods *h* and *i* as well as the levers at *k* and *l*.

The spindles of the steam-valves are hollow, and have stuffing-boxes at their upper ends; whilst the spindles of the eduction-valves being longer, are made to work through the steam-valves, and through the stuffing-boxes so as to be steam-tight. The valves are opened by the action of the eccentric wheel, and are closed by weights, which have been omitted, to render what is shown more intelligible.

The condenser *m* is kept exhausted by the air-pump *n*; the water delivered by the latter into the hot well *o* being conveyed to the boiler by the hot-water pump *p*. The cold water necessary to maintain the vacuum within the condenser is supplied by the cold-water pump *q*. The governor *r* is set in motion by bevelled wheels, driven by the engine, and it is supported in an upright position by a frame or bracket. Instead of a sliding collar there is a perforated ball at the top of the governor, and which rises or falls according as the balls of the governor diverge or collapse. A vertical rod extends from the top of the said ball, and it communicates with the throttle-valve by means of a horizontal rod *r*, situated above, as well as by another upright rod, also marked *r*, depending from the latter. At the two points where the various rods join, there is a bell-crank lever that serves to connect them; and it will be observed, a ball is attached near the lower end of the rod next the throttle-valve: the use of this ball, as likewise of the other one immediately above the governor, is to keep the several rods between them stretched, as otherwise each rod would require to be so strong as not to yield by bending. The balls are made to balance each other; and, therefore, according as either is elevated or depressed, the other ball becomes at the same time influenced in the opposite direction.

139. The power of a steam-engine is dependent on the tension or pressure of the steam employed, and on the surface of the piston.

Assuming the steam to have a tension equal to the pressure of the atmosphere, and the surface of the piston to be 1,378 square inches, the latter will, according to § 77, be pressed downwards with as much force as if it were loaded with 20,000 pounds. Supposing, however, the pressure of the steam to be trebled or quadrupled, the power of the engine will likewise increase in the same degree.

Engines in which steam of low pressure is employed are called *low-pressure* engines, while those that are worked with steam of great pressure are termed *high-pressure* engines.

It must not, however, be imagined that low-pressure engines are less powerful than those of high-pressure. The cylinders in the latter are smaller, by which the difference in pressure is compensated for; the force exerted by the pressure of *one* atmosphere on a piston, the surface of which measures *four* square feet, being evidently equal to that of *four* atmospheres on a piston measuring *one* square foot.

The high-pressure engine *consequently* occupies the smaller space, particularly if the steam on the one side of the piston is not removed by condensation, but allowed to escape into the atmosphere. The condenser and the various pumps are not required in that case, and the whole engine becomes much more simple in consequence. [Fig. 102 represents the high-pressure

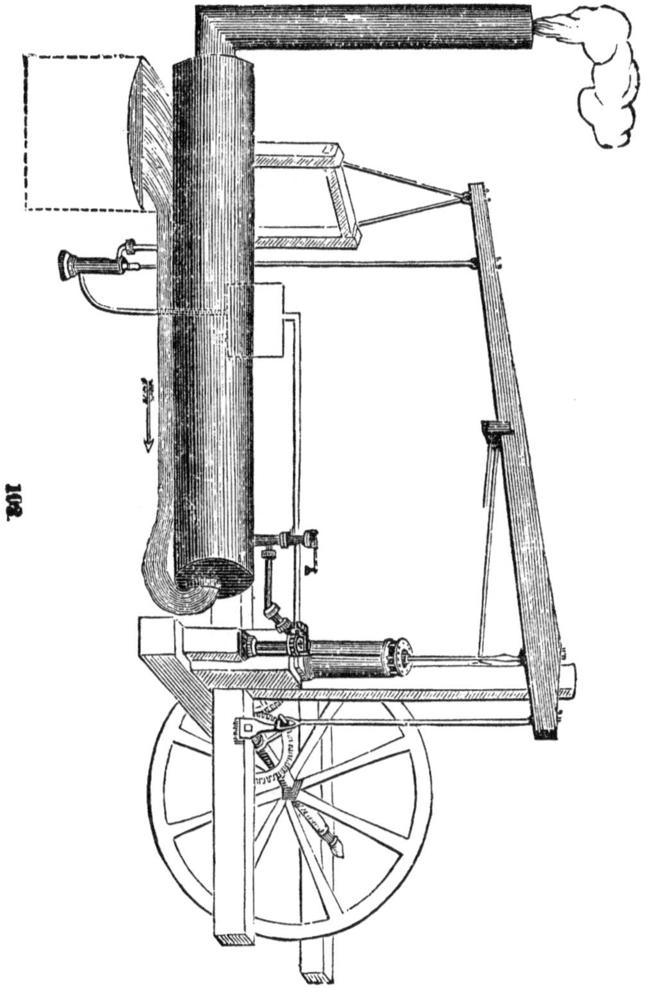

102

engine invented by Oliver Evans, of Philadelphia, in 1784.] This kind of engine is employed for *locomotives*, on account of the small space it occupies.

140. An engine, working at high pressure, requires, in an equal space of time, about the same amount of steam as a low-pressure engine of equal power. The former must, however, be so arranged as to be capable of converting a large amount of water into steam, in a very confined space, and in a short time. This is accomplished by allowing the air, heated in the furnace, to pass through a series of iron tubes which are surrounded by water, as shown in figs. 103 and 104, which represent a longitudinal and a transverse section of a locomotive.

In fig. 103, A A represents the fire-place, which is closed by the door in front. From the fire the heated air has no other channel of escape, than through the series of horizontal tubes which extend from A to D; from D the heated air, together with the smoke, passes through the funnel into the atmosphere. Fig. 104 shows the relative position of these tubes passing through the boiler filled with water, which, moreover, surrounds on all sides the fire-place itself. The water is thus exposed to an extremely large heated surface, which causes at every moment the generation of a great quantity of steam. The steam collects in the space B C above the surface of the water; and from the chamber C passes by the tube *c* into the cylinder. If the position of the mouth of the tube be too low, the rapid ebullition carries a considerable quantity of water mechanically into the tube; but in order to obviate this inconvenience, the chamber is elevated as shown at C. The tube *c* divides into two branches, *d d*, fig. 104, one of which is only seen in fig. 103. Each of these tubes communicates with a chamber from which the steam passes into the cylinder F. On each side of the carriage there is one horizontal cylinder, in which the piston moves in the same direction.

From the chamber *i*, into which the steam is passed by the tubes *c d*, lead two canals communicating with the opposite ends of the cylinder. Upon the bottom surface of the chamber *i* is a sliding valve, which moves backwards and forwards, and whose central part forms a kind of chest *o*, which is open at the bottom. In the position shown at fig. 103, the two canals are closed by this valve. Let us imagine the slide to be pushed so far towards the left hand, that the left canal is no longer closed, but in communication with the cavity *o*, the right hand canal will then be in connexion with the steam chamber *i*; while the slide is in this position, the steam will enter the right-hand end of the cylinder, and drive the piston towards the opposite end of the cylinder, whilst the steam passes from the left-hand side of the piston, and thence by the tube *q* into the funnel. If, however, the slide is at the right-hand end of the chamber, the steam contained in the latter will pass by the left canal into the cylinder, and escape through the right-hand canal into the cavity *o*. The piston-rod is fixed in such a manner that it can move only in a straight line. Fastened to the piston-rod is the connecting-rod, which moves the crank *n* around the axle *m*. The middle wheels of the carriage are fastened to the axle *m*, so that the wheels perform an entire revolution every time the piston moves backwards and forwards, and the carriage is likewise propelled to a distance corresponding to the circumference of the wheel.

To the axle *m* is also fastened the eccentric disc by which the slide is set in motion. As is seen in the figure, the X-shaped end of the rod, which is

103.

104.

fixed to the ring of the eccentric disc, grasps the upper extremity of a lever whose fulcrum is seen at *s*. By the motion of this lever the rods *t t*, and the slide which is connected with them, are moved backwards and forwards.

In order to reverse the motion of the engine, it is necessary to raise the lever N. The fulcrum of this lever is at P, where its axis passes obliquely over the whole carriage. Upon each side of the carriage is fastened the arm of a lever, whose directions run parallel to the elongation of N P. From these arms of the levers descend two vertical rods, to the X-formed ends of the rods which are connected with the eccentric disc. It is now evident that by raising the lever-arm N, the X on each side of the carriage will be pressed down, so that the rod grasps the lower end of the lever whose fulcrum is seen at *s*. According as the rod grasps above or below, the wheel must necessarily revolve either in the direction of the arrow or in the opposite direction.

H and L represent safety-valves; *l* is a whistle used for giving signals.

[*Note.*—The drawing given on the preceding page merely represents the general construction of locomotives. The engines at present in use on the English railways are furnished with a regulator in the pipe *c*, by which the steam passes from the boiler to the cylinders. The use of the regulator is to modify the supply of steam.—Ed.]

141. Machines, set in motion by steam, were already constructed in the seventeenth century. They were, however, exceedingly imperfect, and it was not till the year 1763 that James Watt constructed the steam-engine, identical, in the most important points, with that now in use. The first successful steam-vessel, on a large scale, was constructed by the American, Robert Fulton, in 1807.

The power of the steam-engine is usually compared with horse-power, and it is assumed that the power of one horse will raise 1500 pounds to the height of 3·7 inches in a second of time.

The fuel generally employed for steam-engines is coal or coke. A stationary engine of one-horse power requires about 20 pounds of coal in an hour. In the same period of time an engine of

2	horse power requires	31	pounds of coal.
10	"	100	"
20	"	166	"
100	"	555	"
200	"	1100	"

The locomotive and steam-boat engines require proportionately a much larger amount of coal.

Transmission of Heat.

142. It is well known that a body, to which a high degree of heat is imparted, gradually loses it, or, in other words, cools down; as also, that a body possessing a low temperature gradually acquires a higher one, when exposed to the influence of heat. Heat may, therefore, be said not to be enclosable in any substance, as it endeavours continually to maintain itself

in equilibrium with the surrounding objects; it is, therefore, in perpetual motion.

The transmission of heat takes place in two ways. In the first place, heat may be transmitted through the whole mass of a body by communication from one particle to another, until all have attained an equal temperature. This is transmission by *conduction*. Secondly, heat is transmitted through the air, emanating from bodies in rays, similar to light and sound; it is then called *radiated* heat.

143. All bodies do not transmit heat with equal rapidity through their mass. A piece of iron wire, or a knitting-needle, cannot be held by one end, when the other is heated to redness, without the fingers being burnt, while a shorter piece of wood may burn at one end and be held by the other without the slightest inconvenience. Some bodies are, therefore, good, others are bad *conductors of heat.*

Heavy bodies, such as the metals, are the best conductors of heat, while substances of less density only allow a very slow transmission of heat through their mass. This is particularly the case if the bodies are very porous and loose. Stones, earth, earthenware vessels, and glass are, therefore, numbered amongst the imperfect conductors of heat; while wood, straw, hair, the fibres of plants, and the articles manufactured therefrom, are classed amongst the bad conductors.

Many of the most common phenomena are the results of the various conducting powers of bodies: thus, for instance, water boils sooner in metal vessels than in earthen ones; a piece of red-hot coal soon ceases to glow when placed upon an iron plate, while it retains its heat for a long time when placed upon wood; the cold sensation produced on touching metal, is likewise owing to the rapidity with which the latter conducts away the heat of the hand.

We dress ourselves in bad conductors of heat, such as woollen cloths and furs, in order to prevent too great a decrease of animal heat by radiation or conduction. For the same reason we employ moss, hay, and feathers for the construction of warm resting-places, and envelop trees and plants in straw, to protect them from the cold.

Air and water are likewise bad conductors of heat. The air in cellars and wells maintains nearly the same temperature, summer and winter; and we have already seen, at § 125, that water and air transmit heat rapidly, only because they are set in motion by it. Ice and snow likewise belong to that class of bodies that conduct heat badly. Most winter crops would perish by the frost, if they were not protected by a covering of snow.

144. On approaching a fire, we become sensible of a feeling of warmth—of the rays of heat which emanate from it. That heat reaches us in the form of rays, is proved by placing a screen between ourselves and the fire, when we shall be protected from its influence. The heat of the sun likewise reaches the earth in the form of rays, which warm the air only slightly in their course; for the upper strata of the atmosphere are always found to be extremely cold.

The rays of heat, like those of sound, are refracted, or *deflected*, when they pass from one portion of matter to another of unequal density; they are also *reflected*, when they encounter solid substances. These phenomena are most strikingly exhibited by *burning-glasses* and *reflectors*.

We shall describe the burning-glass in the chapter on light. Reflectors are concave mirrors of polished brass. In fig. 105, which represents the original contrivance by Sir Humphry Davy, two mirrors of this description are situated opposite each other. All the heat-rays that fall on the surface of a reflector, in a direction parallel to its axis, are reflected thereby in such a manner, that they meet at a certain point in front of the mirror, at the point indicated by the bulb of the thermometer. The total amount of heat-rays collected by the reflector are united in this one point; it is, therefore, called the focal- or burning-point. If an object that emits heat be placed in the focal-point of a concave mirror, the whole of the heat-rays that fall upon the latter are reflected in a parallel direction.

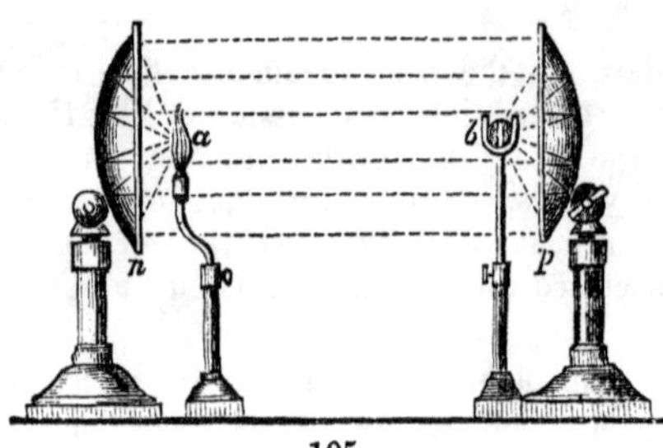

105.

These properties of reflectors have been proved by the following experiments. Two mirrors are placed opposite each other, as in fig. 105, and in the focal-point of one of the mirrors is placed a red-hot iron ball, or a ladle filled with red-hot coals. If we now place a piece of tinder in the focal-point of the other mirror, which may be removed from 18 to 20 feet, the tinder will be inflamed, as all the rays which proceed from the red-hot body are collected by one of the mirrors, and thrown in a parallel direction to the other mirror, which collects them in its focal-point, and by this means sufficient heat is produced at this point to ignite inflammable bodies. A thermometer, held slightly out of the focal-point, or in any place between the two mirrors, will show that the heat-rays produce no appreciable change of temperature at any other point than that above-named.

The temperature of the focal-point depends upon the size of the reflectors and the temperature of the source of heat. Reflectors have been constructed by means of which a temperature may be obtained by the collection of the sun's rays at the focal-point, sufficient to melt and ignite substances, upon which the fiercest fires are scarcely capable of producing the same effect.

The velocity of the rays of heat is equal to those of light, which travels at the rate of 195,000 miles in a second.

145. The relations exhibited between different bodies, and the heat-rays falling upon them, are exceedingly various. Some bodies allow all the rays of heat to pass through them, without retaining or absorbing a single particle: this is the case with air, and also with several solid bodies, as, for instance, rock-salt. These are, however, exceptions to the rule, as all other solids retain a greater or smaller amount of the heat-rays which fall upon them.

As a general rule, the denser the body, and the lighter its colour, the smaller is the amount of heat which it will absorb, and *vice versâ*. Thus lamp-black will retain nearly all the heat-rays that fall upon it, while polished silver or iron reflect them almost completely. If one thermometer be covered with white cloth, and another with black, and both are equally exposed to the sun, the one in the black covering will indicate a higher temperature than the other. Snow will melt more rapidly when covered with a black cloth than it will under a white covering. It is intelligible from this, why white or light-coloured dresses should be preferred in summer, and dark ones in winter.

These two classes of bodies are likewise opposed to each other in their *radiating* power. Dense bodies only possess this power to a slight degree, while it is much greater with porous bodies. Thus, a hot liquid, as tea or coffee, will cool much more slowly in a bright metallic vessel than in a vessel of earthenware, which is coated with lamp-black.

Latent or Combined Heat.

146. We have seen in § 130, that water, when it has once been heated to the boiling point, cannot attain a higher temperature, even if continuously exposed to a greater heat. In that case a portion of the heat passes over continually to the vapour, and the thermometer will indicate 100° C. (212° F.), whether it be immersed in the water or the steam. If snow or ice, the temperature of which is exactly 0° C. (32° F.), be placed in a vessel on a stove, the water produced by its melting will likewise indicate a temperature of 0° C. (32° F.). All the heat imparted in both cases appears merely to serve for the conversion of solid water into liquid, and of the latter into steam, without the water produced by melting indicating a higher temperature than the snow, or the temperature of the steam being higher than that of the boiling water.

Bodies are, therefore, capable of absorbing heat without altering in temperature; they are, however, converted thereby from the denser to the lighter state. The heat thus absorbed, that is, rendered imperceptible to the sense of feeling, is said to be *latent* or *combined*. The steam produced at 100° C. (212 F.) is consequently water of 100° C. (212° F.) + latent heat.

In all cases when a body passes over from a denser to a lighter condition, a certain amount of heat is always absorbed or rendered latent. This heat is abstracted from the surrounding objects, the temperature of which is consequently reduced. If, for example, water be poured on the ground, on a hot summer's day, it will pass over into vapour, abstracting thereby a large amount of heat from the surrounding air and earth, which will be felt to be much cooler in consequence. If two thermometers be suspended together, the bulb of one being moist and the other dry, the former will indicate the lower temperature, as the water, evaporating on its surface, abstracts a portion of its heat.

147. Gaseous bodies, however, in their transition to the fluid, or from that to the solid state, part with their latent heat. This liberation of heat generally occurs under circumstances where it cannot be well perceived; there are, however, a few very striking examples of the conversion of latent into sensible heat, one of which is the disengagement of heat in pouring water over unslacked lime: the nature of this experiment will be more fully explained in the section on Chemistry.

148. On heating equal weights of different substances of the temperature of 0° C. (32° F.) to + 1° C. (33°·8 F.), it will be observed that the quantity of heat required is very different. If water, oil of turpentine, iron, and mercury be employed for the experiment, it will be found that the quantities of heat required by these bodies to raise their temperatures from 0° to + 1° C. (32° to 33°·8 F.) stand in the relation of $1 : \frac{1}{2} : \frac{1}{8} : \frac{1}{33}$. Oil of turpentine requires, therefore, only one-half, iron one-eighth, and mercury only one-thirty-third of the heat required by water to attain the same temperature. If two vessels, perfectly similar, are procured, the one containing one pound of water, and the other one pound of oil of turpentine, both of equal temperature, it will be necessary, in order to heat them both to an equal number of degrees, to place under the vessels containing the water *two* flames of equal size to the *one* that is required by the oil of turpentine.

The relative quantities of heat required by different bodies to attain an equal increase in temperature are termed their *specific heats.* For comparative purposes the specific heat of water is fixed at 1.

It may be concluded from these statements that as every body possesses a peculiar density, so likewise all bodies contain a certain quantity of heat that cannot be indicated by the thermometer, and on the amount of which depends their capacity for absorbing a farther quantity, or as it is termed, their *capacity for heat.*

149. The *distribution* of heat on the surface of the earth is very unequal; various parts thereof are well known to possess temperatures varying very much from those of other parts. It has been already mentioned that the sun must be considered as the principal source of the heat of the earth. The sun's rays do not, however, fall in equal directions on every point of the earth's surface: in the vicinity of the equator their direction is nearly *vertical,* while in the countries approaching the poles they fall obliquely; in fact, their direction becomes more oblique in proportion to the distance from the equator. All heat-rays that fall upon a body at an angle are, however, reflected at the same angle, and only those that fall perpendicularly are perfectly absorbed. Hence the temperature at the equator is much higher than at any other part of the globe: in consequence of this difference of temperature, the earth has been divided into a torrid or tropical zone, the two temperate, and the two cold zones or polar regions.

The difference between summer and winter in the temperate zones is occasioned by the greater length of the days in the first-named season, and by the sun's rays reaching the earth in a direction more approaching the perpendicular than at any other time. In the winter, when the sun is nearer to the earth by about four and a half millions of miles than it is in the summer, the rays fall in a very oblique direction.

150. By the *mean temperature* of a day is understood the mean of the highest and lowest temperatures observed throughout its duration. To arrive at the correct number, observations should, properly speaking, be made from hour to hour, or even at still shorter intervals. Experience has shown, however, that the mean temperature of a day may be arrived at with sufficient accuracy by observing the thermometer in the morning at 7 o'clock, again at noon, and at ten in the evening, and calculating the mean of these observations. The mean temperature of the day furnishes, by calculation,

that of the month, and that of the year is obtained from the temperature of its twelve months.

It is evident that the mean temperature of various places must be exceedingly different, and by way of illustration we may subjoin a few examples:—

Place.	Latitude.	Mean Temperature.		Place.	Latitude.	Mean Temperature.	
		C.	Fahr.			C.	Fahr.
Melville Island	74°	—18°	0°	Vienna..........	48°	10°·1	50°·2
St. Bernards...	45	— 1	30·2	London..........	51	10 ·4	50 ·7
St. Petersburg	59	+ 3	37·4	Paris............	48	10 ·8	51 ·4
Königsburg....	54	6	42·8	Constantinople.	41	13	55 ·4
Berlin..........	52	8	46·4	Rome	41	15	59 ·0
Munich.........	48	8	46·4	Canton..........	23	21	69 ·8
Frankfort-on-the-Maine....	50	9	48·2	Calcutta........	22	28	82 ·4

Although the greater number of the above temperatures confirm the rule, that the temperature of countries increases in proportion to their vicinity to the equator, yet we find several exceptions to this among the number quoted. These arise from the great influence exercised over the temperature by the nature of the earth and of the surrounding objects. Thus, countries under the same latitude will be found to be colder the higher they are situated, the more they are exposed to cold currents of air, and the farther they are distant from large masses of water. Low countries, sheltered from cold winds by chains of mountains, and particularly with barren surfaces, are the hottest. The temperature of land is much decreased by a luxuriant vegetation, partly because plants radiate a large amount of heat during the night, and partly because the evaporation of water occasioned by them renders a large amount of heat latent.

Comparatively small tracts of land, nearly or entirely surrounded by large masses of water, as England, Italy, and the smaller islands, possess most uniform temperatures, partly because the water requires a large amount of heat for the formation of vapour, and partly because it radiates much less heat during the night than does the land. The temperature of England is, indeed, much more uniform than that of Germany; and although the mean temperature of the two countries is the same in many parts, yet, on the Continent, the summers are hotter and the winters colder than on our island. Hence many plants live through the winter here that would perish in Germany, while, on the other hand, grapes and other kinds of fruit do not ripen here as they do abroad, because the heat of the sun never attains a sufficient power.

III. Light.

"Joyful be those
Who breathe in the rosy light."—*Schiller.*

151. The cheering phenomena of light arise from various allied causes, and in this sense we shall speak of the different sources of light. As such we shall consider:—1. The sun and the fixed stars. 2. Heat, since all

objects as soon as they are exposed to a certain temperature appear luminous, it being immaterial whether it be the result of mechanical or chemical action (the latter, however, is most common). 3. Electricity. 4. Many animals of the lower classes which possess the property of appearing luminous, and of which the glow-worm is the most familiar example. Many plants, particularly the Rhizomorpha, frequently found in mines, likewise possess this property in a small degree. 5. The decay of animal matter, particularly of fish, and the dry rot of wood, which give rise to a feeble luminosity. The most important of all these sources of light is the sun. Next to this, the light produced by the chemical process of combustion exercises the greatest influence.

In all other cases besides those above mentioned, when light is observed to proceed from any object, it does not originate with the latter, but has been previously communicated to it from some of the above sources. Bodies are, therefore, *luminous* or *non-luminous*. The light of the moon is derived from the sun, the former being non-luminous, like the earth and most other bodies.

152. Light occurs so frequently in company with heat, and corresponds with the latter in so many of its properties and in so remarkable a manner, that they have been considered by many as inseparable, or more properly speaking, as one and the same thing in different degrees of intensity. They may, however, be distinguished and separated; for there are many powerful kinds of light, for instance, that of the moon and of several luminous insects, that are unaccompanied by any heat, or at any rate by any perceptible amount, and, on the other hand, many substances may be found that will retain a large amount of heat without becoming luminous.

153. Light is distributed only in rays, proceeding from the luminous body in all directions. The velocity with which light travels is extraordinary: it passes over 195,000 miles in a second of time, and occupies, therefore, only eight minutes and thirteen seconds in travelling from the sun to the earth.

The rays of light, when they meet with substances, exhibit a similar behaviour to those of sound and heat, the resulting phenomena, however, being naturally different in appearance. We will notice three cases in particular.

(1.) The rays of light are more or less perfectly intercepted or *absorbed* by the bodies which they meet.

(2.) They are thrown back or *reflected.*

(3.) They pass through bodies.

154. When all the rays of light falling upon a body are absorbed, they disappear altogether, or become invisible: the body that has thus absorbed them appears perfectly *black.* A body of this description does not take up light by continued exposure, as it might heat, in such a manner as to distribute it again in any way. Thus, a want of light or *shadow* is produced on the side of the body opposite to that which is exposed to the rays of light. Lampblack is the substance that most completely absorbs light.

By far the greater number of bodies partly reflect the light as it falls upon them, and absorb another portion. Dense bodies, particularly bright metals, reflect light most perfectly. The reflecting power of other bodies decreases proportionately to their porosity, and consequently bear an inverse ratio to their density. There is likewise a want of light, or shadow, produced behind those bodies that reflect light.

All bodies become visible only by their reflecting the rays of light; it is highly important, for the proper comprehension of all phenomena of vision, to bear in mind continually, that rays of light proceed in all directions from *every visible point* of a body, and that the body is rendered visible to us by one of these rays reaching our eyes.

155. Such bodies as reflect light perfectly are called ***mirrors.*** Without regard to the material of which they consist, we distinguish — 1, *plane* or common mirrors; 2, *concave* or hollow mirrors; 3, *convex* or raised mirrors.

A plane mirror s s' fig. 106, reflects the rays that fall upon it in such a manner that the incident ray r i forms the same angle with the perpendicular p i as the reflected ray i d, whence it follows that the rays diverge from a mirror in such a manner as though they issued from one point, situate as far behind the surface of the mirror as the luminous point lies before it. Hence the image appears to be situated as far behind the surface of the mirror, as the object is placed before it; and it is reversed in such a manner that the left side of the object becomes the right side of the image, and *vice versâ.*

106.

156. The common mirror consists of a glass plate, possessing surfaces as smooth and parallel as possible, one of which is coated with an amalgam of tin and mercury.

Mirrors, the surfaces of which are not parallel, and which are otherwise uneven and not clear, produce distorted images, and, therefore, cannot be used.

If two mirrors be placed opposite and parallel to each other, the image of one mirror will be seen in the other, and an endless number of images is thus obtained. If, however, the mirrors are so placed as to form an angle, the number of mutual reflections will be diminished, and indeed proportionately to the extent of the angle formed by the mirrors.

The construction of the *kaleidoscope* is based simply on the multiplication of an image by two mirrors inclined towards each other.

The mirror has not only become an indispensable article of furniture, by the ordinary uses made of it, but has also been applied in the construction of many optical instruments.

157. A *concave mirror* may be represented by a bright soup-ladle or the reflector of a lantern. The important applications of this mirror render a slight study of its properties necessary.

A concave mirror may be considered as a segment of a hollow sphere, V W, fig. 107. The central point C, and the semi-diameter O C may be termed respectively the *geometrical centre,* and the *radius.* The point F in the centre of the radius is called the *focus,* and the line passing through the centre C, and the focus F, is termed the *optical axis.* The point O of the mirror which is met by the prolongation of the axis is called the *optical centre.*

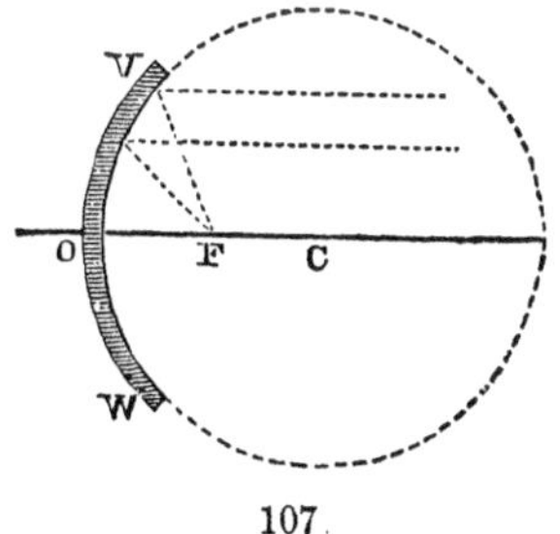

107.

All rays of light that fall *perpendicularly* upon this mirror are reflected in the same direction, so that they pass through the centre of C. All rays that are parallel with the optical axis are reflected by the mirror towards the focus F, and are there collected (comp. § 144).

158. On approaching the concave mirror to any object, various images are obtained, according to the distance between the two. If an arrow, for example, be placed between the focus and the mirror, a *magnified* image thereof will be obtained, appearing, however, to be situated at the back of the mirror, as was the case with the plain mirror. On placing the arrow between the focus and the geometrical centre of the mirror, a *magnified* image will be likewise produced, appearing, however, to be situated in front of the mirror.

Let us endeavour to account for these phenomena by the aid of fig. 108.

If the ray A n passes from the object A B at right angles upon the mirror, it will be reflected in the direction n A C; the ray A e proceeding parallel with the axis of the mirror will be reflected towards the focus F. These two reflected rays will never meet in front of the mirror. If, however, we imagine their direction to be prolonged at the back of the mirror, they will intersect each other at the point a, and the object A will appear to the eye to be situated at that point. The whole of the rays of light passing from A B will be similarly reflected, and thus the magnified image a b is produced at the back of the mirror.

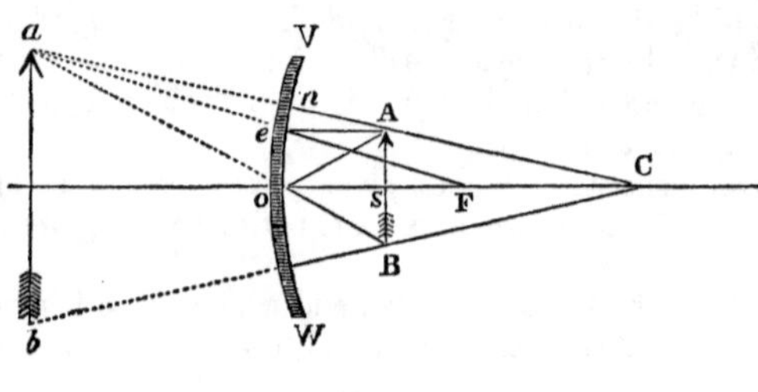

108.

In fig. 109, where the arrow is placed between the focus and the geometrical centre, the ray A u falling perpendicularly on the mirror is reflected in the same direction, whilst the ray A c, that is parallel with the axis of the mirror, is reflected to the focus F. The point A of the object A B must, therefore, appear to occupy that position where, by the prolongation of the two reflected rays, they appear to intersect each other, which is the case at a, as seen in the figure. Rays falling on the mirror from other points of the object would be similarly reflected, and thus the magnified but reversed image would appear situated in the air in front of the mirror.

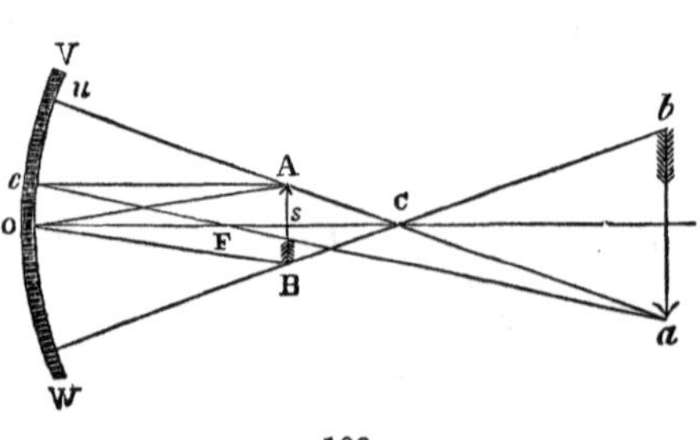

109.

It may easily be proved that this image really is in the air, for on holding a sheet of white paper at a b, the rays will be intercepted, and the image will be distinctly visible on the paper.

159. The concave mirror has found a most important application in the telescope; the so-called *reflecting telescopes* have been constructed by which enormous magnifying effects are produced, such as those obtained with Herschel's celebrated gigantic telescope, which measures five feet in diameter. This kind of telescope has of late met with few applications, as its construction and management are attended with great difficulties. It has been already stated in our chapter on Heat, that concave mirrors may be used as reflectors. They afford likewise excellent means for increasing the power of light, as all rays thrown upon a concave mirror by a light placed within its focus, are reflected in a parallel direction; hence this mirror has been applied to lanterns, magic-lanterns, and lighthouses.

160. The *convex* mirror is of less interest than the former. It is also called the *dispersing* mirror, as all the rays of light that fall upon it are reflected in a diverging direction. It produces *diminished* images of objects, such as may be observed in polished raised metal buttons, or large glass globes, &c.

Refraction of Light.

161. It has been observed at § 153, that some bodies allow of the passage of rays of light through their mass. Such bodies are — air, water, glass, and, in fact, all such as are called *transparent*. It is well known that all bodies do not possess this property to an equal degree. There are semi-transparent and translucent bodies, and others that are only translucent when their mass is extremely thin. Thus, even that dense body, gold, is translucent, when beaten out into thin leaves. In the study of light, however, only those bodies are of importance that are perfectly transparent.

As long as the rays of light pass through the same medium or kind of matter, for instance through the air, their direction remains perfectly straight and unaltered. If, however, a ray of light fall upon a transparent body of greater or less density, it will no longer continue its motion in the original direction, but will follow another which forms a greater or smaller angle with the first.

In such a case the ray of light is said to be *broken* or *refracted*, and the angle denoting the amount of refraction is termed the angle of refraction.

The more common phenomena of refraction are observed when light passes from the space of the universe into the denser atmosphere of our earth, or when it passes from air through water or glass.

It is a well-known fact that a straight stick, when partly immersed in water, appears to be broken at the point of immersion. This is in consequence of the rays of light that pass from the stick to the eye following a different direction when they emerge from the water. Thus, we should not be able to perceive the object m in the vessel $v\ v'$, fig. 110, if the latter were empty, and the eye were situated at o. When, however, water is poured into the vessel, the rays passing from m to $i\ i$ are refracted on emerging from the water, and the object will now appear to the eye to be situated at n, much higher,

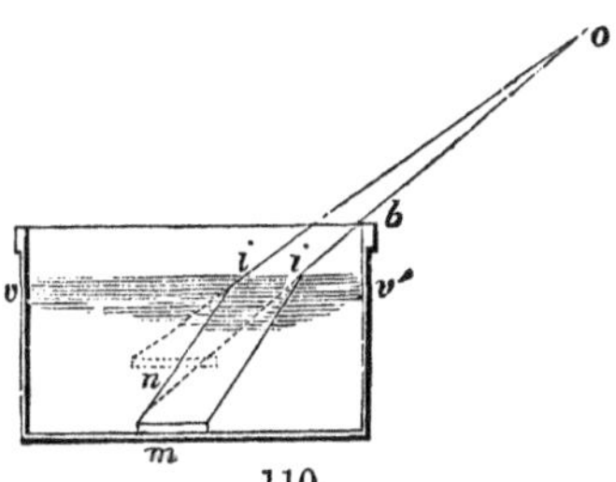

110.

therefore, than its real position. Hence, any objects lying in water appear to be nearer its surface than is really the case.

162. On allowing a ray of light to pass through a thin body with two parallel surfaces, it undergoes scarcely any perceptible alteration. This is observed in window-panes, through which objects appear in their true position.

The case is, however, very different, if the surfaces of the body, through which the light passes, are not parallel.

In experiments on this subject, curved glasses are always employed which have received the name of *lenses*, as some of them possess the form of a lentil. They are of great importance in the construction of telescopes and powerful microscopes.

163. Lenses, like mirrors, are distinguished into those that collect the rays of light and those that disperse them.

The collecting lenses are always thickest in their centre; they are called *double convex lenses.* These likewise contain a focus, a geometrical central point, and an axis, like the convex mirror: the kind of image obtained by this lens is dependent on the position of the object. All rays passing through the central point of these lenses remain unaltered, while those whose direction is parallel with the axis are refracted by the glass in such a manner that they unite at one external point.

The focus of a lens may easily be found by allowing the rays of the sun to fall perpendicularly on one side of it, whilst a sheet of paper is held on the other. A bright ring of light will be observed on the latter, diminishing or increasing in size according to the distance of the paper from the glass. If the former be held in such a manner that the ring of light is reduced to a dazzling luminous point, it is then situated in the focus of the glass. The heat-rays that accompany those of light are likewise united at this point, which is found, in consequence, to possess a high temperature, frequently sufficient to ignite substances. The double convex lens has hence been also called the *burning-glass.*

We will now proceed to examine the phenomena produced by convex glasses.

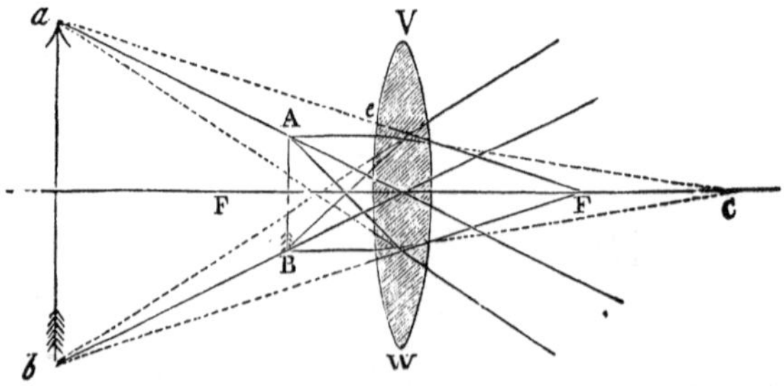

111.

Fig. 111 represents a lens V W, and an object A B, situated between the glass and its focus F. The ray A *c* is now so refracted as to appear to the eye, on the other side of the lens, to come from *a*. The ray coming from B behaves in a similar manner; so that a magnified image of the object is obtained on the same side of the lens.

If, however, the object is farther removed from the lens than the focal-point F, as in fig. 112, an inverted magnified image of the object is obtained on the opposite side of the lens, and may be allowed to fall upon paper.

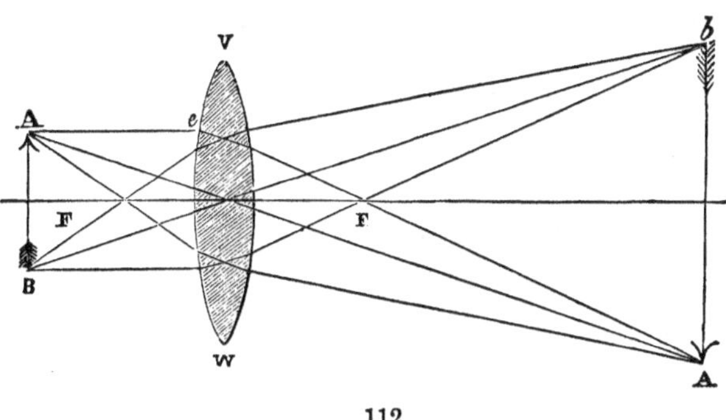

112.

164. The *concave lens* may be also called the hollow lens, as it is spherically hollowed out on both sides (fig. 113). Its properties are widely different from those of the convex lens, all the rays that fall upon it in a direction parallel with its axis being so refracted that they diverge, on emerging from the lens, as though they issued from the point F.

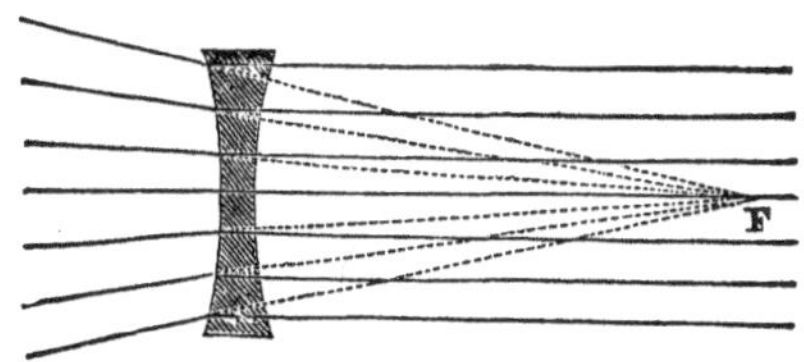

113.

It *converging* rays fall upon a concave lens, they will emerge either in a parallel direction, fig. 113, or, if they converge only slightly, as in fig. 114, they will diverge on passing out.

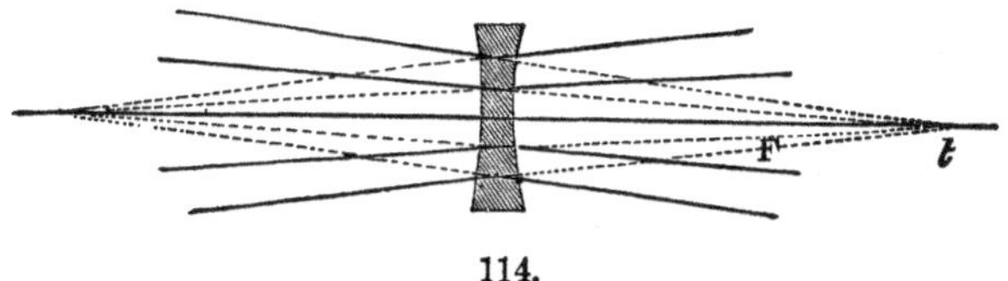

114.

Concave lenses are hence called *diverging* glasses.

165. A very great importance is given to polished glasses by the proper-

ties we have just described. Thus the double convex lens by itself is the magnifying glass in its most simple form; it passes under the general name of lens, and is employed by watch-makers, engravers, mould-cutters, &c. It is likewise indispensable to botanists and anatomists. By an appropriate combination of lenses, microscopes are constructed, capable of furnishing images of the objects observed through them, magnified from 100 to 1,000 times. By means of these instruments, myriads of minute living creatures have been discovered, of the existence of which no conception was previously entertained, and the most important discoveries have been made regarding the structure of plants and the larger animals.

These glasses have, however, not only served to increase the visual powers of the human eye with regard to objects in its vicinity, but they have become the key to the infinite space of the heavens, and far-distant worlds have been brought by them within the range of our vision. Such combinations of lenses as serve for observations in the distance are termed *telescopes:* the general principle of their construction is, that the rays of light proceeding from a distant object are collected by a very large lens, termed the *object-glass*, or by a large concave mirror, and the image thus obtained is magnified by a second lens or the *eye-glass.*

It is to telescopes of this description that we are solely indebted for our knowledge of the wondrous construction of the moon's surface, of the satellites of Jupiter, of Saturn's ring, and of many other important astronomical phenomena. The telescope is likewise indispensable to land-surveyors, mariners, military men, &c.

Finally, we have to call attention to a particular application of the images produced in the air by lenses, as in fig. 112. If an image of this description be allowed to fall upon a white surface, in a dark chamber (camera obscura), it may easily be traced thereon by means of a pencil. If the object be very powerfully illumined by a double convex lens, a highly-magnified image may be obtained on a white surface: such images as these are exhibited by the *magic lantern*, and more particularly by the *solar* microscope.

The art of preparing lenses of glass was first practised in Holland. They were, however, at first only used for spectacles, until towards the close of the 17th century, the microscope was invented by Leuwenhoeck. The invention of the telescope is ascribed to Galileo. Both instruments have been gradually very much improved, the latter particularly by Keppler, Herschel, Newton, Fraunhofer, and several others.

Vision.

166. Of no other organ of sense is the purpose of each individual part so accurately known as of the *eye.* It is, indeed, nothing more than a tolerably simple optical instrument, which may be most easily comprehended by a careful examination of the eye of an ox. On cutting one open, and removing the so-called *crystalline lens*, which consists of a gelatinous substance, it will be found to behave itself exactly like a convex lens cut out of glass.

The Physicist views the apple of the eye as a small round chamber (camera obscura), with a black interior coating, surrounded by membranes, and filled with a perfectly-transparent gelatinous substance, which is called the *vitreous humour.*

The front part of the membrane enclosing the eye, the *tunica sclerotica,* is transparent, and more strongly curved than the rest of the globe: it is called the *cornea,* and forms, with the clear liquid it contains, the *anterior optic chamber b.* The rays of light pass into the eye from any object, for instance, from *l l'* through a small round opening *s s,* called the *pupil;* they undergo a refraction by the crystalline lens *c c',* by which an image of the object is formed on the *retina m m',* a net-like membrane, which is situated at the back of the eye: we become conscious of this image through the *optic nerve.*

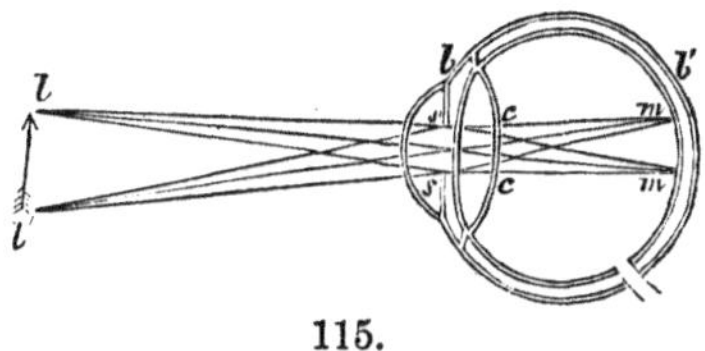

115.

The rays of light proceeding from the object *l l',* are first refracted in the anterior optic chamber *b,* and afterwards again undergo refraction by the lens *c c'* by which a diminished image of the object is produced between *m m'.*

That this is really the case may be shown with the eye of an ox, namely, by removing carefully the back portion of the membrane in scales or layers, so that it becomes thin and translucent, and then holding an object, for instance a burning candle, before the pupil of the eye; a small image of the candle will then be distinctly visible on the retina.

It is hence explicable why *inverted* images are obtained of all objects presented to the eye, why, for example, we see in fig. 115 the point *l* at *m,* and the point *l'* at *m',* and why, in the experiment with the eye of an ox, the diminished image of the candle appears inverted.

As we are accustomed from our earliest youth to observe simultaneously with the senses of vision and feeling, the observation made by the former is immediately rectified by the latter.

It is clearly proved by children and by persons who are born blind and receive their sight in later years, that we only arrive at a correct conception of the situation of objects and of distance, by our sense of feeling and by the movements of our body.

167. Every one, in reading a book, holds it at such a distance from his eyes, as will enable him to see it most distinctly. This distance is called the *distance of distinct vision,* and it generally amounts to eight or ten inches in a perfectly sound eye. At this distance, a sharply-defined image of every letter falls exactly upon the retina, the rays proceeding from every point of the object being so refracted in the eye that they reunite at one point of the retina, as seen in fig. 115, and then produce a perfectly-distinct image. If we assume the eye to retain the exact arrangement exhibited in the above figure, and approach the object closer to the eye, the rays proceeding from one point of the former will diverge so strongly, that they will not become sufficiently refracted by the production of a distinct image on the retina. Indeed, the image must fall at the *back* of the retina, only an *indistinct* image being then produced (fig. 116). If the object be removed beyond the distance of distinct vision, the rays proceeding from it will converge to such an extent as to be united before they arrive at the retina, and in this case an indistinct image is likewise produced (fig. 117).

Hence every object that is closer to, or more remote from, the eye, than the distance of distinct vision, must appear indistinct. This is, however,

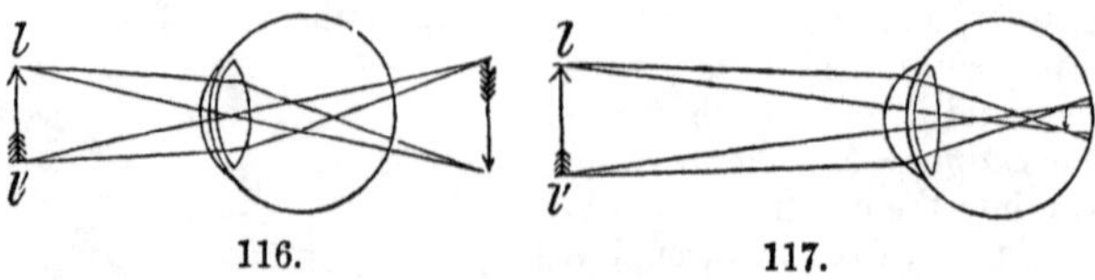

116. 117.

not the case with a perfectly sound eye; any object at a distance is distinctly visible to it, and will remain so, when approached, to a certain limit. The reason of this is, that the arrangement of the refracting portions of the interior of the eye is not unalterable, but may be modified for distant or close vision. If, on viewing an object close at hand, the tunica sclerotica, or forepart of the eye, becomes more strongly curved, it will receive a greater refracting power, whereby the image is made to fall on the retina. When the eye observes remote objects, this portion of the eye becomes flattened, and the distance at which the rays unite, in front of the retina, is thereby diminished.

This capacity of the eye to suit itself to viewing distant or contiguous objects, is called its power of *adaptation* or *accommodation.* This power is, however, not common to all eyes. By frequently or continually looking at objects too close, particularly in one's youth, the forepart of the eyes will soon acquire a *permanently-increased* curvature, and they will thereby lose their power of adapting themselves to distant objects, which they will therefore see only indistinctly: this defect in vision is called *short-sightedness.* The eye is *long-sighted* if it is incapable of adapting itself to view objects that are closer to it than the usual distance of distinct vision, which is eight or ten inches.

The defective vision of a short-sighted person is, therefore, the result of too powerful a refraction of the rays of light by the eye, while with a long-sighted person the reverse is the case. Both defects may be artificially remedied, by employing lenses, which, if convex, will assist in collecting the rays, and if they are concave will assist in their dispersion.

168. *Spectacles*, therefore, afford us means of properly adjusting the refraction of the rays of light, so as to produce a well-defined image on the retina: a long-sighted person must be supplied with spectacles with convex lenses, while short-sighted people require concave spectacles.

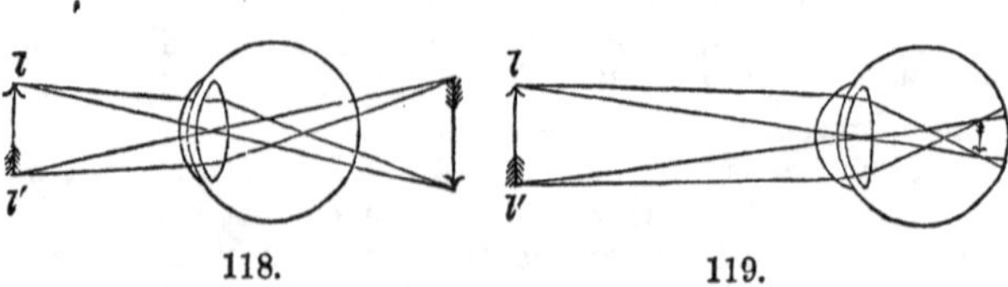

118. 119.

Fig. 118 represents a long-sighted, and fig. 119 a short-sighted eye, neither of which is capable of producing a distinct image of the object *l l'*; as, in the one case, it will fall at the back, and, in the other, in the front of the retina If these eyes are, however, supplied with the appropriate spectacle-glasses *m* and *n* (figs. 120 and 121), the convex lens will effect a greater

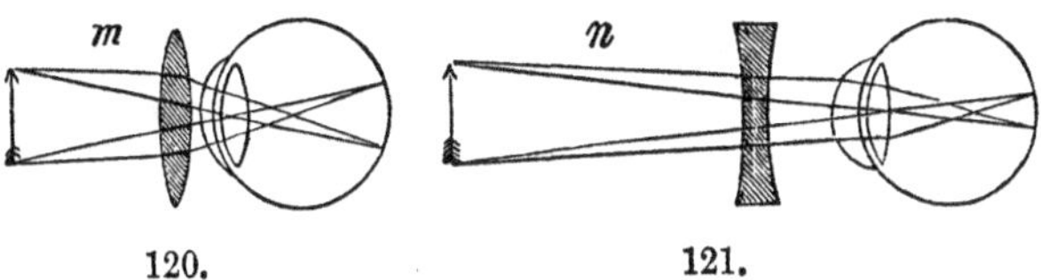

120. 121.

refraction of the rays, and the concave a less-powerful refraction, so that in both cases the image of the object will fall exactly on the retina, and will consequently be well defined.

It is evident that the concavity or convexity of the spectacle-glasses must be regulated according to the magnitude of the defect in the vision.

A person may become blind by an injury sustained by the optic nerve: this kind of blindness is incurable, and is called the incurable cataract, or *amaurosis*. Blindness is more frequently occasioned by *common* cataract, in which case the lens of the eye becomes dim or opaque. This disease may be cured by making, with a steady and practised hand, an incision at one point in the membranes of the eye, by means of sharp and pointed instruments, and then either extracting the lens through the pupil, or pressing it down, so that light may be able to pass into the chamber of the eye. After the operation, the eye is supplied with spectacles containing very powerfully refracting double-convex lenses, in order that the dispersed rays of light falling on the eye may be refracted and fall together on the retina.

The eyes of the higher orders of animals, namely, the mammalia, birds, amphibious animals, and fishes, correspond with the human eye in the most important parts of their structure. Of the more imperfect animals, some possess no eyes, and others have eyes of a peculiar construction (fig. 122). A great number of small hollow cones *a b c d*, stand rectangularly upon the convex retina, *f g*, and through which the rays of light, proceeding from the various points of an object, fall upon the retina. These animals can only see contiguous objects, which appear to them as an object does to our eyes when viewed through wire-work. Each small cone is covered at the upper extremity with a transparent membrane; and an eye of this description presents to us the appearance of a hemisphere, with numerous small surfaces, amounting to from 12,000 to 20,000. All insects, for instance the common flies, have eyes of this description. Many, however, in addition to these plane-surfaced eyes, have lens-eyes, as is the case with spiders.

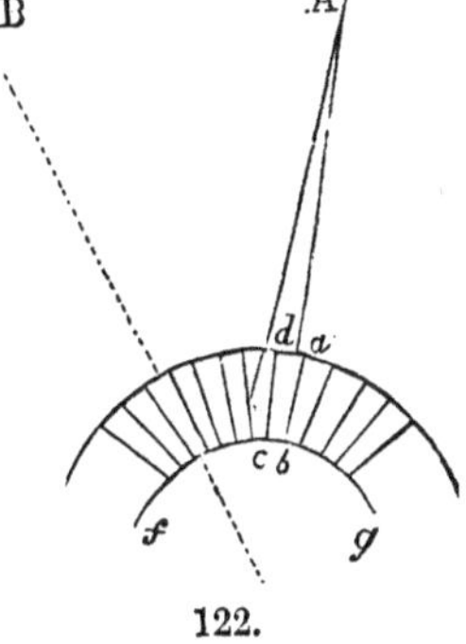

122.

169. Under certain circumstances, Nature herself gives rise to the conditions required to produce remarkable *reflections* of objects in the air, and to which phenomena the names *air pictures*, *fata morgana*, and *mirage* have been given.

For the production of these phenomena, large planes are necessary, over which extends an exceedingly calm stratum of air, so that, after sunrise, the lower portions rise only very gradually as they become warm, and mix with the denser upper portions. If any lofty objects are situated on the plane, as in fig. 123, two images of these will reach the eye of the observer, under the above circumstances; the one produced by the rays that proceed directly from h to p, the other resulting from a ray, proceeding from h being refracted by the less dense strata of air, c, c', c'', c''', to such an extent that it appears to proceed from the direction z; thus a second but *inverted* image of the object is seen in that direction. A stratum of air is situated between the two images, so that now the impression produced is the same as if a row of objects, as trees, hills, spires, &c., were visible and reflected by the water of a lake or sea.

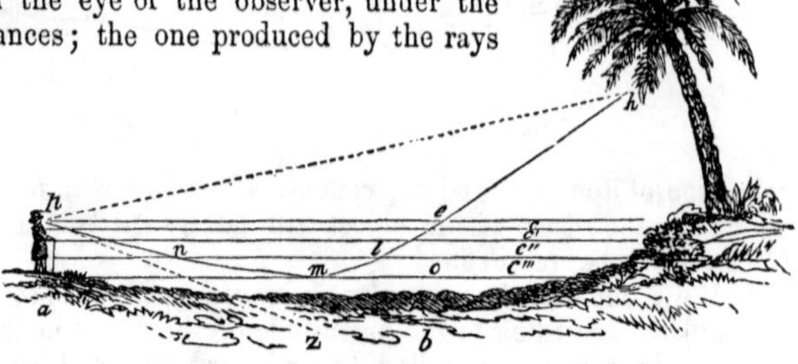

123.

These phenomena are most frequently observed in the deserts of Egypt: travellers are often most painfully disappointed by the sudden disappearance of what seemed to them refreshing waters in the midst of the scorching sand.

Some varieties of these reflections have also been observed, although but rarely, over seas and other places.

Halos round the moon, as also *mock suns* and *moons*, may be seen occasionally, when these bodies are viewed through very thin strata of clouds, which cover the heavens. These phenomena are likewise considered as resulting from the refraction and reflection of light.

Colours.

170. A ray of light, when directed, by means of a mirror m, fig. 124, into a darkened room, through an opening o in the window-shutter, will produce on the opposite wall t of the room a round white image g. If, however, the ray be received upon a triangular piece of glass a so-called *prism*, of which p is a section), on its immediate entrance through the opening, it will not merely diverge considerably from its original path, but will likewise produce an elongated

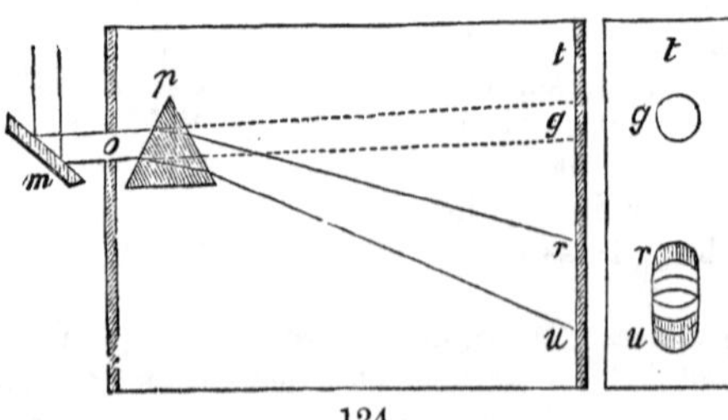

124.

streak of light upon the wall, between r and u, composed of beautiful colours, the lower end at u being *violet*, which is followed successively by stripes of *indigo-blue*, *blue*, *green*, *yellow*, *orange*, and *red*. These are the same colours, and arranged in the same order, as those observed in the rainbow; they are called *prismatic* or rainbow colours, or colours of the solar spectrum.

The white solar light is, therefore, not only refracted by the prism, but also *decomposed* or dissected into seven luminous rays of different colours. The white rays are, therefore, called compound or *mixed* light, because they are composed of the *seven* simple rays. The possibility of decomposing light is based upon the circumstance, that its component parts possess *various degrees of refrangibility*. If the solar spectrum be examined, it will be seen that the red light is situated nearer than the violet light to the position which the non-refracted spot of white light would occupy; the former possesses, therefore, the least, and the latter the greatest refrangibility. The difference in refrangibility arises from the unequal length of the waves of light composing the simple rays, it being analogous to the difference in sound, caused by the unequal length of the sound-waves.

If the seven coloured rays proceeding from the prism be collected by means of a convex lens, they will be reunited at its focal-point to *white* light. This phenomenon may be observed by simply pasting in a circle upon the upper part of a peg-top, pieces of paper of equal size and various colours, resembling as much as possible the prismatic colours, and then spinning it; the impression made upon the eye by the various colours will become mixed, and the variegated upper surface of the top will appear white.

Those bodies, therefore, that refract all the rays of light in their original mixture, are *white*, while those that absorb the rays are *black*. There is, however, scarcely a body existing that possesses one or other of these properties in its full extent: hence result the various shades from white, through gray, to black.

There exist likewise bodies, the particles of which are so arranged that they only check the vibrations of certain waves of light, while they refract the remaining waves unaltered. Thus, a *red* body absorbs all the coloured rays of the white light that fall upon it, with the exception of the *red* rays, which it reflects. All other colours of substances, such as blue, green, yellow, &c., are accounted for in the same manner.

171. Many substances only appear coloured when they are seen in large masses; glass or ice, for instance, appear colourless when in thin layers, while they have a green or blue appearance when viewed in larger masses. Even the air, when viewed in a mass of the height of the atmosphere, has a beautiful blue colour: assuming the absence of the atmosphere, the space of the heavens would appear black. Indeed, the air, when viewed from many high mountains, appears dark-blue, because the black of the universal space above penetrates through the less dense and high stratum of air. On level ground even, the air appears to us darker over our heads than at the horizon, as, in observing the latter, we have to look through a mass of air of far greater extent than that situated over our heads. The blue appearance of distant hills is imparted to them by the large mass of air, situated between them and our eyes.

The *red* and *yellow* colour of the heavens, known by the name of *evening* and *morning red*, is ascribed to the property possessed by the aqueous vapour in the air, particularly when it passes over from the state of fog into real vapour, of allowing the passage of red and yellow light only. This production of vapour generally takes place in the morning or evening.

The Rainbow.

172. This phenomenon of Nature is so remarkable for the splendour of its colours, that it requires our particular notice. Though rain and sunshine are pretty generally known to be the necessary conditions for the production of the rainbow, the precise explanation of its formation cannot be given in a few words; we shall, therefore, confine ourselves here to an endeavour to lead to the proper comprehension of its nature.

A comparison of the rainbow colours with those of the solar spectrum produced by the prism (§ 170), which will be found to correspond with them in shade and arrangement, must lead to the conclusion that the formation of the rainbow is owing to the refraction and decomposition of light.

Drops of dew or rain, suspended to grass or bushes, may be frequently found to appear to the eye of a bright-red colour: by slightly shifting the position of the eye, the colour of the drop may be made to appear successively yellow, green, blue, and violet, and also colourless. This proves that the rays of light, falling in a certain direction upon the drop of water, are refracted thereby and decomposed into the coloured rays which become visible to the eye when it is situated in the direction of the emerging rays. We may, therefore, imagine the seven prismatic colours to reach our eyes simul-

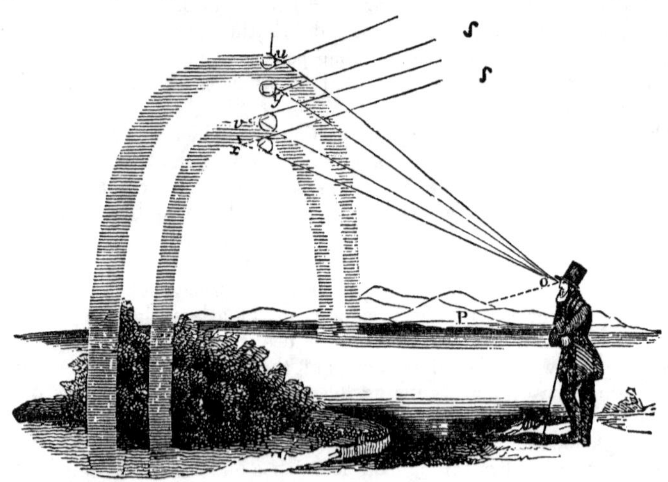

125.

taneously from seven different drops, provided the proper relative position between the latter and the former exists. This is frequently the case when the sun shines upon a quantity of drops falling from waterfalls, fountains, paddle-wheels, &c.

The rainbow is always observed to be situated in the west in the morning and in the east in the afternoon, so that in looking at it we must always stand with our backs to the sun, and have the cloud of rain before us. It is, however, necessary, for the production of a rainbow, that the height of the sun above the horizon should not exceed 42 degrees. Hence we generally observe this phenomenon in the morning or towards evening; and it is only in the winter, when the sun stands very low, that the rainbow is sometimes seen at hours approaching noon. The form of the latter is in reality that of an enormous circle, of which the half that is situated below the horizon is invisible to us. Circular rainbows are visible, however, under certain circumstances, particularly from the masts of vessels. As rays of light reach the eye from all parts of a rainbow, the former may be considered as the point of a cone, the base of which is the rainbow itself, and whose axis is represented by a straight line, passing from the centre of the bow through that of the eye, and, if prolonged, would touch the centre of the sun.

We usually observe a second rainbow close to the first, the colours of which are, however, much paler. This phenomenon is the result of a second refraction of the once-refracted rays by other drops of water, whereby the light becomes much fainter. It must also be observed that in the second rainbow, the order of colours is reversed, the red forming the outer largest circle, and violet the inner circle.

III. PHENOMENA OF CURRENTS.

Electricity—Magnetism.

173. If it were in our power to collect in this work all the observations made, and facts discovered, in the departments of electricity and magnetism, we should be filled with surprise and wonder at the industry and penetration displayed by natural philosophers. The description of all that has been done in this branch of Physics, since the middle of last century, would furnish volumes sufficient to fill a whole library.

But, notwithstanding the multiplicity of electrical and magnetical phenomena, it is a matter of great difficulty to trace their ultimate cause; it is, indeed, scarcely possible for us to form even a general conception thereof from individual effects, as we are able to do with heat, sound, and light.

The ether by which all matter is penetrated appears capable of being set into peculiar motion, which we term the *motion of currents*, possessing a characteristic tendency to return upon itself, in a manner analogous to circular motion. These currents may be considered as moving either in aggregations or in surfaces, giving rise to various phenomena, which become perceptible to us as electricity and magnetism. Some particular phenomena are the results of the mutual approach of two currents of this description from various directions. Thus, parallel currents attract each other, while those meeting from opposite directions repel each other.

The relations of bodies themselves to this kind of motion of ether may vary just as much as they do with the undulatory motion. Manifold effects are thus produced, of which we shall here mention only the most important.

The terms employed in the description thereof do not, however, bear any reference to the above mode of viewing them, it not being sufficiently well grounded to be applied in the consideration of all electric and magnetic phenomena.

I. Electricity.

174. Electrical phenomena are produced, 1, by *friction* between different bodies; 2, by placing in *contact* bodies differing from each other, either in their structure, temperature, or chemical character; 3, by the transition of bodies from one condition to another; 4, by the chemical metamorphosis of bodies; 5, by various animals, either voluntarily or involuntarily.

The most important electrical phenomena arise from the first, second, and fourth causes.

175. (1.) *Frictional Electricity.* — A piece of sealing-wax, resin, or sulphur, when rubbed with wool, acquires the property of attracting light bodies, such as scraps of paper, hairs, &c., from a little distance. This is the most ancient electrical phenomenon, it having been known to the Greeks, who perceived it on rubbing amber, which they called *electron*, and from which the name electricity has, therefore, been derived. A glass tube, when rubbed forcibly with a silk handkerchief, acquires the same property. These substances are said to become *electrical* by friction, and the cause of their attractive power is the *electricity* imparted to them.

A great number of bodies do not possess the above property: they have, therefore, been termed *non-electric*, in opposition to *electric*, bodies. The former class of bodies may be represented by the metals, and the latter by the above-named substances. Accurate observation has, however, shown that there exists, strictly speaking, no perfectly non-electric substance, all bodies being liable to conversion into an electric state, although this property is possessed by some only to a very slight extent.

If glass or resin be forcibly rubbed in the dark, their surfaces will present a luminous appearance: on approaching the knuckle of a finger or any metallic object to them, when in this state, a brilliant *spark* will pass over to the former, accompanied by a crackling noise, and produce a slight pricking sensation at the point where it enters the finger. This phenomenon is called the *electric spark*.

Electricity exists always only on the *surface* of the electrified body, and is only abstracted from those points of glass or resin that are actually touched. If the rubbed glass or resin be approached by a metallic object, the electricity passes over to the latter, which is then possessed of all the electrical properties; it attracts light bodies and emits sparks. It is, however, remarkable that metals lose their electricity immediately and entirely, when they are touched only at one single point. Such bodies as abstract the electricity from electrified resin or glass, thereby becoming electric themselves, are called *conductors*, and other bodies that do not possess these properties are termed *non-conductors*.

Metals are the best conductors of electricity. Liquids, aqueous vapour, the bodies of men and animals, and fresh plants, are likewise very good conductors. Glass, resin, wool, silk, and *dry* air do not conduct electricity at all, or at least only to a very slight extent. If an object of glass be brought near to electrified resin, glass, or metal, it does not remove a trace of electricity. Hence the latter may be retained in any substance by surrounding it with good non-conductors. Thus, for instance, any metallic body, placed upon a disc of resin or plate of glass in *dry* air, and then electrified, will only part with its electricity on the approach of a conductor. When bodies are surrounded on all sides by non-conductors, they are said to be *insulated;* and the latter are, therefore, also called *insulators.*

If a small ball of cork be suspended to a silken thread (fig. 126), and a piece of rubbed sealing-wax be brought towards it, the ball will be attracted until it touches the wax; the moment, however, that this is the case, the cork will be forcibly repelled. It has now taken up a portion of electricity from the wax. On again approaching freshly-rubbed sealing-wax to the ball, it will no longer be attracted; on the contrary, it will fly from the wax in an opposite direction: hence it appears that the two bodies charged with electricity derived from the sealing-wax mutually repel each other. If a glass tube be now rubbed with a piece of silk, and held to the cork, it will be observed that the latter will move towards the glass even from a considerable distance, being *attracted* by the electricity of the glass.

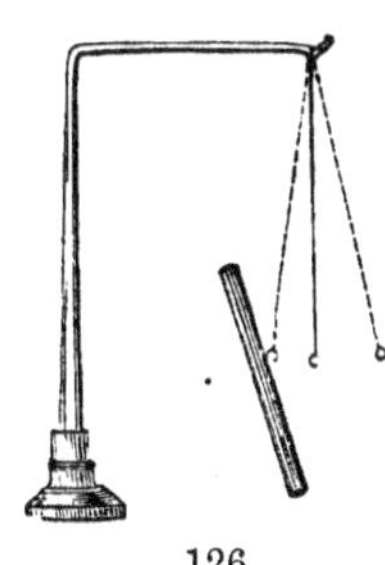
126.

If a ball of this description is charged with electricity from resin, and another with electricity from glass, and these be then approached until they attract or touch each other, they will be found, after having been in contact, neither of them to possess any electrical properties whatever.

The following facts are deduced from the above simple experiments:—

(1.) There are two kinds of electricity; first, that obtained by the friction of glass, which is termed *positive* or vitreous electricity, as also + electricity; secondly, that procured by the friction of resin, to which the name *negative* or resinous electricity has bhen given, and which is also designated as — electricity.

(2.) Bodies, charged with the *same kind* of electricity, *repel* each other, while those containing opposite electricities *attract* each other.

(3.) The opposite electricities always endeavour to unite. When once this is effected, *neutral* electricity ensues, *i. e.*, the two electricities mutually neutralize each other's properties, and electricity is no longer perceptible.

(4.) All bodies contain both electricities in the *combined* state; these may be separated from each other by various means, for instance, by friction. If, then, the rubbed body becomes positively electrified, the substance with which friction is applied becomes negatively electric.

176. *Electricity by Induction.*—The horizontal metal rod $c\,c'$ (fig. 127) is insulated by being fixed upon a glass stand. A couple of cork balls are attached to each end by means of slender metallic wires. A rod of resin r, rendered negatively electrical by friction, is then brought near to one pair of the balls. It may be easily conceived that the negative electricity of the resin will attract the positive electricity of the metal and repel its negative electricity; the combined electricities in the latter are thus *separated*, the + electricity being situated at c', and the — electricity at c. This is rendered perceptible by the behaviour of the balls. The two balls situated at c', both containing + electricity, repel each other; as is likewise the case

with the other two balls at *c*, which have become negatively electrified. On removing the rod of resin *r*, the separating cause is done away with, and the separated electricities in the metal will immediately reunite, which is proved by the balls falling together again.

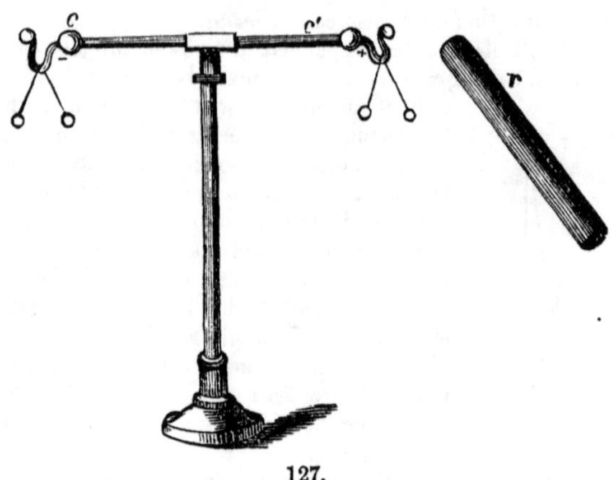

127.

If the metal is touched with the finger at *c*, while the stick of resin *r* is still held near *c'*, the — electricity contained in the former extremity will be conducted off by the finger, while the + electricity collected at the other end will remain combined with the — electricity of the resin. On removing the finger first, and afterwards the resin, the whole rod will be charged with + electricity, as will be indicated by the mutual repulsion of the balls.

If we had employed rubbed glass instead of resin exactly the same phenomena would have taken place, except that in the above description all the electricity marked + and — should be changed, the + made — and the — made +.

This induction of electricity, therefore, affords us a means of charging any isolated body with + or — electricity at pleasure.

177. The *electrophorus* (fig. 128) is a very simple instrument, capable of affording an abundant supply of electricity by means of induction. A mixture of two parts of shellac and one of turpentine is poured into a plate of metal, of about one foot in diameter and one finger-breadth in height, so that the mass yields, on cooling, a cake possessing as even a surface as possible. This is made electric by rubbing it with a cat's skin; a metal cover, furnished in the centre with a glass handle is then placed upon it. We will now proceed to examine the action of the electrophorus. It is assumed that the electricity of the cake has been separated by friction, so that — electricity is collected on its upper surface, while the + electricity is collected on the lower one. In placing the metal plate upon the cake an induction of electricity likewise takes place,

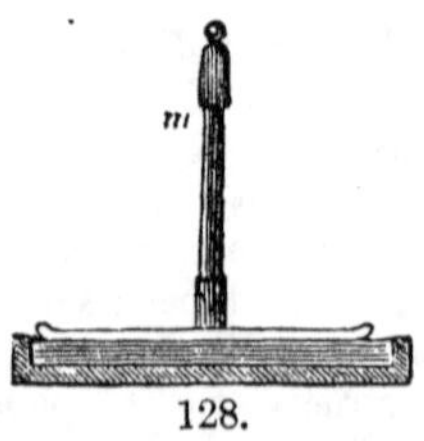

128.

since its + electricity is neutralized by the — electricity of the cake. On now touching the cover whilst in this position with the finger, its free — electricity is conducted away by the body. If the finger be removed, and the cover then lifted by its insulated handle, it will be found charged with free + electricity, which may be then employed for any experiments, in which glass or resin was previously made use of. If this apparatus be properly constructed, a very bright spark may be extracted from the charged cover on approaching the knuckle of a finger.

When its electricity has been thus abstracted, it may again be charged as above described. It is remarkable that a spark may even be obtained from the plate, on lifting it up after the lapse of weeks or even months.

178. The *Leyden jar* (fig. 129) is a common glass jar, coated internally and externally with tinfoil to the height $a\,a'$. The opening is closed by means of a bung or piece of wood $g\,g'$, through which passes a rod t, furnished with a brass ball at the upper end terminating at the lower extremity in a chain, which should touch the jar. On bringing the interior metallic coating by means of the ball in contact with any source of electricity (for example, the cover of the electrophorus) it will receive a charge of + electricity. The latter exerts through the glass a dispersing action upon the electricity contained on the exterior coating, by *combining* with the — electricity, and *repelling* the + electricity, which is conducted by the object on which the jar stands towards the earth, over the surface of which it distributes itself, and thus disappears.

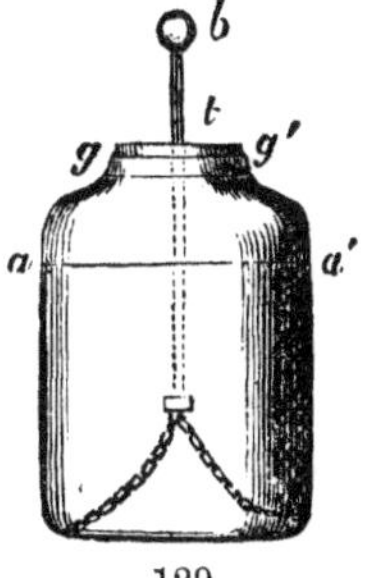

129.

The inner and outer coating of the jar are, therefore, charged with opposite electricities, which are prevented from combining by the glass situated between them. These will unite, however, at the moment that the two coatings are connected by a conducting body. If this connection be effected by touching the ball with one hand and the exterior coating with the other, the electricities will pass through the body, and a peculiar concussion, which is termed the *electric shock*, will be felt, particularly in the joints. Its intensity depends upon the charge of electricity in the jar; forty to fifty sparks, allowed to pass from the cover of the electrophorus into the jar, yield a sufficient charge to produce a very sensible shock. If several persons form a chain by joining hands, and the first one touches the knob, while the person at the other extremity touches the exterior of the charged Leyden jar, a shock of equal force will be *simultaneously* felt by every person, however large the number of persons who form the circle.

The electricity may also be discharged from the jar without the production of a shock, by employing a *discharging rod* (fig. 130), constructed of brass, and provided with a glass handle. By laying hold of the latter, and touching the ball of the jar with one ball of the discharger, and the exterior coating with the other ball, the electricities will be united with the production of a very brilliant spark.

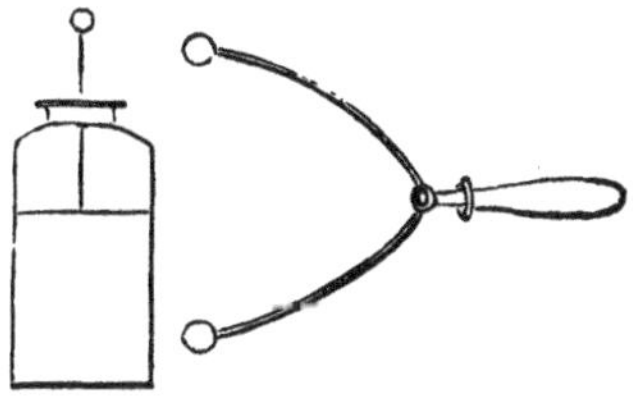
130.

179. A combination of several jars is

called an *electric battery* (fig. 131): this is capable of producing tremendous shocks according to the intensity of its charge. The sparks may be made to pass over at the distance of several inches, and are accompanied by a sharp report. Animals may be killed by such discharges. If the charge be allowed to pass through a long wire, interrupted at any point, a spark will pass over the space, provided it be not too great. The same phenomenon is observed if a wire be arranged with several small spaces, and very pretty and striking phenomena of light may be thus produced.

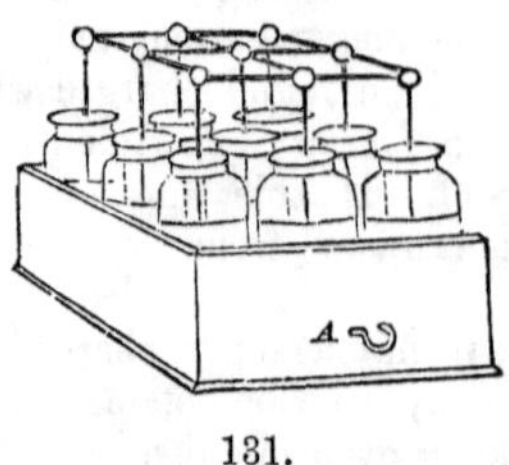

131.

180. *Electrifying machines* (figs. 132 and 133) are employed for the production of powerful electric phenomena. The one in most general use, called the *plate* machine (fig. 132), consists of a glass plate, or disc, $\frac{1}{4}$ to $\frac{1}{2}$ inch in thickness, and 2 to 4 feet in diameter. It is moveable round its

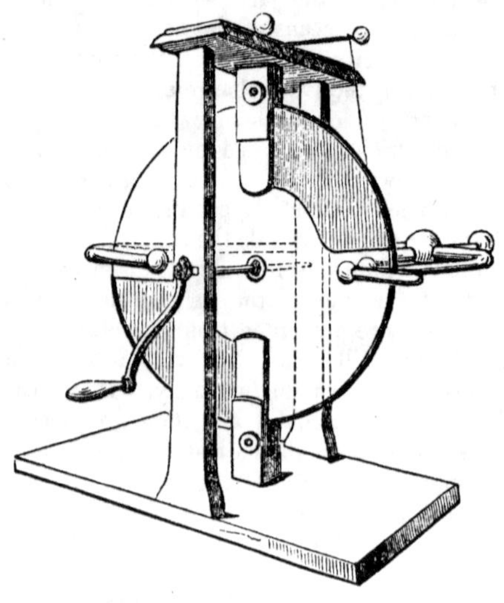

132.

axis, and, when turned round, rubs against four cushions, which are covered with an amalgam of tin and mercury, or, still better, with a coating of bisulphuret of tin. The + electricity, thus liberated, is collected by the *conductor*, which consists of a hollow polished cylinder of brass plate which is insulated by means of a stout rod of glass.

Fig. 133 represents a *cylinder machine.*

Such machines are employed specially for charging batteries, and also for performing a large number of experiments, which are partly of scientific interest, and partly of a popular and entertaining character.

181. As a general rule, it is highly essential that the atmosphere should be warm and dry, when electrical experiments are made, as the conducting

property of moist air prevents the collection of a sufficient amount of electricity for the production of striking effects. In the winter, the experiments succeed best when performed near a fire; and it is advisable to place the apparatus in front of the fire for some time before it is employed.

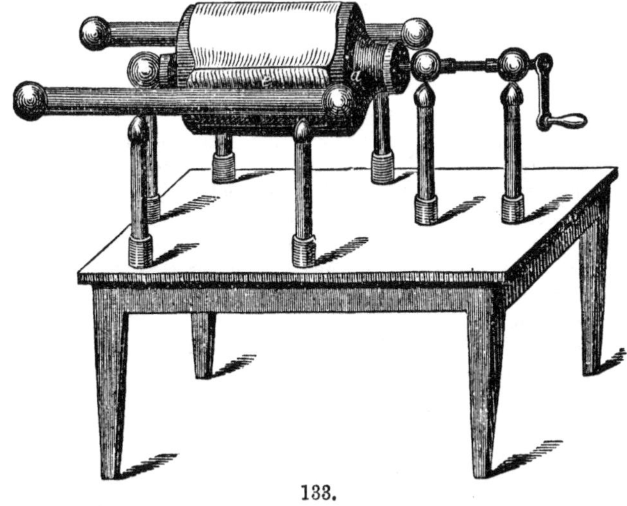

133.

182. The most striking and stupendous electrical phenomena are produced by Nature herself. Thus, the dazzling forks of lightning that break forth, flash after flash, from the clouds, followed by tremendous peals of thunder re-echoing through the skies, are nothing more than immense electric sparks, often miles in length. These discharges pass from one cloud to another, or to the earth, and are accompanied by a report corresponding to the crackling noise which each small spark makes as it passes from the electrophorus.

Although we are unable to form any accurate conception of the manner in which *free* electricity is collected in the different clouds, its existence therein was clearly proved by Franklin, in the year 1752, by means of a kite raised in the air, during a storm; the string, to which it was attached, being possessed of sufficient conducting power to exhibit electrical phenomena. These would naturally be rendered more evident, by enclosing a wire in the string. It has since been proved that the atmosphere is frequently in an electrical state without any thunder-storms being observed; and from this we may with certainty assume, that electrical currents are universally distributed, and produce many effects that still appear to us as enigmatical.

A cloud, for instance, charged with free electricity, on approaching the surface of the earth, acts by induction on the electricity of the latter; and the negative electricity will pass from the earth to the cloud until the two electricities have neutralized each other. In this manner most electrical clouds pass over the earth, without being accompanied by any striking phenomena.

If the electric cloud is very close to the earth, and there are lofty objects on the surface of the latter, such as trees, steeples, mountain summits, &c.,

from which a strong discharge of electricity takes place, the combination of the two electricities at those points is accompanied by a powerful flash; and hence we say that objects are struck by lightning.

183. Thunder-storms are rendered far less dangerous by the use of *lightning-conductors*, which continually conduct the opposite electricity from the earth to the electric cloud, thereby neutralizing or diminishing the electricity of the cloud to a considerable extent. Should, however, a flash be emitted from the cloud even under these circumstances, it will pass over in preference to the elevated iron rod or wire of which the conductor is made; and as the latter is always constructed outside a building, and passes into the ground, the electric current will follow this good conductor, without touching the building. A good lightning-conductor may be considered as capable of protecting a space around it of about 40 feet in diameter.

As sound travels so much more slowly than light, the thunder is always heard after the lightning has been seen. It is only when a storm is just over our heads, and particularly when any object close to us is struck by lightning, that the thunder is heard simultaneously. The greater the interval between lightning and thunder, the greater is the distance of the storm. When the latter is very far off, no thunder is heard; we only see the lightning, which we then term *sheet lightning.*

The effects of lightning are always exceedingly powerful, and sometimes terrific. It annihilates all objects that lie in its path; fuses metals, ignites combustible substances, and destroys men and animals. But in the bodies of persons destroyed by lightning no external injury is in general perceptible. The electric discharge is always accompanied by a peculiar, suffocating, sulphurous smell, which is sometimes noticed in a slight degree to emanate from powerful electrifying machines.

As electricity collects most readily in pointed objects, it is always advisable to avoid trees, steeples, high chimneys, &c., during storms. Single trees or clusters of trees on open fields are particularly dangerous: and unfortunate beings are constantly falling a sacrifice to lightning on such spots, to which they have fled for shelter from the storm and rain.

2. Electricity by Contact.

184. It has already been mentioned that substances, differing from each other either chemically or in their temperature or structure, produce electricity when brought into contact. This property is exhibited especially by metals. We shall choose copper and zinc from among these for our consideration, partly because they are powerful exciters of electricity, and partly because they are the two metals most generally employed for this purpose.

185. *Elementary experiment.*—If two extremely smooth and well-polished discs, one of copper and the other of zinc, each provided with an insulated handle, be placed upon each other, so that the polished surfaces are in contact, and again separated, the zinc will be charged with + electricity, and the copper with — electricity. The charges are, however, very slight, and can only be indicated by the most delicate electrometers, of peculiar construction. The plates themselves undergo at least no perceptible change.

The following is an experiment of a similar nature: two sheets of gold-paper are pasted together back to back, and in a similar manner two of silver-paper. They are then cut into discs of about the size of half a crown, which are piled upon each other in such a manner that gold and silver paper follow alternately: the column thus obtained is slightly compressed and introduced into a glass-tube, the ends of which are then closed with corks, through which are pressed pieces of wires. Piles of from 500 to 2000 pairs may be thus constructed, the wires of which will be found, on examination, to be charged with opposite electricities. This apparatus is called the *dry pile*, or Zamboni's pile, and, under favourable circumstances, retains its power for years.

These two experiments afford almost the only instances in which electricity is produced by simple contact. In most other cases, chemical decomposition acts simultaneously with contact in the production of electricity.

186. Fig. 134 represents the *voltaic* or *galvanic pile*, called after Galvani, its discoverer, and Volta, the founder of the phenomena produced by contact. It is sometimes placed in a stand, the upper and lower parts of which are made of wood, and connected with each other by three glass rods. A disc of copper is placed at the bottom of the pile, and next to it one of zinc; these two discs being generally soldered together, by which the construction of the pile is much simplified. Upon the zinc disc is placed one of pasteboard, woollen cloth, or felt, previously soaked in water, and then pressed. More discs, of the different substances, are then placed upon these exactly in the same order; and thus a pile of from 20 to 40 pairs may be constructed, terminating at the top in a plate of zinc.

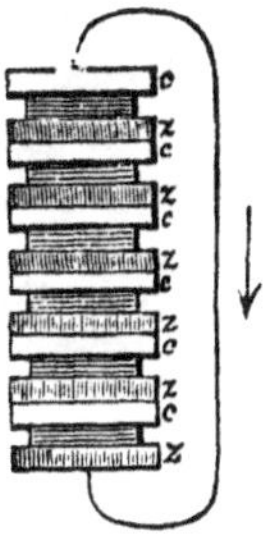

134.

The *zinc end* of the pile is called the *positive pole*, and the *copper end* the *negative pole*, as the respective opposite electricities, produced by the contact of the pairs of plates, are found collected at the extremities. On soldering wires to the terminating plates, as in fig. 134, they will form the two poles of the pile.

When these two wires are in contact, the circuit is said to be *closed*. No sign of electrical excitement is then visible; the action, nevertheless, continues in the interior of the pile. The opposite electricities collected at the poles, in particular, neutralize each other perfectly on meeting; every trace of electricity must therefore vanish, as when a Leyden jar is discharged, if a fresh quantity were not continually produced by every pair of plates: when the circuit is closed, two electrical currents are continually passing through the pile in opposite directions, and partially combine at every point of the *closing wire*. If, therefore, the latter be disconnected at any point, as seen in fig. 134, a continuous spark will pass from one wire to the other. The same takes place if the wires are severed at several points. It is of course requisite that the space between the wires should be of inconsiderable size.

187. The actions of the current, circulating in the pile, merit our special attention. Their results may be classed under three heads; 1. Phenomena of heat and light; 2. The excitation of nerves and muscles; 3. Chemical decompositions.

If a piece of fine wire of any metal be fixed from one conducting wire to the other, so that the electric current must necessarily pass through the wire, it will become hot, red-hot, and even heated to whiteness. Iron-wire burns under these circumstances, while wires of platinum, the most difficultly fusible metal, will melt into small globules. The intensity of the phenomena depends upon the power of the pile. In some instances a platinum wire, 20 inches in length, has been kept at a red-heat by the electrical current. On fixing a point of carbon to each wire, and approaching them until they nearly touch, the passage of the electricity from one pole to another is accompanied by the production of a dazzling white light, rivalling the light of the sun.

188. Assuming the circuit of the pile to be closed, on taking a wire in each hand and breaking contact, a peculiar concussion will be felt in the joints of the arm and hand, accompanied by a slight contortion of the muscles, increasing to a very violent shock, which is repeated every time fresh contact is made. The concussion of the nerves of the body is, therefore, produced by the entrance and exit of the currents of electricity; for they evidently must pass through the body the moment it forms the connecting link between the two poles. By a particular arrangement, the circuit may be closed or interrupted at pleasure, and in such a manner that the current may be made to pass alternately through the wires and the body; the latter being thus exposed to a series of shocks, which are considered particularly adapted for the cure of diseases arising from the injury or derangement of the nervous system, as, for instance, in cases of asphyxia, deafness, &c.: the results, however, of this curative method, have not in general answered the expectations which were at first entertained. Numberless arrangements have been at various times proposed for the construction of medico-galvanic machines; but the one combining the most advantages is shown in figs. 135 and 136, which is composed of two batte-

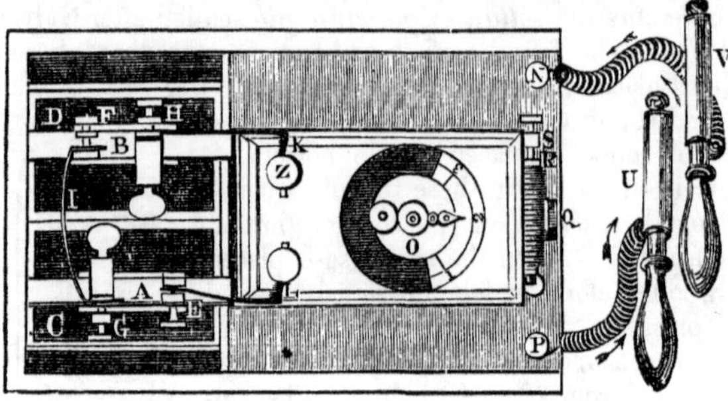

135.

136.

ries A B, with their respective cells C D. Each battery consists of a central thin plate of platinised silver, separated from the outer, or zinc plates, by means of a frame of wood. The binding screws, E F, after passing through the frames, are soldered to the silver plates, and the zinc plates are retained in their respective positions by means of the binding screws G H. The copper band I is used to connect the zinc plate of one battery with the silver plate of the other, and the wires K L are to afford a path by which the electricity may enter and leave the other parts of the apparatus. To the binding-screws, marked X and Z, are attached wires, leading into the interior of the coil machine. The indicator, O, is for the purpose of regulating the *quantity* of the current. The bundle of iron-wires, Q, serves to increase the *intensity* of the current. The contact-breaker, R S, is for the rapid making and breaking the battery contact, and the binding screws, P N, are for attaching the conducting wires of the directors U V, by means of which the current is transmitted to the patient.

189. The chemical action of the electrical current can only become intelligible to us after having studied chemical phenomena in general. At present it will suffice to say that the current exerts a tendency to decompose all chemical compounds, through which it is passed, into their elements. *Electro-metallurgy* is an application of this property of the electrical current.

190. We have made ourselves acquainted with the voltaic pile in its most simple form. It has at various times undergone a great number of alterations with regard to its elements as well as to its construction. The action of the pile is greatly increased by moistening the cloth, placed between the plates, in a solution of salt, or in dilute nitric acid, instead of in water, or by placing the pairs of plates in receivers containing such fluids, and connecting them properly by wires. In this case the electricity is increased to an extraordinary degree with the commencement of chemical decomposition. The power of a pile increases in general proportion to the size and number of its elements. Several piles may be combined, and thus have their power united, as is the case with a battery of Leyden jars.

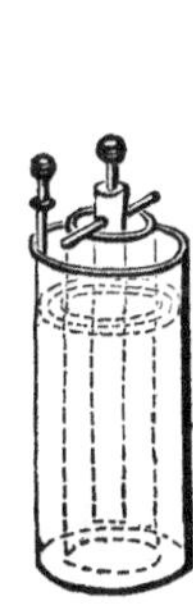

137.

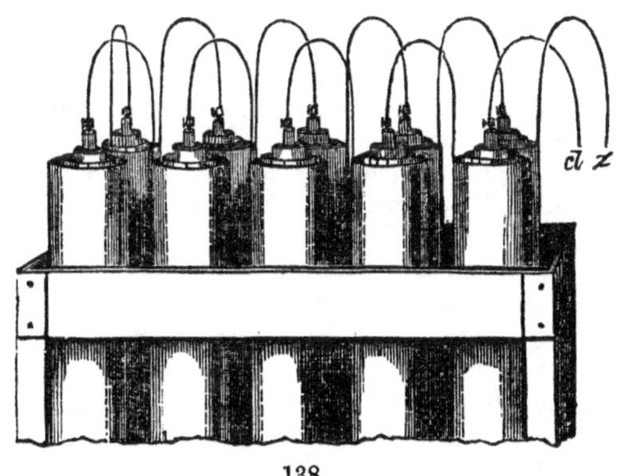

138.

Daniell's *constant* battery, fig. 137, consists of a cylinder of copper, containing a porous cell, in which is placed a solid rod of amalgamated zinc.

The copper cylinder is furnished with a perforated shelf upon which crystals of sulphate of copper are placed, in order to keep the battery in constant action. This battery is excited by the solution of sulphate of copper in the outer cell, and dilute sulphuric acid, containing one part of acid to ten of water, in the inner cell. Fig. 138 represents ten of Daniell's batteries in a mahogany tray, with connectors suitably arranged for obtaining either *quantity* or *intensity*.

Smee's battery, fig. 139, consists of a plate of platinised silver, S, having a bar of wood fixed at the top, to prevent contact with the zinc, and is furnished with two binding screws. A stout plate of amalgamated zinc, Z, is placed on each side of the wood, and both are retained in their position by the binding screws. This combination is immersed in a jar, A, containing dilute sulphuric acid, when, if a metallic communication is made between the poles or screws, an active galvanic current is obtained. Fig. 140 represents a compound Smee's battery.

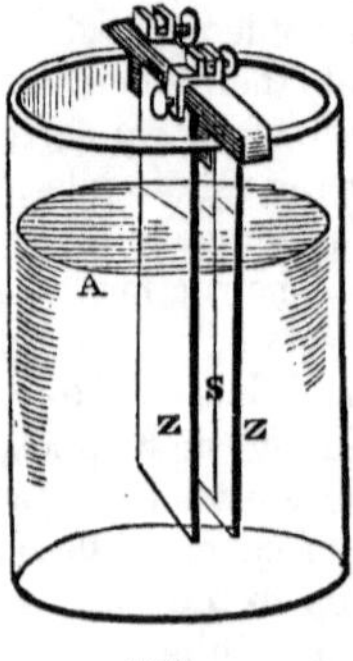

139.

140.

The most powerful galvanic arrangement is shown by figs. 141, 142, and is the invention of Professor Grove. It consists of a slip of platinum, D, placed in a porous cell, C, each cell being surrounded by a thick zinc cylinder, B B, contained in a glass vessel, A A. The platinum in each cell is attached to the zinc of the adjoining cell by binding screws, E F; but at the extremities or poles, the platinum forming the one pole terminating in the screw F, is united by the wire A, and the zinc forming the other pole, and terminating in the screw E, is connected by the wire B. This battery is excited by filling the outer cell with dilute sulphuric acid, the inner porous cell with strong nitric acid.

191. The powerful action of electricity by contact on the nervous system gave rise to its discovery in the year 1789. Galvani, on suspending some frogs' legs, from which he had removed the skin for anatomical purposes, to an *iron* railing, by means of *copper* hooks, observed that they underwent remarkable contortions. The phenomenon when more carefully studied, particularly by Volta, led to an immense number of discoveries with regard to electricity, and their source is evidently not exhausted yet.

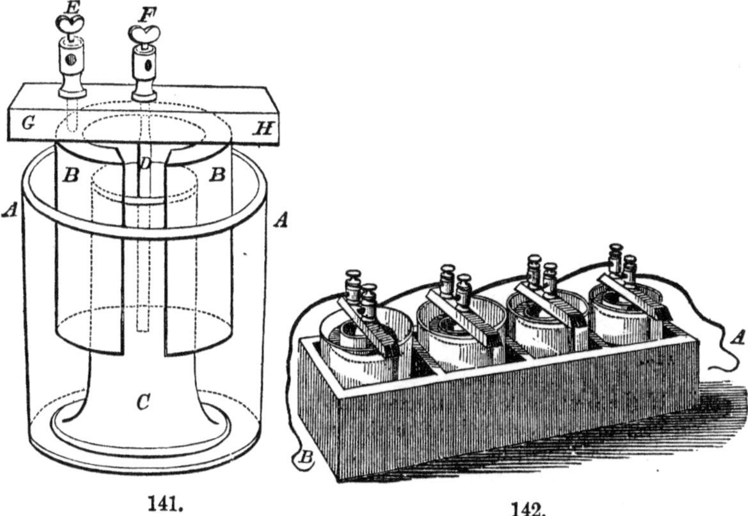

141. 142.

Entire series of phenomena, of too complicated a nature to be explained in a brief outline like the present, are based upon the above observations; we shall therefore confine ourselves, in the following pages, to an examination of the reciprocal action between electricity and magnetism.

2. Magnetism.

192. An iron ore, pretty generally distributed in Nature, possesses the peculiar property of attracting small particles of iron, such as filings, and retaining them on its surface. This observation had already been made by the ancients, and the name of the phenomenon is derived from the viilage of *Magnesia*, where it is said to have been first noticed. The above mineral exists in Sweden to such an extent that it is worked for iron. It is called the *loadstone* or *magnetic iron ore.* This mineral attracts nickel as well as iron; but as the former can only be obtained, with the greatest difficulty, in the pure metallic state, we shall confine ourselves here to the consideration of the behaviour of iron with the magnet.

193. The magnetic property of loadstone may be easily imparted to *steel*, by rubbing the latter in a certain manner with a piece of the mineral. It is then called an *artificial magnet;* and, as it may be made in any form, it is employed for all magnetic observations. A thin and long piece of magnetized steel is termed a *magnetic needle;* and we will first proceed to make ourselves acquainted with the behaviour of this instrument.

If a magnetic needle be strewed over with iron-filings, a great number will adhere to both ends, while the centre will not attract a single particle. The terminating points of the needle, which are possessed of the highest attractive power, are termed its *poles*, while the place where no attraction exists, is called the *equator* of the magnet. The same may be found in all natural and artificial magnets, whatever may be their form. In magnets of regular form, the poles are generally situated at the two opposite ends, and the equator exactly in the centre.

194. If a magnetic needle be arranged so as to revolve easily on its vertical axis, it will always, when set in motion, oscillate from side to side, until it remains stationary in a certain position, to which it invariably returns, in whatever other direction it may be placed. One of the poles always points towards the north, and is called the *north pole* of the magnet, while the other necessarily points to the south, and is termed the *south pole.* This property of the magnet has led to its application as a *compass*, by which simple instrument the direction of any place may be determined when all other means of indication are wanting, as, for instance, on the open sea, in large forests, and in mines.

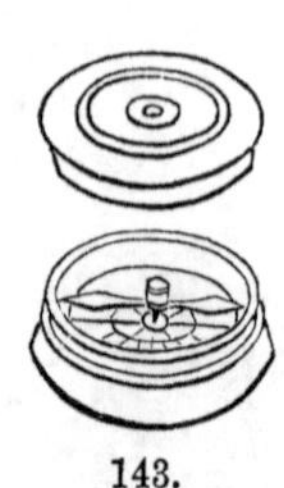
143.

195. If the south pole of a magnetic needle, supported as at fig. 143, be brought near to the south pole of another magnet, the extremity or point of the movable needle will be repulsed. If, on the other hand, its south pole be brought near to the north pole of another magnet, it will be attracted by the latter until they come in contact, and will then cling to each other. Thence we see that *similar* magnetic poles repel, while *opposite* poles attract each other, as is the case in electricity.

196. Although iron and steel are in most respects so similar, they differ very much in their relations to magnetism. Both contain the two kinds of magnetism in combination. As long as this is the case, they are not observed to possess magnetic properties. In iron, the separation of the two kinds of magnetism may be easily, but only transitorily effected. The magnet, therefore, attracts it powerfully, converting it, however, only into a *temporary* magnet. The two kinds of magnetism are more difficultly separated in steel, hence the latter is but slightly attracted by the most powerful magnets. When once effected, however, the separation is *permanent*, and the steel becomes a perfect magnet.

Iron may be made magnetic by *induction*, in the same manner as electricity was shown to be produced by induction. If, for instance, a piece of iron be attached to the north pole of a magnet, its magnetism will be decomposed in such a manner that the south pole of the iron is at the point of contact, and its north pole at the opposite extremity. On holding a small piece of iron to this end, it will be attracted, and likewise acquire polaric properties. Thus a small chain of little rods of iron may be formed, which will, however, fall to pieces as soon as the first piece is no longer under the influence of the magnet.

Steel becomes magnetic by being *rubbed* with a natural or artificial magnet. The north pole of a magnet is placed on the centre of a bar of steel and repeatedly drawn over it towards one extremity; the other half is subjected to a similar treatment with the south pole of the magnet; the bar is thus rendered magnetic, and only loses this property when strongly heated.

As we do not view magnetism as a substance, but as a peculiar current proceeding in a certain direction, it is obvious that an infinite number of magnets may be made by means of one artificial magnet, without the latter losing any of its magnetic properties whatever.

If we assume the action of the magnet to be, like that of the galvanic pile, the result of an excitation of every one of its particles, the sum of which appears to be collected at the two poles, it will not be a matter of surprise to find, on cutting a magnetic wire in half, that each piece will represent a perfect magnet, with two opposite poles and an equator. The case is the same as if we took from the pile several or only one pair of plates, each of which forms a small battery, possessing all the main properties of the larger one.

197. A steel knitting-needle, of uniform thickness, when suspended at its centre by a thread, will be in equilibrium, and occupy a *horizontal* position. If it be converted into a magnet, as described above, and again suspended, it will no longer appear to be in equilibrium: one end will exhibit a very perceptible downward inclination, just as though a weight were attached to it. The thread must be approached to the extremity of the needle that is inclined downwards, in order to re-establish the equilibrium.

This experiment, together with the circumstance above mentioned, that the needle always points in one direction towards the north and south, lead us to the conclusion that some cause must exist for these phenomena. The earth may, in fact, be considered as a large magnet. Its magnetic poles are, however, not in exactly the same situation as the geographical poles; hence its magnetic equator does not coincide with the central line of the earth. The magnetism of the earth imparts to the magnetic needle not only its direction, but also the attraction that alters its equilibrium. As the magnetic north pole of the earth attracts the south pole of the needle, the extremity of the latter that points towards the *north* should properly be called its *south pole.*

In pursuing the northerly direction indicated by the magnetic needle, we should of course not ultimately arrive at the north pole of the earth, as its situation is not identical with that of the magnetic north pole. By extending in our imagination the direction indicated by the needle, we should obtain a circle round the whole earth, which is called the *magnetic meridian.* The latter intersects the meridian passing through the poles of the earth, at a certain angle, which indicates the amount of *declination* of the direction of the needle to the west of the true north pole.

The attractive power exercised by the magnetic poles of the earth must be very unequal at different parts. If the compass be situated at the magnetic equator, its north and south poles will be attracted with equal force by the magnetic poles of the earth, and the needle will, therefore, occupy a perfectly *horizontal* position. On approaching the magnetic north or south pole, the compass will assume a certain *inclination*, increasing proportionably as the distance from the pole diminishes. The magnetic north pole has, in fact, been so nearly approached as to give to the needle a position almost vertical to the surface of the earth.

198. To the influence of the earth's magnetism may, therefore, be ascribed the circumstance that objects of iron and steel become endowed with magnetic properties to a slight extent, when strongly rubbed, beaten, or stamped, particularly if they are at the same time held in the direction corresponding to the declination and inclination of the needle. Thus, scarcely any imple-

ment will be found in the workshop of a smith or locksmith, to which small iron filings or scales will not adhere.

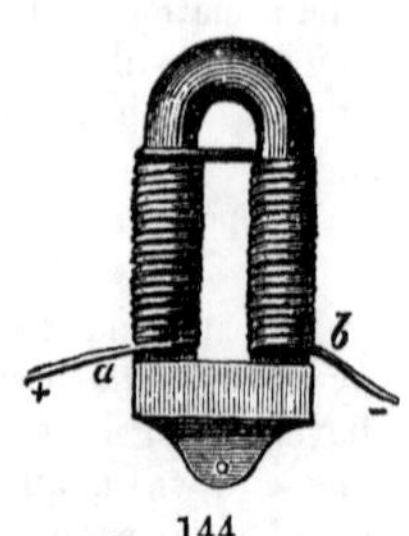

144.

199. The reciprocal action between electricity and magnetism is exceedingly remarkable. If a piece of iron, in the form of a horse-shoe, fig. 144, be wound round with copper-wire, and an electrical current then passed through the latter, the iron will exhibit the most powerful *magnetic* properties, which it loses, however, the moment the current is interrupted. If steel needles be employed in this experiment, they will become permanently magnetic. The conducting wires employed in these experiments are wound round closely with *silk*, in order that they may be insulated in coming in contact with each other, or with other metals, thus permitting the current to pass in their interior in one direction only.

On covering the ends of a non-magnetic piece of iron (fig. 145) with coils of wire, and imparting to the magnet *a b*, which is placed below, a rapid motion round its vertical axis, in such a manner as to cause the poles to approach each end of the iron alternately, an *electrical* current will be established in the wire, by means of which all the electric phenomena already mentioned may be produced.

145.

If an electrical current be passed through a spiral coil of wire, suspended in such a manner as to be moved round its vertical axis, the wire will assume the position of the magnetic needle, and exhibit all its characteristic properties.

By this we prove the existence of an intimate reciprocal relation between the two kinds of currents, and this is termed *electro-magnetism*, a force to which has been attributed the common cause of these phenomena.

The fact of a piece of iron being endowed with a high magnetic power, so long as an electrical current is allowed to pass through a wire coiled round it, as shown by fig. 144, has led to experiments having for their object the application of electro-magnetism as a *motive power;* but hitherto no practical results have been obtained.

On the other hand, the application of electricity by contact to *electric telegraphs* has become of the highest importance, since its practical application was first demonstrated by Professor Morse, in 1837. The following observations will furnish an idea of the principle of this invention:—If the two ends of the wire, wound round the horse-shoe-formed iron, are greatly extended, so as to reach to a spot, at a distance of some miles, where a galvanic pile is situated, the piece of iron may be made alternately magnetic and non-magnetic, by closing the circuit of the battery or breaking contact. By this means, the horse-shoe may be made to attract, at intervals, a piece of iron placed close at hand. Thus, (fig. 146,) in Morse's Patent, a lever, armed at one end with a blunt point, is alternately attracted and repelled by the horse-shoe, producing on the slips of paper dots and lines, which repre-

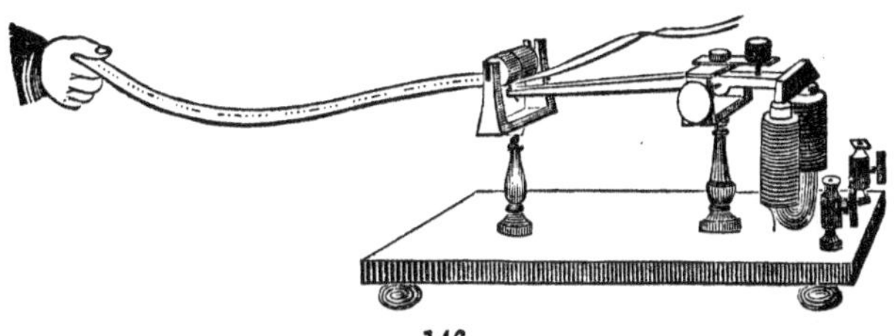

146.

sent letters. The paper is made to pass slowly under the roller, against which the point moves; and this, in the machines now in use, is produced by a clock apparatus. Fig. 147 represents the instrument usually employed to break or complete the circuit, causing the motion of the lever at the other end of the telegraphic line. A less convenient mode, sometimes used in Europe, communicates this motion, by a proper mechanical contrivance, to an index moving over a disc, upon which are marked the letters of the alphabet. A certain position is given to the index, so that, for instance, it points to the letter A on the first closing of the circuit, moving to B on the breaking of contact, thence to C by the second closing, and so on: thus, by making and breaking contact the appropriate number of times, the index may be made to point to any letter, and words or sentences are thus telegraphed from one place to another. Various other instruments have been made for facilitating the use of this important agency, such as Bain's, in which, by chemical affinities, the signs are produced by the discoloration of prepared paper; and House's Printing Telegraph, in which letters cut on the edges of a steel wheel, are printed upon a slip of paper passing over it as it revolves. The complication of machinery by which these effects are produced, renders it unnecessary to dwell upon them, especially as the principle which produces the motive power in all of them is the same—viz.: the alternate breaking and connecting of the magnetic circuit.

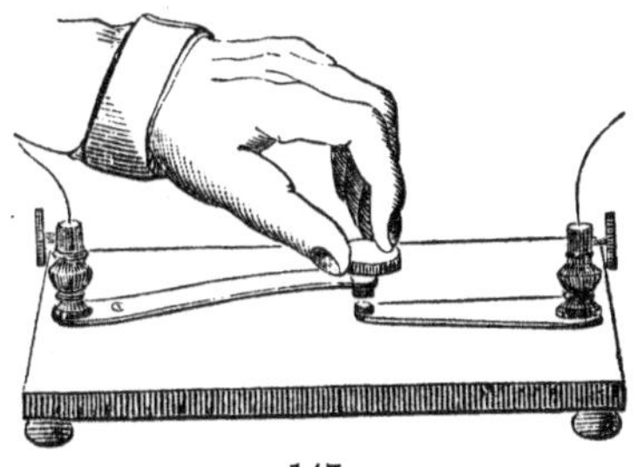

147.

Electric telegraphs are frequently constructed along railways: they combine the advantages of increased certainty and rapidity, over the old telegraphs, with that of cheapness and of being perfectly unimpeded in their operations by night or fog.

Thus as heat and light are most wondrously associated together, so that one seldom appears unaccompanied by the other, and as every increased degree of heat leads to the production of light, so electricity and magnetism may likewise be more frequently dependent upon each other, than experiments and researches have hitherto shown.

The Northern Lights.

200. One of the most brilliant nocturnal phenomena, the *Northern Lights* (Auroræ boreales), appears to have some connection with the magnetism of the earth, as a peculiar oscillation is imparted to delicate magnetic needles, on the appearance of a very powerful northern light, and as the latter is seen in a direction corresponding with that of the magnetic North Pole. This phenomenon of light has also been observed at the South Pole; but it most generally appears in the direction of the North Pole, which is situated nearer to us and is better known.

In its greatest brilliancy the Aurora borealis presents itself to us as an immense belt, consisting of fiery rays, and extending in a semicircle over the horizon, its extremities appearing to touch the earth. It exhibits the greatest variations in the brilliant changes of its colours, and the continued increase and disappearance of its rays. In the long dreary nights of the polar regions it diffuses over the spacious vault of heaven a thousand different lights of the most resplendent beauty. In more civilized regions, its yellowish-red appearance has not unfrequently excited the terror and alarm of the ignorant and superstitious, and even the more enlightened members of society have imagined the phenomena to be portentous of great events, and the harbingers of war, pestilence, and famine, whilst timid imaginations have sometimes shaped them into aerial conflicts.

"Fierce fiery warriors fight upon the clouds
In ranks and squadrons, and right form of war."
Shakspeare.

ASTRONOMY.

"Hail, mighty Sirius, monarch of the Suns!
May we in this poor planet speak with thee?
Say, art thou nearer to His throne, whose nod
Doth govern all things?—Hast thou heard
One whisper through the open gate of Heaven,
When the pale stars shall fall, and yon blue vault
Be as a shrivelled scroll?" *Sigourney.*

1. Astronomy is the science which treats of the heavenly bodies and of their motions. In reference to its object it forms a branch of Physics but the importance and the extent of astronomical phenomena demand for this science an independent consideration. The phenomena of motion exclusively arrest our attention. The laws on which these motions depend are precisely the same as those which are partly explained in Physics, in the doctrines of Equilibrium and Motion; hence Astronomy has been, not unaptly, called by many the *Mechanics of the Heavens* (Celestial Mechanics).

2. The scene on which the phenomena of Astronomy are represented is called the firmament, or the heavens; and the objects that appear in this space or firmament are called the heavenly bodies, or more commonly stars. In the same manner as we have in § 2 of Physics defined space as something infinite, so we may consider the heavenly bodies as innumerable. This incomprehensible only partially unveiled, these immeasurable distances and

immense masses of matter together with rapidity of motion equally inconceivable confer upon the phenomena of Astronomy, and consequently on the science itself, a great elevation and solemnity which do not belong to the other branches of Natural Science.

"The survey of unlimited distances and of immeasurable altitudes, the view of the great ocean spread out at the foot of man, and the greater ocean, the canopy of the heavens, spread out over his head, liberates the spirit from the confined limits of the actual, and from the oppressive shackles of physical life."

Although in these words of Schiller we find the elevating character of astronomical phenomena efficiently represented, still we do not agree with what is maintained by many, viz., that Astronomy is the first and the noblest of all the natural sciences. To the natural philosopher to whom the whole extent of nature belongs, all the individual branches of science constitute the links of an endless chain, from which not a single link can be detached without destroying the harmony of the whole. Erroneous views regarding the growth of the most insignificant plant are, to the truth-seeking mind, as unworthy as the absurdities of the antiquated ideas of the motions of the heavenly bodies.

3. The science of Astronomy is greatly dependent on Mathematics. The relations of space, number, and time, are the important problems to be solved. How large and how far, or how long and how often? These are the primary problems which this science proposes to solve.

Only the science of Mathematics, and especially the higher branches of Geometry and Trigonometry are capable of answering these questions; and it is a fact that the constant, progressive, and increasing demands of Astronomy have been the external propulsive cause to which mathematical science has been mainly indebted for its present high development.

Although it is impossible to follow exactly the course by which astronomers have been able to establish the most important truths of astronomical science, without a considerable knowledge of Mathematics; still the discoveries made by the learned in the laborious way of calculation, and the laws that have been deduced therefrom, may be represented in simple terms, so as to be intelligible even to those whose knowledge of Mathematics is not very profound.

Astronomy especially requires a frequent application of comparisons, in order to make her phenomena more easily comprehensible. It is manifestly difficult to form a conception of the magnitude of the earth, but it is still more difficult to imagine the exceeding vastness of the sun's dimensions, at least a million of times larger than our globe. On the other hand, we can more easily estimate these relative magnitudes, if we represent the earth by a grain of millet, and the sun by a skittle-ball. But how can we form an idea of endless space, with the innumerable heavenly bodies moving therein? This also may be compared to the space of a room, in which countless myriads of atoms whirl around each other as seen in one single sun-beam, which finds its way into the room.

4. The history of Astronomy is as ancient as that of the human race. For thousands of years the same star-bespangled heavens, which now surround us, like an enormous canopy, have awakened the attention of men and excited their admiration. We may here observe that the uncivilized

tribes of the desert, and the nomadic inhabitants of the wide-spread steppes, watch the phenomena of the heavenly bodies with more attention than the inhabitants of our cities. For to those the stars serve as time-piece, sign-post, compass, barometer and calendar, hence they are compelled to direct their attention to the motions of the heavenly bodies; whilst the inhabitants of more civilized countries are not under the same necessity.

We are therefore indebted for a series of highly important observations to those of the ancients who, little advanced in science, but in the capacity of hunters and shepherds, were obliged to contemplate the starry heavens in order to determine the place and time.

5. It cannot be disputed that a preference is to be given to Astronomy over all other branches of natural science, because it can be studied to a certain extent without the aid of many artificial means. As soon as the glorious orb of day has set, the twinkling stars shine forth in the darkening firmament, the larger ones appearing first, and after a time the smaller succeed, until at last myriads of distant worlds appear as a beautiful canopy before the astonished gaze of man. The nocturnal starry heavens afford to every one an accessible field of observation, on which by attentive consideration many important phenomena may be beheld without the aid of any kind of instruments whatever.

While the prosecution of natural philosophy requires a number of artificial and expensive instruments, and Chemistry, a large supply of materials and preparations, Astronomy merely requires her votary to elevate his eye to the firmament above him when he finds himself at once in the midst of celestial phenomena.

If, however, one series of astronomical truths is so accessible, there is a still more considerable number invisible to the unassisted eye. An accurate investigation of astronomical phenomena can therefore only be made with the aid of instruments, and the purchase and erection of these are attended with so considerable an outlay as to render personal observation accessible to a few individuals only. It is this fact which accounts for a certain degree of incompleteness of the astronomical knowledge of the ancients, and it was only from the time when art lent new powers to the eye, by the invention of the telescope, that the field of observation was widened, and by the continued improvements of the instruments the results of observation were rapidly accumulated.

6. The evident influence of the sun upon the surface of the earth as the animating source of light and heat, the remarkable changes of the moon in form and time of rising must, in earlier times, have given to these two luminaries a high degree of importance in the estimation of the ancients, of which the divine honours they received, are, in some measure, a convincing proof to this day. It was also natural to ascribe even to the smaller celestial bodies a relation to the earth and its inhabitants, although this is not so conspicuous as in the case of the former bodies.

We can therefore easily conceive that, at a time when illusory conceptions, in reference to the stars and their phenomena, were prevalent, another influence was generally attributed to them, namely, that they were intimately connected with the destinies of the human race. For every great event, for every remarkable personage, for everything which the benighted and fettered mind of the vulgar could not rationally account, a solution and reason were sought in the stars.

Thus, it was this strange mixture of arbitrary assumptions, illusions, and errors, regarding the nature of the stars, that gave birth to Astrology, which for hundreds of years mystified and perplexed instead of enlightening and enlarging the human mind. It was this, in connexion with superstition and knavery, that brought contempt and persecution upon science, and continually retarded its progress, until the human mind, based on unprejudiced observations, tore asunder its shackles, and learned that the earth is truly a point of space, but not the central point: that the stars are independent worlds, not mere marks and signs for illustrating the destinies of the passing generations of this little earth.

7. In our endeavour to give in the following pages an exposition of the most important astronomical phenomena, we shall not accomplish our task without previously giving an explanation of a number of aids which this science requires in order to render its study more clear. Geometry is the branch of science from which most of these aids are derived, and if we assume them partly to be generally known, a brief outline of this science is requisite to insure an adequate comprehension of the following. After we have in this manner become, in some measure, acquainted with the astronomical method of observations, language, and expressions, we shall proceed to the consideration of those phenomena, which by day as well as by night are unceasingly displayed in the heavens. Hereby we shall acquire a true insight into the arrangement of the heavenly bodies, and be able to divest ourselves of the erroneous notions of former times.

The subject is divisible into the following sections:—

I. Aids to Astronomical Observation.
II. General Astronomical Phenomena.
III. Special Astronomical Phenomena.

I. AIDS TO ASTRONOMICAL OBSERVATION.

Angle.

8. On a plane, a sheet of paper, for example, we describe two lines *a b* and *c d* (fig. 1), which intersect each other in the point *m*; thus the plane is divided into four parts.

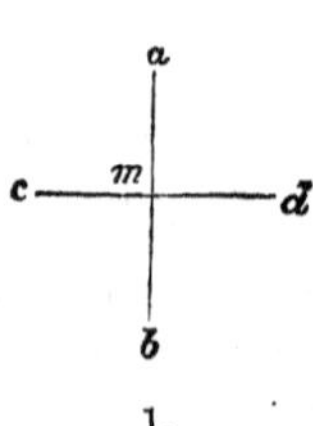

1.

Each of these parts is called an *angle*, and the two lines by which each angle is contained or included, are its *sides*, and the point where they cut each other or intersect, is called the *vertex* of the angle. Thus *a m* and *c m* are the two *sides* of the angle *a m c*.

If we cut out with a pair of scissors the four angles situated about the point *m*, and on applying them to each other, find that they all are exactly of the same size, that is, that the four sections exactly cover each other, we call these angles *right* angles; and in this case the lines *a b* and *c d* cut each other at right angles, or are perpendicular to each other.

Again, if we consider fig. 2, we see at a glance that the lines *a′ b′* and *c′ d′* do not intersect at right angles, but that the plane is divided into four very unequal angles. On cutting out and comparing one of these with an angle of fig. 1, it is evident that the angle a' m' c', fig. 2, is smaller than the right angle a m c, fig. 1, and that the angle a' m' d' is considerably larger than a right angle.

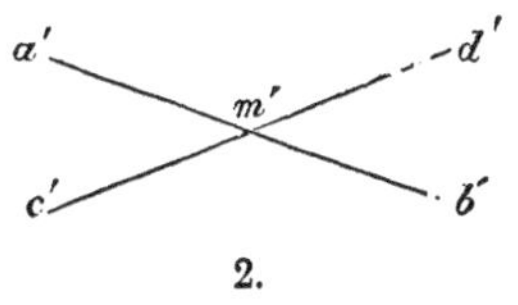

2.

Angles which are smaller than a right angle are called *acute*, and such as are greater are called *obtuse* angles. Around the point m' there are the two acute angles a' m' c' and d' m' b', as well as the two obtuse angles a' m' d' and c' m' b'. Hence we deduce, that round a given point no more than four right angles can be constructed, and only three obtuse angles; and, on the contrary, that an infinite number of acute angles may be formed round the same point; and further, that of the four angles represented in fig. 2, the two opposite vertical angles are equal, and the two *adjacent angles*, a' m' c' and a' m' d', unequal to each other, are together equal to two right angles.

These relations are perfectly independent of the length of the sides which include the angle. For if we suppose that the lines a b and c d (fig. 1), or a' b' and c' d' (fig. 2), are extended indefinitely, still the angles m and m' formed at the point of intersection, remain unchanged.

9. The mutual inclination of the lines including the angle is always determined by the magnitude of the angle. Thus the situation of a point in relation to a plane is partly determined, if we know the angle, formed by a line drawn from that point to any point of the plane. This principle renders the angle so exceedingly important, that it is capable of being employed as the key to the most important truths; for a great part of the actual observations of astronomers are dependent on the study of angles.

The next object is to determine the magnitude of the angle.

To determine the size of an angle the circle is employed. Suppose we describe a circle (o p q r o) about the point of intersection m of the lines a b, c d, which cut each other at right angles, there is opposite to every one of the four right angles a curve-line or arc of a circle, which is exactly a fourth part of the circle; for example, over the angle a m c is the quadrant or fourth part of the circumference o p. That the magnitude of the circle is indifferent, is shown by the dotted lines; for o'' p'' and o' p' are quadrants as well as o p.

3.

The acute angle c m f is hence equal to half a right angle, because the arc by which it is subtended is an octant, the eighth part of a circle, and the obtuse angle a m f is equal to one and a half right angle, because its subtending arc is equal to three-eighths of the circle.

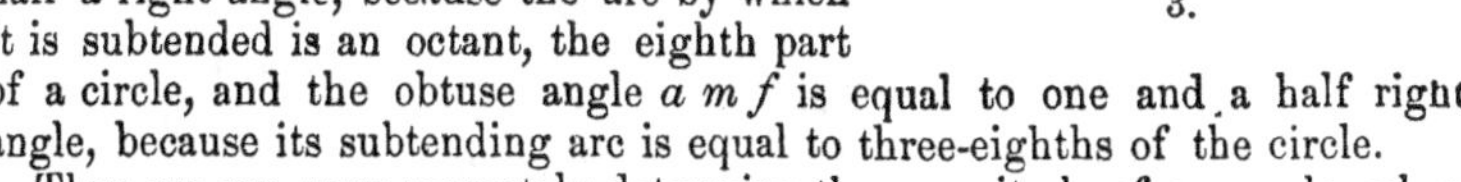

Thus we can very accurately determine the magnitude of an angle, when we state the portion of a circle which the arc of that angle forms.

For this purpose the circle is divided into 360 equal parts, each of which is called a *degree*. And every degree is again divided into 60 equal parts, called *minutes*, and every one of these again into 60 *seconds*.

Hence, when we speak of an angle of 90 degrees, we necessarily mean a right angle, since 90 degrees are the fourth part of the 360 degrees of the whole circle. Every angle less than 90 degrees is an acute angle; and every angle of more degrees is an obtuse angle.

For accurately measuring angles, a simple instrument called a *protractor* is employed, and this is generally made of brass.

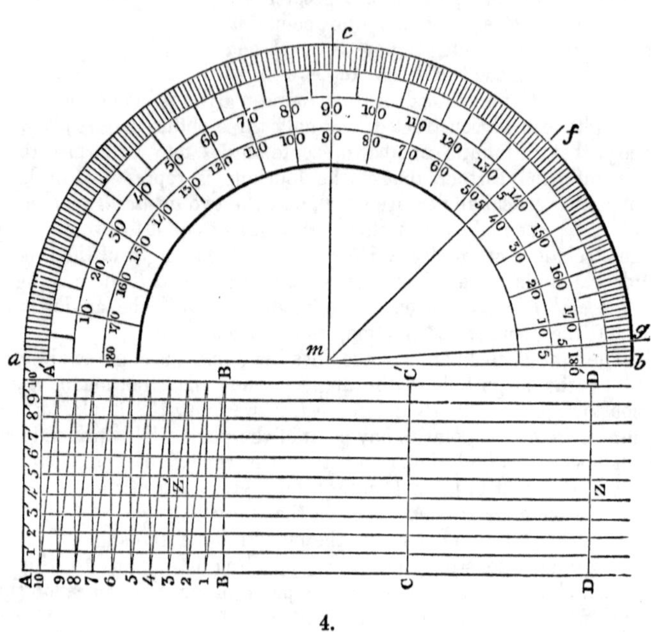

4.

The protractor (fig. 4) is a section called a semi-circle, which is divided into 180 degrees. If by this instrument we wish to measure the angles *a m c*, *a m f*, *c m f*, and *g m b*, we place the protractor so that the centre of the semi-circle and the vertical point of the angle may coincide, and then read the number of degrees. We thus find that *a m c* is equal to 90 degrees, and, therefore, a right angle; that *a m f* is equal to 135 degrees, and, therefore, an obtuse angle: also *f m b* is an acute angle of 45 degrees, or half a right angle; and, finally, *g m b* is a very acute angle of only 5 degrees.

In accurate mensuration, the minutes and even seconds of a degree are measured. The number indicating degrees is distinguished by a small cypher (°), the minutes by a dash (′), and the seconds by two dashés (″); thus, for example, an angle = 90° 35′ 16″ signifies an angle of ninety degrees, thirty-five minutes, and sixteen seconds.

10. Only a *drawn* angle can be measured by the protractor. When an angle in which only imaginary lines intersect each other is to be measured, another instrument is employed.

For example, if the angle formed by the lines extending from two distant steeples, A and B, to the eye of the observer, where they meet in C (fig. 5), is to be determined, the simplest apparatus for this purpose is the *angle instrument* (fig. 6). This is constructed of a metallic ring, the rim of which is divided into degrees, and called the *limb*. In the centre, C, of this circle, there is a pivot about which a rod or bar, RR, called the index-arm, revolves in a similar manner to the hand of a clock. The instrument is placed horizontally upon a small table, so that its centre, C, is situated exactly in the place where the lines drawn from A and B are supposed to intersect.

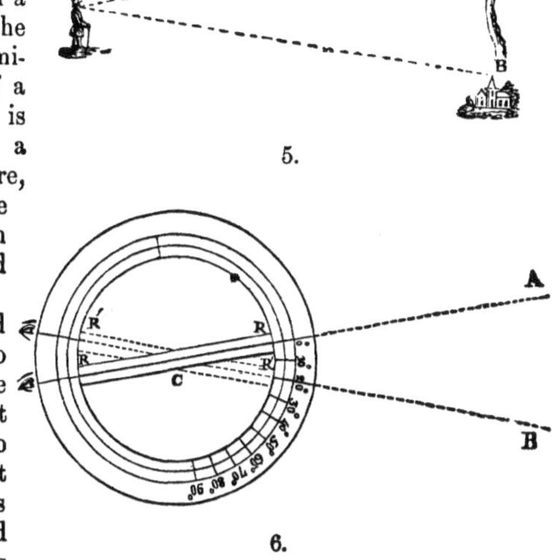

5.

6.

The index is next directed to the part of the limb marked with 0°, and the instrument so adjusted that the point A may appear to the eye in the same straight line as the index-arm. This is subsequently moved round the pivot till the point B is in its direction, which is the case if it has the position R′ R′; in this manner the index-arm describes an arc which is measured on the graduated limb of the instrument, which in the present case is 20°; consequently the angle at C over which this arc is situated is 20°.

This is the fundamental arrangement which we find with more or less variation in all astronomical instruments for measuring angles.

It is evident that, according as the angle to be measured is either vertical or horizontal to the surface of the earth, the circle of the instrument must be placed either parallel with or vertical to it. This latter position of the instrument must be adopted in measuring the angle formed by an imaginary line drawn from the top of a tower to a point on the surface of the earth with the surface.

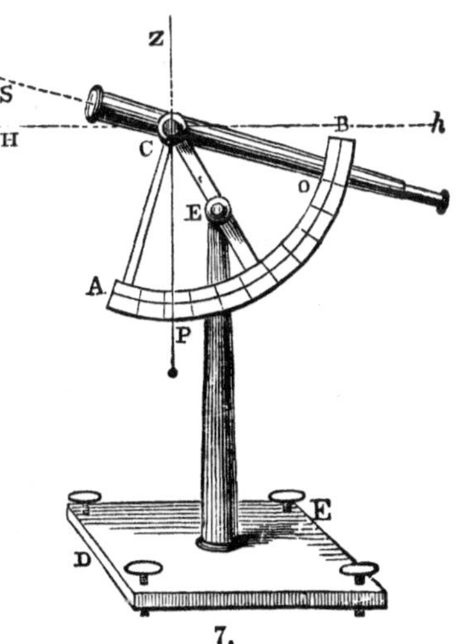

7.

In cases where angles are to be measured, the extent of which does not exceed that of a right angle, or an angle of 60°, it is more convenient to employ a quadrant or a sextant than an entire circle.

Fig. 7 represents a quadrant moveable round the point E. A B is the limb, and C the centre of the quadrant. The instrument is so disposed that a telescope which is attached to one of its sides may be directed to a point in the horizon H, in the line H h, and the other side, C A, may coincide with the line of the plummet P attached to C; after this adjustment the telescope is directed to the star S, when the plummet which retains its vertical position marks off on the limb of the quadrant the number of the degrees of the angle, which a line drawn from the star to the observer makes with the horizon.

The construction of angle instruments has now reached to such a high degree of perfection, that an angle of one second, and even of half a second can be measured. The angle of one second is but $\frac{1}{324000}$ of a right angle. To realize the idea of an angle so excessively minute as one second, we may suppose a line drawn from the upper and under side of a human hair to a point three feet distant: these two lines would contain an angle of a second.

Circle.

11. Suppose we fix a nail in a table, and attach to it a thread, and to the other end of the latter a black-lead pencil. With this we describe a line round the nail; keeping the thread equally stretched during the operation. A *circle* is thus described, with this essential quality, that every point in this line so drawn is equally distant from the point on which the nail is fastened, and which is termed the *centre* of the circle. A straight line drawn from the centre of a circle to a point of its circumference, such as is in the above example described by the stretched thread, is called the *semi-diameter*, or *radius*, of the circle; and it is evident that all the half diameters or radii of a circle are equal. If the radius is extended till it meet the opposite part of the circumference, it will form the *diameter* of the circle, which is evidently the double of the radius. All diameters also of the same circle are therefore equal. (See fig. 8.)

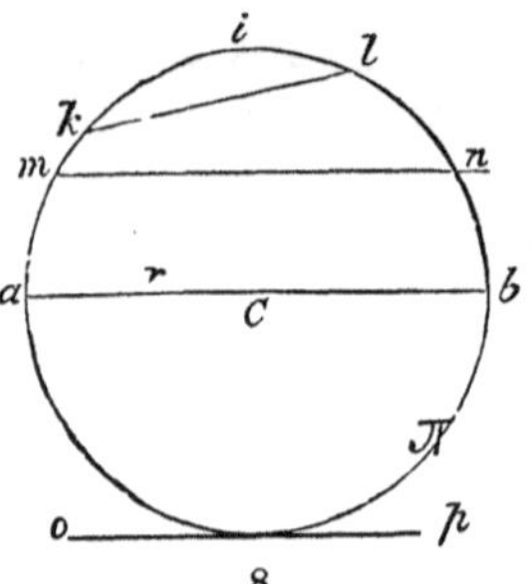

8.

c = centre.
$a\,c$ = semi-diameter = r.
$a\,b$ = diameter = $2\,r$ = d.
$k\,i\,l$ = arc of the circumference.
$k\,l$ = chord.
$m\,n$ = secant.
$o\,p$ = tangent.
$d\,\pi$ = circumference, $\pi = 3{\cdot}14$.

Any portion of a circumference, $k\,i\,l$ for example, is called an *arc;* and the straight line $k\,l$, uniting its two ends, is called the *chord* of that arc. A line $m\,n$, cutting the circle in two points, is called the *secant;* and a line $o\,p$, outside a circle, touching the circle in one point only, is called the *tangent.* The circumference is denoted by $d\,\pi$ or $2\,r\,\pi$, the Greek letter π representing the number 3·14, the circumference being 3·14 times longer than the diameter. Suppose the length of the diameter to be 4 inches, that of the circumference will be $4 \times 3{\cdot}14 = 12{\cdot}56$ inches.

The superficial contents of the circle is equal to $r\,r\,\pi$, which shows that it is found by multiplying the semi-diameter by itself, and the product by the number 3·14.

SPHERE.

12. Particular attention must be paid by the student to the sphere, which is a body with a convex surface, and every point of whieh is equally distant from a point within the sphere, called the *centre.* A straight line drawn from the centre to any point of the surface is a *semi-diameter*, and the extension of this line to the opposite surface of the sphere is called the *diameter.* As in the circle, so also in the sphere, all the semi-diameters and diameters are equal.

Let us suppose a sphere intersected by planes which pass through its centre, these planes will represent the *great circle* of the sphere, whose radius is equal to the radius of the sphere.

The *superficial contents* of a sphere, or its superficies, is found by multiplying the superficies of one of its great circles by four, and may be expressed by the formula $4 \pi r r = \pi d d$. The surfaces of two spheres have the same relative proportions to each other as the squares of their diameters.

The *cubic contents* of a sphere are found by multiplying one-third part of the radius by the superficial contents, and may be represented by the formula $\frac{1}{3} (4\pi r r r) = \frac{1}{6} (\pi d d d)$. The relative contents of two spheres of unequal magnitudes are to each other as the cubes of their diameters, or as their diameters three times multiplied by themselves.

It appears desirable to give some examples illustrative of the foregoing statements in reference to the circle and the sphere, and we adopt for both a diameter of twelve inches:—

Diameter = 12 inches.

Semi-diameter = r = 6 inches.

Circumference = $12 \times \pi = 12 \times 3{\cdot}14 = 37{\cdot}6$ inches.

Area of the circle = $r \times r \times \pi = 6 \times 6 \times 3{\cdot}14 = 113$ square inches.

Superficies of the sphere = $4 \times (r \times r \times \pi) = 4 \times 113 = 452$ square inches.

Cubic contents of the sphere = $(\frac{1}{3} \times r) \times 4 (r \times r \times \pi) = 2 \times 422 =$ 904 cubic inches.

The superficial contents of a sphere of 6 inches diameter and one of 12 inches diameter are, according to the above rule, as 6×6 to 12×12, or as 36 to 144, and their cubic contents as $6 \times 6 \times 6 = 216$, to $12 \times 12 \times 12 =$ 1728.

ELLIPSE.

13. The *ellipse* and its properties are much less generally known than the circle. This is also a figure contained by a curve line, which is produced in the manner following:—Suppose two pegs fixed on a plane (fig. 9.) A thread, longer than the distance between the pegs, is fastened by one end to the first peg, and by the other to the second peg. If we now stretch the thread by means of a lead-pencil and draw a line around the two pegs as wide as the stretched thread will allow, we describe an oval figure which is called an *ellipse.*

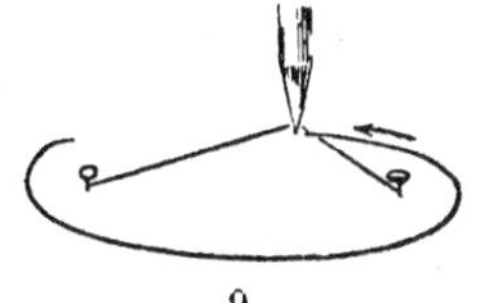

9.

This figure has a long axis $a\ b$ (fig. 10); and perpendicular to this a short axis $d\ e$, passing through the centre c. The two points S S′ are called the *foci* of the ellipse; also, as is evident from the construction of the figure, any two lines drawn from the two foci, to any point of the circumference, for instance, S *m* and S′ *m* or S *m′* and S′ *m′*, &c., which represent the thread when the pencil is at *m* or *m′*, are together equal to the larger axis of the ellipse. These lines, and we may imagine an infinite number of such, are called *radii vectores*. The distance of the foci S or S′ from the centre *c*, is called the *eccentricity* of the ellipse. It is evident that the smaller the eccentricity is, the nearer the figure approaches to that of the circle. The superficies of the ellipse is found by multiplying the two half axes, *a c* and *d c*, by each other, and this product by the number 3·14.

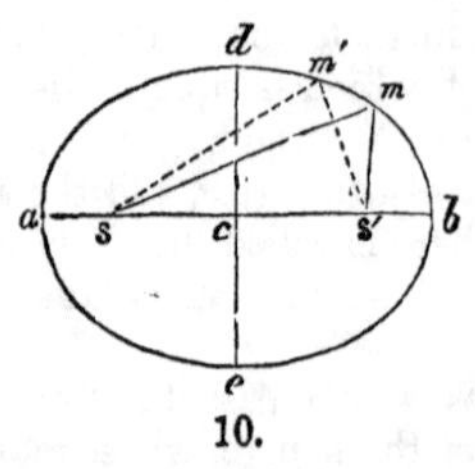

10.

The ellipse has special claims on our attention, inasmuch as it is the path described by most of the heavenly bodies, as, for example, that of the earth, which is nothing but an ellipse.

Parabola.

14. Another curved line, having peculiar properties, is the *parabola*. This figure is most easily represented by the aid of a cone, by which also several other curved lines, commonly called conical sections, may be represented. Thus, if we make diagonal sections of a cone parallel to the base, as, for example, *a b*, we obtain only circular planes; but on the other hand, oblique sections through both sides of the cone, as *a c* and *a d*, form ellipses. If the cone is cut by a plane parallel to one of its sides, as in *a e* and *m n*, the plane obtained is circumscribed by an entirely different curved line, namely, a *parabola*, the peculiarity of which consists in the fact of its ends never meeting, as in the circle and the ellipse, but continually becoming more distant from each other, even if continued *ad infinitum*.

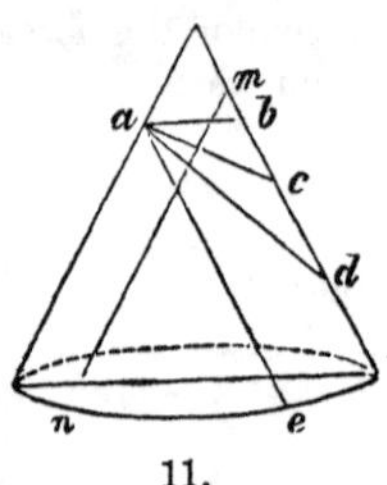

11.

The orbits of some of the heavenly bodies are parabolas; as, for example, those of several of the comets, which, consequently, can never appear again, unless in the lapse of time they alter their direction.

Mensuration.

15. By Mensuration is understood the most accurate division of any line, surface, or space by a given measure. The result of mensuration informs us how many times this measure is contained in the object to be measured.

In the Physical portion of this work (§ 7) we have given a comparative view of the smaller measures of length, and have assumed the *meter* as unit. This measure is obtained when the fourth part of a great circle, the plane of which cuts the earth at the poles, is divided into ten millions of equal parts. This measure bears to the English imperial yard the relation of—

Meter.		Yard.
1·	=	1·093633
0·91438348	=	1·

Again, the circumference of the earth at the equator is divided into 360 degrees.

Distance — Diagonal Scale.

16. If we suppose one definite point in space determined, then every other point is *distant* from that assumed point; and the straight line which can be drawn, or which may be imagined to be drawn, from the one point to the other, is called the shortest distance, or simply their *distance*. As space is boundless, no measure and no number can limit distance.

We speak of *commensurable* and *incommensurable* distances. The first are such as we can either measure directly by the application of a measuring instrument, or by calculation; and different measures or scales are employed, according to the magnitude to be measured. Thus we express the distances of the heavens by the distances of the stars, of the sun, and by the semi diameter of the earth. We measure the surface of the earth by degrees, miles, rods, &c., and objects of less extent by feet, inches, and lines.

Incommensurable distances are such as we can neither determine by our senses nor by our instruments. For example, we say that the distance between one atom and another is incommensurably small, and the distances of most of the fixed stars and of the Milky Way incommensurably great.

All distances greater than the eye of sense can reach we bring within the range of our spiritual optics by the powers of imagination. But sometimes even these are insufficient, for the enormous distances of the heavenly bodies are beyond the sphere of imaginative power.

In such cases the *diagonal scale* (fig. 12) is an essential means in aiding the imagination, since by the use of this instrument we can make diagrams which represent the same ratios upon a place which can easily be seen.

In this instrument, constructed on mathematical principles, the lines A B, B C, &c., represent given spaces, as miles; A B is divided by ten parallel lines into tenths of a mile, and from these points, 1, 2, 3, 4, &c., lines are drawn to the right hand, diagonally, to A′, B′, intersect the parallels 1′, 2′, 3′, 4′, &c., in such a manner, that from every tenth of a mile, again the tenth part is marked off. The marked-off section amounts to $\frac{1}{10}$ upon the parallel 1′, $\frac{2}{10}$ upon 2′, to $\frac{3}{10}$ upon 3′, to $\frac{9}{10}$ upon 9′, so that by means of a compass, any magnitude required may be measured in miles, tenths, and hundredths of miles. For example,

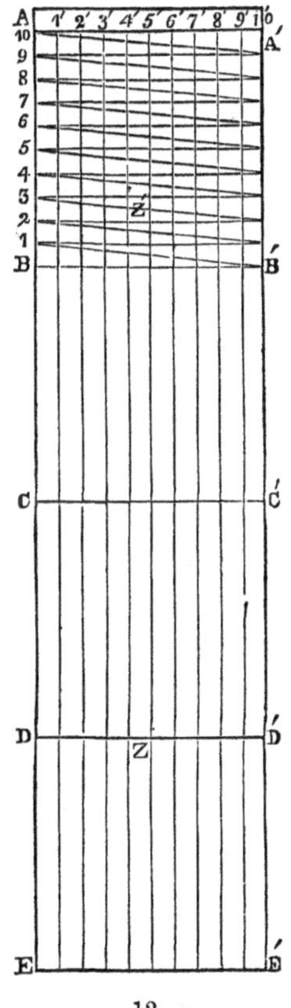

12.

$2\frac{1}{4}$ miles, or 2·25, is laid down from the scale, thus—place the one point of the compasses at Z, and extend the other to the point of intersection of the diagonal 3, and the parallel 5′ at Z′, and the space between the points of the compasses corresponds exactly to two entire miles two tenths and five hundredth parts. A diagonal scale of this description is frequently appended to the bottom of the instrument called the protractor, as in fig. 5.

Angle of Vision—Apparent and Actual Magnitude.

17. In our Physical section we have shown that from every object that we see, rays of light penetrate the eye and form an image of the object upon the inner coating (*tunica reticulata*) of this organ; on the magnitude of this image, made perceptible to us through the optic nerve, the apparent magnitude of the object depends. Let us suppose, for example, lines drawn from the two extremities *a b* (fig. 13) of an image formed on the retina corresponding to the object, these lines intersect each other, and form the visual or optic angle, whose magnitude is dependent on that of the image on the retina. It may, therefore, be said that the apparent magnitude of an object is expressed by the magnitude of the angle of vision under which it appears. It is a general rule, that the greater the visual angle the greater is the apparent magnitude of an object.

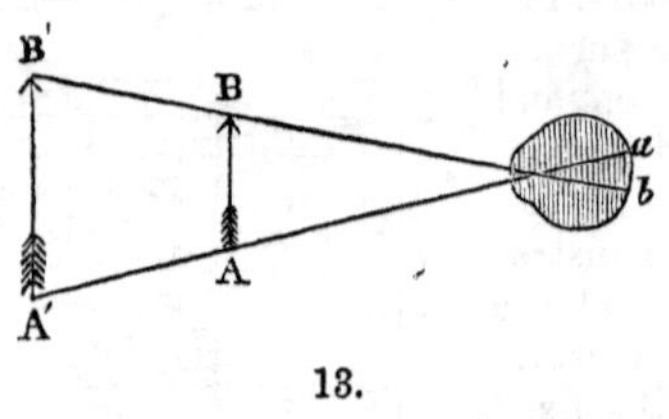

13.

The magnitude of the angle of vision evidently depends on two things, the first is the actual size of the object, and the second is its distance from the eye. And in reference to the latter this law is prevalent, viz., that the angle of vision, under which an object is seen within certain limits, decreases with the increase of the distance of the object. The same object at double the distance will appear to have only half, and at three times the distance only a third of the magnitude which it has in the single distance.

For the same reason, the trees of two parallel rows appear to approximate more and more according to their remoteness, because their relative distance appears to the eye under a smaller angle. Illusions of different kinds depend on this principle; and we have only by experience gradually acquired the habit of determining the distance of known objects by their apparent magnitude. In the twilight, or in a fog, which renders the outlines of objects indistinct, a distant church steeple or a tree may easily be mistaken for a man close to us, or *vice versâ*, because the angle of vision of the lofty but distant object may appear the same as that of an object which is of less height, but nearer to the observer.

Two consequences can be deduced from the foregoing principle, of the utmost importance in the science of astronomy, namely, first, when the apparent magnitude and the distance of an object are known, its actual magnitude can be determined; and, second, when the actual and apparent magnitudes of a body are determined, the distance of the body itself can be ascertained.

Determination of Distance.

18. Only short distances are in general measured by actual measurement with a rule or chain; consequently there is no necessity for explaining this

process, inasmuch as these practices are seldom employed, even in measuring large distances on the earth, and never applied in determining the distances of the heavenly bodies.

Here we do not deal with distances *measured*, but *reckoned*. For this purpose we require from geometry some principles regarding the similarity of triangles, and a few laws from trigonometry.

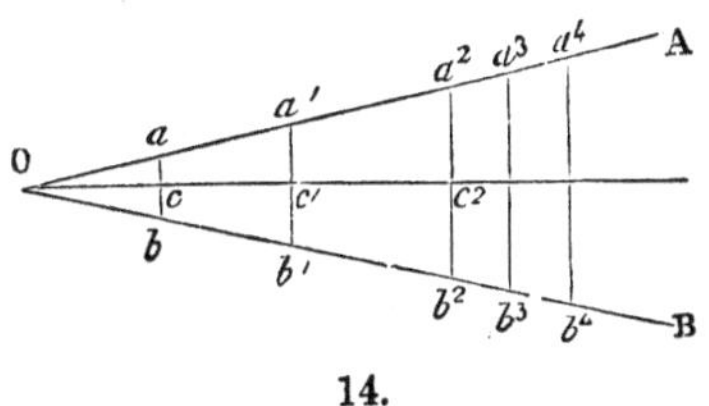

14.

In fig. 14, we perceive between the sides A *o* and B *o* of the angle *o*, the parallel lines *a b*, *a' b'*, &c. It is evident that these lines are the longer the farther they are distant from the angle *o*, and it can be proved that *a' b'* is as many times longer than *a b*, as *o c'* is longer than *o c*, and as many times as *o a'* is longer than *o a*, and as many times as *o b'* is longer than *o b*. The same remarks apply to all the other drawn or imaginary parallels between the sides *o A* and *o B* in relation to *a b*, or between any two of these parallels. Thus a^4 b^4 is as many times longer than a^3 b^3, as *o* a^4 is longer than *o* a^3, &c.

This simple principle is applicable to the mensuration of perpendicular distances or heights, as well as of horizontal distances. For example—

Let *a'' b''* (fig. 15) be a tower, the height of which is to be ascertained. We first measure accurately a good ground or base line *b'' o*, then set up a staff *a b*, over the top of which the eye can see the summit of the tower *a''*. Let a second staff *a' b'*, be so placed between the tower and the observer that its top *a'* may appear to the eye in a straight line with *a''*. By drawing a line connecting these four points, *a''*, *a'*, *a*, *o*, we obtain a diagram corresponding exactly to fig. 14, and from the above principle it follows that *a'' b''* is as many times longer than *a' b'* as *b'' o* is longer than *b' o*. Suppose, for illustration, that *a' b'* is 15 feet high, and *b' o* 30 feet long, then must also *a'' b''* be half as long as the measured base line. But this line is 120 feet, therefore the height of the tower is 60 feet.

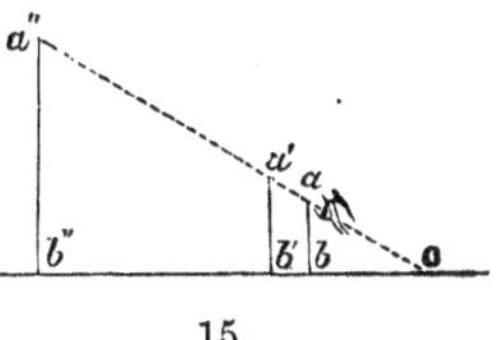

15.

By the length of the shadows thrown by two objects, we can ascertain the height of the objects by which they are cast; and this affords us a very simple method of determining the altitude of objects. For example, we measure a staff fixed in the ground *a' b'* (fig. 15), and also its shadow; we then measure the shadow of a tower *b'' o*. Hence, so many times as the staff is longer or shorter than its shadow, so many times the height of the tower longer or shorter than the length of its shadow.

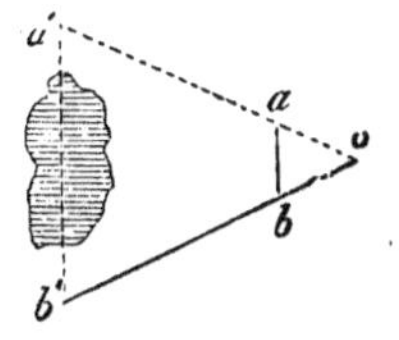

16.

We apply the same principle with suitable modifications to the determination of the mutual distance of two points (*a' b'*, fig. 16), which we cannot measure directly, as, for instance, when a wood or lake intervenes. In this case it will be sufficient to ascertain the distance $o\ b'$ in order to determine that of $a'\ b'$ as well as $a'\ o$. Let two staffs be fixed in the ground at the point a and b, which are in the same straight lines with a' and b', and with the eye of the observer at o; draw $a\ b$ parallel with $a'\ b'$, find the measure of the triangle $a\ b\ o$, then as many times as $o\ b'$ is longer than $o\ b$, so many times is $a'\ b'$ longer than $a\ b$.

Trigonometrical Mensuration—(Measuring of Angles.)

19. We occasionally find on certain elevated positions, as, for example, on the tops of hills and mountains, erections of wood or stone, of greater or less altitude, and an inscription sometimes is added, importing that this is a *trigonometrical station*. It is generally known that such stations are employed to survey the surface of the country, and that the latter is by this means divided into a number of triangles, spread out like a net. These triangles being measured, their sum gives the contents of the surface surveyed.

It is difficult to convey to the uninitiated in mathematical science a clear notion of the process whereby these surveys are made; we will, however, endeavour to render it comprehensible.

The angle A (fig. 17) is contained by the sides A B and A O. From the extremity B of the side A B let a perpendicular B O fall upon the side A O. The line A B is supposed to be of an unchangeable length, and hence it is called the *constant*, and we assume that it is moveable round the point A. We raise the constant A B till it occupies, for example, the position A B′. Thus we see that both the angle at A, and also the perpendicular, let fall from the extremities of the constant, must increase. The angle B′ A O is evidently greater than B A O, and B′ O′ longer than B O; this increasing line is called the *sine* of the given angle A.

17.

Again, let us suppose in the same angle A (fig. 18), that the side A O is invariable, and on the end O erect a perpendicular O B, and extend it till it cuts the other side A B. As the angle at A is increased, so also is the perpendicular, which we call the *tangent* of the angle A.

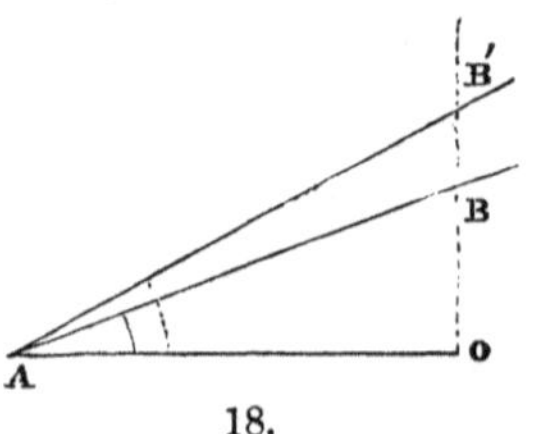

18.

We hence understand that the sine and the tangent are two lines, which bear a certain relation to a given angle, and increase with the enlargement of the angle. It is easy to perceive that the tangent of the angle A is susceptible of a much greater increment than the sine, and a law has been discovered, and trigonometrical tables have been constructed, in which the proportion of the sine and tangent to the constant of every angle is given. For example, if we look in the table for the sine of the angle of 30°, we find the number 0·5 is given: that is, the sine of this angle is only half as great as the constant.

From what has been above stated, the important practical application is clear, viz., that from the given magnitude of an angle and one of its sides, the sine or the tangent can be found, with the aid of the trigonometrical tables, as may be thus exemplified:—

Let it be required to determine the height of a tower O B (fig. 19). By previous admeasurement, the base A O is found to be 430 feet, and the angle A 35°. O B is the tangent of the angle A, which by the tables is equal to 0.7; that is, the tangent O B is 7-10ths of the constant A O, and 1-10th of 430 being equal to 43, O B is equal to 7 × 43 = 301 feet.

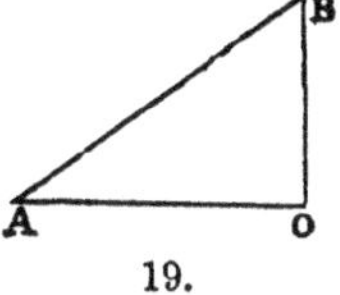

19.

Distance and Magnitude of the Heavenly Bodies.

20. The methods which have been described in § 18 are never applied to measure vertical or horizontal distances on the surface of the earth; trigonometrical calculations are always employed. These last are the only means possible for ascertaining the distances of the heavenly bodies. As in this case the semi-diameter of the earth is taken as the base line, the length of this must first be determined, which is done in the following manner:—Let us suppose the earth to be represented by the circle fig. 20, and two observers by a and a', being distant from each other just the length of the arc a a', which by accurate admeasurement is known to be 138·2 miles. Each of these observers simultaneously takes notice of a fixed star, perpendicularly over his head s s', the two lines drawn from the star to the observers will, if extended, meet in the earth's centre and form the angle c. We cannot measure this angle, because the centre of the earth is inaccessible, the distance, however, of the fixed stars from the earth is so excessively great that it makes no perceptible difference whether the angle, formed by the lines uniting the two stars s and s' with the observer's eye, be measured from the centre or from a point c' on the surface of the earth. To employ an illustration—it is of as little influence as if a mite in the centre or on the surface of a millet-seed were to look at the summits of two distant mountains. Without sensible error, we therefore assume the angle c to be equal to the angle c', and measure the latter. If this is equal to two degrees, we know that the arc a a', equal to $138\frac{2}{10}$ miles, stands over an angle of two degrees, and consequently that $69\frac{1}{10}$ miles = 1°, which for the whole circumference of the earth, amounting, as is known, to 360°, is $360 \times 69\frac{1}{10} = 24{,}876$, or more correctly, 24,897 miles. But as (§ 11) the circumference of a circle is 3·14 times as great as its diameter, the diameter of the

20.

earth is consequently $\frac{24897}{3{\cdot}14.} = 7929.$

If two persons, A and C (fig. 21), from different stations, observe the same point M, the visual lines naturally meet in the point M, and form an angle, which is called the angle of *parallax*. If the eye were at M, this angle would be the angle of vision, or the angle under which the base line A C of the two observers appears to the eye. The angle at M also expresses the apparent magnitude

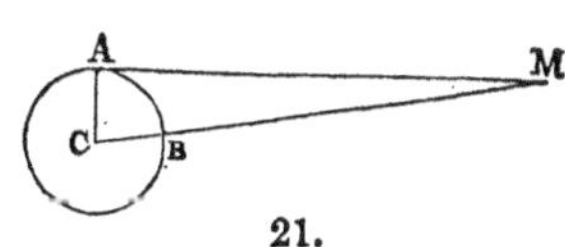

21.

of A C when viewed from M, and this apparent magnitude is called the *parallax* of M.

Let M represent the moon, C the centre of the earth represented by the circle, then A C is the parallax of the moon; that is, the apparent magnitude the semi-diameter of the earth would have if seen from the moon. If the moon be observed at the same time from A, being then in the horizon, and from the point B, being then in the zenith, and the visual line of which when extended passes through the centre of the earth, we obtain, by uniting the points A C M by lines, the triangle A C M.

Therefore, as A M, the tangent of the circle (§ 11), stands at right angles to the radius A C, the angle at A is a right angle, and the magnitude of the angle at C is found by means of the arc A B, the distance of the two observers from each other. As soon, however, as we are acquainted with the magnitude of two angles of a triangle, we arrive at that of the third, because we know that all the angles of a triangle together equal two right angles (180°). The angle at M, generally called the moon's parallax, is thus found to be 56 minutes and 58 seconds. We know that in the right-angled triangle M A C the measure of the angle M = 56′ 58″, and also that A C, the semi-diameter of the earth = 3964 miles. This is sufficient, in order by trigonometry, to obtain the length of the side M C; that is, to find the moon's distance from the earth. A C is the sine of the angle M, and by the table the sine of an angle of 56′ 58″ is equal to $\frac{1652}{100000}$; or, in other words, according to § 19, if we divide the constant M C, the distance of the moon, into 100,000 equal parts, the sine A C the earth's semi-diameter = 1652 of these parts. And this last quantity being contained 60 times in 100,000, the distance of the moon from the earth is equal to 60 semi-diameters of the earth, or 60 × 3964 = 237,840 miles.

In a similar way the parallax of the sun has been found = 8″, 6, and the distance of the sun from the earth to be 95,000,000 miles.

22. Having ascertained the actual distance of the sun and moon, and their apparent magnitudes, their actual magnitudes may be thence readily calculated. Let us assume, for example, A C (fig. 21), to be the moon's semi-diameter, and A M the moon's distance from the earth, then A C will be the trigonometrical tangent of the angle M, if we make A M the constant. But now it has been found by observation that the apparent diameter of the moon, or the angle of vision under which it is seen by the observer at M = 31′ 16″. The apparent magnitude of the semi-diameter of the moon amounts therefore to 15′ 38″; but the trigonometrical tangent of an angle of 15′ 38″ stands to the constant as 454 : 100,000. As the constant A M is = 237,840 miles, we obtain for A C, = $\frac{454 \times 237840}{100000}$, 1080 miles, and for the actual diameter of the moon, which is equal to twice A C, 2160 miles. In the same manner we calculate from the apparent diameter of the sun, which is = 32′ 0″ 88-100th, and from his distance the actual diameter at 882,270 miles.

II. GENERAL ASTRONOMICAL PHENOMENA.

(A.) THE EARTH.

Figure.

23. We presuppose the reader to have a general notion of the spherical form of the earth and heavenly bodies, and of their motions in space; we, therefore, reserve the proofs for a subsequent portion of the work.

The following facts are confirmatory of the spherical form of the earth. We can only see a very small portion of its surface from any station whatever; if the earth were a plane, our extent of view would not be so limited as in fact it is. If we observe a ship receding from our sight on the apparently flat ocean, the first part which disappears is the hull, and lastly the masts and pennon. An exactly similar appearance is observed when a person walks up and over a hill, his feet disappear first and his hat last, and, *vice versâ*, in approaching our station his hat appears first. Voyages and travels by land and by water have shown indisputably that it may be travelled or sailed round by constantly proceeding from one point in the same direction, and that the traveller will at last arrive at the very place whence he set out on his journey. We farther conclude, from the circular appearance of the earth's shadow, as seen in a lunar eclipse, that the body casting this shadow is spherical. Finally, by actual observation, we know that the other heavenly bodies are spherical.

Notwithstanding the sphericity of the earth, the surface appears to us as a plane, this appearance being a consequence of its great extent. Even from the tops of mountains of 10,000 feet in height, the eye can survey only the 1-4000th part of the earth's surface, and hence this little space appears as a plane.

Magnitude of the Earth.

24. It has been already shown, § 20, that it is possible to measure a body even of so great magnitude as the earth. A tabular view of the relative terrestrial magnitudes is given below.

Diameter of the earth	=	7,929	miles.
Circumference	=	24,897	miles.
Superficial contents	=	197,408,788	square miles.
Solid contents	=	260,875,713,342	cubic miles.

It is evident from these numbers, that the elevations on the surface of the earth, viz., the mountains, have no influence at all upon its general figure Indeed, if we suppose that the earth is represented by a globe of 16 inches diameter, the highest mountains would resemble small grains of sand of $\frac{1}{100}$ inch in height attached to the surface of this globe.

Division of the Earth.

25. A skittle-ball rolling upon a bowling-green has another motion in addition to that of the course it follows. We perceive that the grains of

sand adhering to its surface describe, according to their position, smaller or larger circles around two opposite points of the ball, and we term the imaginary line passing through the centre of the ball and these points, the axis of rotation, or, briefly, the axis of the ball.

It has been proved that the earth (fig. 22) likewise turns round an axis, N S, the two extremities of which are named the *Poles*. The one, N, is called the *North Pole*, and the other, S, the *South Pole*, and the great circle A Q, drawn round the globe equally distant from the two poles, is called the *Equator*, as it divides the earth into two equal parts, viz., into the northern and southern hemispheres.

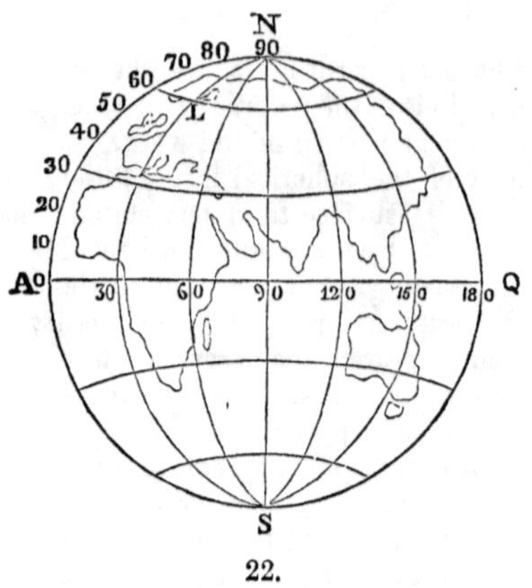

22.

The equator is divided into 360 equal parts or *degrees*, every one of which, as has been already shown in § 20, is $69\frac{1}{10}$ miles long. We may imagine a circle drawn through each of these divisions round the globe, and passing through the poles, so that the globe appears encircled with 180 rings, of which we here can only represent a few — as 30, 60, 90, &c., These vertical circles passing through the equator and the two poles are called *meridians*, and of course have all the same magnitude. At the equator a meridional degree is $69\frac{1}{10}$ miles long; but, as is evident, this continually diminishes towards the poles, where they all meet. In reckoning meridians we commence at a certain point called the first meridian, as, for instance, at A (fig. 22), which was formerly on the island of Ferro, on the west coast of Africa, then supposed to be the westernmost point of land. In England the meridional degrees are calculated from Greenwich.

The distance of any meridian from the first meridian is termed the *Longitude*, and it is employed in describing the situation of a place on the earth's surface. Suppose L (fig. 22) a city, its longitude will be 30°, since it lies on a meridian which is 30° from the first. So, for example, the longitude of Oporto is 8° 37′ west, Paris 2° 22′ east, Vienna 16° 16′ east, Bagdad 44° 45′ east, Surat 73° 7′ east, Java 110° east, Mount Hecla 350° east, reckoned from the meridian of Greenwich, and so on until we return to the first meridian, or the point where we began to reckon. At the 180th degree we have proceeded half round the globe, and reached the farthest distance from the first meridian, and are now on the opposite side of the earth, and proceeding farther we ultimately arrive at the point whence we started.

" It will readily be perceived that a knowledge of the longitude alone is not sufficient to determine the situation of a place on the earth's surface. When we say, for example, that the longitude of a place is 30°, it may lie on any point whatever of the whole hemisphere, N L S (fig. 22). This point must therefore be determined more accurately, and hence the first meridian is divided into 90 equal parts north and south of the equator towards the poles. These are called *degrees of latitude*, and the lines drawn through these round the globe, parallel to the equator, are called circles or *parallels of latitude*, and diminish as they approach the poles.

Hence, by the *latitude* of a place we mean its distance from the equator towards the poles, and we speak of north and south latitude according as the place is situated in the northern or southern hemisphere.

So, for example, the point L (fig. 22), which has 30° longitude and 60° north latitude, is in Sweden.

For greater precision, these degrees of latitude and longitude are farther divided into minutes and seconds. These divisions of the earth's surface are made very intelligible by means of a ball, whereon the principal lines above mentioned and the outlines of the continents, as well as some of the most important places are marked. An arrangement of this description is called a *terrestrial globe*.

By way of example we give the *longitudes* and *latitudes* of several places in the following table:—

PLACE.	Longitude from London.			Longitude from Ferro.		North Latitude	
London	0°	0′		18°	6′	51	31′
Athens	23	52	East.	41	32	38	5
Augsburg	10	17	,,	28	33	48	21
Berlin	13	26	,,	31	3	52	31
Cologne	6	29	,,	24	35	50	15
Constantinople	28	53	,,	46	36	41	1
Darmstadt	8	9	,,	26	15	49	56
Frankfort-on-the-Maine	7	55	,,	26	1	50	7
Göttingen	9	30	,,	27	36	51	32
Hamburg	9	32	,,	27	38	53	33
Königsburg	20	4	,,	38	10	54	43
Leipzig	11	55	,,	30	1	51	20
Mannheim	2	1	,,	20	7	49	29
Munich	11	8	,,	29	14	48	8
Paris	2	25	,,	20	0	48	50
Petersburg	30	19	,,	47	59	59	56
Prague	14	15	,,	32	5	59	5
Rome	12	32	,,	40	38	41	54
Riga	23	41	,,	41	47	56	57
Stralsund	23	6	,,	41	12	54	19
Vienna	16	28	,,	34	2	48	12
Worms	7	55	,,	26	1	49	38

(B.) DIVISION OF THE HEAVENS.

27. The earth is the station from which the eye of man beholds the Universe. We might presume, without any precise knowledge of astronomy, that many things would appear under a different aspect if the eye beheld them from the moon or the sun, or from one of the most distant stars. Therefore, we must divide the firmament surrounding us, and define the particular points, lines, and spaces in the same, without which it would not be possible to describe the phenomena occurring in it with any degree of precision.

The spherical form of the earth does not admit of a top and a bottom, and hence every observer assumes that his station is the highest. Let us suppose, for example, that we are stationed on the point *o* of the earth's surface (fig. 23); an inhabitant on the opposite point is under our feet; but an inhabitant of the earth at *o'* would have as good a reason for considering himself as over us.

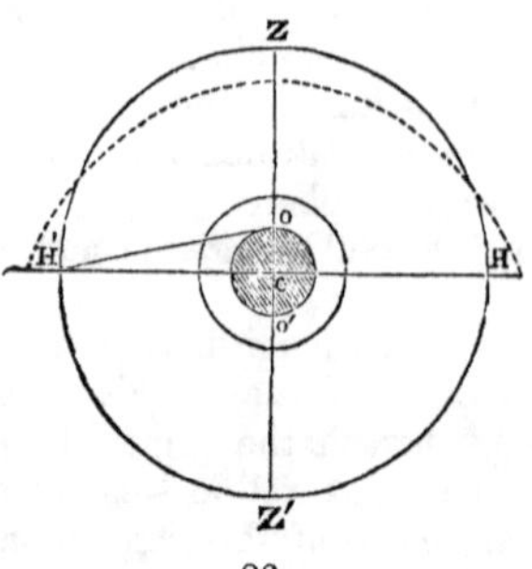

23.

From the station of the observer at *o* let a line be drawn perpendicularly; if this line be prolonged indefinitely through the centre *c* of the earth to the point Z, which is over the observer's head, and to the opposite point Z', the former Z will represent the *zenith*, and the opposite point Z' the *nadir* of the observer.

Let us suppose one of the heavenly bodies, for example the sun, in the station Z, we say that such body is in the zenith of the observer at *o*. But the heavenly bodies at the nadir Z' cannot, of course, be seen at the same time by the observer.

28. If we look from *o* on the starry vault of heaven, the stars glittering in it appear to the eye as if all were equally distant. We have an impression of being surrounded by an enormous dome, on the inner ceiling of which the stars appear to be attached. The apparent firmament which surrounds the earth is represented by Z H' Z' H Z, and the distance from *o* to Z is to be assumed as infinitely great. It is further to be noticed that, in consequence of an optical deception, the concave heavens do not appear hemispherical, but rather flattened, as the dotted line indicates.

Apparent and Real Horizon.

29. If the observer, instead of surveying the firmament above him, looks around over the surface of the earth, he appears to be bounded on all sides by a circle, of which he himself is in the centre. This appearance is represented more completely when the point of observation is on the smooth, open sea, or on an elevated point, as the summit of a mountain. The circle which limits the view on all sides is called the *visible*, or *apparent horizon*, and meets, and apparently supports, the vaulted arch of the heavens, which seems to rest thereon. It has already been stated that the eye cannot see more than 1-400th part of the earth's surface from the top of a mountain 10,000 feet high, and from a height of 25,000 feet, the greatest elevation yet reached by man, the semi-diameter of the circle of vision amounts to 198 miles.

From the summit of a mountain (fig. 24), at the base of a tower, we perceive the distant point P as distinctly as from the top of the tower. The altitude of the latter is too little to have any perceptible effect on the appearance of a far-distant object, or to extend the range of our vision. For observing proximate objects, the height of the tower has an influence, as is proved by the point P', being visible from the top of the tower, but not from its base.

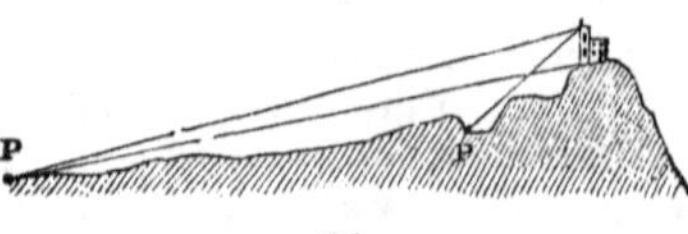

24.

The distance of the nearest of the heavenly bodies from the earth is so enormously great that it is immaterial from whatever part of the earth, whether from its surface or from its centre, they be observed. The semi diameter of the earth *o c* (fig. 23) is, compared with those immense distances, an insignificant magnitude; and it is certain that an observer, whom we may suppose to be stationed at the centre of the earth *c*, can see no larger a portion of the heavens, than he who is situated on its surface at *o*. Indeed, a star at H′ is just as visible from *o* as from *c*, hence a plane H′ *c* H, which cuts the earth through the centre perpendicularly to another, cutting the earth through the zenith and nadir (Z Z′) of the observer at *o*, will be the *true horizon* of the observer at *o*. This plane, which divides the heavens into two equal portions, the one above and the other below the horizon, is the *horizon of Astronomy*. It is evident that objects below the horizon are invisible.

Apparent Motion of the Heavenly Bodies.

30. When we are moved or carried with a considerable velocity, as, for example, in a railway carriage, it appears to us that all the objects which we pass, contiguous to the line of motion, are moving rapidly in an opposite direction. That this motion is only apparent is so well known that it would scarcely deceive a child.

We daily experience, however, a similar illusion, in consequence of the rotatory motion of the earth around its axis. It appears to us that we are at rest in the centre of the vast concavity of the firmament, which, with its stars, seems to revolve round the earth. This was indeed the opinion prevalent for thousands of years, and there was no little difficulty in establishing the correct view.

We shall, however, in our consideration of celestial phenomena, treat the subject in the first instance as if the earth was really the fixed centre of the firmament. Therefore, whenever the rising or setting of the sun or stars forms the subject of description, such motions are to be understood as only apparent. In common life all the expressions regarding apparent motion have been retained, and the greater part of Astronomy consists, as it were, in the translation of apparent celestial phenomena into the actual.

31. The attentive observation of the starry heavens, even during a single night, will convince us that all the visible stars describe circles which are the smaller, the nearer the stars are to a certain point of the heavens P (fig. 25). In close proximity to this point there is a tolerably bright star called the *Pole Star*, which has scarcely any motion, but appears to the eye as always occupying the same position. Hence a line P P′ drawn from this star, through the centre of the earth *c*, represents the axis around which all the heavenly bodies perform their apparent motions. The part of the celestial axis P P′ passing through the earth, is the earth's axis; the north pole, of which *p* is on the same side as the pole star, and the south pole *p*′ is on the opposite side.

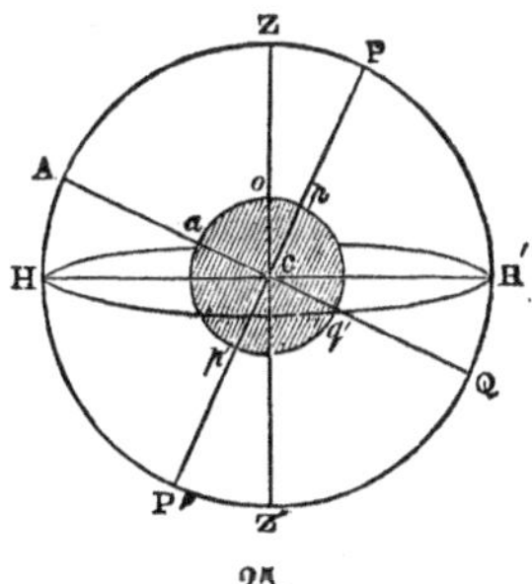

25.

We have, therefore, by the aid of the stars, determined the position of the earth's axis, and by this latter we can assign to the equator its proper place. For if $p\,p'$ be the earth's axis, $a\,q'$ is the greatest circle drawn round the earth, equally distant from both poles, and the plane of which cuts the earth's axis at right angles.

Furthermore, let us suppose the plane of the equator to be extended till it reach the celestial concave; we thus find the place of the celestial equator A Q, or *equinoctial*, as it is generally termed in opposition to the equator, which always means the terrestrial equator. The equinoctial divides the heavens into the northern and southern hemispheres. We cannot actually describe the equinoctial and make it visible, but we can imagine its line of direction by observing those stars through which it passes.

We are now in a condition to assign to an observer different stations in relation to the earth's axis on the earth's surface, which will essentially modify the aspects under which celestial phenomena are represented. One of these stations may be supposed to be at one of the two poles, for example, at *p*, or at any one point of the equator, as at *a*, or, finally, on any portion of the surface of the earth which lies between the pole and the equator, as, for example, *o*.

As the last is the station naturally occupied by most observers, and by all Europeans, we will first describe the phenomena as they appear to an observer placed at the station *o* (fig. 25). This is 50° from the north pole, and corresponds to the latitude of Frankfort and Central Germany.

DIURNAL PHENOMENA.

32. If, on the 21st March, a little before six o'clock in the morning, we look towards the brightest part of the horizon, we perceive at the point O (fig. 26), the *rising* of the sun. We call the exact point where this phenomenon occurs, the *East*, and that point W, of the horizon directly opposite, and distant 180° from the East, we call the *West*. If we turn our back to the East and look to the West, the point of the horizon on our left, distant 90° from the West, is the *South*, H, and the point opposite, on the right is the *North*, H'.

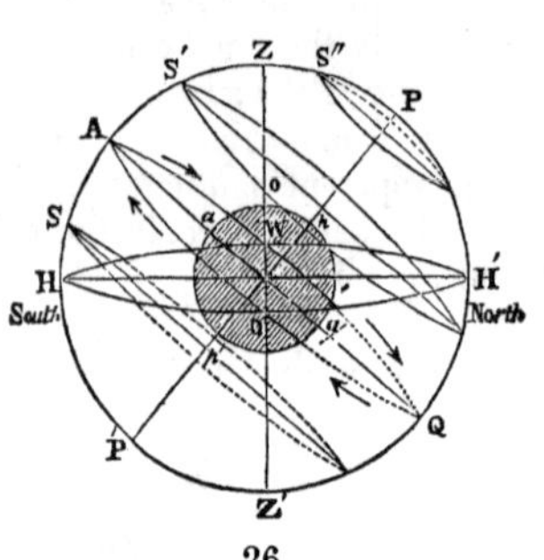

26.

These four points are called the *cardinal points*, and the straight lines which unite two opposite cardinal points intersect each other at right angles in the centre of the earth. The line H H' which unites the north and the south is named the *meridian*.

33. The rotation of the earth round its axis is in the direction from West to East, contrary to the apparent motion of the sun and stars. Consequently we see the sun, after his rising at O, progressively advancing more and more in the direction of the arrow towards the meridian in an arc which cuts the horizon in the point of the angle O A W (fig. 26), which is called an *oblique* arc. In this manner the sun finally reaches the highest point A of the heavens, which is called the *point of culmination*, and the time at which

this takes place is called *mid-day.* From this instant we perceive the sun progressing in the direction of the second arrow, descending towards the horizon, and disappearing or *setting* in the west point W. While the sun is above the horizon, his dazzling brightness illumines the surface of the earth and the atmosphere above the observer, in such a manner as to outshine all the other heavenly bodies, and to render them invisible. The period elapsing between the sun's rising and setting we call *day,* and the arc O A W, which the sun describes, the *diurnal arc.*

As soon as the sun has set, the day is terminated; the twilight appears, and is succeeded by night, which veils the earth in darkness. The concave vault of heaven is then bespangled with the gradually emerging stars, sometimes accompanied by the moon, the light of which considerably diminishes the darkness of the night. The arc W Q O, which the sun describes under the horizon, is named his *nocturnal arc.* At Q he reaches his lowest point, which is called his *inferior culmination.*

The time which the sun requires in this manner to describe his apparent motion from O to A W Q, and back again to O, is termed a *mean solar day,* or, briefly, *day,* and is divided into 24 hours.

By inspecting fig. 26, we perceive that the sun's course through the diurnal and nocturnal arcs O A W Q O on the 21st of March, is the same line which we already (§ 31) have described as the equinoctial, or celestial equator; on this day the sun therefore passes through the equinoctial. We also know that the diurnal arc O A W is equal to the nocturnal arc W Q O, and, consequently, that both day and night have an equal duration of 12 hours each. The period when this phenomenon occurs is called the *vernal equinox.*

The duration of the day and night, it is well known, varies considerably in the course of the year; therefore the sun during the whole year cannot remain on the equinoctial. Some weeks after the vernal equinox, the sun appears to the observer at *o* at mid-day some considerable distance higher above his horizon H H′, and nearer to the pole P, and he continually approximates to the pole till the 21st of June, when he reaches his greatest altitude at S′, which is then $23\frac{1}{2}°$ above the equinoctial. It is evident that on this day the diurnal arc described by the sun is longer than his nocturnal arc, and, consequently, the day is considerably longer than the night. Therefore, on the 21st of June we have the longest day, and the sun is said to be in the *summer solstice.*

From this day, the arcs described by the sun again gradually approach the equinoctial A Q, which he enters on the 22nd of September, and we have again equal day and night, or the *autumnal equinox.* From this time, the southern distance of the sun from the equinoctial gradually increases, his diurnal arc becomes smaller and smaller, and the days consequently shorter and shorter, till, on the 21st of December, he has arrived at the *winter solstice,* when we have the shortest day. From this point the sun again daily approaches the equinoctial, to which he returns on the 21st of March.

The time which elapses during these observations, and which is employed by the sun in ascending from the equinoctial to the highest point S′, and in descending to the lowest point S, and, finally, again entering the equinoctial, is named a *year,* and is exactly 365 days, 5 hours, 48 minutes, and 48 seconds.

We also see that the sun, to an observer at *o,* does not rise and set every day in the same point of the horizon, but that, while the days increase, the sun rises and sets at a point more northerly towards H′, and more towards the south H, when the days decrease. The point O where the sun rises at the equinox is also termed the *vernal point.*

The Ecliptic.

34. From what has been previously said, it is evident that the sun has a twofold apparent motion, viz., a circular motion obliquely ascending from the horizon, which is explained by the rotation of the earth, and by our position *o* to the earth's axis *p p′*, and also by a rising and setting motion between the solstitial points S and S′, which causes the inequality of the days and nights. Independently of the daily motion of the sun, we observe that at the summer solstice on the 21st of June, at mid-day, the sun is at S′, and one-half year later, viz., on the 21st of December, at midnight, the sun is at *s*, from which he arrives again in the space of half a year at S′; so we are able to represent this annual motion of the sun, by a circle, the diameter of which is the line S′ *s*. This circle is called the *Ecliptic.*

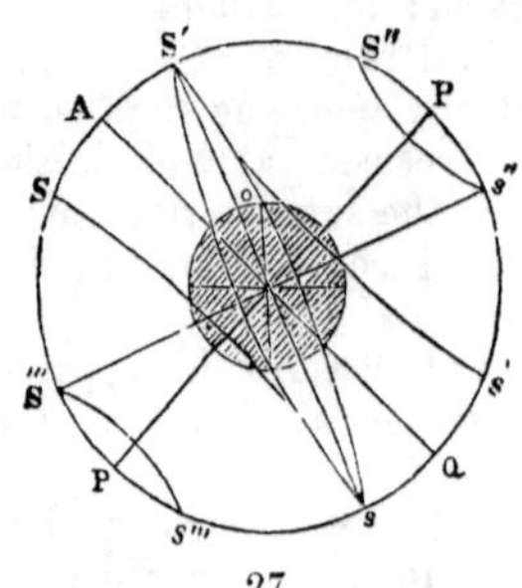

27.

The plane of the ecliptic S′ *s* cuts the plane of the equinoctial A Q at an angle of 23½°, and the axis of the ecliptic S‴ *s″* makes the same angle with the axis of the heavens P P. The two parallel circles, S′ *s′* and S *s*, include a zone, extending on both sides of the equinoctial, and beyond which the sun never passes. These circles are called the *Tropics*, from τρέπω, *I turn*, because the sun turns back at these points and again approaches the equinoctial. The parallel circles S″ *s″*, and S‴ *s‴* described by the poles of the ecliptic S″ *s″* about the celestial poles P P, are called the two *arctic circles.*

Nocturnal Phenomena.

35. The stars, as well as the sun, in describing their courses in the heavens, reach an upper point of *culmination* (S A S′ S″, fig. 27), and a lower point, which is situated upon the opposite side of the celestial sphere. But we can actually perceive both these points of culmination only in those stars which, as S″, are closer to the pole, P. These stars never set to us; and in the vicinity of the north pole they may be seen by day, for example, when the sun is totally eclipsed. The more distant stars, S′ A S, complete their daily course partly under the horizon, consequently; they rise and set. Some, which are very remote from the north pole, barely rise above the horizon, and speedily disappear. Finally, those nearer the south pole, as S‴, describe their revolution round about the pole without being at any time visible to the observer at *o*. We never find the fixed stars, like the sun, change their position relatively to the equinoctial and the poles. A star on the equinoctial at A to-day, will describe, every following night of the entire year, its course on the equinoctial; and all the other stars are subject to this general law, for example, we find S S′ S″ the whole year through, and, at the same time, always in the same relative position.

36. Very different celestial phenomena from the above-described, are, however, observed when the place of observation is at the equator, or at one of the poles of the earth. If we suppose our station to be at the north pole, *p* (fig. 28), the pole star will necessarily be in the zenith Z, and the plane of the horizon will coincide with that of the equinoctial A Q. When the sun is above the horizon, he describes a circle round the horizon without setting. The stars S S′ likewise describe circles which are parallel to each other and to the horizon A Q, and hence to the observer at *p* they neither rise nor set.

28.

As will be afterwards shown, the sun is for half the year constantly above the horizon of those who live in the vicinity of the north pole, and the day is consequently six months long. The night which follows is of equal duration, the sun being under the horizon, and then the sun is visible at the south pole during a period of six months.

37. If an observer is placed on the terrestrial equator at the point *a* (fig. 29), the earth's axis *p p′* being extended, its extremities will lie in the horizon P P′ of the observer. Whilst the pole star at P in the horizon appears immoveable, all the other stars, for example, S, S′, Z, S″, S‴, rise in a perpendicular direction over the horizon P P′, and describe semicircles above it. The sun also there rises and sets perpendicularly to the horizon. Hence, it is evident that the lengths of every arc described above the horizon are equal to those described below it; therefore at the equator the sun and the stars are visible as long as the time during which they are invisible, consequently the days and nights have an equal duration of 12 hours.

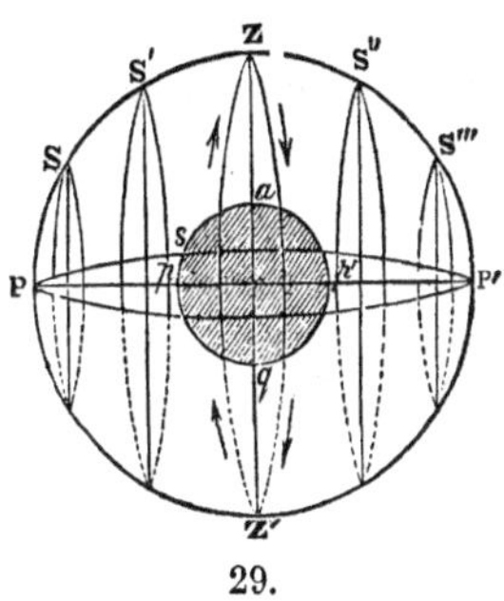

29.

Polar Altitude.

38. The distance of the north pole P (fig. 30) from the horizon H′ of an observer is called the *polar altitude* of the latter.

So, for instance, the polar altitude, viz., the height at which the pole star at P appears to an observer at *o*, is expressed both by the arc P H′, and also by the angle P C H′.

By *equatorial altitude* is meant the distance of a star at A on the equinoctial from the horizon H of the observer, and is expressed both by the angle A C H, and also by the arc A H.

The arcs of the polar and equatorial altitudes of one and the same place make together always an arc of 90°, that is a quarter of a circle, or a quadrant. In London, for example, we see the pole-star is elevated to an

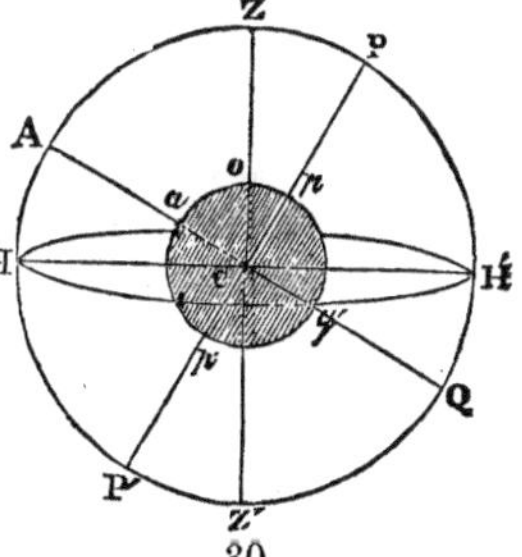

30.

angle of 51° 30′ above the horizon, which elevation we call its altitude. If we subtract this number from 90°, we find that 38° 30′ is the equatorial altitude of the place. Since the place does not change its relative position on the surface of the earth, the polar altitude remains always the same, that is, the pole-star is always at the same height from the horizon.

On the other hand, an *observer* can change his position on the earth. If, for example, he advances in the direction from *o* to *p*, the pole-star is more and more elevated to a greater height above his horizon, or, in other words, the polar altitude of the observer is increased in the same ratio as the equatorial altitude is diminished.

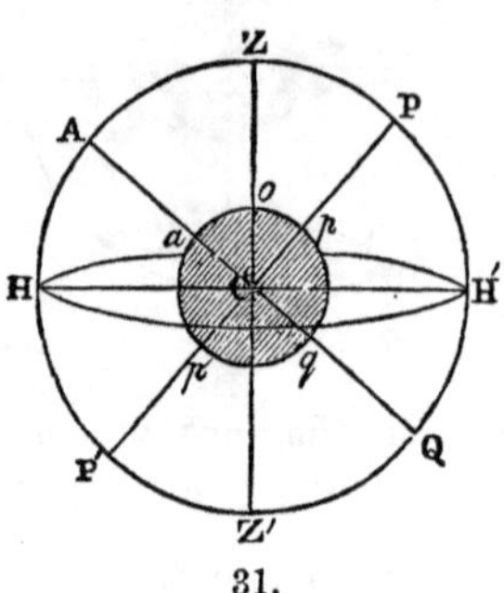

31.

If he reaches *p*, viz., the north pole, his polar altitude is 90°, and the pole-star is in his zenith, whilst the equator coincides with his horizon, and consequently the equatorial altitude is zero. (See fig. 28.)

If, on the contrary, a journey be made in an opposite direction from *o* towards the equator *a*, the pole-star gradually descends towards the horizon, consequently the polar altitude continually decreases in the same ratio as the equatorial altitude increases. When the traveller has arrived at the equator *a*, the polar altitude is = 0°, and the pole-star appears in the horizon, whilst the equinoctial is in his zenith. (See fig. 29.)

It is easily understood that the polar altitude of a place is the same as we have already explained in § 26 to be its *latitude*, namely, the distance of the place from the equator.

The fact that the polar altitude of a star increases or decreases, according as we approach the equator, or the north pole, is a striking proof of the spherical form of the earth.

Altitude of the Stars.

39. By the altitude of a star we understand its distance from the horizon of an observer. To express this altitude, *vertical circles* are employed, Z R and Z R′ (fig. 32), which are supposed to be drawn from the zenith through the stars S and S′ perpendicularly to the horizon H H′. The arcs S R and S′ R′ are therefore the altitudes of the stars S and S′ for the observer at *o*. The arcs S Z and S′ Z, which with the altitudes of the stars S and S′ make the quadrant or 90°, are called the *zenith distance* of these stars.

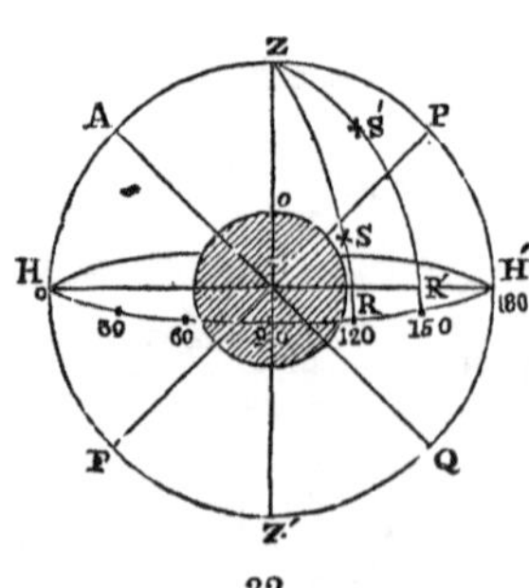

32.

To define accurately the position of a star in reference to the horizon, the whole space from H south to H′ north, is divided into 180°, and the distance of the circles of altitude of a star from the south point, expressed in degrees, is called the *azimuth* of this star. Thus the azimuth of the star S is the arc R H = 120°, that of S′ is the arc R′ H = 150°. All stars that are on the same vertical circle have evidently the same azimuth; and, according to the side of the heavens on which the star is, the azimuth will be named either east or west.

The same star will appear at different altitudes if observed from different points of the earth at the same time. Consequently, if the altitude of a star at a given place and time is known by a voyager, he can, from the altitude of the same star observed from another place, find the situation of the position he is in. The determination of the altitudes of the heavenly bodies is of the utmost importance to seafaring men, who at an early period of their lives are trained to make these observations with accuracy and despatch.

Meridian.

40. If we suppose the circle Z H′ Z′ H Z (fig. 33) drawn through the zenith Z, and the nadir Z′ of the observer at *o*, and also through the celestial poles P and P′, this circle will represent the *meridian* or *noon circle* of the observer at *o*. This circle is so termed from the circumstance already stated (§ 33) that the observer has mid-day or noon when the sun enters it. At this moment the sun reaches his highest or culminating point; and when a star, or when several stars (for many stars may be supposed on the arc H A Z P), appear on the meridian, we name this their point of culmination.

In the diagram (fig. 33) the meridian is the only one of the celestial circles which lies in the plane of the paper, while the horizon, the equinoctial, and the vertical circles are to be imagined as projecting from this plane, which position is not easily represented. The plane of the meridian cuts the horizon of the observer at right angles in the line H H′, which has been already described (§ 32) as the *meridional line*. And as the polar altitude and the horizon are different for every place on the earth's surface, so every place has its own special meridian.

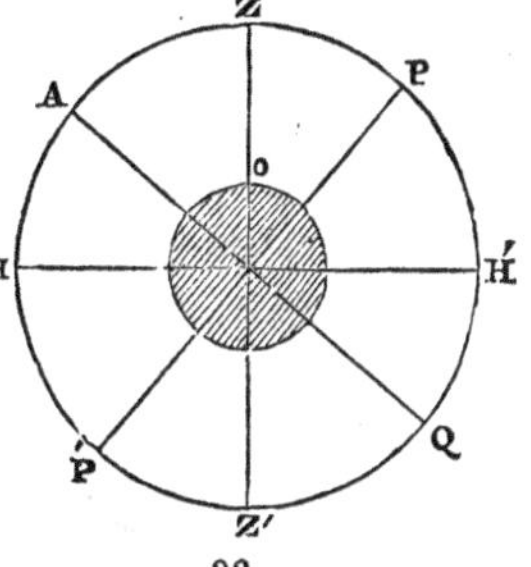

33.

If, for instance, the observer at *o*, while contemplating the aspect of the nocturnal starry firmament, turns his back to the pole-star P, and looks exactly towards the south point H, he has thus placed himself in the direction of his own meridian. If in this position he observes a star which is on the meridian, this star by the rotation of the earth after some time will not remain on the meridian, but appear as proceeding towards the West, while others have entered the meridian. If the time of transit of a star through the meridian has been noted by the observer, he will find it on the meridian again exactly 24 hours afterwards.

On an artificial celestial globe the meridian is represented by a brass ring, in which the globe is moveable.

It is difficult to determine exactly by the eye the precise place of the meridian in the heavens. For more accurate observations a telescope is employed which is moveable around its small axis, so carefully adjusted that its longitudinal axis lies in the direction of the celestial meridian. Through this instrument the stars can be seen only during their transit through the meridian, and hence an instrument of this kind is called a meridian telescope or transit instrument.

41. All the lines and points hitherto named give the station of a star only

for a definite place on the earth's surface. For the determination of a star's precise position in the heavens, other lines are drawn which always preserve the same place relative to the same star.

The equator is such a line. This indicates first of all whether a star is on the northern or southern hemisphere. Through the equator, commencing at the vernal equinox O, 180 circles are drawn which divide it into 360°. The distance of any such circle from the point O, is called the *right ascension* of a star which has its place in that circle. For example, the arc O D of 30°, and O D′ of 60°, are the right ascensions of the stars S and S′.

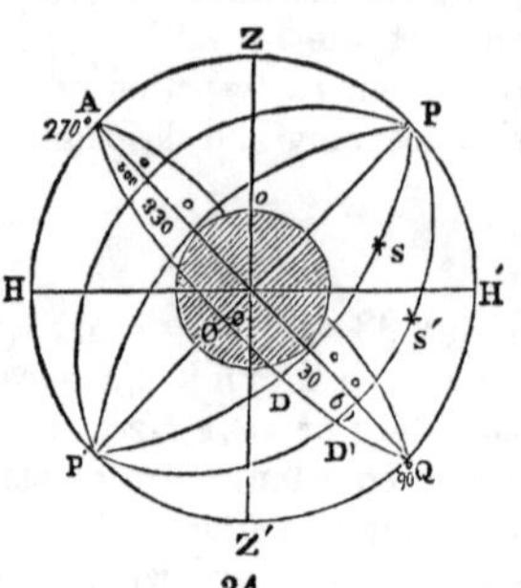

34.

The distance of a star from the equator is called its *declination*, which is either North or South. The arcs D S and D′ S′ express the northern declination of the stars S S′. Hence all those circles drawn through the equator, viz., P D P′ and P D′ P′ are called *circles of declination.*

It may hence be observed, that the right ascension and declination of a star being known, its position on the celestial globe is readily found in the same manner as places are found on the terrestrial globe by the longitude and latitude.

Celestial Globe.

42. We have in the preceding section named and described such a considerable number of points and lines, that it appears desirable to give a connected

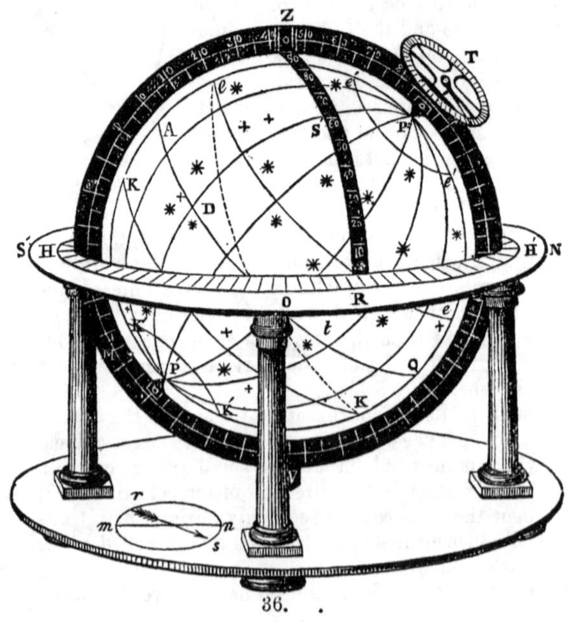

36.

view of them. It is always difficult, and, in some cases, impossible, to represent those points and lines on the heavens, without some such aid as that which is afforded by a celestial globe. This may be obtained at every mapseller's from 4 to 36 inches in diameter, and at prices varying, according to the size and construction, from 5*s.* upwards; and though the larger are preferable, a very clear apprehension of astronomical phenomena may be acquired from the smaller-sized globes.

The best construction of a celestial globe would be that of a smaller ball which represents the earth, surrounded by a larger hemisphere representing the concave vault of heaven on which the stars and their courses might be described. Such a mechanical contrivance being impracticable, the student is to remember that his position is supposed to be in the interior of the globe upon a small terrestrial globe.

43. Points and Lines on the Celestial Globe.

Z Zenith of the Observer (§ 27).
P North Pole (§ 31).
P′ South Pole.
S′ South (§ 32).
N North.
O East.
(West, being opposite, is invisible.)
e e Northern Tropic of Cancer (§ 34).
K K Southern Tropic of Capricorn.
e′ e′ Northern Arctic Circle.
h′ k′ Southern Arctic Circle.
M Meridian of the Observer (§ 40).
T Horary Circle (§ 152).
P H′ Polar Altitude of the Observer (§ 38).
A H Equatorial Altitude of the Observer (§ 38).
P P′ Celestial Axis (§ 31).
A Q Equinoctial (§ 31).
H H′ Horizon (§ 29.)
e K Ecliptic (§ 34).
S Star.
S R Height of the Star (§ 39).
S Z Zenith distance of the same (§ 39.)
R H Azimuth of the same (§ 39).
S D North declination of the same (§ 41).
D A Right ascension of the same.
S P Polar distance of the same.

The celestial globe rests in the first place by two pivots fixed to its poles, P P′, in a brass ring, M, which represents the *meridian* of the observer, and which is about half a line distant from the surface of the globe, leaving it just sufficient space for free motion round its axis.

The meridian rests in suitable notches in a horizontal frame H H′ and in the support V which allow the globe as required to be placed in different positions relative to the horizon. The horizontal ring represents the true *horizon* of the observer.

From the point A of the *equinoctial* A Q, the meridian is divided both in the direction of the north and of the south pole, into 90°. The *declination* of a certain star is found on the meridian by bringing it under the meridian. In like manner the meridian is employed to place the globe in the polar altitude of the observer.

The *horizon* is divided from the southern point S′, into 360°; and on this the azimuth of a star is read off.

At the point Z of the meridian, which corresponds to the zenith of the observer, a brass quadrant Z R can be screwed, which rises from the horizon, and is divided into 90°: from this the altitude and zenith distance of a star is read off.

Above all things the globe must be placed in a position corresponding to the situation of the observer upon the earth; that is, the meridian of the globe H H′, must be in the meridional line of the observer, and the pola-

altitude P H′ must also correspond to that of the observer. The latter is very simple, for example, an inhabitant at the equator, the polar altitude of which is = 0° (§ 37), rectifies the globe, so that both the poles, P P′, lie in the plane of the equator. In the neighborhood of London the globe is to be placed or rectified, so that the arc P H′, the height of the pole above the horizon, may be 51° 30′.

We determine the meridional line of the observer by the compass which for this purpose is appended to every large globe. For example, we draw on the base or pedestal of the globe the line *m n* parallel with the meridian H H′ of the globe, and place on this line, so drawn, the magnetic needle *r s*, the point of which assumes a northerly direction. We then turn the pedestal of the globe till the line *m n* coincides with the needle. It has been, however, shown in our Physical section (§ 197), that the direction of the needle is not exactly north, but varies somewhat from it. We correct this variation of the needle by turning the pedestal till the needle makes an angle with the line *m n* of 18°, which is the amount of the westerly variation of the needle; and consequently the line *m n* is now exactly in a northerly direction, and is parallel with the meridian H H′.

44. Another contrivance appended to the globe is the *horary circle* T (fig. 35), which is divided into 24 equal parts or hours, corresponding to the 24 hours of day and night. The horary circle is immoveable, but through its centre passes a prolongation of the axis of the globe to which an index is fastened, and which passes over a space on the ring as soon as the globe is turned round. If the globe makes a complete rotation, and therefore the 360 degrees of the equator pass under the meridian, the index also describes the whole circle of 24 hours, consequently the globe makes, for every hour which the index traverses, a rotation of 15 degrees. The index, however, is not of the same piece as the axis, but can be turned round it by means of a screw or other suitable contrivance in such a manner that the hand can be pointed to any number of the horary circle without at the same time turning the globe. The importance of the horary circle for the use of the globe will immediately become evident by its application.

After the globe is put in a correct position in relation to the polar altitude and cardinal points, it must be placed in a situation corresponding to the time of observation in reference to the stars which are then visible. This will be rendered clear by the following observations:—Every day at 12 o'clock the sun stands in the meridian of the observer (see § 40), hence we first bring that point of the globe under the brass meridian on which the sun stands at 12 o'clock at noon. This point is of course situated on the ecliptic, and in the beginning of spring on the 21st of March at the point whence the ecliptic intersects the equator, from which point the latter is divided into 360 degrees. On every following day the sun travels almost exactly one degree farther, as, for example, after the lapse of 204 days, that is in the middle of October, the straight *ascension* of the sun (§ 41), that is its distance from the vernal point, amounts to 204 degrees. If, therefore, we bring this degree of the equator under the meridian, the position at which the latter intersects the ecliptic is the position of the sun at mid-day.

The hand of the horary circle is now placed upon the one number 12, and the globe turned round till the hand points to the other number 12, making thus half a revolution. All the constellations on the globe have now the position which the stars occupy at midnight at the place of the observer. For example, we thus find that at this hour, the constellation of *Cassiopeia* is in the meridian. If we afterwards turn the globe to the right or left, the hand can be brought upon every hour desired before or after midnight, in which case the stars then visible present themselves on the globe.

Numerous problems which suggest themselves to the student, or which are found in the small treatises sold by the map-sellers, may be solved by the aid of the celestial globe.

In the commencement there is some little difficulty to transfer the picture of the heavens to the globe and *vice versâ*. The student must suppose himself to be in the centre of the globe, and from thence imagine straight lines drawn through the stars which are represented on the globe, and prolonged to the heavens where they will reach the corresponding stars.

It is best for the student to commence his observations in the twilight of evening or on moonlight nights, because then the larger and more conspicuous stars only are visible, so that he is not confused by the large number of stars which are visible on dark nights. When the larger stars are known, the smaller are easily found.

(C.) CLASSIFICATION OF THE HEAVENLY BODIES.

45. Of all the celestial bodies, the *sun*, this brilliant star of day, and the *moon*, distinguished by the changeableness of her form, merit our special consideration.

These two celestial bodies, by their apparent magnitude, present themselves amongst the other stars as universal lords, an idea which, however long it may have prevailed, has been materially injured by the observations of astronomy.

Also, amongst the stars themselves, we find by accurate observation many differences. We perceive that by far the greater number of the stars appear to us always to occupy the same points of the firmament, when we observe them at the same stated times; and it is on this account that they have received the name of *fixed stars.*

Some stars change their positions in the heavens so remarkably, that at definite periods they occupy certain particular positions, being sometimes to be seen in one, sometimes in another quarter of the heavens: these were hence named wandering stars, or *planets.* The number of these stars or planets at present known is only upwards of thirty.

Finally, the *comets* are still more remarkable, both by their being accompanied by a more or less extended luminous appendage, which follows the star like a tail, and by the changes of position, which are still more considerable than those of the planets, since some comets often suddenly appear and again disappear, and others only present themselves again after the lapse of a great many years.

We shall commence with a description of the fixed stars, these being most important for the geography of the heavens. We will afterwards explain the relation of the earth to the sun and moon as being of particular importance regarding time and climate, and, finally, through the study of the planets and comets pass to a more general consideration of the arrangement of the universe.

Fixed Stars.

46. By successive and repeated observations of the fixed stars, with the asssistance of the globe and star charts, we readily acquire a facility in finding their places in the firmament. We observe, furthermore, that these bodies, otherwise a maze of complicity, are grouped or arranged in a very definite manner, with which we gradually become so familiar, that the least change of the heavenly bodies cannot escape us.

When the sun disappears below the horizon, the stars appear as so many sparkling points, dispersed here and there, through the spacious firmament, during the continuance of twilight. Their number is increased with the increasing darkness; and, by the assistance of a telescope, myriads are observable in the immense incomprehensible regions of space. Places which to the unassisted eye appear only like nebulous spots or streaks, by the armed eye are distinctly recognised as groups of countless stars; and the *Milky Way*, as it is termed, is found to be composed of countless millions of such bodies.

The apparent magnitude of the stars is very different. Whilst some glisten and shine with a lustre which far surpasses others, some can scarcely be recognised as luminous points. By their apparent magnitudes, as visible to the unassisted eye, the stars are divided into six classes. There are 18 stars of the first magnitude, 60 of the second, 200 of the third, 380 of the fourth, and with the two following classes, in all about 5,000; of telescopic stars about 70,000 have been observed; and from reasons which cannot be here stated, the probable number of stars in the universe is estimated at 500,000 millions.

The fixed stars appear, even through the most powerful telescopes, invariably as small luminous points: hence we may judge of their enormous distances. This is confirmed by another circumstance, viz., that two stars of proximate mutual distance always appear to us equally distant from whatever part of the earth's orbit they may be observed. Although the most distant points of the earth's orbit are 195 millions of miles asunder, it is possible to ascertain, with certainty, the parallax of only a few of the fixed stars; that is, the angle of vision under which the semi-diameter of the earth's orbit $= 97\frac{1}{2}$ millions of miles, would appear to an eye placed on one of the fixed stars. The merit of the greatest exactness in determining the parallax of the fixed stars is awarded to the observations of the renowned astronomer, Bessel,* of Königsburg, who succeeded in ascertaining the parallax of No. 61 in the constellation of the Swan; which is found to be 0·3136 second. By this parallax the sun's mean distance from this star, 61 of the Swan, is calculated to be nearly 62,672,712 millions of miles. Light, which moves at the rate of 195,000 miles in a second, would require $10\frac{3}{10}$ years to pass through this space; and a locomotive steam-engine, which travels at

* *Bessel*, the Professor of Astronomy at Königsburg, was born at Minden in 1784, and died in 1846. To great natural powers of observation he united the rare and profound knowledge of theoretical mathematics, which he applied, in a way hitherto unknown, to the reduction of errors in the results of observations, surpassing in accuracy all that had been accomplished before his time. In this respect he will be regarded as an example to the astronomers of all subsequent ages.

the rate of 920 miles per day, would be 200 millions of years in reaching this star.

A stellar parallax, greater than a second, has not yet been accurately determined. Hence it is a well-founded assumption that the nearest of the fixed stars is 200,000 times farther from the earth than the sun; consequently, about 19 billions of miles is the assumed distance of the nearest fixed star from the earth.

To conceive such a stellar distance surpasses the utmost range of human imagination, and to form any adequate conception of this enormous extent of space is utterly impossible; but we may approximate to a somewhat clear apprehension by comparison. Light, as above stated, moves with the celerity of 195,000 miles in a second; yet three years, at least, would elapse ere light from the nearest of the fixed stars could reach the earth.

This is by no means the utmost extent of the distances of bodies in celestial space. On the contrary, it has been assumed, with feasibility, that stars have been observed, the distances of which amount to 1½ million times that of the sun, and the light from which would be many years in reaching our earth.

It may naturally be assumed that bodies, which are visible at such inconceivable distances, are also of enormously great magnitude; and we are justified in assuming that none of the fixed stars are in this respect inferior to the sun, and that most of them surpass him in magnitude.

Stars visible in Europe.

47. Even in the earliest ages stars that appeared to be in close proximity were grouped together, and by the aid of a lively fancy their outline was supposed to resemble certain well-known objects. Hence originated the names of the constellations. The seven stars of the Great Bear were sometimes called Charles's Wain, the Plough of the North, &c. In most of the constellations, however, a wide field is left to the imagination, for it is seldom that we are enabled to discover any relation between the outlines of the groups and their names.

48. The eye directed towards the heavens does not at every place and at all times perceive the same stars; but, on the contrary, essential differences in the appearance of the heavens are observed according to the point of the earth and to the season and hour at which the observation is made. An observer at the north pole has in his zenith the *pole-star*, and he sees from there the whole northern hemisphere, and consequently all its stars. An inhabitant at the equator sees half the northern and half the southern hemispheres of the heavens, and the pole-star appears to him in the horizon.

The greater number of Europeans dwell between the 40th and 70th degrees of north latitude, and to them all the stars of the northern and more or less of the stars of the southern hemisphere are visible according as they are more or less distant from the equator.

Under all circumstances, we never perceive at the same time more than half of the starry heavens; but it is easy to imagine that, after a time, we see a greater number of stars, in consequence of the rotation of the earth, since there are continually stars setting in the west and others rising in the east.

49. We will now pass to the consideration of the constellations, and it is best to commence with those which are near the pole-star, and which are visible every evening and during the whole night, since they never set.

It is most convenient to proceed from the *Great Bear*, because this is the most remarkable group of stars, which every one is acquainted with, even those who are not engaged in the study of astronomy. It consists of seven stars, six of which are of the second magnitude; four of them form a square, the other three stand in an arc in the tail of the Bear. If we imagine a line drawn through the two latter stars of the Bear, its prolongation will reach a star of the second magnitude standing alone, and which is the pole-star belonging to the Little Bear. The importance of this star has already been several times mentioned; as it is only $1\frac{2}{3}$ degree distant from the pole, it may be regarded as the point around which the whole hemisphere of the heavens turns.

One of the most extensive constellations is the *Dragon*, which winds itself around the Bear, and is formed of many stars of the third and fourth magnitude, which define nearly half the polar circle. Opposite to the Great Bear, on the other side of the pole, we perceive five stars of the second and third magnitude, forming a W. This constellation, half of which is in the Milky Way, is called *Cassiopeia*. If we unite this group of stars with the Great Bear by a line, and draw through the middle of this another line at right angles, we see on the right hand of this line *Capella*, a star of the first magnitude, in the constellation of the *Waggoner*, and on the left hand *Weger* of *Lyra*, which is also of the first magnitude.

Of the other groups worthy of mention situated within the Tropic of Cancer we may mention *Bootes*, in which is *Arcturus*, shining as a star of the first magnitude, and to which a straight line drawn through the two lower stars of the Great Bear leads. Near to Cassiopeia is *Perseus*, with a star of the second magnitude, standing on a brilliant part of the Milky Way. From this we readily find the three bright stars of *Andromeda*, as well as *Perseus*, recognisable by four stars of the second magnitude, forming a square.

Constellations of the Ecliptic.

50. We now come to a portion of the heavens which is bounded by the two tropics, and which is of especial interest, since within these limits we find the constellations of the ecliptic.

Of all the celestial zones, or circles, the ecliptic is the only one which we find distinguished in the firmament by a series of constellations. The ecliptic has been divided into twelve equal divisions by twelve constellations, or signs, supposed to be equally distant; and each constellation contains 30°, the circle being divided, as usual, into 360°. As we shall subsequently have to consider the important relations of these constellations to ourselves, we shall, for the present, only give their names and characteristic signs Since the equator cuts the ecliptic in two points, one of these two sections is on the north and the other on the south hemisphere of heaven. Hence we divide the constellations of the ecliptic, or signs of the zodiac, as they are commonly called, into the northern and southern constellations, and supply their names and ancient marks, or signs, as under.

I. Northern Constellations of the Zodiac.			II. Southern Constellations of the Zodiac.		
1. The Ram	♈	Aries.	7. The Balance	♎	Libra.
2. The Bull	♉	Taurus.	8. The Scorpion	♏	Scorpio.
3. The Twins	♊	Gemini.	9. The Archer	♐	Sagittarius.
4. The Crab	♋	Cancer.	10. The Goat	♑	Capricornus.
5. The Lion	♌	Leo.	11. The Water-bearer	♒	Aquarius.
6. The Virgin	♍	Virgo.	12. The Fishes	♓	Pisces.

As an illustration of the position of the ecliptic in the heavens, we refer to the diagram of the celestial globe.

We commence with the northern constellations of the ecliptic at the vernal equinox, viz., where the ecliptic cuts the equator, and the first is the *Ram*, known by the three large stars in the head; the brightest is of the second magnitude. Next follows the *Bull*, under Perseus and the Waggoner (Auriga), easily known by the V, which is formed by a group of four stars in the Bull's head, and called the *Hyades*, or rainy stars. The star of the first magnitude at the upper end of the V, to the left, is *Aldebaran*. On the back of the Bull are seen the Pleiades, a group of small stars, very close together.

In the *Twins* the ecliptic reaches its greatest northern altitude. We perceive two bright stars of the second magnitude, *Castor* and *Pollux*, in the head of the constellation, and four stars of the third magnitude at the feet forming together an oblong.

This region of the heavens is distinguished by remarkable brilliancy, owing to the proximity of several constellations, amongst which we notice *Orion*, the most beautiful of all the stars, which is placed on the southern side beneath the Bull and the Twins. Two stars of the first magnitude especially attract our notice, these are *Betelgeuze* on the east shoulder, and *Rigel* on the west foot. Between these stars three others of the second magnitude, standing together, form the girdle of *Orion*, which is also termed *Jacob's Staff*. Near to the girdle we notice the remarkable spot of Orion. *Betelgeuze* forms with two other stars of the first magnitude a regular triangle, namely, with *Procyon* of the *Little Dog*, and with *Sirius*, the most lustrous of stars, standing at the head of the Great Dog, and hence it is also called the *Dog-star*. This constellation can be seen during the dog-days (from July to August) rising and setting with the sun, which at this season of the year has reached its greatest height, and therefore diffuses the greatest heat.

The direction of the ecliptic is now through the invisible constellation of the *Crab*, composed of faintly-glimmering stars, to the *Lion*, distinguished by four principal stars forming a large trapezium : : (figure of four sides), of which *Regulus*, the chief ornament of this constellation, is a star of the first magnitude. Next succeeds the *Virgin*, conspicuous for five stars, forming an anchor with rectangular flukes, and also for the star of the first magnitude called the ear of corn of the Virgin (Spica Virginis).

Here the ecliptic is again cut by the equator, and we now descend to the southern constellations, where we first meet with the *Balance*, with four stars, which form a pretty regular square.

In the *Scorpion*, Antares appears as a star of the first magnitude, which the *Archer* follows, visible only in the lower part of the southern horizon: it is easily recognized by four stars, forming a rectangular figure. The ecliptic here has reached its most southern declination, and recommences its ascending course to the equator, meeting first the constellation of the *Goat* under the *Eagle*, distinguished by *Atair*, a star of the first magnitude, and the *Water-bearer*, easily known by two stars on his shoulders, and three at some distance to the south-east of the former.

The *Fishes* conclude the orbitual path of the sun round the vault of heaven. This sign contains no remarkable star, and its position is most easily determined by Pegasus, below which it is situated. But between the water-bearer and the fishes, and lower in the south, is Fomalhaut, a star of the first magnitude in the constellation of the southern fishes.

III. SPECIAL ASTRONOMICAL PHENOMENA.

Sun and Earth.

50. Suppose on the two ends of a rod there be fixed two balls, a and b, fig. 36, and the ball a to be three times the magnitude of the ball b; the centre of gravitation must be, consequently, nearer the greater magnitude: and from Physical section, (§ 47), we know that if we divide the distance between the centres of the two balls into four equal parts, the common centre of gravitation lies at one-quarter of the distance, namely at c. Then if we multiply the distance 3 by the mass $b = 1$, we have 3; and if we again multiply the mass 3 by the distance 1, we have the same result; and hence the two bodies, if supported at c, will be equilibrium. If we suppose these two bodies in motion round the centre of gravitation, we see in the dotted lines the orbits described by both balls, and also that the smaller mass, b, describes a circle round the larger mass a.

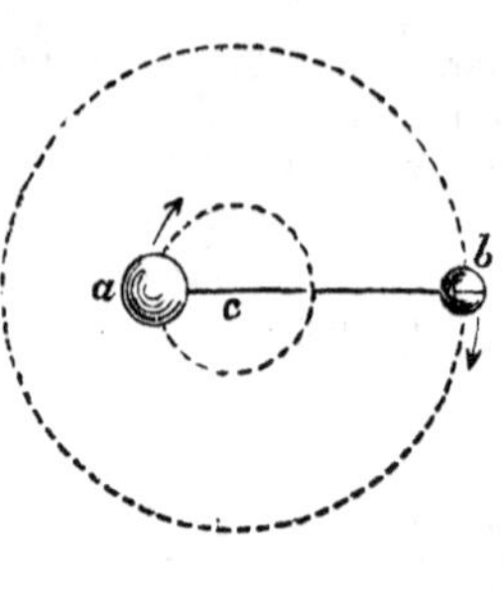

36.

If we throw into the atmosphere two unequal masses similarly connected, we shall find that they assume a rotatory motion around their common centre of gravitation, and the smaller mass constantly describes an orbit around the larger.

If, in the example fig. 36, the mass of the ball a were ten times or a hundred times the mass of b, the common centre of gravitation would fall within the greater ball; and we should find that this ball would describe a circle round a point in the interior of itself, whilst the smaller ball would describe a circle round the greater.

52. The sun and the earth are two bodies or masses of a spherical shape, and have similar relations to each other as the two masses, fig. 36, only their difference is much greater, as the following table shows:—

TABLE of the RELATIVE MAGNITUDES of the SUN and EARTH.

	Earth.	Sun.	Ratio of the Earth to the Sun.	
Diameter .... Miles	7,926	887,580	1	112
Surface .... Square Miles	197,336,595	2,296,080,000,000	1	12,577
Contents .... Cubic Miles	260,692,177,925	399,815,355,000,000	1	1,410,000
Mean Distance { Miles	95,447,700	......		
Mean Distance { Radii of the Earth	24,000	......		

If we imagine these two bodies to be connected by any means whatever, their common centre of gravitation would fall within the body of the sun, and in truth very near to its centre. If these were slung into the immensity of space, they would describe revolutions like the balls in the above example, the sun about his own axis, and the earth in an crbit round the sun.

This is actually the case, although the sun and earth are not connected by any material bond, like the bodies in the example, but by a peculiar combination of forces.

The force which maintains the connection of the sun and the earth, is the mutual attraction which affects all bodies, and which we have already, in Physics, explained as the force of gravitation.

That the sun and earth preserve their respective distances, and do not progressively approach each other till a collision takes place, is owing to the operation of a second force, which acts at right angles to the gravitating tendency, and produces the compound motion of the earth. (Comp. Phys., § 52.)

53. The enormous mass of the body of the sun is not without motion. We perceive this by means of certain dark places on the luminous surface of the sun, and which we call *spots* on the sun's disc. These do not always appear in the same places. For it has been observed that they traverse the sun's disc from the one margin to the other, where they finally disappear; thus passing over the opposite surface of the sun, they emerge again, after some time, on the same part of his margin, where they first appeared. This phenomenon proves that the sun revolves on its axis; and the time elapsing during one rotation, is twenty-five days and a half, while the earth's rotation is completed in one day.

It is a difficult matter to explain the cause of the dazzling brightness and of the reanimating heat which proceed from the sun. The assumption that the sun is a burning body, in a chemical sense, is untenable. Every body constantly emitting light and heat by combustion is liable to a continual decrease; and this must have happened to the sun in a sensible degree, notwithstanding the prodigious immensity of its bulk. But, on the contrary, the sun appears to be the source of an unvarying amount of light and heat.

It is the opinion of most philosophers that the sun is a dark body, surrounded by a peculiar atmosphere, which is kept in a state of continual vibration by the enormous velocity of the sun's revolution, and thus becomes evident to us as light and warmth. Sometimes there are to be seen breaks, originating in unknown causes, in the sun's atmosphere, and through these breaks or chasms, which we call spots, we can see the dark body of the sun.

That friction can be a source of light and heat, some well-known phenomena testify. Let, for example, a piston which tightly fits a cylindrical tube, be pressed down the tube rapidly and forcibly, both light and heat will be gene rated at the same time, and the last in sufficient quantity to kindle tinder, if attached to the end of the piston. This apparatus is called a *pneumatic tinder-box.* We also find that when mercury is shaken in an exhausted glass tube, it produces a vivid light; and from these facts it may be concluded, that it is possible that light and heat may be produced without adopting an assumption contradicted by all our experience of terrestrial bodies.

54. The path in which the earth moves, in its course round the sun, is an *ellipse* (§ 13) of very small eccentricity, approaching almost to a circle. The long axis, or line of the *apsides*, is 189,051,000 of miles. In one of the foci is the sun, and the earth reaches its greatest distance from this luminary, when it is at the one end of the axis of the ecliptic, where the distance is 96,969,583 miles, which is on the 2nd of July. This point is the sun's greatest distance, or as it is called, *aphelion.* On the opposite point of the great axis of the ecliptic, the earth reaches the point nearest to the sun, or its *perihelion*, on the 1st January, when it is 93,763,878 miles distant from the sun. By taking the half sum of the greater and less distance of the earth from the sun, we ascertain the mean distance of these two bodies to be 95,447,700 miles.

The earth's orbit may in most cases be considered circular without occasioning any sensible error. Its semi-diameter would hence be 94,200,000, and its circumference about 585,597,000 miles; and this space is traversed by the earth in 365 days and a few hours: consequently the earth traverses a space of eighteen miles and a half in a second. Hence, the velocity of the earth's orbitual motion is much greater than the velocity of its diurnal motion, which at a point in the equator, is only at the rate of about 1,430 feet in a second. If we could travel with a velocity equal to that of the earth's orbitual motion, we might accomplish a journey round the earth of 24,849 miles in twenty-two minutes and a half.

This assigned velocity is only the *mean* of the earth's actual velocity. The elliptic figure of its orbit has an essential influence in modifying it, either retarding or accelerating: the celerity is augmented when the earth is approaching its perihelion, and is retarded while drawing towards its aphelion. From this circumstance, as will be hereafter shown, there is a difference between the duration of the summer and winter half-years, the former being seven days and three-quarters longer than the latter.

Position of the Earth's axis to the plane of the Earth's orbit.

55. We suppose a plane passing through the centre of the sun, and extended on all sides, having the earth moving within it. This may be represented by a round piece of pasteboard having a circular and central hole into which a small ball may be half inserted. This ball or globe represents the sun; the flat pasteboard represents the plane of the earth's orbit, which can be described on the paper by a circle having the sun for its centre. The earth itself may also be represented by a smaller ball inserted in a similar circular hole, or into several made in different parts of its orbit.

It is very difficult, in some cases impossible, to illustrate satisfactorily the phenomena, to be described in the following paragraphs, by means of diagrams alone.

These are only calculated to represent objects that are adequately illustrated on a flat surface; but many of the phenomena of motion can only be explained by a model which cannot be conveniently represented by a diagram.

If we describe on a small ball, which represents the earth, the usual circles, viz., the equator, the tropical, and the polar circles, together with the poles themselves, it is easy to perceive that we can give to this ball very different positions to the plane of the earth's orbit. We may place it so that both poles, and consequently the earth's axis, may be in the plane of its orbit; or it may be placed with its axis perpendicular to the plane; and, finally, it may be made to assume an oblique position to it, so that its axis may make an acute angle with the plane of the orbit.

It is now to be shown that these three different positions produce most important changes upon the phenomena observable on the earth's surface. The comprehension is much aided by placing a light to represent the sun on the centre of a round table. On the margin of the table, at an equal height with the flame, we place a small globe, whose axis may be made to assume any one of the three above-mentioned positions. Instead of a globe, a little wooden ball may be used, moveable about a knitting needle, which serves for its axis. The needle may be elevated to the same height as the candle, by being stuck into a cork in a bottle, and it may be either perpendicular to, or parallel with, or inclined to the plane of the table. The requisite parallel circles and the equator are described on the ball. Finally, the circumference of the table is divided into four equal portions by two lines intersecting each other at right angles in the centre. With the aid of this simple arrangement, the following statements will be more easily and clearly comprehended than they could be by any diagrams whatever.

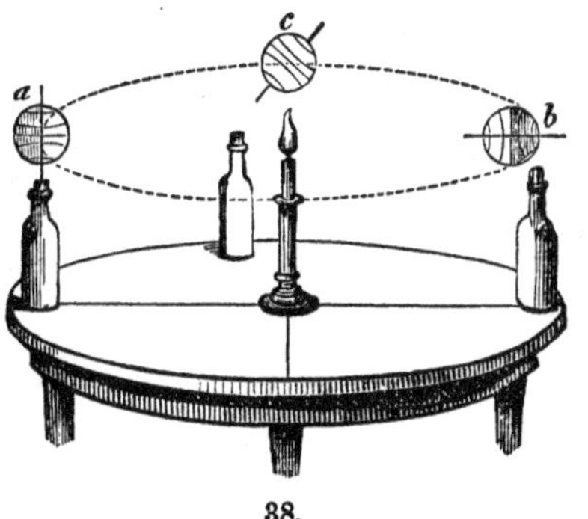

38.

56. In the first place we assume that the earth's axis is perpendicular to the plane of its orbit, as in *a*, fig. 38.

In this condition, every portion of the earth during the whole year, would have the duration of the days and nights equal. The sun's rays falling thus perpendicularly on the equator, would burn up the regions situated near it, and render them uninhabitable. The countries situated between the circles somewhat more distant from the equator would be more fortunate, since in consequence of the oblique direction of the sun's rays they would enjoy the temperature of a mild spring, which would be continuous during the whole year. But the inhabitants of those countries would be deprived of the charms of the successive changes of season which we enjoy. Many plants could not reach their full development under these circumstances. But the condition of the regions at a considerable distance from the equator, or near the poles, would be very dismal. Partly on account of the obliquity of the sun's rays, and partly through their interception, an eternal winter and continual desolation would be prevalent in countries where millions of human beings now lead comfortable and happy lives. If, therefore, the earth's axis were placed perpendicularly to its orbit, the greater portion of its surface would be an uninhabitable desert.

Still more conspicuous phenomena would be produced, if the axis of the earth, as in *b*, fig. 38, were parallel to its orbit, so that its poles continually remain in the same direction. In this case the entire northern hemisphere would be enlightened once a year; the light would fall perpendicularly upon the north pole, and the day would be 24 hours long. On the opposite side, at *a*, the southern hemisphere would be enlightened and heated in a similar way; and a sharp alternation of heat and cold would be the result, unmitigated by the gradations which are actually experienced. This would render the earth a far more incommodious habitation than it would be under the former supposition.

It is well known that our earth neither has that uniformity of light and heat which would be occasioned by the perpendicularity of its axis, nor that abrupt change which would be the consequence of its parallel position to the plane of its orbit; hence, its inclination to its orbit must be an acute angle. (Comp. *c*, fig. 38.)

This is really the case, and hereby we are in a condition to explain a series of phenomena which are as important as they are well known.

57. Let us now consider the earth in its four principal positions relatively to the sun. In fig. 39, S is the sun, T the earth, the axis of which, *s* N, in all the representations remains parallel. It is evident, that only that portion of the earth which is opposite to the sun can receive the benefit of his light and warmth: the shaded portions represent the dark sides, and the unshaded the *enlightened halves* of the globe in these positions. T represents the position of the earth on the 21st of March, when the sun's rays fall perpendicularly on the equator. In this case the circle of illumination passes through both the poles *s* and N, consequently there is day both on half the northern and half of the southern hemispheres at the same time; and as the earth turns on its axis *s* N, every part of its surface describes one-half of its daily rotation by day, and the other half by night. While the earth is in this portion of her orbit, the day and night are equal all over the earth, and hence its name *vernal equinox* (spring equal night). The same phenomenon appears at the *autumnal equinox*, represented by T″, where the diagram represents the unenlightened, or night appearance of the earth.

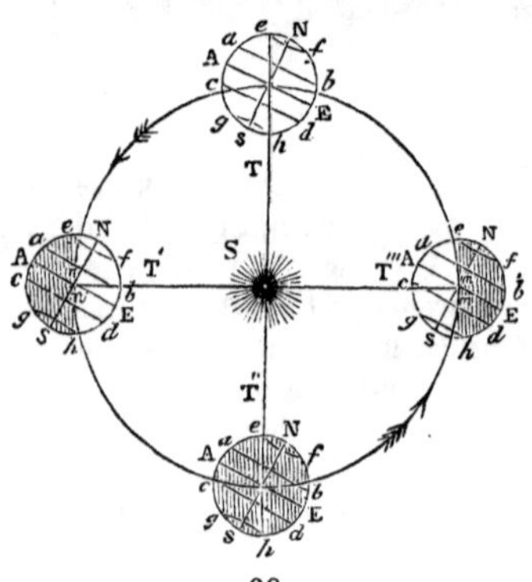

39.

When the earth in her course has traversed the next quadrant of her orbit, on the 21st of June she enters the *summer solstice*, T′. We perceive that the north pole, N, and a considerable part of the earth's surface contiguous to it, remains enlightened during the entire daily rotation of the earth round its axis. Within the north polar circle, *e f*, at the latitude of $66\frac{1}{2}°$, or $23\frac{1}{2}°$ from the pole, the sun shines for 24 hours, and the nearer the pole the longer is the duration of sunshine. The portion lying in a higher latitude than $66\frac{1}{2}°$ is named the northern polar, or arctic, or frigid zone.

The reverse of all this occurs at the southern polar zone, *g h*, where, on the same day, the sun is not visible, but the night lasts for 24 hours.

On the equator the duration of both day and night is equal; for the illuminated portion *n* E, of this circle is equal to the darkened portion *n* A. On every point north of the equator the day will be longer than the night, since the illuminated portion *m b*, of the parallel circle *a b*, is evidently greater than the unenlightened portion *m a*; consequently, an inhabitant of this region will be longer in the illuminated than in the darkened part during the earth's diurnal rotation. All who live on the northern side of the equator have, on the 21st of June, their longest day and their shortest night.

That phenomena, in direct contrast to the above, should occur on the southern side of the equator, may be easily conceived.

The parallel circle, *a b*, on which the sun's rays fall perpendicularly on the 21st of June, is called the *tropic of Cancer*. Whilst the earth continues its orbitual course, the length of the days gradually decreases; and when, on the 23d of September, she enters the *autumnal equinox*, T'', day and night are again equal. From this point by farther progression, the day is continually shortened, till, on the 21st of December, the earth has reached the *winter solstice*, T''', where the sun is perpendicular to the *tropic of Capricorn*, *c d*. Here the diurnal arcs *m a* are evidently shorter than the nocturnal arcs *m b*, to all the inhabitants of the northern hemisphere. We have at this season our shortest days and longest nights; and our antipodes in the southern hemisphere enjoy their longest days.

TABLE of POLAR ALTITUDE and DURATION of SOLAR ALTITUDE.

Polar Altitude.	Duration of the Longest Day.
0° 0′	12 hours.
16 44	13 ,,
30 48	14 ,,
49 22	16 ,,
63 23	20 ,,
66 32	24 ,,
67 23	1 month.
73 39	3 months.
90 0	6 ,,

From the winter solstice to the vernal equinox, the day constantly increases and the night decreases; until at the latter point they are again equal.

Thus we see that, on this obliquity of the earth's axis to the plane of its orbit, the *apparent* annual course of the sun, its passage across the equator twice a year, and progress to the tropics, described in § 34, can be explained.

The greatest altitude and declination of the sun is indicated by the tropical circles, which are $23\frac{1}{2}°$ north and south of the equator; because in these points the farther progress of the sun is arrested, and his subsequent progress is backwards to the equator.

58. To the inhabitants of the regions of the earth lying on each side of the equator, and within the tropics, called the tropical or torrid zone, the sun during the whole year is either perpendicular, or almost perpendicular. Hence

they have greater heat and less diversity of season than the inhabitants of other portions of the globe. Plants and animals, even man himself, under the united effects of light and heat, assume peculiar forms and qualities.

Between the tropics and polar circles, on both sides of the equator, are situated the two *temperate zones*. In these regions the sun's rays never fall perpendicularly on the earth; and some portion of their calorific power is not absorbed, but reflected, and the temperaturee never reaches the maximum.

The entire surface of the torrid zone is estimated at 68½ millions of square miles; the two temperate zones at 102 millions; and the two frigid zones at 17 millions of square miles.

In the course of the year, the effects of the sun upon our northern temperate zone *a b e f*, (fig. 39), are very dissimilar. During the summer solstice (at T′), the sun's rays meet the earth at a much less oblique angle than at the time of the winter solstice, when the sun is on the southern side of the equator, and when his rays fall so obliquely that a large portion of their calorific influence is intercepted and dissipated in the surrounding atmosphere. Besides this, there is the longer duration of the sun above our horizon, and consequently a greater absorption of heat by the surface of the ground. This is the cause of the great range of temperature experienced by us in the space of a year; hence the change of seasons, the transition from an ungenial season to the mild expansive influence of spring, followed by the ripening warmth of summer, when finally the autumn, with a decrease of both light and heat, opens the gate to icy winter.

What advantages, what attractions for mankind, are connected with this perpetual change of season! what an endless variety of charms to awake our attention and to excite our gratitude! The loveliness of flowery spring, the glowing splendour of summer, the exuberance of autumn, and the stern uniformity of winter, have been the subjects of painting and poetry from the earliest ages to the present day.

59. Were the earth's orbit actually a circle, as in fig. 39, the periods between the equinoxes and solstices would be exactly equal; and the summer half-year from the vernal to the autumnal equinox would be of the same duration as the winter half-year.

This, however, is not the case; and the reason is, that the earth's orbit is elliptical, and the sun's place is in one of its foci.

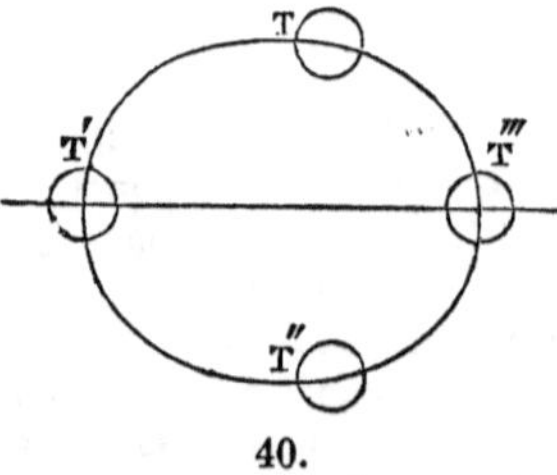

40.

If T and T″ (fig. 40) are the equinoctial points, the portion of the arc of the winter half-year, T T‴ T″, lying between the two, is smaller than that portion of the orbit of the summer half-year, T T′ T″; and besides this, the velocity of the earth, in the winter portion of her orbit, is greater than in the other portion, because the earth is then nearer to the sun. Both causes co-operate; and their united effect is, that the summer half-year is 186 days and 12 hours long, and the winter half-year consists of only 178 days and 18 hours; consequently, the former is longer than the latter by 7¾ days.

Though the perihelion falls in mid-winter, and we are then 3,205,705 miles nearer the sun than we are at the time of the summer solstice, this greater proximity has no effect on the temperature of the earth's surface, being modified by the greater obliquity of the sun's rays and the shortness of the days, as has already been shown.

60. Suppose we observe the setting of the sun, on any evening, and remark at the same time the position of a star or of a constellation near the place where the sun disappeared below the horizon, on the following evening we shall perceive the same star or constellation in the same position near which we perceive the sun set. If, however, this observation is repeated or continued for several days, we may perceive that the sun approaches nearer to the star; and subsequently the latter sets at the same time as the sun, and is not of course perceptible after sunset. The same observation with another star may be repeated in a similar manner. On the eastern part of the horizon, also, we find a similar phenomenon. A star as near as possible to the sun, and which rises only a short time before him, will, after several days, rise earlier and be at a greater distance because the sun has travelled from it. Thus, we may observe the perpetual progression of the sun among the fixed stars from the west to the east, and we can describe his path when we remark the constellations in the vicinity of which he appears or disappears.

These constellations compose a *girdle* or zone among the fixed stars, so named probably from ζώννυμι, *I girdle*, or from ζῶον, *a living creature*, because most of the constellations of the *Zodiac* bear the name of animals. The zodiac, or constellations of the ecliptic, is bounded by two parallel circles of from seven to eight degrees' distance from the ecliptic. When the sun appears in the neighbourhood of one of these constellations, we say that *he is in that constellation.* By twelve equally-distant constellations, the names and signs of which we have given in § 49, the ancients divided the zodiac into twelve equal portions. The sun passes from one constellation of the zodiac to another, a distance of 30°, in the space of from 28 to 31 days, which is called a *month.* After the sun has completed his course in the space of twelve months from one constellation to another, he appears again in the constellation where he was first observed; and this revolution completes the year. During every successive month the sun is in another constellation.

About 3,000 years since, when the zodiac was assumed, the sun at the vernal equinox was in the constellation of the Ram (Aries), and the succeeding months with their constellations were as follow:—

March	– Aries, the Ram.	September	– Libra, the Balance.
April	– – Taurus, the Bull.	October	– Scorpio, the Scorpion.
May	– – Gemini, the Twins.	November	– Sagittarius, the Archer
June	– – Cancer, the Crab.	December	– Capricornus, the Goat.
July	– – Leo, the Lion.	January	– Aquarius, the Waterbearer.
August	– Virgo, the Virgin.	February	– Pisces, the Fishes.

In consequence of a slow retrogression of the nodal point where the eliptic and the equinoctial cut each other (called the *precession* of the equinoxes), this relation between the sun's actual course and the constellations has been altered. The sun, for example, is not in Aries on the 21st of March, but in the constellation of Pisces; and also in the succeeding months the sun is in the constellation corresponding to the preceding sign. In order to avoid confusion, the ancient signs are still placed on celestial charts and globes; and a distinction is made between the *constellation* and its *sign* or mark

The latter are nothing but twelve marks, by which the ecliptic is divided; the former are the actual groups of stars. If, for example, the sun or a planet is said to be in the sign of the Crab (Cancer), we look on the globe or chart for the sign ♋, and find there the preceding constellation, viz., that of the Twins (Gemini). (See fig. 41.)

As has been already stated, the ecliptic cuts the equator at an angle of $23\frac{1}{2}°$ in two opposite points distant 180°. These are the points which we call the equinoctial points, or the equinoxes: the sun at the vernal equinox, on the 21st of March, is in the constellation of the Fishes (Pisces), and in the sign of the Ram, and at the autumnal equinox, on the 23rd of September, he is in the constellation of Virgo, and in the sign of the Balance (Libra).

61. This apparent motion of the sun we must now refer to its real cause, viz., the motion of the earth.

To assist us in comprehending this motion, we again employ a round table, with a light in the centre to represent the sun. We now place the table in the centre of a circular room, round the wall of which the signs of the ecliptic are described at equal distances, and on the same level with the light on the table. In fig. 41 the inner circle represents the table, and the outer the

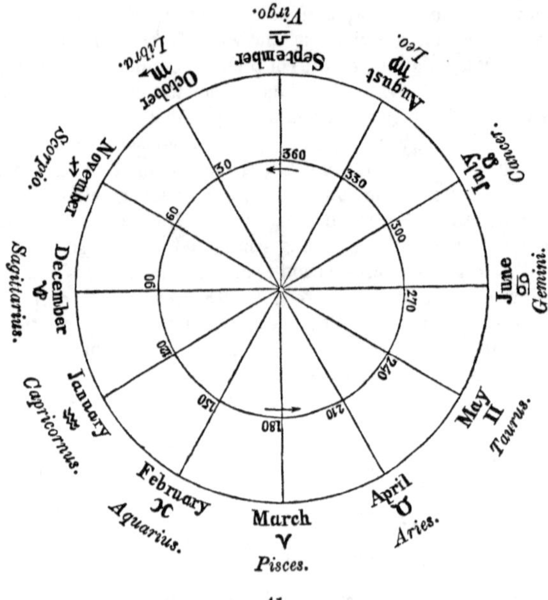

41.

circumference of the room. The observer's eye is supposed to be on a level with the light, and in the place indicated by the arrow (←o) at 360°, where we suppose the earth to be commencing her motion on the 21st of March in the direction of the arrow (o→). At this precise time the sun appears in the sign Aries Moving along the margin of the table, which is divided into twelve equal parts, in one such part farther on, we perceive the sun in the sign of Taurus, and he appears to have described an arc of 30° in a direction precisely opposite to ours. Thus we proceed in our course round the sun, and perceive him passing from one sign to another till he appears again in that of the Ram, and the year is completed.

Before the motion of the earth round the sun was established on certain data, the earth was believed to be in the centre of the ecliptic, *i. e.*, in the place where the sun really is, fig. 41. In fact, the phenomena are the same, if we place ourselves in the centre of the table and cause a light representing the sun to be carried round it, beginning at the lower arrow. We see the light passing through all the signs.

That the ecliptic cuts the equator at an angle of 23½°, is merely a result of the inclination of the earth's axis towards its orbit.

In fig. 42 we see the sun surrounded by an inner circle which represents the earth's orbit, and by an outer circle which is formed by the stars of the ecliptic. If the axis of the earth *n s* were perpendicular to the plane of both these circles, the ecliptic would coincide with the plane of the equinoctial *a q*. The actual position of the axis is, however, inclined towards both these circles, as N S, in which case A Q is the equator, the plane of which evidently cuts the plane of the ecliptic under the same angle which the imaginary perpendicular axis *n s* forms with the inclined axis N S.

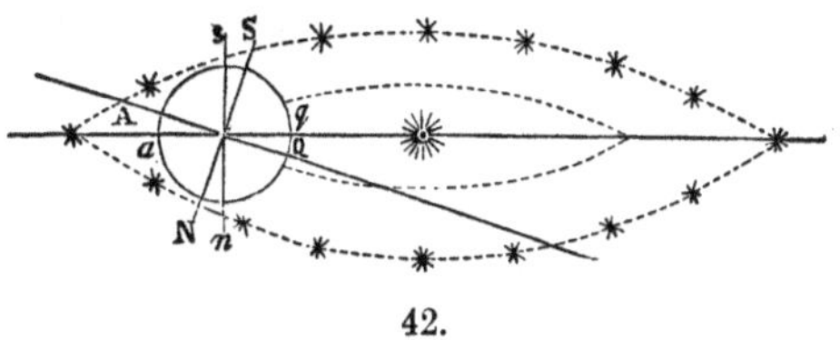

42.

Equation of Time.

62. The earth rotates with perfect uniformity around its own axis in 23 hours, 56 minutes, and 4 seconds. This period is called a *sidereal day*. Like the solar day it is divided into 24 equal parts, and each such part is called a *sidereal hour*. Astronomers make use of this time because they can examine it with the greatest facility and accuracy, and can, by its means, easily determine the position of a star.

On the other hand, the time which the sun requires from one transit through the meridian of a certain place to the following transit is called a *solar day*. This is about 4 minutes longer than a sidereal day, because the sun appears to have removed about 1 degree every day towards the east. It is similar to the minute-hand of a watch, which after having been directly over the hour-hand must make somewhat more than one revolution to reach the hour-hand again, since the latter has, in the mean time, traversed a certain distance in the same direction.

The solar day has always been divided into 24 hours. A well-constructed and rightly-situated sun-dial always indicates the hour correctly.

The solar days, however, are not of equal duration, since, as we have seen, they depend upon the unequal motion of the earth in her elliptical orbit, which causes the apparent motion of the sun; and also because the sun does not appear to move in the plane of the equator, but in the ecliptic, which is inclined 23½° towards it.

But as a good clock ought to have a perfectly uniform movement, it cannot of course indicate the inequalities of solar time; hence the so-called mean solar time has been introduced. Besides the sun itself, we may imagine another sun which moves with uniform velocity in the plane of the equator, and which always passes simultaneously with the actual sun through the vernal equinox.

The imaginary sun sometimes precedes and sometimes follows the actual sun, and several times they pass simultaneously through the meridian. A watch which points always to the hour of twelve when the imaginary sun passes through the meridian indicates the mean solar time which is so termed in contradistinction to the true time indicated by the sun-dial. The difference between the mean and true solar time is called the *equation of time.* The following table shows the equation of time for the different months accurately to one minute. If it be desired to regulate a watch according to the sun-dial, we are obliged to add to or subtract from the time indicated by the dial as many minutes as are indicated by the table.

If, for example, the sun-dial, on the 26th of March, indicates 10 hours 17 minutes, the watch must indicate 10 hours 17 minutes + 6 minutes, or 10 hours 23 minutes; and also for the 7th of September, if the sun-dial indicates 8 hours 55 minutes, the watch must point to 8 hours 55 minutes — 2 minutes, or 8 hours 53 minutes.

EQUATION OF TIME.

	Min.		Min.		Min.		Min.
January 1	+ 4	April 1	+ 4	August 2	+ 6	Nov. 3	— 16¼
4	+ 5	5	+ 3	11	+ 5	9	— 16
6	+ 6	8	+ 2	17	+ 4	17	— 15
8	+ 7	12	+ 1	21	+ 3	21	— 14
11	+ 8	15	0	25	+ 2	25	— 13
13	+ 9	20	— 1	29	+ 1	28	— 12
16	+ 10	25	— 2	Sept. 1	0	Dec. 1	— 11
19	+ 11			4	— 1	3	— 10
23	+ 12	May 11	— 3	7	— 2	6	— 9
27	+ 13	15	— 4	10	— 3	8	— 8
		29	— 3	13	— 4	10	— 7
February 2	+ 14			16	— 5	12	— 6
13	+ 14½	June 5	— 2	19	— 6	15	— 5
20	+ 14	10	— 1	22	— 7	17	— 4
27	+ 13	15	0	25	— 8	19	— 3
		20	+ 1	27	— 9	21	— 2
March 4	+ 12	24	+ 2	30	— 10	23	— 1
8	+ 11	29	+ 3	Oct. 4	— 11	25	0
12	+ 10			7	— 12	27	+ 1
16	+ 9	July 4	+ 4	11	— 13	29	+ 2
19	+ 8	11	+ 5	15	— 14	31	+ 3
23	+ 7	20	+ 6	20	— 15		
26	+ 6			28	— 16		
29	+ 5						

EARTH AND MOON.

63. A relation similar to that between the sun and the earth exists also between the earth and the moon; the latter is attached to the earth by the

invisible bond of attraction, and, as its satellite, accompanies it in its path round the sun.

On comparing these two bodies, the moon and the earth, we find the moon's diameter to be 2,157 miles, or 3·67 times smaller than the diameter of the earth. The surface of the earth is about 14 times larger than that of the moon, and, in solid contents, is 50 times greater. To an observer in the moon the earth must appear 3·67 times larger than the moon appears to us. The apparent diameter of the latter is 31′ 16″.

The distance of the moon from the centre of the earth is 237,840 miles, or 60 semi-diameters of the earth, an insignificant space when compared with the distance of the sun, and especially when contrasted with the distances of the fixed stars. Indeed the moon is of all the heavenly luminaries the nearest to us, and it is owing to this that she apparently surpasses in magnitude all other celestial bodies, except the sun, and that, in appearance, she is almost of dimensions equal to him.

This proximity enables us to make important observations on the body of the moon, which being magnified 500 times, or brought nearer by a powerful telescope, affords a spectacle as surprising as it is beautiful. When with the unassisted eye alone the moon is viewed, we perceive large dark parts to which fancy and tradition have often assigned a human or other appearance; the armed eye, however, represents these in a most definite manner, and we have in general acquired tolerably well-grounded views respecting the condition of the moon's surface.

In the half-moon, while the enlightened border towards the sun is circular and smoothly rounded off, the opposite border is indented and jagged, with deep recesses and prominent points. That certain clear points in the moon are mountains there is no reasonable doubt, from the long-projecting shadows that their unenlightened sides cast behind them; as the altitude of the sun increases they shorten, and at full moon disappear. By admeasurement, it has been discovered that some of these mountains are as high or even higher than any terrestrial mountains. Annular mountains (*Ringgebirge*) are the most common form of lunar mountains: sometimes these enclose an extensive plain, sometimes a crater of great depth, having sometimes a conical elevation in its centre called the central mountain. Besides these, there are groups and chains of mountains traversing the moon in every direction; so that by far the larger portion of the lunar surface is occupied by these diversified mountain ranges. This may be discovered through a moderately good telescope.

On comparing the appearance of the lunar mountains with those of the earth, and with the idea which we entertain of the origin of terrestrial mountains, a *volcanic* origin is with good grounds ascribed to the former.

According to the most exact observations, it appears that the moon has no atmosphere similar to ours, that on its surface there are no great bodies of water like our seas and oceans, so that the existence of water is doubtful. The whole physical condition of the lunar surface must, therefore, be so different from that of our earth, that beings organized as we are could not exist there.

It would be ridiculous to waste time in refuting the assertion, that edifices and even living creatures might be seen on the moon. If we were in a condition to apply telescopes magnifying a thousand times, the moon would appear in that case no other than a place 50 miles distant appears to the naked eye; yet who can discern a house or a living creature of any sort at such a distance?

64. The lunar orbit is an ellipse having the earth in one of the foci, and its eccentricity is greater than that of the earth's orbit, that is, it varies in a greater degree from the circular figure.

Hence the moon is not always equidistant from the earth, but has its *apogee*, its *perigee*, and mean distance, similar in this respect to the relations existing between the earth and the sun (§ 53), already described. Hence its apparent magnitude is not uniform: its greater apparent diameter is 33 20″, and the smaller 29′ 12″, and the mean 31′ 16″, according to its distance from the earth. The celerity of the moon's motion is the greater, the more it approaches the earth.

But since the moon moves at the same time with the earth around the sun, its motion is very complicated, being that of a spiral line about the earth's orbit, the calculation and determination of which are attended with very great difficulties.

But these vanish when we first of all submit to consideration the relation of the moon to the earth, assuming the earth as the centre of the lunar orbit.

The path traversed by the moon in the heavens is certainly within the zodiacal circle, yet it does not exactly coincide with the sun's apparent course, the ecliptic, but cuts this at an angle of a little more than 5°, in two opposite points, which are called the moon's *nodes*, or nodes of the lunar orbit. The one half is therefore north, and the other half south of the ecliptic.

If the position of the moon, in respect to any known star, be observed on one evening and repeated the next, the moon will be found to have moved a little more than 13° from west to east from that star. As the whole circle of her orbit is 360°, accurate calculation has proved that this space is traversed by the moon in 27 days 7 hours 43′ 12″, after which time she has returned to the same star. This time is called the moon's *periodic* time or periodicity.

During the moon's course round the earth in the above stated period, she turns once on her own axis, which is almost perpendicular to the ecliptic, so that the lunar equator nearly coincides with it, and, consequently, in the moon the same phenomena relative to the sun will be observable which the earth would have presented if, as in § 56, the earth's axis were perpendicular to the plane of the ecliptic.

One consequence of this protracted period of lunar rotation is, that the one-half of the moon will have the sun's rays for nearly 15 days, and the other side during this period would be in darkness, were it not for the reflected light she receives from the earth.

From our earth only one side of the moon, or one-half of the lunar surface, is ever visible, *i. e.*, the moon always presents the same face to the earth. This is occasioned by the coincidence of the period where the moon revolves round the earth and that in which she moves round her own axis. Her revolution and rotation are accomplished in the same period. This fact may be proved experimentally. Let us imagine a candle placed upon a round table; if we now walk round the table, keeping the face always turned towards the light, we do not merely pass round the table, but in the mean time, turn round our own axis.

SUN, EARTH, AND MOON.

Phases of the Moon.

65. No other heavenly body shows such remarkable changes in its aspect as the moon. This is so striking, that the phrase, "changeable as the moon," is proverbial.

For an explanation of the different aspects, or *phases of the moon*, we must have recourse to the sun, for these are the result of the changes of the mutual positions of the sun, the earth, and the moon.

We have first to remark that, on account of the great distance of the earth and the moon from the sun, and the great magnitude of the last, all the rays of light that proceed from the sun fall in a parallel direction upon the earth and moon, and it is indifferent at what portion of their orbits they receive these rays.

Therefore let T, fig. 43, represent the earth, and *c c*.... the moon in the various positions she assumes in her orbit, and S S .... the rays of light proceeding in a parallel direction from the distant sun. It is evident that the surfaces both of the earth and moon opposite to the sun will be completely enlightened, and to an eye placed in the sun these two bodies would present the appearance of constantly enlightened, perfect discs. The reverse side, viz., that which is not opposite to the sun, is naturally dark.

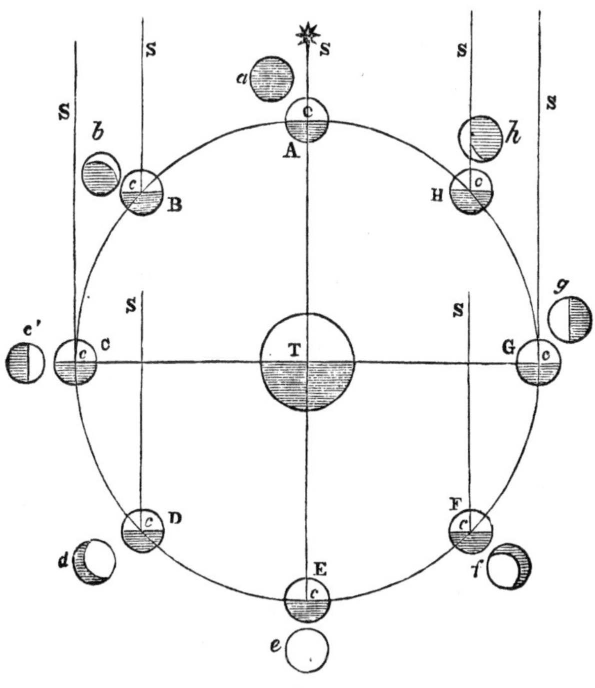

43

Suppose the sun, the moon, and the earth to be in one straight line, in the order of sun, moon, and earth (S A T, fig. 43), this position is called *conjunction;* and when the earth is between the sun and the moon, it is called *opposition*, as S T E. The two positions C and G are called the moon's *quadratures.* From the earth, only that half of the lunar surface which is turned towards us is visible, that is, that part of our diagram which is cut by the circle representing the orbit of the moon. Whilst, therefore, A B C D E F G H represent the moon as she would appear if viewed from the sun, the figures in the juxtaposition, viz., *a b c' d e f g h*, represent the phases of the moon as they actually appear to an eye on the earth observing them in these several positions.

In the lunar conjunction at A the unenlightened disc of the moon is turned towards the earth, and we have then *new moon* as it is termed. At this period the moon is scarcely visible, but in some states of the atmosphere she appears as a pale ash-gray body, reflecting the little light borrowed from the earth. After a few days she appears to us at B, as a shining crescent *b*, the points of which are turned from the sun. In the quadrature C she increases to the *first quarter c'*, where she presents her semi-lunar shape. When she reaches the opposite point of her orbit, and is in opposition, we have what is called *full moon.* By a similar gradual decrease she returns to that part of her orbit, where she is again in conjunction.

The following simple operation will afford a satisfactory view of the lunar phases. In the centre of a table, place a rather large globe to represent the earth, about which, a smaller globe representing the moon may be carried, preserving an equal distance from the centre. At a suitable distance from both, place a light to represent the sun, and at the same height as the two globes. In this experiment it is usual to colour the lunar globe white, that the exact shadow line may be sharply defined. If from the large globe we now look at the lunar globe, during its revolution, we shall obtain a very accurate view of the different phases of the moon.

66. Since the moon daily describes an arc of 13° in the heavens, from west to east, it is certain that her rising or appearance above the horizon will be later every successive night; and in this respect she differs from the fixed stars, which preserve to a minute the exact period of rising and setting. As the rising or setting of the moon can be exactly calculated, and is besides a matter of considerable importance, both this, as well as her different phases, are given in the Almanac; but with greater fulness in the Nautical Almanac.

Tides.

67. As the attraction between the different portions of matter is always mutual, the moon is not only attracted by the earth, but the latter is also attracted by the moon. Lunar attraction is most powerfully and sensibly felt on those portions of the earth's surface that are nearest to the moon, which is the case when the moon passes through the meridian of these places. Attraction is strongest on the equator — because the moon is always nearly perpendicular to this part of the surface of the earth.

On the continental parts of the earth, lunar attraction exerts scarcely any perceptible influence; whilst, on the contrary, the waters of the ocean which cover the greater portion of the earth's surface, by their mobility, more easily follow the attracting influence, and are elevated in the direction of the meridian where the moon is present.

This elevation of the waters of the seas and oceans, at stated periods, is called the *flow*, or flux of the *tide*, and, as has been shown, is always greatest at the equator, and gradually decreases with the increase of latitude. For example, at St. Malo it amounts to 50 feet, while on the northern part of the Norwegian coast, it is scarcely perceptible.

Even the centre of the earth is susceptible of attraction in this direction, and in some degree yields to it; hence the waters on the opposite side of the meridian are elevated, because in consequence of their inertia they are not in a condition instantly to obey the motion of the attracted earth. Thus the flood-tide forms a belt or ring, encompassing the whole globe, passing through the poles, attaining its greatest elevation at the equator, and gradually diminishing towards both poles, where it altogether disappears. The direction of the tidal wave is from east to west, regulated by the moon's gradual motion to the meridians of the different places.

Consequently at any one place, during the space of 24 hours, there are two tides, which are 12 hours apart, and at the periods when this phenomenon occurs in our locality, the sea is also elevated in the locality of our antipodes.

But, again, if the oceanic wave is elevated at the same period in opposite parts of the earth, and, by its cumulative process, occasions, what is termed, high water at these opposite points, at the intermediate points the water must naturally in the same measure be lower, and occasion the *ebb* or reflux tide; and this reflux must be greatest at those points equally distant from the points of high water or flood-tide. All places lying under the same meridian have ebb or reflux tide at the same time; and this tidal depression forms a concave circle which, in the poles, cuts the circle of the high tide at right angles.

On the sea-shore we perceive, during six hours, the waters flowing towards the land, accumulating on the sea-beach, or covering the flat sands, flowing up the estuaries of tidal rivers, or dashing themselves to foam and spray on the lofty banks or steep rocky barriers of the ocean: when they have reached their maximum height, they appear quiescent for the space of a quarter of an hour; they then flow back to the sea during six hours longer, when they recommence their fresh reiterated attacks on the firm barriers of the stable ground.

There does not exist a more sublime and fearfully awful spectacle, than the sea affords when agitated by the combined influence of both tide and storm.

The howling of the tempest, the roar of mighty waves, the rushing sound of the broken waters, vainly struggling to pass their appointed bounds, form a scene difficult to be imagined, and impossible to be described.

As the moon appears on the meridian, the following day, about 50 minutes later than on the previous day, and as the time of high water at every individual place corresponds with the lunar motions, the phenomena of ebb and flow, or of high and low water, can be ascertained for every haven—an object of the utmost value in navigation.

In general, however, the tides do not occur so simply as has been above described. Besides local peculiarities, such as the configuration and position of the shore, occasional causes, as winds, &c., disturb the regular progress of the tide. And besides these, the sun has an important effect on the flow and ebb, according to his relative position to the earth and moon.

If the sun and moon be in conjunction (see fig. 43), by their combined influence the tides are higher, but if they be in opposition, they counteract each other, and the tides are lower. The sun's influence is least, when the moon is in her quadratures.

Eclipses.

68. Eclipses of the heavenly bodies are merely the shadows of certain opaque bodies thrown upon others coming within the verge of their darkened sides. If the luminous body A, fig. 44, be of larger dimensions than the

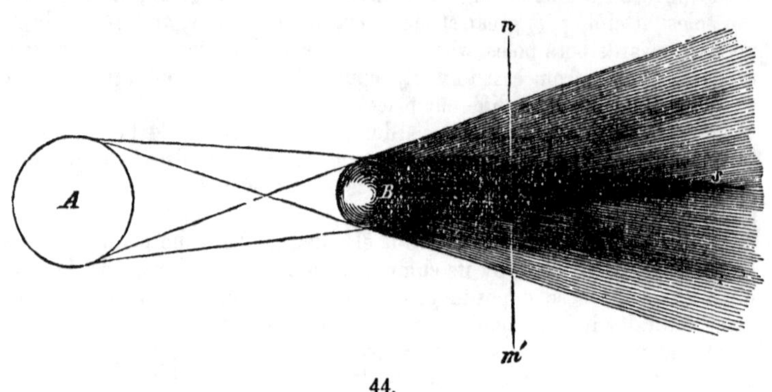

44.

dark body, B, there originate, in consequence of the rectilinear propagation of light, two sorts of shadows. The *umbra* is that sort of shadow in which no part of the luminous body is perceptible; it forms a cone, the apex of which is behind the dark body. As soon as the eye is placed on the umbra, it can perceive no part of the source of light A, which appears to be eclipsed. On the other hand, the *penumbra* originates in that locality where only a portion of the light proceeding from a luminous object can fall; hence an eye in the *penumbra* would see a part, but not the whole of the illuminating body. This shadow, also, forms a cone, which, if extended, the apex will fall before the opaque body. If we receive the shadows so projected at *m n*, for example, on a white sheet, we have in the centre a dark circle, which is the umbra, surrounded by the penumbra, which gradually decreases in intensity towards the exterior (see fig. 45). The farther we hold the sheet from the body producing the shadow, the umbra decreases, and the penumbra is enlarged.

45.

Lunar Eclipse.

69. Let A, fig. 44, be the sun, and B the earth, the length of the umbra of the latter will exceed 108 diameters of the earth. Since the moon is only about 30 terrestrial diameters distant from the earth, and as the diameter

of the earth's shadow, at this distance, is nearly three times as large as the apparent diameter of the moon, it follows that when the latter enters this shadow, she must be totally eclipsed.

If the moon's orbit was coincident with the ecliptic, or if both moon and earth moved round the sun in the same plane, there would be an eclipse at every conjunction, and at every opposition, (see § 65), *i. e.*, a solar eclipse would happen at every new moon, and a lunar eclipse at every full moon. But we have seen that the lunar orbit cuts the ecliptic only in two points (Nodes, § 64); consequently, an eclipse of the moon is possible only when, at the time of opposition, the moon is in one of her nodes, or in close proximity to it, which can only occur 29 times in the space of 18 years.

70. A lunar eclipse begins on the eastern margin of the moon, and is either *total*, when her whole disc enters the umbra, or *partial*, when only part of her disc is in the shadow. A total eclipse may last for two hours.

Eclipses of the moon are visible at all points of the nocturnal hemisphere of the earth, if the moon be above their horizon, and the eclipse will be of equal duration and equal magnitude. If, however, the places of observation lie at a considerable distance east and west of each other, the commencement and termination of the eclipse will be perceived at different times; and hereby we have the means of determining the longitude, *i. e.*, the distance of the observer from the first meridian (see § 25). The greater the distance between two places, the greater will be the difference of time at which an eclipse will begin or end at the two places. Suppose for the one place the eclipse begins at 10 P.M., and at a place farther to the west at 11 P.M., we know that the difference of the longitude of the two places is 15°. The circular outline of the earth's shadow on the moon, is a notable proof of the sphericity of the earth.

Solar Eclipse.

71. When the moon and the sun are in conjunction, the moon's place may be represented by M, fig. 46, between the earth T, and the sun S. If this conjunction occur when the moon is in one of her nodes, or within 16° of it, the shadow of the moon will fall upon the earth, and the sun will be eclipsed. This can only happen 41 times in 18 years; and it will presently be shown that, at any one place, an eclipse of the sun is three times less frequent than an eclipse of the moon.

The lunar umbra extends from the moon a space about equal to her distance from the earth, and hence only a small portion *d* of the earth's surface enters the lunar umbra. To the inhabitants of this part of the earth the sun will be totally eclipsed, and the eclipse will be annular if only the margin of the sun's disc remain uneclipsed by the lunar shadow. This is only possible when the moon is in her apogee, or greatest distance from the earth, where her apparent diameter is less than that of the sun, which it cannot, in general, exceed more than 1′ 38″. Hence the duration of a total eclipse cannot be more than $3\frac{1}{4}$ minutes.

On the contrary, the penumbra of the moon is diffused over a much larger portion, *n m*, of the surface of the earth, since its section is five-ninths of the earth's diameter. The inhabitants of this portion of the earth do not

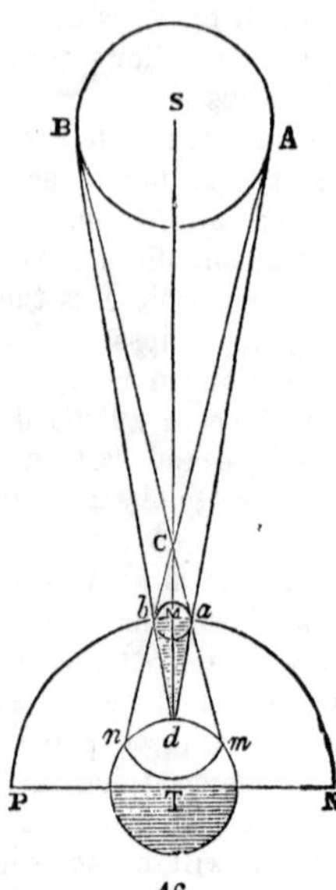

46.

receive light from all parts of the sun, consequently a *part* of this luminary is invisible to them, and the eclipse is said to be *partial*.

Solar eclipses commence on the western margin of the sun, and advance to the eastern. On account of the proximity of the moon to us, an eclipse of the sun is, in all places above the horizon of which the sun appears, visible neither at the same time, nor is it of equal duration, nor of equal extent: in some parts it may not be visible at all. In favourable situations, the diameter of the umbra, where it reaches the earth, amounts to about 167 miles, and in this small strip of the earth's surface only can the sun appear totally eclipsed.

Planets.

72. It has been already stated (§ 45) that, on an attentive observation of the heavenly bodies, certain stars are observed which obviously change their positions in relation to the fixed stars, and which have therefore been called planets, or wandering stars.

If examined through a telescope, they appear considerably magnified, with commensurable discs illuminated by the sun, whose light they receive and reflect. In these respects they differ essentially from the fixed stars, which even under the greatest magnifying power appear only as small luminous points, and are considered to be self-illuminated bodies, or suns, at enormous distances.

Compared with the fixed stars, the planets are at moderate distances, and insignificant in number, but in other respects they are invested with a remarkable interest.

The planetary motions are confined to the portion of the heavens called the Zodiac (see § 60). But how essentially different are their orbits from those of the sun and moon! Whilst these preserve a uniformity of motion, describing equal arcs in definite spaces of time, advancing from west to east, from one constellation to another, till they have completed a whole circuit of the heavens, we perceive that the case is widely different with the planets. Sometimes they advance rapidly, then relax their apparent speed, then stand for some days perfectly still, and then reverse their motions, and again describe an irregular line, somewhat like the representation in fig. 47. The planet's course, W V, in the direction of the sun's path, is called its *direct* motion, and its reverse motion, V S, is called *retrograde*, and between these two kinds of motion the planet is always for a time stationary. We also perceive that half of a planet's course is on the north and half on the south side of the ecliptic, E C; consequently their orbits cut the ecliptic at two opposite points, termed *nodes*, similarly to the moon's.

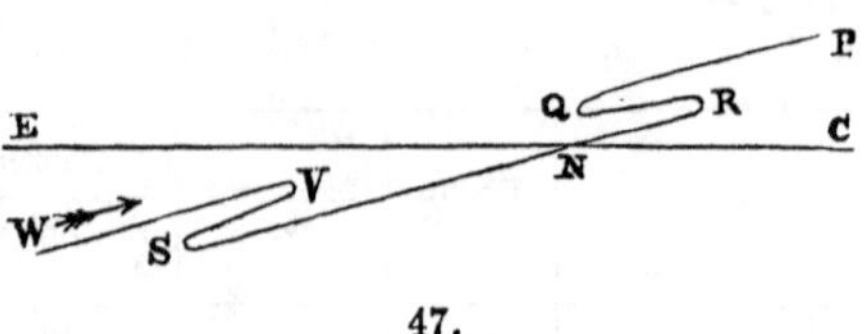

47.

Before we arrived at the correct knowledge of the planetary courses, and the relation of these bodies to the sun, nothing was more difficult than the *explanation* of their peculiar motions. All the attempts of the earlier erroneous systems of astronomy were wrecked by the planets, and thereby proved at once their inaccuracy or insufficiency.

73. The sun is not only the centre of attraction for our earth, which describes its elliptic course around him, but also for a great number of other heavenly bodies, the first of which are the planets, among which the earth itself must be classed.

We know at the present day 33 planets, and from recent discoveries we have ground for the assumption that more planets are discoverable.

The planets present essential differences in magnitude, distance from the sun, celerity of movement, and in physical characters; they all agree in form, opaqueness, and in the ellipticity of their orbits around the sun, which lie almost in one plane. A rotatory motion on their axes has been observed in so many, that it is a fair assumption that they all possess this property.

74. The planets may be systematically represented, relatively to each other and to the sun, by drawing them of proportionate magnitude, and at proportionate distances, on a table, or even on a sheet of paper. The sun is, of course, to be assumed as the fixed and common centre of attraction, around which the orbits of the planets may be described either as circular or elliptical.

A tolerably satisfactory diagram of the relative distances of the planetary bodies may be constructed by assuming the mean distances of these bodies from the sun, as the radii of a succession of concentric circles, each one representing the orbit of a single planet. In order to describe their ellipticity, the larger diameter and eccentricity (§ 13) must be given.

The planets situated nearer than the earth to the sun, of which there are

only two, Mercury and Venus, we distinguish by the title *inferior* planets; those moving in orbits, lying on the outside of the earth's orbit, we call *superior* planets, which include all the other planetary bodies.

By the term *ancient* planets, we understand those that have been known since the most remote ages, viz., Mercury, Venus, the Earth, Mars, Jupiter, and Saturn; whilst the rest, discovered since the invention of telescopes, are styled *modern* planets.

The following tables comprehend the most important relations of the planets:—

I.

PLANETS.	Signs	Known since	Discovered by	Diameter.		Solid Contents.	
				English Miles.	Greatest apparent.*	Millions of Cubic Miles.	Earth = 1.
1. Mercury ...	☿	Antiq.	....	3,123	13″	10,195	$\frac{1}{17}$
2. Venus	♀	"	....	7,702	64″	223,521	$\frac{10}{11}$
3. Earth	♁	"	....	7,916	....	260,775	1
4. Mars	♂	"	....	4,398	23″	48,723	$\frac{1}{7}$
5. Ceres	①	1801	Piazzi	1,024	....	20,783	....
6. Pallas	②	1802	Olbers	2,099	4″·2	....	$\frac{1}{1661}$
7. Juno	③	1804	Harding ...	1,425	0″·4	1,372	$\frac{1}{9842}$
8. Vesta	④	1807	Olbers	238	0″·5	98	$\frac{1}{17638}$
9. Astrea	⑤	1845	Hencke	....	....	....	....
10. Hebe	⑥	1847	Hencke	....	....	....	....
11. Iris	⑦	1847	Hind	....	....	....	....
12. Flora	⑧	1847	Hind	....	....	....	....
13. Metis	⑨	1848	Graham	....	....	....	....
14. Hygeia	⑩	1849	DeGasparis	....	....	....	....
15. Parthenope	⑪	1850	DeGasparis	....	....	....	....
16. Victoria ...	⑫	1850	"	....	....	....	....
17. Egeria	⑬	1850	DeGasparis	....	....	....	....
18. Irene	⑭	1851	Hind	....	....	....	....
[19. Eunomia..	⑮	1851	DeGasparis	....	....	....	....
20. Psyche	⑯	1852	"	....	....	....	....
21. Thetis	⑰	1852	Luther	....	....	....	....
22. Melpomene	⑱	1852	Hind	....	....	....	....
23. Massalia ...	⑲	1852	Chacornac .	....	....	....	....
24. Fortuna	⑳	1852	Hind	....	....	....	....
25. Lutetia	㉑	1852	Goldschmit	....	....	....	....
26. Calliope ...	㉒	1852	Hind	....	....	....	....
27. Thalia	㉓	1852	"	....	....	....	....
28. Phocea	㉔	1853	Chacornac .	....	....	....	....
[29.	㉕	1853	DeGasparis	....	....	....	....
30. Jupiter	♃	Antiq.	....	91,522	49″·2	343,125,828	1,491
31. Saturn......	♄	"	....	76,068	20″·3	245,089,877	772
32. Uranus	♅	1781	Herschel ...	35,112	4″·3	19,727,774	87
33. Neptune....	♆	1846	Adams and Leverrier	......	2″.6	....	77
Sun..........	☉	....	....	882,270	32′·34″	399,839,629,687	1,415,225
Moon	☽	....	....	2,160	31′·16″	5,274	$\frac{1}{50}$

* The apparent diameter is expressed by the number of seconds contained in the angle under which the planet is seen from the earth at its shortest distance.

The smaller and recently-discovered planets are usually called Asteroids. For these, recent admeasurements prove that the above-assigned diameters are too large.

II.

PLANETS.	Mean Distance from the Sun, or Half the greater Axis of their Orbits.		Eccentricity in parts of its Semi-major Axis.	Time of Revolution round their Axes.		Time of Revolution round their Orbits.	Celerity of Orbitual Motion, or Space passed over in a Second.
	Miles.	Earth's Distances.					
	1	2	3	4		5	6
				Hrs.	Min.	Days.	Feet.
1. Mercury ..	36,000,000	0·3	0·205	24	0	88	162,611
2. Venus......	68,000,000	0·7	0·006	23	21	225	118,960
3. Earth	93,000,000	1·0	0·016	23	56	365	101,173
4. Mars	142,000,000	1·5	0·093	24	39	687	81,963
5. Flora.......	209,856,610	2·2	0·156	....		1,194	....
6. Victoria...	....	......	....	....		1,303	....
7. Vesta	225,000,000	2·3	0·093	....		1,335	65,813
8. Iris	223,034,070	2·3	0·207	....		1,344	....
9. Metis	....	......	....	....		1,346	....
10. Hebe.......	223,771,830	2.3	0·182	....		1,380	....
11. Parthenope	....	......	....	....		1,401	....
12. Astrea	245,305,200	2·5	0·188	....		1,511	....
13. Egeria	....	......	....	....		1,478	....
14. Juno	253,000,000	2·6	0·255	....		1,591	61,909
15. Ceres.......	263,000,000	2·7	0·078	....		1,681	60,821
16. Pallas	265,000,000	2·7	0·245	....		1,682	60,820
17. Hygeia	....	......	....	....		2,042	....
18. Irene.......	....	......	....	....		....	....
19. Jupiter	485,000,000	5·2	0·048	9	56	4,333	44,362
20. Saturn.....	890,000,000	9·2	0·056	10	16	10,758	32,757
21. Uranus ...	1,800,000,000	19·2	0·045	7	5	30,687	23,093
22. Neptune...	3,446,722,500	36·1	0·008	....		....	....

75. The two inferior planets, *Mercury* and *Venus*, have phenomena in some respects similar to those of the moon. As they move between the orbit of the earth and the sun, they enter with these bodies, at certain times, into a twofold conjunction, viz., in an *inferior conjunction*, when the planet is between the sun and the earth, and in a *superior* when it is beyond the sun, and in the same straight line with the earth. During the superior conjunction, which frequently occurs in the planet Mercury, caused by the rapidity of its orbitual motion, we occasionally obtain a view of this body, as a dark, round speck passing over the sun's disc. This passage over the sun is called the *transit* of Mercury, and it affords a convincing proof that the planets derive their light from the sun.

In certain positions towards the sun, when viewed through a telescope, this planet clearly exhibits certain alterations of form, which are called phases. Venus, at certain periods, and especially in the morning, after being for some time invisible, appears as a bright sickle. Venus is in general readily recognised by her brilliancy and considerable apparent magnitude, as well as by her proximity to the sun. In consequence of this proximity she is visible always at the time of sunrise and sunset, and hence she has received the name of *morning* and *evening star* (Lucifer and Hesperus). An atmosphere and lofty mountains have been observed in this planet, and a rotatory motion about her axis, which lies nearly in the plane of her orbit.

76. The superior planets describe their paths around the sun and earth, and, consequently, they enter into conjunction, opposition, and quadrature to these bodies (see § 65). The nearest to us, viz., the planet *Mars*, is distinguished by a remarkable dusky-red light (colour), which has been ascribed to a very high and dense atmosphere.

Mars is likewise remarkable for his oblateness, which is produced by the motion round his axis, as well as for the bright spots observed in the vicinity of his poles, forming the so-called *snow-zones*, which decrease when the pole, where this phenomena is observed, is turned to the sun; similar to the phenomena observed on the polar regions of the earth.

Jupiter is distinguished both by his splendour and by his magnitude, being the largest of the planets, as has been shown in Table I., as well as by different belts or zones which are parallel with his equator. An atmosphere has been attributed to this mighty planet. The velocity of its rotatory motion is enormous, being accomplished round its almost perpendicular axis in the space of 10 hours, or at the rate of 28,000 miles an hour. Its oblate figure is (Com. Phys., § 56) a consequence of the celerity of its rotation; its diameter at the poles compared with that of the equator is as 13 : 14.

This stupendous planet is accompanied by four *moons* or *satellites* which present similar appearances to the inhabitants of Jupiter, as the moon to us. Although these moons are considerably larger than ours, they are only visible by telescopic aid. They are remarkable as affording data for calculating the velocity of light. As these moons revolve around Jupiter, they enter from time to time in the umbra of that planet, and are eclipsed. After the moment of immergence and emergence had been exactly calculated, it was found that at the time of conjunction, when the earth and Jupiter are 193,662,000 miles distant, the eclipses of Jupiter's satellites appear considerably *later* than when the same phenomenon takes place at the time of their opposition, when the two planets are nearer to each other. The last rays of a satellite, disappearing in the shadow, reach us some time after the body is actually eclipsed, consequently the light requires a certain time to travel to the earth, and this time amounts to a second for 195,000 miles.

77. The planet *Saturn* is peculiar for an annular disc which surrounds it in the neighborhood of its equator, and rotates freely round the planet. It is only visible to the aided eye in certain positions, viz., when Saturn is in the signs of Aries and Cancer (fig. 48). By attentive observation, this disc is discovered to consist of three rings, which like the mass of the planet are solid, and cast a shadow, clearly visible on the surface of the planet. This ring may be represented as consisting of a large number of small satellites arranged in a contiguous annular form, and performing their revolutions round the planet in the same time.

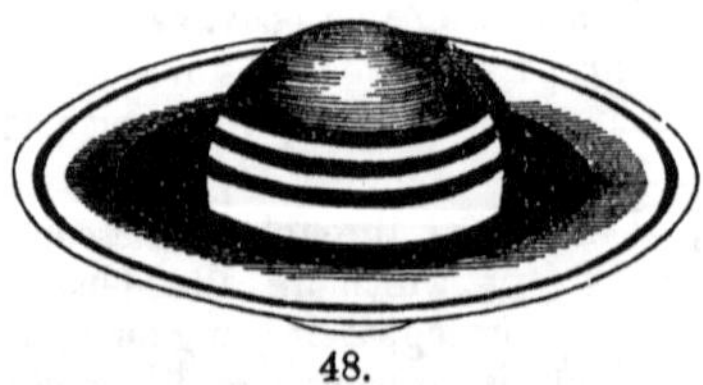

48.

Besides the ring, Saturn is accompanied by seven moons revolving round him at greater distances, and are likewise only visible by the aid of a powerful telescope.

78. Till lately *Uranus* was the most remote planet of our system; it is scarcely visible to the naked eye, and was unknown to the ancients. It is attended by six satellites, of which only two have been accurately observed.

The recently discovered planets we shall notice below.

Planetary System.

79. The renowned Ptolemy, who lived about the middle of the 2nd century of our era, and who belonged to the celebrated Alexandrian school, made the first attempt to classify and explain the phenomena of the heavenly bodies, by laws founded on observation. Antiquity solved all such questions as might originate in an enlightened curiosity on mythic principles, poetical and fanciful, sometimes beautiful, but very illogical and unscientific.

According to the Ptolemaic system, the earth is in the centre of 11 hollow spheres, arranged concentrically within each other, and consequently placed at different distances, and of correspondingly increased magnitudes. In each one of these hollow spheres, which were necessarily supposed to be of the purest crystal, the heavenly bodies were arranged in the following order, viz., the Moon, Mercury, Venus, Sun, Mars, Jupiter, and Saturn: in the eighth crystalline sphere the fixed stars were supposed to be placed. The last three were reserved for the explanation of certain other phenomena.

It is evident that this system is decidedly contradicted by many phenomena, and as this was then manifest, the *Egyptian* planetary system was proposed as an improvement. Mercury and Venus were made satellites of the Sun, who still continued his journey around the earth. Still many remarkable phenomena were unexplained, and especially the peculiar movements of the planets described in § 72. This portion of the science appeared so enigmatical, that its votaries were compelled to take refuge in many fantastical assumptions.

The true system of the universe was undiscovered till near the middle of the 16th century, when Copernicus, who was born in 1473, and died in 1543, comprehended this vast problem, and originated the happy idea of the true solar system, an idea which he cherished during the whole course of his life, and laboured to establish on the sure basis of reckoning and observation. He maintained that the sun was the centre of the system, that the planets moved around the sun in circular orbits, and he farther taught that the daily motion of the heavenly bodies was only apparent, and caused by the rotation of our earth.

The persecution of Galileo, the eminent Italian astronomer, is a proof that the spreading of such new cosmical doctrines was not unattended with danger to their supporters and abettors. This great man, who adopted and farther developed the Copernican system, was compelled to recant his real opinions, and to profess his belief in the immobility of the earth, because the whole system stood in verbal opposition to some passages in the Holy Scriptures.

80. There were still several inexplicable phenomena, such as the change of planetary velocity, at certain periods, and the evident alterations of their

apparent magnitudes, both appearances inconsistent with the assumption of their moving in perfectly circular orbits.

At this period appeared the great Keppler, born at Weil, in Wurtemberg, 1571, who availed himself of all the hitherto ascertained facts connected with Astronomy, and especially of the observations of his distinguished contemporary, Tycho Brahe; by these means Keppler developed the ever-memorable laws, which have rendered his merits unsurpassed and his name immortal. This illustrious man had to maintain a fearful struggle with the common domestic miseries of life, and with the outward calamities of war, was driven from one place to another, with no earthly possession, but his own elevated conceptions.

81. Keppler's laws are the following:—

1. The orbits of the planets are *ellipses*, which have a common focus wherein the sun is placed.
2. Equal areas are described by the planets in equal times; that is, the radii vectores drawn from the focii (§ 13) to the planet, will always stretch over an equal space in the same duration of time in which the planet itself moves, it being indifferent what portion of its orbit the planet may in the meanwhile traverse.
3. The squares of the times of revolution of any two planets are to each other in the same proportion as the cubes of their mean distances from the sun.

The world-renowned Newton placed the key-stone upon the noble edifice founded by his great predecessor. By the discovery of the law of gravitation, he completed the theoretic view of the planetary system. He demonstrated that the cause of all the motions of the heavenly bodies originates in their mutual attraction towards each other; and also that this attractive power increases in proportion to the masses of the bodies attracted, and diminishes the farther the attracting bodies are distant from each other. (Physics, § 24.)

The Newtonian laws explain how all the planets, whose united magnitudes are not equal to that of the sun, are bound to the latter by the invisible bond of attraction, and how the satellites, as our moon, with those of Jupiter and Saturn, are connected with their primaries.

82. By the establishment of these laws, astronomers were in a condition to supply many deficiencies, and to correct many errors which still existed in the science; every discovery, and every new and careful observation, served to confirm the truth of these principles.

The extensive space between the orbits of Mars and Jupiter led to the idea, that an unknown planet must exist between them; the consequence was that four small planets, viz., *Pallas, Juno, Ceres*, and *Vesta*, were discovered, and they are supposed to be fragments of a greater planet. Concerning the newly-discovered asteroids we have not yet obtained very satisfactory accounts.

There is no doubt that the planets have a mutual attraction for each other, which in certain parts of their orbits, where they approach, is sensibly felt. The irregularities apparent in the motion of certain planets have been referred to this cause; they have been named *disturbances* or perturbations, and have been in some cases exactly calculated.

From inexplicable perturbations of the planet Uranus, it was conjectured that another planet must be in existence, and its place was even determined by calculation: thus the recently-discovered planet Neptune, which in consequence of the feebleness of its light would probably still have remained a long time unobserved, was shown to exist.

Comets.

83. On the nocturnal heavens, from time to time, there appear luminous bodies consisting of a more brilliant star-like portion, called the *head*, which is commonly followed on the side turned from the sun by a luminous *tail*, which frequently measures millions of miles in length.

These bodies are called *comets*, and were long deemed supernatural prognostications of great events, or perhaps the harbingers of terrible calamities. It is not long since the appearance of a comet was considered a cause for general alarm.

But since the nature of these irregular visitants of our skies has been investigated by astronomers, and the periodicity of some ascertained, they have ceased to be objects of terror and superstitious dread.

84. Comets are material bodies deriving their light from the sun. Their substance is of such extraordinary tenuity, that even through their nucleus the light of distant fixed stars is plainly visible. They are certainly attracted by the sun, as their motions are accelerated and their brightness increased when nearest to this luminary.

Like the planets they are subject to great irregularities in their orbits, only in a much higher degree: and they also differ from the planets in not being limited to the plane of the ecliptic, but moving in all imaginable directions, sometimes approaching so near the sun as to be absorbed in his splendour, and on their reappearance receding from the sun till they are gradually lost in the immensity of space. Hence a comet is visible only for a few days, or weeks, or months; they are never seen for longer periods.

By very accurate observation it has been ascertained that their orbits like those of the planets are elliptical, but of greater eccentricity, so great, indeed, that their periodicity is of very long duration; and some of the most remarkable and beautiful comets, as those of 1680 and of 1811, are expected to return in from 1,500 to 8,000 years.

Some, on the other hand, reappear after shorter intervals, as those named after Halley, Encke, and Biela, which have been accurately calculated by these astronomers. The first has been determined to complete its revolution in from 75 to 76 years, the second in three years and 115 days, and the last in 6 years and 270 days, and they have been several times observed after these intervals.

Hitherto about 500 comets have been seen, of which number not probably more than 150 have been accurately observed. According to astronomical observations, the greater part of them appear to describe orbits which are neither circular nor elliptic, but *parabolic* (§ 14), and, consequently, their return is impossible, being lost in infinite space, and they are no longer to be considered as constituting a part of our solar system. It has been, however, conjectured that the number of comets belonging to our system may amount to about a million; and since they present themselves in all directions, we may assume the realm of the sun to be not a circular plane, in the centre of which is placed the sun, and in whose circumference the planets move, but we must imagine the occupied space of our solar system to be of a globular form. If it be desired to convey an idea of the solar system by a model, this may be easily accomplished by means of a great number of hoops of different diameters, inclined to each other in all directions around a common centre; the diameter of the exterior being not less than 400 diameters of the earth's orbit, therefore upwards of 73,776 millions of miles.

System of the Universe.

85. After it had been satisfactorily determined that the sun has a rotatory movement about his axis, the conjecture was entertained that this body has also a progressive motion at the same time. We have indeed satisfactory accounts of observations confirmatory of this fact, viz., that the sun moves towards a point in the firmament which is situated in the constellation of *Hercules*. His real path or orbit is, however, of such exceedingly enormous extent that the progress of the sun cannot be ascertained till after a lapse of many years, and especially as all the bodies belonging to the solar system necessarily accompany him in this progress.

It may at all events be admitted, that there is a point in the heavens about which our entire solar system revolves, in the same manner as Jupiter and his satellites move round the sun.

More extensive observations of the heavenly bodies have confirmed the conviction, that the fixed stars constitute the centres of innumerable systems, which are in part like that of our sun, and in part composed only of two stars which at a short distance from each other, revolve round their common centre. These are named binary or *double stars*, and the number hitherto observed amounts to 4,000.

According to Herschel,* the sun is a portion of a system of a higher order, which may be represented as of a lens form, fig. 49. Here the position of our system is indicated by the little circle o. It is evident that the heavens will present to our view fewer stars when we look upwards or downwards, than when we look in the direction $m\,m'$. In the latter case we have a view through layers of stars placed behind each other, and forming a thickly studded zone around us which we have in § 46 described as the Milky Way. It must, however, be admitted that the above-mentioned view regarding the arrangement of our solar system is by no means unquestioned.

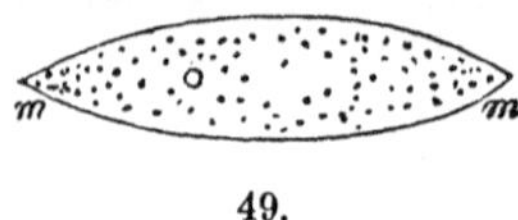

49.

* Herschel (born in 1738, died in 1822) came to London in 1759, as a musical composer and professor. He subsequently devoted himself to the study of astronomy, and engaged in the construction of telescopes, with the view of procuring funds for the erection of a larger instrument than had hitherto been employed. He was so successful, that finally he acquired the means of possessing one of 40 feet focus, viz., the gigantic telescope which surpassed in power all instruments previously constructed. Wherever Herschel turned his instrument, new celestial wonders, not hitherto even surmised, disclosed themselves to his admiring eyes. He has the honour of being the discoverer of the world of fixed stars. The telescope is no longer used, and has been converted by his distinguished son, Sir J. Herschel, into a monument in memory of his illustrious parent.

86. But if we consider the nebulous specks that are dispersed among the constellations, many of which by means of very powerful telescopes have been resolved into groups of stars, while others cannot be so identified on account of their vast distances, ought we not to conclude that these very remote and indiscernible bodies form the Milky Ways of other stellar systems?

When we consider that the nearest of the fixed stars is, at the very least, 200,000 times the radius of the earth's orbit distant from us, and that three years would elapse during the passage of light from that body to our globe, it may be assumed that a period of 25000 years would be requisite to bring to our eyes the light from one of the most remote nebulous spots, and that consequently the distance of this remote object must be 152,163 billions of miles.

Thus we have from the little beacon of our earth, on which we have been placed by an Almighty Hand, taken a comprehensive survey of the solar system; we have also seen that this forms only a part of an infinitely higher order, which last may only be a small part of the infinite whole. Here we find ourselves beyond the bounds of the comprehensible, and are aware that imagination herself is lost in these wonderfully-sublime speculations.

The majesty and omnipotence of the Most High are displayed to our wondering gaze and to our bewildered minds, and we are ready to exclaim with the prophet: *"Lift up your eyes on high, and behold who hath created these things."*

[Sir Isaac Newton.]

CHEMISTRY.

1. Chemistry is the science of those phenomena which are attended by an essential *change* of the objects in which the phenomena are observed, or in those which serve for their production.

When a piece of wood or a fragment of coal is burned, or a bar of iron rusted, these objects, in fact, suffer an essential change, and a series of phenomena must be exhibited in order to restore these various bodies to their original condition.

An object changed by chemical action has naturally acquired new properties, otherwise we could not say that it is changed at all. Hence chemical phenomena are characterised by this important distinction, namely, that their results are always the production or appearance of a body endowed with new qualities. The rust observed on the iron, which is the result of chemical action, is essentially very different from the iron itself.

But we shall be in a better position to ascertain the changes a body undergoes by acquiring a precise knowledge of the properties it possessed before it suffered the chemical change. Hence the object of chemistry is to ascertain, first, the essential nature of bodies, then the changes which they undergo, and, finally, the characters of bodies endowed with other properties, the results of this change.

2. We have been taught by the science of Physics (§ 11) that every body is assumed to be composed of an agglomeration of exceedingly minute atoms. If, now, we examine different bodies, we find that the atoms or molecules which constitute their mass are in most cases of *dissimilar* qualities. There are two processes whereby we are enabled to prove this. The preparation of the beautiful crimson colour known under the name of *cinnabar*, or vermilion, is conducted in manufactories in the following manner: 16 parts by weight of sulphur are fused, and then 100 parts of mercury are gradually added, when a black mass is produced. This is placed in a covered jar, and exposed for a long time to a high temperature. On breaking the jar, when it is cold, we find at the upper part of it a red mass which, when finely pulverized, forms the vermilion of commerce. In carefully conducted and successful operations we obtain an amount of vermilion nearly equal in weight to that of the sulphur and mercury employed. Hence we may justly assume that in the vermilion there is only sulphur and mercury present. If we mix 116 parts by weight of vermilion with 28 parts of iron filings, and heat it in a retort, we obtain in the receiver nearly 100 parts by weight of metallic mercury (see Phys., § 129). In the retort remains a black mass amounting to 44 parts by weight, and which is called *sulphide of iron*. In addition to the 28 parts of iron which have been added, it contains the 16 parts of sulphur which had previously formed with the mercury the vermilion.

These two simple experiments teach us that in the minutest particles of vermilion two different elements are present, namely, mercury and sulphur, and although they cannot be distinguished by the best microscope, we can easily prove the fact by the above-mentioned process. In the following pages many other instances of chemical affinities will be adduced.

There are, therefore, bodies whose minutest constituent particles possess *different* properties; such bodies are called *compound bodies*.

We shall be frustrated in all our attempts to obtain sulphur by the mutual fusion of non-sulphurous bodies. In a piece of pure sulphur, on the other hand, it will be equally vain to seek for the least particle of any substance but sulphur alone. The same is the case with many other bodies; for example, we are unable by the aid of the most powerful microscopes to find in gold or iron the least particle of any substance but gold or iron.

Those bodies which are constituted of perfectly *identical* particles are called *elementary* bodies, or briefly *elements*.

3. The number of elements at present known is 66; but many of these are of little importance and rare occurrence. The tabular view annexed affords a statement of such bodies as are of more frequent occurrence, arranged according to their properties. We merely give the names of the others.

The greater number of elements are lustrous bodies, and these we term *metals*. Those which do not possess this property we term *metalloids*, or, more properly, *non-metallic elements*. We also distinguish solid, liquid, and gaseous elements, and amongst the metals such as have only a trifling specific gravity, and others which are more dense.

TABULAR VIEW OF ELEMENTARY BODIES.

I. NON-METALLIC ELEMENTS.			II. METALLIC ELEMENTS.					
	I.*	II.		I.	II.		I.	II.
a. Gaseous.			*a. Light.*			*b. Heavy.*		
1. Oxygen........	O.	8	14. Potassium..	K.	39	21. Iron.........	Fe.	28
2. Hydrogen	H.	1	15. Sodium	Na.	23	22. Manganese	Mn.	27·6
3. Nitrogen......	N.	14	16. Calcium	Ca.	20	23. Cobalt	Co.	29·5
4. Chlorine	Cl.	35·5	17. Barium	Ba.	68·5	24. Nickel......	Ni.	29·6
5. Fluorine (?) ..	Fl.	19	18. Strontium..	Sr.	43·8	25. Copper......	Cu.	31·7
			19. Magnesium	Mg.	12·2	26. Cadmium...	Cd.	56
b. Liquid.			20. Aluminum.	Al.	13·7	27. Bismuth....	Bi.	213
						28. Lead	Pb.	103·7
6. Bromine	Br.	80				29. Tin	Sn.	58
						30. Zinc	Zn.	32·6
c. Solid.						31. Chromium.	Cr.	26·7
7. Iodine.........	I.	127·1				32. Antimony..	Sb.	129
8. Carbon	C.	6				33. Mercury....	Hg.	100
9. Sulphur	S.	16				34. Silver	Ag.	108·1
10. Phosphorus ..	P.	32				35. Gold	Au.	197
11. Arsenic	As.	75				36. Platinum...	Pt.	98·7
12. Silicium.......	Si.	21·3						
13. Boron	Bo.	10·9						

* The letters under I. indicate the symbols of the elements: the numbers in the second row, II., are the proportionate weights in which the elements combine with each other. (See § 15 and 16.)

The names of the rarer elements are as follows:—Aridium, Cerium, Didymium, Donarium, Erbium, Glucinum, Ilmenium, Iridium, Lanthanum, Lithium, Molybdenum, Niobium, Norium, Osmium, Palladium, Pelopium, Rhodium, Ruthenium, Selenium, Tantalum, Tellurium, Terbium, Thalium, Thorium, Titanium, Tungsten, Uranium, Vanadium, Yttrium, Zirconium.

4. *An element by itself is incapable of change.*—We may select any one of the simple substances above mentioned, and so long as it is kept from external contact with other bodies it will retain unaltered its own essential property or character. Sulphur may be, by heat, fused and converted into vapour, but in both conditions it retains its essential properties. Light, electricity, or magnetism are, *per se*, also incapable of changing an element.

5. *Chemical phenomena can be produced only by the contact of at least two dissimilar elements.*—Iron, exposed to moist air, rusts; sulphur and mercury, united by heat, entirely lose their properties, whilst a third body, with new properties, viz., vermilion, appears in their place.

6. The following mode of illustrating the different chemical combinations has been adopted. Simple substances are composed of the minutest particles of matter, which are perfectly homogeneous. Thus the fragment of sulphur, A. fig. 1, is composed of exceedingly minute particles of sulphur, *a* . . . . . . and the piece of mercury, B, fig. 2, consists of similar minute particles of mercury *b* . . . . . . Between the particles of one body and the particles of another, a mutual *attraction* takes place, which is termed *chemical affinity*

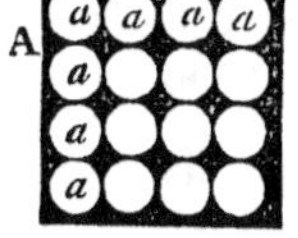

1.

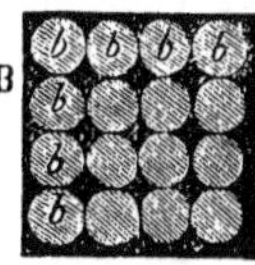

2.

In consequence of affinity, a particle of one body is brought into the closest contact with one particle of the other body. During this intimate contact of the different particles their peculiar properties disappear, and a compound substance appears, with new qualities. Thus, in fig. 3, the particles of sulphur, *a*, appear in connection with the particles of mercury, *b*, and compose the compound particles *a b*, of the vermilion.

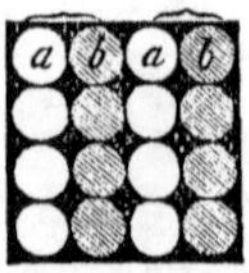

3.

The particles united by chemical attraction appear, as it were, to be combined together, wherefore the body produced is termed a compound body, or a *chemical compound*, and the different simple elements uniting to compose such a body are called the *constituents* of the compound.

7. Although all bodies have a mutual affinity to each other, still the measure or degree in which different elements are capable of combining, is very *dissimilar*, and in the present state of our knowledge we are unable to account for this difference. Suppose, for example, we bring into contact sulphur, iron, and mercury, all of which have a mutual affinity for each other, yet the sulphur will unite with the iron and not with the mercury. And hence the important deduction has been established, namely, that when certain substances are brought into contact with each other, those always first unite which have the greatest mutual affinity.

When simple substances have been thus combined, they remain in this condition till some external operative cause dissolves the union and separates again the different particles that were in intimate connection. It is comprehensible that, in this case, the qualities of the compound body disappear, and that its constituent parts again appear, each with its peculiar characteristics. We signify the separation of the particles of the compound by the term *decomposition.*

8. There are various causes which induce a *decomposition* of chemical combinations. In many compounds the mutual attraction of their constituent parts is so small that little more than a shake is required to effect their separation. For example, a gentle blow on *fulminating silver* is sufficient to cause its instant explosion or decomposition.

Heat is likewise an influential agent in the production of chemical decomposition. While it possesses the property of expanding bodies and of diminishing the cohesion of their particles, it has a tendency to counteract chemical attraction in all cases, and in many to overcome it. When common limestone is burned, that is, when submitted to intense heat, it is essentially changed. A gaseous body (carbonic acid) that previously existed in combination with it, is separated by the influence of the heat. The decomposition of many combinations by *light* is not so easily explicable.

If a *current of electricity* be conducted through a chemical compound, the attraction of the particles is diminished to such a degree, that at present no combination is known which can resist the decomposing influence of a powerful stream. We shall have an opportunity in the sequel of directing our attention more especially to these phenomena.

In the majority of cases of this kind, the *stronger affinity* which one substance has to another, is the active cause of the decomposition of chemical compounds. Suppose, for example, we heat, as shown in § 2, vermilion, which consists of sulphur and mercury particles (HgS), with iron (Fe), the latter combines with the sulphur by reason of its stronger affinity for this element. The particles of iron attract the sulphur-particles from the mercury, and the latter is consequently *released* from its combination, and set at *liberty*, as in figs. 4 and 5.

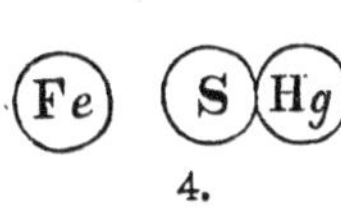

4.

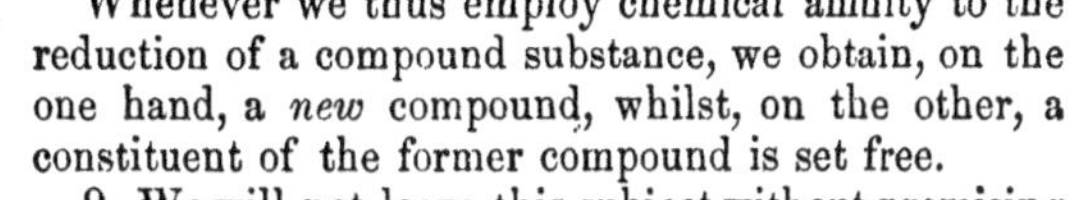

Whenever we thus employ chemical affinity to the reduction of a compound substance, we obtain, on the one hand, a *new* compound, whilst, on the other, a constituent of the former compound is set free.

9. We will not leave this subject without premising a few reflections intimately connected with a just and perfect comprehension of Nature, and especially of the earth and its manifold aspects.

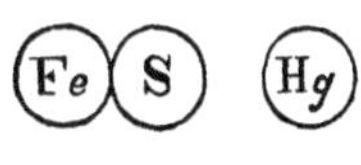

5.

The earth, together with its atmosphere, forms an entire whole, consisting of a certain number of elements. These elements are present in very unequal quantities, and mostly only in mutual combinations. In this manner have been produced the infinitely-diversified forms and qualities of the objects that surround us. For as, by the various combinations of a few alphabetical signs or letters, an endless series of words that compose the different languages of mankind can be formed, so the few elements, combined in different groups, without exception, constitute the immense variety of objects which everywhere surround us.

There is never so much as a single particle of matter belonging to the earth, nor of any object in or about it, that can be utterly lost. If we burn a piece of wood, we only change or alter the condition of its constituent parts. During the process of combustion, these elementary constituents, instead of remaining solid and ligneous, assume new gaseous and other invisible forms of combination; they disappear to us, but pass not beyond the sphere of our terrestrial atmosphere. When we come to the treatment of the food of plants, we shall prove that the constituent parts of the burnt wood which enter the atmosphere, in the form of new combinations, are again capable of reduction, and of being once more placed in a condition to form ligneous matter.

10. Hence, no particle of matter is ever entirely *annihilated*, and from this it also follows, that we are utterly incapable of *producing*, or of creating, the least material atom. When, therefore, we speak of the *preparation* or *production* of a body, we mean merely the separation of a body from a chemical compound, in which it already exists, or else the formation of the same, from its constituents in certain definite proportions.

A particle of sulphur ever remains the same individual indestructible atom of sulphur; and only in chemical union with other bodies, does it disappear to us, and is incapable of detection by the perceptions of the senses. But when we dissolve this chemical union, it appears again, with all its essential characteristics, being liberated from the combining influence of other substances.

11. Chemical affinity does not manifest itself, under all circumstances, between different elements. There are bodies which have powerful affinities for others, that can remain in contact for years without entering into combination. *Cohesion* is the most powerful obstacle to the operation of chemical attraction. That power which holds the individual particles of a simple body in connection, counteracts the power of affinity, and prevents these

particles from losing their coherence, and consequently from entering into combination with other bodies. Hence, it is a general rule, that the greater the power of cohesion, the less the tendency that exists between any two bodies, to enter into chemical combination. All causes which diminish the cohesion of bodies, promote their capacity for chemically combining with each other. Therefore, heat, which is in very many cases the most efficient medium of weakening the power of cohesion, is brought forward in aid of affinity. This agent reduces many bodies to the fluid state, and renders their particles easily moveable, whereby they are in a condition to follow the action of affinity, and to unite themselves with the particles of another body. *Fluid bodies* are already in this favourable position; hence, they are in a high-degree peculiarly susceptible of chemical union. We shall subsequently see that *water* is a very powerful agent in the reduction of bodies to a fluid condition; that is, to *dissolve* them, or hold them in a state of solution, by which their particles are maintained in the requisite degree of mobility.

12. The *gases*, being bodies or substances possessed of little or no cohesiveness, might be supposed to be peculiarly susceptible of chemical attraction, and to combine together with the greatest facility. The case, however, is different from what we should imagine; for example, oxygen and hydrogen, or chlorine and hydrogen, may be brought into mutual contact; yet, except under peculiar circumstances, they are incapable of chemical combination; still they have, notwithstanding, a strong mutual affinity, and their particles being gaseous, possess no cohesion. Consequently, gaseous particles appear to be too widely separated to allow chemical attraction to operate on both with energy sufficient to unite them. Most combinations containing a gaseous element may be decomposed by a higher temperature which increases the expansibility of the gas, and finally overcomes the influence of chemical attraction. We also perceive that the same cause, viz., heat, is in certain cases an auxiliary of affinity, and in others, it counteracts and finally destroys it.

Different Kinds of Combinations.

13. Heretofore we have assumed that chemical combination consists in the union of a particle of one simple body with a particle of another simple body. Although hereby indeed a great multiplicity of combinations can be produced, yet this is not the only possible way in which bodies can unite. In a great number of chemical compounds, there are *three*, in others *four*, and in some, *five* different particles in combination. Examples of a greater number of different elements, united in chemical combination, are exceedingly rare.

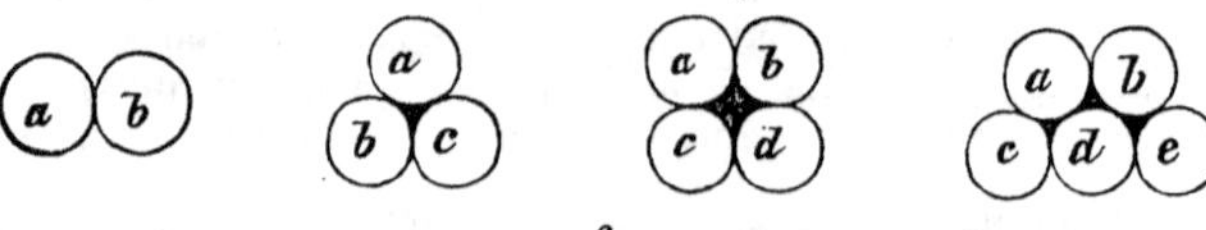

6.

Fig. 6 represents combined, or rather grouped, particles which consist of 2, 3, 4, and 5 simple molecules. It is to be remarked, that by far the greater number of chemical combinations, consist only of two or three dissimilar particles. Those containing four or five are by no means numerous.

It would, however, be erroneous, and contrary to the fact, to infer that the multiplicity of simple materials, capable of uniting with each other, is exhausted in the above-cited examples of combination. An infinite series of chemical compounds is disclosed to our view by the capability of the particles chemically to unite, not only in pairs, but in several other relative proportions. Thus, *one* particle *a* combines not only with one particle *b*, but also with 2 *b*, 3 *b*, 4 *b*, *n b*. Moreover, *several* particles of *a* can combine with *several* of *b*, for example, 2 *a* with 3 *b*, 5 *b*, 7 *b*, &c. Indeed, frequently we find several particles of three, four, or five different elements grouped together in one chemical compound. To assist the comprehension, we will represent such a group, and then prove the fact by examples. The two elements, oxygen O, and sulphur S, form the following *series of compounds:*—

Hyposulphurous Acid. Sulphurous Acid. Sulphuric Acid.

It will be now easy to understand what is meant by the expression *different degrees of combination* of bodies. A glance at the above series will show why sulphurous acid is said to be a *lower*, and sulphuric acid a *higher*, degree of combination of oxygen and sulphur. It is much more difficult to imagine such groups of compound bodies, which consist of *several* particles of *three* or *four* different elements. Before proceeding farther, we may mention, as an example, that an atom of *cane sugar* is to be considered a group of twelve particles of carbon, eleven of hydrogen, and eleven of oxygen.

14. A compound body may admit of combination with a second body of equally complex composition; hence, there is formed a compound of the *second order*. Thus, sulphuric acid unites with potassa, and forms a sulphate of potassa (KO,SO_3). When different combinations of the second order are re-combined, there arise those of the *third order*, of which alum ($Al_2O_3,3SO_3 + KO,SO_3$) is an example. The latter combinations are, however, of unfrequent occurrence, and in the course of describing the individual compounds, we may obtain gradually a clearer comprehension of their nature.

15. In order to express chemical compounds, a number of *symbols* have been introduced, which are extremely convenient in the study of chemistry. The initial letters of the Latin names of the elements have been chosen, of which examples are given in the tabular view (§ 3) in the column I. In chemistry, the letter S represents an atom of sulphur, Hg an atom of mercury, and so on. Hence, if the symbols HgS are placed together they represent an atom of a chemical compound of mercury and sulphur, which is called vermilion, in the same manner, as if an atom of mercury and an atom of sulphur HgS were, as in § 8, placed in contact with each other. HgO is the compound of an atom of mercury, with an atom of oxygen (oxide of mercury); SO_2 is a combination of *one* atom of sulphur with *two* of oxygen (sulphurous acid); SO_3 indicates the higher proportion in which these elements combine to produce sulphuric acid, consisting of *one* part of sulphur, and *three* parts of oxygen, &c.

16. The elements combine with each other in definite unalterable *propor-*

tions by weight. The tabular view of the simple substances given in § 3 represents in column No II. these proportionate weights. They are the result of many experiments, conducted with the greatest care and persevering energy. They are termed the *equivalents, atomic*, or *proportionate weights* of the elements.

The cause of combination in definite proportions by weight depends chiefly on the principle stated in § 6, viz., that even the smallest particles of bodies have definite weights, varying much from each other. Accordingly, those numbers express nothing more than the weight of one of the minutest particles of each of those simple substances.

Consequently when an equivalent of sulphur, that weighs 16 parts, combines with a particle of mercury that weighs 100 parts, a compound particle of vermilion is produced, which weighs 116 parts. In fact, if we decompose 116 ounces of vermilion into its constituents, we obtain 100 ounces of mercury, and 16 ounces of sulphur. Again, as water consists of one equivalent of oxygen, which weighs 8, and one equivalent of hydrogen weighing 1, the two combined with each other, represent 9 parts by weight of water. Assuming, therefore, the water to be perfectly pure, it follows that 9 parts will invariably contain 8 parts by weight of oxygen, and 1 part of hydrogen.

If we place the symbol S, which denotes an equivalent of sulphur that weighs 16, and Hg, a particle of mercury, weighing 100, HgS will then represent the compound of the two elements, weighing 116 parts. Hence, chemical symbols have a double value, for they do not merely express of what, and of how many equivalents a compound is composed, but, in addition to this, they indicate the *proportionate* weights in which the elements are held in combination. This may be farther illustrated by an example. The symbol HgO, oxide of mercury, signifies not merely that this compound consists of one equivalent of mercury and one equivalent of oxygen, but also, that 100 parts by weight of the former are combined with 8 parts of the latter, to form 108 parts of the oxide of mercury. SO_3 represents *sulphuric acid* as a compound of one equivalent of sulphur, with three equivalents of oxygen, or of 16 parts by weight of sulphur with $3 \times 8 = 24$ of oxygen, which, together amount to 40 parts by weight of sulphuric acid.

As we know at a glance by these symbols, that in 116 parts by weight of vermilion, 100 parts of mercury are combined with 16 parts of sulphur, so we may easily calculate how much of each of these elements is contained in 100, or in 30, or in any assigned quantity by weight of vermilion. Suppose 100 lbs. of vermilion are to be prepared, how many pounds of mercury and sulphur are required for this purpose?

(1.) The quantity of sulphur x is to 100 as 16 is to 116, or:

$$x : 100 = 16 : 116; \text{ hence } x = \frac{100 \times 16}{116} = 13{\cdot}7.$$

(2.) The required quantity of mercury y is to 100 as 100 to 116: thus:

$$y : 100 = 100 : 116; \text{ hence } y = \frac{100 \times 100}{116} = 86{\cdot}3.$$

Therefore, in preparing 100 lbs. of vermilion, we employ 13·7 lbs. of sulphur and 86.3 lbs. of mercury. These numbers express the *percentage* weight of sulphur and mercury contained in 100 parts of vermilion.

The knowledge of the proportional numbers in which simple substances mutually combine presents still another advantage. Suppose we are required to state how much vermilion can be obtained from 30 lbs. of mercury, when the same is combined with sulphur.

The required quantity of vermilion x stands to the given proportion of mercury, 30 lbs., as 116 : 100, consequently:

$$x : 30 = 116 : 100; \text{ therefore } x = \frac{30 \times 116}{100} = 34{\cdot}8.$$

Thus, if the combination is properly effected, 34·8 lbs. of vermilion ought to be obtained from 30 lbs. of mercury; hence 4·8 lbs. of sulphur are requisite. If less than this quantity of sulphur be employed, the whole of the mercury will not be converted into vermilion. If more than 4·8 lbs. of sulphur be used, the *superfluous* sulphur does not combine with the mercury, but it either remains *mixed* with the vermilion, or it is volatilized by the heat applied during the process of combination. Only those who are ignorant of the law of definite proportions, whereby the elements are capable of combining with each other, could assert that from 30 lbs. of mercury more than 34·8 pounds of vermilion can be prepared. This law of chemical combination is as certain as that 3 and 4 added together amount to 7 and not to 9 or any other number.

Several significant letters placed in contiguity and representing a compound are called a chemical *formula*, the meaning of which, after what has been stated, can present no difficulty to the student. The formula SO_3, therefore denotes the following:—

Composition of Sulphuric Acid.

Formula.		Number of Equivalents.	Constituents.		Combining Proportion.	Percentage Weight.
S	=	1	Sulphur	=	16	40
O_3	=	3	Oxygen	=	24	60
SO_3	=	1 equivalent of Sulphuric Acid		=	40	100

General Properties of Chemical Compounds.

17. While we direct our attention here to the general properties of chemical compounds, we are not to understand thereby those general properties of bodies which have been already described in Physics (§ 16). On the contrary, we intend to indicate their most general *chemical* characters, particularly the manner in which they deport themselves towards other bodies; if any, and what kind of changes are produced in them.

Three kinds of compounds have been distinguished from an early period in the history of this science, viz., *acids*, *bases*, and *neutral* bodies.

Acids are chemical compounds which have an *acid taste*, impart a *red* colour to vegetable blues (for example, violet and iris), and *lose* their qualities when mixed with a sufficient quantity of one of the compounds of the following class.

Bases (from *basis,* foundation) are distinguished by an *alkaline* taste. A mixture of wood-ashes and lime, with water, produces a substance which has this alkaline property in a high degree. The bases have the power of changing vegetable blues into *green,* and, what is very remarkable, the blue vegetable colour which had been *reddened* by the presence of an acid recovers its *blue tint* on the immission of a sufficient quantity of an alkaline base. On the other hand, the bases entirely lose their basic characters if allowed to combine with acids.

It must, however, be observed, that there are many acids and bases which either do not possess these properties at all or only in a very slight degree. Insoluble acids, such as silicic acid, and insoluble bases, as the heavy metallic oxides, have no taste, and do not affect vegetable colours. The term *strong* acids and bases is usually applied to such as possess the above-mentioned characters in a remarkable degree.

Thus we perceive that acids and alkalies are bodies possessed of opposite characters, yet in consequence of their mutual affinity, enter into combination with each other, whereby they become neutralized and form new bodies which are neither acid nor alkaline, and are commonly called *salts.*

Such bodies as are neither acid nor alkaline are termed also *neutral* bodies. But the salts are not the only neutral compounds. There is a very numerous class of neutral bodies procured from animal and vegetable substances, such, for instance, as sugar, spirit of wine, albumin, &c.; these latter are likewise called *indifferent* substances, because they exhibit no particular action upon, or affinity to, other substances.

18. We are, however, under the necessity of confining our consideration of the *general* chemical deportment of bodies within a brief compass, until we arrive at the enumeration and description of the individual substances. Still we may be allowed to allude to the important distinction between a mechanical mixture of different substances and a chemical compound of the same, from the confusion of which an erroneous opinion may be frequently formed. However intimately different substances may be mixed together, we may readily distinguish, either by the naked eye or by the aid of a magnifying-glass, the particles of those substances beside each other, whilst in chemical combinations no power whatever will enable us to detect the least difference between the particles of the combined mass. The detection of mixtures of fluids or gases is impossible by vision alone, still the mechanical nature of the mixture may be determined by other means, since the individual components of the mixture *retain* their original qualities, which is by no means the case in chemical combinations.

Division of the Subject.

19. Chemical phenomena have always been divided into *two* principal groups. The reason of this twofold division of the subject will be described hereafter. It is very natural to consider, in the first place, the *simple* and afterwards the more *complicated* combinations: of these we have given examples in § 13, when showing the distinction between the manner in which *two* elements combine to produce vermilion, and *three* to form sugar.

Hence we divide Chemistry into two principal sections, of which the first comprises the combinations of the *simple* groups, and the second the combinations of the *compound* groups.

With few exceptions the latter compounds are either met with in animal or vegetable substances, or are prepared from materials derived from them. Hence the second division of Chemistry is frequently termed *Organic*, or Animal and Vegetable Chemistry, in contradistinction to the first branch, which is called *Inorganic* Chemistry.

The following table will give an idea of the farther division of this branch of natural science: —

(A.) COMBINATIONS OF THE SIMPLE GROUPS. (INORGANIC CHEMISTRY.)	(B. COMBINATIONS OF THE COMPOUND GROUPS. (ORGANIC CHEMISTRY.)
I. *Elements and their Combinations.* (1.) Non-Metallic. (2.) Metallic. II. *Peculiar Decompositions of these Compounds.* (1.) By Electricity. (2.) By Light.	I. *Compound Radicals and their Combinations* (1.) Acids. (2.) Bases. (3.) Indifferent Substances. II. *Peculiar Decompositions of these Compounds.* (1.) Spontaneous Decomposition. (2.) Dry distillation.

(A.) COMBINATIONS OF THE SIMPLE GROUPS.

(INORGANIC CHEMISTRY.)

20. In this section we shall become acquainted with the elements themselves, and of their most simple combinations. These bodies are partly met with in Nature under the form of *minerals*, and are partly prepared by artificial processes (§ 10), in which latter case they are called chemical *preparations*. As the composition of these compounds is tolerably simple, their decompositions and the new *products* thereby produced may be easily understood and predetermined.

I. ELEMENTS AND THEIR COMBINATIONS.

21. At the present time we are acquainted with 66 simple substances; but as every year new members are discovered, we are entirely ignorant of the number actually in existence. It may be remarked that even those substances which we now regard as simple elements may be likewise compounds, and that only a very limited number of bodies are really elementary. Still it is very improbable that we shall ever be able to resolve them into simpler forms of matter, and so long as this cannot be effected we must continue to regard them as simple bodies. A great number are so extremely rare that many chemists have never seen them. It is possible that in the interior of the earth large masses of these bodies occur. We shall, however, refrain from alluding to them, since the majority are entirely foreign to ordinary phenomena.

(1.) NON-METALLIC ELEMENTS.

22. Including Oxygen, Hydrogen, Nitrogen, Chlorine, Bromine, Iodine, Fluorine, Sulphur, Phosphorus, Arsenic, Carbon, Silicium, and Boron.

I. OXYGEN.

Symbol: O = 8; Specific Gravity = 1·026.

Oxygen is met with in Nature, either combined or merely mixed with other substances. It may be readily obtained in the pure state from several of its compounds by the influence of heat alone. The red oxide of mercury is one of the substances which readily part with their oxygen. To prepare oxygen from this compound, a portion of the oxide is introduced into a small tube of hard glass (fig. 7) closed at one extremity, and into the other end

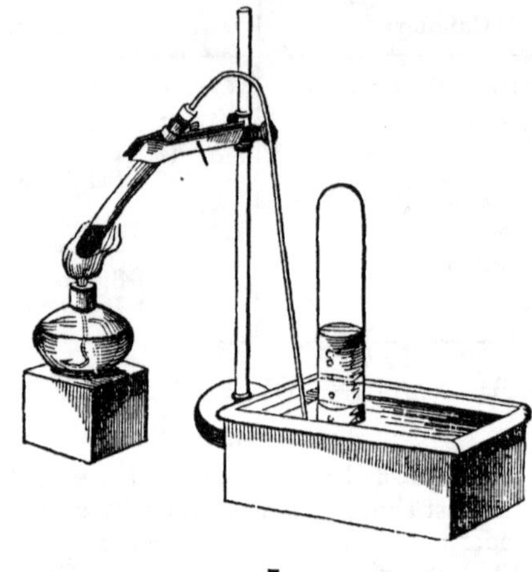

7.

of which is fastened, by means of a cork, a delivery tube. On applying the heat of a small charcoal furnace, or spirit-lamp, as shown in fig. 8, the oxygen

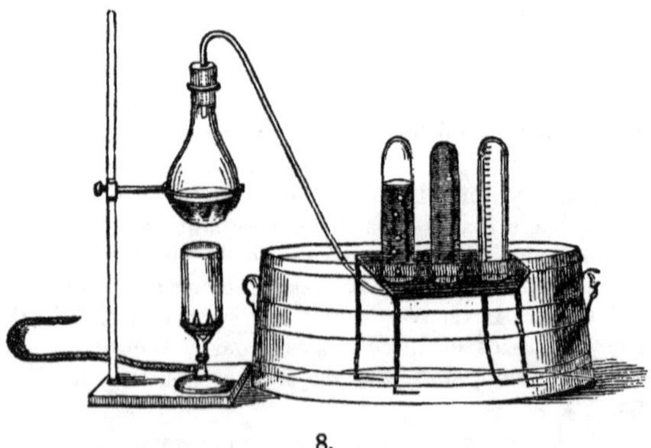

8.

is disengaged, and may be collected in the receiver, which is filled with water, and inverted over the pneumatic trough.* The change may be represented by the following equation:—

Oxide of Mercury.		Mercury.		Oxygen.
HgO	=	Hg	+	O

Oxygen may be likewise very conveniently prepared, in a state of perfect purity, by heating chlorate of potassa (KO,ClO_5) in the same apparatus, the decomposition being expressed as follows:—

Chlorate of Potassa.		Chloride of Potassium.		Oxygen.
KO,ClO_5	=	KCl	+	O_6.

But when this gas is required in very large quantities, it is usual to prepare it from the binoxide of manganese, an oxide occurring abundantly in Nature. This oxide requiring a high temperature, is heated in a retort placed in a furnace (fig. 9), and to which is attached a tube, passing into a wash-bottle,

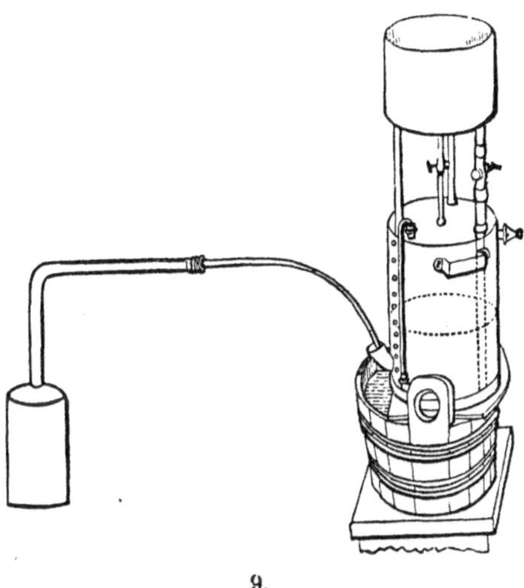

9.

containing a little lime-water for the purpose of absorbing carbonic acid, with which the oxygen may be contaminated. The gas is then collected in the usual manner.

The binoxide of manganese, however, does not part with more than one-third of its oxygen, a mixture of protoxide and sesquioxide of the metal being left in the retort. The following equation represents the change produced by heat:—

Binoxide of Manganese.		Protoxide.		Sesquioxide.		Oxygen.
$3(MnO_2)$	=	MnO	+	Mn_2O_3	+	O_2.

* A similar arrangement to this is made use of for collecting gases in general.

All the green parts of plants evolve oxygen when exposed to the *light of the sun;* a fact which may be readily demonstrated by placing a leafy branch, which is still connected with the parent plant, or a number of fresh leaves, under a stoppered funnel filled with water, and then exposing them to the influence of solar light. After a short time small air-bubbles, consisting of pure oxygen, collect in the upper part of the funnel. The elimination of oxygen observed in many of the so-called *infusoria,* may be also ascribed to plants.

Oxygen is a gas as colourless and odourless as the surrounding air; it is, however, readily distinguished by the extraordinary vivacity with which inflammable substances burn in it. If, for instance, a scarcely-kindled match be plunged into a cylinder filled with oxygen, it instantly bursts into flame, and burns with the greatest rapidity. Phosphorus burns with a dazzling white light, rivalling the sun in brilliancy, whilst sulphur burns with a beautiful blue flame. Pieces of charcoal, and thin strips of steel, to which are attached pieces of amadou [spunk] dipped in sulphur, if previously ignited at the extremities, and then introduced into this gas, as in figs. 10 and 11, throw off the most beautiful scintillations, and are entirely consumed.

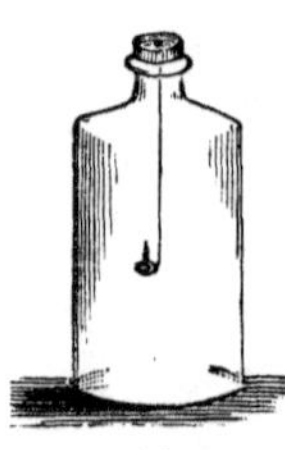
10.

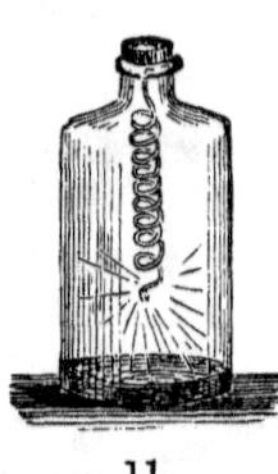
11.

These phenomena depend upon the powerful affinity of oxygen gas for those substances. Hence combustion itself is nothing more than the effect of their combination with the latter element. The compounds formed in the above-mentioned experiments are carbonic acid (CO_2), sulphurous acid (SO_2), phosphoric acid (PO_5), and sesquioxide of iron (Fe_2O_3).

Oxygen is not only the most extensively-diffused element, but it occurs in the largest quantity. It is contained in by far the greatest number of minerals, and forms from 30 to 50 per cent of the entire mass of plants and animals, whilst 112 lbs. of water contain 100 lbs., or eight-ninths of its weight of this gas. It may be said to constitute a third of the known crust of the earth.

It is also important to remark, that the principal mass of the atmosphere is a *mixture* of oxygen with another gas, viz., nitrogen. Five measures contain one of oxygen, and hence it forms one-fifth of the whole atmosphere.

From this it will be seen that all bodies existing in the air are exposed to the influence of the oxygen therein, which exhibits a continual tendency to produce chemical compounds with those substances which are not at all, or only partly, in combination with this gas. Hence it is the cause of an endless series of chemical phenomena which are ever going on around us, and within our bodies. If circumstances are particularly favourable, chemical combination takes place with a rapidity sufficient to generate a large amount of heat, and finally light, or, in other words, those phenomena occur that are ordinarily termed *combustion.* But in by far the greater number of cases, the combination of oxygen takes place more slowly, and unattended with the phenomena of ignition. Heat, however, is undoubtedly generated, but becomes less evident in consequence of being distributed over a greater space of time. The rusting of iron, formation of verdigris on copper, fermentation, putrefaction, decay, moulding, disintegration, respiration of men and animals, are all phenomena primarily induced by oxygen. In all these cases new oxygen-compounds are produced; but if the oxygen were excluded, none of these changes could be effected, any more than a body could burn without the presence of the atmospheric air which contains so large an amount of oxygen.

23. Combination with oxygen is also termed *oxidation.* To *oxidise,* therefore, is to unite with oxygen, and the result of the combination is named an *oxide* or oxygen-compound. But as oxygen is capable of combining in several proportions with most of the above elements, the different *degrees of oxidation* are distinguished by a particular name, as is seen in the following examples.

Oxygen, in combination with non-metallic elements, chiefly forms *acid,* with metals, *basic,* oxides. An elementary body combining with oxygen, and forming therewith an oxygen-compound, is generally designated by the term *radical* of such a combination; for example, sulphur is the radical of sulphuric acid ($S\,O_3$).

The general properties of oxygen-compounds are most conveniently exhibited in the following Table:—

SYNOPSIS OF OXYGEN-COMPOUNDS.

1. BASES.

Degree of Oxidation.		Examples.	Formulæ.	General Properties.
1	*a.* Suboxides...	Suboxide of Mercury Suboxide of Copper..	Hg_2O Cu_2O	Feeble bases; are separated from their combinations by most of the other oxides; absorb oxygen with avidity from the atmosphere, and are converted thereby into higher oxides.
	b. Protoxides...	Protoxide of Iron..... Protoxide of Manganese	FeO MnO	
2	*a.* Protoxides...	Protoxide of Mercury Protoxide of Potassium .... Protoxide of Sodium	HgO KO NaO	Strong bases; frequently caustic; do not pass into a higher state of oxidation when exposed alone to the air. The oxides of the heavy metals are insoluble in water.
	b. Sesquioxides	Sesquioxide of Iron.. Sesquioxide of Manganese................	Fe_2O_3 Mn_2O_3	
3	Binoxides ...	Binoxide of Manganese .... Binoxide of Lead	MnO_2 PbO_2	Neither acid nor basic; decomposed by heat into lower oxides and oxygen.

2. ACIDS.

	c. First degree	Hyposulphurous Acid	S_2O_2	
1 (4)	Second degree	Sulphurous Acid...... Nitrous Acid .... Chlorous Acid .... Phosphorous Acid	SO_2 NO_3 ClO_3 PO_3	Feeble acids; separated from their combinations by most of the other acids; attract oxygen from the air, and become thereby converted into acids of the fourth degree of oxidation.

Degree of Oxidation.		Examples.	Formulæ.	General Properties.
	d. Third degree	Hyposulphuric Acid	S_2O_5	
2 (5)	Fourth degree	Sulphuric Acid .... Nitric Acid............. Chloric Acid .... Manganic Acid	SO_3 NO_5 ClO_5 MnO_3	Strong acids; frequently caustic; mostly unchangeable in the air, some being decomposed by heat like the following.
3 (6)	Highest degree	Perchloric Acid........ Permanganic Acid ...	ClO_7 Mn_2O_7	Feebler than the foregoing acids; readily decomposed by heat into oxygen and a lower degree of oxidation.

24. In addition to these six principal degrees of oxidation, chemists are acquainted with a number of intermediate compounds which in general are feebler acids, and more readily decomposed; examples of this kind are adduced under *c* and *d*, namely, hyposulphurous acid (S_2O_2), and hyposulphuric acid (S_2O_5). In the same manner we find amongst the metallic oxides a number of intermediate combinations possessing no definite chemical characters.

Although the non-metallic elements, in combining with oxygen, give rise in general to the formation of *acids*, we nevertheless meet with a number of inferior oxides possessing properties neither acid nor basic, as, for example, water (HO), protoxide of nitrogen (NO), carbonic oxide (CO), and many others. On the other hand we find that while most of the metallic oxides are *bases*, some of the higher oxides comport themselves as acids, as manganic acid (MnO_3), chromic acid (CrO_3), antimonic acid (SbO_5), &c.

From these examples it will be seen that the name and position of the oxide are determined not by the *number* of equivalents of oxygen, in combination with the radical, but by its *chemical* properties; as, for instance, sulphuric acid, containing only *three* equivalents of oxygen, is a stronger acid than nitric acid, which contains *five* equivalents of the same element.

25. An opinion was long prevalent that oxygen was the only acidifying principle, and from this supposed quality its name was derived. But as it has subsequently been ascertained that there are very strong acids which contain no oxygen, and also that this body, in combination with metals, forms the strongest bases with qualities directly opposed to acids, the term has lost the major part of its signification. On this account the acids which contain this element are now distinguished by the term *oxygen-acids*.

Oxygen is, however, justly accounted the principal, the most important and influential of all elementary bodies. It merits this preference by its abundance, its powerful affinities, and by its manifold combinations with other substances.

2. HYDROGEN.

Symbol: H = 1; Specific Gravity = 0·0688.

26. Hydrogen occurs abundantly in nature, although it is never met with in the free state. It is found in the greatest quantity united with oxygen, forming a compound (HO) termed *water*, which, as is well known, is extensively diffused over the surface of our globe. We invariably avail ourselves of this compound in preparing the pure gas.

Hydrogen is obtained by heating water in a small flask, and passing its vapour through a red-hot gun-barrel, filled with iron nails (*a b*, fig. 12), to

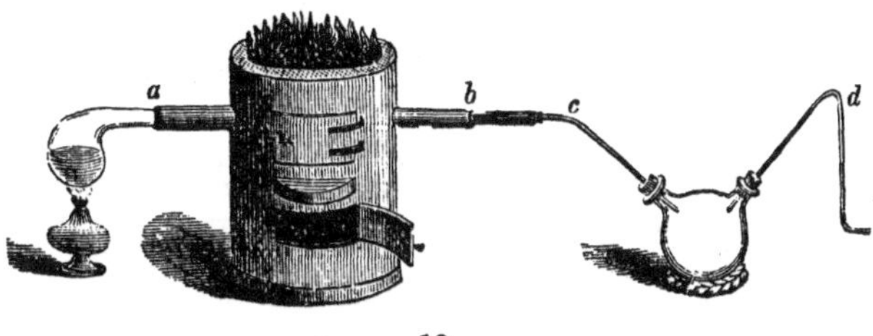

12.

which is attached, by means of a cork, a delivery-tube, *c d*. The oxygen of the water combines with the iron, and produces sesquioxide (Fe_2O_3), while the hydrogen escapes at the curved extremity of the delivery-tube, *c*, and may be collected in the usual manner. The decomposition of the water is thus represented by an equation:—

Water.		Iron.		Sesquioxide of Iron.		Hydrogen.
$3HO$	+	$2Fe$	=	Fe_2O_3	+	$3H$.

Hydrogen is, however, more conveniently prepared by introducing pieces of granulated zinc into an apparatus (fig. 13) which is termed an evolution-flask, and pouring over them a mixture of water and sulphuric acid. The products formed from Zn, HO, and SO_3, are hydrogen, H, evolved in the form of gas, and sulphate of zinc, ZnO,SO_3, which remains in the flask.

Zinc.		Hydrated Sulphuric Acid.		Sulphate of Zinc.		Hydrogen.
Zn	+	HO,SO_3	=	ZnO,SO_3	+	H.

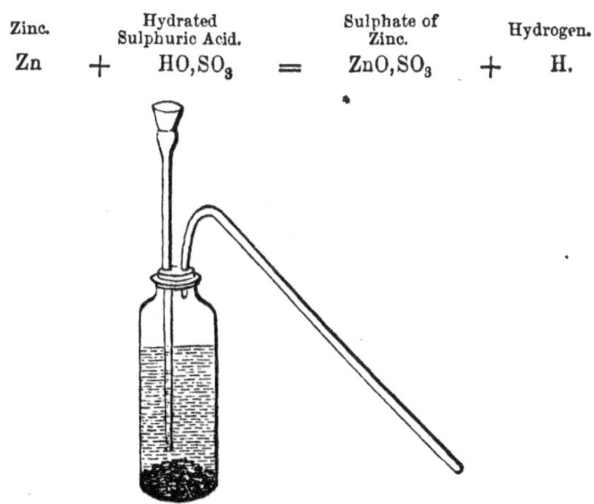

13.

In these two cases the decomposition of water depends upon the affinity of oxygen for iron and zinc.

Hydrogen is a colourless, odourless gas, that *ignites* when approached by flame, and *burns* with a feeble light, but with development of much heat. It thus combines with the oxygen of the atmosphere and produces water HO. As one volume of hydrogen weighs fourteen times less than an equal bulk of atmospheric air, it follows that silk balls that are filled with this gas will ascend in the atmosphere, precisely in the same manner as a cork will rise in water. For the purpose, however, of inflating the larger air-balloons, the cheaper carburetted hydrogen (coal-gas) is generally employed.

Hydrogen has at present received no particular application in the arts, although it is sometimes employed for increasing the intensity of the forge-fire. If we sprinkle water upon red-hot coals it is thereby decomposed, the oxygen combines with the carbon to form carbonic acid, while the liberated hydrogen burns and developes a very high degree of heat.

When hydrogen is passed over an ignited metallic oxide, for instance over protoxide of copper (CuO), it combines with the oxygen of the latter, producing water, which escapes in the form of vapour, whilst the pure metal remains behind. This mode of withdrawing oxygen is termed *deoxidation*, and is frequently employed by chemists.

Compounds of Hydrogen.

27. Hydrogen combines chiefly with the non-metallic elements, scarcely any combinations of this element with metals being at present known. From 5 to 6 per cent. of hydrogen is found in all vegetable and animal matters.

With chlorine, bromine, iodine, fluorine, sulphur, and some other bodies, this element produces acid compounds, which have received the name of *hydrogen-acids*. Its most important combination, however, is:—

Water.

Formula: HO = 9; Specific Gravity = 1.

28. When 12 parts by weight of hydrogen and 100 of oxygen, or, what is the same, two measures of the former gas and one of the latter, are mixed together, no combination occurs, for under these circumstances they are incapable of uniting. Their union, however, is instantaneously effected when the mechanical mixture is brought into contact with an ignited body. The combination is attended with a violent explosion, that is, a flash and loud report, both occasioned by the aqueous vapour being enormously expanded by heat at the moment of its formation. This gaseous mixture has therefore received the name of *explosive gas*, and to avoid the danger attending experiments it should always be prepared in small quantities. By means, however, of a suitable apparatus, a larger quantity of this explosive gas may be burned, and the water, formed during the combustion, collected in sufficient quantity to convince the experimenter that it possesses all the properties of the purest water.

As we are well acquainted with most of these properties, partly through daily experience and partly through physics, we intend to state here only the *chemical* qualities of water. Although neither acid nor basic, but in a high degree neutral or indifferent, water nevertheless possesses a powerful affinity for many chemical compounds, and more especially for acids and bases. Its compounds with these bodies are termed *hydrates*. In the formation of hydrates a development of heat generally takes place, and is occasioned by the water passing into a denser condition, a portion of its combined heat being simultaneously evolved (Physics, § 146). Examples of this kind are the development of heat in mixing strong sulphuric acid with water, and in the slaking of lime.

The acids are more frequently employed in the form of hydrates, as, for example, hydrated sulphuric acid (HO,SO_3) than in the anhydrous condition; and when the latter are not specially indicated, the hydrates are usually understood to be meant when speaking of acids. The *water of hydration* does not admit of being separated from acids by heat, but only by the superior affinity of a metallic oxide.

The bases, or metallic oxides, occasionally acquire peculiar colours in combining with water. Sesquioxide of iron is red, whilst its hydrate is brown; protoxide of copper is black, its hydrate a beautiful blue. Most oxides part with their water of hydration on application of heat, some at a lower, others at a higher temperature. Hydrate of potassa, KO,HO, and hydrate of soda, NaO,HO, however, do not lose their water when exposed even to the strongest red-heat.

Water combines also with salts, forming with their particles solid crystals, and in this state it is termed *water of crystallization*. We perceive in salts and in hydrates that water may be reduced to the *solid* condition not only by low temperatures, but also by chemical affinity; *anhydrous* salts are therefore distinguished from such as contain water of crystallization. The compound NaO,SO_3 is anhydrous sulphate of soda, while NaO,SO_3+10HO is the same salt combined with ten equivalents of water. The greater number of salts, however, part with their water in dry air or when exposed to a temperature of 100° C. (212° F.) In this case the particles of water escape from between the molecules of the salt, which then crumbles down, and exhibits the phenomena termed *efflorescence* of crystals.

29. Water possesses the remarkable property of *dissolving* a great variety of substances; but solution appears to be less the result of chemical affinity than of the great attraction the water-atoms possess for those of the soluble body. The former penetrate through the particles of the latter, and destroy their coherence. Solution appears not to induce any change in the chemical properties of a substance, for on application of heat the water is expelled, and we recover the particles of the dissolved substance, with all its original cohesive properties unchanged.

When to the solution of any substance a new portion of the same is added, without becoming dissolved, the solution is said to be *saturated*, but in general the liquid takes up an additional quantity of the soluble substance, if the temperature be increased. If this solution be now cooled, a portion of the dissolved substance is usually separated in *crystals* of definite form (Physics § 19). Solution is therefore the means of obtaining bodies in the *crystallized* state. If, on the other hand, a dissolved body is suddenly made to pass from the liquid to the solid state, as, for example, when a hot saturated solution is suddenly cooled, the salt does not separate in the form of distinct crystals, but as an *amorphous precipitate*. The latter form is also produced on adding to the solution a substance which produces an *insoluble* compound. If to a solution of baryta (BaO), in water, we add sulphuric acid, the two compounds combine to produce the insoluble sulphate of baryta

(BaO,SO_3), which is immediately deposited at the bottom of the vessel, in the form of a white precipitate.

It is upon the solubility of some compounds, and insolubility of others, the possibility of separating many substances from each other depends, and hence their deportment with water is to the chemist a most important characteristic.

30. The solvent properties of water are the true causes why we never obtain this universal and important fluid in natural and domestic economy in a state of *purity*. It constantly participates in the properties of the manifold sources whence it is derived, or through which we obtain it. Whenever it is in contact with the soil, it invariably dissolves the soluble constituents; and hence it follows that water springing from rocks which are only slightly soluble, as sandstone and granite, is very pure, and is called *soft water*, while that which is derived from calcareous formations is termed *hard water*, and contains a deal of lime, which produces an incrustation on the sides and bottom of the vessel wherein it is boiled. The water of springs which have their source at a greater depth possesses a higher temperature, reaching in some instances to the boiling heat; these sources have received the name of *thermal springs*. If water meets on its passage through the soil, with carbonic acid, hydrosulphuric acid, salts, &c., a portion of these compounds enter into solution, and impart to the water peculiar properties, such as are exhibited in the waters of *mineral springs*. Sea-water contains in solution so many salts, especially common salt and sulphate of magnesia, as to be entirely unfit for the ordinary purposes of life.

Water, distilled from a retort (Physics, § 129), is free from all non-volatile substances, and next to it in point of purity ranks that which is distilled in Nature's laboratory, viz., rain. The latter is therefore especially employed in many of the arts which require pure water, as in dyeing, washing, &c.

3. NITROGEN.

Symbol: N = 14; Specific Gravity = 0·976.

31. Five volumes of common air contain four of nitrogen, mixed with one of oxygen; this element, therefore, constitutes four-fifths of the entire atmosphere. The proportion of nitrogen in the solid portion of the earth is very small; it is rare in mineral, and only sparingly found in vegetable substances; but it is more abundant in animal bodies. Nitrogen may be easily prepared in the following manner: A large flat cork is floated on the surface of the water in the pneumatic trough. On this is placed a small porcelain capsule, containing a fragment of phosphorus, which is ignited and then immediately covered over by a large bell-jar as shown in fig. 14. The jar being immersed about an inch deep in the water, prevents the air from escaping. The burning phosphorus combines with the oxygen of the air contained in the bell-jar and produces phosphoric acid (PO_5), which is dissolved by the water, while nitrogen, amounting to four-fifths of the air in the bell-jar, remains.

14.

It is, however, more convenient to employ, instead of the phosphorus, a few drops of naphtha or spirit of wine, since the vapours of phosphoric acid remain some time before they are dissolved by the water, while the little carbonic acid produced by the combustion of the naphtha in no way interferes with the results of the experiment.

This gas is odourless and colourless, and not injurious to health, for large quantities are continually taken into the stomach and lungs in the processes of respiration and deglutition. If a burning body be introduced into a cylinder of pure nitrogen as in fig. 15, it is instantly extinguished, and animals placed therein soon die for the want of oxygen which is indispensable to their respiration.

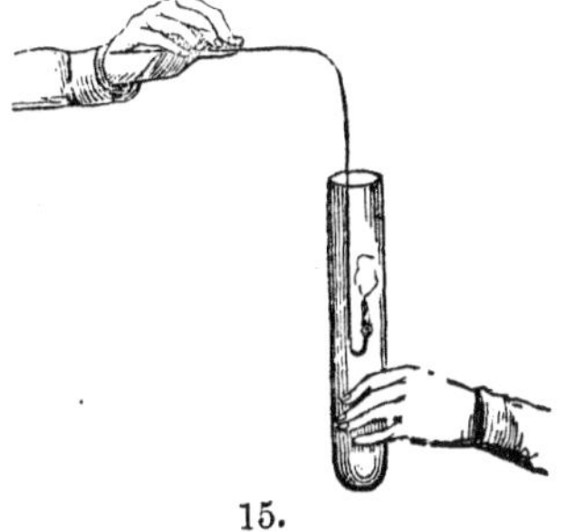

15.

32. The *atmosphere* contains, moreover, many volatile substances, such as *carbonic acid*, to the extent of 4 volumes in 10,000, and aqueous vapour, which varies in quantity according to the temperature (Physics, § 132). On the other hand, many impurities, such as those arising from the exhalations of men, animals, and decaying matter, escape into the almost illimitable atmosphere. The presence of these substances can, therefore, only be detected and chemically ascertained at the place of their formation.

Compounds of Nitrogen.

33. Nitrogen possesses only a feeble affinity for other substances. With many, especially with metals, it does not appear to combine, and its compounds with the other elements are all very readily decomposed.

Nitric Acid, HO,NO_5.—This acid is obtained in the form of hydrate, by distilling in a glass retort (fig. 16), 1 lb. of nitre with an equal weight of sulphuric acid. The pure acid is colourless, of peculiar odour, and caustic acid taste; it imparts a yellow colour to vegetable and animal substances, and finally destroys them. It also dissolves most of the metals, a property dependent upon the readiness with which its oxygen combines with other elements, hence nitric acid is frequently employed by the chemist as a *means of oxidation.* In processes of this nature, the acid loses three equivalents of oxygen, a compound NO_2 being produced, which is a colourless gas, and is called *binoxide of nitrogen.* This gas has the remarkable property of instantly absorbing oxygen from the air, and becoming thereby converted into the brownish-red vapour of *nitrous acid*, NO_3, which possesses a highly-suffocating odour. Nitrous acid in contact with water decomposes into binoxide of nitrogen and nitric acid, as is shown in the following equation:—

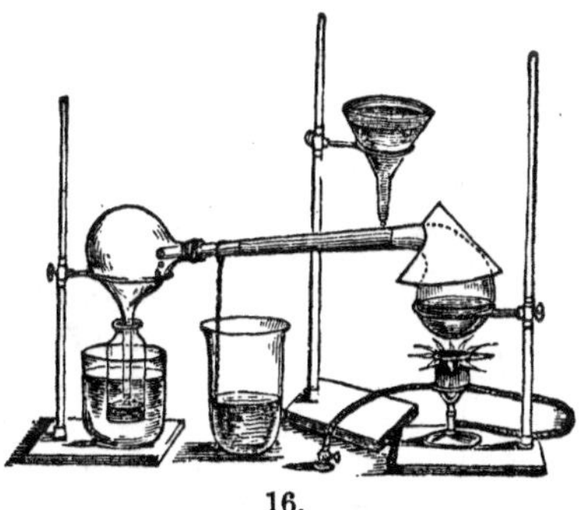

16.

$$3NO_3 + nHO = NO_5 + 2NO_2 + nHO.$$

The peculiar behaviour of binoxide of nitrogen in contact with the air and of nitrous acid in the presence of water, is of great practical importance in the manufacture of sulphuric acid, as will be subsequently shown.

Nitric acid is employed in medicine as a caustic, also in dyeing, and for dissolving and separating metals. The acid of commerce, termed *aquafortis*, is never perfectly pure, and is, to a certain extent, diluted with water.

Protoxide of Nitrogen (NO). This, the lowest oxide of nitrogen, is prepared in the following manner: — Nitrate of ammonia is heated in a small glass retort (fig. 17), furnished with a bent glass tube dipping into a pneu-

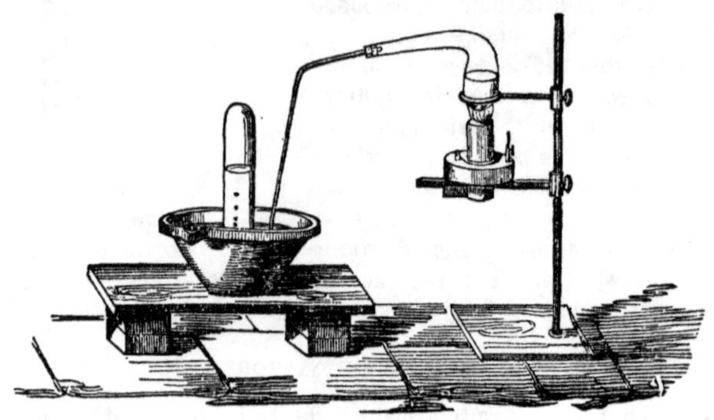

17.

matic trough filled with *warm* water. The substance fuses and enters into ebullition, evolving a large quantity of gas which may be collected in the usual manner. The decomposition will be rendered intelligible by the following equation:—

Nitrate of Ammonia.		Protoxide of Nitrogen.		Water.
NH_4O,NO_5	=	2NO	+	4HO.

The protoxide of nitrogen is a colourless, odourless gas, having a somewhat sweetish taste. It is a powerful supporter of combustion, and a piece of ignited charcoal will burn in it almost as brilliantly as in oxygen. When respired this gas produces a kind of intoxication of a most exhilarating character, accompanied by very agreeable sensations: hence it has commonly received the name of *laughing-gas*.

34. *Ammonia*, NH_4O. — This compound of nitrogen and hydrogen possesses all the properties of a powerful base; it will be therefore described with the metallic oxides.

4. CHLORINE.

Symbol: Cl = 35·5; Specific Gravity = 2·44.

35. Chlorine occurs almost exclusively in the mineral kingdom, and mostly in combination with sodium, with which it produces the compound known to every one as *culinary salt*, and termed by chemists chloride of sodium,

NaCl In the free state, chlorine is obtained by heating hydrochloric acid with binoxide of manganese, as shown in fig. 18.

18.

Chlorine differs remarkably from the gases hitherto described It possesses a slightly greenish-yellow colour, and a peculiarly suffocating odour. When inhaled, it attacks the lungs violently, and hence, it must be considered as highly pernicious; and all experiments with this gas should be conducted with the greatest care. Chlorine is soluble in water, to which it imparts its properties (chlorine-water).

Compounds of Chlorine.

36. Chlorine possesses a remarkably powerful affinity for other substances, exceeding, in many cases, even that of oxygen. It attacks gold and all the other metals, and is especially distinguished by its great attraction for hydrogen. Wherever it meets with this element, in combination with other substances, it displays a remarkable tendency to withdraw it, and to produce hydro-chloric acid (HCl.); and as all vegetable and animal substances contain hydrogen (§ 27), they are destroyed without exception, when exposed to the influence of this gas, but if in contact for a shorter period, the surface only is attacked. This pernicious property of chlorine, however, admits of many highly-valuable applications. Most of the colouring matters of the vegetable kingdom, as well as the fetid exhalations, so prejudicial to health, which arise from decaying animal and vegetable substances, contain hydrogen, and if brought into contact with chlorine, are immediately destroyed by the withdrawal of their hydrogen.

This property, therefore, renders chlorine available in the process of bleaching and in that of purifying air, a subject to which we shall again return.

(1.) *Chloric Acid* (ClO_5) and *Chlorous Acid* (ClO_3).—These acids are employed only in combination with bases, and will be subsequently described.

(2.) *Hydrochloric Acid* (HCl.)—This compound is often in solution when common salt is treated with sulphuric acid, and the evolved gas passed into water, until the latter is saturated. In order to prepare the liquid acid, equal parts of common salt and concentrated sulphuric acid, diluted with a third of its weight of water, are introduced into a large flask (fig 19), and

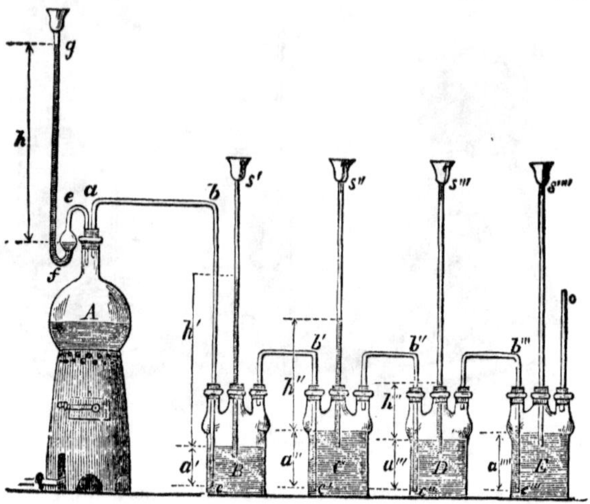

19.

the mixture heated on a charcoal furnace. The flask is connected by means of a glass tube, with a wash-bottle, containing a small quantity of water, in order to retain a little sulphurous acid, with which the gas may be contaminated. In connexion with this are two other tubulated bottles of larger dimensions, and three-fourths filled with cold water, by which the gas is condensed. This method of preparing hydrochloric acid is thus expressed in an equation:—

Chloride of Sodium.		Hydrated Sulphuric Acid.		Sulphate of Soda.		Hydrochloric Acid.
NaCl	+	HO,SO_3	=	NaO,SO_3	+	HCl.

The liquid thus obtained possesses the odour and taste of a strong acid, but is less destructive in its effects than either sulphuric or nitric acid. In the manufacture of soda, this acid is obtained in enormous quantities as a waste product, and usually possesses a yellow colour, which is caused by contamination with iron. Its applications are very numerous, being used in medicine, in many chemical operations, and especially in the preparation of chlorine. When mixed with nitric acid, it forms the so-called *aqua regia*, which is employed for dissolving gold.

When equal measures of chlorine and hydrogen are mixed together, and exposed to the direct light of the sun, they instantly combine, and give rise to a violent explosion. In the shade, however, or by candle-light, these gases may be mixed in a flask without danger. This is one of the most beautiful chemical experiments.

5. BROMINE.

Symbol: Br = 80; Specific Gravity = 2·966.

37. Bromine is one of the rarer elements, being found only in small quantities, combined with sodium and magnesium, in the salts of sea-water, and of many saline springs, especially those of Kreutznach, in which it occurs in the largest quantity.

When prepared in the pure state, it forms a dark-brown, reddish liquid, of peculiar odour, resembling that of chlorine. It has, at present, received no application in the arts; but it appears to impart particular medicinal properties to the waters in which it is found, and for which reason it deserves to be mentioned.

6. IODINE.

Symbol: I. = 127·1; Specific Gravity = 4·97.

38. Iodine occurs more frequently than the body just described, but it is nevertheless considered as one of the rarer elements. It is found in combination with sodium and magnesium, in sea-water, and in almost all marine plants and animals. It is also contained in many springs. This element is the first solid body we have to describe; its colour is grayish-black, and it is almost as lustrous as black-lead; it possesses a peculiarly disagreeable odour, somewhat similar to that of chlorine, and it imparts a brown colour to the skin and to vegetable substances when left in contact for a considerable time. By heat it is converted into a beautiful violet vapour, which, on cooling, solidifies again into small black plates. Iodine is likewise distinguished by producing with starch a deep violet colour, which furnishes us with an excellent test for recognising the presence of the one or the other.

Iodine is poisonous in the free state as well as in combination with metals, but it nevertheless forms an important remedial agent which exerts a specific influence in diseases of the glands, bronchocele, and scrofula. The medicinal properties of cod-liver oil and burnt sponge are chiefly due to the presence of iodine. If iodine be dissolved in spirits of wine, and the solution mixed with aqueous ammonia, a black precipitate is obtained, consisting of iodine and nitrogen. When this compound is dried, the slightest friction instantly decomposes it into its constituents, with violent explosion. In making this experiment, it is therefore necessary to operate on the small scale and to proceed with the greatest care.

7. FLUORINE.

Symbol: Fl = 19; Specific Gravity = 1·28.

39. Fluor-spar is a mineral occurring in many places, but not in large quantities; it is a compound of fluorine and calcium (CaFl.) The element fluorine is a gaseous body, extremely difficult to prepare, on account of the great facility with which it combines with other substances; it is especially distinguished by its powerful affinity for silicic acid, with which it instantly combines when brought into contact. All glass contains silicic acid, and is attacked and decomposed by most of the fluorine compounds: we therefore avail ourselves of this property in etching upon glass, a process conducted in the following manner.

A plate of glass is covered with a thin coating of wax, and blackened by holding it over the flame of a candle, the design being then traced upon the surface with a needle. The plate thus prepared, is now placed over a leaden vessel of sufficient size, containing a mixture of pulverized fluor-spar and sulphuric acid, which is gently warmed. The pungent, acid-smelling vapour of hydrofluoric acid (HFl) is evolved, and attacks the glass wherever it is bare. After 10 or 20 minutes, the plate is removed, and gently warmed, in order to free it from wax, when the etching becomes distinctly visible. The vapours of hydrofluoric acid are, however, very pernicious, and attack even the skin: the greatest care is therefore required.

Bromine, iodine, and fluorine form with oxygen and with hydrogen classes of compounds analogous to those of chlorine.

8. SULPHUR.

Symbol: S = 16; Specific Gravity = 2.

40. In Sicily and the neighbourhood of Naples, are found large masses of pure *native* sulphur, between limestone and marly clay. As obtained, however, it is never perfectly free from earthy matters, and it has therefore to be *refined* or purified.

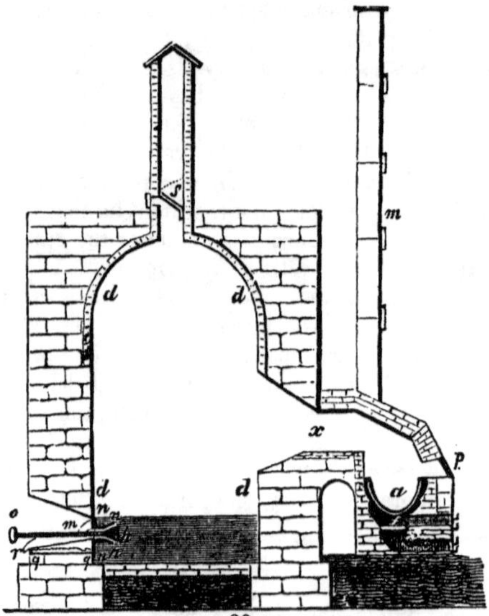

20.

This process is effected in a retort of brass or iron, *a*, fig. 20, communicating by the arched channel *x*, with a large brick chamber, *d,d,d,d*, which serves the purpose of a receiver. The retort is placed over a furnace. The vapour of the sulphur generated in the retort passes through the channel *x* into the chamber, where it condenses in the form of a fine powder, which is known as *flowers of sulphur*. The chamber is furnished with a valve, *s*, to allow the heated air to escape, and at the same time to prevent the ingress of the external air of the atmosphere. In the arrangements formerly in use, it was necessary, in order to charge the retort, to open the door, whereby explosions were frequently occasioned by the mixture of air with the heated vapour of sulphur. This danger is now avoided, by placing outside the furnace a reservoir, which is heated by the hot air of the furnace during its passage to the chimney, *m*. This vessel is connected with the retort by the pipe, closed by a plug. The crude sulphur, as it melts, becomes deprived, to a certain extent, of foreign matters, which settle to the bottom, the fused sulphur, already partly purified, being admitted through the tube into the retort. When the operation is completed, the fused sulphur on the floor of the chamber is drawn off through the small channel, *r*, whose aperture had been closed by means of a plug, *h o*. The sulphur is then cast into cylindric wooden moulds, as shown in fig. 21, and in this form constitutes the roll sulphur of commerce.

Sulphur is also frequently met with in other places, chiefly, however, in combination either with metals, as in iron pyrites (FeS_2), copper pyrites (CuS), &c., or combined with oxygen, as sulphuric acid in sulphate of lime (CaO,SO_3), which forms entire mountains. It is, moreover, frequently met with in vegetable and animal matters, particularly in all albuminous substances, or generally in such as evolve the odour of rotten eggs when suffering decomposition.

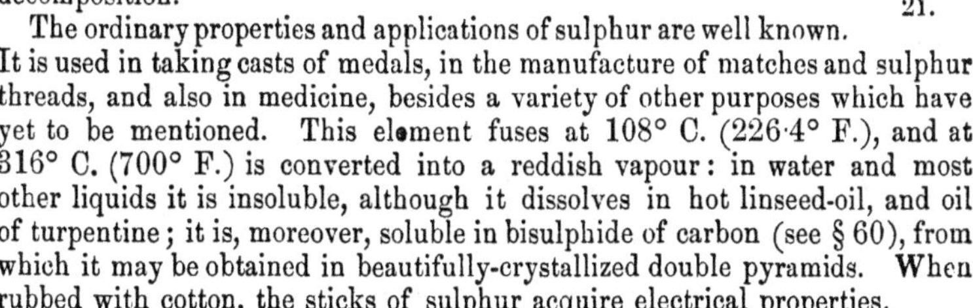

21.

The ordinary properties and applications of sulphur are well known. It is used in taking casts of medals, in the manufacture of matches and sulphur threads, and also in medicine, besides a variety of other purposes which have yet to be mentioned. This element fuses at 108° C. (226·4° F.), and at 316° C. (700° F.) is converted into a reddish vapour: in water and most other liquids it is insoluble, although it dissolves in hot linseed-oil, and oil of turpentine; it is, moreover, soluble in bisulphide of carbon (see § 60), from which it may be obtained in beautifully-crystallized double pyramids. When rubbed with cotton, the sticks of sulphur acquire electrical properties.

Compounds of Sulphur.

41. Chemistry and the arts are indebted to sulphur for one of the most important compounds.

(1.) *Sulphuric acid.*—This acid is always employed in the form of hydrate, HO,SO_3, (§ 28). Its preparation is carried on in extensive manufactories, where sulphurous acid ($(SO)_2$), nitrous acid (NO_3), and aqueous vapours (HO) are mixed together in large leaden chambers.

Sulphurous Acid.		Nitrous Acid.		Water.		Hydrated Sulphuric Acid.		Binoxide of Nitrogen.
SO_2	+	NO_3	+	HO	—	HO,SO_3	+	NO_2.

$$SO_2 + NO_3 + HO - HO,SO_3 + NO_2.$$

The above equation illustrates the formation of *hydrated sulphuric acid*, which collects on the bottom of the chambers while *binoxide of nitrogen* remains. If at this stage of the process an additional quantity of steam, sulphurous acid, and atmospheric air, be admitted into the chamber, the binoxide of nitrogen absorbs oxygen from the air, and is converted into nitrous acid (see § 33). We thus again obtain the requisite mixture for the farther formation of sulphuric acid. In this manner the process may be carried on without intermission. The acid, however, as prepared in the leaden chambers, is diluted with too large an amount of water, and is, therefore, afterwards heated in a platinum-still, when the water is expelled, and a concentrated acid remains, which at the ordinary temperature has a specific gravity of 1·85, and boils only at 326° C. (618·8° F. Although the stills of platinum employed for this purpose are very costly, varying in value from 1000*l.* to 2000*l.*, they are, nevertheless, preferred to glass retorts, on account of their durability.

The hydrate of sulphuric acid is a colourless, odourless, highly caustic, acid liquid, and is distinguished by its power of combining with a farther quantity of water. It withdraws water from moist air, as well as from vegetable and animal substances, whereby the carbon contained in the latter becomes at once evident. Almost all organic substances, when acted upon by sulphuric acid, are instantly blackened, and forthwith entirely carbonized and destroyed. It is, therefore, in the hands of the careless and inexperienced, a very dangerous liquid.

Sulphuric acid dissolves most of the metals, and possesses so powerful an affinity for the metallic oxides, that it is capable of displacing almost all the other acids when they are in combination with bases. It is, therefore, employed in the preparation of most of the acids, for example, of nitric, phosphoric, acetic, hydrochloric, and many others. It may be considered as the basis of all chemical manufactures; and so important is it in the arts, that, in the year 1840, Great Britain was on the point of declaring war against Naples, when she beheld, for the moment, her entire industry endangered by the restrictive measures of the government of that country, which burdened sulphur with excessive export duties. An idea may be formed of the extraordinary consumption of this acid, when it is mentioned that in a single manufactory in Glasgow, that of Messrs. Tennant & Co., upwards of 6,000 tons are annually produced. The price of soda, soap, hydrochloric acid, chlorine, matches, stearin candles, calico, paper, &c., stand in the closest connection with that of sulphur; and it may be justly asserted, that the total consumption of this acid in any country is a sure test of its industrial capabilities. As the acid was first manufactured in England [by the process described above], it is termed on the continent *English* sulphuric acid.

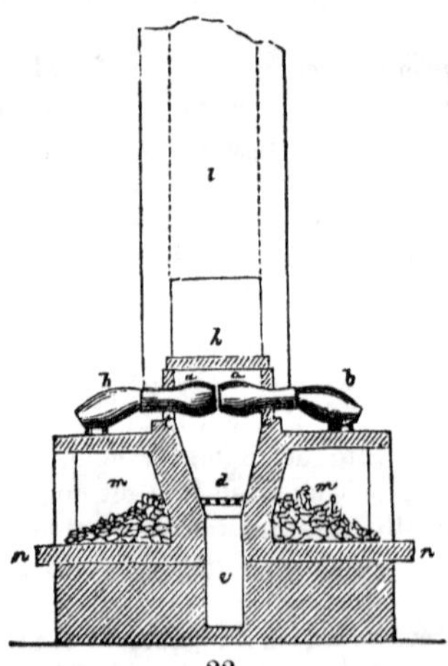

22.

Fuming sulphuric acid, which is a mixture of anhydrous acid and the hydrate, $= SO_3 + HO,SO_3$, distils over when sulphate of protoxide of iron (or, as it is usually termed, green vitriol) is first roasted, and then strongly heated in an earthen retort. In the neighbourhood of the Hartz Mountains where this acid is chiefly manufactured, the dried vitriol is introduced into earthen retorts (*a*, fig. 22,) several of which are arranged in a furnace, and gradually heated. As soon as white vapours appear, the receivers, *b*, containing a small quantity of common concentrated sulphuric acid, are firmly luted to the retorts, and the process continued until no more acid passes over. The acid thus obtained is a brownish-coloured, oily liquid, and was therefore formerly termed oil of vitriol. Exposed to the atmosphere, it evolves vapours of anhydrous sulphuric acid, and by this property, as well as by the power it possesses of dissolving indigo, it is distinguished from the hydrate. The fuming acid is also termed *Saxon* or *Nordhausen* sulphuric acid.

42. (2.) *Sulphurous Acid*, SO_2.—When sulphur is heated in the atmosphere it burns with a blue flame, and forms this pungent, suffocating, colourless gas, which slowly attracts oxygen from the air, and is thereby converted into sulphuric acid. If a sufficient quantity of sulphur be burned in a cask, the sulphurous acid formed removes the whole of the oxygen of the enclosed air, and consequently destroys its power of acidifying wine or beer that may be afterwards introduced into it. This process, termed *sulphurizing*, or burning out of casks, is practised chiefly with the view of removing oxygen. Sulphurous acid is, moreover, employed as a remedial agent in various diseases of the skin, and for bleaching straw, wool, and feathers.

43. (3.) *Hydrosulphuric Acid*, HS.—This acid is a colourless, fetid-smelling gas, which is evolved on treating a metallic sulphide, such as sulphide of iron (FeS), with dilute sulphuric acid. It is, moreover, formed by the putrefaction of vegetable and animal matters containing sulphur, such as night-soil, &c., and may be easily recognized by its odour, which is abundantly evolved from rotten eggs. This gas is highly poisonous, and proves instantly fatal when breathed in the pure state. Many serious accidents have happened to workmen who have incautiously entered sewers and other places where animal matter is in a state of decomposition. In such cases the careful inhalation of chlorine, mixed with atmospheric air, has been found to produce very beneficial effects.

Hydrosulphuric acid is soluble in water, to which it imparts its properties, as is observed in the *sulphur springs* in which this fetid gas is contained. The deportment of hydrosulphuric acid towards the *heavy* metals and their oxides is highly important to the chemist, for when a current of this gas is passed into a solution of a metallic oxide, such as oxide of lead, the sulphur combines with the metal, producing an *insoluble* compound, which is immediately thrown down as a precipitate of *peculiar colour*.

This gas is capable of precipitating all the metals from their solutions, in the form of *sulphides*, and it furnishes us with a valuable means, not only of discovering the presence of metals in a liquid, but of effecting their complete separation.

COLOURS of METALLIC SULPHIDES.

	Black.	Brown.	Orange.	Flesh-colour.	Yellow.	White.
Sulphide of	Lead.	Copper.	Antimony.	Manganese.*	Arsenic.	Zinc.*
"	Bismuth.	Tin (Proto-			Tin.	
"	Mercury.	salts).			Cadmium.	
"	Silver.					
"	Cobalt.*					
"	Nickel.*					
"	Gold.					
"	Platinum.					
"	Iron* (FeS)					

The metals in the first column are mostly precipitated from *dilute* solutions of a *brown* colour, which, however, slowly passes into *black*; those marked * are thrown down by hydrosulphuric acid from alkaline, the others from acid solutions.

The peculiar colour imparted to silver spoons used in eating eggs and fish, and the blackening of white-lead paint in stables, &c., is solely due to the formation of metallic sulphides.

9. PHOSPHORUS.

Symbol: P = 32; Specific Gravity = 1·75.

44. Although phosphorus is pretty generally diffused, and is everywhere met with in the soil, in the form of phosphates, it nevertheless occurs always in very small quantity, and hence belongs to the rarer elements. From the soil the phosphates are absorbed by many plants constituting the food of animals, and from which the phosphorus contained in the animal organism is derived. The animal body, indeed, forms, as it were, the store-house of phosphorus, for it is met with in eggs, in the brain, nerves, and flesh, and especially in the flesh of fishes. The greatest quantity, however, is containe in the bones, that consist of phosphate of lime ($3CaO,PO_5$), from which tl phosphorus of commerce is principally derived.

This element is invariably prepared from *phosphoric acid*, which obtained by treating bones, burnt to whiteness (bone-ash), with sulphur acid. The acid combines with the lime to form insoluble sulphate of lime (CaO,SO_3), and thus liberates the phosphoric acid which is concentrated by evaporation, mixed with pulverized charcoal, and ignited in an earthen retort. The carbon combines with the oxygen of the phosphoric acid, forming carbonic oxide, while the liberated phosphorus distils over, and is condensed in the receivers, which are filled with water.

Phosphorus, when perfectly pure, is a colourless, transparent body, as soft as wax, and is easily cut with a knife. When exposed to the light it speedily acquires a yellow colour, and becomes opaque; in the air it evolves white vapours, which are luminous in the dark, and possess the odour of garlic. This luminosity appears to be due to oxidation, as the fumes emitted are found to consist of phosphorous acid (PO_3). At 35° C. (95° F.) phosphorus fuses; and at 70° C. (158° F.) inflames, with formation of anhydrous phosphoric acid, that appears as a snow-white powder which rapidly attracts moisture from the atmosphere, and is thereby liquefied. The facility with which phosphorus inflames renders it a highly-dangerous body; the warmth of the hand, especially if accompanied by friction, being sufficient to ignite it. For this reason it is always preserved in vessels filled with water. Experiments made with phosphorus require the greatest precaution, the neglect of which has already occasioned many serious accidents.

But, on the other hand, the facility with which phosphorus ignites by slight friction renders it very suitable to the manufacture of the common *lucifer matches*, and its importance and preparation have been very much increased by the extensive consumption of the above-mentioned useful commodity.

The history of phosphorus is of remarkable interest, it having been accidentally discovered in 1669, by an alchemist of the name of Brandt, while engaged in the process of transmutation. On account of its scarcity, it was sold at first for its weight of gold, but at the present time the price has fallen to about three shillings per pound. The existence of manufactories in which upwards of 100 lbs. of phosphorus are daily prepared, offers a remarkable proof of what improvement the manufacture is susceptible, whilst it incontestably shows that by the increased consumption the price has become proportionably diminished, and the quality of the preparation improved.

Of the compounds of phosphorus, we have already mentioned phosphorous acid (PO_3) and phosphoric acid (PO_5). The latter is a powerful, although

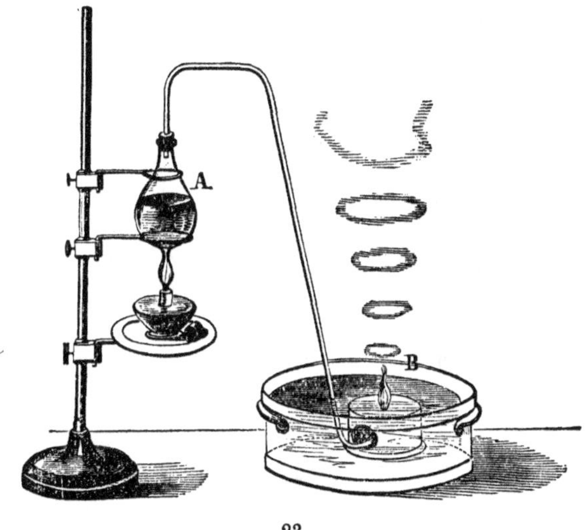

23.

not a caustic acid, and is employed in medicine both in the free state and in combination with soda.

Phosphide of Hydrogen, PH_3.—This gas, commonly termed phosphuretted hydrogen, is obtained by heating, in a flask (fig. 23), small fragments of phosphorus with milk of lime, or solution of caustic potassa. It possesses a disagreeable garlic-like odour, spontaneously inflames when brought into contact with atmospheric air, and produces most beautiful ringlets of smoke.

10. ARSENIC.

Symbol: As = 75; Specific Gravity = 5·7.

45. Arsenic has so many properties of the metals, that it appears to form the connecting link between the non-metallic and metallic elements, and is by many classed with the latter bodies. It generally presents a gray, metallic appearance, and possesses a considerable specific gravity. Hence we did not hesitate to classify it in § 43, with the metallic sulphides.

Arsenic is found partly native and partly in combination with sulphur, and with metals, such as iron, copper, nickel, and cobalt. Being a volatile substance, it is readily separated from the latter bodies by sublimation. (Phys. § 129).

Compounds of Arsenic.

46. (1.) *Arsenious Acid.*—This compound is formed when arsenic is heated in a current of air. It is then evolved as a white vapour of a strong *garlic* odour, and may be collected as a fine powder, which is usually termed

white arsenic, or *arsenious acid*. It is odourless, tasteless, and in the highest degree poisonous. The latter property it is that unfortunately often leads to its employment for criminal purposes, cases of poisoning by this substance being by far the most common. They are in general characterized by vomiting and pains in the bowels, terminating in frightful convulsions and death. As a remedial means, the promotion of vomiting, on the first appearance of poisoning, is the most judicious treatment. A substance, however, has been discovered which has the property of immediately counteracting the effects of arsenic, viz., the hydrated sesquioxide of iron ($Fe_2O_3 + 3\,HO$), which forms a perfectly insoluble compound, that has no poisonous influence upon the system. This remedy has been already employed in many cases with the most happy results.

In judicial inquiries it is important to decide whether death has been occasioned by arsenic, and this can only be done by actually finding the poison, and proving its presence beyond a doubt. By carefully searching the bowels and the ejected food, it is by no means difficult to discover the particles of arsenic, which, on account of their weight, are readily deposited. A particle as large as a needle-point is sufficient to show whether the poison met with is arsenic or not. For this purpose it is introduced into a glass tube (fig. 24), and covered by small fragments of charcoal, *b c*, which is

24.

made red-hot, and the point of the tube then heated. If the substance under examination be actually arsenic, its oxygen will combine with the ignited charcoal, while a brilliant ring of the metallic element is deposited on the cool part of the tube, as seen at *d*. When the arsenic is no longer to be met with in the form of powder, it is more difficult to detect, but in such cases science has pointed out secure methods of proving its presence.

Notwithstanding its dangerous properties, arsenious acid is employed in many arts, as in the manufacture of glass, in dyeing, agriculture, for the destruction of obnoxious vermin, such as rats, &c., and in the preservation of wood.

(2.) *Sulphide of Arsenic*.—Arsenic combines in two proportions with sulphur. The *yellow* sulphide of arsenic, called *orpiment*, is found as a mineral, and is sometimes employed as a beautiful yellow pigment. The *red* variety, which is termed *realgar*, is obtained when sulphur and arsenic are fused together; it is employed as a colour in dyeing, and, in pyrotechny, as a component of the Bengal white-fire, which consists of 24 parts by weight of nitre, 2 of sulphur, and 7 of realgar, finely pulverised, dried, and intimately mixed together.

11. CARBON.

Symbol: C = 6.

47. This element, which usually occurs in a lustreless form, claims in many respects particular attention. On the one hand, the remarkable diver-

sity of condition which carbon can assume, and the properties resulting from such assumptions; on the other hand, its relation to the animal and vegetable kingdoms, both in the free state and in combination, evince that carbon, next to oxygen, is the most important element in the economy of Nature. No substance furnishes us with a more remarkable confirmation of the principle enunciated in our chapter on Physics (§ 11), viz., that all matter is a conglomeration of smaller material particles, and that the properties of individual bodies are determined, not merely by the nature of these particles, but also by their *arrangement* or relative position. The variable forms of carbon, therefore, render it necessary to describe them individually; for the present it is enough to remark, that although crystallized carbon, vegetable carbon, animal carbon, and the various kinds of coals, exhibit a remarkable difference in their physical properties, they nevertheless so far agree as to allow us to designate carbon under all conditions a solid, tasteless and odourless, infusible and non-volatile body, which is insoluble in every substance with the exception of fused cast-iron.

48. Crystallized carbon is known as diamond, and from the earliest times has attracted the attention of even the rudest nations by its extreme hardness and transparency, as well as by its extraordinary brilliancy, and its power of decomposing light into its prismatic colours. These characteristic properties, as also the rarity of its occurrence, have elevated it to the rank of the most costly of all the precious stones. Its specific gravity is greater than that of any other form of carbon, being equal to 4·0, its hardness superior to that of all other substances, and it can only be cut or abraded by a second portion of the same material. It is, moreover, brittle, and admits of being cleaved in certain directions. The crystalline form of the diamond is that of the regular octohedron, or some figure geometrically connected with these (fig. 25, 26, 27).

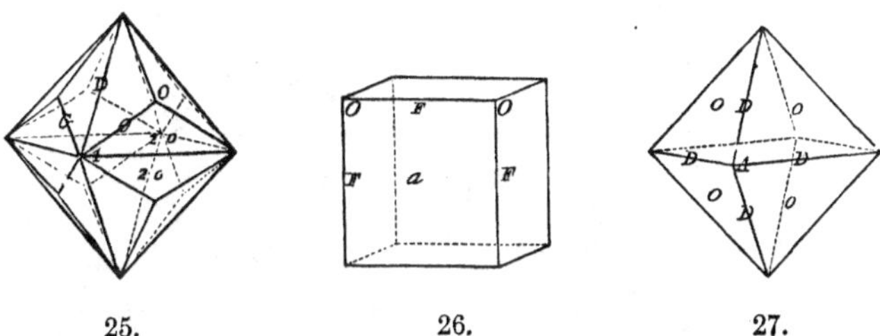

25. 26. 27.

The diamond is found in the alluvial soil of Golconda, in the West Indies, Peru, Brazil, and more recently in the Ural Mountains, and also in the drift-sand of their rivers.

With the conditions under which carbon crystallizes or the diamond forms, we are entirely unacquainted, and it is only barely probable that we shall ever be able to imitate these conditions, and produce diamonds artificially. It is possible that the vast masses of coal occurring in the laboratory of Nature have been exposed for many hundreds of years to an intense heat. of which we can hardly form a conception, and that the carbonaceous particles have, under such conditions, arranged themselves in a regularly crystalline form.

A long time elapsed before the identity of two apparently so dissimilar substances as charcoal and diamond was discovered. Accident, however, first led to the supposition, and in an experiment made with the view of fusing several small diamonds together, they were found to have entirely disappeared. A close investigation showed that they had been *burned*, or, in other words, had combined with oxygen to form carbonic acid (CO_2), a compound that is produced, of precisely the same properties, in the combustion of ordinary coal. If a diamond be heated in a closed vessel, with exclusion of air, it remains perfectly unaltered.

This precious stone is not merely used for ornamental purposes, but supplies us with a valuable means of cutting, or rather determining the fracture of glass, for which purpose its hardness renders it peculiarly adapted.

None of the other varieties of carbon are so free from foreign admixture as the diamond, and hence we consider it as the purest condition under which this element occurs.

49. The origin of *vegetable* or *wood*-charcoal is indicated by the name. All substances of vegetable origin, without exception, contain carbon, which can be separated by a great variety of processes. Moreover, as carbon, oxygen, and hydrogen constitute the principal elements of plants, it follows that we may represent their composition by the general formula x (CHO). On burning wood, &c., with limited access of air, the two latter elements are expelled in the form of water, while a residue remains, consisting of carbon. This process is carried out on a large scale in the preparation of *wood-charcoal* from the denser kinds of wood, especially that of the beech-tree, which is arranged in piles, as in fig. 28. The wood is piled in horizontal layers,

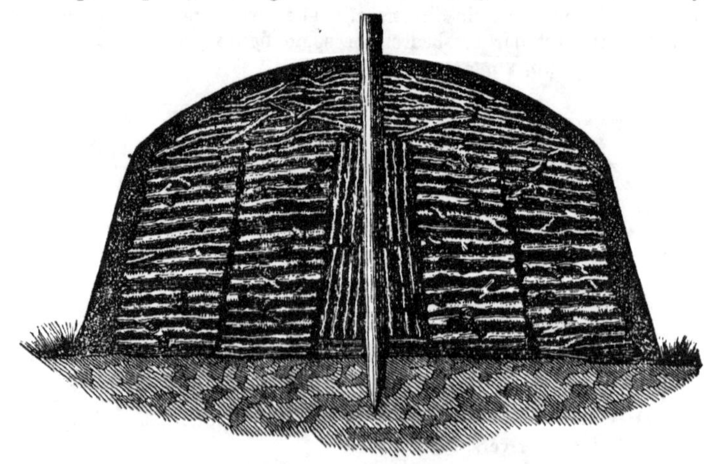

28.

covered over with turf and mould, and kindled in the interior, small openings being here and there made for the purpose of admitting a little air. The whole mass slowly becomes ignited, but only the oxygen and hydrogen of the wood are expelled as products of combustion, while the unconsumed carbon remains. Notwithstanding all precautions, a considerable loss of carbon is experienced, varying in quantity according as the process is more or less complete. To avoid this loss, the carbonization is now frequently continued for a less space of time, and in this manner is obtained a variety which is distinguished as *red* or *brown charcoal.*

We may assume that 100 parts by weight of wood dried in the air contain —

20	per cent.	of water enclosed in its pores.
40	"	oxygen and hydrogen.
40	"	carbon.
100 parts, by weight, of wood.		

Accordingly, we have in 100 pounds of dried wood 80 of actual wood, and in the latter 40 pounds of carbon. But when the process is conducted most successfully, it yields only about 25 pounds; in general not more than 20 pounds are obtained from 100 pounds of wood.

Wood-charcoal is exceedingly porous, and, consequently, its specific gravity is ordinarily very small. That of beech-wood charcoal is 0·187; a cubic foot, interstices included, weighing not more than from 8 to 9 pounds. It possesses in a high degree the power of attracting and condensing, within its pores, air and aqueous vapour, which sometimes leads to its heating and spontaneous combustion. If impure water, containing hydrosulphuric acid and ammonia, be agitated with the powder of freshly-ignited charcoal, both gases are completely removed, and the water is rendered fit for the purposes of life. Wood-charcoal likewise removes colouring matters, but only to a slight degree, as will be described under animal-black.

Wood-charcoal is applied to a variety of technical processes, particularly to produce strong fires in a limited space. It is, moreover, of great importance as a means of deoxidation, *i. e.*, of removing oxygen from metallic oxides, and combining with it to produce carbonic acid. Nearly all the metals, and particularly iron, are prepared by igniting their oxides in contact with carbon. Its use in the manufacture of gunpowder is likewise one of the most important of its applications.

At the ordinary temperature, carbon is only slightly affected by exposure to the atmosphere, and is almost unaltered when placed either in water or in the soil. We advantageously avail ourselves of this property by charring the ends of piles that are to be driven into the earth, and likewise by carbonizing the interior of casks in which water is preserved during long sea-voyages. *Soot* is a vegetable carbon in a finely-pulverized state, and is employed in the preparation of a fine black colour known as Indian ink. To obtain the particular kind of carbon used for this purpose, resin, resinous woods, and such-like substances, are burned with imperfect access of air, and the smoke evolved passes into a hood in which the soot is deposited. The variety known as *Frankfort-black*, or *Printers'-black*, is obtained, in a very finely-divided state, by the carbonization of wine-yeast; it is mixed, however, with salts of potassa.

The varieties of vegetable carbon here described are by no means to be considered as pure, as may be readily proved by the quantity of ash they yield when burned. The charcoal from 100 pounds of wood will of course contain the same amount of ash as would have been obtained in the combustion of the wood itself. One hundred pounds of beech-wood is found to yield about 0·03 pounds of ash; on the other hand, lamp-black which has been thoroughly ignited appears to be almost chemically pure carbon.

50. The black mass which is left on charring animal substances is termed *animal carbon:* it differs very considerably from the foregoing, in its physical as well as chemical properties. Independently of animal fat, which is in all respects analogous to the fatty substances found in plants, we include under the general title of animal products muscular flesh, the skin (leather), cartilage, osseous gelatin, and blood. We refer, moreover, to these substances in the dry or anhydrous condition. Their principal mass in the dry state consists approximately of—

55	parts, by weight, of	carbon.
22	"	oxygen.
7	"	hydrogen.
16	"	nitrogen.
100	parts, by weight, of	animal matter.

They contain besides a minute quantity of phosphorus, sulphur, and inorganic salts. When heated, these substances first swell up and fuse, then cake together, and finally yield a dense, slaggy, lustrous charcoal. This, of course, is not to be considered as pure carbon, for, in addition to phosphates and sulphates, it contains a considerable quantity of nitrogen, so that we may with propriety term it *nitrogenous* carbon. The presence of this element renders it well adapted for the preparation of the chemical compound which forms the basis of the manufacture of Prussian blue, and will be described farther on, under the name of cyanogen.

51. *Bone-charcoal,* termed also bone- and ivory-black, is an animal carbon, which is obtained by burning bones imperfectly. We must regard a bone in its entire mass as a structure consisting of two cellular substances interwoven with each other, as may be represented by figs. 29, 30, and 31, where *a a* represent a soft texture termed gelatin, whilst *b b* are particles of a hard texture, which is incombustible, and consists of phosphate of lime. When bones are ignited with free access of air, the gelatinous particles *a a* are *completely* consumed, and there remains only a white, dense, calcareous tissue (fig. 31), which is bone-ash. If, on the other hand, a bone is digested in hydrochloric acid, the lime-salts only are dissolved, while the gelatin is unattacked, and remains as represented in fig. 30. When the gelatin, extracted by hydrochloric acid, is carbonized by itself, the carbonaceous particles cake together, and we obtain a compact carbon, differing in no respect from the nitrogenous variety above described. If, on the other hand, the gelatin of the bones is carbonized by ignition with a limited supply of air, the calcareous particles prevent the cohesion of the carbon, and we obtain from the bones thus burned an animal-black in a very finely-divided state.

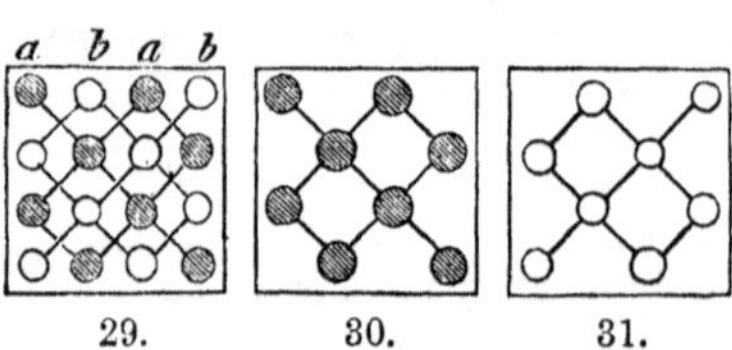

29. 30. 31.

Bone-charcoal is particularly distinguished by its power of combining with dissolved colouring matters and removing them completely from their solutions. If red wine or red ink be agitated with a few spoonfuls of bone-carbon, we obtain, after some time, a transparent liquid as colourless as water. This property is of considerable advantage in the manufacture of sugar; for, when the brown-coloured cane-juice is treated with bone-black, it is rendered perfectly colourless, and a brilliant white sugar is thus obtained. Many other chemical preparations may, by this means, be likewise decolorized, or deprived of the colouring matters which are mixed with them.

Bone-black, as is well known, is also used in the manufacture of blacking, which is usually prepared by mixing four parts with one of sulphuric acid, and then adding four parts of syrup and a little water.

52. *Graphite*, termed also black-lead, is a mineral belonging to the primitive rocks, and occasionally consists of pure carbon; in general, however, it contains a portion of iron. It may be also artificially prepared by the fusion of iron in the smelting furnaces of iron-works. It possesses a grayish-black colour and metallic lustre, and produces a mark when rubbed on paper; a property on which depends its application to the manufacture of lead-pencils. *Anthracite*, a less pure form of carbon, is more allied to coal, and, when burned, leaves an earthy ash. Both varieties will be more minutely described in the chapter on Mineralogy.

Coal and turf are carbonaceous formations, derived from the spontaneous decomposition of plants. The origin of these substances will be considered hereafter.

Compounds of Carbon.

53. Carbon combines with oxygen in several proportions.

Carbonic acid (CO_2) is a colourless, odourless gas, which is contained in the atmosphere in the proportion of 1 measure to 2,500 measures of air. It occurs, moreover, in many minerals, combined with metallic oxides, particularly with lime, forming a compound of which entire ranges of hills are composed. This acid is produced incessantly by the combustion and decay of carbonaceous substances, and by the process of fermentation and the respiration of animals. Its quantity would, therefore, be continually on the increase, were it not that plants remove it from the atmosphere, and thus preserve the equilibrium in a very remarkable manner. We shall still have occasion in a subsequent section to point out with greater precision the important relation existing between carbon and the animal and vegetable kingdoms.

In the preparation of carbonic acid we may avail ourselves most conveniently of carbonate of lime or chalk (CaO,CO_2), which is decomposed by either of the stronger acids, generally by hydrochloric acid. The carbonic acid is set free and evolved in bubbles, producing a lively effervescence, which is the characteristic deportment of all carbonic acid compounds when treated with a strong acid.

If a burning taper be immersed in a vessel filled with carbonic acid, it is immediately extinguished, and men and animals that inhale the pure gas die almost as suddenly; it is therefore to be considered as a highly-dangerous poison when inhaled. The specific gravity of this gas being 1·5, or half as heavy again as air, it will sink in this medium precisely in the same manner as syrup will fall to the bottom of a vessel of water, and mix with the latter fluid only very gradually. If therefore a lighted taper be placed on the bottom of a cylinder (fig. 32), and carbonic acid be slowly poured into it from a vessel filled with this gas, the light will be extinguished immediately the gas reaches to the height of the flame. In cellars where large quantities of wine and beer ferment, the lower stratum of air invariably consists of almost pure carbonic acid, and it not unfrequently happens that workmen lose their lives by stooping down and incautiously inhaling the gas. To obviate this danger, it is usual either to insure a sufficient change of atmosphere, or to mix up caustic lime with water, and sprinkle about the milky liquid, which speedily removes the carbonic acid from the floor. For those who have been suffocated by carbonic acid, the careful inhalation or smelling of ammonia has been recommended as the most efficacious antidote.

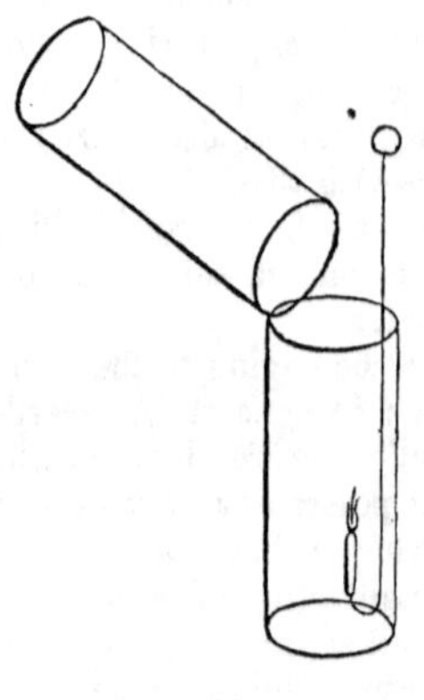

32.

From the lower strata of earth, where, in many places, carbonaceous substances are continually undergoing decomposition, streams of carbonic acid gush forth in a manner similar to springs of water; and if holes of some depth be dug, particularly in volcanic districts, the carbonic acid is heard to rush in with considerable noise: hence it frequently collects at the bottoms of wells and mines, and there causes fatal accidents. In the neighbourhood of Naples there is a cave, termed the Grotto del Cane, in which occurs a stratum of carbonic acid, several feet in height, issuing from the soil. Dogs and other animals die immediately they are placed in it, whilst men may walk erect therein without danger. In Java there is a valley called the Poison-valley, or the vale of death, surrounded by a chain of mountains. The air of this valley contains so large an amount of carbonic acid that men and animals who enter it never return alive.

Carbonic acid is soluble in water, and imparts to it an agreeably-refreshing and slightly-acid taste: nearly all waters occurring in Nature contain a portion of this gas in solution. Whenever springs of water and carbonic acid come in contact in the earth, a large quantity of gas is dissolved, and the water then receives the name of *acidulous* water, such as Selters' water, and many others. Carbonic acid, moreover, is contained in many liquids that are derived from fermentation, as new wine, beer, and champagne; and as the internal use of these liquids is within certain bounds uninjurious, it would appear that carbonic acid has no poisonous action on the stomach, but only exerts its pernicious influence when taken into the lungs.

When carbonic acid is compressed in a suitable apparatus, it is converted into a liquid, which, on removal of the pressure, evaporates with extreme rapidity, absorbing so much heat (Phys. § 146) that a cold is produced of —80° C. or —90° C. (—112 F. or —130 F.), a portion of the liquid acid being thereby frozen. Carbonic acid, therefore, affords an important example of the principle, enunciated in the chapter on Physics, that the condition of matter is essentially dependent upon temperature.

Carbonic acid is extensively employed in the manufacture of white-lead and of the artificial effervescing drinks.

Carbonic oxide (CO) is the name applied to the lowest product of the oxidation of carbon, which is formed when this element is ignited, with limited access of atmospheric air. This gas burns with a beautiful blue flame, as frequently observed in charcoal fires, and gives rise to the formation of carbonic acid. It is likewise irrespirable, and, in conjunction with its product of combustion, is the cause of the fatal accidents which sometimes occur when charcoal is burned in closed rooms.

Carbides of Hydrogen.

54. In all cases where vegetable matter, which we always represent by the general formula x (CHO), (§ 49), suffers decomposition, a portion of the carbon combines with hydrogen, and produces gaseous compounds. If the vegetable matter contains a large quantity of carbon, as is the case in resins, fats, &c., and the decomposition takes place under a high temperature, the carbo-hydrogen = CH is produced, which burns with a highly-luminous flame, and is hence termed *illuminating* gas. But if the decomposition of the vegetable matter is effected at a lower temperature, as, for instance, when the remains of plants decay in marshes or at the bottoms of mines, there is formed an inferior carbide of hydrogen = CH_2, which is therefore termed *marsh-gas*, or the gas of mines.

Marsh-gas, when pure, is colourless and odourless, and burns with a slightly-luminous flame. Its specific gravity is 0·5. When mixed with atmospheric air and then kindled, an explosion takes place similar to that which is produced by the ignition of explosive gas (§ 28). In coal-mines an enormous quantity of this gas is continually generated; it there becomes mixed with the air of the mines, and causes frightful explosions when accidentally kindled by the lights of the workmen. A large number of miners have already lost their lives by this gas, which is technically called *fire-damp*. The numerous fatal accidents have led to the discovery of the *safety-lamp* (fig. 33), an instrument consisting of an ordinary oil-lamp surrounded by fine wire-gauze. If a lamp of this kind is introduced into a mixture of explosive gas, the gas enters by the openings of the gauze, and burns in the interior; the flame, however, is so much reduced in temperature, by the cooling influence of the metallic wire, as to become extinguished before it is communicated to the external gas. This cooling power of wire-gauze may easily be demonstrated by holding it over the flame of a candle, which will be found not to pass through.

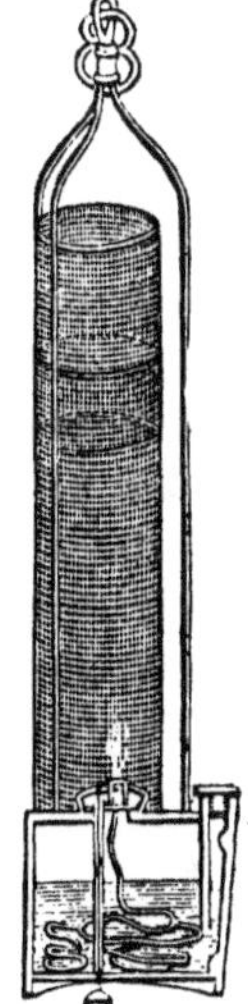

°3.

The gas of mines is one of the constituents of the ordinary coal-gas, which is employed in illumination and in filling balloons.

55. The *luminous gas* (CH) is obtained when bodies rich in carbon and hydrogen, and deficient in oxygen, are ignited in closed vessels. It is a colourless gas, burning with a beautifully-luminous flame, and is the chief component of all our artificial means of illumination. It is either consumed at the spot and in the moment of its formation, as is the case in the burning of candles and lamps, or it is collected in a peculiar vessel, termed a *gasometer*, and thence distributed by iron pipes to our streets and houses.

The preparation of luminous gas is most simply effected by dropping fats or resins into red-hot iron cylinders, and for this purpose are selected the cheapest varieties, which can scarcely be used for other purposes. These substances are decomposed, and yield a gaseous mixture that burns with a remarkably beautiful and bright luminous flame: this mode of manufacture, however, appears not to admit of general adoption in consequence of the high price of the material, but when coals are employed, as is generally the case in this country, the price of production is considerably diminished.

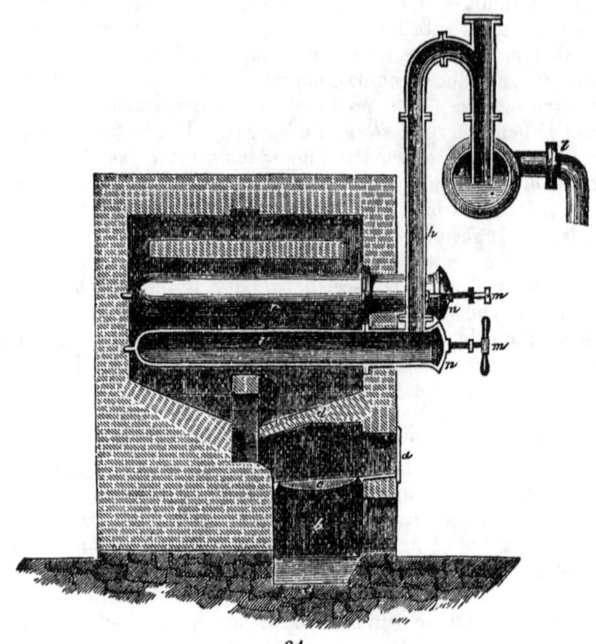

34.

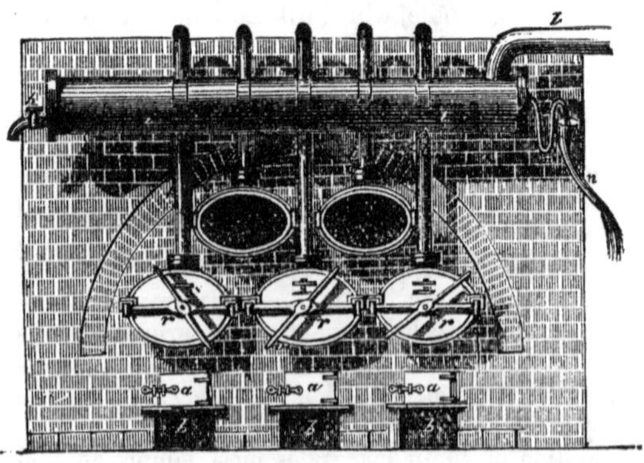

35.

56. The manufacture of coal-gas is divided into three processes, viz., its *formation*, *purification*, and its *collection* and distribution. Its formation is always effected in longish round retort-cylinders of iron, arranged in the manner shown by *r r r* in figs. 34 and 35. Figure 34 represents a section of a furnace, and fig. 35 a front view of the same.

The fire is placed around the retorts upon the grate *c*. The ash-pit is at *b*. The whole apparatus is so arranged that the greatest degree of heat may be produced at the least expense of fuel. The cylinders are closed at the posterior end, and open in front, being each provided with a door which is made to fit air-tight by means of screws and cement. In these cylinders the coal is distilled, and as soon as the evolution of gas has ceased, the doors are opened and the glowing coke raked out and allowed to cool in the vaults.

The gas as it issues from the cylinders passes through the iron pipes *h i* into the hydraulic main *i*, which is half filled with water. The pipes *i i* dip below the surface of the water in order to prevent the gas returning into the retorts when the doors are opened.

In the hydraulic main a considerable quantity of matter volatilized with the gas is deposited. From the upper part of the main passes a pipe, *l*, which first descends into the ground, and then runs in a horizontal direction. Through this pipe the gas escapes. At the lowest part of this horizontal pipe there is another descending-pipe which is open at the bottom, and dips into a cylindrical vessel, encompassed by a third vessel.

The liquid deposited in the hydraulic main *i*, during the distillation, con-

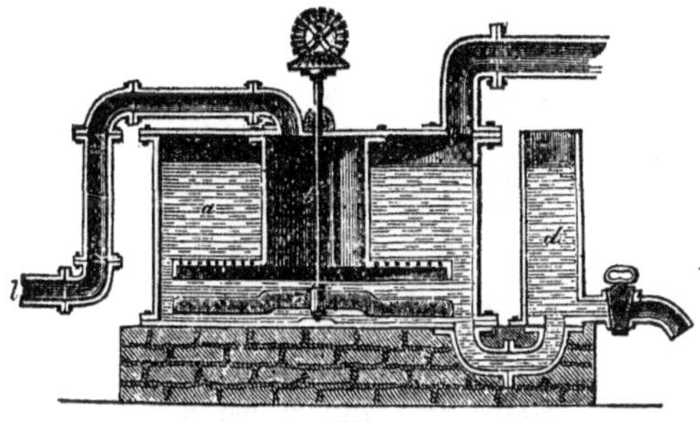

36.

tinually runs over with the gas by the pipe *l*, and enters the condenser; it there fills the surrounding cylinder, and afterwards runs over into the vessel it is placed in, from which it can be removed at pleasure.

Thence the gas pursues its course through the pipe *l* and arrives at the lime-purifier, fig. 36. This consists of a large cylindrical vessel, made perfectly air-tight, and having an inverted funnel fixed in its top. A rod *b* passes through the neck of the funnel, and an agitator is made to revolve by means of a winch and toothed wheel. The bottom of the rod is connected either with a wheel or frame of cross-bars. The vessel *a* is two-thirds filled with a mixture of lime and water, which is introduced by the pipe *d*. The gas passes by the pipe *l* into the funnel, presses down the lime-water to the edge of the funnel, and then escapes in bubbles through the surrounding liquid. The gas is thus freed from sulphuretted hydrogen and carbonic acid. when it appears necessary to renew the purifying mixture, it is allowed to run out by a stopcock and a fresh portion introduced by the tube *d*.

As the gas escapes from the purifier by depressing the liquid in the funnel, it is necessarily in a condensed state in the pipe between the vessel and the retorts; the extent of the pressure is equal to the weight of the water that stands higher on the exterior than in the interior of the funnel. It is therefore necessary that the pipes from the hydraulic main *i* to the retorts should be raised as shown in figs. 34 and 35, otherwise upon opening a retort the liquid in the hydraulic main *i* would be forced back through the pipes *i h*.

We have thus traced the progress of the gas from the retorts wherein it is produced to the purifier in which it is deprived of its impurities; we have next to consider the mode of collecting and distributing it. The gasometer, fig. 37, which is sometimes as much as 30 or 40 feet in diameter, is a

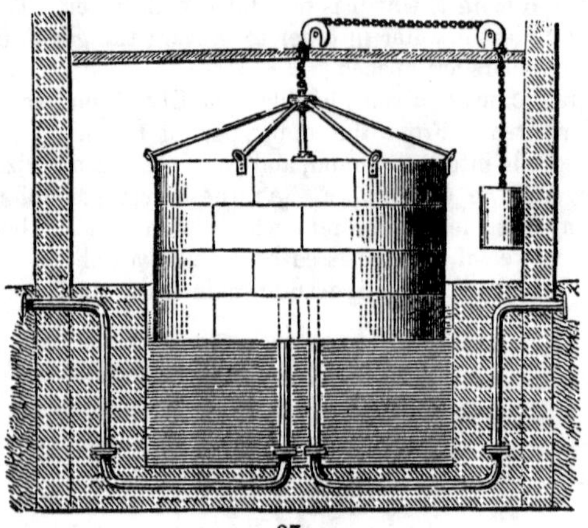

37.

cylinder of iron closed at the top, open at the bottom, and dipping into a second vessel filled nearly to the edge with water. The gas-holder is supported by a chain which passes over the two wheels, and is counterbalanced by a weight. As the gas enters, the gas-holder rises in the water until perfectly filled with gas.

When the gas is to be distributed, a cock is opened, and the gas-holder depressed by means of suitable weights placed on the top. The gas then flows through a pipe, whence it is distributed to its destined place of consumption.

57. Coal-gas is always a mixture of luminous gas (more commonly called olefiant gas), marsh-gas, carbonic oxide, and hydrogen, in variable proportions, depending upon the nature of the coal and of the process of manufacture. In the beginning of the distillation, the olefiant gas, which, of course, is the most valuable constituent, forms approximatively one-fifth of the entire volume, but towards the end of the process, or by too strong a red-heat, its quantity considerably diminishes, while that of the hydrogen increases. We may consider that an ordinary gas-flame hourly consumes from 1 to 1½ cubic

feet of gas. From one pound of coal we obtain from 5 to 6 cubic feet of gas, and coals of the best quality sometimes yield from 7 to 9 cubic feet; while from one measure of oil we obtain from 600 to 700 measures, and from 1 lb. of resin from 14 to 23 measures of gas are produced.

In the retorts remain the *coke* which is employed as a very excellent fuel.

Finally, it may be remarked that coal-gas is employed, in the place of hydrogen, for filling balloons. A ball of three feet diameter filled with the former weighs 11 ozs. less than one containing an equal volume of air, while, if filled with hydrogen, it weighs about 17 ozs. less; the cost of hydrogen, however, is 20 times as much as that of coal-gas.

58. In addition to the two carbo-hydrogens here described, a large number of chemical compounds are known, which consist only of these two elements. They form, however, more compound groups, and will therefore be considered in another part of this section.

Bicarbide of Nitrogen (Cyanogen).

59. Carbon combines only with difficulty and under particular circumstances with nitrogen. When the nitrogenous carbon, described at § 50, is ignited in contact with a metal, the two elements combine together, producing a new substance, termed *cyanogen* (C_2N), which enters into combination with the metal. When a compound of mercury and cyanogen (Hg Cy) is heated, the latter is obtained as a colourless gas, of penetrating odour. When kindled it burns with a beautiful peach-coloured flame. In its mode of combination, this body presents such a remarkable similarity to chlorine, bromine, iodine, and fluorine, as to have induced chemists to class it with these elements; its formula instead of being expressed by C_2N is usually represented by the symbol Cy. The name cyanogen signifies to generate blue, and this compound was so called in consequence of its forming with iron the beautiful blue pigment, known as *Prussian blue.* Cyanogen combines with hydrogen and produces hydrocyanic or prussic acid (H Cy), which is prepared by the distillation of cyanide of mercury with hydrochloric acid.

$$HgCy + HCl = HCy + HgCl.$$

This acid is a colourless gas, of a peculiar odour, strongly resembling that of bitter almonds; it is soluble in water, and imparts to it its properties. Particularly in the anhydrous state it forms a deadly poison, but when diluted with water it is extensively employed as a remedial agent. The kernels of stone-fruit, and especially those of the bitter almond, as well as the leaves of the cherry-laurel, which contain a small quantity of prussic acid, are likewise employed in medicine as well as in confectionary, and in the preparation of laurel-water.

Bisulphide of Carbon.

60. When wood-charcoal is heated to redness in a tube of iron or earthenware, and sulphur is introduced through an opening in the tube, the vapour of the latter in passing over the carbon combines to produce a volatile substance which is condensed in an apparatus (Phys. § 129, fig. 89) connected with the tube. This compound, which is a colourless transparent liquid, is termed *bisulphide of carbon,* and offers one of the most remarkable examples

of the destruction of the peculiarities of elements by chemical combination. From the *solid* yellow sulphur that combines with the *solid* black charcoal, we obtain a *liquid* transparent body of extreme volatility and disagreeable odour. It refracts light so powerfully, that on looking through a vessel containing it, we observe the most beautiful prismatic colours. Bisulphide of carbon is heavier than water, and dissolves with facility sulphur, phosphorus, and several resins, but is scarcely ever employed.

12. SILICIUM.

Symbol: Si = 21·3.

61. Silicium never occurs in the free state, but in combination with oxygen, as *silicic acid* (SiO_3), which is the principal constituent of most minerals. Next to oxygen, silicium may be said to constitute the chief mass of the crust of our earth.

When separated from its oxygen, silicium forms a grayish-brown powder, which is non-volatile, and when heated in an atmosphere of oxygen combines again to produce silicic acid of snowy whiteness.

In the consideration of the compound *silicic acid* (SiO_3), we have to distinguish it under several conditions and in various states of purity.

Rock crystal which is frequently found in the caverns of St. Gothard, crystallized in beautiful six-sided prisms, terminating in pyramids with six faces (fig. 38), is pure silicic acid. White *quartz* is nearly pure silicic acid, containing scarcely a trace of foreign matter, whilst flint, agate, cornelian, jasper, and many other precious stones with which we shall become acquainted in the section on Mineralogy, contain a considerable quantity of other substances. These minerals are distinguished by the hardness peculiar to silicic acid, which imparts to them the property of emitting brilliant sparks when struck with steel. Silicic acid is fusible only in the strongest fires, but when heated to redness with the oxides of the light metals, it combines to produce a series of important compounds, such as glass, porcelain, earthenware, &c.

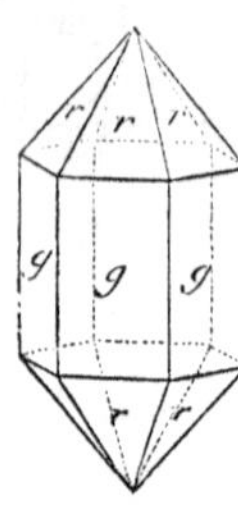

38.

If silicic acid be heated to redness with an excess of caustic alkali, as potassa, soda, or lime, it combines to produce salts which are soluble in water, and from which the weak silicic acid may again be separated in the form of a white gelatinous mass, by the addition of a stronger acid. The liberated acid is soluble in pure water, but loses this property when ignited.

In this soluble form, silicic acid is contained in almost all springs, whence it enters into the organisms of plants, being as essential to their nourishment as salt is to animals. Most plants, particularly the grasses, contain so large a quantity of silicic acid that it may readily be detected in the ash after they are burned. Moreover, the property of cutting, possessed by many grasses (carex, for example), depends upon the accumulation of small hard crystals of silicic acid in the cells of their leaves. It may also be remarked, that the shells or scales of many infusoria, as well as some of the molluscs and polypi, consist of silicic acid.

Silicic acid is not acid to the taste, and is endowed with very feeble affinity; hence it is sometimes designated by the term *silica*.

13. BORON.

Symbol: Bo = 10·9.

62. Boron belongs to the rarer elements, being found only in some lakes of volcanic origin, in combination with oxygen, as boracic acid (BoO_3). In the free state it forms a brownish-green, insoluble, and infusible powder; so that both silicium and boron offer, in reference to their external properties, some points of agreement with ordinary carbon.

Boracic acid is deposited from the water of those volcanic districts in the form of a white powder, and, when purified, is obtained in colourless crystalline plates, which are soluble in alcohol, and to the flame of which the acid imparts a beautiful *green* colour; a property which is frequently made available in coloured illuminations.

A compound of boracic acid with soda ($NaO,2BoO_3$), termed *borax*, is frequently employed, since it may be fused for a long period at a high temperature, and without being altered in its properties. In fusing metals it is frequently added with the view of facilitating the union of the metallic particles, and partly to protect them from the oxidizing influence of the atmosphere. An impure variety of borax occurs as a mineral, and is known under the name of *tinkal*.

(2.) METALS.

63. The metals, with the exception of mercury, are solid bodies, which, however, *melt*, or assume the liquid form, at high temperatures, and, when exposed to a still more intense heat, are converted into vapour. The clean and polished surfaces of metals reflect light and have considerable lustre, which is termed the *metallic lustre*. The greater number possess a high specific gravity, and their particles exhibit a very powerful cohesion, which renders them ductile and malleable, and allows of their being drawn out into wires. They are excellent conductors of electricity.

The metals possess a remarkable affinity for oxygen, and by far the greater number occur in Nature combined with this element. The metallic oxides, contrary to the oxides of the non-metallic bodies, are pre-eminently compounds with *basic* properties. A very limited number of the higher metallic oxides have the characters of acids, and are therefore termed *metallic* acids (§ 23). Their affinities for bases, however, are much less powerful than those of the strong acids of sulphur, nitrogen, and phosphorus, and also of hydrochloric acid. Most of the metallic oxides are insoluble in water.

The metals combine readily with *chlorine*, producing *neutral* compounds, which are termed *chlorides*, and possess the properties of the salts that are formed by the union of metallic oxides with oxygen-acids. The chlorides are mostly soluble in water, and are proportionately seldom met with in Nature. The elements *iodine*, *bromine*, *fluorine*, and the compound radical *cyanogen* (§ 59), exhibit an analogous deportment towards the metals, and, owing to their faculty of producing with the metals saline compounds, they are called *salt-formers* (halogens), and their salts, *haloid-salts*, in contradistinction to the oxygen-salts, or salts of the metallic oxides.

Next to oxygen, sulphur is the element with which the metals are most frequently found in combination. Its natural compounds with the heavy metals have a metallic and, usually, brass-yellow appearance; while those which are artificially prepared are powders of various colours (see § 43). The combinations of sulphur with the metals are termed *sulphides*, and generally have strongly *basic* properties. Some of the higher sulphides, however, deport themselves as acids, and unite with the inferior combinations to form peculiar *sulphur salts*. The sulphides exhibit so powerful an affinity for oxygen that many absorb it even in the air or in water, and become transformed into sulphates of the metallic oxides, whilst others combine with oxygen only when exposed to a high temperature. When treated with an acid, the sulphides yield hydrosulphuric acid and a salt of the oxide.

Classification of the Metals.

64. The metals admit of being readily distinguished by the following table, in which they are presented in several groups, according to their peculiar properties, and each distinguished by a particular name: —

Metals.	Properties of the	
	Oxides.	Sulphides.
(A.) *Light Metals.* Specific gravity from 0·8 to 1 never occur in the uncombined state.	Powerful bases; possessing strong affinity for water, and form with it hydrates. They yield their oxygen to carbon only at a white heat.	Powerful bases, which oxidise in the air, and form sulphates; when treated with acids evolve hydrosulphuric acid.
(a.) *Alkaline Metals.* 1. Potassium. 2. Sodium. (Ammonium.)	Highly caustic; powerful bases, separate all other oxides from their combinations with acids; are very soluble in water, and do not lose their water of hydration at the highest temperatures; attract carbonic acid rapidly from the air.	Caustic; strong bases; very soluble in water, and dissolve a large quantity of sulphur, which is separated on addition of an acid as a white powder, termed *milk of sulphur;* they were formerly termed *liver of sulphur.*
(b.) *Metals of the Alkaline Earths.* 3. Calcium. 4. Barium. 5. Strontium.	Caustic; strong bases; slightly soluble in water; lose their water of hydration at a moderate heat, and powerfully absorb carbonic acid.	Caustic; strong bases; dissolve sulphur, and are partly soluble in water, and partly insoluble.
(c.) *Metals of the Earth proper.* 6. Magnesium. 7. Aluminum.	Feebly caustic. Not caustic. } Weak bases. insoluble in water.	Insoluble in water.
(B.) *Heavy Metals.* Specific gravity from 5 to 21; are found chiefly in combination with oxygen, and frequently with sulphur and arsenic; some are native.	Feebler bases than the foregoing, some are acids; insoluble in water, and lose their water of hydration at a moderate heat.	Neutral compounds; insoluble in water; antimony and several of the rarer metals produce compounds with sulphur, which deport themselves as acids.

Metals.	Properties of the Oxides.	Properties of the Sulphides.
(a.) *Common Metals.* Become oxidised in the air. 8. Iron. 9. Manganese. 10. Cobalt. 11. Nickel. 12. Copper. 13. Bismuth. 14. Lead. 15. Tin. 16. Zinc. 17. Chromium. 18. Antimony.	With few exceptions are soluble in acids, and, when ignited with carbon at a red-heat, yield their oxygen; are, for the most part, fusible and non-volatile.	Those occurring in Nature are somewhat brass-like in appearance, and are termed *pyrites* and *blendes*. Those which are artificially prepared have peculiar colours, as mentioned at § 43; by heat they are converted into sulphates.
(b.) *Noble Metals.* Unchangeable in the air. 19. Mercury. 20. Silver. 21. Gold. 22. Platinum.	Have more the properties of acids than of bases; are decomposed by ignition into oxygen and metal.	With the exception of sulphide of mercury, they leave the pure metal when ignited.

(A.) LIGHT METALS.

14. POTASSIUM.

Symbol: K = 39; Specific Gravity = 0·8.

65. When carbonate of potassa (KO,CO_2) and charcoal, finely pulverized and mixed, are exposed to a white heat in an iron retort *a*, fig. 39, the oxygen of the potassa combines with the carbon whilst the potassium is volatilized as a greenish vapour. The vapour condenses in the form of metallic globules

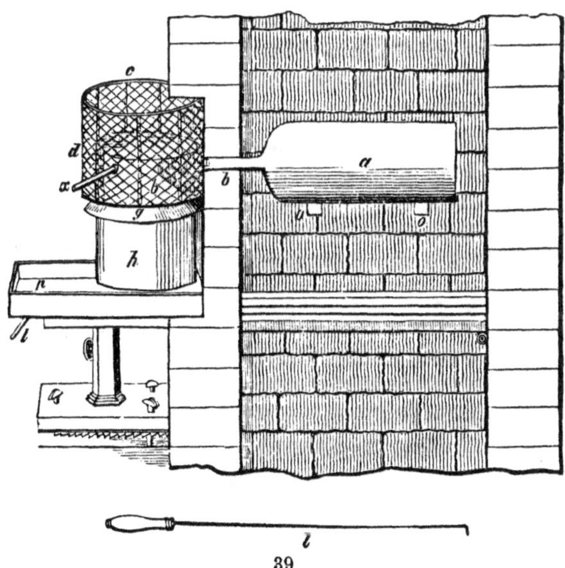

39

of the size of peas in the copper receiver *h*, which is half-filled with mineral *naphtha*. To facilitate the condensation of the potassium, the receiver is surrounded by a wire basket *b x c d*, filled with ice. Although the materials employed in the preparation of this element are by no means costly, it nevertheless retains its high price, owing to the difficulties of the operation and the small quantity obtained.

Potassium exhibits the lustre of silver, and is sufficiently soft to admit of being cut with a knife. Its most remarkable property, however, is the powerful affinity it possesses for oxygen; for, when exposed to the air, it immediately attracts this gas, and becomes covered with a gray coating of oxide of potassium. It abstracts oxygen with the greatest avidity from all bodies containing it, and therefore it can only be retained in the metallic state by preserving it in mineral naphtha, which consists only of carbon and hydrogen.

One of the most beautiful chemical experiments may be made by throwing a fragment of potassium upon water contained in a plate. The metallic globule immediately combines with the oxygen and developes a temperature sufficiently high to inflame the evolved hydrogen, to which the vapour of the burning potassium, simultaneously liberated, imparts a beautiful violet-colour The burning metal floats about with a hissing noise upon the surface of the water until it is entirely converted into oxide of potassium, which dissolves in the water.

Hitherto, potassium has received no application in the arts, although the chemist avails himself of its powerful affinity in separating oxygen from many other oxides, such as silicic acid, boracic acid, magnesia, &c.

Compounds of Potassium.

66. *Oxide of potassium* (KO), usually termed potassa, is obtained in the form of hydrate (KO,HO) when the carbonate of potassa is boiled with caustic lime until it has lost the whole of its carbonic acid (§ 79), which may be readily ascertained by the non-effervescence of a filtered portion of the liquid on addition of hydrochloric acid. The solution, after it has become clear by standing, is evaporated to dryness and ignited, when the dry *hydrate of potassa* is obtained in the form of a white hard mass, which is commonly called *caustic* potassa.

Solution of potassa is in the highest degree alkaline (§ 17) and caustic It dissolves all vegetable and animal substances, particularly fats, and is therefore to be considered as a highly-dangerous substance. Moreover, as it attacks all vessels of which silicic acid is a constituent, it is necessary to employ either iron or silver vessels in all operations in which it is fused, and likewise in its preparation.

Hydrate of potassa is employed in medicine as a caustic; its solution is used in the *manufacture of soap*, and, in a very diluted state, for the purpose of washing. Exposed to the air it rapidly attracts carbonic acid, being slowly converted into carbonate, whereby it loses its caustic properties.

67. *Sulphide of potassium*, which claims our particular attention, is the pentasulphide (KS_5) which is formed when a pulverized mixture of carbonate of potassa and sulphur is gently heated. We thus obtain a fused mass of a fine liver-colour, which is termed *liver of sulphur*, and is almost as alkaline

as caustic potassa. The solution of sulphide of potassium is yellow, and evolves hydrosulphuric acid on addition of an acid, a portion of sulphur being at the same time deposited as a very fine white precipitate, which is termed *milk of sulphur.* When exposed to the influence of the atmosphere it rapidly attracts oxygen and moisture, and is converted into sulphate of potassa. The sulphide of potassium is employed in medicine, particularly for sulphur baths, and in chemistry as a means of deoxidation. Its solution is capable of dissolving a considerable quantity of sulphur.

68. *Carbonate of potassa* (KO,CO_2) is the compound of potassium, from which all the others are prepared. It is obtained by exhausting wood-ashes with hot water, evaporating the brown liquid to dryness, and igniting the residue. The gray mass thus obtained is commonly known by the name of *potashes;* it contains in admixture a variety of other salts.

Carbonate of potassa has a mild, alkaline taste, and communicates a blue colour to reddened litmus-paper; the carbonic acid being insufficient to neutralize the highly-basic properties of the potassa. From the atmosphere it absorbs moisture with avidity, and is ultimately liquefied.

The ashes of different plants afford very dissimilar quantities of potashes; 1000 lbs. of different vegetable substances have been found to yield as follows: pine-wood, 0·45 lb.; beech-wood, 1·45 lb.; oak-bark, 4 lbs.; straw, 5 lbs.; beech-bark, 6 lbs.; the bean-plant, 20 lbs.; nettles, 25 lbs.; thistles, 35 lbs.; and wormwood, 93 lbs. of potashes. Manufactories of this important substance exist in the woody districts of Germany and Russia, and particularly in the immense forests of America.

Potashes are employed in the preparation of all the other compounds of potassa, and particularly of alum, soap, and glass.

69. A most important salt of potassa is the *nitrate,* (KO,NO_5), which is commonly known under the name of *saltpetre.* In the formation of this compound the requisite quantity of nitric acid is produced by the decomposition of nitrogenous organic compounds. As we have seen at § 33, oxygen and nitrogen combine together to produce nitric acid, only under particular circumstances. This formation takes place principally when nitrogenous animal matters are suffered to decay in contact with metallic oxides; the nitric acid produced combines with the oxides, as is observed particularly in stables and in the neighborhood of dung-heaps, where animal substances suffer decomposition. Walls are frequently observed to be coated with small crystals of nitre, possessing a bitterish cooling taste. When animal matters, manure, &c., are intentionally heaped together with moist earth, containing lime and potassa, we have all the conditions required for the formation of saltpetre. The saltpetre beds are exhausted with hot water, and the salt purified by repeated crystallization, when it is obtained in beautiful six-sided columns. The manufacture of saltpetre has considerably diminished since the discovery, in Chili, of large natural beds of nitrate of soda (NaO,NO_5), which is known in commerce as *Chili saltpetre,* and admits of being employed in many cases instead of the ordinary compound of potassa.

Saltpetre has a cooling, saline taste, and is frequently used as a remedial agent, and in the preparation of nitric acid. Exposed to a high temperature, it fuses, and if combustible substances be then brought in contact with it they combine with its abundant store of oxygen, and burn with brilliant vivacity. On this property depends the important application of saltpetre to the manufacture of gunpowder.

Gunpowder is a mixture of 76 parts of saltpetre, 11 of sulphur, and 13 of carbon, separately ground, and mixed into a paste with water. The mass is then compressed by a sieve, to obtain it in small grains, which are afterwards polished by revolving them in a vessel with pulverized charcoal. The manner in which gunpowder acts is readily explained: it is a solid body, decomposing at the moment of inflammation into several gaseous compounds, which are enormously expanded by the heat produced, and are thereby capable of overcoming the most powerful resistance and of producing very formidable effects. From the *solid* gunpowder, which may be represented by the formula $KO, NO_5 + C + S$, are formed by combustion nitrogen, carbonic oxide, and sulphurous acid $= N + CO + SO_2$, all of which are *gaseous* bodies, whilst potassa, (KO), in combination with sulphurous acid, remains behind; or, if the gunpowder be very inferior, sulphide of potassium (KS) is likewise formed.

70. *Chlorate of potassa* (KO, ClO_5) is obtained in the form of beautiful brilliant plates when chlorine is passed into a saturated solution of potassa. This salt, containing so large a proportion of oxygen, burns with combustible substances still more vividly than saltpetre, and is, therefore, a very dangerous compound. It is employed as a constituent of the paste used in the manufacture of matches, in pyrotechny, and for the preparation of oxygen.

In combination with *silicic acid* (§ 61), potassa occurs in a large number of minerals, but particularly in *felspar* ($KO,SiO_3 + Al_2O_3,3SiO_3$), which contains, moreover, silicate of alumina. By the disintegration of this mineral the potassa becomes diffused in most soils, and there forms an essential constituent of the food of almost all plants, from the ashes of which it is subsequently prepared.

Artificial silicate of potassa is prepared by igniting three parts of sand with two of potashes. The fused mass is dissolved in water, and used, under the name of *water-glass*, for the purpose of coating combustible substances, and protecting them from the danger of fire.

When potassa is fused with a larger excess of silicic acid, a glass is obtained which will be more minutely described with the soda glasses.

15. SODIUM.

Symbol: Na = 23; Specific Gravity = ·972.

71. This metal is obtained from *carbonate of soda* (NaO,CO_2), precisely in the same manner as potassium from carbonate of potassa. It possesses all the properties of potassium, with the exception of not inflaming when thrown upon water; although it occasions rapid decomposition. If, however, a fragment of sodium be placed upon moist blotting-paper, it immediately ignites, and burns with a beautiful yellow flame. Moreover, the oxide of sodium (NaO), which is termed *soda*, and the sulphide of this metal, present in their preparation, properties, and applications, so great a similarity to the corresponding compounds of potassium that it is unnecessary here to describe them. We therefore pass at once to the consideration of those compounds of sodium possessing particular characters.

72. *Chloride of sodium* (NaCl) is better known under its familiar name of culinary salt, which we shall therefore adopt. Every one will acknowledge the importance of this body, which forms an indispensable constituent of the

food of man and of many animals: without its presence the digestion of food would be impossible. It has received an important application in agriculture, and is the exclusive source whence we derive *chlorine* (§ 35), which is so important to the arts and manufactures; it is, moreover, the compound containing the chief constituent of soda (§ 73).

Culinary salt is by no means too abundantly distributed in Nature. Hence many disputes have arisen between nations with reference to this necessary compound, and many states have secured its cheap acquisition by commercial treaties. It is found partly in the solid form, as *rock salt*, and partly dissolved in the waters of *saline springs;* and, lastly, it is an invariable constituent of *sea-water.* To obtain it from these various sources, different modes are adopted. The rock-salt is obtained chiefly from the mines of *Salzburg.* To prepare it from the saline springs, the waters are evaporated until sufficiently concentrated to allow the salt to crystallize. If the waters contain from 15 to 20 per cent. of salt, they are at once evaporated in the boiling pans; but if only a small percentage of salt is present, it is customary, with a view of saving fuel, first to evaporate or *graduate* them by exposure to the air. For this purpose the brine is allowed to percolate through high stacks of thorny faggots, called *graduating works;* by which means the air passing over the distributed liquid readily evaporates a large quantity of water. This process is frequently repeated until the brine is worth boiling. From the boiling pans the salt is obtained in the form in which we daily see it at our tables.

Sea-water contains, on the average, about 2½ per cent. of salt. In some parts of the coast of England the water of the sea is let into large shallow ponds, termed *salterns*, where, by the influence of sun and wind, it is slowly evaporated. The salt that is deposited is farther purified by re-solution and evaporation, but even then is inferior in quality to the salt obtained from salt brines.

The salt-works of Germany, particularly those of Luneburg, Reichenhall, Wimpfen, Rappenau, and Durrheim, are very rich, and yield from 23 to 25 per cent. of salt.

73. In the neighbourhood of saline springs and of the sea, grow the so-called salt-plants (Salsola), which yield, when burned, an ash consisting principally of *carbonate of soda* (NaO,CO_2), or, as it is commonly termed, *soda.* The same salt, although less pure, is likewise obtained by the combustion of several marine plants. By far the greater quantity of soda, however, is at present prepared, in large manufactories, from the chloride of sodium. For this purpose, the chloride is first converted into sulphate of soda (NaO,SO_3) by heating it with sulphuric acid, hydrochloric acid (§ 36) being obtained as a secondary product. The sulphate of soda is then ignited with charcoal and carbonate of lime, by which means an insoluble oxisulphide of calcium and soluble carbonate of soda are formed. The carbonate is finally extracted by warm water, and brought into commerce in fine hydrous crystals, as *crystallized* soda, and partly in the anhydrous state, called soda-ash.

In its chemical properties this salt exhibits the greatest similarity to carbonate of potassa (§ 68); and for most of the purposes to which these salts are applied they may be mutually substituted. Soda, however, does not attract moisture from the atmosphere. Its principal use is in the manufacture of hard soap, glass, and in dyeing; its cost, moreover, is less than that of potashes. The crystallized soda, containing 63 per cent. of water of crystallization, is of course much cheaper than that which is calcined.

74. *Sulphate of soda* (NaO,SO_3), which contains a large quantity of water of crystallization, is obtained, as above mentioned, in the fabrication of soda. This salt, which is frequently employed as an aperient, was discovered in the seventeenth century, and named, after Glauber, its discoverer, *the miraculous salt of Glauber* (sal mirabile Glauberi). It is employed in large quantities in the manufacture of glass. When 14 parts of *crystallized* Glauber's salt are finely pulverized, and mixed with 6 parts of sulphuric acid and 4 of water, the temperature sinks to 8° or 10° C. below zero (17.6° to 14° F.). If water contained in a narrow vessel be immersed in the mixture, it is very rapidly frozen. The cause of this phenomenon is due to the absorption of heat by the water of crystallization in passing from the solid to the liquid form, a change which is induced by the sulphuric acid (see Physics, § 146).

75. In the mineral kingdom, soda is found in combination with *silicic acid* less frequently than potassa; but the minerals, natrolite, albite, and other silicious compounds containing soda, are by no means rare. We shall, however, first of all consider the artificial silicate of soda, which is called

Glass.

By this term is understood the transparent artificial compounds of silicic acid with metallic oxides. Glass never contains one oxide only, but several of these invariably occur together, and hence we may term it a mixture of silicates. The principal constituents employed in the preparation of glass are, *silicic acid* (sand), *soda*, *potassa*, *oxide of lead*, and *lime* (CaO), besides the colouring oxides, which are always added only in very small quantities. The kind of glass is determined by the prevailing oxide, and we distinguish in commerce the different varieties under the names of soda-glass, potassa-glass, lead-glass, &c., which differ essentially in their properties.

Potassa-glass is the hardest and most difficult to fuse; moreover, it is the most colourless and transparent, and constitutes the chief mass of the magnificent *Bohemian crystal-glass.* The *soda-glass* was formerly manufactured principally in France, and is, therefore, called *French-glass;* it is softer and more easily fused, and has a bluish-green colour; it is principally used for windows. *Lead-glass* is the heaviest and fuses most readily, whereby it may be recognised without difficulty. The inferior kinds of it have a somewhat cloudy appearance, yet vessels which are made of them have a fine lustre, and they are particularly adapted for those glass-wares which are pressed between hot metallic plates. On the other hand, the purer kind of lead glass, termed *English flint-glass,* is distinguished by its transparency and remarkable power of refracting light, and is consequently employed in the manufacture of lenses. *Lime-glass* is a constituent of all kinds of glass, particularly of the green and yellow bottle-glass, which it renders more fusible. If a larger proportion of lime be used, a semi-transparent and white glass is produced, which is usually termed *milk-glass.*

76. In the preparation of glass, the constituents which are always mixed with broken glass are finely pulverized, dried by ignition, mixed according

to the kind it is wished to produce, and then gradually projected into the melting pot. As many as six, eight, or ten of these crucibles are placed in an arched oven kept continually at a red-heat by a fire which is burning year after year. After the lapse of twelve hours, the mass melts, and at the expiration of twenty-four hours it is ready for working, a process which varies greatly, according to the purposes for which the glass is required. The principal tool of the glass-blower is the so-called *blow-pipe*, consisting of an iron tube from three to four feet long, which he dips into the melted mass, and then blows out the adhering glass, precisely in the same manner as we make bubbles of soap. By suitable rolling, stretching, bending, and moulding, the workman gives to his ball all possible shapes, and cuts with a pair of scissors the soft glass wherever he deems it necessary, exactly as we cut a piece of paper. If it is intended to make sheet or window-glass, a long hollow cylinder is blown, which is first cut open at the lower extremity and then in a longitudinal direction. The sheets are then stretched in a particular kind of oven, and polished. Large plates for mirrors are cast, and then submitted to the tedious and troublesome processes of grinding and polishing, which make this kind of glass exceedingly dear.

77. Coloured glass is obtained by the addition of certain metallic oxides to the melted mass, and these we will mention with the corresponding colours. Black glass is produced by a mixture of protoxide of iron, binoxide of manganese, protoxide of copper, and oxide of cobalt; blue, by oxide of cobalt; violet, by binoxide of manganese; green, by protoxide of copper, or sesquioxide of chromium; bottle-green, by protoxide of iron; purple-red, by oxide of gold with binoxide of tin; ruby, by suboxide of copper; flesh-colour, by sesquioxide of iron; and yellow, by teroxide of antimony and protoxide of silver.

Transparent, highly lustrous, coloured lead-glass, termed glass-flux or strass, is employed in the fabrication of the artificial precious stones, and the brilliant glass pearls. An addition of binoxide of tin renders the white or coloured glass opaque, in which case it is called enamel, and is used for necklaces and all kinds of ornaments.

The art of painting on glass consists of two different processes — either differently-coloured pieces of glass are united by means of lead, or coloured glass-flux is burnt into the surface of the glass; the colour is then on certain parts ground or etched out by hydrofluoric acid (§ 39), and other glass-fluxes burnt in, whereby the required designs are produced. Those colours which are capable of standing the least heat are placed on last. This noble art has been particularly investigated by the chemist, and at the present time the most magnificent colours are obtained.

Ammonium.

78. As will be shown in the subsequent part of this work, we find in all liquids obtained in the dry distillation of nitrogenous bodies, a volatile compound of nitrogen and hydrogen which possesses all the properties of a powerfully basic metallic oxide, and has received the name of *ammonia* (NH_4O). This combination is obtained in a state of purity when chloride of ammonium (NH_4Cl) is heated with caustic lime, and the evolved gas passed into water.

Solution of ammonia (NH_4O), usually termed *spirit of sal-ammoniac* or hartshorn, is a pellucid liquid of penetrating odour and taste, producing a powerfully irritating effect upon the eyes. The abundant formation of ammonia from decaying animal refuse is amply testified by the powerful odour continually emitted by these bodies during decomposition, particularly in moist weather. The formation appears to depend chiefly on the presence of a large quantity of moisture, for when, by suitable arrangements, the liquid contents of cesspools and sewers are allowed to drain off, the generation of this compound is greatly retarded.

Chloride of ammonium (NH_4Cl) is obtained when the alkaline liquid produced in the distillation of animal matters is saturated with hydrochloric acid, and the solution evaporated and sublimed. It occurs as a white salt, commonly termed *sal-ammoniac*, in consequence of having been originally imported from the province of Ammonium in Egypt, where it was prepared by distillation of camel's dung.

Carbonate of ammonia (NH_4O,CO_2) crystallizes from the above-mentioned alkaline liquid, and is purified by frequent solution and recrystallization.

All the compounds of ammonia possess a peculiarly sharp taste, and evolve when mixed with lime the pungent odour of the liquid compound. They are highly valuable remedial agents, acting particularly upon the cutaneous system, and when taken internally, produce the effect of powerful sudorifics. Their *volatility*, and the facility with which they are expelled from other substances render them of great importance in chemistry, and peculiarly fit them for the purposes of many chemical analyses. The ammonia compounds display a remarkable analogy to the corresponding combinations of potassa and soda; and hence we observe that a similar series of phenomena are produced in certain cases when ammonia is substituted for potassa or soda, or when the carbonate of ammonia or sulphide of ammonium is employed in the place of the carbonates of potassa and soda or the sulphide of potassium.

Moreover, the compounds of ammonia are highly important in their relation to the vegetable kingdom. It may be assumed that all the *nitrogen* of plants is derived from the ammonia which they absorb from the soil and from the surrounding atmosphere.

The similarity of ammonia to the metallic oxide has led to the conjecture that all its combinations contain a *compound* metallic body, which has received the name *ammonium* (NH_4); but no one has yet succeeeded in its preparation, although by peculiar processes it may be obtained in the form of an amalgam.

16. CALCIUM.

Symbol: $Ca = 20$.

79. This metal forms a considerable part of the solid crust of the earth, entire mountains consisting of the carbonate of its oxide (chalk); it is also a never-failing constituent of plants and animals. In the free state it offers little interest, and owes its importance chiefly to its combinations. We shall first consider —

Oxide of calcium, or *lime* (CaO), which is obtained by the ignition of carbonate of lime (CaO,CO_2), when the carbonic acid is evolved. On the large scale the process is carried on in furnaces called *lime-kilns*.

The properties of lime are familiar to every one. It possesses a grayish-white appearance, and when moistened with water it combines, with considerable development of heat (Phys. § 147), to produce hydrate of lime (CaO,HO), which is ordinarily termed *slaked lime*. The caustic lime when thus treated swells up and cracks, and finally crumbles to an impalpable powder. On addition of a farther quantity of water, a milky liquid is produced, which is commonly termed *milk of lime*, and from which is deposited a portion of the lime in form of a pasty mass, whilst the clear supernatent liquid is found to be a solution of lime in water, and is called *lime-water*.

Lime is powerfully caustic, hence called *caustic lime*, and attracts carbonic acid with great avidity from the air, whereby it is again converted into carbonate and completely deprived of its caustic properties. If a paste of lime be exposed to the atmosphere, it becomes in a short time converted into hard carbonate of lime, a property on which depends its important application to *mortars* and cements.

Caustic lime is employed in white-washing, and for the purpose of depriving skins of hair in the process of tanning (technically called unhairing), as well as in many chemical operations.

80. *Carbonate of lime* (CaO,CO_2), like silicic acid and carbon, occurs in Nature under a variety of forms. *Calcspar* is colourless, transparent, and crystallized; *marble* is white, granular, and hard; whilst *chalk* is soft, and leaves a mark when drawn across a coloured surface. Other limestones, moreover, are coloured by the admixture of metallic oxides; thus we meet with gray, yellow, black, brown, red, and even with variegated limestones, such as many of the beautiful kinds of marbles. But, notwithstanding their diversity of form and appearance, they, one and all, are characterised by giving rise to a powerful evolution of carbonic acid, when treated with hydrochloric acid, and by yielding caustic lime by ignition.

Carbonate of lime, in all its forms, is an important material, not only for the sculptor, but also as a building-stone and cement for masonry; its comparatively trifling hardness, however, renders it ill adapted for the purpose of constructing roads.

Carbonate of lime is the main component of the shells of the crustacea, of corals, and of the shell of the egg; it enters likewise into the composition of bones, and hence we must regard it as one of the necessary constituents of the food of animals. Although this salt by itself is insoluble, it is nevertheless an almost invariable constituent of the waters we meet with in Nature, containing, as they always do, a portion of carbonic acid, which has the power of dissolving carbonate of lime. But when gently warmed, the volatile gas is expelled and the carbonate of lime deposited in the form of a white incrustation upon the bottom of the vessel. Every household daily affords us opportunities of witnessing deposits of this nature, which are particularly observed on the bottoms of tea-kettles, and if the water contains a large quantity of calcareous matter, even our water-bottles and drinking-glasses become covered with a thin film of carbonate of lime. These depositions may readily be removed by pouring into the vessels a little dilute hydrochloric acid, or some strong vinegar, which in a short time dissolves the carbonate of lime.

81. *Sulphate of lime* ($CaO,SO_3 + 2HO$) is found in considerable masses, and is commonly known under the name of *gypsum*. It occurs either crystallized or granulated, and of dazzling whiteness resembling sugar; in the latter form it is termed *alabaster*, which is so soft as almost to admit of being cut with a knife, and is admirably adapted for various kinds of works of art. Gypsum, as shown by the formula, contains water of crystallization, which is expelled at a gentle heat. But when ignited, ground, and mixed into a paste with water, it acquires the property of entering into chemical combination with it, and forming the original hydrate which in a short time becomes perfectly solid. Thus it offers to the artist a highly-valuable material for preparing the well-known plaster figures, and by its use the noblest statues of ancient and modern art have now been placed within the reach of all.

Gypsum, moreover, has received a valuable application as manure, to which we shall again return in our consideration of the nutrition of plants. In water it is slightly soluble, and imparts to it a disagreeable and somewhat bitterish earthy taste.

Phosphate of lime constitutes the principal mass of the bones of animals, and is extensively employed in the preparation of phosphorus; in the form of ground bones it is likewise used as a manure. It appears to belong to those mineral constituents which are essential to the nutrition of animals, being found in the seeds of all the cereals, from which, expecially those used in bread, is derived the phosphorus contained in the animal organism.

Silicate of lime we have already become acquainted with as a constituent of glass. A number of minerals and mineral remains contain silicic acid and lime: we shall, however, allude here only to the compound known under the name of *hydraulic mortar*, or cement, the principal constituents of which are silicic acid, lime, and alumina. It occurs in nature as the so-called *strass*, or it is prepared artificially. When finely pulverized and mixed into a paste it quickly hardens, even under water, and hence it is employed with great advantage in the construction of masonry under water, and for the purpose of protecting many buildings against the action of water.

Chloride of Lime.

82. When chlorine is passed over hydrate of lime (§ 79), thinly spread upon trays, there is formed a mixture of lime (CaO), chloride of calcium ($CaCl$), and hypochlorite of lime (CaO,ClO). This compound is met with in commerce in the form of a moist white powder, smelling slightly of chlorine, and is generally known under the name of chloride of lime, or *bleaching-powder*.

Chloride of lime evolves chlorine very abundantly when treated with the weakest acids, and even the carbonic acid of the atmosphere suffices to decompose it; hence it offers at the same time the most convenient and frequently-used substance for preparing this very important element. Whilst chloride of lime is employed in enormous quantities in bleaching establishments, we continually avail ourselves of its disinfectant properties in our dwellings, and particularly in anatomical rooms, hospitals, &c. For the latter purpose we place about a table-spoonful of the powder in a saucer, and add to it an equal quantity of hydrochloric acid diluted with a little water, taking great care to avoid the inhalation of the pure chlorine. The doors and windows of the rooms must be previously closed, and opened again after some hours. If, however, the chlorine is needed in an inhabited room, it is advisable to add from time to time only a few drops of hydrochloric acid, always bearing in mind that too much chlorine is very pernicious. If it be desired to bleach written papers, soiled engravings, &c., a filtered solution of the chloride of lime is decomposed with a few drops of hydrochloric acid, and the object immersed in this liquid until the desired effect is produced. The paper is then frequently rinsed and allowed to remain for some hours in a large vessel of pure water, and afterwards dried between folds of blotting-paper. Ink-spots are removed by this process with equal facility.

17. BARIUM.

Symbol: Ba = 68·5.

83. This metal occurs much less frequently than the one we have just described. Its most important compound is the so-called *heavy-spar* or *sulphate of baryta* (BaO,SO_3) which is a white, compact crystalline mineral, and is distinguished from all the other earthy compounds by its great specific gravity, which is = 4·44. When ground to a fine powder, it is employed as a white paint; all the inferior kinds of white lead are largely adulterated with heavy-spar. The sulphate of baryta is perfectly insoluble in water.

Nitrate of baryta (BaO,NO_5) is used in pyrotechny for preparing a green fire, for which the following mixture is employed: 20 parts by weight of sulphur, 33 parts of chlorate of potassa, and 80 parts of nitrate of baryta.

18. STRONTIUM.

Symbol: Sr = 43·8.

84. This somewhat rare metal is distinguished by imparting to flame an extremely beautiful crimson colour, and on this property depends its only application. If we dissolve the *chloride of strontium* ($SrCl$) in spirits of wine, it imparts to the flame a beautiful red tint.

We may obtain a splendid red fire by burning the following *dry* mixture: 10 parts of nitrate of strontia; $1\frac{1}{4}$ part of chlorate of potassa; $3\frac{1}{4}$ parts of sulphur; 1 part of sulphide of antimony; and $\frac{1}{2}$ part of charcoal.

19. MAGNESIUM.

Symbol: Mg = 12·2.

85. Magnesium is frequently met with in combination, and occasionally forms one of the principal constituents of certain mountains. Its soluble compounds are distinguished by a bitter taste and aperient effect, and are almost exclusively employed in medicine. Its oxide is termed *magnesia.*

Chloride of magnesium ($MgCl$) is a constituent of sea-water, to which it imparts its disagreeable taste, and renders it unfit for the ordinary purposes of life. This salt is likewise contained in many saline springs.

Sulphate of magnesia (MgO,SO_3) occurs in sea-water, and in very large quantities in many saline springs, as in those of Epsom, Seidschütz, Kissingen, and many others, from which it is obtained.

Carbonate of magnesia (MgO,CO_2) forms with carbonate of lime a compound called *dolomite*, a rock which occurs in masses of considerable size. In the pure state it is prepared by decomposing a hot solution of sulphate of magnesia with carbonate of soda. When dried it forms an extremely light, flocculent, white powder, which is insoluble in water, and, therefore, tasteless. By ignition it loses its carbonic acid, and is then pure oxide of magnesium (MgO), which is employed in medicine, under the name of *calcined magnesia*, particularly for acidity of the stomach.

20. ALUMINUM.

Symbol: Al = 13·7; Specific Gravity = 2·6.

86. This metal forms a considerable part of the crust of our earth, since its oxygen-compound (Al_2O_3), which is termed *alumina*, constitutes, next to silicic acid and lime, the mass of the greater number of minerals. Like several other bodies, which we have already become accquainted with, alumina presents itself in a great variety of forms. (*Mineralogy*, § 43.)

Crystallized alumina is found under the same circumstances as crystallized carbon, and hence the *sapphire*, consisting of pure alumina, and distinguished by its hardness, lustre, and infusibility, is numbered amongst the precious stones. The minerals *corundum* and *emery*, which are alumina of a less degree of purity, likewise possess considerable hardness, and owing to this property they have received an important application in grinding and polishing other substances.

Pure alumina may be chemically prepared by precipitating a solution of alum by ammonia. The gelatinous precipitate, when washed and dried, forms a white, insoluble, and infusible mass, which strongly adheres to the tongue.

Alumina is distinguished by its great affinity for vegetable fibre and colouring matters. If we place some threads, or a piece of cotton or linen texture, in a solution, and precipitate the alumina, the oxide is found to enter into intimate combination with the fibre; and if the cloth thus prepared be now immersed in a solution of a colouring matter, the alumina fixes a portion of the colour upon the fibre, which then appears to be permanently dyed. This property renders alumina an important material in the process of dyeing. The insoluble precipitates which alumina forms with vegetable colouring matters are known under the name of *lakes*.

40.

87. *Alum* is a compound of sulphate of alumina with sulphate of potassa ($Al_2O_3,3SO_3 + KO,SO_3 + 24HO$), which is found in Nature, but is chiefly prepared artificially. It possesses a sweetish, astringent taste, crystallizes in large colourless double pyramids (fig. 40), and is soluble in

water; it is employed in enormous quantities in dyeing, and in the preparation of other alumina-compounds, particularly of the *acetate of alumina.*

The compounds or mixtures of alumina and silicic acid perform an important part in the economy of Nature and of man. A number of hard minerals consist of silicate of alumina, and give rise, by their disintegration, to an earthy mass, which is commonly termed *clay.* According as they are mixed with other metallic oxides, the clays possess various colours, and are distinguished by particular names; thus we have the white Cologne pipe-clay, fuller's-earth, porcelain-earth, gray clay, yellow clay or loam, and brown and red clays. All these kinds of clay have the general property of adhering more or less strongly to the tongue, and possess a peculiar odour, termed the clay-odour, which is probably due to the continual absorption of ammonia from the atmosphere. Clay produces with water a soft, plastic mass, which retains moisture with extraordinary power, a property which renders it of the greatest importance to agriculture, and secures to plants the moisture needed for their growth.

The plasticity of moist clay has led to its employment from the earliest times in the manufacture of pottery. When the soft vessels of clay are ignited, or, as it is commonly termed, *fired,* they acquire considerable hardness. The names by which they are distinguished depend upon the fineness and purity of the clay.

Porcelain.

88. Porcelain, which has long been known to the Chinese, was discovered in Germany in the year 1701, by Böttcher, a chemist of Meissen, who, by the command of Prince Joachim of Saxony, engaged in the attempt to make gold. This chemist mixed and fused together a variety of substances, and finally his labours were crowned with the discovery of a beautiful semi-transparent substance, which we term porcelain, and which indeed, has proved a true mine of gold to the kingdom of Saxony.

41.

A variety of clay, called porcelain-earth, which is free from iron, is found in many localities, and is the principal constituent required in the fabrication of porcelain. This clay is finely ground, and intimately mixed with a portion of pure silicic acid or gypsum. From the mass thus prepared the vessels are formed, partly by hand on the potter's wheels, and partly by the aid of moulds, upon which these plates of clay are pressed by means of a soft sponge. After the vessels have been slowly dried in the air, they are submitted to the first process of burning, and, in order to prevent them being soiled, they are put into clay capsules, and placed in the coolest part of the potter's kiln (fig. 41). The vessels thus become hard and perfectly white, but their appearance is dull and earthy, and, as the mass imbibes water very powerfully, they adhere strongly to the tongue. The porcelain now requires to be *glazed*, for which purpose it is immersed in a liquid consisting of finely-levigated porcelain-earth, which is rendered more easily fusible by addition of gypsum. When thus covered with glaze, the vessel is a second time fired, at a heat approaching to whiteness.

The superior kinds of porcelain are perfectly white, very hard, and produce sparks when struck with steel. They exhibit a lustrous and conchoidal fracture, and are semi-transparent. Vessels of porcelain which are very thin produce a tone almost as clear and pure as that of metal.

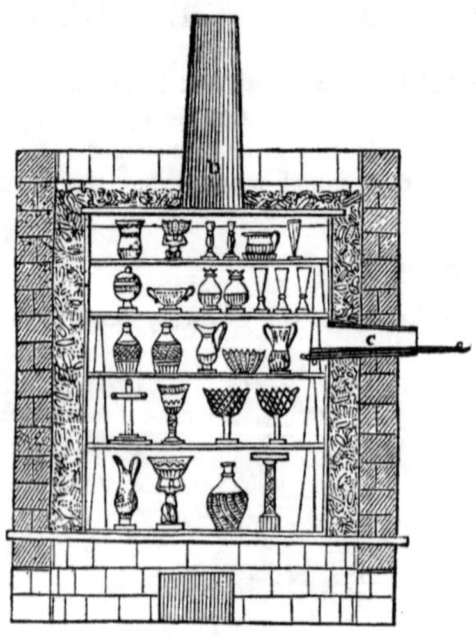

42.

In painting porcelain, a mixture is used consisting of oil of turpentine and coloured glass (§ 77), which is laid on the vessels already glazed, and then burnt in, at a very gentle heat, in the muffle-oven (fig. 42).

The superior Fayence porcelain exhibits a white earthy fracture, and is glazed with the most readily-fusible lead-glass. But vessels of inferior quality present a gray, yellow, or red fracture, and in that case they are glazed with a white glaze of lead-glass and binoxide of tin.

Earthen-ware, or earthen vessels, are made of coarser clay, and are either unglazed, as flower-pots, or they receive a coating of lead-glass, and it not unfrequently happens that, in the attempt to save fuel, the oxide of lead required for the glaze is not perfectly vitrified, and thus the food preserved in such vessels occasionally acquires poisonous properties; it is, therefore, necessary to select well-burned, clear-sounding, and highly-glazed vessels.

Another kind of pottery, which is called *stone-ware*, and is especially used in making bottles, preserve-pots, &c., is glazed by means of chloride of sodium, which is projected into the red-hot oven containing the various vessels. The salt volatilizes, and covers the interior as well as the exterior of the wares with a coating of readily-fusible soda-glass.

An inferior kind of clay is manufactured into tiles and bricks, which generally present a red colour, due to the presence of sesquioxide of iron.

89 The rare mineral known under the name of *lapis lazuli* forms, when finely ground, the magnificent blue colour called *ultramarine*. Chemical

investigations have shown that this mineral consists of sulphide of sodium (§ 71) and silicate of alumina; by igniting these substances together in proper proportions this magnificent colour is now artificially produced. Hence the price of ultramarine, which formerly was equal to that of gold, is now so low as to admit of this substance being employed in painting, in the manufacture of paper-hangings, and for many other purposes.

(B.) HEAVY METALS.

21. IRON (FERRUM).

Symbol: Fe = 28; Specific Gravity = 7·8.

90. We commence our description of the heavy metals by giving an account of iron, which is the most important and valuable of all the metals. Of this we fabricate the plough, with which we till our fields, and the sword, wherewith to defend them. History affords us many proofs that by the possession of a surplus of gold industry becomes in a measure suspended; whilst on the other hand, the possession of iron, the true source of wealth, has led to the boundless developement of arts and manufactures.

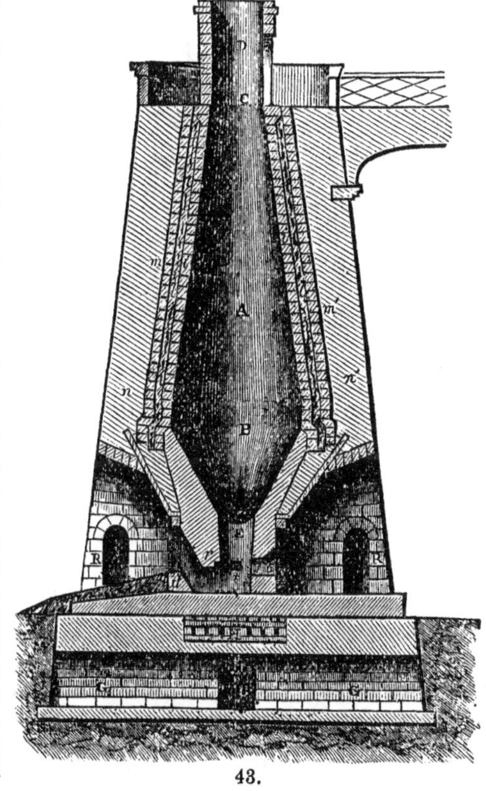

43.

In our section on Mineralogy we shall describe a number of ores from which iron is obtained, and which are particularly abundant in this country, and also in Germany and Sweden. The essential constituents of these ores are *iron* and *oxygen*, from which the latter element has to be separated. For this purpose the ores are broken in small fragments, mixed with limestone and coal, and introduced into the blast-furnace (fig. 43). The cone of the furnace A, is surrounded by fire-bricks, *i i*, which is again enveloped in a casing, *l l*, formed of broken scoriæ, and which separates the internal lining of the furnace from the external coating of fire-bricks, *m m'*, supported by a mass of masonry, *n n'*, formed either of stone or bricks. The opening C, at the top of the furnace, is called the *throat*, or *tunnel-hole*, and is surmounted by a chimney D. The lower cone B, is known by the name of the *boshes,* and is constructed generally of fire-stone. At the commencement of the process, the bottom of the furnace is filled with wood and coal which is ignited, and the fire is afterwards maintained in a state of intense ignition by a powerful and continuous blast of air. As soon as the ore has become thoroughly ignited, its oxygen unites with the carbon to produce carbonic acid, which escapes, whilst the metal itself fuses, and flows to the bottom of the furnace, whence it is from time to time allowed to run out. As the lower stratum fuses, the one above falls down, and by the continual addition of fresh quantities of ore and coal to the upper part of the furnace, the process is continued year after year without interruption, until at last the heat seriously injures the walls, which then require either to be rebuilt or repaired.

Iron, however, is not the only product of the blast-furnace. By far the greater number of ores contain, moreover, silicic acid, alumina and lime, which by the heat required for the separation of the iron, and by the limestone added for the purpose of removing the silicic acid and alumina, become fused to a dark-coloured glass, termed *slag,* which flows with the melted metal to the bottom of the furnace. The slag, being much lighter than the iron, floats upon the surface, and is from time to time removed by rakes, and then solidifies to a vitreous mass. The slag which covers the surface of the melted iron protects it from the atmosphere, which would otherwise oxidize a considerable quantity of metal: hence the necessity of slag in the blast-furnace process; when the ores do not contain those constituents necessary for its formation, it is usual to introduce such minerals, and especially lime, as produce a readily-fusible slag.

Varieties of Iron.

91. Carbon has the property of entering into chemical combination, and of being *dissolved* by iron; and according to the proportion in which it is present we obtain the three principal varieties, namely (1.) Cast-iron, containing a considerable quantity of carbon. (2.) Wrought-iron, free from carbon. (3.) Steel, or iron which is combined with a very trifling quantity of carbon.

(1.) The metal which is immediately drawn from the blast-furnace is termed *pig* or *cast-iron.* 100 pounds contain about 5 pounds of carbon, which is either in perfect chemical combination or only *partly* dissolved. In the former case, the iron is white, lustrous, and forms the variety distinguished as *specular-iron,* which, on account of its tenacity and difficulty of fusion, is unsuited for casting, and is employed in the preparation of the other kinds of iron. In the latter case the iron possesses a grayish or blackish-gray colour, as observed in the ordinary cast-iron or gray pig-iron. This variety fuses at 1000° C. (1832° F.) to a mobile liquid mass, which readily flows into all parts of the moulds of sand. On cooling, it contracts only to the extent of about 1¼ per cent., and therefore it is admirably adapted for all kinds of castings, particularly for furnaces, hearth-plates, and for numberless objects of art. This kind of iron, which exhibits a granulated fracture, is extremely hard and brittle, and does not admit of being worked in any other way.

(2.) *Bar* or *wrought iron* is found to be almost pure iron: it is prepared from the foregoing by powerful ignition, in contact with the atmosphere, whereby the carbon it contains is burned, until scarcely a trace remains. The most remarkable property of this kind of iron is extreme tenacity, which allows it to be wrought with facility, and drawn into fine wires, or rolled into plates, but, owing to its trifling hardness, it is little suited for the manufacture of cutting instruments. Its fracture is gray and jagged, and, when worked, its surface acquires considerable polish, and has then a white colour. Bar-iron fuses only at the strongest white heat, at about 1600° C. (2912 F.), and hence the difficulty of joining two pieces together by fusion; but at a red-heat the iron becomes sufficiently soft to admit of being intimately united by hammering, or, as it is commonly termed, *welded* together.

(3.) Steel contains from 1 to 2 per cent. of carbon. It is either prepared from cast-iron, by the removal of only part of its carbon, or from bar-iron, to which some carbon is again added. The steel prepared by the first process is called *raw* or cast-steel. In the second process, the bars of iron, surrounded by pulverized charcoal, are for some time ignited in earthen vessels, whereby the carbon slowly combines with the iron, and converts it into the so-called *cement-steel*. Larger masses of iron, when treated in a similar manner, have their surfaces only converted into steel, or, as it is commonly termed, *cemented*.

Steel offers one of the most remarkable examples of the *dissimilar* properties one and the same body may acquire by the different arrangement of particles. By itself it possesses nearly all the characters of bar-iron: it is soft and malleable, but it is more readily fusible, since it fuses at a temperature of from 1200° C. to 1400° C. (2192° F. to 2552° F.); its colour likewise varies from gray to grayish-white, but it is susceptible of an extremely fine polish, and acquires thereby a high lustre. If, however, the red-hot steel be suddenly cooled by plunging it into cold water, it becomes entirely changed in its nature, being then extremely brittle and unmalleable, and harder than any other substance, with the exception of the diamond and crystallized alumina. It scratches glass and flint, and is chiefly employed in the fabrication of instruments, in which great hardness is required, such as files, needles, &c.

When *hardened* steel is heated and allowed to cool slowly, it loses its properties, and acquires again the softness and tenacity of raw steel. The stronger the heat employed, the more completely is this remarkable change produced; and by employing suitable temperatures, intermediate qualities of steel may be obtained, which, in addition to greater hardness, acquire at the same time considerable flexibility; a property which is absolutely indispensable for most of the purposes for which it is employed, and particularly for the fabrication of cutting instruments. By heating or *annealing*, the polished steel changes its colour, becoming first of a pale yellow, then dark yellow, orange, red, dark red, violet, blue, and finally blackish-blue, the darker colours being produced by the higher temperatures. These changes of colour observed in steel afford, therefore, an excellent means of judging of the temperature to which it must be exposed when the steel is required for certain purposes. This series of colours may be distinctly seen by holding a knitting-needle in the edge of a candle-flame, when at the hottest part the needle will appear of a black colour, passing through all the other tints towards the cooler extremity.

In most manufactories of steel, the objects are first formed of the soft raw steel, then hardened, and subsequently, to a certain extent, annealed, according to the purpose for which they are required, as we will illustrate by the following examples: *pale yellow* for the finest knives; *golden yellow* for razors and pen-knives; from *brown* to *purple-red* for scissors, axes, chisels, and ordinary knives; *bright blue* for swords, watch-springs, and gimlets: and, finally, *dark blue* for the blades of saws.

Compounds of Iron.

92. In general, the compounds of iron which are soluble in water possess a peculiar *chalybeate* taste, which any person may become acquainted with by tasting ink. They have, moreover, the property of forming a dark-blue, or violet compound (ink), with an infusion of gall-nuts or of oak bark, and with all substances containing tannic acid. In most of its compounds iron possesses medicinal properties, and acts especially upon the blood.

(1.) *Protoxide of iron* (FeO) is only known in combination. Its hydrate (FeO,HO), which is prepared by precipitating a solution of sulphate of iron, or green vitriol, by potassa, is white, but becomes in an instant green, then yellow, and finally brown, passing slowly into the higher oxide.

(2.) *Sesquioxide of iron* (Fe_2O_3) occurs frequently as a mineral, called red iron-stone, and is obtained as a residuary product in the manufacture of fuming sulphuric acid (§ 41). When pulverized, it appears of a dark brick-red colour, and is employed in polishing plate, &c., under the name of *English rouge.* The colour of red-ochre, red-chalk, and red-sandstone, is due to the presence of this compound. The hydrate of the sesquioxide ($Fe_2O_3,3HO$) is frequently met with in Nature under the name of brown iron-stone. It varies in colour from yellow to brown, and imparts to loam, tripoli, &c., their peculiar tints. In the pure state it is prepared by precipitating a solution of sesquichloride of iron by ammonia, and is employed in medicine as an antidote for arsenic (§ 46). It constitutes, moreover, the rust which is seen on iron exposed to the influence of moist air.

(3.) *Bisulphide of iron* (FeS_2), occurring in Nature, and commonly known as *iron pyrites,* is crystalline, and exhibits a metallic lustre, and brass-yellow colour. The ordinary black sulphide (FeS), which is frequently employed in the preparation of hydrosulphuric acid (§ 43), is prepared by gently igniting equal parts by weight of sulphur and finely-divided iron.

(4.) *Chloride of iron* ($FeCl$) is formed when iron is dissolved in hydrochloric acid. It is deposited from a concentrated solution in the form of pale, greenish-blue, hydrated crystals. The sesquichloride of iron (Fe_2Cl_3) is obtained in reddish-brown hydrated crystals from a concentrated solution of iron in aqua regia (§ 36), and is extensively employed in medicine.

(5.) *Cyanide of iron* forms, with cyanide of potassium, a remarkable compound ($FeCy,2KCy$), known under the name of *prussiate of potash* or ferrocyanide of potassium. It is produced when nitrogenous carbon (§ 50) is strongly ignited with potassa, and the mass so obtained subsequently boiled with metallic iron. The concentrated and filtered solution deposits, on cooling, beautiful yellow crystals of ferrocyanide of potassium of the above-mentioned composition, containing, moreover, three equivalents of water of crystallization. A solution of this salt produces, with the soluble compounds of protoxide of iron, a pale-blue precipitate, which in a short time acquires, by exposure to the atmosphere, a beautiful dark-blue colour; but with a solution of the sesquioxide of iron, it immediately forms a fine dark-blue precipitate of *Prussian blue*, which is a compound of cyanogen and iron. The inferior and paler varieties of this much-employed pigment are prepared by adding to the blue deposit, whilst still moist, a portion of finely-levigated white clay. Although this compound contains cyanogen, it nevertheless appears to produce no poisonous effect upon the animal economy. It may be remarked, that the ferrocyanide of potassium is employed in the preparation of hydrocyanic acid and most of the other cyanogen compounds. (Compare § 59.)

93. (6.) *Sulphate of protoxide of iron* (FeO,SO_3+7HO), or green vitriol, forms beautiful green hydrated crystals. It is obtained in large quantities by the oxidation of iron pyrites, and is one of the cheapest salts. The most important purposes to which it is applied is the preparation of Prussian blue, ink, violet, and black dyes, fuming sulphuric acid, and most of the preparations of iron.

(7.) *Carbonate of protoxide of iron* (FeO,CO_2) is obtained by precipitating a solution of the preceding salt with carbonate of soda. Its colour is first white, but rapidly changes to green and brown from the absorption of oxygen and partial conversion into the sesquioxide. Although insoluble in water, it is nevertheless found in numerous springs which contain much *carbonic acid*, being held in solution by this gas: the waters which hold the iron in solution by this means are commonly termed *chalybeate* waters.

22. MANGANESE.

Symbol: $Mn = 27{\cdot}6$; Specific Gravity = 8.

94. Manganese is, next to iron, the most diffused of all the heavy metals, although it is only rarely met with in considerable quantities. There is scarcely an iron ore that does not contain manganese, and hence the iron of commerce almost invariably contains a portion of this metal, occasionally amounting to 4 or 6 per cent.

The metal itself is extremely difficult to prepare in a state of purity, and so hard to fuse that it at present has received no useful application. Its most important compound is the *binoxide of manganese* (MnO_2), which yields a portion of its oxygen with great facility, and is, therefore, extensively employed as a means of oxidation, and for the preparation of oxygen (§ 22). It is used, moreover, in the arts for decolorizing glass, and in enormous quantities for preparing chlorine (§ 35).

Protoxide of manganese (MnO) is employed for imparting a violet colour to glass.

When the binoxide is ignited for a considerable time with potassa, and the mass subsequently treated with water, a beautiful green solution is obtained, consisting of *manganate of potassa* (KO,MnO_3), the colour of which, on farther dilution and exposure to the atmosphere, changes to a beautiful purple-red, the *permanganate of potassa* (KO,Mn_2O_7) being then contained in the liquid. This compound, however, likewise slowly decomposes, and the solution finally becomes colourless. On account of these peculiar changes of colour, the green compound has received the name of *mineral chameleon.*

23. COBALT.

Symbol: Co=29·5; Spec. Gravity=8·7.

24. NICKEL.

Symbol: Ni=29.6; Spec. Gravity=8·8.

95. These two metals occur mostly together, and in a similar state of combination, as ores, which contain besides a portion of sulphur and arsenic. To remove these latter substances the ores are ignited with potassa and nitre, whereby we obtain the soluble arseniate and sulphate of potassa, whilst the oxides of the metals remain behind, and are then employed for the preparation of their respective compounds. Both metals are hard, brittle, difficultly fusible, and attracted by the *magnet.*

Oxide of cobalt produces, with silicic acid, a deep-blue vitreous compound (§ 77), which acquires a light-blue colour when finely pulverized, and then forms the pigment known as *smalts.* The salts of cobalt possess a rose-red or blue colour; and it may be remarked, that the chloride is used as a sympathetic ink. If paper be written upon with a solution of this salt, the writing remains invisible, but when gently warmed it appears of a beautiful blue colour. If to the cobalt solution a few drops of chloride of iron be added, the writing then acquires a splendid green colour.

The most important application of nickel is in the preparation of the alloy it produces with zinc and copper, which is called *German-silver* or argentine and possesses properties closely allied to those of silver. The salts of nickel have a beautiful green colour.

25. COPPER.

Symbol: Cu = 31·7; Specific Gravity = 8·9.

96. Copper possesses a beautiful red colour, and is very tough and malleable; it possesses moderate hardness, and requires a very high temperature for fusion. This metal is frequently met with in the native state, and hence it became known to the ancients long before iron, which is difficult to reduce to the metallic form. It frequently occurs, moreover, in combination with oxygen or sulphur.

Sheet copper, as well known, is worked into a great variety of domestic utensils, particularly tea-kettles, sauce-pans, stills, &c.; and it possesses the great advantage over iron that it is little affected by exposure to the atmosphere. With other metals it combines to produce a series of alloys, which are used for many purposes. The most important of these alloys are the following: 1. *Brass,* which consists of 71 parts of copper and 29 parts of zinc, has a bright yellow colour, and is commonly employed in castings. 2. *Red brass,* termed also tomback or similor, consists of 85 parts of copper and 15 of zinc. When beaten into thin leaves it constitutes the spurious leaf-gold, the powder of which is used in imitative gilding and bronzing. 3. *Bronze,* which was especially used in antiquity for the fabrication of utensils and works of art of every kind, consists of from 85 to 97 parts of copper, and from 15 to 3 of tin. 4. *Gun-metal* contains 90 copper with 10 tin. 5. *Bell-metal* is 75 to 80 parts copper, and 25 to 20 tin. 6. *German-silver,* or argentine, consists of 2 copper, 1 nickel, and 1 zinc. 7. *Coinage silver* and *plate*, and likewise *coinage gold*, invariably contain a small quantity of copper, for the purpose of imparting additional hardness.

Compounds of Copper.

97. The compounds of copper, in so far as they are soluble, are distinguished by a nauseating metallic taste, which is evident when an object of brass or copper is placed in contact with the tongue. Taken internally they act as poisons, and for this reason the vessels of copper are now, as far as practicable, abolished in domestic economy. But, nevertheless, cases of poisoning by copper frequently occur; and, as a remedial means, it is usual to administer, in the first place, an emetic, and afterwards copious draughts of sugared water. The prevailing colours of the compounds of copper are blue and green.

(1.) *Protoxide of copper* (CuO) is formed as a black mass when metallic copper is ignited in the atmosphere. The hydrate of this oxide (CuO,HO) is obtained in the form of a beautiful blue precipitate when a solution of sulphate of copper is decomposed by potassa; by a gentle heat, however, it loses its water, and is converted into the black protoxide.

(2.) *Sulphate of protoxide of copper* (CuO,SO_3), or blue vitriol, with water of crystallization, is one of the most beautiful salts, and is obtained by heating metallic copper with sulphuric acid. It is employed for making many other preparations of copper, and is likewise extensively used for protecting wheat from the depredations of insects, which is done by merely digesting the seed-corn in a solution of the salt.

(3.) *Carbonate of protoxide of copper* (CuO,CO_2) is a bluish-green precipitate, which is formed when a solution of the preceding salt is decomposed by carbonate of soda. This compound, which is employed as a colour, is formed particularly when copper or alloys of this metal are alternately exposed to the influence of water and air, and is commonly termed *verdigris*.

(4.) *Arsenite of protoxide of copper* is the main ingredient of the beautiful Schweinfurt green, which, however, on account of its poisonous properties, is seldom or never used.

Of the *acetate of protoxide of copper*, or the true verdigris, we shall again have occasion to speak.

26. BISMUTH.

Symbol: Bi = 213; Specific Gravity = 9·8; Fusing-point = 246° C. (474°·8 F.).

98. This metal, the colour of which is reddish-white, is neither of frequent occurrence nor is it possessed of properties of any particular value. It may, however, be remarked, that when fused and allowed slowly to cool, it exhibits a remarkable tendency to crystallize. It is employed as a constituent of the fusible alloys (see Tin), and its oxide is used medicinally, and as a white paint.

27. LEAD (PLUMBUM).

Symbol: Pb = 103·7; Specific Gravity = 11·5; Fusing-point = 322° C. (611°·6 F.).

99. Lead is commonly found in combination with sulphur as a grayish-white, lustrous mineral called *galena*. When this ore is heated in the atmo

sphere, or, as the workmen term it, roasted, the sulphur is burned with formation of sulphurous acid, whilst the lead unites with oxygen to produce the oxide from which the metal is subsequently prepared by fusion with coal.

This ponderous and soft metal, which admits of being cut with a knife, is familiar to every one; it is rolled into plates and drawn out into tubes, and is, moreover, used for many kinds of casting, amongst which balls and shot are not the least important. It is likewise a constituent of many alloys which will be considered under tin.

100. The compounds of lead are poisonous, and have the effect of producing violent pains in the bowels, termed *lead-colic*, against which the sulphuretted waters are frequently employed. Poisoning by lead is frequently occasioned by the use of imperfectly-burned earthenware (§ 88), and tin vessels containing lead.

(1.) *Protoxide of lead* (PbO), which is termed also *litharge*, or *silver-litharge*, is formed when lead is heated in the atmosphere, and is thus obtained as a waste product in the separation of silver. It consists of small shining plates of yellowish-gray colour, and is employed in the preparation of other compounds of lead, particularly of glass and glazes (§ 75), and of varnishes and plasters. A mixture of the protoxide and binoxide of lead forms the well-known *minium*, or red-lead, which is used as a paint, and for the same purposes as the protoxide.

(2.) *Carbonate of protoxide of lead* (PbO,CO_2), or *white-lead*, is one of the most important colours, and is most simply obtained by passing a stream of carbonic acid into a solution of acetate of lead. It possesses in a high degree the property of imparting *body* to colours, and hence is used as the basis of most other paints. The inferior kinds of white lead are largely adulterated with heavy-spar (§ 83). The genuine white-lead should dissolve entirely in pure *dilute* nitric acid.

28. TIN.

Symbol: Sn = 59; Specific Gravity = 7·3; Fusing-point = 228° C. (442°·4 F.)

101. Next to silver, tin is the most beautiful of white metals, and on account of its lustre and stability in the atmosphere, is employed in the fabrication of many utensils for the table. It is most frequently met with in combination with oxygen, forming the so-called *tin-stone*, from which the pure metal is obtained by fusion with coal. Occasionally tin contains arsenic, or it is intentionally adulterated with lead, and hence in both cases it is highly dangerous.

This metal is employed in casting, and for preparing *tin-foil* and the spurious *leaf-silver*. It is likewise extensively used for protecting sheet-iron from the oxidizing influence of the atmosphere. The sheets of iron when thus coated, or rather alloyed with tin, constitute the well-known tin-plate which is a highly valuable material, and is employed for numberless purposes. Copper vessels are also *tinned*, and may then be employed without danger for cooking food, as the tin is not in the least degree affected by the materials used in cooking. Some of the tin-alloys have been already described under copper; of the others the most important are:—

(1.) The *solder* of the tinman, which consists of 2 parts of tin and 1 of lead. 2. *Fusible alloy*, formed of 8 parts of bismuth, 5 lead, and 3 tin, fuses at 100° C. (212° F.), and that which consists of 4 parts bismuth, 1 lead, and 1 tin, fuses at so low a temperature as 94° C. (201°·2 F.)

Of the compounds of tin we shall describe:—

(1.) *Protoxide of tin* (SnO), which is formed by heating the metal in contact with the atmosphere, and is principally employed in the preparation of enamel (§ 77), and of the glaze for the Fayence porcelain (§ 88).

(2.) *Protochloride of tin* ($SnCl$) is obtained in colourless crystals when metallic tin is dissolved in hydrochloric acid. In consequence of its property of heightening many colours, it has received an important use in the printing of cotton.

(3.) *Sulphide of tin*, which is prepared by gently heating for some time scrapings of tin with sulphur, is a golden-yellow compound of metallic lustre, and is employed as a gold paint under the name of *Mosaic gold*.

29. ZINC.

(Symbol: Zn = 32·6; Specific Gravity = 6·8; Fusing-point = C. 753°·6 F.)

102. Zinc is a bluish-white brittle metal, principally obtained from a mineral, known under the name of *calamine*, which is a *silicate of protoxide of zinc*. It is used for castings, and, when rolled into sheets, for covering roofs and many other purposes. As we have already seen, it is a constituent of brass and of German silver; and is, moreover, employed by the chemist principally for preparing hydrogen.

The compounds of zinc when taken internally act as poisons, producing a nauseating effect upon the stomach, but several of them, and especially the white *protoxide* (ZnO) and the *sulphate* (ZnO,SO_3), which is also termed white vitrol, are employed with great benefit in many diseases of the eyes.

30. CHROMIUM.

Symbol: Cr = 26·7; Specific Gravity — 5·9.

103. This metal is less generally known than the foregoing, although it is one of the most interesting with which we are acquainted. Almost all its compounds are distinguished by a beautiful colour; and hence it has derived its name from the Greek word χρῶμα, which signifies *colour*.

It is found chiefly in the *chrome iron-stone*, which consists of protoxide of iron and sesquioxide of chromium (Cr_2O_3). By igniting the pulverized mineral with potassa, chromic acid (CrO_3) is formed, and combines with the potassa to produce the *chromate of potassa* (KO,CrO_3), which is a yellow salt, soluble in water, and is employed in making all the other compounds of chromium.

The metal itself, like manganese and pure iron, is extremely difficult to fuse; at present it has received no important application. We shall, therefore, pass at once to the consideration of its compounds.

(1.) *Sesquioxide of chromium* (Cr_2O_3) is obtained in the form of a beautiful green powder, when chromic acid is reduced by gently warming a solution of chromate of potassa with sulphide of potassium. It may be likewise prepared by a variety of other processes, but is always more or less of a fine green colour; it is employed as a pigment, and especially in the painting of glass and porcelain (§ 77).

(2.) *Sesquichloride of chromium* (Cr_2Cl_3) is a crystalline compound occurring in brilliant peach-coloured scales. It has, however, received no application.

(3.) The double salt of *sulphate of sesquioxide of chromium* and *sulphate of potassa* ($Cr_2O_3,3SO_3 + KO,SO_3$) forms beautiful garnet-red crystals. It is termed *chrome-alum*, and is without application.

(4.) On the other hand, the *chromate of lead* (PbO,CrO_3), in its various modifications, is much employed as a yellow pigment, and is obtained on mixing a solution of a lead-salt with chromate of potassa.

(5.) Amongst the numerous other combinations of this metal, which our space will not allow us to describe, the most important is, perhaps, the *chromate of mercury*, which is distinguished by its beautiful vermilion-red colour. All the compounds which are soluble produce a poisonous effect upon the animal economy.

31. ANTIMONY (STIBIUM.)

Symbol: Sb = 129; Specific Gravity — 6·8; Fusing-point = 425° C. (797° F.).

104. We observe in antimony one of the most brittle metals, since it admits of being readily pulverized. It has a bluish-white colour and fine-grained fracture, and is but little altered on exposure to the atmosphere. An alloy, consisting of one part of this metal and four of lead, is used in type-founding.

The compounds of antimony are remarkable for their medicinal effects, and therefore rank amongst the most important remedial agents. In large quantities they induce sickness, and sometimes act as poisons, but in small doses their effects are powerfully sudorific. The most important of these compounds employed in medicine are the *tartrate* of teroxide of antimony and potassa, which is termed also *tartar-emetic*, and the tersulphide (SbS_3), which occurs native as a black crystalline lustrous mineral, whilst that which is artificially prepared forms a beautiful orange-red powder (§ 43). Antimony likewise combines with more oxygen, producing antimonious acid (SbO_4) and antimonic acid (SbO_5).

MERCURY (HYDRARGYRUM).

Symbol: Hg = 100; Specific Gravity = 13·5; Boiling-point = 360° C. (680° F.).

105. With this metal we commence the series of the noble metals, which remain unaltered by exposure to the atmosphere.

Mercury exhibits the remarkable property that, whilst it is one of the heaviest bodies, its particles adhere so slightly together that it remains fluid at the ordinary temperature of our atmosphere. Its important application to the barometer and thermometer has been already alluded to in the section Physics.

It possesses, moreover, other properties, which have led to highly-important applications of this metal; amongst these, perhaps, the most remarkable is, its power of overcoming the cohesion of the particles of, and dissolving other metals, producing semi-fluid compounds termed *amalgams*.

Such an amalgam of tin and mercury is employed as a coating for the glass used for mirrors. The amalgam for electrical machines consists of two parts of mercury, one part of tin, and one of zinc. Mercury is likewise indispensable in the *parting* of gold and silver, and in the process of gilding.

This metal is found either native or in combination with sulphur, and is prepared from the latter by mixing it with iron-filings, and submitting it to distillation. It is met with in small quantities in Rhenish Bavaria in Germany, but the chief quantity of that which is met with in commerce is imported from Spain, South America, and more recently it has been imported from China.

106. The *compounds* of mercury generally are powerful poisons, and even the vapours of the metal itself are highly pernicious, inducing, in the first place, a copious flow of saliva. In small doses, however, several of these compounds are employed as remedies which produce remarkable effects upon the organism.

(1.) *Protoxide of mercury* (HgO) is obtained as a brilliant brick-red powder, by igniting the nitrate. It is chiefly employed in preparing oxygen, and in medicine as a constituent of eye-salves.

(2.) *Chloride of mercury* ($HgCl$) is likewise termed *corrosive sublimate*, since it is obtained by the sublimation (Physics, § 129) of common salt with sulphate of protoxide of mercury. It is one of the strongest poisons, exerting its destructive power both upon plants and animals. Hence its solution is employed as a preventive against the propagation in timber of a peculiar fungus known as *dry-rot,* which often makes enormous ravages in woodwork. This process is named, after its discoverer, *Kyanizing.* Sublimate is, moreover, employed as an external remedy for ring-worm and other obstinate diseases of the skin.

(3.) *Subchloride of mercury* (Hg_2Cl), or *calomel,* which is obtained by subliming a mixture of the chloride and metallic mercury, is one of the most frequently employed medicines, acting chiefly as a purgative.

(4.) *Sulphide of mercury*, or *vermilion* (HgS).—We have already several times mentioned this compound, which is known also by the name of *cinnabar.* Although this beautiful crimson colour occurs in Nature ready formed, it is, nevertheless, artificially prepared by subliming one part of sulphur with six parts of mercury, and subsequently triturating the mass obtained to an impalpable powder. A very magnificent kind of cinnabar is prepared by the Chinese.

33. SILVER (ARGENTUM).

Symbol: Ag = 108·1; Specific Gravity = 10; Fusing point = 1000° C. (1832° F.)

107. Silver, although it is not the most costly, is, nevertheless, one of the most beautiful metals, and the bright lustre of plate, and the numberless objects into which it is worked, universally excite our admiration; it is, moreover, exceedingly malleable and ductile, and admits of being wrought into the most beautiful works of art, and drawn out into thin wires; it is also the best known conductor of heat and electricity.

Silver is found in the metallic state, and frequently alloyed with lead, as in the argentiferous galena. From this ore the silver is prepared by roasting in a smelting furnace, whereby the lead is volatilized in the form of oxide, whilst the pure silver remains behind.

18

In some countries, as in Saxony and South America, recourse is had to another process, that of amalgamation, which depends on the easy solubility of silver and other metals in mercury. The ore, after being reduced to a fine powder, is mixed with common salt, and roasted at a low red-heat, whereby any sulphide of silver the ore may contain is converted into chloride. The mixture is then placed, with some water and iron filings, in a barrel which revolves round its own axis, and the whole agitated for some time, during which process the chloride of silver becomes reduced to the metallic state. A portion of mercury is then introduced, and the agitation continued. The mercury combines with the silver, and the amalgam is then separated by washing. It is afterwards pressed in woollen bags to free it from the greater part of the mercury, and then heated, when the last trace of mercury volatilizes and leaves the silver behind.

108. *Nitrate of silver* (AgO,NO_5) is obtained in splendid white crystals when metallic silver is dissolved in nitric acid. It acts as a powerful caustic, readily destroying the animal tissues, and is extensively employed in surgery, as an external remedy, under the name of *lunar caustic*. When in contact with soluble organic substances it communicates to them, after a short time, a black colour, which is due to the reduction of a portion of the silver; hence it is employed as the basis of the indelible inks used for marking white linen.

Chloride of silver ($AgCl$). When to a solution of silver is added chlorine, or any chlorinated compound, we obtain this compound as a white precipitate, which, on exposure to the light of the sun, speedily acquires a violet colour, which finally passes to black. The *iodide of silver* is even more rapidly altered by light; to this, however, we shall again have to return.

34. GOLD (AURUM).

Symbol: Au = 197; Specific Gravity = 19·5; Fusing point = 1200° C. (2192° F.).

109. Gold is the most beautiful of all the metals, and by the ancients was termed the sun, or the king of metals. It appears, to be pretty generally diffused in Nature, but never occurs in large masses, and hence it is also of higher value than any of the other metals. It is most frequently found in South America, California, Australia, East Indies, Africa, Hungary, and in the Ural Mountains. In general it is met with in the metallic state, partly in large fragments, but more frequently disseminated in small grains through various rocks. From the disintegration of these rocks is derived the gold-sands of many rivers, and from which the gold, on account of its high specific gravity, is readily separated by washing. But from poor ores it is generally obtained by amalgamation with mercury, which dissolves the gold, and which is afterwards separated by distillation, when the mercury is volatilized, and the pure gold remains behind.

The most remarkable property of gold is its extreme ductility. A single grain may be drawn into a wire 500 feet in length. It allows of being beaten into leaves which scarcely exceed $\frac{1}{200000}$ of an inch in thickness. It is, therefore, employed for gilding a great variety of objects, the process being effected either by coating them with the leaf-gold, as in the case of picture-frames, or by painting the metallic objects with a solution of gold in mercury, and subsequently exposing them to a high temperature whereby the mercury is volatilized. Objects of art are also frequently coated with gold by the electrotype process (§ 113).

With regard to the chemical properties of gold, it may be remarked that it is attacked by none of the individual acids; it is, however, dissolved by free chlorine. To obtain this metal in solution it is usual to employ a mixture of nitric and hydrochloric acids (§ 36), which is known under the name of *aqua regia*.

This metal being pretty soft and very costly, is never employed in the pure state. For coins and objects of art it is usually alloyed with silver or copper, which impart to it considerable hardness.

35. PLATINUM.

Symbol: Pt = 98·7; Specific Gravity = 21.

110. This metal has been known only since the discovery of America, the greater part occurring in commerce was exclusively imported from the Southern portions of this Continent, until within the present century it was found in the Ural Mountains. It is invariably met with in the metallic state of a whitish-gray colour; it is, moreover, pretty soft and highly ductile, and, like gold, is only attacked by free chlorine, which in the form of *aqua regia* readily dissolves it. It is distinguished from gold by being infusible in the strongest fires, a property which renders it a highly-valuable material in the fabrication of many chemical vessels, such as crucibles, dishes, &c. As we have already seen (§ 41), the stills employed in the rectification of sulphuric acid are made of this metal, and sometimes cost from one to two thousand pounds. In Russia, platinum is coined into money; but the infusibility of this metal renders it extremely difficult to work.

In the finely-divided state it forms a gray and very porous mass, which is known as *spongy platinum*, and possesses the remarkable property of condensing gases within its pores. Hence, when a jet of hydrogen is directed upon a piece of spongy platinum, the heat caused by its condensation suffices to inflame the gas. This singular power has been applied to the construction of a very beautiful apparatus, known as Döbereiner's lamp (fig. 44), which consists of a glass jar *a*, covered by a brass lid *e*, which is furnished with a suitable stop-cock *c*, and in connection with a small bell-jar *f*, in which is suspended, by means of a wire, a cylinder of metallic zinc *z*. When required for use, the outer jar is two-thirds filled with a mixture of one part sulphuric acid and four parts of water, and the stop-cock opened to allow the escape of atmospheric air, the spongy platinum contained in the small brass cylinder *d* being covered by a piece of paper. The stop-cock is then closed, and the bell-jar *f* allowed to fill with hydrogen, and after it has been filled and emptied several times, the paper is removed from

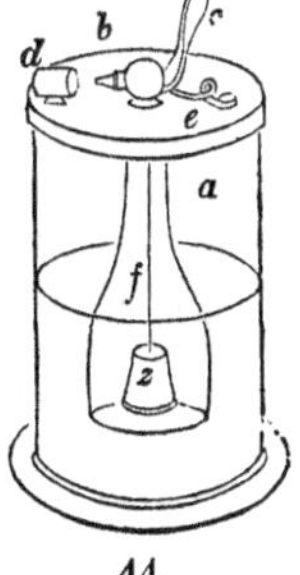

44.

the platinum and the cock is again opened, when the gas, which escapes first, makes the metal red-hot, and finally inflames.

II. Peculiar Decompositions of Simple Chemical Groups.

(1.) DECOMPOSITION BY ELECTRICITY.

111. When an electrical current (Phys. § 186) is passed through a liquid chemical compound, a decomposition is found to take place, if the stream is sufficiently powerful, and providing the two electrodes are not placed too far from each other. In decompositions of this nature we observe the peculiarity that one constituent of the compound is evolved at the *positive pole*, whilst the other appears at the *negative pole*. Hence the former is termed the *electro-negative*, and the latter the *electro-positive* of the compound.

If the electrodes are constructed of a metal possessing the property of combining with the evolved bodies, we observe that such an union takes place, as when the wires are made of copper and an oxygen compound is decomposed, the oxygen unites with the copper to form the protoxide of this metal. Hence the conducting wires are generally made of platinum, a metal which is affected only by a few bodies.

In the decomposition of salts, the acid makes its appearance at the + pole and the base at the — pole. If, therefore, a solution of sulphate of soda (NaO,SO_3) coloured blue by a little infusion of violets or blue cabbage, is introduced into the V tube, fig. 45, and a stream of electricity is passed into it by the two wires *c*, *z*, the sulphuric acid is liberated at the + pole, and colours the liquid in that branch of the tube red, whilst in the other branch the liquid is coloured green by the soda, which is set free at the — pole. As soon as the current is interrupted, the acid again combines with the base, and the liquid thus rendered neutral regains its blue colour (comp. § 17).

45.

If the two inverted tubes, fig. 46, be filled with water, and a powerful current of electricity passed through them, the water is decomposed, and we obtain in the one tube oxygen, and in the other a double volume of hydrogen (§ 28).

112. With regard to the elements already known to us, it may be remarked, that under all circumstances oxygen is eliminated at the + pole, and potassium at the — pole. The other simple bodies, however, sometimes appear at the one pole, and sometimes at the other.

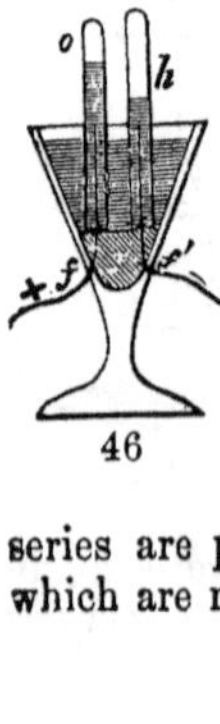

46

In the following *electrical* series, the elements are so arranged that each substance deports itself electro-negatively towards those which follow, and electro-positively to those which precede it. As, for example, chlorine, when in combination with oxygen, is evolved at the — pole, and from its compound with hydrogen, at the + pole. Those elements, which in this series are placed farthest apart, have stronger opposite affinities than those which are nearer to each other

Electrical Series of the Elements.

—Oxygen,	Carbon,	Copper,	Aluminum,
Sulphur,	Chromium,	Bismuth,	Magnesium,
Nitrogen,	Boron,	Lead,	Calcium,
Chlorine,	Antimony,	Cobalt,	Strontium,
Bromine,	Silicium,	Nickel,	Barium,
Iodine,	Gold,	Iron,	Sodium,
Fluorine,	Platinum,	Zinc,	+Potassium.
Phosphorus,	Mercury,	Hydrogen,	
Arsenic,	Silver,	Manganese,	

The importance of these facts to science is unmistakeable, and, indeed, many attempts have been made to explain, from the electrical condition of the elements, the nature of chemical affinity, and of chemical phenomena in general.

The Electrotype Process.

113. This is one of the most beautiful applications of decomposition by the electric stream. A solution of a metallic oxide, such as sulphate of *protoxide of copper,* when submitted to the influence of the electric current is decomposed, the oxygen being separated at the positive, and the copper at the negative, pole. But as metals do not readily combine with each other, the copper in this instance forms a coating upon the surface of the electrode. It is, however, perfectly indifferent what form we give to the pole, so that it may terminate either in a wire, a ball, or a plate with a plane or a partly convex and concave surface; the coating of copper thus deposited by the electric current necessarily assumes the form of the corresponding pole. By this process, then, the most accurate casts of medals, engraved copper plates, &c., may be prepared.

Gilding and *silvering* by the galvanic process depend upon the same principles. But in this case a solution of gold or silver is introduced intc the liquid, and the object to be gilt forms itself the negative pole on which the liberated noble metal becomes deposited.

2. DECOMPOSITION BY LIGHT.

114. In addition to its luminous properties, the light of the sun manifests an important influence, especially upon chemical affinity and the vital power. We have already seen (§ 22) that the leaves of plants evolve oxygen only when exposed to the solar rays; and that chlorine and hydrogen (§ 36) do not combine unless subjected to the same influence. In the section Physics (§ 88) we have defined light as the vibration of æther; and we perceive therein a certain means of exciting the activity of material particles, of which, however, we cannot form a clear conception, nor can we prove it by experimental evidence.

Daguerreotype Process.

The beautiful daguerreotype portraits, or photographic pictures, which are obtained by the decomposition of chemical compounds by solar light, have of late acquired considerable celebrity. The process may be explained as follows:—

Iodide of silver is a compound which is highly susceptible of the influence of light. For daguerreotype experiments it is most conveniently obtained by exposing a polished plate of silver to the vapour of iodine until it becomes covered with a pale yellow film of iodide of silver. As is well known (Phys. § 143), the lighter-coloured bodies, or lighter parts of bodies, reflect more light-rays than darker substances. If, therefore, the iodized silver-plate be introduced into a camera obscura, and the image of an object produced by a compound lens be allowed to fall upon it, the iodine will be separated from the silver on those parts of the plate upon which the light-rays from the object fall. This decomposition is effected more rapidly and completely upon those parts where most light falls. In a few seconds this decomposition is completed; it is not, however, sufficient to produce a distinct picture. The plate, therefore, is afterwards exposed to the vapours of mercury, which amalgamate with those parts of the surface which are freed from iodine, and thus the picture is developed. The plate is then immersed in a saline solution, which removes the excess of iodide of silver, and thus prevents any further action of the light upon the plate. Daguerreotype pictures consist of a dark ground, upon which, in certain places, minute bright globules of mercury are deposited. The picture, however, in this state may be readily rubbed out, and in order to protect it from injury, it is coated by the galvanic process with an exceedingly thin film of gold, and afterwards put in a frame and glass.

The discovery of this process, which gives pictures of wonderful fidelity, was made in Paris in 1839, by *Daguerre*, who received from the French nation a handsome recompense for his labours.

(B.) COMBINATIONS OF THE COMPOUND GROUPS.

(ORGANIC CHEMISTRY.)

115. As we have already shown at § 13, the compounds now to be considered differ very materially from those hitherto described. This becomes at once evident by a comparison of the individual formulæ which the simple and compound groups of chemical compounds present to us.

SIMPLE GROUPS.		
	Formulæ.	
Water.......................... =	HO	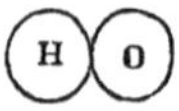 H O
Carbonic Acid .... =	CO_2	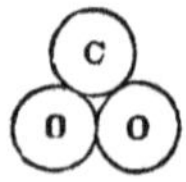 C O O
Sulphuric Acid............... =	SO_3	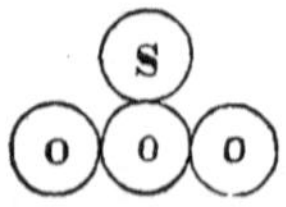 S O O O
Sulphate of Soda .... =	NaO, So_3	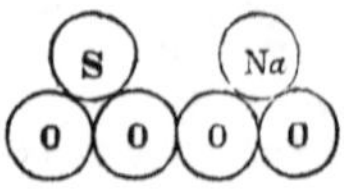 S Na O O O O

COMPOUND GROUPS.

	Formulæ.	
Acetic Acid (Anhydrous)... =	$C_4H_3O_3$	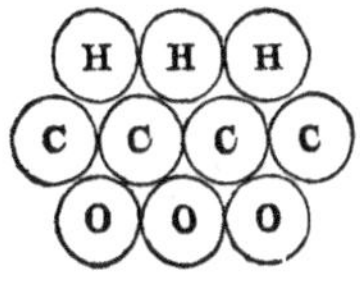 H H H C C C C O O O
Spirit of Wine .... =	$C_4H_6O_2$	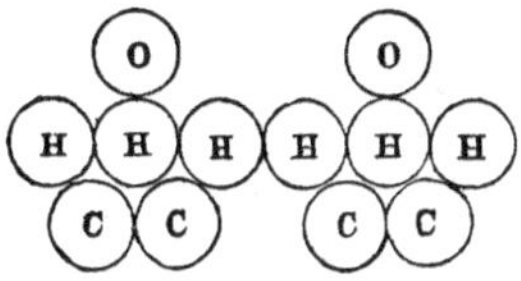 O O H H H H H H C C C C
Sugar (Anhydrous) .... =	$C_6H_5O_5$	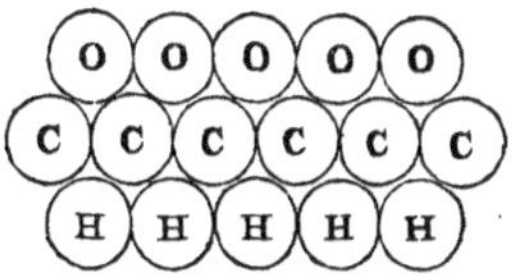 O O O O O C C C C C C H H H H H

From this it will be seen that a water-equivalent is a group of two individual particles, an equivalent of sulphuric acid of four, and that an equivalent of sulphate of soda consists of six particles. On the other hand, an equivalent of acetic acid is formed of ten individual particles, an equivalent of sugar of sixteen, and many other substances occur which are composed of even a still larger number of particles.

It would be impossible for us here to elucidate the reasons which have led chemists to the conviction that these compounds actually consist of such complex groups of simple particles. It will suffice to mention that all past experience leads to such a conviction.

116. In reference to the compounds of these complex groups, we have arrived at the following general facts:—

(1.) The elements which combine together to produce these compounds are—*carbon*, *hydrogen*, *oxygen*, *nitrogen*, *sulphur*, and *phosphorus*. Some compound bodies consist of two of these elements, namely, of carbon and hydrogen, but the greater number contains three—carbon, hydrogen, and oxygen; a large number consists of four—carbon, hydrogen, oxygen, and nitrogen; and only a few contain five or six, including, with the last-mentioned elements, sulphur and phosphorus. Many organic compounds, which are however comparatively of less importance, contain, in addition to the above-mentioned elements, chlorine, bromine, iodine, arsenic, antimony, &c.; hence we may assume that every element may occur as a constituent of organic compounds. It will be remarked that carbon is an invariable constituent of all these combinations.

(2.) The great multiplicity of these combinations arises from the fact that, generally *several* equivalents of each of these simple bodies unite together, as has already been shown in the case of acetic acid, spirit of wine, and sugar.

(3.) It is difficult and in most cases impossible to unite such a great number of equivalents of simple bodies by merely bringing them into contact. In the vegetable and animal organisms, however, the elements are, by the co-operation of several forces, placed in such favourable circumstances, that they combine to produce an extensive series of chemical compounds, which are called, in reference to their origin, *organic* compounds.

(4.) Under the influence of a variety of causes, such as heat, light, electricity, chemical affinity, and frequently even mechanical action, the organic combinations are destroyed and separated into more simple compounds. Thus, for instance, anhydrous grape-sugar ($C_6H_6O_6$) is easily split into alcohol, ($C_4H_6O_2$), and carbonic acid ($2CO_2$). The property of passing through entire series of metamorphoses is characteristic of organic compounds.

(5.) In almost every complex organic combination, we are able to prove the existence of a more simple compound of greater stability, which is generally termed the *radical* of the combination. The nature of these radicals will be subsequently described.

(6.) Finally, if we carefully consider the simple substances, detailed in (1.), which enter into the composition of organized bodies, we cannot overlook the fact that with oxygen they may all form gaseous combinations. If, therefore, an organic body be ignited with access of air, it is *completely consumed, and generally after it has been converted into a black carbonaceous mass.* This property of blackening, which is due to the presence of carbon, is a sure characteristic of an organic compound.

(7.) Those organic bodies which consist only of carbon, oxygen, and hydrogen, are easily distinguished from those which contain also nitrogen or nitrogen and sulphur. The presence of these two latter constituents may be recognised in the spontaneous decomposition or dry distillation of the organic bodies, by the offensive odour of the products evolved. These products consist chiefly of ammonia and hydrosulphuric acid. Hence any nitrogenous substance may be detected by burning it; it then disengages vapours which have the odour of burnt hair or feathers; or the substance under examination may be heated with hydrate of lime, when, if nitrogen be present, a distinct odour of ammonia will be evolved.

1. Compound Radicals and their Combinations.

117. By the reaction of several substances upon alcohol we are enabled to obtain an entire series of combinations, which, in reference to their composition, stand in a remarkable relation to each other, as well as to the alcohol from which they are derived. We must here confine ourselves to the names and formulæ of these substances, the greater number of which possess merely a scientific interest; only a few of them being employed in medicine.

Name.	Composition.
Alcohol	C_4H_5O, HO
Ether	C_4H_5O
Chloride of Ethyl	C_4H_5Cl
Bromide of Ethyl	C_4H_5Br
Iodide of Ethyl	C_4H_5I
Sulphide of Ethyl	C_4H_5S
Carbonate of Ethyl	C_4H_5O, CO_2
Oxalate of Ethyl	C_4H_5O, C_2O_3
Nitrite of Ethyl	C_4H_5O, NO_3

It will be observed, that in this series, the number of equivalents of carbon and hydrogen is the same in all these combinations, with the exception of the alcohol itself. This leads to the assumption that, in all the above-mentioned substances, there exists a combination, C_4H_5, which presents, in its chemical behaviour, the greatest similarity to a simple body. This compound has, therefore, been considered as the *radical* of the series, and is termed *ethyl*, for which the symbol A*e* has been adopted.

Let us once more examine this series and notice how it presents itself after the introduction of A*e* instead of C_4H_5. To assist the comparison we will write, in juxtaposition, a corresponding series of the combinations of a simple body:—

Compound Radical.	Simple Radical.
C_4H_5 = Ae = Ethyl	K = Potassium
Ae + O = Oxide of Ethyl (Ether)	K + O = Oxide of Potassium (Potassa)
Ae + Cl = Chloride of Ethyl	K + Cl = Chloride of Potassium
Ae + I = Iodide of Ethyl	K + I = Iodide of Potassium
Ae + Br = Bromide of Ethyl	K + Br = Bromide of Potassium
Ae + S = Sulphide of Ethyl	K + S = Sulphide of Potassium
Ae O + HO = Hydrate of Oxide of Ethyl (Alcohol)	KO + HO = Hydrate of Oxide of Potassium (*Caustic* Potassa)
Ae O + CO_2 = Carbonate of Ethyl	KO + CO_2 = Carbonate of Potassa
Ae O + C_2O_3 = Oxalate of Ethyl	KO + C_2O_3 = Oxalate of Potassa
Ae O + NO_3 = Nitrite of Ethyl	KO + NO_3 = Nitrite of Potassa

The opinion that this series of combinations is produced by other simple and compound bodies combining with the compound organic radical ethyl, has been strengthened by the fact, that also in acetic acid, benzoic acid, formic acid, fusel-oil, and several other organic combinations, we have proved the existence of such radicals which give rise to series of combinations perfectly analogous to those of the radical above mentioned.

Although it is the object of many chemical investigations made at the present day to discover in all organic combinations the corresponding radicals, still there are many organic substances of great importance, the radicals of which have not yet been discovered.

We can here only allude to these remarkable relations. In the following pages we shall, without regard to theoretical opinions, classify the organic combinations, according to their general chemical properties, into *acids*, *bases*, and *indifferent bodies*.

(I.) ACIDS.

118. The organic acids are mostly contained in the sap or in particular parts of plants, and especially in fruits. Without being corrosive, they have a pure acid taste, and none, with the exception of oxalic acid, exerts a poisonous influence on the animal economy. All these acids possess a feebler affinity than sulphuric acid, and are, therefore, separated by this acid from the bases with which they may be combined. They are either volatile or non-volatile, and are usually prepared by saturating the liquids containing them with lime, evaporating the solution of the *lime-salt* thus obtained to

dryness, and subsequently decomposing it by sulphuric acid, when the organic acid which is thus liberated is either distilled off or separated by filtration.

Another common mode of preparing the non-volatile acids is to combine the acid with protoxide of lead, and to decompose an aqueous solution of the lead-salt by hydrosulphuric acid. In this manner we obtain an insoluble precipitate of black sulphide of lead, whilst the acid is held in solution in the water, and is obtained by filtration in a state of purity. Of the large number of organic acids, we shall describe only the most important—namely, acetic, tartaric, citric, malic, oxalic, tannic, formic, lactic, and the fatty acids.

1. ACETIC ACID.

Formula $= C_4 H_3 O_3$; Symbol $= \overline{A}$.

119. Only a limited number of vegetable juices in their natural condition contain acetic acid; it is, however, readily formed when spirit of wine, or vegetable juices capable of undergoing alcoholic fermentation, is exposed, under certain circumstances, to the influence of the atmosphere, or when vegetable matter, especially wood, is submitted to dry distillation. Both these processes will be more minutely described farther on.

The purest and most concentrated acetic acid forms at 5° C. (41° F.) beautiful transparent crystals, which, however, liquefy at a temperature of 16° C. (60·8° F.). When dissolved in a large quantity of water, they have an agreeable refreshing odour and taste, and hence are frequently used at table as vinegar. Of the salts of this acid we shall mention only the following:—

Acetate of protoxide of lead ($PbO,\overline{A}$). This salt is obtained by dissolving oxide of lead in strong vinegar, and crystallizing the salt which is thus formed. It has a sweetish taste, and is therefore termed *sugar of lead.* The solubility of this salt in water renders it peculiarly adapted to the preparation of most of the other compounds of lead, such as the chrome-yellow and white-lead (§ 99), and, therefore, to the purposes of dyeing. A solution of sugar of lead is employed in medicine as an external remedy, under the name of *Goulard's Extract*, and when more diluted it forms the well-known *Goulard's water.* An addition of sugar of lead promotes, in a high degree, the drying of oil-colours. Acetate of lead is, moreover, a powerful poison.

Acetate of copper ($2CuO,\overline{A}$), commonly called *verdigris,* is produced by placing sheets of copper in contact with acetic acid. It has a bluish-green colour and is likewise poisonous.

Acetate of potassa and *acetate of ammonia* are very frequently employed in medicine, particularly for promoting the healthy functions of the skin.

2. TARTARIC ACID.

Formula $= C_8 H_4 O_{10}$; Symbol $= \overline{T}$.

120. This acid is contained especially in the juice of the grape, and when perfectly pure it forms colourless tabular crystals of strongly acid taste. Its most important compound is the *bitartrate of potassa* ($KO,HO,\overline{T}$),

which is deposited as an incrustation upon the bottoms of casks in which new wine is stored. The purified salt is beautifully white, and its powder is employed in medicine under the name of *cream of tartar*. In dyeing, it is frequently used as a mordant. The double salt of tartrate of potassa and tartrate of teroxide of antimony, called *tartar-emetic*, is much employed as an emetic.

3. CITRIC ACID.

Formula = $C_{12} H_5 O_{11}$; Symbol = $\bar{C}$.

121. Citric acid is found in the free state, chiefly in the citron and lemon, and also in gooseberries, currants, and other fruits. It is distinguished by an agreeably acid taste; it forms columnar crystals, which, like the preceding, are frequently employed in dyeing.

4. MALIC ACID.

Formula = $C_4 H_2 O_4$; Symbol = $\overline{M}$.

122. This acid is contained in almost all fruits, particularly in apples, and most abundantly in the berries of the mountain-ash, from which it is commonly prepared. It is crystallizable and highly acid, but is without application.

5. OXALIC ACID.

Formula = $C_2 O_3$; Symbol = $\overline{O}$.

123. The saps of common sorrel and of wood-sorrel contain *oxalate of potassa* ($KO, 2\overline{O}$), which is obtained from these vegetable juices in colourless crystals, and is commonly called *salt of sorrel*. This salt, as well as the acid itself, forms a readily-soluble compound with the oxide of iron, and hence its frequent application for removing spots of ink; it is likewise used in dyeing. We may remark that this acid is artificially prepared in large quantities by gently heating sugar with nitric acid. In consequence of its simple constitution it may be also arranged with the simple groups. The acid and its soluble salts are poisonous.

6. TANNIC ACID.

Formula = $C_9 H_3 O_5$; Symbol = $\overline{Qt}$.

124. This acid is diffused to a great extent throughout the vegetable kingdom, and we may assume that all vegetable matters which possess an astringent taste contain tannic acid. It occurs, however, most abundantly in the bark of the oak, and in gall-nuts. When prepared from these substances it forms a yellowish powder of highly astringent taste. Its acid properties are very feeble. In medicine it is employed as an astringent, both internally and externally, especially for arresting hæmorrhage, &c.

The most remarkable property of tannic acid is that of producing with the oxides of iron a deep violet or black compound, which under the name of *ink* is, incontestably, one of most important requisites of the present age.

Ink is prepared by boiling together, for some time, 3 oz. of bruised galls and 1 oz. of sulphate of iron, with 2 or 3 pints of water, to which is then added 1 oz. of log-wood, and finally, 1½ oz. of gum-arabic, for the purpose of rendering it somewhat thicker. A similar solution is employed for dyeing various kinds of cloths of a black, gray, or violet colour. If we desire to ascertain whether a liquid, as for instance water, contains iron, we macerate a gall-nut in water or brandy, and add a few drops of the tincture thus prepared to the water, which instantly becomes of a violet colour, if it contains only a trace of iron. If fruit be cut with a knife a portion of the iron becomes dissolved by the acids always present, and subsequently combines with the tannic acid, contained principally in the rind, and appears as a blue or black coloured compound. Wine, which contains tannic acid, when mixed with a chalybeate water, likewise imparts a violet colour to the mixture.

Tannic acid has derived its name from the property it possesses of forming with hides, a compound which is insoluble in water, and commonly known as *leather*, hence it is an essential requisite in the process of tanning, which we shall describe farther on.

7. FORMIC ACID.

Formula $= C_2 HO_3$; Symbol $= \overline{F}$.

125. Ants contain a somewhat caustic acid, which may be used by these small insects as an important weapon of defence. The properties of this acid, however, have been accurately known only since the discovery of a mode of artificially preparing it by the distillation of a mixture of sugar, binoxide of manganese, and sulphuric acid. In the concentrated state, formic acid is a colourless volatile liquid of penetrating odour and caustic properties, for when placed upon the skin it almost instantly raises a blister similar to that produced by burning.

8. LACTIC ACID.

Formula $= C_6 H_5 O_5$; Symbol $= \overline{L}$.

126. Lactic acid is present in many vegetable and animal substances, partly already formed, and partly only subsequently produced by the process of decomposition. Fresh meat invariably presents a feebly-acid reaction, due to the presence of a minute quantity of lactic acid which the juice always contains. It is met with in urine, and as a product of decomposition in sour milk, in the juice of sourkraut, and other pickles, such as ghirkins, &c. It is uncrystallizable, and has a strongly acid taste; at present it is applied to no particular purpose. The efficiency, however, of sour whey, in removing stains from table-cloths, is due to this acid.

9. FATTY ACIDS.

127. These acids will be more minutely considered when we speak of their natural compounds called *fats*, which comport themselves as indifferent bodies.

(2.) BASES.

128. Certain vegetable substances, by their singularly bitter taste and remarkable effects upon the animal system, have from an early period excited attention, and have claimed the character of valuable remedial agents. We may mention as examples the quina-bark and opium. Recent investigations have shown, however, that not the entire mass of these substances possesses the same medicinal qualities, but that the greater part of them consist of inefficacious substances, such as woody fibre, resin, gum, &c., whilst the peculiar active constituent forms only a very minute share of their weight.

A German chemist of the name of Sertürner, in 1804, was the first who succeeded in extracting the active principle from opium. Shortly afterwards similar substances were discovered in other plants, and when prepared in the pure state it was observed that they comport themselves as *bases*, and produce, with acids, fine colourless and distinctly-crystallizable salts. All the vegetable bases contain nitrogen, and in general possess the following properties: — They are colourless and odourless, but of extremely bitter taste. In water they are insoluble, but on the other hand are soluble in spirit of wine, and many also in ether. Even in very small doses they produce a powerful effect upon the systems of plants and animals, the greater part of them being potent poisons. They are employed exclusively in medicine, to which they have proved of the greatest importance. Whilst formerly it was necessary in ague and other diseases of an intermittent character to take many ounces of pulverized quina-bark to effect a cure, it is now only requisite to take a few grains of quinine to eradicate the same disease. By the use of quinine, moreover, we gain another advantage, namely, we avoid the above-mentioned vegetable matters, which not unfrequently destroy the effects of the base. For example, the quina-bark contains a large quantity of astringent tannic acid, and opium a variety of principles which render the application of it impossible where its base may be administered with great advantage.

The vegetable bases are usually prepared in the following manner: — The parts of plants which contain them are boiled with water, containing an admixture of sulphuric acid. In this manner is obtained a soluble sulphate of the base, which is decomposed by the addition of ammonia. The latter produces with the sulphuric acid a soluble sulphate of ammonia, while the base is precipitated. The base, which is generally somewhat coloured, is redissolved in dilute sulphuric acid, boiled with animal charcoal, and again precipitated by ammonia; the operation being repeated until the base is perfectly colourless. From many substances the bases are extracted by boiling alcohol, decolorized by animal charcoal, and purified by crystallization Simple as this process may appear, it nevertheless presents many difficulties in practice, especially as regards the removal of colouring matters, and it requires much care and experience.

The most important organic bases are the following:—

Quinine (formula $C_{20}H_{12}NO_2$) is contained in the different kinds of quina-bark, and, as above mentioned, is employed as an active remedy in febrile diseases. 100 parts of the best bark yield approximatively 3 parts of quinine.

Morphine (formula $C_{35}H_{20}NO_6$) is the active and highly-poisonous base of opium. 100 parts of opium yield about 12 parts of morphine.

Strychnine (formula $C_{44}H_{22}N_2O_4$) is found in several poisonous fruits and barks of trees growing in South America, particularly of the nux-vomica (*Strychnos nux-vomica*), from which it is usually prepared. It is one of the most powerful poisons, of which a few grains are capable of destroying life, its action being characterized by a powerful influence on the spinal marrow.

Coneine (formula $C_{16}H_{15}N$), which is prepared from the hemlock (*Conium maculatum*), is distinguished from the foregoing bases by being fluid and volatile. Its action is highly poisonous, whilst it instantly paralyses the activity of the spinal marrow.

The great importance and the high commercial value of the organic bases, several of which, as quinine and morphine, are endowed with remarkable medicinal properties, have induced chemists to attempt the artificial formation of these compounds, hitherto exclusively produced by vital processes. These endeavours have not as yet been crowned with success; but even now they have elicited a series of very important results, which clearly show that the progress of chemical science cannot fail to solve the problem. From these results it appears that a very close connection may be traced between the organic bases, all of which contain nitrogen and ammonia, which we have considered in a former part of this work (§ 78). We there stated that ammonia consists of one equivalent of nitrogen and three equivalents of hydrogen, and that its composition may be represented by the formula NH_3. Now it has beeen proved that the various hydrogen-equivalents may be replaced, atom for atom, by various hydrocarbons obtained from very different sources. In the new substances thus produced, the fundamental character of ammonia, namely, its power of combining with acids, is retained. In this manner, by gradually removing the various atoms of hydrogen from ammonia and replacing them by a hydrocarbon C_4H_5 which is called *ethyl*, because, as we have seen, it forms part of ordinary ether, the following series of organic bases or compound ammonias have been obtained:—

Ammonia.	Ethyl-Ammonia.	Diethyl-Ammonia.	Triethyl-Ammonia.
$\left.\begin{matrix} H \\ H \\ H \end{matrix}\right\} N$	$\left.\begin{matrix} C_4H_5 \\ H \\ H \end{matrix}\right\} N$	$\left.\begin{matrix} C_4H_5 \\ C_4H_5 \\ H \end{matrix}\right\} N$	$\left.\begin{matrix} C_4H_5 \\ C_4H_5 \\ C_4H_5 \end{matrix}\right\} N$

All these substances are volatile, like ammonia itself, and differ in this respect from quinine, morphine, &c., which are of a fixed nature. However, Dr. Hoffmann, to whom most of these results are due, has lately discovered a series of analogous bodies, still closely connected with ammonia, but which like most of the natural bases have ceased to be volatile. The latter class of substances is likely to become of particular importance; they exhibit the most remarkable properties, several of them combining, in fact, the bitterness of quinine with the causticity of potassa and soda. These compounds may, probably, be themselves endowed with valuable medicinal properties; at all events they appear to pave the way to the artificial formation of the natural alkaloids

(3.) INDIFERENT SUBSTANCES.

129. As these bodies have neither acid nor basic properties, and cannot be compared to the salts, they are termed *indifferent* substances. They are of

great importance, both in the arts and in medicine, and are indispensable to the existence of man and animals, since they compose the principal part of animal nutriment. We divide the indifferent substances into those which contain no nitrogen, and those in which this element is present. The latter generally contain also sulphur.

a. NON-NITROGENOUS INDIFFERENT SUBSTANCES.

130. We may assume that these substances, which constitute the principal part of the food of men and animals, contribute but little to the direct increase of the body, but are rather to be regarded as the means of maintaining the natural warmth—in fact, as a sort of fuel, and as the material whereby respiration is supported: to this we shall farther allude in our chapter on nutrition.

While we pass over a large number of the less important compounds, we shall consider only the following more minutely, viz.: starch, gum, sugar, spirit of wine, ether, fats, ethereal oils, resins, gum-resins, colouring matters, woody-fibre, vegetable mucilage, and gelatin.

1. STARCH.

Formula = $C_{12} H_{10} O_{10}$.

131. Starch is contained in many parts of plants, particularly in the seeds of the cereals, in many tuberous roots, such as those of the potato, dahlia, artichoke, &c., in the pith of the palm, in many fruits, as in apples, and in smaller quantities, even in the bark and wood of trees.

If these parts of plants be ground and agitated with water, the starch is separated as a white deposit, which is purified by repeatedly washing; it is then subsequently dried.

Starch is insoluble in cold water and in spirit of wine; but in hot water it swells up into a gelatinous mass, which is known as paste. In a large quantity of hot water it perfectly dissolves. Although little qualified to combine with other substances, it nevertheless forms with iodine a remarkable compound of deep-violet colour. This colour is so remarkable that the minutest trace of iodine may be detected by means of starch, and *vice versâ.*

Starch is employed as food, as a paste, for thickening the colours in calico printing, for stiffening linen cloth, for sizing paper, &c. Several kinds of starch are distinguished according to the plant from which they are derived, such as *potato-starch, wheat-starch, sago* (from the pith of the palm), *arrow-root* (from the root of Maranta arundinacea, and *tapioca*, which is likewise obtained from an American root. All these kinds of starch, however, agree perfectly with each other in their essential properties.

Starch has derived considerable importance from its products of decomposition: when gently heated, or rather roasted, it is in part converted into a kind of gum, which is termed *leucom*, and is employed in calico printing For the same purposes is used the starch-gum or *dextrin*, which is formed when starch is moistened and heated for some time with very dilute sulphuric acid; it possesses almost all the properties of gum-arabic. If the action of the acid upon the starch be continued longer, it is finally converted into *starch*, or *grape-sugar*, which has a sweetish taste, but is not crystallizable

As a remarkable fact it may be mentioned that germinated corn contains a substance, termed *diastase*, which has the property of transforming starch into gum and sugar, in the same manner as we effect the transformation by the aid of sulphuric acid (see § 155).

2. GUM.

Formula = $C_{12} H_{11} O_{11}$.

132. Although gum is found in numerous plants, still it is obtained only from a few Eastern trees belonging to the family of Mimosa, and from which it flows in drops that harden in the air, and are generally known under the name of *gum-arabic*. The purest gum is colourless, soluble in water, and insoluble in spirit of wine. It is chiefly employed for pasting, for mixing with colours, lacquering, &c.; it is, however, now frequently replaced by starch-gum, which possesses nearly all its properties. It must be remarked that also other vegetable juices are termed gum; but, in a chemical point of view, we understand by this term only the compound here described.

3. SUGAR.

Formula = $C_{12} H_{11} O_{11}$.

133. Sugar is diffused to a great extent throughout the vegetable kingdom. The greater number of fruits, many roots, and stalks, contain sugar; but it is the small quantity in which it is present, or its admixture with other substances, which prevents, in general, its extraction. It is found, however, most abundantly, and in the purest condition, in the juice of the sugar-cane, in beet-root, and in a species of maple (*Acer saccharinus*). In the sugar plantations of the East and West Indies the canes are crushed and pressed, and the juice, containing about 10 per cent. of sugar, mixed with some milk of lime; after being heated, it is allowed to get clear by standing, and then evaporated as quickly as possible, in order to avoid fermentation. The addition of lime is made for the purpose of removing the albumen and vegetable acids of the juice. In this manner is obtained *raw sugar*, which, according to the care displayed in the operation, presents the appearance of a yellowish or brownish moist powder, possessing at the same time a somewhat unpleasant odour and taste. This, which is caused by the impurities of the sugar, is afterwards removed by the process of *refining*, which is generally performed in Europe and the United States.

The colour of raw sugar is due partly to the presence of colouring matters, and partly to the conversion of a portion of the sugar during evaporation into a brown-coloured, non-crystallizable kind of sugar, which is termed *molasses*. The sugar is, therefore, dissolved in the smallest possible quantity of water, and boiled for some time with animal charcoal (bone-black, § 51), being thus almost perfectly decolourized. The syrup is afterwards filtered through bags of flannel or canvas to separate the particles of carbon. But as a portion of the charcoal passes through the filters, the sugar-solution is afterwards boiled with white of egg, or blood which contains albumen. By the coagulation of the albumen all the impurities remaining suspended in the solution are removed, and the liquid then appears perfectly clear, and is finally evaporated in the boiling-pan to the point of crystallization, when it is run into earthenware moulds of a conical shape, which have an opening at the narrow extremity. The sugar soon hardens into small granular crystals, whilst the non-crystallizable portion formed during the ebullition drains into a vessel placed beneath to receive it, and forms the dark-brown, sticky substance, which is known as *treacle*, and used for a great variety of purposes. But as a portion of this colouring syrup always remains in the sugar, the loaves are washed by allowing water to percolate through them very slowly. When this is accomplished, the moulds are taken off, the sugar dried, and afterwards brought into commerce as *white* or *refined sugar*. If the sugar-solution is less evaporated, and placed in a warm room, it forms large yellow or brown crystals, and in this form it is termed *sugar-candy*.

The principal point in the manufacture of sugar is to produce the least possible quantity of molasses, the value of which is very trifling. To accomplish this, the evaporation is conducted with the greatest celerity, with exclusion of atmospheric air, and at a lower temperature, by removing the steam, as it is formed in the closed pan, by means of an air-pump. Hence a refinery requires, besides a considerable working capital, a great stock of expensive apparatus.

The separation of sugar from beet-root is conducted in precisely the same way; but the purification is more difficult, and requires greater care, since the beet-juice contains far more impurities than the juice of the cane, and, moreover, contains a less percentage of sugar. This circumstance, combined with the high price of fuel, the greater value of other field produce, and the improvement of the sugar process in hot climates, have led to a diminution of the cultivation of beet-root for the sake of its sugar on the continent of Europe.

The properties and uses of sugar are sufficiently well known; it may, however, be remarked, that sugar is a substance which undergoes no decomposition by itself, but, on the other hand, is even capable of preventing decomposition in other substances; and hence it is frequently employed for preserving fruit, &c.

4. GRAPE-SUGAR.

Formula $= C_{12} H_{14} O_{14}$.

134. This term is applied to the sugar contained in grapes, in fruit, and in honey, as well as that which is obtained by the decomposition of starch (§ 131). It has a less sweet taste than cane-sugar, and were it possible to convert it into the latter, to which it is so closely allied in regard to its composition, it would, indeed, be a discovery of incalculable value, since Europe would then be able to manufacture from the starch of the potato all the sugar required.

Milk-sugar ($C_{12}H_{12}O_{12}$) is a peculiar crystallizable kind of sugar, contained principally in milk: it is distinguished from cane-sugar by being less soluble and of inferior sweetness.

All kinds of sugar, under certain circumstances, suffer *fermentation;* a peculiar decomposition, by which the very important product, spirit of wine, is formed.

5. SPIRIT OF WINE.

Formula = $C_4 H_6 O_2$.

135. Spirit of wine or alcohol never occurs ready formed in Nature; but it is under all circumstances a product of the decomposition of sugar by fermentation, a process we shall more minutely describe farther on. When the spirit is formed in the fermented liquids, its separation is effected by distillation in a suitable apparatus (Phys. § 129). The spirit of wine, being more volatile than water, distils over first, and by repeated distillation over burnt lime it is entirely deprived of water, and in that form is termed *anhydrous* or *absolute alcohol.*

Spirit of wine is a colourless liquid, of an agreeably-refreshing odour and burning taste. Its specific gravity is 0·79, and its boiling-point 78° C. (172·4° F.). Many substances, as, for instance, salts which are soluble in water are not dissolved by spirit of wine; but, on the other hand, it dissolves most of the resins and ethereal oils, which are insoluble in water. Spirit of wine burns with a feebly-luminous flame, without smoke, and is, therefore, frequently used as a fuel, particularly on the Continent. For water it exercises a very powerful affinity, absorbing it even from the atmosphere. Moist vegetable or animal matters, when placed in spirit of wine, are deprived of all their moisture, being thus, as it were, dried and protected from decay. The burning sensation produced by spirit of wine upon the mouth and stomach is due to the separation of water from the mucous membranes of these organs. It produces also upon the nervous system a remarkable effect, which is known as intoxication.

47.

Spirit of wine is miscible with water in all proportions. A mixture, containing from 80 to 85 per cent. of alcohol, is commonly termed *spirit; brandy* contains only from 49 to 50 per cent. In commerce it is of the greatest importance to possess a ready method of determining the strength of such mixtures, *i. e.*, the quantity of alcohol contained in them. For this purpose is employed an instrument, called a *hydrometer* (Phys., § 88). Since spirit of wine has a less specific gravity than pure water, it follows that this instrument will sink lower in absolute alcohol than when it is placed in water. The hydrometer, which consists of a glass bulb-tube (fig. 47), is plunged into water, and the point cutting the surface is marked 0°. It is then placed in absolute alcohol, and the point to which it sinks is marked 100°. A series of mixtures are made, containing from 1 to 99 per cent. of alcohol. The more alcohol the liquids contain, the deeper of course will the hydrometer sink. It is now successively introduced into each of these mixtures, and the point to which it sinks marked upon the tube. In this manner we obtain a scale, which accurately indicates the percentage of alcohol that may be contained in any spirituous mixtures, the strength of which we wish to ascertain.

The instrument thus marked is termed the percentage volume hydrometer, and was invented by Gay-Lussac and Tralles: it is now chiefly used on the Continent for determining the quantity of absolute alcohol in spirits. Unfortunately, this convenient division has not always been adopted; Cartier, Baumé, Beck, Sykes, and several others, have divided the scale into an arbitrary number of degrees. A detailed description of these instruments and of their construction would occupy too much space; we shall, therefore, merely give a comparative table of some of the hydrometers now in use.

Specific Gravity.	Percentage Volume (Tralles).	Percentage Weight, at 60° F.	Degree, according to Cartier.	Degree, according to Beck.	Degree, according to Baume.
1·000	0	0	10	0	10
0·991	5	4·0	...	...	...
0·985	10	8·0	12	...	...
0·980	15	12·1	...	3	13
0·975	20	16·2	...	...	...
0·970	25	20·4	14	5	...
0·964	30	24·6	15	6	15
0·958	35	28·9	...	...	16
0·951	40	33·4	...	9	17
0·942	45	37·9	18	...	...
0·933	50	42·5	...	12	20
0·923	55	47·2	21	14	...
0·912	60	52·2	...	16	24
0·901	65	57·2	24	19	...
0·889	70	62·5	27	...	28
0·876	75	67·9	...	24	...
0·863	80	73·5	30	27	32
0·848	85	79·5	35	30	35
0·833	90	85·7	...	34	38
0·815	95	92·4	40	38	42
0·793	100	100·0	44	44	48

When very dilute alcohol, or any liquid containing spirit, is exposed for some time at a temperature of 45° C. (113° F.) to the influence of the air, it absorbs oxygen, and becomes converted into acetic acid.

Spirit of wine, moreover, forms a very extensive series of products of decomposition, which, however, are of little value in the arts. The most important of these compounds is *chloroform*, which is a transparent liquid, of a specific gravity = 1·48; so that when dropped into water it sinks to the bottom. It is prepared by distilling dilute alcohol with chloride of lime (§ 82). The compound thus obtained has an agreeable odour, resembling that of ripe apples, and boils at so low a temperature as 60° C. (140° F.). If 20 or 30 drops of chloroform are placed in a handkerchief that is held before the mouth and nose, and the vapours thus inhaled, it produces in most persons a state of perfect unconsciousness and insensibility to pain; and hence it is now extensively employed for inducing this state during surgical operations. The composition of chloroform is expressed by the formula C_2HCl_3.

If 11 parts of alcohol of 85 per cent. be gently heated with a solution of 1 part of mercury dissolved in 12 parts of nitric acid, a lively decomposition, and after a short time a deposition of white crystals, takes place. This new compound is termed *fulminating mercury*, because when struck or rubbed it is decomposed with a violent knell, and it is therefore used as one of the ingredients in the manufacture of percussion caps. The fulminating mercury is a compound of *fulminic acid* ($C_4N_2O_2$), with two equivalents of protoxide of mercury.

6. ETHER.

Formula = $C_4 H_5 O$.

136. Ether, which is also commonly termed sulphuric ether, is a product of the decomposition of spirit of wine. When alcohol, the formula of which is represented by $C_4H_6O_2$, is mixed with sulphuric acid and distilled, it loses one equivalent of HO, and we obtain the compound C_4H_5O, or ether. This compound is a transparent, highly-volatile liquid, which boils at 35° C. (95° F.), and possesses an extremely penetrating odour. The specific gravity of ether is 0·713; it does not mix with water, nor dissolve any of the salts, but on the other hand, it takes into solution nearly all the resins, ethereal oils, and fats. The inhalation of the vapour of ether produces the same state of insensibility as chloroform.

7. FATS.

137. The fats occur ready formed in organic bodies, and we are still incapable of producing them by any artificial means. They are either solid or liquid, and in their chemical deportment display a remarkable similarity, whether they be obtained from plants or animals. Every kind of fat consists of an acid constituent, the *fatty acid*, in combination with an indifferent body termed *glycerine*.

The fatty acid, if liquid, is termed *oleic acid*, and, if solid and crystalline, *stearic acid*. The greater number of fats are mixtures of the compounds of these two acids with glycerine; and the solidity or fluidity of these bodies depends entirely on the preponderance of either the one or the other of these constituents. If it be stearic acid, then the fat is solid; but if oleic acid prevail, the fat is liquid.

For man the fats are of the greatest importance, since they form in his food the chief constituent for the development of animal heat; and hence it follows that an enormous quantity of fat is required as food by the inhabitants of northern climes. The fats are divided into the following groups, according to the purposes to which they are applied:—

As *food*, are used olive-oil, poppy-oil, nut-oil, butter, lard, suet, and several others.

As *fuel:* rape-oil, hemp-seed oil, palm-oil, cocoa-nut oil, train-oil (fat of marine mammiferous animals), tallow, &c.

For *soap:* olive-oil, rape-oil, hemp-seed oil, palm-oil, cocoa-nut oil, train-oil, and tallow.

For *plasters:* olive-oil and lard.

For *varnishes* and *oil-colours:* linseed-oil and nut-oil.

The fats are distinguished by their insolubility in water, spirit of wine, and in acids: they are, however, soluble in ether and caustic alkalies, and are perfectly non-volatile. Under the influence of heat, and of many chemical agents, the various fats give rise to the formation of peculiar volatile fatty acids, which have a strong and highly disagreeable rancid odour. The peculiar odour of the different kinds of fat always depends upon the presence of particular volatile acids, of which *butyric acid* is most common.

The greater number of oils and fats is unchanged by exposure to the air, and remains unctuous for years; some, however, solidify, by the absorption of oxygen, to a resinous varnish, and are, therefore, termed *drying oils.* The most important of these is linseed-oil. Oils expressed from seeds invariably contain certain quantities of water and vegetable mucilage, which are highly prejudicial to the use of these oils in burning. By long standing, or by agitation with a portion of sulphuric acid, and afterwards allowing it to stand till it becomes clear, a refined oil is obtained, which is perfectly free from those impurities.

SOAPS.

138. The soaps are compounds of fatty acids, with potassa or soda. In commerce we distinguish two kinds, viz., *soft soaps*, consisting of oleic acid and potassa, and *hard soaps*, which contain stearic acid in combination with soda. Their preparation is essentially the same. As the affinity of the fatty acids is not sufficiently powerful to remove the carbonic acid from the soda, the soap-boiler first prepares a caustic *ley* (§ 66), by pouring water over a mixture of burnt lime and carbonate of soda (§ 73). By continued boiling of the ley with the tallow, the process of saponification is accomplished, a gelatinous mass being produced, containing a quantity of water, from which it has to be freed. For this purpose common salt is added, to form, with the water, a concentrated solution, which sinks to the bottom. On this saline stratum swims the soap, which, on cooling, becomes solid. The solidity and hardness of the soap depend upon the completeness of the saponification, and on the separation of the soap from the lees. When these conditions have been perfectly fulfilled, the product is called *perfect* soap. From 10 to 50 per cent. of water or weak ley may be added, and stirred into the soap during cooling, and in this way the yellow or ordinary soap is produced, which, of course, is deteriorated in value exactly in proportion to the amount of water in its composition. This renders the real value of soap so difficult to be ascertained, and leads to many frauds in its manufacture and sale. Mottled and other coloured soaps are prepared by mixing colours with it during its preparation; but this is unattended with the least practical advantage.

Lead plasters are compounds of oleic acid with protoxide of lead, which are obtained by heating oil with either litharge or minium. By employing a low temperature the white-lead plaster is formed; but at a stronger heat is produced the brown variety, which is known under the name of *brown diachylon.*

The compound of stearic acid with *lime* is solid and insoluble in water. If, therefore, a soda-soap be placed in a calcareous water (§ 80), an insoluble lime-soap is produced, which coagulates in white flakes. Waters of this kind are consequently unsuited for the purposes of washing; they may, however, be rendered fit for use by mixing with them a little milk of lime, drawing off the clear liquid, and adding to it a solution of soda till no farther turbidity is produced.

STEARIN CANDLES.

139. These candles are made of pure stearic acid. For this purpose a lime-soap is first prepared by saponifying tallow with milk of lime. The

stearate of lime thus produced is decomposed by sulphuric acid, which combines with the lime to produce sulphate of lime, and sets the stearic acid free. The acid is then freed by pressure from any adhering oleic acid; it then presents the appearance of a beautifully-white crystalline mass, which has lost its greasy character, and, after the addition of a portion of wax, is ready for forming candles. Stearic acid reddens blue vegetable colours, and hence the spots from stearin candles frequently attack the colour of cloths. The composition of this acid is $= C_{68}H_{68}O_5$.

8. WAX.

140. This substance is allied in its general properties to the fats. It is met with as a product of the vegetable kingdom in the pollen of flowers, and many other parts of plants; it is, however, frequently coloured green, brown, or red by being associated with resin or colouring matters. Bees also have the power of producing wax from the honey by the digestive process; and this wax so produced, together with what they collect from the farina of flowers, they use in the construction of their cells. By melting the honeycomb we obtain the crude wax, of a yellow colour, both of which are partly due to the presence of honey. Thin plates of this impure wax, when moistened and exposed to the influence of solar light, become perfectly bleached. When thus purified it is colourless, odourless, and tasteless, insoluble in water, difficultly soluble in boiling alcohol, but pretty soluble in hot ether.

The specific gravity of wax is 0.96, and its fusing point 68° C. (154·4° F.). Like the fats, it chiefly consists of a substance saponifiable by potassa-ley, namely *cerin,* and another body called *myricin.* Wax is used in medicine, in the manufacture of candles, and for many other purposes. Tree-wax, which is sometimes termed Chinese or Japanese wax, is obtained by exhausting with boiling water the bark and fruit of several trees; it agrees in all its essential properties with bees'-wax.

9. VOLATILE OILS.

141. The volatile or *ethereal* oils occur in the vegetable kingdom, and are in general the cause of the peculiar odours of different parts of plants, particularly of the flowers, leaves, and fruits, in which they commonly exist in droplets enclosed in the cellular tissue. These oils are all volatile, and, when pure, generally colourless. They possess a penetrating and, with few exceptions, an agreeable odour and burning taste. On paper they cause a temporary greasy stain, which, however, disappears as the oil becomes volatilized. They are almost entirely insoluble in water, but, on the other hand, they readily dissolve in spirit of wine, ether, and fats. With regard to their chemical composition, it may be remarked that they form two principal groups, of which the first consists only of carbon and hydrogen, whilst the members of the second group contain, in addition to these two elements, oxygen, and a few of them sulphur or nitrogen.

The volatile oils absorb oxygen from the atmosphere, whereby they solidify, and are finally converted into resinous bodies. When exposed to a low temperature, many of these oils deposit a solid crystalline substance, which has received the name of *stearoptĕne.* The application of the volatile oils is manifold. The substances in which they are contained are frequently employed as aromatics, and in the preparation of spirituous drinks, liqueurs, &c. They are, moreover, frequently used in the preparation of medicinal waters, and as active remedial agents; for the latter purpose the oils themselves are in like manner employed.

The volatile oils are generally prepared for distilling a large quantity of the odorous herb with a comparatively small portion of water. The oil is thus volatilized, and is found floating upon the surface of the distillate.

142. The following oils are particularly worthy of being mentioned:—

Turpentine-oil ($C_{10}H_8$) is found in all the various species of fir. This oil is particularly important, from its power of dissolving many resins, and forming with them rapidly-drying *varnishes*. Turpentine is likewise extensively employed for dissolving and thinning oil-colours which are used in painting. Like most other volatile oils, it is highly inflammable, and burns with a strong smoky flame.

As constituents of perfumery, the following are principally used;—*Lemon-oil*, obtained from the rind of the lemon; *bergamot-oil*, from the rind of the bergamot-citron; *orange-flower oil; clove-oil*, from cloves; *cinnamon-oil; lavender-oil; bitter-almond-oil* and *rose-oil* (otto of roses), the latter being prepared chiefly in the East, and is exceedingly costly.

Juniper-oil, aniseed-oil, fennel-oil, cumin-oil, cinnamon-oil, clove-oil, and *peppermint-oil* are chiefly employed for flavouring spirits and liqueurs.

The *oil of chamomile*, which is distinguished by its beautiful blue colour, is employed as a remedial agent.

From the volatile oil of a tree (*Laurus camphora*) growing in the East Indies, a solid white substance separates, which is known under the name of *camphor*. This substance is employed as a perfume; and likewise in medicine, both as an internal and external stimulant.

The peculiar odour of spirit prepared from corn and from potatoes is due to the presence of a volatile-oil, called *fusel oil*, or hydrated oxyde of amyl ($C_{10}H_{11}O,HO$).

Bitter almonds yield a volatile oil, which possesses the peculiar odour of hydrocyanic acid, and is extremely poisonous. A pungent oil containing sulphur is found in mustard and in onions. The chemical characters of these oils will be more minutely described hereafter.

10. RESINS.

143. The resins are products of the vegetable kingdom, and are observed to exude from many plants when they are cut or wounded. In general they are mixed with a volatile oil, which stands in intimate chemical relation to the resins. The resins have generally a yellow colour, and are devoid of crystalline structure. The oil, in admixture, imparts to them peculiar odours and tastes, and when burned, many of them emit agreeably-smelling products of combustion, and hence are frequently employed for fumigations. The resins are insoluble in water; but, on the other hand, they readily dissolve in alcohol, ether, and the volatile oils. If these solutions of resins be thinly spread upon wood or any other substance, and exposed to the air, the solvent is slowly volatilized, and there remains a brilliant coating of the resin, which is called *varnish* or *polish*. It has already been mentioned that the resins are non-conductors of electricity. With regard to the chemical characters

of resins, we may remark that they deport themselves as weak acids, and form with strong bases a series of compounds similar to those of the fatty acids; such bodies are the resin-soaps, some of which are employed in the arts. These resinous acids are readily separated from their combinations by stronger acids, and are thus obtained in a colourless, odourless, and crystalline form. The following are the most important resins:—

144. *Turpentine*, which exudes from the various pine or fir trees, particularly from the larch, is a mixture of volatile oil and resin. By distillation with water the turpentine-oil is volatilized, while a brown resin remains, which is known under the name of *colophony*. When the turpentine is dried in the air, we obtain the *yellow-pine resin*. By agitating the fused colophony with a portion of water, the two combine to produce the brown opaque *pitch*. The numerous applications of these resins is well known.

Copal is imported from the East Indies in bright-yellow pieces. When fused and dissolved in hot linseed-oil it forms the well-known copal-varnish, which is the most durable of all the varnishes, since it is not affected by spirit of wine.

Mastic and *sandarach* are resins consisting of white or bright-yellow tears, which form transparent varnishes when dissolved in spirit of wine. They are chiefly employed, with benzoin and storax, in fumigations.

Shellac exudes from the punctures made by an insect allied to the cochineal in the barks of several trees growing in the East Indies. It is much employed in the manufacture of sealing-wax, and when dissolved in spirit of wine it forms the common polish (French polish) of the cabinet-maker. It may be perfectly decolorized by chlorine, and afterwards employed as a colourless varnish.

Jalapresin, which is obtained from the jalap-root, is much used in medicine as a powerful purgative.

Caoutchouc, or *Indian-rubber*, is contained in the milky juice of many plants, as, for instance, that of lettuce. It is, however, prepared only from the juice of some trees, growing in South America and the islands of the Indian Archipelago. The extreme elasticity of this interesting substance has led to its employment in the manufacture of water-proof cloth, which was first introduced by Mackintosh of Glasgow. For this purpose the caoutchouc is dissolved in coal-tar naphtha (§ 17), which is obtained as a secondary product in gas-works.

Gutta-percha has been imported into Europe, from the East Indies, only since 1843. It is obtained from a large tree, growing in Singapore, Borneo, and other islands, partly by collecting the milky juice, and partly by removing the layers of inspissated sap from the bark of the tree. It occurs in commerce in two forms—in small pieces, resembling the shavings of leather, and in blocks of a whitish-gray colour, which have the appearance of decayed wood. Gutta-percha is insoluble in water, spirit of wine, soda and potassa-ley, and in weak acids; but is partly soluble in ether, and readily soluble in turpentine-oil. Its most important property is that of becoming, in boiling water, soft and as plastic as wax, so that we may form with it objects of every possible shape, and take impressions of works of art, since it perfectly retains, after cooling, the form which is given to it. Gutta-percha is extremely tough, but is not elastic. This latter property, however, may be readily imparted to it by the addition of a portion of caoutchouc.

Amber is a resin occurring in the mineral kingdom. Its origin appears to stand in intimate connection with the submerged forests which now yield the brown-coal of the Continent. This beautiful yellow and hard resin is worked into many objects of art; and when fused by heat, and dissolved in hot turpentine oil, it forms a very durable and frequently-used varnish, which is not affected either by soap or spirit of wine.

11. GUM RESINS.

145. These substances are mixtures of resins, gums, volatile oils, and occasionally other substances. They exude from various plants in tropical climates, and are of high importance principally by reason of their medicinal qualities. The most important are:—*Gamboge*, which is employed as a beautiful yellow paint; *ammoniacum; assafœdita*, termed devil's dung (*Stercus diaboli*), on account of its remarkably disagreeable odour; *myrrh; aloes*, a bitter and drastic purgative; *opium*, and many others.

12. COLOURING MATTERS.

146. From the endless variety of colours displayed by the vegetable kingdom, we derive comparatively few colouring matters, since the greater part, particularly those of flowers, are rapidly destroyed by light and air. The more durable colouring matters manifest so variable a deportment, that it is impossible to depict them in general, and to describe them in detail would occupy too large a share of an elementary work. Some of these colouring matters are soluble in water, spirit of wine, or ether; they partly combine, like acids, with bases, and particularly with alumina (§ 86); they are all destroyed by chlorine. A few combine immediately with wool, silk, and cotton; others only when these materials are previously *mordantized, i. e.*, impregnated with alum, or some other body which has the power of fixing the colour upon them. Since most of the colouring matters are devoid of crystalline structure, their chemical characters are less known than those of the above-described indifferent organic substances. The most important colouring matters used in dyeing are the following:—

Yellows: Woad (Isatis tinctoria); *fustic; yellow oak; yellow berries*, or Persian berries; *turmeric*, or yellow root; and *annatto*.

Reds: Dyers' red, or *madder*, a root which is indisputably one of the most important materials employed in dyeing, and yields very durable red, violet, and brown colours; blue or *Campeachy wood;* red or *Brazil wood; saffron-wood; cochineal*, an insect living in South America upon various kinds of cactus, and from which the beautiful purple-coloured carmine is prepared; *archill* and *cudbear*, prepared from lichens; and, lastly, *dragons' blood*.

Greens: Only a few of these are known; however, the sap of the buckthorn is employed under the name of *sap-green*. The green leaves of plants owe their colour to the so-called leaf-green or *chlorophyl*, which is of a resinous nature, but is unsuited to the purposes of dyeing.

Blues: To these belong *litmus*, which is obtained from certain lichens. It is employed by the chemist in the preparation of test-papers, which are used for ascertaining the acid or alkaline nature of bodies (§ 17).

The most important of all the blue colours is *indigo*, which is a nitrogenous body, and is prepared from several plants growing in the East Indies

Its chief superiority consists in the extreme durability of its colour, since it is not reddened even by the strongest acids.

13. VEGETABLE MUCILAGE.

147. Mucilage is contained in many vegetable substances, to which it imparts the property of forming with water an adhesive slimy liquid, which is employed for many purposes, especially as a palliative in hooping-cough and diseases of the chest. Substances which consist almost entirely of dry mucilage, or contain a very large quantity, are — *tragacanth-gum*, *cherry-gum*, *salep-root*, *carrageen-moss*, *linseed*, *quince-seeds*, *marsh-mallow roots*, and many others.

14. VEGETABLE GELATIN.

148. This substance, which is termed also *pectin*, and is closely allied to the foregoing, is contained in the juice of most fruits and roots. If such a juice, as, for instance, that of the raspberry, be boiled with sugar or mixed with spirit of wine, the gelatin will be found to deposit in the form of a transparent mass.

15. VEGETABLE FIBRE.

149. The principal mass of plants consists of woody fibre, which is formed partly of small hollow tubes and partly of cells. Within these tissues are enclosed various other substances with which we have already become acquainted, namely, starch, chlorophyl, sugar, colouring matter, &c., which, however, may be completely separated by washing with water, spirit of wine, acids, and other solvents. The composition of the woody fibre thus purified may be expressed by the formula $C_{12}H_{10}O_{10}$, or, in other words, 100 parts contain 44·4 carbon, 6·2 hydrogen, and 49·4 oxygen.

Bleached cotton, flax, hemp, and paper prepared from linen, are tolerably pure woody fibre, which is neither soluble in water nor in any other liquid without decomposition. On the other hand, when immersed in liquids, it has the power of imbibing them, a property on which depends the nutrition of plants. When woody fibre, saw-dust, or straw, is treated with dilute sulphuric acid, it is first converted into a kind of gum, and finally, by long ebullition, into grape-sugar. If heated with concentrated solution of potassa, the elements of the fibre become grouped into oxalic, acetic, and carbonic acids, which unite with the potassa and produce salts.

When cotton-wool is submitted to the influence of fuming nitric acid, it suffers a remarkable change, and afterwards, when properly dried, possesses the property of exploding with great violence either by the blow of a hammer, or when heated to a temperature of from 60° C. to 90° (140° to 194° F.). This new compound, which is known under the name of *gun-cotton*, is now sometimes used for fire-arms, and more frequently for blasting in mines; but, though acting with great force, is scarcely a safe substitute for gunpowder, owing to its easy inflammability. The mode of preparing it is to immerse cotton-wool for a space of four or five minutes in a mixture of 1 part by weight of fuming nitric acid with 1½ to 2 parts of sulphuric acid, and subsequently washing it in pure water and drying it at a temperature of 50° C. (122° F.)

With many basic salts, particularly those of alumina and sesquioxide of iron, as well as with colouring matters, vegetable fibre has the property of combining in such a manner, that these substances form upon it a more or less durable adhesive coating. On this property is based the process of dyeing linen and cotton cloth (comp. § 86).

Wood, the principal mass of which consists of vegetable fibre, is not only of the highest importance as a building material, but is of essential value as a fuel. In the latter respect we shall submit it to a closer examination when we speak of the decomposition of organic bodies. On that occasion, too, we shall describe the carbonaceous products, such as humus, peat, turf, brown-coal, and coal, which are produced, under different influences, from the decomposition of vegetable fibre.

b. Nitrogenous Indifferent Substances.

150. Under the non-nitrogenous organic compounds, such as starch, woody fibre, gum, and the various kinds of sugar, we have become acquainted with a series of bodies, which show by their composition and certain phenomena of decomposition that they mutually stand in intimate relation. The fats likewise offer to us a group of similarly-composed bodies, which when mixed together in various proportions, constitute the different fatty substances of the vegetable and animal kingdoms. The fact that all these bodies consist only of three primary elements, viz., carbon, hydrogen, and oxygen, and that moreover by their chemical deportment they may be readily prepared in the pure state, has rendered it possible for us perfectly to elucidate their composition and the metamorphoses they suffer under certain influences.

In a similar manner, we find now in vegetable and animal substances another group of bodies, which exhibit a remarkable concordance in their chemical constituents and properties. These bodies, which are generally termed *albuminous* compounds, are—white of egg, or *albumen*, *fibrin*, and *casein*, the substance of cheese. These three bodies contain, in addition to carbon, hydrogen, nitrogen, and oxygen, a portion of sulphur and phosphorus. Our knowledge of the composition of these substances, however, is at present very imperfect, partly because we cannot readily prepare them in a state of purity, and partly from the extreme difficulty of determining accurately the proportions of nitrogen, sulphur, and phosphorus, which occur only in comparatively small quantities. But we know that the proportionate weights of the constituents of albumen, casein, and fibrin are very nearly the same, and hence they have hitherto been regarded as identical. Recent investigations have, however, not confirmed this supposition. We shall here confine ourselves to the description of their well-known general properties, and give the composition which has been assigned to them by the most recent investigations.

100 parts by weight of these bodies contain on the average 53 carbon, 7 hydrogen, 22 oxygen, and 16 nitrogen. The proportion of sulphur and phosphorus, however, varies in these different substances from ½ to 2 per cent. The greatest quantity of the former element is found in the albumen of the egg, in which it amounts to from 1·7 to 2 per cent.

151. The general properties of albuminous bodies are the following: they are not crystallizable, but appear in the moist state as a white mass, which presents, when dry, a semi-transparent horn-like appearance. In the systems of plants and animals they are held in solution by water, and hence occur in the liquid state. But under the influence of vitality, of heat, by mixing

their solutions with a weak acid or spirit of wine, they become converted into an insoluble modification. In the latter form, they are insoluble in water, spirit of wine, ether, and fats. They dissolve, however, in weak solutions of the caustic alkalies, and are again partly precipitated unchanged by acids. The albuminous bodies dissolve in concentrated hydrochloric acid, with a beautiful dark-blue colour; they are likewise slowly dissolved by the acid liquid of the gastric juice. If the albuminous bodies are left in the moist state to spontaneous decomposition, *i. e.*, to putrefaction, they evolve an extremely offensive odour, which is due to the elimination of carbonate of ammonia, sulphide of ammonium, and butyric acid. It is worthy of remark, that these bodies, when undergoing spontaneous decomposition, have the property of causing a peculiar decomposition of sugar into carbonic acid and spirit of wine, whenever they are brought into contact with its solution.

The albuminous bodies are of the highest importance as constituents of food, since the solid parts of flesh, blood, brains, and many other animal substances, consist chiefly of these compounds. Hence we consider those alimentary substances which are rich in albumen, fibrin, and casein, as the most nutritious, and suited to the formation of flesh, blood, &c.

1. ALBUMEN.

152. Albumen is a constituent of all those vegetable and animal juices which coagulate when heated. If any green vegetable matter, such as the leaves of cabbage, &c., be crushed and pressed, we obtain a green liquid, from which the albumen separates on the application of heat. The albumen thus prepared has a greenish colour, due to the presence of chlorophyl (§ 146), which may, however, be readily separated by means of spirit of wine. When beet-root and potatoes are sliced and digested for some time in water, the albumen these substances contain will enter into solution, and, on heating the water, will be found to separate in white flocks. Albumen, in the purest form, is contained in the egg, and likewise in blood. When fresh blood is allowed to stand some time, it is observed to separate into two parts, namely, into a solid called the *coagulum*, and a fluid termed *serum*, on which the former swims. The latter contains in solution the albumen, which coagulates when the serum is heated.

The essential properties of albumen are the following: it is contained in the juices of plants and animals in the *soluble* condition, which it loses when heated to the temperature of boiling water. It separates then in the form of a white flocculent mass, which is not again dissolved by water, and in that form is commonly termed *coagulated* albumen. By coagulation of the albumen it envelops other substances which may be contained in the liquids, and thus removes them; hence all albuminous juices are well adapted for clarifying turbid beer, wine, and other liquids, and are employed particularly in the fabrication of sugar (§ 133). When an albuminous liquid is mixed with spirit of wine or an acid, the albumen is at once precipitated.

2. FIBRIN.

153. *Fibrin*, like albumen, is known in the solid and fluid conditions. The red mass which constitutes the flesh or muscle of animals is solid fibrin. It is contained in a soluble state in blood, and separates on cooling of the latter into the so-called *coagulum*. In this form the fibrin is coloured by a

red substance contained in the blood, which, however, may be easily removed by washing. Vegetable fibrin (or *gluten*) is prepared by placing wheaten flour in a bag, and kneading it with fresh portions of water until the latter no longer becomes milky. The water removes the starch contained in the flour, and leaves a tenacious gluey mass, which is known as *gluten*, and when purified, deports itself in a similar manner to animal fibrin.

3. CASEIN.

154. Milk is a mixture of fat (butter) with a solution of *casein* in water. When the milk, freed as much as possible from butter, is heated, a white pellicle is formed upon the surface, and becomes renewed as often as it is taken off. This skin which forms upon the milk is casein. Casein also coagulates by heat, not suddenly like albumen, but only slowly; it may, however, be instantly coagulated, when to the heated liquid containing it a few drops of acid are added. When beans, peas, or leguminous fruits generally, are bruised and macerated with water, the casein becomes dissolved; by heating the solution it is separated as a white pellicle, which exhibits the greatest similarity to the casein obtained from milk. If milk be allowed to stand for some time it becomes sour, from the conversion of the sugar it contains into lactic acid (§ 126), which then induces the coagulation of the casein. The most remarkable effect upon casein is produced by the so-called *rennet*, which is a certain part of the stomach of a young calf. If a small quantity of this rennet be introduced into milk, the casein is forthwith coagulated, but in what manner this change is induced we are as yet unable to offer a satisfactory explanation.

Casein, when mixed with the cream of the milk, constitutes the fat cheeses, whilst the poor or thin cheeses are prepared from skimmed milk. In the ripe or decayed cheeses the casein has partly passed into a state of putrefaction, and consequently is changed in its chemical characters.

4. DIASTASE.

155. When barley is moistened with water, it begins after some days to germinate. The germinated barley, when dried, is termed *malt*, and differs essentially from the barley which yields it. If we mix ground malt with water, and add to the filtered liquid a portion of spirit of wine, the *diastase* will be precipitated in admixture with albumen and gum. This substance is distinguished by the remarkable property of transforming starch into gum and sugar, in the same manner as we have seen, at § 131, this change can be effected by acids. Hence malt contains but little starch, the greater part being transformed by the diastase into gum and sugar, as is proved by the sweet taste which malt possesses. This property of diastase is turned to advantage in the preparation of saccharine fluids, which are employed for the manufacture of beer, brandy, and vinegar (see Fermentation, § 160).

Gelatin (Glue).

156. Various parts of the animal body, particularly the skin, cartilage, and the soft portions of the bones (comp. § 51), dissolve completely by long ebullition in water, and produce a liquid which solidifies on cooling to a jelly, which, after being dried, is termed *gelatin*. Hence those parts of the animal

body are also termed the *gelatinous* formations. The application of common gelatin or *glue* as a cement is well known.

The purest gelatin is prepared by dissolving isinglass in boiling water, whereby we obtain a colourless, odourless, and tasteless liquid. The gelatin, when dry, is unaltered by exposure to the air, but when boiled for some time with dilute sulphuric acid it is converted into an exceedingly sweet sugar, which is termed *gelatin-sugar*. A remarkable property of gelatin is the power it possesses of forming with tannic acid a compound which is insoluble in water. If a solution of this substance be mixed with a decoction of oak-bark or nut-galls, a large flocky precipitate is immediately produced.

Leather.

157. The animal skin can be transformed into such a peculiar condition, that whilst it withstands the putrefactive process, it at the same time affords, by its toughness and pliability, a highly-valuable material for different purposes. The skin of animals in this form is termed *leather*, of which three principal kinds are known in commerce, viz., Morocco, shamois, and Russian, besides several others.

Sole-leather, or shoe-leather, is nothing more than an insoluble compound of skin with tannic acid. In the preparation of this variety, the hides are first sprinkled with salt and piled upon each other in pits, where they spontaneously *heat*, or as it is technically called, *sweat*, and admit then of the hair being easily removed. The hides are afterwards placed in running water until they are soft and porous, and then they are thrown into pits containing the tan liquor, which is prepared by extracting oak-bark with water. The more perfectly this liquid penetrates through the skin, the more completely will the latter be transformed into leather. Several months are commonly required to complete the process.

The hair and fat adhering to the skin may also be removed by treating the hides with caustic lime. After the process is completed, and the lime removed by the aid of a weak acid, the properties of leather are given to the hides by maceration in a solution of alum and salt, as in the preparation of *white leathers;* or they are converted into shamois leather by frequent immersion in oil and pressing them, the excess of oil being finally removed by a solution of a caustic alkali.

II. PECULIAR DECOMPOSITIONS OF ORGANIC COMPOUNDS.

158. From what has been advanced, we know that the body of a plant or that of an animal is an agglomeration of different substances, with which, both in reference to their properties as well as to their chemical composition, we are already acquainted. Thus the chief mass of the animal body consists of fibrin, gelatinous tissues, albumen, and fat, independently of phosphate of lime, which forms the solid constituent of bones. The substance of a plant is composed of ligneous fibre, chlorophyl, albumen, gum, starch, oil, &c.; and it is to be remarked, that most of these animal and vegetable substances are either held in solution by water or mollified and penetrated by it, as, for instance, the fibrin, which constitutes the muscle. Hence water is to be considered as a principal constituent of these bodies. We know,

moreover that carbon, hydrogen, oxygen, nitrogen, sulphur, and phosphorus, are the elements that enter into the composition of these substances, which represent highly-complicated compound groups.

Thus the bodies of plants and animals are organizations of wondrous complexity and diversity of *material* and *structure;* and so long as the breath of life, the animating principle, is present, so long is the body preserved from internal decay, and protected from the external effects of wind and weather. But as soon as the vital principle has quitted the corporeal structure, the constituent parts obey the law of chemical attraction. The highly-complex groups of the body can no longer exist as such; they separate or fall to pieces, and their molecules arrange themselves in simpler combinations, which appear as products of decomposition. Still the decay of the body is not merely occasioned by the highly-complex nature of its internal structure, but the influence of the surrounding oxygen and the water of the atmosphere likewise contribute essentially thereto, and give for the most part the primary and principal impulse to decomposition.

This process is still more rapidly and completely effected by the joint influence of a higher temperature. If the influence of external air be excluded, the process of decomposition receives the name of *dry distillation,* whilst the transition of organized bodies into simple combinations, by the action of air and water at the common temperature, is called *spontaneous decomposition.*

It is evident that all the products resulting from the decay of organic bodies must be of more simple composition than the bodies themselves, that they can contain only the same simple materials which we find in those organic bodies, and that the sum of their weight can only exceed the weight of the decomposed body, when, during the process of decomposition, oxygen and water have been absorbed from the atmosphere.

(1.) Spontaneous Decomposition.

159. The resolution of organic bodies into simple compounds, at the ordinary temperature, is called spontaneous decomposition. This process, however, under different circumstances has received different appellations. If the decomposed body contained sugar, and if alcohol be found among the products of decomposition, the process is called *fermentation.* If putrid odours are evolved during the decomposition, it is termed *putrefaction.* When an organic body is destroyed by the combined influence of atmospheric oxygen, light, and moisture, it is said to be *rotted* or *decayed.*

Fermentation.

160. In all the saccharine juices of plants, as, for instance, in the juice of the grape, of fruit, of the sugar-cane, of the beet-root, in an infusion of malt (§ 155), there is found, in addition to sugar, a nitrogenous substance, in general, albumen or vegetable fibrin. When such a liquid is exposed to the air, there first commences a change in the nitrogenous constituent, which absorbs oxygen, and slowly separates from the liquid in the form of a brownish precipitate, called *yeast* or *ferment.* It appears as if this change, going on at every point of the entire liquid mass, gives the first impulse to the decomposition of the sugar; for as soon as the process has commenced, the group of particles forming the sugar arrange themselves in two other

groups, viz., into alcohol and carbonic acid. The latter, which at every point of the surface of the liquid rises in small bubbles, occasions the frothing or rising of the liquid, whereby the fermentative process is so readily recognised.

The decomposition of sugar into alcohol and carbonic acid may be represented by the following formula :—

1 atom of anhydrous grape-sugar $= C_{12}\,H_{12}\,O_{12}$ decomposes into
2 atoms of alcohol $= C_8\,H_{12}\,O_4$ and
4 atoms of carbonic acid $= C_4\,O_8$.
$\Big\} = C_{12}\,H_{12}\,O_{12}$

The fermentation is completed when all the sugar is converted into alcohol; the liquid is then put into a still and the alcohol separated by distillation.

The yeast, separated as a deposit during the process of fermentation, possesses the property of exciting the decomposition of a new portion of saccharine liquid, with which it may be mixed, a very minute quantity of yeast being sufficient to cause the fermentation of a very large quantity of sugar. Finally, however, the yeast loses the power of exciting fermentation, by the completion of its own decomposition.

The fermentation of saccharine liquids, however, does not take place under all circumstances. The contact of atmospheric air, and a temperature of from 20° to 30° C. (68° to 86° F.) is necessary. Under 10° C. (50° F.) fermentation does not proceed. Certain substances when added to fermentable liquids, only in very minute quantities, have the power of preventing decomposition; such are, for instance, volatile oil of mustard, sulphurous acid, nitrous acid, and several others.

Yeast loses its power of exciting fermentation when perfectly dried or heated to a temperature of 100° C. (212° F.), or if mixed with alcohol, acids, or alkalies. Artificial yeast, or *leaven*, is prepared by exposing a piece of dough for some days to a moderate temperature, until it acquires a vinous odour.

Spirituous Drinks.

161. These liquids are all products of the fermentation of saccharine fluids, and are either prepared by subsequent distillation, as spirit of wine, and the various kinds of brandy; or without distillation, as wine and beer.

Distilled spirituous liquors, of course, contain only volatile constituents, their chief bulk being alcohol and water. In general, they are distinguished by different, and more or less agreeable flavours, according to the substance from which they are derived. The cause of this is, that during the fermentation of these substances a peculiar volatile oil or ether is formed, which possesses a characteristic odour, and imparts it to the spirit. Thus the spirit prepared from potatoes and corn owes its odour and flavour to the presence of fusel-oil (§ 142). *Rum* is prepared from cane-sugar, and *arrack* from fermented rice. On the table-lands of Asia the inhabitants prepare a highly-intoxicating beverage from milk-sugar.

Starch is converted into grape-sugar, both by means of sulphuric acid and also by diastase (§ 155), hence we in general avail ourselves of amylaceous vegetable matters for the preparation of spirit. Mashed grain, or boiled potatoes, are for this purpose mixed in the fermenting vat with the mash and afterwards distilled.

Various amounts of alcohol are contained in wine, according to the quantity of saccharine matter in the grapes. Whilst the ordinary wines of Germany contain only about 8 to 10 per cent. of alcohol, and the strongest Rhenish wine from 12 to 14 per cent., we find in the wines of the south of France, Spain and Portugal, from 18 to 20 per cent. The wine, besides alcohol, contains those constituent parts of the grape-juice which are soluble in the spirit. In addition to colouring matters, wine, especially Rhenish wine, contains bitartrate of potassa (§ 120), which imparts to it an acid taste. We also find in many wines, especially those of the south of Europe, sugar, which occurs naturally in it, or sometimes is intentionally added to it. The bouquet of wine is due to the presence of peculiar ethereal liquids. Red wine contains, besides the colouring matter, a portion of tannic acid, which imparts to the wine an astringent flavour.

Beer is prepared by infusing germinated barley (malt) in hot water, and boiling the sweet-wort thus obtained with hops; it is afterwards placed in a wide exposed vessel called a cooler, where its temperature is reduced as quickly as possible. The cooled liquid is then conveyed to the open fermenting tun, in which it undergoes a slow process of fermentation until nearly all the sugar is converted into alcohol, when the beer is either drawn off for immediate use or barrelled for the cellar.

The constituents of beer are, besides water, from 4 to 5 per cent. of alcohol, sugar, gum, which imparts to the beer its viscidity, the bitter principle of the hops, and carbonic acid, which is the cause of its frothing. Beer very readily becomes what is called sour or stale, that is, its alcohol is easily converted into acetic acid; and the weaker the beer the more readily is this change induced. This acidification is retarded by the bitter principle and volatile oil of the hops, and, consequently, strongly-hopped bitter beer can be preserved in a potable condition for a longer period than sweet beer. A low temperature, however, is essential to the preservation of the beer, and therefore it is generally placed in cellars where the temperature even in summer does not exceed 8°, or at most 10° C. (46° to 50° F.).

Acetic Fermentation.

162. Acetic fermentation depends upon the conversion of alcohol into acetic acid, by the influence of atmospheric oxygen. One equivalent of spirit of wine ($C_4H_6O_2$), combines with four equivalents of oxygen, and forms one equivalent of acetic acid $C_4H_4O_4$), and two equivalents of water (2HO). Acetic acid is manufactured by exposing alcoholic liquids, at a temperature of from 28° to 35° C. (80 to 95° F.) to the air. A great variety of substances are employed in the manufacture of acetic acid, such as the refuse obtained in making beer and wine. In general, however, a fermented mash (§ 161) is used and placed at suitable temperature in partially-closed vessels. The alcohol is thus slowly transformed into vinegar, the process being completed as soon as the liquid becomes clear.

48.

Alcohol may be very readily converted into acetic acid by allowing dilute spirit of wine to percolate several times through a vessel filled with shavings of wood (fig. 65). A very large surface of spirit being thus exposed to the influence of the oxygen of the atmosphere, the process is much facilitated.

PUTREFACTION.

163. This process yields products of a character very different from the foregoing. Here also it is necessary to bear in mind the elements of vegetable and animal bodies before we can pretend to form any precise idea of the products that result from their putrefaction. These are not the same under all circumstances, but vary essentially according as the putrefactive process takes place at a lower temperature and in the presence of water, or at a higher temperature with exclusion of moisture. Furthermore, animal substances yield, in consequence of the large proportion of sulphur and nitrogen which they contain, certain products in larger quantities than do vegetable substances, which are not so rich in these elements.

We may generally assume that, when the putrefactive process takes place at a lower temperature and in the presence of much water, *hydrogen* compounds are chiefly formed; whilst at a higher temperature and with less water, *oxygen* compounds are produced.

The following view may assist in rendering this mode of decomposition more intelligible: —

PRODUCTS of the DECOMPOSITION of VEGETABLE and ANIMAL MATTERS.

With much Water and at a lower Temperature.		With little Water and at a higher Temperature.	
Water	HO	Water	HO
Carbide of Hydrogen (Marsh Gas)	CH_2	Carbonic Acid	CO_2
Sulphide of Hydrogen (Hydrosulphuric Acid)	HS	Sulphuric Acid	SO_3
Phosphide of Hydrogen (Phosphuretted Hydrogen)	PH_3	Phosphoric Acid	PO_5
Ammonia	NH_3	Nitric Acid	NO_5
x (O C S P N H).		x (H C S P N O).	

It is not, however, to be inferred that these products are so exclusively formed as is represented in the above table. On the contrary, the products of the one series are more or less produced among those of the other, according to circumstances. Frequently at the commencement of the process, when there is still much water present, there appears more of the first series, and towards the termination there is more of the other, or the first pass subsequently even into the oxygen-compounds. The products which are formed likewise combine with each other, and produce more complex compounds, such as carbonate and nitrate of ammonia, sulphide of ammonium, and many others.

The medium surrounding the decomposing body itself has great influence on the nature of the products formed during spontaneous decomposition. If strong bases be present, particularly potassa or lime, acids are chiefly formed which unite with these bases. On this depends the formation of nitric acid, as already noticed (§ 33).

All the above-mentioned products of decomposition exist in manures, whether solid or liquid, and on their presence depends chiefly the nutritive quality of these agents as food of plants. But as these combinations, without exception, are volatile, manures lose their efficiency by exposure to the atmosphere. Hence many attempts have been made, by the addition of substances such as lime, clay, gypsum, sulphate of iron, sulphuric acid, &c., to fix those volatile acids and bases, and to retain them in the manure.

164. Putrefaction is prevented by excluding the influence of water or of the air, or by a very low temperature. All thoroughly-dried animal and vegetable substances are not susceptible of putrefaction. Drying is accomplished either by exposure to the atmosphere, by artificial heat, or by the application of such substances as have the property of abstracting the water on account of the greater affinity they have to this fluid. Such substances, for example, are common salt and sugar; and on this principle depends the process of curing by means of these substances. Spirit of wine has the same effect on substances which are immersed in it. If meat, vegetables, and similar kinds of provisions be put into tin vessels which are filled with hot water, and on which is soldered a perfectly air-tight lid, and if then they are heated for some hours in boiling water, such provisions can be kept more than a year without their undergoing any change. This mode, discovered by Appert, is indeed adopted in preserving food for long sea-voyages or for winter store. The success of this process altogether depends on the complete exclusion of the oxygen of the atmosphere.

A mammoth, an animal which is now extinct, has been discovered in Siberia frozen in the ground. The hide, hair, and flesh, were found to be in a perfect state of preservation, so that the flesh was eaten by dogs. This animal must have remained at least several thousand years in this condition, and it affords a very remarkable and convincing proof that cold prevents the process of putrefaction.

Many substances which arrest fermentation prevent or delay also putrefaction, such as creosote, pyroligneous acid, and likewise arsenic and corrosive sublimate. The preparation of mummies depends on this principle, viz., that of drying the body as much as possible, and subsequently introducing a variety of antiputrescent substances.

Slow Carbonization.

165. When the remains of plants, for example, wood, stems, roots, moss, &c., under partial or complete exclusion of atmospheric air and water, are submitted to spontaneous decomposition, their oxygen and hydrogen are slowly eliminated from the mass in the form of carbonic acid, water, and carburetted hydrogen (marsh-gas), while the residue becomes continually richer in carbon. This change is easily recognised by the colours of the bodies, which are so much the darker the more completely the carbonization has been effected. The change produced may be also proved by chemical investigation. The products which remain are ligneous earth, mould, turf, peat, and the different varieties of coal. All these substances are distinguished by the extent to which decomposition has taken place. The most important member of the series is common coal.

In ordinary cultivated soils there is always present a large portion of partially-decomposed vegetable remains, termed *humus*, which frequently communicates to the soil a darker colour than is possessed by the uncultivated subsoil.

In consequence of the gradual decomposition of vegetable substances, we find in certain localities different kinds of carbonaceous materials, accumulated in such large masses as to be available as fuel. In fact, the forests growing on the whole surface of the earth, would be insufficient for our daily consumption, if we could not have recourse to the treasures which for thousands of years have been accumulated in the bowels of the earth. The vast importance of combustible substances, renders a more detailed account of them expedient.

166. *Turf* is undoubtedly the most recent of the carbonaceous formations. It owes its origin principally to the turf-moss, as it is called, (*Sphagnum palustre,*) which frequently covers the whole surface of extensive moist moors. When the roots and under parts of the moss perish, there grows up a new covering of moss, which also decays in the following year, and thus the vegetable mould increases by successive annual depositions, which in the course of from eighty to one hundred years become a considerably deep accumulation. The carbonizing process is incessantly active; the under layers increase in blackness and become consolidated by the pressure of the superincumbent mass. Hence the best turf is the oldest: its black appearance and great density scarcely allow us to recognise it as a vegetable product. The more recent turf is, on the contrary, brown, of a looser texture, and evidently appears to be a formation of vegetable mould, half-decayed stems of mosses and of roots, and dead parts of all sorts of plants that generally grow in such places.

Under particular circumstances, the turf is more or less mixed with earthy matter. Sometimes the latter substance is found in scarcely appreciable quantities, while occasionally it amounts to from 30 to 40 per cent. of the whole. In the latter case, the greater specific gravity of the turf is no certain proof of its good quality; therefore, in determining the value of the turf, we must take into consideration the amount of ash which it yields.

167. The formation of *brown-coal* (a species of coal which occurs in many parts of Germany) is ascribed to a period anterior to the history of the human race. More or less large masses of wood have been suddenly buried, or gradually concealed and changed in appearance, by the constant accumulation of earthy deposits. Brown-coal presents the remarkable transition-process between ordinary coal and mere wood, and this, of course, differs according to the circumstances under which the coal has been formed. In brown-coal are found stems with the woody annular rings quite apparent; also seeds, leaves, and bark. Some specimens of this formation, on the contrary, are earthy, or black and solid, affording no indications of a ligneous or vegetable origin. The brown-coal, the name of which is derived from its colour, has considerable density, acquired by the pressure of the mass of earth under which it has been formed. We can form an idea of this enormous pressure from the fact that trunks of trees originally cylindrical have been flattened and pressed into an elliptical shape. This kind of coal is an excellent fuel, though sometimes associated with sulphide of iron, which gives to it a disagreeable odour when burned.

168. The origin of our common coal must be ascribed to a still earlier period. This, as well as brown-coal, is undoubtedly of vegetable origin, being formed from stems of trees and other ligneous matter. But these, in a long series of years, and by constant pressure, have been so much altered,

that, for a long time, the vegetable origin of coal was doubted. This doubt, however, has been removed, on the one hand, by the fact that turf and brown-coal form a transition-series between the vegetable matter and common coal, and, on the other hand, by the circumstance that different remains of plants or vegetable fossils are everywhere associated with the coal. Even stems of well-known forms of vegetation have been discovered. The microscope also plainly reveals the cellular structure, even in the most solid coal.

The difficulty of accounting for such astonishing masses of coal, sometimes found in layers of 40 feet thick, is still unresolved. It is certain that the carbonization of such enormous masses of wood must have been a process of many thousands of years' duration.

Coal is compact, black, and shining. Its specific gravity is 1·3, and if compared with the density of wood and of charcoal (§ 49, and Physics, § 34,) it becomes evident that the same bulk of coal contains a far larger quantity of combustible matter. On this account it is an excellent fuel, but being denser, it is more difficult to kindle, and requires a greater supply of air to keep it in combustion than either wood or charcoal.

We are not, however, entitled to consider coal as pure carbon. It always contains oxygen, hydrogen, and a small quantity, viz., from 1 to 2 per cent., of *nitrogen*. Moreover we meet with certain mineral constituents, particularly *sulphur* in combination with iron. It is evident that the dense superincumbent mass of earthy matter on the carbonaceous strata has prevented their complete carbonization. The carbonization, however, can be accomplished by a process analogous to that used in the carbonizing of wood (§ 49). In this process the sulphur, which is so prejudicial to the use of coal, is in the mean time separated from it: the product obtained is called *coke*. As this material, with the exception of its mineral constituents, consists entirely of carbon, and possesses a great density, it forms the most valuable of all fuels when a high degree of heat is required in a small space. Hence it is almost exclusively employed in generating steam in locomotives. Coke has a gray shining, almost metallic, sometimes a slaggy, appearance, and is so dense that it sounds when struck with a hard body. Coal is found under a great variety of aspects, and of very unequal composition and quality, as the subjoined tabular view shows very conspicuously. It is evident that it is of less value the more mineral, and consequently incombustible, materials it contains. The different kinds of coal, when pulverized and heated, comport themselves in three ways. They either swell up and finally cake together, and are therefore distinguished as *caking-coal*, this kind being particularly adapted for forges and for gas-lighting: or the particles of pulverized coal sinter together, and this coal is therefore called *sinter-coal;* whilst the so-called *sand-coal* remains powdery. The latter is much less valuable than the other varieties. One of the best kinds of coal occurring in England is the *cannel*, or *candle-coal*, which burns with a beautifully clear flame, hence its name. This property and the applicability of coal for gas-lighting depend chiefly on the amount of *hydrogen* it contains.

169. Now that we have in the preceding sections become acquainted with wood, turf, brown-coal, and coal, we will subjoin some general considerations in reference to the value of these various combustibles, as materials for fuel All our modes of obtaining artificial heat depend on the combination of carbon and hydrogen with oxygen, which produces the phenomena of combustion.

Hence it may be stated as a rule that those bodies which contain in an equal weight the largest quantity of unoxidized carbon and hydrogen are the most valuable fuels. In 100 lbs. of green wood we have only 20 lbs. of carbon, while 100 lbs. of dry wood contain 40 lbs.

The heat which fuel yields is entirely dependent on the manner of its combustion, since equal weights of coal under similar circumstances, when perfectly consumed, yield an equal supply of heat. A perfect combustion, however, is such wherein no particle of carbon escapes without being converted into the highest oxygen compound, namely, carbonic acid.

An evident loss of heat is experienced in every furnace from which unconsumed gas and vapour, in the form of smoke, or inflammable gas (carbonic oxide, which burns with a blue flame), escapes into the atmosphere.

In the use of fuel the following points are of importance, viz., the quantity of carbon, hydrogen, water, and mineral substances which they contain; then the density; and finally, the most perfect combustion by a sufficient draught of air.

COMPARISON of VARIOUS FUELS.

Dried at 100° C. (212° F.)	Density.	100 parts, by weight, contain			
		Carbon.	Hydrogen.	Oxygen.	Mineral Constituents.
Charcoal	0·187	99·07	...	...	0·03
Coke	1·08	95	...	...	to 5
Caking-coal	1·28	87	5	5	1·3
Cannel-coal	1·31	67	5	8	2·5
Brown-coal (best quality)	1·37	66	4·8	18	2·7
Turf (best quality)	...	58	5·9	31	4·6
Brown-coal (ligneous)	1·27	51	5	30	1·29
Beech-wood	0·728	49	6	44	...
Ditto (dried in the air)	...	40	...	...	...

The above table clearly shows that the proportion of oxygen decreases in the same ratio as we proceed towards older carbonaceous formations; whilst in wood we find 44 per cent. of oxygen, the quantity in many kinds of coal decreases to about 5 per cent.

(2.) DRY DISTILLATION.

170. The materials which are submitted to this process for the sake of the products obtained, are coals, wood, and the flesh of animals. The process is conducted in large manufactories, where the materials to be decomposed are heated in iron vessels of various forms, and to which suitable arrangements are appended for condensing and collecting the volatile products.

The combinations formed during the distillation depend chiefly on the composition of the bodies submitted to this process.

The following table affords a view of the different nature of the products obtained:—

PRODUCTS obtained from the DRY DISTILLATION of—

COAL.		WOOD.		ANIMAL SUBSTANCES.	
Water	HO	Water	HO	Water	HO
Ammonia	NH_3	Naphtha	$C_2H_4O_2$	Sulphide of Ammonium	NH_4S
Volatile Tar Oil	CHO	Acetic Acid	$C_4H_4O_4$	Cyanide of Ammonium	NH_4Cy
Tar	CHO	Volatile Tar Oil	CHO	Carbonate of Ammonia	NH_4O,CO_2
Naphthaline	$C_{20}H_8$	Tar	CHO	Volatile Tar Oil	CHON
Carburetted Hydrogen	CH_2	Creosote	$C^{14}H_8O_2$	Tar	CHON
Olefiant Gas	C_4H_4	Carburetted Hydrogen	CH_2	Carburetted Hydrogen	CH_2
Sulphurous Acid	SO_2	Carbonic Acid	CO_2	Phosphuretted Hydrogen	PH_3
Carbonic Acid	CO_2	Carbonic Oxide	CO	Carbonic Acid	CO_2
Carbonic Oxide	CO			Carbonic Oxide	CO
As Residue:		As Residue:		As Residue:	
Coke		Charcoal	C	Nitrogenous Carbon	NC
x	C,H,O,S,N	x	C,H,O	x	C,H,O,S,N,P

Here, as well as in the putrefactive process, the products of the one series appear among those of the other series, though always subordinate in quantity.

In general the hydrogenated products appear first, such as acetic acid, naphtha, volatile oils, and water containing ammonia, which, however, are soon partly decomposed, and thus give rise to simpler combinations, such as carburetted hydrogen, carbonic acid, and carbonic oxide. The tar which appears in each of these cases is a body of no definite chemical composition, but rather a mixture of many substances, particularly of volatile oils, and is coloured black by carbon. Several of the substances found in the tar, on account of their properties and practical utility, have become objects of manufacturing industry; thus, for instance, is obtained from this substance, by distillation with water, the volatile tar-oil which is employed as an illuminating material and as a solvent of caoutchouc.

The tar and tar-oil obtained from animal substances are, however, on account of their penetrating and offensive odour, scarcely fit to be applied to any useful practical purpose.

The employment of carburetted hydrogen as an illuminating material has already been noticed in § 56. *Naphthaline* is a constituent, especially of the coal-tar, crystallizing in nacreous plates. It possesses a peculiar and not unpleasant odour, characteristic of lamp-black, which always contains a portion of this substance. *Creosote* is an oily, colourless liquid, which is obtained also from tar, and possesses in a high degree the odour of smoke. It has an extremely hot taste, and is in some degree a preventive of putrefaction and fermentation.

Ammonia and its important combinations obtainable from animal substances by the process of distillation have been already described in § 78. The impure distillate which contains the ammonia is employed in medicine under the name of *spirit of hartshorn*. *Pyroligneous acid* is used in the preparation of acetic acid and of acetates, particularly of acetate of lead

This kind of vinegar, on account of its creosotic flavour, is never employed in domestic economy. Like nearly all the products of dry distillation, it possesses the property of arresting or preventing putrefaction and fermentation. Naphtha, or hydrated oxide of methyl (C_2H_3O, HO), obtained in the dry distillation of wood, possesses properties analogous to those of ordinary alcohol. Its radical, termed methyl (C_2H_3), yields a class of compounds possessing peculiar interest, and presenting the most complete parallelism in properties and composition to those of ethyl. Naphtha is colourless and of not unpleasant odour, and is employed in Great Britain as a fuel for lamps, being less expensive than the highly-taxed spirit of wine.

Natural Products of Distillation.

171. We are taught from the structure and origin of the crust of the earth that at different epochs the upper stratum has been ruptured by streams of glowing mineral substances proceeding from the interior of the earth. In places where this melted matter came in contact with those strata, the latter have been more or less altered in their qualities. If this action took place, for example, in the vicinity of coal, this material, through the influence of intense heat, might have been altered in the same manner, and might have yielded exactly such products as if submitted to dry distillation. *Anthracite* (§ 52) is justly considered as the result of the action of heat upon coal, since it contains as little oxygen and hydrogen as coke, from which it differs merely in its non-porosity, which is to be accounted for by the pressure to which it was subject during the process of its formation. The artificially-prepared coal-tar is replaced by *petroleum* or stone-oil (CH).

In many districts, particularly on the borders of the Caspian Sea, at Amiano in Italy, and at Rangoon in Burmah, an oily substance called *rock-oil*, or petroleum, is found to exude from the soil, and is met with floating on the surface of the water of springs. Some kinds are of a pale colour and very fluid, while others are dark and semi-solid at the ordinary temperature. The latter varieties when distilled yield a colourless naphtha which has the formula C_6H_5; its principal application is in the preservation of potassium, sodium, and the metals of the alkaline earths. The residue remaining after the volatile oil has passed off contains a considerable quantity of *paraffine*—a substance said to be obtained in considerable quantity in the distillation of Irish peat, and to be admirably adapted, when mixed with a suitable proportion of wax, to making candles.

In like manner naturally-formed tar, which has received the name of *asphalt* or *Jew's pitch* (bitumen), is found sometimes in an indurated condition, and sometimes more or less soft. This is employed for many purposes, particularly for tarring, as fuel, cement, black paint, or varnish for wood, iron, &c. Mixed with coarse sand it is used in the preparation of roofing-felt, and for paving, flooring, &c. The artificially-prepared tar may be employed for similar purposes after it has been deprived of its oil by distillation with water.

Herewith we conclude our description of chemical phenomena, several of which have been but slightly noticed, and more not mentioned at all. To those who wish to study chemistry more profoundly, either for professional, artistic, or manufacturing purposes, we recommend the many excellent works on this subject in our own and the continental languages.

MINERALOGY AND GEOLOGY.

1. MINERALOGY is the science which treats of MINERALS, or those constituents of the earth which are of similar composition through their entire mass.

All parts of the same Mineral are alike. In none of them do we observe those peculiar structures which we term *Organs*, and which, in Plants and Animals, fulfil functions that are indispensable to the existence of the individuals to which they belong. Minerals are consequently also called *Inorganic* substances. It is immaterial whether the mineral subjected to examination be large or small; in either case it presents to us the same structure. A small specimen of sandstone gives us as good an idea of its properties as would be given by a large block or mountain of the same material. A rock crystal a line long is as perfect as one that measures a foot.

2. In the section Chemistry (§ 3 and § 9) we have already seen that the entire mass of the earth is composed of only a few more than 60 simple substances or elements. By virtue of the chemical affinity possessed by these bodies they are found to exist in the greatest varieties of combination, and only seldom occur as simple substances. Proceeding from this view, Mineralogy might be termed the science of the chemical compounds occurring in Nature, and this is, to a certain extent, really the case. We have already, in studying the science of Chemistry, become acquainted with a number of such natural compounds, and have been referred to this section for a description of some others.

Chemical affinity, however, is not the only power by which the elements are influenced in the great laboratory of Nature. Its action is accompanied by that of a number of forces and influences, producing a series of mineralogical formations which cannot be considered simply from a chemical point of view, nor explained by chemical affinity alone.

3. Minerals may, therefore, be classed in two principal groups, which are readily distinguishable from each other. Those of the first class possess all the properties of perfect chemical compounds, are definite in their chemical composition, and equally definite in their crystalline form. These bodies are the true or *simple* Minerals, and the science that treats of them is MINERALOGY.

The other series of minerals has an essentially different character. The objects composing it are either evident mixtures of simple minerals, or, if they agree with simple minerals in chemical composition, they differ by the absence of definite crystalline form. Hence they do not occur as well-defined individuals, but in amorphous masses. These substances are called *Mixed Minerals*, *Stones*, or *Rocks*. The study of their individual properties, of their relations to each other and to the mass of the earth, and the investigation of their origin and mode of aggregation, constitute the subject of that division of this science which is termed GEOLOGY.

I.—MINERALOGY.

4. The first condition required of Mineralogy is that it shall furnish us with means to recognise Minerals and determine the classes to which they belong. Minerals may be distinguished and classified by certain characteristics. These are, principally, 1, their *Form;* 2, their *Physical*, and 3, their *Chemical*, properties. With the aid of these characteristics we can make an attempt to describe minerals.

1. FORM OF MINERALS.—CRYSTALLOGRAPHY.

5. We have already remarked in Physics (§ 20), and in Chemistry (§ 29), that the smallest particles of chemical compounds attract each other and arrange themselves in certain directions, producing regularly-formed bodies, which are called *crystals*. These forms exhibit *faces* or *planes; edges* or

lines of contact of two planes, and *points* or *angles* formed by the meeting of three or more planes. There is no form of crystal exhibiting less than four planes, six edges and four angles, and most crystals are composed of a larger number.

As every mineral, with few exceptions, always crystallises in one definite primary form, the observation of their forms is naturally a very important and certain mode of discriminating minerals. The forms of crystals are, however, exceedingly numerous. On examining a collection of minerals, hundreds of different forms are presented to the eye; yet these varieties may be traced back to a few fundamental forms, from which they are all derived. Of these fundamental forms there are six, which, with the various secondary or derived forms, constitute six families or systems of crystallisation, the study of which forms a particular branch of science termed *Crystallography*. It is not possible for us to enter into the details of this science, but we will endeavour to make ourselves acquainted with the primary forms, with the most important secondary forms, and with the manner in which a secondary crystal is described and traced back to its primary form.

Primary Forms of Crystals.

6. The *regular octohedron* (fig. 1). This crystal is limited by eight equal equilateral triangles, and has twelve edges and six angles. An imaginary line, extending from one angle to the opposite one, represents what is called the *axis* of the crystal. The octohedron has therefore three such axes, which are all equal and intersect each other at right angles. The whole form of the crystal is dependent upon this relation of the axes. If we construct a cross with three knitting-needles of equal length, so that they cross each other at right angles, their ends will represent the angles of a regular octohedron.

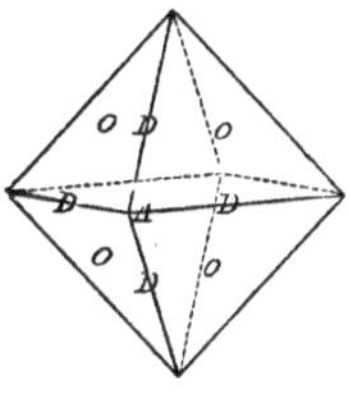

1.

Irregular octohedrons, which are likewise primary forms, may easily be represented by such crosses. The axes are either of unequal length, or they do not intersect each other at right angles, or they may exhibit both of these deviations.

In examining and describing a crystal, it is always placed in such a position that one of the axes is situated vertically in front of the observer; this is called the *principal axis*, whilst the others are termed *secondary* axes. When the axes of a crystal are equal, any one may be adopted as the principal axis, but when they are unequal the longest is generally chosen as the principal axis.

7. The *secondary* forms of the octohedron, as of all other crystals, are produced by the real or imaginary removal of certain portions of the primary form in a regular manner. We will give a few examples of this, which may be rendered more lucid by the use of prepared models or by cutting the requisite forms out of a piece of potato or turnip. On removing the angles from the octohedron (fig. 2) by parallel sections, a cube will at last be obtained. The *cube*, or six-faced solid (fig. 3), has six square planes of equal magnitude, eight angles, and twelve edges. On removing the angles of this crystal, as in fig. 4, the regular octohedron is obtained. The crystal repre-

sented by fig. 5 is intermediate between those shown by figures 2 and 4, or between figures 1 and 3. It is evident that these forms bear certain definite relations to each other, and therefore they are said to belong to the same system of crystallisation, which has been called the *regular* system.

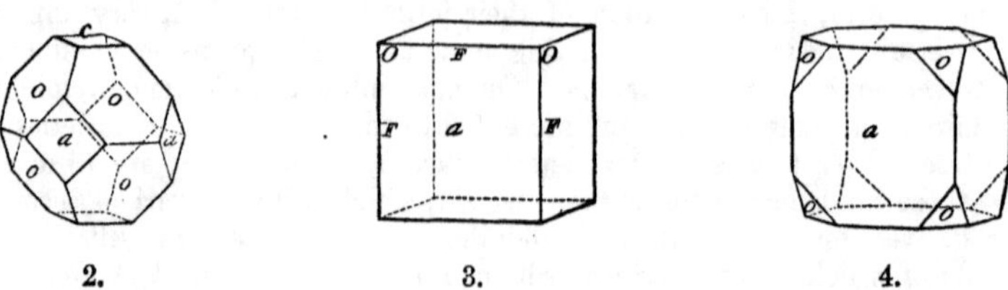

2. 3. 4.

A number of secondary forms may be obtained by truncations that remove the angles and edges of the primary forms. Thus, fig. 6 is a cube deprived of its edges and angles. On the removal of the edges of the cube in a regular manner the *rhombic dodecahedron* is obtained (fig. 7), of which the twelve equal planes are rhombs.

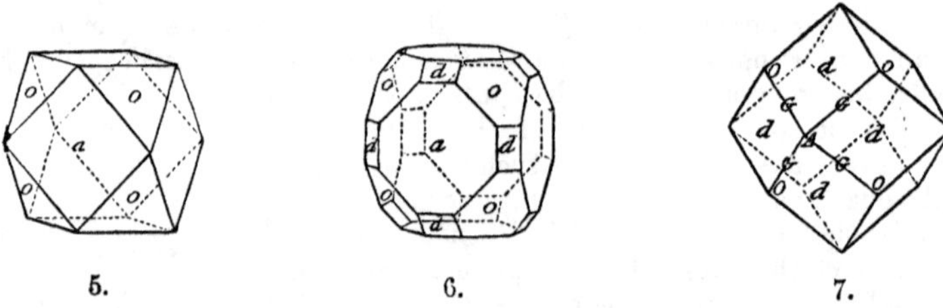

5. 6. 7.

Another series of secondary forms—the *hemihedral* forms — is produced by removing, not the whole of the angles or edges of a primary form, but only the alternate angles or edges which are situated opposite to each other. The three-sided pyramid, or *tetrahedron* (figs. 8 and 9), is thus obtained from the octohedron. The *pentagonal dodecahedron* (fig. 10) is a secondary form obtained in a somewhat similar manner.

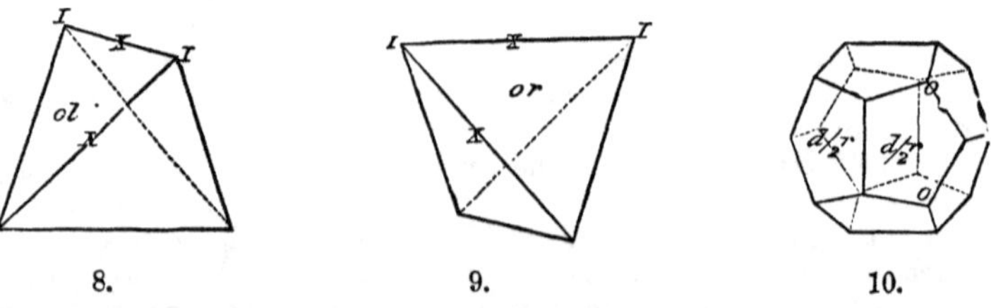

8. 9. 10.

The *second* primary form is the *quadratic octohedron* (fig. 11): this form has three axes intersecting each other at right angles, two of which are equal, while the third is longer or shorter than the others. The horizontal section of this octohedron is a square. The vertical section is a rhomb. By truncation of its lateral edges the prism (fig. 12) is obtained. The latter may have its edges and angles replaced by various modifications.

The *third* primary form is the *rhombic-octohedron* (fig. 13), the axes of which cross each other at right angles, but are all unequal. The three sections of this octohedron are rhombs. This is one of the crystalline forms of sulphur. The rhombic *prism* is obtained by the truncation of the lateral edges of the octohedron, namely, those that are marked *g* in figure 12.

The *fourth* primary form is an octohedron with three axes of unequal length, two of which intersect each other at an oblique angle, but are placed

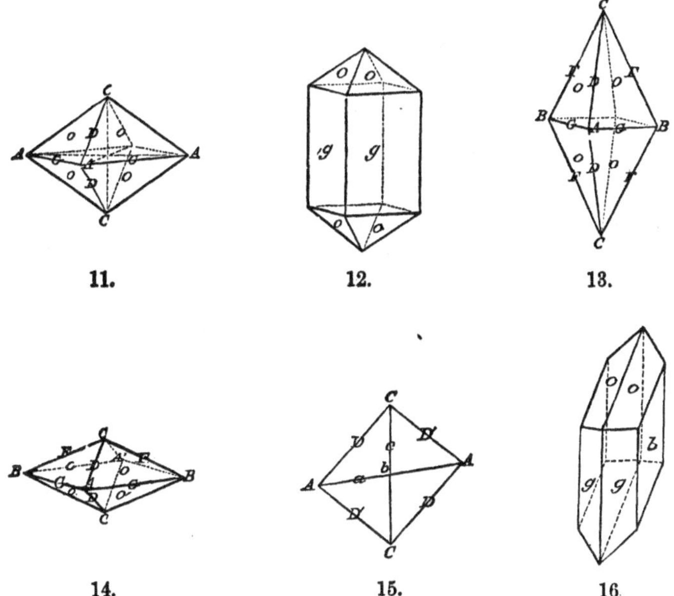

11. 12. 13.

14. 15. 16.

at right angles to the third axis, as shown in figs. 14 and 15. This octohedron generally occurs in its secondary forms, particularly in oblique rhombic prisms, as in gypsum (fig. 16).

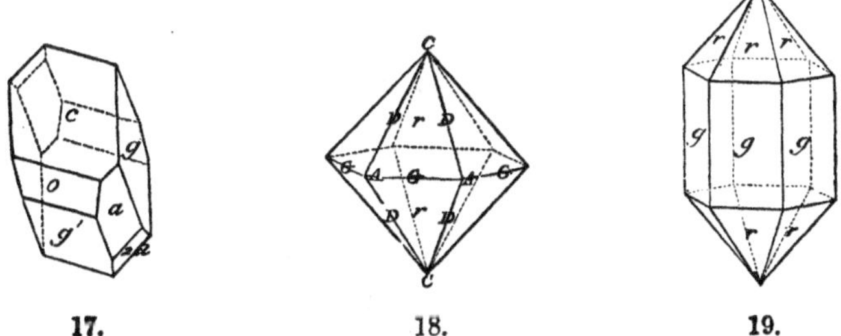

17. 18. 19.

The *fifth* primary form is an octohedron of which all the axes are unequal, and all intersect each other at oblique angles. This octohedron only occurs in its secondary forms, such as is exhibited by fig. 17, which is the crystalline form of axinite.

The *sixth* primary form is the *hexagonal dodecahedron* (fig. 18), a double six-sided pyramid. This system, which is termed the *hexagonal system*, is the only one which has four axes: three of these are equal, and intersect each other at acute but equal angles. The fourth or principal axis is unequal to the others and intersects them at a right angle. Among the secondary forms of this system may be mentioned the beautiful hexagonal prism (fig. 19), and the rhombohedron (fig. 20), which is enclosed by six equal rhombs.

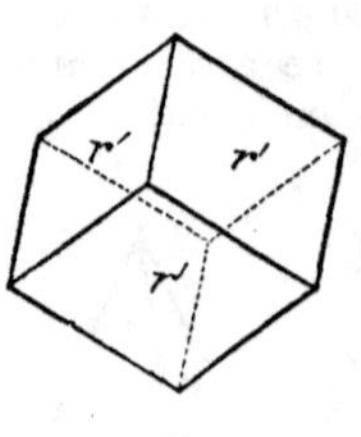

20.

9. The same mineral frequently occurs in very different crystalline forms, which, however, will always be found to belong to one of these six systems, that is to say, they may always be traced back in some way or other to primary forms included in these systems. The determination of the form of the crystal is frequently attended with considerable difficulty. This arises in part from the similarity which many forms have to each other, so that they can frequently be distinguished only by the most accurate measurements of the edges and angles of the crystals. Sometimes the difficulty is caused by the imperfect nature of the crystals that are to be examined; for crystals so regularly and distinctly formed as they are usually exhibited in diagrams, are of rare occurrence. In attempting to account for the irregularities of natural crystals, it may generally be assumed that there were obstacles present at the instant of their formation which did not permit the crystal to be equally and perfectly developed on all sides. Thus, it is frequently observed that only one-half, or only an edge, or an angle, or a plane of the crystal is formed, the remainder of the form being entirely wanting or merged in an extraneous adhering mass (see the figure at page 260). The most regular forms frequently appear to be perfectly irregular, the necessary conditions for the formation of the crystal having been favourable only on one side of the mass. The difficulties attending the examination of crystals may, however, be overcome by practice. Models of crystals, which may easily be procured, are of great assistance in the study of crystallography.

A variety of familiar names are given to irregular crystalline formations, such as tables, plates, needles, &c.

A mineral appears as a *crystalline* mass or aggregate when it consists of small crystals irregularly and closely arranged together. Thus, for instance, calcareous spar is distinctly crystallized, and marble only crystalline, carbonate of lime. When a mineral exhibits no crystalline arrangement of its particles, it is said to be massive or amorphous. Cavities in many masses of rocks are sometimes filled with groups of crystals. These are called *geodes* or *drusic cavities* (comp. § 81).

2. PHYSICAL CHARACTERS OF MINERALS.

10. As minerals cannot always be distinguished by their form, other characteristic properties are called into aid, such as the cohesion, the specific

gravity, and the colour of minerals, and their relations to light, electricity, and magnetism. These are termed the *physical characters* of minerals.

Cohesion.

11. There are only two liquid minerals; the greater number is solid, and with these special regard is paid to their cleavage, fracture, and hardness.

A mineral is cleavable when it is possessed of crystalline structure. In such a case its particles are arranged in a certain manner, so as to exhibit less cohesive power in one direction than in another, in the same manner as wood is more easily cleavable in the direction of its fibre than across the grain. There are, of course, various degrees of *cleavability;* thus, mica is cleavable into the thinnest laminæ. Cleavage surfaces are more or less plane.

Fractures, or fractured surfaces, are produced by the forcible disintegration of minerals that are not cleavable, or of cleavable minerals in any other direction than that of their cleavage. The appearance of the fracture is very characteristic of many minerals; it is either *even* or *uneven*, or it may be *conchoidal*, as for example, in the case of flint. It is also *splintery*, or *jagged*, and very frequently *earthy*, as in chalk and many other minerals.

12. In the description of a mineral, particular attention is always paid to its *hardness*. Many minerals are sufficiently hard to resist the best files, while others are so soft as to admit of being scratched with the finger-nail. There are between these two extremes various degrees of hardness, which cannot be so easily described. Other means have, therefore, been resorted to for the determination of the degree of hardness of different minerals with tolerable accuracy. Of two minerals, that one of course is the hardest which will scratch the other without being scratched itself. A scale of hardness has been constructed by Mohs, consisting of ten well-known minerals, so arranged that each one will scratch that which precedes it, and may be itself scratched by all those which follow it in the scale. Thus, ten degrees of hardness are obtained between the softest mineral, which is talc, and the hardest, namely diamond: these degrees are represented by the corresponding numbers; they are as follows:—

Degree of hardness		Degree of hardness	
1=Talc.		6=Felspar.	
2=Gypsum.		7=Quartz.	
3=Calcareous spar.		8=Topaz.	
4=Fluorspar.		9=Corundum.	
5=Apatite.		10=Diamond.	

If, therefore, the degree of hardness of a certain mineral is 7, we know it to be equal to that of quartz. It may easily be remembered that a high degree of hardness is represented by a high number, and *vice versâ*. The best way of trying the hardness of a mineral is to rub it on a hard fine-toothed file in comparison with the minerals that constitute the scale, pieces of which are reserved for that use. The scratching of minerals by one another is liable to several fallacies.

Specific Gravity of Minerals.

13. The density or specific gravity of a body, as was shown in Physics (§ 58), is the weight of a certain volume, compared with that of an equal

volume of water. Thus, the density of lead is = 11, since 1 cubic inch of this metal weighs 11 times as much as 1 cubic inch of water. We have already spoken of the value of a knowledge of specific gravities; the fact of substances always possessing the same density under uniform circumstances, furnishes an important means of recognizing them, particularly in the case of minerals. Hence the determination of their specific gravities has been made and repeated with the greatest care, generally at a temperature of 15°·5 C (60° F.). From what has been said in Chemistry, it may in general be assumed that minerals of high specific gravity, contain the heavy metals.

Relations of Minerals to Light.

14. As minerals are a very extensive and diversified class of bodies, they exhibit an exceedingly varied behaviour under the influence of the rays of light. Many minerals permit these rays of light to pass through them, refracting or deflecting them in the passage. Others reflect the light in a peculiar manner. These properties give rise to the transparency, the refracting power, the lustre, and the colour of minerals.

Transparency is either perfect or imperfect. We meet with the former chiefly in highly-developed crystals; and when this character appears in conjunction with the absence of colour, it is termed simply *transparent.* Imperfect transparency is indicated by the terms *semi-transparency* and *translucency;* pellucid at the edges. The term *opaque* means that no rays of light are transmitted by the mineral.

Refracting power (Phys. § 137) is only perceptible in perfectly transparent crystals. It varies exceedingly in different minerals; thus the precious stones are highly refractive, while other minerals possess this property in a slight degree. What is called *double refraction* is a very peculiar phenomenon. Many minerals not only refract the incident ray, but divide it into two parts, each proceeding in a different direction, so that two images are seen of any object, such as a black line, when viewed in a certain direction through the crystal. Iceland spar is a mineral which exhibits this doubly refractive power with great distinctness.

15. The *lustre* of minerals is dependent on the nature of their surfaces; and the more these approximate to the reflecting surfaces of mirrors, the more perfect it is. Minute flaws, inequalities, all give rise to certain peculiarities of lustre, which have received various easily intelligible denominations, according to their nature and vividness.

Thus we distinguish: *metallic lustre, adamantine lustre, vitreous lustre, waxy* or *fatty lustre, pearly* or *nacreous lustre,* and *silky lustre.* Some minerals are also described as *splendent, shining, glistening, glimmering,* and *dull;* those of earthy fracture, for instance, are distinguished by the latter term.

The *colours* of minerals are expressed by the terms generally adopted for denoting the impressions they produce on the eye. The principal colours are *white, grey, black, blue, green, yellow, red,* and *brown;* besides these there is a variety of mixed colours of all possible shades. A scale of colour, similar to the scale of hardness, has been constructed, the colour of a certain mineral being distinguished by a particular name.

The *streak* of a mineral is also a remarkable characteristic; it is the colour that appears on rubbing or streaking a mineral on a white body, or on scratching it with a harder substance. The streak is, generally speaking, lighter than the colour of the mineral, thus, for example, manganite is nearly black, whilst on paper it produces a brown streak. The colour of a mineral often agrees with that of its streak, yet lively-coloured minerals frequently yield very pale or even colourless powders. The streak of a mineral, that is the colour of the powder produced by scratching it, is a much more trustworthy character than its external colour.

There are many other phenomena of colour, such as *opalescence* and *iridescence*, which, however, occur less frequently. Some minerals under certain conditions, for instance when they are heated, or exposed for some time to the rays of the sun, possess the property of becoming slightly luminous in the dark. This property is called *phosphorescence.*

Relation of Minerals to Electricity and Magnetism.

16. Physics has taught us (§ 151) that all bodies are classed into two groups, one comprising those that become electrical by friction, which are called *electric bodies*, the other formed of those bodies that do not exhibit this property, and which are therefore termed *non-electric.* The electric bodies are non-conductors, and the non-electric bodies are conductors of electricity. It may readily be ascertained to which group a mineral belongs, by rubbing it, and then approaching it to an electrometer. Generally speaking, those minerals that contain heavy metals belong to the class of non-electrics or conductors, while minerals that consist of the nonmetallic elements, and the compounds of the lighter metals, become electric by friction, and are non-conductors or imperfect conductors of electricity.

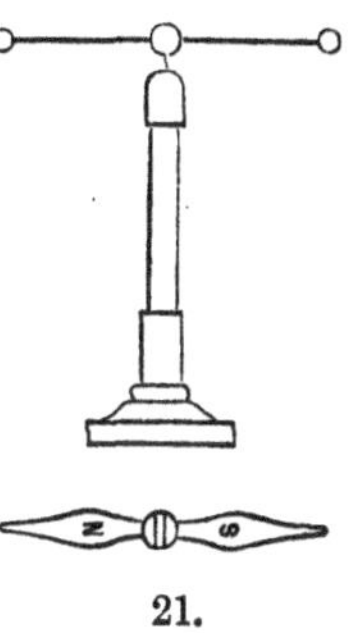

21.

Comparatively few minerals, and only those which contain iron (comp. Phys. § 168) exhibit *magnetic* properties. The magnetic deportment of a mineral may easily be detected by placing it in juxtaposition to a magnetic needle. Fig. 21 represents an electrometer mounted on a point. Below it is a magnetic needle adapted to the same support.

Odour, Taste, and Feel of Minerals.

17. Most minerals have no *odour*. Some have a very characteristic odour, which generally arises from the presence of foreign substances, particularly of mineral naphtha (Chem. § 170); sometimes, however, the odour becomes perceptible only on striking, rubbing, or breathing on the mineral. Several minerals, such as those containing sulphur and arsenic, evolve peculiar odours when heated, these odours being due to chemical changes.

Taste is only possessed by such minerals as are soluble in water, of which there are comparatively few. Its nature is of course dependent on the composition of the mineral; thus the taste of rock-salt is *saline*, that of salts of magnesia *bitter*, that of nitrates *cooling*, &c.

The *touch* or perception experienced on handling many minerals is very characteristic, some being *rough*, as lava; others *fatty* or *unctuous*, as soap-stone or talc, whilst others, such as the precious stones, produce a sensation of *cold* when touched. Several minerals possess the property of absorbing water, and some with such power as to adhere firmly to the tongue or a moistened finger, when brought in contact with it; clays exhibit this property in a remarkable degree.

3. CHEMICAL PROPERTIES OF MINERALS.

18. As we have already described minerals as chemical compounds occurring in Nature, they must necessarily be possessed of properties bearing a certain relation to their constituents, and becoming particularly evident when the minerals are decomposed. Chemical formulæ are also employed with great convenience in distinguishing those minerals which have a definite chemical composition. It is therefore of advantage to have become already acquainted with Chemistry, since in Mineralogy we have to refer to that science at every step.

When structure and physical characteristics are insufficient to enable us to recognise a mineral or determine its nature, we must have recourse to chemical action. The mineralogist has then to solve two problems by means of Chemistry; first, the *nature* of the substances contained in the mineral, and then the *quantity* in which each substance is present. To arrive at a knowledge of the latter it is necessary to effect a perfect separation of the mineral into its constituents, and accurately to weigh them. This operation is called *quantitative analysis*, and requires much time and care.

Qualitative analysis merely makes us acquainted with the various substances contained in a body, and, generally speaking, may be conducted with greater expedition, particularly by the mineralogist, who has other auxiliary means at his disposal, for recognising a mineral. He therefore confines himself, as far as possible, to the most simple chemical agents, which he can easily take about with him, and have continually at command. He avails himself especially of the decomposing power of heat, and the solvent property of water and acids. The submission of a mineral to the former is termed its investigation in the *dry way*, and to the latter its examination by the *moist way*.

Action of Heat on Minerals.

19. The Mineralogist applies heat in various degrees of intensity, from gentle warming to th most powerful ignition. For the latter purpose he

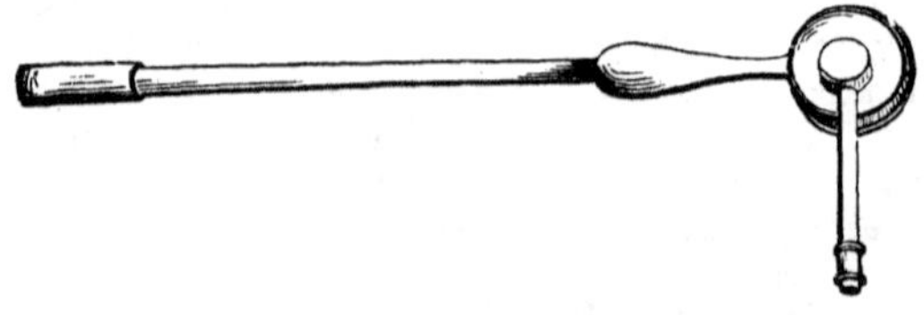

22.

makes use of the *blow-pipe* (fig. 22,) which is a tube of metal, terminating in a point with a narrow orifice. The lower end is the mouth-piece. The blowpipe is made 7 or 8 inches in length, acccording to the eyesight of the experimenter. On forcing, by means of the blowpipe, a jet of air into the

24.

flame of a lamp (fig. 23), we obtain on a small scale the same effect which the smith produces by the bellows of the forge, namely, an intense heat in a confined space. The blowpipe imparts to the flame a conical form; into this flame small fragments of the mineral to be examined are introduced, being either held by a small pair of forceps with platinum points (fig. 24),

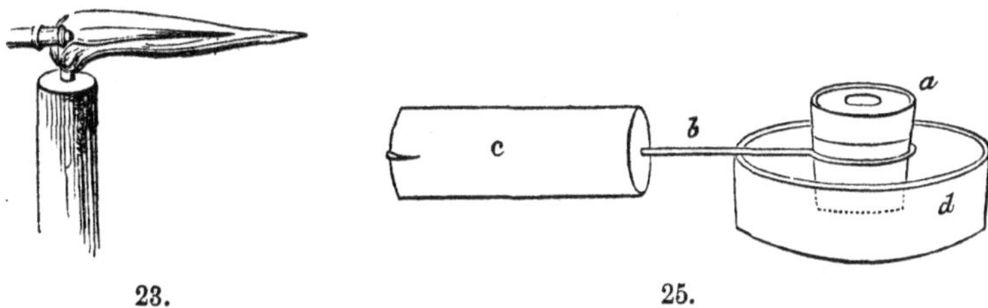

23. 25.

or placed upon a piece of well-burnt charcoal, or a charcoal pastile (fig. 25.)* When the specimen is to be only gently heated, it is frequently heated in a glass tube by means of a spirit-lamp without the aid of the blowpipe.

20. In performing these experiments, the particular points to which attention is directed, are the fusibility and volatility of the substance, as also the particular colour which it may impart to the blowpipe flame.

The *fusibility* of minerals varies exceedingly. Some fuse at a gentle heat in the ordinary flame of a lamp, as salts, for instance; others are fused only by the application of the most intense heat; and others again are perfectly infusible. The different degrees of fusibility are expressed by the terms easily fusible, difficultly fusible, infusible, &c.

The fusion of substances is attended by other phenomena worthy of notice; thus some minerals fuse quietly, others swell up or intumesce, or decrepitate, &c. The fused mass presents itself in the form of a glass, a slag, a scoria, an enamel, or a metallic bead, the latter being generally formed when a heavy metal is present.

Volatile substances are very often expelled from minerals by the application of heat. Thus aqueous vapour is almost always evolved, and it is necessary to observe whether this water be merely accidental, or chemically combined as water of hydration or of crystallisation (Chem. § 28). Many minerals disengage various gases, as, for instance, chalk evolves carbonic acid, and binoxide of manganese evolves oxygen. New compounds are often produced during ignition, by the combined action of heat and the oxygen of the air.

* Fig. 25, *a*, represents a charcoal pastile of the full size; *b*, an iron-wire handle; *c*, a cylinder of cork; *d*, a porcelain capsule. The lower part of the pastile is chiefly of clay, and is incombustible; the upper part of charcoal. Another variety of blowpipe pastile contains soda and borax among the charcoal, and is used when metallic ores are to be reduced.

Thus, lead ores become easily coated with a yellow crust of oxide of lead, ores of antimony with white oxide of antimony, sulphuretted ores yield sulphurous acid, which is easily recognised by its suffocating odour, and arsenical ores evolve the peculiar garlic odour of arsenic.

The *colour of the blowpipe flame* is often an excellent means of distinguishing a mineral. Strontia imparts to the flame a purple tint, lime a bright red, potassa a violet, soda a bright yellow, boron and copper a green tint, &c.

21. We have hitherto spoken of the test examination by the blowpipe flame alone. The co-operation of chemical substances is frequently employed, by which peculiar phenomena are produced. Such substances are, the oxygen of the air, the carbon of the *interior* of the blow-pipe flame, carbonate of soda, and borax or biborate of soda.

We have already seen in § 20 that the oxygen of the air exerts an oxidising influence, and it must here be remarked, that the point of the blowpipe flame is the only portion which allows the oxygen to have access to the substance: it is therefore called the *oxidising flame* of the blowpipe. If the substance under examination be introduced into the wide interior portion of the flame, which is not luminous, and still contains unconsumed carbon, the latter exercises a reducing action, if the substance contains an oxygen compound. This portion of the flame is hence called the *inner* or *reducing flame.* Thus, for instance, a piece of tin may easily be converted into white oxide in the outer flame, and reduced again to a metallic bead in the inner flame.

22. Carbonate of soda and borax, when added to the specimen under examination before the blowpipe flame, are called *fluxes*, since they produce easily fusible compounds. Carbonate of soda when fused with compounds rich in silica, forms an easily fusible soda-glass; it likewise serves for the production of soluble salts of arsenic, sulphur, manganese, &c., which are converted into acids by exposure to a high temperature. In borax (Chem. § 62), the boracic acid that withstands the action of fire, combines with metallic oxides, forming peculiarly coloured glasses, which correspond pretty well in their colours with those of the glass fluxes with which we have previously become acquainted (Chem. § 77). The result obtained in this experiment is dependent on the part of the flame in which the fusion is effected, since the lower oxides frequently yield glasses which differ in colour from those produced by the higher oxides, as is shown by the following examples (see page 325).

The mixture of borax and the substance to be tried is melted on the end of a fine platinum wire, bent into a ring of one-eighth of an inch in diameter.

Similar coloured beads are produced by fusing metallic bodies in a glass formed of microcosmic salt (the double phosphate of soda and ammonia). A crystal of this salt is fused on a charcoal pastile, fig. 26, till it has the form of fig. 27. It is then mixed with the metallic body and again fused, and the heat is continued till the charcoal capsule burns away and leaves the bead exposed, as shown in fig. 28.

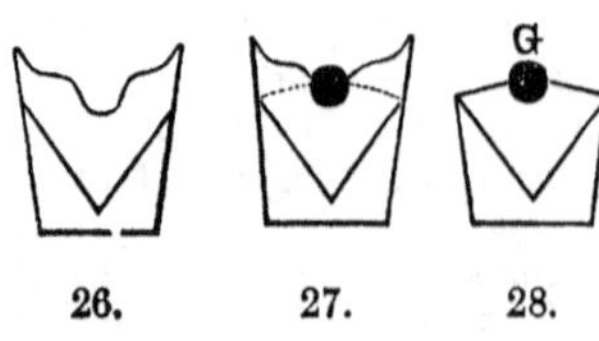

26. 27. 28.

Oxides.	Colour of the Borax Glasses.	
	In the Oxidising Flame.	In the Reducing Flame.
Chromium..	Emerald-green........................	Yellowish-brown, colourless on cooling.
Manganese.	Violet..................................	Colourless.
Antimony..	Bright-yellow	Turbid and greyish.
Bismuth....	Colourless............................	Grey and turbid.
Zinc	Colourless, a white enamel with much zinc.........................	
Tin..........	Colourless	Colourless.
Lead........	Yellow, colourless on cooling....	Reduced to metallic beads.
Iron	Dark red, becoming lighter and nearly colourless on cooling..	Bottle-green, blue-green.
Cobalt.	Blue	Blue.
Nickel.......	Reddish-yellow, lighter on cooling	Greyish.
Copper......	Blue	Colourless, cinnabar-red and opaque on cooling.
Silver........	Milky white on cooling............	Greyish.

23. In finally availing ourselves of the co-operation of water and acids as solvents of minerals, we enter at once into the range of those chemical phenomena, which are followed out in all their details in special works on analytical chemistry.

It therefore only remains to be observed, that these solvents are generally applied in a certain order; namely, water first, then hydrochloric acid, then nitric acid, and finally a mixture of the two (Chem. § 36.) Hydrochloric acid is most frequently employed, in order to observe whether the minerals effervesce; that is, whether they contain carbonic acid, which escapes as gas when the mineral is put into this acid.

24. We have now made ourselves acquainted with all the preliminary knowledge required to enable us to proceed to describe Minerals. It must, however, be remarked, that of all sciences Mineralogy is the one in which mere description, even of the best kind, is least available. In this science self inspection is absolutely necessary. The object proposed is not a purely theoretical knowledge of minerals, but a practical acquaintance only attainable through the medium of our senses; a facility in combining into one conception of all the different qualities of such objects, whereby the characteristics are permanently, indissolubly, and unceasingly associated in our minds with the bodies which are so characterised.

It is, therefore, advisable that the student who intends to engage in the pursuit of Mineralogy, should avail himself of those minerals which are furnished by the neighbourhood in which he is living. Even the poorest districts have some minerals, and the examination of these will aid him in forming a conception of others. It is by no means difficult to obtain gradually the most important minerals by exchange or purchase, and thus to form a small collection. Small systematic collections of specimens of minerals can now be purchased for a trifling sum. In all institutions where this branch of natural science is embraced in the course of study, it is necessary above all things to excite an interest for the science by the aid of a collection of the most important minerals. In the study of natural history, the best description may be considered merely as a crutch, which is cast aside directly the student has an opportunity of inspecting the objects personally.

Classification of Minerals.

25. A mineral which may be distinguished from all others by its peculiar chemical composition and properties, is acknowledged as a distinct *Species.* The number of minerals thus established amounts to four or five hundred, and is rapidly increasing.

Minerals may be arranged according to various systems. Either their form is principally considered, and they are then arranged according to the systems of crystals, or their arrangement is based upon their density and hardness. Since, however, it has been more clearly shown that all these properties are dependent on the chemical constitution of the minerals, the latter has become the directing clue to their arrangement. In this classification particular regard is paid to that constituent which either predominates in quantity, or in its particular character, and which therefore furnishes the name for the formation of the group. The order of succession of the minerals, in this arrangement, is nearly the same as that of the elements and their compounds in chemistry, although gaps are found to exist here and there in the system.

The acquirement of a knowledge of chemistry is of course presupposed, whereby a number of difficulties will vanish, which would render the study of mineralogy, according to outward characteristics alone, exceedingly laborious.

26. The nomenclature of minerals has been formed gradually, without any scientific basis, and is consequently imperfect. The names of genera and species are derived from many sources; as, for example, from popular or vulgar names, from the locality where they were first noticed, and from the names of celebrated naturalists; and but few names have been derived from their properties and chemical constituents. An alteration in the nomenclature cannot however be effected, as it would give rise to the greatest confusion. The old names are retained as a matter of convenience, just as, in chemistry, the names water and potash are still employed, instead of the more systematic names of oxide of hydrogen and oxide of potassium.

4. DESCRIPTION OF MINERALS.

27. A considerable space would be required for the description of all the minerals that are now known. We must therefore content ourselves with describing the most important, and even these only briefly. A sufficiently detailed account has been given of several; for instance, of the different kinds of coal, in the chemical section of this work: of these, therefore, the mere enumeration will suffice.

Most of the simple minerals occur in comparatively small quantities, though some which are aggregated in large masses form a considerable portion of the earth's surface. These will be referred to in the chapter on Rocks.

In the following descriptions, H. signifies the hardness, and Sp. Gr. the specific gravity, of the minerals:—

Synoptical Table of Minerals.

1st Class. Non-metallic Bodies.	2nd Class. Metals.		3rd Class. Organic Compounds.
	1st Order. Light Metals.	2nd Order. Heavy Metals.	
Group.	Group.	Group.	Group.
1. Sulphur.	5. Potassium.	13. Iron.	29. Salts.
2. Boron.	6. Sodium.	14. Manganese.	30. Earthy resins.
3. Carbon.	7. Ammonium.	15. Cobalt.	
4. Silicium.	8. Calcium.	16. Nickel.	
	9. Barium.	17. Copper.	
	10. Strontium.	18. Bismuth.	
	11. Magnesium.	19. Lead.	
	12. Aluminum.	20. Tin.	
		21. Zinc.	
		22. Chromium.	
		23. Antimony.	
		24. Arsenic.	
		25. Mercury.	
		26. Silver.	
		27. Gold.	
		28. Platinum.	

FIRST CLASS.—MINERALS OF THE NON-METALLIC ELEMENTS.

1st Group—SULPHUR.

28. The primary form of crystallized Sulphur is the rhombic octohedron occurring with various truncations of the edges and angles (figs. 29, 30). Sulphur occurs more frequently in the semi-crystalline or granular, and the earthy state, and less frequently in the fibrous condition. Its cleavage is imperfect; its fracture conchoidal and uneven; H = 1.5 to 2·5; it is brittle and fragile; Sp. Gr. = 1·9 to 2·1. The chemical properties of sulphur and its application have been described in the section Chemistry (§ 40).

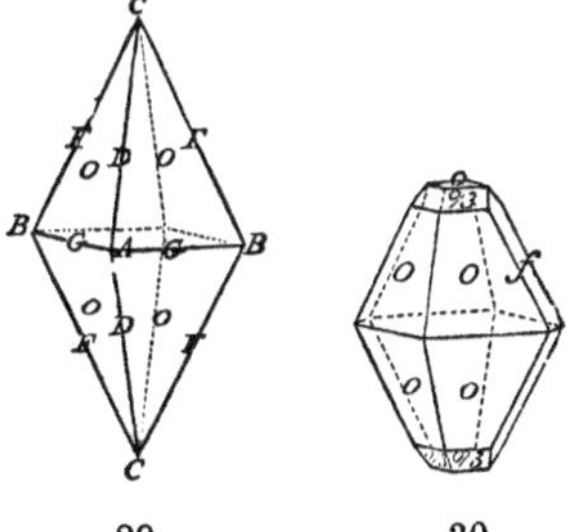

29. 30.

The most important locality of sulphur is Sicily, where it is found in the tertiary formations, associated with calcareous spar and celestine; at Girgenti, Fiume, &c. Moreover, the strata of earthy sulphur in Poland are likewise very considerable. In addition to these localities, there are many places in Germany and the rest of Europe, as also in other parts of the globe, where sulphur is found. [Sulphur is found as a deposit about the sulphur springs of New York, Virginia, &c., and occurs also in coal deposits and elsewhere, where sulphuret of iron is undergoing decomposition; also in microscopic crystals at some of the gold mines of Virginia. It occurs in masses in limestone on the Potomac, 25 miles above Washington.] But the sulphur derived from these sources is far less pure than the sulphur of Sicily.

2ND GROUP—BORON.

29. This element occurs only in combination with oxygen, as Boracic acid ($BO_3 + HO$), which crystallises in scales, and is found as a crust upon the surface of the earth in the neighbourhood of volcanic springs. It is friable, of Sp. Gr. = 1·48, translucent, white, bitter and acid to the taste; it is easily fusible, and imparts a green colour to flame; it is soluble in water and alcohol. Boracic acid is deposited at the margin and at the bottoms of volcanic springs or lakes, particularly in those of Sasso (hence the name Sassolin), Castelnuovo, and others, in Tuscany.

3RD GROUP—CARBON.

30. (1.) *Diamond.*—This mineral occurs crystallised in regular octohedrons, or in some of the geometrically allied forms (figs. 31, 32, 33). It

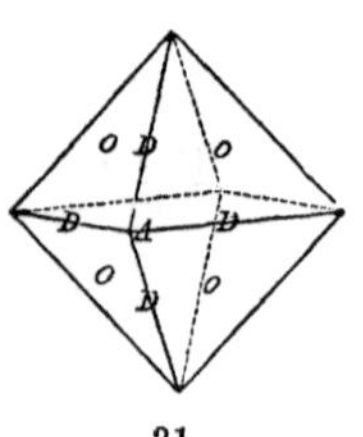

31.

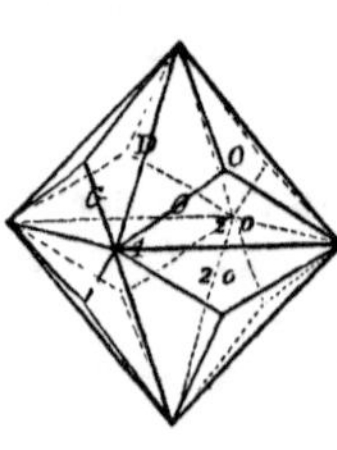

32.

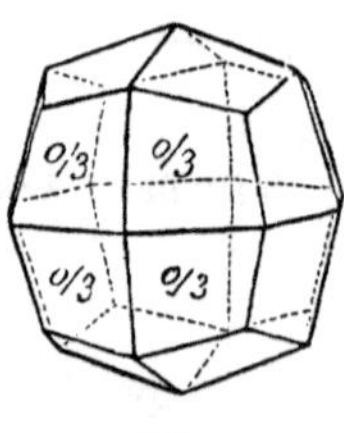

33.

is possessed of the greatest hardness, which is = 10; Sp. Gr. = 3·5 to 3·6; it is mostly cleavable, transparent, generally colourless, highly lustrous, refracts light very powerfully, and is the most valuable of all the precious stones. It occurs principally in alluvial soil and in rocks of secondary formation, in the East Indies (Golconda), and in Brazil. It has also lately been discovered in the sands of the rivers which have their sources in the Uralian mountains: [and several have been found in North Carolina and Georgia.] 1 carat (= 4 grains) of small diamonds, employed for polishing the larger ones, for cutting glass, &c., costs from 20*s.* to 25*s.* A polished diamond (brilliant) weighing 1 carat, is valued at from 8*l.* to 10*l.*; the prices of diamonds increase to such an extent with their size, that a brilliant weighing 5 carats may cost as much as from 150*l.* to 250*l.* The largest diamond at present in Europe is one in possession of the Queen of Portugal. It weighs 215 carats, and is valued at upwards of 150,000*l.*

(2.) *Graphite* (Plumbago) is found in tabular crystals, belonging to the hexagonal system, but generally it occurs in scales and small laminæ. H = 1 to 2, Sp. Gr. = 1·8 to 2·4; it is cleavable, steel-grey to black, unctuous to the touch, and produces a black streak. It is found embedded in various rocks at Passau, in Bavaria; the finest quality, however, is met with at Borrowdale, in Cumberland. The graphite from the former place is generally employed for crucibles and for blacking stoves, and that from the latter locality for the best black-lead pencils. [Graphite is also found in many localities in the United States; the chief of which are Stockbridge, Mass., Ticonderoga, N. Y., Brandon, Vt., Wake, N. C., and Attleborough, Pa.]

(3.) *Anthracite* occurs in large masses, having a conchoidal fracture. H = 2 to 2·5, Sp. Gr. = 1·4 to 1·7; it is greyish-black, and leaves but little ash when burned. It is found in strata, occasionally of very considerable thickness, in the primitive rocks; as, for instance, [in Pennsylvania,] in Wales, and in the Hartz mountains. It is employed as a fuel for strong blast or wind furnaces, &c.

Coal, brown-coal, and *turf* must be mentioned as varieties of carbon, since this element forms their chief constituent. Their most important characters and properties have already been detailed in § 164 of Chemistry. We shall, however, more minutely describe the nature of their stratification in the chapter on Geology.

4th Group — SILICIUM.

31. By the term silicia the Mineralogist recognises the compound, which chemists call silicic acid (SiO_3, Chem § 61). The number of silicious minerals is exceedingly large; silica, however, generally occurs in combination with alumina, hence the greater number of silica compounds is mentioned in the alumina group. It may in general be remarked, that the hardness of the purer kinds of silica is very considerable, sometimes amounting to 8·9; hence it produces sparks when struck with steel, whilst its specific gravity rarely exceeds 4·5. It possesses mostly a vitreous lustre, its prevailing colour being white. Silica, when chemically pure, or merely coloured by small quantities of different oxides, is termed *quartz.*

Quartz Family.

Its crystals belong to the hexagonal system, and occur most frequently as double six-sided pyramids (fig. 18), but which are generally subjected to the

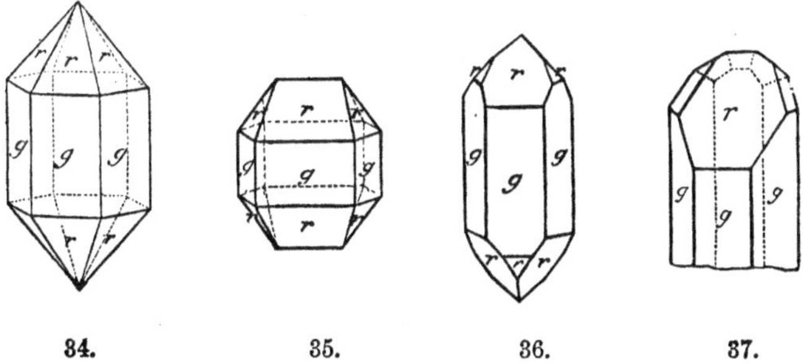

34. 35. 36. 37.

modifications and irregularities spoken of in the article on Crystallography, and in the part represented in the figures 34 to 37. Quartz also occurs frequently in crystalline, compact, or granular masses. Its fracture is conchoidal; H = 7; Sp. Gr. = 2·5 to 2·8. It is either perfectly transparent, or white; it occurs likewise of all colours, and of every possible shade. It is insoluble in all acids, with the exception of hydrofluoric acid (Chem. § 39); it yields with carbonate of soda, before the blowpipe, a transparent *glass;* and when struck with steel it emits brilliant sparks. The following are the principal varieties of quartz:—

(1.) *Rock-crystal*, which is found in beautiful, transparent, six-sided prisms of considerable size, in the various primitive mountains. The crystals obtained from the caverns of St. Gotthardt are remarkably fine; they have also been found of extraordinary size and purity in Madagascar, where blocks of from 15 to 20 feet in circumference occur. Rock crystal is employed in jewelry, and as a constituent of pure glass fluxes. It is often slightly coloured, and frequently contains various foreign minerals, either in small scales or in other forms.

(2.) *Amethyst* is quartz that is more or less intensely coloured [purple or bluish-violet] by protoxide of manganese. It occurs rarely in perfectly formed crystals, but more frequently as crystals lining drusic cavities. It is often found in the cavities of porphyry and amygdaloid, and, as it is by no means a rare mineral, is extensively employed as a jewel of small value. The amethyst was worn by the ancients as a charm against drunkenness.

(3.) Silica is called *common quartz*, when it does not occur in regular crystals, but only crystalline, granular, and compact. In this state it is often found in considerable masses, which are called quartz rock; it also forms compound rocks with other minerals, of which granite offers a familiar example. It is very extensively dispersed over the surface of the earth. Its purer kinds are employed in the manufacture of glass, porcelain, &c. It is generally white and translucent; some varieties of it, altered in colour or otherwise, have received different names, as *rose quartz;* the blue variety, *siderite; schiller-spar; cats-eye*, so called from its peculiar iridescence; *avanturine*, containing yellow and reddish laminæ of mica, which render it a very beautiful and ornamental stone.

(4.) *Chalcedony* is an opaque kind of quartz, occurring in spherical, botryoidal, and nodular masses, possessing the most varied colours and curious markings. It is employed extensively for making snuff-boxes, buttons, marbles, &c. Red or yellow-coloured chalcedony is called *carnelian*, and the green-coloured, chrysoprase; both are much prized for seals, and other raised and engraved ornamental works of art.

(5.) *Flint*, the properties of which are well known, is found in large irregular masses, in many parts of England and about Paris. Its application as a promethean apparatus has diminished considerably since the invention of lucifer-matches and percussion-caps. It is extensively used in potteries.

(6.) *Hornstone* is a variety of quartz somewhat similar to flint, but has a more splintery fracture, and bears a remarkable resemblance to horn.

(7.) *Jasper* is opaque, dull, and only slightly lustrous, on account of the larger amount of alumina and oxide of iron which it contains. It occurs of all colours; but red, yellow, and brown are most frequent.

(8.) *Flinty slate* is a mineral consisting of quartz, alumina, lime, and sesquioxide of iron, coloured black by carbon; it is employed as a whet-stone and touch-stone.

(9.) *Agate* is, generally speaking, a beautifully-marked mineral, consisting of a mixture of various kinds of quartz, particularly of amethyst, chalcedony, and jasper. It is extensively employed by lapidaries for making a variety of ornamental objects, and also for mortars, which are employed for pulverising very hard substances.

32. This mineral is a particular variety of quartz, containing water in chemical combination. It does not occur crystallized, but in compact vitreous masses, and is distinguished by the brilliant and changeable reflections of light exhibited by some of its varieties; whence the term *opalescent* is derived. *Noble opal* possesses this property in a very high degree, and is therefore much prized as a jewel. *Semi-opal*, or *common opal*, is less remarkable for its change of colours. *Hydrophane* is a mineral, possessing the peculiar property of becoming transparent and iridescent only when moistened with water.

Silicious sinter and *mountain meal* are likewise varieties of quartz, containing water; the former is deposited in a variety of forms by hot springs, particularly by the Geyser of Iceland. The latter is an earthy deposit from silicious waters, and, when examined under the microscope, is found to consist almost entirely of the shells of infusoriæ. Another kind is called *polishing slate*, and is employed by lapidaries for polishing stones.

SECOND CLASS.—MINERALS CONTAINING METALS.

FIRST ORDER—LIGHT METALS.

5th Group—POTASSIUM.

33. The most important and indeed the greater number of minerals containing potassium, likewise contain alumina, as an essential constituent: we shall therefore describe them in the aluminous group. Of natural potassa salts, we have only to mention the nitrate and the sulphate of potassa.

Nitrate of potassa, or *nitre* (KO,NO_5), crystallises in regular rhombic prisms, but is found, in many localities, in the form of crusts of acicular and capillary crystals (comp. Chem. § 69). [In Madison County, Kentucky, it is found scattered through the loose earth, covering the bottom of a large cave. Other similar caverns in the western part of the United States also contain it.]

Sulphate of potassa (KO,SO_3) belongs to the same crystalline system, and is found occasionally in volcanic lava.

6th Group—SODIUM.

34. (1.) *Nitrate of soda* (NaO,NO_5) crystallises in the hexagonal system as obtuse rhombohedrons, and occurs in crystalline masses of considerable magnitude; which, in the districts of Atakama and Tarapaca, in Peru, extend over a space of nearly 200 miles.

(2.) *Rock-salt*, chloride of sodium ($NaCl$), crystallises in the cubical system; it generally occurs, however, in tabular crystalline masses, and is easily cleavable in a direction parallel to the planes of the primary form; its fracture is conchoidal, H = 2; Sp. Gr. = 2·2 to 2·3; its colour is generally white, but it is also found of a red, green, yellow, and blue colour; its chemical properties and applications are detailed in Chemistry, § 72. Rock-salt occurs in secondary Rocks, in masses of considerable magnitude, often in company with gypsum, alumina, and saline clay. [In the United States, it has been found forming large beds with gypsum, in Virginia, Washington Co., 18 miles from Abingdon, and in the Salmon River Mountains of Oregon.] The salt-works of Cheshire, of Hallein in Saltsburg, and of Wielitzka, in Gallicia, are particularly celebrated: in the latter is found the *decrepitating salt*, which dissolves in water with a decrepitating noise and disengagement of numerous bubbles of hydrogen gas. The gas is enclosed between the crystalline planes of the salt. A number of other minerals containing soda are found, but are of less importance than the foregoing. Of these may be mentioned anhydrous and hydrated sulphate of soda (Thenardite = NaO,SO_3, and Glauberite = NaO,SO_3+10HO); carbonate of soda, containing a large quantity of water (Soda = NaO,CO_2+10HO), and another kind containing little water, called *trona* ($2NaO,3CO_2+4HO$), which occurs in the interior of Barbary in considerable quantities, as a crust on the earth, and is applicable to the same purposes as soda.

Biborate of soda ($NaO,2BO_3+10HO$), as a mineral, is called borax or tincal, and is found at the bottom and on the borders of a lake in Thibet.

7TH GROUP—AMMONIA.

35. Since the combinations of ammonia, as we have seen in § 78 of Chemistry, are of a volatile nature, they occur only in inconsiderable masses, though not unfrequently, in the mineral kingdom. They are met with principally as crystalline coatings or crusts; for instance, in cavities and the fissures of lava of active volcanoes, in brown-coal works, particularly in the neighbourhood of burning and spent heaps of coals.

8TH GROUP—CALCIUM.

36. This metal forms an extensive group of minerals, which possess a low degree of hardness and density, and are generally of a pure white colour. The most remarkable are—

(1.) *Fluorspar* (CaFl), which crystallises in various forms of the regular system, but most frequently as cubes. It is perfectly cleavable; its fracture is conchoidal; H = 4; Sp. Gr. = 3·1 to 3·17; it is transparent and gradually passes into translucency, and seldom occurs white, being generally tinted faintly violet, green, yellow, &c.; regarding its chemical properties, see Chemistry, § 39. Fluorspar is a mineral of frequent occurrence, though never in considerable masses. The same mineral occurs amorphous, as *compact fluor* and *earthy fluor*.

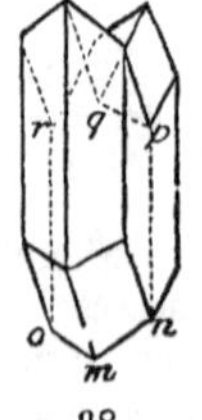

38

(2.) *Anhydrite* (CaO,SO_3), or anhydrous sulphate of lime, is found generally associated with gypsum and rock-salt. It occurs crystallised, and also in radiated, granular, and compact masses.

(3.) *Gypsum* (CaO,SO_3+2HO), or hydrated sulphate of lime, occurs most frequently in tabular crystals, which may be cleaved into very thin laminæ; they belong to the system of the fourth primary form (fig. 16); H = 2; Sp. Gr. = 2 to 2·4. It frequently occurs in double or twin crystals, of the form represented in fig. 38. It is possessed of double refractive power, vitreous ustre, and generally has a white colour. This kind of gypsum is called *elenite;* there are, besides, other varieties, viz., *fibrous* gypsum; *compact* or *granular* gypsum, which is called *alabaster*, and *earthy* gypsum. Regarding its application, see Chemistry, § 81.

(4.) *Apatite*, sometimes called asparagus-stone, on account of its beautiful pale-green colour, consists of phosphate of lime, fluoride and chloride of calcium. It crystallises in the hexagonal system, often like fig. 41, and s frequently embedded in various kinds of rocks.

(5.) *Pharmacolite* is arseniate of lime ($= CaO,AsO_5$).

(6.) Carbonate of Lime (CaO, CO_2).

37. This mineral exhibits the remarkable peculiarity of crystallising in forms belonging to two different systems; hence its varieties form two families, namely, those of Calcareous spar and Arragonite.

(1.) *Calcareous spar* crystallises in the hexagonal system, and more particularly in modifications of the rhombohedron (fig. 20). These are so exceedingly numerous, that 1,700 different forms have already been distinguished. Figures 39 to 44 represent some of the chief forms of carbonate

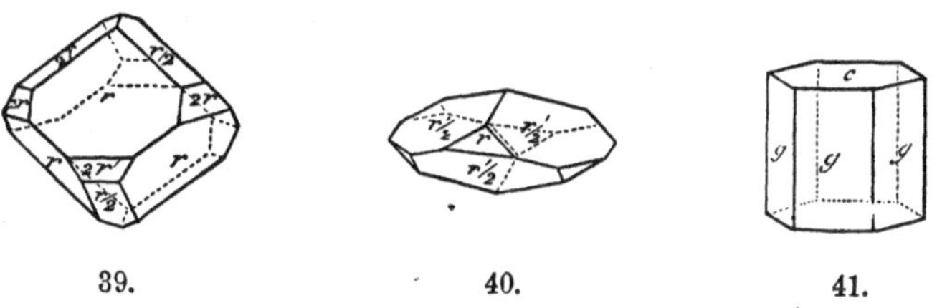

39. 40. 41.

of lime, which we shall briefly describe, as they give much insight into the mysteries of crystallography. Fig. 39, r shows the planes of the primitive rhombohedron (obtainable from *all* the crystals of calcareous spar by cleavage), combined with $r\frac{1}{2}$, a more obtuse rhombohedron, and r 2, a more acute rhombohedron. In fig. 40, the primary rhombohedron, r, is almost entirely obliterated by the large planes of the obtuse rhombohedron, $r\frac{1}{2}$. In fig. 41

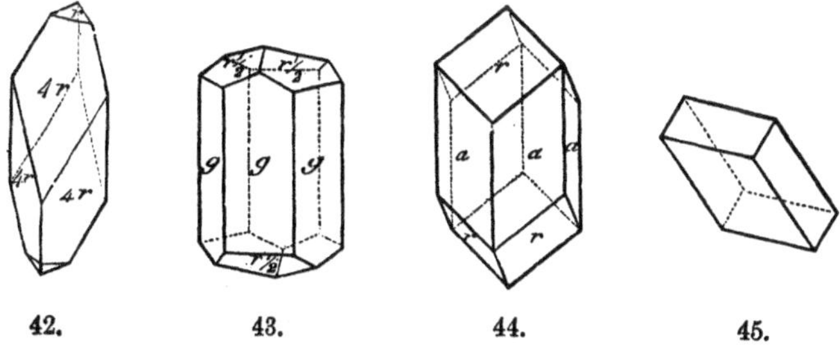

42. 43. 44. 45.

we have a regular six-sided prism, such as forms the middle portion of the crystal represented by fig. 19. Fig. 42 represents small faces of the primitive rhombohedron, *r*, combined with a predominant and very acute rhombohedron, *r* 4. In fig. 43 we have the obtuse rhombohedron, $r\,\frac{1}{2}$, terminating a regular six-sided prism, *g* (fig. 41), and in fig. 44 the inverse, but equal six-sided prism, *a*, terminated by the regular rhombohedron, *r*. Crystals of all these forms are readily procured among the minerals of Cumberland and Derbyshire.

Fortunately the remaining properties of calcareous spar are such as to admit of its easy recognition. It is very easily cleavable into the primitive rhombohedron (fig. 20), and into tables such as shown by fig. 45. It has a conchoidal, splintery, and uneven fracture; H = 3; Sp. Gr. = 2·6 to 2·17; it becomes electric by friction, is soluble in the mineral acids with evolution of carbonic acid, and is converted by exposure to a red-heat, into caustic lime (Chemistry, § 79). Its varieties are :—

(*a.*) *Crystallised calcareous spar*, called also Iceland spar, or *doubly refracting spar*, because it is possessed of double refractive power in a high degree (§ 14). It most generally forms tabular, transparent, colourless crystals of vitreous lustre, often occurring in all varieties of formations, particularly in drusic cavities and in metallic veins. The double refracting spar found in Iceland is celebrated for its beauty. (*b.*) *Fibrous limestone*, which occurs principally in stalactitic formations, in the cavities of chalk-hills. (*c.*) *Marble*, or granular carbonate of lime, which is most esteemed when it is perfectly white, fine-grained, compact, and free from coloured veins. It is employed in that state by sculptors, for their most beautiful productions. The most celebrated marble quarries are those of Carrara, in Italy, and of Paros, in Greece. Coloured marble, frequently containing variegated spots and veins, is much more common; it is employed for pedestals, columns, &c.; it is one of the most beautiful building materials, and is often imitated with coloured and polished gypsum (stucco). (*d.*) *Schiefer spar.* (*e.*) *Aphrite*, or *earth-foam.* (*f.*) *Compact limestone*, in which no crystalline structure is perceptible, and which generally occurs in large masses, forming entire limestone-hills. It is found in all later mountain formations, in the most varied forms and colours, as *stinkstone, marl, oolite* (*Roestone*), *calcareous tufa*, &c. (*g.*) *Chalk*, well known as the fine earthy white writing material, occurring in masses in the tertiary formations, particularly in England and in France (Champaigne).

(2.) *Arragonite*, the crystals of which belong to the rhombic system (fig. 13), and generally occur as rhombic prisms. The crystals are sometimes isolated, and often grown together, groups being thus frequently produced, which have the appearance of hexagonal prisms. Arragonite is cleavable; its fracture is conchoidal and uneven; H = 3 to 4; Sp. Gr. = 2·9 to 3; it is transparent, vitreous, and colourless. It is not unfrequently found in the vesicular cavities of basalt and other rocks. It occurs in groups of hexagonal prisms in Arragonia, whence its name is derived. Besides crystallised arragonite, we also find radiated and fibrous arragonite.

9th Group — BARIUM.

38. (1.) *Heavy spar*, or sulphate of baryta (BaO, SO_3), crystallises in rhombic prisms, of which there exist about 73 modifications; fig. 46 represents one of the tabular forms in which this mineral crystallises. It is perfectly cleavable, and exhibits an imperfect conchoidal fracture; H = 3 to

3·5, Sp. Gr. = 4·3 to 4·58, whereby it is easily distinguished from spathic minerals of nearly similar forms. It is transparent, and possesses double refractive power and vitreous lustre; it imparts a green colour to the blowpipe flame. A piece of heavy spar, when warmed, or heated to redness, will remain luminous in the dark for some time afterwards.

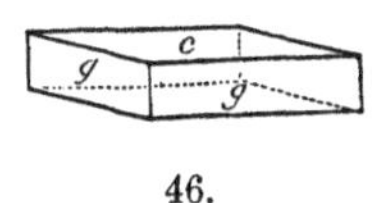

46.

Crystallised *heavy spar* is a mineral of frequent occurrence in mineral veins. It is employed as a white paint, and used to adulterate white-lead (Chemistry, § 83). Heavy spar also occurs radiated, fibrous, granular, compact, and earthy.

(2.) *Witherite*, or carbonate of baryta (BaO,CO_2), crystallises in regular rhombic prisms, and is principally found in this country. It is employed as the source of many of the other compounds of baryta; as, for instance, of chloride of barium, nitrate of baryta, &c.

10th Group — STRONTIUM.

39. (1.) *Celestine*, or sulphate of strontia (SrO,SO_3), crystallises in the rhombic system (fig. 13), the rhombic prism being the prevailing form. Its cleavage is perfect; its fracture conchoidal or uneven; H = 3 to 3·5; Sp. Gr. = 3·8 to 3·96; it is transparent, double refractive, colourless or white, of vitreous lustre, and imparts a *crimson colour* to the flame of the blowpipe. It does not occur very frequently. The varieties of this mineral are: — *celestine-spar*, *radiated celestine*, and *fibrous celestine*, which has a blue tint, and is found at Jena; and compact celestine, which contains from 8 to 9 per cent. of carbonate of lime. These minerals are employed for the preparation of strontia-salts (Chemistry, § 84).

(2.) *Strontianite*, or carbonate of strontia (SrO,CO_2), is of less frequent occurrence than the preceding mineral, and crystallises in the same system.

11th Group — MAGNESIUM.

40. This metal forms a rather larger group of minerals than the preceding metals. Among these may be mentioned *periclase*, which is nearly pure magnesia (MgO); hydrate of magnesia (MgO,HO); *boracite*, or phosphate of magnesia; and *hydroboracite*, containing, besides the latter substance, phosphate of lime and water. All these minerals occur but rarely, and in inconsiderable masses. *Sulphate of magnesia* (MgO,SO_3), is of more frequent occurrence; but, on account of its solubility, is only found as thin crusts or films of crystalline fibres in the clefts of rocks. In the Siberian steppes, however, whole districts are found covered with this and other magnesian salts. It is contained in large quantities in magnesian mineral waters, particularly in those of Epsom, Seidlitz, Eger, and Seidschütz.

Magnesite, carbonate of magnesia (MgO,CO_2), occurs either crystallised, as *magnesite spar* (talc-spar), or as compact magnesite. The former crystalltses in the hexagonal system, and is found in the form of obtuse rhombohedrons; H=4; Sp. Gr. = 3. The magnesian limestone, consisting of lime, magnesia, and carbonic acid ($CaO,CO_2 + MgO,CO_2$), is a mineral occurring in larger masses. Its crystalline variety is called *bitter spar*, and sometimes *brown spar*. It occurs in obtuse rhombohedrons, nearly resembling fig. 20, which are easily cleavable, and of conchoidal fracture; H = 3·5 to 4; Sp. Gr. = 2·8 to 3. It is semi-transparent, has a vitreous lustre, and is white, or frequently coloured yellow or brown by the presence of iron or manganese. It is principally found in clefts and cavities of the granular magnesio-calcite, called *Dolomite*. The white crystalline variety of Dolomite resembles marble, the coloured kinds are like common varieties of limestone; and as it occurs in large masses, it is employed for similar purposes.

The combinations of magnesia with silicic acid, form a particular class of minerals, of which *Talc* is a prominent member. This mineral contains 62 per cent. of silicic acid, 30 per cent. of magnesia, and occurs principally in aggregates of imperfect crystals. It is smooth and unctuous to the touch, is very soft, and is white or faintly coloured. It is found in quantities as chlorite slate. A variety of this mineral, called pot-stone, which may be cut and turned, is employed for the manufacture of various vessels. Besides the above, we shall mention, in connection with magnesia, the serpentine and augite minerals, which may be grouped into families.

1st Family — Serpentine.

41. This class comprises soft minerals, which may be cut with a knife, their hardness rarely exceeding 2·3. They do not occur in crystals, but are mostly opaque, difficultly fusible, and but slightly lustrous. They principally consist of magnesia and silicic acid, generally coloured by oxide of iron. To this family belongs the unctuous Steatite, or soap-stone, which is employed for removing grease-spots, or as a soft polishing powder, as also for the manufacture of a great variety of objects of art. The most common varieties are French chalk, and the well-known meerschaum, which is used for the manufacture of tobacco-pipes. *Serpentine*, which is called ophite, or snake-stone, on account of its green-spotted appearance, resembling the skin of a snake, forms compact masses of granular fracture, occurring as rocks. Its hardness is 3; it is employed for the manufacture of a number of objects, particularly columns, boxes, mixing-mortars for chemists and druggists, &c. There is moreover a large number of minerals resembling serpentine, which may be classed in this family.

2nd Family — Augites.

These minerals possess a hardness between 4·5 and 7, and a specific gravity of 2·8 to 3·5. Their prevailing colours are dark-green and black; they are fusible before the blowpipe. Their principal constituents are silica and magnesia, but some of them also contain considerable quantities of other oxides, such as sesquioxide of iron and alumina, which render it difficult to classify these minerals according to their chemical constituents. The augites occur in peculiar crystalline forms, and not unfrequently in considerable masses. They are also contained in many varieties of rocks, such as lava, basalt, &c. The most important members of this family are augite and hornblende, of which the various kinds are again distinguished by different names.

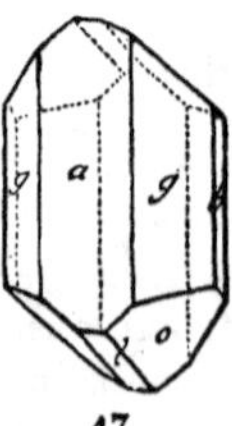

47.

Augite crystallises in prisms belonging to the fourth system; fig. 47 represents one of its usual forms: its different varieties occur principally in volcanic formations and their vicinities. The most notable are — *diopside, diallage, bronzite, hypersthene,* and *kokolite.*

Hornblende belongs to the same crystalline systems as the preceding mineral, with which it likewise exhibits similarity in its chemical composition and colour. *Asbestos, amianthus,* and *mountain cork,* must be viewed as varieties of hornblende, crystallised in exceedingly fine needles. The most pliable kinds of asbestos are mixed with flax, and woven into stuffs and cloths, from which the flax may be removed by simple ignition, and thus incombustible cloths are prepared, which may be worn in case of danger from fire. The dead bodies of the rich were, in ancient times, enveloped in such garments, and then burned; by which means their ashes were preserved.

12TH GROUP—ALUMINUM.

43. This group is exceedingly large and numerous, and must therefore be subdivided into families. Of these minerals there are only a few which contain the sesquioxide of aluminum, or alumina, as the chief constituent. It forms, however, the principal compound when in combination with silicic acid; and the large amount of the latter substance in a mineral, frequently renders it doubtful whether it should not rather be classed among the silicious than the aluminous group. This class contains a large number of minerals, which are important to the arts and to agriculture; it likewise includes the most precious jewels, next in value to the diamond itself.

1ST FAMILY—CORUNDUMS.

44. These minerals, consisting of pure alumina (Al_2O_3), occur in various forms. (1.) The crystallised variety is *sapphire,* which is found in various modifications of the hexagonal system. It is cleavable, and of conchoidal fracture; Sp. Gr. =4; H. =9; it is perfectly transparent, possesses a highly vitreous lustre, and beautiful blue colour; it is, however, also found of a red, green, yellow, and white colour; the red variety, which is called *ruby,* being very highly prized. [The yellow variety is called *topaz;* and the green, *emerald.*] The above properties render sapphire a very valuable gem: it occurs in small crystals in Germany, but the finest specimens are found in the East Indies, in diluvial soils and in the sand of rivers, which have their source in such formations. [A fine blue variety of sapphire occurs at Newton, N. J.; and well-defined crystals of bluish and pink colours are found at Warwick, N. Y.]

(2.) *Common corundum* is found in rough, scarcely translucent, dull, or dirty-coloured crystals, embedded in granitic rocks; being possessed of great hardness, it is reduced to powder, and employed for cutting and polishing other precious stones. (3.) *Emery* occurs in compact or granular masses, which are found in Saxony, in Greece, and in other localities, embedded in mica-slate. It is but slightly lustrous, and has a bluish-grey colour Its powder is frequently employed for cutting and polishing.

2ND FAMILY—ALUMS.

45. (1.) *Aluminite* (Al_2O_3,SO_3+9HO) is basic sulphate of alumina, and is found in small quantities as a white earthy mass. (2.) *Sulphate of*

alumina ($Al_2O_3,3SO_3+18HO$), termed also feather-alum, occurs in fibrous crystalline crusts, or in porous and compact masses. (3.) *Alum-stone*, consisting of alumina, potassa, and sulphuric acid, crystallises in the hexagonal system as rhombohedrons, and is found particularly in the vicinity of Rome, where it is employed for the preparation of Roman alum; which, as it contains no iron in chemical combination, was for a long time particularly prized, until the progress of Chemistry made us acquainted with other methods of preparing alum free from iron. (4.) *Alum* ($KO,SO_3+Al_2O_3,3SO_3+24HO$), with which we have become acquainted in the section Chemistry, § 87, occurs likewise in Nature, crystallised in regular octohedrons. It is an interesting fact, that various minerals exist which have a composition corresponding to that of alum, in which the potassa is replaced by other bases, without the form of the crystal being in the least altered. Thus we are acquainted with :—

Potassa-alum	=	$KO,SO_3 + Al_2O_3,3SO_3 + 24HO$.
Soda-alum	=	$NaO,SO_3 + Al_2O_3,3SO_3 + 24HO$.
Ammonia-alum	=	$NH_4O,SO_3 + Al_2O_3,3SO_3 + 24HO$.
Manganese-alum	=	$MnO,SO_3 + Al_2O_3,3SO_3 + 24HO$.

a series of compounds, the formulæ of which present the greatest similarity. Such compounds as the above, containing different constituents, but crystallising in the same form, are termed *isomorphous*, that is, of similar form: we shall meet with several other examples of isomorphism as we proceed.

Phosphate of alumina is likewise found in the crystalline form, and is called *Wavellite.*

3rd Family—Spinels.

46. These minerals are combinations of alumina and magnesia, and are represented by the formula MgO,Al_2O_3, in which the alumina occupies the place of an acid. They crystallise in regular octohedrons and in modifications of this form; they are distinguished by their hardness (H.=8; Sp. Gr.=3·8), lustre, and transparency, and are prized as valuable gems. Various kinds of spinel are distinguished by the colour: the scarlet variety, which is called *spinel ruby*, is the most highly prized; it occurs in the East Indies. Besides this variety, we are acquainted with blue, green, and black spinels

4th Family—Zeolites.

47. The *Zeolites*, or *boiling stones*, so called on account of their containing water, with which, when heated before the blowpipe, they part under *intumescence*, are mostly white, vitreous, and transparent; they possess a hardness of 3·5 to 3·6, and a specific gravity of from 2 to 3. Their principal constituent is silicate of alumina, which, in the different varieties, is combined with variable quantities of silicate of potassa, soda, and lime, and with water of crystallisation often in considerable quantities. Although these minerals are interesting on account of their chemical composition, and particularly the variety and peculiarity of their crystalline forms, there is no member of the family that is of any importance with regard to frequency of occurrence or technical application. We must confine ourselves to mentioning a few of the best known zeolites, such as *analcime*, *harmotome*, or cross-stone, so

called from the crystals often crossing each other at right angles, *stilbite*, *chabasite*, *mesotype*, *natrolite*, *prehnite*, *Thomsonite*, &c. Very beautiful specimens of all these minerals are found in cavities in the basaltic rocks near Kilpatrick and Kilmacolm, on the Clyde.

5TH FAMILY—CLAYS.

48. By the term *clay* is understood a chemical combination of silica with alumina (Al_2O_3,SiO_3), as has already been mentioned in Chemistry, § 87. The minerals of which clay is the principal constituent are either crystallised, possessing a hardness of about 7·5, transparent, and of vitreous lustre, or they are compact or earthy. All varieties of clay are difficultly fusible or perfectly infusible before the blowpipe. The more remarkable are:—

(1.) *Andalusite*, which occurs in regular rhombic prisms: H=7·5; Sp. Gr.=3·1 to 3·2: it is infusible and generally flesh-coloured. (2.) *Chiastolite*, so called (from the Greek) in allusion to its being marked with the Greek letter chi (X), visible on the cross-sections of the crystals. (3.) *Disthène*, which crystallises in columns, belongs to the 4th system, and acquires a bluish luminosity when gently heated: H. = 5 to 7; Sp. Gr. = 3·5 to 3·6.

The following are earthy clays, coloured red, yellow, or brown, by sesquioxide of iron or its hydrate: *Yellow ochre*, which is used as a colour. *Tripoli*, employed for polishing. *Bole*, or Lemnian earth, is a red clay, unctuous to the touch, and adheres to the tongue; it was formerly used in medicine, and is now employed as a colour, particularly for earthen utensils. *Terra de Sienna* is a brown clay, employed as a colour by artists and printers. *Lithomarge* occurs in fissures of various rocks.

The most valuable of all clays is the *porcelain earth*, or Kaolin, ($3Al_2O_3$, $4SiO_3 + 6HO$,) which, as will be seen hereafter, consists of disintegrated felspar, and forms large earthy masses, which are white, or only faintly tinted, and perfectly free from iron. This valuable material, which is used in the manufacture of porcelain, is found, though not frequently, in layers in granite and other rocks. Superior kinds are obtained from Cornwall, Schneeberg, Meissen in Saxony, Passau, Carlsbad, Limoges in France, and from many other places. That this earth is found in China and Japan is proved by the importation of the first porcelain from these empires, and also by the name Kaolin having been given to this mineral.

49. Common *clay* is, however, of far more importance to mankind than even porcelain earth. When somewhat similar to the latter, it is called porcelain clay; or pipe clay, if it is white; Potter's clay, if coloured and of coarser quality. All clays are unctuous to the touch and adhere to the tongue, since they absorb and retain water with great avidity. They absorb fat and oil still more powerfully, and are hence employed for removing grease-spots. Clay is also possessed of a peculiar odour, which arises from its property of absorbing ammonia from the atmosphere. Clay is infusible, and blocks of burnt clay are therefore employed, under the name of fire-bricks, for building structures, which are to sustain a high temperature, such as porcelain furnaces, blast furnaces, glass furnaces, &c. Earthy clay is employed for the manufacture of various kinds of pottery (Chemistry

§ 88). When clay contains lime in admixture it loses its peculiar properties, particularly its infusibility; it then passes into marl and loam.

In concluding our description of this family, mention must be made of *agalmatolite*, a clay-stone, out of which the Chinese carve their idols (Pagodas), and produce figures which give us anything but a sublime conception of a deity.

6TH FAMILY — FELSPARS.

50. The name *spar* is very old, and was probably chosen to indicate a cleavable crystallised mineral. The minerals of this class bear a great similarity in their composition to the zeolites, if the water contained in the latter be disregarded. Their hardness reaches to 7, their specific gravity to 3·3. They are mostly possessed of vitreous lustre, are generally coloured, and difficultly fusible before the blowpipe. The most remarkable are as follow:—

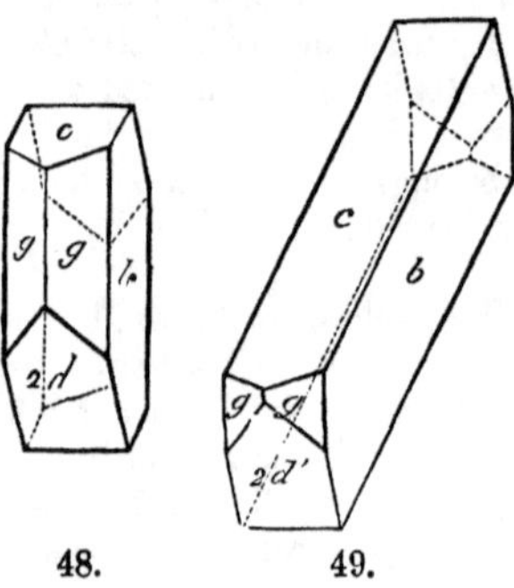

48. 49.

(1.) *Felspar* ($KO,SiO_3+Al_2O_3,3SiO_3$), which crystallises in prisms of a great variety of forms, belonging to the oblique rhombic system of crystallisation (fig. 14). Figs. 48 and 49 represent two of its usual crystals. It is easily cleavable, and has an uneven fracture; H.=6; Sp. Gr.=2·5: it is transparent, of vitreous lustre, white or flesh-coloured, and occasionally green. It occurs in aggregations of well-defined crystals, as also in large crystalline masses. It is found most frequently as a constituent of various kinds of rocks, particularly of granite, gneiss, and syenite, which renders it of particular importance. A bluish-green felspar, of peculiar internal nacreous lustre, is termed *adularia*, or *moonstone*. The amorphous, compact felspar is called felspar rock, or *felsite*. This forms likewise a principal constituent of various rocks.

(2.) *Albite* ($NaO,SiO_3+Al_2O_3,3SiO_3$) is felspar, containing soda instead of potassa. It is likewise an important constituent of many rocks. *Spodumene*, or oligoklase, is similar in composition. *Labradorite* is remarkable for its opaline reflections, of a blue, yellow, or red hue, somewhat resembling the colours observed on the breasts of pigeons, and on many butterflies. Besides these varieties, we may mention *anorthite*, *leucite*, *nepheline*, *sodalite*, and *hauyne*.

(3.) *Lazulite*, or *Lapis-lazuli*, is distinguished by its magnificent blue colour. It is found in Siberia, Thibet, and China, and is extensively employed in jewellery for ornamental works; and, when properly prepared, is used as a beautiful pigment, under the name of *ultramarine*. Since, however, chemists have become accurately acquainted with the constitution of this mineral, they have succeeded in preparing the above colours artificially. (Chemistry, § 89.)

The following minerals appear to be mixtures of silicic acid and felspar, which have become fused together, by a high temperature, to vitreous, slaggy, or spongy masses. *Obsidian* occurs in black, blue, or greenish-black vitreous masses, and is employed for the manufacture of ornaments, such as boxes, buttons, &c. The South Americans employ this mineral for the manufacture of knives, weapons, &c. *Pumice-stone*, which is found in stream-like layers in the vicinity of volcanos, is very porous, fibrous, and vitreous, and is employed, as is well known, for cutting and polishing, particularly softer objects, since its hardness is only = 4·5. *Pearlstone* and *pitchstone* likewise belong to this family.

7TH FAMILY — GARNETS.

51. This family embraces minerals of very remarkable crystalline forms; they do not, however, occur in large quantities, and are not applicable to the arts, excepting to jewellery. Their hardness varies from 5 to 7·5; their Sp. Gr. from 2·6 to 4·3. They are mostly coloured and fusible before the blowpipe. Besides *Wernerite* and *Axinite*, the latter remarkable for the peculiar form of its crystals, fig. 17, *Tourmaline*, or schorl is particularly worthy of mention. The latter crystallises in very complicated forms, which are derived from an obtuse rhombohedron of the hexagonal system. The usual forms are six-sided prisms, so much distorted as to resemble three-sided prisms, generally perfect only at one end. Its chemical composition cannot be well expressed by a formula; it contains many constituents, among which are boracic acid, alumina, and silicic acid. It is worthy of mention, that a crystal of tourmaline, when warmed, becomes negatively electric at one extremity and positively electric at the other. Tourmalines are found of all colours: the transparent green and brown crystals are employed in the investigation of certain phenomena of light.—It may be remarked of *Staurolite* that its crystals frequently occur in regularly-formed crosses (fig. 50).—The best-known mineral of this group is *Garnet*, which crystallises in beautiful rhombic dodecahedrons (fig. 51), belonging to the regular system. It consists of silicate of alumina, combined with another silicate of a metallic oxide, generally lime or iron, but which varies exceedingly, so that a whole series of different garnets are known, like the alums (§ 45), corresponding pretty accurately in their physical characters; and many of them occurring together in the same mass. Garnets are very imperfectly cleavable, their fracture is conchoidal, H. = 6·5 to 7·5; Sp. Gr. = 3·5 to 4·2; they are mostly transparent, and occur of all colours. The beautiful deep-red garnet (*Precious* Garnet) is the most highly-prized variety, and in great request for necklaces, ear-rings, &c. The greater number of garnets come from the neighbourhood of Kulm in Bohemia. *Pyrope*, *Idocrase*, and *Epidote* are other remarkable minerals which belong to this family.

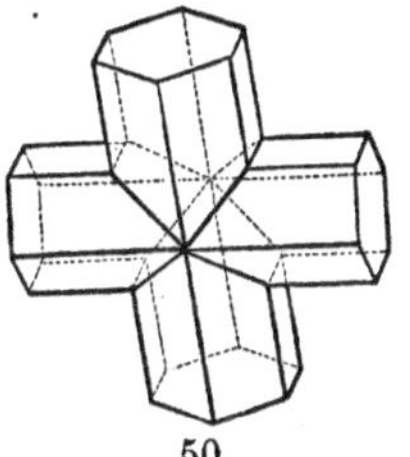

50.

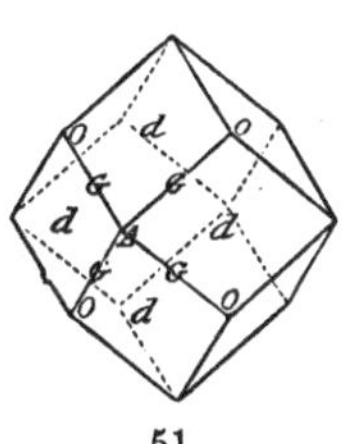

51.

8TH FAMILY—MICA.

52. The greater number of the minerals of this family are crystallised in small thin laminæ, of pearly lustre. These laminæ are very cleavable, pliable,

and possessed of a low degree of hardness; hence the varieties of mica are smooth and unctuous to the touch. Their chemical composition cannot be expressed by a formula: silica and alumina are the predominant constituents; many of the varieties contain, however, a considerable quantity of magnesia. Mica is often colourless, sometimes coloured, particularly green and black.

Common or *Potassa Mica* is very largely distributed, particularly in various rocks—for instance, in granite, gneiss, and mica-slate, in which it is observable as lustrous laminæ. It occurs in Siberia in very large plates, which are employed instead of glass for windows. Of the various kinds of mica we may mention *chlorite,* remarkable for its fine green colour, which it imparts to those kinds of stones of which it is a constituent, for instance, to *chlorite slate. Lepidolite,* or Rose Mica, which contains lithia, belongs to this family.

9TH FAMILY—GEMS.

53. This class embraces all minerals that possess properties which adapt them to the purposes of the jeweller—hardness, beauty of colour, brilliancy of lustre, rarity, &c. We have already spoken of the diamond, the ruby, and the sapphire. The other minerals of this family have a hardness of from 7·5 to 8·5, and a Sp. Gr. of from 2·8 to 4·6: they are transparent, difficulty fusible or infusible, and generally exhibit beautiful colours. Among them may be mentioned *topaz,* which is generally of a fine yellow colour; *pale green chrysoberyl: emerald,* remarkable for its beautiful green colour; and *zircon,* of which the hyacinth-coloured variety is most prized, and has received the name of *hyacinth.* The crystals of the two first-named minerals belong to the rhombic system, and those of the emerald to the hexagonal system. Fig. 41, is the usual natural form of the emerald.

SECOND ORDER.—HEAVY METALS.

13TH GROUP—IRON.

54. Iron forms a very important group, both from the great number of ferruginous minerals that exist and from the large masses in which they occur. Their Sp. Gr. ranges to 8·0; the greater number is opaque and coloured, and possesses the hardness of quartz. They are attracted by the magnet, and yield, with borax, a dark-red glass in the outer blow-pipe flame, and a bottle-green glass in the inner flame. Regarding their application to the production of iron, sufficient details have been given in the section Chemistry (§ 90). The most important minerals of this group are:—

(1.) *Native Iron,* occurring rarely in layers or veins of inconsiderable thickness, or in grains and laminæ. The most remarkable variety is the *meteoric iron,* consisting of masses of native iron which have fallen from the atmosphere, and which weigh from 171 to 3000, or even 14,000 pounds. Mention may be made here of the *meteoric stones,* which contain, with few exceptions, native iron, besides other earthy constituents, such as augite, hornblende, olivine, &c. [Native Iron, supposed to be of terrestrial origin, has been observed at Canaan, Conn., where it occurs in a vein two inches thick.]

(2.) *Magnetic Iron Ore* ($FeO+Fe_2O_3$), *Oxidulated iron,* crystallises in regular octohedrons (fig. 1, and often in macles, fig. 52). It is remarkable for its magnetic properties: it also occurs in compact masses of considerable magnitude, forming entire mountain strata. It is one of the most highly-prized ores of iron, being used chiefly for the production of steel. [Nearly all the celebrated iron mines of Sweden consist of magnetic iron. Very extensive beds of it occur in New York, and in the mountainous districts of New Jersey and Pennsylvania.]

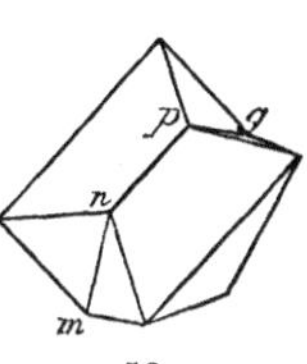

52.

(3.) *Red Iron Ore, Specular Iron Ore, Sesquioxide of Iron* (Fe_2O_3), or *Red Hæmatite*, crystallises in the hexagonal system as a rhombohedron and its derivatives. It is possessed of bright metallic lustre and red streak, and likewise yields a red powder. It occurs in various forms, as crystallised *iron glance*, micaceous iron, fibrous hæmatite, bloodstone, and also as compact, scaly, and earthy red ironstone, the latter of which is also called *red iron ochre*. If it contains an admixture of clay, it is called in Germany *red clay ironstone;* but this is not the important ore which is called *clay ironstone* in Scotland. These minerals are important as iron ores, and are also employed in small quantities as polishing materials and as colours.

(4.) *Brown Iron Ore* (Hydrated Sesquioxide of Iron, $Fe_2O_3 + 2HO$) does not occur in a distinctly crystalline form. The fibrous brown ironstone, however, consists of fine capillary crystals, radiating from a centre, and forming spherical and botryoidal masses. Besides this variety there is the compact and earthy brown ironstone, which, by containing clay, forms the transition member to the brown and yellow clay ironstones, of which we may mention the yellow ochre and umber, both used as colours. *Pea iron ore*, and *Morass ore*, the ironstone which is deposited in morasses, belong to this class; the latter is less valuable for the amount of iron it contains than the foregoing.

55. Iron occurs combined with sulphur in various proportions, generally as fine crystallised minerals, of a brass-like lustre, which are called *pyrites*. Of these we may mention:—

(5.) *Magnetic iron Pyrites* ($Fe_2S_3 + 5FeS$), which crystallises in six-sided prisms and is attracted by the magnet.

(6.) *Iron Pyrites* (FeS_2), crystallises in the regular system, particularly as a pentagonal dodecahedron (fig. 10) and its modifications; its Hardness is = 6 to 6.5, hence it produces sparks when struck with steel. It occurs very plentifully, and sometimes in very fine laminæ and grains, in coal for instance, and yields protosulphate of iron when oxidised by exposure to the air, particularly in the presence of water (Chemistry, § 93). This salt occurs in the mineral kingdom under the name of *Green Vitriol*.

56. The remaining ferruginous minerals, of which there is still a large number, are most of them of little importance with regard to the quantity in which they occur, and likewise in their applications; we will therefore limit ourselves to a few of the most remarkable: — *Vivianite*, or blue iron ore (phosphate of iron), *green ironstone*, which is the same chemical compound, containing water of hydration, and the series of combinations of arsenic with iron, called *arsenical pyrites*, which possesses a white metallic

lustre. Of the latter may be mentioned *arsenical iron*, *scorodite*, *pharmacosiderite*, and arsenical iron pyrites, which is also termed *mispickel.*

Carbonate of Iron (FeO, CO_2) occurs in larger quantities; when crystallised it is called *Spathic ironstone.* It forms very obtuse rhombohedrons. This ore is admirably suited for the production of steel. It is also found in the fibrous form, and is then called *sphærosiderite.* The *Clay ironstone* of the Scotch metallurgists consists of carbonate of iron, in combination with variable quantities of carbonate of lime, clay, &c. It is a mineral of great importance.

The *green earth*, which is employed as a colour under the name of *Veronese green*, is silicate of sesquioxide of iron with lime and a little magnesia. *Chrome iron* ($FeO + Cr_2O_3$), which consists of sesquioxide of chromium and protoxide of iron, occurs generally massive, granular, or crystalline, and is important, as being the mineral from which the compounds of chromium are prepared (Chemistry, § 103).

14th Group — MANGANESE.

57. This metal generally occurs as oxide; and, in addition to its being the principal constituent of several minerals, is found in many others in smaller quantities as their colouring matter. The fused minerals are generally coloured violet, whilst the massive minerals are usually brown or black. The most important varieties are:—

Pyrolusite (Binoxide of Manganese, MnO_2), which occurs crystallised in regular rhombic prisms, but is most generally found in crystalline masses consisting of aggregates of acicular crystals. Its colour and streak are black; its Hardness is = 2 to 2·5; its Sp. Gr. = 4·9. The valuable application of this mineral to the preparation of chlorine has already been referred to (Chemistry, § 35).

Hausmannite (Proto-sesquioxide of Manganese, $MnO + Mn_2O_3$), which crystallises in quadratic octohedrons, is brownish black or black, produces a brownish-red streak, and occurs generally associated with pyrolusite.

Braunite, or Protoxide of Manganese, has the same crystalline form as hausmannite; its colour and streak are both dark-brownish black. The value of pyrolusite is naturally much decreased by an admixture of these two minerals; hence, in purchasing this mineral for practical purposes in the arts, particular attention must be paid to the colour and streak.

Nanganite (Hydrated Oxide of Manganese) is of little importance in the arts. Sulphide of Manganese, or prismatic *Manganese Blende*, Silicate of Manganese, Carbonate of Manganese, or Red Manganese, and many other minerals of this family, have not received any application in the arts.

15th Group — COBALT.

58. The minerals of this scarce metal are mostly sulphuretted or arsenical compounds. They are opaque and coloured, and furnish a blue glass with borax before the blowpipe. The most important are: Sulphide of Cobalt (Cobalt Pyrites, Co_2S_3), possessing a white colour, a metallic lustre, and crystallising in regular octohedrons; *Arsenical Cobalt* (Speiscobalt, $CoAs_2$), occurring in cubes, of a white colour, and metallic lustre, in the Erzgebirge in Saxony; *Arsenical Cobalt Pyrites* ($CoAs_3$); *Cobalt Bloom*, or hydrated arsenite of Cobalt; *Cobaltine*, or white cobalt ($CoS_2, CoAs_2$),

crystallising as pentagonal dodecahedrons, with metallic lustre, and pinkish colour; and, finally, *Earthy Cobalt*, occurring massive or earthy, and of a black colour. The latter contains a mixture of oxide of cobalt, with a considerable quantity of oxides of manganese, copper, and iron. All these minerals are employed for the preparation of cobalt, and especially of the cobalt glass called Smalts (Chemistry, § 95).

16th Group—NICKEL.

59. The minerals of this group are not of more frequent occurrence than those of the preceding group, and they usually occur under similar circumstances. They also generally contain a small admixture of cobalt, sufficient to furnish a blue glass with borax. The most important are:—

Sulphide of Nickel (NiS) which occurs in capillary or acicular crystals; *Red Arsenical Nickel* (Kupfer nickel NiAs), occurring but rarely crystallised, generally massive, dendritic, or botryoidal, and possessing a copper-red metallic lustre; *White Arsenical Nickel* ($NiAs_2$), of tin-white metallic lustre; *Nickel Ochre*, or arseniate of nickel; *Nickel Glance*, or white nickel ore ($NiS_2 + NiAs_2$) of grey metallic lustre. Nickel also occurs in combination with several metals; for instance, it is associated with antimony as antimonial nickel (NiSb), antimonial nickel pyrites ($NiS_2 + NiSb_2$), *bismuth nickel pyrites*, and nickel iron pyrites.

All these minerals are but impure chemical compounds, containing always more or less iron, copper, cobalt, lead, &c. Nickel ores are employed for the production of nickel, which is extensively used in the manufacture of German silver. They are found in the Erzgebirge, and also at Riechelsdorf in Hesse.

17th Group—COPPER.

60. This metal forms a large group of minerals, as it occurs not only in great masses, but also in the most manifold combinations. Only a comparatively small number, however, are employed for the production of copper. The Hardness of the minerals of this group ranges from 2 to 4, and their Sp. Gr. to 6; they yield metallic copper before the blowpipe. The following are the most important:—

(1.) *Native Copper*, which seldom exhibits a crystalline form, but generally occurs in peculiar arborescent or moss-like formations. It is frequently found in considerable masses, and is worked for copper. [Native copper is found throughout the red sand-stone region of the United States, particularly in Massachusetts, Connecticut, and New Jersey: but no known locality of the world exceeds the Lake Superior copper region in the abundance of native copper. One large mass recently laid open at the "Cliff Mine" has been estimated to weigh 80 tons.]

Red Oxide of Copper (suboxide of copper, Cu_2O) crystallises very beautifully in distinct crystals of many forms of the octohedral system, namely, the cube (fig. 3), the octohedron (fig. 1), the rhombic dodecahedron (fig. 7), the triakisoctohedron (fig. 55), and in many combinations of these forms, as in fig. 53, where the dodecahedron predominates over the octohedron, and fig. 51, where the octohedron predominates over the dodecahedron. Fig. 2 also presents one of the numerous varieties of this mineral.

This mineral has a beautiful red colour, but it is generally coated with green. It yields a very fine copper [and has been observed crystallized and massive at Schuylers, Somerville, and Flemington copper mines, N. J.].

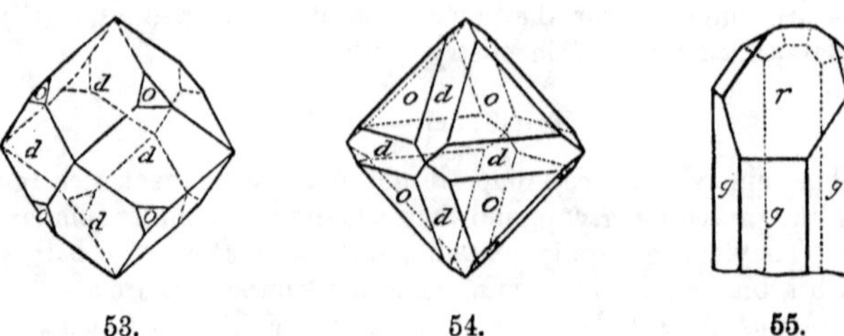

53. 54. 55.

Vitreous Copper (Sulphide of Copper, CuS) [or *Copper Glance*] occurs in tabular rhombic prisms of blackish lead-grey metallic lustre, and is worked for copper.

The soluble salts of copper produced in small quantities by the decomposition of other copper ores, particularly of sulphide of copper, are of little importance. They are found principally in the neighbourhood of volcanos, from the fissures of which vapours issue containing hydrochloric and sulphurous acids. Of these salts may be mentioned: sulphate of copper (blue vitriol CuO,SO_3), various phosphates and arseniates of copper, chloride of copper, &c.

The two following may be classed among the most beautiful productions of the mineral kingdom:—

(1.) *Malachite*, or Carbonate of Copper (CuO,CO_2+HO), which crystallises in oblique rhombic prisms, generally uniting into fibrous radiating groups, possesses a fine emerald-green colour, and silky lustre. It also occurs massive and earthy, and is employed for ornamental purposes, and as a pigment; and where it occurs in larger quantities, as in Australia, it is worked for copper.

(2.) *Blue Carbonate of Copper* (azure copper ore) is carbonate of copper combined with hydrated oxide of copper, and occurs either in short prismatic or tabular crystals, or massive and earthy. This mineral is remarkable for its beautiful blue colour, and is hence employed as a pigment. The *Silicate of Copper* ($3CuO,2SiO_3$), Chrysocolla, has a fine green colour.

The minerals in which copper exists in combination with other metals, and in which sulphur is usually a constituent, form a far more numerous group, of which we may mention Bismuthic Sulphide of Copper (needle ore), Antimonial Sulphide of Copper and Lead (Bournonite), Tin Pyrites and *Purple Copper* (Buntkupfererz). The last is a mixture of sulphides of copper and iron. It crystallises in regular octohedrons, and in the forms represented by figs. 3, 52, 2, 4, and 5. It has the lustre of brass, but generally presents the most beautiful variegations of blue and red. The *Sulphide of Copper* (Copper Pyrites $CuS + FeS$) crystallises in quadratic octohedrons, and bears much similarity to the last-mentioned mineral. It is the most abundant of all the ores of copper, and, like the purple copper, is frequently smelted.

In concluding our enumeration of copper minerals, we may mention ***Fahl***

Ore (grey copper ore), which crystallises in the regular octohedral system, but usually occurs in very complicated hemihedral combinations, of which the double tetrahedron (fig. 56) is one of the simplest. It possesses a grey metallic lustre: its principal constituents are copper, antimony, sulphur, and arsenic, with variable quantities of iron, zinc, and silver. Hence several varieties of this mineral are produced. They are all worked for copper, and the richer specimens for silver.

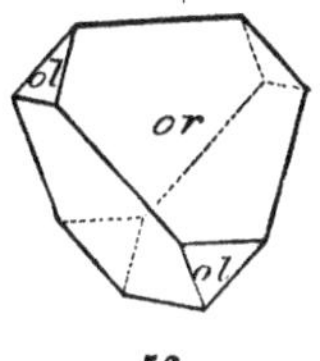

56.

18th Group—BISMUTH.

61. The minerals of this metal are of secondary importance with regard to their distribution and number. Some of the most important are:—*Native Bismuth*, which occurs in regular octohedrons, possessing a reddish silvery lustre; H. = 2 to 2·5; and Sp. Gr. = 9·7; *Bismuth Ochre*, or sesquioxide of bismuth, (Bi_2O_3,) occurs in company with the former, particularly in the mountains of Saxony; *Bismuthine*, or sesquisulphide of bismuth (Bi_2S_3) crystallises in rhombic prisms, of a lead-grey metallic lustre. Bismuth Blende consists of silicate of bismuth, and possesses the highest specific gravity of all the ores of this group (5·9). Bismuth has met with but few applications. It is a usual ingredient of fusible alloys.

19th Group—LEAD.

62. This metal rarely occurs in the native state, but generally in combination either with oxygen or sulphur in minerals of low degrees of hardness, but of high specific gravity (4·6 to 8). These combinations yield metallic lead, or the yellow oxide, with great facility before the blow-pipe. Many of the minerals of this group occur only in inconsiderable quantities, such as *native lead*, *minium*, or lead ochre, *chloride of lead*, and many others.

On the other hand the *Sulphide of Lead*, or *Galena* (PbS), is the most abundant mineral of this group, and is the one which is principally worked for lead. With the applications of this metal we have already become acquainted. Galena crystallises in the regular system, particularly in tubes, octohedrons, and trakisoctohedrons, and the various modifications of these forms; it likewise occurs in compact masses, which are more or less finely granulated or dense. This mineral is always distinguished by its high specific gravity (reaching to 67·), its grey colour, brilliant metallic lustre, and easy cubical cleavage.

Galena frequently contains silver, in sufficient quantity to render it worth extracting (Chem. § 107). It is likewise occasionally found to contain gold, antimony, iron, and arsenic.

[The most extensive deposits of Galena in the United States are met with in Missouri, Illinois, Iowa and Wisconsin.]

An extensive series of minerals is formed by the combination of lead, antimony, and sulphur, in various proportions. Of these we may mention *Zinkenite*, *Jamesonite*, Sulphide of Antimony and Lead, &c., most of which are named after the discoverers.

Of the native Salts of Lead we may mention sulphate of lead (PbO,SO_3), which crystallises in rhombic prisms, and is distinguished by its brilliant lustre and white colour; White Lead ore, or Carbonate of Lead, which crystallises in regular rhombic prisms, and is remarkable for its adamantine lustre and double refractive power. We shall pass over the combinations of lead with the rarer elements, merely mentioning Chromate of Lead (Chem. § 103), which occurs in a beautiful crystalline form in the Uralian mountains.

20TH GROUP—TIN.

63. Tin does not occur native, but generally as *Tinstone*, which is the binoxide of this metal (SnO_2). This mineral crystallises in quadratic octohedrons, the modifications of which are frequently found in twin crystals. They vary from semi-transparency to opacity, possess a high lustre, are sometimes white, but more generally coloured, and sometimes even black. *Fibrous Tin Ore*, which likewise consists of binoxide of tin, occurs in much larger masses, of delicately fibrous structure. Cornwall and the East Indies are particularly rich in tin ores, the metal from which may easily be obtained by fusion with charcoal.

21ST GROUP—ZINC.

64. Oxide of Zinc is occasionally found in the form of crystalline masses of a red colour, and is called *Red Oxide of Zinc.* [Red zinc ore occurs at Franklin and Stirling, N. J.] A much more plentiful mineral of this group is *Zinc Blende*, which consists of zinc and sulphur (ZnS). It crystallises in the regular system, its most usual forms being the rhombic dodecahedron (fig. 7), the cube (fig. 3), the octohedron (fig. 1), the tetrahedrons (figs. 8 and 56), the macle (fig. 52), and the complex form represented by fig. 57, in which the cube is modified by the planes of the rhombic dodecahedron (fig. 7), and the tetrahedron (fig. 9). The fracture of zinc blende is conchoidal; H. = 3·5 to 4; Sp. Gr. 4·1; it possesses an adamantine lustre. Its colour is green, yellow, red, brown, or black. It is worked for zinc, and occurs laminated, fibrous, radiated, and massive.

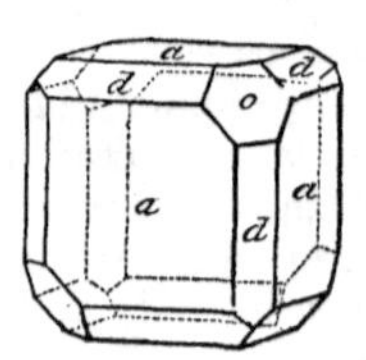

57.

Sulphate of Zinc (ZnO,SO_3) is also found, though only in small quantities, but the Carbonate of Zinc, or *zinc spar*, occurs more frequently. The latter crystallises in the hexagonal system, in the form of rhombohedrons; it possesses a vitreous lustre, and is generally white or only slightly coloured. It is employed chiefly in the manufacture of brass; *Calamine* (silicious oxide of zinc) is the most common mineral of this group, and is employed for the same purpose; it consists of oxide of zinc and silicic acid, and crystallises in rhombic prisms. This mineral is possessed of a remarkable lustre, and is either white or slightly yellow. When heated, the crystals of this mineral exhibit polaric electricity in a remarkable degree, and likewise acquire luminous properties by friction.

22ND GROUP—CHROMIUM.

65. It is highly remarkable that this metal, of which the chemist prepares a great number of the most beautifully coloured compounds, should only occur in a comparatively small number of natural combinations. This may in some measure explain the circumstance of chromium having been dis-

covered so recently as 1797. In addition to Chromate of Lead (§ 61), and Chrome Iron ore (§55), already referred to, we have only to mention *Chrome Ochre* (sesquioxide of chromium, Cr_2O_3), which occurs but rarely and in small quantities. There are, however, several other minerals which contain a small quantity of chromium.

23RD GROUP—ANTIMONY.

66. The minerals of the antimony-group are possessed of Hardness reaching as high as 6·6; and a Sp. Gr. = 4. Before the blowpipe they yield white vapours, which form a bluish-white incrustation upon charcoal. The rarer minerals of this group are:—*Native Antimony, White Antimony* (teroxide of antimony, SbO_3), and *Antimonial Ochre* ($SbO_4 + AO$).

The *Tersulphide of Antimony* (SbS_3) occurs more abundantly, and is a combination of antimony with sulphur, which crystallises in the prismatic system. Its crystals are mostly long, columnar, and acicular, aggregated together, and generally possess a lead-grey metallic lustre. This mineral is employed in the preparation of metallic antimony, and is also used in medicine.

Red Antimony is a compound of oxide with sulphide of antimony, and is distinguished by its cherry-red colour, and the adamantine lustre of its acicular crystals; it is one of the rarer ores of this metal.

24TH GROUP—ARSENIC.

67. This poisonous metal occurs in many metallic compounds, with the greater number of which we have already become acquainted, for example with Arsenical Iron, Arsenical Cobalt, Arsenical Nickel, &c. The minerals of the arsenic-group yield white fumes before the blowpipe, which have a powerful odour of garlic. The white fumes consist of the highly poisonous arsenious acid. The odour is produced by vaporised metallic arsenic. The most remarkable minerals of this group are:—

Native Arsenic, which is not of unfrequent occurrence; it is generally found in nodular masses not crystallised. It posssesses a tin-white, or grey-metallic lustre, but soon becomes black by exposure to the air; H. = 3·5; Sp. Gr. 5 7. It frequently occurs mixed with antimony and silver.

Oxide of Arsenic (AsO_3) may be considered as a product of the preceding mineral, occurring only in inconsiderable quantities, and generally in irregular forms, having an adamantine lustre and whitish colour.

Realgar (AsS_2), is the lower sulphide of arsenic; it crystallises in oblique rhombic prisms, but also occurs in compact masses. It has a pearly lustre, a bright red colour, and gives a yellow streak. It is employed as a colour, and as a constituent of the white fire in pyrotechny. *Orpiment* (AsS_3) is the higher sulphide of arsenic, which is rarely found in the crystallised state, but generally in uniform masses; its lustre is pearly, and its colour bright lemon yellow; it is hence employed as a pigment (Chem. § 45).

25TH GROUP—MERCURY.

68. Although liquid, this metal occurs native, and is found in the form of larger or smaller globules in the cavities and fissures of clay slate, and carboniferous sandstone, as, for instance, at Moshellandsberg in Rhenish Bavaria. The greater quantity of mercury, however, is obtained from

Native Cinnabar (HgS), which occurs in botryoidal and compact masses, H. = 2·5; Sp. Gr = 8. Cinnabar is opaque, and of adamantine lustre; it possesses a carmine colour, and gives a bright scarlet streak. It becomes black on being heated, but reassumes its red colour on cooling. The principal localities in which it is found are Rhenish Bavaria, Almaden in Spain, Idria in Carniola, Mexico, China, and California.

Native Chloride of Mercury, $HgCl$, is a mineral of less frequent occurrence. The mixture of cinnabar, carbon, and earthy matter, occurring in Idria, is called liver ore, or hepatic cinnabar.

26th Group — SILVER.

69. This is one of the more frequent metals, occurring native, as well as in a great variety of minerals, alloyed with other metals, or combined with arsenic and sulphur. Silver ores yield metallic silver when heated before the blowpipe alone, or with carbonate of soda.

Native Silver occurs either in small crystals, of the cubical system, in crystalline groups, or in a great variety of curious forms, sometimes arborescent or like moss, as also in laminæ, irregular masses, and grains. H. = 2·5 to 3; Sp. Gr. = 10·3. It possesses the common properties of silver; it is, however, generally tarnished of a yellowish or brown colour. It is found in most countries; in Germany it occurs with other silver ores, particularly in the Saxon Erzegebirge. The most important ores that are worked for silver are the following:—

Sulphide of Silver, or Vitreous Silver (AgS), crystallises in the cubical system, but occurs more frequently in irregular forms, of a grey or black colour, and metallic lustre. It is also found as an earthy mineral, under the name of *Black Sulphide of Silver.*

Antimonial Silver, containing from 70 to 80 per cent. of silver, occurs in modifications of the rhombic prism. It has a silvery or yellow metallic lustre, but is more generally coated with a black tarnish.

Brittle Sulphide of Silver is a combination of the sulphides of silver and antimony, containing about 70 per cent. of silver. It occurs in regular rhombic prisms and irregular masses, possessing a metallic lustre and an iron-black colour. The most important silver ore, however, is *Ruby Silver*, which consists of silver, antimony, sulphur, and arsenic. It crystallises in modifications of the rhombohedron, has an adamantine lustre, a colour ranging from iron-black to crimson, and produces a beautiful crimson streak. H. = 2·5 to 3; Sp. Gr. = 5·5 to 5·8. It contains from 58 to 64 per cent. of silver.

Sulphide of Silver and Copper contains about 52 per cent. of silver, and occurs in blackish-grey crystals of the rhombic system, possessing metallic lustre.

Besides these we may mention the names of several minerals, which occur more rarely, and are therefore of secondary importance. Chloride of silver (hornsilver), bromide of silver, carbonate of silver, bismuthic silver, sternbergite, polybasite, and many others.

27th Group — GOLD.

70. It is indeed highly remarkable, that the more precious the metals the more they appear to be isolated and separated from the other mineral sub-

stances of common occurrence, in the same manner as men of a higher order of intellect, seek to stand aloof from those endowed with capacities of a lowet cast. Thus gold is generally found native, either crystallised in the several modifications of the regular system, as represented by figures 1 to 9, and 58, 59, and 60, or in the most varied shapes, such as dentritic, capillary,

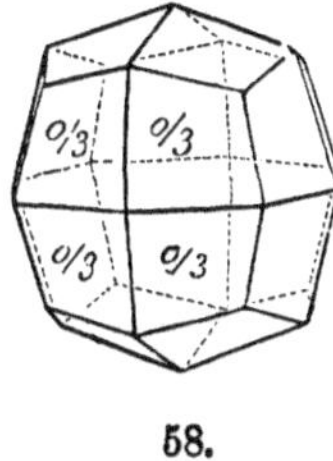

58.

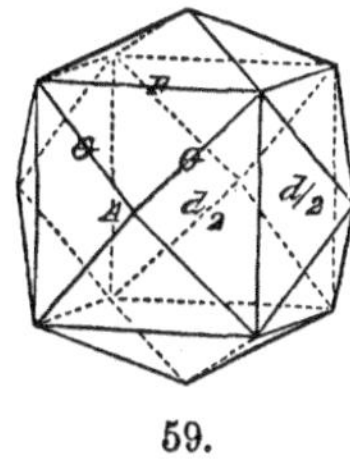

59.

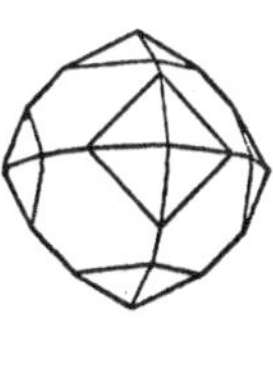

60.

arborescent, foliaceous, &c. It is likewise found in irregular masses and grains, and finally as sand and dust; it exists in the two latter forms disseminated in various kinds of rocks, such as granite, &c., and owing to their disintegration, it finds its way into the sand of rivers, and the rubble-stones of alluvial soils.

As the specific gravity of gold in this state is as high as 19·4, the smallest grains may be separated from sand by washing, the gold being immediately deposited.

Silver is the metal which occurs most frequently associated with gold; natural alloys of these two metals are found, containing from 0·16 to 38·7 per cent. of silver, which causes a considerable difference both of colour and density. In addition to this alloy, we may mention *sylvanite* (graphic tellurium) which contains, besides gold and silver, one of the rarer metals, viz., tellurium.

Europe in general is poor in gold; the only rich gold mines are at Kremnitz, in Hungary. The East Indies, South America, California, Australia, and the Ural mountains, are rich in this metal, pieces of gold of considerable size having been found in these localities: in the year 1842 a mass weighing 86 pounds was found in the gold-sand district of Alexandrowsk, near Miask, [and still more considerable masses have recently been furnished by California and Australia.] Pieces of 23 to 24 pounds weight are not unfrequently met with. The most important rivers of Germany, in which gold is found, are the Rhine, the Danube, the Isar, and the Inn.

28th Group — PLATINUM.

71. Platinum is likewise found only in the native state; it generally occurs in nodular pieces and grains, and but rarely in the crystalline form, as cubes. It is frequently alloyed with other metals, more particularly with iron, of which as much as from 5 to 11 per cent. is sometimes present. The specific gravity of native platinum is from 17 to 18; its colour is steel-grey. It was first discovered in Spanish America, where it received the name of platina, signifying *similar to silver* (plata being the name of silver). It was afterwards found in quantities in the Ural mountains, where it occurs

in alluvial formations, but more frequently in the rubble-stones of serpentine rocks. Masses weighing from 10 to 20 pounds have been found in these localities.

THIRD CLASS. MINERALS OF ORGANIC COMPOUNDS.

29TH GROUP — SALTS.

72. As belonging to this small group of minerals we may mention *Humboldtine* consisting of oxalate of protoxide of iron; and *honeystone* or mellite, a combination of alumina with an acid, consisting of carbon and oxygen (of the formula C_3O_4), which has been named after the mineral mellitic acid. This mineral has received its name from its peculiar honey-yellow colour; it crystallises in transparent, quadratic octohedrons, similar to figures 61 and 62. Both minerals are of rare occurrence, and of little practical importance

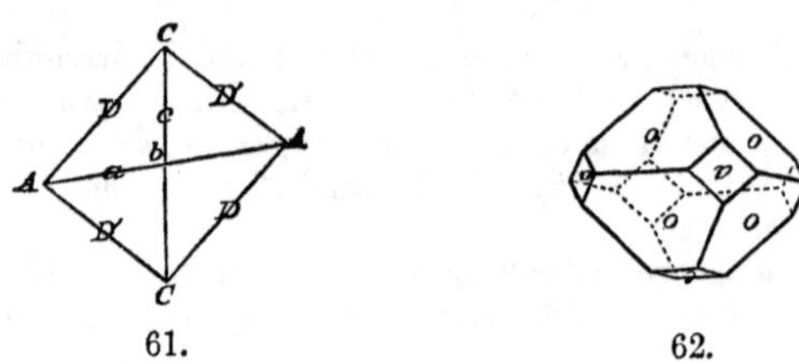

61. 62.

30TH GROUP — EARTHY RESINS. (BITUMENS.)

72*. This group comprises solid and liquid organic compounds, the most important properties of which have been described in the chemical section of this work, among the resins and volatile oils (§ 138). They consist of more or less metamorphosed products of the vegetable remains of a former period, as we have already stated in our chapter on the dry distillation of vegetable matters (Chem. § 169). They occur in the latest formations of the earth's crust. The most remarkable are:—

Amber, a fossil resin, occurring principally in brown-coal formations, and generally in the brown-coal itself. The greater quantity is found in detached pieces on the sea-shore, where it has been washed by the waves, or in the sand and loam, more or less distant from the beach. Amber is fished and dug for more particularly on the east coast of Prussia, from Dantzic to Memel. Pieces of amber are found adhering to fragments of wood and bark; other specimens contain insects, pine-needles and cones enclosed, which leaves no doubt that it originates from a fossilized or an extinct species of pine. Regarding its other properties and applications, see Chemistry, § 141.

Other rarer members of this group are, fossil copal, retinite, mountain or earth wax, elastic bitumen, mountain tallow or Scheererite, idrialite, &c.

Mineral or *Persian Naphtha*, a colourless semi-fluid liquid, is described in Chemistry, § 170, where we have also given a description of *Asphaltum* or *Bitumen*.

II.—GEOLOGY.

73. In the extensive series of minerals hitherto contemplated, we have not unfrequently met with such as excited our attention, not merely by their individual properties, but by their being dispersed in considerable masses, through the crust of the earth. Thus quartz, lime, dolomite, and many other minerals, have a limited extent as regularly crystallised objects, but as amorphous formations, they occur in many parts and in immense deposits. Here other more important relations, totally different from those of form, lustre, hardness, or colour, attract our attention. We no longer contemplate those minute and nicely-adapted ornaments of that gigantic structure, the crust of the earth, but have to examine the mighty foundations, walls, and columns, which constitute its fabric.

It is requisite, first, to investigate the materials of this edifice, and after that, its manner of construction.

74. We assume as an established fact that the earth is a spherical body, flattened or depressed at its poles, the diameter from pole to pole being 7,916 miles. The surface of this globe is calculated at 211,000,000 square miles, of which about 150,000,000 are covered with water, and 61,000,000 appear as land. The water, by the law of gravitation, and by the mobility of its parts, assumes a level surface, which appears spherical only when contemplated in its entire mass. If, on the other hand, we examine the solid parts of the earth, it presents itself to the eye in the most varied forms. From the plains stretching out like the ocean, there arise gradually or suddenly considerable heights, sometimes in consolidated masses, sometimes in single

chains or isolated peaks, and these, with steppes, prairies, extensive deserts, table-lands, hills, mountains and mountain vales, abysses and precipitous mural and rocky eminences with craggy summits, lost in the clouds, offer us endless charms by a successive variety of beautiful and sublime scenery.

75. The diversity of the component parts of these mountain masses is, however, scarcely less wondrous than are the remarkable changes of their external forms. A person born and come to maturity amongst volcanic rocks and plutonic formations, accustomed to the daily aspect of granite, basalt, and porphyry, will view with lively surprise the first prospect of the regularly stratified aqueous formations, with their tabular lime and sandstone rocks, containing innumerable petrifactions of organic beings. Hence observation has unceasingly been applied in acquiring a knowledge of the rocky masses. The crust of the earth up to the altitude of 24,000 feet, and down to depths of from 1,700 to 3,000 feet, has been examined in every direction of its accessible parts, particularly within the last 50 years. The indefatigable geologist has successfully applied his hammer to aid his investigations, and everywhere has he collected information until the science has gradually obtained such a standing as to enable us to form a somewhat definite conception of the structure of the earth, and to account for the co-operating causes of its present form.

Although a more accurate investigation of rocks and their arrangement has, until now, been undertaken only in England, Germany, France, the adjoining countries [and the United States], yet sufficient is known of North and South America, and of various parts of Asia, to warrant the assumption, with tolerable certainty, of the following important principle:—*The crust of the earth consists of only a proportionally small number of different rocks, and these are similar to each other at the most distant points of our globe, both as to species and arrangement.*

Thus the various kinds of rock are distributed equally over the entire earth, and the granite blocks of South America, of Heidelberg, and of the most northern latitudes are exactly alike; while on the other hand, plants and animals of the equator, of the temperate zones, and of the polar circles, exhibit the greatest and most striking differences.

76. Next to this general view of the surface of the earth, a few glances at its interior structure are particularly significant. We have seen that man has penetrated beneath the surface only to a depth most insignificant in proportion to the radius of the globe. Opportunity has nevertheless been afforded by this for making observations, which lead to important inferences. We have noticed in § 127 of Physics, that the average temperature of Germany is from 9° to 10°C. (48° to 50° F.), and that at the equator it is 27° C. (80·6° F.), by which, of course, the temperature at the level of the sea is understood, since the higher elevations always have an inferior temperature. It is a striking fact that a thermometer placed in any locality four feet below the surface of the ground, no longer indicates the change of the daily temperature, but merely that of the year. Again, at a depth of 60 feet it indicates everywhere and all times the same temperature, which is never affected by the hottest summer or the coldest winter.

Hence this constantly-equal temperature is held to be the specific heat of the earth, independent of that imparted by the sun. Proceeding from this point still deeper, about 120 feet for example, the centigrade thermometer

(Physics, § 98) will rise one degree. This remarkable increase in the temperature of the earth towards its centre, amounting to one degree for every 120 feet, has been proved to be the same at the most varying points of the globe, and at all depths.

Now, if the increase of heat progresses in the same ratio towards the deeper and unknown parts, it must attain, at the depth of 36 miles, 1,800° (3,272° F.), a temperature at which iron would melt; at 54 miles a heat of 2,700° (4,892° F.) would prevail, in which all known substances would become molten liquids. Hence it seems but natural to conclude that the interior of the earth is one burning mass of liquid fire surrounded by a crust, that has cooled down gradually and become hardened. We shall see, in the following pages, that there are many other reasons for such a conclusion; we may merely allude here to thermal springs, the waters of which are the hotter the deeper their source may be.

77. A diligent and attentive investigation of the crust of the earth has been undertaken, especially in Germany, where Werner, Professor of Mining at Freiberg, gave the first impulse to the study. We owe, however, the above-mentioned important discovery of the exact similarity of the various kinds of rock, to the illustrious traveller Alexander v. Humboldt, and to the indefatigable Leopold v. Buch.

78. In order correctly to distinguish any kind of rock, we must of course first consider it mineralogically, *i. e.*, its chemical constituents, its hardness, its density, &c., then we have to regard the form of the rock; and although we have no crystals to contemplate in this case, yet when considered in their entire mass, the rocks present, each in its kind, a very peculiar form. Next to this, the peculiarity of their arrangement and stratification is of great importance; and finally, the numerous animal and vegetable fossils enclosed in many of these rocks, contribute most essentially to characterise and distinguish them. Thus we may arrange the subject in the following divisions: — 1. *Description of rocks.* 2. *Structure of rocks.* 3. *Stratification* and *superposition of rocks.* 4. *Organic remains.* These four branches constitute DESCRIPTIVE GEOLOGY. After having elucidated these, we may proceed to the consideration of the structure of the earth's crust, the formation of the various chains of mountains, and their connexion with one another, which constitute what may be termed SYSTEMATIC GEOLOGY.

DESCRIPTIVE GEOLOGY.

A. DESCRIPTION OF ROCKS.

79. In endeavouring to distinguish the different kinds of rock, we meet with the same difficulty as in the study of minerals (§ 24). Here, likewise, ocular examination, collecting of specimens, observing the deportment of the rock under the hammer, attentive consideration of the mountains, vales, water-courses, quarries, mines, &c., are absolutely necessary to form a correct conception of the entire subject.

The following description of rocks may, therefore, more correctly be called a mere outline or sketch of the more important members. A collection of the various kinds of rock is much easier to make than one of minerals, as the former generally occur in great masses, and may therefore be obtained at a less cost.

80. The minerals which form a considerable part of the earth's crust are termed, in general, *rocks*. These rocks, in their internal structure, are of two kinds: either they consist purely of minute particles, for instance, of crystals, grains, laminæ, &c., of one and the same mineral, or they consist of two, three, or four different minerals mixed with each other. There are accordingly two principal classes or divisions, viz., *simple* rocks, and *compound* rocks. Thus, for instance, marble, consisting of nothing but grains of carbonate of lime, is a simple rock. Granite, on the contrary, in which we find quartz, mica, and felspar, is a compound rock.

81. Many terms that have become habitual to us in the description of minerals will have to be repeated also in that of rocks. Granular, spathous, fibrous, foliated, compact, earthy, &c., are terms that have already been frequently used. There are, however, several peculiarities observable in the construction of compound rocks, which we must first notice, before we proceed to describe them. The component parts are combined either in the *crystalline* form, or they are held together in an amorphous state by a non-crystalline mass, in the same manner, for instance, as mortar combines the stones of a wall. In many the cohesion is very great, in others but slight, and these latter are called *loose* rocks, as, for instance, rubble-stones, gravel, marl, &c The mixture is either distinct and discernible by the naked eye, or it is indistinct, and can be detected only by the help of glasses or by chemical means. A rock is called *slaty* when it splits easily in one direction, which is commonly the case whenever one of the component parts, or all of them, have the form of small laminæ arranged in parallel layers. The structure of the *porphyry* class is very peculiar. This comprises rocks of a given substance enclosing crystals of other minerals, which impart to it a spotted appearance. If a rock contains vesicular cavities filled partly or entirely with another mineral, similar in shape to an almond, it is called *amygdaloidal;* if, however, these cavities occur frequently in it, and are empty, the rock is called *slaggy*. *Geodes,* or *drusic cavities*, are hollow nodules, enclosed in the larger masses of rocks, which are lined inside with beautiful crystallisations. Finally we must mention the *accidental* constituents of rocks, in which occasionally single crystals may be observed; these, however, occur in inconsiderable quantities, and do not in the least alter the specific nature of the entire mass. Thus, for instance, in granite single garnets are sometimes found, the presence of which, however, does not at all affect the character of this species of rock.

Classification of Rocks.

82. Rocks may be classified in various ways; for instance, into granular, spathous, foliated rocks, &c.: it is, however, highly essential that such an arrangement does not separate those rocks that are chemically allied to each other.

The character of a rock is frequently more uncertain than that of a mineral, particularly as one kind or species frequently makes a transition into another; thus, for example, compact limestone passes into granular limestone, and granite into gneiss.

In the following description we shall retain the general division mentioned in § 80, of simple and mixed or compound rocks, and will merely enumerate the most important kinds, with a description of their most striking characteristics.

I. SIMPLE OR UNIFORM ROCKS.

83. These have already been described in the first part of Mineralogy. We will therefore merely recite here the names of those which are most important.

1. *Rock-salt*, § 34.	9. *Felsite*, § 50.	17. *Red Ironstone*, § 54.
2. *Gypsum*, § 36.	10. *Quartz*, § 31.	18. *Magnetic Ironstone*, § 54.
3. *Limestone*, § 37.	11. *Augite Rock*, § 42.	19. *Graphite*. § 30.
4. *Dolomite*, § 40.	12. *Hornblende Rock*, § 42.	20. *Anthracite*, § 30.
5. *Spathic Ironstone*, § 55.	13. *Talc Slate*, § 52.	21. *Coal*, § 30.
6. *Pitchstone*, § 50.	14. *Chlorite Slate*, § 52.	22. *Brown Coal*, § 30, § 23.
7. *Obsidian*, § 50.	15. *Serpentine*, § 41.	23. *Peat*, § 30.
8. *Pearlstone*, § 50.	16. *Brown Ironstone*, § 54.	24. *Asphaltum*, § 72.

II. MIXED OR COMPOUND ROCKS.

a. Crystalline Rocks.

25. Clay-slate.

84. This rock is an indistinct mixture of very minute particles of mica, a little quartz, felspar, and talc, containing sometimes particles of coal, hornblende, or chlorite, and having mostly the appearance of an uniform mass. It is distinctly slaty, and has a fracture varying from splintery to earthy. It occurs of a greenish-grey, bluish-grey, violet, red, brownish-black, and, when decayed, sometimes yellowish-grey colour. When pulverised it is mostly white, but when coal is present it is black. Chiastolite, staurolite, garnet, tourmaline, and iron pyrites, are accidental constituents of this rock.

Varieties: common clay-slate; greywacke-slate; dark-grey slate, which is used for covering roofs, for writing-slates, &c.; whetstone-slate; pencil-slate, which is used for slate-pencils and for drawing. The latter containing a considerable quantity of coal, is sufficiently soft to impart its colour to paper, and is employed as natural black chalk. Alum-slate, containing a considerable quantity of coal, iron pyrites, and alumina, is used for the manufacture of alum.

26. Mica-slate.

85. Mica-slate is a distinct admixture of mica and quartz in alternate layers, the mica frequently enclosing small laminæ of quartz. It occurs slaty, grey, white, yellowish, reddish, brownish, and lustrous. Among the accidental constituents are more particularly—garnet, talc, chlorite, felspar, hornblende, tourmaline, staurolite, iron pyrites, magnetic iron-ore, and graphite. It passes over into gneiss, clay-, talc-, and hornblende-slates. The mica is sometimes replaced in this rock by other minerals. The following kinds of rocks being thus produced: talc- and iron-mica-slate; itacolumite, or flexible sandstone, from the mountain Itacolumi in the Brazils; also tourmaline-slate.

27. Gneiss.

86. This kind of rock has received its name from the language of the miners, without any particular meaning; it is a mixture of quartz, mica, and

felspar. The quartz and felspar form granular layers, separated by laminæ of mica; it is slaty, grey, whitish, yellowish, reddish, greenish, &c. It forms transitions into mica-slate, granite, &c. Accidental constituents are: garnet, tourmaline, epidote, andalusite, iron pyrites, graphite, &c.

[Talcose gneiss contains talc in the place of mica; and if hornblende be superadded to quartz, felspar, and mica, it forms syenitic gneiss.]

28. Granite.

87. The granular aspect of this rock acquired for it, at an early date, the above name, which is derived from the Latin *granum* (grain). Granite is a mixture of quartz, felspar, and mica, in which, however, the laminæ of the latter do not lie parallel to each other, thus preventing a slaty structure; it is grey, reddish, yellowish, greenish, and white. Accidental constituents are: tourmaline, hornblende, andalusite, pinite, epidote, garnet, topaz, graphite, magnetic iron ore, tin ore, &c. It forms transitions into gneiss, syenite, and porphyry.

The following are varieties of this rock:—*Porphyritic granite*, containing single large crystals of felspar: *graphic granite*, so called on account of its marks, which bear a resemblance to writing, and which are formed by the close intermixture of the quartz and felspar; *protogine*, a mixture of quartz, felspar, and talc; *granulite*, mostly a slaty compound of felspar and quartz; *greisen*, a mixture of quartz and mica, mostly containing tin ore and arsenical pyrites.

Granite is particularly adapted for constructing roads on account of its hardness; it is less suited for building, being rather difficult to work. The city of Aberdeen is built of granite. It is frequently employed in large blocks for bridges, foundations of buildings, monuments, &c. Disintegrated granite yields a productive soil.

29. Syenite.

88. Syenite is a distinct mixture of felspar and hornblende, frequently associated with quartz and mica; the entire mass might, therefore, come under the denomination of hornblende-granite. An admixture of very minute crystals of titanite is likewise characteristic of this rock; it is granular, reddish, or greenish. Its accidental constituents are the same as those of granite. It forms transitions into granite, hornblende, and porphyry. *Porphyritic* and *slaty syenite* are varieties.

Syenite is applied to the same purposes as granite, to which it is, however, preferred for ornamental architecture, on account of its being more finely marked. The numerous and great architectural monuments in Upper Egypt are constructed of a reddish syenite, from *Syene*, from which locality the name of the rock is derived.

30. Greenstone.

89. This rock, likewise designated as *greenstone-slate* (trap, diabase, whinstone), is either a distinct or indistinct mixture of amphibole (bronzite, hypersthene, schillerspar), with felspar, and is either granular or compact, slaty and porphyritic; sometimes it is vesicular or amygdaloidal, the vesicular cavities being filled with calcareous spar. The colour varies from green to black; sometimes it is dark-grey. The most frequent accidental constituents are: iron pyrites, quartz, mica, garnet, epidote, and magnetic iron ore.

The amygdaloidal and other greenstones that occur abundantly on the banks of the Clyde, in Scotland, abound with beautiful minerals belonging to the zeolitic class. The localities of Kilpatrick and Kilmacolm are particularly famous for phrenite, Thomsonite, cubicite, mesotype, harmotome, stilbite, and other minerals of this class. Its varieties are: *diorite*, a distinct compound of hornblende and albite, frequently with iron pyrites (the same rock of slaty structure is called *diorite slate*); *aphanite*, a compact and apparently uniform mixture, containing amphibole and albite, sometimes amygdaloidal, and when there is a preponderance of separate crystals of albite or hornblende, forming a transition into aphanite-porphyry; *gabbro*, a granular mixture of labrador and diallage, sometimes containing titanic iron and serpentine; *wacke*, a brownish or dirty-greenish rock, from compact to earthy, sometimes vesicular, slaggy, or amygdaloidal, originating most likely in the decomposition of various kinds of greenstone. These species of greenstone are used for building, and some of them, which partly pass over into the porphyry variety, are employed in works of art under the name of *porfido verte antico*. Greenstone, on account of its extreme toughness, offers a valuable material for the formation of macadamised roads.

31. Porphyry.

90. Porphyry is a compact felsite mass, containing single crystals of felspar, quartz, more rarely mica or hornblende, and more accidentally garnets or iron-pyrites. Its structure is porphyritic (comp. § 81); it occurs of a reddish, yellowish, and brownish colour, and variegated. Several works of art constructed by the ancient sculptors in stone, designated by this term, do not agree with what is now termed porphyry.

All kinds of porphyry are much used for building, for roads, &c. By disintegration they generally yield a very productive soil, containing potassa. The different varieties are: *quartz-phorphyry*, or red porphyry (*porfido rosso antico*), consisting of a compact mass of felsite, with crystals of quartz or felspar, and mostly yellow, red, or brown; *mica-porphyry*, a mass of compact felsite, with crystals of mica and felspar; *syenite-porphyry*, a mass of compact or crystalline felsite, with crystals of felspar and hornblende; *pitchstone-porphyry*, fundamentally composed of pitchstone, blended with crystals of vitreous felspar and quartz.

It is worthy of remark that several of the finely-spotted porphyries are employed in the construction of works of art, such as columns, slabs, vases, urns, bowls, &c., not unfrequently of extraordinary size. The most celebrated are the porphyry works of Elfdalen, in Sweden, and of Kolywan, in Asiatic Russia.

32. Melaphyr.

91. This rock may be called augite-porphyry, or black porphyry, and also amygdaloid. It is a compact, or somewhat crystalline, and mostly indistinct mixture of augite and Labrador felspar, frequently porphyritic, with single crystals of Labrador and augite, which impart to it a dark-brownish, greenish, or black colour. Accidental constituents of this rock are mica and iron pyrites, but *never* quartz. We may mention as varieties the compact, *porphyritic melaphyr*, and likewise *amygdaloid*. In the latter the principal and generally uniform mass contains vesicular cavities, partly or wholly filled

up. These cavities are either quite irregular in shape, spherical or oblong in one and the same direction, or they are pear-shaped with the tapering extremity undermost. No doubt can be entertained that these cavities originated in an evolution of gas from the interior of the rock. The contents of the vesicular cavities consist of calcareous spar, chalcedony, agate, quartz, zeolites, chabasite, &c. The layers or nodules of these crystals are in some cases parallel to the sides of the cavities; in others in irregular masses. The uniform contents assume either botryoidal or stalactitical forms.

Melaphyr is likewise used for building and for roads. It does not easily decay, but by disintegration it yields a very productive soil.

33. Basalt.

92. This rock is generally an indistinct mixture of augite and felspar; it is also called *basanite,* and some kinds of it have received the name of trap. The above constituents are generally associated with olivine and magnetic iron ore.

Basalt is compact, porphyritic, granular, amygdaloidal, and slaggy; its colour is either black, greenish, greyish, or brownish-black. It is commonly hard and heavy. A distinction is made between the common basalt, which is compact and apparently uniform in mass, and *dolerite,* a distinctly mixed basalt, in which we recognise especially augite and felspar. The accidental constituents are nepheline, leucite, mica, and iron pyrites, besides olivine and magnetic iron ore. The *amygdaloidal basalt* possesses vesicular cavities. Basalt furnishes the best material for paving roads. For building, the compact basalt is too heavy, while on the other hand the porous basalt is well adapted for this purpose; it is not applied to finer works of art. The latter kind is met with in Germany, in the vicinity of extinct volcanos, especially in the seven mountains, of which the Drachenfels is the most celebrated; it is found likewise in the most southern parts of the black forest (Kaiserstuhl), and in Bohemia, where it is used as dry building stone, and the lighter variety in the construction of cupolas and vaults. The porous basalt, from the quarries in the neighbourhood of Coblentz (at Neidermending), is much celebrated, and is employed for millstones. When disintegrated by atmospheric influences, basalt yields a highly productive soil, which is particularly warm on account of its dark colour.

34. Phonolite.

93. This rock is called klingstein, or sounding stone, from its property of producing a clear sound when struck with a hammer, and though apparently uniform, it is a mixture of felsite and natrolite; it occurs compact, laminated, porphyritic, from crystals of felspar, but rarely vesicular. The fracture varies from splintery to conchoidal, and from vitreous to earthy. The colours of this rock are greenish-grey, grey, and blackish-grey. A peculiarity of this kind of rock is, that nearly all its exposed surfaces are coated with a white crust of the disintegrated stone. The accidental constituents are: hornblende, augite, magnetic iron ore, titanite, leucite, and mica. The drusic and vesicular cavities generally contain zeolites. This rock passes over into trachyte, and approaches on the other hand to basalt. As varieties we may distinguish compact phonolite, porphyry slate, and the decomposed phonolite, which is a soft almost earthy rock, and yields a kind of porcelain earth, like

the above-mentioned white crust of disintegrated rock. This rock, which frequently splits into plates, is used in building, sometimes even for roofing, and also frequently for paving. The clay soil resulting from its decomposition is but little favourable to agriculture.

35. Trachyte.

94. Trachyte is an indistinct, indefinite, mostly granular mixture, in which felspar predominates. It is nearly always porphyritic, from the presence of vitreous felspar crystals, and generally contains scales of mica and needles of hornblende. It occurs granular, porphyritic, compact, slaggy, and earthy. The fundamental mass is grey, yellowish, reddish, or greenish. For building purposes this rock may easily be dressed with the hammer and other suitable tools; but it decays easily, as has been proved, for instance, in the cathedral at Cologne, the more ancient part of which is constructed of trachyte, from the Siebengebirge. It yields a productive loamy soil for agriculture.

36. Lava.

95. This is an indistinct mixture of augite and felspar, frequently associated with leucite and magnetic iron ore, more rarely with mica, olivine, &c. It occurs granular, compact, porphyritic, and slaggy. Its colour is either dark, brown, grey, reddish, greenish, yellowish, or black. All the glowing masses in general that are emitted in streams from volcanos during eruptions, independent of their composition, are called lavas. The different varieties are — the *basaltic lava*, very similar to basalt, though rougher; *doleritic lava; leucite lava; porphgritic lava; slaggy lava;* and lastly the *volcanic scoria*, consisting of detached fragments, and called *lapilli*, or volcanic sand. Lava is particularly distinguished for the remarkably fruitful soil it yields by slow decomposition. This may be a consequence partly of its chemical constitution, partly of its dark colour, and of the evolution of heat and carbonic acid proceeding from the ground near volcanos still in action.

b. Mechanically Mixed Rocks.

I. *Distinctly Mixed Rocks.*

37. Breccia.

96. Breccia is a combination of angular portions of rocks, enclosed within another mass, which may be termed the uniting medium or cement. These breccias receive different names, according to their enclosed fragments, or uniting medium. Thus we distinguish, *e. g.* granite-, porphyry-, limestone-, and bone-breccias. From the supposition that some breccias have arisen through the forcible trituration of a liquid mass against a solid one, they are called *trituration-breccias*, as, for example, a mass of porphyry with fragments of clay-slate.

When the uniting medium of the breccia is sufficiently hard, it may be used for building material. A few breccias, which, from the admixture of variegated and differently-formed fragments of rocks, present a very beautiful appearance, particularly when polished, are applied in ornamental architecture, and receive different denominations, answering to their appearance

Thus a breccia, consisting of granite, porphyry, and diorite, is called *breccia verde d'egitto,* and the various marble breccias are named *violetta antica, dorata, pavonazza,* &c.

38. Conglomerates.

97. *Conglomerate* is distinguished from breccia by the *rounded* rocky fragments which are cemented together by an uniform mass. They have received various names, according to their constituent fragments: gneiss-conglomerate, basalt-conglomerate, *greywacke, nagelfluh,* &c. Conglomerates may be used for building and road-making. They, as well as the breccias, yield on disintegration a soil, the productive quality of which must, of course, depend upon the nature of the rocks composing them. Thus greywacke conglomerate yields a strong, and therefore loose, clayey soil. The red conglomerate has a sandy or clayey-combining medium, containing layers of porphyry, gneiss, granite, mica-slate, clay-slate, &c., which remain undecayed in the clayey and sandy soil. Basalt-conglomerate generally yields a very fertile loam- and clay-soil.

39. Sandstone.

98. This rock, so universally distributed and so well known, is a combination of minute and mostly spherical particles, held together by a uniting medium which is scarcely to be distinguished. The particles are principally quartz, and the cement is generally clay, marl, or oxide of iron, more rarely hornstone. We distinguish accordingly *clayey, calcareous, marly, ferruginous,* and *silicious sandstone.*

We call it *conglomerate* sandstone, if it contains isolated and large rubble-stones. Besides grains of quartz, it sometimes contains scales of mica or grains of felspar, hornblende, or green earth. The latter imparts a green colour to it, and hence the name *green sandstone.* There are various other admixtures in sandstone, of which we will merely mention the globular concretions of clay, which are termed *clay-galls.*

Many other names given to sandstone, such as keuper sandstone, lias, &c., refer to the systems of stratification, which we shall describe further on.

In sandstone we possess one of the most valuable materials for manifold uses; it is particularly adapted for building, being very workable. Sandstones of finer grain and uniform colour throughout offer an excellent material for sculpture, and have been employed particularly in the rich and magnificent ornaments of our ancient cathedrals. The colour of sandstone ranges from white through yellow, greenish yellow, to brownish and brown, —the latter variety being found of great beauty, particularly in Würtemberg. Besides these, red sandstone is also frequently found.

Sandstone is but an indifferent material for road-making; but the hardest kinds are used for mill-stones, grinding-stones, and many in the form of flags are used for roofing and paving.

The soil it produces by decay is one of the most unproductive, since it is totally destitute of potassa and soda, and incapable of retaining moisture. Sandstone, in which clay and marl preponderate as a cement, is, of course, more favourable to agriculture.

40. Debris. Gravel. Sand. Crumbled Rocks (Gruss).

99. The term *debris* is applied to a loose accumulation of rocky fragments, like breccias, without cement, whilst by *gravel* or *rubble-stones* we understand a collection of rounded fragments of rocks, that may be regarded as conglomerate, which is not united by a binding material. *Sand* is a loose accumulation of grains of minerals, mostly of quartz. *Gruss* signifies the loose, unconnected constituents of any compound rock, *e. g.* granite-gruss consists of an uncombined mixture of grains of quartz, mica, and felspar.

II. *Indistinctly Mixed Rocks.*

41. Marls.

100. Although apparently uniform, marls are an amorphous mixture of carbonate of lime and of clay occurring of all densities, from compact to earthy, also slaty, but rarely of a fine grain; the colour of marls is either grey or yellowish, reddish, greenish, bluish, black, white, or variegated. They crumble to pieces in the air, generally very rapidly, and effervesce feebly with diluted hydrochloric acid. According to the preponderance of one or the other constituents, or the admixture of other minerals, we distinguish *common marl, calcareous marl, clayey marl, silicious marl, sandy marl,* and *bituminous marl,* which is mixed with bitumen (asphalt), and frequently occurs slaty. Finally, we meet with *cupriferous slate,* a bituminous marly slate of black or dark-grey colour, which is famous for its abundance in those copper ores, mentioned in § 59, and which contains besides cobalt-, nickel-, and silver-ores.

Marl is totally unfit for building purposes, in consequence of its rapid disintegration; it is, however, on this account, the more valuable in agriculture. Marl soil is considered the most fruitful, although it must be observed that it should not contain under 10 nor above 60 per cent. of carbonate of lime. Poor land and calcareous soils are improved by a dressing of marl. The marl containing a larger proportion of lime, is also burned and used as hydraulic lime or cement (comp. Chemistry, § 81). Marls are particularly found in districts of the more recent formations, *e. g.* in Suabia.

42. Clay.

101. *Clay,* though apparently uniform, is a mixture of alumina with a little lime and silica (comp. Chemistry, § 87). It occurs compact, earthy, soft, and friable; it softens in water and is exceedingly plastic. It is found of all colours, and sometimes even black, owing to the presence of bitumen. We distinguish besides pale common clay, yellow loam, and a loose earthy mixture of clay, lime, and sand (löss), of yellowish-grey colour, distributed more particularly throughout the valleys of the Rhine. *Saline clay* is mixed with rock-salt, and has a dark colour, which is due to the presence of carbon.

Only the clay of the more ancient formations, hardened into stone, is used as a building material. Respecting the use of plastic clay, we have given comprehensive information in § 88 of Chemistry.

43. Fullers' Earth.

102. This term denotes a soft friable mass, probably derived from the decomposition of greenstone; it possesses an uneven fracture, from coarse to fine earthy, and is unctuous to the touch. Its colour varies from grey, greenish, yellow, to white. It forms with water a thin, unmouldable paste, which is used by manufacturers for extracting the greasy matter from woollen fabrics. It contains about 10 per cent. of clay and up to 60 per cent. of lime, and is closely related to the boles.

44. Tufa.

103. Under this name several kinds of rock, not accurately defined, are comprehended, containing rather loose and partly earthy combinations of clayey, calcareous, and sandy constituents. Their colour is mostly grey or yellowish; sometimes they also enclose a mixture of debris or fragments of compact rocks. Amongst other tufas we notice the following, viz., *trass*, a volcanic tufa, which, mixed with 1½ to 2½ parts of lime, forms cement which sets under water (Chemistry, § 81), and hence has been applied to many important purposes. The trass from the neighbourhood of Andernach is the most celebrated in Germany. The volcanic tufa of Italy, *pausilipp tufa* and *peperine*, or pepper-stone, are partly applicable for building; but they are sometimes much injured by the influence of the weather. In the neighbourhood of Naples there exist antique buildings, grottos, &c., constructed of this rock; its disintegration produces an extremely fruitful soil.

45. Humus.

104. Arable or cultivated soil is the superficial stratum of the earth's crust. It is a soil mineralogically undefined, and the product of vegetable and animal nature upon the soil yielded by disintegration of any kind of rock. The remains of decaying organic substances (comp. Chemistry, § 164) are intimately mixed with the particles of the crumbled rock, and impart to it mostly a darker and sometimes a black colour, and highly fertilising properties. Some localities of the earth, however, are entirely destitute of this mould; for instance, where pure lime- or quartz-rock forms the surface, vegetable life, in consequence of the deficiency of nutrition, is either totally absent, or, if present, it is developed so imperfectly, that humus or organic matter cannot be formed on such soils.

B. STRUCTURE OF ROCKS.

105. When a mass of any variety of rocks is before us, there are two modes of considering it with reference to its form; firstly, its configuration and relation to external objects, and secondly, its interior structure. We accordingly distinguish the internal and external forms of rocks.

Internal Forms of Rocks.

106. We do not anywhere find masses of rock of any extent equally coherent throughout. Even in the most compact and hard kinds we observe divisions and separations which are formed by chasms and fissures. The origin of the latter may easily be illustrated by a mass of moist clay. As it dries, fissures and cracks appear on the surface, while the interior parts

contract, as may frequently be perceived on a large scale in all clay-soils during hot summers. The above rocks must, therefore, have formerly been soft, and, contracting as they hardened, must have split in various directions, thus forming larger or smaller divisions. In the former case the rocks may be called *irregularly massive*, and in the latter split or *fissured* rocks.

The strata of some rocks are often disposed with a wonderful regularity, presenting a mural appearance as if actually constructed of gigantic masonry. This is exhibited by the Cyclopean granite walls, which occur in prodigious masses on the summit of Goatfell, in the Island of Arran, and in those at Land's End, Cornwall, (fig. 1), where vertical cliffs, appearing

1.

like artificial walls, formed of gigantic masses of granite, sometimes rise to the height of 100 feet. There are also rocks enclosing globular concretions, arising from the circumstance that the hardening of the mass has taken place in different central points at once, round which further deposits were formed in concentric layers. Thus when trap-rock is exposed to the weather, the surface undergoes decomposition, and peels off, in thin layers, like the concentric coats of an onion, often exhibiting large round masses on the surface of the rock.

2. Decomposing Surface of Trap-Rock at Corrie, in Arran.

Occasionally the rounded masses are so small, that the rock has the appearance of a quantity of pea-iron ore. More frequently rocks are split up into pillars, having generally the form of hexagonal columns. Such columnar formations are beautifully illustrated by the basaltic columns of Fingal's Cave, in the Isle of Staffa (fig. 3) [which has now been worn out by the action of the Atlantic breakers], and by the Giant's Causeway, on the west coast of Antrim, in Ireland. Similar formations occur near Stolpen, in Saxony, and at Unkel, on the Rhine, where columns of the length of from 30 to 80 feet have been observed. These columns frequently have horizontal joints (fig. 4), at which they split into smaller pieces. They are usually accompanied by smaller columns, decreasing in

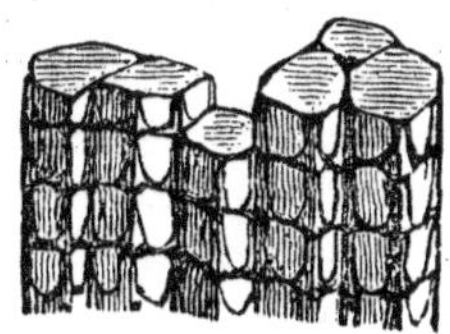

4.

3. Fingal's Cave, Isle of Staffa.

regularity of form, so as sometimes to appear rather as three-sided than as hexagonal columns.

The most common structure of rocks, however, is that of flat or tabular masses. These divisions are, moreover, less regularly defined. They are frequently so massive as to form immense blocks, or they appear as tabular slabs, gradually attenuating to flags and slates.

Stratification.

107. Rocks separated into strata, frequently give peculiar evidence by their structure, that the superincumbent layers did not originate at one and the same period, but that their deposition, solidification, and contraction took place, gradually and successively. This is rendered particularly evident by the circumstance, that between strata of the same kind, intermediate layers are often observed; for instance, beds of limestone are separated by others of marl. We have abundant evidence that rocks stratified in this manner, arose by a gradual settlement of their particles, formerly suspended in water, according to their greater specific gravity. Similar formations of layers or strata may be perceived on a smaller scale on the banks of brooks or rivers. Having in the following pages to return to the origin of stratification, we will first consider some peculiarities of the strata, or of their relative position and direction.

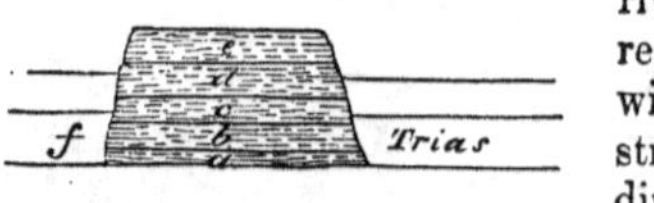

5.

The different layers of a stratified rock, as shown in fig. 5, have a parallel position like the leaves of a book. The thickness or *depth* of the individual strata is exceedingly unequal; for some of them, as represented by lines in the diagram, measure scarcely a quarter of an inch, and are interposed between others that measure in depth from 20 to 30 feet. The direction of these strata is either horizontal, *i. e.* parallel to the surface of the earth, as in fig. 5; or in an inclined position, as the strata *a* to *g* in fig. 6. Various strata are likewise occasionally observed to have a vertical position, as in fig. 7, in which case they are called upright strata. The course in which water poured on an inclined stratified layer would descend, is called, in geological language, the fall or *dip* of the strata. The direction of various strata is designated by the term *strike.*

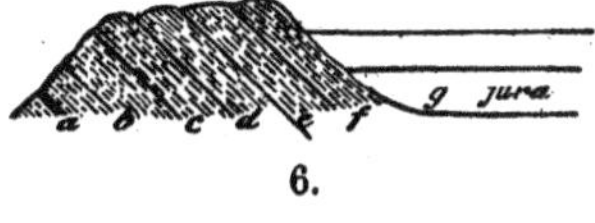

6.

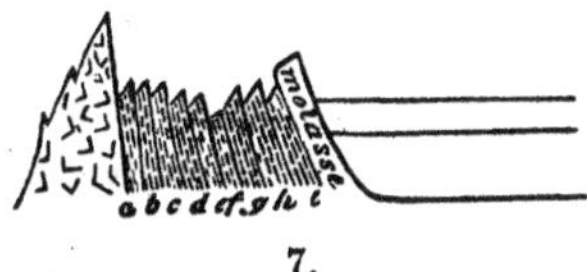

7.

When various strata come to the surface of the earth, as shown in figs. 5, 6, and 7, they are said to *crop out* or *basset.* The exposed or superficial parts of the erect and inclined strata, as in figs. 6 and 7, might be called their *heads.* The horizontal layers become exposed mostly by the action of currents of water, rivers, &c., as in fig. 8, or by the action of the sea; by making rail-roads, quarrying, and mining.

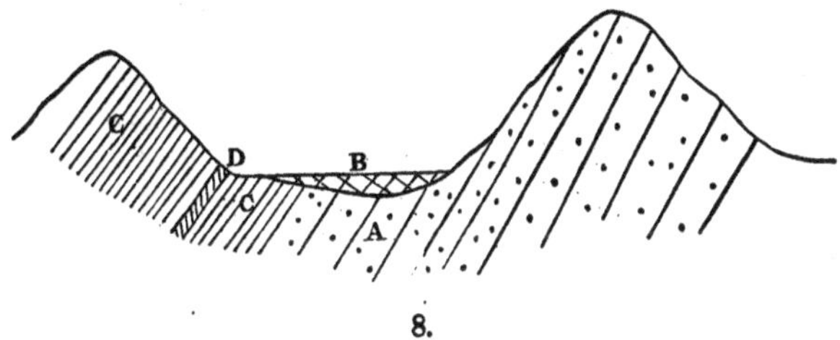

8.

Fig. 8. Denudation of Glen Shirrag, Island of Arran. A, the old red sandstone on the north of Glen Shirrag: B, the alluvial hollow of the Glen: C, the carboniferous formations, with limestone strata: D, apparently unconnected with the old red sandstone.

Various strata are frequently observed to taper off, and to decrease considerably in thickness in one direction, finally either ceasing entirely, or extending further in scarcely recognisable laminæ between the other rocks. This occurs especially with beds of coal, the discovery of the wedge-like end of which frequently leads to a bed of greater thickness.

From this it will be evident that various strata may appear in one place to be in almost immediate contact, whilst at a short distance further they are separated from each other. The erect or inclined strata are evidently not in their original position, but have been forced out of it by some cause acting subsequently to their formation. This is, however, not the only alteration which certain strata have suffered, for their regular and parallel course is often more or less interrupted, and in that case they appear no longer equally super-imposed like the leaves of a book, but are bent, twisted, broken up, and intermingled.

External Forms of Rocks.

108. If we contemplate the general aspect of rocks in relation to surrounding objects, they present themselves under three different forms, namely, as *Stratified* rocks, *Massive* or *Unstratified* rocks, and as *Veins.*

Most commonly several strata of different kinds of rock are perceived to overlie each other, and form in this manner systems of stratification, frequently of very considerable magnitude. Limestone, Dolomite, Coal, Sandstone, Clay, and Marl, afford special examples of such stratification.

The structure of the massive rocks never exhibits the slightest appearance of stratification, but merely an irregular division or cleavage, or the fissures mentioned in § 106. They are rarely spread over any considerable space, but occur as isolated precipitous masses breaking through the stratified rocks, and interrupting more or less their regular arrangement. Granite, syenite, porphyry, basalt, &c., exist merely as massive rocks, and never occur stratified.

Veins penetrate not merely through the stratified, but also through massive rocks: their form may be readily understood, if we study their origin. In the chasms and fissures that arose during the process of hardening, of the one kind of rock, there penetrated afterwards the semi-fluid masses of the other kinds, which, in course of time, likewise hardened. These veins are rather irregularly distributed, but their dip and strike are likewise taken into consideration. These veins must, however, be distinguished from the mineral or metallic veins, which are generally of inferior thickness, but of more importance since they contain valuable minerals and ores, and are therefore frequently mined.

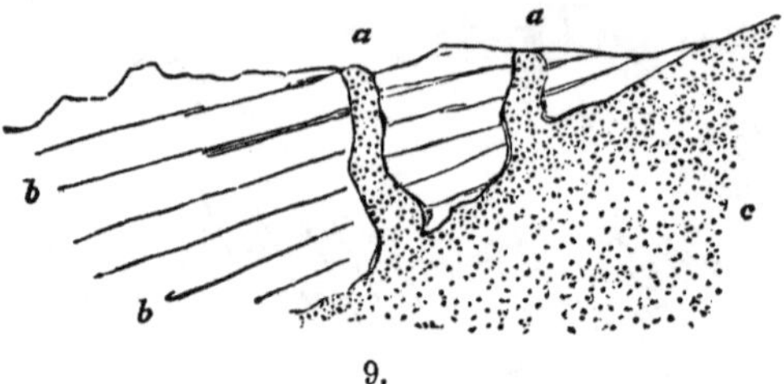

9.

Vein of Granite penetrating Mica-slate near Wicca Cove, Cornwall.
a, Granite Veins. *b*, Slate. *c*, Main mass of Granite.

Special Forms of Rocks.

109. As such we have to mention formations frequently observed in the caverns of several parts of England, particularly Somerset and Derby. These are called *Stalactites* (fig. 10), if pendent from walls, and increasing downwards like icicles, or *Stalagmites,* if arising from the ground, and increasing or growing upwards by the accumulated droppings from above. They generally arise from water, holding lime in solution, which trickles through the roofs and sides of caverns, and on evaporating leaves the lime behind in the most singular and varied shapes. *Incrustations* are formed by the evaporation of waters, holding minerals in solution, upon any object, which thus becomes covered with coatings of various thickness. We find frequently tra-

10.

Stalactites and Stalagmites.

cings resembling trees or mosses between slabs or plates of rocks, forming *Dendrites* (fig. 11), which may easily be imitated, and their origin illustrated by placing some finely levigated clay between two plates of smooth glass, or stone, and pressing them slightly together. A variety of ramified designs are thus obtained, similar to the hardened formations occurring in Nature, which may easily be mistaken for petrified moss or other vegetable objects.

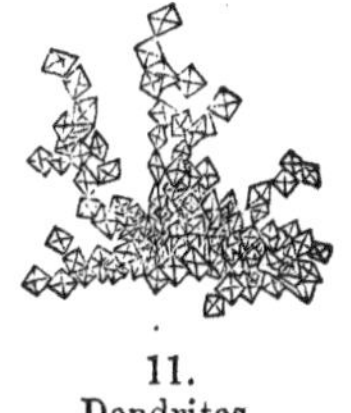

11.
Dendrites.

C. SUPERPOSITION OF ROCKS.

110. From the relative position and combination of the strata, masses, and veins, we are enabled to identify the different periods of their formation, or the ages of the deposits.

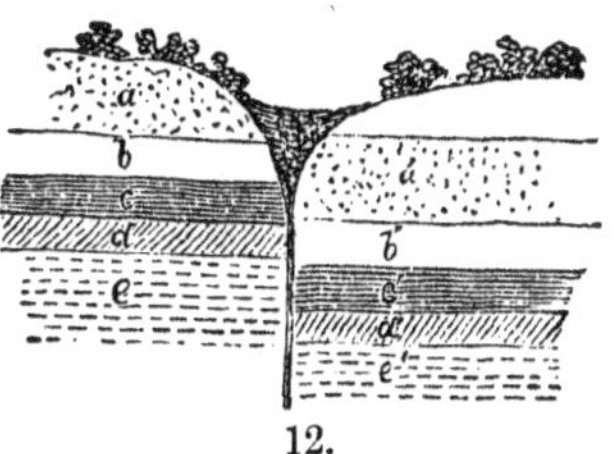

12.

The relative position of the strata to each other, may be very different. For instance, they may be lying horizontal and parallel to each other (fig. 12), or they may assume an inclined or vertical position (fig. 13), covered by parallel horizontal stratifications.

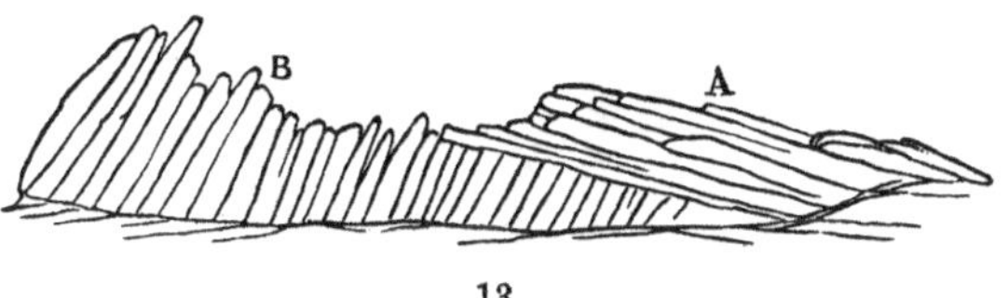

13.

Massive rocks generally are found rising side by side, and it rarely happens that one kind of rock is covered over to any extent, by the horizontal layer of another. Trunk-shaped and *fragmentary* rocks are often partially or entirely surrounded by a layer of another rock; as, for example, granite by gneiss (fig. 14), which often occurs when the interior rock, in its eruptive ascent, breaks off, and carries along with it fragments of the other which it entirely encloses.

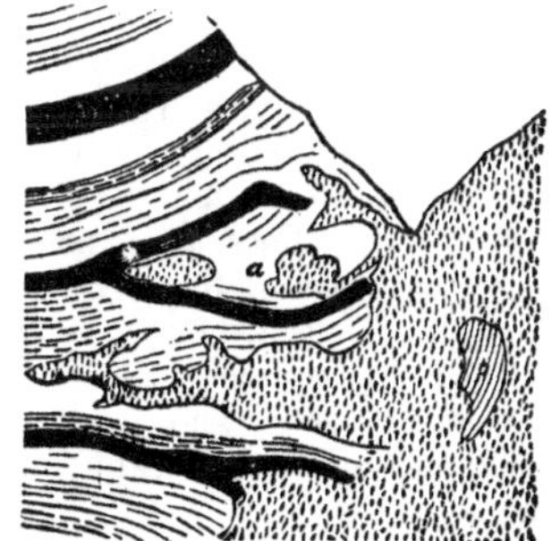

14.

Veins generally stand more in a vertical direction towards the interior of the earth, than in horizontal or oblique directions. They are frequently found to pass through the rock almost perfectly parallel with each other. By a subsequent displacement or disturbance of the position of the main rock, these veins are of course likewise displaced and broken up, which gives rise to great difficulties in mining, in following up a rich vein of ore. The lodes also cross and pass through each other The coal measures of Great Britain are frequently seen to have been dislocated by *faults.* This will be easily understood by referring to figs. 12, 15, 16, in which the dark-coloured strata represent coal measures, which have been displaced from their original position by subterranean disturbing influences.

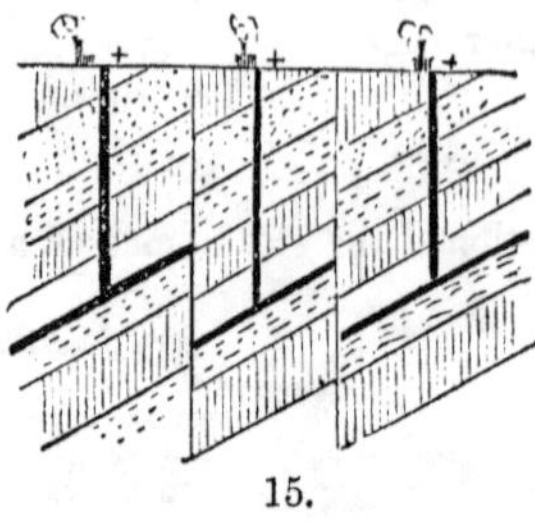

15.

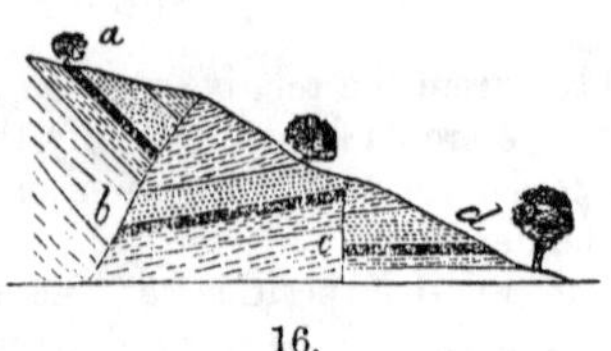

16.

Fig. 17 represents a very remarkable example from the mountains of Jura, where, owing to the flexibility of the strata, they have suffered great contortion, without becoming ruptured, so as to produce faults.

17.

111. From a closer observation of the above-mentioned relative position of rocks, we gather the most important conclusions, as to which of them is the older, or, what amounts to the same, which formation was hardened first. The following principles may be accordingly accepted as perfectly established. The upper strata are newer, or of more recent date than those which are below them; rocks which have disturbed the position or stratification of the adjacent formations are more recent than these; rocky masses in the middle of other rocks from which they are separated by sharply-defined lines, are generally of more recent formation than the latter; rocks which enclose fragments or disjointed layers are younger than those to which these detached pieces belong; veins and lodes are more recent than the beds of rocks in which they are found, and younger than the veins which they cross or intersect; and, finally, if one stratum of rock is younger than a second and older than a third, the second must be likewise older than the third.

D. ORGANIC REMAINS.

112. Many deposits of rock enclose forms which are called petrifactions, and which may be recognised at a glance, as not being of mineral origin, but to have belonged formerly to the vegetable or animal kingdom. Hence it follows that the origin of the rocks themselves must be dated from the same period in which those plants and animals existed. The petrifaction of these bodies has not been the result of a transformation of their chemical constituents into those of a mineral character, since that would be impossible, as has been shown in Chemistry (§ 10). On the contrary, these plants and animals, when on the surface of the earth, became enveloped, during its great revolutions, in the semi-fluid substance of the rocks in which they are now found, and which subsequently hardened. It is evident that under such violent processes the softer and more perishable parts could not be preserved, and hence, in general, only the more durable parts of plants, such as bark, wood, and ligneous fruits, or the calcareous shells of corals, mussels, and snails, as well as the bones of the higher class of animals, have been preserved. The more perishable organised formations, consisting of carbon, hydrogen, and oxygen, have undoubtedly been sooner or later decomposed, since they are never found in the rock. Nevertheless, under favourable circumstances, many a token or evidence of these formations has been preserved in the midst of destruction. Delicate leaves, and minutely articulated insects enveloped in the semi-fluid mass, have at least left behind impressions in the hardened rocks, from which their formation and class may often be clearly traced. In other specimens the innumerable little interstices or cavities of their bodies have been gradually filled up with the mineral fluid, which, upon hardening, preserved likewise their internal structure.

113. Difficult as it was at first to explain the appearance of an innumerable host of organic remains enclosed in rocks at great depths, and at altitudes of 12,000 feet, these petrifactions became at a later period most essential, as characteristic of the various rocks in which they occur. The following facts have resulted from accurate observations of these remains.

Petrifactions are found only in *stratified* rocks, which have been deposited from water, and never in unstratified or igneous rocks. The number of species, both of petrified plants and animals in the various strata, is very unequal: those occurring in the upper strata, approximate more closely to the still-existing species of the animal and vegetable kingdoms: these, however, decrease in the lower strata, so that the more perfectly developed animals and plants gradually disappear whilst the lower orders prevail, and the existing species become more and more rare. In the lowest and oldest strata, only such fossil remains, of organised beings, are met with, as are now no longer to be found in the recent state.

If the formation of two beds of rock, in different localities, has for other reasons been recognised as contemporary, they must contain the same petrifactions; and, on the other hand, we conclude from the exact similarity of the species of fossils existing in these rocks that they must be of coëval formation. Hence petrifactions have become of the utmost importance in ascertaining the age of the several strata, and in some cases they are the easiest, and even the only means of deciding that question: as we find in the various strata a widely-differing vegetable and animal world, we conclude that the climate and condition of the surface of the earth, at the various periods of its formation, must have been very dissimilar. Again, the fossils of the oldest strata give evidence of the animal creation having been much more equally spread over the surface of the earth than it is at present; and hence the great difference of temperature at the poles and the equator seems not to have been so remarkable formerly, as it is at the present period.

114. The total number of fossil plants and animals is exceedingly great, and has become the object of two special sciences, namely *Fossil Botany* and *Palæontology.* Their correct description requires of course a comprehensive knowledge of botany and zoology, and therefore, in treating of these sciences, we have paid proper regard to these petrifactions. However, we will introduce here a concise review of the plants and animals which occur as fossils, beginning with the lower or more imperfect orders.

Of *fossil plants,* we find the following orders: algæ; lichens; and mosses; *Equesetaceæ* occupying the oldest up to the mediæval strata. Lycopodiaceæ, tree ferns, particularly abundant only in the old strata; Liliacea; palms, stems, fruits, and foliage; *pines* and *dicotyledonous trees;* the latter occur only in the more recent strata.

Fossil Animals.—*Infusoria* are found in many strata; polypi or *corals* occur most frequently in the oldest formations. Radiata and echinodermata, amongst which are found encrinites, star-fish, and the common sea-urchin (*Echinus esculentus*), and *mollusca;* these are the most frequent of all, and to the geologist the most important. There are found, beginning in the old strata, and most plentifully in the middle strata, not only bivalve shells, but also univalve snails, and among the latter especially several important genera now perfectly extinct, as ammonites and belemnites. Annellata or fossils of the worm kind are rare; *crustacea* are likewise not of frequent occurrence. *Insects* occur distinctly only in beds of brown-coal, especially in amber: they are on the whole but rare. *Fishes* are exceedingly numerous, upwards of 800 species having already been recognised in the various strata. *Amphibious animals* are represented by the batrachia or frog tribe, though rare; and the ophidia or snake tribe are replaced in great number by saurians or the lizard tribe, now and then of gigantic size, but at present totally extinct. *Birds* are but seldom found in the older strata; *mammalia* exist only in the uppermost strata. There are, however, several extinct species of gigantic size, including the mammoth, megatherium (page 309), dinotherium, &c. Monkeys are exceedingly rare. Traces of human remains are not contained in any of those strata that have been subjected again at a later period to a general destructive influence. Man, therefore, did not appear on earth until its crust was sufficiently stable, and suffered no longer any general revolution.

SYSTEMATIC GEOLOGY.

Origin and Structure of the Crust of the Earth.

115. This wondrous edifice, inhabited by man, did not receive at once its present form. Let us trace, from the preceding statements, founded on experience and facts, the history of its origin and progress.

There was a time when the whole earth must have been a liquid glowing mass rolling its onward course through space. The elements or simple substances which it contains then united with each other only in such combinations as could exist at a high temperature. The gases formed the atmosphere which surrounded the firmer nucleus as a covering; with this was associated the vapours of an immense number of volatile compounds which could not remain in a solid or liquid state at such a temperature. The ocean was then in the form of vapour. Thus the earth in its first phases of formation appears to have been a soft, red-hot nucleus, enveloped by an immense and very dense atmosphere which surrounded it or followed its course, perhaps in the manner that the vapoury sphere or tail of the comets and nebulous stars appear now to accompany these bodies through the illimitable universe.

But by continually radiating heat into infinite space, the earth suffered a decrease of temperature at least on its surface. The difficultly fusible chemical compounds, such as silicate of alumina and magnesian clay-slate (mica-slate), &c., began gradually to separate in the form of finely laminated crystals, and by continued cooling to settle upon the surface of the nucleus of the earth, forming the first thin coating or crust over the red-hot liquid mass, and thus separating it from its vapoury atmosphere. This was the commencement of the earth's crust, which might now be increased in firmness more rapidly since the immediate influence of the internal heat was arrested, and as the combinations, existing in form of vapour, might now be deposited thereon, at least partly, in the form of liquids.

116. At that time organic life could not exist. The crust was still too hot to admit of plants taking root and growing; the existence of vegetation, however, is indispensable to animal life, and indeed those lower slaty strata, consisting of mica-slate and clay-slate, contain nowhere the least trace of animal or vegetable matter. If water had gathered already at that period upon the crust of the earth, it must have possessed a much higher temperature than at present; hence it was capable of dissolving numerous chemical compounds; and while the ocean at present contains only the easily soluble common salt, &c., the ocean of that period may have held in solution great quantities of silicates, sulphates, and carbonates. It also broke up again a portion of the solid crust, and formed therewith a muddy liquid, which, as the earth cooled, again gradually deposited its solid parts in granular strata, forming what is now known as sandstone.

117. Thus we behold acting continually, in concert and by turns, the laws of chemical affinity and of gravitation, in obedience to the latter of which the more compact substances endeavoured to occupy the lowest place. Had this mode of formation thus regularly continued, the surface of the earth must have assumed a tolerably symmetrical shape; the eye would have beheld neither elevations nor depressions; the main body of the earth would have been covered all round by a shallow ocean, and this in its turn would have been enveloped by the atmosphere. The surface of the earth, however, is differently formed. Repeated disturbances gave to it a more varying exterior. And what may have been the cause? The very same powers of Nature, which, by the same laws, prevail up to the present day, and which, acting under the peculiar circumstances, existing at that period on a grander scale, produced phenomena now scarcely conceivable.

118. The more compact parts that were deposited first are justly called

fundamental or *primitive* rocks; what was formed next in strata, is designated as *stratified* formations, consisting generally of several different strata, which form together a stratified system. Whatever rocks originated within the same period we call *coeval formations*, and hence we speak of the oldest, the mediæval, and the modern formation, which follow each other in consecutive order.

The crust of the earth, upon hardening and contracting, split into fissures and chasms similar to what we perceive frequently on a considerable scale in parched clay soils. The water entered these chasms, widening them more and more by its solvent power, and penetrated at last through the thin crust to the still glowing interior mass. The result of the sudden contact of an immense body of water with a red-hot surface, would be the formation of a vast body of steam, which would attain simultaneously an extraordinary expansive force from the high temperature. These vapours pressing in every direction with an irresistible force, raised the crust of the earth, puffing it up here and there in vesicles of immense size; they tore it up finally, with awful force, and from the opened abyss there poured forth the red-hot liquid mass. Convulsively propelled by the vapours thus liberated, it spread over the neighbouring surface or was formed into mountains surrounding the opening of the eruption.

119. Let us cast a glance on the present surface of the earth. How different do we find it from that regular form described in § 117! From the uplifted portion of the earth's crust the waters have flowed to the lower parts. The solids have separated from the liquids; the former appearing as *continents* surrounded by islands, the latter as the *sea*. The main land itself consists partly of stratified rocks, partly of an irregularly shaped mass, which has been forced up from the interior and slowly solidified, and which hence presents the appearance of an irregular mass of unstratified rock. The fissures that arose here and there in both formations were filled up with the softer rocks or ores, and in this manner originated *veins*. (Comp. § 108.)

We have now recognized *water* and *fire* as the two causes of the above forms, and hence we name the latter from the mythological representatives of the former: Neptunic, or water formations, and Plutonic, or volcanic (fire) formations.

120. The mountains of this period of primitive formation were not of considerable altitude, nor the seas of any great depth. The localities which had become dry were gradually covered with plants, and perhaps coeval with these animals were created. Considering the thinness of the earth's crust at that period, both land and water must have possessed a higher temperature than at the present time, and hence only such beings were created as were capable of existing under such conditions. Ferns, polypi (corals), are the essential remains of the first living creations that are found in the oldest strata, then formed.

121. It is uncertain how long after this first revolution the earth's crust remained in the condition then acquired. It may have been hundreds or thousands of years. The thickness of the strata gradually deposited, and the successive generations of animals, the remains of which lie over each other in the later formations, afford only relative indications with respect to this subject.

It is, however, certain that the first revolution was not the only one.

Although the crust of the earth increased in thickness by its continual cooling, still the same causes have effected later eruptions, the essential phenomena of which we have already described. The tension and pressure of the vapours must, however, have become much greater from the increased thickness of the crust that confined them, and consequently the now compact strata that have been raised to a much greater height, and the quantity of massive rock forced up through the openings has been much greater, and piled up higher than on their first formation.

The massive rocks of the earlier formation must likewise have been frequently pierced by those of the subsequent periods, whereas the reverse of course could not take place. The waters destroyed at the same time a great part of these rocks and deposited them again in strata, while the vegetable and animal world was overwhelmed in the ruins, and here and there buried and petrified. (§ 112.)

122. Thus several revolutions followed each other at increasing intervals of time. For each later one a greater lapse of time was required in proportion to the still increasing thickness of the crust of the earth, before new fissures, penetrating into the interior, could give access to water. The result was, however, all the more powerful, and the displacement of the strata previously formed, as well as the rising masses of Plutonic rocks, were so much the more considerable. It is an ascertained fact that the *highest* mountains of the earth, the Andes, Cordilleras, Alps, &c., are at the same time the most recent, that is to say, the latest which have been upheaved.

123. Each of these struggles of formation was terminated by the closing up of the fissures and chasms in the crust of the earth, partly through the continued cooling of the interior mass, partly by being covered by aqueous deposits on the outer surface. In some places this was effected perfectly, in others less so, and probably in the latter a new eruption was occasioned at a later period.

But even with the termination of the last general upheaval not all the fissures, leading to the interior, were perfectly closed. In isolated localities where these chasms happened to be very wide, or where mighty rocks accidentally presented gaps between their parts, these openings into the interior were preserved and exist up to the present day. They might properly be compared to the shafts of our chimneys which lead from the exterior of a house to a fire-place.

Such openings in the earth are called *volcanos*, fig. 18. Their operations and effects are pretty well known and easily understood from the previous statements. If their shafts were empty we should be able to look down them to the glowing bowels of the earth; but these hollows or craters are covered with cooled and hardened masses of rocks called *lava*, and with other *volcanic* formations.

From time to time the waters, in a manner not very difficult to explain, find access to the interior of these volcanos. The steam suddenly rises. bursts open large fissures, and causes earthquakes, that thus convulse a large extent of country, and generally precede an eruption. For the increasing tension of the steam will at last force the glowing mass upwards, together with its solid cover. The repeated rising and falling of the great volumes of steam, their partial escape, and the violent commotion and vibrations of great masses of the earth, are always attended with terrific noise, which may be compared at times to the continued rollings, and occasionally to the single

18. View of the Cone of Cotopaxi.

claps of thunder. The red-hot and liquid mass being forced up finally to the mouth of the crater, its cover is immediately burst and thrown up

19. Crater of Vesuvius in 1829.

towards the heavens, its fragments and dust being scattered in the air, and carried by the winds, as volcanic ashes, often to a distance of many miles, fig. 19. The glowing mass or stream of lava overflows unimpeded the margin of the crater, fig. 20, and in its progress down the sides of the mountain destroys irresistibly every thing it meets.

20. Stream of Lava from Vesuvius in April 1822.

This terrific revolution of Nature possesses, however, at the same time, the conditions of its termination. The steam having escaped, the calm in the interior is restored, and the ejected lava-stream flows slower outside the mountain; finally the progress of the stream is interrupted, and the lava begins to harden, while the interior mass sinks down again to its original level. Only steam, sulphurous vapours, &c., still escape from the crater, and hot fountains spring forth in its neighbourhood, indicating that all below is still glowing. A. von Humboldt truly designates volcanos as the safety-valves of the earth's crust.

124. The environs of volcanos are covered with older and more recent streams of lava, which by decomposition yield a most productive soil, and hence a most luxuriant vegetation surrounds the bases of all volcanoes. In spite of the dangerous proximity, several villages have been built near Mount Vesuvius within the reach of its destructive activity. Moreover, in the neighbourhood of volcanos minerals are now in daily progress of formation, either crystallising from the glowing mass, or being formed by the decomposing influence of the rising acid vapours upon other rocks. Hence in these localities a large number of minerals is to be found.

In course of time, however, all volcanos seem to become extinct, as is the case already with many. Thus, for instance, the so-called Eifel, between the river Aar and Treves, consists of a group of volcanic elevations. Lake Laacher, near Andernach, is the crater of an extinct volcano, filled with water, the whole surrounding country bearing characteristic evidence of volcanic origin.

The external form of volcanos is very peculiar, and generally *conical.* They are, in fact, gigantic air or steam vesicles, which have been upheaved from below, and finally elongated to an apex, at the termination of which the steam and gas broke through. But such a disruption has not taken place in every case. We find a great many conical mountains that never were active volcanos: in these cases the force acting from below was not sufficiently powerful to pierce through the crust; the glowing mass was hardened inside without even reaching the surface. Indeed, we frequently find in the centre of such conical elevations, consisting of stratified rocks, a mass of Plutonic rock, particularly basalt.

125. In Europe there are no active volcanos of importance, with the exception of Mount Vesuvius, Etna, and Stromboli, in Italy, and of those in Iceland, among which Mount Hecla is the most celebrated. The eruptions of the above-named volcanos following each other at continually greater intervals of time, though still formidable to the nearest neighbourhood, do not now extend over any considerable extent of country. History, however, records several instances of terrible volcanic disturbances, which proved destructive to entire districts, and even to whole countries. Thus in the year A. D. 79 the flourishing and rich cities of Herculaneum and Pompeii were buried beneath volcanic ashes. Lisbon was destroyed by an earthquake in the year 1755, and even at more recent dates formidable destruction by earthquakes has taken place in South America. In that part of the world entire groups of volcanos are found still active, from the position of which L. von Buch points out, that they stand on the fissures of former disruptions of the earth's crust, and have interior connection with each other. The most celebrated volcanos of South America are—the Jorullo, which arose in 1758, and the Cotopaxi, of the chain of Andes. The latter volcano, which is 17,662 feet in height, now and then sends forth great masses of mud and quantities of fish, thus proving in a remarkable and convincing manner its internal connection with the waters.

126. Hitherto we have directed attention only to one of the phenomena that appeared during the early revolutions of the earth, namely, its volcanic disturbances.

Let us now return to other phenomena, and consider the development of animal and vegetable life. It is clear that organic growth could proceed in a proportionately larger scale, the longer the periods were that elapsed between the succeeding disturbances. Plants and animals made their appearance not only more plentifully but also in greater variety. Palms and coniferous plants appear in addition to ferns and equiseta, and batrachians and other amphibious animals, in addition to fishes. Intermingled with these the crustacea appeared in immense numbers. Thus the more perfect creatures followed in proper order upon the imperfect, since the existence of the latter formed the indispensable condition of that of the former. A certain change likewise took place with regard to the formation of rocks. The deposition of the insoluble and difficultly-fusible combination of silica and alumina in the primitive rocks was followed by the gradual deposition, amongst the mediæval rocks, of beds of limestone, gypsum, rock-salt, and of coal, the remains of the destroyed vegetable kingdom of earlier ages.

127. Consequently, it is natural that, in penetrating the crust of the earth, we should meet with a series of strata differing in character according to the period at which they were individually formed, and as in all essential points the same phenomena had occurred over the whole surface of the earth, it follows that the coeval formations of its crust must be everywhere equal or similar. Experience has, on the whole, confirmed this inference, though, in some instances, the proof is often difficult and sometimes impossible to obtain. Thus, everywhere, slaty rocks form the lowest or oldest strata: nevertheless, many deviations exist. In many localities entire systems or series of rocky masses, which we find at other places, are wanting: however, this is after all but a local deficiency, and, therefore, of minor importance. We shall see that water was frequently the cause of the destruction of such systems in some localities, while they were preserved in others.

Classification of Formations.

128. The term *formation* in Geology is applied to any portions of the earth's crust, of lesser or greater thickness, which arose under the same contemporary influence. Formations, which, in consequence of their close proximity, stand in mutual relation to each other, are considered by the geologist as connected groups; the separate layers constituting a formation are called its *members*.

129. The coeval formations of the various Neptunic and Plutonic rocks, cannot be easily ascertained, on account of their different external and internal condition, although a subsequent aqueous formation must correspond with a preceding igneous formation. Greenstone and porphyry which have broken through granite are certainly of later production than granite, as greywacke and coal that overlie the slaty rocks are newer than those rocks.

It would, perhaps, be most conformable to our purpose to designate the different periods of formation by those Plutonic rocks, which were then produced, and thus to classify the total construction of the earth's crust into the periods of the elevation of granite, of greenstone, of porphyry, of melaphyr, of basalt and of volcanos, and treating, intermediately, of the aqueous formations as they were slowly and successively deposited. In all geological systems, however, the terms have been chosen from the stratified rocks, partly because the latter were first examined scientifically, partly because the Plutonic rocks are not everywhere defined with desirable certainty.

130. In the following Table we meet with peculiar terms, some of whicn are merely accidental, without particular meaning, while others indicate an essential member of the group, as, for instance, the names — marl, red sandstone (new and old), lias, fossiliferous limestone (muschelkalk), &c.

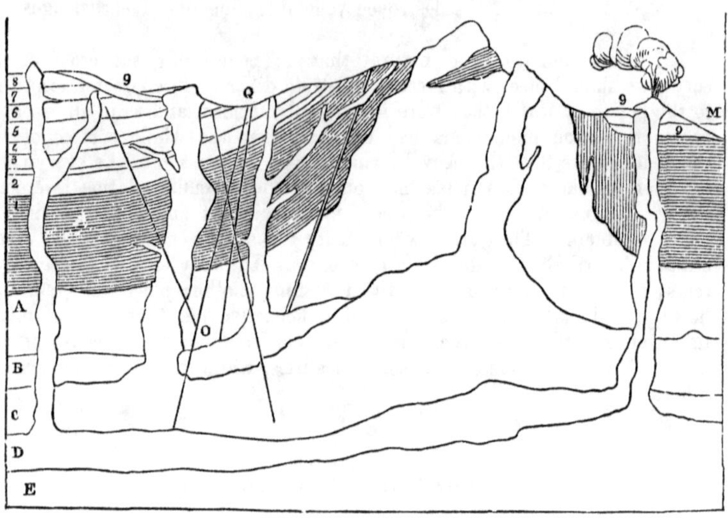

21. Illustration of the Arrangement of the various Groups of Rocks.

Stratified Rocks.	Quaternary Rocks ...	9. Diluvial and Alluvial	Deposits.
	Tertiary	8. Molasse (comp. § 142).	
	Secondary..............	7. Chalk.	
		6. Jura.	
		5. Trias.	
		4. Zechstein.	
		3. Coal.	
	Transition Rocks.....	2.. Greywacke.	
	Primitive Rocks	1. Slate.	

Interior Mass of the Earth.

Massive Rocks.	A. Granite.
	B. Greenstone.
	C. Porphyry.
	D. Basalt.
	E. Volcanic Rocks.

M. The Sea.
O. Mineral Veins.

SYSTEMATIC ARRANGEMENT of the FORMATIONS (beginning with the oldest).

Aqueous Formations (Neptunic, Normal or Stratified Formation; Stratified Rocks).			Igneous Formations (Plutonic or Volcanic, Abnormal Formation; Massive Rocks).	
Groups.	**Formations.**	**Classes.**	**Groups.**	**Most important Rocks of these Groups.**
I. Slate-Group.	Clay-Slate, Mica-slate, Gneiss.	1. Primitive or Metamorphic Rocks.	A. Granite-Group.	Granite, Granulite, Syenite.
II. Silurian-Group.	Upper and Lower Greywacke.	2. Transition or Palaeozoic Rocks.	B. Greenstone-Group.	Greenstone, Serpentine.
III. Carboniferous Group.	Old Red Sandstone, Coal-beds, Mountain-Limestone, Coal Sandstone.			
IV. Permian-Group.	Magnesian Limestone, or Zechstein.	3. Secondary or Mesozoic Rocks.	C. Porphyry-Group.	Felsite-porphyry, Pitchstone-porphyry, Melaphyr.
V. Trias-Group.	Keuper, Muschelkalk, Variegated Sandstone.			
VI. Oolitic, or Jurassic-Group.	Lower Oolite, Middle Oolite, Upper Oolite, Lias.		D. Basalt-Group.	Basalt, Phonolite, Trachyte.
VII. Chalk-Group.	Wealden, Green Sand, Chalk.			
VIII. Molasse-Group.	Eocene, Meiocene, Pleiocene.	4. Tertiary, Supra-cretaceous, or Cainozoic Rocks.	E. Volcanic Group.	Lava, Scoria, Volcanic Mud.
IX. Diluvial and Alluvial Groups.	Alluvium, Newer Pleitocene, Older Pleitocene, Diluvium or Drift.	5. Quaternary Rocks.		

22. Configuration and Arrangement of the various species of Rocks.

Fig. 22 will afford a general idea of the configuration and arrangement of the various species of rocks and veins.

1. Granite.	13. Shale.
2. Gneiss.	14. Calcareous Sandstone.
3. Mica-slate.	15. Ironstone.
4. Syenite.	16. Basalt.
5. Serpentine.	17. Coal.
6. Porphyry.	18. Gypsum.
7. Granular Marble.	19. Rock Salt.
8. Chlorite Slate.	20. Chalk.
9. Quartz Rock.	21. Amygdaloid.
10. Greywacke.	A A. Primary Mountains.
11. Sandstone.	B B. Secondary Mountains.
12. Limestone.	*a a.* Veins.

131. In the study of the stratified rocks the only correct method will be to proceed from the oldest to the most recent formation: first, because this method corresponds with the progress of the development of the earth and of its products; and, secondly, because the description of later conglomerates, if they contain displaced fragments of older stratified rocks, previously undescribed, could not be rendered perfectly clear. By inverting the progress from the more recent to the older groups, the former would appear as if suspended in the air, because the supporting strata, on which they are resting, would not be known.

A.—AQUEOUS FORMATIONS.

Neptunic, Normal, or Stratified Formations.

1st Group—SLATES.

Primitive or Metamorphic Rocks.

132. The slate-group has been entered in the table of classification § 130 amongst the aqueous formations, although, from the way in which it originated, we ought perhaps to class it amongst the igneous formations. [Rocks of this group appear to have been originally deposited from water, and to have been subsequently altered by the combined action of heat, pressure, and other causes. Hence they are called *altered* or *metamorphic* rocks.] We class the slates among the stratified rocks because they were designated in § 115 as the *first compact layer* or crust of the once entirely fluid globe, which was however soon broken through by granite. Hence the slate rocks ought to be met with everywhere, if immense bodies of the stratified formations had not covered them in. They are however distributed over the whole surface of the earth, and constitute the principal part of a great number of mountains.

Other massive rocks frequently penetrate through this slate-group, especially greenstone, porphyry, and granite. They contain, not unfrequently, veins of ore.

The four principal kinds of this group are clay-slate, mica-slate, [crystal line marble,] and gneiss.

Clay-slate (§ 84), of which the common roofing and writing slate is the purest form, occurs in great variety. It is not so rich in mineral veins, and is less generally distributed than the other kinds. Great masses of it occur in Wales, in Cumberland, about Loch Lomond in Scotland, and in many parts of Germany. [It is usually dark-coloured, but varies from a greenish or bluish-grey to a lead colour.]

133. Mica-slate (§ 85) is very important from the mighty masses which exist of it. This rock forms large mountains with projecting ridges or

23. Mountains of Mica-slate and Granite, Glen Sannox, Island of Arran.

craggy tops and precipitous ravines. A great part of the *Swiss* and *Tyrol* Alps consists of this rock, which is moreover the prevailing constituent of the *Sudets*, the *Riesen-*, *Erze-*, and *Fichtel-Gebirge*. It is very abundant

24. Contorted Mica-slate, Island of Arran.

in Scotland, in the mountains that extend from Argyleshire up towards Aberdeen. In the neighbourhood of the places where granite and porphyry break through it, it contains rich veins of ore, which lead to important mining operations.

[*Crystalline marble*, which was originally coral, chalk or tuff, has been crystallized by the action of heat under enormous pressure. When pure, it constitutes the white granular marble used in sculpture.]

Gneiss, which holds an intermediate position between mica-slate and granite, occurs in a great variety of forms, and is rich in mineral veins, particularly where it is penetrated by porphyry. This rock forms entire mountains in many parts of the continent of Europe, especially in the alpine districts, where it is commonly associated with granite; [with which it is identical in composition, but differs from it in being stratified.] It is also abundant in Scotland. [Vermont, the western parts of Massachusetts, and Connecticut furnish interesting examples of metamorphic rocks: and the strata of the Allegheny mountains have been extensively altered by the action of the same metamorphic causes.

The amount of change exhibited by the rocks of this group differs exceedingly in degree. Some are but slightly crystalline; and their fossils, though indistinct, are not obliterated. Others have lost nearly all traces of their sedimentary origin, and their fossils are mostly obliterated. Others again are wholly crystalline in their structure, and entirely destitute of organic remains.]

2nd Group—GREYWACKE.

Transition or Silurian Rocks.

134. The term trantition rocks, applied to this group, shows, that we have arrived at the confines of the decidedly-stratified formations. These rocks exhibit, in fact, the character of the first crust of the earth, which we have, in § 118, designated as primitive rocks.

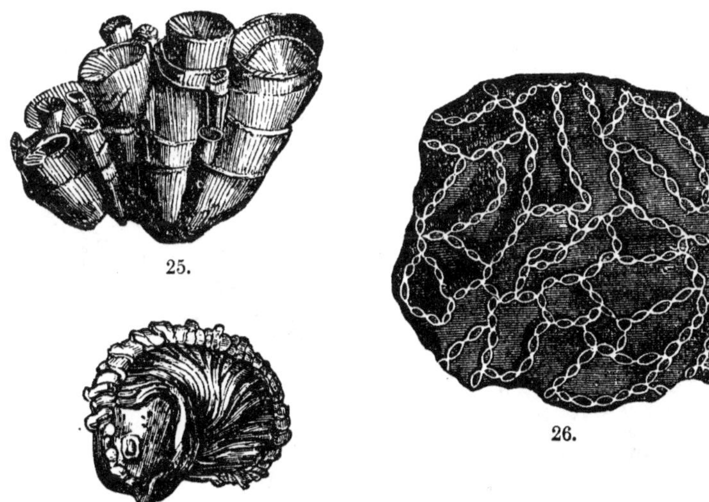

25.

26.

27.

[The name of *Silurian* was first proposed by Sir Roderick Murchison, from the name of the place where it was first successfully investigated, *i. e.*, that part of Wales and some contiguous counties of England which once constituted the kingdom of the *Silures*, a tribe of ancient Britons.]

The most important members of this group are *greywacke-slate* and *greywacke-sandstone*, which are associated, particularly in the upper parts, with masses of limestone and dolomite. The name of this group is derived from a species of finely-grained sandstone, of grey colour, detached and compact pieces of which lying about on the fields are called "Wacken."

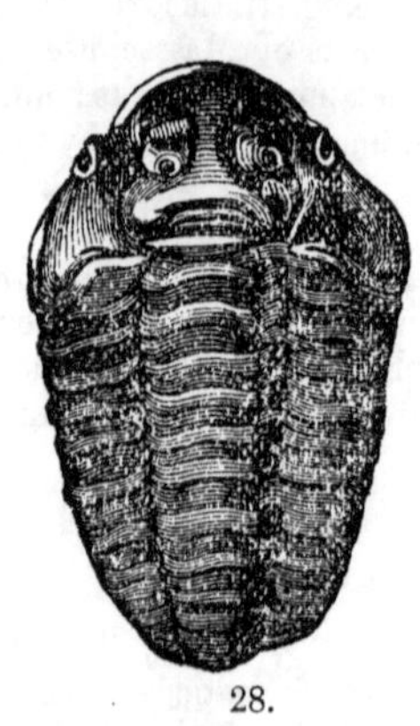

28.

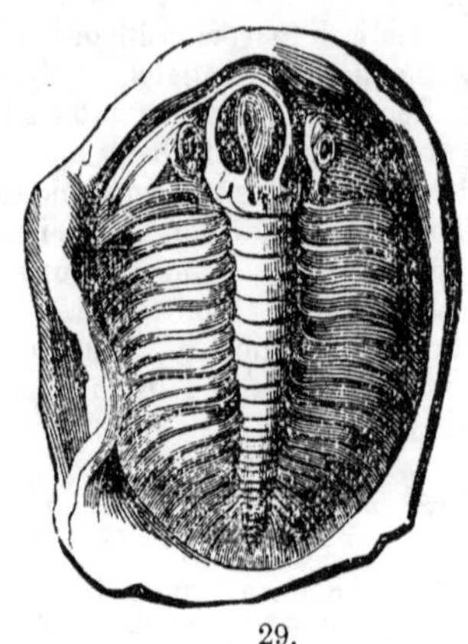

29.

Greywacke has been found distributed in large masses through various parts of Europe, especially in the interior of Bohemia and in the Tyrolese Alps. It occurs likewise in several other quarters of the globe. It is abundant in the south of Scotland at Leadhills. The valleys of the greywacke-group are mostly very winding, as, for instance, that of the Mosel and of the Aar.

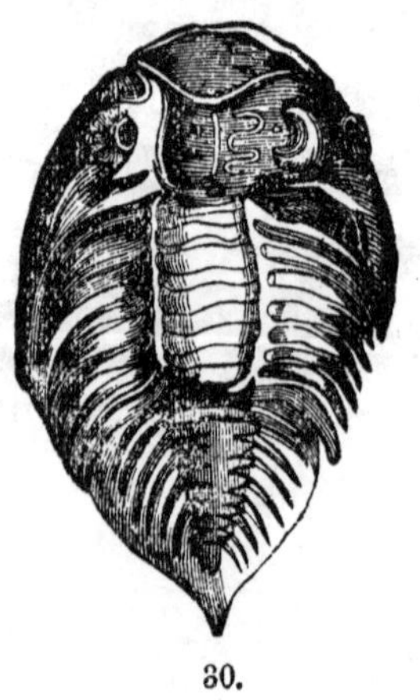

30.

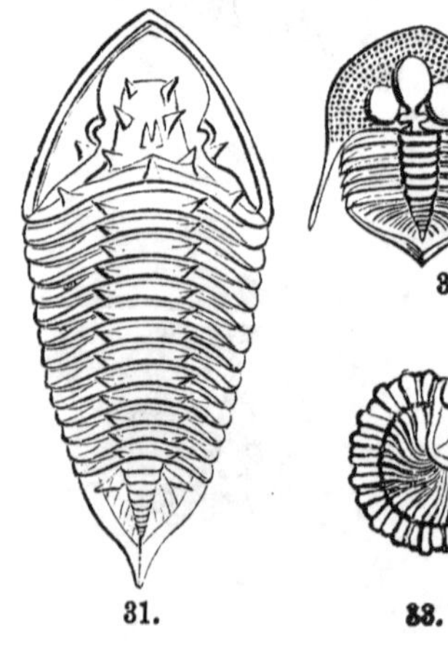

31. 32. 33.

The *greywacke-slates* constitute a part of the slaty mountains of the Rhine, and form, in some places, a transition into common slate, fit for roofing. This formation contains, especially in England, *Anthracite* (§ 30), a coal that takes fire with difficulty, and possesses a perfect mineral appearance.

Fossils are found abundantly in the upper members of this group, while the lower contain but few. They are chiefly Polypi, Mollusca, and the so-called *Trilobites, i. e.*, extinct crustacea of the isapodous and decapodous families. [The crinoideans and corals (figs. 25 and 26) were well represented. The family of Trilobites (figs. 27—33) was more fully represented in this than in any other period.] Fishes and plants appear here more rarely. [All the vertebrated animals except fishes are wanting.]

3rd Group—COAL FORMATION.

135. We have now to consider one of the most important of the various formations, namely, that which includes coal as its essential member, a mineral which as fuel has become indispensable to man for domestic and industrial purposes. This group begins with a coarse conglomerate, consisting of the fragments of older rocks, and never containing basalt, limestone, or flints, and which, on account of its peculiar colour, is called *Old Red Sandstone.* This attains to the thickness of even 3000 feet, and occurs sometimes on the flanks of high mountains, and sometimes constituting by itself mountainous masses, as in the Thuringian forest and the Hartz mouutains. Very few impressions of plants are found in this rock.

Upon this old red sandstone follows the *coal formation* properly speaking. It consists of beds of coal from a few inches to 20 feet (and rarely more than 40 feet) in thickness, and between which there is frequently interposed a peculiar *sandstone* (coal sandstone, new red sandstone), and a dark coloured *slate-clay* (coal schiefer). In this order from 8 to 120 beds of coal frequently overlie each other, of which however only the few thicker ones repay the trouble of working. Beneath the coal lies the *greywacke* of the preceding group. The sandstone is exceedingly diversified, and often of fine quality, and well adapted for building purposes.

34.

The outcropping of the coal formation at the surface of the earth seems, in some measure, to depend upon the rising of the mountains; for, in extensive plains, it is generally not discovered, or, in such localities, the beds are too far below the surface to be discoverable or even to be reached by boring.

Coal seems likewise not to have been formed equally in all places during the period in which it originated. The remains of plants, [of which about 1000 species have been described, being more than half of the entire number occurring in the fossil state], found in this stratum lead to the inference, that, during that period there existed an exceedingly vigorous and crowded vegetation, principally confined to equisetaceæ and ferns, of which the *Sphenopteris Hibberti* (fig. 34), *Pecopteris Bucklandi* (fig. 35) and *Neuropteris Loshii* (fig. 36), are amongst the most beautiful that have yet been discovered. [Not less than 250 species of ferns have been already obtained from the coal strata; a somewhat singular result, because the whole of Europe affords at present no more than 50 indigenous species.] These remarkable plants must have presented an aspect essentially different from that

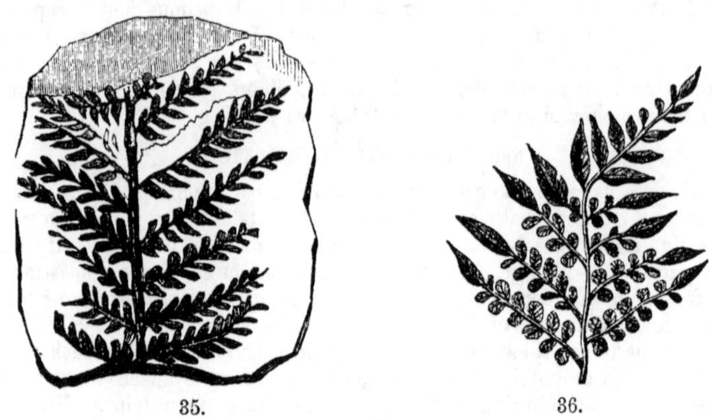

35. 36.

of our present forests. Most likely, however, such coverings of vegetation were not everywhere equally crowded together to give rise by their destruction to beds of coal. Hence it is very possible, nay, even probable, that, in some localities, the other members of this group may be found in succession without any beds of coal between them.

[Fig. 37 represents the Fauna and Flora of the Carboniferous period].

37.

It has been generally observed, that the beds of coal are partially surrounded by hills as in a sort of trough, similar to the position of the molasse (§ 142), from which it would appear, as if those forests of vegetation were particularly developed only within these mountain gorges, and could only have formed considerable deposits of coal at those places. The preceding statements afford indications to guide us in searching for coal wherever we may suspect its presence. If the part of the country be composed of primitive mountains or of Plutonic rocks, which we have designated in fig. 21 under letters A to E, we may, with certainty, conclude on the absence of coal. If stratified formations of great thickness be present, it is not likely that we shall find coal at an accessible depth; such is more probable, however, where the aqueous formations, bordering upon the massive rocks, have been elevated and uplifted by these, in such a manner that the lower strata approach the surface or even become exposed to our view.

Our search after coal is particularly encouraged by the presence of red sandstone and grey-wacke, because these formations generally border on beds of coal. If, moreover, the surrounding hills of massive rock should form a basin, the hope of finding coal is all the more well founded, and repeated boring should be resorted to.

136. The coal-beds of Germany are not very numerous, nor is the coal of the best quality. It is in Great Britain that the best coal is most abundantly found, particularly in the neighbourhood of Newcastle-on-Tyne, in Staffordshire, and in Lanarkshire. Coal is also met with in Belgium and the neighbouring parts of France, and at Dombrowa, in Poland. The members of the coal-group have been found generally spread over America, Asia, and even Australia. In South America coal was discovered by Humboldt at a height of 8,000 feet above the level of the sea. The total amount of coal raised annually in Europe exceeds 700 millions of cwts., of which England alone contributes about 450, and Germany about 40 millions. [There is a rich bituminous coal-field in Nova Scotia and a small anthracite coal-field in the eastern part of Massachusetts; but the largest explored coal-field in the world has its north-east extremity west of the Delaware River, in New York, and extends through Pennsylvania into Ohio westward, and to Alabama on the south-west. It covers more than 100,000 square miles, and contains more than one million of million tons of bituminous coal. A much less extensive but rich field of anthracite coal lies in the eastern part of Pennsylvania, west of the Delaware River. The central region of Michigan constitutes another large coal-field. Another covers most of Illinois, the south-west part of Indiana, and the adjacent part of Kentucky. The carboniferous system is found in Vancouver's Island and in New Mexico; and in South America, in Chili.]

The *mountain limestone*, which accompanies the coal formation, is a mineral of considerable importance. It usually includes extensive metallic deposits. This is the case in Belgium, in Derbyshire, and in Scotland. Near Glasgow, it is accompanied not only by coal, but by immense masses of clay ironstone, and in the smelting of iron from that ore, the carboniferous limestone is used as a flux. It forms very beautiful dark-coloured marbles which admit of a fine polish. Organic remains are very abundant in it, of which figures 38–42 may be cited as characteristic specimens.

[Among the vegetation of the carboniferous era, may be mentioned Sigillaria (figs. 43 and 44) and Stigmaria, which were once supposed to be distinct plants. But it is now established that the former is the stem and the latter the root of a large tree. The roots are found abundantly in a deposit of clay, which invariably underlies the coal, and is therefore called *underclay*. The trunks are generally in a horizontal position, but they are

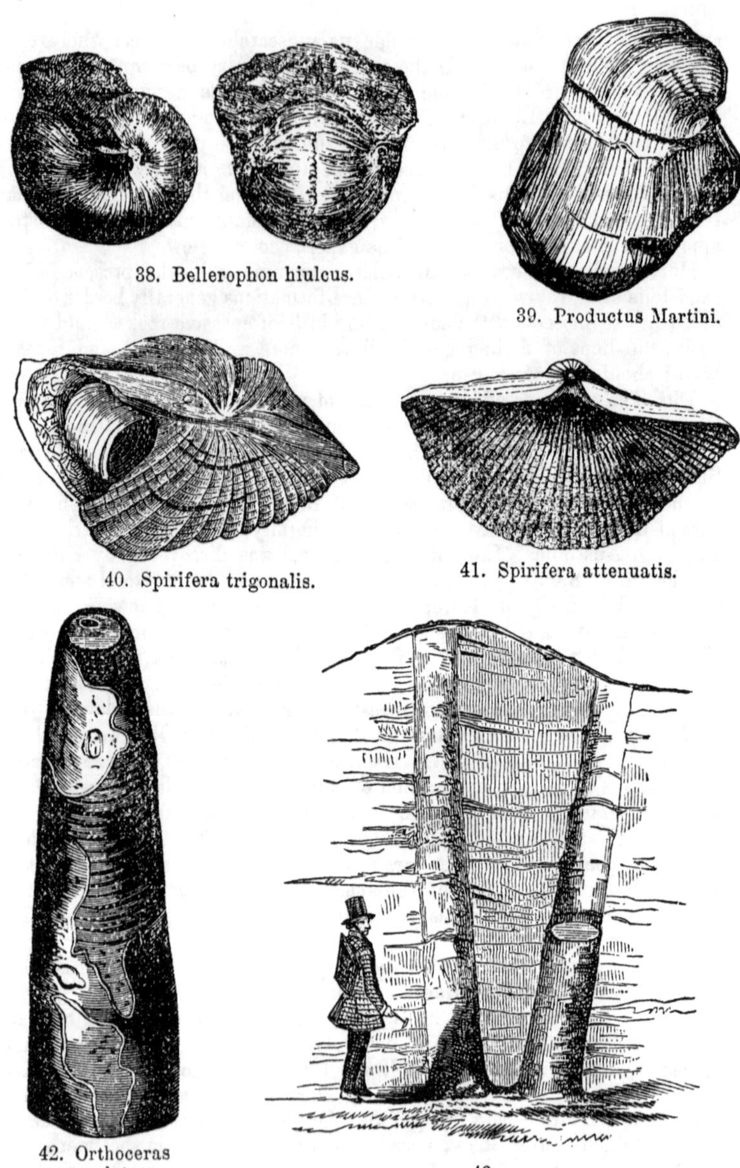

38. Bellerophon hiulcus.

39. Productus Martini.

40. Spirifera trigonalis.

41. Spirifera attenuatis.

42. Orthoceras undatum.

43.

occasionally found erect, as was exhibited (fig. 44) in the Killingworth Colliery, Newcastle district. Not less than 150 species of fishes of this period have been preserved; and a majority of these (94 species) belonged to the families of the shark and ray. Some of these fish are very remote in their

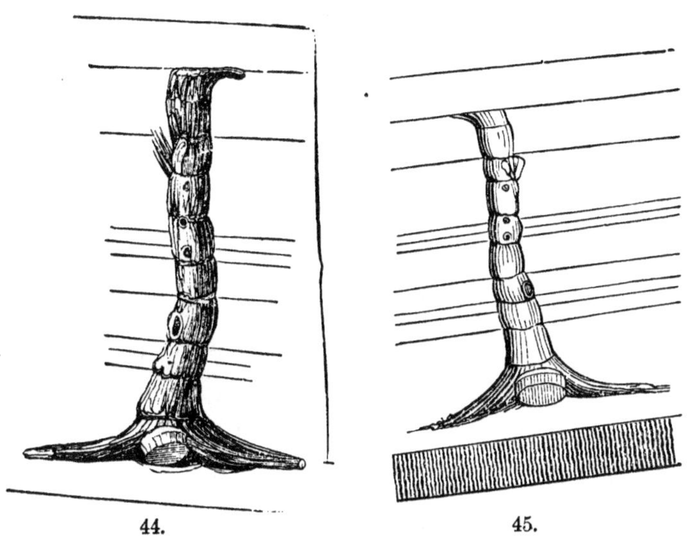

44. 45.

organization from any now living, especially those of the family called *sauroid* by Agassiz; as *Megalichthys*, *Holoptychius*, and others, which are often of great size, and all predaceous. These were doubtless more highly organized than any living fish.]

4TH GROUP—ZECHSTEIN, OR PERMIAN SYSTEM.

137. Of all the formations constituting the crust of the earth, that of the Magnesian limestone or Zechstein has been found up to the present time the least distributed. [Sir Roderick Murchison has proposed for it the name of *Permian*, from Perm, a Russian government, where these strata are more extensively developed than elsewhere, occupying an area twice the size of France, and containing an abundant and varied series of fossils. It is also well developed in England and France; but it is in Germany especially that it appears with many well-marked subdivisions.] In the north-east of the latter country, and especially in the county of Mansfield, in Saxony, between the sandstone of the preceding group and the conglomerate of the following, there lies, sharply separated, this group, the most essential member of which is a dark bituminous marl-slate rich in copper ores, whence it has obtained the name of *Copper-Slate*. This is worked in many mines. The Zechstein-group contains but few species of fossils; but these few occur in great quantities. [The species of fossil plants are not numerous, and most of them are identified with those of the carboniferous group. Of fossil animals, 166 species are known, being chiefly corals, shells and fish. The trilobites have disappeared.]

The upper members of the Zechstein formation occasionally contain *gypsum*, which occurs in some localities in considerable masses, as, for instance, on the south of the Hartz mountains. It is often also accompanied by *rock-salt:* the salt-works of Northern Germany depend, therefore, upon the produce of the Zechstein formation. In the neighbourhood of Eisleben and Eisenach many caverns are found within the gypsum beds, which probably arose from the previous existence of rock-salt in them, which, in course of time, was removed by the action of water.

5th Group—TRIAS, or New Red-Sandstone.

138. The name of this group is derived from its consisting of three members. They occur in Thuringia and Swabia; the entire Black Forest belongs to it, as do the opposite Vosges Mountains, between which the Rhine has excavated its gigantic bed. [In England, it is principally developed in the valleys of the Dee, Mersey and Weaver. In the United States, it extends from Vermont, in the valley of the Connecticut River, through Massachusetts and Connecticut, and from New Jersey to North and South Carolina.]

Gypsum and *Rock-salt* are characteristic of this group, the upper member of which, called *Keuper*, contains them in great abundance. Thus in Wirtemberg all the salt-works are supplied from this member, as likewise are those of Halle, Fredericshall, Dürrheim, Wimpfen, &c.

Another member of this group is *Muschelkalk*, or shell-limestone, thus called from the great quantities of the shells it contains in separate layers. [This member is wanting in England.]

The lowest and most abundant member of this group is the *Variegated Sandstone*, which is of a red, yellow, and white colour, and is very abundantly distributed over the continent of Europe. [It was from this member that Dr. Buckland proposed the name of "Poikilitic" or *variegated*, for the whole group.] The thickness of its beds varies from 400 to 600 feet, and occasionally reaches to 1,000 feet.

The decrease of fossils in the trias-group is very remarkable. The keuper

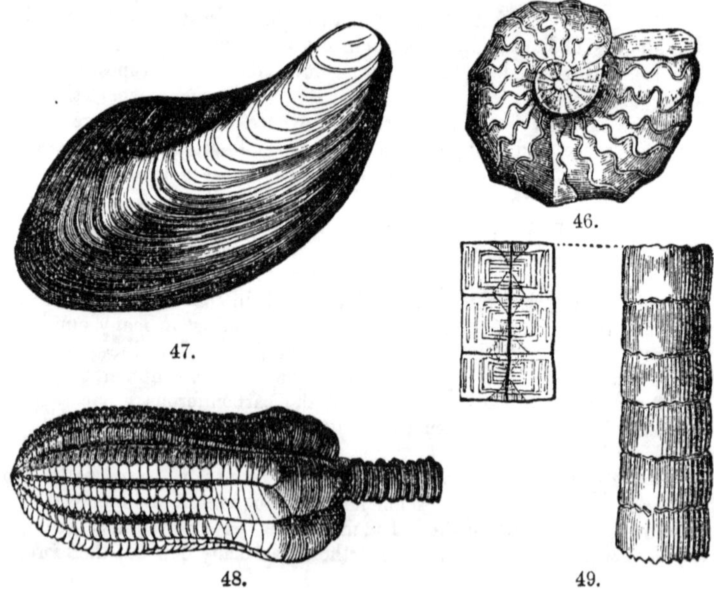

46.

47.

48.

49.

and the variegated sandstone are especially poor in these remains. They are numerous in fossiliferous lime (muschelkalk), but less rich in the number of species than in Jura. Bivalve shells predominate, and the ammonites and belemnites, so frequent in the latter, are here entirely wanting. We must mention, however, the ceratites [a genus allied to the ammonites], as belonging exclusively to muschelkalk. [Fig. 46 represents the *Ceratites nodosus*. *Aricula socialis*, fig. 47, which ranges through the keuper, Muschelkalk and variegated sandstone, is very characteristic of the Muschelkalk in Germany, France and Poland. The abundance of the heads and stems of lily encrinites (*Encrinites moniliformis*, fig. 48) shows the slow manner in which some beds of this limestone have been formed in clear sea-water. The lily encrinite was remarkable for the elegance and symmetry of its form and for its complicated skeleton, which consisted of not less than twenty-six thousand pieces. The body was supported on a slender stem, of which a drawing on a larger scale is seen in fig. 49, and which was attached at the base to some hard substance in the sea.] Of fossil plants we find ferns, and the various species of equisetaceæ, in all the members of this group, down to the variegated sandstone. Remains of fish and amphibious animals are rarely met with.

In certain layers of the variegated sandstone there have been discovered hardened footprints, of which it is doubtful whether they belong to mammalia, to birds, or to amphibious animals, which latter is the most probable. At Hessberg, near Hildberghausen, in Saxony, unmistakable impressions of the feet of quadrupeds have been discovered in the grey sandstone of that neighbourhood. (See fig. 50.) [From the resemblance of these foot-

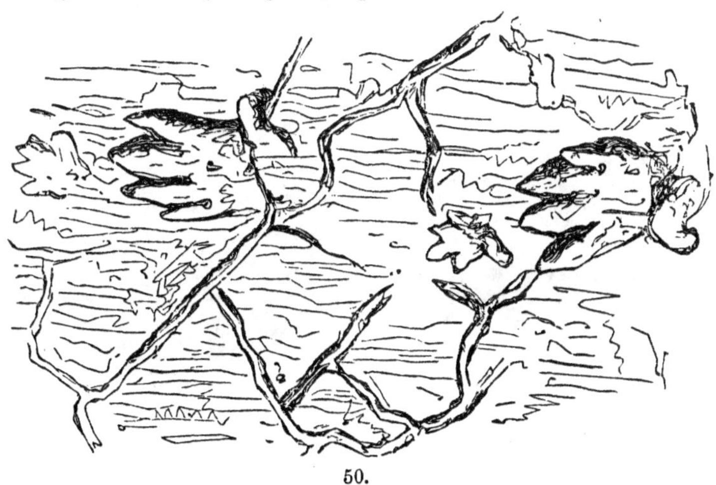

50.

prints to the form of the human hand, the animal by which they were impressed has been called Cheirotherium or *Handbeast;* but they are now generally assigned to the Labyrinthodon, an animal whose bones are found in the same series of deposits. Professor Hitchcock has discovered, in the sandstone of the Connecticut valley, footprints of about 50 species of animals, of which 12 were quadrupeds, and 32 bipeds. Of these last, 8 were probably birds with three thick toes, 14 birds with three or four slender toes, and 8 may have been biped reptiles. Of the remaining species some were invertebrate animals, and others wholly doubtful.]

6TH GROUP—JURA.

139. The Jura mountains, which rise from 4,000 to 5,000 feet, have given their name to this formation, which has been found pretty abundantly distributed all over Europe. [The group consists of four members, namely, the *upper*, the *middle*, and the *lower Oolite*, and the *lias*. The whole group is sometimes called the "Oolitic," and has been so named because in the countries where it was first examined, the limestones belonging to it had an oolitic structure, *i. e.* were composed of numerous small egg-like grains, resembling the roe of a fish, each of which has usually a small fragment of sand as a nucleus, around which concentric layers of calcareous matter have accumulated.] Limestone is its principal rock, occurring alternately with dolomite, marl, clay, and sandstone. In the upper strata a lighter coloured limestone prevails, which turns white when exposed to the air, and contains corals, while among the lower strata dark-coloured limestones and marls are predominant.

In Germany, the Swabian Alps, extending through Bavaria and Franconia up to Saxony, belong especially to the Jura-group. This formation is famous for its numerous caverns, containing deposits of bones. It also contains those compact tabular limestones which are important in their application as lithographic stones. These are found at Solenhofen in Pappenheim.

The lowest member of the Jura-formation has received its name, *lias*, from the corruption of the word layers.

51. Ammonites Bucklandi.

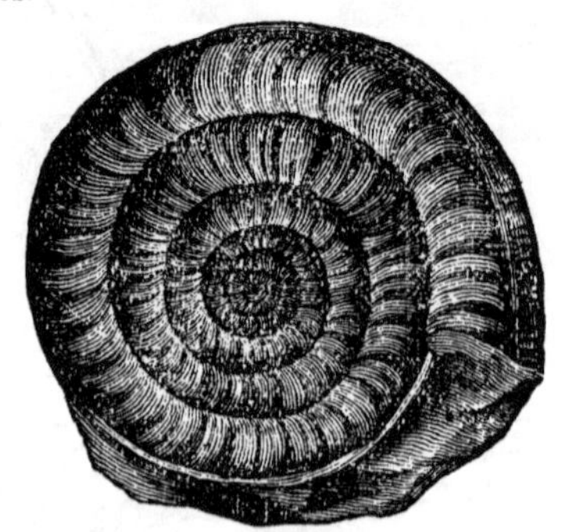

52.

Fossils are exceedingly plentiful throughout the entire formation, particularly mollusca, amongst which there are many *Ammonites* (figs. 51 and 52) and *Belemnites* (fig. 53), fish and saurians; of which the winged lizard (*Pterodactylus*, fig. 54) is perhaps the most remarkable member. [Of the marine saurians in the

53. Belemnites mucronatus.

Oolitic members, the *Pliosaurus* and *Cetiosaurus* were the most remarkable. The *Megalosaurus* was the largest of the terrestrial saurians. The

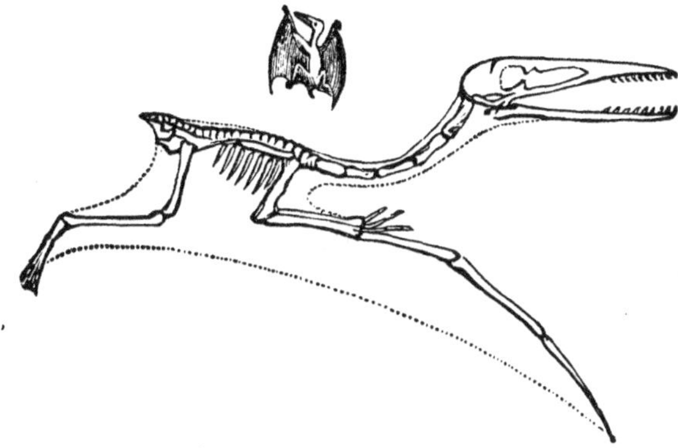

54. Pterodactylus longirostris.

most characteristic fossils of the Oolite, however, are the remains of the marsupial quadrupeds, found in the Stonesfield slate; and which furnish the earliest proofs of the existence of mammals on the surface of our planet.] In the lower strata, marine plants are found.

[The Fauna and vegetation of the Lias are shown in fig. 55. This liassic

55.

member is characterized by the most remarkable animal remains of the whole fossiliferous strata. The reptiles belong mostly to two genera: the *Icthyosaurus*, whose skeleton is shown in fig. 56, and restored outline in

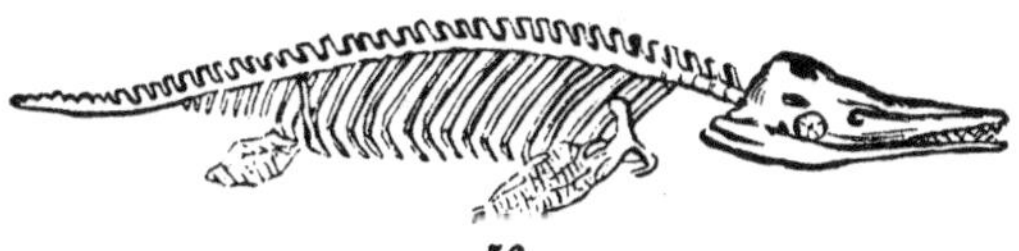

56.

fig. 57, and the *Plesiosaurus*, whose skeleton is seen in fig. 58, and restored outline in fig. 59.

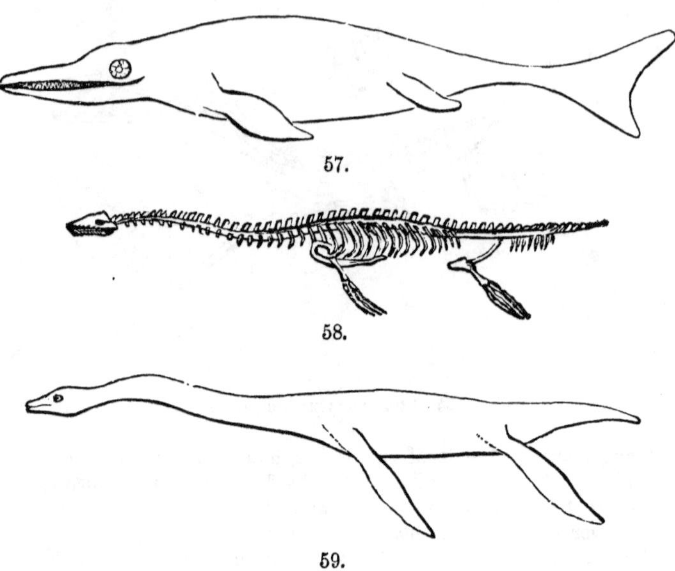

57.

58.

59.

We have ample and curious evidence of the voracity of the Ichthyosaurus and the nature of its food, which appears to have been fish and small reptiles; for the half-digested remains of these animals are found in the fossil feces or Coprolites (fig. 60) of the ichthyosaur.

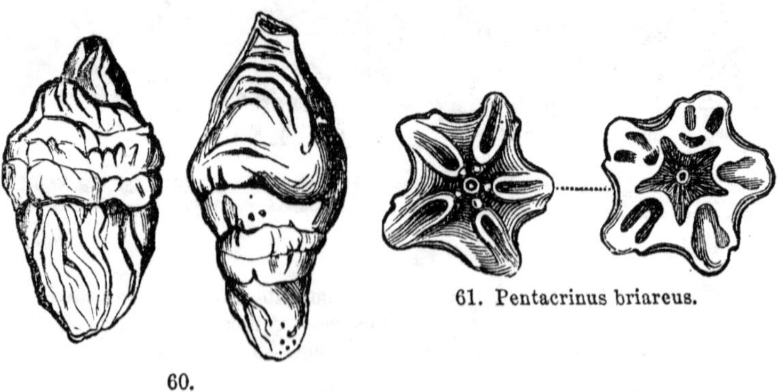

61. Pentacrinus briareus.

60.

Corals were rare; but their place was supplied by the crinoideans, particularly by the genus *pentacrinus*. The P. briareus is shown in fig. 61.]

The soils produced from the Jura-formation are fruitful, with the exception of those from the limestone and dolomite mountains.

7th Group—CHALK.

140. While the formations of the preceding groups make their appearance more in dispersed localities, and particularly where the natural conditions of alluvial and diluvial action existed on a more or less grand scale, we find the members of the cretaceous group much more independently and continuously spread. It consists of a defined series of Lime-, Marl-, Sand-, and Clay-strata, the uppermost of which contain the fossils of marine animals, and the lowermost those of terrestrial plants and of fresh-water animals.

Chalk includes a series of groups, to which the Zechstein, Trias, and Jura groups belong, and which Werner designated as *Secondary* mountain formation. The most striking characteristic of the secondary mountain formation is the absence of the fossils of birds and mammalia, which indicates that it originated under physical conditions essentially different from the later and present formations.

The Chalk-group has been found not only in almost all countries of Europe, but also in various parts of Asia, Africa, and America. Europe, during its formation, seems to have been almost entirely covered by the sea. The rocks of this group form a hilly or undulated country, without producing high mountains.

141. The most distinguished and characteristic member of the group is *Chalk*, which attains a thickness of from 600 to 900 feet. It passes from white chalk into chalk-marl and limestone, of different degrees of hardness and impurity. Chalk-soil is generally barren, and particularly in France where there are extensive plains of high and waste table-land entirely covered with it.

It is remarkable that *Flints* are invariably associated with chalk, which encloses them as nodules of various sizes and forms. A closer investigation proves them to be agglomerates of the silicious shells of infusoria. The fossils of this group are exceedingly numerous, especially those of deep-sea animals.

Among the lower members of the chalk-group important strata of sandstone make their appearance, known in England as *greensand*, from being coloured by grains of green earth. In Germany it is termed Quadersandstein, on account of its splitting naturally into large square masses. It is found on the surface of the earth, particularly in Saxony, where it forms the remarkable and picturesque ravines and precipitous rocks of the district near Dresden, known as the Saxon Switzerland.

Fossils of the Chalk-Group.

[Fossil plants are rare in the cretaceous rocks; but sponges and corals are numerous, white chalk being composed mostly of their remains.

The echinoderms are very abundant, the prevailing genera being *Spatangus* (fig. 62), *Ananchytes* (fig. 63), and *Galerites* (fig. 64).

The fossil shells are also very numerous, and belong mainly to the salt-water species: the most common being *Terebratula* (figs. 65, 66, and 67) and *Ostrea* (fig. 68).

Of cephalopoda, the genera Ammonites (fig. 69) and *Belemnites* (fig. 70) are largely developed, though less so than in the oolite rocks. The genera *hamites* (fig. 71), *baculites* (fig. 72), *scaphites* (fig. 73), and *turrilites* (fig.

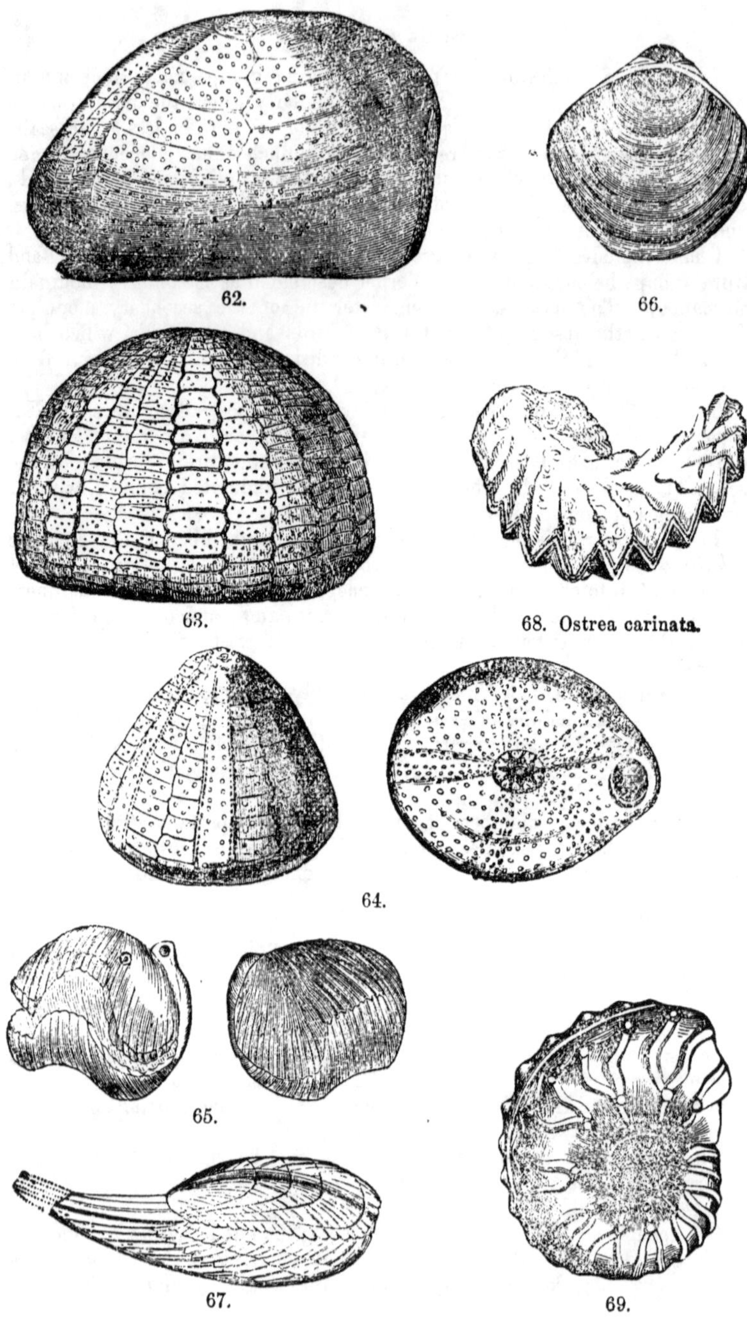
62.
66.
63.
68. Ostrea carinata.
64.
65.
67.
69.

74), are numerous, and characteristic of this system; a few only being found in the oolites.

The limestones which, in the countries bordering on the Mediterranean, are the equivalents of the cretaceous rocks of the north of Europe, have received the names of hippurite and nummulite limestone, from the abun-

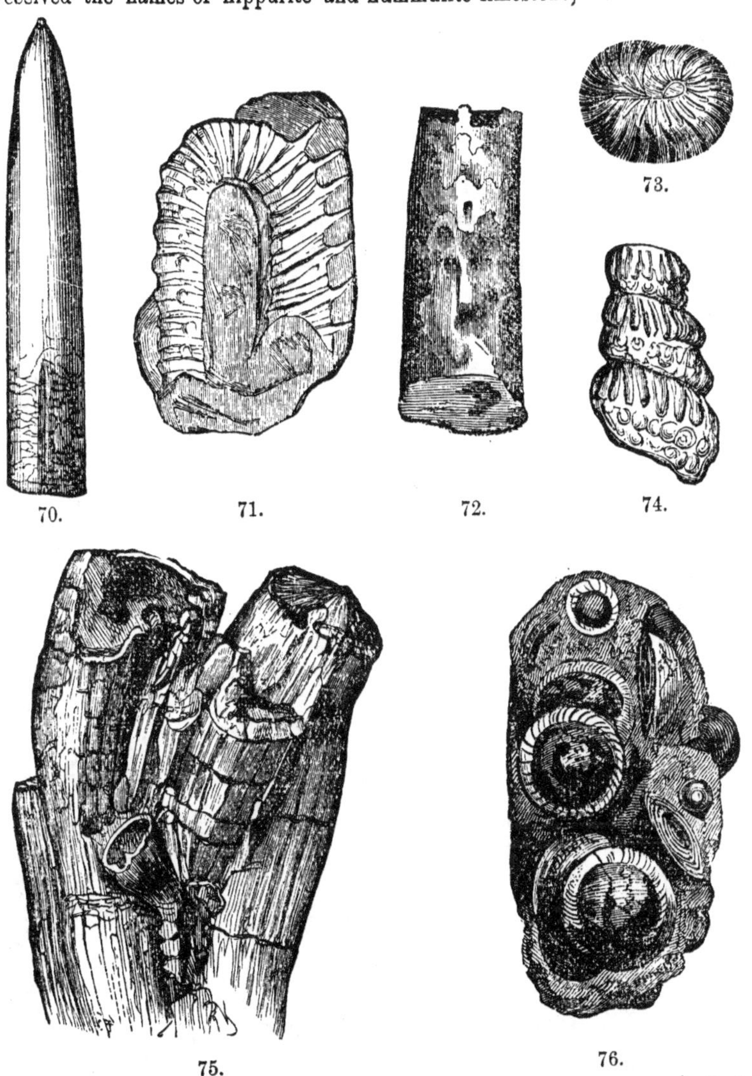

70. 71. 72. 73. 74.

75. 76.

dance of the remains of these two genera contained in them. The shell of the hippurite (fig. 75) is unlike that of any genus of mollusc now existing. The nummulite (fig. 76) is a discoid chambered cell, which derives its name from its resemblance to a piece of money.]

8th Group — MOLASSE.

Tertiary Rocks.

142. The appellation of this group is derived from a coarse and loose sandstone belonging to it, and occurring in Switzerland, where it is called Molasse: it contains frequently large fragments of other rocks, firmly cemented to a compact mass, named "*Nagleftuh*," and which rises, for instance, on the Rigi, to a height of 6,000 feet. Alternating with strata of *Brown-Coal* and *Calcareous Rocks*, this group forms the margin of the Alps.

During the period when this group was formed, several large bays or gulfs of the sea seem to have been gradually filled up, in which sand, gravel, and marl, with fossils of fresh-water animals, form the principal portion of the upper strata, while in the middle strata a coarsely-grained limestone, termed *Grobkalk*, and an admixture of granular green earth, and a variety of terrestrial and marine fossils prevail. The lower strata are composed of *Clay* and *Brown-Coal*. In different localities, however, various deviations occur from this succession.

It is worthy of remark, that several capitals, such as London, Vienna, Mayence, and Paris, are situated in the centre of such filled-up basins. Amongst the fossils of the Mayence basin, the Dinotherium is the most remarkable which has yet been discovered. It is a gigantic animal, similar to an elephant, with two large tusks curved downwards from the lower jaw (fig. 77). In the London basin clay predominates, whilst the basin of Paris furnishes an excellent material for millstones. In the gypsum quarries, near Paris, a large number of marine fossils occur, amongst which about 1,400 extinct species of mollusca have been enumerated. [Fig. 78

77.

78.

represents the Fauna and vegetation of the epoch of the Paris basin. A high temperature is indicated by the prevalence of palms intermixed with conifers and other exogenous trees approaching the character of existing species. Extinct genera of the pachydermatous order of mammals abound; of these, the *Anoplotherium commune*, as restored by Cuvier, is seen on the left, and behind him are *Palaeotherium magnum* and *P. minus;* near the latter is a land-tortoise; and it appears from recent discoveries that monkeys might have been represented gambolling on the boughs, and boas coiled around the trunks of the trees. Birds of which some traces occur in older strata are now abundant. The volcano in the distance represents the craters of Auvergne, at present dormant, some of which commenced their action towards the close of this era.

The epoch of the Paris basin belongs to the *Eocene,* or older tertiary of Lyell.]

143. Except in Switzerland, the Molasse does not rise to any considerable altitude. In the north of Germany, in Bohemia, in Wetteravia, &c., the Brown-coal formations predominate, while the middle stratum of Grobkalk is wanting. In the place of the latter a characteristic associate of the lower section deserves our notice; it is a *Sandstone,* distinguished by its great compactness, and as being distributed in large blocks, often strikingly rounded off, over all the north of Germany.

Brown-coal occurs more frequently in level countries and nearer the surface than in the higher grounds, where greater masses of alluvial and diluvial deposits cover it, though even there it is found sometimes uplifted to the surface by massive rocks. In the neighbourhood of Basalts it is considerably altered, probably from the influence of heat. Its ligneous structure disappears almost entirely, and it assumes greater resemblance to ordinary coal. (Chem., § 166.)

79.

It has already been mentioned that well-preserved trunks of trees, leaves, fruits, and also amber enclosing insects, &c., are found in the beds of Brown-coal. Earthy Brown-coal, containing an admixture of clay and sulphide of iron, is worked for alum. (Chem., § 86.)

[The Fauna and vegetation of the middle tertiary or *Meiocene* of Lyell, are represented in fig. 80. This epoch is sometimes called the elephantoid In the foreground are seen the elephant, rhinoceros and hippopotamus (pachyderms of existing genera but extinct species), which commenced with the meiocene or middle tertiaries, and disappeared from Europe at the erratic block or *drift* period; in the background are placed the stag, ox, and horse, to intimate the extensive development of those genera during the *Pleiocene* or later tertiary era. The hyena entering his den indicates the increase of carnivora during this period, and the accumulation of mammalian bones in caverns. The forests consist of oak, fir, birch, poplar and other trees, closely approaching, if not identical with indigenous European species. The distant volcano represents the greater part of the eruptions of Central France, of the Rhine, Catalonia and Hungary, which appear to have taken place during the Meiocene and Pleiocene epochs.

The tertiary rocks of Europe are found principally in basins, and appear to have been deposited in lakes and estuaries of limited extent; and of these, the Paris basin (§ 142), the basin of the Thames, and that of Vienna, furnish examples which have been well studied.

In the United States, the tertiary rocks are found upon the Atlantic seaboard and the Gulf of Mexico. Its western limit is at the first or lowest falls of the principal rivers, and is generally marked by the long-leafed pine, whose distance from the shore is limited by this formation.]

9th Group—ALLUVIAL AND DILUVIAL DEPOSITS.

144. Alluvial Formation, or a deposition of soil from water, still takes place every day under our own observation. Brooks and rivers continually tear away from mountains and valleys more or less of their marginal projections, in proportion to the solidity of the rocks and the power of the fall of water. Thus the elevations of the earth are continually, though imperceptibly, diminished.

The dislodged particles are deposited again in the state of mud, gravel, and pebbles, wherever the streams flow more calmly. Amongst these we find such mineral substances as were distributed in veins through the mountains, and which, on account of their greater specific gravity, were deposited sooner than other less ponderous minerals. Thus gold and precious stones, and also tin-ore, are congregated in many localities of the alluvial and diluvial formations, and may there be searched for with success, while in the mountains whence they come they would be far more difficult to find.

The greatest alluvial deposits from the mud and sand of great rivers are the so-called *Deltas*, triangular islands formed at the mouths of those rivers, and dividing them into many branches, as is the case with the Nile, the Rhine, the Danube [and the Mississippi].

Great lakes have been gradually filled up with alluvial deposits.

The sea also continually destroys (figs. 80, 81, 82, and 83) one line of coast and reconstructs another, and in some localities the formation of a new marine sandstone or limestone has been observed going on gradually from the deposits of evaporated sea-water, and from the remains of finely divided shells. This is the only kind of rock which has hitherto been found to contain the remains of man; a human skeleton having been discovered embedded in this rock on the island of Guadaloupe.

Calcareous Tufa, a rock of by no means inconsiderable extent, belongs likewise to the present period. The carbonate of lime copiously held in

80.

81. Action of the Waves on Precipitous Rocks.

82.

83. Examples of Rocks worn by the Sea

solution by the waters of many brooks, lakes, and swamps, containing an excess of carbonic acid, is deposited, when a portion of the carbonic acid escapes into the air (Chemistry, § 52). A coating of carbonate of lime is thus deposited upon all the objects in the water, a rock being gradually formed, which is at first loose and soft, but hardens by exposure to the air, and in this state forms an excellent building material. Such is the famous *Travertine* found in a swamp near San Philippo, in the neighbourhood of Rome, where a layer of this rock attaining a depth of 30 feet has been formed within 20 years. Silicious springs, like those near Karlsbad, and the famous hot-springs of Iceland, the Geysers (fig. 84), deposit *Silicious Sinter.* Moreover, the layers of *Bog Iron-ore* (*Raseneisenerz*) deposited from chalybeate waters, and the saline crusts formed on the shores of the sea, or on the banks of lakes, marshes, and swamps, by their partially drying up, are by no means inconsiderable.

145. Of greater importance, however, are the *Turf* or *Peat Bogs,* the origin of which, falling within historical times, has already been described in the Chemical section of this work (§ 165). They occupy the lower levels, such as the plains of Ireland, Holland, Prussia, Hanover, and Denmark. Sometimes considerable patches are found in hollows on the summits of primitive mountains. Weapons, and other articles made by man, are sometimes found deeply imbedded in peat bogs,—for example, Celtic weapons; and on one occasion, the wooden bridge, constructed by Germanicus when penetrating through the Netherlands into Germany, was so found. The

84. The Geysers of Iceland.

origin of Peat may be traced back to the period of diluvial and molasse formations, forming there a transition into Brown-coal.

The *Beds of Infusoria* must be considered in a similar light. An invisible world of the most minute animalculæ, with shells or shields around them, consisting of silicic acid, with the remains of an innumerable host of Infusoria, are deposited in layers, which form a friable mass of silicious rocks, known by the names of *Tripoli*, *Polishing Slate*, and *Kieselguhr*. The annexed diagrams (figs. 85 to 89) represent a few of the best-defined

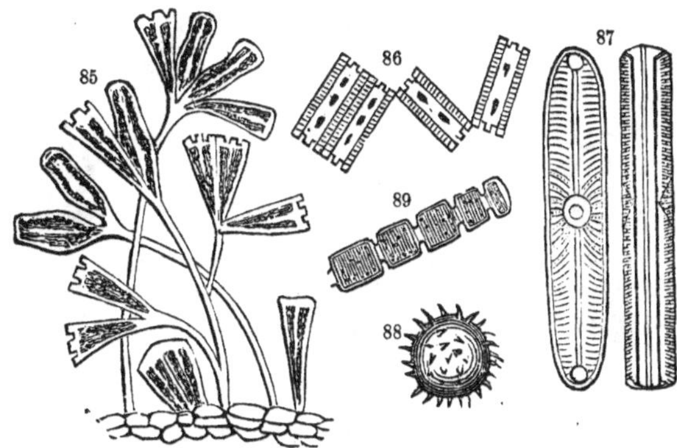

85. Gomphomena lanceolata. 88. Xantidium ramosum.
86. Bacillaria vulgaris. 89. Gallionella distans.
87. Navicula viridis.

species which have been recognised by M. Ehrenberg, who has calculated that the space of a single cubic inch would contain upwards of 35,000 millions of such remains. In the ocean this formation is represented by the beds of corals which are built up from the bottom by Polypi, and gradually approach the surface of the water with their calcareous ramifications, thus appearing above the surface of the sea as coral reefs, and frequently constituting coral islands (fig. 90), which abound in the Pacific Ocean.

90. Whit-Sunday Island in the Pacific.

Among the Polypi which help to form coral reefs, we may cite the following:—

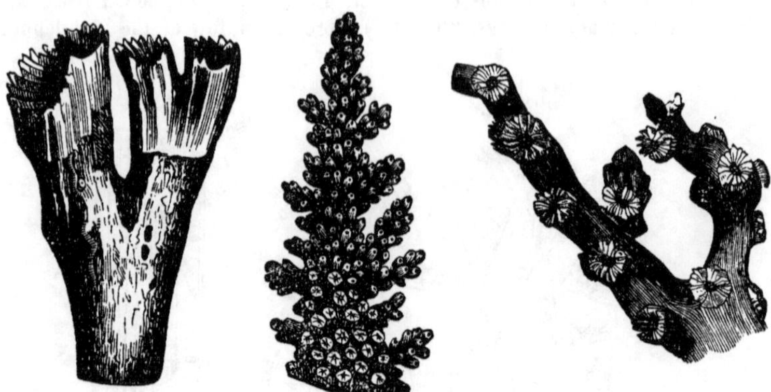

91. Caryophyllea fastigiata. 92. Madrepora muricata. 93. Oculina hirtella.

On the whole, the alluvial formations never reach a considerable thickness above the level of the sea, and they enclose only the remains of still existing plants and animals.

146. Diluvial Formation.—This constitutes even more mighty masses. It arose in pre-historical times as a deposit from a general inundation before the existence of mankind; for it never encloses human skeletons or bones. We find among all nations obscure traditions of mighty floods, which, like the *Deluge*, described in the Bible, had covered a great part of the earth.

The deposits which arose from this flood are of much greater depth than the alluvium deposited from seas and rivers. They are nearly 200 feet thick; they are generally elevated about 1000 feet, and sometimes as much as 2000 feet above the level of the ocean. The whole of the lower countries of Europe, as well as some plains of smaller extent in its highlands, consist of this formation. Thus the whole valley of the Rhine is filled up with diluvial deposit, which consists of a fruitful marly or sandy loam, which is called *Löss*, because, being too stiff to be washed away gradually by intersecting brooks, it allows itself to be undermined, and breaks downward vertically, or loosens in masses.

Diluvial deposits enclose many remains of animals, not only of the existing kinds, but also of several extinct species. Among the latter we find particularly large terrestrial animals, such as the mammoth, the cavern bear (*Ursus Spelæus*), &c. The accumulation of such fossil bones in many caverns is very remarkable; for instance, at Muggendorf in Bavaria, Gailenreuth in Franconia, in the Baumanns and Biels caverns of the *Hartz*, in the Nebel cavern near Tübingen, and in several other localities. These may have arisen from the caverns having been the places of resort of various carnivorous animals, or from the action of the floods carrying the bones thither.

147. Certain migrations of detached masses of rock may likewise have occurred at this period of great floods, as otherwise they would be as incon-

ceivable as they are incongruous with the present state of things. In the great plains of northern Germany, we find large blocks of rounded stone, principally of granite, lying about singly all over the diluvial deposits, and which we thence call, *Erratic Blocks* or *Boulders*. No granite can be discovered far and wide in their neighbourhood, nor at any depth below the surface. It is certain that these blocks must have been transported over sea, from Scandinavia or Finland, where mountains of the same kind of rock still exist, and it is probable that they were conveyed by immense icebergs, which detached them on breaking up. The descriptions given by northern travellers, of the size of the icebergs still floating about in the polar regions, renders this not at all improbable.

IGNEOUS FORMATIONS.

Plutonic and Volcanic: Abnormal Formations. Massive Rocks.

148. In this division we have classed the groups of granite, greenstone, porphyry, basalt, and volcanic rocks, which are indicated in fig. 21, page 380, by the letters A, B, C, D, and E.

The massive rocks, not overlying each other in regular strata, but occurring only wedged, as it were, beside and into each other, it is generally much more difficult to separate the different groups accurately; moreover, the fossils which so much facilitate the distinction of the stratified groups, are entirely wanting in these rocks.

The massive rocks distributed over the surface of the earth are more unifrom in their constitution than the sedimentary rocks, a circumstance which may be explained by supposing them to have been upheaved from the interior of the earth, and consequently less subjected to external and local influences than the substances of the stratified formations.

A. Granite-Group.

Primitive Rocks.

149. *Granite* was long considered to be the true primtive or fundamental rock, an opinion which extends even beyond the circle of scientific geologists. According to our previous statements, however, we consider it merely as the first of a series of igneous rocks, which in various subsequent periods, sufficiently remote from each other, broke through the crust of the earth.

This rock occurs likewise in many varieties, of which granite, granulite, and syenite, are geologically considered the more important. *Granite* (§ 87) is less distributed than the slaty rocks. It occurs principally in the form of mountains, and is rarely found in plains. The external configurations of granite are various, but peaked mountains and rugged isolated craps prevail, piled upon each other in great quantities into picturesque groups of apparent ruins. Peculiarly characteristic are the large blocks, like woolsacks, which often abound on the surface of granitic districts. These are large fragments of granite, the angular edges of which, having been worn off by gradual decomposition, they remain as rounded blocks. Mineral veins are not frequent in granite, yet iron-stone and tin-ore must be men-

94. Mountains of Granite, and Mica-slate, seen from the summit of Goatfell, in the Island of Arran.

95. Granite Boulder near Neufchatel.

tioned as occurring in this rock; accidental admixtures of several precious stones and laminæ of gold are likewise occasionally found.

Granite abounds in the north of Scotland, in the island of Arran, in Wales, and in Cornwall.

Granulite (§ 87) is found to a less extent, but under interesting circumstances, at the northern foot of the Erzgebirge, in Germany.

Syenite (§ 88) is found less widely distributed in Europe than granite, but is said to extend over large tracts of country in Chili, and at Mount Sinai.

Syenite is often found ruptured by granite, whence it is thought to be of earlier formation than the latter rock.

The cut (No. 96) exhibits another remarkable peculiarity in the scenery of granite mountains, namely the occurrence of a lake that fills what appears to resemble a volcanic crater.*

---

* We borrow from Professor RAMSAY the following description of such a scene:—

"Before descending to the coast, let the geologist turn aside to see a solitary mountain tarn, in the silent recesses of Beina Mhorroinn. This little sheet of

96. Corrie-an-Lachan, Island of Arran.

B. Greenstone-Group.

Trap Formation.

150. Differing from the rocks of the preceding group, greenstone never occurs in extensive masses, nor forms entire mountains, nor even considerable parts of mountains. It forms, on the contrary, small irregular masses, hillocks, blocks, and intricate veins or dykes, particularly in the substance of granite, slate-rocks, greywacke, and sandstone. In general, greenstone,

---

water is by far the most picturesque of all the lochs of Arran, and is situated deep in a hollow, called Corrie-an-Lachan. The place is perfectly lonely; not a tree is near; and, except the brown heath on its margin, and a few stunted rushes by the brook, the surrounding hills are almost bare of vegetation. The water is dark and deep, and the stormy blasts of the mountain never reach its still and unruffled surface. From its edge, on all sides but that toward the sea, rise the naked hills, whose sides are either formed of massive granite blocks, which, though surely yielding to decay, yet offer a stronger resistance to the destroying influences of time than the softer portions of the mountain, where the decomposing rock may almost be seen slowly crumbling away.

"A remarkable feature of the granite hills of Arran, is the Corries (one of which is represented in the cut). These may be frequently observed in the ridge between Brodick and Sannox, and in the hills of the interior. They generally present the appearance of a volcanic crater, part of one side of which has disappeared; and the masses of granite which compose the encircling hills are frequently arranged in layers diverging from the centre of the Corrie according to the angle of inclination of the hill. For obvious reasons it will be evident to the most inexperienced observer, that there is no analogy between the Corries (Corrie = Cauldron?) and modern volcanic craters; and it is probable that they owe their origin to the softer nature and earlier decay of the rock, with which at remote periods they may even have been nearly filled. May not even the great glens owe their origin to the same cause?"—*Geology of the Island of Arran*, 8vo, Glasgow, 1841, p. 50.

when it appears on the surface, constitutes small rounded summits, which in districts of clay-slate, may be recognised even at a distance. The internal cleavage of greenstone is chiefly either nodular or spherical, being rarely seen split in the form of columns and slabs. Of the many varieties of greenstone those of *Diorite* (§ 89) and *Serpentine* (§ 41) occur to the greatest extent. Mineral veins are rarely met with in these rocks, but they contain frequently ores, for instance of iron, copper, and tin, as accidental components, sometimes in sufficient quantities to render them worthy the attention of the miner.

C. Porphyry-Group.

151. According to Leopold v. Buch, the various porphyries must not merely be considered as a frequent cause of mountainous upheavals, since they also rise up frequently by themselves as considerable mountainous masses. They have been found in all parts of the globe, under the same relative arrangement, breaking in trunk-like masses, or in wide-spreading veins, through the granite and slate formations, and through the greywacke and carboniferous groups of the secondary rocks. In their external appearance, the porphyries appear to be peculiarly adapted for the formation of rocky mountains, and frequently they constitute isolated hills in the midst of other rocks. They cleave into angular fragments, and frequently split into multiform pillars and slabs. In their point of contact with other rocks, *Breccias* frequently occur (§ 96).

A great many varieties of porphyry exist, amongst which, *pitchstone porphyry*, *melaphyr*, and *amygdaloid*, are the most important.

Pitchstone porphyry occurs only in isolated masses. *Melaphyr* and *amygdaloid* are more widely distributed; they do not however constitute extensive districts, but form small trunk-like masses and irregular veins in Upper Silesia, Bohemia, Saxony, Scotland, and in many other localities.

D. Basaltic Group.

152. This upheaved group exhibits so decided a character that it is easily

97. Basaltic Columns.

recognisable even by the unpractised eye. Being of much later date than most of the secondary formations, or than the above-named massive rocks, it is found to have broken through them and penetrated even up to the molasse-group. Only the diluvial and alluvial formations have been formed since the appearance of the basalt.

Basaltic rocks frequently form lines of spreading hilly country, independent of chains of mountains; or, very characteristically, they constitute single dome-shaped elevations or conical hills in the flat regions of the stratified formations. They are distributed all over the globe, and in Germany they form a very remarkable basaltic zone, running from east to west.

Isolated basaltic cones sometimes attain a height of 1000 feet, and present to the eye the most varied and graceful cleavage; the basalt itself consisting mostly of regular hexagonal or pentagonal columns.

The more important varieties are *Phonolite* (§ 93) and *Trachyte* (§ 94); which are however rather rare, and occur mostly associated with the common basalt.

The rocks of this group are not penetrated by veins of ore.

Wherever the basaltic rocks border on other kinds of rocks, the most remarkable phenomena have originated at the period of their upheaval as a glowing liquid mass. In such localities these latter rocks have undergone great alteration still distinctly visible, being partly fused or reduced to mere slag, similar to the effects of volcanos, still in activity, or to the process of our smelting furnaces, where such igneous formations are constantly produced

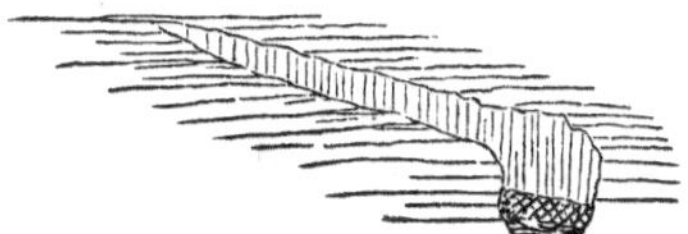

98. Sunk Trap Dyke.

99. Raised Trap Dyke.

100. Basaltic columns on the border of the river Volant in Ardèche, France.

on a smaller scale. The appearance produced by the junction of the trap-rocks with sandstone, slate-rocks, &c., can be easily examined at Dunòon, in the Island of Bute, or in numerous other localities on the Clyde.

When a trap dyke is more durable than the penetrated strata, the rock which it traverses being worn away by the action of the elements, the trap dyke is left above its surface in the form of a wall, fig. 99. But when the dyke is more perishable than the rock which it pierces, the trap decomposes and leaves a hollow, bounded on each side by a perpendicular wall of sand stone, fig. 98.

E. Volcanic Group.

153. We have already explicitly described in § 123 the activity and the influence of volcanoes upon their surrounding neighbourhood. According to modern views, all upheaved massive rocks might be considered as extinct volcanoes, some of which are of immense extent. However, it is only with the group of basalt, immediately preceding the volcanic group, that we find a considerable approximation in character to the present volcanic formations.

A characteristic feature of volcanos is the conical form of their summits, which appear sometimes isolated and sometimes in groups or chains. A farther characteristic is the formation of a funnel-shaped crater at their summits. The rocks which we meet with in volcanos, and in their immediate neighbourhood, consist of *lava, slags,* and *trachyte* (§ 94), in which no mineral veins are present.

101. Extinct Volcanos of Auvergne.

CONCLUSION.

154. On taking a retrospective glance at what has been stated under the heads of Mineralogy and Geology, we find ourselves progressing most remarkably from the minute and elementary to the greatest and most complicated phenomena.

First. Mineralogy teaches us, in the simple mineral specimen, the chemical combinations formed by Nature, the determination of which, as well as of their form of crystallisation, is properly considered a part of Chemistry. These minute crystals do not, however, occur merely isolated, but in aggregations of great number united to continuous masses. We also frequently find the crystals of different minerals intermingled and closely united in greater masses, when their definite form of crystallisation is often interfered with by the mechanical actions of friction, pressure, admixture, and by partial or entire fusion or solution. Thus from the consideration of the simple and compound rocks, Geology leads us on to the contemplation of still greater masses, and their arrangement in successive strata.

155. In describing so many most useful mineral substances, the importance of the science here treated must have become evident to every one.

The mineralogist teaches us not only to *distinguish* such minerals as sulphate of baryta and sulphate of strontia, limestone, salt, sulphur, coal, and the best of ores, so indispensable to man, but he also informs us under what local circumstances we may expect to *find* them.

Besides this, the knowledge of the mineralogist enables him better to judge of the nature of soils produced by decomposition; and, indeed, this knowledge of soils, so essential to agriculture, has been made the subject of scientific treatment, founded on Mineralogy. Geology, again, has lent its aid for another important purpose,—to procure one of the most indispensable necessaries of life, viz., water. In the section *Physics* (§ 60), it has been shown how this liquid, while endeavouring to find its level, springs up as a fountain, wherever it can force its way. Experience has taught us, however, that we can assist its course in this respect, that we can make channels for it in certain localities, or, in other words, that we may form artificial springs by boring.

ARTESIAN WELLS.

156. The possibility of forming such a well, named *Artesian*, after the department Artois, in France, where the attempt was first made, depends upon certain geological conditions, tolerably well ascertained, according to which a well-informed geologist may easily judge whether in certain localities boring is practicable, with the probability of success.

This would be the case under the following circumstances:—

(1.) Water must be continually absorbed and collected on an elevated point, higher than the place where the boring is to be tried.

(2.) This water must, from the nature of the formations below, find access beneath the point of boring by subterraneous channels.

(3.) It must have no other artificial or natural egress, to an amount equal to the quantity at the collecting points, neither at nor below the level of the boring point.

These three general conditions may actually be fulfilled in various ways. Most commonly, however, they are realized in the stratified formations by the peculiar position and alternating quality of the several strata. If, for instance, a sandy stratum, acting as a filter, (*a b*, fig. 102,) occupies a somewhat inclined position between two other strata impervious to water, such as clay, the water being absorbed by the superficial parts at *a b*, which may be of very great extent, will penetrate through its whole depth, and finding no egress below, on account of the basin-like form of the stratum, as in fig. 102, or from its resting at the lower termination upon a compact rock, the water will collect, under sufficient pressure, to form an artesian well. The overlying strata need only be bored through, as shown in the centre of the

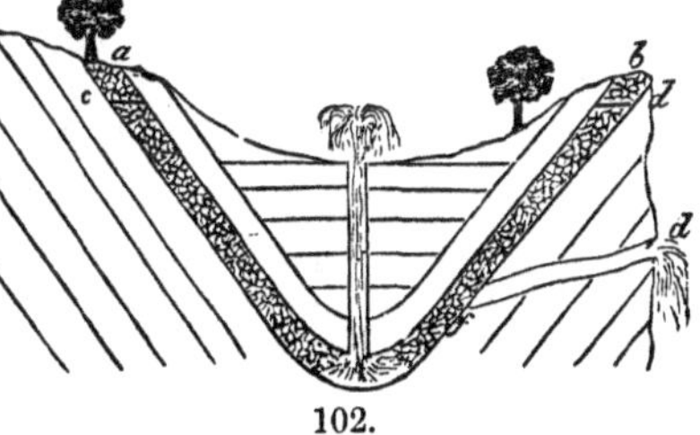

102.

figure, to obtain the desired spring. The passage *f d*, in fig. 102, explains the manner in which a natural spring, *d*, may be supplied with water from a porous bed through a fissure in the rocks. Similar conditions may exist in localities where massive rocks prevail, by means of fissures and cavities, although these are of rarer occurrence, and do not admit of a decided judgment beforehand.

Hence, while in stratified formations, we may predict frequently with great certainty the success of boring for an artesian well, such an undertaking will, on the whole, be very hazardous in localities where slaty or massive rocks predominate, and, consequently, the desired result would not be at all probable.

Artesian wells from a great depth possess a high temperature, as, for instance, the water of the artesian well at Grenelle, near Paris, which is 1,663 Parisian feet (= 540 met.) in depth, possesses a temperature of 28° C. (82·4 F.) This opens up a speculative view of making the immense store of subterraneous heat available for our domestic purposes. Should the stratified formations, from which the artesian spring rises, contain mineral substances soluble in water, in such case it would appear as mineral water. Thus in the Keuper and Zechstein (§ 137 and 138), so rich in beds of rock-salt, saline springs, for the manufacture of common salt, have been frequently found by boring.

MINING.

157. In order to procure for man the comforts and necessaries of life by the assistance of gold and silver, by that of iron, coal, salt, and other minerals, the MINER unceasingly performs his laborious task with steady perseverance.

Miners are generally a poor but an honest and industrious class of people, quiet and earnest at their work, but cheerful and fond of musical entertainment in their hours of recreation. Separate manners, habits, and dress, as well as a peculiar language for everything concerning their occupation, make the miners a characteristic set of men, strongly distinguished from agriculturists, sailors, or townsmen.

With his tools, consisting of a pickaxe, hammer, and crowbar, and provided with a safety-lamp, the miner proceeds either to work shafts vertically down into the ground, forming deep pits, or he carries out galleries in horizontal directions, and by combining these two ways he penetrates the rocks in search of ores which run through them in veins or form entire beds in separate strata, as, for instance, coal or rock-salt. Mines are sometimes of immense extent, for some shafts have been sunk to the depth of 3000 feet: the greatest depth, however, below the level of the sea amounts only to from 1300 to 1600 feet, which would make only about $\frac{1}{14800}$ of the radius of our globe (V. Humboldt's Cosmos). The galleries extend in some mines to an astonishing length, as, for instance, the George-gallery in the Harz, which requires three hours to pass through, and the celebrated Christopher-gallery in Salzburg, 10,500 feet long. These galleries, though mostly of a height sufficient for a man just to walk through, frequently admit of access only in a stooping or creeping position.

158. The calling of the miner, besides being very toilsome, is, next to that of the sailor, exposed to the greatest amount of danger. There are

many mines, in which, out of 1000 workpeople, an average of 7 annually lose their lives, while about 200 suffer more or less personal injury from accidents. In others, it is stated, that an average of even from 12 to 16, out of 250 people, perish annually. Sometimes, a sudden irruption of water from below or laterally, sometimes the fire-damp (Chem. § 54), which explodes on taking fire, or suffocating gases, especially carbonic acid gas (Chem. § 52), choke damp, prove destructive to them. At times, also, the roof of the mine itself gives way, either from negligence in propping, or from unavoidable concussions, and buries the miners alive. This frequently happens, particularly in South America, where earthquakes are still of common occurrence. All these circumstances contributed much in former times to make the miners a particularly superstitious class of people, abounding in fictions and traditions of jealous mountain sprites, dwarfs, and hobgoblins, dwelling in the interior of the mountains, and watching over their ores and treasures, which they grudge mankind, and for taking of which they assail the miner, and seek to do him harm. On the other hand, they believed in benevolent fairies and protecting spirits, that aided and assisted them.

The progress of science and education has, however, cleared away much of this prejudice and ignorance: the better-informed miner of the present time knows how to distinguish truth from fiction, and while trying to avoid dangers by needful precautions, he puts his trust in God, the ruler of all things.

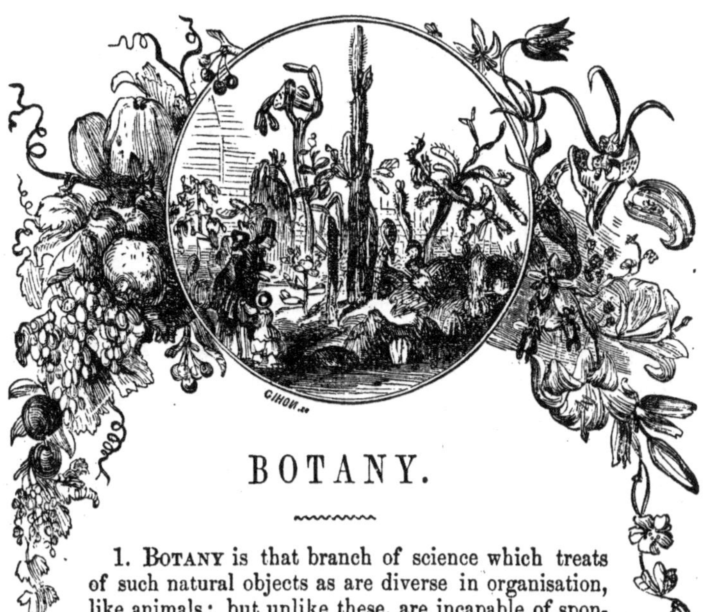

BOTANY.

1. **Botany** is that branch of science which treats of such natural objects as are diverse in organisation, like animals; but unlike these, are incapable of spontaneous movement. The diversity of their organisation consists in this, viz., that in every plant certain parts are present which display essential distinctions as well in external aspect as in internal structure.

The simplest form in which vegetation appears to us, is in that of minute vesicles, consisting of a peculiarly thin membrane called tissue, or cellulose, containing a fluid, and occasionally some greenish granules. The tissue, the fluid, and the solid contents of the little cell (cellule), are different, both in their formation and in their chemical composition. A still greater and more obvious diversity is perceptible in an entire plant, which is only an aggregation of an infinite number of similarly constituted cells. But the distinction is far more striking, supposing a larger plant, a tree, for instance, to be the subject of comparison. Here the variation in the form and consistence is so remarkable, that the dissimilarity of the different parts of the entire object, is not easily to be mistaken, even by a child.

If we compare a simple mineral with a plant (Min. § 3), for example, a crystal of quartz with a laurel, we find every particle of the crystal composed of minute atoms of quartz; in other words, the mineral is homogeneous, of the same consistency and composition throughout its entire mass. Neither the eye nor the chemical analysis of the object can discover the least difference. On the other hand, the external form and internal structure of the root, the stem, the leaves, the flowers, and the fruit of the laurel, are altogether dissimilar. There are, indeed, some minerals, granite, for example, that have the appearance of a diversity in their formation, yet in these *compound rocks*, as they are called, it is easy to perceive that they are nothing more than a mixture of simple minerals.

2. If we make a series of observations on a particular plant, under suitable circumstances, we cannot avoid perceiving the peculiar changes which it successively undergoes. Another phenomenon of the utmost importance is, that the fluid substance which fills the elementary and simplest organic forms in which plants appear, exhibits *motion*. Further, it is to be observed that the plant increases in size and weight, or *grows*, that is, it receives from the surrounding soil and atmosphere the materials necessary for this increase, and assimilates or adapts them to the production and extension of the ever-varying forms, under the infinite multiplicity of which all vegetation exists. Finally, a period ensues when the plant ceases to exert this self-formative energy, yields to the power of chemical laws, falls to pieces, decays, and is forthwith resolved into its primary elements.

Here another very remarkable fact deserves notice — viz., that the materials absorbed or inhaled by a plant during the term of its growth, are, in chemical combination, form, and qualities, altogether different from the substances which we meet with in the body of the plant We never find in the soil the material which communicates the green colour to the leaves; nor is the starch, which so abundantly is formed in the seeds, sometimes also in the tuberous parts of plants, to be found in the ground where they grow. The plant, therefore, has the power of *assimilating* the materials absorbed by it; and this is true, both in respect of their chemical combination as well as of the external forms which they are made to assume.

In this respect the mineral exhibits a remarkable contrast. It indeed does possess the capability of appropriating new portions, of increasing its mass, of growing. But this can only be accomplished when its media are of exactly the same nature as itself. For example, a crystal of calcareous spar can only enlarge itself in a fluid medium which contains the carbonate of lime. The crystal is, however, incapable of forming, from this material, either any other form or any other chemical compound, than the one appropriate to itself; it grows without either changing its form or its substance.

3. This capability of increase by the assimilation of heterogeneous materials, we call the *vitality* of plants; and those parts by which this assimilating process is conducted, are named the *organs of vegetation*. In the simpler forms of vegetable life, *i. e.* in plants of an almost homogeneous structure, all the organs act equally in the process of assimilation. In the more highly-organised orders, the various distinct organs perform separate and independent parts in the economy of vegetation, and hence are called dissimilar organs.

The mineral has no organ — it belongs to the division of unorganised objects.

4. It has already been stated in § 2, that plants possess an internal vital motion. Externally, however, we can perceive no appearance of this capability. Indeed, the newly-formed organs or parts take their place without apparent motion; and if the branches, twigs, and leaves were unmoved by the breath of heaven, they might seem without vitality altogether. The roaring of the wind among the trees of a forest is the voice of the storm, not of the woods. The plant cannot change its place nor alter the circumstances of its existence. It appears wherever accident or design has placed its seed, and it perishes, if the conditions necessary to its life be not within

its reach; it possesses no power to obtain them by changing its original station.

It is true, that many blossoms open and shut their petalous cups at certain times, that the sensitive mimosa folds its leaflets, and its branchlets droop if only touched by the softest finger; and that the stamens of certain plants exhibit remarkable appearances of mobility. But all these phenomena are produced by external causes. It was either the sun, or moisture, or a touch, which caused the motion, which without one or other of these causes would never have been produced at all.

A plant, therefore, is an organised body without external voluntary movement: and hereby it is essentially distinct from an *animal* with which, in organisation, it is closely connected. The primary elementary principle, or simplest form of the animal as of the plant, is that of a minute vesicle or cell, containing a fluid in which are some granular substances. And at this stage it cannot be distinguished from a plant in a similar condition, except by the faculty of voluntary movement, the power of changing its place. The animal has a locomotive power; sometimes, indeed, it is a very limited sphere to which it is confined; yet it may change its place for another more conducive to the exigencies of its being.

It is sufficient for the present to have shown the most general characteristics by which plants are distinguished from the other objects that, with them, compose the great kingdom of Nature. A precise and clear apprehension of their varied forms and wonderful phenomena, can only be obtained by a careful analysis of the nature and structure of the subjects of the vegetable kingdom. This we will endeavour to supply in the following sections.

I. The Internal and External Structure of Plants (Anatomy and Organography).
II. Vitality of Plants (Physiology).
III. Classification of Plants (Systematic Botany).
IV. Description of Plants (Descriptive Botany).

I. THE INTERNAL AND EXTERNAL STRUCTURE OF PLANTS.

ANATOMY AND ORGANOGRAPHY.

5. In water which has for a considerable time remained stagnant, green flocculous bodies are produced, which, to the naked eye, appear like highly attenuated and tender threads. When viewed through a microscope they present the appearance of rows of small globular or ovate vesicles, like beads strung on a thread. Similar threads, possessing a beautiful blue colour, and consisting partly of spherical and partly of oval vesicles, may be seen, even with the unassisted eye, and very distinctly under a weak magnifying power, when we examine the hairs which invest the stamens of *Tradescantia virginica*, (Spider-wort), an ornamental plant with tripetalous violet-blue flowers, which is frequently cultivated in gardens.

Although, on a cursory view, some parts of plants have the appearance of a more or less dense, uniformly simple, solid conformation, yet by the aid of magnifying glasses we find that such is not the case. The microscope shows, that even the compactest and hardest portions of vegetables, the woody parts, and the indurated and stony shells of fruits, are a combination of an infinite number of minute forms, identical with the primary element above mentioned, and capable of being resolved into cells like those of which the flocculous matter of the above-mentioned algæ is composed. It is true that a great diversity, both in form and magnitude, is apparent; nevertheless, the most accurate observations have shown, that these diversities are only variations or modifications of the vesicular minute forms constituting the water-plant above noticed. This elementary principle has received the name of *plant-cell*, or briefly the *cell*.

Hence, the cell is properly regarded as the *elementary* or *fundamental organ* of vegetation; and the knowledge of the origin, the structure, the functions, and the metamorphoses which this organ undergoes during the period of its life, constitutes the foundation of scientific Botany. The title, *compound organs of vegetation*, is applied to those peculiarly formed parts, which are present in most plants, and which have special functions assigned to them in the economy of vegetation. They are, for example, the leaves, the blossoms, &c.

a. SIMPLE ORGANS OF VEGETATION.

6. An infinite number of parts, selected from different plants, has been examined by the aid of the microscope, and all of these parts so examined have been found to consist of innumerable small cavities, which in figure vary so considerably, that they have been distinguished by peculiar names. Farther observations have, however, shown that they are all in fact but modifications of the one elementary form—viz., the plant-cell, which first of all claims our attention as the origin or basis of all the simple organs of vegetation; the most important modifications or varieties of this primary organ are the *vascular* and *woody tissues*, the *cambium cells*, and *lactiferous ducts*, or *milk-sap vessels*. In addition to these we have to investigate the *cellular tissue*, cellulose or membrane, that originates in the connexion of the cells, together with the intercellular passages, interposed between the cells or vascular tissues.

The Cells.

7. Without entering upon the obscure subject of the origin of the cell, a matter not yet satisfactorily explained, we find that its simplest form is globular, and that its diameter varies from the 1-300th to the 1-50th part of a line. This vessel is composed of a membrane, colourless, and of extreme tenuity: every vessel is a distinct individual, apparently incapable of further structure or extension, and without any visible *perforations*. The internal wall of the living cell is lined with a viscid, mostly yellowish-coloured fluid, which seems not unfrequently to be endowed with a peculiar motion, and which is called the *circulation* of the cell-sap. Between the cellular tissue of the cell and the above mentioned fluid, a new layer is deposited, which increases the thickness of the cell. Upon this there is formed a third or even a fourth new layer; and sometimes these internally formed layers amount to the number of thirty: in which case the internal cavity of the

cell is completely filled up with these internal layers so deposited. The most remarkable phenomenon connected with these formations, is, that these new cellular linings are not all equally deposited upon the tissues previously formed. Hence the tissue appears in some parts clearer or more transparent than in others, where the internally deposited layers are more complete. The matter forming these interior membranes is called protoplasma, and its more or less complete development produces the cellular modifications called *porous*, or dotted, *barred*, *annular*, or *spiral* or *recticulated* cells. The dotted cells were named *porous cells*, when these transparent parts of the cells were believed to be real perforations of the cellular tissue.

The regular form of these recent or subsequent additions to the cell appears to be the following, viz., that of spiral elastic filaments deposited on the internal surface of the cell-wall in close or open coils as the case may be, but frequently in lateral contact, and even cohering, so as to form a tube of spiral coils. On this principle the above-mentioned forms of the tissue are explicable.

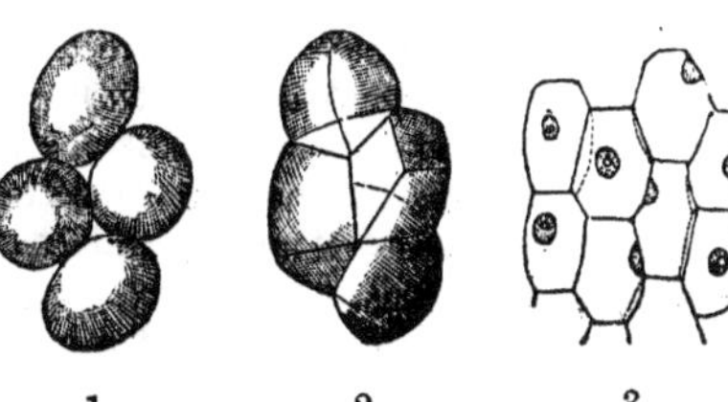

1. 2. 3.

8. As this appears to be the law of the internal structure of the cell, we have next to consider its internal formation and aspect. In the fleshy parts of plants, and especially in many fruits, as the apple, pear, &c., and in the water-plants (algæ) mentioned in § 5, the cells assume a globular shape as represented in fig. 1.; and through their mutual pressure on each other they become angular: a section shows that they are mostly hexangular, as represented in fig. 2. The tissue may be compared to the bubbles formed by the agitation of soapy water; and their mutual pressure, whereby they assume the hexagonal shape, may be very exactly represented by a number of globules of moist clay more or less compressed. In this manner every individual cell assumes a polygonal shape corresponding to the form of the cells represented in fig. 3; and which disposition is, in many plants, preserved with the utmost regularity. Such cells as are, with tolerable equality, extended in all directions, are named *parenchyma*, and of these are composed the tuberous parts of plants, as the potato, dahlia-roots, &c., and especially the soft spongy part of fruits, the pith, the fleshy portions of the leaf, bark, &c. Over and under or around these cells are arranged the elongated pointed cells, which are denominated *woody fibre* or ligneous tissue (*prosenchyma*), fig. 4. These, which are also hexangular, are very compactly disposed, and constitute the chief portions of the more solid parts of plants, as the ligneous parts of trees, shrubs, &c. The very long, flexible cells, or tissue of fibres, which constitute flax, hemp, and the inner bark of many trees, are called the internal *cortical layers*, and appear under the microscope as round threads of uniform thickness, whereas all fibres of cotton wool, when magnified, present the appearance of flattish bands with somewhat

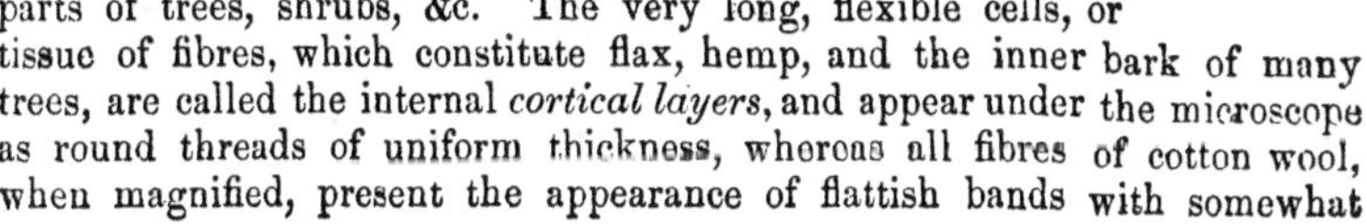

4

rounded margins. By these marks, the union of flax and cotton in the same web or piece of cloth may readily be detected.

In particular places, the tissue assumes occasionally very abnormal shapes, as the stellate or star-formed cells. These are generally described as *irregular cells.*

The Contents of the Cells.

9. We very often find in the interior of the cells a colourless transparent fluid, which is called the *cellular sap.* This fluid, which consists chiefly of water, holds in solution more or less of certain soluble vegetable substances, such as gum, sugar, albumen, mucilage, acids, and salts, and many other substances, which we have already, in Chemistry (§ 118—146), shown to be productions of the vegetable kingdom.

But in addition to these constituents above mentioned, we often meet with solid substances in the cells—as, for example, small regularly-formed crystals separated from the sap, sometimes roundish granules, in which form the *starch* and the *leaf-green,* the colouring matter of the leaves (Chlorophyl, p. 250), most commonly appear as in fig. 5, in which *c* represents the cells containing chlorophyl, and *r r* the Raphidian cells. The starch is easily distinguished by assuming a violet colour on the application of a solution of iodine. Round particles of fatty matters or of volatile oils are also perceptible in the cellular contents of many parts of plants; and the sap itself often appears coloured by the agency of some colouring matter which it retains in solution. Atmospheric air is, besides, frequently found in the cells; and especially when these are old and contribute but little to the vital activity of the plant.

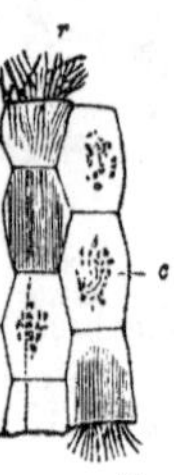

5.

In young cells, universally, are found cellular nuclei or nucleal vesicles (cytoblast), which are intimately connected with the origin of the cell, and at a later period mostly disappear.

The Functions of the Cells.

10. As the magnitude of every plant, whether small or great, is only an aggregate of all its individual cells, so, also, the entire life of a plant is nothing else but the sum or aggregation of the activities of all the cells of which it is composed. The special province of the cells is to receive from the soil or atmosphere the water necessary for the various vegetative purposes, together with the nutritious materials dissolved in the watery and aerial fluids, and to circulate or disperse them through the whole body of the plant. The vegetable circulation is not carried on through the agency of the tubular channels existing in plants, but only by the passage of sap in all directions from one cell to another.

Since the cells have no openings, it is somewhat difficult to explain in what manner the fluid can enter into the plant from without, and by what means it can, from cell to cell, maintain an internal circulation. This action, however, is dependent on the peculiar quality both of vegetable and animal tissues and fibres, viz., that they are permeable by many fluids, without being dissolved by them. Experiments show that this permeative action is carried on and regulated by definite principles. When, for example, two fluids of *unequal densities*, as an aqueous solution of sugar and mere water, are separated from each other by a diaphragm of pig's bladder, we perceive a constant tendency on both sides to restore the equilibrium in the density of the two fluids. A portion of the water penetrates the bladder mixing with the solution, and a portion of the latter finds its way to the former by the same medium. In this experiment one important fact is to be observed, viz., that the fluid of less density always passes through the separating medium more rapidly than the denser of the two; consequently, in this experiment more water passes through the bladder to the saccharine solution, and less of the latter to the water. This permeative capability of the tissue of vegetables and animals is called *endosmose*.

The fluid contents of the cells are always denser than the mere water which is in external contact with the roots or leaves; consequently, the latter, urged by the law of transudation, or *endosmose*, enters the most contiguous cells, whence it passes further into the circulation of the plant. This operation, however, would soon restore the equilibrium between the water within the plant and that which is supplied from without, and thus prevent any further supply, if an agency lodged in other organs, for evaporating the superfluous fluids, were not constantly engaged in maintaining the relative densities of the cellular contents, and of the external nutritive materials.

11. The cells, however, not only in this manner circulate the sap through the whole plant, but also further essentially alter the nature of the sap contained in the cells; so that, both in different plants and in different parts of the same plant, and even in the same parts of the same plant, at different times, we find substances essentially differing in character from each other.

The circulation of the sap through the cells is accomplished with moderate celerity. This is ascertainable by remarking in spring the time occupied, by the sap, in reaching incisions made at different distances in the stems of trees. It may also be calculated by observing the time which elapses during the restoration of a drooping plant, which has been placed in water for this experiment.

The force with which the cells absorb and circulate fluids may be ascertained by the following experiment. In spring let the freshly-cut end of a vine-branch be inserted into a vertical glass tube, and closely bound to the same by means of a piece of skin or caoutchouc. The water passing out from the cut surface of the shoot will ascend in the glass tube even to the height of from 30 to 40 feet; and hence it is inferred that the ascent of the sap in vegetables is impelled by a force which is somewhat greater than the pressure of the atmosphere. (Phys. § 84.)

VASCULAR TISSUE (FIBROUS TISSUE).

12. This somewhat inappropriate name has been given to a variety or modification of the cells, which are never observed in very young plants, nor in certain parts of plants during any period of their existence, but are of later origin, being developed by a change in the direction or extension and functions of the original cells. These forms, called vascular tissue, are composed of bundles of cylindrical-shaped cells, either pointed at their extremities and overlapping each other, forming conical cells, or terminating at their points of contact; these are the usual forms of woody tissue, fibres of flax, &c.

Accordingly, as these vascular organs are provided with perforations, rings, or spirals, they are distinguished by the names of *porous*, or rather *pitted*, *scalariform* (like the steps of a ladder), fig. 6; *annular*, or *ring-formed*, fig. 7 *a;* and *spiral-formed*, fig. 7 *b*.

13. We have already stated, in § 7, that there is a spiral fibre coiled up on the inside of the cellular membrane, and that this spiral lining by successive layers of the same nature became stronger than the cell itself. Hence it was originally supposed that the spiral vessels consisted of minute fibres wound around the cell, like a metallic wire around a violin-string. Only in a more recent period has the true cellular membrane been detected, which is composed of pure cellulose matter covering the spirals or tracheæ. The spiral elastic fibres are easily discoverable in the leaf-stalk of a geranium or of any other fibrous and fleshy petiole, by making a slight incision around the stalk, and pulling the parts gently asunder, when the fibres or bundles of fibres will be visible even to the unassisted eye, like the fine threads of a spider's web. But their true construction can only be satisfactorily seen by the aid of a powerful microscope. In a section these vessels appear either round, or, more frequently, hexangular (as in figs. 6 and 8).

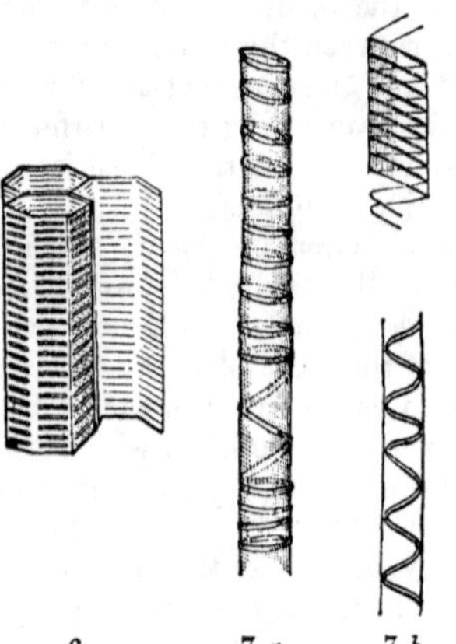

6. 7 *a* 7 *b*

13. The contents of these vessels is atmospheric air, and they take no part in the circulation of the sap. Their forms also are complete; that is, they are not, like the cells, capable of further modification. On this account they are of subordinate importance in the general economy of vegetation; and this is evinced by the fact that the lower and less highly-developed families of plants have no vascular organs, but are entirely composed of cells, hence they derive the name of *cellular plants* (plantæ cellulares). To these families belong the Fungi, the Algæ, the Lichenes, the Hepaticæ, the Musci* (the mushroom tribe, the sea-weeds, the lichens, liverworts, and mosses), which are the simplest objects of the vegetable kingdom both in structure and organisation. Where the vascular tissue is present the form is more highly developed. The vascular organs appear simple only at their first formation; they subsequently undergo modifications, and receive accessions of newly-formed vessels, and become what are *bundles of vascular tissue.* A union of these together, or a ramification of one from another, is never met with; nor do they ever exclusively constitute any portion of a plant; they are rather in the midst of or surrounded by the cells.

CAMBIUM CELLS.

14. External to the bundles of woody and vascular tissue of many plants there is a layer of cells, containing a mucilaginous semi-fluid matter, and

* The latter are not entirely cellular plants; they have some vascular tissue.—ED.

forming a tissue called *cambium*. This organ is in constant activity, either in forming new cells, which are added to those already in existence, or else in continuing the growth of such as have been previously formed. This layer is interposed between the wood and the bark.

Laticiferous Cells (Lactiferous, or Milk-vessels).

15. If we tear a leaf or stalk of Celandine, Poppy, Spurge, &c., there appear on the lacerated parts several drops of a thick orange, or milk-white sap, called *latex*, of which caoutchouc always forms a constituent portion (Chem. § 140), and hence its clammy or viscid nature. This sap is yellowish in the Œnanthe crocata (water hemlock or dropwort), and in a few plants it assumes a red or a blue colour.

These vessels are tubular and branched, conveying the latex or milk-sap into all parts of the plant. Their mode of development shows that they originate in the most recently-formed cellular tissue of the lactiferous plants before the existence of the spiral vessels. These passages or channels contain a fluid, colourless at first, but subsequently producing granules, and finally milky sap; and they are at first formed only out of the intercellular interstices, but gradually acquire a peculiar lining of remarkable tenuity, which finally becomes a moderately strong membrane.

The erroneous opinion that this sap circulates in the vegetable similarly to the circulation of the blood, has been corrected by experiment and observation. Its peculiar function in the economy of the plant is not satisfactorily ascertained; only its agency seems subordinate, from the fact that in most plants it is not present.

Cellular Tissue.

16. This tissue originates in the union of the cells, and varies materially both in form and function, being mainly dependent on the prevalent cellular formations.

One sort of tissue, which derives its origin from cells of the simplest form, and which is universally found in all plants, is called *parenchyma* (see § 8). When the cells have an incompact or lax position on each other, the tissue is imperfect, whilst in the perfect tissues the cellular walls are united to each other as completely as possible. The elongated, regular, or articulated tissues have an obvious relation to the form of the simple cell: this tissue is called *prosenchyma* (woody tissue), and is composed of the thickened and extended membrane of the woody cells (§ 8).

The bundles of vascular tissue, on the contrary, are a combination of the variously-formed vessels which constitute both this and the woody tissue, and are easily distinguished by the mass of parenchyma which surrounds them. They exhibit various peculiarities both in their arrangement and in their further development, and by these diversities large families and classes of plants are conveniently grouped. In one of these groups or divisions of plants, viz., the Filices (Ferns), the bundles of vascular tissue are produced almost simultaneously, or they exhibit little or no increase during the existence of the plant. In the palms and grasses they receive an enlargement for a certain time, but their growth terminates long before the plant has reached maturity. In our forest trees this tissue is continually increasing while the life of the plant endures. The first mode of increase in these vessels is named *simultaneous*, the second *limited*, the third *unlimited* development.

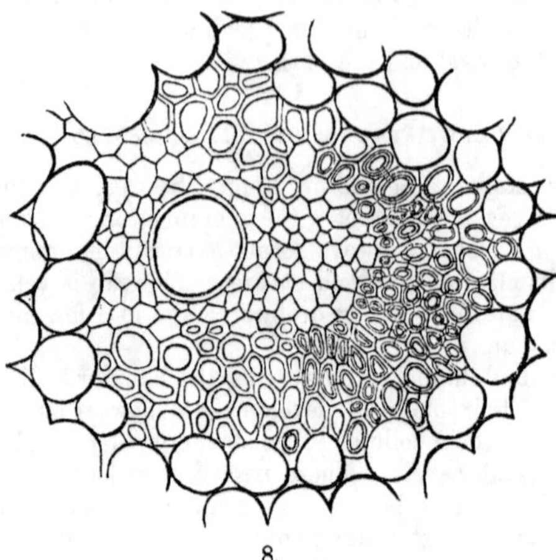

8.

In a cross section, represented by fig. 8, there is seen a large opening or passage composed of, or having its membranes formed of, the *woody tissue* by which it is surrounded; on these there is a layer of cambium-cells (§ 14), and on the latter a layer of *cortex* (inner cortical layers or bast-cells, § 8). The whole is surrounded by the lax or round uncompressed cells of parenchymatous tissues.

17. The tissue of the cuticle or *epidermis*, which externally covers all parts of the plant while they remain green, or are in a growing condition, is of a peculiar nature, and demands special consideration. This organ is formed of a series of flattish cells, very much compressed, and in close contact, with the exception of some portions, where the *stomata*, or mouths or

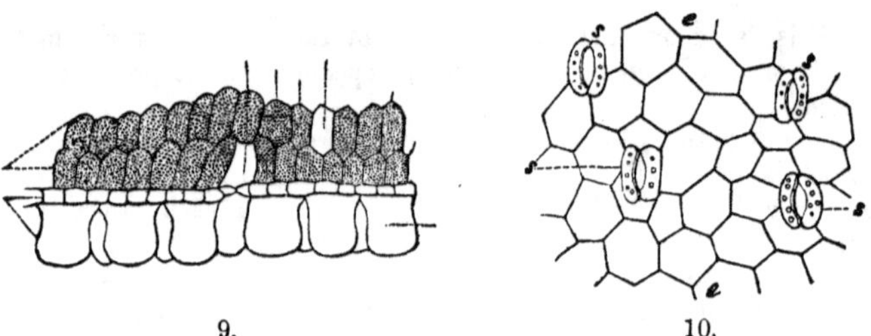

9. 10.

apertures are placed. In fig. 9 a section of a leaf is represented, the large transparent empty cells of the epidermis, and above these the parenchymatous cells of the leaf filled with greenish-coloured granules. In four places, fig. 10, stomata (*s s s s*) are seen, which have their openings surrounded by parenchymatous cells disposed in semilunar forms. Under each stoma (mouth) there is seen a hollow space connected with the intercellular passages of the leaf. These stomata, above represented, are so numerous on the upper side of the leaf, that hundreds have been counted in the space of a square line. Through these minute organs an intimate connection exists between the interior of the plant and the external air.

18. The epidermal cells not unfrequently exhibit very abnormal formations. For example, they are often externally projected from the surface of the leaf or stem, and become hairs not seldom branching; and in many plants, as in the stinging-nettle, they contain an irritating sap. Bristles, prickles, glands, warts, and especially the substance which forms the well-known cork, are all due to the metamorphoses of this exterior integument.

Intercellular Spaces.

19. The round and angular cells are never so closely arranged as to leave no empty spaces. In lax tissue these are tolerably large, but in that which is compressed they are almost entirely invisible. The *passages* formed by these intercellular spaces are mostly triangular, in intimate combination with each other, and are either filled with air or with a watery fluid.

We find besides, in the stems of many plants, and especially in aquatics, between the masses of cellular tissue, numerous and sometimes very large and regular channel-tubes which contain air. These air-cells or passages traverse the whole extent of the stem, and in a section of the Spanish reed (Arundo donax), and in the stem of the water-lily, are perceptible by the naked eye.

By decay and by rupture of the cellular tissue there are frequently formed in the inside of stems *lacunæ* or hollows, which, as in grasses and umbelliferous plants, sometimes occupy the whole interior of the culm or stem.

In these empty spaces, produced by the rupture and decay of the cellular membrane, *receptacles* of various forms are found which are filled with oil, resin, gum, and other vegetable secretions.

B. COMPOUND ORGANS OF VEGETATION.

20. These, which constitute the larger and more conspicuous parts of plants, are divided into *organs* of *nutrition* or *vegetation*, those concerned in the nourishment and growth of the plant, and *organs* of *increase* and *reproduction*, whose function is the production of new individuals. In our description, these organs assume a threefold aspect, viz., their external form, their internal structure, and their functional agency in the general economy of the vegetable kingdom.

Organs of Nutrition.

21. In the more highly-organised classes, the *root* is deemed one of the essential organs, inasmuch as it contributes, by absorption or imbibition, the principal part of the nourishment necessary for the growth of the plant. Besides this organ, the *stem* and *leaves* perform a more or less important part in the nutritive processes, and are also included in this section. The stem, so long at least as it remains in a green pulpy state, is likewise capable of receiving the materials of nutrition from without, and in all states and stages is the active medium of communication between the root and the leaves. These last named organs contribute but little direct external nutriment, but their indirect influence on the growth and health of the plant, by their capacity of evaporating the excess of watery fluids by accelerating the motions of the sap from below upwards, and by elaborating the various vegetable secretions, is indispensable to the healthy existence of every one of the vegetable organs.

Root, or Descending Axis.

22. With the exception of the lower families of the less highly-organised plants, some Fungi, Lichens, or Algæ, for example, which consist merely of a mass of cellular tissue without any definite shape or arrangement, or are composed of a succession of flocculous or crustaceous *layers*, all plants have a tendency to a direction which is always perpendicular to the surface of the earth. This line of direction is called the *axis* of the plant, and is either upwards, forming the stem, or downwards, forming the root or descending axis.

The radical part possesses two tendencies: the one is to grow towards the earth's centre, and the other is to avoid the light. The stem, on the other hand, possesses two precisely opposite tendencies, viz., to grow upwards and to come to the light. The limit between the root and the stem is called the *collum* or *neck*, and when this part is distinguished by a swelling, as in the Carrot, Turnip, &c., it has received various names expressive of its form or structure.

The lateral parts of plants, such as branches, that grow round about or out of the axis, are called *secondary axes* or *lateral organs.*

23. In reference to their external appearance roots are either *simple* or *compound.*

The simple root is either *entire* or *divided.* In the latter state it has a greater or less number of branches. The *tap-root* is a prolongation of the central axis or principal root which descends perpendicularly. The lateral roots are called *ramifications* of the tap-root: both forms are represented in fig. 12.

The commonest forms of the root are the *fibrous* or thread-shaped root; the *cylindric*, fig. 11; the *spindle-shaped*, fig. 12; the *conical*, or tapering root, fig. 13; the *globular*, or turnip-shaped, fig. 14. The *granular*,

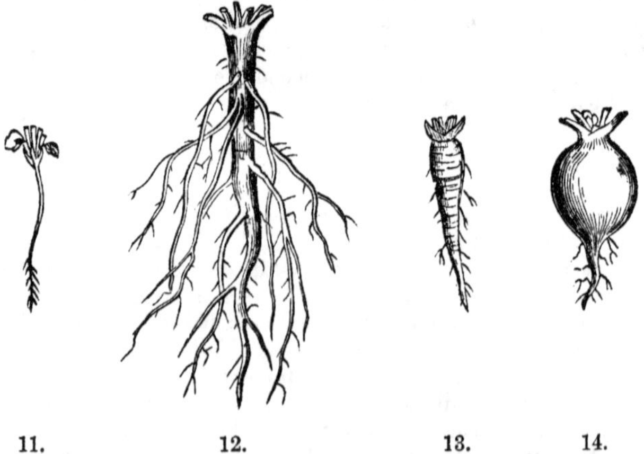

11. 12. 13. 14.

tubercular, and the *palmate* forms; the three last are exemplified by the roots of Saxifraga granulata (saxifrage), Solanum tuberosum (potato), and the last by several of the Orchids.

The compound roots originate in a multiplication of the simple roots, and are either *fibrous* or *fasciculate*, the latter owing its origin merely to an enlargement of the fibres. The accompanying fig. (15) represents the compound root with its rootlets invested with hairy appendages called *fibrils*.

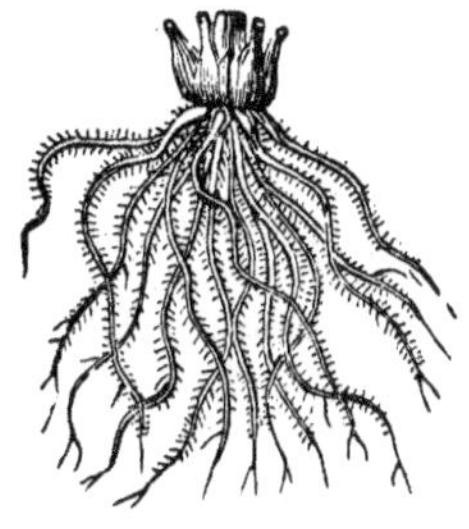

15.

Whilst the majority of roots penetrates the soil, there are not a few plants, especially acquatics, which develope these organs in the water: these are called *floating* or *swimming roots.* Also many plants, particularly trees that grow in the torrid zone, develope from different parts of their stem roots instead of branches. These *ærial* roots as they are termed, are prolonged till they reach the surface of the earth, when they strike root in the soil.* In Ivy, Dodder, and other plants of a similar nature, the roots form what are called *suckers.*

The interior structure of the root agrees in all essential characteristics with the stem, and consequently does not require à special description.

Functions of the Root.

24. Roots fix the plants, either in the soil or to other bodies or places, by some peculiar means of attachment. At all times the plant derives its prin cipal supply of nutriment through these organs, and at certain times, viz., during the infancy of the plant, it is nourished exclusively through them. All parts of the root are capable of imbibing the water in its immediate vicinity, together with the materials held in solution by this fluid. Insoluble substances cannot enter into the systems of plants. The roots are always developed in the direction of those places whence they derive their chief supply of food; that is, they accommodate themselves to the nature of the medium wherein they are developed. Sometimes they penetrate the hardest soil, and insinuate themselves into the rents and clefts of rocks in search of congenial nutriment.

Roots are said to have also the power of ejecting unsuitable matters, namely, such as they cannot assimilate for nutrition and growth.

---

* Perhaps the most remarkable instance of this kind is the banyan-tree (Ficus Indica). One of these trees, at present existing on the banks of the Nerbudda, has branches propped by adventitious stems, which spread so far as to afford a shaded space of 2,000 feet in circumference. Mr. Forbes states that the hanging roots, changed into stems in this tree, are 3,500 in number. The banyan-tree is thus beautifully alluded to by Milton, in his *Paradise Lost:*—

——————" There soon they choose
The fig-tree, not that kind for fruit renowned;
But such as at this day to Indians known,
In Malabar or Decan spreads her arms,
Branching so broad and long, that in the ground
The bended twigs take root, and daughters grow
About the mother-tree, a pillared shade
High over-arched, and echoing walks between."—Ed.

The Stem.

25. We have already mentioned, in § 22, that the stem is that part of the plant which has a tendency to elongation in a direction contrary to the root, and always towards the light. In many examples, however, the exterior form and manner of extension do in nowise correspond to our idea of a longitudinal axis perpendicular to the earth's surface. It is frequently so short as scarcely, or at all, to become visible above ground, and in this case it is distinguished by the name of *subterranean* or under-ground stem.

Two forms of the stem are especially to be distinguished, viz., the lower under-ground root-like stem, which is called the *Stock* (Rhizome, or root-stock), and the elongated cylindric above-ground stem, which is the *stem-proper.* The forms of the stems comprehended in both of these principal divisions vary considerably from each other.

Forms of the Rhizome or root-stock are:—

1st. The *bulbous*, a very abbreviated, orbicular, or globular stem, surrounded by thick parenchymatous leaves, which in their axils produce buds: *ex.*, the Onion.

2nd. The *pseudo-bulb*, similar in shape to the bulb, but without the leaves and leaf-buds: *ex.*, the root of Orchis.

3rd. The *root-stock*, or Rhizome proper, is only a variety of the last or under-ground stem, and is distinguished from the true root by the production of buds: *ex.*, roots of Iris, &c.

Forms of the stem-proper are:—

1st. The stem of *mosses* is *filiform* (thread-like), leafy, sometimes simple, sometimes branched, but never attaining to any considerable size or strength.

2nd. The *culm*, which bears the fructification in the grass-tribe, is a cylindrical, hollow, mostly quite simple, and usually jointed organ.

3rd. The *palm-stem*, which is peculiar to this magnificent plant and to the tree-ferns, mostly occurs as a simple cylindrical stem, of uniform thickness, and marked on the exterior of its circumference by the scars of the leaves with which it was once surrounded.

4th. The *stalk*, which is usually characterized by a green, herbaceous appearance; its duration is mostly limited to the space of one year. This modification of the stem is peculiar to an immense number of plants, and is susceptible of a vast variety of forms. The mode of its development, both external and internal, and the disposition of its secondary or lateral axes (branches, leaves, &c.), are of great importance in systematic and descriptive Botany.

5th and last. The *ligneous* or *woody-stem* is the most complete of all the forms of this organ, and is especially distinguished by its hardness and durability. It occurs in all trees and shrubs, with the exception of palm and tree-fern stems, which have been noticed above.

26. In describing all or any of the above-mentioned varieties or forms of the stem, particular attention should be paid to the individual peculiarities which distinguish this organ in different plants. Such, for example, are its *substance*, *direction*, *situation*, and *duration.*

The solidity and strength, as well as the external aspect and internal structure of the stem, are naturally dependent on its substance, and these diversities are precisely and intelligibly indicated by the following terms or epithets: — The stem is, accordingly, either *solid* and *firm* or *lax*, or *soft*, *hollow*, *tubular*, *woody*, *fibrous*, *herbaceous*, *fleshy*, *juicy*, *flexible*, *fragile*, *rigid*, *tough*, *easily pliable*, *weak*, &c.

The *direction* is described as *upright*, *procumbent*, or trailing on the ground, *decumbent*, *incumbent*, *arched*, *creeping*, *clasping*, &c.

In reference to *situation*, the stem is either *above* or *below* the ground, *floating* or *swimming*, climbing or clinging, like Ivy and Dodder, *winding* to the *right* or *winding* to the *left*.

The duration of the stem is generally equal to the duration of the plant, and either survives the production of the blossoms and fruit, or perishes when the object is effected.

Hence plants are divided into, A — *annual*, or summer-plants, and distinguished by the sign ⊙, or (1); B—*biennial* plants, such as produce blossoms usually in their second year — these are distinguished by the sign ♂, or ⊖ (2); C—*perennial*, or more permanent plants, are distinguished by the sign ♃ or (o-c).

Internal Structure of the Stem.

27. The inner structure of the stem is totally independent of its outward form. The diversities which we perceive in its structure are entirely attributable to the mutual relations of the cellular tissue and the bundles of vascular tissue which constitute the mass of all stems; and, above all, to the position and arrangement of the vascular tissues in reference to each other.

All plants, as we shall subsequently explain, are divided into three groups or grand divisions called classes, which are distinguishable from each other by distinctions in their embryos or seeds, in their blossoms, and in the interior structure of their stems. These groups are the following:—

1st Group or division comprehends the *Acotyledonous* plants, viz., such plants as have no visible blossoms or seeds, but reproduce themselves by means of embryonic cells or spores; and the vascular tissues of their stems are simultaneously produced, and are located either in the middle of the stem, or in very large masses in different parts.

2nd Group or division comprehends the *Monocotyledonous* plants, producing blossoms and seeds which germinate with only *one* embryonic leaf (or seed-lobe, Cotyledon). Their bundles of vascular tissue are not simultaneously produced, but they are deposited without any regular arrangement in the cellular tissue of the stem. The nervation of their leaves is parallel.

3rd Group or division comprehends the *Dicotyledonous* plants, which, like the second group, produce blossoms and seeds. They develope *two* embryonic leaves, sometimes more. The duration of the growth of their vascular tissue is unlimited, and the latter is regularly deposited on the stem in concentric layers. The nervation of their leaves is ramified and reticulated (comp. § 16)

Stem of Acotyledonous Plants.

28. To this division belong the Equisetaceæ, the Lycopodiaceæ, the *Musci*, in which the bundles of vascular tissue occupy the centre of the stem (fig. 16); the *Filices*, whose vascular system is arranged partly in large and partly in small groups (fig. 17). A section of the frond of the Eagle-fern (Pteris aquilina), especially if cut aslant and near the root, affords a mode-

rately correct representation of a double eagle with expanded wings. This is the vascular tissue of the frond represented in fig. 18; and generally these vessels are so disposed in this group, that every family forming a part of it may be with certainty recognised by this characteristic.

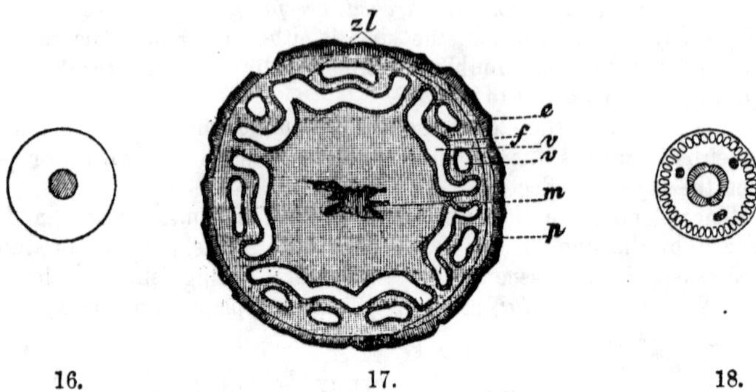

16. 17. 18.

It is further deserving of notice, that in acotyledonous plants the additions are always made in an upward direction, only on the summit of the plant, either by the formation of new vessels or by the elongation of such as have been already formed.

Stem of Monocotyledonous Plants.

29. To this class belong, among many others, the grasses, sedges, rushes, and bulbous plants. The stem of the palm, however, is best adapted for exhibiting the peculiarities by which this class is distinguished from the other two. If we examine a section of this stem, fig. 19, we perceive a great number of separate bundles of vascular tissue dispersed without order among the cellular tissue of the parenchyma. The growth of stems belonging to plants of this class is effected, not by the increase of the fibres already formed, but by vascular and other tissues which are produced at the circumference and reach to the summit, and hence such stems increase in length as well as in circumference.*

19.

Stem of Dicotyledonous Plants.

30. As this kind of stem is peculiar to all our common trees, and to a vast majority of plants belonging to the vegetable kingdom, it requires a more detailed illustration.

In all these stems the bundles of vascular tissue are regularly arranged in concentric layers around a common axis or centre, which is formed of parenchymatous cells, and is called the *pith*, or the substance enclosed in the medullary sheath. The increase or growth of the stem is effected by successive additions of vascular tissue to the circumference or outside of the tree.

* Authors are not agreed regarding the development of the monocotyledonous stem.—Ed.

On examining the section of a one-year old dicotyledonous stem, magnified as in fig. 20, we perceive several parts clearly distinguishable from each other.

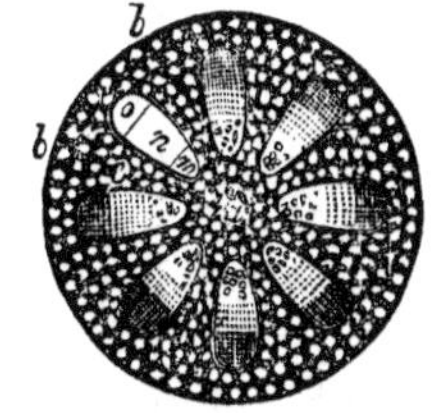

20.

In the cellular tissue there is perceived a series of vascular bundles, flattened and arranged round the axis of the stem, and forming the medullary sheath or tube containing the *pith*, a parenchymatous substance, *a*. The tissues on the circumference, *b b*, form the *bark*, and the parenchymatous tissues, *c c*, surrounding the woody layers and forming a communication between the pith and the bark, are *medullary rays*.

Among the bundles of vascular tissue (pleurenchyma) there are several distinct parts to be distinguished. The interior part forms, as above noticed, the medullary sheath, *m*, round which the woody layers, *n*, are deposited, and towards their circumference there is a layer of cambium cells, *o*, which, as already mentioned in § 14, constitute a series of tissues that are in a constant state of vigorous activity. This portion of the stem consequently acts the most important part in its further development, for through its layers almost exclusively the upward and downward motions of the sap are effected and the diameter of the stem increased. In many plants belonging to this family there occur the liber, or inner cortical layers (§ 8,) which constitute what is termed *bast*.

We thus distinguish the three chief constituent parts of the stem, viz., the *pith*, the *wood*, and the *bark*.

31. The growth of a permanent dicotyledonous stem is continued by a successive annual deposition of woody layers on that formed the previous year. And every new layer is deposited between the former and the cortical layers, or bast or inner bark, and this deposition is effected in the cambium layers, *o*, and consequently between the wood, *n*, and the inner bark.

Thus every year a new layer is deposited between the previous formation and the bark; and a section will exhibit these concentric rings of wood obviously distinct from each other; and as one year is requisite for the formation of a single layer of wood, these depositions are named *annual*

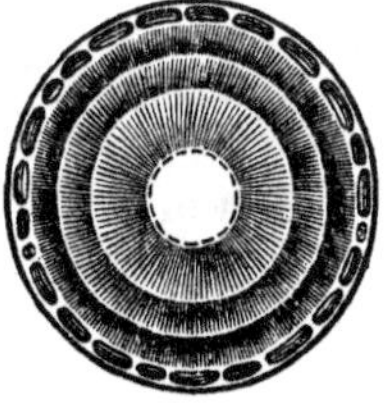
21.

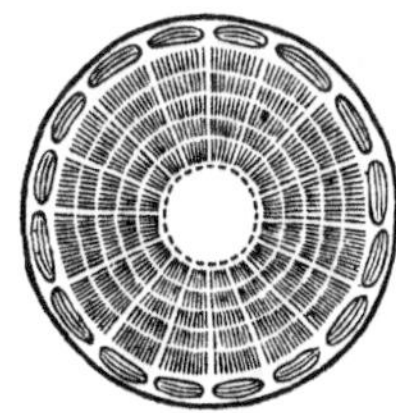
22.

layers or *rings*. In fig. 21 we have a representation of a stem three years old, and in fig. 22 one of five years of age.

As the cortical layers and the parenchymatous materials, of which the outer bark is composed, are but slowly increased, and form altogether but an inconsiderable portion of the bulk of the stem, their annual increase cannot be ascertained. But the number of annually-deposited woody layers, or concentric rings; is a certain indication of the age of the tree.

The pith and medullary rays obtain little or no increase during the life of the tree; and after a considerable period has elapsed the pith is no longer visible.

The medullary rays, however, are not obliterated, but are to be distinguished in stems of the greatest age. To these are attributed the longitudinal fissility of the wood, and they possess a shining close appearance, from which they have been named by carpenters, the *silver grain* of the timber.

32. In the course of the first year, in which the woody and other fibrous tissues are formed, their sap is dried up and they become hardened or *lignified*. These tissues subsequently take no part in the vital functions of the plant, which are carried on only in the cambium of the outermost layer of fibrous tissue, which consequently performs the most important part in the economy of the plant.

By degrees the external part of the rind dies, splits in many trees, and assumes a brownish colour, and in this condition is called *bark*. The series of layers commencing with the suberous parts in an old stem are the following: viz., the bark, the rind, the bast (of which matting is frequently made), the cambium, the wood, and the pith.

Functions of the Stem.

33. The stem, as above stated, § 21, is the medium of communication between the most remote parts of the plant, viz., the root and the leaves. But the entire duty of maintaining this communication devolves upon it only during the first year of its existence: at a later period this function is performed almost solely by the cambium-layers of the newly-formed bundles of woody tissue, and by the layer immediately under the rind. Our old hollow oaks, elms, and willows sufficiently prove this fact. In these, the whole, or almost the whole of the wood is decayed; but they still continue to live and have a green and vigorous old age.

But let us suppose that the bark is removed, and that the sappy cambial layers are exposed to the effects of the sun and atmosphere, we shall soon perceive that these shrink, shrivel, and dry up, and are no longer in a condition to afford a passage for the sap. If the rind be removed all round about the stem, the death of the tree is the inevitable consequence. Hence carpenters usually bark the freshly-cut willow poles about a finger's breadth, before placing them in the ground, to prevent them from taking root afresh and producing new leaves. These sap-conveying layers are, besides, the abode of the larvæ of many insects, which often devour the cambial tissues all round the tree, and thus occasion the destruction of entire woods and forests.

If, however, the tree be accidentally deprived of only a portion of its bark, and when the denuded part does not extend all round the stem, the bark may be renovated by the activity of the tissues; and this will be considerably promoted and accelerated by protecting the wounded parts from the injurious effects of solar and atmospheric influences by a plaster of clay, marl, or any adhesive compost.

Leaves.

34. The lateral developments surrounding the stem or branches, viz., organs which assume an expanded, flattened development, in contrast with the cylindrical form of the root and stem, are called *leaves*. Both air and light are necessary for their development, and they are consequently never found perfectly formed on the subterranean parts of plants. They are distinguished by peculiar names which signify their position or situation on the stem or branch. Commencing with the lowermost, we have, 1st. The *embryonic leaf* or seed-lobe (Cotyledon), which generally falls off after the development of the other leaves. 2nd. The *radical* or *root-leaves*, which grow next to the root, and are generally distinguished by a form differing in some respects from the upper leaves. 3rd. The *stem-leaves*. 4th. The *stipules*, which grow at the base of the stem-leaves in certain families of plants. 5th. The *Bracts* or *floral leaves*, which appear on the upper part of a stem or branch, and bear in their axils (axis, the angle formed by their own axis and the axis of the branch or stem on which they grow) a flower- or fruit-bud. Bracts or floral leaves are distinguished from the stem-leaves by a difference or modification of their form, and sometimes by their colour and consistence.

The leaves developed on the very extremities of a chief or lateral axis vary from other leaves so remarkably, both in shape and functions, that they receive a different name, viz., blossoms, and are described as independent organs. All the above-mentioned forms of foliage do not exist on every plant; and as the stem-leaf is the most important of these foliaceous appendages, this organ is meant when we speak of the *leaf*.

35. Sometimes the leaf appears at its base, *i. e.*, the place nearest its point of attachment, as a semicircular investment of the stem, sometimes it entirely embraces the latter organ and is named a *sheathing leaf*. We find examples of this in the family of grasses, the leaves of which are all furnished with sheaths enveloping part of the stem. The leaf in general is connected by its base with the stem or branch through the intervention of an organ called a *petiole* or leaf-stalk; and from this petiole the *lamina* (blade) or leaf-proper is developed. When the petiole is not present, the leaf is said to be *sessile* or *sitting*; and in this latter case the leaf often forms a semicircular sheath at its base, half surrounding the stem. The angle formed between the leaf or leaf-stalk and the stem is called the *axil* of the leaf.

36. The manifold diversities and modifications of leaves, both in form and arrangement, are so manifest as not to be overlooked; they are obvious even to the most heedless observers. They not only afford characteristic marks which distinguish certain genera and species of plants, but even whole families can be certainly identified by their means alone. Therefore the botanist pays especial attention to this part of the subject, comparing and discriminating the similarities and dissimilarities which occur among these infinitely-numerous and extremely-diversified objects, but of which only a slight sketch can be given in the present work.

In studying this organ, special notice must be taken of the distribution of the bundles of vascular tissue which constitute the nerves, as also of the form or shape of the leaf, the nature of its margin, of its point or extremity, and of its base, &c.

The bundle of vascular tissue proceeding from the stem, and constituting the more solid part of the petiole when present, forms the *nervation*, or nervous system of the leaf. The nerves are easily to be distinguished from the rest of the leaf by their lighter colour and closer consistency.

The way in which they are distributed in the *lamina* or blade is two-fold. In the first case they are separated at the base of the leaf-blade into several *parallel* or *curvilineal nerves*, which extend longitudinally and again unite or come together, or approach towards the apex (extremity or point of the leaf). Examples of this peculiar nervation occur in most monocotyledonous plants, as Grasses, Orchids, &c. (Compare § 27.)

In the second case there is usually a *principal nerve*, or *middle* or *median nerve* (mid-rib), which oxtends to the extremity of the leaf, and sends out *ramifications* or lateral nerves. These lateral nerves are either *parallel* (pinnate-nerved), or form a sort of network over the whole blade, and are hence called *reticulate* (disposed somewhat like the meshes of a net). This mode of nervation is peculiar to dicotyledonous plants, and forms one of the characters by which this class is most readily distinguished.

In all the forms above mentioned, the petiole and the blade form only one plane. There are some leaves, however, named *peltate* (like a shield or buckler), in which the leaf-nerves form an angle with the petiole. This form is exemplified by the leaf of Hydrocotyle, Indian cress, &c.

Such terms as *three-*, *four-*, *five-nerved*, *palmate-nerved*, need no explanation. When the central nerve is very short, and the lateral nerves are strong and subdivided, the nervation is called *pedate*.

Forms of Leaves.

37. The shape or form of these organs is always regulated or modified by the divergence, ramification, and greater or less extension of the divisions of the primary nerve or mid-rib, and also by the position and length of the branching or secondary nerves. When the median nerve and its divisions or its branches diverge in the same plane, the leaf is flat and thin; when the divisions or the ramifications lie in different planes, or diverge in different directions, the leaf is either *orbicular* or *peltate*, or sometimes *palmate*, *digi-*

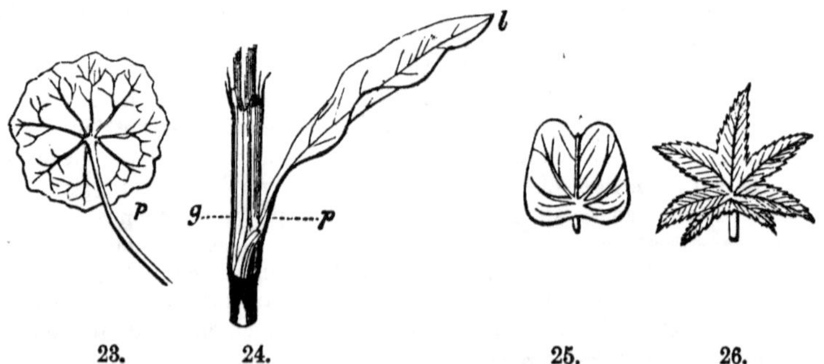

23. 24. 25. 26.

tate, and *pedate* forms are produced (see figs. 23, 26, 27, 28), or else succulent leaves, like those of *Sedum acre* (see figs. 29, 30). The complete leaf consists of two parts—first, the *petiole* or leaf-stalk, which connects the

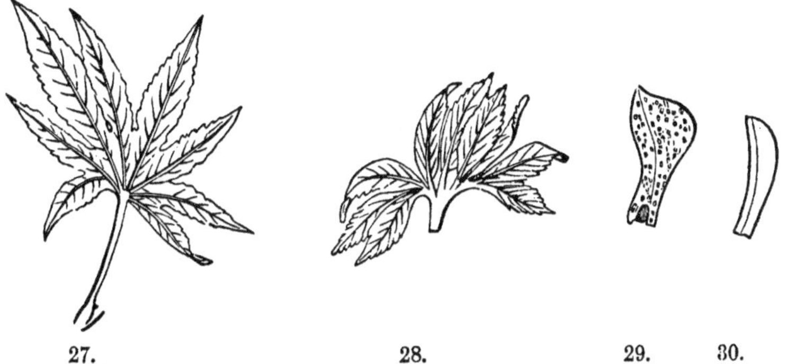

27. 28. 29. 30.

flattened or expanded portion to the stem or branch, and, second, the *lamina* or blade of the leaf (see fig. 24 *l*). The petiole is composed of the united bundles of vascular tissues; the blade is formed by the extension, divarication, and reticulation of the vascular bundles, the interstices being filled up with cellular tissue (*parenchyma*), and the whole covered by the epidermis. The petiole is not always present; and when it is absent, the leaf is *sessile* (*sedeo*, I sit). When sessile leaves embrace the stem they are called *amplexicaul* (*amplecti*, to embrace, and *caulis*, a stalk).

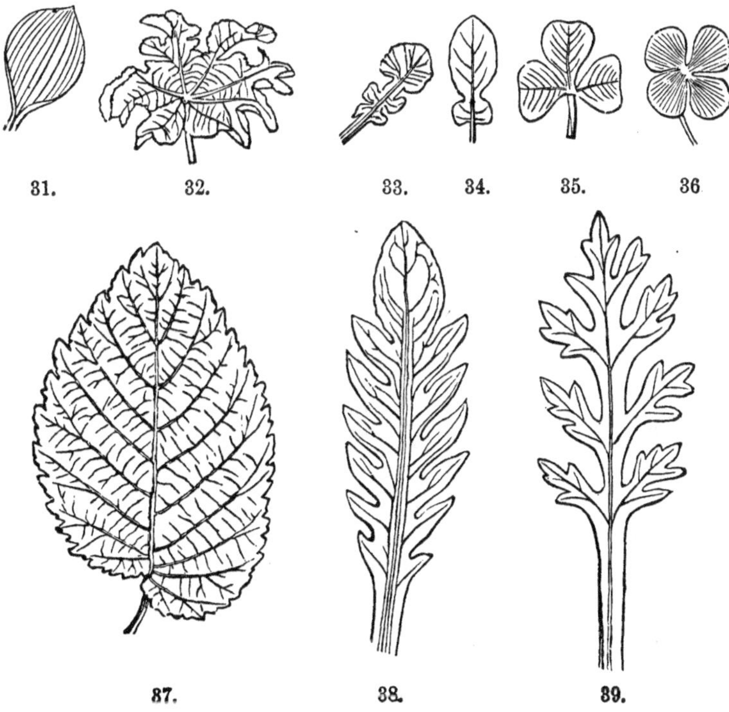

31. 32. 33. 34. 35. 36

37. 38. 39.

38. The most obvious division of leaves is into simple and compound. In the former case the blade of the leaf consists of but one piece, either entire or variously cleft or parted (see figs. 33, 34, 35, 36, 37, 38, 39). Compound leaves are composed of one or several pieces called leaflets, jointed or articulated to the common petiole (see figs. 64, 65).

39. *Simple leaves.*—It has already been stated that the figure of the leaf is modified by the divisions of the medium or primary nerve, and by the divergency and length of the secondary or branching nerves. When the parenchyma is equally developed on each side of the mid-rib or leaf-stalk, the leaf is called *equal* (fig. 41), if otherwise, the leaf is *unequal* or *oblique* (fig. 37). The common and dog violets afford examples of equal leaves, elm and Begonia of unequal or oblique leaves. When the nerves have only a very slight divergence, and proceed from the base to the apex in lines nearly parallel with the mid-rib, the leaf is *acicular*, as in the pine tribe, or *linear* as in the grasses (fig. 46). When the divergence or the length of the secondary nerves is small, and the leaf tapers at each end, it is called *lanceolate*, (*lancea*, a spear), (fig. 49.) If the middle, secondary, or branching nerves only slightly exceed in length the other lateral nerves, and if the base and apex be convex, the leaf is said to be *rounded*, *elliptical*, or *oval* (figs. 47, 53, 41); if the basal nerves be the longest, the leaf is *ovate* or egg-shaped (fig. 44); on the contrary, if the nerves at the apex be the longest, the leaf is *obovate*, or inversely egg-shaped. The *cuneate* and *spathulate* (wedge-shaped and spathula-like forms) are only modifications of this latter disposition of the nerves (see figs. 55, 40). When the nervation is prolonged downwards at an obtuse angle with the mid-rib so as to form two rounded lobes, the leaf is *cordate* or heart-shaped, as in the sweet and dog violets (fig. 45); when the parenchyma is deficient at the apex, and similar rounded lobes are formed at the summit, the leaf is said to be *obcordate*, or inversely heart-shaped, as in the leaflets of white clover (fig. 35); when the base is strongly lobed, and the apex broadly rounded, the leaf is said to be *reniform*, or kidney-shaped (fig. 52); when the lobes are extended downwards and terminate in acute angles, the *sagittate* or arrow-shaped leaf is produced, as in Sagittaria sagittifolia (fig. 48). Succulent leaves are produced, as already stated, by the divergence of the nerves in different planes with a large development of cellular tissue, and their forms are usually *conical*, *prismatical*, *ensiform* (*ensis*, a sword), *acinaciform* (*acinaces*, a scimi-

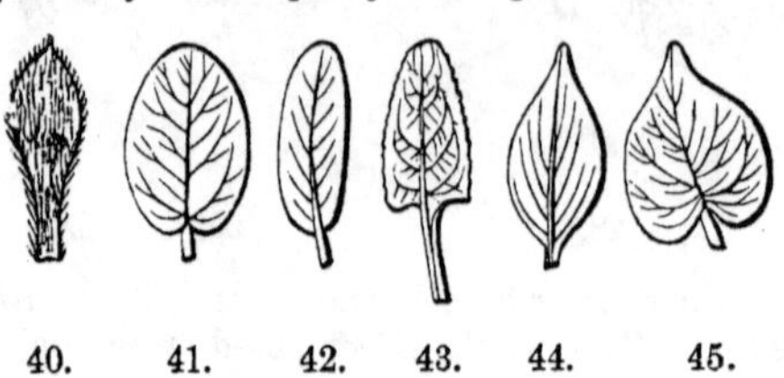

40. 41. 42. 43. 44. 45.

46.

47. 48. 49. 50. 51.

tar), or *dolabriform* (*dolabra*, a hatchet) (figs. 29, 30). When the lobes of the base are united so as to surround the stem, the leaf is *perfoliate* (fig. 56); when two leaves grow together at the base, and thus surround the stem, the leaf is *connate*, as in Honeysuckles; when the parenchyma is developed so as to fill up more than the interstitial places in the reticulation, the leaf is said to be *crisp*, *wavy*, or *curled*, as in rheum undulatum (fig. 32), also in many species of Rumex (Dock) and Mallow; when the leaves surround the stem in a radiating manner, as in the various Galliums, the leaf is *whorled*, (fig. 51); when the leaf ends abruptly in a straight margin, either at the apex or base, the leaf is *truncate* (figs. 54, 43); when the apex is only slightly notched, the leaf is called *emarginate* (fig. 25); when the depression is very slight, it is called *retuse* (*retusus*, blunt), fig. 57); when the point of a leaf is very long, it is called *acuminate* (fig. 59); when the point is very hard and sharp, it is called *mucronate* (*mucro*, a point), (fig. 60).

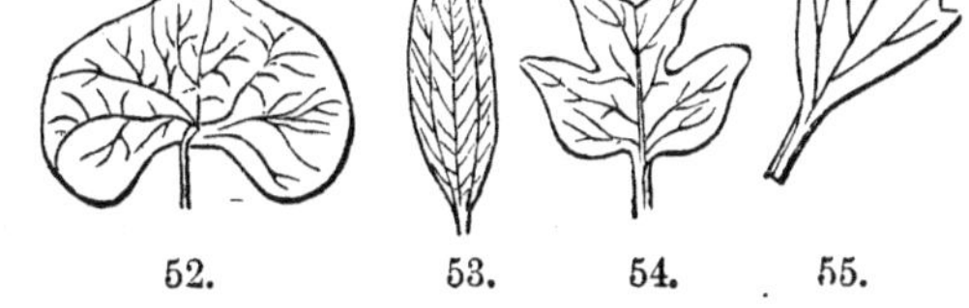

52. 53. 54. 55.

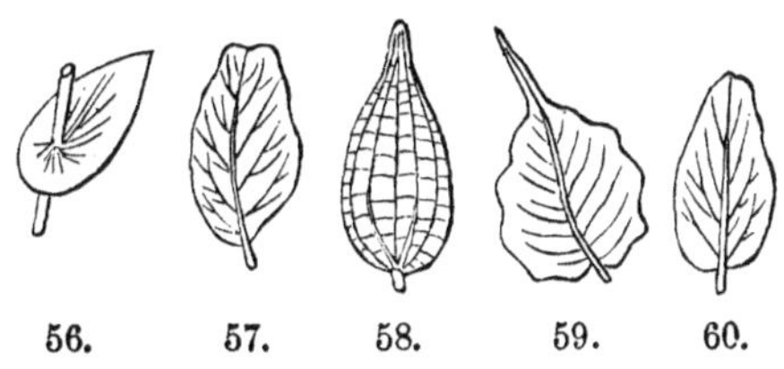

56. 57. 58. 59. 60.

40. The margin of the leaf is either entire or it is variously parted, cleft, notched, crenated, crenulate, or sinuous. When there is no projection nor incision in the margin, the leaf is called *entire* (figs. 41–5); when the margin is furnished with rounded prominences, it is either crenated or crenulate, according as the projections are greater or smaller, and the indentations of greater or less depth (fig. 59). If the projections are pointed and diverge at right angles to the mid-rib or base, the leaf is *dentate* (*dens*, a tooth) (fig. 55.) When the projections point towards the summit, the leaf is *serrate* (*serra*, a saw). If there be two series of teeth on the margin, *i. e.* if the primary teeth are also serrated, the leaf is then *doubly serrate* (fig. 61). When the projections or prominences are far apart, the margin is said to be *sinuous* or *flexuous* (figs. 62, 57, 59). If the incisions reach half-way, or nearly half-

61. 62. 63.

way, from the margin to the mid-rib, the leaf is said to be *cleft*, or *divided* (fig. 38), and separated portions are called *lobes;* when the incision reaches near to the mid-rib, the leaf is *partite*, or parted (fig. 39). *Hastate, auriculate, lyrate,* and *panduriform* leaves are merely varieties of the cleft or partite leaf, the sinus or portion of the leaf not filled up with parenchyma being wider (figs. 63, 33, 34). The difference between the hastate and the auriculate leaf consists solely in the lobes of the former being horizontal, as in Rumex acetosella, in the latter these are directed towards the apex (see fig. 63). The *palmate, digitate*, and *pedate* forms of foliage are dependent on the number of divisions of the mid-rib or petiolary vascular bundles, and bear names indicative of the number of their lobes or partitions, as *trifid* (three-cleft), *quadrifid* (four cleft), *quinquefid* (five-cleft), and so on (figs. 26, 27, 28). When the lobes or partitions are arranged in a winged manner, or forming angles with the mid-rib, the leaf is *pinnatifid* (*pinna*, a wing, and *findo*, I cleave) (fig. 39); when the nervation is radiating, and not in the same plane as the petiole, the leaf may be either *orbicular*, as in *Hydrocotyle*, or *peltate* (*pelta*, a buckler), as in *Ricinus Palma Christi*, as already stated (figs. 23, 27).

41. *Compound Leaves.*—When the incisions of the leaf extend from the margin to the mid-rib, and when each portion of the compound leaf is separately jointed to the common petiole or mid-rib, such a leaf is compound, whether it consists of only one leaflet, as in Orange, or of an indefinite number, as in Acacia. When there is only one series of leaflets on each

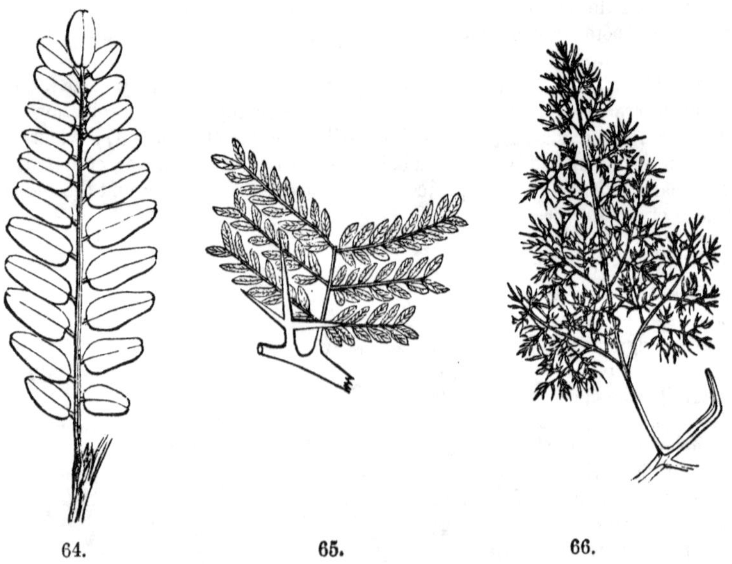

64. 65. 66.

side of the mid-rib, the leaf is *simply pinnate* (*pinna*, a wing) (fig. 64); when the leaflets or pinnæ are again subdivided, forming a secondary series of leaflets, the compound leaf is *double-* or *bi-pinnate* (fig. 65); when these secondary leaflets, or *pinnulæ*, are subdivided a third time, the leaf is *thrice-* or *tri-pinnate*, or *decompound* (fig. 66). This figure also represents a *supra-decompound* leaf, in which the subdivisions are still further extended.

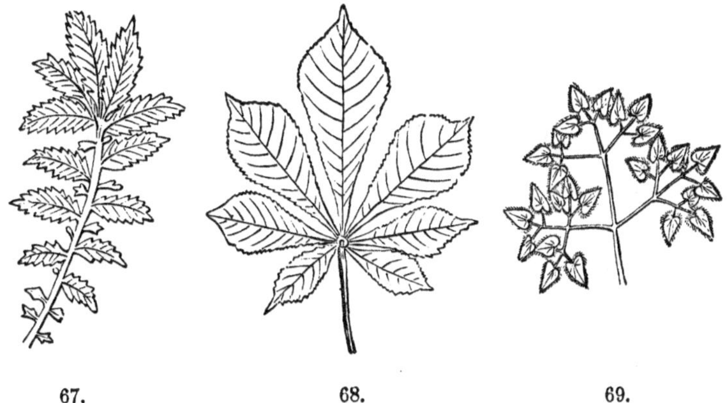

67. 68. 69.

When the leaflets are opposite, without the intervention of a small or rudimentary leaflet, and without a terminating odd leaflet, the leaf is called *pari-pinnate*, or equally pinnate (fig 65); when otherwise, *imparipinnate*, or unequally pinnate (fig. 64). When the pinnæ are of different sizes, or deficient, the leaf is interruptedly pinnate (fig. 67). When all the leaflets originate in the same point of the common petiole, the leaf is *trifoliate*, *quadrifoliate*, *quinquefoliate*, *septennate*, accordingly as the number of leaflets may be, viz., three, four, five, or seven (figs. 35, 36, 68). The compound leaf may also be *bi-ternate*, *tri-ternate* (fig. 69), a form abundantly illustrated by Archangel and several umbelliferous plants.

Function of Leaves.

42. The great importance of these organs in the economy of vegetation may be understood from the fact, that a tree constantly deprived of its leaves is ultimately destroyed, and that even their temporary or partial removal essentially retards its healthy development.

The function of the leaves, chiefly carried on through the stomata, described in § 17, is twofold, viz., first, the evaporation of the excess of moisture, or the superfluous water; second, the absorption and separation of different gases.

43. Plants do not assimilate the whole of the water absorbed by their roots, but exhale more than two-thirds through the medium of their leaves. The sap remaining in the leaves is thus rendered exceedingly concentrated, since it now contains the non-volatile mineral constituents which the water had absorbed from the soil. Indeed, the leaves, when burned, yield a large proportion of ash. The copious evaporation taking place from the surface of the leaves has a sensible effect on the temperature of the atmosphere, which is sensibly lower, where it is exposed to the influence of extensive woods or even of fields covered by luxuriant crops. It has been observed

that a tree of moderate size exhaled, in the space of 10 hours, 15 lbs. of water through its respiratory organs.

44. Under the influence of solar light the leaves exhale oxygen, whilst, on the contrary, during the night they inhale oxygen and exhale carbonic acid. It is also true that the leaves are capable of inhaling both carbonic acid and aqueous vapour from the atmosphere for the nutrition of the plant, although this process is generally accomplished through the agency of the roots.

It only remains to be noticed, that all the functions described in this paragraph, and attributed to the agency of leaves, may be performed by any other green portions of the plant, provided that these portions be furnished with stomata.

ORGANS OF INCREASE AND REPRODUCTION.

45. If the subjects of the vegetable kingdom had not been originally endowed with a marvellous capability of continually renovating and reproducing themselves, it is very evident, from the prodigious amount of destruction effected through the various accidents to which they are liable, as well as through their incessant consumption by both man and beast, that they must long ago have vanished from the earth, and have left its surface a cheerless desert. Every plant, however, is created with a reproductive power, which, in fecundity, far surpasses the most prolific of animals; and every plant, so produced, is again capable, under favourable circumstances, of producing a race of plants as numerous as that of its parent.

If, on a transient view, these multiplicative and reproductive organs of different plants appear so diverse that it may be deemed impossible to comprehend them all under one common type, we should do well to reconsider what has been already stated in § 5, in reference to the life of the cell, and its importance as the primary and most essential organ of the vegetable kingdom. If the above-cited section be well studied and truly apprehended, the propagation of plants will be divested of all its apparent difficulty and complexity.

Many plants, at special periods of their life, produce, in certain parts, *embryo-cells*, or *spores* or *buds*, which are easily detached from their parent-plant. These, falling into the soil in their vicinity, commence an independent existence, and thus secure the perpetuation of the individual species. This is the case with all the lower orders, which have been denominated *acotyledonous plants* (see § 28). In the other classes of plants we likewise find similar embryo-cells, which have a more complicated mode of production and a more complete development. Those very peculiarly-constructed organs called *stamens*, which exercise so important an influence on the other reproductive organs, both secrete and contain the *pollen cells*, or farina or pollen-dust, as it is often called. This cell, or powdery granule, is not essentially different from the embryo-cells of acotyledonous plants.

It differs, however, circumstantially: for example, it is not capable of development when it comes in contact with the soil or water, or any other media in which the embryo-cells or spores of acotyledonous plants will germinate For the *staminal* or *seminal* embryo-cell a special organ is provided, which receives it on its separation from the cells of the anther, and in which alone it can be farther developed. Besides, its development even here is very much circumscribed, for the most part only becoming a very small but perfect plant, which is called the *embryo;* and in this condition it remains stationary, until the decay of the organs by which it was protected and nourished is complete, and then it receives the name of *seed.* It is well known that seeds, under circumstances suitable to the exigencies of their nature, are developed into perfect plants, and that, although the active powers of the seed may have been long dormant, they do not lose their vitality, especially if kept dry, and preserved from the injurious effects of the atmosphere and other contingencies.

Finally, many individual parts of plants, when removed from their parent and placed under favourable circumstances, are capable of producing plants similar in all respects to those from which they were taken. This property is possessed by the buds which we find on the branches, or on the leaves, or in tubers and bulbs.

In the following paragraphs we shall investigate the nature and properties of the bud, as well as those of the blossom and the fruit.

Buds.

46. The rudiments of future and more extensive development are to be met with, not only on the extremities of the principal axis, but also on its circumference and on its secondary or lateral axes. These rudimentary parts or buds present the appearance of very-much abbreviated axes, consisting of a series of closely-imbricated leaflets, the exterior parts of which are of a brownish colour and of a scaly structure. Such a miniature axis is named *bud* or *eye*, and is represented in fig. 70. It is called a terminal bud when formed on the extremity of the principal axis *b t*, and a lateral bud when produced on a lateral axis, *b a*, *b a*, *b a*. The buds produced on the periphery of a principal or lateral axis are always found on the axil of a leaf, and hence they are termed *axillary buds*, and the arrangement of branches may be as easily ascertained as that of leaves. (Comp. § 41.)

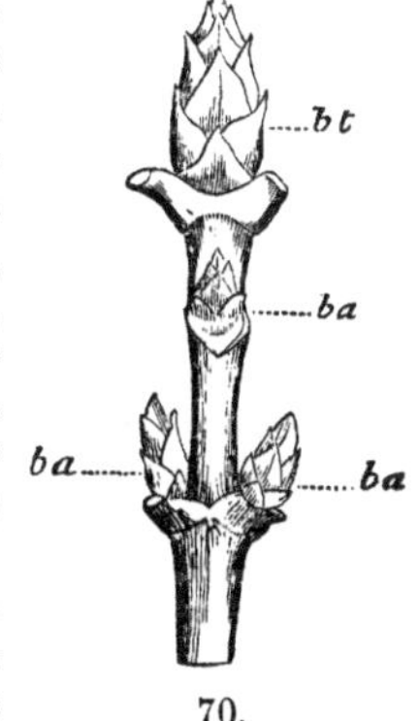

70.

The bud is developed, and constitutes an independent axis under laws peculiar to itself, and the imbricated, crowded, rudimentary leaflets appear at distances commensurate with the more or less elongation of the internodes, which of course is dependent on the more or less vigorous growth of the plant, and in the course of time new buds are again formed in their axils.

The differences of buds will appear on their sectional examination. For example, we can ascertain whether or not the future axis, developed from the bud, will produce a blossom, and so terminate the growth of the plant in that direction, in which case it is called a *flower-* or *fruit-bud;* or, if we find only the rudiments of a leafy twig, it is a *leaf-bud.*

The bud may either be farther developed immediately after its appearance, or its future development may be retarded for a considerable period, during which it remains in an apparently dormant condition. This occurs in our fruit trees, whose buds, formed during the previous summer, are not developed till the spring following. Hence these hybernating buds are enclosed in leathery (coriaceous), clammy scales, whereby they are defended from the cold. This protection is not necessary for buds which are expanded soon after their formation, and the colour of their leaflets or scales is green like other leaves.

47. Buds possess the remarkable property, even when separated from the mother plant, of developing themselves on another plant, if placed in a situation where they can appropriate to themselves the nutriment necessary for their growth. On this principle the process of budding is dependent. To accomplish this successfully, the bud is transferred to a plant which very closely resembles the parent, in order that the coalescence of the two may be effected as speedily as possible. When a bud only is transferred from one tree to another, the operation is called *inoculation* or *budding*, and when a portion of the wood is employed, with one or more buds on it, we call it *grafting*. The bud or graft thus transferred produces, even on another tree, an axis or branch which possesses all the qualities of the mother-plant. This practice is an invaluable medium for increasing the most estimable flower- and fruit-bearing plants and trees, which are thus capable of producing fruit upon the wild, natural plants, whose produce otherwise would be worthless.

Inoculation, or Budding.

48. This operation is chiefly performed on the wild- or dog-rose tree, which is commonly used for this purpose on account of its luxuriant growth and durability.

The stock or wild rose is planted in a garden, or in some spot where it is meant to be an ornamental object, and suffered to grow in its new situation about a year previous to the operation of budding it. For this purpose there is, first of all, an incision made in its bark similar to the letter T (fig 71). A bud is abstracted, with the leaf, in the axil of which the bud is produced, and a portion of the wood under the rind, from a branch bearing valuable roses, the whole being of the form of a little shield (see fig. 72). The rind of the section of the wild rose is slightly raised up with the flattened handle of the budding-knife, to permit the easy application and insertion of the bud and bark which have been previously deprived of the small portion of wood cut off from the parent rose-stem; it is then moved upwards that it may be in close contact with the cross-cut of the incision, for it is at this point that incorporation or coalescence first commences; it is then closely tied round with a piece of bast (matting) or woollen cloth (fig. 73). The wild rose is subsequently cut away above the inserted bud, and all the shoots formed on the stem sedulously rubbed or

71. 72. 73.

broken off; nothing is suffered to remain but the new axis produced by the inserted bud, and if the operation be performed in spring, roses are often produced in the course of the succeeding summer. After midsummer inoculation is practised with the dormant eye or bud, which remains undeveloped till the following spring, when the stock is cut away above the inserted eye, which then becomes a shoot and produces roses in summer.

Grafting.

49. In this operation a single bud is not employed, but a small twig or branchlet, bearing three or four buds. This is called the *graft*, slip, or scion. Whether the wild stock on which it is to be inserted be a young plant, or an old tree, in either case a cross section is made either of the young stem, or of a branch, if the tree be large. A strong cleft is made (fig. 74) with a sharp-pointed wedge or strong knife, so that the graft cut to the shape of a wedge (fig. 75) may exactly fit the cleft made for its reception in the wild stem (fig. 76). The cleft is subsequently protected from the light, the air, and moisture, by a composition of loam or sort of compost, and the graft is bound to the stock with bast or cloth in such a manner that the inner bark of the one may exactly coincide with the same part of the other.

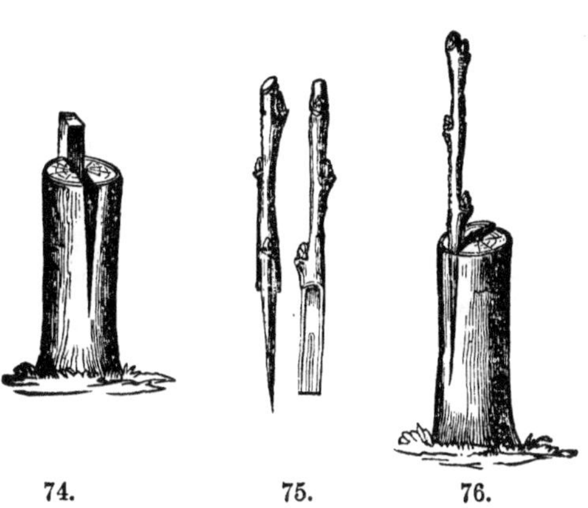

74. 75. 76.

Occasionally a cutting, with a tongue of bark attached, is inserted in the stock like a bud, as described above. This mode has the advantage of preserving the stock, which can be budded again in case of failure: if the split grafting is unsuccessful, the decay of the stock is unavoidable. Another method of grafting is by *approach* or *inarching*, when two growing plants are united together, and when adhesion has been effected, the one is severed from its own stock and left to grow on the other.

These operations may be performed in a great many ways, and all may be more or less successful. The essential requisite in all of them is, that the recently-cut bark of the slip or scion to be grafted, intimately coincides with the same part of the plant on which it is grafted, otherwise no adhesion can take place. Grafting is generally performed in the spring, when the sap-conducting layers are in the greatest activity.

The bud, however, will not grow on any stem whatever, but in general only on the stems of plants belonging to the same genus; the white rose and apricot cannot be grafted on the oak.

Bulb.

50. A bud, whose bracts are moderately large, thick, or fleshy, and full of

sap, is named a bulb. Such buds or bulbs are generally formed on subterranean stems, but the bulb-bearing lily and the garlic are examples of bulbs being produced on aerial stems; still their position in either case is in the axils of the leaves. The bulb when severed from its parent, possesses the capability of prolonging its axis in the two opposite directions, in the development of both root and leaves. It retains this power at least for a year, provided it be preserved from the effects of moisture, which speedily produces rottenness in its fleshy integuments.

The bulb is in a condition to produce new lateral bulbs around its axis, which new productions either adhere to the bulb, or are detached, forming independent plants. With their development the destiny of the mother-bulb is fulfilled; its leaves, bereft of their sappy contents, shrivel and wither, and subsequently perish.

Tuber.

51. The buds in the tuber are also capable of independent development, although around their axes we do not usually discover a vestige of such leafy appendages as surround the bulb. We find instead of these an abundant supply of nourishment lodged in the parenchymatous tissue, which chiefly consists of water, starch, sugar, &c.

Tubers generally possess several eyes or buds, which in some plants, as in the dahlia, are not perceptible till they begin to shoot. If preserved from putrescence, these retain their vitality at least one year.

Blossom.

52. We justify the botanist who prizes certain inconspicuous parts of a flower unnoticed by the multitude, above those showy, splendid, graceful, odorous, gorgeously-coloured organs which are the pride and admiration of the florist. The taste and admiration, however, of the man of science for these beautiful productions are no more sacrificed to his scientific views of their nature and origin, than our enjoyment of a highly-artistic work is diminished by our knowledge of the principles upon which it was executed. It is one thing to gaze and wonder, it is another to understand, admire, and enjoy.

By the term *blossom* we understand those peculiarly-formed leaves arranged in verticils or whorls around the summit of a principal or lateral axis, which have been termed *floral leaves*, floral integuments, envelopes, &c., but which in the following section will be generally expressed by the term floral verticils or whorls, and the particular organs by the terms calyx, corolla, sepals, petals, &c.

In external form these leaves are essentially different from the other leaves of the plant, and in the regularly-developed perfect blossom constitute *four series or verticils* of *floral leaves*, which are all different and arranged within each other.

The two external verticils take no part in the reproductive process, hence they are not indispensable parts of the blossom. One or both are frequently absent, and their absence does not in any way frustrate the object of the floral functions. Hence these two external organs are frequently called *floral-envelopes.*

The presence of both of the inner series of floral verticils is, on the contrary, necessary, and they are therefore regarded as indispensable parts of the blossom.

Proceeding from the exterior to the interior, or rather, more accurately, from the inferior to the superior, we have the four following series of separate floral verticils:—

1st. The *calyx;* 2nd. The *corolla;* 3rd. The *stamens;* 4th. The *pistil:* which in the more recent nomenclature are called the calyx-leaves, the corolla-leaves, the stamen-leaves, and the carpellary or fruit-leaf or leaves.

1. Calyx.

53. In colour and consistency the calyx-leaves closely approximate to the stem-leaves. In many plants, however, the colour of the calyx considerably varies from the usual colour of leaves, as, for example, in the fuchsia, the calyx of which is scarlet. It is often wanting, as in the vine; or it is caducous, as in the poppy. When there is but one series of external floral verticils, and it is uncertain whether it is to be deemed a calyx or a corolla, it is designated by the comprehensive name of *envelope*, of which the tulip affords an example.

The calyx-leaves are either free and form a *polyphyllous* (polysepalous) calyx, or they are laterally connected by their margins, and form a *monophyllous* (monosepalous) calyx.

In the polyphyllous calyx the number of the individual leaflets, with their form and position, are described. In the monophyllous calyx the form or shape, and the margin or border, which is mostly toothed, are the chief objects of consideration. The lower part is called the *throat* or tube.

In form the calyx is either *tubular* or *cylindrical* (fig. 77), or *clavate* (club-shaped) (fig. 78); *turbinate* (top-shaped) (fig. 79); *campanulate* (bell-shaped) (fig. 80); *funiculate* (funnel-shaped) (fig. 81); *urceolate* (urn-shaped); (fig. 82); *globose* (globular) (fig. 83); *vesiculate*, &c.

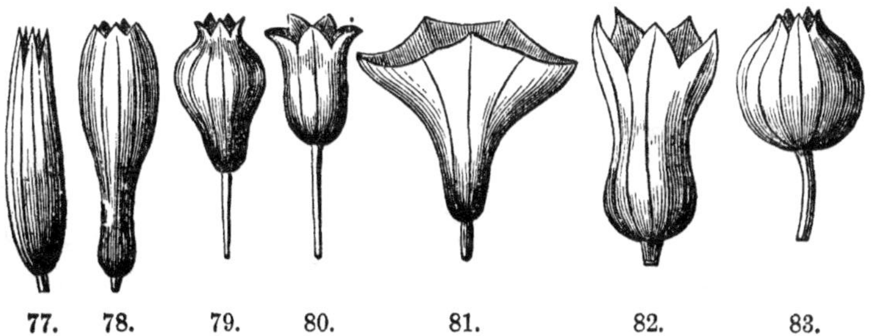

77. 78. 79. 80. 81. 82. 83.

The throat of the calyx is either naked or clothed with hair; it is sometimes closed with these excrescences.

The calyx is said to be *regular* when all its separate leaflets are perfectly similar, and when they are not so, it is *irregular*. A common example of an irregular monophyllous calyx is the *bilabiate* form, which is divided into two lobes or lips by a rather deep cleft. This form is found in salvia (sage).

2. Corolla.

54. The leaflets of this organ display more remarkable variations from the stem-leaves than those of the calyx. Its symmetry, delicacy, and oftentimes splendid colours, form one of the most attractive features of the vegetable kingdom; and for its sake flowers have been cultivated in all ages. They are the special favourites of the human race; they ornament our feasts, deck our bridal solemnities, and are strewed over our graves.

The corolla is in many respects analogous to the calyx, like it being composed of one or of more than one leaflet, and it is also regular or irregular.

In the corolla we distinguish the upper developed portion, which is called the *limb* or lamina, and the lower portion, which in many blossoms, as the pink, for example, is like the petiole of a leaf, and termed the *claw* (unguis).

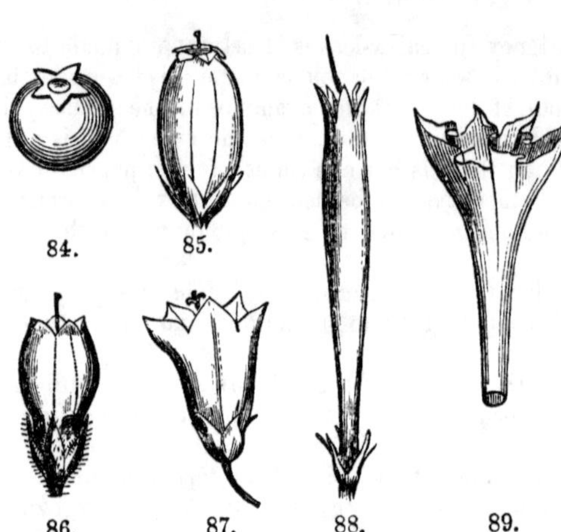

84. 85. 86. 87. 88. 89.

Many forms of the monophyllous (monopetalous) corolla agree with the forms of the calyx described in § 53, and are recognised by the same names. As special forms we cite the following, viz., the *globular* (fig. 84); *urceolate*, urn-shaped (fig. 85); *ovate* (fig. 86); *campanulate*, bell-shaped (fig. 87); *tubular* (fig. 88); *infundibuliform* (fig. 89); *hypocratiform* (fig. 90); *rotate*, radiate (fig. 91.)

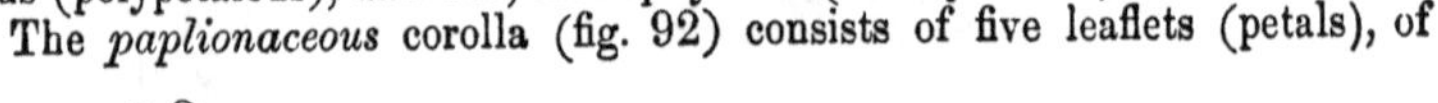

55. Two forms of the irregular corolla are common, viz., one, polyphyllous (polypetalous), and one, monophyllous (monopetalous).

The *paplionaceous* corolla (fig. 92) consists of five leaflets (petals), of

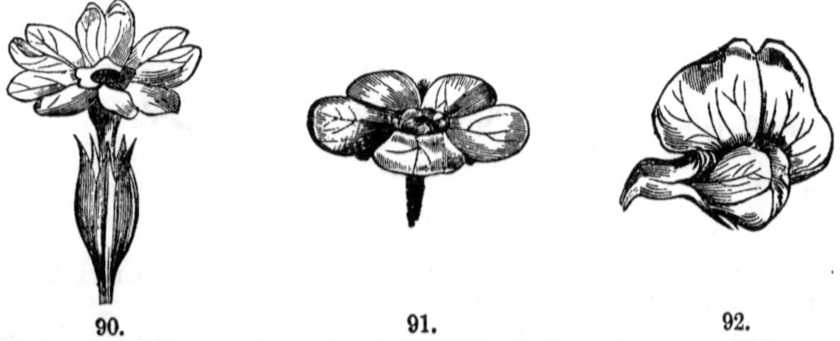

90. 91. 92.

which the upper one is called the *vexillum* or standard; the two lateral leaflets are the *alæ* or wings, and the inferior two, partially or entirely covered by the wings, and often slightly cohering, are called the *carina* or keel. These blossoms are peculiar to the pea, the bean, and many other plants, which form a large proportion of the *leguminiferous* order.

The *labiate-formed* or lip-shaped corolla (fig. 93) is divided by a section of its limb into the upper and under lip. The first is sometimes arched, and is named *galea*, or helmet; the under part is generally divided into three parts or lobes, and is called *labium* or lip; the tubular part of the corolla is called the throat. When the helmet and lip are much separated by a large hiatus or gap, the corolla is said to be *ringent* or gaping. When the lower lip is pressed against the upper so as to leave only a chink, as in the common snapdragon, &c., the flower is called *personate* or masked. All these corollas of labiate and personate forms originate in the union of the normal number of petals usually found in this class—viz., in labiate flowers two petals united form the helmet, and three the lip; in ringent flowers two form the lip, and three the helmet. The plants bearing labiate and personate flowers constitute the great and important order of the *Labiatæ*, and a portion of the family *Scrophulariaceæ*.

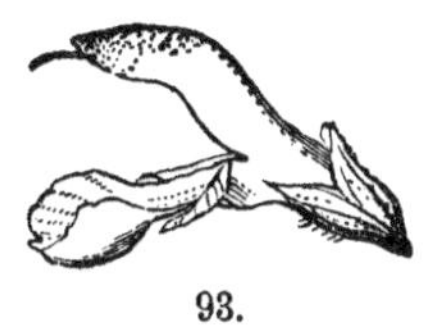
93.

3. Stamens.

56. The third series of floral verticils varies so remarkably from the common form of leaves as to have received the name of *filaments*, or threads. They appear generally so unlike leaves that their real character would never perhaps have been discovered, if the transition of the stamens into petals and leaflets had not clearly established this fact.

If we examine, for example, the corolla of the water-lily or of the pink or double rose, we find the petals gradually diminishing in size towards the centre, and finally they appear crowned with a yellow point, and become partially *filamentous*, or thread-shaped (fig. 94); finally the real stamens appear (figs. 95 and 96), which are more or less slender and extended, and mostly colourless.

57. In the stamen we distinguish two distinct parts, the under, mostly *filiform* (thread-shaped), and hence designated the *filament*, or thread; and the upper, which forms an elliptical or globular and celled organ, containing a powdery substance, is called the *anther*. The latter is the essential part. The filaments are often very much abbreviated, and sometimes altogether wanting or united with some other parts, in which latter case the anther is *sessile*.

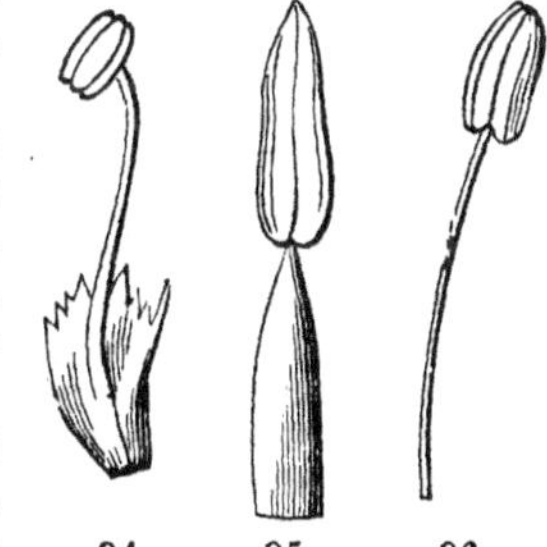
94. 95. 96

The stamens afford important characters whereby plants are classified and described. Groups of families are distinguished by the number of the stamens, by their length, their position, and by their coherence. When the stamens are all connected by a web-like membrane at their base, they are said to be *monadelphous;* when in two bundles, *diadelphous;* when in three or more, *polyadelphous.* The geranium, the pea, and St. John's wort, afford examples of these three modes in which the stamens are united.

58. In the anthers or pollen-sacs we find the minute powdery matter called *pollen*, which is mostly yellow, but sometimes also red, brown, violet, or green. These pollen-grains have a diameter of from $\frac{1}{20}$th to $\frac{1}{300}$th part of a line; and when examined by the aid of a powerful microscope, they appear to consist of a series of small vesicles of a round form, and filled with a granular fluid matter. Those pollen-grains which are united in fours, or in multiples of four, are the reproductive cells; not, however, like the spores of ferns and other kindred orders, immediately attaching themselves to the soil, and germinating, but by being received into another organic portion of the plant prepared for their reception, which part is named the *pistil*. This latter organ is found in the fourth floral verticil; and to this the reproductive cell must be conveyed in order to commence its processes of development, which we are to consider more accurately when describing the seed.

At the proper time the anther or pollen-bag is ruptured, and shakes out a small cloud of pollen-granules, some of which reach the place of their destination; and in general the stamens are so situated in relation to the pistil, that the latter can easily receive the pollen-grains. Sometimes, however, this is not the case, from the shortness of the stamens, or from their growing on a different part of the plant, or even on a different plant altogether. In these cases the wind or insects, chiefly the bees, are the means whereby the contents of the anther are conveyed to the pistil.

If a blossom is deprived of its anther, it will produce no fruit. Varieties of flowers and fruits are produced by shaking the pollen of one plant upon the flowers of another deprived of its stamens. Many esteemed sorts of tulips and pinks have been produced by this process.

4. Pistil.

59. The fruit-leaflet or *pistil* constitutes the fourth and last floral verticil, and is placed in the centre and forms the extremity of the axis, the growth of which is terminated by the production of the fruit. This part in its formation remarkably approximates to the form of the stem-leaves, partly in the green colour of the ovary, and partly in the coherency and growth of the fruit. The leafy origin of the fruit is represented by fig. 97, viz., a carpellary leaf of the double-flowering cherry, the margins of which are inclined inwards, and finally unite, while the mid-rib or petiole is prolonged, and forms what is termed the *style*. The place of coherence is called the *suture* or seam; and on this seam or suture the future fruit is generally developed. At this period it is called the *ovule*, and will subsequently be the subject of a closer examination.

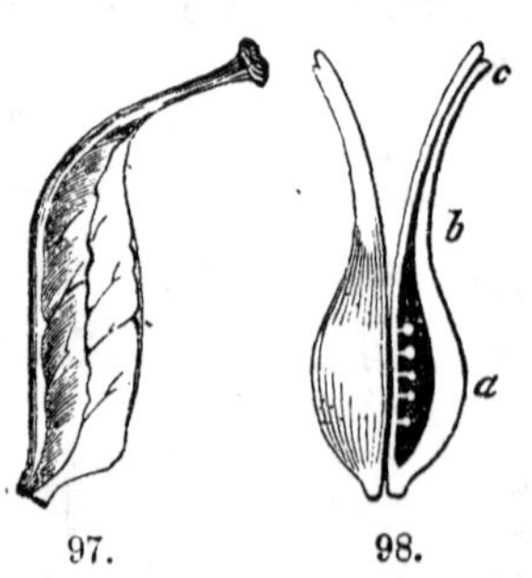

97. 98.

The pistil is composed of three distinctly different parts. The under part, more or less distended, which forms the receptacle of the future fruit or seed, is called the *ovary* (fig. 98 *a*), and is prolonged into a thread-shaped tubular portion, called the *style* (*b*), which is terminated by the *stigma* (*c*), which sometimes assumes a feathery appearance, and sometimes is provided with a cavity or hollow filled with a viscid fluid. The style is frequently absent, and in this case the stigma is said to be *sessile*.

60. The ovary is either composed of one leaflet or of several. In the latter case every individual leaflet forms an individual separate pistil, or the leaflets are united by coherency, and apparently form, by the process of cohesion, only one pistil, but we can generally ascertain, by the number of styles or stigmas, how many leaflets have been united. The manner in which this process of cohesion has been effected occasions several modifications of this organ which materially affect the form of the fruit, and will again come under our consideration.

Mutual Relations of the Floral Verticils.

61. Besides the organic parts of blossoms, already described, they present many other peculiarities which afford important distinguishing characteristics. To these latter belong especially the relative position of the floral envelopes and that of the fructification.

The summit or vertex of the stem on which the flowers and fruit are produced is called the *axis of the inflorescence*, and generally assumes a rounded outline, as in fig. 99, and the four series of floral verticils occupy a station accordantly with their mode of development. Each external envelope of the flower or of the fruit is truly developed under its inner and proximate verticil, and consequently all the remaining series of envelopes are under the carpellary envelopes which form the innermost series. If the blossom actually assumes this, normal position, it is said to be *hypogynous*, all the parts

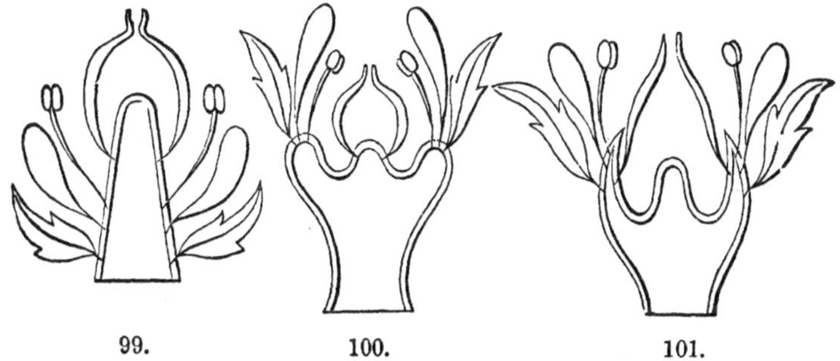

99. 100. 101.

being under the pistil or innermost verticil. Frequently, however, the under part of the floral axis is elevated, forming at its extremity a sort of ring (fig. 100) or disk, on which the external verticils are laterally placed round the pistil, and at about the same height as its base. This position is called *perigynous*. If this ring bearing the verticils is elevated above the extremity of the axis or ovary, then the position is named *epigynous* (fig. 101).

62. Sometimes one series of floral verticils is united with its proximate series, as in the rose, apple-blossom, &c.; and sometimes the stamens and pistil are united, as in the orchis.

Flowers in which both stamens and pistils are present, are called *hermaphrodite*; those containing only stamens are called *male flowers;* those containing only pistils, *female flowers.* When both these organs are absent, the flowers are said to be *neutral.*

There are plants which produce separately male and female flowers on the same stem; these are called .*monæcious.*

Those which bear the same essential parts on different stems are called *diæcious plants.* The willow, hemp, and hop are examples.

Occasional or Accidental Parts of the Blossom.

63. Under this term we include such unessential parts as occur only on certain flowers; as, for example, the *crown*—an intermediate form, partaking both of the character of the petals and stamens, as in the common daffodil, the white narcissus, &c. Sometimes this forms a scaly process, as, for example, under the limb of the corolla of Myosotis palustris (Forget-me-not). These formations may be considered as lateral leaflets of the corolla (§ 54).

The *honey-pores* or nectaries of the corolla are filled with a saccharine sap, and often assume the form of a spur or horn.

Inflorescence.

64. Having now described the individual constituent parts of flowers, the arrangement, or relative position of the whole, both to each other and to the stem or axis on and around which they grow, remains for consideration. This relationship of the entire aggregated flower is called *inflorescence.*

That part of a principal or lateral axis on which the floral verticils are developed is named the *peduncle.* If this part be very short or absent, the flower is *sessile.* If the blossom or flower is on the extremity of a principal axis, the blossom is called *terminal.* In every other case the blossom is lateral. *Axillary* blossoms originate in the axils of the leaves.

A perfectly simple stem produces only *one blossom,* which is terminal, as the tulip.

A branching stem produces *more than one blossom,* of which pinks and lilies are examples.

65. When the individual blossoms appear on different parts of the plant without any obvious or striking arrangement, the inflorescence is said to be *scattered* or *dispersed;* when they assume a proximate or condensed, or some definite form, it is indicated by some term corresponding to the form, &c.

In the condensed mode of inflorescence we generally find, next to the common peduncle, which is sometimes called a rachis (*rach*), a series of small leaves (bracts), in the axils of which the flowers, either pedicelled or non pedicelled, are produced. Sometimes the under bracts are without flowers in their axils, and then they form a densely-imbricated arrangement, which is called *involucrum* or involucre. This is exemplified in the sun-flower.

66. The inflorescence is principally distinguished by the length, thickness, and breadth of the rach or common peduncle, and by the form and consistency of the bracts or floral leaves. By these we distinguish the following varieties of inflorescence:—

1st. The *spike* or *ear* (fig. 102), in which sessile or short-pedicelled flowers are arranged along the rach, in the axils of the bracts. When lateral ears or spikes originate in the axils of the bracts, the ear or spike is said to be *compound*. 2nd. The *catkin* (fig. 103), a pendent spike, which falls off

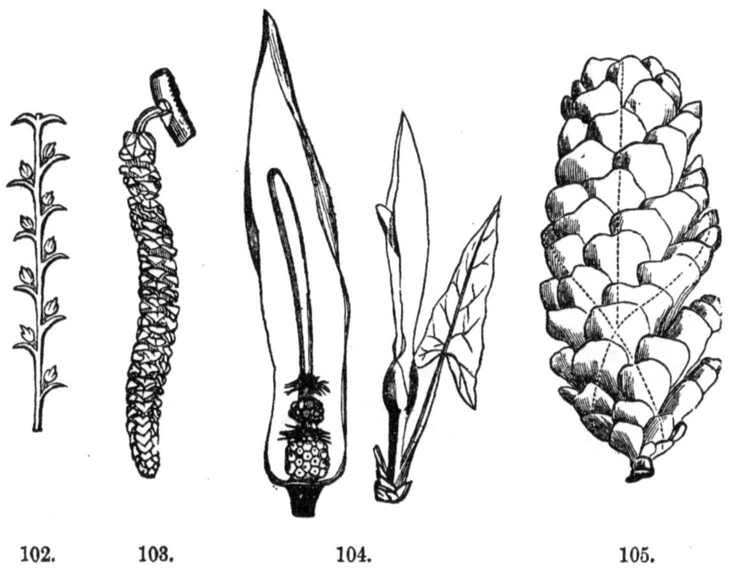

102. 103. 104. 105.

after the blossoming has been accomplished, as in hazel. 3rd. The *spadix*, or succulent thick spike (fig. 104); *ex.* Arum and Calamus. 4th. The *cone*,

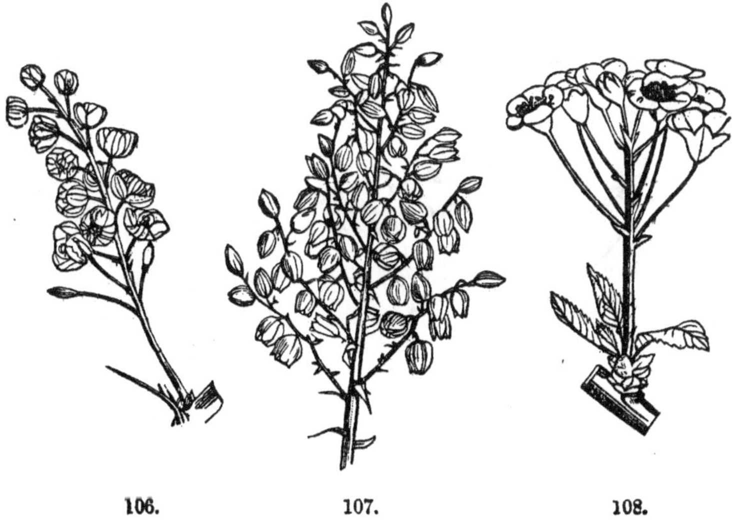

106. 107. 108.

composed of indurated woody or scaly bracts; *ex.* the pine tribe (fig. 105). 5th. The *cluster* or raceme, with the flowers on longer or shorter peduncles, as in the currant (fig. 106). 6th. The *panicle* is a branched *raceme* (fig. 107). 7th. The *thyrsus* is a panicle, with the lateral branches longest in the middle and shortened at both ends; *ex.* lilac, loose-strife, &c. 8th. The *cyme* (fig. 108), where the principal axis is shortened, and the lateral axes lengthened; *ex.* iberis, laurustinus, &c. 9th. The *corymb* like the cyme, but with branching lateral axes; *ex.* snow-ball, senecio, &c. 10th. The *umbel* (fig. 109), in which the principal axis is so shortened that all the lateral floral axes radiate from a common point surrounded by the bracts, which thus form a verticilled involucre (§ 41). When the rays or lateral axes bear smaller *umbels*, the umbel is *compound* (fig. 109).

109. 110.

This very characteristic mode of inflorescence is found in the extensive family of *Umbelliferæ;* to which, among many others, the carrot, the parsley, &c., belong.

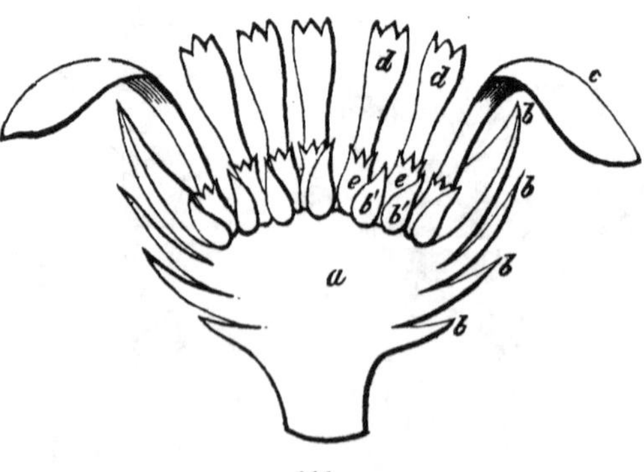

111.

11th. The *capitulum* or head (fig. 110) consists of small flowers (florets), either with very short pedicels, or quite sessile, densely arranged on a very much shortened rach or axis; *ex.* scabious, clover, &c.

If the axis be considerably thickened and extended, either vertically or horizontally, there result a very peculiar kind of inflorescence, which distinguishes an exceedingly numerous natural order of plants. It is illustrated by fig. 111.

Here we see the enlarged rach or disk, *a*, surrounded by several verticils of bracts, *b b*, which together form a common involucrum. The small bracts, *b' b'*, which stand upon the disk, and which, on account of their scarious nature, are called chaff, bear in their axils the quite sessile florets *c* and *d*, which rarely have a calyx *e*. The florets are either all of the same form, or they are partly *tubular*, *d*, partly *linguiform*, or *ligulate*, *c* (tongue or strap shaped).

The disk, however, is not always flat; it is frequently hemispherical, rounded, conical, or concave. When no bracts nor chaffy scales appear on the disk, it is said to be naked, *nudate*. The florets arranged round its margin are called *florets of the ray*; those in the centre, *florets of the disk*.

This kind of inflorescence occurs in all the flowers called *compound*, and is the distinguishing characteristic of the great family of the *Compositæ*, to which the sun-flower, the tansy, the dandelion, and many other genera of plants belong.

FRUIT.

67. The destiny of the flower is fulfilled as soon as the transmission of the pollen-grains into the ovary of the pistil has been effected. From this period the entire growth of the plant is arrested; it henceforth withers and decays. The ovary, on the other hand, with its contents, is developed, and the ovules are thus ultimately changed into seeds. Not seldom, however, do the bracts and the calyx also assume a new form during this process of transformation.

The seed must, of course, be regarded as the essential part of the fruit, as being the developed ovule of the ovary or carpellary integument; this latter part, however, has a great influence on the external appearance of the fruit, and gives origin to a number of names by which the different sorts of fruit are distinguished.

The internal arrangement of the various parts of the fruit depends on the number, the position, and cohesion of the pistils; consequently we have to reconsider this important organ under another aspect.

68. We now understand that the pistil or pistils are placed on the summit of the floral axis, which, on account of its participation in the production of the fruit, is also called the axis of fructification. This axis either terminates with one pistil (fruit-leaf) or with several. In the former case the ovary is simply one-celled (§ 59); in the latter case the manner of cohesion determines the number of the cells of which the ovary is to consist.

The accompanying figures represent a section of different ovaries, part formed of one leaf turned in and cohering at the margin (112 and 113) part consisting of several leaves in combination with the fruit-axis.

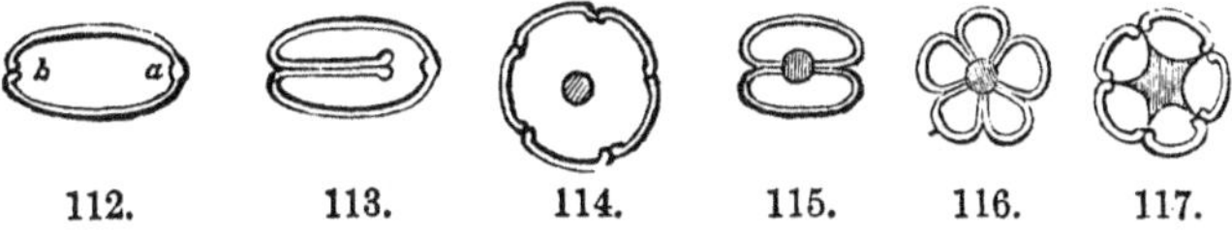

112. 113. 114. 115. 116. 117.

In fig. 112 is shown the section of a one-celled ovary formed out of one fruit-leaf; *a* is the mid-rib, or principal nerve of the leaf; and *b*, the margins in a state of cohesion. In fig. 113 the bending or turning-in of the carpellary leaf is greater, and the ovary becomes an imperfectly two-celled ovary.

The *single-celled ovary* (fig. 114) consists of five carpellary leaves, united by lateral cohesion round the fruit-axis. Hence, when the leaves turn inwards equally, and cohere to the fruit-axis, there results, in accordance with the number of the carpellary leaves, a two-, three, or five-celled ovary (figs. 115 and 116). An external extension of the fruit-axis may also produce a many-celled ovary (fig. 117).

Thus the external forms of the future fruit are discoverable in the ovary, or are indicated by its structure. Also the rupture of the carpels or capsules, when the seed is ripened, follows the law of carpellary union, *i. e.*, the *dehiscence* of the carpellary envelope is generally by the suture, where the original junction was effected (§ 59).

Exterior Forms of Fruit.

69. The carpellary leaves take the principal share in the formation of the fruit. They form the immediate *domicile* of the seeds. The fruit-envelopes, or pericarps, however, are not seldom formed by a further development of the corolla or of the calyx, and sometimes even originate from a metamorphosed bract.

The peculiar external forms of the fruit depend on those transformations which these parts of the blossom undergo during the process of fructification. Thus we find some carpels leafy, some leathery, some stony, some pulpy or fleshy, &c. The external covering is frequently a mass of parenchymatous matter, containing starch, sugar, mucilage, oils, acids, &c., which are often of more value for the purposes of life than the seeds themselves.

The most important forms of fruit are the following:—

a. Unilocular or Monocapsular Fruit.

70. (1.) The *cone*, where the seed lies naked in the axils of the ligneous bracts, where it is produced without the intervention of the pistil. The Coniferæ are examples.

(2.) The *legume*, which is formed of one carpellary leaf, and on the suture, formed by the union of the two margins (fig. 112 *b*), the seeds are attached. The Leguminiferæ, viz., pea, bean, &c., are examples.

(3.) The *follicle*, a kind of carpel, similar to the legume, but dehiscing by its ventral suture; as larkspur, marsh-marigold, &c.

b. Capsular Fruit.

71. (4.) The *capsule-proper* consists of two or more leaves, united either by the margins, forming a one-celled capsule (fig. 114), or turned in and extending towards the axis of the fruit, forming an imperfectly multilocular fruit, or uniting with the axis, forming a perfect many-celled capsule; as in violet, reseda, balsam, &c. (5.) The *pod* or *silique* consists of two fruit-leaves united, with a very thin membranous dissepiment, separating it into two parts: examples — stock, wall-flower, &c. The *silicle* or pouch is like the pod, only much shortened; as shepherd's purse, &c. (6.) The *cariopse*, a one-seeded fruit, with a non-dehiscent membranous pericarp, either attached

to or closely investing the seed: oats, ranunculus, labiate plants, &c. (7.) The *achænium*, a dry, brittle, non-dehiscent fruit: rose, strawberry, &c. (8.) The *nut*, an indehiscent indurated fruit, with one seed: hazel-nut, acorn, &c. The *nucule* is a small nut, with a coriaceous or shelly pericarp, as buckwheat, &c. (9.) The *berry*, bacceate fruit; the external covering is soft, and the interior pulpy: currants, lemons, &c. The cucumber and melon are to be regarded as peculiar varieties of the bacceate fruits. (10.) The *stone-fruits*, the external parts of which are fleshy, the internal stony: plums, peaches, &c. (11.) *Pomaceous* fruits: apple-like fruits. These consist of several folliculous carpels, surrounded by an unusually thick parenchymatous substance, formed while the seeds are approaching maturity: apples, pears, medlars, &c.

The strawberry, raspberry, and mulberry, are to be considered as compound fruits.

Seed.

72. The axillary buds appear on the stem as abbreviated lateral axes, which, either directly or after a considerable interval, are capable of further extension; so, also, on other parts of perfect plants, there are buds with a peculiar development, destined for the production of seed; and hence these are called *seed-buds.*

The position of the seed-bud is always at the end of the plant-axis, whether principal or lateral; and with the production of the seed-bud the growth of that part of the plant is terminated.

The seed-bud appears at first as a very small cellular white object, called the ovule. In the interior of this is a cell, called the embryo-sac (fig. 118).

The seed-bud is unable by itself to form a seed; myriads of them perish undeveloped. This can only be effected through the medium of the reproductive pollen-grain, which must find its way to and penetrate the embryo-sac before it can be developed into a perfect plant.

73. In many plants, the *Coniferæ*, for example, the position of the ovule is very analogous to that of the common bud. It lies in the axils of the condensed scaly or ligneous leaflets, without a covering; hence these are called naked ovules. At a later period we find the seeds developed, without any carpellary covering except the scaly bracts forming the cone. These are very conspicuous in the fruit of the pinus pinifera, which bears edible seeds.

But the far greater proportion of plants produces their seed-buds (ovules) in particularly-constructed leafy cells, which have been already described (§ 59) under the name of pistil or carpellary leaf. We have seen that this organ consists of an enlarged basal part, called the ovary; and in the cavity or in the cells of the ovary are the ovules, to which, through an opening called the stigma, sometimes immediately, sometimes through the intervention of the style, the pollen-grains reach.

74. As the ovule in different plants presents several peculiar modifications in its structure, these, therefore, require special consideration. There is formed around the ultimate particle which we call the nucleus of the ovule sometimes a single, sometimes a double *membranous sac*, which does not quite enclose the nucleus, but leaves a portion at its upper end open, which opening is the *foramen*, or mouth of the ovule. When the nucleus of the

ovule is so situated that the foramen is opposite to the hilum or placenta, its direction is said to be orthotropal; when, through the curvature of the ovule itself, or by the prolongation of the umbilical cord, the foramen approaches the hilum, the direction is campylotropal (crooked); when its position is reversed, it is said to be anatropal. For illustration of the technical expressions employed in this and the two foregoing paragraphs, see the accompanying diagram (fig. 118) of a highly magnified ovule.

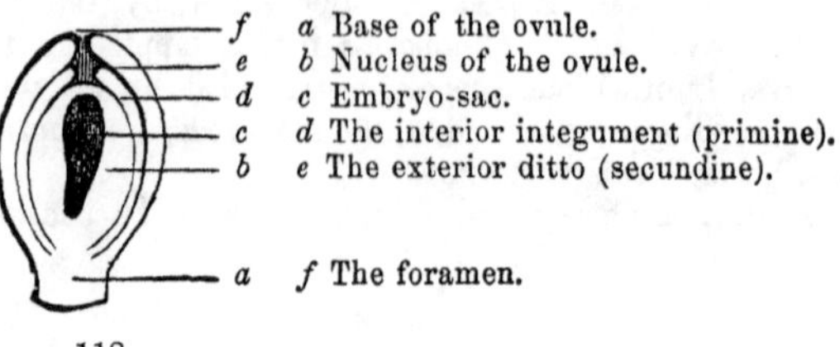

118.

75. When a pollen-grain comes in contact with the stigma, the former is observed to swell and to protrude, through one of its apertures, a delicate tubular cell, called the *pollen-sac*. This body passes by the stigma, through the tubular style, if present, into the ovary, and finally enters the embryo-sac of the ovule through the aperture in its linings, called the foramen. While the outer portion of the pollen-sac decays, the part which entered the ovule forms a new tissue, which gradually assumes a new form, provided with a leafy bud and rootlets, and to which the term *embryo* or *germ* has been applied.

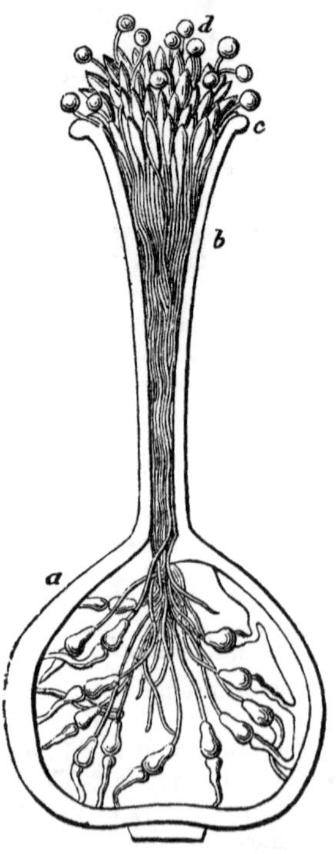

119.

Fig. 119 is a highly magnified representation of a pistil having the stigma, *c*, filled with pollen-grains, *d;* and the pollen-sacs of the latter, lengthened, are observed extending downwards through the style, *b*, into the cell or cavity of the ovary, *a*, and penetrating the numerous ovules there contained.

It deserves to be remarked, that the point of the pollen-sac which thus makes its way into the ovule forms the plumule or terminal bud of the embryo, whilst the opposite end is developed into the rootlets.

76. With the changes consequent on the discharge of the pollen into the stigma and embryo-sac the ovule also is transformed, and its protective appendages are gradually increased by the tissues constituting the *albuminous substances*, of which some seeds are almost entirely, others only partially composed. The tissues contain besides albu-

men, sugar, gum, starch, oil, or other fatty products, substances which, independently of their utility in domestic economy, &c., are destined to supply nutriment to the embryo necessary for its further development. There are some seeds which contain no albuminous compounds, but are entirely composed of the embryo. We recognise in the episperm, or seminal integument, the external envelope of the ovule, although very considerably changed in its appearance.

On examining a pea, a bean, or a horse-chestnut, we may easily perceive the hilum by which the ovule was attached to the placenta; we find also the embryo surrounded by the albuminous substances, with its radicle and plumule, which are very conspicuous at an early stage in the future development of the seed.

The germ or embryo differs from the common bud chiefly in its constituting a very minute axis, provided with a root, which derives nourishment entirely from the various substances contained in the seed, and stored up therein for that purpose, till the roots are in a condition to suck nutriment from the soil.

The embryo, when thus developed, is in a condition to continue the life of the plant, and to increase the total amount of vegetation; and though in itself individually a perishable being, is nevertheless in a condition to prolong its duration indefinitely by means of its reproductive energy.

II. VITALITY OF PLANTS.

(VEGETABLE PHYSIOLOGY.)

PHENOMENA OF LIFE IN GENERAL.

77. By the term *vitality*, or life, we mean the principle or the cause of the entire series of the activities of all the organs existing in plants and animals, together with the phenomena resulting therefrom.

The cause of these activities is *vital power*. It is, however, uncertain whether or not this is a self-existent independent power, or the sum of all the known natural powers, which, operating under special relations, and being mutually limited by peculiar conditions, produce what we in general terms ascribe to the agency of life.

There can be no doubt of this, viz., that the forces we have become acquainted with in Physics and Chemistry, as attraction, and especially chemical attraction, have a most important influence on the phenomena of life. And this subject has been most successfully investigated by explaining, as far as possible, the vital phenomena on principles deduced from the operation of the recognised general laws of Nature, and by ascribing as little as possible to the vital power. And this is the only mode of investigation whereby we shall either succeed in determining the independent reality of this power, and the laws by which its operations are regulated, or be able to show that it is only a combination of natural causes.

78. Vital power is peculiarly and exclusively distinguished by its capability of appropriating the simple chemical substances, and of applying these to the production of bodies, such as we, with all our resources at command, are utterly unable to effect, and probably ever will be

It is true that we can combine, *in the due proportions of weight and volume, all the chemical constituents* which are contained in the sap of plants: but life alone is able to construct either a cell or an organ from these materials.

79. The fundamental work of life appears to be its power of forming the vegetable or animal cell through the absorption or assimilation of new matter from without; and also by means of the *nutritive matter*, causing an increase in all directions; or, in other words, it possesses the *power of growth.*

The growth of bodies thus constituted is, however, limited in space and duration. Nature, in all her productions, is regulated by laws and conditions of necessity, concealed from human ken. We know this only, that she produces an infinite variety of individual beings, which are limited in form and extension.

Whenever an individual being has reached to the extent of measure and duration assigned to it by the law of its own nature, all further development ceases, even under the most favourable circumstances. The activity of life, manifested with incessant accelerative power, has reached to a point whence its progressive decay is as rapid, until it is finally reduced to its primary constituents. We denominate this cessation of power the death of plants and animals. From the moment that vitality has ceased, the once living form becomes subject to the laws of the general forces of Nature alone, and principally to those of chemical affinity, by which the perishable structure of the body is destroyed, and decomposed into a series of chemical combinations (Chemistry, § 157).

80. The variety, also, of terrestrial objects produced by the vital power is limited. So far as we know by experience life only reproduces the same forms, though from new materials, and these new productions are subject to the same laws.

The number of individuals is also limited by the laws which regulate the supply of nutriment; it is, however, exceedingly great.

The mass of animated nature is inconceivably small compared with that of the earth. It covers, however, the greatest portion of the surface of the terrestrial globe.

The time requisite for the perfect development of these living objects is very unequal. Some of the simplest-formed animals and plants have only a few hours' existence. Some trees, on the contrary, live for thousands of years.

81. We should always remember, as a fundamental principle, that life has no power to create, not even the smallest particle of one of its own little cells. Its power is limited to the assimilation of materials, afforded as the media out of which it produces organic forms. None of the simple chemical substances which we meet with in plants are produced in them, but have been selected from without, and, by the power of vitality, made to assume a certain form or combination.

82. In the selection and reception of new materials from without, to be employed in the formation of organic parts, vitality is somewhat analogous to the power of attraction which is manifested in the origin and production of crystals (Physics, § 20; Chemistry, § 29).

The laws which regulate the formation of organised and inorganised bodies are however, essentially different; for while we have shown in Mineralogy,

§ 5, more precisely, that the forms of all crystals are developed with flat surfaces, with rectilineal sides and angles of regular construction, plants and animals have rather a cylindrical or spherical figure: the rounded shape, in some one or other of its varieties or modifications, may be said to be generally prevalent. We may remark that the angular cells of plants were originally spherical, and that this their first form was changed by pressure (§ 8).

The crystal also increases in magnitude, or grows by the successive deposition of layers of similar matter applied equally to all parts of its surface; otherwise it does not undergo the slightest change. Plants and animals, on the contrary, receive their nutriment or materials of growth internally, and change both the form and chemical character of these substances. Hence minerals are frequently distinguished as *exogenous* objects, and organised bodies as *endogenous* objects.

The crystal, besides, is only limited in form; it is unlimited in extent, and would increase for ever if the necessary materials were afforded it.

External influences of various kinds operate more or less powerfully in changing or destroying the original activity of organs. When we observe a change of the ordinary or normal vital phenomena, we designate the unnatural condition so produced by the name of *disease*. If these disturbing influences be of long duration or of considerable intensity, death is the general result.

VITAL PHENOMENA OF PLANTS.

83. In the foregoing general considerations we have pointed out the most prominent principles on which the life both of plants and of animals is dependent; and in reference to the life and functions of plants, we have already, in the sections devoted to Organography, incidentally communicated much information.

The nutritious materials applied to plants is a subject of the highest importance, and requires further and more extensive illustration; for a knowledge of this branch of the subject is greatly conducive to the successful cultivation of plants, the various branches of agrarial and horticultural science, on which the existence and well-being of millions of men and beasts are dependent.

NUTRITION OF PLANTS.

84. An accurate comprehension of this department of the science is attainable only through a right understanding of the various organs of vegetation and of their functions, as well as through that of the nutritive media received from without, and the subsequent change of the latter into vegetable substances.

What, then, are the nourishing media or food of plants?

We can only satisfactorily and precisely answer this question by stating what are the simple chemical component parts of the different vegetable objects; for it is an established fact, that the smallest particle of their whole mass is not, and cannot be, self-produced (§ 81); therefore everything which they contain must be derived from without.

We have already seen (§ 6) that the principal mass of every plant is composed of cellular tissue, vascular tissue, or of woody fibre; also that there are contained in the cellular membrane partly solid substances, as starch, chlorophyl, resin, salts, &c., and partly a watery sap, holding in solution sugar, gum, acids in union with metallic oxides, albumen, &c.; to which are to be added, as the contents of many plants, volatile and fixed oils, with other fatty matters.

Daily experience also shows that the chief mass of every plant, by combustion, passes into gaseous combinations; it disappears, and only the non-volatile metallic oxides and salts remain as *ash*, which forms an inconsiderable proportion of the weight of the plant.

Are we, therefore, to infer that starch, woody fibre, sugar, oil, albumen, &c., are the nourishing media of plants?

If so, the soil, the water, and the atmosphere, wherein plants pass their lives, should contain these bodies, in order that the plants might therefrom simply receive them, and convey them to their proper place.

But such is not the case. We never meet with woody fibre, starch, sugar, albumen, &c., but in the plant itself; it must consequently possess the means of assimilating them, of combining them out of the simple chemical substances.

Consequently the nutritive media of plants are simple chemical substances, out of which are composed all the various organs, simple and compound, with their contents, which altogether constitute the entire mass of a plant.

85. Chemistry also informs us (§ 115, &c.) what these simple substances are which, in combination, constitute vegetable bodies. These originate in or are formed from:—

Carbon and Hydrogen	The volatile oils.
Carbon, hydrogen, and oxygen . . .	The vegetable acids, woody fibre, starch, gum, mucilage, sugar, fats, chlorophyl, resin, colouring matter.
Carbon, hydrogen, oxygen, and nitrogen	The organic bases.
Carbon, hydrogen, oxygen, nitrogen, sulphur, and phosphorus	Vegetable albumen, fibrin, and casein.

All these materials may be perfectly consumed by combustion, and therefore we term them the *combustible* constituents of plants, in contradistinction to those parts which remain as ashes after combustion, viz., the *solid, mineral* vegetable constituents.

If we submit the ashes of the most opposite kinds of plants to the test of experiment, we discover the following constituents:—

Acids.	Metallic Oxides.
Carbonic acid.	*Potassa.*
Silicic acid (Silica).	*Soda.*
Phosphoric acid.	*Lime.*
Sulphuric acid.	*Magnesia.*
Nitric acid.	Alumina.
	Sesquioxide of iron.
	Oxide of manganese.

To which are to be added *chloride of sodium* (common salt), chloride of potassium, and in marine plants iodide of sodium and iodide of magnesium.

The acids and metallic oxides above mentioned in *italics* are found in every vegetable ash, and are therefore to be regarded as essential constituents of plants; whilst the remaining substances are only found in certain individuals, or appear in so insignificant a quantity as not to be considered as essential constituents of their being.

The mineral substances do not constitute any of the organic tissues, but are either held in solution by the sap, or are lodged in a solid form within the cells (§ 9). For example, the cells of many grasses contain so great a number of silicious crystals on the margin of their leaves, that these parts are capable of cutting like a knife. The *Equiseta* or shave-grass plants have a large quantity of this earth; and hence their utility in the polishing of wood, &c.

The *carbonates* of metallic oxides are not found in living plants. The carbonic acid originates on the combustion of the plant, and in the destruction of the vegetable acids (the oxalic, tartaric, &c.). This is also the case, in some degree, with a portion of the sulphuric and phosphoric acids.

86. Every individual plant may be compared to a magazine or store, which contains many different simple materials in very unequal quantities. No one of these materials can be produced in the interior of the plant; consequently it must have absorbed them from without. If the materials necessary for the healthy development of a plant are not to be had within its reach, it either perishes or prolongs a miserable existence.

All plants do not contain the same constituents in equal proportions; but for any one genus or species of plants, these constituent parts are requisite in a certain quantity.

Nature universally supplies the means necessary for the development of plants, but in very unequal proportions. The barest rocks, the deep morass, the shifting sand, the deep seas, the ploughed fields, the rubbish heap and trim garden—all these support plants, and are adorned therewith. But the plants themselves are not similar. They differ as much as do their localities.

The cultivation of plants, the science of agriculture, consists solely in this, viz., to prepare the soil in such a manner that the plants to be produced therein may find within their reach such nutritive materials as may be most conducive to their full development.

As it is impossible to convey any satisfactory knowledge of these external conditions of vegetable life without some accurate notions of the constituent parts of plants and of their various formations, we shall in the following sections treat, first, of the assimilating process in reference to combustible constituents of plants; and, secondly, of their mineral constituents.

Assimilation of the Combustible Constituent Parts of Plants.

87. In these we find the following simple materials:—1st. Carbon. 2nd. Hydrogen. 3rd. Oxygen. 4th. Nitrogen. 5th. Sulphur.

1. Assimilation of Carbon.

Carbon, by itself, is totally insoluble in water, and hence cannot, through this medium, be introduced into the circulation of the plant. Neither can it be assimilated in its solid form, because, in accordance with the law of vegetable absorption (§ 10), a plant is incapable of receiving any body into its circulation, which is not in a fluid condition. All the carbon which is met with in plants must have been received by them in the form of a com pound, which is soluble in water. This body is *carbonic acid,* which (comp. Chem., § 52) consists of carbon and oxygen.

Hence we consider carbonic acid as one of the chief nutritious constituents of the food of plants.

This material is principally received into the system of the plant through the *roots,* and partially through the *leaves;* and the carbonic acid is decomposed in the plant itself. Its carbon is applied to the formation of the vegetable organs; its oxygen is allowed to escape by the leaves.

The *root* (§ 24) sucks up the water in its neighbourhood. All the water of both land and sea holds carbonic acid in solution. It is produced from the never-failing supply of dead and decaying animal and vegetable matter on the surface of the earth, and also by the respiration of man and animals.

During the development of the embryo, and while the stem does not appear above ground, and further till the leaves are produced, the root is exclusively the medium of supplying carbonic acid to the plant.

The development and growth of plants are remarkably promoted by an abundant supply of *humus* (Chem., § 164), a substance produced by decayed vegetable substances, and consequently containing a large supply of carbonic acid.

For plants, whose growth is of long duration, as trees, for example, every soil contains an ample supply of carbonic acid necessary for their existence and growth. Annual plants, on the other hand, which have a rapid and luxuriant growth, as cabbages, turnips, &c., require soil specially rich in humus. For such crops the ground is either improved by spreading on it and mixing with it vegetable and animal manure, or rich earth brought from the woods or commons; or else by frequently repeated ploughings and harrowings, in order that the oxygen of the atmosphere may unite with the carbon of the decaying substances, and so form carbonic acid.

By itself humus is just as insoluble in water as carbon; and hence it is not a medium of nutrition for the plant till it has gradually been converted into carbonic acid: but, like vegetable charcoal, it possesses in a high degree the quality of attracting carbonic acid and aqueous vapour from the atmosphere; and it is this quality chiefly which renders humus so valuable a nutritious material for plants.

The presence of humus in the soil can be recognised by the dark colour of the earth. The quantity may be ascertained by igniting a portion of the soil, whereby the combustible humus is destroyed or dissipated, and the mineral constituents of the soil remain.

88. The leaves inhale through their stomata or breathing pores (§ 17) carbonic acid from the atmosphere, and exhale the oxygen, which, when separated from the carbon, is never retained in vegetable bodies. The separation of the oxygen only takes place during the day, and goes on with greatest rapidity when the plants are exposed to the full action of the solar rays (Chem. § 22).

The atmosphere contains, in 5,000 measures of air, two measures of carbonic acid, which plants are continually abstracting from it. The equilibrium is as continually restored by the breathing of animals, by combustion, and by the decomposition of carbonaceous bodies.

Although the carbonic acid of the air appears only very insignificant, yet on account of the prodigious extent of the atmosphere, it is sufficient to yield an ample supply of carbon for the development of every plant on the face of the earth.

All the phenomena of the vegetable kingdom confirm this view, viz., that the great mass of carbon is received from the atmosphere, either directly by the roots, or indirectly by the leaves; and this view cannot be questioned in reference to such plants as cactus, house-leek, &c., which grow on bare rocks, or walls and roofs; or in such as grow in water, as forget-me-not, hyacinth, water-cress, &c.

89. During the night, and in darkness (in cellars, for example), there is no assimilation of carbon by the leaves, and no separation of oxygen by the respiratory process. The plant, even in this condition, can form new parts, not certainly from materials supplied externally, but out of its own substance; as is clearly shown by the sprouting and extension of the stems of potatoes in a dark cellar.

If during the night a plant be covered by a bell-glass, in the morning the atmosphere about the plant will contain a larger measure of carbonic acid than before. This is occasioned by the oxygen of the air surrounding the plant effecting an oxidising operation on its surface, and thus occasioning the formation of a certain quantity of carbonic acid: the amount, however, is very unequal in different plants. It is most abundantly produced by such as contain a large portion of easily oxidisible volatile oil in their glandular vessels.

2. Assimilation of Hydrogen and Oxygen.

90. In most of the parts of plants which contain hydrogen and oxygen, the weight of these two bodies is in the same proportion to each other as in water, viz., of 8 of oxygen to 1 of hydrogen. (Chem. § 28).

Hence, these two bodies exist in the form of water, and are received into the plant almost exclusively through the root. But, since there are many vegetable substances, as, for example, the volatile oils, resins, &c., which contain indeed hydrogen, but which contain either no oxygen, or, at all events, a less proportion than that above mentioned, it follows that plants possess the power of assimilating into their constituents a portion of the elements of water received by them. The hydrogen in this case is assimilated, the oxygen is exhaled.

Hence, the presence of water is absolutely indispensable for the development of the plant. It, however, absorbs much more than it applies to the enlargement of its mass. The superfluous portion is again evaporated by the leaves.

Moreover, the leaves possess the capability of absorbing water in the condition of vapour, otherwise the dew could not have the beneficial influence on vegetation which it certainly possesses.

We will recur to this part of the subject when we treat of the assimilation of the mineral constituents of plants.

3. Assimilation of Nitrogen.

91. Though the leaves of plants are constantly surrounded by nitrogen, which amounts to four fifths of the atmosphere, yet it is never absorbed by them.

All the nitrogen which we meet with in plants has been received by their roots from the soil, and in the form of a chemical combination of nitrogen with hydrogen, as *ammonia*. (Chem. § 78.)

We know that, in the decomposition of nitrogenous substances, as of animal bodies for example, ammonia, easily distinguishable among the other gaseous products by its penetrating odour, is copiously evolved. Hence, this gaseous substance is diffused through the atmosphere, which, however, retains so small a part of it that it is scarcely to be detected. The ammonia is soluble in water, and consequently returns to the earth with every shower of rain, and thence is absorbed by the roots of the plants.

Besides carbon, several minerals possess in a remarkable degree, the property of attracting ammonia from the atmosphere: among these, clay and sesquioxide of iron absorb this substance from the air with as great avidity as a sponge imbibes water, and consequently contribute essentially to the procuring of nitrogen for the plants.

92. Plants do not retain much nitrogen. It is found chiefly in the sap, in the seeds, and in the tenderest parts or shoots. In 2,500 lbs. of hay there are 984 lbs. of carbon, and only 32 lbs. of nitrogen.

We artificially facilitate the assimilation of nitrogen by increasing the ammoniacal contents of the soil. This is effected by scattering animal manure on the ground; and as the ammonia is very volatile, in order to prevent its escape, it is quickly ploughed into the soil.

A great part of the ammonia, especially that which is contained in fluid manure, is lost; for the ammonia alone, as well as when in combination with carbonic acid (carbonate of ammonia) is volatile.

On the other hand, the sulphates and phosphates of ammonia are not volatile at the common temperature, and it is the presence of these two salts which renders liquid manure so valuable. If the manure or compost heap receives from time to time diluted sulphuric acid, this prevents the escape of the ammonia by combining with it, and hereby it is reserved for the nourishment of the plant.

93. *Gypsum* is also of great utility in combining the ammonia with the soil. If gypsum (sulphate of lime, Chem. § 81) be scattered upon the land, the sulphuric acid of the gypsum unites with the ammonia, which is present, whereby the volatility of the latter is prevented, and its fertilising properties retained.

The effect of gypsum as a fertiliser is so striking, that Franklin, who had learned its good qualities in Europe, was desirous of introducing it to the notice of his fellow-citizens in America. They, however, lent an incredulous ear to his recommendations, and disbelieved the marvellous effects of a few bushels of gypsum sown on the land. Franklin posted on a declivity of a field manured with gypsum the words, "*The effects of Gypsum.*" The luxuriant growth of the crop emphatically told the wayfarers that gypsum was a manure of surpassing importance, and it needed no further commendations.

Assimilation of Sulphur.

94. Sulphur is found in plants in still smaller proportions than nitrogen. It is, however, always present in albumen, in fibrin, and in casein, the latter of which (comp. Chem. § 149) contains from one-half to two per cent. of substance.

All sulphur found in the plant reaches it by the roots, and always in the form of sulphuric acid, which we consequently are to regard as one of the nutritive media of plants. This acid, though in small proportions, is met with in every soil, and chiefly in combination with lime, forming gypsum. This salt is soluble in water, and through this medium is well adapted for assimilation. Moreover, all manures contain sulphate of ammonia, a salt which, by its richness in nitrogen and sulphur, is specially conducive to the growth of those parts of plants which contain these materials.

Hence, the scattering of gypsum on the land is also valuable on account of sulphur it contains, and it is especially beneficial in promoting the growth of leguminous plants, clover, &c.

Assimilation of Mineral Constituents.

95. The mineral constituents of plants are combinations of silicic acid, phosphoric acid, and sulphuric acid, with potassa, soda, lime, and magnesia; and, moreover, chlorides of potassium and sodium. Alumina, oxides of iron and manganese, nitric acid, and iodine are more rarely found in plants.

The sum of these incombustible materials contributes but a very small proportion of the weight of the plant. 100 lbs. of the following vegetable substances yielded the annexed quantities of ash: pine-wood, $\frac{8}{10}$ lbs.; oak-wood, 2½ lbs.; wheat-straw, 4½ lbs.; limetree-wood, 5 lbs.; potato-haulm, 15 lbs.

Different parts of one and the same plant contain unequal quantities of mineral constituents. They are generally far more abundant in the leaves, in the seeds, and in the bark than in the stem and roots: 100 lbs. of pine-leaves gave 8 lbs. of ash, and the same quantity of oak-bark and leaves yielded from 8 to 9 lbs.

The quantity of ashes yielded by different plants is not only unequal, but the composition also, as the following table shows, which is drawn up from an analysis of the ashes of the under-mentioned plants: —

100 parts of ashes of: —	Potassa- and Soda-Salts.	Lime- and Magnesia-Salts.	Silicic Acid.
1. Wheat { Straw	22·00	7·00	61·00
2. Wheat { Grain	47·00	44·50	0·5
3. Barley { Straw	20·00	20·20	57·0
4. Barley { Grain	29·00	32·5	35·5
5. Peau-haulm	27·82	63·74	7·81
6. Clover	39·20	56·00	4·90
7. Potato { Haulm	4·20	59·40	36·40
8. Potato { Tubers	85·81	14·19	...
9. Red Beet-root	88·00	12·00	...
10. White Beet-root	81·60	18·40	...

From this table we plainly perceive the difference in the composition of ashes yielded by these different plants, as well as the difference in the different parts of the same plant; for while the ashes of pea-haulm contain $63\frac{74}{100}$ of salts of lime, the straw of wheat has only 7, and the grain $44\frac{50}{100}$. Hence we may with certainty conclude that every plant must have a definite amount of mineral substances in its composition. These materials, held in solution by water, can only be received into the system of the plant through the medium of the roots.

If the soil does not contain these materials, or contains them in proportions inadequate to the necessities of the plants, certain parts cannot be developed at all, or only imperfectly.

This has been ascertained by accurate experiments. In pure quartz-sand, for example, the pea germinates and grows, but produces no seed. The same thing occurs when salts of lime and potassa are added to the sand.

96. So long as there is present in the soil an abundance of carbonic acid, water, and ammonia, which convey the carbon, hydrogen, oxygen, and nitrogen to the plant, so long do the mineral constituents of the plant display the greatest inequality in their distribution.

The soil, as we know by mineralogy, is nothing else but disintegrated rock; consequently, the nature of the soil depends on the composition of the rocks which form its constituent parts. Pure limestone or quartz would, by atmospheric influences, be converted into soil containing only lime or silica, and hence the potassa necessary for the plant could not originally be in the ground. The compound rocks, on the contrary, such as granitic, basaltic, porphyritic rocks, clay-slate, greywacke, lava, and many others, contain all the mineral constituents found in the ashes of plants, and hence, by the decomposition of such rocks, the most fertile soils are produced. (Comp. Miner. § 84—104.

97. In the seeds of grasses, and in most other seeds, lime and magnesia are always preseut in combination with *phosphoric acid.* One hundred pounds of the ashes of wheat yield 45 lbs. of yellow peas, 34 lbs. of phosphoric acid. The phosphoric acid is originally found combined with lime as a mineral forming *apatite* (Min. § 36). The phosphate of lime is assimilated in the seed, and animals, by its consumption, derive the necessary supply for the formation of their bones. (Chem. § 44.)

98. In many plants one of the mineral constituents occurs much more abundantly than the others, as (comp. § 95) silica in wheat, lime in the pea, potassa in the roots of beet, &c.

Hence plants may be separated into alkaline, calcareous, and silicious plants.

To the *alkaline plants* belong wormwood, spinach, mangold-wurzel, turnip, and maize.

To the *calcareous plants,* the lichens, cactus, clover, bean, pea, and tobacco.

To the *silicious plants,* wheat, barley, rye, oats, and grasses generally, as well as heath, broom, and acacia.

By far the greatest portion of plants is capable of being classed by the prevalence of these constituents in their seeds, or in their stems or roots, under some one or other of these three groups, and such plants are generally capable of a wider distribution.

99. After we have ascertained the importance of the mineral constituents in the economy of plants, we shall have no difficulty in accounting for the appearance of many plants in certain localities only. As, for example, we find the *wild celery* and the *salsolas* only in the neighbourhood of the sea, or of saline springs, because they require a considerable portion of soda which they cannot find except in such places. The *borage* and *thorn-apple,*

on the contrary, are always found in the vicinity of human habitations, both plants requiring a larger supply of saltpetre which is derived from the decomposition of excrementitious animal substances. (Chem. § 69.)

Certain plants altogether disappear in some places that are very plentiful in other localities. In the argillaceous soils of the banks of the Wey and Thames the purple heath and yellow broom are looked for in vain, while at the distance of a few miles, on St. George's Hill, Esher and Dartford Heaths, the soil of whole woods and hangers are completely covered with these plants.

The presence or absence of these characteristic plants affords the surest test of the nature of the soil, which is thus readily known without the trouble of submitting it to a chemical analysis.

100. The presence of *water* in the soil is not only necessary as a conducting medium for the carbonic acid and the ammonia, but also for dissolving and holding in solution the other mineral constituents which are thus rendered absorbable by the roots of plants.

A sufficiency of water is indispensable to the existence of plants. A soil may contain abundance of humus, ammonia, and salts; but these constituents are a sealed and unavailable treasure in the absence of water, which is necessary to dissolve them, and reduce them to a fit condition for assimilation.

The capability of the soil to attract and to retain moisture is dependent on its *argillaceous* contents. (Min. § 49.)

But too much clay is as detrimental as a deficiency of this material. In that case, the soil is either constantly wet, cohesive, and inaccessible to atmospheric influences, or it is too hard, and consequently impenetrable by the roots of plants. Only rushes, reeds, and other worthless weeds appear on such soils, and they are hence called clay plants.

MANURE.

101. It has been found by experiment that a field of 4 acres, or 5,760 square yards, cropped or cultivated with wheat, yielded 130 lbs. of potassa-salts, 67 lbs. of lime-salts, and 260 lbs. of silicic acid, or altogether 357 lbs. of mineral constituents. Of these, 112 lbs. were phosphates. If a rotation of similar crops be taken for several years in succession from the same field, it is evident that a considerable portion of these minerals must be derived from the soil, which consequently gradually impoverishes its surface, and diminishes its fertility.

In fact, after a few years of such cropping, the productive quality of the soil is so far diminished, that the land barely returns the seed. The cause of this is, that the plants can no longer find in the soil those mineral constituents which are requisite for their full development.

If we must have an uninterrupted succession of crops, we must be careful to restore to the land, by the process of manuring, as large a quantity of these mineral substances as we have taken from it.

The dung of cattle, night-soil, and other animal products, contain phosphates and sulphates. If these are laid on the field, it will again be in a condition to nourish the plants cultivated thereon. Such manures are besides beneficial in furnishing carbonic acid and ammonia during the process of decomposition.

It is also clear that a number of substances are applicable as manures, if the former cannot be conveniently procured.

Coprolites, gypsum, bone-dust, wood-ashes, turf and coal-ashes, soap-lees, burnt lime, and the ammoniacal rejectamenta of various manufactures, form manuring materials of very considerable value.

The more accurately we know the component parts of soils, the more efficiently we can manure the land. And the addition of a few bushels of the proper manure, supplying exactly what the soil wants, is better than whole loads of dung applied indiscriminately.

FALLOW.

102. A soil impoverished by cropping is often renovated and fertilised without dung, by leaving it uncultivated for a longer or shorter period. This operation is named fallowing; and, in many countries, where the population is not dense, is exclusively practised as a means of restoring fertility to the land, without the expensive process of manuring.

This remarkable phenomenon is explicable on these principles, viz., that during the time of fallowing, the air and water uninterruptedly act upon the soil, and occasion a farther decomposition, or disintegration of its particles. By the same process the soluble mineral constituents of the soil are again in sufficient abundance for a future crop, and in a condition to be dissolved by water, and absorbed by the roots of plants. For the better understanding of this, it should be recollected, that the most of the salts that enter into the composition of vegetable substances are very difficultly soluble, and therefore they require a considerable period in order that the water of the soil may dissolve them.

Only a few soils which are naturally very fertile, as disintegrated lava, for example, [or the rich loam and alluvial lands of North America,] will bear successive cropping, without either manuring or fallowing.

ROTATION.

103. In § 95 we have seen that different genera of plants not only extract different mineral constituents from the soil, but also that they extract these in very unequal proportions. While a field of four acres, by a wheat crop, is deprived of 112 lbs. of phosphates, a crop of turnips only takes from the land 38 lbs. Hence it is clear that this field will produce three crops of turnips without being more exhausted than by one crop of wheat.

It is also clear, that a soil which for one sort of crop is exhausted, may be well suited for the production of two or even three crops of a different kind. Without fresh manuring, a crop of clover, or of potatoes, may be taken after a crop of wheat, because these demand a less quantity of phosphates for their growth and development.

A rotation of crops, however, cannot be very precisely prescribed, as it must be entirely regulated by the nature of the soil, which varies in different places. But generally on a well-arranged system of rotation, after a thorough manuring, a field will bear several successive crops without fallowing, which, to a large extent, is not practicable in densely-populous countries.

AGRICULTURE.

104. This, the most important of all our industrial occupations, has hitherto been practised only empirically, hence its scientific treatment must necessarily be productive of very advantageous results.

The prosperity of agriculture is surely to be deemed more conducive to the welfare of a nation than that of any branch of manufacturing industry whatever. From the fact that the Emperor of China annually ploughs a portion of a field, and that the famous Emperor Joseph once, on his travels through Bohemia, drew a furrow with his own hand, we perceive the vast importance that these potentates attached to this science.

105. Plants afford an ample remuneration for the labour and care bestowed on their cultivation. Only let us compare the tubers of the wild potato, not usually larger than a pea, growing on the mountains of Mexico, with the gigantic tubers of our fields, some averaging nearly a pound in weight — or the wild carrot root, no thicker than a quill, and hard as wood — with the large juicy vegetable cultivated for our tables, or finally, the sour crab-apple of our woods and hedges, with the delicious ribstone-pippin; and we shall have a convincing proof of the almost miraculous effects of cultivation.

We may, perhaps, be permitted to relate the following incident, as a further confirmatory proof of the public and private advantages of planting:— In *Wallerstadten*, a small village near *Darmstadt*, a French soldier, sick, wounded, and poor, was left behind, during the Seven-years' War, and through the hospitality and care of the kind villagers recovered his health and strength. Being attached to the people and to the place, he determined to pass his life among them, and to support himself by his labour. The care of all the cows of the village was entrusted to him, and whilst he tended the herd, he planted with apple and other fruit-bearing trees all parts of the common pasture suitable for their growth. The plants he reared at home and carried with him, and put them into the soil, or dressed or pruned them when his charge permitted him leisure for so doing. The effect of his labour is, that the whole common pasture of this village has become an orchard, which yields a considerable annual sum to the community. Thus one good action was recompensed by another!

PARASITICAL PLANTS.

106. There are many plants which do not grow immediately from the earth, but strike their roots into certain parts of other plants. Their roots are generally united with, or developed on, the cortical layers of the plants on which they grow; thus evidently abstracting a portion of their sap and retarding their growth. The *misletoe* is a plant of this kind, and is usually ound growing on fruit trees or on the white-thorn, poplar, &c. Many para·tes also grow on the roots of other plants, as the *broom-rape* (orobanche), *ithræa* (tooth-wort), *yellow bird's nest* (monotropa); and many other plants belonging to the order Schophulariceæ, as *rhinanthus*, *euphrasia*, &c., have been recently discovered to be of a parasitic nature. On flax, beans, clover, furze, &c., several species of *cuscuta* usually grow; a curious genus of pretty climbers.

DURATION OF PLANTS.

107. While only a few hours are permitted for the development of myriads of the minute or microscopic fungi, some fungous plants live for days, months, and a few of the more woody kinds, still longer. In § 80, we have shown that the duration of the more highly-organised forms of vegetable life is much longer; indeed, with the exception of *annual* and *biennial* plants, all others live to a very advanced period.

By the number of annually deposited rings or woody layers it has been satisfactorily proved that there are many trees of upwards of 2000 years of age, and these still growing vigorously. On the banks of the Senegal there are trees of the *baobab*, or monkey-bread kind, that are not less than 6000 years old!

Generally, but not universally, the circumference or extent of growth of a plant corresponds to its age. A large diameter indicates a great age. While our red-pine attains a height of from 160 to 180 feet, and a diameter of 6, there are palms which, without being thicker, reach to the immense altitude of 250 feet. There are many of the winding plants of South America which have stems of only about an inch in diameter, and which reach the astonishing length of 1,500 feet. On Mount Etna there is an ancient chestnut tree, the circumference of which amounts to from 60 to 80 feet.

An elm, at Worms, called the Luther tree, is 116 feet high, and 35 feet in circumference. Its age may be from 600 to 800 years. The baobab tree, just mentioned, reaches to the height of only from 60 to 80 feet, with a diameter of 27 feet.

[Still larger trees, both in regard to girth and altitude, than any of the foregoing, are to be found in northern California, and in Oregon. A prostrate tree was found to measure 250 feet in length, and 58 feet in circumference at the base.]

The retention of their vitality by seeds is also very unequal. Many lose it in the course of a year. And seeds of barley, produced during the time of the irruption of the Arabs into France, have retained their vitality ever since, a period of 600 years. Indeed, it has been affirmed, that corn found in the sepulchres of the ancient Egyptian kings, has germinated, and such corn cannot be less than 2000 years old.

DISTRIBUTION OR DISPERSION OF PLANTS.

108. The surface of the earth is very unequally covered with plants. Towards the Poles, plants gradually diminish both in number and in size, so that the lofty pine, in the inhospitable wastes of high latitudes, becomes a stunted shrub. Lichens and mosses are almost the only covering of the cold rocky surface; and in the regions of perpetual frost and snow all vegetable life ceases. On the other hand, in the regions which lie towards the equator, vegetation assumes the richest and most gorgeous aspect, appearing under various and often gigantic forms, yielding the fairest blossoms, the most exquisite perfumes, and the most delicious fruits.

Plants are, in general, confined to certain regions of the earth, or even to more limited localities, where they find what is necessary for their healthy existence. Imaginary lines may be laid down on the surface of the earth which will show the limits of the different countries where the olive, the vine, the wheat, the maize, the rice, and many other plants, can be successfully cultivated.

These lines of equal temperature (isothermal lines) are not parallel with the equator, as we have shown in Physics, § 126, that local influences have a consideral effect in altering the temperature.

In the temperate climate of England many plants from Australia and Polynesia, which would be frozen in Germany, grow in the open air, whilst the grape and peach rarely ripen in Great Britain, because they require a higher summer temperature than the insular situation of that country permits them to enjoy. These, however, ripen in Germany, because the summer temperature there is proportionably higher. Lofty mountains in the warm regions of the world produce at different altitudes plants of the most unequal climates. For while palms and orange-trees flourish at their base, their lofty rocky summits are clothed with lichens or eternal snow.

109. Within natural limits, Nature has abundantly provided for the dispersion of plants. She has supplied some of them with feathery or downy-covered crowns, whereby they are wafted from place to place with every breeze, or even breath of wind; others are provided with sharply-hooked appendages, whereby they attach themselves to the woolly coverings of animals, and thus are conveyed to considerable distances. The birds, the herbivorous mammals, the floods, the rivers, and even the sea, are active agents in distributing plants to very remote stations.

The riches of the vegetable world in both hemispheres, in America, Asia, Australia, New Zealand, have been disclosed to us through the enterprising and successful expeditions of modern travellers and discoverers. Every year brings an accession of new plants, many of which are acclimatised, which, on their introduction, were supposed to require the protection of a conservatory. Many are even self-propagated. The beautiful evening primrose (Œnothera), which in 1614 was first introduced, now grows freely and blossoms in our hedges. Also the Canadian flea-wort, which, since the discovery of America, was accidentally introduced among rye, has become a common weed in many fields contiguous to the sea, or to a sea-port.

By the *Flora* of a country or district we understand an enumeration or catalogue, descriptive or otherwise, as the case may be, of all the plants growing spontaneously in that country or district.

III. CLASSIFICATION OF PLANTS.

SYSTEMATIC BOTANY.

110. In classifying, as well as in distinguishing, the great body of plants composing the vegetable kingdom, very definite and permanent characteristic marks should be employed. For example, if we were to classify by magnitude into herbaceous, frutescent, and arboreous plants (herbs, shrubs, and trees), we must place the willow in every one of these classes, for on the mountains it appears *herbaceous* (Salix herbacea), in osier holts, *frutescent* (Salix viminalis), and on the plains and meadows as *arboreous* (Salix cinera).

For the most prevalent artificial method of classifying plants we are indebted to Linnæus, a Swede, born in 1707, to whom has been assigned, by universal consent, the first rank among the most distinguished naturalists.

Linnæus followed two different methods in the classification of plants. In the one he founded the classes and orders upon certain peculiarities of the floral organs. In the other he classified all plants, by certain general resemblances which exist among plants, into what are called natural orders or families. This latter method was very much improved by Jussieu, Curator of the Jardin des Plantes, Paris, and more recently by A. P. Decandolle, of Geneva, and Dr. J. Lindley, of London. This is called the *natural method*, or natural system, of botany, whilst the former is termed the *artificial* or *Linnæan system*.

111. Those plants which correspond in all essential and unvarying mark or characters belong to one *sort* or *species*.

All plants corresponding in certain more comprehensive marks or characters form a *kind* or *genus*. These generic marks are chiefly certain parts of the blossom.

All plants constituting a genus bear the name of the genus, which is called the generic name, and also a second name, called the specific name, which distinguishes the species. Thus the genus *Viola*, violet, includes the species *Viola odorata*, sweet violet; *Viola canina*, dog violet; *Viola tricolor*, heartsease; and many more species besides.

It is necessary to give the Latin names in describing plants, because the same plant does not bear the same name in every country, nor always in the same country; for there are provincial names of things as well as provincial dialects: hence the Latin, which is universally understood by the learned and scientific, is always employed in the nomenclature of botany, and indeed in most other sciences.

Orders are formed on still more comprehensive characters than genera, of which an order contains several, sometimes a great number, of genera. These ordinal agreements are called *relations*, and one genus is related to another by means of the common character of greatest similarity. This principle is in complete contrast with chemical relations, for in this science bodies are related which have the least similarity.

The sun-flower, the tansy, the aster, and the dahlia, are, for example, plants of different genera, but they belong to the same order.

That all plants are divided into three principal groups, namely, Acotyledonous, Monocotyledonous, and Dicotyledonous, we have already shown in § 27.

These general ideas are most readily and impressively exemplified by observation and diligent perseverance in the collection, discrimination, and classification of plants.

THE ARTIFICIAL OR LINNÆAN SYSTEM OF BOTANY.

112. According to this system all plants are divided into twenty-four classes. The twenty-three first contain all the monocotyledonous and dicotyledonous plants indiscriminately. The twenty-fourth only the acotyledonous.

The characters of the classes are founded on the number, situation, relative length of the stamens, and also on their union with each other, or with other parts of the blossom, and, lastly, on their absence.

Every class is divided into several orders, which, in the thirteen first classes, are distinguished by the number of the styles or stigmas.

Tabular View of the Linnæan System of Classification.

A.—Flowers present.

I. Hermaphrodite, stamens and pistils in every flower.

1. Stamens free.

a. Stamens of equal length	Class 1. Monandria.
	" 2. Diandria.
	" 3. Triandria.
	" 4. Tetrandria.
	" 5. Pentandria.
	" 6. Hexandria.
	" 7. Heptandria.
	" 8. Octandria.
	" 9. Enneandria.
	" 10. Decandria.
	" 11. Dodecandria.
Stamens inserted on the calyx	" 12. Icosandria.
" on the receptacle	" 13. Polandria.
Four stamens of different length, two long and two short	" 14. Didynamia.
Six " four long and two short	" 15. Tetradynamia.
Two stamens united by the filaments in one bundle	" 16. Monadelphia.
" " in two bundles	" 17. Diadelphia.
" " in more than two bundles.	" 18. Polyadelphia
" by the anthers	" 19. Syngenesia.
" with the pistil	" 20. Gynandria.
II. Unisexual Flowers.	
Stamens and pistils in different flowers on same plant.	" 21. Monœcia.
" " on different plants	" 22. Diœcia.
III. Stamens and pistils in the same or in different flowers, on the same or on different plants	23. Polygamia.
B.—Flowers absent	24. Cryptogamia.

Tabular View of Classes and Orders.

Classes.	Orders.	Examples.
I.—Monandria	Monogynia.......... one style	Hippuris.
One stamen.	Digynia.............. two styles	Callitriche.
II.—Diandria	Monogynia.......... one style	Syringa.
Two stamens.	Digynia.............. two styles	Anthoxanthum.
III.—Triandria	Monogynia.......... one style	Iris.
Three stamens.	Digynia .... two styles	Hordeum.
	Trigynia............. three do.	Holosteum.
IV.—Tetrandria	Monogynia.......... one style	Scabiosa.
Four stamens.	Digynia.............. two styles	Gentiana.
	Trigynia............. three do.	
V.—Pentandria	Monogynia.......... one style	Borago.
Five stamens.	Digynia.............. two styles	Fœniculum.
	Trigynia............. three do.	Sambucus.
	Tetragynia.......... four do.	Parnassia.
	Pentagynia.......... five do.	Linum.
	Polygynia .... many do.	Myosurus.

Tabular View of Classes and Orders—*continued.*

Classes.	Orders.	Examples.
VI.—Hexandria..........	Monogynia..........one style	Lilium.
Six stamens.	Digynia ....two styles	Oxyria.
	Trigynia.............three do.	Rumex.
	Tetragynia..........four do.	
	Polygynia ....many do.	Alisma.
VII.—Heptandria.........	Monogynia..........one style	Trientalis.
Seven stamens.	Digynia ....two styles	
	Trigynia ....three do.	
	Heptagynia..........seven do.	
VIII.—Octandria...........	Monogynia...........one style	Daphne.
Eight stamens.	Digynia...............two styles	Chrysosplenium.
	Trigynia..............three do.	Polygonum.
	Tetragynia...........four do.	Paris.
IX.—Enneandria.........	Monogynia...........one style	
Nine stamens.	Trigynia..............three styles	
	Hexagynia ....six do.	Butomus.
X.—Decandria	Monogynia...........one style	Pyrola.
Ten stamens.	Digynia...............two styles	Dianthus.
	Trigynia..............three do.	Silene.
	Pentagynia ....five do.	Lychnis.
	Decagynia ....ten do.	
XI.—Dodecandria	Monogynia...........one style	Lythrum.
Twelve to nineteen stamens.	Digynia...............two styles	Agrimonia.
	Trigynia..............three do.	Reseda.
	Pentagynia...........five do.	
	Dodecagynia.........twelve do.	Sempervivum.
XII.—Icosandria..........	Monogynia...........one style	Prunus.
Twenty or more stamens inserted on the calyx.	Digynia...............two styles	Cratægus.
	Trigynia..............three do.	Sorbus.
	Pentagynia ....five do.	
	Polygynia ....many do.	Rosa.
XIII.—Polyandria..........	Monogynia...........one style	Papaver.
Many stamens inserted on the receptacle (base of the flower).	Digynia...............two styles	Pæonia.
	Trigynia..............three do.	Aconitum.
	Tetragynia...........four do.	
	Pentagynia ....five do.	Nigella.
	Hexagynia	
	Polygynia ....many do.	Ranunculus.
XIV.—Didynamia..........	Gymnospermia.fournaked seeds	Lavandula.
Two long and two short stamens. Labiate and Personate Flowers.	Angiospermia..seeds in capsules	Linaria.
XV.—Tetradynamia	Siliculosa, broad pouch and short style	Capsella.
Four long and two short stamens. Cruciferous Flowers.	Siliquosa, long pod, stigma sessile.	Brassica.

Tabular View of Classes and Orders—*continued.*

Classes.	Orders.	Examples.
XVI.—MONADELPHIA....... Stamens united in one bundle.	Pentandria ....five stamens	Erodium.
	Enneandria.........nine do.	
	Decandria ....ten do.	Geranium.
	Dodecandria ....twelve do.	Malva.
	Polyandria ....many do.	
XVII.—DIADELPHIA .... Stamens united in two bundles, one containing nine (generally) and one free.	Pentandria.........five stamens (two above and three below.)	
	Hexandria .... six do. (three right, three left, or three above and three below.)	Fumaria.
	Octandria ....eight do. (four above and four below, all united at the base.)	Polygala.
	Decandria.............ten do. (one above and nine below, united in a cleft surrounding the ovary.)	Pisum, Trifolum, Genista.
XVIII.—POLYDELPHIA ...... Stamens united in more than two bundles.	Pentandria.........five stamens	
	Decandria ....ten do.	
	Polyandria ....many do.	Hypericum.
XIX.—SYNGENESIA .... Five stamens, filaments free, anthers united, flower monopetalous, florets united on a disk. Compositæ.	Polygamia equalis, florets equal	Lactuca.
	Polygamia superflua, ray florets with styles only.	Aster.
	Polygamia frustranea, ray florets without both stamens and styles.	Helianthus.
	Polygamia necessaria, florets of the disk with stamens, ray with styles.	Calendula.
	Polygamia segregata, a common calyx including all the florets, and a distinct calyx for each.	Echinops.
	Monogamia	
XX.—GYNANDRIA........... Stamens and pistils united.	Diandria ....two anthers	Orchis.
	Triandria ....three do.	
	Tetrandria..........four do.	
	Pentandria ....five do.	
	Hexandria...........six do.	Aristolochia.
	Decandria...........ten do.	
	Dodecandria.....twelve to nineteen do.	
	Polyandria...twenty or more do.	
XXI.—MONŒCIA............. Stamens and styles in different flowers and on the same plant.	Monandria...........one stamen	Arum.
	Diandria..............two stamens	Lemna.
	Triandria.............three do.	Carex.
	Tetrandria ....four do.	Urtica.
	Pentandria...........five do.	Amaranthus.
	Hexandria ....six do.	
	Heptandria ....seven do.	
	Polyandria..more than seven do.	Quercus.
	Monadelphia..stamens united	Pinus.

Classes.	Orders.	Examples.
	Syngenesia...stamens united by their anthers.	
	Gynandria, stamens and styles united.	
XXII.—DIŒCIA............ Stamens and styles in different flowers on different plants.	Monandria.........one stamen	Salix.
	Diandria............two stamens	
	Triandria...........three do.	Ficus.
	Tetrandria.........four do.	Viscum.
	Pentandria ....five do.	Cannabis.
	Hexandria ....six do.	Loranthus.
	Octandria ....eight do.	Populus.
	Enneandria.........nine do.	Laurus.
	Decandria...........ten do.	
	Dodecandria....eleven to nineteen do.	Stratiotes.
	Polyandria......many do.	
	Monadelphia....stamens united	
	Syngenesia......stamens united by the anthers.	
	Gynandria ......stamen and style united.	
XXIII.—POLYGAMIA...... Flowers with stamens and styles separately, and with flowers containing both on the same or on different plants.	Monœcia, unisexual flowers on the same plant.	Acer.
	Diœcia, unisexual flowers on different plants.	Fraxinus.
	Triœcia, hermaphrodite and unisexual flowers on three plants.	
XXIV.—CRYPTOGAMIA.... Organs of fructification concealed.	....	Aspidium filix-mas, Fucus.

113. The artificial system possesses the great advantage of clear, simple characteristics, by which it is generally easy to ascertain the class and order of a plant. It may be recommended to beginners as an introduction to the natural system.

NATURAL SYSTEM (JUSSIEU'S).

Classes.			
I. Acotyledones		....	1st Class
II. Monocotyledones		Monohypogynæ (stamens hypogynous)...........	2nd "
		Monoperigynæ (stamens perigynous)...............	3rd "
		Monoepigynæ (stamens epigynous).................	4th "
III. Dicotyledones.	Monoclines, flowers hermaphrodite.		
	Apetalæ (no petals)	Epistamineæ (stamens epigynous)	5th "
		Peristamineæ (stamens perigynous)................	6th "
		Hypostamineæ (stamens hypogynous)............	7th "
	Monopetalæ (petals united).	Hypocorollæ (corolla hypogynous)..................	8th "
		Pericorollæ (corolla perigynous).....................	9th "
		Epicorollæ (corolla epigynous). Synantheræ (anthers united)	10th "
		Epicorollæ (corolla epigynous). Chorisantheræ (anthers free)	11th "
	Polypetalæ (petals distinct).	Epipetalæ petals epigynous)...........................	12th "
		Peripetalæ (petals perigynous).......................	13th "
		Hypopetalæ (petals hypogynous)......................	14th "
	Diclines, flowers unisexual or without a perianth..........................		15th "

114. It may be observed that this system, being founded partly on individual organs, is also, in some degree artificial. Rigid, precisely scientific distinctions, are not found in Nature, which seems to prefer gradual or almost imperceptible transitions from the simplest to the most complex of her developments.

IV. DESCRIPTION OF PLANTS.

DESCRIPTIVE BOTANY.

115. The marvellous variety, both in form and organisation, of the subjects of the vegetable kingdom may be inferred from the fact, that already above 100,000 plants have been observed; and every day increases the vast amount. These, however, occupy the surface of the whole earth; only a small proportion of the whole is produced in any given country. In Germany there are probably about 7,000. In the British isles a much smaller number.

The description of plants is to be found in works exclusively appropriated to botanical science. These works either comprehend all plants, or those of a greater or less extent of territory, or only of a district. Those devoted to the universal Flora are generally composed in Latin, which is a language more universally understood than any other.

In reference to the *Flora of Germany*, which has been often written, we, out of the many works on this subject, mention only Koch's Synopsis of the German and Swiss Flora, and the compendium of the German Flora by the same author, and the work of Kittel. Also the following descriptive local Floras, for example, that of Frankfort-on-the-Maine, by Fresenius; of Baden, by Gmelin; of Würtemberg, by Schübler; and also Marten's Flora of the same place; of Hesse, by Schnittspahn; Flora of the Rhine, by Döll; Austria, by Schultes; Silesia, by Wimmer; Berlin, by Schlectendal; the Prussian Flora, by Ruthe; Brunswick, by Lachmann, &c.

Besides the English Flora by Sir J. E. Smith, which will always be regarded as the standard of descriptive British botany, and the works of Balfour, Babbington, Irvine, and others, the following local Floras are recommended: Dr. Johnston's Flora of Berwick-on-Tweed, Leighton's Flora of Shropshire, Jones's of Devon, Murray's Northern Flora, unfortunately only a fragment, but a valuable relic, especially to such as knew the amiable author, who was prematurely cut off in the zealous discharge of the duties of his profession. Besides these, there are various county catalogues of plants, more or less complete, and the ancient local lists of Blackstone, Jacobs, Warner, &c., together with the interesting itineraries of Johnson, the precursor of all British local botanists.

[As regards American plants, the principal authorities are Bigelow, U. P. C. Barton, Darlington, Rafinesque, &c. Gray's Botanical Text-Book may be recommended as a standard and valuable work.]

Some work of this nature, in which the plants are described and arranged either on the artificial or on the natural system, is indispensable to the student of botany, in order to enable him to identify the plants which he may collect, by comparing them with those described in books. The only method of learning botany is by collection, comparison, discrimination, and identification. Without this constant practice, which demands the exercise of accurate and persevering observation, it is impossible to impress on the memory the manifold forms of vegetable objects, or to obtain a comprehensive idea of their arrangement.

The following is not so much a description as an enumeration of the principal plants employed in the arts or in medicine, or which are applicable to nutritive purposes, as food for man or domestic animals, or are remarkable in any other respect. We adopt the natural arrangement, commencing with the less highly organised forms of vegetable life.

A. ACOTYLEDONS.

116. We have already shown that this extensive group comprehends all such plants as have no visible floral organs, and do not produce real fruit. Their reproduction is accomplished by means of *spores*, or embryonic granules or cells, which appear in the form and consistency of a remarkably minute powdery matter. These individual granules have the power of self-development, and are often so impalpably small that they are diffused everywhere. In every place accessible to the air these minute reproductive corpuscles are to be found, and we need not marvel that the plants produced by them are apparently of spontaneous origin.

The spores are produced in great numbers densely packed on each other, as, for example, on the reverse or dorsal side of a fern-frond (leaf), where they form small protuberances (sori), or they are found in small receptacles called spore-cases, but have various names in the various orders. In the mosses, the organs bearing spores are of an urceolate form, generally with an operculum or lid, and have a very neat appearance.

To this group of plants belong the Algæ, the Lichens, the Fungi, the Musci, which are merely cellular plants (§ 18). Also the Equiseta, Ferns, and Lycopods, which, though vascular plants, are of a less perfect organization than the other orders of vasculares.

117. Algæ. *The Sea-weed tribe.*—To these almost exclusively water-plants belong the *confervæ*, which are produced in standing or stagnant water, and the very numerous genera of marine plants, known by the name of *tangle, fuci*, &c., the ashes of which produce the kelp and barilla of commerce; these likewise produce iodine (Chem. § 38). The *gigantic fuci* of the South Seas are reported by navigators to be from 500 to 1,500 feet in length, and afford nutriment and shelter to many thousands of marine animals. The mucilaginous substance prepared from *sargassum* is a remedy in pulmonary diseases, and some of the fuci have *vermifugal* properties.

118. Lichenes. *The Lichen tribe.*—These are spread over the trunks and branches of trees, old palings, barns, walls, rocks, &c. They are dry and coriaceous, mostly of a yellow or white colour, usually very much ramified, sometimes foliaceous and spreading, covering large spaces of the ground, rocks, walls, trees, &c. Cetraria islandica (fig. 120), or *Iceland moss*, is common in high northern latitudes, where it forms the principal food of the Laplander's wealth, the reindeer. It contains much amylaceous matter, and is consequently very nutritious. It is also a remedy in pulmonary complaints. *Litmus* is prepared from a species of *Lecanora*. Another species of the same plant yields *Cudbear*, the famous red dye of the Glasgow

manufactures. *Archil*, or Orchil, a beautiful purple dye, is obtained from Roccella tinctoria, which is a production of the Canary Islands.

120. Cetraria Islandica.

119. FUNGI. *The Mushroom tribe.*—The smallest objects of this tribe, even the common grey mould, which is frequently produced on decaying and other substances, together with the myriads of microscopic fungi, which at certain times and in certain localities are so prevalent, are not without some claims to admiration, on account of their regularity of form and not seldom beauty of colour.

The larger sorts of fungi are usually found in woods that are moist and shady, as well as in meadows, and frequently on trees. The *Agaric* (fig. 121) is distinguished by the delicate tender gills on the under side of the pileus, and in this genus we find the varieties of the *edible mushroom* and *champignon.* The *fly mushroom,* Agaricus amanita, a very beautiful

121. Agaricus Campestris.

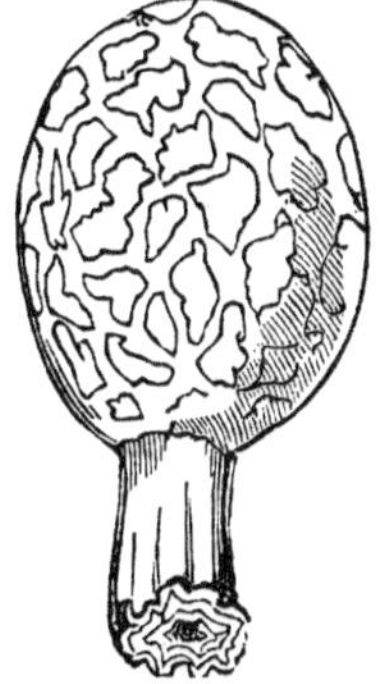

122. Morchella esculenta.

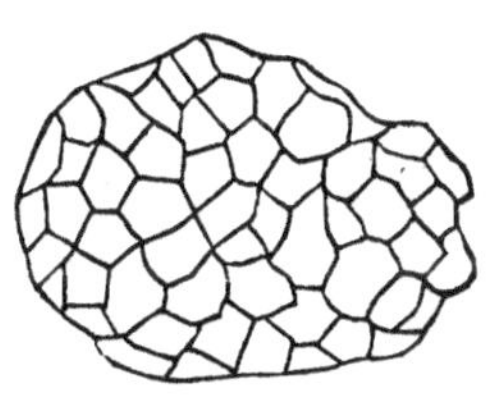

123. Tuber cibarium.

species, is highly dangerous. As this tribe contains a vast number of species, very difficult to distinguish from each other, great care should be employed in selecting such as may safely be employed in culinary preparations. It may be recommended to those who are not perfectly acquainted with the varieties and modifications of the agarics, never to eat any but such as have been cultivated.

The *Boletus,* or porous fungus, is provided with pores instead of gills on the under side, in which also the reproductive bodies or spores are lodged. Some of these are eatable (with caution), and many are very poisonous.

The *Polypori* grow mostly on trees, and from several of them tinder is prepared, called German tinder. The white and intensely bitter fungus of the Larch is employed as a cattle medicine. Many fungi grow on wood, which they rapidly destroy. A partial remedy for this has been recom mended and practised to a certain extent, viz., the *Kyanizing process* (steeping the wood in a solution of corrosive sublimate). A more recently-discovered process is the injection of certain antiseptic substances into the porous parts of the wood.

Finally, the morel, *Morchella* (fig. 122), and the subterraneous delicious *truffle*, Tuber cibarium (fig. 123), belong to this family.

120. MUSCI. *The Moss tribe.*—In this tribe we first meet with the peculiar green colour of plants and with the formation of a stem whereby these form the connecting link between the foliaceous lichens and the more perfectly-developed forms of vegetation. These pretty minute plants compose a numerous family universally dispersed, and not without utility in the general economy of Nature. The *turf-moss* has been already mentioned as the material of which the soil of bogs is constituted. (Chem. § 165.)

121. EQUISETACEÆ. *Horse-tail tribe.*—These plants are remarkable for the abundance of silex which they contain. So that when the whole plant has been submitted to the process of combustion, a perfect skeleton of the form remains, as has been noticed in § 85. They, on this account, possess the quality of a file, and are used for polishing wood, &c. They commonly grow in damp situations, on sandy fields, and in woods and marshy places.

122. FILICES. *Fern tribe.*—These plants constitute an extensive group, which in external appearance approaches nearer to the more highly-developed plants than any of the above-mentioned acotyledonous orders. Their most conspicuous organ is the leaf, *frond*, which is beautifully cut or incised at the margin, and almost always pinnate (feathered). They bear spores on the dorsal side of the frond.

The *Eagle-fern* (Pteris aquilina), and the *Shield-fern* (Aspidium filix mas), occur generally in our woods and hedges; the beautiful *Adiantum* (Lady's-hair) (fig. 124), and *Asplenium* (Maiden-hair), grow on rocks and on old brick walls, &c.

124. Adiantum capillus-veneris.

The ferns of the South Sea Islands are distinguished by their gigantic size, frequently constituting the woods and forests of these fertile islands. We have shown in Mineralogy, § 114, that the organic remains of the ancient Flora are remarkably rich in petrified ferns.

123. LYCOPODIACEÆ. *Club-moss tribe.*—In woods and upland wastes we generally meet with these plants. Their thecæ (spore cases) are filled with a yellow powder, very minute and highly inflammable. This powder is employed in pyrotechny, and in producing an imitation of lightning in theatres.

B. MONOCOTYLEDONS

124. Are plants germinating with only one seed-leaf or lobe (cotyledon), their woody and vascular fibre being disposed irregularly, and with parallel-nerved leaves.

125. GRAMINEÆ. *Grass tribe.*—The individuals of this numerous family, mostly comprehended in the third class of the Linnæan system, on account

of their great similarity to each other, are very difficult to describe and to distinguish.

Independently of their beauty wherewith they adorn our meadows, pastures, parks, and lawns, they are, as being the principal food of our flocks, cattle and horses, of the utmost importance. Of fodder and grazing grasses the following are the most valuable, viz:—

Aira flexuosa, hair-grass; *Poa pratensis*, meadow-grass; *Festuca pratensis*, fescue-grass; *Phleum pratense*, timothy-grass; *Alopecurus pratensis*, meadow fox-tail; *Anthoxanthum odoratum*, sweet-scented vernal-grass; *Lolium perenne*, rye-grass; *Bromus racemosus*, brome-grass; *Agrostis*, bent-grass; *Dactylis glomerata*, cock's-foot grass; and the beautiful *totter-grass*, Briza media.

The fodder-grasses contain much silex and potassa (§ 98), and need an abundant supply of water to dissolve the silicious and alkaline substances which are requisite for their nutriment.

Another portion of the grasses is distinguished by the abundance of amylaceous substances and phosphates, which they produce; and hence they are so important as the nutritive materials of human food. These are generally called corn or cereal grasses, and are distinguished not only by the perfection which they have attained, but also by the number of varieties which are in greater or less estimation. The culture of corn is as ancient as history itself. To this division of grasses belong *Triticum*, wheat, *Secale*, rye, *Hordeum*, barley, *Avena*, oat. These have been so extensively distributed by human agency that all trace of their native country has disappeared.

Besides these, the following form part of this extensive order, viz.:—*Phalaris canariensis*, the canary-grass of commerce; *Lolium temulentum*, to which stupefying properties are ascribed; *Millium, Millet, Zea*, maize or Indian corn, chiefly produced in America; *Oryza*, rice, the produce of the watered fertile plains of the Ganges, &c., and constituting the principal subsistence of the Orientals; *Arundo phragmitis*, reed-grass; *Arundo donax*, Spanish reed, which is extensively employed in various wicker-work fabrics, and sometimes used in schools (cane); *Bambusa*, bamboo, a large reed useful for building purposes, for which its strength and lightness render it very suitable. One of the most valuable grasses, *Saccharum*, sugar-cane, is a native of the East, and thence planted in the West Indies. It yields the sugar, molasses, and rum, of commerce. The cultivation of sugar under the tropical heats is one of the severest labours which the original curse has imposed on the human family, and when we enjoy the luxury of this article, we should remember at what expense of toil and suffering it was produced.

126. CYPERACEÆ. *Sedge tribe.*—Among these we enumerate the *Carex*, sedge, a numerous genus, with a triangular solid stem, and with flowers in spikes, either simple or branched. They are neither adapted for fodder nor grazing, and generally disappear when the land is drained and well manured with ashes. One or two of these plants are extremely useful in binding the sand by their roots, and so forming a natural barrier to the encroachments of the sea. Various kinds of rush, *Scirpus*, &c., as well as *Eriophorum*, cotton-grass, belong to this family.

127. ARACEÆ. *The Arum tribe.*—Plants distinguished by their floral spadix (§ 66). The principal are the *Arum* or *Indian turnip* (fig. 125)

of our meadows and road sides, indicating by the large expanding leaf and flower the approach of genial weather: the *Calamus*, sweet-reed, the root of which was formerly in repute as a medicinal substance: the *Calla*, of the sunny lands of the south, which has so long been a favourite on account of its large pure white blossom, and still retains its place in the greenhouse. Its native country is Africa.

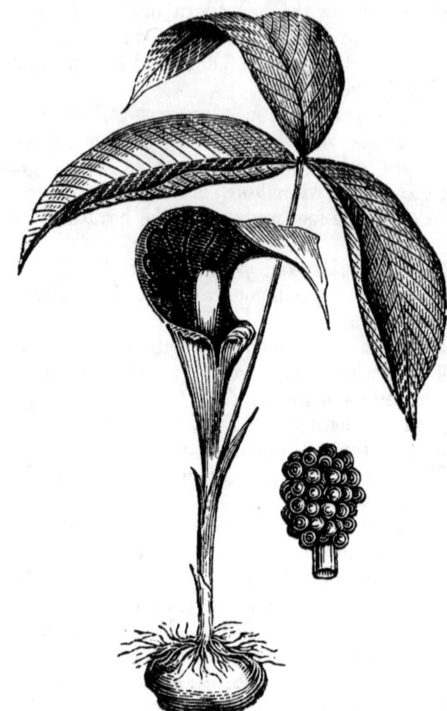

125. Arum triphyllum.

128. Typhaceæ. *Reed-mace tribe.*—These tall handsome plants, with their long cylindrical inflorescence, grow in ponds, and cannot be easily overlooked. Less conspicuous is the bur-reed, *Sparganium*, which is, however, distinguished by its round prickly head, and grows commonly in ditches. The broad leaves of these plants are used by coopers as layers for closing the joints of casks.

129. Alismaceæ. *Water-plantain tribe.*—A small family containing the genera *Alisma*, water-plantain (fig. 126), *Sagittaria*, arrow-head, so named from its arrow-shaped leaves. These all grow in ponds, ditches, or watery places.

130. Melanthaceæ. *The Colchicum tribe.*—An acrid property is possessed by the seeds and roots of many individuals of this family, and they are consequently of a poisonous nature. The *Colchicum* (fig. 127) and *White Hellebore* (Veratrum album, fig. 128) are used in medicine.

131. Asparagineæ. *Asparagus tribe.*—Besides the well-known *Asparagus*, which often grows wild in sandy fields, &c., and when well manured with nitrogenous materials yields the delicious vegetable of our tables, the following belong to this order: the *Lily of the Valley* (Convallaria majalis), the *Herbparis*, one berry (poisonous), and the *Dioscorea*, yam, which in the warmer regions is cultivated as an esculent.

132. Liliaceæ. *Lily tribe.*—A tuberous or rather bulbous root distinguishes all the plants of this tribe. *Allium*, leek, is well known by its abounding in mucilaginous matter, and by its exciting, penetrating, disagreeable odour, which is owing to the presence of a volatile sulphuretted oil. Several species of this genus are extensively cultivated, as the onion, garlic, &c., famous for their culinary properties. The following are in much

estimation for their flowers:—*Ornithogalum*, star of Bethlehem; *Muscari*, clustered or grape-hyacinth; the precious *Hyacinth* of the East, one of the

126. Alisma plantago.

127. Colchicum autumnale.

1. Closed capsule. 2. Open do. 3. Styles. 4. Section of capsule. 5 Seed.

128. Veratrum album.

129. Various species of aloes.

most prized of florists' flowers; the gorgeous *Tulip;* the magnificent *White Lily,* said to have been originally brought from the Holy Land; the *Mar-*

tagon Lily or turban, Turk's-cap; the stately but poisonous *Crown imperial*, and many others. To these may be added the different sorts of *Aloes* (figs. 129 and 130), containing a bitter and drastic juice, which is imported from the warmer parts of America and other quarters. The *New Zealand flax* (Phormium tenax) produces in its long leaves a fibrous material of wonderful tenacity, stronger than hemp.

133. AMARYLIDACEÆ. *Amaryllis tribe.* — In this order we meet with the *Narcissus*, one of our earliest flowering spring-plants; and the *Snowdrop*, which blooms before the winter has past. The *Leucojum*, or summer snowflake, and the splendid exotic *Amaryllis*, belong to the same family.

134. IRIDACEÆ. *The Iris tribe.*—An order of highly-ornamental plants, bearing yellow, blue, and variously-coloured flowers. Their roots are mostly tuberous and fibrous; a few are bulbous. *Iris florentina*, of Southern Europe, produces violet-scented roots, which on this account have been employed as a dentifrice. The *Saffron*, yellow crocus, was formerly much cultivated for the sake of its pollen-grains, which were an esteemed specific in arthritic complaints. Saffron Walden, in Essex, is said to have derived one of its names from the extensive culture of this plant in its vicinity.

130. A. socotrina.

135. BROMELIACEÆ. *Pine-apple tribe.* —*Bromelia ananas*, the pine of our stoves, is a native of America. Its fruit has been much improved by cultivation, and it is highly esteemed for its rich strawberry flavour. The tree Aloe, *Agave Americana*, is a native of the same country. It is cultivated here in large garden-tubs, and is very tardy in blossoming, some say only in 100 years. The flower and flower-stalk are from 20 to 30 feet high, bearing thousands of blossoms; the plant dies after blossoming.

136. PALMÆ. *Palm tribe.* — These gigantic monocotyledons, the princes of the vegetable kingdom, as they were named by Linnæus, sometimes attain a height of nearly 200 feet. Their long slender stems and broad arching leaves have an imposing effect on the landscape of the regions where they grow, and have often been described in glowing colours. We honour them as the symbol of peace, and value them as supplying food, clothing, and shelter. The Date-palm (*Phœnix dactylifera*), the Coco-palm (*Cocos*, fig. 131), are known by their large fine-flavoured nuts. The Sago-palm (*Sagus*, fig. 132) supplies in its pith a farinaceous, nutritious substance, called sago. Several yield fatty substances; and the violet-scented palm-oil is obtained from the Oil-palm (*Elais gui-*

131. Cocos nucifera.

132. Sagus rumphii.

133. Elais guineensis.

neensis, fig. 133), and is exported from Africa in considerable quantities. The *Cabbage-palm* bears edible leaves, and from the sap a beverage called toddy is prepared. Finally, the *Areca palm* produces a nut which is wrapped up in betel leaves, and chewed by the natives of India.

134. Zingiber officinale.
a. Flower. *b.* Stamen.

137. ZINGIBERACEÆ. *The Ginger tribe.*—Natives of warm regions, with aromatic stimulative properties resident in their roots and seeds, of which *Ginger* (Zingiber officinales, fig. 134) and *Cardamoms* are examples. *Maranta* yields the well-known arrow-root of commerce. *Curcuma longa*, a native of Eastern Asia yields the well-known turmeric, which is used as a condiment and as a yellow dye. It contains a yellow colouring matter, called *curcumin.*

138. MUSACEÆ. *Banana tribe.* —We not unfrequently observe in green-houses a plant resembling in growth a palm, and bearing gigantic leaves. This plant is the *Pesang*, or Fig-tree of Paradise, termed also *Banana* (Musa sapientum, fig. 135); a tree which is of the same importance to millions of the natives of the torrid regions of Asia and America, as the various kinds of corn, the potato, the date-palm, &c., are to the inhabitants of other lands. Besides the delicious fruit of the Banana,

135. Musa sapientum.

the leaves, which attain a length of from 8 to 10 feet, are employed for many purposes of life. *Musa textilis* yields a kind of woody fibre, which is used in India in the manufacture of fine muslins. Manilla Hemp is the produce of *Musa textilis.* The woody tissue of many species of Musa is used for maufacture in warm climates. The young shoots of the Banana are used as a culinary vegetable. *Urania speciosa*, or *Ravenala,* is the Water-tree of the Dutch, so called on account of the great quantity of water which flows from its stem or leaf-stalk when cut across.

139. ORCHIDACEÆ. *The Orchis tribe.*—The fleshy tubers of most of these plants yield *salep*, which, dressed with water, forms a mucilaginous nutritious dietary article. The highly curious and beautiful flowers of the *Wood*, the *Spotted*, and the *Meadow Orchises* are not uncommon. The beautiful *Lady's Slipper* is very rare. The *Bee*, *Butterfly*, and *Fly Orchises* are of rather rare occurrence. *Vanilla* (fig. 136), one of the most precious aromatics known, and used in the culinary preparation of the most delicious dishes prepared for epicurean taste, is a member of this family. The parasitic orchids of the warm regions of America, when cultivated in our stoves and conservatories, are, from the beauty of their colours and the singularity of their forms, objects of attention and special admiration.

136. Vanilla aromatica.

C. DICOTYLEDONS.

140. Plants with two or more cotyledons or seed-leaves, or lobes, concentric layers of woody fibre arranged regularly, leaf-nerves ramified and reticulated.

141. CONIFERÆ. *The Fir tribe.*—These trees are readily distinguished by their wood, which is destitute of medullary rays, by their leaves, which are mostly linear and sharp-pointed, and by their cone-shaped fruit. They are also distinguished by the utility of their wood, as timber, and by the resinous, oleaginous, and aromatic substances which they produce. (Comp. Chemistry, § 141.) These secretions consist of pitch, turpentine, resin, balsams, oil, astringents, &c.

The most common trees of this order are the *Yellow* or *long-leaved* Pine (Pinus palustris) the *Red Pine* (Pinus abies), the *White Pine* (P. picea), the *Larch* (P. larix), the *Scotch Pine* (P. sylvestris, fig. 137). The seeds of the *Pinaster* and the *P. pinea* of Italy taste like almonds, with a slight flavour of turpentine. The *Cedar*, the *Yew*, the *Cypress*, and the *Juniper*, are also of this order.

137. Pinus sylvestris.

142. AMENTACEÆ. *The Poplar tribe.*—After the coniferæ, the ament or catkin-bearing trees constitute the largest portion of our woods and forests, and also yield the largest quantity of wood both for timber and fuel. Among these we find the *Oak* (Quercus), with its majestic top, the symbol of Saxon energy and firmness; the *smooth-barked Beech* (Fagus); the *Birch* (Betula); the *Alder* (Alnus); the *Hazel* (Corylus). The seeds of this order are either oleaginous, like those of the beech and hazel, or amylaceous, as in the edible *Chestnuts* (Castanea), and the *Acorn*, which is too acrid to be eatable, except by swine.

The bark of these trees contains tannin, and the willow contains a bitter substance called salicin, possessed of tonic properties. The Poplar is a tree which gives a singular aspect to the landscape of many parts of the country. The fruit of *Myrica* (Gale) contains a waxy substance, sometimes used as a cattle medicine.

143. URTICACEÆ. *The Nettle tribe.*—Plants with a highly developed vascular fibre, which forms the staple of many of our manufactures. *Cannabis*, the hemp plant (fig. 138), secretes a greenish oil; and the fibrous bark of the *Stinging-nettle* (Urtica) is manufactured into nettle-cloth. The venomous nature of the sap contained at the base of the sting, is not to be compared with the fearful poisons of some East Indian species. The Hop contains in its floral integuments an aromatic bitter substance, on which account it is extensively used in the brewing of beer. Hemp also contains an aromatic principle, which is possessed of narcotic properties. One of our most useful trees, the *Elm*, belongs to this order, and also the *planes* which are often selected to ornament our squares and other public places. One specially important group of this order contains the *Bread-fruit tree* (Artocarpus) of the South Sea Islands; the *Fig* (Ficus), celebrated in all ages; and the *Mulberry* (Morus), prized for its delicious fruit. Here also are found the most deadly poisons in the world. The *Upas*, or *Upas-antiar*, is used by the Javanese for poisoning their arrows. The milky sap of *Ficus elastica* becomes the article Caoutchouc, and the *Galactodendron utile*, or famous Cow-tree of Demerara, is daily tapped for a supply of milk.

138. Cannabis Sativa.

144. CHENOPODIACEÆ. *Goose-foot tribe.*—In the vicinity of the sea, on the saltings or land occasionally flooded by salt water, we find the Salsolas (*Salsola* and *Salicornia*), the importance of which plants as a source of soda, was greater in a former period than it is now (Chem. § 73). The various kinds of Goose-foot (*Chenopodium*) are very common in England upon rubbish-heaps. Many plants of this order are of considerable value as objects of horticulture and agriculture, of which *Beet*, *Spinach*, and *Mangold-wurzel* are common examples.

145. EUPHORBIACEÆ *Spurge tribe.*—The numerous plants of this order, with few exceptions, abound in juice, which is possessed of very caustic qualities applied externally; internally exhibited, it is poisonous.

The most familiar example of this family is the *Spurge*, many of which are among the commonest of weeds. The *Manchineel* (Hippomane) also produces a very acrid juice, which is dispersed by boiling, and then the roots yield a nutritious dietary article. The *Jatropa manihot* is rendered eatable by the same process, and the farinaceous article derived from both of these plants is the *tapioca* of commerce; in the West Indies commonly eaten by the negroes.

Croton oil, one of the most violent drastics, is prepared from a plant belonging to this order, and the *Ricinus palma Christi* (fig. 139) yields

139. Ricinus communis.

a. Stamens. c. Stigmas. e. Seed.
b. Anther. d. Capsule. f. Embryo.

castor-oil, which is so famous for its mild aperient properties. The beautiful Box, the favourite ornament of our lawns, belongs to the Euphorbiaceæ, and affords a remarkably hard and dense wood, which is admirably adapted to the purposes of the wood-engraver. Several American trees of the same family, especially *Syphonia elastica,* yield a milky juice, which on evaporation furnishes India-rubber.

146. ARISTOLOCHIACEÆ. *Birth-wort tribe.*—The plants of this small family are mostly climbers, and possessed of bitter or acrid tonic stimulating qualities. *Aristolochia sipho,* with large cordate leaves, is valued as an ornamental plant. *Serpentaria* and *Assarum* are used in medicine.

147. THYMELIACEÆ. *Mezereon tribe.*—The most common plants of this order are *Daphne laureola,* not rare in chalky woods and hedges; and *D. mezereum* (fig. 140), the beautiful flowering shrub of our gardens, the flowers

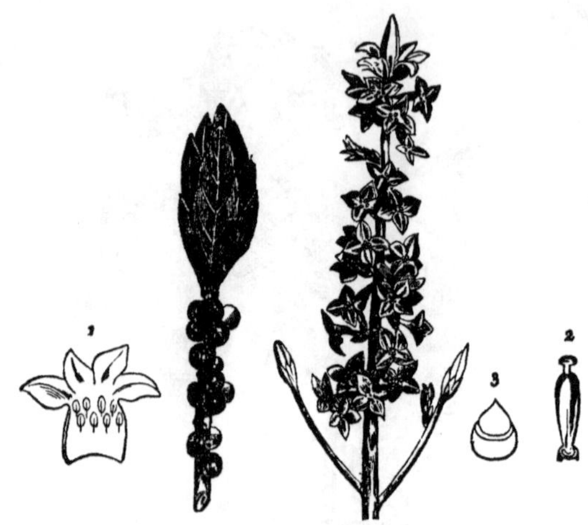

140. Daphne mezereum.
1. Stamen. 2. Pistil. 3. Part of berry and seed.

of which appear in March. The juice of its rind is so acrid that it will speedily raise blisters on the skin.

148. MYRISTICACEÆ. *Nutmeg tribe.*—The tree (Myristica moschata, fig. 141,)) from which we derive the nutmeg, which is an important object of commerce, belongs to this family. The nut is enveloped in an integument which is called mace. Some species produce a fixed oil of a fatty consistence. The beautiful *Tulip-tree* (Liriodendron tulipifera) belongs to this order.

149. LAURACEÆ. *Cinnamon tribe.*—This highly-aromatic family is chiefly confined to the East Indies. It includes, among many other plants, *Laurus cinnamomum* (fig. 142), which produces the fine Ceylon cinnamon; and the *Laurus cassia,* which yields the aromatic bark from which cinnamon-oil is extracted. The *Victor's Laurel* (Laurus nobilis) not only supplies wreaths for our poets and artists, but the leaves also lend a spicy aroma to our condiments, and the oil of the same is employed in medicine. *Camphor,* the produce of *Laurus camphora,* has various applications. (Com. Chem. § 139.)

150. POLYGONACEÆ. *Buck-wheat tribe.*—The plants of this tribe have triangular seeds in a hard shelly perisperm, and are used for nearly the same

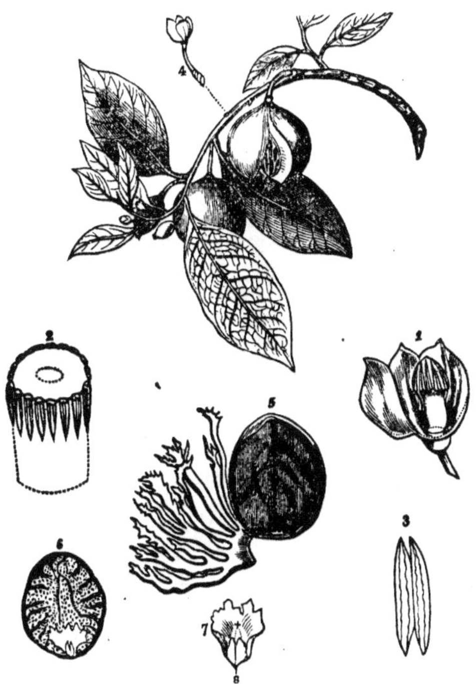

141. Myristaca moschata.

1. Calyx and stamens. 3. Anthers. 5. Nub.
2. Stamens. 4. Female flower. 6. Seed divided.
7. Embryo.

purposes as oatmeal, and can be produced on the poorest soils. The species of *Dock* (Rumex) contain oxalic acid, and some of these are cultivated as salad plants. The famous *Rhubarb* is obtained from *Rheum* (figs. 143, 144, and 145), which grows on the steppes of Northern Asia, and usually reaches Europe through Russia.

150. Labiatæ. *Libate tribe.*—The very numerous members of this family are known by their labiate or ringent blossoms, and by their four stamens, two of which are shorter than the other two. They are also mostly distinguished for secreting a highly volatile aromatic oil, which is partly used in medicine, partly as a perfume. *Mint, Rosemary, Thyme, Marjoram, Hyssop, Sage, Lavender,* &c., are examples. As non-aromatics, the *Dead Nettle,* the *Ground Ivy,* and several others may be mentioned.

152. Ericaceæ. *Heath tribe.*—A great number of plants, besides *Calluna vulgaris,* or Common Heath, belongs to this family; but the greater part of them is imported from Africa, and they are all highly prized for the neatness of their habit, and the abundance of their pretty globular, urceolate, or campanulate flowers. Heath forms almost the only surface-covering of our mountains; and extensive, dry, barren, sandy flats are covered with

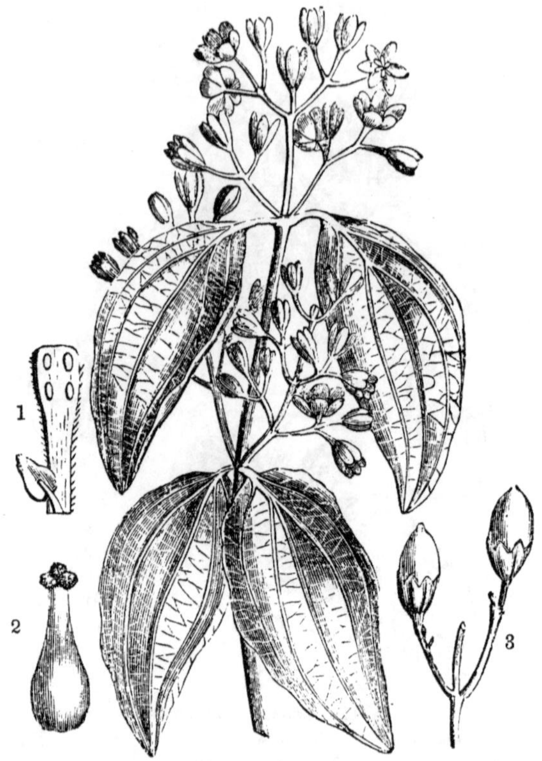

142. Laurus cinnamomum.

1. Perfect Stamen, with an Abortive one at Base. 2. Pistil
3. Fruit.

143. Rheum emodi.

144. Rheum compactum

145. Rheum pulmatum.

them. They are of some value in affording a rich supply of honey to the bees. The *Rhododendron*, or Alpine Rose, is found near the summits of the lofty mountains; and the exotic plants of this genus, with Azaleas, Kalmias, &c., are the great ornaments of our lawns in early summer. The *Bilberry* (Vaccinium myrtillus) grows in woods, and produces an insipid berry, which, however, is used for culinary purposes; and the *Cowberry* (V. vitisidæa) is also eatable; and the *Cranberry* is imported in vast quantities from Canada, &c.

146. Digitalis Purpurea.

153. SCROPHULARIACEÆ. *Figwort tribe.*—Among many unimportant plants belonging to this family, such as *Scrophularia* (Figwort), *Euphrasia* (Eye-bright), formerly of some repute as an officinal plant, and the *Veronicas*, some of which are ornamental, and many of them worthless weeds, we may notice *Digitalis* (fig. 146), a beautiful plant, and much esteemed as an effective remedial agent in various complaints. The beautiful calceolarias, commonly called ladies' slippers, are members of this family.

154. SOLANACEÆ. *Night-shade tribe.*—The individual plants composing this important order are easily referable to it by their external characters. They have a monopetalous rotate corolla, and five stamens. The most of them are also distinguished by their narcotic qualities, which are mostly resident in their roots and seeds.

147. Datura stramonium.

148. Atropa belladonna.
1. Stamens. 2. Styles. 3. Stigma. 4. Berry and Seed.

As poisonous plants, we mention the *Thorn-apple* (Datura, fig. 147), *Hyoscyamus, Atropa belladonna* (fig. 148), which has too often allured children to eat its poisonous black shining berries. It is, however, of rare occurrence. The *Woody* and *annual Nightshades* (Solanum nigrum and Dulcamara are suspected plants.

Tobacco (Nicotiana) loses a small part of its narcotic qualities by drying and preparation. This plant, now so common an article of commerce and consumption, was introduced from America in 1540.

We are indebted to the same quarter of the world for the *Potato* (Solanum tuberosum), which was first brought to England in 1586, by Sir Walter Raleigh, or rather by some colonists led by him to Virginia, who soon returned and brought the potato along with them. This valuable esculent, which now yields food for millions of human beings, was not cultivated as an article of general consumption till about 100 years ago. As it is exceedingly prolific, and can be produced on the poorest soils, it has much diminished the risk of famine with which this country was occasionally visited. The potato-culture is still susceptible of improvement, both in the quality and in the quantity of the tubers. Potatoes which have been allowed to sprout in pits or cellars are dangerous. Frozen potatoes may be rendered catable by laying them for a considerable time in cold water. The potatoes may be taken out when a crust of ice has been formed on the water, and lodged in a cellar for immediate consumption. In wet seasons the potato does not secrete a due quantity of farinaceous matter, and consequently is more liable to decomposition, especially if the heaps where they are stored be too large. The cause of a disease which for the last few years has destroyed a vast quantity of potatoes, is still but little known.

Among the other members of this family are the *Egg-plant* (Solanum oviferum), and the *Love-apple* (Solanum lycopersicum), both ornamental plants. *Physalis*, or Winter Cherry, and *Capsicum*, or Spanish Pepper, also *Mullein* (Verbascum), sometimes used as an expectorant.

155. Boraginaceæ. *Borage tribe.*—The plants of this order have rough hairy stems and leaves, with monopetalous rotate corollas, and five stamens; sometimes the petals are disunited. They secrete mucilage; and several of them, especially *Borage* (Borago), requires for its growth a soil containing nitrates (§ 99. The common plants belonging to this family are *Comfrey* (Symphytum), *Bugloss* (Lycopsis), *Gromwell* (Lithospermum), *Ox-tongue* (Anchusa), *Alkanet* (Anchusa tinctoria), the root of which yields a red dye; the *Viper's bugloss* (Echium), *Forget-me-not* (Myosotis), which loses its hairy habit when growing in water.

149. Gentiana lutea.

156. Convolvulaceæ. *Bindweed tribe.*—This small order comprehends *Convolvulus sepium* and *C. arvensis*, the hedge and field convolvulus;

32

the Jalap plant (C. Jalapa), whose resinous root is medicinal. *C. Batatas* yields a large farinaceous root employed as potatoes.

150. Menyanthes trifoliata.

157. GENTIANACEÆ. *The Gentian tribe.*—A family of plants distinguished by the intense blue colour of their blossoms, and by their exceedingly bitter roots. They are *Gentiana acaulis*, and *verna*, both Alpine plants; and *G. lutea* (fig. 149), used in medicine as a tonic; and also the pretty *Erythræa* and the handsome *Menyanthes* (fig. 150).

158. APOCYNACEÆ. *Dogbane tribe.*—This tolerably large order is mostly composed of exotic plants, many of which are dangerous, as *Strychnos* nux vomica (fig. 151), whose seeds are called crow's eyes, or St. Ignatius' beans, and contain the poisonous alkaloid which is termed Strychnine. (Com. Chem. § 148.)

Upas tieute, an East Indian tree, yields a juice with which the natives poison their arrows. The evergreen *Vinca* (Periwinkle) and *Asclepias* of Europe are harmless.

159. JASMINIACEÆ. *Jasmin tribe.*—A family of favourite plants; among many others the sweet-scented *Jessamine*, the *Syringa* (Lilac), and *Privet* are distinguished. It contains the famous Olive-tree (fig. 152), the pride of Italy and Greece, and the symbol of peace. The *Ash* (Fraxinus) of warmer climates yields a substance called *manna*. The well-known blistering insects (Spanish flies) are found only on the plants of this family.

151 Strychnos nux vomica.

160. CAPRIFOLIACEÆ. *Honeysuckle tribe.*—In this family we find the choicest plants for covering the arbours, and for ornamenting the verandahs and other parts of our dwellings. The flowers and berries of the *Elder* (Sambucus nigra) have long been an esteemed sudorific; and the *Snow-ball* (Viburnum) is one of our most ornamental shrubs.

161. DIPSACEÆ. *Teazel tribe.*—The most important plant of the order is the *Teazel* (Dipsacus fullonum), cultivated for its capitula or heads; used by cloth manufacturers for raising the nap on cloth. The *Scabious* adorns our meadows in the late summer, and the sweet scabious is still retained as an ornament in our gardens.

152. Olea europæa.
1. Corolla. 2. Calyx. 3. Drupes.

162. COMPOSITÆ. *Compound tribe.* — This exceedingly numerous family, with compound flowers, is separated into four sub-orders: —

1st. CICHORACEÆ. *Chicory sub-tribe.*—This sub-order is distinguished by the linguiform florets, and by a bitter milky sap, of which our well-known salad-plant, *Lettuce* (Lactuca), *poisonous Lettuce* (Lactuca virosa), *Chicory* (Cichorium), *Endive*, &c., are examples. *Chicory* is used to adulterate coffee, and to colour porter. *Dandelion* (Leontodon taraxacum) is used medicinally, and *Scorzonera* was once famous as a pot-herb.

2nd. CYNAROCEPHALÆ. *Artichoke sub-tribe.* — The plants of this sub-order are known by their bitter juices. Our *Lady's Thistle* (Carduus benedictus), the *Corn-flower*, the *Knap-weed*, and the *Clot-bur*, are familiar examples. The latter, by the hooked bracts, takes firm hold of everything softer than itself. The *Artichoke* is an esculent of less repute than formerly, and *Safflor* (Carthamus) is esteemed for the red but not permanent colour which it yields.

3rd. EUPATORINEÆ. *Hemp Agrimony sub-tribe.* — The most common plants of this sub-tribe are the *Tussilago*, the yellow blossoms of which appear early in spring; the leaves not till late in summer. It is an expectorative plant. The *Everlasting* (Gnaphalium), of which the Germans and French make funereal wreaths; the *Tansy*, *Artemisia*, or *Wormwood*, a reputed anthelmintic; hence its name.

4th. RADIATÆ. *Ray-flowered sub-tribe.*—The *Daisy*, the first prize of infancy, is sufficiently characteristic of this sub-order; to which, among many hundreds besides, the following belong: —

Milfoil, the *noble Chamomile*, distinguished from the baser sort by its hollow disk, and more obviously by its rich fragrance, especially when bruised by the passing steps of the wayfarer. The *Asters* of China and the *Dahlias* of Mexico are the most ornamental of our late-flowering garden-plants, and the stately *sun-flower;* a species of the latter yields the well-known esculent called Jerusalem artichoke, which some fondly fancy to be nearly equal in value to the potato. The seeds of Madia yield a savoury oil.

163. VALERIANACEÆ. *Valerian tribe.*—The field salad, *Fedia olitoria*, or *Lamb's Lettuce*, is one of the earliest and welcomest plants of this tribe.

The *Common Valerian* is a medicinal plant, the root of which has a peculiar odour, very agreeable to cats.

164. RUBIACEÆ. *Madder and Peruvian Bark tribe.*—The different genera of this important family are not distinguished by any obvious discriminative characters, either external or internal. The genus *Cinchona,* or *Peruvian bark,* yields the famous febrifuge so well known. At its first introduction into Europe in the 17th century, its value was estimated at its weight in gold. It yields the quinine of the Pharmacopœia (Chem. § 148), and is the common specific in cases of intermittent fever.

Cephælis (fig. 153) yields the *Ipecacuanha* of the shops. *Coffee* is a native of Africa, but has been long cultivated in Arabia, in the East and West Indies, &c., and forms an important item in European imports.

153. Cephælis ipecacuanha.

The first coffee-houses were established in Constantinople in 1554; in London, in 1652; in Marseilles, in 1671. The annual production of coffee is estimated at 500 millions of pounds; the value of this article imported into Europe is estimated at about seven millions of pounds sterling. Coffee contains a substance, called *caffeine,* that can be crystallised; this product has been discovered both in tea and cocoa.

Madder (Rubia) produces the precious dye called Turkey-red, and is, consequently, an object of culture in many countries. The *Galium* grows in our hedges, and, like the Clot-bur, sticks to the clothes and woolly covering of animals. The pretty *Asperula* (Woodruff) is used in the preparation of the favourite "maiwein" of the Rhine.

165. UMBELLIFERÆ. *Umbellate tribe.*—All the plants arranged in this order have five stamens, and belong to the 5th class, Pentandria, of the Linnæan system. Their umbellate inflorescence and many-parted leaves are obvious distinguishing ordinal marks. Their seeds are small, and abound in volatile oil, and for this property they are partly used in medicine, and partly in culinary preparations. Several form juicy saccharine roots, as the *Carrot* and *Parsnip.* The leaves of *Parsley, Celery,* &c., are also edible. *Fennel, Caraways, Anise, Coriander* (fig. 154), &c., are aromatic.

Together with these plants, the roots, or leaves, or seeds of which afford eatables or condiments, there are some highly poisonous, of which the following are examples, viz.: *Conium maculatum* (Hemlock, fig. 155) and *Æthusa cynapium* (Fools' Parsley). The mistaking of these plants has

154. Coriandum sativum.

1. A portion of an umbil in fruit.
2. A fruit magnified.
3. Transverse section of the same.

155. Conium maculatum.

a. Vertical section of fruit. *c.* Fruit.
b. Transverse do. do. *d.* Flower.

often produced fatal accidents, as they are very liable to be collected instead of several of the above-named eatable species.

On this account we will give a precise description of these two poisonous plants.

The Hemlock has a spotted, round, hollow stem, usually from 3 to 4 feet high. Its leaves are smooth tripinnate; the leaflets, lanceolate, incised with pointed teeth. The involucre has five bracts, and the involucel three pendent bracts; the petals are small and white. The fruit is oval, and the seeds are provided with five ribs (*vittæ*).

The whole plant has an unpleasant smell, when wetted or rubbed between the fingers.

The Parsnip is distinguished from the Hemlock by its yellow flowers and the want of the involucre and involucel. The Hemlock can only be mistaken for Parsley when it is young and before it has produced its stem. The leaves of the Parsley then afford a good discriminative character, in being oval, incised, and toothed, and in yielding an agreeable odour when rubbed.

The Fool's Parsley has bipinnate leaves, with small leaflets. The umbels have no involucre, and the umbellules have an involucel of three pendent bracts, half surrounding the peduncle. The fruit is roundish, and the seeds are furnished with five rather thick ribs.

This plant, Fool's Parsley, often grows in gardens, and might be mistaken for Chervil or Parsley. Its *smaller, inodorous leaflets,* however, precisely distinguish it from both these edible plants.

The *Water Hemlock* (Cicuta virosa, fig. 156) is still more dangerous than either of the two above-described poisonous species, only it grows in water and at a distance from human habitations, and therefore is less likely to be

156. Cicuta virosa.

1. A flower. 2. Fruit.

gathered for domestic purposes. [The *Cicuta virosa* is common to Europe, and is also found in Canada; but the *Cicuta maculata* (fig. 157) is found in all parts of the United States, growing in wet places, and flowering in July and August.]

The poisonous effects of Conium are paralysis, convulsions, palsies, &c. When inadvertently taken, warm water and oil should be swallowed as soon as possible, in order to produce evacuation of the stomach. And this general remedy may be employed in similar cases, if medical aid be at a distance, or until such can be procured.

Some Persian umbelliferous plants contain a milky juice, which, on eva-

157. Cicuta maculata.

158. Narthex assafœtida.

poration, yields gum resins (Chem. § 142): as familiar examples, may be mentioned assafœtida and gum-ammoniacum [the former of which is obtained from the *Narthex Assafœtida* (fig. 158), which is a native of many parts of Persia].

166. GROSSULACEÆ. *Gooseberry tribe.*—We must not neglect to mention this little tribe of plants which produce our numerous varieties of Gooseberries and Currants.

167. CUCURBITACEÆ. *Gourd tribe.* — This family is distinguished by its huge fruit; and contains the *Melon*, the *Gourd*, the *Cucumber*, the *Bitter Colocynth*, [Cucumis colocynthis, fig. 159,] the *White Briony*, &c.

159. Cucumis colocynthis.

168. CACTACEÆ. *Cactus tribe.*—More than 400 distinct species of this order are found in different parts of America. In outward appearance they depart so widely from the normal form of plants, that they have more the aspect of deformed monsters or mere abortions than of definitely-organised bodies. They consist chiefly of a very fleshy stem, sometimes globular or ovate, with angles and deep depressions, sometimes cylindrical, sometimes triangular, sometimes flat, sometimes lobed; but always armed with dangerous spines or prickles. Their blossoms are of marvellous beauty, and generally very large; and the contrast between these and the grotesque stems further excites our admiration. Some of them grow in the south of Europe. The *C. opuntia* bears edible fruit, and *C. coccenelifera* yields food for the cochineal insect, which produces the beautiful scarlet dye. In hot climates their sap affords a refreshing drink, and they form impassable hedges. *C. speciosus*, *C. flagelliformis*, and *C. phyllanthoides* are cultivated as ornamental plants.

169. MYRTACEÆ. *The Myrtle tribe.*—All these plants secrete a volatile oil, and are found only in warm climates. We frequently, however, cultivate them as ornamental objects, especially the *Myrtle*, whose green, shining leaves, and pure white blossoms appear so lovely on the ringlets of a bride. Among other productions of this family are the *Clove* [the unexpanded flower of *Caryophyllus aromaticus*, fig. 160], the *Cajeput-oil* [which is derived from the *Melaleuca cajuputi*, fig. 161], and the *Allspice*. The *Guavas* and *Rose-apples* are pulpy edible fruits. They are all natives of the East Indies.

170. ROSACEÆ. *The Rose tribe.* — In this order we meet with a great number of well-known and very useful plants. Many diversities and anomalies are indeed prevalent in this family; but we may be convinced by an

160. Caryophyllus aromaticus.

161. Melaleuca cajuputi. 162. Indigofera tinctoria

attentive consideration of their blossoms, that the *Rose*, the queen of flowers, has a just claim to represent her numerous relations, and to lend her name to her immediate descendants. In this place it would be superfluous to praise a flower which has been celebrated by the poets of all nations and of all times. In Persia and other oriental lands the precious attar of roses, or rose-oil, is extracted from its petals.

The species, sub-species, and varieties of the *Rose* amount to thousands, and it is not the only plant of the family which has a numerous progeny. We reckon by hundreds the varieties of *Apples*, *Pears*, *Plums*, and *Cherries*, which have in the progress of horticultural science been amazingly improved as well as increased, though originally derived from the *Crab*, *Wild Pear*, *Sloe*, and *Wild Cherry*. The *Strawberry*, *Raspberry*, &c., have given rise to multitudes of sorts, all more or less prized. The leaves of the *Laurel*, the fruit of the *Almond-tree*, and, in general, the sap of all these plants, contain a small portion of prussic acid. The *Hips* and the *Haws*, the fruits of the Wild Rose and Hawthorn, afford winter-food for the immense flocks of Field-fares which annually visit England in October.

The *Cratægus* forms a thick and durable hedge-fence.

171. LEGUMINIFERÆ. *The Legume-bearing tribe.*—In this extensive order, well characterised either by the papilionaceous blossom (§ 55), or by the leguminous pericarp, or, finally, by the pinnate foliage, a great number of very useful plants are to be met with. Their seeds contain much starch, and are especially rich in nitrogenous fibrin and phosphate of lime, and are on these accounts considered as the most nutritive of all plants.

The *Bean*, the *Pea*, the *Kidney-bean*, with their many varieties, are employed in various ways as articles of human diet. The *Trefoil*, *Sainfoin*, and *Lucern*, are estimable fodder-plants. The Melitot, when dry, has a pleasant smell, like green cheese, and is used to scent snuff.

The *Indigo plant* [Indigofera tinctoria, fig. 162] produces one of the most valuable of colours, celebrated for its beauty and durability. This highly-important plant is chiefly cultivated in India. It is prepared by macerating

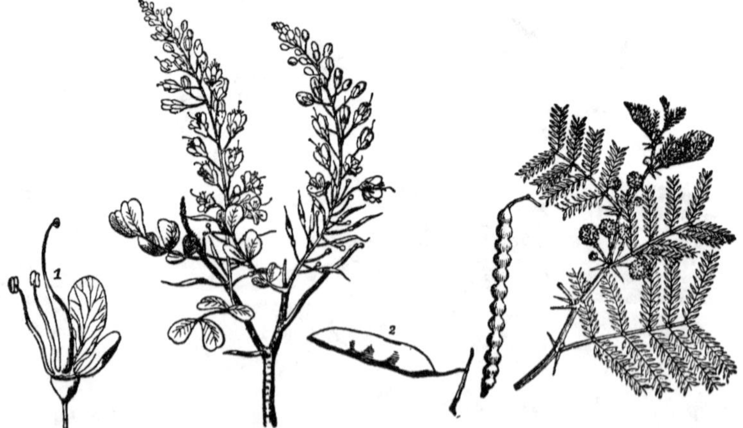

163. Hæmatoxylon campeachianum. 164. Acacia arabica.

the plants, or only their leaves and tops, in water for several days, and then taking off the coloured scum which rises during the operation of steeping:

this process is repeated several times, till all the colouring matter is extracted; the slimy product is then dried and packed for exportation. Other plants of this family, as the *Hæmatoxylon* [or Logwood, *Hæmatoxylon campeachianum*, fig. 163] and the *Cæsalpinia*, yield dye-stuffs: the former, blue, violet, and black; the latter, a red colour.

The number of plants in this family producing medicinal substances is still greater. Among these, we may mention the different sorts of *Mimosa*, which produce *Gum-arabic* (fig. 164), the *Senna-plant* (figs. 165 and 166),

165. Cassia canceolata.
1. Separated flowers. 2. Seed. 3. Legume.

the *St. John's Bread-tree*, the *Tamarind* (fig. 167), the *Liquorice* (fig. 168), the *Gum-tragacanth*, the *Copal*, the *Balsam of Tolu*, and many others.

Finally, many of these plants form the most conspicuous and permanent ornaments of our gardens and pleasure-grounds. Among these may be mentioned the *Laburnum*, the *mytisus*, the lovely *Wisteria*, and many sorts of *Broom*, &c.

172. TEREBINTHACEÆ. *The Sumach tribe.*—This numerous tribe, mostly composed of plants produced in warmer regions than ours, is remarkable for the resinous substances, gums, and oils, which are its chief productions. The *Sumach*, of which there are many species, yields stringent matter, used in tanning and dyeing. It also yields the celebrated varnish. The *Poison-oak*, another individual of the Sumach genus, is reported to be so poisonous that it is dangerous to tarry even in the vicinity of the tree. Its effects, however, are not the same on all persons. The *Walnut-tree* is celebrated for its fruit, and the wood is used in preparing models. During the wars of the French Revolution many Walnut trees were planted in England to supply musket-stocks, which are made of this wood.

173. RHAMNACEÆ. *The Buck-thorn tribe.*—The black pulpy berries of the *Buck-thorn* (Rhammus catharticus), mixed with lime-water and dried, form the vegetable colour called sap-green. The carbon obtained from *R. frangula* is preferred for the manufacture of gunpowder.

174. RUTACEÆ. *The Rue tribe.*—In this there are many sub-tribes

166. Cassia acutifolia.
a. Detached Flower.

167. Tamarindus indico.
a. Set of stamens. b. Style. c. Pod.

168. Glycyrrhiza glabra.

which might almost be considered as distinct orders. Of these, the *Rue* is remarkable for yielding a powerfully aromatic and volatile oil. The *Dictamnus* is an ornamental flower, with rich purple blossoms; sometimes in warm nights the plant emits a sort of phosphorescent light. The *Quassia* (fig. 169), an extraordinarily bitter drug, and the *Guaiacum* (fig. 170), used in medicine, are members of this family.

169. Quassia excelsa.

1. Male flower.
2. Flower expanded.
3. Fertile flower.
4. Drupe.

175. VITACEÆ. *The Vine tribe.*—This tree, with a few other less notable plants, forms a small but highly important order. Though originally a native of Persia and of the East, it has become acclimatised in the whole of southern Europe, and is the common and useful ornament of the cottages in the southern counties of England [and in the Middle and Southern States of this country], where every one may sit under his own vine, if not under his own fig-tree.

176. ACERACEÆ. *The Sycamore tribe.*—A small order, mostly trees, producing light useful timber and fuel-wood. From one of this species *Acer saccharinum*, the Canadians extract large quantities of sugar.

170. Guaiacum officinale.
1. Corolla and stamens. 2. Seeds. 3. Fruit.

177. AURANTIACEÆ. *The Orange tribe.*—These dark-leaved trees of the south of Europe and other sunny lands are remarkable for the abundance of aromatic volatile oil, which they produce in every part of their substance, as well as for their beautiful fruit, which is partly composed of citric acid and partly of sugar. There resides in the rind of the fruit an aromatic bitter material. The principal species are the *common Orange*, the *Lime*, the *Lemon*, and the *Shaddock*, and there are numerous varieties.

178. CAMELLIACEÆ. *The Camellia tribe.*—Besides the Camellia, or Japan Rose, one of the choicest ornaments of the conservatory, this tribe includes the Tea-shrub, a native of the Celestial Empire. The different sorts of tea originate rather in the season at which the leaves are plucked off, and in the manner in which they are prepared, than in any specific difference in the shrubs on which this article is produced. Tea as well as coffee contains a crystallisable matter. A Russian ambassador first introduced tea from China about the beginning of the 17th century. Its annual consumption is now reckoned at 700 millions of pounds.

179. BYTTNERIACEÆ. *Cocoa-tree tribe.*—The regions of Mexico produce the plants from which the well-known cocoa of commerce is obtained; a substance from which chocolate is prepared. [These plants belong to the genus *Theobroma*, which are all small trees, one of whose species is shown in fig. 171.] This contains, like coffee and tea, as above mentioned, a crystallisable product, [*theobromine.*]

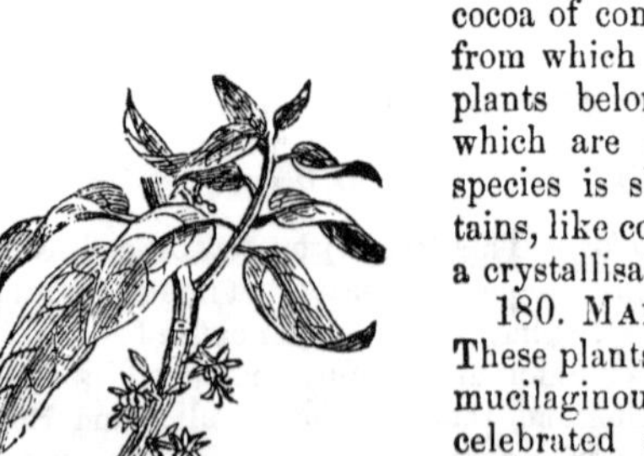

171. Theobroma cacao.

180. MALVACEÆ. *The Mallow tribe.*—These plants produce abundance of a viscid mucilaginous material, and have been long celebrated as totally destitute of all unwholesome qualities. Emollient fomentations are prepared from the roots of *Althæa*, *Malva*, &c.

One of the most important plants of this order is the *Cotton-plant* (Gossypium), whose parent land is Africa, whence it has been transferred to America and to the East Indies: it is also planted and thrives in the south of Europe. The wool is produced in the carpels, just as a similar substance is formed in the catkins of *Poplar*, *Willow*, &c., and in the capsules of *Epilobium* (French-willow herb). This wool is manufactured into stuffs of infinite variety, both in texture and colour, and supplies more clothing than all other vestiary materials put together; and its cultivation and fabrication form the employment of millions of the human race, aided by the most ingenious machinery that has ever been invented.

181. Linaceæ. *The Flax tribe.*—This order, next to the one above described, is the most important, as supplying a greater amount of clothing material than any other family of the vegetable kingdom, with the above exception. Its greater tenacity and absorbency, as well as its applicability to the manufacture of paper, render it more valuable on the whole than cotton.

182. Caryophyllaceæ. *The Pink tribe.*—In all gardens we meet the *Pink*, *Carnation*, and several *Silenes*. The *Soap-wort plant* (Saponaria), when its leaves are bruised or crushed, makes a lather with water, and was formerly used for the same purposes as soap. The *Corn-cockle* (Githago) also belongs to this order.

183. Violaceæ. *The Violet tribe.*—This small order is composed chiefly of the numerous species of the genus *Viola*, to which the *Sweet-scented Violet* and the *V. tricolor*, which has recently acquired much celebrity as a florist's flower, belong. *Field Violet* (V. arvensis) is a common application in the case of cuticular or skin diseases; and the roots of many are emetic. The other plants related to this genus are unimportant.

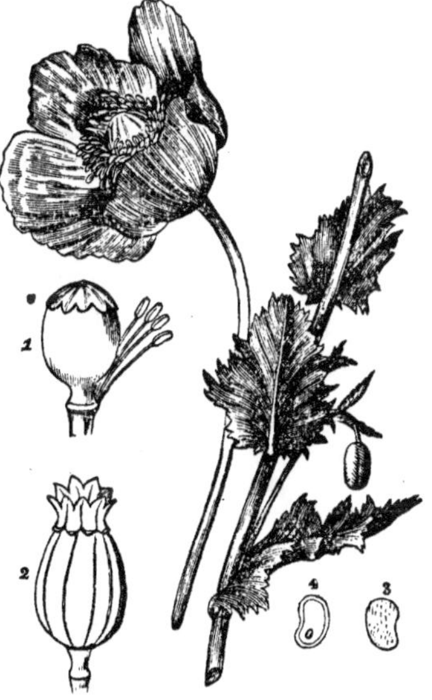

172. Papaver somniferum.
1. Capsule of P. officinale. 2. Do. of P. somniferum. 3, 4. Seeds.

184. Cruciferæ. *The Cruciferous tribe.*—This is one of the most numerous and distinct families of the vegetable kingdom. It is wholly included in the Linnæan class Tetradynamia, having six stamens, four long and two short. The petals are four, with a cruciate arrangement, and the fruit is either a pod (silique), or a pouch (silicle). All parts of these plants secrete a stimulating, sulphurous, volatile oil; and their seeds are especially oleaginous. Some of them, as the Horse-radish and Mustard, are very hot and acrid; their acridity, when dispersed by cultivation, renders them nutritious and succulent. The *Cabbage*, *Cauliflower*, *Brocoli*, *Sea-kale*, *Turnip*, *Radish*, &c., are examples The *Woad* (Isatis tinctoria) is employed in the preparation of a dye-stuff

similar to indigo. With this plant it is supposed that the ancient Britons stained their naked bodies — *quo hostibus terribiliores essent,* as Cæsar relates.

185. PAPAVERACEÆ. *The Poppy tribe.*—The most important plant of this family is the *common Poppy* (Papaver somniferum, fig. 172), which yields a juice that, when inspissated and dried, becomes opium. For this purpose the plant is widely cultivated in Turkey and in the East Indies. The juice of the Poppy is narcotic and poisonous; it is used by the Orientals as an intoxicating medium, and has injurious consequences. Opium is a mixture of caoutchouc, resin, and several vegetable acids and bases, of which morphine (Chem. § 148) is the most important.

173. Helleborus niger.

The *Field Poppy* and two or three kindred species grow commonly in our corn-fields, and *Celandine* by the road-sides, lanes, &c., mostly near habitations

186. NYMPHÆACEÆ. *The Water-lily tribe.*—We mention the *White Water-lily* as the ornament of our lakes, ponds, and stagnant waters, and as nearly related to the celebrated *Lotus* of the river Nile, the seeds and roots of which are eatable, and the same flower is often adopted as the memorial or symbol of the riches and fertility of Egypt. The most magnificent of all plants whatever is, perhaps, the *Guiana Water-lily* (Victoria regia), with its white and rosy blossoms, and its leaves, which are 4 feet in diameter and 15 feet in circumference.

174. Aconitum napellus.

187. RANUNCULACEÆ. *The Crowfoot tribe.*—The numerous plants of this order belong mostly to the class Polyandria. They are all more or less acrid, and some are poisonous.

The most remarkable and common plants of the order are the *Butter-cups, King-cups*, &c., the *black* (fig. 173) *and green Hellebores*, the *Hepatica*, an early flowering plant, and the *Eranthis*, which appears with the *Snow-drop;* the *Anemone*, which blossoms in all seasons, the *Aconite*, or *Wolf's-bane* (fig. 174), the *Larkspur*, the *Columbine*, the *Nigella*, or *Jack-in-the-Green*, and the *gorgeous Peony*. The many eminently beautiful species of *Clematis*, most of them climbing plants, belong also to this order.

CONCLUSION.

The Vegetable Kingdom is divided into about 300 families, of which, in the foregoing outline, we have enumerated and partly described 69. There are many of the unnoticed orders, however, of no less botanical interest than those families which we have selected as illustrative of our subject. We have, however, preferred such plants as are either well known and most readily procurable, or such as are best adapted for the exemplification of the science. Others are important on account of their relation to mankind, and consequently merited special notice. Sometimes a section of an order has been quoted, in order that a particularly important plant might be introduced to the reader's notice, when it was inexpedient to notice the order at large.

Our limited space, and the elementary objects of the work itself, precluded all reference to changes of nomenclature and natural sequences of the orders in the systematic arrangement. These and all other exclusively botanical details, necessary for such as desire to be more profoundly acquainted with the science, can be obtained by consulting the works we have recommended at page 479.

Java Upas, or Poison-Tree.

ZOOLOGY.

1. Zoology is that branch of natural science which treats of those terrestrial beings or objects which are endowed with the capability of self-nourishment, of sensation, and of external spontaneous movement. Such objects are named *animals*, and the science which describes their organisation, &c., is called *Zoology*.

Animals are beings furnished with distinct and different parts, limbs, or members, viz., with every appurtenance requisite for the fulfilment of the object of their creation, as well as for their own individual preservation and reproduction; and of these they cannot be deprived without prejudice to their symmetry, health, or even to their existence. In this they are distinguished from plants, most of which can be pruned or lopped without injury, many with advantage to their health and beauty. In our section on Botany, we have already described these dissimilar parts as *organs*, and have shown that they do not exist in the mineral kingdom.

Animals are endowed with the power of motion, which is effected by changing the position of their motive organs, and this they do spontaneously, and independent of those accidental, external influences, which produce motion in certain plants, as in the *Sensitive Plant*, Mimosa pudica, Hedysarum gyrans, &c., which, on the slightest touch, fold up their leaflets and suffer their branches to droop down by their sides, as if really actuated by a voluntary impulse. With the exception of this and similar motions already noticed, plants are endowed only with an inward movement of their fluids, viz., the ascent and descent of the sap.

2. A further and more important distinguishing characteristic of the animal is its *faculty of sensation*. It has been already shown that every animal

is excited by a natural impulse to place itself in the most favourable circumstances for fulfilling the end and conditions of its being. Besides this, every external interference injurious to its life or comfort is speedily and keenly felt, and often avoided or resisted. The animal, unlike the plant, does not receive all kinds of treatment with patient endurance, but always seeks the means either of escape or of resistance, and sometimes, indeed, of retaliation.

The percipient capacity of animals is also susceptible of considerable enlargement by domestication or intercourse with the human race. It is well known that their susceptibility and perceptibility can be improved so far that they are able to comprehend precisely the motions, the tone, and even the looks of their owners, and readily comport themselves accordingly.

The capability of any animal of assuming a deportment corresponding to external relations and circumstances we designate by the term *will*, and hence the movements of animals are said to be *voluntary* or *spontaneous*.

3. The relative perfection of an animal is in proportion to the number and development of its organs. There are animals whose whole body consists of one single organ, and these, consequently, bear the strongest analogy to the plant-cell; others, on the contrary, are composed of a great number of very distinct, dissimilar organs.

Hence a knowledge of all the animal organs is necessary for the understanding of their individual organisation; and as in the human body the combination and development of the individual organs are the most complete, an acquaintance with human anatomy will materially assist the student of animal organography in general, by affording him a standard with which he may compare the structure and functions of analogous parts in animals of an inferior grade.

The proximity of our own bodies, and our familiarity with their external organisation, but, above all, our more intimate acquaintance with the internal springs of all our activities, supply the means of acquiring, with greater facility and precision, a more correct comprehension of the animal economy than can possibly be obtained by studying the structure of animals in general. Therefore, we commence with the study of the anatomy and physiology of the human body; and in our comparison of the same with the structure of the bodies of inferior animals, we advance from a knowledge of the known to the unknown.

4. The entire province of Zoology forms two principal divisions. The first treats of animal organs and their functions; the second treats of the internal and external characteristics of animals, their nomenclature and description.

I. ORGANS AND THEIR FUNCTIONS.

ANATOMY AND PHYSIOLOGY.

5. The different parts of the human body are obviously diverse in *form* and *substance*, in *situation*, and in *functional purposes*. In reference to form and material, we evidently perceive that the body consists partly of fluid and partly of solid substances. The fluids are either absorbed or are surrounded by the solid parts, and receive different names, corresponding to their properties, as will be shown hereafter.

The solid portions of the animal body are in general distinguished by the term *tissue*, although, in most cases, they do not possess even a remote similarity to what is generally understood by this term.

6. In the investigation of the internal structure of plants, the microscope shows us that their internal organisation originates in modifications and alterations of the simple cell, and that all their simple organs are referable to this type. A similar analogy is not prevalent in the animal body; on the contrary, microscopic analysis proves that animal tissues are composed of at least four different primary forms, which are apparent whether they be viewed individually or collectively, and between which there is no transition-state perceptible, as is the case in the modifications of the cellular into the vascular tissue in plants (Botany, § 12). This greater multifariousness of primary forms is proof of the higher development of animals.

The *cellular tissue*, more properly spongy parenchymatous matter, *muscular fibre*, *nervous fibre*, and the *osseous system*, or bony tissues, are generally distinguished as the elementary forms and constituents of the more highly developed animal body.

7. Thus one part of the animal body is cellular, consisting of perfectly-enclosed microscopic vesicles, containing various kinds of fluids. These cells are present in the cuticle or epidermis, and in the finer pellicle composing the mucous membrane; and their walls are formed of horny or cuticular substance. We may regard the fat as an aggregation of albuminous cells, which are filled with an oleaginous substance. When these cells contain coloured particles, they form the pigmentary matter upon which the different coloured skins of animals depend.

Cellular tissue is also found among dissimilar masses of different tissues, as in the gristly or cartilaginous parts of many bones, &c.

Another series of tissues consists of very fine cylindrical filaments, or fibres, which are found in the mucous membranes, and the capsular ligaments of joints, &c.

8. The *muscles*, or flesh, of animals, consist of flattish threads, or fibres, which are divided into two classes. The first class is distinguished by transverse lines, or striæ, upon the surface; the other by roundish or elongated formations, called nuclei. The former are found in the red muscles of the trunk, limbs, and heart; the latter in the bladder and in the membranous investments of the alimentary canal.

9. The *nerves* and the whitish substance forming the brain and the spinal chord, contain another kind of tissue or fibre, within which an oily matter is enclosed in a homogenous, pellucid membrane. Cellular forms of a peculiar kind, called *ganglia*, or *ganglionic centres*, appear in the gray-coloured mass of the nervous system.

10. The *bones* of animals consist of a laminated substance, in which the spindle-shaped, osseous particles are imbedded. A number of reticulated passages, traversing the bone, and filled with marrow, are always present. The smallest portion of the dental mass, viz., the root, or fang, of the tooth, exhibits the same structure as the other bones. The interior solid matter of the tooth consists of a uniform or fibrous mass, penetrated by a system of microscopic tubes or channels, called the dental channels. The enamel of the tooth consists of a very dense coating of prismatic fibres, arranged in a closely-compacted form.

11. The *local relation* of organs in the body is, for the sake of convenience in describing and classifying them, distinguished by the following terms, viz., external and internal, superior, inferior, anterior, posterior, &c.

By *superior* and *inferior* we signify higher or lower in respect to the *summit of the head;* by *anterior* and *posterior* we denote the situation of the parts as nearer to the fore or hinder surface of the body. *Inner* and *outer*, the relation of any given part to an assumed line bisecting the body into lateral halves, passing through the middle of the head and trunk, and continued between the inferior extremities; *inner* denotes an approach to *outer* a removal from, this median line. *External* and *internal* are generally used in describing cavities.

The great framework of the body is called the *trunk;* and, besides the neck and head, four members or limbs proceed from its extremities.

The *head* is distinguished from the trunk as being the superior part of man and the anterior in the beast. In the animal kingdom, we observe striking diversities in the number of limbs, sometimes these being very numerous, and frequently altogether absent.

In the trunk, we distinguish the upper part as the *thorax*, and the lower part as the *abdomen.* Both these cavities, containing certain organs known by the name of *viscera*, are so completely filled as to leave no empty space.

The thorax is separated from the abdomen by a strong muscle called the *diaphragm;* in the former are placed the *lungs*, with air-cells, and the *heart*, with the principal arteries; in the latter are the alimentary or digestive organs, viz., the *stomach*, with the *intestines*, the *liver*, the *spleen*, the *kidneys*, and the *bladder*.

12. The organs are classified neither by their form nor by their position in the body, but solely by their functions; consequently they are divisible into *organs of motion*, *organs of nutrition* or *digestion*, and *organs of sensation.*

Inasmuch as many organs of different kinds co-operate in the performance of a common function, and are hence to be treated as mutually dependent upon each other, they are, therefore called a system; for example, we employ the terms osseous system, alimentary system, circulatory system, generative system, &c.

1. ORGANS OF MOTION.

13. The organs destined for movement are — 1st, the *bones;* 2nd, the *muscles;* 3rd, the *nerves.* These different systems are never isolated, but always in mutual combination and reciprocal operation. They form the motive system, which is not found in plants.

1. THE BONES.

14. The bones constitute the only truly solid portions of the body, being the basis of the muscular and tegumentary systems, affording the means of attachment to the softer parts, and by their solidity maintaining those definite and distinct forms which distinguish the higher classes of animals. The bones also serve to protect the most delicate and sensitive of our bodily organs, forming, as it were, a case for the brain, a cavity for the heart and lungs, and a canal for the spinal cord.

The skeleton of an animal is an anatomical preparation of all the bones which constituted its framework; and as every part external to the bones is only to be regarded as a filling-up or rounding-off the cavities and sharp outlines of the osseous structure, this latter is considered, both on account of its durability and as affording the most permanent characteristics, to be the first and most important branch of anatomy. It is only by studying the internal structure of animals that we obtain any real acquaintance with their nature and economy, just as we judge of the stability of a roof by its interior construction, rather than by the material or form of its exterior covering.

15. The bones are composed of layers of animal tissue, in which phosphate and carbonate of lime are deposited (Chem. § 50). In 100 lbs. of fresh bones there are 33 lbs of tissue, which may be extracted as glue or gelatin by boiling. The rest consists of 58 lbs. of phosphate of lime and 9 lbs. of carbonate of lime. The bones of cartilaginous fishes, and also certain parts of bones generally, contain less lime and frequently no trace of this material. Such bones, or parts of bones, are consequently soft, and are named *cartilage*, or gristle. The hardest of all the osseous formations, viz., the teeth, are very rich in lime.

The employment of bones in the preparation of glue, bone-black, phosphorus, &c., has been already explained in Chem. §§ 44, 155, and in Botany, § 97.

The entire osseous system is divided into bones of the trunk, bones of the limbs, and bones of the head (see fig. 3, p. 520).

a. Bones of the Trunk.

16. The most important part of the trunk is the *vertebral column*, which is composed of a series of small bones, called *vertebræ*, amounting in the human skeleton to 33; viz., 7 *cervical* (vertebræ of the neck), 12 *dorsal* (vertebræ of the back), 5 *lumbar* (vertebræ of the loins), 5 *sacral*, which subsequently unite to form the sacrum, 4 *coccygial*, which are also united in the adult.

The spine, or vertebral column, consisting of the above-mentioned bones, is situated in the direction of the axial line of the body. The distinct bones of this organ are all more or less firmly jointed together, hence the spine is flexible, a property it could not possess if composed of but one bone. The individual vertebræ have an articulating surface, *a*, fig. 2, where they come in contact with each other, and behind this the spinous process *b*, and the transverse processes *c;* and in the centre of each vertebræ, where these spinous processes root, is the opening or spinal canal, by which the nervous chord is enclosed, protected, and conveyed along the spine.

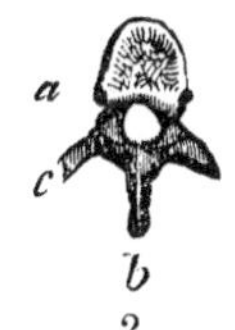

2.

Many animals have fewer vertebral bones than man, and *vice versa*. Serpents have 150, and some even a larger number than this.

17. The *ribs* are attached in pairs to the bodies and transverse processes of the twelve dorsal vertebræ; consequently there are twenty-four ribs in the human skeleton. The seven upper pairs are longer, and are named the true or pectoral ribs, which unite the vertebral column with the sternum; the five lower pairs are shorter, and hence named the short ribs.

Frontal bone.
Parietal bone.
Orbit
Temporal bone.
Lower jaw
Cervical vertebræ
Clavicle.
Scapula
Humerus
Lumbar vertebræ
Ilium
Ilium.
Ulna
Radius
Carpus
Metacarpus
Phalanges
Femur
Patella.
Tibia
Fibula
Tarsus.
Metatarsus.
Phalanges.

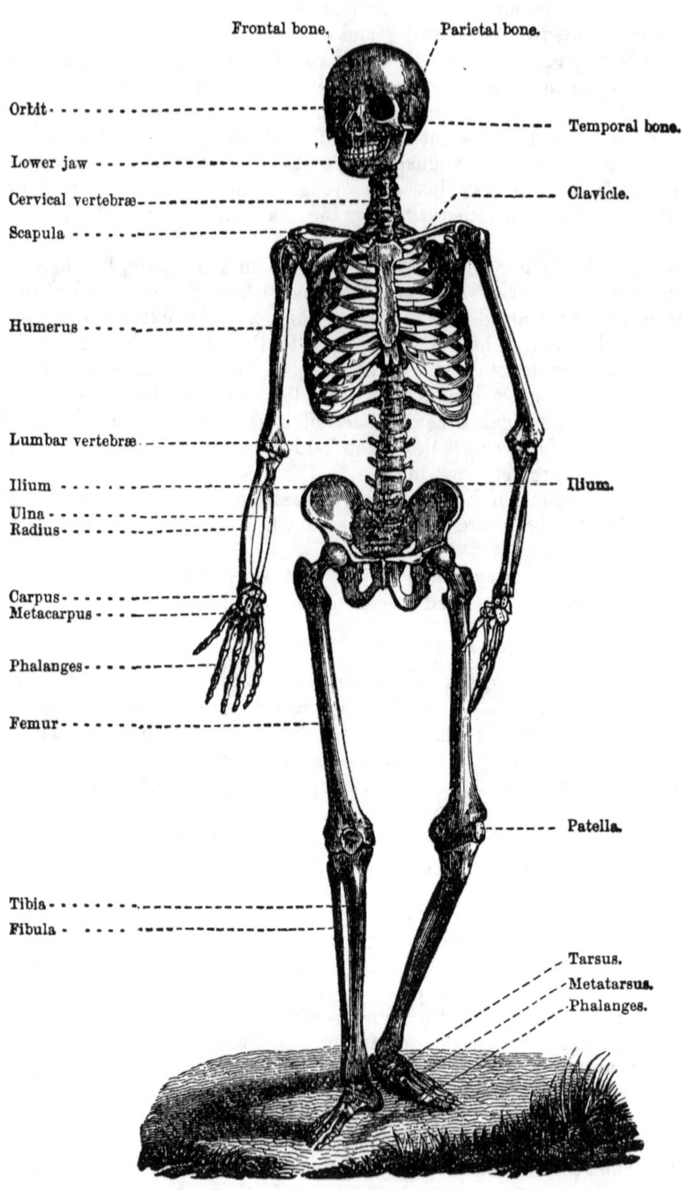

3.

The ribs, as above mentioned, are united anteriorly with a long flat bone, called the *breast-bone* (sternum), and thus the system of the *thorax*, or chest, is completely enclosed.

b. Bones of the Limbs.

18. The limbs are always arranged in pairs, and each individual limb of the pair in every respect exactly corresponds to the other. They are divided into superior and inferior in men, whose posture is erect, and into anterior and posterior in animals, whose posture is horizontal.

The bones of the upper limbs are—

The scapula, or *blade-bone*, which is a large triangular flat bone of considerable breadth lying on the back, and forming the posterior part of the shoulder, attached by an articular surface to the clavicle (*collar-bone*), which connects the blade-bone with the sternum, and with which it is united.

The scapula is attached to the humerus (upper arm-bone), by a ball and socket-joint (a concave articulating surface, fitted for the reception of the convex head of the *humerus*).

The fore-arm is formed of two bones; the one situated in the direction of the thumb, viz., the anterior or outer bone, is named *radius*, and the other, in the direction of the little finger, viz., the posterior or inner bone, *ulna*.

The *hand* is composed of three parts, viz., the *wrist* (carpus), the *hand* (metacarpus), and the *fingers* (phalanges).

The *wrist* is formed of eight small cube-shaped bones, arranged closely together in two series. By these little bones the hand is capable of bearing a great strain, and of moving with ease and celerity. These carpal bones resist, with comparatively little injury, violent and sudden collision; for example, the injurious effects of a fall are much lessened by falling on the hands.

The *hand* is composed of five tolerably long and equal bones.

The *fingers* have three bones, viz., one for each joint, and the thumb two.

On the whole, there are in both arms, with the hands, sixty-four individual or distinct bones.

19. The bones of the lower or inferior limbs have in number, form, and situation, a great analogy to those of the superior limbs. The pelvis, a large, somewhat basin-shaped bone, united with the lower vertebral bone (os sacrum), forms the upper portion of the lower limbs.

The pelvis is composed of three separate bones, which have united, viz., the *hip-bone* (os ilii), the *sitting-bone* (os ischii), and the *anterior-bone* (os pubis), which corresponds to the collar-bone.

At the connective point of these three bones there is a deep concave articulating surface, into which the head of the thigh-bone is inserted, which is the longest bone of the human body. At the lower end of the thigh-bone there lies, in front of the knee-joint, anteriorly, a small, flat, triangular bone, called the *knee-cap*, or patella. The upper end of the tibia is articulated by the knee-joint with the lower end of the femur; the fibula is joined to the tibia only, and has no connection with the femur, but assists at its lower end in forming the ankle-joint.

The foot is composed of seven bones; the *centre bone* (astragalus) is articulated to the lower end of the tibia, and behind and beneath this is situated the *bone of the heel* (os calcis), in front of which one single navicular bone and four other tarsal bones are arranged.

The *metatarsal bones* and the *bones of the toes*, in number and situation, correspond with the bones of the hand.

Since the pelvis is a union of three bones, the osseous system of the lower members consists in the whole of only sixty-one separate bones.

c. Bones of the Head.

20. The bones of the head are more complicated, on account of the irregularities in their shape and arrangements. They originally consist of a large number, but after a certain period in the life of the individual many of them become connected together.

These bones are divided into those of the head and face: the first are the cranial bones, the latter the facial or maxillary bones. In the human subject the cranium is the upper, and the jaws or maxillæ are the lower part of the system.

21. The *brain-case* posteriorly is formed by the occiput, which rests on the first bone of the vertebral column; it is provided with a protuberance, and, in many animals with a crest. In this bone is the *aperture* (foramen) which affords a passage for the spinal chord, which here passes out of the cavity of the skull. To the skull also belong the *frontal, parietal,* and *temporal bones,* united by suture, and enclosing the brain.

The following bones are united to the above-mentioned, and contribute to the structure of the internal part of the head, viz., the *sphenoid,* with its winged processes, the *ethmoid,* the *vomer,* the *lachrymal,* and the *nasal* bones, which form the foundation of the nose.

22. In man the *jaws* form the lower part of the head, in other animals, the forepart of the same. They are divided into the upper and under jaw, or maxillary bones. The *superior maxillary bone,* or upper jaw, is composed of three parts, which are united, viz., the anterior portion, which has two incisor teeth, and the two processes with which it coheres, and which have one canine tooth and five other teeth each. The upper jaw is formed by the two superior maxillary bones, united in the centre by suture.

The *under* or *lower jaw* in the human subject is formed of one piece, connected by a joint to the temporal bone beneath each ear. In birds, fishes. and reptiles, this bone is not jointed, but joined to the temporal bone. In insects the lower jaw and temporal bones are quite separate, and act like a pair of tongs.

23. The *teeth* are placed in hollow cavities of the jaws, which they exactly fit. Their number is thirty-two, being sixteen in each jaw. These dental organs are divided into four sorts, viz., two incisors, one canine tooth, two anterior and three posterior molar or grinding teeth on each side.

The upper and free portion of the tooth is called the *crown,* the under parts are the *neck* and the *roots.* The front teeth have a simple, the back teeth a two-, three-, or four-fanged root.

The substance of the teeth is harder than that of the rest of the bones, and the exterior part, or *enamel,* is the hardest. In many animals of the herbivorous families this forms only a thin layer over the softer part of the tooth, and is pretty rapidly worn away. The *enamel* of the molar or grinding teeth of many quadrupeds is very durable, being indigitated into the substance of the tooth, or imbedded in a *cement,* not found in simpler forms of these organs.

Every tooth at the lower extremity of the root is furnished with a small opening, through which a blood-vessel and a nerve pass, supplying nutriment and sensibility to the tooth.

The perfect development of the teeth is only accomplished at a comparatively late period in the life of the animal; in some not till mature age. The first teeth fall out between the sixth and tenth year, and are changed; but if the second teeth are lost, they are never replaced.

All animals do not possess the above-named sorts of teeth, for example many want the molars or grinders. The canine teeth are often enormously enlarged, and in this condition are named the fangs or tusks. Teeth form the most important marks whereby the higher orders of the mammals are distinguished, indicating with certainty both the natural economy of the animal, and also its age, size, and other particulars.

24. The total number of bones in the skeleton of man, exclusive of the teeth, is 207. The number is greater in the undeveloped infant, whose skeleton is partly composed of cartilage, which is ossified only at a subsequent period of its life. The dry skeleton of an adult, freed from fatty and other matters, weighs from 9 lbs. to 12 lbs., and, consequently, constitutes from 1-16th to 1-17th of the entire weight of the body, which at an average is about 137 lbs.

25. Only in the more highly-developed forms of animal life do we find bones or cartilage enclosing a brain and spinal chord, hence the presence of a vertebral column is a distinguishing characteristic; and by the presence or absence of this organ the whole animal kingdom is divided into two principal groups, viz., the vertebrata and invertebrata—the vertebrate and the invertebrate animals; to the first belong the *mammals* (mammalia), *birds* (aves), *fishes* (pisces), and *reptiles* (reptilia); to the second the *crustaceous animals* (crustacea), *insects* (insecta), *worms*, *polypi*, &c. (annulata).

26. The bones are covered with a fine, mostly very susceptible, membrane called *periosteum*. Very few nerves are found in the bones, with the exception of the teeth. They are, however, traversed by a series of very minute blood-vessels, which supply them with nutriment. Within they are generally less dense than towards the surface. They are frequently porous, or even quite hollow, and in the latter case are filled with a fatty substance called *marrow*.

The calcareous matter in the bone increases with age, and the marrowy substance decreases, so that at a later period of life the bone becomes brittle and more easily fractured than at an earlier period. The bones of birds are nearly all hollow, whereby great strength is combined with the least possible weight. The concussion of the bones against each other is prevented by the gristly, very smooth, elastic substance which lines every part of the joint, both in the joints adapted for motion, as the shoulder-joint, &c., and also in the immoveable, or partially moveable joints, as those connecting the vertebræ; besides this cartilaginous ligament, by which they are united and held in their place, they are supplied with an oleaginous substance called the synovia, whereby the motions of the joint are promoted and the friction altogether prevented.

2. THE MUSCLES.

27. We have already in § 8 stated that the muscles are composed of the union of very fine fibres, which possess the power of contraction, or of

shortening themselves. In 100 lbs. by weight of dried muscle we find the following chemical substances: 54 lbs. of carbon, 7 lbs. hydrogen, 21 lbs. oxygen, 15 lbs. nitrogen, with minute quantities of sulphur, phosphorus, and alkalies (1·4 per cent). The fresh muscle contains 77 per cent. of water. The muscles of the higher reptilia, birds, and mammiferous animals are red, those of fish are white. In the invertebrata the muscles are only imperfectly developed, but are present in some form or other even in the lowest of these. In common language, the muscular part of animals is called *flesh*.

28. The muscles completely invest the bones, which, except the teeth, are never visible in the living subject. As a general rule a muscle is thickened in its middle, and attenuated at each end, and enclosed in a peculiar membrance which separates it from the other muscles which are in contiguity with it.

The thin part of the muscle is remarkably tough. It has various names as *tendon*, *sinew*, &c., and is always attached to the bone. The muscles are either covered by a more or less thick layer of fat, or immediately by the skin. In the muscular system there are numerous blood vessels which supply nourishment to the muscles; there are, besides, many nerves of motion and sensation lodged in the same organs, so that the injury of a muscle is always attended with acute pain.

The union of the muscles with the bones is so arranged that one muscle is always attached between two bones. For example, the brachial muscle is attached by its upper end to the humerus, and running to the inner side of the arm towards a process of the ulna, or inner bone of the fore-arm, is fastened to it by its lower end. When this muscle is thickened in the middle by its contractile power, the lower part of the arm is bent upwards. The length and power of the muscles are very different.

Every movement is accomplished by means of some muscle whose function it is to produce this motion, and sometimes several muscles contribute to the production of one motion. Hence the dividing of a muscle either perfectly arrests motion, or weakens it, or changes its direction. If, by the action of a muscle, any limb or part of the body has its position changed, the same muscle cannot restore it to its former position; but, for this purpose, there is a second muscle present, which acts in exactly the opposite direction. Hence the muscles are divided into flexor or bending, and extensor or extending muscles. The former pass down in front of the joint, the latter behind it.

29. From what has been advanced, it is evident that the number of the muscles is considerable, and also that they are arranged in pairs. The number of pairs of muscles in the human body is about 238. The numbering and describing the muscles belong to anatomy, and form a special branch of that science which is termed Myology.

The expanded muscle, provided for the movement of the skin in animals, is one of peculiar structure and mechanical interest. In many animals, as the hedge-hog and the porcupine for example, the muscular arrangement for raising the spines or quills is very powerful, and invests the greater part of the body. We have an example of this organ in the human subject, *i. e.* in that muscle by which the skin of the head is moveable.

3. NERVES.

30. The matter of which the nerves are composed, as already stated in § 9, is very peculiar, both in form and composition. It has the appearance of a white, caseous, *marrowy substance.* In several parts it is present in large masses, and there it is surrounded by a gray substance; in other parts it assumes the form of threads or chords, which are mostly reticulated.

Under the microscope a mass of nerves presents the appearance of a gray and white fatty or albuminous substance. One hundred parts by weight contain 66 parts of carbon, 10 of hydrogen, 19 of oxygen, 2 of nitrogen, and 0·9 parts of phosphorus. This nervous substance is distinguished from all other corporeal substances by the large proportion of phosphorus which it contains.

31. The *brain* constitutes the great nervous mass, which is enclosed on all sides by the very solid bones of the *skull* (cranium), and immediately below this it is further protected by the hard *brain-membrane* (dura mater). Its form is hemispherical, and its magnitude is nearly that of the upper part of the head: it is divided into two halves by a deep section. The surface is very unequal, occasioned by the irregularities of its folds, which are called *cerebral convolutions,* and which occasion numerous eminences and corresponding depressions. That portion of the brain, which occupies the anterior and upper part of the skull, is termed the *brain* (cerebrum), and is separated by a deep fissure from the *little brain* (cerebellum), which is lodged in the posterior part of the cranial cavity. Under this latter, the substance of the brain is continued into the *medulla oblongata,* which through the *foramen magnum,* formed by the occipital bone and its processes, connects the spinal chord with the nervous substance of the brain. The weight of the human brain is about 2½ lbs., and that of the whole of the nerves together amounts to 3 lbs. The cerebral organ is nourished by an arterial system dispersed all over it.

32. In all directions from the cerebrum and spinal chord proceed the nerves, which are fine white filaments, arranged at their origin in bundles, gradually diverging, separating, and ramifying the further they proceed from the original source or centre. In their course they appear to receive branches, and to unite with each other so as to form a kind of net-work. Their dispersion is so general that a slight puncture in any part of the skin touches a nerve, which instantly communicates to the sensorium the sensation of pain. All parts of the body that possess feeling owe this faculty to the presence of the nerves.

33. The nerves are divided into two systems, according to the duties they have to perform in the animal economy; firstly, into such as serve the purposes of sensation and motion, viz., nerves of sense and nerves of motion; and, secondly, vital and nutritive nerves. The first system originates posteriorly in the brain and spinal chord, whence they are diffused over the body from within the vertebral column, while the other system is disposed anteriorly, and external to the vertebræ, and these are appropriated to the viscera.

a. Nerves of Sensation and Motion.

34. In enumerating and describing the nerves the chief only are noticed. In the diagram, fig. 3, they are represented as cut off at a short distance

from their main source. They originate either in the brain, *a*, or proceed from the elongated cerebral process, *f'*, or from the spinal marrow, *f*. No nerve originates in the cerebellum, *e*. The nerves, like the muscles, are always present in pairs.

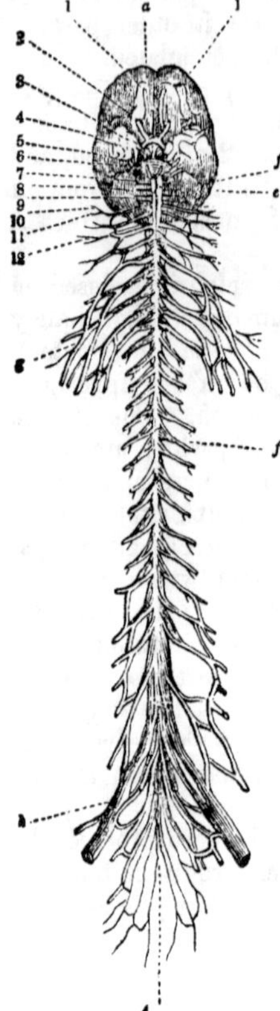

The *cerebral nerves* consist of twelve pairs,* which in fig. 3 are indicated by corresponding numbers. They are — 1. The olfactory nerves. 2. The optic nerves. 3. The motor nerves of the eye. 4. The pathetic nerves, for turning up the eye. 5. The trigeminal nerves, divided into three branches, which are again subdivided into branches, the most remarkable of which are the lachrymal nerves, the nerves of the palate and teeth, and the gustatory nerves, which bestow the sense of taste upon the tongue. 6. The abducent nerves to the outer muscle of the eye. 7. The facial nerves. 8. The auditory nerves.

The four remaining nerves, which originate in the medulla oblongata, are only distributed partially in the head, but send out branches to the other parts of the body, viz., to the viscera, and, in particular, to the stomach and intestines. Many remarkable phenomena are explicable hereby; as, for example, the presence of worms in the intestines is inferred from the tickling sensation in the nostrils; and headache is one of the usual concomitants of a derangement of the digestive organs.

The *spinal nerves* amount to thirty pairs, of which eight are cervical, twelve dorsal, five lumbar, and five sacral, corresponding to the divisions of the vertebral column.

The fifth to the eighth cervical nerves form a ramified system, or plexus, *g*, fig. 4, in which the nerves of the arm originate. The five lumbar nerves in like manner, *h*, form the great femoral system of nerves from which the nerves of the lower members of the body proceed.

b. Nerves of the Viscera.

Nervous System of the Alimentary, Respiratory, and Circulatory Organs.

35. All the spinal nerves transmit branches anteriorly from the vertebral column to supply the nervous system of the viscera. These are united into plexuses, and receive besides several branches from the cerebral nerves that supply the viscera, viz. the eighth pair. There are also two long nervous trunks on the anterior part of the vertebral column, extending from the head to the extremity of the spine, forming *ganglia* at regular distances, from which, as from a centre, nerves branch out to every part of the viscera.

---

* The arrangement here adopted of the nerves differs from that of the English anatomists who make but nine pairs of cerebral nerves.—Ed.

Among these nervous centres, or ganglia, the following are most important, viz., the upper and lower cervical, the thoracic or pectoral, the large and small splanchnic nerves, the solar and the renal plexuses.

It is a remarkable characteristic of the nerves that belong to the nutritive or *digestive* system that they do not ramify with countless divarications as the nerves of sensation and motion do, but that they all proceed in different directions from ganglia, or nervous centres, and are again united in other ganglia or plexuses, and in this manner form a sort of reticulated system.

Such nervous centres have received the name of *ganglia*, and therefore the whole system of these nerves has been termed the *gangliar system*.

It is further remarkable that these visceral nerves are the cause of motions and functions, which are performed independently of our will: the respiratory, the digestive, and the circulatory processes are functional operations not only performed independently of us, but even while we are asleep and unconscious of any such activities being in operation at all. Although the stomach, the intestines, and the arteries and veins are all provided with numerous nerves, yet we are not conscious of the food in the former, nor its motion in the intestines, nor even of the circulation of the blood in the arteries and veins. The case, however, is very different in those parts of the body provided with sensitive and motive nerves, which not only perform their duties as quick as lightning, but through their instrumentality we are immediately conscious of the slightest external impressions.

36. The nervous system is pretty equally developed in the mammiferæ, birds, reptiles, and fishes. In insects nervous centres or ganglia are arranged longitudinally in their bodies, sending out lateral nerves (fig. 4). Even in the molluscous animals a nervous system is perceptible. No animal is altogether without a nervous system. Traces of nerves are even discernible in the gelatinous polypi.

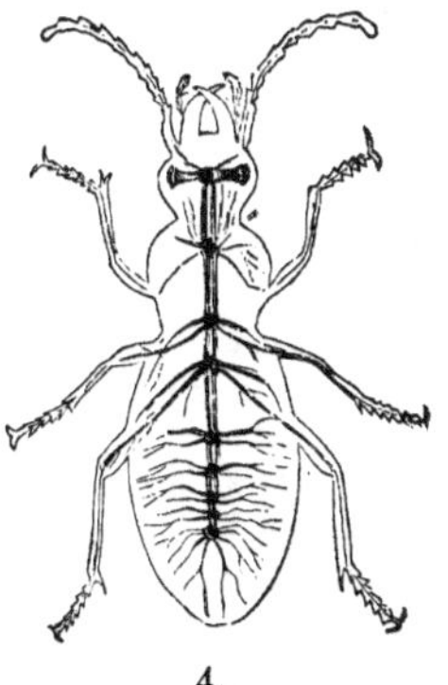
4.

37. The *brain* seems to be the centre of sensation, as it constitutes the chief mass of the nervous substance. It is, moreover, generally believed to be the seat of intelligence, for every injury of the brain is accompanied by a corresponding injury of the intellectual activity. By mere compression of the brain of an animal all motion and sensation cease, and a longer continuance of the same cause produces death. Pressure on one side of the brain occasions partial paralysis. The lesion of the brain is always dangerous, and especially an injury of the elongated cerebral process, from which so many of the nerves of the head originate, and upon which the respiratory system depends, so that a serious injury in this locality is followed by certain death. If a section is made in the place where this organ proceeds from the skull, or above the first cervical vertebra (in the nape of the neck), the most gigantic and vigorous body falls down a lifeless mass as if struck by lightning.

In ancient warfare, when the wounded elephant, maddened with pain, turned round and made a furious onset on the ranks of his owners, his driver thrust a sharp poniard or knife into the upper part of his neck, thus speedily and effectively disabling the powerful and destructive animal

An injury done to the spinal chord is nearly equally dangerous.

Internal as well as external accidents to this organ are perilous to life. An impulse of blood to the head often obstructs the activity of the nerves, and occasions what we call apoplexy. Several causes produce an excess of cerebral excitement, which is followed by a subsequent depression; such as ardent spirits, opium, strychnine, &c., and, above all, prussic acid. Giddiness, vertigo, frenzy, stupor, rigidity, and death, are the gradations which manifest the inward operations of cerebral complaints.

38. The intimate connection that exists between our intellectual and nervous life is evident from the influence which purely spiritual impressions are capable of exerting upon the nervous system. Anxious thought produces headache; very strong feelings of joy or grief, or any other violent emotions, have an effect on the brain similar to what is produced by external causes. Unconsciousness, stupidity, madness, and death, not unfrequently accompany violent mental or spiritual excitements.

Hence some have entertained the idea that a development of the cerebral organ is always accompanied with a corresponding development of the intellectual and moral faculties; that the various cerebral folds and convolutions, prominences and depressions, indicate the disposition and intelligence of the individual; and inasmuch as the cranial bones accommodate themselves to the various elevations and depressions of the brain, the character of persons while alive may thus be determined. This idea, aided by the ingenuity of its supporters, Gall, Spurzheim, and Combe, has become a sort of science, namely, Phrenology, which has excited but little attention or respect in England, and is comparatively only lightly esteemed in Germany, where it originated.

Motion.

39. Movement is produced by a peculiar and combined portion of the nerves, muscles, and bones. The last-named organs contribute to this activity by affording the basis on which the muscles, sinews, tendons, &c., are attached. The muscles are the immediate cause of motion, by means of their extensibility and contractility, and this capability they possess solely in virtue of their intimate relations with the nerves, for by the section or lesion of the latter the power of the muscles to effect movement is impaired or destroyed; consequently, the nerves are the original exciting cause of motion in the human body, the muscles and bones merely the immediate motive agents.

40. Accurate researches have taught us that the different portions of the nervous system contribute very unequally to the phenomena of motion. The following are the essential distinctions of these organs:—The nerves, which govern or communicate voluntary motion and sensation, originate in the *brain* and *spinal chord*. Some of these, as the third, fourth, sixth, seventh, and eleventh pairs of cerebral nerves, exclusively regulate motion, whilst the others serve the purposes both of motion and sensation; but, strictly speaking, this is incorrect. Every bundle of nerves that proceeds from the spinal chord consists of several threads or fibres, which do not anastomose, or even unite, but extend directly to their source. To some of these threads is appropriated the production of sensation, to others that of motion; and although in the bundles themselves they are incapable of being distinguished,

yet their individuality may be ascertained by a careful examination of the bundles in the source in which they originate. All nerves proceeding from the spinal chord originate in two roots; the anterior roots are nerves of motion, the posterior are nerves of sensation. If the posterior roots of the nerves are cut through, the whole body is deprived of sensation, but not of motion; if the anterior roots of the nerves be cut through, the power of motion ceases, but sensation remains.

The *cerebellum*, and the parts of the cerebrum contiguous to it, have less to do with the communication of motion than with the regulation and direction of that motion. By peculiar sections of these parts we have learned that animals injured in this way lose the power of moving, except in certain directions, as forwards, backwards, laterally, &c.

The *elongated cerebral process* (medulla oblongata) is supposed to be the source of those movements which may take place as well with as without the influence of the will, as in the respiration, &c.

The visceral nerves, or gangliar system, regulate the activities of the muscles of the digestive organs, and these, as well as the nerves of circulation and respiration, act independently of our will.

41. It is still undetermined how and by what means the nerves are capable of causing the contraction of the muscular fibre. In 1789, Galvani made the discovery that a stream of electricity is capable of exciting this contractility, precisely in the same manner as this is done by the intervention of the nerves (Physics, § 167). Consequently, views were long entertained that electricity was the cause of all muscular movements. There are, however, weighty reasons contradictory of this explanation of the phenomena of motion, and it is still admitted that the precise nature of the operation of the nerves on the muscular system has not yet been satisfactorily explained.

42. The contractile force of a muscle is only of limited duration. Sooner or later a period arrives when the most powerful muscular organ is incapable of exerting contraction any longer. This condition we term *exhaustion*. After a certain time spent in sleep, which we call *rest*, the muscles are again capable of exerting their contractile forces.

The motive energy is entirely regulated by the amplitude of the active muscle, and by the will, which is the motive cause. To what an extent the latter power can influence the muscular force, we learn from examples of the enormous energy which is called forth by danger, passion, and madness.

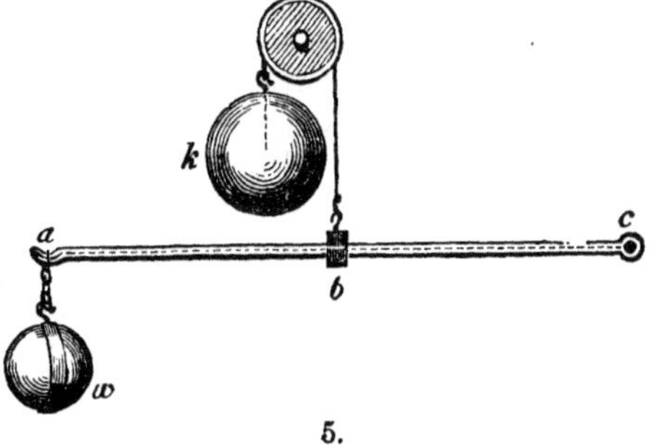

5.

43. Most of the limbs in their common motions are represented by a simple or single-armed lever, and are, in truth, such as we see in fig. 5, having its fulcrum at *c*, while the weight at the opposite extremity, *a*,

presses downwards, and the lower end of the upward-drawing muscle is fixed at a point between the two extremities of the simple lever.

Thus, for example, the fore-arm, fig. 6, may be considered a lever of this kind, having the fulcrum, or point of resistance, in the joint *a*, and at the extremity of the weight *w* pressing downwards, while at the point *b* the upward-drawing muscle is attached. From the physical laws illustrated in § 34 of Physics, it is evident that we are able to sustain a greater weight the nearer we place it to the fulcrum at *a*; as, for example, we can support a heavy basket in the joint of the arm which we could not hold out in our hand. Let us assume that the distance from the joint to the middle of the hand is 15 inches, and that at 1 inch distant from the fulcrum of the joint a weight of 2 lbs. is placed, if the same weight is placed in the hand, it will press downwards with a force of $15 \times 2 = 30$ lbs.

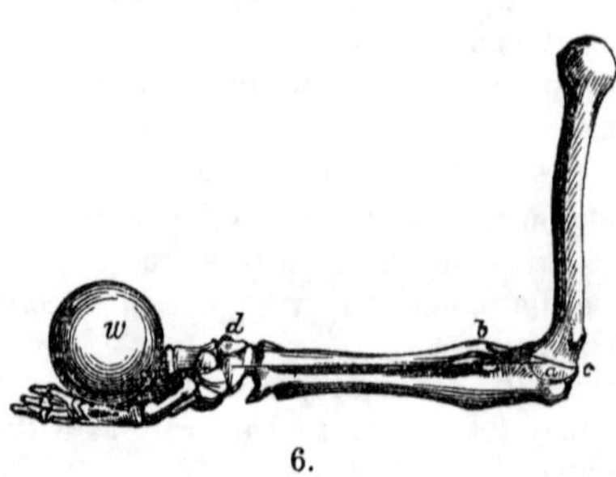

6.

II. ORGANS OF VITALITY.

44. To the vital organs belong the alimentary, the circulatory, and the respiratory. In the lower order of animals these exist only as individual or simple organs; in the higher orders they are very numerous, complex in form and position, and form systems of organisation arranged under these three above-named classes.

1. Alimentary Organs.

45. By the term alimentary we understand the activities of all the organs which reduce or change the condition of the substances received for the nutrition of the body, in such a manner as to render them suited to form new parts of the body, or to be assimilated.

All the organs immediately contributing to the production of this effect are alimentary or digestive organs.

These organs have the still further function of rejecting many of the innutritious and indigestible substances which have been received into the body, along with the alimentary materials.

46. The simplest form of the alimentary organ is that of a cylindrical-shaped bag or pouch. Its upper orifice, adapted to receive the food, is called its *mouth* (cardiac orifice), the lower part is called the *pylorus*, or pyloric orifice, by which the food, when triturated and sufficiently pulpy, is emitted into the intestines; the enlargement of this sac between the two openings is called the *stomach*. In addition to this, in the more highly organised animals, there appears a series of contiguous and combined organs, which are represented by fig. 7, in which the natural position of the stomach is somewhat altered, through the elevation of the liver from over the gall-bladder and stomach, which otherwise would be unseen in the diagram.

47. The separation of the aliments commences in the mouth, where the

food is both divided and partly masticated by the teeth. The chewing apparatus is of an exceedingly powerful description, the under jaw acting on the upper like one limb of a double lever or pair of nut-crackers, where the joint is the fulcrum: the tongue serves to place the food between the molar teeth, and at the same time acts as the organ of mastication, supplied with moisture by the *salivary* glands, three pairs of which are present, viz., the sub-lingual, under the tongue; the parotid, near the ear; and the sub-maxillary, situated on the inside of the lower jaw.

The *saliva* is a colourless, watery fluid, which holds in solution about one per cent. of a more solid material; its office is to moisten the food and to make its deglutition more easy. Although the saliva has scarcely a greater solvent power than water, yet experiments prove that chewed food is more nutritious than that which is unchewed. Fresh saliva has some alkaline properties (Chem. § 17).

48. From the mouth the food passes through the *œsophagus*, which is also called the throat, into the stomach. This is a strong membranous bag, which lies across the cavity of the abdomen, close under the *diaphragm*,

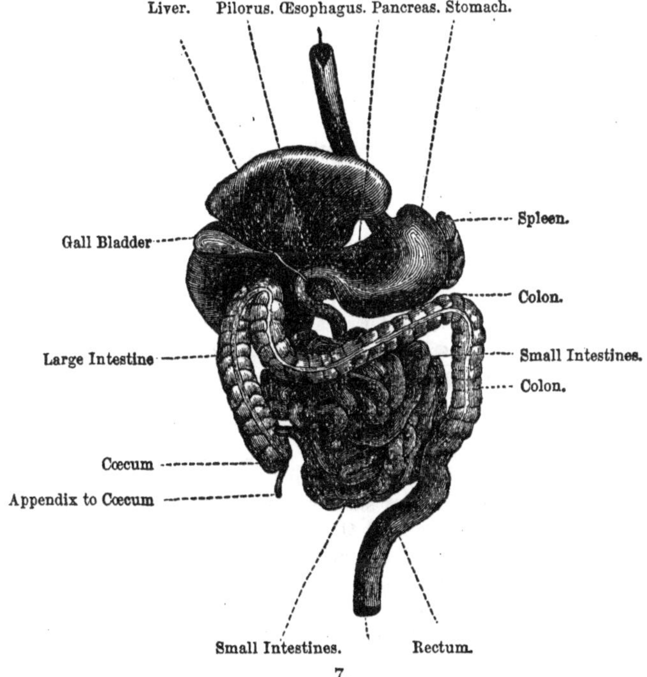

7.

and is covered by the liver. At the left, where the œsophagus enters and forms *the mouth of the stomach* (cardiac orifice), this organ is enlarged, and it is again contracted at the lower end on the right, where is the passage, called *pylorus*, into the lower stomach or intestinal canal. Both this passage and also the mouth of the stomach are drawn together, or constricted, by an annular muscle, and remain shut during the progress of digestion. Behind the left part of the stomach lies the *spleen*, an organ apparently formed of the fine ramifications of an artery; its functions are unknown.

The inner membrane of the stomach is lined with a muscular fibrous layer, by means of which it can be contracted. This is in many animals, and especially in domestic fowls (the gizzard), very powerful and capable of crushing and grinding very hard substances. When the stomach is empty, its membrane is relaxed and interiorly furnished with many plaits or folds, which are diminished when the organ is again distended. Its inner coat is covered with a slimy membrane, called the mucous membrane, which secretes an acid fluid called the gastric juice.

49. The gastric juice is a fluid containing 98 per cent. of water, which holds in solution some common salt and hydrochloric acid. The early opinions on the agency of the digestive organs were, that the food was macerated between the hard coats of the stomach; but the most accurate experiments prove that this is not the case. The food is dissolved by the gastric juice, and this is easily shown to be a fact, by employing the gastric juice taken from slaughtered animals, warming it to the proper temperature, and placing in it small chopped pieces of food, which it soon acts upon and dissolves. An artificial fluid has been prepared which possesses the same solvent properties as the gastric juice; but it has always been found that the process is accomplished with greater celerity by this fluid when taken from the stomach. Even a mixture of the natural and artificial fluids accelerates the dissolution of the food. It is now the general opinion that the gastric juice contains a peculiar, organic, digestive material.

50. The gastric juice reduces the food into a thick pulpy mass named *chyme* (chymus).

When the food is in this state, it passes into the part of the alimentary canal called the intestines. This is on the whole about 30 feet long, and is closely folded together in the lower part of the abdominal cavity. The intestinal canal is not all of uniform capacity, and is distinguished by appropriate names. The upper part into which the chyme passes from the stomach is called the *duodenum*, because it is about 12 finger-breadths in length.

The alimentary process is still continued in the duodenum where the chyme is brought into contact with the pancreatic juice, derived from the pancreas (*salivary glands* of the stomach), which lie near (see fig. 7), and secrete a fluid which has a great similarity to the saliva of the mouth. Here also, simultaneously, the *bile* from the *gall-bladder* mingles with the chyme. The bile is a clear, green, very bitter fluid, and feels soapy and is employed in the place of soap in washing many fine articles of wearing apparel. Its chemical composition explains this, for it is a combination of a fatty acid with soda (Chem. § 134), forming thus a real natural soap, possessing the weak alkaline qualities of other soaps.

51. The *liver* is the organ in which the bile is secreted. Its size is very considerable, and with its two lobes is the largest of all the visceral organs. The substance of the liver consists of a combination of small, firm, granular particles, interpenetrated by a great number of blood-vessels, and containing, besides, small tubular channels conveying the bile into the duodenum and gall-bladder. The liver consequently contains much blood, and is of a dark reddish-brown colour.

52. The chymification or digestive process is finished on the mixture of the bile and the chyme, and the aliments are henceforth separated into two portions, the one solid the other fluid. The former is not adapted for assimilation with the body and is therefore rejected. The fluid portion, on the contrary, contains all the matter of the food applicable to the nutrition of the body, and is named *chyle*. This substance is colourless; and, with this exception, is very similar to the blood, as we shall show when we describe the latter fluid.

53. The contents of the duodenum now pass into the small intestines, which are narrow, extended, and disposed in complex coils, and their passage through the latter is an operation which lasts some considerable time. The subsequent elimination of the intestinal contents is effected through a peculiar vermiform movement called the peristaltic motion. Along the intestinal canal there are numerous absorbent vessels originating in spongy cellular processes; and by these vessels, or lymphatics, as they are called, the chyle is absorbed and conveyed to the thoracic duct, where all these unite. The chyle subsequently passes into the veins and so mixes with the blood. The further the contents of the intestines proceed in their downward course, the less nutriment they yield, and, finally, when they have reached the *large intestine* (colon, fig. 7), as it is termed, their nutritious matter is altogether absorbed. In this latter stage they become more solid, begin to putrefy, and are finally ejected from the body.

54. All kinds of food are changed or digested in a similar way during their passage through the digestive canal. In general, solid nutritive substances are less digestible than such as are of a softer or looser nature. If, within a certain time, any substance is not digested, it passes on, together with the digested aliments, and numbers of such substances are ejected from the body totally unchanged. Such materials, of course, contribute no nourishment, and their presence in the intestines is frequently productive of pain or uneasy sensations.

Both accurate investigations as well as common experience teach us, that easily digestible food only requires from one hour to an hour and a half in the process. The following are a few of such alimentary substances, viz. :— Asparagus, spinach, celery; the pulp and parenchymatous portions of different sorts of fruit; preparations of cereal grains, such as oats, rye, barley, rice, maize; also peas, beans, chestnuts; bread, one day old; turnips, potatoes, veal, mutton, fowls, soft-boiled eggs, milk, and boiled fish.

Less digestible substances, or such as are not chymified, or only incompletely so, in the given time, are: — Salads, lettuce, water-cresses, chicory, white cabbage, onions, horse-radish, carrots, walnuts; newly-baked bread, patties; pork of all kinds, fresh, salted, or cured; hard-boiled eggs, and omelettes.

Substances nearly or altogether indigestible are the following: — Mushrooms, kernels of all sorts of stone fruits, oily and fatty matters of plants and animals, the husks of peas, beans, &c., rinds and skins of fruit; the skinny, gristly parts of meat, cartilaginous and osseous parts, &c.

Warm food is more easily digested than cold; the latter dimishes the heat of the stomach, which acts more powerfully when of a certain temperature.

2. Organs of Circulation.

55. The organs by which the blood is circulated are called *vessels*. They are a series of cylindrical tubular channels, always filled with a fluid, and, in combination, form the *vascular system*.

They are, according to the nature of their fluid contents, divided into *arteries*, where the fluid is a bright red; *veins*, where it is of a dark red; and lymphatic vessels, where the fluid is without colour. The red-coloured fluid is called *blood*.

56. The function of circulation is essentially of a threefold character in the animal economy. First, it conveys the digested aliments all over the body for its nutrition. Second, it eliminates or separates from the different organs those portions which have been exhausted and are no longer serviceable to these organs. Thirdly, the blood serves to maintain and distribute an equal temperature over the whole body.

The Blood.

57. The average weight of a man of 40 years of age is estimated at 137 lbs. (com. Physics, § 51), of which the blood amounts to about 30·5 lbs.

Blood is a non-transparent, bright-red fluid, mostly consisting of water, in which the following materials are contained as its relative constituents:—

Constituent Parts of Blood.	100 Parts contain:
Water	78·2
Blood-globules	13·5
Fibrin	0·3
Albumen	6·7
Saline substances	0·9
Fatty matter	0·4
	100·0

These numbers express the average relative proportions, according to which these materials are combined to form blood; age, occupation, and health do, however, exercise a modifying influence on the composition of this fluid.

But besides the solid and fluid constituents above mentioned, there are in the blood several gases, as *oxygen*, *nitrogen*, and *carbonic acid*.

When viewed through a microscope, the blood appears as a clear, pale yellowish fluid, in which an infinite number of minute red particles swim about, which are named *blood-globules*, and communicate to the blood its red colour. It is to be observed that the colouring matter of the blood contains *iron*, of which it is calculated that the amount is 0·06 per cent., which in 30·5 lbs. is about a quarter of an ounce. A portion of the corpuscles contained in the blood, viz., the *lymph corpuscles*, is without colour.

If fresh blood is suffered to remain at rest for a short time, it coagulates, that is, separates into two parts, viz., the solid part, which *floats* on the surface, and is called *coagulum*, or clot; and the watery yellowish part, which is called *serum*.

On cooling, the fibrin coagulates in the form of a flocculent matter, and combines with the globules, so that both together form the red-coloured solid mass called coagulum, which swims upon the serum. If the fresh blood be briskly agitated with the hand, or a brush, the fibrin is separated, but is not again capable of combining with the globules. The blood retains its red colour, but loses its coagulating property. The fibrin (Chem. § 151) is colourless, and is found in the form of white threads hanging to the small brush with which the blood was agitated.

58. If the serum be heated to ebullition, the *albumen* is coagulated (Chem. § 151), hence all the blood used in cookery becomes solid. If we mix blood with a liquid which is rendered thick and turbid by the presence of minute particles of foreign matters, and heat it to ebullition, the albumen of the blood during coagulation envelopes these particles, and renders the liquid perfectly clear. In sugar-refining, bullock's blood is used for the process of clarification.

The saline matter of the blood is principally *common salt* and *phosphate of lime*, of which last material the bones are chiefly composed.

There are, besides the above, several other substances in the blood, but in so small quantities, that, though known, their proportion is scarcely determinable. The most important of these is *fat*, which is perceived in the form of small globules swimming in the blood.

59. From the above we learn that in the blood is present all the materials of which the various parts of the human body consist, viz.: fibrin and albumen, which form the muscle and the skin; phospate of lime, which forms the solid substances of the bones; fatty and other substances found in smaller quantities, and constituting the smaller parts, as the brain, &c. Consequently the blood is the fluid nutritive material of our bodies; and we may affirm with certainty that every portion of the same originates in the blood, and was formerly in a fluid condition.

But in order that the blood may be in a condition to perform its function of renewing the waste of the body, it must be provided with the means of reaching every part of the system, and this is accomplished by the different vessels, which altogether form the vascular apparatus, provided for the circulation of the blood.

1. The Arteries.

60. The arteries are small tubes whose walls are possessed of great elasticity, and therefore do not collapse when empty. They originate in the *heart* (see fig. 8), which is a hollow muscular organ situated in the cavity of the chest and divided into several compartments.

In the arteries we find the bright red-coloured blood; and their function is the distribution of this fluid to all parts of the body.

From the left ventricle of the heart arises the principal blood-vessel, which is named the *aorta* (figs. 8 and 9), giving off several branches. Of these the carotid arteries, situated on the right and left sides of the neck, convey blood to the head. The *subclavian* arteries are next given off to the upper extremities on each side.

Then the aorta, forming an arch nearly directly backwards, descends on the left side of the vertebral column, giving off in its course branches to the different organs of digestion, and then bifurcates or divides into two for the supply of the lower extremities.

All these main channels or branches are divided and again subdivided until finally they are lost in a series of exceedingly minute reticulated vessels, only visible by the aid of a powerful microscope, and are then called the capillary vessels. Here is the commencement of the veins.

The larger arteries lie chiefly on the inner side of the limbs, and most of them are rather deeply situated and are well protected by the surrounding muscles. When they lie near the surface, the motion of the blood is externally perceptible by a slight motion of the contiguous parts: this is the case with the carotid arteries in the neck. This motion is still more perceptible as a slight throb or stroke (the pulse), felt on applying the finger gently to the radial artery in the wrist, as is the usual mode of feeling the pulse.

A wound in the large arteries is very dangerous, because the blood being impelled with considerable force from the heart, hemorrhage is easily produced. In accidental injuries of the arteries, till surgical aid can be obtained, the efflux of blood is to be prevented by compression, ligatures, bandages, or any other mechanical means.

2. The Veins.

61. The veins are also tubular channels of a laxer consistency than the arteries, and being more flaccid collapse when empty. They originate in the infinitely numerous capillary vessels which connect the arteries and veins. The union of the capillary vessels constitutes larger veins, and the combination of the latter forms several principal branches or venous trunks, which ultimately are reduced to two principal veins, called the venæ cavæ, which conduct the blood into the right auricle of the heart (see fig. 8).

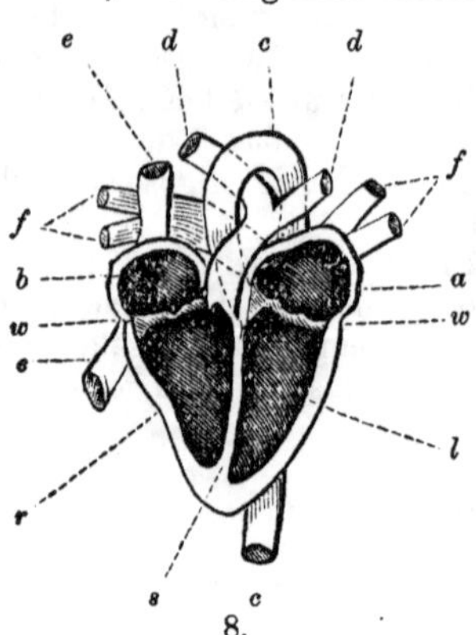

8.

The venous blood has a much darker colour than the arterial.

The pulsation of the blood, dependent on the action of the heart, is lost in the capillary vessels; and consequently, in the veins, no pulsation is felt. Many veins lie close to the surface, and are distinguished by their blue colour appearing through the semi-transparent skin. If the return of their contents to the heart be impeded, they swell to a great size: this is often observable in the veins that pass over the back of the hand.

A small longitudinal incision made in a vein closes again with celerity and ease. In the practice of blood-letting, or phlebotomy, an incision is made with a sharp-pointed instrument, called a lancet, in a large vein on the front of the arm, whence the required quantity of blood is drawn; a slight bandage is sufficient to close the opening again.

3. Absorbent and Lymphatic Vessels.

62. In almost every part of the body, both immediately beneath the skin and deeper, *lymphatic vessels* are found. By this name we designate a system of very thin-walled transparent canals, which in extremely delicate ramifications take their rise in the interior of the various organs. In their

progress from the place of their origin, these minute channels ramify and again unite, thus forming larger vessels which in several places discharge their contents into the veins.

The contents of the absorbent and lymphatic vessels constitute what is called *lymph*, generally a yellowish transparent fluid, in which are discovered, by the aid of the microscope, round colourless corpuscles, similar to the blood-globules, but not so large.

The lymphatic vessels which originate in the intestines are of special importance. It has been already stated in § 53 that numerous spongy cellular formations are found situated along the smaller intestinal canal. These are the mouths of the lymphatic system of the intestines or *lacteals*, consisting of numerous minute, sometimes united channels, whose functions are most intimately connected with the process of digestion. If during the digestive operation the contents of these vessels be examined, they appear to be of a cloudy whitish colour, and milky appearance; and hence the principal vessel where they all finally unite is called the *thoracic lacteal duct*, because it ascends along the vertebral column upwards into the cavity of the breast, direct to the place where the left jugular vein and subclavian vein unite; there it passes into the veins, and its contents are mingled with the blood.

The portion of the lymphatic vessels originating in or on the intestines undoubtedly performs the function of absorbing the nutritive substance (chyle) produced during the digestive process, and hence they are called *absorbent vessels*. They are at first widely spread through the mesenteric folds, investing the intestines, and from these they gradually combine to form the thoracic duct.

In this manner the milky substance absorbed from the intestines is continually undergoing a successive series of changes which assimilate it more and more to the blood. Before its entrance into the veins it has a pale-red colour, which is heightened when it has been exposed to the action of the air in the lungs. It, like blood, possesses the property of coagulating as it cools. Hence, it may be considered as colourless blood; and in a large proportion of the invertebrata the contents of the blood-vessels are always colourless.

Circulation of the Blood.

63. The heart is the centre from which all the motion of the blood proceeds. A section of this organ is represented by fig. 8, which is somewhat simplified for the sake of perspicuity. The heart is longitudinally divided by a partition, *s*, into the *right* and *left ventricles* or chambers, viz., *r* and *l*; each of these divisions has also a *superior cavity* (auricle) *a*, *b*, also separated by a flap or valve *w*, so that each ventricle or cell has a communication with its auricle.

The heart is a hollow muscle which by its power of contraction can diminish the capacity of its cavity. If we assume that this organ is filled with blood, its contraction will forcibly impel the blood into the tubular channels which open into the heart. Eight of the larger are represented in the diagram, but the blood is not impelled by the contraction of the heart into all of them, but into two only. The cause of this is to be attributed to the presence of *valves*, which shut the apertures or openings of the arteries as well as those of the veins. These valves, like the valves of a pump (Physics, § 83), only open when the fluid presses against one side, and are kept closed when the fluid comes in an opposite direction. By the contraction of the heart the valves of the arteries, *c* and *d*, are forced open, and permit the entrance of the blood, whilst those of the veins, *e* and *f*, which are attached in an opposite position, remain closed.

The contraction of the heart, like that of every other muscle, is only exerted for a short time, after which it again expands; and, as soon as this occurs, the valves of the arteries are immediately closed, and those of the veins simultaneously opened, and the blood allowed to flow into the heart.

This alternate contraction and dilatation of the heart is the peculiar movement which we call *the beating of the heart.*

On an average, the heart performs seventy of these beats in a minute; and they may be ascertained either by external feeling of the breast in the region of the heart, or more accurately by counting the corresponding number of pulsations which may be felt in the wrist. In children, and in men when in a state of excitement, or when affected by various diseases, especially in fevers, the pulsations amount to as many as one hundred in a minute.

64. The heart discharges two functions at the same time—first, it distributes the purified blood, with renovated nutritive power, into all parts of the body; and, second, it impels the dark-red blood into the lungs, where it comes into contact with atmospheric air, whereby its bright-red colour is restored. The former is called the general, and the latter the pulmonary circulation.

65. The general circulation of the blood is accomplished by the left division of the heart. By its contraction the *bright-red blood* is forced into the aorta *a*, and distributed through its branches in all directions. By the dilatation of the heart the dark-red blood is returned to the right auricle through the large veins, *e*, which open into it, and thence it passes into the right ventricle of the heart.

66. The *pulmonary circulation* of the blood is between the heart and the lungs, and proceeds from the right ventricle simultaneously with the general circulation. The ventricle propels the dark-red blood it contains through the pulmonary artery, which, dividing into two branches, *d d*, conveys the blood to both lobes of the lungs. By another dilatation of the heart, the blood returns purified and of a bright-red colour through the pulmonary veins, *f f*, into the left auricle, whence it passes into the left ventricle which is immediately beneath it, in order, at the next contraction of the heart, to enter the general circulation.

From the above we are taught that the entire mass of blood in our bodies is constantly in motion, and alternately undergoing the process of the general and pulmonary circulations.

67. The discovery of the circulation of the blood, one of the most intricate as well as one of the most important branches of anatomical knowledge, explanatory of many of the phenomena of life, we owe to our renowned countryman, Harvey (1619).

The observation made in § 60, that the finest ramifications of the arteries, the capillary vessels, form the transition immediately to the same vessels of the veins, can be satisfactorily proved by viewing with a microscope the transparent skin which lies between the toes of a frog. The motion of the blood-globules through the capillary vessels from the arteries to the veins can be clearly observed.

Organs of Respiration.

68. The *lungs*, together with the connected channels or passages that lead to and from them, are called the organs of respiration. Fig. 9.

The mass of the lungs consists of the very fine ramifications of three different kinds of channels, of which the first is the trachea, or *wind-pipe*, the

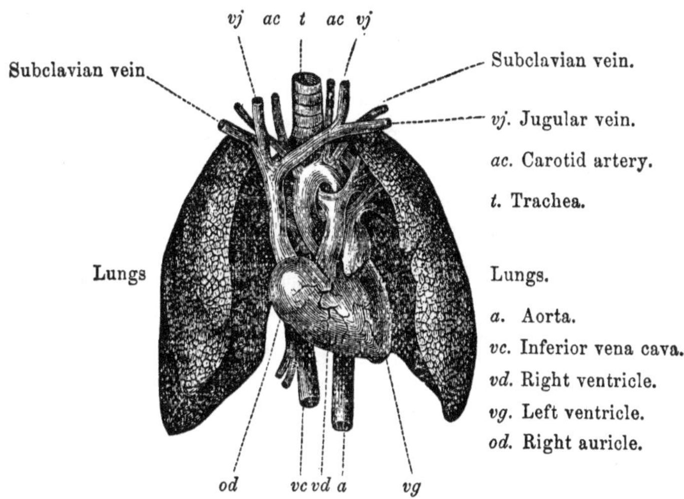

9. Lungs, heart, and principal vessels of man. (Comp. § 60 and 61.)

second the pulmonary artery, and the third the pulmonary veins. This organ is of considerable size, occupying, with the heart, which it surrounds on both sides, the whole extent of the thoracic cavity, and consists of two tolerably equal lobes.

The office of the lungs is to bring the dark-red blood through the pulmonary artery into contact with the air.

69. The *trachea*, or *wind-pipe*, *t*, which opens into the mouth, and is thereby connected with the nose, consists of about twenty hard gristly rings, which are all united by membrane. At the upper part of the trachea is situated the larynx, where the trachea, or wind-pipe, by an aperture called the *glottis*, opens into the pharynx or superior part of the œsophagus.

To prevent the passage of any portion of food or drink into the wind-pipe, the latter is protected by a cartilaginous valve called the epiglottis, which closes the opening of the trachea during the deglutition of the food. It remains open, on the contrary, for breathing, speaking, &c. It often happens that during the process of deglutition particles of food, liquids, &c., do enter the wind-pipe, and a violent irritation or coughing is the consequence, and by this means the irritating matter is expelled.

In the thorax the wind-pipe is divided into two principal branches, which extend through the lungs, divaricating in all directions, and terminating in small cells filled with air: these cells are again encompassed with the very fine ramifications of the arteries, which are also dispersed over the lungs.

Thus the lungs always contain a large quantity of air. When taken from an animal, and the air expelled, they collapse, and may be again distended to their full dimensions by the injection of air through the wind-pipe.

70. The act of respiration or breathing is accomplished by a particular muscle which expands the chest, so that a quantity of air passes through the trachea into the rarefied space within the thorax. When the muscles of the chest relax, a quantity of air, corresponding to the diminished space, escapes or is forced out. The average bulk of air breathed by a man at every inspiration is about 33 cubic inches. In an adult the number of inspirations amounts to 18 in a minute; in children the number is greater. There are on an average 3.8 pulsations to every respiration.

Effect of Respiration upon the Blood.

71. We have seen in § 65 that the blood having, by the general circulation, been distributed to all parts of the body, is returned again through the *venæ cavæ* into the right auricle of the heart, that it thence passes into the right ventricle, and by the next contraction of the heart is forced into the bifurcated pulmonary artery, which carries the blood into both lobes of the lungs.

An important change in the condition of the blood is now effected through its contact with the air. This contact is not, however, immediate. Both are separated by the very fine membrane of the pulmonary air-cells and of the capillary vessels. There appears to be a similar interpenetration of these membranes containing the air and the blood, as we have described in Botany under the name of *endosmose* (§ 10), viz., the absorption of the sap by the plant-cells.

72. A comparison of the atmospheric air inhaled by the lungs, with that which is exhaled from the lungs, will show us the result of this contact of the blood with atmospheric air.

The air inspired is atmospheric air, and of course is of the same temperature, an average of 51° Fahr., and contains the same proportion of water; the air expired is of the same temperature as the body, or on an average of 99° Fahr., and contains a corresponding proportion of aqueous vapour, amounting to about one grain at every expiration. The following tabular view will exemplify the change which the air has undergone by passing through the lungs:

Contents of the Air in	Before Inspiration.		After Expiration.	
	In 100 Measures.	In 100 Parts by Weight.	In 100 Measures.	In 100 Parts by Weight.
Oxygen........	20·815	23·001	16·033	17·373
Nitrogen......	79·185	76·999	79·587	76·081
Carbonic acid	A trace.	A trace.	4·380	6·546
	100·000	100·000	100·000	100·000

This table, founded upon numerous observations and experiments, teaches us that the nitrogen suffers little or no change: it is returned to the atmosphere in the same condition as when it was inhaled by the lungs.

The case is different with the oxygen. Its quantity appears to be diminished 4·38 per cent. by the process of respiration, and the expired air or breath contains a corresponding quantity of *carbonic acid* (Chem. § 53). Hence it appears that a certain portion of oxygen is withdrawn from the air, and a corresponding portion of carbonic acid mixed with it.

What has become of the oxygen which has disappeared?

It unites with the carbonaceous matter of the dark-red blood, and forms carbonic acid, which is expired. After this process has been accomplished, the blood recovers its bright-red colour, and returns through the pulmonary veins into the left auricle, and thence into the left ventricle, to recommence its circulatory course.

73. In this manner the body of an adult produces at every respiration a certain quantity of carbonic acid, amounting in an hour to about 44 grammes. (1½ ounces.) This carbonic acid contains 12 grammes of carbon, consequently the body must yield by the process of respiration, in the course of 24 hours, 288 grammes, or about 10 ounces of carbon.

One natural consequence of this is, that we must supply our bodies with the requisite amount of carbonaceous materials, in order that it may be in a condition to support respiration. And in fact this is done by means of the food, which consists of animal and vegetable matter, both containing carbon. A considerable portion of the food daily consumed serves merely to support respiration. With every breath we draw the body loses a definite portion of its weight, and this loss must be supplied. A famishing person is self-consumed by constant respiration. If we could exist for weeks or months without breathing, we could dispense with food for a corresponding period. There are animals, such as serpents and toads, which can live for many weeks without sensible respiration, and it is known that these can dispense with food for an equal period. In the hybernating animals, or those which sleep during the winter, breathing is suspended, and during that time they require no food.

Animals that pass the winter in a dormant state, like the badger, marmot, and many others, breathe, indeed, but very feebly. Consequently, during this time they consume a considerable portion of their bodies; for these animals at the beginning of their winter-sleep are swollen with fat, and at its termination are very lean. A longer duration of this condition would be impossible.

74. Chemistry (§ 22) informs us that when oxygen combines with other materials, a certain amount of heat is evolved; and this becomes the more perceptible the larger the quantity that combines within a given time. It is well known that if a piece of coal is burned in the atmosphere, it communicates a certain amount of heat, and we can apply this heat for producing very different effects.

Now if, as has been shown above, the process of respiration is nothing else than the chemical combination, taking place in our bodies, of carbon with other materials, a certain amount of heat must be generated and felt. This is, in truth, the case. We can decidedly affirm that the essential object of respiration is the production of heat—that this heat is communicated to the blood, and by this fluid it is quickly, equally, and universally diffused over every part of the body. The heat of the blood, and consequently that of all parts of the body, is 99° Fahrenheit. It is higher in children, and lower in persons of advanced age. And in the whole mammiferous class it is pretty nearly the same as it is in man. In the denizens of the Polar regions, it is something higher, and in all birds it amounts to about 108° Fahrenheit. Fishes and reptiles have the same warmth as the temperature of the media by which they are surrounded.

Physiological Inferences.

75. From what has been stated in the previous sections respecting the organs of digestion, circulation, and respiration, there are several inferences to be drawn which are explanatory of the various phenomena of life. Among these the phenomena of nutrition are the most important, as on this process depends not only the preservation, but also the improvement or civilization of the human race.

76. If we compare the substances constituting the nutriment of men and other animals with the food of plants, we find that there is an essential difference not merely in the organs of absorption and assimilation, but also in the material that is received into the system. Nutrition in the vegetable kingdom is not limited to a single organ, as is the case in animals; we find that the whole surface of the former, viz., the leaves, the root, and the bark of herbaceous plants, is adapted to the reception of their food; whilst, with few exceptions, animals can receive nutriment only by a single aperture—the mouth.

But the difference appears greater and more essential when we compare the nutritive substances themselves. Plants are supported entirely on *inorganic* materials; for water, carbonic acid, and ammonia are the three chief component parts of the food of the vegetable world (Botany, § 87, &c.), and these materials are all produced by the general influence of natural forces operating upon the constituents of the earth and atmosphere; but, notwithstanding, they are inanimate, inorganic bodies like minerals, and are totally dissimilar to the parts of plants which they are employed to produce. Plants, therefore, have the power of assimilating the inorganic parts of the substance of the earth, and also of forming these into organic bodies. From water, carbonic acid, and ammonia the plant forms woody fibre, starch, sugar, vegetable albumen, and many other materials, which, as we have already seen (Chem. § 119—§ 124), are constituents of the vegetable kingdom.

77. This capability is not possessed by the animal. From these three materials which constitute the food of plants, it can neither form its own albumen, nor muscular fibre, nor fat. On the cold, lifeless breast of inanimate nature the animal would pine away, and soon perish. It requires for its existence an agent to convert the requisite materials into an organic body, and this agent is the plant.

When we compare the chemical combination of albumen, casein, fibrin, and the fatty matter of plants (Chem. § 149), with the analogous materials which are found in the bodies of animals, we find that the animal receives, in the plants on which it feeds, all the materials already formed which are necessary for the development of the various parts of its body.

78. Hence the process of digestion in animals is simple, and more easily

intelligible than that of plants. The animal does not form, from the required elements, its muscle, fat, &c., but by means of its alimentary organs, dissolves or chymnifies these very materials already prepared in the plant, and through the organs of circulation conveys and applies them to all parts of its body.

This is still more evident in the case of carnivorous animals, or in such as live on the blood of other animals. It is evident that these subsist entirely on the identical materials which form their own bodies. The digestive organs only effect a modification, not a chemical change, of the materials on which they subsist.

It is a fact that the function of digestion is the easier, the more analogous the food is to the constituents of our own bodies. The digestive process in the herbivorous animals is in many respects different from that of carnivorous animals. The latter consume merely what may be assimilated into the flesh of their own bodies, consequently the digestive process is more rapid; their nourishment is contained in smaller compass, and is speedily consumed; and the separation of the excrementitious from the nutritious portion of their food is less complicated than it is in herbivorous animals.

The hay and grass on which the ox feeds contain but a small proportion of albumen, fibrin, and fat applicable to the nourishment and growth of the beast; and, on the other hand, such food is rich in woody fibre, which is not appropriate for his nutrition. Consequently, this animal spends a very long time in eating, most of which time he employs in separating the unsuitable part of his food from that which is suited to his nature. A longer time is spent in dissolving the materials, and in separating the woody fibre, than is requisite for the entire digestive process of the flesh-eating beast.

In the herbivorous animal the food remains a very long time in the stomach, even after being soaked and macerated in a particular part of it, and it must be returned to the mouth, where it is chewed a second time, mixed with saliva, and rendered suitable for digestion. The intestinal canal in both beasts and birds of the rapacious orders—the cat and kite, for example —is disproportionately short.

79. The average weight of an adult man neither increases nor diminishes. But there are exceptions, such as a great accumulation of fat, and the wasting of the body by sickness and disease. And from the period when our bodies have attained their full development, all the food which we consume only serves to maintain or support our bodies, but not to enlarge them. The weight of every particle of solid and fluid substances which we receive during a year can be calculated as exactly as the weight of what is separated and rejected from our bodies. Independently of that portion of our food which passes through the alimentary canal, and is rejected partly in a solid and partly in a fluid form, we have also to take into consideration the perspiration through the pores of the skin, and the exhalations from the lungs.

80. All kinds of food taken into the body are not used for the same purpose. Starch, sugar, gum, spirits, and fat are materials that we constantly make use of. None of these contain nitrogen. Hence these substances cannot in the slightest degree contribute to the support and increase of such parts of our bodies as contain nitrogen, such as albumen and muscular fibre. Yet neither the lives of men nor of beasts can be preserved without them. They are essentially necessary to the maintenance of respiration, and their office in the animal economy is to contribute carbon, which is exhaled from

the body; and in the process of respiration there is a constant and equal development of heat, and consequently all nutritious substances of the nature of starch, gum, sugar, alcohol, and fat, may be designated the supporters of animal heat.

81. For the formation of nitrogenous constituent parts, we require nitrogenous food; and these are albumen, fibrin, and casein, either vegetable or animal. Only such foods as contain one or more of these substances can supply to the blood those constituents which this fluid conveys into all parts of the body, either for its increase or renovation. Hence, these may be considered as being devoted to the formation of blood, and they are what is commonly understood by nourishing aliments (Chem. § 150).

82. Suppose an animal fed on perfectly pure starch and albumen—he receives all that is necessary for the support of respiration and the formation of muscular fibre; yet he will not enjoy health, but must sooner or later die, because in these foods he receives no *phosphate of lime* from which the mass of the bones is formed, and no *salt*, which is also indispensable for the secretion of gastric juice, the most important of the digestive fluids.

If a beast be foddered with turnip, oil-cake, potatoes, distillery refuse, &c., which contain little or no lime, he is not supplied with the materials necessary for the formation of his bones; and, consequently, these remain weak while other parts of his body become so disproportionably enlarged that the bones break in consequence of being unable to support the weight. This fearful disease, called softening of the bones (Mollites ossium), cannot affect cattle plentifully supplied with clover and hay, which contain much lime salts (comp. Botany, § 98).

Fowls and pigeons eagerly seek and greedily swallow whatever contains calcareous substances (Mortar, Chem. § 79). This is, indeed, indispensable to all birds, and especially to domestic poultry, which lay so many eggs; sometimes from the deficiency of lime the egg is without a proper shell, but is, instead, enclosed in a soft membranous bag.

Men and other animals unconsciously seek for nutriment containing salt, which is indispensable for them. And in addition to the salt with which most natural springs, and many vegetable and animal substances, are more or less impregnated, we use salt with almost all our food; a practice which has been from the earliest times considered as conducive to digestion.

83. The kinds of food most conducive to health and growth are such as contain the necessary constituents for the development of heat, the formation of blood and bones, and these are, especially, the seeds of cereals (various kinds of corn), leguminous and other fruits, milk, meat, eggs, and blood.

84. From the Table on page 545, we learn, that the cereals, wheat, rye, &c., contain both the materials requisite for supporting respiration, as starch, the nitrogenous substances, as fibrin, to form blood, and phosphate of lime to form the bones. Bread and water are sufficient to support a man whose labour is not immoderately exhausting. Rye and barley contain from 18 to 24 per cent. of woody fibre useless as food, and in the proportion of starch and fibrin which they contain hold the next rank to wheat. The last mentioned, however, contains but a small portion of lime salts, so small that a pigeon fed with wheat exclusively becomes rickety. In the cereals, and especially in wheat, the nitrogenous constituent is mostly contained in the exterior layer, whilst the interior is almost pure starch. Hence the removal

of this exterior layer renders the flour considerably whiter, but it contains proportionally less nutriment. In rice and in potatoes we find a large portion of starch, but very little of what is requisite for nourishing the blood. Hence large quantities of such food must be consumed in order to supply the body with a sufficient portion of nitrogen. It is a well-known fact that the inhabitants of Ireland consume immense quantities of potatoes as diet, and the Negro can eat an equal quantity of rice. In both cases so much starch is conveyed into the stomach, that a part of it is rejected undigested and consequently unchanged.

TABULAR VIEW of the CHEMICAL CONSTITUENTS of the following Dietary Articles:—

100 Parts by Weight of the following Nutritive Substances—contain	1. Non-Nitrogenous or Calorific Substances.			2. Nitrogenous or Sanguifying Substances.*			3. Substances supplying Osseous Matter.	
	Starch.	Sugar.	Fat.	Albumen.	Fibrin.	Casein.	Phosphate of Lime.	Water.
Rye	40	2	..	..	8	..	?	10
Wheat	74	4	..	..	11	..	0·08	10
Barley	32	5	..	..	5 (?)	..	0·24	11
Rice	85	Trace.	Trace.	..	3.6	..	0·4	6
Potatoes	15	Gum 4	..	1·4	..	..	..	75
Beans	42	Trace.	0·7	..	..	18·20	1·0	23
Peas	42	2	..	..	..	18	2·0	13
Meat	..	..	..	..	23	..	..	77
Milk	..	4	3·	..	..	5·	0·5	87
Blood	..	..	0·4	6·7	13·8	..	0·9	78
White of Egg	..	..	..	12–14	..	..	..	88–86
Yolk of Egg	..	..	29·	17	..	..	..	54

*Compare Chemistry, § 152, 153.

Peas and beans are the most nutritious of vegetable substances, on account of the very considerable amount of nitrogenous casein which they contain, and approximate to flesh. The latter (flesh) which consists entirely of blood-producing fibrin, is preferable to beans and peas in being more easily digestible. Alone, the flesh does not contain sufficient carbon to support respiration, but it is generally accompanied with fat which is productive of heat.

In no kind of food, however, do we meet with a more favourable combination of nutritious constituents than in milk, which contains sugar, fat, casein, the requisite salts in solution; and hence it is the only food provided naturally for the young of *all* the mammifera, as well as for those of the human race.

85. As all the substances assimilated in the body must be reduced to a fluid form, the constant presence of a certain quantity of water is necessary in order to effect the solution of, and to convey the nutritious particles. This watery fluid is partly contained in the food itself, and is partly taken as drink. Milk is the only food which, with so much nutritive matter, also contains the requisite amount of water.

Our bodies like plants require more water for dissolving solid food than can be assimilated, and there is consequently a portion of fluid to be separated. This process is accomplished in three different ways; but on an average it may be assumed that, of the entire quantity of water which is to be removed, one-fifth passes away by the lungs, one-fifth through the skin by perspiration, and three-fifths as urine.

86. The renal artery (artery of the kidneys) conducts the blood in its circulation through the *kidneys*, which are two glandular organs placed in the abdominal cavity, and their function is to separate or secrete from the blood a portion of superfluous water together with several other substances which it holds in solution. These are used-up particles or detritus of the body, which the blood in its course takes up, especially from the muscles, and are with the urine conveyed from the kidneys into the bladder whence they are ejected from the body.

87. The quantity of food necessary for the support of a man depends both on the temperature and moisture, or dryness of the atmosphere, and also on the circumstances of the individual himself. As a general rule it may be stated, that the colder and moister the climate, the more nourishment is requisite. This greater appetite for food is occasioned by the loss of caloric expended in respiration, which deficiency must be supplied by an increased consumption of food.

It is a fact generally known, that the inhabitants of warm countries require considerably less food than those of temperate and cold climates; and that the inhabitants of the frigid zones, especially, consume large quantities of calorific materials (comp. § 80). The Laplanders, for example, drink train oil in large quantities. Hence the stronger appetite of the natives of the north, which appears to us so enormous, is by no means to be accounted gluttony or excess, but what the exigencies of their circumstances fully justify. The excessive cold of their climate can only be endured by their receiving copious supplies of warmth-producing food.

88. In every muscular motion, there is a portion of the muscle so moved used up or spent. This loss of muscular substance must be repaired or renewed in order that the muscle may be in a condition to repeat the motion. No muscular motion can be perpetual; perpetual movement or friction would speedily diminish the substance of the body, and in time would wear it out. In all animals, after long and continued exertion or expenditure of muscular force, a feeling of lassitude is apparent, which is succeeded by a period of repose, which we call *sleep*. In man the average period of muscular motion is seventeen hours a day; and seven hours are generally spent in rest or sleep. During the latter period his muscles are restored by a sufficient increase of fibrous substance, and are thus prepared for a subsequent expenditure of muscular energy.

Hence it is clear that those who endure severe and long-continued bodily exertions, and thereby expend a more than ordinary proportion of muscular substance, require proportionally a larger supply of food whereby this loss may be compensated: and for this purpose they should receive the most nutritious kinds of food, as bread, meat, leguminous fruits, cheese, and similar aliments.

III. ORGANS OF SENSE.

89. The organs of sense do not consist of a simple formation, but of a union of the several parts we have before described. In them we find bones,

muscles, nerves, and blood-vessels, and in this respect they may be viewed as compound organs.—We distinguish five organs of sense, viz., the skin, the tongue, the nose, the ear, and the eye.

1. The Skin.

90. The skin is the organ of feeling, and covers the entire surface of the body. It consists of three different skins or layers—namely, of the skin proper, the muscular layer, and the cellular tissue.

(*a.*) The skin forms the exterior covering of the whole body; and is evidently composed of three distinct layers, viz., the epidermis or cuticle, the rete mucosum, and the cutis vera or true skin.

The *epidermis* is a thin, transparent membrane, without sensibility. It may be perforated by a sharp-pointed instrument and raised up. In some places by friction and pressure it is thickened, and forms *callosities*, or corns, as they are commonly termed.

The *pores* are the very numerous and minute apertures of the skin; and in similar depressions are the roots of the hair. Both these organs will form the subject of further consideration.

Beneath the epidermis is the *rete mucosum*, which is properly the under part of the epidermis. This layer exhibits no organised structure, and is chiefly remarkable for assuming, under certain climatic influences, peculiar colours, whereby the inhabitants of different regions of the earth are distinguished; as, for example, the black or swarthy complexion of the Negro, brown of the Malay, the copper colour of the American Indians, the yellow complexion of the Chinese, and the pale or colourless skin of the Whites, as they are called. With the whites of temperate climates the red blood-vessels lying immediately under the skin shine through the upper, and impart to the surface a red colour, as in the lips and cheeks.

The *cutis vera* forms the essential part of the *vascular skin*, and consists of a thick, tough layer of fibres, vessels, and nerves thickly interwoven. When this is freed from the upper layers and hairs, it is [in the case of some animals, after being subjected to the process of tanning] employed as leather.

On examining the cutis of man with a microscope, an infinite number of minute *papillæ* or prominencies are discovered, consisting of bundles of fine nervous threads which terminate in them, and are the seat of sensation. They are easily perceived on the inner surface of the fingers, forming linear elevations.

91. (*b.*) The *muscular layer* consists of a thin layer of muscular fibres extended under the skin, and in the human subject is present only in certain parts, as on the neck and head. In many animals, as the hedge-hog, this layer is drawn over the whole of the body (comp. § 29).

(*c.*) The *cellular layer*, which is also called cellular tissue, constitutes the third layer of the covering of the body, and in many places where the muscular layer is wanting, the second. It consists of a loose tissue filled with fat, and is slightly developed in lean subjects, but abundantly in those who are fat.

92. The hair, the nails, the scales, the feathers, and horns belong to the skin.

The hairs are inserted by roots or bulbs, into depressions of the skin. They grow only from the roots, possessing neither nerves nor any other vascular organisation, so that they can be cut without any perceptible pain. The hairs are hollow, and, like the rete mucosum, are filled with a fluid which communicates to them their peculiar colour.

The nails, scales, and feathers may be considered as highly-developed hairs growing together from their roots: they are also devoid of feeling and grow from their roots. The same remark applies to the horns; and when these in many animals are less perfectly developed, as, for instance, the horn of the rhinoceros, they may be distinctly shown to consist of agglutinated hairs. All these cuticular excrescences agree in their chemical constituents; 100 parts contain 51 parts of carbon, 7 of hydrogen, 18 of nitrogen, 24 of oxygen, with a small portiou of sulphur. By reason of the large proportion of nitrogen which they contain, they are extensively employed in the manufacture of Prussian blue (Chem. § 92).

93. The numerous capillary vessels, spread all over the vascular skin, bring the blood which they contain into close proximity to the entire surface of the body and with the atmosphere, which only by the walls of these vessels and epidermis is prevented from immediate contact with them. For since the skin is not impermeable, portions of the constituents of the blood are evaporated and appear through the small apertures of the epidermis as the moisture which we call *sweat* or *perspiration.*

The perspiration is chiefly composed of water. It contains, however, many volatile substances distinguished by a peculiar odour. The quantity, on the whole, amounts to one-fifth of the fluid matter which is separated from the body. This evaporation by the skin is essential to the health of the body, and a decrease of this activity of the skin is always injurious. Animals, when their pores are stopped by a coating of varnish spread over the skin, speedily perish. An increased perspiration is occasioned by all causes which excite a copious flow of blood to the skin, also by external heat, powerful exertion, warm drinks, &c. The skins of the carnivora have no pores; consequently they do not perspire, and need smaller quantities of water.

2. The Tongue.

94. The tongue is the organ of *taste.* This organ, which may be considered a distinct and highly-developed portion of the skin, is provided, all over its surface, with small prominences called the gustatory papillæ, which are distinctly discernible. The muscular skin is present in the form of two powerful muscles which give mobility to the tongue, and assist in the operations of macerating and swallowing the food. The tongue performs also an important part as one of the principal vocal organs, and hence it may be also termed the organ of speech as well as that of taste.

Only such bodies as are soluble in water affect the organ of taste. Perfectly insoluble substances are called tasteless, such, for example, as flint, coal, &c. Hence the power of tasting possessed by the tongue is constantly supported by its contiguity to the salivary glands (§ 47), which secrete the aqueous saliva, whereby the substances put into the mouth are partly dissolved and hence made perceptible to the taste.

The tongue is met with as a visible organ in the vertebrata and in many of the invertebrata. But though in many of the lower animals this organ is wanting, yet the sense of taste is certainly possessed. This is evident from their selection of particular kinds of food, as is the case with caterpillars, which prefer one plant and reject another.

3. The Nose.

95. The nose is the organ of *smell*. Its essential part is *the turbinated bones*, which consist of thin convoluted plates, covered by the mucous membrane of the nose or *pituitary membrane*. By means of a secretion of mucus it is kept continually moist, and this condition is necessary for the perception of odours, since the same membrane when dry is deprived of the sense of smell. The same incapacity for smell is also occasioned by a too abundant secretion of mucus, as, for example, during a cold. In a very limited space, the pituitary membrane exposes a surface of several square feet to the influence of odoriferous objects, and may be compared to a rolled-up sheet of paper, which in a small space has the same extent of surface as before.

Such substances alone are odoriferous as possess the property of assuming a gaseous form — all others are termed inodorous. It is remarkable what very minute particles of matter may be perceived by the smell: if a grain of musk be placed in a room, the odour fills the whole space, and after a time pervades every part of the house. Yet we do not find after weighing it in the finest and most delicate balance, that any sensible diminution of its weight has taken place. This organ is, therefore, one of the most important, as it informs us of the presence of much of which our other senses can give us no intimation. It is known that the savage can smell smoke for many miles; that camels in the parched deserts smell the water long before they approach it, and perceptibly quicken their speed that they may the sooner reach the watering-place; that the hound, guided by the scent alone, will follow the game or his master for many hours without intermission.

96. In men, the nasal cavity opens into the cavity of the mouth by two passages placed behind the palate, so that the air can be drawn in through the nostrils for respiration, and through which it generally enters during sleep. This organisation is found in mammals, birds, and reptiles; but in fishes it has a different situation.

The lower orders of animals have no visible organs of smell. Yet they are not all totally destitute of this sense; for example, the carrion-beetle (Todtengräber) scents the decomposing bodies on which it preys, and moths avoid strong-smelling substances.

4. The Ear.

97. The ear is the organ of *hearing*. It is always double, consisting of the external and internal ear. The external ear (fig 10), is contracted into the *meatus auditorius externus*, or external passage, which is terminated by a very elastic membrane (Membrana tympani) behind which lies the *tympanum*. The cavity of the tympanum is connected with the mouth by a tube, which admits of the entrance of air. This explains the reason why deaf persons open their mouths when listening. In the cavity of the tympanum there is a series of small bones, which are named from their shapes, viz., the *hammer* (malleus) fig. 11 *a* and fig. 12 *d*. The *anvil* (incus) *b*, the os orbiculare, *c*, and the *stirrup ring d* (stapes). The labyrinth (fig. 10) is

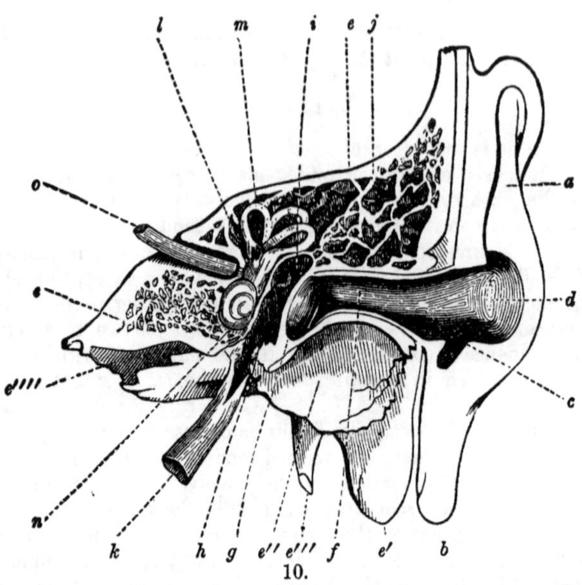

10.

[This figure represents a vertical section of the auditory apparatus, of which the interior parts are slightly magnified to render them more distinct: *a*, the tragus; *b*, the lobe of the ear; *c*, the little eminence called antitragus; *d*, the conch of the ear, the end of which is continuous with the external auditory meatus, *f*; *ee*, portion of the temporal bone called the petrous portion, in which is lodged the auditory apparatus; *e'*, the mastoid process of the temporal bone; *e''*, portion of the glenoid fossa of the temporal bone, in which the lower jaw is articulated; *e'''*, the styloid process of the temporal bone, serving for the attachment of muscles and ligaments of the os hyoides; *e''''*, extremity of the canal which the internal carotid artery passes through to enter the cavity of the cranium; *f*, the external meatus auditorius; *g*, the membrana tympani; *h*, the tympanum from which the small bones have been removed; *i*, opening leading from the cavity of the tympanum to the cells in the petrous bone; in the internal wall of the tympanum are perceived the two openings called fenestra ovalis and rotunda; *k*, Eustachian tube, leading from the tympanum to the back of the pharynx; *l*, the vestibule; *m*, semicircular canals; *n*, the cochlea; *o*, the auditory nerve.]

a b c d

11.

a Malleus.
b. The Incus.
c Os orbiculare
d. The stapes.

composed of the *cochlea*, *n*, and the *vestibule*, *l*, the *fenestra ovalis*, and the semicircular canals, *m*. The cochlea and the vestibule are full of a watery fluid in which the fibres of the *auditory* nerve, *o*, are expanded.

Without any precise scientific knowledge of these individual organs and their functions, a general idea may be formed of the process of hearing, viz., that the waves of sound are collected by the external ear, and conveyed to the membrane of the tympanum, which is thereby set in motion, and this is communicated through the small bones to the fluid of a labyrinth, and thus to the auditory nerve.

The most essential portion of the organ of hearing is the nerve. The tympanum may be injured, and the series of small bones deranged, without being followed by a total

[This figure represents the external wall of the typanum, the membrana tympani, the small bones of the ear and their muscles, the whole magnified; *aa*, cavity of the tympanum; *b*, the membrana tympani; *c*, the manubrium of the malleus, of which the extremity rests upon the membrane of the tympanum; *d*, the head of the malleus articulating with the incus; *e*, process of the malleus giving rise to the anterior muscle; *f*, internal muscle of the malleus; *g*, the incus articulating with *h*, the os orbiculare; *i*, the stapes articulating with the orbicular bone, and resting upon the fenestra ovalis; *k*, the muscle of the stapes.]

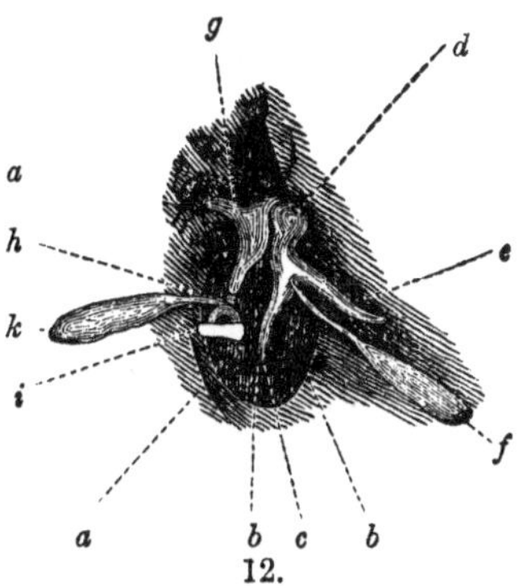

12.

loss of hearing. In many animals, crabs for example, this organ consists merely of a vesicle filled with fluid through which the auditory nerve is spread out.

The mammifera alone have an externally visible ear. In reptiles and fishes the ear is covered over with the skin, and in birds there is but a simple aperture. In the lower orders, with few exceptions, this organ is unknown.

5. The Eye.

98. The eye is the organ of *sight*. We will first describe its individual parts, and subsequently its functions. The eye, with all its integuments, is named the *eye-ball*, represented by a lateral section, fig. 13. Considering the eye from the inside to the outside, we find that its interior consists of a transparent ball, the substance of which is gelatinous, and is called the *vitreous humour*, *v*. This transparent ball is enveloped by three coats, the innermost of which is the *retina*, *r*, which is an expansion of the *optic nerve*. The retina is covered by the *tunica choroides*, *c h*, which derives its name from the numerous blood-vessels which are present, and communicate to it their red colour. Its anterior portion terminates with the brown, grey, or blue coloured *iris*, *i*. In the centre of the iris is the *pupil*, *p*, and beneath the iris are the *ciliary vessels*, *p c*. The whole inner surface of the tunica choroides is covered with a *black pigment*, and the eye is similar to a small dark chamber only lighted by the pupil. Occasionally, this pigment is wanting, so that the red vessels appear through the transparent membrane, and communicate a red colour to the eyes. Men with such eyes are called *Albinos*. They cannot easily bear the light. This is also the case with ferrets and white rabbits, &c., whose eyes are red.

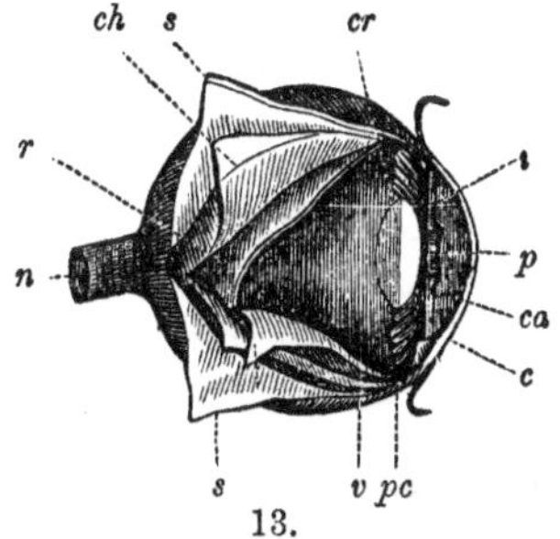

13.

The third and outermost coating or membrane of the eye is called the *sclerotic tunic* (tunica sclerotica), *s*. It is like porcelain, white and strong and protects the softer and inner parts. The fore part is the *cornea*, *c*, some what more convex and perfectly transparent. Between the cornea and the iris is situated the *chamber c a*, which is filled with a colourless transparent fluid.

The *crystalline lens*, *c r*, is situated just behind the pupil, and consists of a gelatinous perfectly transparent substance, more solid than the *vitreous humour*, *v*, which fills up the posterior chamber of the eye. All these parts may be clearly seen in the dissection of a bullock's eye. From this the crystalline lens may be abstracted, and by inspection any one may convince himself that it possesses the properties of a convex lens prepared from glass or crystal; and also that the structure and functions of the eye (the *sight*), are in perfect accordance with the principles of optics, which have been explained in our treatise on Physics (§ 142).

II. CLASSIFICATION AND DESCRIPTION OF ANIMALS.

99. In the foregoing brief outline of anatomy and physiology, we have selected the human subject, because the body of man is composed of a greater number of organs, in a higher state of development, than is to be found in any other terrestrial animal. Adopting the human body as the standard, we compare with this all other animals, and assign to them their relative places in the animal kingdom, either higher or lower, according as they approach this standard, or are remote from it.

Animals approaching nearest to man, either in the number or the development of their individual organs, occupy a higher place in the systematic arrangement than such as exhibit a greater or less deficiency either in the number or development of their organic apparatus.

Notwithstanding, the practical distinction of animals is not unattended with considerable impediments; inasmuch as the external forms of analogous organs in many animals vary very considerably from that of the human species. For example, the respiratory organ in the insect-class is merely an elongated air-cell passing through the whole body, and bears no resemblance to our lungs, except in function.

From the manifest difficulty there is in estimating the importance of diagnostic characters, there are different views entertained in reference to classification. Some naturalists assign a higher rank to the molluscous orders than to insects, whilst others place them lower. Upon the whole, however, they are all agreed upon the fundamental principles of a systematic arrangement, and it will be of far greater importance for us to learn the distinguishing characteristics of the different animals than to balance the merits of the various systems proposed for their systematic classification.

At the present time, about 48,870 *genera* of animals are known and accurately described, and it may be assumed that the number actually existing is not fewer than 88,000, which, with the addition of petrified remains of animals not hitherto found in a recent state, viz., 12,000, will make a grand total of probably above 100,000 genera. It has been already stated in § 25 that they are all divisible into two principal groups, viz., animals that have no vertebral column, *invertebrata*, forming the one group; and such as have a vertebral column, *vertebrata*, forming the other.

These two principal *groups* are divided into *classes;* the classes are divided into *orders*, and subdivided into *families;* these contain, as in botany, several species of a similar kind, which constitute a *genus*, or *family*.

It is evident that an adequate description of this immense number of living creatures far exceeds the limits of any elementary work. The present is only intended to show the importance of classification, and to exemplify the classes and orders by a general description of the most remarkable animals in each. The student who desires to follow up the subject is referred to special works on the science of Zoology. The following table exhibits a view of the classes and orders of the animal kingdom:—

Tabular View of the Animal Kingdom.

A.—Vertebrata.

Animals with an interior osseous jointed apparatus (skeleton), containing the brain and spinal chord, which is conveyed through the vertebral canal, with red blood contained in a vascular system of arteries, veins, and absorbent vessels.

Classes.	Orders.
I. *Mammalia.*	
Red, warm blood; heart with two auricles and two ventricles; with lungs; producing their young alive, and nourishing them with their milk; bodies hairy, with few exceptions. Number of known genera = 1500.	1. Bimana. 2. Quadrumana. 3. Cheiroptera. 4. Carnivora. 5. Marsupialia. 6. Rodentia. 7. Edentata. 8. Pachydermata multungula. 9. Solidungula. 10. Ruminantia. 11. Pinnipeda. 12. Cetacea.
II. *Aves* (*Birds*).	
Red, warm blood; heart with two auricles and two ventricles; with lungs; lay eggs; bodies covered with feathers; anterior members, wings. Number of known genera = 6000.	1. Rapaces. 2. Incessores. 3. Rassores, *seu* Gallinaceæ. 4. Cursores. 5. Grallatores. 6. Natantes.
III. *Amphibia* (*Reptiles*).	
Red, cold blood; heart with two auricles and with a simple or imperfectly divided ventricle; breathe through lungs and partly through gills; lay eggs; skin scaly or naked. Number of known genera = 1500.	1. Chelonii—turtles. 2. Sauri—lizards. 3. Serpentes—serpents. 4. Batrachia—Frogs.
IV. *Pisces* (*Fishes.*)	
Heart with one auricle and one ventricle; red, cold blood; breathe through gills; lay eggs; have members adapted for swimming, and a scaly skin. Number of genera = 5000.	1. Plagiostomi. 2. Eleutherobranchi. 3. Cyclostomi. 4. Pectognathi. 5. Lophobranchi. 6. Malacopterygii. 7. Acanthopterygii.

B. Invertebrata.

No brain nor spinal chord; either with smaller ganglionic centres or knots united by nerves, or with a simple nerve, or with no traces of a nervous system.

Classes.	Orders.
V. *Crustacea.*	
Limbs jointed with more than three pairs of feet; with mostly two feelers (antennæ); eyes mostly compound, with gills or gill-sacs.	1. Decapoda. 2. Stomapoda. 3. Amphipoda. 4. Læmedipoda. 5. Isopoda. 6. Cladocera. 7. Phyllopoda. 8. Copepoda. 9. Ostropoda.
VI. *Insecta* (*Insects*).	
Head and trunk separated by a neck; jointed members; three pairs of feet; one pair of feelers (antennæ); eyes compound; with pulmonary tubes; with metamorphosis.	1. Coleoptera. 2. Orthoptera. 3. Neuroptera. 4. Lepidoptera. 5. Hemiptera. 6. Diptera.
VII. *Arachnida* (*Spiders.*)	
Head and trunk not separated by a neck; generally four pairs of limbs; simple eyes; no feelers; breathe through pulmonary sacs and tubes; without metamorphosis.	1. Pulmonary arachnidans. 2. Tracheal arachnidans.
VIII. *Annulata* (*Worms*).	
Bodies considerably elongated, composed of a succession of annular segments; without limbs; breathe by pulmonary sacculi (sacs); generally with red blood; aquatic, except the earthworm.	1. Dorsibranchiata. 2. Annelida. 3. Tubicola.
IX. *Mollusca* (*Mollusks.*)	
Bodies soft, with slimy skin; a complete vascular system; mostly enclosed in one or two calcareous shells.	1. Cephalopoda. 2. Pteropoda. 3. Conchifera. 4. Gasteropoda 5. Brachiopoda 6. Acephala. 7. Tunicata.
X. *Radiata. Echinodermata.*	
Mostly radiated bodies with a coriaceous or calcareous integument, in which the mouth and anal apertures are attached; marine locomotive animals.	1. Fistularia. 2. Echinida. 3. Asteroida. 4. Crinoidea.

Tabular View of the Animal Kingdom—*continued.*

Classes.	Orders.
XI. *Entozoa.* Bodies soft and transparent, various in structure and figure; with no tentaculi: live in other animals.	1. Filiformes. 2. Echinorynchi. 3. Sterilmintha. 4. Cœlelmintha.
XII. *Acalepha.* Marine aquatics with gelatinous pellucid bodies; with a vascular system; filiform tentaculi; traces of nerves; floating freely.	1. Pulmonigrada. 2. Cilograda. 3. Physograda. 4. Cirrigrada. 5. Diphyda.
XIII. *Polypi.* Bodies gelatinous or fleshy, mostly attached; mouth provided with radiating filiform tentaculi; whole interior consists of an alimentary sac; increasing by germs and divisions.	1. Sea anemonies. 2. Corallidæ. 3. Tubular horny polypi. 4. Sea-pen. 5. Hydræ.
XIV. *Infusoria. Polygastrica.* Bodies gelatinous, pellucid; composed of numerous alimentory sacs or tubes; their fluids have a kind of circulation; no nervous system; microscopic animals; moving freely.	1. Anentera, without an intestinal canal. 2. Enterodela, having a complete alimentary organ.

A.—VERTEBRATA.

100. The vertebral column is the essential distinguishing mark of the more highly-developed classes of the animal kingdom: this forms the cartilaginous or bony covering of the spinal chord, which, united with the never-failing brain, and with the nerves emanating from both, forms the highly-developed nervous system, by means of which sensation and great activity are communicated. The very complicated external organs of sensation in this grand division form a striking contrast with the supposed analogous organs present in animals of the invertebrate sub-kingdom.

The higher rank of the vertebrate classes of the creation is further manifested by their internal jointed skeleton; a complex and curious alimentary canal; a muscular motive system; a system of arteries, veins, and nerves, for the circulation of the fluids and for the communication of sensation. The multiplicity and complexity of their organisation necessarily demand a larger extent of space than the bodies of the invertebrata. The smallest of the vertebrata, even of those whose fineness of organisation is scarcely visible, unless when under a magnifying power, are, when contrasted with the greatest number of the invertebrata, proportionally of gigantic size. In variety and number, however, they are far surpassed by the latter group.

The higher classes, in their relations and analogies to the human race, are more extensive and remarkable than those of the inferior classes. Their ravages are less injurious and more easily prevented, than the invisible depre dations and destructive devastations of many of the inferior grades of animated creatures.

The vertebrata are divided into four classes, viz., mammalia, birds, reptiles, and fishes.

First Class. Mammalia.

101. This class comprehends the most perfect forms of animal life, and presents manifold diagnostic marks of distinction from other classes. The most obvious of these is, that they bring forth their young alive, and nourish them, while young, with their own milk. Their bodies are generally invested with a covering of hair, which, in a very few, is converted by coherence and agglutination into spinous or scaly processes. The organs of sensation are all remarkably developed, and the external ear is almost always provided with a cartilaginous muscle. Their vertebral column is flexible, and the neck is, with few exceptions, composed of seven vertebræ. They are distinguished by four limbs, two corresponding pairs anterior and posterior, the extremities of which separate into five, four, three, or two divisions (toes), and sometimes they are entire, as in the *solidungula*. The trachea, or windpipe, is closed by a valve; the voice, or sound, is not, however, melodious, but mostly harsh or shrill. The development of the organs of sense, of the brain, and of the muscular and nervous systems, in the mammiferous vertebrata, renders them of the utmost importance in the general economy of human life. They not only supply man with the most important part of his nutriment and clothing, but serve him in an infinite variety of ways; some of them, possessed of more than ordinary sagacity, are even often called, and not undeservedly, the associates and friends of the human species.

The distinctive ordinal marks of quadrupeds are mainly derived from the form of the *teeth* and of the *feet*. In reference to their position, the teeth are said to be either *anterior*, in *front;* or *posterior*, in the *further part of the jaw*. In front are four *incisor*, or cutting teeth, and two *canine* teeth; and in the further part of the jaw there are five *molar*, or grinding teeth, on each side, of which the two pairs in each jaw situated next the canine teeth are called *pseudo-molar*, or false grinding teeth; and these are deficient in some animals. The substance of the teeth presents aberrations from the

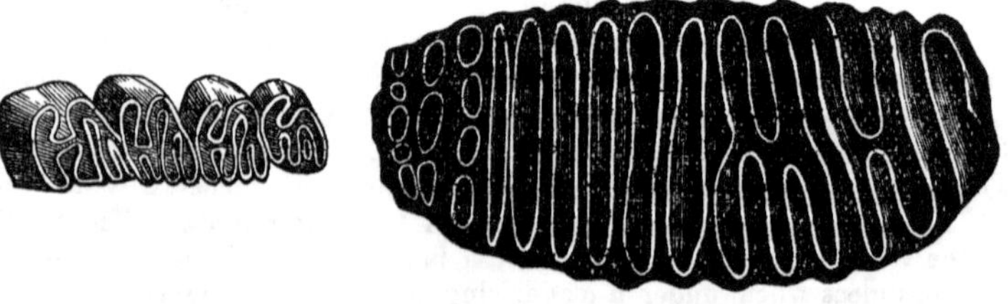

14. 15.

normal type; for example, whilst the front, or incisor and canine teeth, are entirely covered with enamel, this substance forms plaits or folds, penetrating the ivory of the molars (see fig. 14). Some of the latter exhibit on the grinding surface a series of enamel plaits, and a still harder substance, called cement, which interpenetrates the ivory of the tooth, as in the elephant's molar teeth, fig. 15. In many animals, the grinding surfaces of the molar teeth are provided with *prominences* or *ridges*, or with *jags* and *depressions;* the former is the case in man, the latter in animals of the feline and canine genera.

In the form and length of the legs there are great variations, being in both respects adapted to the exigencies of the particular animal, viz., for laying hold of prey, for running, leaping, bounding, grubbing, or swimming. In general, however, the fore legs differ more or less from the hind ones. When one of the toes, as in the ape-family, is situated opposite the other toes, like a thumb, the organ is called a *hand;* in all other cases it is called the *paw.* The extremity of the toe is covered either with a flat or curved nail, or terminated in a sharp-pointed, crooked claw, or is enclosed in a horny blunt hoof.

Terrestrial mammifera are also characterised by their mode of life and general economy. Some, for example, feed exclusively on vegetable substances. Their young are produced with a hairy investment, are in possession of sight at their birth, and are, for a considerable time, exclusively nourished by their mother's milk. Others eat only flesh, and bring forth their young naked and blind. A third kind can live on both flesh and vegetables indifferently.

Division of Mammalia.

A. Anterior and Posterior limbs developed.			B. Anterior and Posterior Limbs imperfectly developed.	
a. With Nails or Claws on Moveable Toes.		*b.* With Hoofs on Immoveable Toes		
With Incisor, Canine, and Molar Teeth.	With a Deficiency of the Normal Number of Teeth.	With Highly-developed Molar Teeth.	Teeth like Carnivora.	Teeth Setaceous, or Bristly.
1. Bimana. 2. Quadrumana. 3. Cheiroptera. 4. Carnivora. 5. Marsupialia.	6. Rodentia. 7. Edentata.	8. Multungula or Pachydermata. 9. Solidungula. 10. Ruminantia.	11. Pinnipeda. Phocæ. Seals, &c.	12. Cetacea. Whales.

First Order. Bimana.

102. The only genus of this order is *man* (Homo sapiens), the structure of whose body we have already described; and in this only he is the standard of comparison in the arrangement of all other animals among which he is classed; while his posture, his capability of speech, his intelligence and reason, elevate him to a station infinitely higher than the other animals, of which he is the sovereign ruler. The peculiar distinctive marks which separate man from the animals that have the greatest similarity to him are—hands at extremities of the superior limbs; teeth of equal length, without large openings between them; an upright posture; less hairiness; and flatter nails than we find in the kindred tribes.

The remarkable diversities that appear among various tribes or divisions of the human family are generally considered to be variations occasioned by time and climate; these varieties, however, do not militate against the original unity of the race. The following are the principal varieties of this exalted order.

(1.) The *Caucasian race*, of fair complexion, with soft hair, and of all shades, from light-brown and flaxen to black; small oval face, with lofty arched forehead. This race, according to our ideas, is the standard of beauty; and it includes all the Europeans, the inhabitants of Western Asia, of the North of Africa, and of North America, &c. (2.) The *Mongolian race;* complexion yellow or tawny; hair black, thin and straight; broad, flat faces, with prominent cheek-bones; nose small and flat, and small eyes, with closely-approaching eyelids. By these marks we recognise the inhabitants of Central Asia, the Kalmucks, Tartars, Chinese, &c. (3.) The *Ethiopian race,* with woolly, crisp, and black hair, small head, and prominent cheek-bones; the forehead is depressed and the chin is protrusive; these marks, with the flat noses and large thick lips, distinguish the inhabitants of Africa, with the exception of those of the Mediterranean coasts. (4.) The *American race* have a coppery complexion, low forehead, prominent cheek-bones, lank and black hair. These are the indigenous inhabitants of America. (5.) The *Malayan race*, with brown or black complexion, black curly hair, flat nose, and forehead somewhat prominent. The South Sea islanders are of this race.

SECOND ORDER. QUADRUMANA.

103. Among all animals, the quadrumana, or *Ape-tribe*, both in external figure and in internal structure, approach nearest to the human family. They have all the three kinds of teeth, and eyes directed forwards; they are also particularly distinguished by their hand-like feet, with a thumb in some degree opposite to the toes or fingers, forming altogether a powerful prehensile organ. They cannot walk upright, because their hind feet have no sole, which is indispensable to the upright posture. Apes inhabit only the warmer regions of the earth, and live socially in the forests, mostly on the trees, which they climb with great dexterity and speed. The monkeys avail themselves of their long and contractible tail in climbing and leaping from tree to tree, often suspending themselves by twisting this muscular organ around the branches. They live principally on fruit; but in confinement they eat all sorts of food, especially eggs, pastry, and similar viands. Some of them prey on insects. Although their bodily organisation be so elevated and their strength so considerable, that they apparently might render important services to mankind, yet they appear to be totally useless to man, whom they represent only under the vilest and most disgusting of caricatures. They are selfish, malicious, deceitful, crafty, and thievish, without the slightest docility, especially at an advanced period of their lives. But the most domesticated is not to be trusted. On account of their droll similarity to humanity, and their ridiculously-ludicrous gestures, they are frequently carried about and exhibited for vulgar amusement.

Of this family there is so great a number of genera, that the most comprehensive zoological works have scarcely exhausted the subject. Consequently, many are very imperfectly known. Their characteristic differences are also so slight, that they are easily confounded and mistaken for each other.

This order is divided into three sections, viz., *apes proper* (Simiadæ), which are distinguished by the absence of tails and cheek-pouches; the *monkeys* of the New World (Cebidæ), distinguished by cheek-pouches, an additional molar tooth, and a long tail, which is used by them as an organ of prehension; and the *lemurs* (Lemuridæ), which have thumbs on the extremities of their fore as well as on their hind limbs. Some of the first bear the closest resemblance to the human form and physiognomy, and are all natives of the Old World. The apes, baboons, and monkeys of the eastern hemisphere are distinguished by having the nasal septa smaller than it is in the other individuals of the order: of these, we may mention the *orang-outang*, which is the largest of the tribe (Simia satyrus), a native of Borneo and Sumatra, and the *chimpanzee* (S. troglodytes), fig. 16, both without tails, and bearing a considerable resemblance to the human physiognomy and form; they are sometimes seen of the height of from six to seven feet, and have given occasion to many fabulous stories of wild men of the woods. The Javanese assert that they can speak, but that they conceal this faculty lest they should be enslaved by the more crafty bipeds. To this section also belong the long-armed apes, *gibbons* (Hylobates lar), and the caudate (tailed) species; for example, the *long-tailed monkey* (Semnopithecus nemæus,) most remarkable for its strange mixture of colours, and the extraordinary length of the caudal appendage; the *green monkey* (Cercopithecus sabæus), and the *macauco* (Inuus cynomolgus, fig. 17); and the *common* or *Barbary*, or *showman's ape* (I. sylvanus), which is found about the rock of Gibraltar, and is the only ape indigenous to the European continent. All these are frequently exhibited by the owners of menageries. In such establishments are also frequently to be seen the *papians* (Cynocephalus,) whose head resembles the dog's; and the *Arabian papian* (Cynocephalus hamadryas), and the *mandrill* (C. maimon), distinguished by its red visage and blue nose.

16.

The individuals of this tribe indigenous to the New World have a larger nasal septum, and hence their nostrils are more lateral than they are in the other members of the family. Many of these employ the end of their tails as the others do their hand, and as the elephant uses his trunk. The most remarkable genera of this tribe are the *howling monkey* (Mycetes Beelzebul), and the *spider monkeys* (Ateles). The *Capuchin ape* (Cebus capucinus), and the *sajou* (C. apella), are frequently found in menageries. Besides these, there are also the *squirrel monkey* (Callithrix sciurea); the *night monkey*, distinguished by its large eyes, and its habit of hunting by night, like the carnivora; and the *silken monkey*, or *uistiti* (Hapale jacchus)

17.

The *lemurs, makis*, &c., form a section of this family, differing from the above in having the general form of the carnivora, though they agree with the rest of the quadrumana in the arrangement of their digital organs. They are social, living chiefly on fruit and insects, and hunt by night, for which they are well adapted by the great size of their eyes. The principal genera are the *lemur* (L. catta), the *indri* (Lichanotus), the *coris* (Stenops), the *galegos*, and the *sarsiers*. They mostly inhabit the Old World, and especially the large island of Madagascar.

Third Order. Cheiroptera (*the Bat Tribe*).

104. These animals, in several respects analogous to certain genera of the rodent animals, particularly to mice, are distinguished by a fine membranous wing, stretched out between the long toes of the anterior limbs, and attached to the posterior legs. Concealed during the daytime in fissures, dark corners, &c., they fly about in the twilight, hunting their insect prey, which they catch with great dexterity. Some are found in the warmer regions of the world, and live on blood, which they suck from living animals; but a few subsist on fruit. The most remarkable are the *nasal-leaf bats* (Phyllostoma), which, during the night, suck the blood of men and other animals when asleep: of this animal marvellous stories have been related. The

most common bats are the *common vampire* (Ph. spectrum), and the *hastate-crested bat* (Ph. hastatus); the *greater* and *lesser horse-shoe bats*, which have these curious nasal leaf-like appendages on both nose and ears; the *flitter-mouse*, or *common bat* (fig. 18) of this country (Vespertilio murinus); and the *red bat* (V. noctula). In the East Indies, in Africa, and in Australia, there are herbivorous bats, called flying dogs, because of the resemblance which their heads bear to those of the canine genera. They are called vampires, and are objects of general aversion and dread. The largest of these (Pteropus edulus) *black rousette* is of the size of a small dog, and its flesh is eatable.

18.

FOURTH ORDER. CARNIVORA (*the Carnivorous Tribe*).

105. In this order we meet with a large assemblage of animals, which prey upon all the rest of the brute creation, and even on man himself; and hence we are engaged in constant hostilities with the whole race where they happen to occupy the same regions as ourselves, to whom they are the most dangerous and formidable neighbours. As their natural food is living animals, we find that they are provided with a powerful apparatus both of claws and teeth; the former for seizing, the latter for holding their prey. The order is separated into three sub-orders, distinguished by their nutritive economy, and by the organisation of their dental apparatus, viz., the insectivora, which have pointed, conical, molar teeth; the carnivora (proper), with sharp, cutting, molar teeth; and the herbivoro-carnivora, which have teeth also adapted to both the kinds of food on which they subsist.

The *insectivora* of this order are distinguished by their broad naked sole, which they place flat on the ground while walking: in size and economy they are very similar to the size of the rodents (family of the rats, mice, &c.) Amongst these are to be noticed the *hedgehog* (Erinaceus), well known by its prickly skin, and by folding itself up, like a ball, when it is attacked; it preys by night on several injurious insects and other animals: the common *shrew* (Sorex araneus, fig. 19); and the *pigmy shrew* (S. pygmæus), the smallest of all mammiferous quadrupeds. Both of these inhabit holes under-ground, and, on account of their strong musky scent, are not eaten by cats.

19.

The *mole* (Talpa Europæ) is provided with a broad, hand like, strong-nailed paw, suited to the necessities of an animal that grubs in the soil, and which preys on earth-worms, larvæ of insects, &c. Some agriculturists regard its operations as injurious, whilst others are of a contrary opinion. The mole-hills are indeed unsightly objects, but, when scattered over the surface, form a tolerable substitute for a top-dressing. The under-ground galleries may occasionally loosen the soil about the roots of plants, but they afford the means of carrying off a great deal of superfluous moisture, and are in fact an efficient system of surface-drainage. Moles are not blind, though this is the vulgar belief; only their eyes are very small, and deeply situated in the head; a provision admirably adapted to their under-ground habits of existence. It is said that the eyelids of the *Cape mole* (T. cæca) are actually coherent. The *golden mole* of the same country (T. inaurata) is remarkable for the yellow or coppery lustre of its fur, and for being the only mammifer known possessing this property, viz., the metallic glance, which is such a remarkable embellishment in many birds, fishes, &c. The *radiated mole* (Condylura) has a peculiarly-formed snout, which is provided with radiating processes like short feelers.

The proper carnivora are all unguicalate, and are chiefly distinguishable from other kindred orders by their dental and digestive apparatus, and by external characters of a more general nature, all of which are exceedingly well adapted to the necessities of creatures which subsist almost exclusively on a flesh diet, and generally seize their prey alive. They are furnished with six incisor, or cutting, teeth in each jaw, besides fangs or tearers, which are separated by dental interstices from the pointed, tuberculated, grinding teeth of the posterior maxillaries.

The animals belonging to the plantigrade section of the carnivora are characterised by naked soles, and by the general prevalence of tuberculated teeth. Their form is elongated, with short bones; and the larger animals of the tribe, which inhabit the northern parts of the world, are all flesh-eaters; while the smaller, which chiefly inhabit warm climates, prey on small animals, and also eat eggs, fruit, plants, &c. None of these are useful to man. The most important members of the ursine, or bear family, are the great *white bear* (Ursus maritimus), or polar bear, an inhabitant of the arctic regions, subsisting entirely on seals and fish; the *brown bear* (U. arctos) is frequently exhibited by bear-wardens, who teach the animal to walk on his hind paws, and to perform several antics and grotesque dances for the amusement of the by-standers. These animals become fat before winter, which they pass in a dormant condition. The *black bear* (U. Americanus) is a native of the New World, and the *racoon* (U. lator) has the singular custom of plunging its food in water before it tastes it. The smaller ursine quadrupeds are the *nasua*, or red cuati, the East Indian *arctitis*, &c.

A very rapacious, bloodthirsty, sub-section of the carnivora is characterised by long slender bodies and short limbs, which are specially adapted to their habits, viz., hunting under-ground. The *badger* (Meles) burrows in deep holes, and hunts small animals by night; it also eats fruit and roots of plants. The *glutton* (Gulo) is an inhabitant of northern countries, and is erroneously believed to be an enormous eater. The *skunk* (Mephitis), dreaded on account of its intolerable stench, is a native of America, the West Indies, and Java. The following are much prized for their valuable furs, viz., the *pole-cat* (Mustela putorius), the *ferret* (M. furo), used for hunting rats and rabbits, the *ermine* (M. erminea), the *common weasel* (M. vulgaris), the *common marten* (M. martes), the *stone-marten*, the *sable marten* (M.

zibellina), and, finally, the *otter* (Lutra), which subsists on fish, and is provided with a membranous expansion, connecting its toes, whereby it is well adapted for swimming and hunting its fishy prey.

Among the family of the Viverridæ are *civets* the *Egyptian rat*, or *ichneumon* (Herpestes ichneumon), celebrated on account of its devouring the eggs of the formidable crocodile, and the *civet* (Viverra zibetha), which yields the powerfully-odoriferous perfume.

The canine family is more extensive than the former. Here we meet with the *fox* (Canis vulpes), so renowned in all ages for crafty devices, that "cunning as a fox" is a proverbial phrase, common to all European languages; also the *arctic fox* (C. lagopus); the *jackal* (C. aureus); the gluttonous, predaceous *wolf* (C. lupus), long extinct in this country, but still common in the northern parts of Europe, and also in alpine tracts further south; the *domestic dog* (C. familiaris), of which the varieties are almost infinite. Some are trained to hunt, others to point **or** set at game, others to watch sheep, premises, &c. They are all more or less attached to man, and are capable of receiving instruction in infinitely diversified forms, and with very different views. The most admirable adaptation of canine strength and sagacity is exemplified in the dogs of St. Bernard, which are trained to rescue unfortunate travellers who may be overtaken by a storm, and buried in Alpine snow.

20.

Finally, to this family belong the *feline* tribe (Felina), the bloodthirstiest, most rapacious, and formidable of all predaceous animals, as well on account of their dexterity and rapidity of movement as of their enormous strength.

21.

They are almost all limited to the warmer climates. The *hyena* (Hyæna, fig. 20) forms the link between the canine and feline races, and it is remarkable for preying only on carrion, and even on corpses grubbed out of and dragged from their graves. The royal *lion* (Felis leo) is found only in the Old World, together with the still more fierce and ferocious *tiger* (F. tigris). The *panther* (F. pardus, fig. 21), *leopard* (F. leopardus), and the *ocelot* (F. pardalis), are remarkable for their beautifully-spotted skins. The *jaguar*, or American tiger (F. onca), is the most formidable of predaceous animals in the New World. The American, or *red lion* (F. concolor) is only a feeble representative of his royal brothers of Asia and Africa. Our *wild cat* (F. domestica) has been reclaimed, and is universally admitted as a member of the social circle. Her mousing propensities and services are generally rewarded by indulgent and generous treatment.

FIFTH ORDER. MARSUPIALIA (*the Kangaroo Tribe*).

106. The animals of this order are found only in the tropical regions of America, the Sunda Islands, and New Holland. In size they rarely exceed hares and rats. They derive their name from a sack, or pouch, formed on the external lower part of their abdomen, in which they often carry their young after parturition. In some genera of this order the marsupial appendage is deficient, but the conformation of their skeleton, and especially the structure of the pelvis, clearly point out their relationship to the other animals of this order. Several members of this family are herbivorous; while others, in their mode of life, are like the martens and weasels. To the marsupial section belongs the *kangaroo* (Halmaturus, fig. 22), which is about the size of a stag, but with much more powerful hind legs. It is the largest indigenous terrestrial animal of New Holland. The *phascolarctos* (Lipurus), or *koala*, which carries its young on its back, is also a native of New Holland. The *kangaroo hare* and the *kangaroo rat* (Balantia), or *kuskus*, are abundant in the Moluccas.

22.

The carnivorous members of this order produce many young ones at a birth, and many carry them on their backs. The *marsupial marten* and the *opossums* are the most interesting. Many sorts of these are prevalent in America, and are formidable enemies to the poultry of the inhabitants. They bear their young fifty days in their sack, and for some time after on their backs. The *common opossum* (Didelphis marsupialis), about the size of a small dog, and the *flying lemur* (Lemur volans), whose head resembles an ape's, also belong to this section.

SIXTH ORDER. RODENTIA (*the Rodent Tribe*).

107. This large order is divisible into several sub-orders or families, as, for example, the *squirrel* tribe (Sciurina), pretty, lively little creatures, that mostly inhabit trees and hollow trunks, and rarely burrow in the earth. They subsist principally on fruits, kernels, &c. The principal of these are

the *climbing rat* (Isodon), the *marmot* or *mountain rat* (Arctomys), the *dormouse* (Sciurus glis), the *hazel* or *oak rat* (Mus quercinus), the *squirrel* (Sc. vulgaris), and the *flying squirrel* (Sc. volitans).

Mice are active little creatures, mostly living in galleries, holes, and nests, either under ground or in dry protected situations on the earth's surface. They go abroad at night in search of food, which is mostly grain or roots of various sorts; but sometimes, though rarely, they prey on small animals, &c. They are themselves, however, more frequently the prey of larger creatures of predaceous nocturnal habits. The following are the most conspicuous animals of this sub-order, viz., the *lemming* or *Norway rat* (Mus Norwegicus), the *ponched rat* (M. bursarius), the *house-mouse* (M. Musculus), the *field-mouse* (M. solvaticus), the *house-rat* (M. rattus), the *brown rat* (M. decumanus), the *water-vole* (M. amphibius), and the *hamster* (M. cricetus), which lays up great stores of corn.

In the family of the leapers (Macropoda) and hares (Leporina) we meet with many genera which have their hind feet remarkably developed, whereby they are able to make extraordinary leaps, and so escape from animals much stronger than themselves. Many of these are important on account of their fine-flavoured flesh, and for their valuable fur. They are chiefly found in warm regions, and mostly feed on plants. Of these we may notice the *jerboa* (Dipus), the *Cape-hare* (Mus caffer), the *chinchilla* (C. lanigera), which produces the most costly fur, the *coney*, or *rabbit* (Lepus caniculus), and the *common hare* (L. timidus).

Other rodentia are distinguished by their natant membranous hind feet, the most important of which is the *beaver* (Castor fiber), which, selecting the banks of rivers for a habitation, constructs his subterranean abode in the shape of a baker's oven, with an entrance under water. The otter constructs his dwelling in a similar way. On the continent of Europe the beaver is almost extirpated; but he is of frequent occurrence in America and Asia. This animal is destroyed for the sake of his fur, which is so extensively employed in the manufacture of hats; and also on account of a peculiar secretion, called *castoreum*, which is a valuable drug.

To this order belongs also the *porcupine* (Hystrix cristata), which is rare in the south of Europe, but far from uncommon in Africa, where it lives in subterranean cavities.

South America produces an endless variety of rodent animals, which are called subungulate, because their broad sheathing nails are somewhat like hoofs. To these inoffensive and savoury-fleshed animals belong the *aguti*, or *common agoutis* (Dasyprocta), the *paca* (Cœlogenys), the *cavia*, very similar to the well-known *guinea-pig*, which last is also a member of this sub-order. It is a remarkable fact that the guinea-pig, which was introduced into Europe from America several hundred years ago, is no longer found wild in its original native land. In size and appearance the *capybara*, or water-pig (Hydrochærus), resembles a small pig.

Seventh Order. Edentata.

108. The animals composing this order are easily distinguished by the absence of teeth in the anterior part of their protruded maxillaries, and also by the partial deficiency of the same organs in the posterior parts of the jaws. Their toes are likewise protected by long claws. They are further

characterised by their sluggish habits and stupid appearance, and are only found in tropical and sub-tropical regions, and never in great numbers. The

23.

most singular is, perhaps, the *duck-billed quadruped* (Ornithorhynchus paradoxus, fig. 23), which has been observed only in New Holland. To this order belong also the *ant eaters* and *ant bear* (Myrmecophaga), the scaly *pangolins* (Manis), the *armadillo* (Dasypus, fig. 24), covered with scaly armour, like some of the amphibians; also the *sloth* (Bradypus), of which the smaller is named *unau*, or two-toed sloth, and the larger, *ais*, or common sloth.

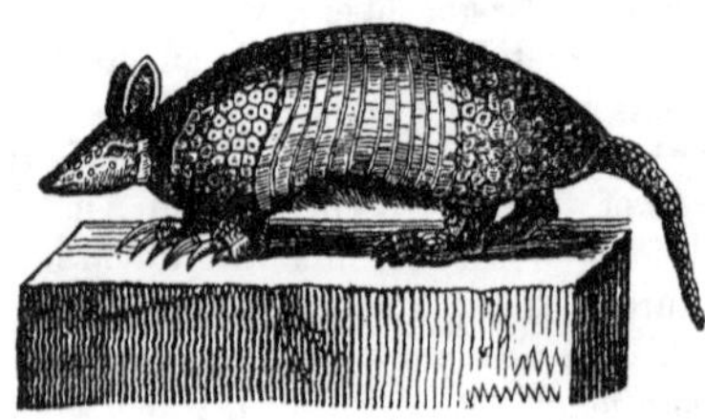

24.

Eighth Order. Pachydermata *seu* Multungula.

109. The thick skins of the animals belonging to this order are only partially hairy, and their toes (from two to five), which are either distinct or coherent, are not moveable, but enclosed in callous or horny cases or hoofs. They are the largest of all terrestrial mammalia, exist principally on vegetable food, and are only found in the old world. Of all the genera of this order the *elephant* (Elephas, fig. 25) is the most remarkable, being equally an object of admiration as well on account of his size, extraordinary strength, sagacity, and wondrous docility, as for the mechanical adaptation of his organs to the necessities of his animal economy. With his trunk he can perform the most minute as well as the most essential offices which would be impossible for any other animal. In fig. 15 we have given a representation of one of the compound molar teeth of the elephant; but he has a still more important organ, viz., his tusks, which are from three to four feet long, and

25.

weigh from twenty to thirty pounds, and supply the valuable material, ivory. The Asiatic elephant is reputed a more tractable beast than his African brother; the latter is further distinguished by long ears, and a more arched forehead. These animals live amicably in troops in the moist forests of Asia and Africa, and are harmless when unprovoked. The most unwieldy of all terrestrial animals is undoubtedly the *river horse* (Hippopotamus, fig. 26), only found in the sluggish and muddy rivers of Africa; with its clumsy head, long barrel-like trunk, and its short legs, it has the least possible resemblance to the symmetry of the noble and finely-proportioned animal whose name it bears.

26.

Our well-known and highly-prized swine belong to a section of this order. The *domestic sow* (Sus scrofa) is one of the most valuable animals, and has been imported into the New World, where it is now abundant. The *Java sow* (S. babirussa) is provided with long curved tusks. The *peccary* (Dicotyles) is distinguished by a glandular secretion which gives to its flesh a disagreeable flavour.

In the next sub-order, *Tapiridæ*, we find the *tapir* characterised by five unequal toes, with a short trunk like the pig. The rhinoceros, whose hide is bullet-proof, sometimes with one, sometimes with two horns, belongs to the same sub-order.

Ninth Order. Solidungula.

110. The whole order is composed of but one family, of which the *noble horse* (Equus caballus) is the representative type, and the most important member; an animal distinguished equally by gracefulness of form, celerity of movement, and tractability and usefulness to mankind. Though so extensively spread over the earth, these animals are never found in a wild or untamed condition, except such as have escaped from domestic servitude, as in America, where enormous troops of wild horses exist in the vast prairies of that country. Many breeds have been produced during the long period of their subjugation. The *mule* is a sort of hybrid, produced between the ass and the mare. Another hybrid is also distinguished, viz., that between the horse and the she ass, but this is less common than the other.

The horse has six front teeth, twelve molars, and two canine teeth in each jaw: the latter are frequently absent. Upper jaw 6 molars, 1 canine, 6 front, 1 canine, 6 molars. Lower jaw 6 molars, 1 canine, 6 front, 1 canine, 6 molars.

27.

The incisor or front teeth have on their cutting surface a dark-brown impression, called a mark, because it is by this that the age of a horse is known, for these marks are obliterated by increasing age.

Africa is the home of three species of this order, viz., the *zebra* (Equus zebra, fig. 27), the *quagga* (Equus quagga), and the *onager*. These are all found in the Cape colony. The *wild ass* or onager (E. asinus) appears in immense troops in the steppes of Tartary, and in the vast tracts of the Ural mountains. The domestic ass is a degenerated descendant of these fleet, spirited animals.

Tenth Order. Ruminantia (*Cud-chewing Animals*).

111. It is universally agreed that this order comprehends the most useful of all mammiferous quadrupeds. They supply us with leather, wool, horn, flesh, milk, butter, cheese, and with solid oil or fat, which is called tallow. Besides this, they are valuable as beasts of burden and draught; and though slow, yet patient and enduring. They have almost all been domesticated,

and consequently there are infinite varieties and aberrations from the common original type. They are all characterised by the cloven or divided hoof, and by the absence of incisor teeth in the upper jaw; with few exceptions they are provided with two horns. They are all herbivorous, and their alimentary apparatus or stomach is separated into four divisions. The first and amplest is called the *paunch* (rumen), into which the half-chewed fodder or herbage first passes; from this the food is conveyed to the second cavity (reticulum), where it is formed into balls, whence it is carried again to the mouth, where it undergoes the process of further mastication. When this has been accomplished, the food passes into the third chamber of the complex stomach, called the *psalterium* (manyplies), which has its mucous-lining membrane disposed in large longitudinal folds, so as to form deep *lamellæ*, like the leaves of a book; it is finally received into the fourth and last stomach or *reed*, where it mixes with the gastric juice (rennet), and becomes aliment.

The ruminant animals form several large families, and of these we first notice the *camel*, which is without horns, but is provided with callosities of a horny nature on the breast and knees. Of this section we distinguish the one-humped camel or *dromedary* (Camelus dromedarius), most common in Arabia and Africa, and the *two-humped camel* (C. bactrianus), with two humps or bunches, chiefly employed as a beast of burden in northern Asia. On account of their almost incredible abstinence, their celerity, strength, endurance, and patient disposition, camels are the most important beasts of transit, both for persons and merchandise, in the extensive barren deserts and steppes of the old world — a more effectual barrier to intercourse than even the sea. Hence the camel is called the ship of the desert. The flesh and milk of the animals are useful as nutriment, and the hair is employed in the manufacture of cloth.

The American camel, or Peruvian sheep, *guanaco* (Camelus lama), is smaller than the former, and has no hump; the *vicugna* also belongs to the New World, and both yield the fine wool called camel hair. The *little lama*, or *paco*, belongs to the same tribe.

The most remarkable of all the members of this family, and indeed of the whole animal kingdom, is the *giraffe* (Camelopardalis, fig. 28), standing eighteen feet high to the crown of the head, which is surmounted by four radiating bony protuberances covered with hairy skin. This brown-spotted, fleet quadruped is a native of the hot regions of central and southern Africa.

An extensive section of the ruminant animals, viz., the *cervidæ* or *deer tribe*, is distinguished by solid, bony horns, which are deciduous, and annually renewed. Among these we find in northern Asia, and especially in Thibet, the *musk deer* (Moschus moschiferus), from which the valuable musk is obtained; the *hart* (Cervus), the *roe* (C. capreolus), the *noble hart*, stag, or red deer (C. elaphus), the *doe* (C. dama), the *rein-deer* (C. tarandus), and the *elk* (C. alces).

Another large division of this order is composed of animals whose horns are permanent and hollow, not solid, as in the last section, but sheathing round a bony nucleus, called the core, which is a prolongation of the frontal bone.

We distinguish the following as being among the most important genera, viz., the *sheep* (Ovis); the wild *Sardinian sheep;* the *domestic sheep* (O.

28.

aries); the *fat-tailed sheep* (O. steatopyga); the *goat* (Capra), to which belong the *stein-bock* (C. ibex); the *wild goat* (C. ægagrus); the *tame goat* (C. hircus); the *Angora* and *Cashmere* goats, which bear the fine wool of which the valuable Cashmere shawls are fabricated; the beautiful alert *antelope*, of which there are numerous species that inhabit the desert and waste places of Arabia, India, and South Africa; among these are reckoned also the *pigmy* or *dwarf antelope* (Antilope pygmæ); the *gazelle* (A. dorcas); the *Arabian antelope*, the *swift antelope* (A. dama), and the *Indian antelope* with twisted horns (A. cervicapra); the *common antelope* (C. rubicapra); and the *gnu*, an animal whose form strikingly resembles that of a small horse, with horns like a buffalo's. The bovine section of the order (*bovidæ*, from *bos*, ox) has been distinguished among all nations and from the earliest ages as the most useful of domestic animals, and as beasts of burden and draught, the usual personification of patience and laboriousness. The *bison* (B. moschatus), the *common ox* (B. taurus), the *common buffalo* (B. Americanus), and the *urochs* (B. urus), still found in Lithuania, are the most conspicuous members of this family.

ELEVENTH ORDER. PINNIPEDA (*the Seal Tribe.*)

112. This order and the following form the connective links between the mammifers and the class of fishes. In organic development and utility to man they are much inferior to the former. The bodies of the seal tribe (fig. 29), are covered with short glossy hair lying flat on the skin; their legs are only partially developed, especially the hind legs, and the toes are connected with a membranous apparatus which is excellently adapted for assisting them in swimming, although out of water they scarcely enable the animal to crawl. They are all inhabitants of the sea and of large estuaries, though occasionally they may be seen basking on the shore. Their food consists of fish, mollusca, &c. The skin, oil, and tusks of these animals are articles of commercial value.

29.

The most remarkable individuals belonging to the genus *Phocidæ* are the *sea-dog* or *sea-calf* (P. vitulina), common in the Arctic Ocean, the *sea-monk* (P. monachus); the *crested seal* (P. cristata); the *sea-lion* (Otaria jubata). The *walrus* (Trichechus rosmarus) sometimes measures 20 feet in length, with a weight of above 2000 lbs., armed with fearful tusks; these formidable animals prey upon the shell-fish-eating denizens of the icy seas, and sometimes engage in deadly conflict between themselves.

TWELFTH ORDER. CETACEA (*the Whale Tribe*).

113. To this tribe belong the largest animals in existence. They are, moreover, distinguished from all other mammifers, not only by their enormous bulk, but also by the total absence of hind feet, and by the development of their anterior members into paddles or swimming paws adapted solely for moving in the water, to which they are strictly limited. In external appearance and habits they are exactly similar to fishes. There is scarcely a trace of hair present, even on their upper lip. The oil, whalebone, and spermaceti which they yield are valuable articles of commerce. Like terrestrial animals, they breathe through nasal apertures, which are in the upper part of their head, by which they eject the water which they inhale along with the air. They inhabit the Northern Ocean, particularly that about Green-

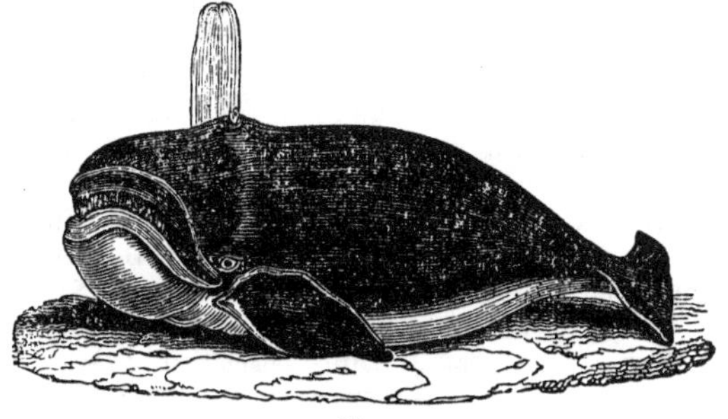
30.

land, but they are also found in the Southern Ocean; and whale-fishing establishments have been planted for several years on the shores of New Zealand, &c. The *Greenland whale* (fig. 30), is from 60 to 80 feet long, and from 50 to 60 tons weight. Instead of teeth, the whale has a fringe of horny fibres resembling stiff hair or bristles, which serves as a gigantic strainer, in which are caught shoals of molluscous animals that swarm sc abundantly in the Northern Ocean. The *spermaceti whale* (Physiter), or cachelot, is sometimes above 100 feet long. This animal affords spermaceti and ambergris.

The *narwhal* (Monodon), the *dolphin* (Dolphinus), aquatic animals of from 8 to 18 feet long, are all members of this family. They are remarkable for the celerity of their movements, and are of very rapacious habits. The above-mentioned live on polypi, molluscous animals, and fish. The following have their anterior limbs more developed, and are herbiverous, viz., the *Arctic marine cow* (Manatus borealis), and the *Atlantic sea-cow* (M. Atlanticus), and the *mermaid* (Halicore, Dügong), which occurs in the seas of the Indian Archipelago.

Second Class. Birds (Aves).

114. The obvious characteristic of all the tribes, families, and individuals of this clas is the feathers, with which the body is covered. In birds, as in mammals, we observe four members, the anterior pair being wings, the posterior legs; also a hard tongue, a bill-formed mouth without teeth, two nasal apertures, and externally open ears, but without the external muscular appendage. Their long neck, composed of from 9 to 23 vertebræ, very much facilitates the movement of their body; the largeness of the brain accounts for their tenaciousness of memory, also for their docility, instinct, and intelligence, which are of a high order, and are remarkably characteristic of many birds. The pulmonary apparatus is highly developed, every part of the body being permeated by the atmospheric air, the body is thereby lightened, and capable not only of supporting itself in the thin medium wherein it is destined to move, but to skim through it with astonishing rapidity. The powerful pulmonary organisation of birds is not only favourable to rapid flight, but also to the high development of their vocal apparatus; and in fact they are the only creatures, except the human, that possess the gift of song. The structure of their bones is hollow, combining the greatest strength with the least weight, and their blood is of a temperature from 10° to 12° Fahr. higher than in the mammifers.

The propagation of the feathered tribes is effected by eggs, which are generally laid to the number of from six to twelve, rarely so many as twenty, before hatching takes place. To the development of the chick or young bird, a period of incubation, which generally lasts three weeks, and a temperature of about 100° are requisite, and after the brood is hatched, the parents with solicitous care provide for the wants and watch over the safety of their offspring. They feed on vegetable food of all sorts, and also on all sorts of fish. They reside either on the water or on the land, and often alternately on both. Birds permanently resident in any country are called *resident birds*, as the sparrow, for example; some are birds of passage, as the *fieldfare*, or *migratory*, as the swallow.

Important distinguishing characters of birds are afforded by the foot and the bill. Some have feet adapted for swimming, some for walking, some for running, some for hopping, some for climbing. The foot has no more than four toes. The femoral bone is short, and both it and the knee are entirely concealed by the strong and massive muscles with which they are covered, and there is only one tarso-metatarsal bone present which forms a continuation of the leg. The bill is sometimes elongated and pointed, sometimes curved at the extremity, sometimes short and thick, and sometimes conical, sometimes compressed horizontally, sometimes laterally, sometimes quite straight and cylindrical, sometimes hooked. In many birds the bill at its base is surrounded by a yellow membrane called the *wax* (cire).

Independently of the beauty of the feathered tribes that delight the senses by the symmetry of their forms, the grace of their varied evolutions, the splendour of their plumage, and the melody of their varied and exquisite notes, they are intrinsically useful on account of their flesh, their eggs, and their feathers. The injury they occasion is very small in proportion to the advantages which they yield. It is rare indeed that the largest and most rapacious of them are formidable to man, and no bird is poisonous.

Birds are divided into two grand divisions, by characters founded on their structure and vital economy. The first group is composed of birds which are hatched blind and callous, must be nourished for a considerable time in the nest, and subsequently live on one sort of food. They hop on the ground, and their flight is rapid and without effort, and they are mostly on the wing. The birds of the second grand division are hatched with open eyes, and with a flocculous or downy covering; and they no sooner leave the egg, than they run about and pick up their food, which is of various kinds. They step, or waddle, or run, seldom fly, and are mostly land birds, but some are aquatic.

115. Division of Birds.

A. Tarsal bone feathered to the spur, or nearly so.	B. Upper part of the tarsal bone only feathered.
1. Rapaces or Raptatores.—With powerful legs and toes, furnished with sharp-pointed hooked talons; bill with strong upper, hooked pointed mandible, and cereous membrane.	4. Cursores.—Legs and feet adapted for rapid motion; wings imperfect, and unsuitable for flight.
2. Incessores.—Toes adapted for hopping or climbing; claws mostly compressed. Bill usually without the cirement.	5. Grallatores.—Legs very long, adapted for wading; toes partially or slightly united by a fold, or quite free; rarely webbed; wings powerful.
3. Rasores.—Toes partially united by a small fold, or quite distinct. Claws not compressed, mostly blunt; upper mandible mostly arched; sometimes with a cirement.	6. Natatores.—Legs moderately long; toes usually connected, forming a swimming-paddle: in some the toes are palmate, or free.

First Order. Raptatores (*Birds of Prey*).

116. These birds are distinguished by powerful feet and claws, strength of vision, and wings adapted for rapid flight, and in general by an organisation suitable for preying upon other animals, though many of them live on carrion. The indigestible portions of their food, such as wool and feathers, they eject. These substances or pellets are firmly rolled up, and

are named coprolites when in a state of petrification. The female birds are generally larger than the males, and they lay only a few eggs, which are hatched in an artlessly-formed nest, usually constructed on inaccessible rocks or on high trees.

31.

Such of this order as prey by day are called diurnal birds of prey, and compose the family of the vultures and falcons, which are clothed with short feathers arranged closely and flatly on the body.

The social *vultures* (Vulturini) are very ravenous, and are distinguished by the want of feathers on the head. Among these we notice the *condor* (Vultur gryphus), the largest of all flying birds; the distance between his extended wings measured from the tips is from 11 to 13 feet. This bird inhabits the lofty Andes in South America. The *carrion vulture* or *Egyptian vulture* (V. pernopterus), the *gray vulture* (V. cinereus), the *white-headed vulture* (V .leucocephalus *seu* fulvus), (fig. 31), are the principal and most common birds of the sub-order Vultu-

32.

ridæ. Between the eagles and vultures naturalists place the *lammergeier* or *bearded griffin* (Gypaëtos barbatus, fig. 32), which is domiciled in the mountains of Southern Europe.

The *falcons* (Accipitrini) constitute a numerous family, distinguished alike by noble aspect, graceful form, intelligence, and courage. Their prey is chiefly living birds, reptiles, and other small animals, among which may be reckoned insects. The largest birds of this tribe are the eagles, of which the most remarkable are the *golden eagle* (Falco fulvus), the *erne* or *great sea eagle* (F. albicella), the *osprey* or *fishing eagle* (F. haliætos); both the latter are expert fishers. Of the smaller birds of the falcon tribe, viz., the falcons proper, several of which were in very high estimation when the science of falconry was one of the chief sources of amusement, and the most beloved of field sports, the following are the most remarkable, viz., the *noble* or *Iceland falcon* (F. islandicus), the *merlin* (F. æsalon), the *kestrel* (F. tinnunculus), the *hawk* (F. palumbarius), the *sparrow-hawk* (F. nisus); also those birds of this family distinguished by fan-tails, as the *kite* (F. milvus), the *buzzard* (F. buteo), and the *glede, harpy,* or *moor buzzard* (F. rufus). The *secretary bird* (Gypogeranus secretarius), a native of South Africa, distinguished by very long legs, in which it resembles the grallatores, also by a tuft of feathers on its head, is highly esteemed by the colonists of the Cape, on account of its incessant warfare with the serpent race, which it preys upon and destroys in vast numbers.

The *nocturnal* or *crepuscular predaceous birds* or *owls,* are covered with loose very soft feathers, with very large eyes, unable to bear the glare of broad daylight, and consequently prey by night, or in the twilight. They devour vast numbers of mice and similar vermin, and their services in this respect are deemed very advantageous. They are followed and persecuted by flocks of little birds during the day if they happen to appear abroad. The best known of this tribe are the *eagle-owl* (Strix bubo), the *horned owl* (S. otus), the *barn-owl* (S. flammea), and *screech-owl* (S. noctua).

Second Order. Incessores.

117. The number of individuals comprehended in this order is so immensely large, that it has been found convenient to subdivide them into several subordinate families. In general their feet are not strong, and they have three toes before and one behind, opposite the three anterior ones. Some of them have the two exterior toes united at their base by a short process, and in some the toes are connected as far as the second joint. In the family of the *Psittacidæ,* the toes are all directed anteriorly; in the climbing birds two are anterior, and two posterior (the exterior toe being capable of assuming a posterior direction). It is in this order that we find the general and peculiar characters of birds in the highest state of development. They are distinguished by rapidity of flight, symmetry, general beauty of plumage, often elegancy and brilliancy, activity, architectural skill, docibility, and especially by their exquisitely melodious vocal organisation.

The birds of this order form either only small tribes, or numerous families. The first is the case in the *night-jar* or *goat-sucker* (Caprimulgus), remarkable for the extensive opening of its mandibles, a conformation well adapted to its predaceous economy, viz., catching insects while on the wing, and the *swifts* (Cypselus), which build their nests in towers and steeples.

The *singing birds* (Canores) compose an entire section of this order, amongst which are reckoned the *swallows* (Hirundo); of these there are the *chimney-swallow,* the *martin,* or *house swallow,* and the *bank swallow* or *sand-martin.* One of these is the *esculent swallow* (H. esculenta), which is found in the Indian Archipelago, and forms its nest of a gelatinous substance, which it finds in the surrounding seas. This is the celebrated delicacy known in commerce by the name "birds' nests." The *black-cap* (Muscicapa), one of the fly catchers, is a bird of passage. The *butcher-bird,* and the *flusher* (Lanius excubitor and collurio), are rapacious, preying on insects, and not seldom on smaller individuals of the feathered creation. In the family of the *thrushes* (Merulidæ), we meet with the beautiful yellow *oriole* (Oriolus galbula), the *mistel-thrush* (Turdus viscivorus), the *field-fare*

(T. pilaris), the *song-thrush* (T. musicus), the *blackbird* (T. merula), and the *spotted thrush* (T. polyglotta). Some of the above named are celebrated as delicate eating, some as singing birds; in the latter quality they are, however, infinitely surpassed by the *songsters* or warblers proper (Sylvidæ), mostly small and sober-coloured birds. The *nightingale* (Sylvia luscinia) is celebrated above all birds for the compass, variety, and melody of its note, and the following also contribute their share to the animation and charm of our woods, groves, and hedges, viz., the *gray linnet* (S. cinerea), the *black-cap* (S. atrocapilla), the *redstart* (S. erithacus), the *redbreast* (S. rubecula), and the *reed-warbler* (S. arundinacia). The smallest of our native birds belong also to this tribe, viz., the *golden-crested* and *common wrens* (S. regulus and S. troglodytes).

Better known than the *Alpine warbler* (Accentor alpinus), and the *pipets* (Anthus), are the beautiful *wagtail* (Motacilla), and the *tree-lark* or *tree-creeper* (Certhia), the pert lively *siskins*, the most common of which are the *great titmouse* (Parus major), the *blue titmouse* (P. cœruleus), the *long-tailed tit* or *bottle tit* (P. pendulinus), which is celebrated for its ingeniously-constructed nest, often suspended over water, sometimes among reeds, and the *nuthatch* (Sitta). The *Bohemian wax-wing* (Ampelis garrula), and the beautiful *yellow chatterer* are of rarer occurrence than the above.

The *raven* tribe (Corvinæ), a family of larger birds, are distinguished by their large and strong bill, and loud, shrill, or croaking voice; they mostly live on fruit or kernels, sometimes on worms, grubs, flesh, &c. To these belong the *jay* (Corvus glandarius), the *magpie* (C. pica), the *chough* or *jackdaw* (C monedula), the *hooded crow* (C. cornix), the *seed crow* or *rook* (C. frugilegus), the *common crow* (C. corone), and the *raven* (C. corax), which occasionally seizes small quadrupeds. These are all known by their mostly black plumage, and by their capacity of uttering distinct sounds. This latter faculty is characteristic of the *starling* (Sturnus vulgaris), and of the *African beef-eater*, which picks out and devours the grubs in the hides of the cattle while grazing. The *bird of paradise* (fig. 33), only found in New Guinea, and highly prized for its beautiful long feathers, also belongs to this section.

33.

The granivorous birds feed their young with insect food, and are also distinguished by their habit of congregating in large flocks, and they occasionally do some damage in the newly-sown fields. There are some of these, however, that form an important item in the dietetic economy. Among these the following are the most important, viz., the *field lark* (Alauda arvensis), the *crested* and *heath larks*, the *yellow hammer* (Emberiza citrinella), the *snow bunting* (E. nivalis), and the delicious *ortolan* (E. hortulana). The *finches* (Fringilla) are among the most common of our birds, particularly the *chaffinch* (F. cœlebs), the *green-finch* or *thistle-finch* (F. carduelis), the *haw-finch*, the *gray linnet* (F. cannabina), the *green-finch* (F. spinus), and the *canary* (F. canaria), the well-known domestic singing bird, originally introduced from the Canary Islands several hundred years ago. All these birds are easily kept in confinement, and are prized for their song, which is not the case with the *sparrow* (F. domestica), whose plumage is more becoming than its other qualities. The following are rather larger birds, viz., the *bullfinch* (Loxia pyrrhula), the *pine-finch* (L. enucleator), and the *crossbill* (L. curvirostra).

In the sub-order tenuirostres are found the smallest of all birds; viz., the *humming birds* (Trochilus, fig. 34), which are natives of South America,

34. 35.

and are very numerous. They are further remarkable for the splendid metallic lustre, or brilliant hue of their feathers; they live on small insects which they pick out of flowers; hence the erroneous notion that they suck the saccharine juices of blossoms. The *hoopoo* (Upupa epops) is larger than the above, and is adorned with a feathery crest or crown. Another sub-section is formed of birds with a tarsal membrane uniting the base of their toes, and whose bill is disproportionately large. Among these are arranged the *hornbill* (Buceros), the *bee-eater* (Merops), and also the *king-fisher* (Alcedo), which has a quadrangular bill.

The climbing birds (Scansores) have their toes arranged in pairs, two anterior and two posterior, as in the *cuckoo* (Cuculus canorus), so remarkable for its monotonous note, and for laying its eggs in the nests of various singing birds, which hatch and feed the intruder at the expense of their own natural offspring. The *honey cuckoo* (C. indicator), which, by its note, bewrays the stores of honey, collected by wild bees, is a native of the Cape, and a member of this sub-order; so also is the *toucan* (Rhampastos), with his enormous bill; and the *woodpeckers*, which seek their insect food in the bark of trees, for which purpose their strong sharp-pointed bills and wiry rigid tongues are admirably adapted. The *black woodpecker* (Picus martius), the *green woodpecker* or *poppinjay* (P. viridis), the *spotted woodpecker* (P. varius), and the *wryneck* (Jynx) belonging to the same tribe.

The great family of the *parrots* and *paroquets* form the last tribe of this large order. These have very large and powerful, curved upper mandibles, the lower short and obtuse, invested at the base with the cereous membrane. These birds are furnished with a thick fleshy tongue, and are able to mimic the human voice; the sounds which they utter are shrill and disagreeable; they are only found in tropical regions, and feed chiefly on fruit, rarely on insects or flesh. There are above 200 species of the parrot tribe (Psittacus), all remarkable for the splendour of their plumage and the drollness of their gestures; the *common gray parrot* (Ps. erithacus), the *cockatoo* (Ps. cristatus), the *blue maccaw* (Ps. ararauna), and the *red maccaw* (Ps. macao, fig. 35), and the *parrakeets* (Ps. pullarius), are pretty generally known.

Third Order. Rasores (Gallinacei).

118. The domestic fowls have a short, rather curved bill, and strong feet peculiarly adapted for scratching; they rarely fly, have a disagreeable shrill cry, but are highly esteemed for their delicate flesh and eggs; the young come out of the shell with the power of sight and motion, and immediately run about and pick up their food; the cock birds are larger and more beautiful than the hens.

Among the pigeon tribe (Columbæ), all of which live in pairs, and feed their helpless young for a considerable period, we notice the *ringdove* (C. palumbus), the *wood pigeon* (C. œnas), the *turtle-dove* (C. turtur), the *rock pigeon* (C. risoria), and the *passenger pigeon* (C. migratoria), which passes from central to North America in such enormous flocks; and finally the *crowned pigeon* (C. coronata).

Under the section of *game birds* (Tetraonidæ) we note the *capercailzie* (Tetrao urogallus), the *black cock* (T. tetrix), the *hazel grouse* (T. bonasia), the *red grouse* (T. scotica), the *ptarmigan* (T. lagopus), which changes its plumage in winter, and prefers alpine localities, and the *common partridge* (T. perdrix), always after the breeding season appearing in little flocks or coveys, under, as it is said, a single cock bird, and lastly the *quail* (T. coturnix).

Among the family of hens proper (Phasianidæ), which originally came from Asia, and are distinguished by the gorgeousness of their plumage, we find the *peacock* (Pavo), a bird proudly conscious of his superiority, and displays his splendour to the admiring beholder, the soberer coloured *domestic cock* (Phasianus gallus), the *common pheasant* (Ph. colchicus), the *gold* and *silver pheasants* (Ph. pictus and nycthemerus), the *argus pheasant* (Argus), the *guinea hen* (Numida meleagris), and the *turkey* of North America (Meleagris gallopavo).

The *Lyre-tailed bird* (Menura), a remarkable bird of New Holland, with a curious tail; and the long extinct *Dodo* (Didus), an immensely huge bird discovered in the Isle of France in 1598.

FOURTH ORDER. CURSORES.

119. This order comprehends the largest birds, scarcely capable of flight because of the shortness or deficiency of their wing feathers. The length of their legs and the structure of their foot, however, qualify them for outstripping the fleetest horse in rapidity of flight. They are excessively edacious, devouring all sorts of food, vegetable and animal. There are only a few birds belonging to this order, the chief of which are, the *kiwi* (Apterix

36. 37.

australis), the *cassowary* (Casuarius indicus, fig. 36), and the greatest of all birds, the *two-toed ostrich* (Struthio camelus, fig. 37), which is from 6 ft. to 8 ft. high, and yields the celebrated ornamental feathers. This bird is common in Central and South Africa, and in the south-west of Asia; it lays its eggs in the sand, and leaves them to be hatched by solar heat. In more temperate regions it hatches its young by incubation. In South America we find the *three-toed ostrich* (Rhea Americana), and in New Holland the *emu* (Rh. Novæ Hollandiæ).

FIFTH ORDER. GRALLATORES.

120. The birds of this order connect the last with the following, viz., the running birds with the natatores. Their long legs fit them for wading, while their webbed or half-webbed toes are well adapted for swimming. These birds constantly fly with outstretched legs, and live in swampy moist places, or on the banks of rivers, lakes, &c. Their food is worms, insects, grubs, snails, slugs, reptiles, and fish, which they meet with in their accustomed haunts.

The *screamer* (Palamedes), a bird of South America, distinguished by strong spurs on the bend of its wings, and the *bustard* (Otis tarda), which is a rare visitant of this country, belong to this order.

Among the family of the herons (Herodii), we place the *crane* (Grus), the various kinds of *herons* (Ardea), as the *common heron* (A. cinerea), the *white heron* (A. ægretta), which produces the beautiful feathers manufactured into artificial plumes; the *bittern* (A. stellaris). Of the genus stork (Ciconia), we notice, in addition to our ancient and well-known intimate friend, the *Indian marabu* and the *African or adjutant stork* (Argala, fig. 38), very large birds, which devour multitudes of noxious animals, and clear the streets and ways of much putrescent matter. The white

39.

38.

tail-feathers of this stork are employed by the orientals in the preparation of plumes. In Africa also we meet with the great *ibis* (Tantalus ibis, fig. 39), and the *sacred ibis* (I. religiosa), which is venerated in Egypt as the harbinger of the annual inundation of the Nile, and was frequently embalmed and mummified. The *spoonbill* (Platalea), remarkable for its broad flat bill and its very long legs; also the *flamingo* (Phœnicopterus), distinguished by its rosy-red feathers and scarlet wings, and an extraordinary length of neck, are members of this family.

The smaller birds of the same order are the *plover tribe* (Charadriadæ), which seek their food mostly on the borders of rivers, &c., as the *golden plover* (Charadrius), the *lap-wing* or *peewit* (Vanellus), the *turn-stone* (Strepsilas), the *oyster-catcher* (Hæmatopus), the *red-shank* (H. rufipes), and the *curlew* (Recurvirostra), with a long recurved bill.

The family of the *snipes* (Scolopacidæ) are furnished with a long, flexible and susceptible bill, employed in searching for worms, snails, &c., in the muddy soil. Among these we meet with the *green-shanks* and *sand-pipers*

(Totanus glottis and stagnatilis), the *woodcock* (Scolopax rusticola), the *common snipe* (Sc. media), and the *tern*, or *ruffe*, of the sea-shore (Tringa).

The *water-hens* (Rallidæ) live entirely in the water, and dive as well as swim, and hereby they approach very closely to the natatores. Among these are included the *water-rail* (Rallus aquaticus), the *moor-hens* (Gallinula), among which we notice the *land-rail* (G. grex), and the *common water*, or *moor-hen* (G. chloropus), the beautiful *purple-rail* (Porphyrio), the *sand-piper* (Parra), remarkable for very long toes and a sharp spur on its wing, and the *black water-coot* (Fulica atra), common in ponds and lakes.

Sixth Order. Natatores.

121. These birds have short legs, and feet adapted for swimming, the toes being connected by a strong membrane. Their feathers are very close, and they are further protected from the water and cold by a downy skin. Except at brooding seasons they live constantly on the water, and mostly subsist on fish, consequently their flesh is generally rank, with an oily flavour. They form several families, as under.

40.

The *divers* (Colymbidæ), owe their name to the dexterity wherewith they immerse themselves in water, as the *crested diver* (Colymbus cristatus), and the *great northern diver*, (C. Septentrionalis). To the polar zone belong the waddling *auks* (Alca), viz., the *great auk*, or *arctic penguin* (A. impennis), the *guillemot* (Uria troile), the *red merganser*, or *goosander* (Mergulus), the *puffin* (Mormon).

The manchots, or *penguins* (fig. 40), of the Southern Atlantic and Pacific Oceans, are furnished with very short wings, ill adapted to support their clumsy fat bodies; their legs are also very short, and so situated that the bird stands almost upright when on its legs. It is notwithstanding, well adapted, by its warm down and thick feathers, as well as by its fatness, for living in water. Both feathers and oil are valuable to the inhabitants of Patagonia and Van Diemen's Land.

41.

The family of the *pelicans* (Pelecanidæ), is distinguished among all aquatic birds by the great extent and power of their wings. The red beak and enormous pouch of the pelican (Pelecanus onocrotalus), (fig. 41), have given rise to the saying that this bird nourishes her young by her own breast. The *sea-raven*, or *cormorant* (Halieus carbo), the *frigate-bird* (Tachypetes, fig. 42), and the *tropic-bird* (Phæton), are members of this tribe.

42.

The *gulls*, gregarious birds (Laridæe), are also remarkable for their extent and power of wing, which is sharply pointed. The *sea-swallow* (Sterna hirundo), the *glaucous gull* (Larus glaucus), the *herring-gull* (L. argentatus), the *mew-gull* (L. canus), and the *robber-gull* (Lestris), are the principal birds of this sub-order.

Among the *petrels* (Procellaria) are included the *fulmar* of the Arctic seas (P. Glacialis), *St. Peter's fowl* (P. pelagica), and the celebrated *albatross* (Diomedea).

The family of the *anatidæ* are upon the whole the most useful of all the aquatic fowls, the feathers of which are so extensively used in the stuffing of beds, &c., and formerly were the staple article in the manufacture of pens. They have recently been superseded by the substitution of a more durable material. Their flesh and eggs are, however, still in estimation. The *goose* (Anser cinereus), the ancient guardian of the Roman capital; the *swan* (Cygnus olor); many species of ducks, particularly the *wild duck* (Anas boschas), the *eider duck* (A. mollissima), famous for its down, and the *goosander* (Mergus), are members of this family.

Third Class. (Reptilia Amphibia).

122. The animals composing this class are either entirely naked or their skin is covered by scales or horny plates. Their nasal aperture is in the throat, and through this they breathe. Some of them at an early stage of their existence have gills, which subsequently disappear; but in several these organs are permanent. The ear, although developed, is not externally visible.

Their blood has the same temperature as the medium wherein they live. Their muscular system is highly developed, separated into bundles by a membranous integument, and they are consequently capable of exerting much force in their motions and general economy. Their capability of reproducing a member, that they may have accidentally lost, is also very remarkable. Their power of utterance seems to be as limited as in fishes, for, with the exception of the serpent's hiss and the croaking of frogs, this class does not possess the organs of sound.

In external organisation they show much diversity. Some have 4 feet, some 2 feet, and some, as the serpents, have nothing analogous to these locomotive organs. With few exceptions they increase by eggs; yet they never produce such an enormous progeny as the fishes do.

The number of genera is small, amounting on the whole to only 1270. In the transformations they undergo in skin, shape, and colour, they approximate to the insect class.

The feeling which the reptile class excites in us is generally that of aversion, disgust, apprehension, or even hatred. This is partly occasioned by their solitary, lurking, predaceous habits; by their preying on the defenceless smaller animals, which they never attack openly, but fall upon them unawares. This is besides the only class of venomous animals, many of which are furnished with the most deadly poisons. Their naked body is also an object of disgust to a higher order of beings. They are all unsocial, devoid of instinctive craft, manifest no attachment to their young, and are of very little practical utility.

123. Division of the Reptilia.

A. Heart with two auricles, and imperfectly divided ventricles; undergo no change; skin covered with scales or plates.		B. Heart simple: *i. e.*, without separate cavities; change; with gills; skin naked.	
1. Chelonii—Turtles.	2. Sauri—Lizards.	3. Serpentes—Serpents.	4. Batrachiæ—Frogs.
4-footed, with united immoveable ribs. Sternum broad; without teeth.	4-footed (rarely 2 or none); with moveable ribs, and under maxillary united.	Without feet; no eyelids; ribs moveable; no sternum; under maxillary united by cartilage.	4-footed (rarely with 2 or no feet); ribs short, or wanting.

First Order. Chelonia (*the Turtle Tribe*).

124. The organisation of the skeleton of this tribe of animals is apparently very anomalous; for the ribs and sternum are placed quite at the exterior of the body, and united so as to form a broad dorsal shield, and an equally strong pectoral plate, in which the animal lives, surrounded by armour more or less perfectly united, the sutures being covered with horny plates or strong coriaceous membrane. These are the most useful of all the reptile class, their flesh and eggs being most delicious and nutritious food. In many places where they are not liable to much disturbance they are found in very considerable numbers.

Their shell, called tortoise-shell, is manufactured into many useful and ornamental articles. Of this tribe the following deserve to be noticed: the *land tortoise* (Testudo græca), the *geometrical tortoise* (T. geometrica), the *snuff-box tortoise* (Cistudo), the *marsh tortoises* (Emys) of the Orinoco, which come in great shoals to the Tortosa Islands to lay their eggs, of which millions are collected and manufactured into oil; the *European tortoise* (E. europæa), the rapacious and gluttonous *river tortoise* (Aspidonectes), with leathery shields; the *marine tortoise*, among which are the *giant tortoise*, (Chelonia mydas), from 6 feet to 7 feet long, which weighs about 900 lbs., and yields the beautiful material called tortoise-shell. These abound about the Mediterranean Sea and the Atlantic Ocean, as well as the *edible tortoise* (Ch. esculenta), so celebrated in the concoction of the famous turtle soup.

SECOND ORDER. SAURI (*the Lizard Tribe*).

125. Of the three sections into which this order is subdivided, we notice first the *armed lizards* (Loricati), whose bodies are covered with bony shields. The *crocodile* (Crocodilus), and other equally dangerous aquatic reptiles, which in internal structure bear a close resemblance to the mammiferous quadrupeds, belong to this section.

The most famous of these is the *crocodile* of the Nile (C. vulgaris, fig. 43), which is from 20 to 30 feet long; and the *gavial*, or *crocodile* of the

43.

Ganges (C. gangeticus), distinguished by its long and slender upper and lower maxillaries or jaws. The American crocodile is called the *alligator*, or *cayman* (C. lucius), and has a wider and less extended maxillary apparatus.

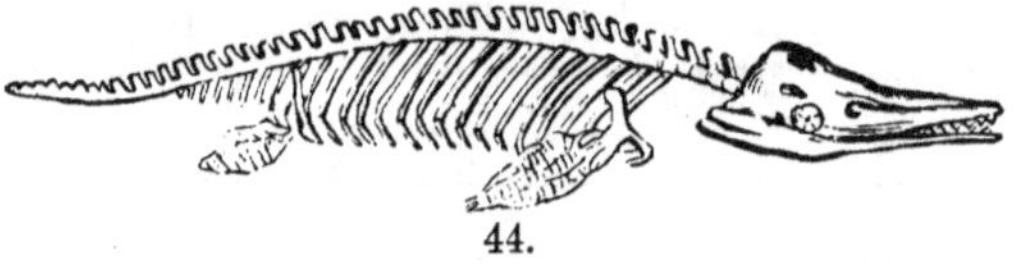

44.

Among the petrified organic remains of similar animals we meet with the *ichthyosaurus*, fig. 44, and *plesiosaurus*, fig. 45, with feet formed for swimming, from 30 to 50 feet long, and with 90 vertebræ.

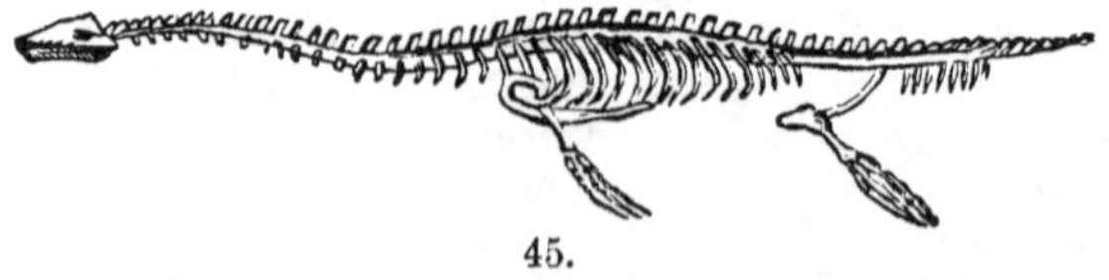

45.

The section of scaly saurians embraces also the family of the *monitors*. The *monitor* of the Nile (M. niloticus), is useful for destroying the eggs and the young of crocodiles. The *monitor* of Guinea (Thorictis dracæna), is about 5 feet long and resembles the crocodile. The *gray* and *green lizards* (Lacerta agilis and L. viridis), are harmless, pretty, little, active creatures. The *chameleon* (Chamæleo Africanus, fig. 46), possesses the faculty of changing its colour in so remarkable a manner, that "changeable as a chameleon" is proverbial.

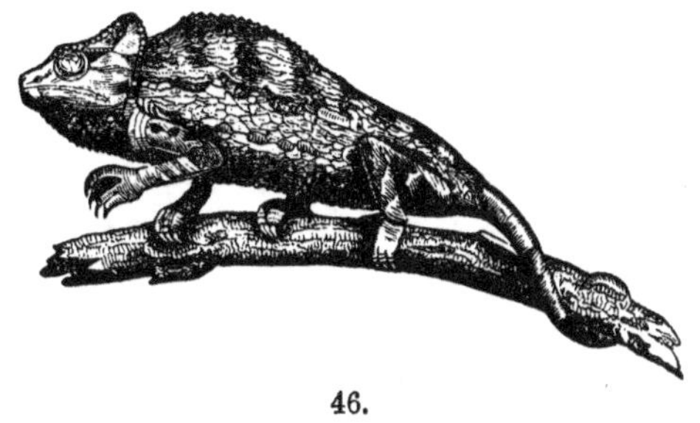

46.

The *flying dragon* (Draco volans, fig. 47), a small Javanese lizard, is characterised by a thick fleshy tongue and a membranous expansion, by which it suspends itself in the air, but it is incapable of rapid or continuous motion

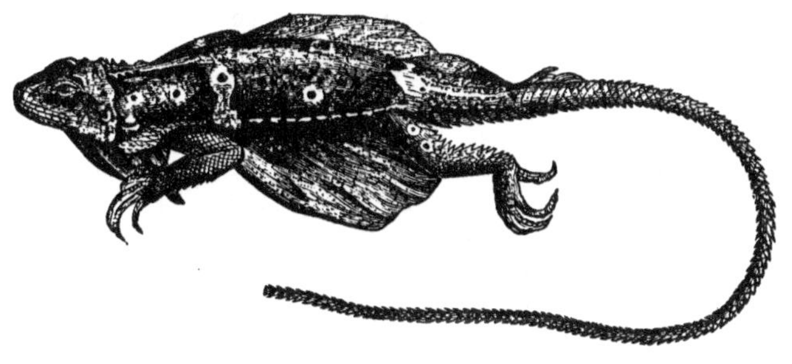

47.

in this element; and the *crested basilisk* (Basiliscus mitratus), the *leguan* (Iguana), several feet long, and affording edible flesh, the lively-coloured *anolis* (Anoli), the *radiate lizard* (Stellio), and finally, the *gecko*, a nocturnal sluggish creature, with peculiarly expansive feet, by which it can crawl up walls, are all members of this sub-order. Of this latter hideous reptile, one species (Platydactylus) is found in the south of Europe.

Among the following, characterised by a forked tongue, and a suppression or a modification of their members, whereby they are apparently similar to the true serpent family, we notice the following: viz., the *pseudopodes*, or *false-foots* (Pseudopus), which have no fore-legs, and only possess the hind feet in a rudimentary condition; the *glass-snake* (Ophiosaurus); the *skink* (Scincus), formerly used in medicinal preparations; and, finally, the *common blind worm* (Anguis fragilis), which brings forth its young alive, and in its whole internal structure differs from the snakes, with which in external appearances it has so great a resemblance.

The *annular lizards*, or *ophiosaurians* (Annulati), with imbricated scaly skins, are the last and smallest section of this sub-order; the *Amphisbean* (Amphisbœna), and many other serpent-like lizards, belong to it.

THIRD ORDER. SERPENTES (*the Serpent Tribe*).

126. There is a great similarity in the internal structure of serpents. Their head is small, but the mouth is very expansible on account of the maxillary bones being separate and only united by an expansive cartilaginous elastic substance. Hence they can swallow objects larger than themselves. Many of them are furnished with hollow teeth, containing a venomous fluid secreted in a peculiar gland, which renders the bite of these animals so dangerous. They frequently slough, or cast their skins, and the most of them are natives of tropical and sub-tropical regions. The following are some of the more important members of the serpent tribe, viz.,

The *South American coral snake* (Ilysia syctale), of a beautiful coral red, variegated with black bands; the *cylindrical coral snake* (Cylindrophis). The monsters of the order, however, are the *boas*, certainly not venomous, but of enormous size, viz., from 30 feet to 40 feet long, and of incredible muscular strength, destroying the most powerful quadrupeds by gradual and continuous pressure in their mighty folds. The *boa constrictor* and the *marine boa* (B. marina), are natives of Brazil; whilst the *tiger boas* (Python tigris and bivittatus) of the East Indies are not uncommonly exhibited in menageries.

The harmless snakes (Coluber), are not uncommon in Europe, as the *common water-snake*, or *collared adder* (C. natrix), which is steel gray, with white and black spots on the belly, and a yellow ring about the neck; the *yellow water-snake*, or *yellow viper* (C. flavescens), from 3 feet to 5 feet long, is frequent in the Sclangenbad of Germany, and the *common ringed snake* is frequent in England.

One of the most beautiful of the tribe is the South American *green tree-snake* (Dryophis).

Among the *venomous serpents* (Venenosi), we find in the Indian Ocean the *sea-snakes* (Pelamys and Hydrophis), with broad, flat, compressed tails, which they employ as rudders in steering their course through the watery element; and in Brazil the cinnabar-red, and black and white ringed *snake*, or *coral viper* (Elaps corallinus); the *spectacled and haje snake* (Naja tripudians), of India, which performs an important part in the idolatrous rites of the natives, and also in the juggling tricks of itinerant mountebanks, is one of the most dangerous of the venomous tribe. This creature when excited has the power of bending its cervical vertebræ into a sort of collar behind its head. The jugglers, before exhibiting their tricks with it, contrive to exhaust the venom by causing it repeatedly to bite a piece of cloth. They also understand how to render the poison innocuous by tapping its head, or by pressure of the brain.

48.

In our own country the *common viper* (Vipera berus), is not an uncommon though unwelcome, intruder in warm sunny places in the vicinity of woods, especially on chalky soil. It is 2 feet long, of a gray-brown colour, with zigzag bands over and along the back. To small animals the viper's bite is mortal, and under certain circumstances it is dangerous to man. In all such accidents, suction, excision, or cauterising of the wound is advisable. The most common of the venomous serpents of the Antilles and Brazil are the *lance-headed vipers*, or *cophias* (Trigonocephalus). The *rattle-snakes* (Crotalus horridus, fig. 48), in South America, and (C. durissus) in North America, are not less formidable. The dry, hard, caudal ringlets, or horny cells, that are attached to their skin, occasion the peculiar rattling noise, when the animal moves, that gives notice of its proximity. The power of charming, or bewildering, or attracting small animals within their deadly fangs, is said to be the effect of a powerful odour which they have the means of diffusing.

FOURTH ORDER. BATRACHIÆ (*the Frog Tribe*).

127. The batrachian reptiles have a naked skin, and they have either no ribs or only these in a rudimentary form. They are developed from the ova in an ichthyous condition, with extended outward gills, and reach their final and perfect form after many transformations and sloughings. In several the gills are permanent.

49.

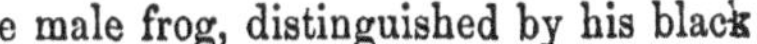

The first section of this order contains the ecaudate (tailless) *frogs*, which have no trace of ribs, but possess very long hind legs, hence their hopping motion. We find here the *American pipa* (Pipa americana), which bears her eggs and young for a considerable time on her back; the beautiful *green tree-frog* (Hyla orborea, fig. 49), which is often seen as an inmate of our houses, generally being kept in wardian glass cases; the male frog, distinguished by his black throat, utters his small croak at any unusual noise or excitement. The *French frog* (Rana esculenta), is not quite a stranger in our island, while the *grass*, or *common frog* (R. temporaria), is very plentiful, and whose black eggs, surrounded by a pale white gelatinous matter, are so abundant in our ditches and ponds in early spring. The slimy, footless, long-tailed young, commonly called *pow-heads*, or *tad-poles*, undergo a change after a few weeks. Only the femora (hind legs) of the green water-frogs are eaten. Of exotic frogs we notice the *glossy frog* (R. micans), the

50.

bullfrog (R. mugiens), and the *horned-frog* (R. cornuta). The transition from the frogs to the toads is formed by the *fire-frog* (Bombina), and the *nurse-frog*, or *obstetric toad* (B. obstetricans), which carries her eggs coiled around her legs. The *toads* (fig. 50), lay their eggs in long strings, and are rather terrestrial than aquatic animals; they are plump, sluggish, nocturnal creatures, with watery tuberculated skins, and in appearance and movement are generally considered disagreeable objects; their only redeeming feature is their beautiful eye, apparently encased in gold. Although ugliness itself be personified by the toad, and though its smell be rank as garlic, it is not poisonous—it is ugly, but not "venomous." The *garlic-smelling toad* (Bufo fuscus), is common, and the *reed*, or *cross toad* (C. calamites), the former common and the latter rare in England. The *common land toad* (B. cinereus), and the *giant toad*, or *bull-frog* of the Anglo-American (B. gigas), are found on the Continent.

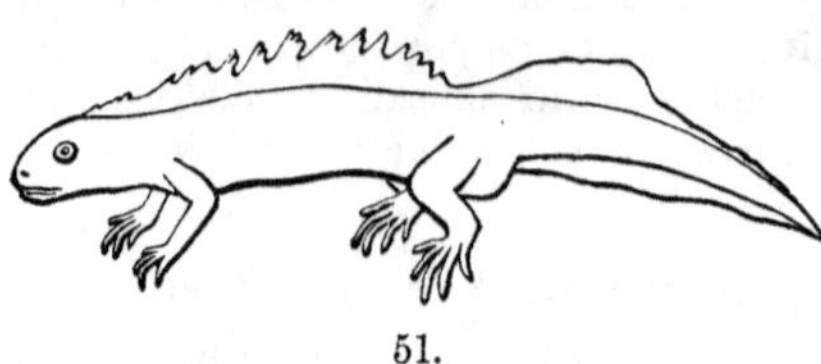

51.

The second section of batrachian reptiles includes the *salamanders* (Claudata). Some of these lose their gills after their metamorphosis has been completed, as the *salamander* (Salamandra), spotted with yellow and black, and erroneously deemed venomous; and the *water newt* (Triton, fig. 51), which has a dentate crest along its back; others retain their gills, or a breathing aperture, during their whole existence, as the *eel-salamander* (Amphiuma), the *gilled salamander*, or *axolotl* (Siredon, fig. 52), the *Proteus anguineus* and the *Sirene*, which inhabit subterranean waters in cavernous recesses of the eagle mountains in the Ukraine.

52.

The last section comprehends the *cæcilia*, so called because its eyes are below the skin. It is without feet, similar to a worm, and is found in America and Java.

The Fourth Class. Pisces: Fishes.

128. Fishes are exclusively confined to the water. They do not breathe by the nose, but by *gills*, which are membranous folds called the branchial arches, situated laterally behind the head. The water swallowed in breathing passes the branchial apparatus, and the atmosphere contained in the water by this means is brought into contact with the blood-vessels; the air thus received with the water is sufficient to support respiration in the fish, without the necessity of its coming to the surface to breathe.

The blood is red, but its temperature is always regulated by that of the water in which the fishes live. They are for the most part provided with a remarkable organ called the swimming bladder, filled with air. This organ is capable of being compressed or extended by a special muscle, whereby the external amplitude of the fish is increased or diminished, and by this apparatus the fish can either rise or sink in the water. The muscles of fishes are white, and not separated into distinct bundles by the skin, hence their movements are imperfect when compared with those of the higher classes.

The skeleton of a fish is not perfectly developed, the limbs are scarcely rudimentary, and their place is supplied by fins. The nature and position of these organs are characteristic of the various subdivisions of the class. The fins are the cervical (neck), the pectoral, the dorsal, the ventral, and the caudal (tail), fins. They are also designated as cuticular, radiate, and spiny fins; and if the fish be one of a higher order, the number and position of the fins correspond to the limbs of the more highly-developed animals.

The skin of the fish is either naked or provided with a scaly imbrication, arranged as tiles on a roof, viz., indurated plates, on which protuberances, lamina, and spines are frequently present. They increase by ova (spawn), which are found in enormously large numbers, the herring having 40,000 ova in its roe, and the stock-fish, or ling, 400,000. The male fish is provided with an organ called *milt*, in which the lacteous food is secreted. The utility of the fish is very great, for independently of the delicious food which they all supply with scarcely any exception, their bones or gristle, their scales, their skin, their swimming bladder, and their fat, are all serviceable in a variety of ways.

129. Classification of Fishes.

A. Cartilaginous Fishes—Skeleton composed of Cartilage.			B. Osseous Fishes—Skeleton composed of Bones.			
Pectoral and Ventral Fins.			Bones of Upper Mandible.			
Present.		Absent.	Immoveable—United.	Moveable.		
				Gills radiated.	Gills Pectiniform.	
1. Order—Mandibles transverse.	2. Order—Gills free.	3. Order—Mandibles round.	4. Order—Gills attached	5. Order—Gills radiated.	6. Order—Soft Fins.	7. Order—Spiny Fins.

First Order. Plagiostomi (*the Shark Tribe*).

130. Among these fishes are arranged the most voracious of all sea monsters, the *sharks* (Squalus). The *white shark* (S. carcharias), and the *giant-shark* (S. maximus), which is 40 feet long. The jaw of the shark is armed with rows of sharp-pointed, strong, and fearful teeth. For days they accompany or lurk near ships in expectation of prey. In many places (for example, in the valley of the Rhine, particularly near Alzei), thousands of shark's teeth are found, the petrified remains of an ancient world. By country people these organic remains are erroneously called serpent's tongues. The reddish and spotted *dog-fish* (S. canicula), is only 2 feet long. The *saw-fish* (S. pristis), is characterised by a very long serrated snout, a formidable weapon with which it attacks the largest fishes.

The *hammer-headed shark* (Zygæna malleus), is distinguished by the singularity of its shape. The tuberculated skin of the shark is manufactured into shagreen, and abundance of oil is extracted from the liver. The family of the *rays* (Raja), is distinguished especially by their broad flat shape, and by the thorny and spinous processes with which many of them are even dangerously armed.

The *skate* (R. batis) is found in the North Seas; and the *electric ray* (Torpedo), whose electrifying organ consists of a number of cellular processes, exhibited in fig. 53.

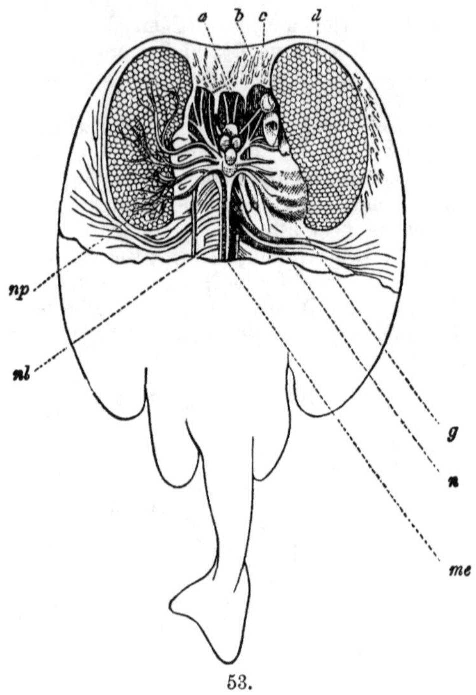

53.

[Electrical apparatus of the Torpedo:—*a*, brain; *me*, spinal chord; *b c*, eye and optic nerve; *d*, electrical organs; *np*, pneumogastric nerves, proceeding to the electric organ; *nl*, branch from the preceding, covering the lateral nerve; *n*, spinal nerves; *g*, gills.]

SECOND ORDER. ELEUTHEROBRANCHI: STURGEONS, &c.

131. In this small order there are some of the most useful fishes, the *sturgeon* for example (Accipenser sturio, fig. 54), and the *great sturgeon* (Acc. huso), both reckoned delicious food; and, in addition, the valuable article *isinglass*.

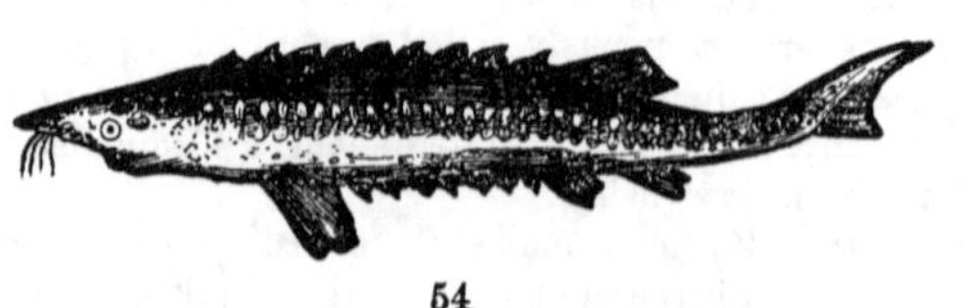

54.

is obtained from their swimming-bladder, and *caviare* from their roe. These fish abound in the Caspian and Black Seas, and in the tidal rivers that flow into them. The capture and cure of the fish are actively prosecuted by the Don Cossacks. They are occasionally caught in the Severn, and also in the Rhine and other large rivers.

THIRD ORDER. CYCLOSTOMI.

132. The gills of these very imperfectly-developed fishes consist of a series of external apertures; and as they live by suction, their rounded jaws are well adapted for this purpose. The *lamprey* (Petromyzon marinus, fig. 55), the *nine-eyed eel* (P. fluviatilis), which is far from uncommon, and is often caught and pickled, the *lamprillon*, or *lamproyon* (P. branchialis), with inconspicuous eyes, and the blind *hag-fish* (Myxine), belong to this order.

55.

FOURTH ORDER. PECTOGNATHI.

133. We find in this order singularly formed fishes, some spherical, some cuneate (wedge-like), frequently with thorny or prickly skins. Some of them can inflate their bodies, and then appear like a floating globe; some can utter a growling sound. They are found only in the tropical seas. The most remarkable are the *hedge-hog fish*, or *spring globe-fish* (Diodon), the *thorn-back* (Tetrodon), the *swimming-head*, or *sun-fish* (Orthagoriscus mola), the *trunk-fish*, or *coffer-fish* (Ostracion), armed with angular plates, and the *unicorn-fish* (Balistes monoceros).

FIFTH ORDER. LOPHOBRANCHI.

134. Fishes with narrow, toothless jaws, mostly consisting of bone and skin, and like the foregoing family more distinguished by the singularity of their form than for any known utility. As examples, we notice the *needle-fish*, the *sea-pony fish* (Syngnathus hippocampus), the *sea-dragon*, *pipe-fish*, &c.

SIXTH ORDER. MALACOPTERIGII.

135. This, the largest of all the orders, comprehends the most important families both of the sea and fresh-water fish, and in the capture, curing, and exportation of which, thousands of men are constantly employed; of all these the *salmon* (Salmo), is the most important. This valuable and delicious fish has two small anterior dorsal fins, the posterior are without rays. Its jaws are large, and mostly furnished with raking teeth. At certain seasons they ascend the rivers from the sea, for the purpose of depositing their spawn. The most valuable of the family is the *common salmon* (Salmo salar), a native of the North Sea, which ascends all our considerable rivers, and forms the most important branch of our fisheries. It is highly esteemed for its rich flavoured red flesh, which is often preserved and sold by the name of *kippered salmon*. The *fresh-water trout*, or *graylins* (S. lacustris), inhabits

the large lakes in Switzerland; and the *common trout* (S. trutta), a fine fish beautifully marked with red spots, lives in the clear, cool, water of mountain streams; the *capellan* (Mallotus), a small sea fish which congregates in enormous shoals, and is the principal food of the cod and ling; the *thymallus*, or *grayling* (S. thymallus), and the *lavarets*, or *gwyniads* (S. lavaretus and maræнula), are common in the Lake of Constance, and are there caught, preserved, and exported.

The herring tribe is also very important. The *common herring* (Clupea harengus) is common in the north seas; and the method of curing them, as the process of preserving is called, was practised by the Dutch about the beginning of the fifteenth century. It was first practised by Beukel in 1397. The estimated annual capture is 1000 millions, and about an equal number is supposed to fall a prey to other fishes. To this section of the order also belong the *anchovy* (C. enchrasicholus), and the *pilchard*, which abounds on the Cornish coast; the *sardine* (C. sardina), and the *shad* (C. alosa), which ascends the rivers in the early part of the summer, and is esteemed a great delicacy, but should be eaten with caution.

The pike-family is composed of little-known fishes, many of which are inhabitants of the sea. The following are the most remarkable, viz., the *river-pike*, the *spear-pike*, the *bony-pike*, the *horn-pike*, and many others. The *common river-pike* (Esox lucius), with triangular flattened head and black spotted fins, is in general estimation as an excellent fish. It is very voracious, long-lived, attaining the length of from 4 feet to 8 feet, and a weight of from 12 to 40 lbs. Its cranial bones are so singularly formed and arranged, that they have been compared to the cross. The *flying pike* (Exocœtus volans), a native of our European seas, is remarkable for its very long pectoral fins, and hence it can move short distances in the air above water.

The *carp* (Cyprinus) is the type of a family distinguished by large, deciduous scales, and jaws without teeth; they have no fins on the opercula of the gills, inhabit muddy ponds, and live on worms.

We find the *loach* or *groundling* (Cobitis) in fresh water, also the *bearded groundling;* the *carp* (Cyprinus), of which there are numerous species, as the *gudgeon* (C. gobio), the *barbel* (C. barbus), the *tench* (C. tinca), also many sorts of white fish, amongst which are the *roach* (C. rutilus), the *bleak* (C. alburnus), fishes only three or four inches long, whose very small silvery scales are employed in the fabrication of glass pearls (beads); the *crucian carp* (C. cerassius), the *gold fish* (C. auratus), imported from China, and frequently kept in vases to ornament saloons, drawing-rooms, &c.; the *common carp* (C. carpio), one of the best and commonest of our fresh-water fish.

56.

The largest of our exclusively fresh-water fish is the *sheet-fish* or *sly silurus* (Silurus glanis), the head of a family, of which we can only mention the *malapterus* of the Nile (S. electricus, fig. 56), and the *armed shad.*

The fish belonging to the family of *cod*, *ling*, &c., are mostly cylindric, either naked or clothed with very thin scales; they are all sea fish, and are all excellent food. The family of *gadus* are the first in point of excellence, among which are the *eelpout* (G. lota), the *hake* or *ling* (G. merlucius), the *haddock* (G. æglefinus), and the *cod* (G. morrhua), three of the most important kinds of fish, partly eaten fresh, and partly preserved as provisions. When salted and dried they form an important article of export and import. From the liver of the cod an oil is obtained which has of late years acquired a high reputation as a preventive of pulmonary diseases. *Soles* (Pleuronectes), remarkable for their flat shape, afford very delicate food, also the *turbot* (Pl. maxima, fig. 57), a delicious fish, and the *plaice* (Pl. platessa, fig. 58).

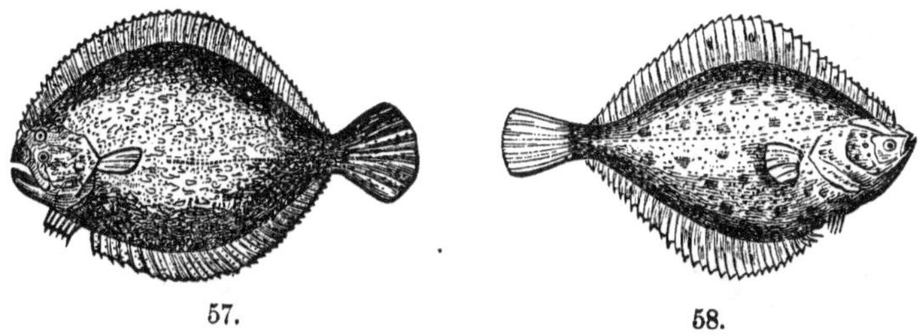

57. 58.

The *remora* or *sucking-fish* (Echineis) is provided with a peculiar kind of gristly head-plate, by which it can adhere firmly to the keels of ships or other objects.

The eel family is distinguished by the snaky form and scaleless, slimy, slippery skin of all the species; the fins are small, and fewer than the normal number. The best known are the *river eel* (Muræna anguilla), the *sea eel* (M. helena), both excellent table fish; the *electric eel* of South America (Gymnotus electricus, fig. 59); the *sand eel* (Amodytes), which is found in the sands on the shores of the northern and eastern seas, used by fishermen as bait, also the *snake-fish*, the *ribband-fish*, &c.

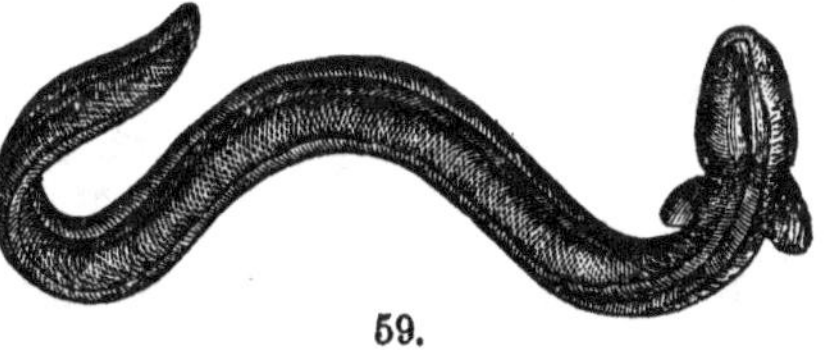

59.

Seventh Order. Acanthopterigii.

136. This order is second only to the last, in the number and importance of the individuals which it embraces, and they are all distinguished by their spinous fin-rays. Among the most remarkable we find the *sea-wolf* or *wolf-fish* (Anarrhichas lupus), a voracious animal from 6 feet to 7 feet long, of great utility in the domestic economy of the Icelanders, the *go* or *sea groundling* (Gobius), common in the lagoons of Venice; said to watch its spawn with jealous care. The most remarkable for the singularity of their appearance are the *spider-fish*, the frightful *sea devil* (Lophius), the *sea-bat* and *frog-fish*, whilst the *parrot-fish* (Scarus), and the *sparus* (Sparus), are distin-

guished by the splendour of their colours; the *perch* (Perca fluviatilis) is on the contrary a fine flavoured river fish, characterised by red breast- belly- and tail-fins, and with black transverse bands on the dark green back; the *pike-perch* (Lucioperca), the *stone-perch* (Acerina cernua), are river fishes worth mentioning.

Among the epicures of ancient Rome, the *mullet* (Mullus surmuletus) was highly prized both for its colour and flavour, and often purchased at enormous sums, 500 florins being sometimes paid for this luxury. The *stargazer* (Uranoscopus) is so named from the position of its eyes being on the crown of its head. In this order we find the vulgar curiosity, the *flying-fish* (Trigla hirundo), and the *flying gurnard* (Dactyloptera volitans). The *stickle-back* (Gasterosteus) devours the ova or spawn of fishes, and is therefore an injurious little river fish, though not much above an inch long. The *mackerel* (Scomber) is an important fish, caught in vast shoals on the channel coasts of England; the *tunny* (Thynnus, fig. 60) is the largest edible sea-fish, being sometimes 15 feet long. It migrates from the Black to the Mediterranean Sea, and forms excellent fishing sport, and no small profit to the fishermen of Greece and the Levant. Some sea-fish of this order are

60. 61.

formidable on account of the enormous length of their sharp-pointed upper jaw, particularly the *sword-fish* (Xiphias, fig. 61), also the constant associate of the *shark*, the *blue boatswain* (Naucrates ductor), and the *surgeon* (Acanthurus), armed with a cutting process at each side.

In another family we find many richly-coloured fishes of the tropical seas, for example, the *horseman* (Ephippus), beautifully spotted and banded; the *beaked chelmon* (Chelmon rostratus), and the *squirting-fish* (Toxotes jaculator). In China and Japan the two latter mentioned dislodge insects from aquatic plants by the jets of water they are able to throw upon them.

In the East Indies is found the *climbing-fish* (Anabas), which is capable of living for a considerable time out of water, and with the assistance of its gills and spinous fins, can even climb up trees.

The last section of this order includes the *great-headed mullet* (Mugil cephalus), found in rivers that flow into the Mediterranean, also the *snipe-fish* (Centhriscus scolopax), which is a well-flavoured fish.

B. INVERTEBRATA (INVERTEBRATE ANIMALS).

137. These are justly said to occupy a lower station in the animal kingdom, inasmuch as they are only furnished with such organs as are indispensable to the most important functions of their economy, and even these organs frequently appear so imperfect, rudimentary, or altogether so partially developed, that for a long time doubts were seriously entertained of their right to a place in the animal kingdom at all.

The intestinal canal or stomach, the alimentary organ, appears at first sight to be the most indispensable; and in fact the very lowest animals are nothing else but a series of canals or cavities permeating the body, and possessing the power of supplying it with aliment: the whole animal is a stomach; but gradually ascending higher in the scale we perceive, in addition to the alimentary canal, which in the higher classes forms a distinct organ, a series of vessels filled with uncoloured sanguinous fluids, and provided with nervous knots, ganglia, or centres of nerves. All the organs which we attribute to man as organs of vitality, are more or less developed in the higher orders of the invertebrata; and hence they might be called animals provided with an alimentary apparatus.

On the other hand the osseous, muscular, and nervous systems which distinguish the higher classes, and which impart to them the variety of shape, beauty, motion, and intelligence, are never conjointly present in the lower orders of the animal creation. Even the faculty of sensation, whereby the animal is vitally connected with the external world, for without sensation it would appear rather to belong to the vegetable than to the animal kingdom, appears to be very imperfect or altogether deficient.

138. The white mass of viscera which mostly compose the bodies of invertebrate animals, is well protected against external injuries; the visceral organs are in some cases enclosed in tough, gristly, or horny envelopes, some being covered with a calcareous shell which is formed of a secretion produced from themselves. The soft condition of their bodies indicates the watery abode, or the aquatic economy of many of these creatures.

One obvious mark characterising this whole group is their general comparative smallness of size. By far the greater portion is visible only by the aided eye. The giant mussel and the cuttle-fish are the only individuals that excite attention, on account of their magnitude.

But if these animals be inferior to the higher orders in size and development, they are very superior in the astonishing multiplicity of genera and species, and in the enormous number of individuals contained in each species. Here Nature appears to us infinite in resources, ever showing by new instances and examples with what ease the same object can be effected by an organisation infinitely diversified in form and mode of application.

139. The individual animals of this group appear very unimportant in their relations to the human race. A cow or a sheep, a horse or a dog, even a hen or a falcon, might not only be the support of a man, but even of a whole family.

The invertebrata are important only by the numbers in which they appear, and in their immediate neighbourhood they are generally rather injurious than profitable. Millions of these creatures are constantly threatening our granaries, our wardrobes, our habitations, even our own bodies, with either destruction or injury, and many of our usages and vital duties are nothing else but an unconscious yet ceaseless conflict with the invisible myriads constantly making inroads on our property, or attacks on ourselves.

Most men would probably be very well satisfied to renounce oysters, honey, silk, wax, and shell-lac, all very important productions of the lower tribes of animals, if they at this cost could purchase exemption from the ravages of the locust, the caterpillar, the moth, the grub, the maggot, the gnat, the mosquito, and the myriads of other vermin that prey upon man in one way or another.

On the whole, however, the destruction of the lower animals would occasion a gap in the creation, and be the cause of the entire loss of whole tribes of higher creatures. The lives of millions depend on the presence of these apparently insignificant creatures; no individual link of the chain of organic life can be abstracted without endangering the safety of the whole.

The utility of even microscopic animals of these classes will be noticed when we come to the treatment of the genera and species themselves.

Instead of four classes, under which we arranged all the vertebrate animals, we divide the invertebrata into nine classes, viz., the Crustacea, the Insecta, Arachnida, Annulata, Mollusca, Radiata, Intestina, Entozoa, Zoophyta, and Infusoria. We hereby omit one class, which under the name *Foraminifera*, is placed between Entozoa and Zoophyta. It comprehends a multitude of small shelled marine animals, scarcely so large as a grain of sand, but their natural history has not yet been satisfactorily investigated.

FIFTH CLASS. CRUSTACEA.

140. The external covering of these animals is either a horny envelope or a crustaceous integument consisting partly of carbonate of lime, whence the name of the class has been derived. The head and trunk are united in one piece, and protected by a shell; both are distinct from the abdomen, which is separated by an indentation or notch, and has usually the appearance of a tail. They breathe through a fringe-like process, or through pulmonary tubes, and possess in a high degree the power of redeveloping an accidentally lost limb.

We place the *crab* at the head of the numerous subdivisions of this class, because it is superior to the remaining orders not only in size but in utility, for it supplies a rich, nutritious, and fine-flavoured food. The following are among the most remarkable of the sea-crabs, viz., the *squills* (Squilla), the

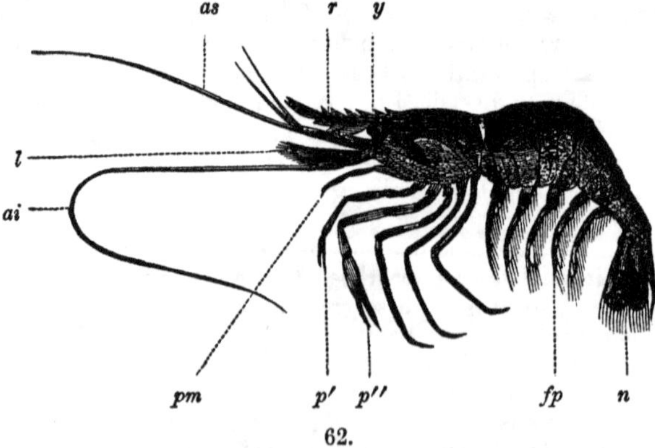

62.

[PRAWN: *as*, antennæ of the first pair; *ai*, antennæ of the second pair; *l*, laminar appendage covering its base; *r*, rostrum or frontal prolongation of the carapace; *y*, eyes; *p m*, external foot-jaw; *p′*, first thoracic member; *p″*, second thoracic member; *f p*, false legs, or swimming members of the abdomen; *n*, tail-fin.]

prawns (Palæmon, fig. 62), the *shrimps* (Crangon), *lobster* (Astacus marinus), which is sometimes found two feet long; the *giant-lobster* (Palinurus), the *hermit-crab* or *Bernhard's crab* (Pagurus), which, having no shell on its posterior parts, places them for protection in an empty snail-shell. In fresh water we find only the *river-crab* or *cray-fish* (Astacus fluviatilis), of a brown colour, but which, when boiled, assumes a lively red. This crab casts its shell from time to time, and forms a new one.

The acaudate or tailless crustaceans compose a special section of this family, and are named *proper crabs*. Like most individuals of the class, they easily lose their claws, which are as easily restored. There are many sorts of these, as the common *sea-crab* (Portunus), the *spider-crab*, the *mussel-crab* (Pinnotherus), the *river-crab* (Telphusa), the *land-crab* (Gecarcinus), which is very common in Jamaica, where they are often seen in immense multitudes, traversing the island to the shore, where they lay their eggs, and return to the mountains accompanied by their young; there are also the *mud-crab* and the *dog-crab*, the latter of which frequently lives on the land, and is said sometimes to climb trees.

The *wood-louse* tribe forms a remarkable section of the crustacean class. These never have claws on their feet, and hence their name, Isopods; they mostly live in water, as troublesome parasites on fish; some of them live in moist, or in dark solitary places. The following are the most remarkable of these—the *whale-louse* (Cyamus), the *spectre-louse* (Caprella), the *branchipus* (Branchipus), the *water-flea* (Gammarus), the *sea-flea* (Talitrus), the *barnacle* (Cymothoa asilus), a great tormentor of fish.

Better known than the above-mentioned are the following, viz., the *cellar woodlouse* (Oniscus asellus); the *armed glomeris* (O. armadillus), which rolls itself up till it is like a pea; the *milliped* (Julus), of which there are several species, with from forty to ninety articulated rings, and an equal number of feet; the *centipedes* (Scolopendra) are similar, but broader, one of which, viz., the yellow, is luminous in the dark.

The *parasitic crabs* (Parasita) compose a larger section. Many of these crustaceans are as minute as infusorial animalcules, and move rapidly, like these, in the water, as the *one-eye* (Monoculus), the *cypris* (Cypris), and many others. Some of these are not above a line long, and prey on different sorts of fish, of which almost every one has a peculiar parasite; for example, the *sturgeon-louse*, the *tunny-louse* (Cecrops), the *carp-louse* (Argulus), &c. Of a similar form is the *Molucca crab*, *limolus* or *king-crab* (Xiphosura), which is one foot long, with spinous caudal processes, from five to seven inches in length, with which the savage Indians point their arrows.

A family of marine animals (Cirripeda), which were formerly classed among the mollusca, has been transferred to the crustacean class. The most of these animals are formed of a series of articulated, segmentary, calcareous rings, which constitute their testaceous habitation; and they fix themselves to rocks, posts, and even to other marine animals, as mollusca, &c. Among these are to be noticed the *lepas* (Lepas), the *balanus*, or *acorn-shell* (Balanus), called also the sea-tulip, many sorts of which are attached to tangle (fuci), crabs, &c. Several adhere to the skin of the cetacea.

Sixth Class. Insecta (Insects).

141. The insect world, which we are next to describe, animates and embellishes every part of Nature's dominions, for, with the exception of frigid rocks, the entire surface of the earth, the water, and the atmosphere, afford them a habitation in some one or other of their wondrous aspects and transformations. Whilst the larvæ conceal themselves in the soil, or move about in the water, or eat into the substance of trees, the complete insect in countless myriads swarms in the atmosphere, or flits from one object to another with unceasing and tireless vivacity.

In order to observe the activities and economy of this world of minute beings, let the spectator seat himself on the green turf of the river's brink in a warm summer afternoon, where he will find himself in the centre of a stage, surrounded by numerous agents or actors, who represent the utmost diversity of character, and exhibit a wondrous multiplicity of external appearances. The little, plain, industrious ant, is evidently engaged in some engrossing labour; the brilliant butterfly, apparently without aim or object, is incessantly flitting from one flower to another, but notwithstanding their apparently aimless and objectless motions, all of them are equally intent upon the serious business of life. There booms and buzzes the chaffer, here the bee is collecting and laying up a store for future wants; the caterpillar is feeding on the green leaf; the flies and gnats are swarming in the atmosphere, acquiring an appetite for their evening meal.

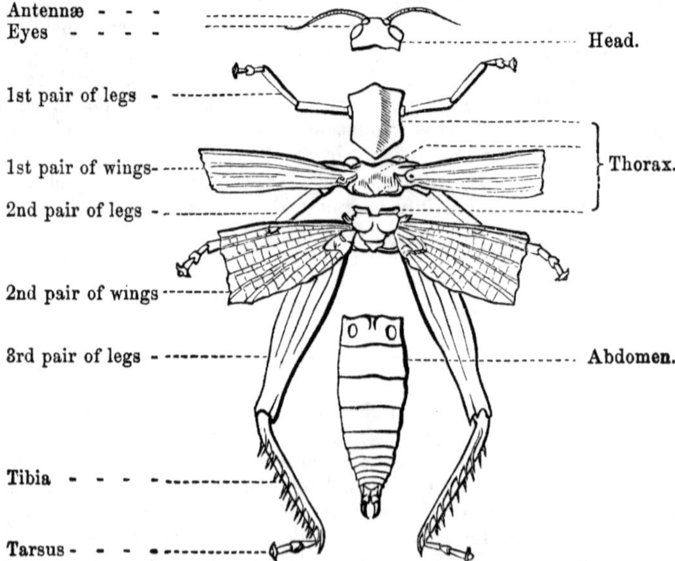

63. Anatomy of the external skeleton of an insect.

The chief character of insects consists in the threefold division of their bodies, which altogether are constructed of ten jointed rings, or segments, of which three form the thorax, or trunk; and at each joint of these three rings there is a pair of legs; consequently an insect is provided with six feet or external limbs (fig. 63). Along the body there is a series of air-conducting tubes (tracheæ), which ramify through the insect, and permeate it in every direction. Besides the vital respiratory, circulatory, and alimentary organs, the perfectly-developed insect has the organ of sight constructed with the greatest complexity. This highly-curious apparatus is an agglomeration of an immense number of facets, which correspond with the nervous filaments that convey sensation to the brain; and although the organs of smell, hearing, and taste be not externally developed, yet these animals are notwithstanding capable in a high degree of exercising even these faculties in a manner correspondent to their necessities and general economy.

The wings of insects are placed on the two posterior segments of the thorax. In several kinds of insects these organs are not present. The alimentary apparatus is developed with wonderful ingenuity; the antennæ (feelers), the proboscis, and the threefold jointed leg, terminating in a series of smaller segments (tarsi), are objects of great complexity and curiosity.

But perhaps the most remarkable phenomena presented by the insect class are the series of changes or transformations which they undergo before arriving at their perfect or fully-developed condition. This is named the *metamorphosis* of insects. From the egg slips out a small maggot, or caterpillar, very edacious and of quick growth, which after a certain period sloughs or casts its skin, and enters into the *pupa state*, in which it is enclosed in a firm, horny, or hard, dense substance, in which condition it exists during

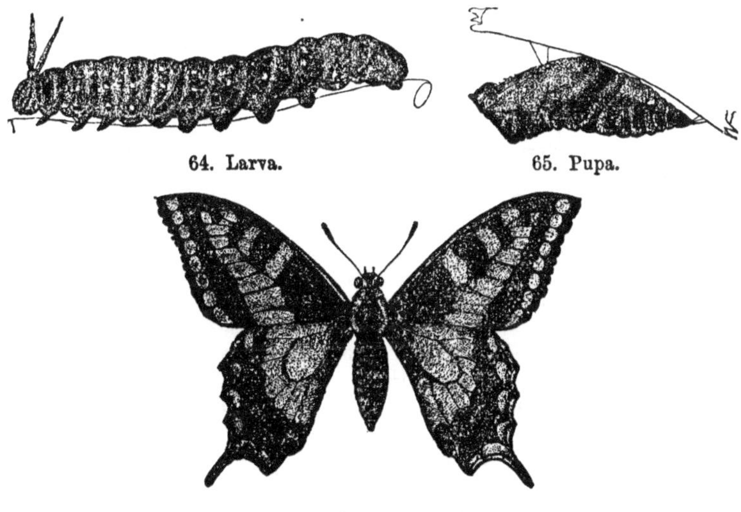

64. Larva. 65. Pupa.

66. Imago.

another period, without nourishment and without movement. Finally, it casts off its tegumentary incumbrance, and flies away as a perfectly-developed insect. The last stage of insect metamorphosis is called the *imago*, or perfect state of its existence (see figs. 64, 65, and 66).

142. Tabular View of the Orders of Insects.

1. Wings enclosed in a horny case; Coleoptera.	2. Wings more feebly organised; Hemiptera.	3. With 2 pairs of wings, the posterior largest. Orthoptera.	4. Wings reticulated; Neuroptera.	5. Wings with scales; Lepidoptera.	6. Naked wings; Hymenoptera.	7. Two-winged. Diptera.
1. Leg formed of 5-jointed segments. 2. Ditto of an unequal number. 3. Ditto of 4 joints. 4. Ditto of 3 joints.	1. Coccus. 2. Cicada. 3. Cimex.	1. Locusta. 2. Gryllus. 3. Blatta.	1. Termes. 2. Ephemera. 3. Libellula.	1. Moths. 2. Nocturnal Lepidoptera. 3. Diurnal ditto. 4. Sphinges.	1. Cynips. 2. Vespa. 3. Apis.	1. Culex. 2. Pulex. 3. Musca.

First Order. Coleoptera (*the Beetle Tribe*).

143. The animals comprehended in this order of the insect class are distinguished by an indurated integument, and by the horny anterior pair of wings, which form a case (elytra) for the posterior pair, when the insect is not flying. The members and head, especially the mouth, are highly developed. Like the papilionaceous order, they pass through all the insect transformations, and, like them, are found of the largest size, and of the most beautiful colours, in warm climates. In India and Brazil only do we meet with the very large and splendid species of coleopterous insects. The larva, and sometimes even the beetles themselves, are herbivorous; the latter generally feed on animal substances, to which they are very destructive.

The subdivision of this order depends on the number of their toes or tarsal joints, as follow:—

(1.) Pentamera, with five joints in all the tarsi.
(2.) Heteromeri, with five joints in the four anterior tarsi, and one joint less in the two hind tarsi.
(3.) Tetramera, with four joints to all the tarsi.
(4.) Trimera, with three joints to all the tarsi.

They may also be distinguished from each other by their more obvious characters of external form and modes of existence. The most important are the *common beetles* (Carabus), predaceous insects, constantly in motion; the *gold-smith*, or *gardener beetle* (C. auratus); the *sycophant* (Calosoma); the *sand-sparkler* (Cicindela); the *bombardier beetle* and the *water beetles*, of which the large *water beetle* (Hydrophilus piceus) attaches itself to fish, and lives upon them by suction; the *short-winged beetle* (Staphilinus); the *leaping beetle* (Elater), which can spring up though laid on its back; the *green chafer* (Buprestis); the *boring beetle*, whose larva bores into trees, and does considerable damage; the *carrion beetles*, among which are the *gravedigger* (Necrophoras), the *bacon-maggot* or *jumper* (Dermestes), and the destructive *museum beetle* (Anthrenus museorum); the *dung beetles*, among which are the *common dung beetle* (Scarabæus); the *pill-chafer* (Birrhus); the *turnip-fly*, or *skip-jack* (Nitidula), which are injurious to the young leaf of the turnip; the *blossom-* and *leaf-chafers*, as the *green shining rose-chafer* (Cetonia); the *stag-beetle* (Lucanus cervus), the *May-*

chafer (Melolontha), the larvæ or grubs of which are very destructive to the roots of wheat, vegetables, &c.

All the above-named beetles belong to the *Pentamerous* order.

Among the *Heteromera*, which does not comprehend a numerous assemblage, we find the *May-worm* (Meloe), the *brimstone-chafer* (Cistela), and the most useful of all the chafers, viz., the *Spanish fly* (Lytta vesicatoria, fig. 67), which is so extensively employed in blistering-plaisters, and is highly poisonous; it is found only on the ash, viburnum, and elder, and is easily discovered by its strong smell.

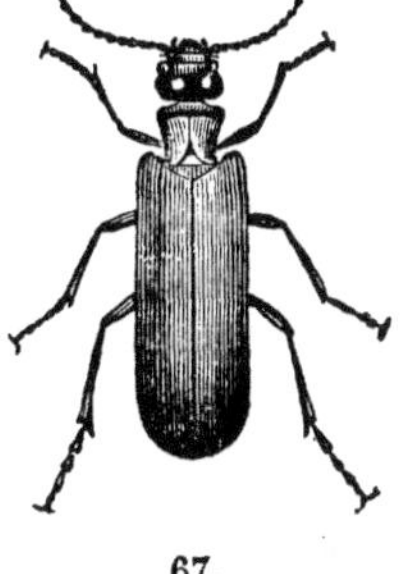
67.

Among the *Tetramerous* beetles we find the *weevils* and *long-snouts* (Curculia and Rhynchænus); the *vine* and *beech beetles* (R. Bacchus and betuleti), both of which are injurious; also the *corn-borer* (Calandra granaria), the *pine-borer* (Cerambix), the *carpenter beetle* (Lamia ædilis), the *bark beetle* (Bostrichus typographicus), the larva of which lives under the bark, and does immense mischief in the pine woods: the *leaf-fretters* (Chrysomelina) are round and beautifully-coloured beetles, with a strong lustre.

Only a few individuals belong to the *Trimerous* section, of which the well-known *lady-bird* (Coccionella septempunctata) is an example.

Second Order. Hemiptera.

144. The insects of this order are characterised by a rigid tubular suctorial organ, serving both as a piercer and sucking instrument, which they use in extracting the juices of plants and animals, on which they live. To this order belong the *cochineal* or *scale-insects* (Coccus), and from the species C. cacti, which feeds on the fig-cactus, the beautiful colour carmine is obtained, which is the basis of scarlet; the *lac scale-insect* (C. lacca), which pierces the bark of the Indian fig-tree, from which there flows sap, which on exposure is hardened into the substance called shell-lac; the numerous sorts of *aphides*, or plant-lice, vermin preying on rose-trees and other shrubs and plants. The exuviæ of these little creatures form a whitish matter, spread over the leaves; their punctures in warm weather occasion the flowing of sap, which being condensed on the outer rind, or cuticle, becomes what is called honey-dew. Some genera of this order are able to produce sounds by the sonorous vibration of their wings or legs: the grasshopper and common cricket are examples. The semi-globular, frothy, saliva-like masses frequently observed on willow leaves are produced by the puncture of one of the cicadæ, and the little animal is generally found in the centre. The *lantern-bearer* (Fulgora), a native of China and America, is said to have a powerfully-luminous head, but this has been contradicted by modern observers. The *head-louse* (Pediculus capitis), and the *common bed-bug* (Cimex), are without wings; these disgusting, troublesome pests, can, however, be dislodged by energetic and persevering habits of cleanliness. The *bugs* with which *plants* and *fruit* are infested have coriaceous anterior, and membranous posterior wings, are very similar to beetles, and have the peculiar disagreeable odour of the house-bug. The *water-bugs*, which move by jerks or starts, and frequently describe various kinds of curves on the surface of

still water, and the *scorpion-bugs* (Nepa), so called from the scissor-like articulations of their anterior legs, and their sharply-pointed tails, belong to this sub-tribe.

Third Order. Orthoptera.

145. In this order the anterior pair of wings is membranous, and the posterior pair is disposed longitudinally, like a fan. They exist only in two states, and the only difference between the insect when it first emerges from the egg and when it attains to its complete or imago state, is that it is winged in the latter but not in the former. To this order belong the *locusts* (Locusta), of which there are several kinds; among many others we notice the *large green locust* (L. viridissima), and the *migratory locusts* (Acridium migratorium), which pass from Asia into Europe in enormous swarms, and eat up every green thing; the *domestic cricket* (Gryllus) is another kind, which frequents the fields, and sometimes inhabits our dwellings, and is well known by its peculiar chirruping sound, which is produced by the vibratory movement of its wings. The predaceous *mantis*, the *earwig*, *cockroach*, and several other similar genera, the females of which are wingless abound in kitchens, bakehouses, &c., where they generally prey by night.

Fourth Order. Neuroptera.

146. These insects are known by their four large gauze-like reticulated wings and great eyes. They do not generally exist in the pupa state, but pass from one state to another by sloughing or changing their tegumentary envelope. Their larvæ are often found furnished with feet, and not less lively and energetic than the perfect insect.

The most remarkable are the following, viz., the *plant-louse lion*, whose larvæ destroy multitudes of plant-lice; the *ant-lion*, which devours the ants (§ 150), which it catches in its lurking-place, a funnel-shaped hole made in the sand; the *termites*, or white ants, which are abundant in India, Africa, and South America. Their grubs and larvæ are without wings, and form, or rather erect, edifices six feet high. In their perfect state, both males and females are winged. These animals are well known and feared as the ravagers and destroyers of everything that lies in the direct course of their predatory expeditions. The larvæ of the *dragon* and *Mayflies* (Ephemera) exist for years in the water, or in empty seed-vessels, or in hollows of wood, &c., and the developed insect lives only for two days, and many die at the end of the first day. In warm days of summer they appear in large swarms, and again suddenly disappear. The best known of the order is the *water-lady*, or *dragon-fly* (Lebellula), which skims about over rivers, ponds, &c., and is distinguished by its beautiful steel-blue, green, and golden hues.

Fifth Order. Lepidoptera.

147. The *butterflies*, as they are generally termed, have four, mostly large, wings, which are covered with minute scales, which can be wiped off like dust. Their larvæ are called caterpillars, and have never more than eight pairs of legs, and generally prepare a cocoon as a receptacle for their young, which is called a chrysalis.

Tabular View of the Lepidoptera.

1 Order. Twilight Lepidoptera. Blattæ—Moths.	2 Order. Nocturnal Lepidoptera. Phalaenæ.	3 Order. Crepuscular (Evening) Lepidoptera. Sphynges.	4 Order. Diurnal Lepidoptera. Papiliones.
1. Tinea. 2. Tortrix. 3. Alucita.	1. Geometra. 2. Noctua. 3. Bombyx.	1. Zygæna. 2. Sesia. 3. Sphynx.	1. Hesperia. 2. Tachyptera. 3. Aëronauta.

Many lepidopterous insects are remarkable on account of their destructive habits. For example, their larvæ destroy hair, feathers, and furs; the *cloth-moth* (Tinea sarcitella), and the *fur-moth* (T. pellionella), deposit their ova in woollen stuffs and in furs; and the *corn-moth* (T. granella) is often a pest in granaries. The *ring-moth* (Bombyx nuestria), the *golden-tailed moth* (B. chrysorhœa), the *apricot-moth* (B. antiqua), and the *damson-plum moth* (B. gognostigma), whose females are without wings, are all more or less injurious to the fruit-trees. The *pine-tree moth* (Noctua piniperda), the *fir-moth* (B. monacha), the *pine-moth* (B. pini and B. processionea), are reckoned injurious in fir and pine plantations. The caterpillars of the various sorts of white and yellow butterflies are destructive to coleworts and other culinary vegetables; of these, the *cabbage-butterfly* (Tachyptera brassica), and the *cabbage-owl* (Noctua brassica), are the most common.

68.

It is difficult to make a selection of those most distinguished for beauty of colour; yet the following may be mentioned, viz., the *red under-wing moth* (N. sponsa), the *blue ash-moth* (N. fraxini), the *brown bear* (B. caja), the *nocturnal peacock's-eye* (B. pavonia, fig. 68), the *evening peacock's-eye* (Sphinx ocellata), the *spurge sphynx* (S. euphorbii), the *privet moth* (S. convolvuli), the *death-head moth* (S. atropos), the *Apollo*, the *swallow-tailed mo'h* (Aëronauta machaon), the *scarce swallow-tail* (A. podaliria), the *white-bordered*

69. Silk-worm Moth. 70. Chrysalis of the Silk-worm

mantle (Antiopa), the *diurnal peacock's-eye* (T. Io), the *admiral* (T. atalanta), the *purple emperor* (T. iris), &c.

The largest of the whole order, viz., the *great Atlas moth* (B. Atlas), is more than two hands in size; a native of China and Java.

148. The most useful insect of all the lepidoptera is the *silk-worm*, which amply indemnifies mankind for the ravages occasioned by many members of this family. This is the famous *silk-spinner* or *mulberry-moth* (Bombyx mori, figs. 69, 70, and 71). This insect was first imported from China by the emperor Justinian; it was subsequently reared in Sicily, and from that island was introduced into Italy, about the year 1130. In France, the culture of silk-worms was first attempted in 1470, and silk was a flourishing manufacture under Henry the Fourth, in 1600. Repeated attempts have been made to introduce the silk-worm into England, and not altogether without success. The total value of raw silk produced in France is estimated at about twenty millions of francs. The silk-worm, or rather caterpillar, feeds on mulberry-leaves, and when arrived at maturity spins a thread about 900 feet long, wound round itself, and forming what is called a cocoon; and from 200 to 400 of these make a pound. From eight to twelve of such cocoon threads are spun together to produce a silken thread of the thickness of a hair, and there are probably about ten pounds of cocoons in one pound of spun silk.

71

Sixth Order. Hymenoptera.

149. Hymenopterous insects are distinguished by four slightly-nerved wings. The *ichneumon* is provided with an *ovipositor*, with which it pierces holes in insects, in which its eggs are deposited, and whereby multitudes of the insect tribe are destroyed. Others, in a similar manner, pierce holes in plants, as the *gall-insect cynips* (Cynips quercus), by the puncture of which the *gall-nut* of commerce is produced. This article is well known as the basis of ink and black dyes.

The proper *wasps* (Vespæ) live in large communities, in dwellings more or less artificially constructed, in which they lay up provision for their young. They eat animal substances, such as insects, &c. The most remarkable are the *hornet* and the *common wasp* (Vespa), the *caterpillar-wasp*, the *mason-bee*, the *timber-wasp*, &c. Among the *ants* (Formicæ), which also belong to this order, the male is winged, and the females, or *working-ants*, are wingless

The most important of the order are the *bees*, which store up honey in waxen cells. These live either solitarily, or in more or less extensive societies The *honey-bees* (Apis mellifica) constitute communities of from sixteen to twenty thousand, the largest portion of which are armed *labourers*. The males, or *drones*, are larger, and have no stings. Of these there are several hundreds in a stock or swarm. There is only one single female, or *queen*, who is the parent, as well as the ruler, of this numerous progeny. Their cells, their provident habits, and their social order, are all equally subjects of wonder and admiration. *Earth-bees*, *wall-bees*, *tapestry-bees*, *tailor-bees*, and *carpenter-bees*, are only a few of this large family. The largest of all the apians is the *humble-bee*, or *humming-bee* (Bombus).

Seventh Order. Diptera.

150. The larvæ and grubs of the *gnat* tribe (Culux) live in water, and hence, in wet swampy places and in rainy seasons, they form an almost intolerable plague, as musquitoes and midges are in hot climates. The *gad-* or *bot-fly* (Oestrus) deposits its eggs on the shoulders and backs of bullocks, horses, and deer, and when the animals lick themselves, these ova are conveyed into their stomachs, so that the grubs are often found in their intestines, nostrils, and in slight swellings on their backs. The well known *flea* (Pulex irritans) produces larvæ scarcely to be distinguished from those of the gnat. It is without wings.

Of the flies which lay their eggs in meat and other provisions, the most destructive are the *carrion-fly*, the *chamber-fly* (Musca domestica), the *cheese-hopper*, the *cherry-fly*, the *stubble-fly*, the *leaf-fly*, the *fungus-fly*, &c. The larvæ of the plant-lice fly destroy myriads of these noxious vermin, which feed on leaves, and the larvæ of the ant-fly make a funnel-shaped hole in the sand, where they entrap the ants. The green *gold-fly* and the beautiful blue and red *spotted flies* deserve to be noticed, while the *harvest-bug* and the *horse-fly* are too well known by the intolerable itching and pain produced by their stings.

Seventh Class. Arachnidæ (*the Spider Tribe*).

151. These animals have, for the most part, a largely-developed abdomen, exceeding in size both the thorax and head, which in this class are united. To the thorax there are attached four pairs of legs, but no wings. Like insects, they are provided with air-tubes, which permeate their body in all directions, and supply the animal with air for breathing, and oxygenised blood, to support the circulatory system. Upon the upper side of the cephalothorax are placed the simple eyes, of which from two to eight, and, in some of the scorpion tribe, from ten to twelve, are present. The arachnidans are divisible into three groups, viz., scorpions, spiders, and mites.

The *scorpion* family is distinguished from the spiders by the greater length of their articulated and slender body, which terminates in a hollow sting, which latter organ is intimately connected with a poison bag or bladder. The sting of the *European scorpion*, which is a native only of the southern parts of Europe, is mortal when inflicted on small animals, and in every case it excites inflammation, and is attended with great suffering. The *Indian scorpion*, which is about four inches long, is capable of inflicting a deadly-venomous wound.

The *spiders* are all predaceous, living on insects, which they ensnare and seize with their fangs, kill, and then suck the whole substance, with the exception of their integuments. Most of them prepare nets of fine threads, which they spin from the posterior part of the abdomen, from a spinning apparatus called a *spinnaret;* others, however, directly seize their prey, by springing upon it, as the *leaping-spider* (Salticus); the *brown wolf-spider* (Dolomedes), which frequently is seen carrying a small woolly bag along with it, in which its ova are enclosed; the *tarantula* (Lycosa tarantula), assumed to be a fearfully-venomous spider, its bite causing the patient to dance and skip like one in a frenzy; this has, however, lately been doubted. The *mining-spider* lurks in an earth-hole, and the *water-spider* (Argyroneta) entraps aquatic insects in a remarkable nest, somewhat like a finger-stall, which she places among the weeds by the river's brink.

The most common of the weaving spiders are the *house-spider* (Aræna domestica), and the *tortoise-shell* (Epeira diadema), the green and gray *garden-spider*, and the very small summer or *gossamer-spider*, which last covers the fields with millions of the finest threads, which hold the morning dews of harvest, and appear in the early morn, when the sun's rays fall obliquely, like myriads of glittering pearls, reflecting all the varied colours of the rainbow. The least breeze dissipates the gay illusion, and destroys the beautiful workmanship of the tiny beings. The *bird-spider* (Mygale avicularia), as large as a man's hand, a native of Surinam, is believed to be the largest of the arachnidans.

The *harvest-man*, or *Harry-long-legs* (Phalangium), which lives after its long legs are torn off. This forms the transition-order between the spiders and the mites, and other little creatures that are frequently found in old books, papers, and collections of plants. The *book-scorpion* (Chelifer) is the representative of these destructive vermin.

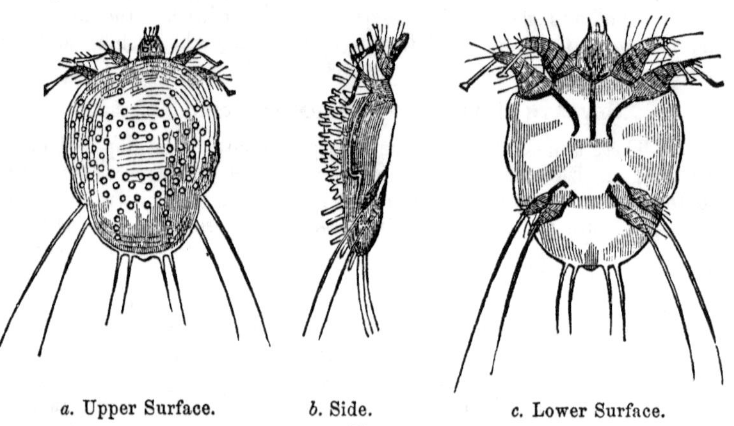

a. Upper Surface. *b.* Side. *c.* Lower Surface.

72.

The *mites* are small insects, that partly consume decaying plants, but are most commonly found among the predaceous vermin of other larger animals. To these belong the *insect mites* (Trombidium); the *ticks* (Ixodes), which suck the fluids of dogs and sheep; the *chicken tick* (Acarus gallinæ); the *chafer mite* (A. coleoptratorum); the *acarus of the itch* (A. scabiei, fig. 72), which produces the aforesaid disease, in the pustules of which they are found; and the *cheese-* and *meal-mites.*

Eighth Class. Annulata (Annelida).

152. The integuments of the animals composing this class consist of a system of *articulated rings*, and hence they are conveniently designated annelidans. These rings are mostly of equal diameter, so that worms have in general an elongated, perfectly cylindrical form, with an oral and anal aperture, one at each end. No sections representing the head, thorax, and abdomen are perceptible in this class. The joints of the rings are generally provided with short bristles or long hairy filaments, but these are never articulated, nor are employed to aid the movement of the animal; but many authors regard these bristly or hairy appendages as in some degree or other conducive to locomotion.

In worms, neither lungs, nor gills, nor air-tubes have been discovered. Their circulatory system is a ramification of blood-vessels in their cuticular integuments; hence the necessary purification of the blood by atmospheric air is effected by the direct contact of the latter. It is remarkable that the vascular system of the greatest part of the annelidans has a red colour, which is not the case in any other class of invertebrate animals. An enlargement of the arterial vessels, which in the higher classes forms the heart, is never perceived in these, but in several a pulsation of the larger arteries is perceptible.

Their habitats are exclusively either the water, or else very moist earth or mud. The greatest part of them inhabit the sea.

Red Worms.

153. Many genera of these inhabit the sea, and most of them are ornamented with threads, hair, and scales, which do not, however, appear to be of much significancy in their general economy. As examples we cite the *nereids* (Nereidæ, fig. 73), the *tufted* and *tasseled worms*, so named on ac-

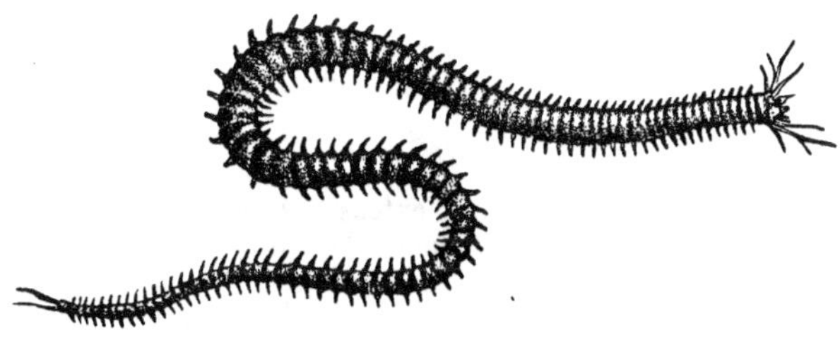

73.

count of the bunches of hair with which their articulations are provided. The *felt-worm* (Aphrodite), the long hairs of which are among the most splendid objects in the animal kingdom, and their effulgence is said to be equalled by that of the humming birds alone. There are besides, the Sabellas, or *pencil*, *fan*, *and comb-worms* (Sabella), and the *giant-worm* (Eunice gigantea), an aquatic native of the West Indies. Several of this tribe constantly inhabit a shell, sometimes composed of several jointed segments, a tegumentary apparatus formed of their own secretions, and sometimes of grains of sand or fragments of shells agglutinated together. The *serpulas* (Serpulæ) are frequently found adhering to stones, mussels, &c., in the north sea.

The *common earth-worm* (Lumbricus terrestris) feeds upon the tender radicles of plants, and often falls a prey to birds and chickens, and is besides used by anglers as ground-bait. For this latter purpose the *sand-worm* (Arenicola), which abounds in sand by the sea-shore, is frequently employed by fishers; in the lobster and crab-fishery as many as from three to four thousand of these worms are attached on hooks to one line.

In stagnant waters abound the *naied-worms* (Nais proboscidea), which have the remarkable character of increasing by mechanical division. Among the smooth-skinned worms, there is the *leech*, the most useful creature of all invertebrata, which by its blood-sucking propensity has saved the lives of many human beings. The leech used in medicine (Hirudo medicinalis) is from three to four inches long and not above one-fourth of an inch thick; its back is black, with eight yellow, black and red stripes, with yellow spots on the stomach. It is now rarely found in the pools and ditches of England, so many thousands having been recently caught for domestic use and for exportation without any provident forethought of the future. The rearing of these important creatures having been thus neglected, millions are now imported annually from Poland, Hungary, Wallachia, and even from Siberia. Many artificial leech-ponds have been recently constructed. It is recommended that all leeches which have been employed in bleeding should neither be cast away nor destroyed, which is too frequently the case, but that they should be preserved and brought to leech-ponds, where among the turfs and clods, they increase so fast, that the very poorest person might avail himself of their aid in cases where such remedies alone are available. Owing to the high price of leeches, persons of limited means must renounce altogether the benefits derivable from their application. The leech lays her eggs in a gelatinous mass about the size of an acorn; after a certain period the young are developed, which are then quite colourless, and are unfit for suction of human blood until they attain to the age of two years. The *horse-leech* is common in England and in all the British isles. It is somewhat larger than the medicinal leech and is of no known utility.

White Worms.

154. These annelidans form an inextensive group of very small animals which, until recently, were classed among the Infusoria. They have obtained the name of *wheel animalcules* (Turbellaria), on account of the whirls they produce in water, by which motion the animalcula on which they live are drawn into their mouths. Their bodies are mostly soft, transparent, provided with a tail, and through union or division they are very variable in their appearance. In many of them red eyes are perceptible. In stagnant waters the *rotate-worm* (Rotifer vulgaris) is frequently met with.

Ninth Class. Mollusca.

155. The vital organs in this class are so perfectly developed that they have been by authors compared to the higher classes of animals, because they are possessed of a trunk similar to quadrupeds, &c., only deprived of the head and limbs.

The molluscs have an alimentary apparatus, which forms a distinct organ, with several convolutions and two apertures, a tolerably large liver and circulatory system which contains a watery fluid, and proceeds from a centre or heart with one ventricle or chamber. The lungs are represented either by lamellæ and vascular ramifications which are called gills, or by pulmonary tubes abundantly furnished with ramified vessels. The nervous filaments which proceed from gangliar rings are only partially present in the higher orders of the class; many of them, however, have tentacula, which they have the power of projecting or retracting at pleasure. Their skin is called the *mantle*, and is not present in all the molluscous orders. This organ is soft and slimy, and covers the mollusk like a sack. By this the muscles are either contracted or expanded, the shells shut or opened; or, if the muscle has an elongated form and is used for locomotion or for piercing, it is called a *foot*. If the muscle be expanded and adapted for crawling, it is called a *sole.*

The greater part of the molluscs secrete a fluid, which by exposure is indurated, forming a shell (testa), which consists of carbonate of lime, and hence they are named *testacea* or testaceous animals (Conchylia). The shell is either one entire piece, as in the snails, or in two pieces, as is the case in the mussels.

They are all inhabitants of the water, and the most beautiful and the largest are only found in the tropical seas. A few inhabit the moist ground. They are almost all eatable, and therefore useful. They generally subsist on vegetable substances; but many of the larger marine testacea live by sucking the juices of other molluscous or fishy inhabitants of the sea. They increase by eggs, which they produce in immense quantities.

On account of the perfect development of their viscera, the molluscs have, by many authors, been placed higher in their systematic classifications than the annular and articulated tribes.

They are, in general, subdivided into two principal groups; in those of the first, a head is more or less developed, and, in the second, this is not the case. Besides they are divided into seven orders of very unequal importance.

156. To the first section of the molluscs belongs the order *Cephalopoda*, thus named because the tentacula or motive organs are appendages to the head; these organs serve the purposes either of seizing prey or of attaching the animal to foreign bodies, or for swimming or crawling; they are remarkable for the number of their suctorial nipples on the borders of their tentacula, by which they can attach themselves so firmly that no force can pull them off without laceration of the limbs themselves. No cupping glass is so firmly attached to the patient's skin as the numerous hollow nipples of the cephalopods are attached to their prey.

The most important animal of this order is the *cuttle fish* (Sepia), which is from five inches to about two feet long. This creature is found in all seas, and its appearance is that of a short-necked flask. The animal is provided with a bag which is filled with an inky fluid of a dark brown colour, which is extensively used by artists under the name of *sepia*. It also produces the *fish-bone* of commerce (os sepiæ), an oval calcareous formation in the back of the mollusk, and celebrated as a dentifrice.

The smaller *sepias*, which often appear in enormous shoals, are the principal food of the cod, and the larger crustaceans. In the Mediterranean sea on the coasts of Greece, the *great cuttle fish* (Octopus vulgaris) is met with; the tentacula of this monster are twelve feet long and very formidable. This animal, which the ancients named *polypes* (many footed), may probably have given birth and currency to the tales of the fabulous monsters (Kraken) of the Norwegian seas, which perform so important a part in many northern sagas.

The above are unfurnished with a shell, but to the testaceous portion of the order belong the *pearly nautilus* (Nautilus, fig. 74), the beautifully

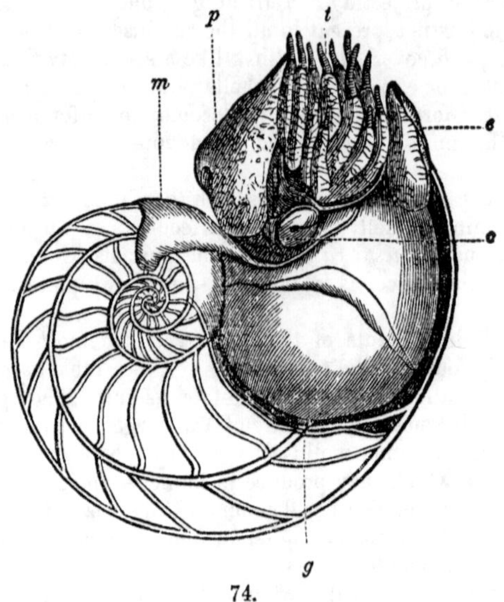

74.

[Pearly Nautilus, with the shell laid open; *t*, tentacula; *e*, funnel; *p*, foot; *m*, portion of mantle; *o*, eye; *g*, siphon.]

convoluted pearly shell of which is formed into drinking-cups, and the *glass-boat* or *paper nautilus* (Argonauta, fig. 75), with a whiter, thinner, beautifully formed shell.

Among the petrifactions of the stratified rocks (Mineralogy § 114) are found many testaceous organic remains which are attributed to this order, though no longer found in a recent state; the principal of these are the *ammonites*, *gryphites*, *belemnites*, &c.

The second order, *pteropoda*, so called on account of the lateral wing-like processes which constitute their locomotive apparatus. They are mostly very small, but appear at certain times in countless numbers. The most remarkable is the *clio* or *whale mussel* (Clio borealis), which is common in the North Sea, and is the principal sustenance of the whale.

156. The *gasteropoda* or *snails* form a very extensive and important order. The greater portion of this tribe has only *one* shell, which in general is convoluted. The muscular part of their body is extended, and forms *one* ventral disk or foot, from which motive organ they have received their name, Gasteropoda. They can, however, likewise swim. Although very languid and

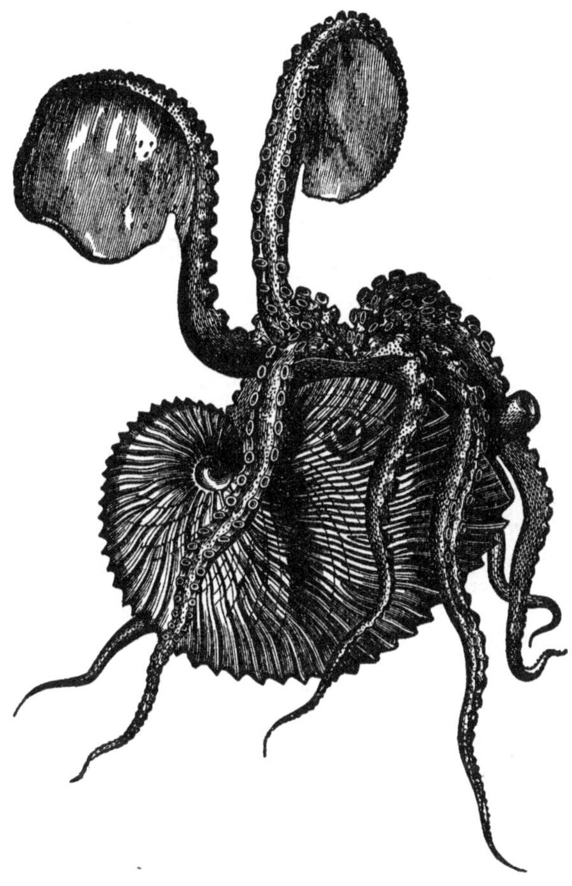

75.

sluggish, they are frequently very injurious to the labours of the horticulturist. Those which have no shelly covering are called *slugs*. The snails are distinguished by a distinct head and tentacula which surround the mouth; and in the warm seas these are remarkable for their size and effulgent colours. Their shells are applicable to many ornamental purposes.

The most important individuals of this tribe are the following, viz.— *Doris Buccinum*, *bladder-snail* (Bulla), the *cup-snail*, *chafer-snail*, the *chiton* (Chiton), *platter-snail* (Patella); the greater part of these live on marine plants. The juice of the *sea-hare snail* (Aplysia depilans) is so acrid that it destroys the hair.

The most common of the terrestrial snails which live on moist earth or in swamps, are the red and brown *common slug* (Limax), the *salad* or *field slug* (L. agrestis), both of which are without shells. The large *edible snail*

(Helix pomatia) has a convoluted shell, and is esteemed delicate and nutritious food; the *garden-snail* (H. hortensis); the large *swamp-snail* (H. stagnalis); the *trencher* or *post-horn snail* (Planorbis); and the common *swamp-snail* (Paludina), belong to this order.

One of the most beautiful marine snails is the *cocklestairs* (Scalaria), which, as a curiosity, is valued at ten dollars; of the genus *turbo,* there is a species in Holland which is salted and used as food.

The following also deserve to be noticed, viz., the *skittle-snail* (Conus); the *roller-snail* (Voluta); the large *cowrie* or *tiger-shell snail* (Cypræa tigris), beautifully spotted and frequently manufactured and mounted as bon-bon boxes, snuff-boxes, &c.; the small *spotted shell* (Cypræa moneta), or *Cowrie,* used in India for ornamenting harness, and also as money; the *egg-snail* (Ovula); the *harp-snail* (Buccinum harpa). The shell of a snail, which, on account of its fire-red mouth, is called the *fiery oven* (Cassis), is employed by lapidaries as a cement. The *trumpet-snail* (Murex tritonis), which is half a foot long, and has its mouth beautifully red-coloured; the *spindle-snail* (Fusus), and the *winged-snail* (Strombus).

Several snails yield, when submitted to heat, a beautiful purple-coloured juice, which anciently was employed in dyeing the most costly stuffs. The famous Tyrian purple is supposed to have been prepared from the sap of a certain kind of snail found in the eastern parts of the Mediterranean Sea.

158. The *Brachiopoda* are distinguished by two long spiral arms placed on each side of the mouth, from which they have received the name of brachiopods; these organs are destined for procuring the animal's food as well as for locomotion. They form a small section of marine mollusks, which are always attached to rocks or other objects. Their habitation is composed of two shells; and the most remarkable are the *terebratula,* multitudes of which are found as petrified remains in various kinds of stratified rocks.

159. The *conchifera* surpass all the mollusks in the amount of human nutriment which they afford. They are like the last order furnished with bivalve shells, which open and shut by a joint or hinge, a motion effected by the mantle of the animal. They commonly live at the bottom of the water, where they move about in the muddy slime by the agency of their expanded muscle or foot, as it is not unappropriately called. The most important are the following, viz.

The *boring-shells,* frequently found on our coasts; the *pholas,* or boring-worm (Teredo navalis), about the size of a quill, which bores into the timber of ships and weirs and occasions much damage; the *stone-pholas* (Pholas dactylus), which by means of its hard siliceous shell, penetrates stones; its flesh is savoury, and shines in the dark; the *razor-shell* (Solen); the *sauce mussel* (Tellina gari), from which an Indian sauce is prepared which is highly esteemed as a delicious condiment; the *triangular mussel* (Donax), and the edible *heart-mussel* (Cardium). Among fresh-water mussels we find the following:—

The large *duck-mussel* (Anatina), the *swan-mussel,* the *painter's mussel* (Mya pictorum), the shells of which are used for keeping painter's colours; the *pearl-mussel* (Mya margaritifera), which occurs in some tidal rivers in England and in the brooks of northern Germany, and from which pearls of considerable value have been obtained.

The following shells and mollusks are confined exclusively to the sea, viz., the *ark-mussel* (Arca), the *giant-mussel* (Chama gigas), which is found in the Moluccas, and is the largest of the whole class, often attaining a circumference of from six to eight feet, and a weight of 200 lbs.; the *gammon-mussel* (Mytilus) is a triangular violet-coloured shell, shaped like a ham, with eatable flesh. A bunch or tuft of silky hair, called *Byssus*, nearly a foot long, is produced on this shell; in the *pinna*, a Sicilian mussel, this byssus is so large, soft, and delicate that the inhabitants manufacture it into stuffs, of which gloves, and other small articles of dress, are sometimes made, and are not infrequent in cabinets of curiosities. On this mussel a small crab, called the *pinna-warder*, is frequently found. The genuine *pearl-mussel* (Margaritifera), which produces the precious pearl, and the mother-of-pearl, as it is called, is caught in the East and West Indies, and especially in the Persian Gulf, by pearl fishers or divers.

The most important of all this tribe is undoubtedly the *oyster* (Ostrea edulis, fig. 76), many sorts of which are obtained on all the coasts of north-

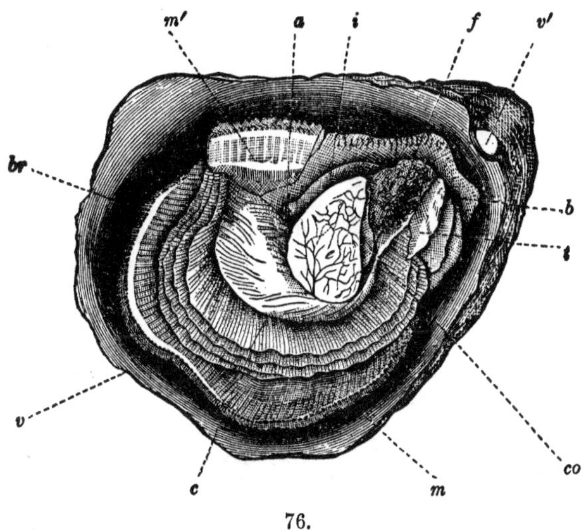

76.

[Anatomy of the oyster: *v*, one of the valves of the shell; *v′*, its hinge, *m*, one of the lobes of the mantle; *m′*, a portion of the other lobe folded back; *c*, adductor muscle; *b r*, gills; *b*, mouth; *t*, tentacula, or prolonged lips; *f*, liver; *i*, intestine; *a*, anus; *c o*, heart.]

ern Europe; and their breeding, catching, and exportation supply labour and subsistence to thousands of families. A single oyster is said to contain two millions of eggs. The *pecten* (Comb) and *scallop* are beautiful shells of the ostracean genus.

160. The last order, *Tunicata*, which includes those mollusks which, instead of a calcareous shell, have an external investment of a coriaceous nature incasing their whole body. They are found agglutinated to rocks, sea-weeds, or other submarine bodies, either individually or in bunches. The *Salpæ* and *Pyrosomæ* are gelatinous and transparent, growing in masses like the above-mentioned tunicated mollusks. The latter has the property of

emitting a brilliant phosphorescent light, whence is derived the name by which this species is distinguished.

TENTH CLASS. RADIATA.

161. The animals composing this class are all inhabitants of the sea, and are distinguished by a coriaceous or calcareous investment on which there are generally found appendages that have the appearance of tufts or feelers. Some, like the *sea-urchins* (Echinodermata), have strong spines, hence the origin of their general name.

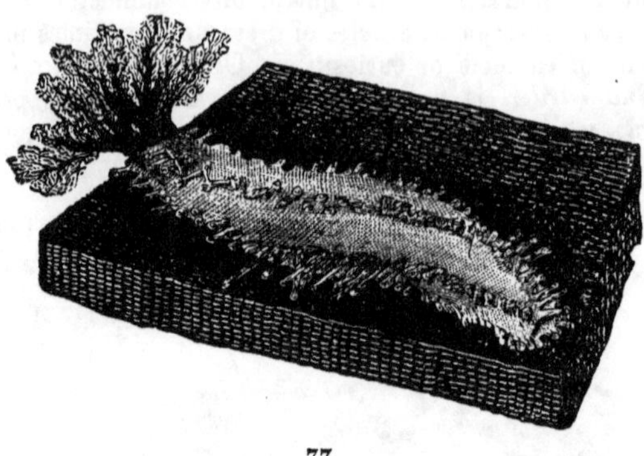

77.

These organs, which the animal can contract or expand at pleasure, partly perform the office of tentacula (feelers) and partly discharge the duties of respiration and locomotion. Their position is regular, being mostly five radiating processes extending horizontally around their mouth. The radiate animals compose three sections or subdivisions; the first are cylindrical and vermicular, the second are globular, and the third radiate.

Among the animals composing the first section, are the *Holothuria* (fig. 77), commonly known by the appellation of sea-cucumbers, which, when taken out of the sea, emit water, like a syringe. H. edulis is esteemed a delicacy among the Chinese.

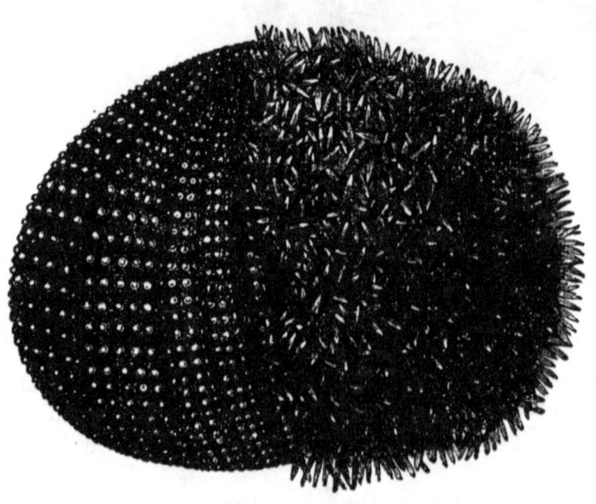

78.

The *sea-urchins* (Echini), are globular, hemispherical or cordate (heart-shaped),furnished with many ridges and spines, somewhat like a melon-cactus; and by the assistance of these spinous appendages they are able to crawl along the shore. The oral aperture is on the under side, the intestinal canal is very long and disposed in several convolutions, and it usually terminates in an anal opening on the upper side. They feed on small crabs and mussels; and the greater portion, especially of the larger sorts, is edible. The most common are the *Turk's cap* (Cidaris imperialis), and the common *sea-urchin* (Echinus esculentus, fig. 78).

In habits and economy the *Asterias* or *Star-fish* is very similar to the animals composing the preceding sections. The *common star-fish* (Asterias) has its five-rayed processes compressed and flattened; in the *Ophiura*, these appendages are vermicular; in the *Gorgonocephalus*, or head of Medusa, they are united by ligaments so as to permit a considerable degree of motion. The *sea-lilies* (Encrinites), and the *sea-pink*, consist of a long often branching stem, which is attached to the submarine soil or rock on which they live; the upper portion of their body resembles the blossom of a flower, which they are enabled to open and shut at their pleasure.

Many of the echini, the asterias, and the encrinites, are found petrified, especially in the calcareous and other stratified formations.

ELEVENTH CLASS. ENTOZOA (CŒLELMINTHA).

162. The animals of this class present the remarkable phenomena of existing in the interior of other animals, as their name implies, and they are chiefly found in the various portions of the viscera. Their organisation is very imperfect. The traces of organs of sensation are imperceptible, even a respiratory apparatus cannot be recognised in these soft, almost homogeneous objects. They certainly live on the fluids of the animals which harbour them, and are not only permanent but often dangerous inmates. About 1500 sorts are known, almost every animal being infested with a kind of intestinal parasite peculiar to itself, and frequently harbouring several sorts at the same time. They are divisible by their form into five chief orders.

The first order is composed of *round worms*, one of which, the *thread-worm* (Filaria), is three feet long and of the thickness of a filament of silk; a terrible pest in tropical regions, where it is developed in the human leg immediately under the skin. In the human stomach is found the *trichocephalus*, from one to two lines long, and more than one species of *ascaris*, viz. (A. lumbricoides) and (A. vermicularis) about three lines long, are frequent in the intestinal canal of children. The *strongilus* is found in the kidneys of men and horses; and the strongilus filaria in the trachea of sheep. The latter excites violent coughing.

Of the two following orders, we only mention the *itch-worm* of swine (Echinorhynchus), and the *liver-worm* (Distoma); the latter is found in the biliary ducts of men and sheep.

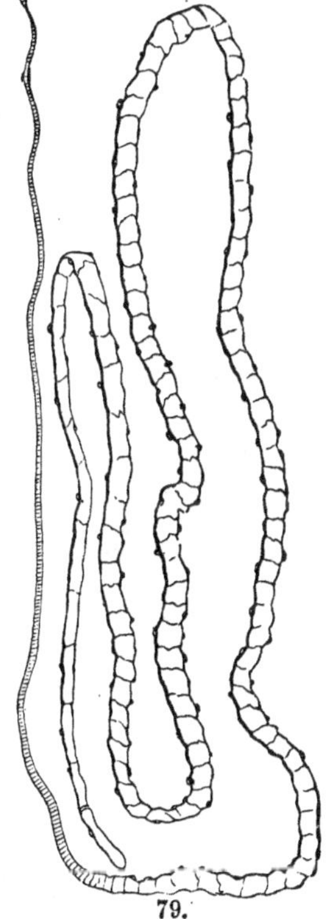
79.

The order of the *tape-worms* contains the *Tænia solium* (fig. 79), one of the most enduring and pernicious parasites of the human subject, being of exceedingly difficult destruction, for if it happens to be broken, the part which is terminated by the head, has the faculty of reproducing itself. The common tape-worm is from four to ten feet long, chiefly found among the inhabitants of Western Europe; the other species (Botriocephalus) is sometimes found of the enormous length of from 20 to 30 feet. It is met with among Eastern Europeans.

The *hyatid* (Cysticercus) is vesiculate in form, with a suctorial apparatus or head. It is found in almost all the viscera of the human body, and especially in swine; in the latter it occasions nuclei of the size of a pea or even of a nut. It is also found in the brain of sheep, and occasions what is commonly called the gids (affection of the brain). It consists of a delicate transparent bladder, and is sometimes as large as a hen's egg provided with an apparatus of hooks and suckers.

Twelfth Class. Acalephæ. Sea Nettles.

163. The lower we descend in our progressive survey of the animal kingdom, the more strikingly does the contrast between the lower and higher types of animated beings excite our wonder and admiration. The lower forms are so abnormal, and exhibit so many and decided aberrations, that their description, either identically or analogically, is not unattended with difficulty.

Organs which in the higher animals are well known, and their functions well defined, are either totally wanting or so peculiarly constructed that we are under the necessity of considering them in another aspect, or under different relations. But besides, as all the living creatures arranged under the following classes are marine, and for the most part impossible to be preserved in a state fit for investigation, a knowledge of their structure, &c., is unattainable without the aid of accurate pictorial representations.

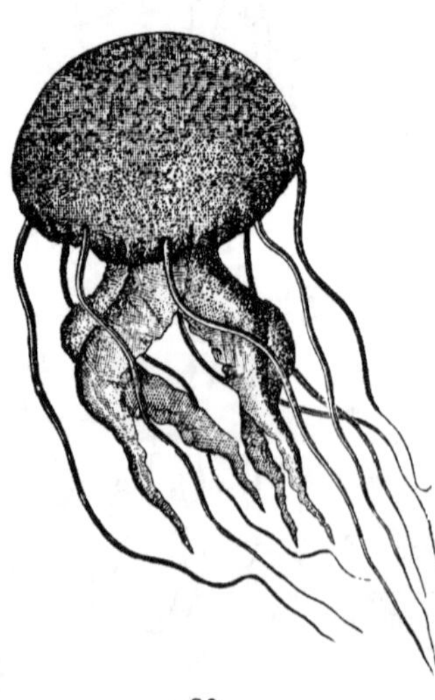

80.

These acalephas or nettle-like animals, a name derived from their stinging properties, are divided into three orders, each of which is characterised by their locomotive appendages, viz., the *pulmonigrada*, the *ciliograda*, and the *physograda*. In general, the animal consists of a membranous bladder, swimming in or on the water, from which flaps or multitudes of filamentous processes are suspended. These are permeated by tubular suctorial passages which convey nourishment to the animal and aid it in moving from place to place. The creature is not furnished with a mouth, but entangles its prey, mostly fishes, in its prehensile organs, and sucks the juices even to the bones. While some of the acalephous genera live, as in the last example, entirely by suction, and are hence called suctorial genera, there are others which have an oral aperture and an alimentary canal, which are analogous to similar organs in animals of a higher rank. Of these there are many sorts, some of which emit, during the night, rays of the most effulgent and variegated colours.

If their tentacula touch any sensitive part of the body, as the hand, for example, a burning sensation is produced similar to that which is felt when stung by a nettle. This is supposed to be caused by a peculiarly acrid juice secreted in their tentacula, and which is probably used by them as a digestive fluid.

The following are the best known of the class, viz., the *girdle of Venus* (Cestum Veneris); the *Portuguese man-of-war* of sailors (Physalia); *Berenice's hair* (Coma Berenicis); the *Rhizostoma*, &c. On the coasts of the east and north seas, during the ebb tide, there is occasionally found the *Medusa aurita* (fig. 80), with a six-inches-broad disk, formed of a milk-white transparent gelatinous mass, with four violet-coloured alimentary and prehensile pendent organs.

When forsaken by the tide and left on the strand, the animal dries up and leaves nothing but a small quantity of transparent cellular substance of only a few grains' weight, although, when in the water, it probably weighed as many pounds. It is of no known utility to man, but may afford subsistence to marine animals.

Thirteenth Class. Polypi.

164. The Zoophytes of earlier authors, or polypi, are gelatinous or membranaceous creatures of various forms, though mostly tubular. In general they have only one aperture, surrounded by from eight to twelve capillary or linguiform tentacula, by which they seize their prey and convey it to the mouth. They increase by ova, or oftener by gemmæ or buds, which, while on the original, are gradually developed till they become perfect polypi, when by natural fissure they are separated from the parent. The best known of these are the *green* and *gray polypi* (Hydra viridis and grisea, fig. 81). The marine polypi are exceedingly numerous; their skin is various, sometimes similar to paper; sometimes it is coriaceous, sometimes calcareous, sometimes the integument is gelatinous, of a more or less firm consistency, and when dried these animal remains may be used like hay for packing. Among others, the following are well known, viz., the *Fungias* or fungoid polypi, which are attached to shallow parts of the bottom of the Mediterranean sea, especially about the Greek islands, whence they are brought up by divers. They are used as a substitute for soap, and are divided into two kinds, viz., the *washing fungia* and the *horse fungia*. The animal part of this

81.

substance consists in the slimy envelope, which exhibits some sensibility. Some authors have denied their right to a place in the animal kingdom.

The branching polypi consist of a gelatinous substance, in which gradually there is formed a nucleus of carbonate of lime. These polypi are firmly attached to the bottom of the sea or to rocks, and generally continue growing till they reach its surface, when they form a family consisting of myriads of millions of beings; their edifices, known by the names of coral banks and reefs, are very perilous to navigation, and are also the origin of numerous islands, particularly in the great South Pacific Ocean.

The forms of these coral edifices are very various, sometimes very beautiful; the most remarkable are the *red coral* (Isis nobilis), which commonly occurs on the coast of Algiers, and is fabricated into many ornamental articles; also the *white coral*, the *sea-feather* (Plumatella), the *marine-fig* (Synoicum), the *sea-cork* (Alcyonium), the *sea-grapes*, &c.

Another tribe of polypi is composed of *Tubiporidæ*, the animal part of which is invested with a calcareous tube or covering provided here and there with orifices through which the creature protrudes its tentacula in search of food. Such as are furnished with numerous small openings are called *millepores*, those assuming more or less an arborescent appearance are named *madrepores*. Several species are named in accordance with their appearance, as *Neptune's ruffles* (Retepora), the *sea-coral*, the *black coral*, which is capable of being fabricated into ornamental articles.

The *marine nettles* (Actinia, fig. 82), are rather large fleshy polypi, of the form of a small flower pot; their large mouth is surrounded with numerous radiating tentacula. If they are touched with the hand, their tentacula exert immediately their retractile and prehensile energy, seize the hand, which feels a burning pain, as if stung by a nettle. Hence these objects have received the name of sea-nettles. They generally remain attached to submarine rocks or to the bottom of the sea. They have, however, the power of locomotion, and they are also said to be eatable.

82.

The softer polypi are eaten by marine animals, especially by fishes and whales. The calcareous stems of others are often burnt into lime, and form excellent mortar. Corals are frequently found petrified, especially in mountains of the ancient formations (Miner. § 114).

Fourteenth Class. Infusoria.

165. If water is poured on some vegetable or animal substance, for example, on leaves, grass, or on a bit of flesh, and the infusion exposed for some days to the ordinary temperature of a sitting-room, a thin pellicle is formed on the surface. Suppose a bit of this to be placed in a drop of water and submitted to a microscope, a multitude of small lively creatures will be seen, of very different magnitudes and shapes, moving about with great energy in the water. Sometimes a single drop of such water contains a thousand of these animalcules. From their origin they have derived the name of *Infusoria* or Infusorial animalcules; they have only been known

since the invention of the microscope, for scarcely any of them are visible to the naked eye.

In stagnant water, and indeed in fluids of every description, where either vegetable or animal substances are undergoing the process of decomposition, these creatures are present; they are found also in the sea and in rivers, but not in pure spring water.

In reference to the origin of these animalcules, the view was long entertained that they were generated spontaneously, that the decaying and dead parts of the vegetable and animal substances were decomposed and resolved into these simple beings. The most accurate experiments, however, have shown us that the infusoria are constantly produced from eggs which are always present in the atmosphere, and which are easily developed when they come into contact with a suitable medium, after which they increase with incredible celerity. These are analogous to the spores or sporidea of the minute or microscopic fungi, and to the unexpected appearance of plants in places where no one ever scattered their seeds (Botany § 99 and 109). If the infusorial matter be strictly secluded from atmospheric influences, or if it be exposed to the same at a very high temperature, no *infusoria* will appear. They are rarely or ever developed on mountains of a certain height, where the atmosphere is pretty free from such substances.

When we consider that these creatures are only 1-1500th to 1·2000th part of a line in diameter, and are only visible when under a powerful magnifier, it may be easily conceived that the eggs, which are 100 times smaller, exist by millions in the atmosphere, though beyond the possibility of detection. Hence, when a stagnant pool has been dried up, the wind carries up, with the dust, the innumerable ova of infusoria, and these re continually floating about in the atmosphere till they meet with circumstances favourable to their development.

These creatures feed partly on vegetable and partly on animal decomposing substances, and occasionally prey on each other. They either catch their food by darting on it with open mouth, or by a rotatory motion of their radiated tentacula with which many of them are furnished, excite a little whirlpool or sort of current in the water which carries the prey into their jaws. These last are named *rotifera;* and as being more perfect creatures than some others of the class, have recently been ranked as a distinct order in the higher class of worms (§ 154).

Though these animalcules be so exceedingly minute, yet they exhibit great varieties of form, and many genera are now distinguished; they seem to have the power of contraction and expansion, and especially of assuming various aspects. The following are the names of a few best-known genera which may serve as a general indication of their form. These are, for example, the *monads* (Monas, Protozoa), *paste eels* (Vibrio), found in diseased grains of wheat (usually called the *brand*), the *screw* and *plate animalcules* (Cyclidium), the *globular*, *navicular*, &c. (Volvox, Navicula), the *trumpet*, the *urn*, and *clock* animalcules. Many infusoria have a calcareous or siliceous investment, over their entire body, serving as a sort of panoply for defence. In some, this defensive covering, in addition to lime and silicic acid, contains sesquioxide of iron, forming a shell surrounding the creature like a lobster- or crab-shell. When the animal dies, the soft part only perishes, the shell remains of its original form, and the remarkable discovery has been made that entire formations of rock are composed of the shells of infusoria alone (Compare Mineralogy, § 145). It is also a remarkable fact, connected with these little beings, that oxygen gas is exhaled by many infusoria, whilst all other animals yield by expiration carbonic acid gas.

Fifteenth Class. Spongia.

Notwithstanding the numerous investigations of sponges, but little is known of their true nature beyond the anastomosing filaments of which their frame-work consists, and which, during the life of the sponge, is overspread with a glairy semifluid matter. The surfaces of sponges are observed to be studded with numerous minute apertures (see fig. 83), leading to interior canals, which, coalescing and forming larger passages, terminate in cavities that finally open by large and projecting orifices upon the surface of the sponge. Through the above-mentioned little apertures the water is absorbed, and on pressing the sponge escapes by the larger orifices.

83.

After their first production, sponges remain permanently fixed to rocks and other objects suitable to their development.

The number of species at present described amounts to one hundred and forty-seven, some of which are inhabitants of our own shores; but the greater number flourishes in tropical seas, where several species are found of great size and beauty.

GLOSSARY.

ABDO'MEN. From *abdĕre*, to conceal. The largest of the three splanchnic cavities. The chief viscera contained in it are the stomach, intestines, liver, spleen, pancreas, kidneys, and bladder. It is lined by the serous membrane, called the peritoneum.

A'BIES. Lat. A fir-tree. Specific name of a tree.

ABNOR'MAL. Not conformed to rule. From the Lat. *ab*, from, and *norma*, a rule.

ACA'CIA. Gr. *ake*, a point; a thorny tree. A genus of the family Leguminósæ and order Minósæ. About 300 species are enumerated; many of them yield gum. The gum Arabic of our shops is chiefly derived from the *A. vera* and *arabicâ*.

ACA'CIA ARA'BICA. Arabian acacia.

ACA'CIAS. Trees belonging to the genus acacia.

ACER SACCHARI'NUM. The sugar-maple.

A'CID. A term given by chemists to those compound bodies which unite with salifiable bases to form salts: for example, a compound of sulphur and oxygen, called sulphuric acid, unites with magnesia, and forms a salt, named sulphate of magnesia, or Epsom salts. The acids which constitute objects of special manufacture for commercial purposes, are the following: — Acetic, arsenious, carbonic, chromic, citric, hydrocyanic (Prussic), malic, muriatic (hydrochloric), nitric, oxalic, phosphoric, sulphuric, and tartaric.

ACI'DULOUS. Sourish; possessing acid properties.

ACOTYLE'DONS. Plants in which the seed-lobes, or cotyledons, are absent, or indistinct. They form a grand division of the vegetable kingdom, including the ferns, lichens, &c., and correspond to the *Cryptogamia* of Linnæus.

ADANSO'NIA. A genus of plants named in honour of Michel Adanson, a famous French botanist, born in 1727. *Adanso'nia digita'ta.* Sour gourd, or African sour-sop. Monkeys' bread or Baobab tree of Senegal, which is considered the largest, or rather the broadest tree in the world. "Several, measured by Adanson, were from sixty-eight to seventy-eight feet in circumference, but not extraordinarily high. The trunks were from twelve to fifteen feet high, before they divided into many horizontal branches, which touched the ground at their extremities; these were from forty-five to fifty-five feet long, and were so large that each branch was equal to a monstrous tree; and where the water of a neighbouring river had washed away the earth, so as to leave the roots of one of these trees bare and open to the sight, they measured 110 feet long, without including those parts of the roots which remained covered. It yields a fruit which resembles a gourd, and which serves for vessels of various uses; the bark furnishes a coarse thread, which they form into ropes, and into cloth, with which the natives cover their middle from the girdle to the knees; the small leaves supply them with food in times of scarcity, while the large ones are used for covering their houses, or, by burning, for the manufacture of good soap. At Sierra Leone this tree does not grow larger than an orchard apple-tree." *Loudon.*

ADHE'SION. A term applied in physics to denote the force by which particles of different kinds are held together, so as to form a *heterogenous* whole, which may be broken up by *mechanical* means. Affinity, on the contrary, unites particles of different kinds, so as to form a homogeneous whole, which is indestructible by mechanical means.

A'DIT. Lat. *adeo*, I approach. A horizontal shaft or passage in a mine, either for access, or for carrying off water. It is sometimes called "the drift."

AFFIN'ITY. The chemical term denoting the peculiar attractive force which produces the combination of dissimilar substances; such as of an alkali with an acid, or of sulphur with a metal. See ADHESION.

AFRICA'NUS. Lat. African; belonging or relating to Africa.

A'GAMOUS. From the Gr. *a*, privative, and *gamos*, marriage. Having no sex. In *botany*, having no visible organs of fructification. A term applied to cryptogamic plants.

A'GATE. A name given to all varieties of quartz which have not a vitreous aspect; are compact, semi-transparent, and whose fracture resembles that of wax. Agates are of various colours, and admit of a fine polish. According to Theophrastus and Pliny, the name comes from the river Achates in Sicily, now the Drillo, on the banks of which the first agates were found.

AIR-PLANTS. A name given to certain parasitic plants which were supposed to be nourished by the air alone, without contact with the soil. There are some species which will live many months suspended by a string in a warm apartment.

ALABA'STER. A stone, usually white, and soft enough to be scratched by iron, or even by the nail. There are two kinds of it: the *gypseous*, which is merely a natural semi-crystalline sulphate of lime, and the *calcareous* alabaster, which is a carbonate of lime. The oriental alabaster is always of the latter kind, and is most esteemed, because it is agreeably variegated with lively colours. It is, moreover, susceptible of taking a marble-polish.

AL'BA,
AL'BUS, } Lat. White.
AL'BUM,

ALBI'NO. Spanish. From the Lat. *albus*, white. Applied to individuals of the human race (and extended also to some other animals) who have white hair; the iris, pinkish or very pale; and the eyes unable to bear much light. Albinos are most frequent in the negro race; but it does not seem to be true that there are tribes of Albinos in any part of the world.

ALBU'MEN. From the Lat. *albus*, white. A chemical term, applied to an immediate organic principle, which constitutes the chief part of the white of egg. Animal and vegetable albumen are nearly the same in composition.

AL'DEHYDE. A substance obtained by depriving alcohol of its hydrogen. The name is formed by taking the first syllables of the words *al*cohol-*dehyd*rogenated.

A'LGA. Lat. Sea-weed.

A'LGÆ. Plural of alga. Name of a sub-class of cryptógamous plants, which is subdivided into three families: the *Phy'ceæ*, or submerged sea-weeds; the *Lichens*, or emerged sea-weeds, and the *Byssa'ceæ*, or amphibious sea-weeds. The algæ or sea-weeds are ágamous plants which live in the air, on the surface or at the bottom of fresh or salt water; they are remarkable for their cellular or filamentous structure, into which no vessels enter.

AL'KALI. A class of chemical bodies, distinguished chiefly by their solubility in water, and their power of neutralizing acids, so as to form saline compounds. The alkalies of manufacturing importance are ammonia, potash, and soda. These alkalies change the purple colour of red cabbage and radishes to a green, the reddened tincture of litmus to a purple, and the colour of turmeric and many other yellow dyes, to a brown. Even when combined with carbonic acid, the three alkalies exercise this discolouring power, which the alkaline earths, lime, baryta, and strontia, do not. The same three alkalies have an acrid taste, and combine with oils, so as to form soap. They unite with water in every proportion, and also with alcohol. Their carbonates are also soluble in water, and they are thus distinguished from the alkaline earths.

AL'KALINE. Having the properties of an alkali.

AL'KALOIDS. A term applied in chemistry to the organic alkalies or bases. Sertürner was the first discoverer of them, having recognized in opium the alkaloid now called morphia.

ALLO'Y. This term formerly signified a compound of gold or silver with some metal of inferior value; but it now means any compound of any two or more metals whatever. Thus, bronze is an alloy of copper and tin; brass, an alloy of copper and zinc; and type-metal, an alloy of lead and antimony. All the alloys possess metallic lustre, even when cut or broken to pieces; they are opaque; are excellent conductors of heat and electricity; are frequently susceptible of crystallizing; and are more or less ductile, malleable, elastic, and sonorous. An alloy which consists of metals differently fusible, is usually malleable in the cold, and brittle when hot, as is exemplified with brass and gong-metal.

ALLU'VIA. Lat. Plural of alluvium.

ALLU'VIAL. Of the nature of alluvium.

ALLU'VION, } From the Lat. *alluo*, I wash upon. Gravel, sand, mud, and other trans-
ALLU'VIUM, } ported matter, washed down by rivers and floods upon lands not permanently submerged beneath water. A deposit formed of matter transported by currents of water.

A'LOE. Name of a genus of plants which includes very many species. The inspissated juice of several of these species constitutes the varieties of the medicine called Socotrine, Barbadoes aloes, &c.

Alpi'na,
Alpi'nus, } Lat. Alpine; belonging or relating to the Alps.
Alpi'num,

Alu'minum, or Alumi'nium. From *alu'men*, alum. The metal which forms the basis of alum; of alumina, or pure argil.

A'madou. The French name of the spongy combustible substance called *spunk*, which is prepared from a species of agaric, the *boletus igniarius*, a kind of mushroom, which grows on the trunks of old oaks, ashes, beeches, &c.

Amal'gam. An alloy in which one of the constituent metals is mercury.

Amalgama'tion. A process used extensively in extracting silver and gold from certain of their ores, founded on the property which mercury has of dissolving these metals as disseminated in the minerals, and thus of separating them from the earthy matters.

Amary'llis. From the Gr. *amarusso*, to be resplendent. A nymph, in ancient mythology. Name of a genus of plants, forming the type of the family of Amaryllídeæ, composed of about sixty species. Generally they are bulbous plants, remarkable for the size and beauty of their flowers.

Am'ber. A fossil resin, found chiefly on the shores of the Baltic, and at Cape Sable in Maryland. It is highly electrical, the term "electricity" itself being derived from its name in Greek, "electron."

A'methyst. From the Gr. *amethustos*, not drunk. The ancients gave this name to a stone in which the wine-red colour was tempered with violet. A violet variety of hyaline quartz.

Amian'thus. A filamentous mineral, called also *Asbestos*.

Ammo'nia. A colourless gas of a peculiar, pungent odour. It causes death when respired; and its strong alkaline reaction distinguishes it from all other elastic fluids. It is liberated from all its chemical combinations by the alkalies. Spirits of hartshorn is a solution of this gas.

Ammo'niac. A gum-resin, the inspissated juice of an umbelliferous plant, the *dorema ammoniacum*, which grows in Persia.

Ammoni'acal. Of the nature of ammonia.

Am'monite. From the Lat. *Ammon*, a name of Jupiter. A fossil so called from a supposed resemblance to the horns engraven on the heads of Jupiter Ammon. In certain parts of England called *snake-stones*. Ammonites are fossil shells, rolled upon the same plane, consisting of a series of separate chambers, like the nautilus.

Amor'phous. From the Gr. *a*, privative, and *morphe*, form. Without definite or regular shape. Said of minerals and other substances which occur in forms not easy to be defined.

Ampeli'deæ. From the Gr. *ampelos*, a vine. Name of the family of Phanerógamous plants, which includes the vine.

Amphi'bious. From the Gr. *amphibios*, two-lived. Having the faculty of living in two elements.

A'mplitude. In astronomy, denotes the angular distance of a celestial body, at the time it rises or sets, from the east or west points of the horizon. It is sometimes used to designate the horizontal distance a projectile reaches when thrown from a gun.

Am'yris. From the Gr. *amuros*, not perfumed. A genus of phanerógamous plants, which is the type of the family of Amyri'deæ, which is allied to the family of turpentines. *Am'yris gileade'nsis*. The Balm of Gilead. *Am'yris kataf*. The myrrh-tree. *Am'yris opoba'lsamum*. The opobalsam, or balsam of Mecca.

Ana'lysis. The art of resolving a compound substance or machine into its constituent parts.

Ana'nas. Portuguese. Pine-apple. Genus of the family Bromeliáceæ, and type of the tribe Ananáceæ.

Andro'meda. Mythological name of a constellation. Genus of the family Ericáceæ, and type of the tribe Andromédeæ or Andromedas.

Ange'lica archenge'lica. Garden Angelica. Roots and seeds used in medicine as an aromatic stimulant.

Angui'nus. Lat. Of the nature of a snake; belonging or relating to a snake.

A'neroid. From the Gr. *a* or *an*, privative, without, and *reō*, to flow. A name given to a kind of barometer which is constructed without a liquid to counterpoise the air. The Aneroid barometer consists of a cylinder of copper with a very thin and corrugated end, partially exhausted of air, and hermetically sealed. The effect of the varying pressure of the atmosphere on the thin end is magnified by a system of levers, so as to affect the index of a dial like that of a watch or clock. This is a French invention, but was patented in England, in the year 1844. See Barómeter.

Anima'lcula. Lat. Plural of Animálculum.

Anima'lcule. A diminutive animal. A term used to designate animals so small that they cannot be seen by the unassisted eye.

ANIMA'LCULUM. Lat. Animalcule.

ANISA'TUM. Lat. Belonging or relating to aniseed. Specific name of the tree which produces star-aniseed.

AN'NUAL. From the Lat. *annus*, a year. Yearly. A plant which rises from the seed, reaches perfection, and perishes within a year, is termed an annual.

ANTA'RCTICA. Lat. Antarctic.

A'NTHER. From the Gr. *anthera*, a flowery herb. In botany, the essential part of the stamen. The small yellowish body, compared to a diminutive leaf folded on itself, which crowns the stamen, and in which the pollen is formed.

ANTIQUO'RUM. Lat. Of the ancients.

ANTISE'PTICS. Substances which counteract the spontaneous decomposition of animal and vegetable substances. These are chiefly culinary salt, nitre, spices, and sugar, which operate partly by inducing a change in the animal or vegetable fibres, and partly by combining with and rendering the constituents unsusceptible of decomposition.

APHE'LION. From the Gr. *apo*, from, and *hélios*, the sun. That point of a planet's orbit most distant from the sun; opposed to *perihelion*.

A'PHIDES. Plural of aphis.

A'PHIS. Gr. A plant-louse; a vine-fretter.

APOCY'NEÆ. From the Gr. *apo*, far from, and *kuon*, dog. Having the virtue of driving away dogs; the plant which kills dogs. Botanical name of a family of which the genus *apo'cynum* is the type.

A'PTERYX. From the Gr. *apteros*, without wings. Name of a genus of birds.

A'QUA FOR'TIS. Strong water. Nitric acid, somewhat dilute, was so named by the alchemists, on account of its strong solvent and corrosive operation upon many mineral, vegetable, and animal substances.

A'QUA RE'GIA. Royal water. The name given by the alchemists to that mixture of nitric and muriatic acids which is best fitted to dissolve gold, styled by them the *King of the Metals*. It is now called *Nitro-muriatic acid*.

A'QUEOUS ROCKS. Are those formed by deposits from water.

A'QUILA. Lat. An eagle. *Aquila albicilla*. The fishing eagle.

AR'BUTUS. Lat. A shrub. A genus of plants.

A'REA OF SUBSIDENCE. A geological expression, used to designate a space which has settled.

ARE'CA. Cabbage-tree. A genus of plants of the family of Palmæ. *Are'ca catechu*. The medicinal or betel-nut palm.

ARENA'CEOUS. From the Lat. *are'na*, sand. Sandy; of the nature of sand.

ARGEN'TEUM. Lat. Silvery; relating to silver.

ARGENTI'FEROUS. From the Lat. *argentum*, silver, and *fero*, I bear. Containing silver.

ARGILLA'CEOUS. From the Lat. *argillo*, clay or argil. Of the nature of clay.

AR'GOL. Crude tartar.

ARGONAU'TA. Lat. From the Gr. *argo*, name of a vessel, and *nautes*, a navigator. Name of a genus of cephalo'podous mollusks.

ARMADI'LLO. Spanish. Diminutive of *armado*, armed. Name of a mammal of the family of edentáta or edentates.

AROMA'TICUS. Lat. Aromatic; spicy.

AR'RACK. A kind of intoxicating beverage made in India, by distilling the fermented juice of the cocoa-nut, the palmyra-tree, and rice in the husk.

AR'ROW-ROOT. A species of starch obtained from the *maranta arundinacea*, a plant which grows in the West Indies.

AR'SENIC. A metal of a shining, steel-gray colour. Heated in contact with atmospheric air, it rapidly absorbs oxygen, and forms *arsenious acid*, which is the poison commonly called arsenic, or *rat's-bane*. Arsenic is found in its metallic state, in the form of oxide or arsenious acid, or white arsenic; and, combined with sulphur, forming orpiment and realgar.

ARTE'SIAN. From *Artois*, name of a province of France where especial attention has been given to a means of obtaining water, which consists in boring vertical perforations of small diameter in the exterior crust of the earth, frequently of great depth. These are termed Artesian wells.

ARTICULA'TA. Lat. From *articulus*, a joint or articulation. Articulated; having joints or articulations.

ASCLE'PIAS. A name of Esculapius. A genus of phanerógamous plants. *Ascle'pias gigante'a*. Mudar of the Hindoos. The milky juice is very caustic; the bark of the root as well as the juice are used in medicine by the Asiatics.

A'SPHALT, ASPHA'LTUM, } From the Gr. *a*, privative, and *sphalto*, I slip, or *asphaltos*, bitumen Used anciently as a cement. A black, brittle bitumen, found on the surface and banks of the Dead Sea, hence called the Asphaltic lake.

ASPHYX'IA. From the Gr. *a*, privative, and *sphuxis*, pulse. Without pulse. Seeming death from suspended respiration, from any cause, such as drowning, strangulation, or suffocation.

ASSAY'. The process by which the quality of gold and silver bullion, coin, plate, or trinkets, is ascertained with precision.

ASSI'MILATE. From the Lat. *ad* and *similare*, to render similar. Assimilation is the act by which living bodies appropriate and transform into their own substance, matters with which they may be placed in contact. In man, assimilation is a function of nutrition.

ASPLE'NIFO'LIA. Compound of *asplenium*, a genus of ferns, and *folia*, leaves. Having leaves resembling those of the asplénium.

A'STER. From the Gr. *aster*, a star. A name given to the plant by the Greeks, in allusion to the radiate form of the flowers. Name of a genus of plants which forms the type of the *asteroides* or asters — literally, *star-flowers*.

ASTRA'GALI. Lat. Plural of Astragalus.

ASTRA'GALUS. Lat. Name of a genus of phanerógamous plants of the family of leguminósæ. Also, a bone of the heel.

A'TOLL. A chaplet or ring of coral, enclosing a lagoon or portion of the ocean in its centre.

ATO'MIC WEIGHTS, or A'TOMS. The primal quantities in which the different objects of chemistry, simple or compound, combine with each other, referred to a common body, taken as unity. Oxygen is assumed by some chemists, and hydrogen by others, as the standard of comparison.

AUCHE'NIA. From the Gr. *auchenios*, belonging to the head or neck. Lat. Name of a genus of mammals, the Llama. Also, a genus of coleópterous insects.

AURI'CULA. Lat. Little ear. A genus of phanerógamous plants of the family of Primuláceæ.

AURI'FEROUS. From the Lat. *aurum*, gold, and *fero*, I bear. Gold-bearing; containing gold.

AU'ROCHS. An alteration of the German *Auerochs*, wild-bull. Their race is now almost extinct; a few individuals are found in the forests of Lithuania, &c.

AU'RUM MUSI'VUM. Mosaic gold. The bisulphuret of tin.

AUSTRA'LE. }
AUSTRA'LIS. } Lat. Belonging or relating to the south.

AZE'DARACH. From the Arab. *Azadaracht*, a name given by Avicenna to a plant.

A'ZOTE. }
AZO'TIC GAS. } From the Gr. *a*, privative, and *zo'on*, life. The name given by chemists to a gas, now also called nitrogen, which will support neither respiration nor combustion. It constitutes seventy-nine per cent. of the atmosphere, and enters into the composition of all animal matter, except fatty substances, and into a certain number of proximate vegetable principles.

A'ZOTIZED. Said of certain vegetable substances, which, as containing nitrogen, were supposed, at one time, to partake in some measure of the animal nature; most animal bodies being characterized by the presence of much nitrogen in their composition. The vegetable products, indigo, caffein, gluten, and many others, contain abundance of azote.

BACCI'FERUM. Lat. Compound of *bacca*, a berry, and *fero*, I bear. Berry-bearing. Specific name of a plant.

BALANCE OF TORSION, or TORSION BALANCE. A machine, invented by Coulomb, for measuring the intensities of electric or magnetic forces, by establishing an equilibrium between them and the force of torsion.

BALÆ'NA. Lat. A whale. Name of a genus of mammals, belonging to the order Cetácea. *Balæ'na mystece'tus.* The common whale. *Balæ'na gibbo'sa.* A kind of whale which has five or six protuberances on its back.

BALSAMS. Native compounds of ethereal or essential oils, with resin, and frequently benzoic acid. Most of them have the consistence of honey; but a few are solid, or become so by keeping. They flow either spontaneously, or by incisions made, from trees and shrubs in tropical climates. They possess peculiar powerful smells, aromatic hot tastes, but lose their odoriferous properties by long exposure to the air. They are insoluble in water; soluble, to a considerable degree, in ether, and completely in alcohol. When distilled with water, ethereal oil comes over, and resin remains in the retort.

We distinguish the *Balsams with benzoic acid*, or the Balsams proper, and the *Balsams without benzoic acid.*

Of the balsams proper, there are only five: — the balsam of Peru, of Tolu, Benzoin, *solid* Styrax, and *liquid* Styrax. Among the balsams without benzoic acid may be mentioned the Copaiva and Mecca balsams.

BARIL'LA. A crude soda, procured by the incineration of the *salsola soda*, a sea-shore plant, cultivated for this purpose in Spain, Sicily, Sardinia, &c. Good barilla usually contains twenty per cent. of real alkali, associated with muriates and sulphates, chiefly of soda, some lime, and alumina, with very little sulphur. The quantity of barilla imported into England, in 1851, was 45,740 cwts.

BA'RIUM. From the Gr. *barus*, heavy. A metal obtained from bary'ta, by Sir H. Davy.

BARK. The outer rind of plants. Many varieties of bark are known to commerce, but the term is commonly used to express either Peruvian bark, a most valuable pharmaceutical remedy, or Oak bark, which is very extensively used by tanners and dyers.

BARO'METER. From the Gr. *baros*, weight, and *metron*, a measure. An instrument for measuring the weight of atmospherical air.

BAROME'TRIC. }
BAROME'TRICAL. } Belonging or relating to the barometer.

BARY'TA, or BARY'TES. One of the simple earths. The earth and its soluble salts are all highly poisonous. The antidote is any soluble sulphate, as the sulphate of soda (Glauber's salt), or the sulphate of magnesia (Epsom salts).

BASA'LT. An Ethiopian word. A black or bluish-gray rock, harder than glass, very tenacious, and consequently difficult to break; it is homogeneous in appearance, although essentially composed of pyroxene and feldspar, with a large proportion of oxide of iron or titanium. Basalt is considered by all geologists to be a product of igneous formation.

BASA'LTIC. Belonging or relating to basalt.

BAS'SORIN. A constituent of a species of gum which comes from Bassora, as also of gum-tragacanth, and of some gum-resins. It is semi-transparent, difficult to pulverize, swells considerably in cold or boiling water, and forms a thick mucilage, without dissolving.

BATRAC'HIAN. From the Gr. *ba'trachos*, a frog. The name given by naturalists to those reptiles which resemble frogs in their organization. Batrachians form the fourth order in the class of Reptiles.

BDEL'LIUM. A gum-resin, produced by an unknown plant, which grows in Persia and Arabia.

BEER. The fermented infusion of malted barley, flavoured with hops, constitutes the best species of beer; but there are many beverages of inferior quality to which this name is given, such as spruce-beer, ginger-beer, molasses-beer, &c.; all of which consist of a saccharine liquor, partially advanced into the vinous fermentation, and flavoured with peculiar substances.

BE'LEMNITES. From the Gr. *belem'non*, a dart. A genus of dibranchiate cephalopods, the shells of which are chambered and perforated by a siphon, but internal. They are long, straight, and conical; and commonly called "thunder-stones."

BEN'JAMIN. See BENZOIN.

BENZ'OIN, or BEN'JAMIN. A species of resin, used chiefly in perfumery. It is extracted by incision, from the trunk and branches of the *styrax benzoin*, which grows in Java, Sumatra, Santa Fé, and in the kingdom of Siam. Benzoic acid is obtained from it by sublimation.

BER'YL. A mineral, allied to the emerald. It is transparent, of a pale green colour, and in Brazil it is sometimes sold under the name of emerald.

BE'TEL. The leaf of the betel or Siriboa pepper.

BE'TULA. Lat. Birch. Name of a genus of plants. *Be'tula nana.* Dwarf birch.

BE'ZOAR. The name of certain concretions, found in the stomachs of animals, to which many fanciful virtues were formerly ascribed.

BIFURCA'TION. From *bis*, twice, and *furca*, a fork. The division of a trunk into two branches; as, the *bifurcation of the trachea, of the aorta*, &c.

BIGNO'NIA. A genus of plants, named in honour of the Abbé Bignon, the Librarian of Louis XIV.

BIS'MUTH. From the Germ. *Wismuth.* A brittle, yellowish-white metal.

BITU'MEN. A combustible mineral, composed of carbon, hydrogen, and oxygen.

BI'XA ORLEA'NA. A plant which produces a colouring matter, called *annotto.*

BLEACH'ING. The process by which the textile filaments, cotton, flax, hemp, wool, silk, and the cloths made of them, as well as various vegetable and animal substances, are deprived of their natural colour, and rendered nearly or altogether white. The term *bleaching* comes from the French verb, *blanchir*, to whiten. The word *blanch*, which has the same origin, is applied to the whitening of living plants, by making them grow in the dark, as when the stems of celery are covered over with mould.

BLUE VI'TRIOL. Sulphate of copper.

BO'A. Name of a genus of non-venomous reptiles.

BOHE'A. Specific name of a tea-plant.

BOM'BAX. From *bombux*, one of the Greek names of cotton. A genus of plants of the family Malváceæ. *Bombax heptaphyllum.* A kind of cotton-tree. *Bombax ceiba.* The cotton-wood tree, much valued for making canoes.

BONE-BLACK, or *Animal charcoal*, as it is less correctly called, is the black carbonaceous substance into which bones are converted by calcination in close vessels.
BORA'CIC ACID. An acid obtained from borax, consisting of boron and oxygen.
BORA'SSUS. From the Gr. *borassos*, a date. A genus of the family of Palms. *Borassus flabellifórmis.* The fan-leaved palm.
BO'RATE. The salt resulting from a combination of boracic acid and a salifiable base, as the borate of soda.
BO'RAX. Tinkal. A natural compound of soda and boracic acid.
BO'RON. A simple or undecomposable substance, the basis of boracic acid and borax.
BOS. Lat. An ox. A genus of ruminating mammals, embracing several species. *Bos urus.* The Urus. *Bos caffer.* Cape buffalo. *Bos buba'los.* Common buffalo. *Bos America'nus.* The Bison. *Bos moscha'tus.* The Musk Ox. *Bos gru'niens.* The Yak.
BOTA'NIC. Belonging or relating to botany.
BO'TANY. From the Gr. *botane.* The branch of natural history which embraces the knowledge and study of plants.
BOUL'DERS, or BOWL'DERS. Rounded masses of stone lying upon the surface, or loosely imbedded in the soil.
BOULDER FORMATION, or Erratic block formation. A geological term applied to a part of the diluvial drift.
BRAC'HIAL. From *brachium*, the arm. Belonging to the arm.
BRAC'TEÆ. Lat. Bracts. Floral leaves, different in colour from other leaves.
BRA'NCHIA. Lat. A gill.
BRA'NCHIÆ. Lat. From the Gr. *bragchos*, the throat. The gills of fishes. They are the breathing organs of fishes; they differ from lungs both in their form and structure.
BRA'NDY. The name given to ardent spirits distilled from wine.
BRASS. An alloy of copper and zinc.
BRAS'SICA. Lat. Cabbage.
BREC'CIA. Italian. A rock, composed of an agglutination of angular fragments. When the fragments are rolled pebbles, it constitutes a conglomerate rock, called *pudding-stone.*
BRIM'STONE. Roll sulphur.
BRO'MINE. One of the chemical elements. It derives its name from its nauseous smell.
BRON'CHIA. From the Gr. *brogchos*, the throat. The Romans used the term *bronchus* for the whole of the trachea; whilst they called its ramifications *bronchia. Bronchia, bronchiæ*, and *bronchi*, now mean the two tubes, with their ramifications, which arise from the bifurcation of the trachea.
BRON'CHIAL. Relating to the bronchia.
BRONZE. An alloy of copper and tin, to which sometimes a little zinc and lead are added. It is much harder than copper, and was employed by the ancients to make swords, hatchets, &c., before the method of working iron was generally understood.
BU'BO. Lat. An owl. A specific as well as generic name. *Bubo maximus.* A kind of owl.
BU'FO. Lat. A toad. *Bufo Agua.* A Brazilian toad.
BUR'SA. Lat. A sack, a purse, or pouch.

CAC'TI. Lat. Plural of cactus.
CAC'TUS. From the Gr. *kaktos*, spiny plant. Name of a genus of the family of Cactáceæ. *Cactus coccine'llifer.* The cochineal cactus. *Cactus opu'ntia.* Indian fig.
CACH'ALOT, or CACH'ELOT. Fr. Name of the spermaceti whale. Used to designate a variety of the order of Cetáceans, which has teeth in both jaws.
CAD'MIUM. A white metal, much like tin. Its ores are associated with those of zinc. Discovered in 1818.
CADU'COUS. From the Lat. *cado*, I fall. In Botany, when a part is temporary, and soon disappears or falls off, it is said to be caducous.
CA'FFEINE. Fr. In chemistry, the name of the proximate principle of coffee.
CA'JEPUT, CAJEPU'TA. A Malay name for a greenish, volatile oil, used as a remedy in rheumatism, &c.
CA'LAMINE. A native carbonate of zinc. *Electric calamine* is the native silicate of zinc.
CALCINA'TION. The act of submitting to a strong heat any infusible mineral substance, which we are desirous of depriving either of its water, or of any other volatilizable substance that enters into its composition; or which we wish to combine with oxygen. *Alum* is calcined to get rid of its water of crystallization; *chalk*, to reduce it to the state of pure lime, by driving off the carbonic acid; and *certain metals*, as mercury, to oxidize them.
CAL'CIUM. From the Lat. *calx, calcis*, lime. A metal discovered by Sir H. Davy, in 1807, which, united with oxygen, forms oxide of calcium or lime.

CAL'CULUS. The stony-looking morbid concretion, occasionally found in the bladder of urine, gall-bladder, cystic duct, kidneys, and other parts of living animals.
CA'LOMEL. The mild or sub-chloride of mercury.
CALO'RIC. From the Lat. *caleo*, I am warm. The term used by chemists to designate *the matter of heat.*
CALORI'FIC. Belonging or relating to caloric.
CAM'BRIAN SYSTEM. From Cambria, in Wales. A name given by geologists to the lowest sedimentary rocks, characterized by fossil remains of animals lowest in the scale of organization, such as corallines, &c. It is also called the Schistose system, on account of its slaty nature.
CAMPA'NULA. From the Lat. *campana*, a bell, from the shape of its corolla. A genus of phanerógamous plants of the family of Campanuláceæ, of which it is the type. 182 species are described.
CAMPHORO'SMA. From the Lat. *cam'phora*, camphor, and the Gr. *osme*, odour. A genus of plants of the family of Chenopodáceæ.
CAM'PHORA. Lat. Camphor. Belonging or relating to camphor.
CANARIE'NSIS. Lat. Belonging or relating to the Canary Islands.
CANDELA'BRUM. Lat. A candlestick.
CA'NINE. From the Lat. *canis*, a dog. Teeth which resemble those of a dog are so called; the canine teeth of the upper jaw in man are commonly called the eye-teeth.
CAOU'TCHOUC. Gum-elastic; India-rubber, a substance obtained from the *Jatro'pha ela'stica*, the *Fi'cus in'dica*, and the *Urce'ola ela'stica.*
CAPE'NSIS. Lat. Belonging or relating to the Cape of Good Hope.
CA'PILLARY. From *capillus*, a hair. Hair-like; small.
CA'RAT. A weight used by goldsmiths and jewellers.
CAR'BON. From the Lat. *carbo*, charcoal. A chemical element, or undecomposed body. The diamond is pure carbon. It is the basis of anthracite, and of all the varieties of mineral coal, and is one of the principal constituents of all organic bodies.
CAR'BONATE. Any compound of carbonic acid and a salifiable base, as *carbonate of lime, carbonate of soda.* The carbonates principally used in the arts and manufactures are, those of *ammonia, copper, iron, lead, lime, magnesia, potash,* and *soda.* Native carbonate of copper is the beautiful green mineral called Malachite.
CARBO'NIC ACID. A compound of carbon and oxygen.
CARBONI'FEROUS. From the Lat. *carbo*, coal, and *fero*, I bear. Coal-bearing; containing carbon. In geology, the term is applied to those strata which contain coal, and to the period when the coal measures were formed.
CAR'BUNCLE. A gem, highly prized by the ancients; most probably a variety of the noble garnet of modern mineralogists.
CARBURET'TED HY'DROGEN. A compound of carbon and hydrogen. Such compounds are called, more briefly, carbo-hydrogens, and are numerous. The more important are, oil-gas, coal-gas, olefiant-gas, marsh-gas, oil of lemon, oil of turpentine, petroleum, naphtha, naphthaline, oil of wine, caoutchoucine, and caoutchouc.
CAR'DIAC. Relating to the heart or the upper orifice of the stomach.
CARNI'VORA. From the Lat. *caro, carnis*, flesh, and *voro*, I eat. Name of a family of Mammals.
CARTILA'GINOUS FISHES. A term used to designate that division of the class of fishes which includes only those having cartilaginous instead of bony skeletons.
CARYOPHY'LLUS. Lat. A garden-pink. A genus of plants of the family of Caryophy'lleæ. *Caryophy'llus aroma'ticus.* The olive-tree.
CA'SPIA. Lat. Belonging or relating to the Caspian Sea.
CASSA'VA. Starch prepared from the root of the manioc (*Jatropha Manihot*). The tree belongs to the natural family of the *Euphorbia'ceæ.*
CAS'SIA. From the Gr. *kassia*, cinnamon. A genus of plants of the family of Papilionáceæ. The genus contains more than 300 species.
CATA'LPA. A genus of plants of the family of Bignoniáceæ.
CAT'ECHU. An astringent extract, used in medicine. It is made from the wood of the *Minosa Catechu*, which grows in Bombay, Bengal, and other parts of India.
CAT'S-EYE. A beautiful silicious mineral, penetrated by fibres of asbestos, which, when polished, reflects an effulgent, pearly light, much resembling the mutable reflections from the eye of a cat.
CAT'GUT. The name, absurdly enough, given to the cords made of the twisted intestines of sheep. It is used for strings of violins and other instruments.
CAUS'TIC. Any chemical substance corrosive of the skin and flesh; as, potash, called common caustic, and nitrate of silver, called lunar caustic, by surgeons.
CA'VIAR. / CAVIARE' (ka-veer). } The salted roe of certain species of fish, especially the sturgeon. This product forms a considerable article of trade, being exported

annually from the town of Astracan alone, upon the shores of the Caspian Sea, to the amount of several hundred tons. The Italians first introduced it into Eastern Europe, from Constantinople, under the name of *Caviale.*

CAWK. The English miner's name for sulphate of baryta, or heavy spar.

CEI'BA. Synonym of *Bombax*, cotton. Specific name of a kind of cotton.

CEL'ESTINE. Native sulphate of strontia, found abundantly near Bristol in England, in the red marl formation. It is used to prepare the nitrate of strontia, which is employed, in theatrical fireworks, for the production of the red light.

CEMENTA'TION. A chemical process, which consists in imbedding a solid body in a pulverulent matter, and exposing both to ignition in an earthen or metallic case. In this way, iron is cemented with charcoal, to form steel, and bottle-glass with gypsum-powder, or sand, to form Reaumur's porcelain.

CEM'ENTS. Substances capable of taking the liquid form, and of being in that state applied between the surfaces of two bodies, so as to unite them by solidifying. They may be divided into two classes: those which are applied through the agency of a liquid menstruum, such as water, alcohol, oil; and those which are applied by fusion with heat.

CEN'TIGRADE. From *centum*, a hundred, and *gradus*, a degree. Consisting of a hundred degrees, as the *centigrade thermometer*, which has the distance between the freezing and boiling points of water divided into 100 degrees.

CERATI'TES. From the Gr. *keratites*, horned. A generic name of certain insects.

CERATO'DES. From the Gr. *keratodes*, formed of horns. A genus of mollusks.

CER'EAL. From the Lat. *ceres*, corn. Applied to grasses which produce the bread-corns; as wheat, rye, barley, oats, rice, &c.

CEREA'LIA. Lat. Name of a tribe of grasses.

CE'RIUM. Named after the planet Ceres. A white, brittle metal, discovered in 1803, by Hisinger and Berzelius.

CE'RUSE. A name of the carbonate of lead, which is now commonly called *White Lead.*

CER'VUS. Lat. A stag. A genus of mammals.

CETA'CEA. From the Gr. *ketos*, a whale. A genus of pisciform mammals that have fins in place of feet, and inhabit the sea. Name of an order of aquatic mammals.

CHALK. Earthy carbonate of lime. *French* chalk is *steatite*, or soap-stone; a soft magnesian mineral. *Red* chalk is a clay coloured with the peroxide of iron, of which it contains about 17 per cent.

CHALYB'EATE. From *chalybs*, steel. The name given in medicine to the preparations of iron. *Chalybeate waters* are waters which contain iron in solution.

CHAMBERED SHELLS. A term used to designate those shells of mollusks which are divided internally into cells or chambers by partitions.

CHAR'COAL. The fixed residuum of vegetables exposed to ignition out of contact of air.

CHEIRO'PTERA. From the Gr. *cheir*, hand, and *pteron*, a wing; signifying the hand has become a wing. Name of a family of mammals, including the bats.

CHELO'NIAN. From the Gr. *chelone*, a tortoise. Applied to reptiles resembling tortoises.

CHI'LI SALTPE'TRE. Nitrate of soda.

CHI'NA INK. A pigment made, according to a description in a Japanese book, from the condensed smoke or soot of burned camphor; and hence, when of the best quality, it has this odour. Most of the China ink is made from oil-lampblack occasionally disguised as to smell, with musk, or with a little camphor-black.

CHLO'RATE. Any compound of chloric acid, with a salifiable base. The only important chlorate is that of potash, which has become the object of a pretty extensive manufacture, in consequence of its application to make matches for procuring instantaneous light, and a detonating powder for fire-arms and blasting.

CHLO'RINE. One of the most energetic of the chemical elements, discovered in 1774, by Scheele. It is used extensively as a bleaching agent; and, as such, requires to be tempered by the quiescent affinity of some alkaline base, as potash or lime. Its leading affinity is for hydrogen. Malaria, or morbific and putrescent miasmata, consist chiefly of hydrogenous matter as their basis, and are best counteracted by chlorine, where it can conveniently be applied. The chlorides of soda and lime are the forms in which it is generally used.

CHLORI'TIC. From the Gr. *chloros*, green. Belonging or relating to chlorite, an earthy mineral found in the cavities of slate-rocks.

CHOC'OLATE. An alimentary preparation of very ancient use in Mexico, from which country it was introduced into Europe by the Spaniards, in the year 1520, and by them long kept a secret from the rest of the world. Linnæus was so fond of it, that he gave the specific name, *theobro'ma*, "food of the gods," to the cacao-tree which produced it.

CHROME, CHRO'MIUM. From the Gr. *chroma*, colour. A whitish, brittle metal, discovered by Vauquelin in 1797. In union with oxygen it forms chromic acid.

Cin'nabar. The native red sulphuret of mercury, and is the most prolific ore of that metal. *Vermilion* is an artificial cinnabar.

Ci'rri. Plural of *cirrus.*

Ci'rro-cu'mulus. A sondercloud; a kind of cloud. The cirro-cumulus is intermediate between the cirrus and cumulus, and is composed of small well-defined masses, closely arranged.

Ci'rro-stra'tus. A wanecloud. The cirro-stratus, intermediate between the cirrus and stratus, consists of horizontal masses separated into groups, with which the sky is sometime so mottled as to suggest the idea of resemblance to the back of a mackerel.

Ci'rrus. Lat. A tendril. A kind of cloud. Applied to certain appendages of animals; as the beard from the end and sides of the mouth of certain fishes. The cirrus cloud consists of fibres or curling streaks which diverge in all directions. It occupies the highest region, and is frequently the first cloud which is seen after a continuance of clear weather.

Clay. A mixture of the two simple earths, alumina and silica, generally tinged with iron. Lime, magnesia, with some other colouring metallic oxides, are occasionally present in small quantities in certain natural clays. Fine porcelain-clay is called *ka'olin,* and consists of nearly equal parts of alumina and silica, being derived from the disintegration of the mineral felspar.

Clay-slate. A rock which resembles clay or shale, but is generally distinguished by its structure; the particles having been re-arranged, and exhibiting what is called slaty cleavage. It is one of the metamorphic rocks.

Cleav'age. The mechanical division of the laminæ of rocks and minerals, to show the constant direction in which they may be separated.

Coal measures. The geological formation in which coal is found.

Co'balt. From the Germ. *kobold,* a devil. A brittle metal of a reddish-gray colour. Its ores are always associated with arsenic.

Co'bra capel'lo. Portu. *cobra,* snake, and *capello,* a caul or hood. Hood-snake, a venomous serpent.

Coccine'lla. From the Gr. *kokkinos,* scarlet. A genus of coleopt'erous insects; commonly called Lady-birds.

Coccine'llifer. From *coccinella* (the diminutive of the Lat. *coccinus,* crimson), a genus of coleopterous insects, and *fero,* I bear. A specific name.

Coc'cus. From the Gr. *kokkos,* a seed which dyes scarlet. A genus of insects of the order Hermip'tera. *Coccus la'cca.* A species of cochineal insect. *Coccus i'licus.* Green oak cochineal.

Coch'ineal was taken in Europe at first for a seed, but was proved by the observations of Leeuwenhoeck to be an insect (*coc'cus cac'ti*), being the female of that species of shield-louse, or *coccus,* discovered in Mexico as long ago as 1518. It is brought to us from Mexico, where the animal lives upon the *cac'tus opun'tia* or *nopal.*

Co'cos. Gr. A genus of palms; the cocoanut. *Cocos olera'cia.* The oil cocoanut.

Cof'fee. The seed of a tree of the natural family *rubia'ceæ.* There are several species of the genus, but the only one cultivated is the *Coffæ'a Arab'ica,* a native of Upper Ethiopia and Arabia Felix.

Coke. Carbonized pitcoal.

Cohe'sion. The force which holds together the *similar* particles of bodies, uniting them into a *homogeneous* whole, which may be broken up by *mechanical* means. See Adhesion, and Affinity.

Colu'briform. From the Lat. *co'luber,* a serpent, an adder, and *forma,* shape. Addershape.

Colum'ba. Lat. A pigeon. A genus of birds. *Colum'ba migrato'ria.* Wild pigeon.

Colum'bium. A metal discovered in a mineral found in Massachusetts by Mr. Hachett, in 1801.

Colu'mnar. In the form of columns.

Combina'tion. A chemical term, which denotes the intimate union of dissimilar particles of matter into a homogeneous-looking compound, possessed of properties generally different from those of the separate constituents.

Combus'tible. Any substance which, exposed in the air to a certain temperature, consumes spontaneously, with the emission of light and heat. All such combustibles as are cheap enough for common use, go under the name of *fuel.* Every combustible requires a peculiar pitch of temperature to be kindled, called its *accen'dible* or *kindling* point. Thus, phosphorus, sulphur, hydrogen, carburetted hydrogen, and carbon, take fire at successively higher heats.

Combus'tion. The combination of two bodies accompanied by the extrication of heat and light. When a body rapidly combines with oxygen, for example, with a disengagement of heat and lignt, it is said to undergo combustion.

COMPARATIVE ANATOMY. The comparative study of the various parts of the bodies of different animals.
COMPO'SITÆ. A family of Monopetalous plants.
CONCH'IFER. From *concha*, a shell, and *fero*, to bear. An animal that produces or is covered with a shell, as the tortoise. It is applied *particularly* to bivalve mollusks.
CONCHO'LOGY. The science of shells and the animals which inhabit them.
CONDENSA'TION. The act of causing the parts that compose a body to approach or unite more closely. *Dew* and *clouds* are formed by the condensation of vapour. Condensation is opposed to *rarefaction* and *expansion*.
CONDUC'TOR. Those substances which possess the property of transferring caloric or heat, and electricity, are termed conductors of heat or caloric, and conductors of electricity.
CON'DYLE. A protuberance on the end of a bone.
CONFER'VÆ. Tribe of plants of the family of Zoospérmeæ. It includes many sea-weeds.
CONGELA'TION. The process of passing from a liquid to a solid state; the act of *freezing* liquids.
CON'GENER. From the Lat. *con*, with, and *genus*, race. Species belonging to the same genus, are termed congeners, or congeneric.
CONGLO'MERATE. From the Lat. *conglomero*, I heap together. Any rock composed of pebbles cemented together by another mineral substance, either calcareous, silicious, or argillaceous.
CO'NIFER. From the Lat. *conus*, a cone, and *fero*, I bear. A tree or plant which bears cones, such as pines, fir-trees, &c.
CONI'FERÆ. A family of plants which includes the conifers.
CONIROS'TERS. A tribe of insessorial birds, including those which have a strong bill of a conical form, as the crows and finches.
COPAL'. A resin which exudes spontaneously from two trees, the *Rhus Copalli'num* and the *Elæocar'pus Copa'lifer*, the first of which grows in America, and the second in the East Indies. A third species of copal-tree grows on the coasts of Guinea, especially on the banks of some rivers, among whose sands the resin is found.
COP'PER. One of the metals most anciently known. It was named from the island of Cyprus, where it was extensively mined and smelted by the Greeks. Its alchemical name was *Venus*.
COP'PERAS. Protosulphate of iron. Called also *Green Vitriol*.
COP'ROLITE. The petrified dung of carnivorous animals.
CO'RAL. From the Gr. *koreo*, I ornament, and *als*, the sea. The hard calcareous support formed by certain polypi. The finest coral is found in the Mediterranean. It is fished for upon the coasts of Provence, and constitutes a considerable branch of trade at Marseilles. Coral-fishing is nearly as dangerous as pearl-fishing, on account of the number of sharks which frequent the seas where it is carried on. Coral is mostly of a fine red colour, but occasionally it is flesh-coloured, yellow, or white. The red is preferred for making necklaces, crosses, and other female ornaments. It is worked up like precious stones.
CO'RALLINE. Belonging or relating to coral.
CORALLI'NEÆ. The corallines, a tribe of calciferous polypi.
CORIA'CEOUS. From the Lat. *corium*, the hide of a beast. Leathery.
CORK. The bark of the *quercus Suber*, a species of oak-tree, which grows abundantly in the southern provinces of France, Italy, and Spain.
CORO'NA. Lat. A crown. A genus of plants.
CORO'NÆ. Plural of corona.
CORRO'SIVE SUB'LIMATE. Bichloride of mercury.
CORU'NDUM. A crystallized or massive mineral of extreme hardness, almost opaque, and of a reddish colour. It is allied to the sapphire, and is composed of nearly pure alúmina.
COTYLE'DON. From the Gr. *kotule'don*, a seed-lobe.
COTYLE'DONOUS. Belonging or relating to a cotyle'don or seed-lobe.
CRA'TER. Lat. A great cup or bowl. The mouth of a volcano.
CRATERI'FEROUS. Containing craters.
CRA'TERIFORM. In form of a crater.
CRETA'CEOUS. From the Lat. *creta*, chalk. Of the nature of chalk, relating to chalk.
CRINOI'DEÆ. From the Gr. *krinon*, a lily, and *eidos*, resemblance. A family of radiate animals.
CROP OUT. When a rock, in place, emerges on the surface of the earth, it is said to crop out.
CRO'TON. A genus of plants of the family of Euphorbiáceæ.
CRUCI'FERÆ. From the Lat. *crux*, *crucis*, a cross, and *fero*, I bear. A family of plants which have flowers in form of a Maltese cross

CRU'CIFORM. In shape of a cross.
CRUSTA'CEA. From the Lat. *crusta*, a crust. A class of articulated animals.
CRUSTA'CEAN. An animal of the class of crustacea; a crab.
CRYPTOGA'MIA. From the Gr. *kruptos*, concealed, and *gamos*, marriage. A class of plants, which are propagated without apparent seeds.
CRYPTO'GAMOUS. Belonging or relating to the cryptogámia.
CRYST'AL. From the Gr. *krustallos*, ice. This term was originally applied to those beautiful transparent varieties of silica or quartz known under the name of *rock-crystal.* When substances pass from the fluid to the solid state, they frequently assume those regular forms which are generally termed crystals. A crystal is any inorganic solid of homogeneous structure, bounded by natural planes and right lines, symmetrically arranged. Many vegetable and animal products, however, are susceptible of crystallization.
CRYS'TALLINE. Relating to, or resembling crystals.
CRYSTALLIZA'TION. The process by which crystals are formed.
CU'CULUS. Lat. A cuckoo. A genus of passerine birds.
CU'LEX. Lat. A gnat. A genus of insects of the family of Dip'tera, and type of the tribe Culícides: *culex pi'piens*, the common gnat.
CU'MULI. Plural of cumulus.
CU'MULO-STRA'TUS. Twain cloud: it partakes of the appearance of the cumulus and stratus.
CU'MULUS. A form of cloud. A convex aggregate of watery particles, increasing upwards from a horizontal base, and assuming more or less of a conical figure.
CUPELLA'TION is a mode of analyzing gold, silver, palladium, and platinum, by adding to small portions of alloys, containing these metals, a bit of lead; fusing the mixture in a little *cup* of bone-earth, called a *cupel;* and then, by the joint action of heat and air, oxidizing the copper, tin, &c., present in the precious metals. The oxides thus produced are dissolved, and carried down into the porous cupel in a liquid state, by the vitrified oxide of lead.
CUR'VIDENS. Lat. *Curvus*, bent, and *dens*, tooth. Having a bent tooth.
CUSPA'RIA. A genus of plants, named after the tree which yields the Angustura bark.
CYANHY'DRIC ACID. Another name for hydrocyanic or Prussic acid.
CYCADA'CEOUS. Belonging or relating to the cycádeæ.
CYCA'DEÆ. A family of plants allied to the cónifers.
CY'CAS. A genus of plants, the type of the family cycádeæ. *Cy'cas revolu'ta.* Narrow-leaved cycas.
CY'CLAS. From the Gr. *kuklos*, a circle. A genus of gasteropods.
CYG'NUS. Lat. A swan. A genus of birds. *Cyg'nus mu'sicus.* The whistling swan.
CYNOCE'PHALUS. From the Gr. *kuon*, a dog, and *kephale*, head. A genus of mammals. Dog-headed monkey or baboon.
CYPERA'CEÆ. Name of a family of herbaceous plants.
CYPRI'NIDÆ. From the Gr. *kuprinos*, a carp. Name of a family of fishes.
CY'TOBLAST. A cell-germ. A primary *granule*, from which all vegetable and animal bodies are presumed to be formed.

DAC'TYLIS. From the Gr. *daktulos*, a finger. A genus of the family of Gramíneæ. *Dac'tylis cæspi'tosa.* Tussock grass.
DAGUERRE'OTYPE. The art of procuring pictures by the action of light, the invention of which is due to M. Daguerre and M. Niepce, two Frenchmen.
DAH'LIA. After Dahl, a Swedish botanist. Genus of plants of the family of Compósitæ.
DALBE'RGIA. After Dalberg, a Swedish botanist. A genus of plants of the family of Papilionáceæ, and of the tribe of Dalbergiæ.
DARWI'NII. The name of Darwin latinized. Belonging or relating to Darwin.
DASYU'RIDÆ. From the Gr. *dasus*, thick, hairy, and *oura*, tail. A family of mammals.
DE'BRIS. Fr. Wreck, ruins, remains. In geology, the term is applied to large fragments, to distinguish them from *detritus*, or those which are pulverized.
DECANTA'TION. The act of pouring off the clear supernatant liquid from any sediment or deposit. It is much employed in the chemical arts, and is most conveniently effected by a syphon.
DEC'APOD. An animal with ten feet or legs.
DECAR'BONIZE. To deprive of carbon.
DECI'DUOUS. From the Lat. *decido*, I fall off. Applied to plants whose leaves fall off in autumn, to distinguish them from evergreens.
DECLINA'TION of any celestial body, is the angular distance of the body, north or south, from the equator.

DECOC'TION means either the act of boiling a liquid along with some organic substance, or the liquid compound resulting from that act.

DECOMPOSI'TION. The separation of the constituent principles of any compound body. The *decomposition of forces* is the same as the *resolution of forces.*

DECREPITA'TION. The crackling noise, attended with the flying asunder of their parts, made by several salts and minerals, when heated.

DEFLAGRA'TION. The sudden blazing up of a combustible; as of charcoal and sulphur when thrown into melted nitre.

DEINOTHE'RIUM. From the Gr. *deinos*, terrible, and *ther*, wild beast. A genus of fossil pachyderms.

DELIQUES'CENT. A term applied to a solid which attracts so much moisture from the air as to become spontaneously soft or liquid; such as potash and chloride of calcium.

DELPHI'NUS. Lat. Dolphin. A genus of aquatic mammals.

DEL'TA. The Gr. letter Δ. The triangular deposits, shoals or islands, at the mouths of rivers are called deltas.

DEL'TOID. From the Gr. letter Δ, and *eidos*, resemblance. Resembling the letter delta.

DEN'SITY. The quantity of matter contained under a given bulk.

DENUDA'TION. From the Lat. *denudo*, a strip. A removal of a part of the land, so as to lay bare the inferior strata.

DEODA'R. A kind of pine-tree.

DEPHLOGIS'TICATED. Deprived of phlogiston, which was formerly supposed to be the common combustible principle. It is nearly synonymous with *oxygenated.* The word, however, should be dropped, since the idea originally attached to it proceeded from a false logic.

DEPOSI'TION. From the Lat. *depono*, I let fall. In geology, the falling to the bottom, of matters suspended or dissolved in water.

DE'TINENS. Lat. Detaining; that which has the power to detain.

DETRI'TUS. A geological term, applied to deposits composed of various substances which have been comminuted by attrition. The larger fragments are usually termed *débris;* those which are pulverized, as it were, constitute *detritus.* Sand is the detritus of silicious rocks.

DEUTOX'IDE. Literally, means the *second* oxide; but it is usually employed to denote a compound containing two atoms of oxygen to one of a metal or other element. Thus we say deutoxide of copper, and deutoxide of mercury. Berzelius has abbreviated this expression by adopting the principles of the French nomenclature of 1787; according to which the higher stage of oxidation is characterized by the termination *-ic*, and the lower by *-ous;* and he writes, accordingly, *cupric* and *mercuric*, to designate the deutoxides of these two metals; *cuprous* and *mercurous*, to designate their protoxides.

DEVO'NIAN SYSTEM. So called because it is largely developed in Devonshire, England. It is synonymous with the old red sandstone formation. It is composed at first of puddingstone, and then passes into sandstone, with which it alternates at different places.

DEW'-POINT. The temperature at which dew begins to be formed.

DEX'TRINE. A gummy substance, obtained from starch by the action of diastase or acids. It derives its name from the circumstance that it turns, more than any other body, the plane of polarization to the right hand.

DIAMAGNE'TIC. If a bar of iron be suspended between the poles of an electro-magnet, it will be attracted by both poles on the line of force. But if a bar of bismuth be suspended in the same manner, it will be repelled by both poles, and rest at right-angles to the line of force. Substances which are attracted by both poles of an electro-magnet are said to be *magnetic*, and those which are repelled by both poles are termed *diamagnetic.*

DIADEL'PHIA. In *botany*, a class of plants whose stamens are united in two bodies by their filaments.

DIAG'ONAL. A right-line drawn from angle to angle of a quadrilateral or multilateral figure, and dividing it into two parts.

DI'APHRAGM. A partition. In *anatomy*, the midriff, a muscle which separates the thoracic from the abdominal cavity.

DI'ASTASE. A peculiar substance, generated during the germination of grain for the brewery, tending to the transformation of starch into sugar.

DIATHER'MANOUS. Freely permeable to heat.

DICHO'TOMA, DICHO'TOMUM, DICHO'TOMUS, } From the Gr. *dichotomos*, equally divided. In zoology, this term is applied to a species of the genus Iris, the body of which is bifurcate. In botany, it is applied to the stem, branches, peduncles, leaves, hairs, styles &c., when they are bifurcated in form.

DICOTYLE'DON. From the Gr. *dis*, two, and *kotuledon*, seed-lobe. A double seed-lobe

DICOTYLE'DONOUS. Relating to dicotyle'don; having a double seed-lobe.

DIDEL'PHIDÆ. A tribe of marsupial mammals.

DIDEL'PHIS. A genus of marsupial mammals.

DIDEL'PHOUS. From the Gr. *dis*, double, and *delphus*, womb. Applied to opossums and other marsupial mammals.

DIDY'MIUM. A metal discovered recently by Mosander. It derives its name from its being associated as a *twin* brother of lan'thanum, in the ores of cerium.

DIDYNA'MIA. In *botany*, the name of a class of plants of four stamens, disposed in two pairs, one being shorter than the other.

DIGAS'TRIC. Having a double belly. An epithet applied to one of the muscles of the neck.

DIGITA'TA. Lat. Di'gitate; spread out like the fingers.

DILLENIA'CEÆ. Proper name. A family of plants.

DILU'VIAL. From *diluvium*, a deluge. Pertaining to a flood or deluge, more especially to the deluge in Noah's days.

DILU'VIUM. Literally, a deluge. In *geology*, a deposit of superficial loam, sand, gravel, pebbles, &c., caused by the deluge or ancient currents of water.

DINO'RNIS. From the Gr. *deinos*, great, terrible, and *ornis*, a bird. A genus of fossil or extinct birds.

DINOTHE'RIUM. See DEINOTHERIUM.

DIONÆ'A. One of the names of Venus. A genus of plants of the family of Droserácea. *Dionæ'a musci'pula.* Venus' Fly-trap.

DIO'SMA. From the Gr. *dios*, divine, and *osme*, smell. A genus of plants of the family of Dios'meæ.

DIO'TIS. From the Gr. *diôtos*, having two ears: referring to the flower. A genus of plants of the family of helianthácææ.

DIP. In geology, direction of the inclination of strata. "To take a dip," is to measure the degree that a stratum inclines or dips from a horizontal line. *Generally*, inclination downwards; as *the dip of the needle*, in magnetism.

DISINFEC'TANT. An agent for removing the causes of infection, as chlorine.

DISIN'TEGRATE. From the Lat. *de*, privative, *integer*, a whole. To separate or break up an aggregate into parts.

DISLOCA'TION. Displacement. In geology, where strata or veins have been displaced from the position where first deposited or formed, they are said to be dislocated.

DISTILLA'TION. From *dis*, asunder, and *stilla*, a drop. The vaporization and subsequent condensation of a liquid. The term, *dry distillation*, is applied to the distillation of substances without the addition of water. *Destructive distillation* is the distillation of substances at very high temperatures, so that the ultimate elements are separated or evolved in new combinations.

The distillation of ardent spirits from wine, beer, &c., was unknown to the ancient Greeks and Romans. It seems to have been invented by the barbarians of the North of Europe, as a solace to their cold and humid clime; and was first made known to the Southern nations in the writings of Arnoldus de Villa Nova, and his pupil, Raymond Lully of Majorca, who declares this admirable essence of wine to be an emanation of divinity, an element newly revealed to man, but hid from antiquity, because the human race were then too young to need this beverage, destined to revive the energies of modern decrepitude. However much he erred as to the value of this remarkable essence, he truly predicted its vast influence upon humanity, since to both civilized and savage nations it has realized greater ills than were threatened in the fabled box of Pandora.

DOC'IMACY. The art by which the nature and proportions of an ore are determined.

DO'LOMITE. Magnesian marble, or granular magnesian carbonate of lime. Named after Dolomieu.

DONA'RIUM. A metal recently discovered by Bergemann. It is named after the Scandinavian god, *Donar*.

DRACÆ'NA. Lat. A genus of Saurians.

DRACÆ'NÆ. Plural of Dracæna.

DRUSE.
DRU'SIC CA'VITY. } A cavity in a rock, having its interior surface studded with crystals.

DRYOBA'LANOPS. From the Gr. *drus*, *os*, an oak, *balanos*, an acorn, and *ops*, aspect. A genus of plants of the family of Dip'terocárpeæ. *Dryoba'lanops ca'mphora.* The camphor-tree of Sumatra.

DUCTIL'ITY. The property of being drawn out in length without breaking. It is possessed in a pre-eminent degree by gold and silver.

DYNA'MIC. From the Gr. *dunamis*, power, force. Belonging or relating to dynamics.

DYNA'MICS. The doctrine of forces as exhibited in moving bodies which are at liberty to obey the impulses communicated to them. The motions of celestial bodies in their orbits, or of a stone falling freely through the air, are embraced in the study of dynamics.

DYNAMOM'ETER. An instrument for measuring force, especially the relative strength of men and other animals.

EARTHS. Formerly, chemists, believing them to be simple bodies, included the following substances under the name of earths: Baryta, Strontia, Lime, Magnesia, Alumina or Clay, Silica, Glucina, Zirconia, and Yttria. Research has shown that all have metallic or metalloid bases.

ECHID'NA. Greek name of a monster, supposed to have the body of a beautiful woman and the tail of a serpent. A genus of mammals of the family of Monotre'mata.

ECLIP'TIC. In astronomy, the great circle of the heavens which the sun appears to describe in his annual revolution.

EDENTA'TA. From the Lat. *e*, without, and *dens*, tooth: without teeth. An order of mammals which are destitute of teeth.

EDUL'CORATE. A word introduced by the alchemists to signify the sweetening, or rather rendering insipid, of acrimonious pulverulent substances, by copious ablutions with water. It means, in modern language, the washing away of all particles soluble in water, by agitation or trituration with this fluid, and subsequent decantation or filtration.

EDU'LIS. Lat. Eatable; that which may be eaten.

EFFERVES'CENCE. When gaseous matter is suddenly extricated, with a hissing sound, during a chemical mixture, or by the application of a chemical solvent to a solid, the phenomenon, from its resemblance to that of simmering or boiling water, is called effervescence.

EFFLORES'CENCE. The pulverulent covering formed on the surface of saline substances from which the atmosphere has removed the water of crystallization. When saline substances give up their water of crystallization to the air, they are said to effloresce. Saltpetre appears as an efflorescence upon the ground and walls in many situations.

ELA'IS. } From the Gr. *elaia*, the olive. A genus of plants of the family of Palms.
ELÆ'IS. } The *Ela'is Guineen'sis* yields the Palm-oil.

ELEC'TIVE AFFIN'ITY. The order of preference, so to speak, in which the several chemical substances *choose* to combine.

ELECTRI'CITY. From the Gr. *elektron*, amber, the substance in which it was first observed. The property acquired by glass and resin from friction to attract light substances. Electricity exists in all bodies, and becomes manifest, at least partially, whenever the natural state of equilibrium of their molecules is disturbed by any cause.

ELEC'TRICUS. Lat. Electric. Belonging to, or relating to electricity.

ELEC'TRO-MAG'NETISM. The phenomena produced when a current of electricity is traversing any substance; or when electricity is in motion, magnetism is at the same time developed.

ELEC'TRO-MAG'NET. An apparatus for exhibiting the phenomena of electro-magnetism.

E'LEMENT. The ancients considered earth, fire, water, and air, as simple substances. The alchemists had three elements: salt, earth, and mercury. In modern science, the term *element* signifies merely a substance which has not yet been resolved by analysis into any simpler form of matter; and it is therefore synonymous with undecompounded.

ELEPHAN'TINA. Lat. Belonging or relating to an elephant; elephantine.

E'LEPHAS. Lat. Gr. name of the elephant. A genus of mammals of the order pachydermata.

ELLIP'TICA. Lat. Elliptic.

ELU'TRIATE. When an insoluble pulverulent matter, like whitening or ground flints, is diffused through a large body of water, and the mixture is allowed to settle for a little, the larger particles will subside. If the supernatant liquid be now carefully decanted, or run off, with a syphon, it will contain an impalpable powder, which, on repose, will collect at the bottom, and may be taken out to dry. This process is called *elutria'tion.*

EMBALM'ING. An operation, in which balsams were employed, to preserve human corpses from putrefaction; whence the name. The ancient Egyptians had recourse to this process for preserving the bodies of numerous families, and even of the animals which they loved or worshipped.

EM'BRYO. From the Gr. *embruon*, from *bruô*, I bud forth. A germ at the early stages of development.

E'MERALD. A mineral of a beautiful green colour, much valued for ornamental jewelry. It consists of silica, alumina, glucina, oxide of chromium, which is the colouring matter, and a trace of lime.

E'MERY. This mineral was long regarded as an ore of iron; and was called by Haüy, *fer oxidé quartzifère.* It is very abundant in the island of Naxos, at Cape *Emeri*, whence it is imported in large quantities. It occurs also in the islands of Jersey and Guernsey, at Almaden, in Poland, Saxony, Sweden, Persia, &c. It has recently been discovered in Minnesota; but nearly all that is used at present in the arts comes from Turkey, near ancient Smyrna. Its colour varies from red-brown to dark-brown; and it is so hard as to scratch quartz and many precious stones. By Mr. Tennant's analysis, it consists of alumina 80, silica 3, and iron 4. Another inferior kind yielded 32 of iron, and only 50 of alumina.

EMPYREU'MA. The offensive smell produced by fire applied to organic matter, chiefly vegetable, in close vessels.

EN'CRINITES. From the Gr. *krinon*, a lily. A genus of fossil *Echi'noderms*. The skeleton of this animal is said to consist of not less than 26,000 separate pieces.

ENTOZO'A. Plural of *Entozo'on*.

ENTOZO'ON. An animal living in some part of another animal.

E'OCENE. From the Gr. *eôs*, dawn, and *kainos*, recent. In *geology*, a name for the older tertiary formation, in which the first dawn, as it were, of existing species appears.

EPACRI'DEÆ. From the Gr. *epi*, upon, and *akros*, an elevated place, a hill. A family of plants.

EP'IPHYTE. From the Gr. *epi*, upon, and *phutos*, a plant. Applied to plants which grow upon other plants.

EP'SOM SALTS. Sulphate of magnesia.

EQUINOCTIA'LIS. Lat. Equinoctial.

E'QUINOX. From *æquus*, equal, and *nox*, night. The time when the sun enters one of the equinoctial points, making the day and night of equal length. The sun enters the first point of Aries about the 21st of March, and the first point of Libra about the 23d of September. These are called the *vernal* and *autumnal equinoxes*. These points are found to be moving backward, or westward, at the rate of 50″ in a year. This is called the *precession of the equinoxes*.

EQUISE'TUM. From the Lat. *equus*, a horse, and *seta*, hair. A genus of plants of the family of Equisitáceæ.

EQUIV'ALENTS, CHEM'ICAL. An expression first employed by Dr. Wollaston, to denote the primary proportions in which the various chemical bodies reciprocally combine; the numbers representing these proportions being referred to one standard substance, of general interest, such as oxygen or hydrogen, taken as unity.

E'QUUS. Lat. A horse. A genus of mammals.

ER'BIUM. A metal, recently discovered.

ERYTHROX'YLON. From the Gr. *eruthros*, red, and *xulon*, wood. A genus of plants.

ESCARP'MENT. From the Ital. *scarpa*, sharp, formed from the Lat. *carpere*, to cut. The steep face often presented by the abrupt termination of strata, where subjacent beds crop out from beneath them.

ESCULEN'TA. Lat. Esculent.

ES'SENCES. Either etherous oils, in which all the fragrance of vegetable products reside, or the same combined and diluted with alcohol.

E'THER. The name of a class of very light, volatile, inflammable, and fragrant spirituous liquids, obtained by distilling, in a glass retort, a mixture of alcohol with almost any strong acid. Every acid modifies the result, in a certain degree, when several varieties of ether are produced. The only one of commercial importance is sulphuric ether, which was first made known, under the name of *sweet oil of vitriol*, in 1540, by the receipt of Walterus Cordus. Froberus, 190 years after that date, directed the chemists afresh to this substance, under the new denomination of *ether*. Its chemical formula is C_4H_5O.

E'THIOPS. The absurd name given by the alchemists to certain black metallic preparations.

ETHNO'GRAPHER. From the Gr. *ethnos*, a nation, and *graphô*, I write. One who cultivates ethnography: an ethno'logist.

ETHNO'GRAPHY. A department of knowledge which treats of the different natural races and families of men. A treatise on the subject.

EUCALY'PTI. Lat. Plural of eucalyptus.

EUCALY'PTUS. From the Gr. *eu*, well, and *kaluptos*, covered. A genus of plants of the family of Myrtáceæ.

EUDIOM'ETER. Any apparatus subservient to the chemical examination of the atmospheric air. It means a *measure of purity*; but it is employed merely to determine the proportion of oxygen which it may contain.

EUPHO'RBIA. Gr. Name of a plant. A genus of plants, of which there are 300 species.

EVAPORA'TION. The process by which any substance is converted into, and carried off in, vapour.

EXCE'LSA. Lat. Noble, tall, stately.

EXCO'RTICA Lat. Without bark.

EXO'GENOUS. From the Gr. *ex*, from, and *geinomai*, I grow. Applied to plants which grow by successive external additions to their wood.

EXPAN'SION. The increase of bulk experienced by heated bodies.

EXTEN'SILE. Having the power to extend itself.

EXU'VIÆ. Lat. The sloughs or cast skins, or cast shells of animals.

FA'GUS. Lat. Beech. A genus of plants of the family of Amentáceæ.
FA'LCO. Lat. Falcon. A genus of birds. *Fa'lco isla'ndicus.* The Gerfalcon.
FA'MILY. In natural history the term is applied to an assemblage of several genera which resemble each other in many respects.
FARI'NA. Lat. Meal.
FAR'INHA. Portu. Meal, flour.
FARINO'SA. Lat. Mealy; belonging or relating to meal.
FAULTS. In *mining*, disturbances of the strata, which interrupt the miner's operations, and put him at *fault*, to discover where the vein of ore or bed of coal has been thrown by the convulsions of nature.
FAU'NA. All animals of all kinds peculiar to a country constitute the *fauna* of that country.
FEC'ULA. Sometimes signifies corn-flour, and sometimes starch, from whatever source obtained.
FE'LIS. Lat. A cat. A genus of mammals of the family of carni'vora. *Felis irbis.* The panther.
FEL'SPAR. A simple mineral, and a leading constituent of granite. It consists of silica 66·75, alumina 17·50, potash 12, lime 1·25, and oxide of iron 0·75 (Rose). Its decomposition furnishes the ka'olin, or porcelain clay.
FENESTRA'LIS. Lat. Belonging or relating to a window or opening.
FER'MENT. Any substance which, when added in a small quantity to vegetable or animal fluids, tends to excite those intestinal motions and changes which accompany fermentation.
FERMENTA'TION. When organic substances, under the influence of water, air, and warmth, are abandoned to the reciprocal operation of their proximate principles (sugar, starch, gluten, &c.), they are entirely changed and decomposed, so that their ultimate principles (oxygen, hydrogen, carbon, &c.) combine in new proportions, and thus give birth to various new compounds. To this process, the general name of fermentation has been given.
FERNS. The filices; an order of cryptogámic plants.
FI'CUS. Lat. A fig. A genus of plants of the family of Moræ'ceæ.
FILTRA'TION. A purely mechanical process for separating a liquid from undissolved particles floating in it. The filtering substance may consist of any porous matter, in a solid, foliated, or pulverulent form; as porous earthenware, unsized paper, cloth of many kinds, or sand.
FIORD. A frith, firth, or furth; a rocky chasm penetrated by the sea; a rock-bound strait.
FLABELLIFO'RME. From the Lat. *flabellum*, a fan, and *forma*, form. Fan-shaped.
FLO'RA. Lat. Name of the Goddess of Flowers. All the plants of all kinds, belonging to a country, constitute the *flora* of that country.
FLO'RIDA. Belonging or relating to flowers; or relating to the State of Florida.
FLUX. Any substance capable of promoting the fusion of earths or metallic ores by heat. *White* flux is the residuum of the deflagration, in a red-hot crucible, of a mixture of two parts of nitre and one of cream of tartar. It is, in fact, merely a carbonate of potash. *Black* flux is obtained when equal parts of nitre and tartar are deflagrated. It owes its colour to the carbonaceous matter of the tartaric acid, which remains unconsumed: the quantity of nitre being too small for that purpose. The presence of the charcoal renders this preparation a convenient flux for reducing calcined or oxidized ores to the metallic state. Limestone, fluor-spar, borax, and several earthy or metallic oxides, are employed as fluxes in metallurgy.
FLY POW'DER. The black-coloured powder obtained by the spontaneous oxidation of metallic arsenic in the air. A *suboxide* of arsenic.
FO'CI. Lat. Plural of focus.
FO'CUS. Lat. A hearth. In optics the term describes the point or space where the rays of light are concentrated by a lens. The apex of a cone of rays of light, or of heat, formed by a lens, or concave mirror.
FOLIA'CEOUS. From the Lat. *folium*. Leafy. Having the form of leaves.
FOO'TSTALKS. In *botany*, the stalks of flowers, or of leaves.
FOR'MULÆ, CHEM'ICAL. Symbols representing the different substances, simple and compound.
FO'SSIL. From the Lat. *fodio*, I dig. Any organic body, or the traces of any organic body, whether animal or vegetable, which has been buried in the earth by natural causes.
FOSSILI'FEROUS. Containing fossils: fossil-bearing.
FRA'GRANS. Lat. Fragrant; odorous.
FRA'GILIS. Lat. Fragile; easily broken.
FROND. Also, *frons*. A name applied to the leaves of palms, and of cryptógamous plants.
FRONDO'SA. Lat. Full of green leaves.

FU'CI. Lat. Plural of fucus.
FU'CUS. Lat. Sea-weed. A genus of aquatic plants.
FU'EL. Such combustibles as are used for fires or furnaces; as wood, turf, and pit-coal.
FUNC'TION. From the Lat. *fungor*, I act. The action of an organ, or system of organs.
FUNE'REUS. Lat. Funereal: belonging to a dead body.
FUN'GI. Lat. Plural of fungus.
FUN'GUS. Lat. A mushroom.
FUSIBIL'ITY. The property by which solids assume the liquid state.

GA'DUS. Lat. A codfish.
GALE'NA. From the Gr. *galene*, lead ore. A mineral composed of sulphur and lead: a natural sulphuret of lead.
GALLINA'CEOUS. From the Lat. *galli'na*, hen. Relating to birds of the order of Gallinácea.
GALL-NUTS, or GALLS. Excrescences found upon the leaves and leaf-stalks of a species of oak, called *quercus infectoria*, which grows in the Levant. They are produced in consequence of the puncture of the female of the gall-wasp (*cynips folii quercus*), made in order to deposit her eggs.
GALVA'NIC. Belonging or relating to galvanism.
GAL'VANISM. From *Galvani*, a distinguished Italian philosopher. That branch of electrical science in which electricity is made manifest by the mediate contact of different metals. Also, the phenomena exhibited by living animal matter, when placed between the poles or extremities of an apparatus for showing electricity by the mediate contact of different metals.
GANGEA'TICUS. Lat. Gangeatic; belonging or relating to the river Ganges.
GANGUE. The mineral substance which either encloses, or usually accompanies any metallic ore in the vein. Quartz, lamellar carbonate of lime, sulphate of baryta, and sulphate and fluate of lime, generally form the gangues; but a great many other substances become such when they predominate in a vein.
GARDE'NIA. After a proper name. A genus of plants of the family of Rubiáceæ; it contains some forty species. The *Garde'nia grandiflo'ra* is the Cape Jasmin.
GAR'NET. A mineral consisting of silicates of alumina, lime, iron, and manganese. It occurs imbedded in mica-slate, granite, and gneiss, and occasionally in limestone, chlorite-slate, serpentine, and lava. There are several varieties of garnet.
GAS. From the Germ. *geist*, spirit. The name given to all permanently elastic fluids, or airs, different from the atmospheric air.
GAS'EOUS. Of the nature of gas.
GEMS. Precious stones, which, by their colour, limpidity, lustre, brilliant polish, purity, and rarity, are sought after as objects of dress and decoration. They form the principal part of the crown-jewels of kings, not only for their beauty, but because they are supposed to comprise the greatest value in the smallest bulk; for a diamond, no larger than a nut or an acorn, may be the representative sign of the territorial value of a whole country, the equivalent, in commercial exchange, of a hundred fortunes acquired by severe toil and privations. Diamonds, sapphires, emeralds, rubies, topazes, hyacinths, and chrysoberyls, are reckoned the most valuable gems.
GE'NERA. Lat. Plural of genus.
GENRE. Fr. Genus, kind, manner, style. In *painting*, it is applied to signify the representation of certain kinds of objects, as landscapes, views, animals, plants, flowers, scenes in common life. Pictures of *genre*, then, are pictures of a genus or kind as to subject; as landscapes, marine views, flower pieces, still-life, &c.
GE'NUS. Lat. A kindred, breed, race, or family.
GEOG'NOSY. A *knowledge* of the structure of the earth. Geology is a *description* of the same. See GEOLOGY.
GEO'LOGY. From the Gr. *ge*, the earth, and *logos*, discourse. That branch of natural history which treats of the structure of the terrestrial globe. It is divided into *descriptive* geology; *dynamic* geology, which treats of the forces by which the surface of the earth has been modified; *practical* and *economic* geology, embracing the application of geological science to mining, road-making, architecture, and agriculture.
GEOTHER'MAL. From the Gr. *ge*, the earth, and *thermos*, heat, temperature. Relating to temperature of the earth.
GERMINA'TION. The process of the development of the seed and the embryo which it contains.
GEY'SERS. From an Icelandic word, signifying raging or roaring. Celebrated spouting fountains of boiling water in Iceland.
GIBBO'SA. Lat. Gibbous; having protuberances or bunches.
GIBRALTA'RICA. Lat. Belonging or relating to Gibraltar.
GIGANTE'A. } Lat. Gigantic, huge.
GIGANTE'US. }

GILEADE'NSIS. Lat. Belonging or relating to Gilead.
GLA'CIAL. Belonging or relating to ice.
GLA'CIERS. Fr. Masses or beds of ice formed in high mountains, derived from the snows or lakes frozen by the continued cold of those regions.
GLAND. An organ formed for the purpose of secreting a peculiar fluid.
GLAU'BER'S SALT. Sulphate of soda.
GLAU'COUS. From the Gr. *glaukos*, blue. Applied to the bluish and pulverulent aspect which certain plants present, such as the leaves of cabbages, &c. Also used to signify the bloom of the colour of cabbage-leaves, sometimes observed on polished bodies.
GLUCI'NA. One of the earths, originally discovered by Vauquelin, in the beryl and emerald. It is the oxide of Gluci'num.
GLUCI'NUM. A metal discovered in glucina, in 1798, by Vauquelin.
GLU'COSE. The name given to grape and starch-sugar.
GLU'TEN. Lat. The viscid elastic substance which remains when wheat-flour is wrapped in a coarse cloth, and washed under a stream of water, so as to carry off the starch and soluble matters. It exists in many plants and in animals. It is the basis of glue.
GNEISS. Germ. A rock resembling granite. It is composed chiefly of feldspar and mica, and is more or less slaty in its structure. Gneiss is used for building and flagging.
GOLD. The most valuable and longest known of the metals.
GONIOM'ETER. A little instrument, made either on mechanical or optical principles, for measuring the angles of crystals. It is indispensable to the mineralogist.
GRÆ'CA. Lat. Greek.
GRAMI'NEÆ. Lat. Grasses. A family of monocotylédonous plants, containing about 3000 species.
GRANDIFLO'RA. Lat. Large-flowered.
GRAN'ITE. A compound rock, composed essentially of quartz, feldspar, and mica, each in *granular* crystals.
GRANI'TIC. Of the nature of granite.
GRANI'VORA. } Applied to animals which feed upon grains, especially to passerine
GRANI'VOROUS. } birds.
GRAN'ULAR. Composed of grains.
GRANULA'TION. The process by which metals are reduced to minute grains.
GREEN'STONE. A rough variety of trap-rock, consisting chiefly of hornblende.
GREEN VIT'RIOL. Sulphate of the protoxide of iron.
GRIT. A coarse-grained sandstone.
GUINEEN'SIS. Latin. Belonging or relating to Guinea.
GUM. A vegetable product, which is tasteless and inodorous, and is distinguished by being soluble in water, and insoluble in alcohol: gum-arabic, for example.
GYMNO'TUS. From the Gr. *gumnos*, naked, and *nôtos*, back. A genus of fishes.
GYP'SUM. Native sulphate of lime. It is converted into plaster of Paris by heat.

HA'BITAT. Lat. He inhabits. Used to designate the place in which animals and plants are naturally found.
HA'LCYON. From the Gr. *halkuo'n*, a king-fisher. A genus of birds.
HEA'VY SPAR. Sulphate of baryta.
HELI'ACAL. From the Gr. *helios*, the sun. Relating to the sun. When a star rises so as to be visible in morning twilight, before the appearance of the sun, it is said to rise *heliacally*.
HELIA'NTHUS. From the Gr. *helios*, the sun, and *anthos*, flower; sunflower.
HE'PAR. A Latin word, signifying *liver*. A name given by the older chemists to some of those compounds of sulphur with the metals, which had a liver-brown colour.
HEPTAPHY'LLUM. From the Gr. *hepta*, seven, and *phullon*, a leaf. Seven-leaved. A specific name.
HERBA'CEOUS. In *botany*, herb-like; that perishes every year. An annual stem. Not woody.
HERBI'VORA. Lat. Herbivorous.
HERBIV'OROUS. From the Lat. *herba*, a plant, and *vorare*, to eat. Plant-eating. Applied to animals which feed chiefly or exclusively on plants or herbs.
HI'BERNATE. From the Lat. *hibernare*, to winter. Animals which retire and sleep throughout the winter, are said to hibernate.
HIPPOPO'TAMUS. From the Gr. *hippos*, a horse, and *potamos*, river. River-horse. A genus of mammals.
HIRSU'TA. Lat. Hirsute; covered with soft hairs.
HO'RARY. From the Lat. *hora*, an hour. The motion of a celestial body, or the space it moves through in an hour, is termed its *horary motion*.
HO'RRIDA. Lat. Horrid; spiny.

HORSE'SHOE MAG'NET. A magnet in form of a horseshoe.

HYDRAN'GEA. From the Gr. *hudôr*, water, and *aggos*, a vessel. A genus of plants of the family of Saxifragáceæ, and tribe of Hydrangéæ.

HY'DRATES. Compounds of the oxides, salts, &c., with water in definite or equivalent proportions.

HYDRAU'LIC. From the Gr. *hudôr*, water, and *aulos*, a pipe. Relating to liquids in motion. Hydraulics is that branch of natural philosophy or physics which treats of the force of water and other liquids in motion.

HYDROSTA'TIC. From the Gr. *hudôr*, water, and *staô*, I stand. Relating to water in a state of rest. Hydrostatics is the science which treats of the equilibrium and pressure of water and other liquids.

HY'DROGEN. From the Gr. *hudôr*, water, and *gennaein*, to generate. A colourless, tasteless, inodorous gas, one part of which, by weight, combined with eight parts of oxygen forms water; combined with sulphur, it constitutes *sulphuretted* hydrogen; and with carbon, carburetted hydrogen, the gas used for illumination.

HYDROM'ETER. An instrument for ascertaining the specific gravities of liquids.

HYMENO'PTERA. From the Gr. *humen*, a membrane, and *pteron*, wing. Systematic name of a class of insects, characterized by membranous wings.

I'BEX. Lat. A wild goat. A genus of mammals.

I'BIS. A genus of birds.

IG'NEOUS ROCKS. Are those rocks whose structure is attributable to the influence of heat, such as granite and basalt. They are distinct from stratified rocks, or those formed by deposits from water.

IGUA'NA. A reptile of the lizard tribe.

IGUA'NIAN. Applied to Saurians which resemble the iguana.

IGUA'NODON. From *iguana*, and the Gr. *odous*, tooth. A genus of extinct or fossil reptiles, of gigantic size, discovered in the south of England.

I'LEX. Lat. The Holly.

IL'ICIS. Lat. Of the Holly; belonging or relating to the holly.

IM'BRICATE. Laid one over another like tiles.

INCONSPIC'UOUS. Lat. Not conspicuous or remarkable.

INCI'SOR. From the Lat. *incido*, I cut. Applied to those teeth which occupy the anterior or centre of the upper and lower jaws, because they are used for cutting the food.

IN'CA. Designation of the aboriginal Peruvian princes; used as a specific name. Also, a genus of insects.

IN'DIAN RUB'BER. The vulgar name of caoutchouc in this country.

IN'DICA—IN'DICUS. Lat. Indian: belonging or relating to India.

INDICA'TOR. Lat. Indicator; one who points out. A genus of birds.

INFUSO'RIA. Animals of infusions; microscopic animalcules.

INFUSO'RIAL. Belonging or relating to the Infusoria.

INORGA'NIC. Without organs or organization.

IN'SECT. From the Lat. *in*, into, *seco*, I cut. Applied to animals whose bodies are cut, as it were, into three parts—head, thorax, and abdomen.

I'ODINE. One of the chemical elements, discovered accidentally, in 1812, by M. Courtois.

IRI'DEÆ. A family of monocotylédonous plants.

IRI'DIUM. From the Lat. *iris*, the rainbow. A grey, brittle, very infusible metal, which is found associated with the ores of platinum. It is so called, because its different solutions exhibit all the colours of the rainbow.

ISLA'NDICUS. Lat. Belonging or relating to Iceland.

ISOCHI'MENAL. From the Gr. *isos*, equal, and *cheima*, winter. Isochimenal lines pass through all places where the mean winter temperature is the same.

IS'OGEOTHE'RMAL. From the Gr. *isos*, equal, *ge*, the earth, and *thermos*, heat. Applied to lines which are supposed to pass through all parts of the earth's structure, on the surface, where the mean heat is the same.

ISOTHE'RMAL. From the Gr. *isos*, equal, and *thermos*, heat. Isothermal lines are supposed to pass through all places where the mean temperature of the air is the same.

ISOTHE'RIAL. From the Gr. *isos*, equal, and *thereios*, having the heat of summer. Isotherial lines are supposed to be drawn through all places having the same mean summer temperature.

JAPO'NICA—JAPO'NICUS. Belonging or relating to Japan.

JAS'PER. A silicious mineral, of various colours; sometimes spotted, banded, or variegated. It takes a fine polish.

JURA'SSIC. Belonging or relating to the Jura mountains. Applied to a system of rocks, of the middle secondary geological period. Also termed oolitic.

KA'LI. The Arabs gave this name to an annual plant which grows near the sea-shore, now known under the name of *salsola soda*, and from whose ashes they extracted a substance, which they called *alkali*, for making soap.
KA'LMIA. A genus of plants of the family of Ericáceæ.
KELP. The crude alkaline matter produced by incinerating various species of fuci, or *sea-weed*.

LABIA'TÆ. From the Lat. *labium*, lip; in allusion to the form of the corolla. A family of dicotylédonous plants.
LAKES. Colours consisting of a vegetable dye, combined by precipitation with a white, earthy basis, which is usually alumina.
LANA'TA. Lat. Woolly.
LANCEOLA'TUS. Lat. Lanceolate; lance-shaped.
LAND'SLIP, or LAND'SLIDE. In geology, the removal of a portion of land down an inclined surface, from its attachment being loosened by the action of water beneath, or by an earthquake.
LAN'THANUM. A metal discovered in 1840 by Mosander.
LA'PIS LA'ZULI. A mineral belonging to the aluminous silicates, of an azure blue colour.
LA'RVA. Lat. A mask. The first state of an insect after leaving the egg.
LA'RVÆ. Lat. Plural of larva.
LA'TENT HEAT. Heat not indicated by the thermometer; that heat upon which the liquid and aëriform conditions of bodies depend, and which becomes *sensible* during the conversion of vapour into liquids, and of liquids into solids.
LAUREA'CEÆ. } LAURI'NEÆ. } From *laurus*, laurel, one of the genera. A family of plants.
LA'VA. In *geology*, substances which flow in a melted state from a volcano. Lavas vary in consistence and texture.
LEGUMINO'SÆ. From the Lat. *legu'men*, a bean. A family of plants.
LEGU'MINOUS. Belonging or relating to the Leguminosæ.
LEONI'NA. Lat. Belonging or relating to a lion.
LEPIDO'PTERA. From the Gr. *lepis*, a scale, and *pteron*, a wing, scaly wings. An order of insects characterized by scaly wings.
LEPORI'NA. Lat. Belonging or relating to a hare.
LEVIGA'TION. The mechanical process by which hard substances are educed to a very fine powder.
LI'AS. Provincial corruption of the word *layers*. In *geology*, a division of the secondary formation. It is also called the Liassic, Jurassic, and Oolitic system of rocks.
LI'CHENS. An order of cryptógamous plants. They include various mosses.
LILIA'CEÆ. A family of plants.
LILIA'CEOUS. Belonging or relating to the lily.
LIMB. In *botany*, the spreading part or border of a leaf or petal. In *astronomy*, the outermost edge of the sun or moon.
LI'RIODE'NDRON. From the Gr. *leirion*, a lily, and *dendron*, a tree. The tulip tree. A genus of plants of the family of Magnoliáceæ.
LITH'ARGE. Semivitrified protoxide of lead.
LITH'IA. One of the earths.
LI'THIUM. A metal.
LIXIVIA'TION. The abstraction, by water, of the soluble alkaline or saline matters present in any earthy admixture; as, from that of quicklime and potashes, to make potash lye.
LLA'NOS. Spanish. Planes.
LOAD'STONE. An iron ore, consisting of the protoxide and peroxide of iron, in a state of combination.
LOAM. A native clay, mixed with quartz sand and iron ochre, and occasionally with some carbonate of lime.
LOBE. A term applied in botany to the more or less profound divisions of a leaf, corolla, or other part of a plant.
LOBELIA'CEÆ. In honour of Lobel, a botanist. A family of dicotylédonous plants.
LON'GIFRONS. Lat. Having a long front or forehead.
LO'TUS. A genus of plants of the family of Leguminósæ.
LU'NAR CAUS'TIC. Nitrate of silver.
LUTE. A pasty or loamy matter, employed to close the joints of chemical apparatus, or coat their surfaces, and protect them from the direct action of flame.
LU'TEUS. } LU'TEA. } LU'TEUM. } Lat. Yellow; dirty; made of clay. A specific name.

MACROU'ROUS. From the Gr. *makros*, great, and *oura*, tail. Having a long or large tail.
MAG'ISTERY. An old chemical term to designate white pulverulent substances, spontaneously precipitated in making certain metallic solutions; as magistery of bismuth.
MAGNE'SIA. One of the alkaline earths.
MAGNE'SIAN. Containing magnesia.
MAGNE'SIUM. A silvery white metal obtained from magnesia.
MAG'NET. Loadstone is the natural magnet, which has the property of attracting iron. Artificial magnets are prepared so as to possess the peculiar attractive properties of the loadstone.
MAG'NETISM. The science which investigates the phenomena presented by natural and artificial magnets, and the laws by which they are connected.
MAGNO'LIA. Name of Magnol, a French botanist. A genus of plants of the family of Magnoliáceæ.
MA'LACHITE. A mineral; native green carbonate of copper.
MALLEABIL'ITY. The property of being beaten out into thin leaves.
MALT. Barley-corn, which has been subjected to an artificial process of germination.
MAM'MAL. Any animal that suckles its young.
MAMMA'LIA. From the Lat. *mamma*, a breast. The name of the class of mammals or animals which suckle their young.
MAMMI'FERÆ. Same as mammalia.
MAN'GANESE. A metal.
MARI'TIMA. Lat. Maritime; relating to the sea.
MARL. Argillaceous carbonate of lime. There are several varieties of marl.
MARSU'PIAL. From the Lat. *marsupium*, a pouch. Any animal having a peculiar pouch in front or on the abdomen.
MAR'TIAL. Belonging to iron: from Mars, the mythological and alchemical name of this metal.
MAS'TODON. From the Gr. *mastos*, a nipple, and *odous*, a tooth. A genus of extinct mammals allied to the elephant.
MA'TRIX. In *geology*, the stony substance or bed in which metallic ores and crystalline minerals are embedded. The *gangue*.
MAURI'TIA. Belonging to the island of Mauritius.
MAURO'RUM. Lat. Of the Moors.
MA'XIMUS. }
MA'XIMA. } Lat. The greatest.
MA'XIMUM. }
MEDU'SA. A genus of marine animals of the class Aca'lepha.
MEGATHE'RIUM. From the Gr. *megas*, great, and *therion*, beast. Name of a fossil quadruped.
MEI'OCENE. See *Mi'ocene*.
MELALEU'CA. From the Gr. *melas*, black, and *leukos*, white. A genus of plants of the family of Myrtáceæ.
MELOFO'RMIS. From the Lat. *melo*, a melon, and *forma*, shape. Melon-shaped.
MER'CURY. Quicksilver. A metal which is liquid at ordinary temperatures.
MESEMBRYAN'THEMUM. From the Gr. *mesèmbria*, the mid-day, and *anthemum*, flowering; so called because the flowers usually expand at mid-day. The fig marigold. A genus of plants of the family of Fico'ides.
METALLI'FEROUS. Containing metal, or metals.
MET'ALLOID. Literally, resembling metal. The metals obtained from the alkalis and earths are sometimes called metalloids.
METAL'LURGY. The art of extracting metals from their ores.
METAMOR'PHIC. From the Gr. *meta*, indicating change, and *morphe*, form. Metamorphic rocks are those which are evidently of mechanical origin, but owing to the presumed action of heat, have undergone change. Altered rocks.
ME'TEORITES. Meteoric stones. Stones of a peculiar aspect and composition, which have fallen from the air.
MIA'SMA. } MIA'SMATA. } From the Gr. *miainô*, I contaminate. Applied to any emanation from animal or vegetable substances, or from the earth, which may prejudicially influence the health of those persons who may be exposed to it.
MI'CA. From the Lat. *mico*, I shine. A mineral, generally found in thin, elastic laminæ, soft, smooth, and of various colours and degrees of transparency. It is one of the constituents of granite.
MI'CA-SCHIST. Germ. (Gr. *schistos*, slaty, easily split.) A lamellar rock, composed of quartz, ordinarily grayish, and a great quantity of brilliant lamellæ of mica, arranged in scales, or extended leaves.
MICROCOS'MIC SALT. Phosphate of soda and ammonia.

MI'DAS. Name of a genus of monkeys; also, of a genus of reptiles.
MIGRATO'RIA. Lat. Migrating.
MILLEP'ORA. From the Lat. *mille*, a thousand, and *pori*, holes. A genus of stony polyps, or corallines.
MIMO'SA. From the Lat. *mimus*, a comedian; in allusion to its numerous varieties. A genus, and a tribe of plants.
MI'NIMUM. Lat. The least.
MI'OCENE. From the Gr. *meiōn*, less, and *kainos*, recent. In geology, a name of a group of rocks of the tertiary period.
MIRA'GE. Fr. A kind of natural optical illusion, arising from the unequal and irregular refraction of light by the lower strata of the atmosphere. The illusive appearance of water in deserts is explained in this manner.
MISPICK'EL. Arsenical pyrites.
MOLLU'SCA. Lat. Mollusks. A branch of the animal kingdom.
MOLLU'SCOUS. Belonging or relating to mollusks.
MOL'LUSK. From the Lat. *mollis*, soft. Applied to certain soft animals which inhabit shells, as oysters.
MOLYBDE'NUM. A white, brittle metal.
MONI'LIFORM. From the Lat. *monile*, a necklace. In form of a string of beads; necklace-like.
MO'NITOR. A genus of Saurian reptiles.
MONOCOTYLE'DON. From the Gr. *monos*, single, and *kotuledon*, seed-lobe. A single seed-lobe.
MONO'CEROS. From the Gr. *monos*, single, and *keras*, horn. Having one horn.
MONOCOTYLE'DONOUS. Relating to monocotylédons.
MO'NODON. From the Gr. *monos*, single, and *odous*, tooth. Name of a genus of aquatic mammals. The Narwhal.
MONOSPE'RMA. From the Gr. *monos*, single, and *sperma*, seed. One-seeded. A specific name.
MORAI'NES. Fr. The name given by geologists to longitudinal deposits of stony detritus, found at the bases and along the edges of all the great glaciers.
MO'RUS. Mulberry. A genus of plants of the family of Urti'ceæ.
MOSASAU'RUS. From *Meuse*, name of a river, and the Gr. *sauros*, a lizard. A genus of fossil reptiles.
MOSCHI'FERUS. Lat. Musk-bearing; containing musk.
MOS'CHUS. Lat. from the Gr. *moschos*, musk. Name of a genus of mammals.
MO'SSES. Cryptógamous parasites of the family of Lycopodeáceæ.
MU'CILAGE. A mixture of gum and water.
MU'RAL. Belonging or relating to a wall.
MU'SA. The banana. A genus of plants of the family of Musáceæ.
MUS'CHELKALK. German. Shell limestone.
MUSCI'PULA. Lat. A fly-trap or mouse-trap. A name of a plant.
MU'SICUS. Lat. Relating to music; musical.
MUST. The sweet juice of the grape.
MYRI'STICA. A genus of plants of the family of Myrista'ceæ; *Myris'tica moscha'ta*, the nutmeg tree.
MYR'TUS. Myrtle. A genus of plants of the family of Myrta'ceæ.

NA'NA. From the Lat. *nanus*, a dwarf. A specific name.
NA'PHTHA. A limpid bitumen.
NARCI'SSUS. Name of a genus of plants of the family of Amarylli'deæ.
NA'TRIUM. A metal; commonly called *sodium*.
NA'TRON. The name of the native sesquicarbonate of soda, which occurs in Egypt, in the west of the Delta; also, in the neighbourhood of Fezzan, in Northern Africa, where it exists under the name of *trona*, crystallized along with sulphate of soda; near Smyrna, in Tartary, Siberia, Hungary, Hindostan, and Mexico.
NEC'TARY. That part of a flower which secretes *nectar* or honey.
NELUM'BIUM. A genus of plants of the family of Nymphæa'ceæ. Sacred bean.
NER'OLI. The name given by perfumers to the essential oil of orange flowers. It is procured by distillation with water, in the same way as most other volatile oils.
NES'TOR. An extinct bird.
NEURO'PTERA. From the Gr. *neuron*, a nerve, and *pteron*, wing. An order of insects
NEUTRALIZA'TION. The state produced when acid and alkaline matters are combined in such proportions that neither predominates; as evinced by the colour of the tinctures of litmus and turmeric remaining unaffected by the combination.
NEW RED SAND'STONE. In *geology*, a system of rocks of the secondary formation.

NICK'EL. A white metal. It is the basis of "German Silver."
NI'GRA. Lat. Black.
NIM'BUS. A rain cloud.
NI'TIDA. Lat. Neat, clean, bright.
NI'TROGEN. A simple, permanently elastic fluid or gas, also called azote; which constitutes four-fifths of the atmosphere, and is the basis of nitric acid.
NIVA'LIS. Lat. Snowy.
NON-CONDUC'TOR. Applied to substances which do not possess the property of transmitting electricity or heat.
NO'PAL. The Mexican name of the plant *cac'tus opun'tia*, upon which the cochineal insect breeds.
NO'RIUM. A newly-discovered metal.
NOR'MAL. Regular; according to an established law, rule, or principle.
NOTOR'NIS. Name of an extinct bird.
NOTOTHE'RIUM. A fossil genus of marsupial mammals.
NUMMULA'RIA. From the Lat. *nummus*, a coin. A family of mollusks. Num'mulites. Fossils, of a flattened form, resembling small coins.

OBSI'DIAN. A glassy lava. Volcanic glass.
OCEAN'ICA. Lat. Relating to the ocean.
ODORA'TA. Lat. Odorous.
ODORATISSI'MA. Lat. Very, or most odorous.
ODORI'FERA. Lat. Odoriferous.
OIL OF VIT'RIOL. The old name of concentrated *sulphuric acid.*
OLD RED SAND'STONE. A system of rocks of the secondary formation.
O'LEA. Lat. Olive. A genus of plants of the family of Olea'ceæ.
O'OLITE. From the Gr. *ôon*, an egg, and *lithos*, stone. A granular variety of carbonate of lime, frequently called *roe-stone.*
O'PAL. A brittle mineral, characterized by its iridescent reflection of light. It consists of *silica*, with about ten per cent. of water.
OPALES'CENT. Resembling opal.
OPHI'DIAN. From the Gr. *ophis*, a serpent. Applied to reptiles of the order of Ophidia.
ORCHID'EOUS. Relating to the genus orchis.
OR'CHIS. A genus of plants of the family of Orchide'æ, named from most of the species being marked by two tubercles.
ORES. Mineral bodies which contain so much metal as to be worth the smelting, or being reduced by fire to the metallic state. The substances naturally combined with metals, marking their metallic characters, are chiefly oxygen, chlorine, sulphur, phosphorus, selenium, arsenic, water, and several acids, of which the carbonic is the most common.
OR'GAN. From the Gr. *organon*, an instrument. Part of an organized being, destined to exercise some particular function; for example, the ears are the organs of hearing, the muscles are the organs of motion.
ORGA'NIC. Relating to an organ. *Organic remains*, are the fossil remains of organized beings.
ORGANIZA'TION. The mode or manner of structure of an organized being.
OR'GANIZED. Composed of organs; having a mode of structure.
ORIENTA'LE. } ORIENTA'LIS. } Lat. Eastern. Belonging to the East.
ORNITHORYN'CHUS. From the Gr. *ornis*, *ornithos*, a bird, and *rugchos*, a beak. A genus of mammals, having the beak of a duck.
OSCILLA'TION. The act of moving backwards and forwards, like a pendulum.
OS'MIUM. From the Gr. *osme*, odour. A metal discovered in 1803, by Tennant.
OTA'RIA. From the Gr. *ôtarion*, a small car. A genus of amphibious mammals, of the tribe of seals.
OUT'CROP. In *geology*, the emergence of a rock in place, at the surface.
O'VARY. In *botany*, that part of a flower in which the young seeds are contained.
OX'ALIS. A genus of plants of the family of Oxali'deæ.
OX'YGEN. The vivifying gas which constitutes about one-fifth of the atmosphere, the presence of which is essential to life.
O'ZONE. From the Gr. *ozô*, I smell of something. The odorous matter perceived when electricity passes from pointed bodies into the air.

PACHYDER'MATA. Lat. from the Gr. *pachus*, thick, and *derma*, skin. An order of mammals—Pachyderms.
PALÆONTO'LOGY. From the Gr. *palaios*, ancient, *on*, a being or creature, and *logos*, discourse. That branch of zoological science, which treats of fossil organic remains.

PALÆOTHE'RIUM. From the Gr. *palaios*, ancient, and *therion*, beast. A fossil genus of pachyder'matous mammals.

PALÆOZO'IC. From the Gr. *palaios*, ancient, and *zoe*, life. Relating to ancient life; belonging or relating to fossils.

PALLA'DIUM. A white, hard, very malleable and ductile metal, which is susceptible of a fine polish. It is more difficult to melt than gold.

PALME'LLA. A genus of plants of the family of Confervâceæ. *Palme'lla niva'lis*, a plant of the snowy regions, which gives colour to the snow amidst which it grows. *Proctoco'c-cus* is the red snow plant.

PA'NICUM. Panic-grass. A genus of plants of the family of Grami'neæ. *Pa'nicum milia'ceum*, millet, a grain used for feeding poultry in England.

PA'PA. Spanish. Pope. Specific name of a vulture.

PAPYRI'FERA. From *papyrus*, a sort of paper, and *fero*, I bear. Paper-bearing.

PAPY'RUS. A genus of plants of the family of Cypera'ceæ. The *Papy'rus antiquo'rum* yields the substance used as paper by the ancient Egyptians.

PARADISA'ICA. Lat. Belonging or relating to Paradise. A specific name.

PAR'ASITE. From the Gr. *para*, near, and *sitos*, corn. A plant which attaches itself to other plants, or an animal which lives in or on the bodies of other animals — so as to subsist at their expense. The mistletoe is a parasitic plant — the louse, a parasitic animal.

PAREN'CHYMA. The texture of glandular and other organs, composed of agglomerated globules, united by areolar tissue, and tearing with more or less facility. Such is the texture of the liver, kidneys, &c.

PARHE'LIA. Plural of parhelion.

PARHE'LION. From the Gr. *para*, alongside of, and *helios*, the sun. A mock sun. A meteor which consists in the simultaneous appearance of several suns, "fantastic images of the true one."

PARNA'SSUS. A genus of lepidopterous insects of the tribe of Parna'ssidæ.

PASS'ERES.
PASS'ERINES.
PASS'ERINE BIRDS. } From the Lat. *passer*, a sparrow. Name of a varied and extensive order of birds, not easily characterized.

PASSIFLO'RA. Abbreviation of *flos*, flower, and *passionis*, of the passion. Passion-flower. So called, from a supposed resemblance between its floral organs, and the instruments of the Passion of our Saviour. An extensive and beautiful genus of plants.

PATAGO'NICA. Lat. Relating to Patagonia. Specific name of a penguin.

PAVO'NIA. Formed from the Lat. *pavo*, a peacock. A specific name.

PEARL'ASH. A commercial form of *potash*.

PEAT. The natural accumulation of vegetable matter on the surface of lands not in a state of cultivation; always moist to a greater or less degree; varying according to the kind of plants, to the decay of which the formation of peat is due.

PEDUN'CLE. In *botany*, the stem or stalk that supports the flower and the fruit. From the Lat. *pes*, a foot.

PELA'GIC. From the Lat. *pelagus*, the sea. Relating to the sea.

PELO'PIUM. A metal discovered by Prof. H. Rose.

PEN'DULUM. From the Lat. *pendo*, I hang. A weight suspended at the end of a rod, so that it may vibrate from side to side in a plane, is called a pendulum.

PENUM'BRA. From the Lat. *pæne*, almost, and *umbra*, shade. In *astronomy*, the partial shadow in an eclipse.

PER'MIAN. After the ancient kingdom of Permia. A name applied by Mr. Murchison to a system of rocks, consisting of an extensive group of fossiliferous strata, intermediate, in their geological position, between the Carboniferous and Triassic systems, the latter being the upper portion of the New Red Sandstone formation.

PERTURBA'TION. In *astronomy*, the deviation of a celestial body from the elliptic orbit which it would describe, if acted upon by no other attractive force than that of the sun, or central body about which it revolves.

PE'TAL. From the Gr. *petalon*, a leaf. A part of the corolla of a flower analogous to a leaf.

PETRO'LEUM. From the Gr. *petros*, a rock, and the Lat. *oleum*, oil. Rock-oil, often called *Barbadoes tar*. A brown, liquid bitumen, found in the West Indies, Europe, &c.

PHANEROGA'MIA. From the Gr. *phaneros*, evident, and *gamos*, marriage. Phanerógamous plants. Applied to plants having distinct flowers.

PHLOX. Gr. Flame. A genus of beautiful plants of the family of Polemoniaceæ.

PHO'CA. Lat. A seal. A genus of aquatic mammals, embracing the common seal or *Pho'ca vituli'na*; the Harp seal or *P. ocea'nica*; the Hare-tailed seal or *P. lagura*; the sea-lion; sea-wolf; sea-elephant; sea-cow; &c., &c.

PHO'CÆ. Lat. Plural of phoca.

PHO'NOLITE. From the Gr. *phoneó*, I resound, and *lithos*, a stone. Clink-stone. A kind of compact basalt which is sonorous when struck.

PHOR'MIUM. From the Gr. *phormos*, a basket. Flax-lily. A genus of plants of the family of Asphodéleæ. *Phor'mium te'nax*, Iris-leaved flax-lily of New Zealand.

PHOS'PHATES. Compounds of phosphoric acid with salifiable bases, as soda, are termed phosphates: Phosphate of soda, for example.

PHOSPHORE'SCENCE. Emission of light from substances at common temperatures, or below a red heat.

PHOSPHORE'SCENT. Having the property of emitting light without sensible heat.

PHOSPHO'RIC A'CID. A compound of phosphorus and oxygen, having the properties of acids.

PHOS'PHORUS. From the Gr. *phos*, light, and *pheró*, I bear. A simple substance which is highly inflammable.

PHOTO'METER. From the Gr. *phós*, light, and *metron*, measure. An instrument for measuring the intensity of light.

PHYSA'LIA. } PHY'SALIS. } From the Gr. *phuse*, a vesicle. A genus of animals of the family of Acalepha. The Portuguese man-of-war belongs to this class.

PHY'SALIS. A genus of plants of the family of Solanáceæ. *Physa'lis e'dulis*, the Cape gooseberry.

PHYSE'TER. A blower. Name of a genus of mammals of the family of Ceta'cea.

PIME'NTO. Allspice; Jamaica pepper.

PIN'NATE. From the Lat. *pinnatus*, feathered. Having leaflets arranged along each side of a common petiole, like the feather of a quill.

PINNATI'FIDA. Lat. Pinna'tifid. A leaf is so called when it is divided into lobes from the margin nearly to the midriff.

PI'NUS. Lat. A pine-tree. A genus of plants of the family of Coniferæ. *Pi'nus a'bies.* The Norway spruce. *Pi'nus canarie'nsis.* The Canary pine. *Pi'nus ce'mbra.* The Riga balsam tree; the Cembran or Siberian pine. *Pi'nus exce'lsa.* The lofty or Nepal pine. *Pi'nus marit'ima.* The maritime pine. *Pi'nus pi'nea.* The Stone pine.

PI'PA. A genus of batrachian reptiles. A kind of toad.

PLAS'TER OF PARIS. Gypsum. Sulphate of lime.

PLA'TINA. } PLA'TINUM. } The diminutive of the Spanish *plata*, silver. A metal of a steel gray colour, approaching to the white colour of silver, to which resemblance it owes its name. It was found in Choco, one of the provinces of Colombia, and brought to Europe, in 1741, by Don Antonio de Ulloa.

PLESIOSAU'RUS. From the Gr. *plesios*, next, and *sauros*, a lizard. A genus of extinct marine animals, allied to the lizard and crocodile, having the neck very long, and the tail short. Also written *Ple'siosaur.*

PLEI'OCENE. } PLI'OCENE. } From the Gr. *pleion*, more, and *kainos*, recent. A term applied by geologists to the newer tertiary formation, because there is found fossilized in it a greater number of existing than of extinct species.

PLUMBA'GO. Black-lead or graphite. A mineral consisting of carbon. A little iron is usually, but not necessarily, an ingredient. Excepting the diamond, it is the purest form in which carbon occurs in nature.

PLUMB-LINE. } PLU'MMET. } From the Lat. *plumbum*, lead. An instrument, consisting of a string with a weight, usually of lead, attached to a straight staff, for the purpose of ascertaining the direction of gravitation, or the perpendicular to the horizon.

PLUTO'NIC ROCKS. Unstratified crystalline rocks, probably formed at great depths beneath the surface by igneous fusion. *Volcanic rocks* are formed near the surface.

POLARIZA'TION. The process by which light is polarized.

PO'LARIZED LIGHT. Light so modified as to possess poles, or sides, having opposite properties. Light by reflection or refraction, when passed through crystals possessing the power of double refraction, becomes modified, so that it does not present the same phenomena of transmission and reflection, as light which had not been polarized.

POLYG'ONUM. From the Gr. *polus*, many, and *gonu*, a knee or joint. A genus of plants of the family of Polygonáceæ.

POLYMO'RPHA. Lat. From the Gr. *polus*, many, and *morphe*, form. Many-shaped. A specific name.

PO'LYPI. Lat. Plural of polypus.

POL'YPUS. From the Gr. *polus*, many, and *pous*, foot. A genus of radiate animals.

PON'TICA. Lat. From *pontus*, the sea. Belonging or relating to the sea.

PORPHYRIT'IC. Of the nature of porphyry.

POR'PHYRY. From the Gr. *porphura*, purple. Originally applied to a *red rock* found in Egypt. A compact feldspathic rock, containing disseminated crystals of feldspar; the latter, when polished, forming small angular spots, of a light colour, thickly sprinkled over the surface. The rock is of various colours, dark green, red, blue, black, &c.

PORT'LAND RED. A name given by geologists to the superior division of the upper óolite or lias system. The "Portland stone" is a kind of limestone found in the south of England, and more particularly in the Isle of Portland. In this series of strata is a silicious sand known as the "Portland sand."

POTAS'SIUM. A metal discovered in potash, by Sir H. Davy, in 1807.

PREDA'CEOUS. Living on prey.

PREHEN'SILE. From the Lat. *prehendere*, to lay hold of. Having the faculty to lay hold of. Applied to the tails of those monkeys, for example, which have the power to suspend themselves by the tail.

PRI'MARY FORMA'TION. A term applied by geologists to designate the different rocks which were formed prior to the creation of plants and animals.

PRI'MUM MO'BILE. That which first imparts motion.

PRISM. A solid bounded by three planes, two of which are equal.

PRISMA'TIC. Belonging or relating to a prism.

PROBOSCI'DIAN. From the Gr. *proboskis*, a proboscis or trunk. Applied to mammals of the family which includes the elephant.

PROCELLA'RIA. From the Lat. *procella*, a tempest at sea. A genus of birds of the family of Palmi'pedes.

PROLI'FERA. Lat. Formed from *proles*, a race or stock, and *fero*, I bear. Prolific.

PRO'TEA. A genus of plants of the family of Proteáceæ. *Pro'tea cyanero'ides*, Artichoke-flowered protea.

PRO'TEUS. Lat. A genus of reptiles.

PTE'RIS. Gr. Name of Fern. A genus of cryptógamous plants. Brake. *Pte'ris escule'nta.* Edible fern.

PUL'MONARY. From the Lat. *pulmo*, the lungs. Pertaining to the lungs.

PUTREFAC'TION. From the Lat. *putris*, putrid, and *facere*, to make. The decomposition of animal bodies, or of such plants as contain nitrogen in their composition, which takes place spontaneously when they are exposed to the air, under the influence of moisture and warmth. During the process there is a complete transposition of the proximate principles, the elementary substances combining in new, and principally gaseous compounds. Oxygen is absorbed from the atmosphere, and converted into carbonic acid; one portion of the hydrogen forms water with the oxygen; another forms, with the nitrogen, carbon, phosphorus, and sulphur, respectively, ammonia, carburetted, phosphuretted, and sulphuretted hydrogen gases, which occasion the nauseous smell evolved by putrefying bodies.

PYR'ITES. From the Gr. *pur*, fire. A term originally applied to the native bisulphuret of iron, in allusion to its giving sparks with steel. Now applied to a combination of sulphur with iron or copper, which presents a yellowish, metallic lustre.

PYROG'ENOUS. From the Gr. *pur*, fire, and *geinomai*, I beget. Applied to rocks which owe their origin to the action of fire, as granite.

PYROM'ETER. The name of an instrument for measuring high degrees of heat, above the range of the mercurial thermometer.

PYROPH'OROUS. The generic name of any chemical preparation, generally a powder, which inflames spontaneously when exposed to the air.

PY'THON. A genus of reptiles.

QUAD'RANT. From the Lat. *quadrans*, a fourth. In *geometry*, the fourth part of a circle, or of its circumference. In *astronomy* and *navigation*, an instrument for taking the altitudes and distances of the heavenly bodies.

QUADRU'MANA. Formed from the Lat. *quatuor*, four, and *manus*, hand. An order of mammals characterized by having four hands.

QUARTZ. Germ. Rock crystal.

QUA'RTZITE. A mineral resembling quartz. Granular quartz.

QUARTZ'OSE. Of the nature of quartz.

QUICK'SILVER. Mercury. A metal which is fluid at ordinary temperatures.

RADIA'TA. Lat. Radiates; the name of a class of zóophytes.

RA'DIATE. From the Lat. *radius*, a ray; furnished with rays; having rays.

RADIA'TION. The emission of the rays of light, or of heat, from a luminous or a heated body.

RA'NA. Lat. A frog. A genus of reptiles.

RANUN'CULI. Lat. Plural of ranunculus.

RANUN'CULUS. From the Lat, *rana*, a frog, because the species inhabit humid places Crow-foot. A genus of plants of the family of Ranunculáceæ.

Rectifica'tion. A second distillation of alcoholic liquors, to free them from whatever impurities may have passed over in the first.
Refra'ction. From the Lat. *refractus*, broken. The deviation of a ray of light from its rectilinear course, caused by passing through a transparent substance. The degree of refraction depends upon the density of the medium through which the ray of light passes.
Reful'gens. Lat. Shining brightly; refulgent.
Reg'ulus. A term introduced by the alchemists, but now nearly obsolete. It means, literally, *a little king*, and refers to the metallic state as one of royalty, compared with the native earthy condition. Antimony is the only metal now known by the name of regulus.
Re'ptile. From the Lat. *repere*, to crawl. A term applied to any animal that moves naturally upon its belly, or on very short legs, as serpents, &c.
Repti'lia. Lat. The class of reptiles: it comprises those vertebrate animals which have cold blood, an aërial respiration, and an incomplete circulation.
Resini'fera. Lat. Containing resin.
Revolu'ta. Lat. Turned back; tumbled.
Rho'dium. From the Gr. *rhodon*, a rose, on account of the rose-red colour of some of its salts. A metal discovered, in the year 1803, by Wollaston.
Rhodode'ndron. From the Gr. *rhodon*, a rose, and *dendron*, a tree. A genus of plants of the family of Ericáceæ.
Rhus. A genus of plants of the family of Terebintháceæ. *Rhus vernix*. The varnish Sumach.
Rock-salt. Common salt, found in masses or beds in the new red sandstone.
Roden'tia. From the Lat. *rodere*, to gnaw. An order of mammals.
Ro'dents. Animals of the order of Rodentia.
Ro'sa. Lat. Rose. A genus of plants of the family of Rosáceæ. *Rosa sinensis*. The Chinese rose.
Ru'ber. Lat. Red.
Rubia'ceæ. A family of plants.
Ru'by. A crystallized gem, of various shades of red.
Ru'minant. An animal that chews the cud.
Rumina'ntia. An order of mammals which are characterized by chewing the cud.
Ru'minate. To chew the cud.

Sal ammo'niac. Muriate or hydrochlorate of ammonia. Its name is derived from Ammon, or the temple of Jupiter Ammon, in Egypt, near which the salt was originally made.
Salines'. Natural deposits of salt; salt-springs.
Sa'lix. Lat. Willow. A genus of plants of the family of Salici'neæ. *Sa'lix lana'ta*. Woolly willow.
Sal prunel'la. Fused nitre cast into cakes or balls.
Salt. A combination of an acid with one or more bases.
Sa'molus. From the Celtic, *san*, salutary, and *mos*, pig. Salutary to pigs. Brook-weed. A genus of plants of the family of Primuláceæ. *Sa'molus valera'ndi*. Common brookweed.
San'darach. A name given by the Arabs to an odorous resin.
Sa'ndstone. Any rock consisting of aggregated grains of sand.
Sapona'ria. Lat. Soapy.
Sa'pphire. A very hard gem, consisting essentially of crystallized alumina. It is of various colours; the *blue* variety being usually called sapphire; the *red*, the oriental ruby; the *yellow*, the oriental topaz.
Satura'tion. From the Lat. *satur*, filled. In *chemistry*, the union, combination, or impregnation of one body with another by affinity, till the receiving body can contain no more; or solution continued till the solvent can contain no more.
Sau'rian. From the Gr. *sauros*, a lizard. Applied to animals of the lizard tribe.
Sau'roid. From the Gr. *sauros*, a lizard, and *eidos*, resemblance. Resembling a lizard.
Sca'ndens. Lat. Climbing.
Scheele's green. A pulverulent arsenite of copper.
Schist. From the Gr. *schistos*, split. Slate.
Schisto'se. Slaty.
Sco'lopax. Lat. A genus of birds; a heron.
Scopa'ria. From *scopa*, a broom. A genus of plants of the family of Scrophulari'neæ.
Sco'riæ. Volcanic cinders. Cinders and slags of basaltic lavas of a reddish-brown and black colour.
Scoria'ceous. Of the nature of scoriæ.

SCO'RIFORM. In form of scoriæ.

SEAMS. In *geology*, thin layers of strata interposed between others.

SE'CONDARY FORMA'TION. In *geology*, the formation which is next in order to the transition formation.

SE'CULAR. From the Lat. *seculum*, a century. *Secular evolutions* are those which take place gradually and imperceptibly, through a long period of time. *Secular tides* are those which are dependent upon the secular variation of the moon's mean distance from the earth.

SE'DIMENT. From the Lat. *sedeo*, I sit. That which subsides or settles to the bottom of any liquid.

SEDIME'NTARY. Belonging or relating to sediment.

SEE'D-LOBE. The envelope in which the seed of a plant is formed.

SE'LENITE. A variety of gypsum, or sulphate of lime.

SELE'NIUM. A non-metallic chemical element, discovered by Berzelius, in 1817.

SE'PAL. That part of the calyx of a flower which resembles a leaf.

SE'PIA. A kind of paint prepared from the cuttle-fish. A genus of mollusks.

SEPTENTRIONA'LIS. Lat. Northern.

SER'PENTINE. A magnesian rock of various colours, and often speckled like a serpent's back. It is generally dark-green.

SERRA'TA. Lat. Serrate.

SER'RATE. From the Lat. *serra*, a saw. Toothed like a saw.

SHAFT. A cylindrical hollow space, or pit, in mines, made for the purpose of extracting ores, &c.

SHALE. An indurated slaty clay, or clay-slate.

SHI'NGLE. Loose, water-worn gravel and pebbles.

SIER'RA. Span. A mountain-chain.

SI'LEX. From the Gr. *chalix*, a pebble. The principal constituent of quartz, rock-crystal, and other *sili'cious* minerals.

SI'LICA. Silicious earth: the oxide of *silicon* (the elementary basis of silica), constituting almost the whole of *silex* or flint. It combines with many of the metallic oxides, and is for this reason sometimes called *sili'cic* acid.

SI'LICATE. A compound of silicic acid and a basis. *Plate-glass* and *window-glass* are silicates of soda and potassa; and *flint-glass* is a similar compound, with a large addition of silicate of lead.

SILI'CIFIED. Petrified or mineralized by silicious earth.

SILI'CIOUS. Containing silica.

SILI'CIUM. } SIL'ICON. } The metalloid which forms the basis of silica.

SILT. The name given to the sand, clay, and earth, which accumulate in running waters.

SILU'RIAN SYSTEM. A series of rocks formerly known as the *greywacke series*. So called after the *Silures* or *Siluri*, the ancient Britons who inhabited the region where these strata are most distinctly developed. They are entirely of marine origin.

SILU'RUS. Lat. A genus of fishes of the family of Siluridæ.

SIL'VA. A forest, or woods.

SIN'TER. Germ. A scale. *Calcareous sinter* is a variety of carbonate of lime, composed of successive concentric layers. *Silicious sinter* is a variety of common opal.

SIPHO'NIA. A genus of plants of the family of Euphorbiáceæ.

SLATE. A well-known rock, which is divisible into thin plates or layers.

SMEL'TING. The operation by which the ores of iron, copper, lead, &c., are reduced to the metallic state.

SO'LAR SPEC'TRUM. Lat. *Spectrum*, an image. In *optics*, the name given to an elongated image of the sun formed on a wall or screen by a beam of undecomposed light, received through a small hole, and refracted by a prism.

SOLFATA'RA. Italian. A volcanic vent, emitting sulphur and sulphurous compounds.

SPAR. (Germ. *Spath.*) Applied to certain crystallized mineral substances, which easily break into cubic, prismatic, or other forms.

SPAR'RY. Of the nature of spar.

SPE'CIES. A kind; a subdivision of genus. According to Dr. Morton, a primordial type. "An animal," says Mr. John Cassin, "which constantly perpetuates its kind, or, in other words, produces itself either exactly, or within a demonstrable range of variation, is a species." Extinct species is a term applied to those kinds of organized beings, whether plants or animals, which are not found living upon the face of the earth.

SPECI'FIC. Relating to species.

SPECI'FIC WEIGHT, OR SPECI'FIC GRA'VITY. The relative weight of one body with that of another of equal volume.

SPECIO'SA. / SPECIO'SUM. / SPECIO'SUS. } Lat. Handsome. A word used as a specific name.
SPE'CULAR IRON. A kind of iron ore of granular structure, and metallic lustre, sometimes shining.
SPECTA'BILIS. Lat. Visible, remarkable, notable.
SPEC'ULUM METAL. An alloy of copper and tin.
SPICA'TA. Lat. Having spikes; eared like corn.
SPINE'LLE, or SPINE'L. Fr. A sub-species of ruby.
SPIRÆ'A. A genus of plants of the family of Rosáceæ.
SPI'RIT OF AMMO'NIA. Properly speaking, alcohol combined with ammoni'acal gas; but the term is often applied to water of ammonia.
SPI'RIT OF WINE. Alcohol.
SPORES. The seeds of lichens, and cryptógamous plants.
SPORU'LES. The diminutive of spores.
SPUMA'CEOUS. From the Lat. *spuma*, foam. Foamy.
STA'MEN. Lat. The male apparatus of a flower.
STARCH. A vegetable substance which exists in many tuberous roots, the stalks of palms, and in the seeds of the cereal grasses.
STE'ATITE. A mineral of the magnesian family. It consists of, silica 44, magnesia 44, alumina 2, iron 7·3, manganese 1·5, chromium 2, with a trace of lime.
STEPPE. Fr. from the Lat. *stipes*, a landmark. A term applied to the savannas of Tartary, of the Crimea, &c., and salt deserts of Northern Asia. A level waste, destitute of trees: a prairie.
STI'GMA. The superior, terminating part of the pistil of a flower.
STRA'TA. Lat. Plural of *stratum*, a layer, a bed.
STRATIFICA'TION. An arrangement in beds or layers.
STRA'TIFIED. Arranged in strata.
STRA'TUM. Lat. In *geology*, a bed of sedimentary rock.
STRA'TUS. A kind of cloud: it consists of horizontal layers, and includes fogs and mists; its under surface usually rests upon the land or sea, and it is therefore the lowest of the clouds.
STRI'Æ. Lat. Diminutive channels or creases.
STRIA'TA. Lat. Striated; marked with striæ.
STRON'TIA. One of the alkaline earths, of which *strontium* is the metallic basis.
STRON'TIUM. A metalloid found in the earth called strontia.
STRU'THIO. Lat. An ostrich. A genus of birds.
STRU'THIOUS. Of the nature of an ostrich.
STRYCH'NOS. A genus of plants of the family of Apocy'neæ. *Strych'nos toxica'ria.* The poison strychnos. The Nux Vomica is the seed of a plant of this genus.
SUBLIMA'TION. The process by which volatile substances are raised by heat, and again condensed into the solid form. The substances so obtained are called *sub'limates.*
SUB'SALT. A salt in which the base is not saturated with acid; as subacetate of lead.
SUB'SOIL. An under soil.
SUBSTRA'TA. Lat. Plural of *substratum*, an under layer or bed.
SU'GAR OF LEAD. Acetate of lead.
SUL'PHATE. Any compound of sulphuric acid with a salifiable base.
SUL'PHURET. A compound of sulphur with another solid, as with iron, forming *sulphuret of iron.*
SUL'PHURETTED. Containing sulphur; as, hydrogen containing sulphur is called sulphuretted hydrogen.
SUPE'RBA. Lat. Superb, elegant.
SYCOMO'RUS. Lat. The Sycamore; applied also as a specific name.
SY'ENITE and SI'ENITE. A granite rock from *Syene* or *Siena*, in Egypt. It consists of quartz, feldspar, and hornblende. It is tougher than granite.
SYL'VIA. Name of a genus of birds.
SYNGENE'SIA. From the Gr. *sun*, together, and *geinomai*, to grow. Linnæan name of a class of plants.
SYN'THESIS. A Greek word, signifying combination. It is applied to the chemical action which unites dissimilar bodies into a uniform compound; as sulphuric acid and lime into gypsum; or chlorine and sodium into common salt.
SY'RUP. A solution of sugar in water.

TAN'TALUM. A metal, remarkable for its insolubility in acids. Called also *Columbium.*
TAR'TAR. Called also *argal* or *argol.* The crude bitartrate of potassa, which exists in the juice of the grape, and is deposited from wines in their fermenting casks; being preci-

pitated in proportion as the alcohol is formed, in consequence of its insolubility in that liquid.

TAR'TAR EME'TIC. The double tartrate of antimony and potassa.

TELESCO'PIC. Relating to the telescope; telescopic objects are those which may be seen by the aid of a telescope.

TELLU'RIUM. A rare metal, found in the gold mines of Transylvania.

TEM'PERATURE. A definite degree of sensible heat.

TEMPORA'RIA. Lat. Temporary; relating to time.

TE'NAX. Lat. Tenacious.

TER'MES. A genus of insects of the order of Neuroptera, and family of Termitidæ. White ants.

TER'RA JAPO'NICA. An astringent medicinal gum, obtained from the Acácia ca'techu.

TER'TIARY FORMA'TION. A series of sedimentary rocks, which are superior to the primary and secondary, and distinguished by the fossil remains found in them.

TEST. A chemical reagent of any kind, which indicates, by special characters, the nature of any substance, simple or compound.

TESTA'CEÆ. From *testa*, a shell. Testáceans; animals provided with an external shelly cover, composed chiefly of carbonate of lime.

TESTA'CEOUS. Consisting of carbonate of lime and animal matter.

TESTU'DO. Lat. Tortoise. A genus of reptiles of the order of Chelo'nians.

THE'A. A genus of plants of the tribe of Came'lleæ. *The'a bo'hea*, Bohea tea; *The'a vi'ridis*, Green tea.

THE'INE. The proximate principle of tea.

THEOBRO'MINE. A chemical principle found in cocoa-beans, and identical with caffein and theine, as obtained from tea and coffee.

THER'MAL. From the Gr. *thermos*, heat. Warm; belonging or relating to heat.

THERMOM'ETER. An instrument to measure temperature.

THORI'NA. One of the earths.

THO'RIUM. A metal obtained from Thori'na, an earthy substance.

TI'DAL. Relating to tides. *Tidal wave* is the elevation of the water of the ocean, produced by the attraction of the moon.

TITA'NIUM. A metal discovered in 1781, by W. Gregor, in a ferruginous sand.

TO'PAZ. A crystallized pellucid mineral, harder than quartz; commonly of a yellow wine colour, but it also occurs white, blue, and brown.

TO'RSION BA'LANCE. See BALANCE.

TOU'RMALINE. A mineral substance, consisting of a bo'ro-si'licate of a'lumine, harder than quartz, but not as hard as topaz.

TRA'CHYTE. From the Gr. *trachus*, rough. A variety of lava. A feldspathic rock, which often contains glassy feldspar and hornblende. When the feldspar crystals are thickly and uniformly disseminated, it is called *trachy'tic por'phyry*.

TRAP. From the Swedish *trappa*, a flight of stairs, because *trap-rocks* frequently occur in large tabular masses rising one above another like the successive steps of a staircase. Applied to certain igneous rocks composed of feldspar, augite, and hornblende.

TRA'PPEAN. Belonging to trap-rocks.

TRI'AS. From the Lat. *tres*, three. Synonym of the triássic system of rocks, consisting of the *Bunter sandstein*, the *Muschelkalk*, and *Keuper*, a group of sandy marls of variegated colours.

TRIDENTA'TA. Lat. Three-toothed; having three teeth.

TRIGONOCE'PHALUS. From the Gr. *treis*, three, *gonos*, an angle, and *kephale*, head. genus of very venomous serpents. *Trigonoce'phalus lanceola'tus*. Lance-head viper.

TRI'LOBITE. From the Lat. *tres*, three, and *lobus*, lobe. A genus of fossil crustáceans.

TU'FA. Italian. A volcanic rock, composed of an agglutination of fragmented scoriæ.

TUNG'STEN. Swedish. *Heavy stone*. A metal which is hard, white, brittle, and difficult to fuse.

TU'RDUS. Lat. A thrush. Name of a genus of birds.

TUR'MERIC. The roots of the *Curcuma longa* and *rotunda*, plants which grow in the East Indies, where it is much employed in dyeing yellow, and as a condiment. The yellow tint of turmeric is changed to a brown-red by alkalies, alkaline earths, subacetate of lead, and several metallic oxides. Hence, it is used as a chemical test.

TU'RQUOISE. A blue mineral, found in Persia; its colour depends on the presence of oxide of copper.

UM'BEL. A form of inflorescence, in which several peduncles expand so as to produce a flower somewhat resembling a parasol when open.

UMBELLI'FERÆ. From *umbélla*, a sun-shade, and *fero*, I bear. Name of a family of plants.

UMBELLI'FEROUS. Bearing umbels. Belonging or relating to the Umbelli'feræ.

UNCINA'TA. Lat. From *uncus*, a hook. Hooked; having hooks.
UPHEAV'AL. The elevation of lands by earthquakes.
URA'NIUM. A metal discovered by Klaproth, in 1789.
U'RENS. Lat. Burning.
URSI'NUS. Lat. Belonging or relating to bears.

VA'CUUM. From the Lat. *vacuus*, empty. A portion of space void of matter.
VANA'DIUM. A silvery-white metal, discovered originally by Del Rio, in 1801, but not admitted until 1830.
VANE'SSA. A genus of butterflies. *Vane'ssa ca'rdui.* The painted lady-butterfly.
VA'POUR. The state of elastic or aeriform fluidity into which any substance, naturally solid or liquid at ordinary temperatures, may be converted by the agency of heat.
VEINS. In *mining*, the fissures or rents in rocks, which are filled with peculiar mineral substances, most commonly metallic ores.
VEIN'STONES. Gangues. The mineral substances which accompany, and frequently enclose, the metallic ores.
VENENI'FLUA. Lat. Flowing with poison.
VENE'TIAN CHALK. Steatite.
VE'NUS. A planet. Also the mythological and alchemical name of copper.
VERMIL'ION. Artificial cinnabar.
VERNICI'FLUA. Lat. Flowing with varnish.
VER'NIX. Lat. Varnish.
VERONI'CA. A genus of plants of the family of Scrophularínæ.
VER'TEBRA. From the Lat. *vertere*, to turn. A joint or bone of the spine. ***Ver'tebral co'lumn***, is the spine or backbone.
VER'TEBRATE. Having vertebræ, or a spine.
VER'TICOSE. Whorl-like.
VILLO'SUS. Lat. Velvety.
VI'RIDIS. Lat. Green.
VIT'RIFIED. From the Lat. *vitrum*, glass. Converted into glass.
VIT'RIOL. From *vitrum*, glass. The old chemical, and still the vulgar, appellation of sulphuric acid, and of many of its compounds, which in certain states have a glassy appearance. Thus, vitriolic acid, or oil of vitriol, is sulphuric acid; blue vitriol, sulphate of copper; green vitriol, sulphate of iron; and white vitriol, sulphate of zinc.
VIVI'PARUM. Lat. Vivi'parous.
VOLCA'NIC. Belonging or relating to volcanoes.
VOLTA'IC. Applied to electricity produced after the manner of Volta, an Italian philosopher.
VUL'TUR PA'PA. The king of vultures.

WACKE. A massive mineral, intermediate between claystone and basalt.
WA'TERSHED. The general declivity of the face of a country which determines the direction of the flowing of water.
WEALD. Name of a part of Kent and Surrey, in England. The *Wealden clay* and *Wealden deposit* are found in this part of England.
WHITE LEAD. Carbonate of lead, or *ceruse*.
WINE. The fermented juice of the grape.
WOOTZ. The Indian name of steel.
WORT. The fermented infusion of malt or grains.

XANTHOX'YLUM. From the Gr. *xanthos*, yellow, and *xulon*, wood. Toothache-tree. A genus of plants of the family of Rutáceæ.
XERA'NTHEMUM. From the Gr. *xeros*, dry, and *anthos*, flower. A genus of plants of the family of Compo'sitæ.

YEAST. The froth of fermenting wort.
YT'TRIA. A rare earth.
YTT'RIUM. A metal discovered by Wöhler, in 1828; it is of a dark-gray colour, and brittle.
YUC'CA. Adam's needle. A genus of plants of the family of Liliáceæ. It yields an esculent root.

ZIRCO'NIA. A rare earth, extracted from the minerals zircon and hyacinth. It is an oxide of zirconium.
ZIRCO'NIUM. A metal found in *zirconia*, an earth, discovered by Klaproth, in 1789.
ZOOL'OGY. From the Gr. *zo'on*, an animal, and *logos*, a discourse. That branch of Natural History which treats of animals.
ZO'OPHYTE. From the Gr. *zo'on*, an animal, and *phuton*, a plant. An animal without vertebræ, or extremities, that attaches itself to solid bodies, and seems to live and vegetate like a plant.

INDEX.

THE END.

www.ingramcontent.com/pod-product-compliance
Lightning Source LLC
LaVergne TN
LVHW011240110826
845149LV00001B/6

* 9 7 8 1 4 1 8 1 8 9 2 4 2 *